REGULATION OF LAWYERS:
Problems of Law and Ethics

ASPEN PUBLISHERS

Regulation of Lawyers: Problems of Law and Ethics

Eighth Edition

Stephen Gillers

Emily Kempin Professor of Law
New York University School of Law

Wolters Kluwer
Law & Business

AUSTIN   BOSTON   CHICAGO   NEW YORK   THE NETHERLANDS

Aspen Publishers
Attn: Permissions Department
76 Ninth Avenue, 7th Floor
New York, NY 10011-5201

To contact Customer Care, e-mail customer.care@aspenpublishers.com, call 1-800-234-1660, fax 1-800-901-9075, or mail correspondence to:

Aspen Publishers
Attn: Order Department
PO Box 990
Frederick, MD 21705

Printed in the United States of America.

1 2 3 4 5 6 7 8 9 0

ISBN 978-0-7355-7969-9

Library of Congress Cataloging-in-Publication Data

Gillers, Stephen, 1943-
  Regulation of lawyers : problems of law and ethics/Stephen Gillers.—8th ed.
      p. cm.
    ISBN 978-0-7355-7969-9
  1. Legal ethics—United States—Cases. 2. Lawyers—United States—Discipline—Cases.
3. Practice of law—United States—Cases. I. Title.

KF306.G55 2009
174'.30973—dc22

2009003049

About Wolters Kluwer Law & Business

Wolters Kluwer Law & Business is a leading provider of research information and workflow solutions in key specialty areas. The strengths of the individual brands of Aspen Publishers, CCH, Kluwer Law International and Loislaw are aligned within Wolters Kluwer Law & Business to provide comprehensive, in-depth solutions and expert-authored content for the legal, professional and education markets.

CCH was founded in 1913 and has served more than four generations of business professionals and their clients. The CCH products in the Wolters Kluwer Law & Business group are highly regarded electronic and print resources for legal, securities, antitrust and trade regulation, government contracting, banking, pension, payroll, employment and labor, and healthcare reimbursement and compliance professionals.

Aspen Publishers is a leading information provider for attorneys, business professionals and law students. Written by preeminent authorities, Aspen products offer analytical and practical information in a range of specialty practice areas from securities law and intellectual property to mergers and acquisitions and pension/benefits. Aspen's trusted legal education resources provide professors and students with high-quality, up-to-date and effective resources for successful instruction and study in all areas of the law.

Kluwer Law International supplies the global business community with comprehensive English-language international legal information. Legal practitioners, corporate counsel and business executives around the world rely on the Kluwer Law International journals, loose-leafs, books and electronic products for authoritative information in many areas of international legal practice.

Loislaw is a premier provider of digitized legal content to small law firm practitioners of various specializations. Loislaw provides attorneys with the ability to quickly and efficiently find the necessary legal information they need, when and where they need it, by facilitating access to primary law as well as state-specific law, records, forms and treatises.

Wolters Kluwer Law & Business, a unit of Wolters Kluwer, is headquartered in New York and Riverwoods, Illinois. Wolters Kluwer is a leading multinational publisher and information services company.

In loving dedication to
Gillian Gillers
and
Heather Gillers

les enfants du paradis

Summary of Contents

Part Four

AVOIDING AND REDRESSING PROFESSIONAL FAILURE 631

Part Five

FIRST AMENDMENT RIGHTS OF LAWYERS
AND JUDICIAL CANDIDATES 855

Contents

Part Two

CONFLICTS OF INTEREST   **211**

Chapter V   Concurrent Conflicts of Interest   **213**

Part Three

Why It's Important:
A Preface for Students

I imagine you're pretty busy and that reading a preface is not at the top of your to-do list. But this one is different. It is written with you very much in mind. And it's short. So give me five minutes.

I want to say four things right off. First, as may already be apparent, this casebook has a personality, a recognizable voice: namely, mine. In that way, it may be unlike other casebooks. Its voice is conversational. And here and there, it takes a position directly, not solely through the words and views of others. Second, this book contains many problems. Some are a paragraph long, others are a page or two. Many are based on real situations that I've heard or read about. Mostly, the problems are dense and messy, like life. They are not stick-figure problems. They are real-people problems. They arose yesterday or will arise tomorrow, in one form or another. Third, the book contains many short essays (i.e., notes). The legal ethics world is best learned not only as a set of abstract doctrines, but also through stories taken from many cases and elsewhere. Detail illuminates nuance and variation and thereby provides a context in which to test the doctrines. I further explain this approach in chapter 1.

Fourth, this is your second most important law school class. *Yeah, right,* you think. It's a bold statement, I know. Here's why I think it's true. Say you become an antitrust lawyer. Your criminal procedure class will fade into a remote corner of memory. Or if you become a criminal defense lawyer, you're unlikely to need to know much antitrust. But whatever work you do as a lawyer, you will practice what you learn in this book and in the class that assigns it whenever you advise a client, argue in court, draft a document, write a brief, or negotiate with an opponent. So antitrust or criminal law or whatever may be your most important legal subject, depending on the direction of your professional life, but this subject is a close second. Here you learn the rules you must live by and the consequences if you don't. Other courses teach lessons that directly bear on your clients' legal problems. This course is for you. One exception: Knowledge of these rules enables you to protect your clients against misconduct of other lawyers — conduct that may violate conflict rules, for example, or rules against communicating with another lawyer's clients.

As you approach the starting line of your legal career, perhaps most important to you are rules that constrain your professional behavior. You will want to know — in such areas as competence, fees, marketing, confidentiality, conflicts of interest, negotiation, and the client-lawyer relationship — what may I do and how may I behave to be confident that my conduct will not land me before a disciplinary committee, create civil liability, invite court sanction, forfeit my fee, or damage my reputation? Even reading this question should alert you that the "ethics" in legal ethics is not merely about being a morally good person. It is about being a professionally safe lawyer. For the fact is that the law business is heavily regulated, and its regulations have grown more complex in recent decades. This has led to new terms — *the law governing lawyers* and *the law of lawyering* — lest anyone be fooled by the word "ethics" into believing that the subject is about how to be a good person.

You make two errors at your peril. First, do not believe that the right way to act — toward clients, courts, adversaries, or colleagues — will be intuitively obvious. Sure, sometimes it will be. But no one needs to teach you not to lie or steal in professional life, and certainly not using hundreds of pages of text to do it. The rules here are often obscure; they may even be counterintuitive, and they can be subtle in application. Application in turn calls for judgment, and judgment is mostly learned through life experience. Indeed, much of what lawyers do for clients is make judgments — about where the law is headed, what a particular judge or court will do, how great may be the risk of a contemplated course of conduct. You develop that judgment across years of practice, but the process begins now. Second, you don't want to make the mistake of assuming that your employer will provide all the protection you need against missteps. Good law offices do have systems to detect and avoid improper conduct and they have people to whom lawyers can turn for advice. But the best systems and resources are still not perfect, and anyway, the professional responsibility of a lawyer cannot be delegated to a boss. Furthermore, you need to know enough about this material to be aware when you have a problem that requires you to seek advice.

Another perspective from which to view the laws and rules that regulate lawyers considers their effect on civil society and the administration of justice. The obligations that lawyers impose on themselves through self-regulation or that are imposed on them by courts and legislatures, taken together, help define the nature and work of the entire profession and therefore the behavior of our legal institutions and the quality of our social justice. For example, a rule that allows lawyers to advertise will influence the conduct of individual members of the bar. But it can also affect consumer demand and (through greater competition) the size of legal fees. A rule that prohibits or requires a lawyer to reveal certain kinds of information about a client in order to protect others from harm will control that lawyer's own behavior, but it may also affect which client populations use lawyers and what information clients are willing to give those lawyers. In short, many rules have social and political consequences (sometimes profound ones) beyond any single representation or practice.

As you enter law practice, you may be more interested in such questions as "How do I behave?" and "How can I stay out of trouble?" than in asking, "What are the consequences to civil society and justice if one or another version of a particular rule is applied to America's more than 800,000 practicing lawyers?" Still, the last question is important and, if not as immediate, will surely arise in the course of your professional life. Many readers of this book will someday be in positions that require them to address the broader question — as heads of law offices, members of bar committees, legislators, government lawyers, and judges.

Asking about the consequences to justice and civil society if a rule is resolved one way rather than another — asking which resolution is best — engenders different, sometimes vehement, responses from practicing lawyers and the public. Why is that? In part, it is because the answers depend on political and moral values more fundamental than the "ethics" that inform various codes. And, of course, the political and moral values of different people differ. In addressing these questions, we should also try to be honest about the interests we mean to protect. Those of society generally? Those of a particular client population? The legal profession's? Our own? Law school and law practice, it is sometimes said, encourage more rather than less self-interest in answering the questions raised here. In transition as you are, your answers may vary from what they would have been before you entered law school, and they will likely be different still five years on.

* * *

This is the eighth edition of the book. I started on the first edition in 1982 shortly before the birth of the two amazing young women to whom all editions have been dedicated. Between editions, I spend an hour or two each week planning the next one. You get to thinking a lot about what a casebook is and can be when you live with one for so long. The book's primary function is to provide information, but that's just the beginning. The minimum editorial task would allow me to pick good cases and other materials, edit them, order them logically, add interstitial notes and questions, and put the product between covers. Voila! A casebook. Of course, one must begin this way, but if nothing more were possible (even if not required), I wonder if I would have kept at it for so long. Luckily, more is possible while still serving the book's objective — to teach the subject.

For starters, we can strive for humor, variety, clarity, and engaging writing. The enterprise will not likely support the extended charm of a Hazlitt essay or the quirkiness of a Vonnegut novel — assuming I had the talent to achieve either (in which case I'd probably be in a different line of work) — but a casebook is a book, after all, and it should have an authorial presence in so far as possible. That's what makes the book mine.

The legal profession is a culture of storytellers and stories. Harrison Tweed (1885-1969), a president of the New York City Bar Association, once said: "I have a high opinion of lawyers. With all their faults, they stack up well against those in every other occupation or profession. They are better to work with or play with or fight with or drink with than most other varieties of mankind." These words are inscribed on a wall at the Association's headquarters. As a young lawyer, I thought Tweed was over the top, if not downright sanctimonious, in making so grandiose a claim. At that time in my life, I was inclined to agree with the character in George Bernard Shaw's play *The Doctor's Dilemma* who said "all professions are conspiracies against the laity." Amen! To some extent, I still find Tweed a bit excessive and Shaw apt, even if hyperbolic. But I now think Tweed had a point. The profession and its members *are* fascinating to study, and its stories *are* fascinating to hear. As with the study of any culture, understanding the bar requires density of information. We must know a thousand small things about life within the society of lawyers, not merely a dozen big things, if we are going to understand it truly.

I invite your views on the book. What was dull? What worked well? How can the book be improved? Have you encountered a quote or story somewhere (true or fictitious) that you think nicely highlights an issue? This edition is indebted to past users who alerted me to interesting sources. Send e-mail to stephen. gillers@nyu.edu. All comments will be gratefully acknowledged.

Stephen Gillers
January 2009

Acknowledgments

Like the first seven editions of this book, written for law students, this edition is also the fortunate beneficiary of the diligent work of a law student, Lisa C. Kerr, NYU LL.M. class of 2009. In compressed time, which overlapped exams and winter break no less, Lisa worked carefully through the nearly 1000 pages of this book. Her labors greatly improved the result. What more can an author ask?

I have been fortunate beyond words to have the priceless administrative help of a single person — Shirley Gray — with the very first word of the very first edition and continuing, meticulously, to the very last word of this one.

This eighth edition builds on the first seven and, therefore, benefits from the work of New York University School of Law students whose energies contributed to its ancestors. They are: Anderson T. Bailey, New York University School of Law, J.D., class of 2006 (seventh edition); Howard Anglin, Cindy Hwang, and Eric R. Womack, J.D., class of 2003 (sixth edition); Leonard A. Ho and David F. Levine, class of 1999 (fifth edition); Julie C. Brain and Maria Lopotukhin, class of 1995 and 1996, respectively (fourth edition); Mary E. McDonald, class of 1993 (third edition); Laura Gilbert and Barbara Quakenbos, class of 1990 and 1988, respectively (second edition); and Patricia C. Hayashi, class of 1983, Virginia L. Richards, class of 1986, and Susan A. Waxenberg, class of 1982 (first edition).

My debt to members of the professional staff of the NYU School of Law Library also continues. Anyone who produces a book like this knows how important librarians are. Exceptionally useful assistance to this and prior editions was repeatedly available from Ronald Brown, Elizabeth Evans, Gretchen Feltes, Leslie Rich, and Jay Shuman.

My colleague Norman Dorsen was my co-author on the first two editions of this casebook. Other demands on his time caused Professor Dorsen to trust succeeding editions to my sole care. Nevertheless, in countless ways this edition, like its predecessors, benefits from Professor Dorsen's early work and advice.

My understanding of the issues raised in the following pages is greatly enhanced by conversations with one person whom I mention last but am grateful to most: Barbara S. Gillers, Esq., whose professional work on lawyer regulation puts her daily on the front lines of most of the developing issues recounted here.

I would like to thank the following for permission to reprint the identified material:

American Bar Association, excerpts from the Legislative History for Rules of Professional Conduct and from ABA Model Rules of Professional Conduct.

Anthony Barkow, Martin Lederman, David Luban, and John Steele, for excerpts from their blog posts in response to the New York Times article reprinted in chapter 8.

Robert S. Caine, A Lawyer's View of Being a Litigant, N.Y.L.J., May 16, 1994, at 2. Reprinted by permission.

William H. Fortune, Richard Underwood, Edward J. Imwinkelried. Modern Litigation and Professional Responsibility Handbook (Aspen 2001). Reprinted by permission.

Marvin E. Frankel, from Partisan Justice by Marvin E. Frankel. Copyright © 1980 by Marvin E. Frankel. Reprinted by permission.

Ronald L. Goldfarb, Lawyers Should Be Judged by the Clients They Keep, Wash. Post, Apr. 6, 1997. Reprinted by permission.

Daniel J. Kornstein, A Tragic Fire—A Great Cross-Examination, N.Y.L.J., Mar. 28, 1986, at 2. Reprinted by permission.

Jonathan R. Macey, Mandatory Pro Bono: Comfort for the Poor or Welfare for the Rich?, 77 Cornell L. Rev. 1115 (1992). Reprinted with permission of the Cornell Law Review.

John B. Mitchell, Reasonable Doubts Are Where You Find Them: A Response to Professor Subin's Position on the Criminal Lawyer's Different Mission, 1 Geo. J. Legal Ethics 339 (1987). Reprinted by permission.

Robert M. Morgenthau, for his letter to the editor of the New York Times and his letter to the author, both in chapter 8.

New York Times, for Doubting Case, A Prosecutor Helped the Defense in chapter 8. From The New York Times, June 23, 2008, © 2008 The New York Times. All rights reserved. Used by permission and protected by the Copyright Laws of the United States. The printing, copying, redistribution, or retransmission of the Material without express written permission is prohibited.

Robert C. Post, On the Popular Image of the Lawyer: Reflections in a Dark Glass, 75 Cal. L. Rev. 379, 379-380, 387-389 (1987). Reprinted by permission.

Deborah Rhode, Cultures of Commitment: Pro Bono for Lawyers and Law Students, 67 Fordham L. Rev. 2415 (1999). Reprinted by permission.

Simon H. Rifkind, The Lawyer's Role and Responsibility in Modern Society, 30 The Record of the Assoc. Of the Bar of the City of N.Y. 534 (1975). Copyright © 1975 by Simon H. Rifkind. Reprinted by permission.

Ann Ruben and Emily Ruben, Letters to the Editor, N.Y.L.J., Apr. 14, 1986, at 2. Reprinted by permission.

Harry I. Subin, Is This Lie Necessary? Further Reflections on the Right to Present a False Defense, 1 Geo. J. Legal Ethics 689, 690-691 (1988). Reprinted by permission.

Harry I. Subin, The Criminal Lawyer's "Different Mission," 1 Geo. J. Legal Ethics 125 (1987). Reprinted by permission.

A Word About Case Editing

No case is reprinted unedited. Omissions are identified with ellipses or brackets, but there is no identification where only case citations or other authorities are deleted. Case citations do not include subsequent history except that United States Supreme Court denials of certiorari are indicated for principal cases.

REGULATION OF LAWYERS:
Problems of Law and Ethics

I

Where Do "Ethics" Rules Come From?

- *Theories and Ideology Behind Lawyer Conduct Rules*
- *Sources of the Rules*
- *This Thing Called "Professionalism"*

As the Preface cautioned, "legal ethics" is something of a misnomer for the subject of this book and the courses likely to use it. The term is fine as a shorthand, but the subject is considerably broader (some would say it is also narrower) than that simple label implies. What you are studying here is all of the law governing lawyers. Rules that govern how members of the legal profession — including judges — may or must behave come from many sources. I will introduce them here but first I want to spend a little time with a few big questions. Even if we can't answer all of the questions now (or even later), just posing them will help to organize the material and clarify our thinking about the issues.

Does Legal Ethics Have a Theory?

Do the various rules and laws subsumed under the title Regulation of Lawyers derive from an overarching Theory of Everything, or at least A Theory of Nearly Everything — one grand design that explains (most of) the rules? For academics (me, your teacher), the answer is kind of easy: Theories "R" Us. They are part of the academic toolkit and what we're paid to produce. How do we debate the right rule without some view of our goals for those rules? And once we identify goals, we have to defend them, which forces us to identify norms and values that each goal serves, and so on until we get a theory that explains it all. Truth be told, either we never find that theory, disagree on what it is, or see our theory disproved by the next generation of academics out to make their mark. We know that, but it doesn't stop us. In asking the questions, we learn a lot.[1]

---

1. To borrow from Rainer Maria Rilke's *Letters to a Young Poet* (1903): "And the point is to live everything. Live the questions now. Perhaps then, someday far in the future, you will gradually, without even noticing it, live your way into the answer."

1

To my mind, searching for a grand design, at least for this material, is not fruitful. It forces us to squeeze every rule or law into the same theoretical mold or, alternatively, to recalibrate our hypothesis in order to accommodate each new development. I do not say that the rules and laws governing lawyers are unmoored from public policy, ideals of justice, and moral values. Quite the contrary. What I do mean is that these policies and values will at times conflict. The conflicts generate some of the most interesting (and heated) professional debates. If you listen in on a bar committee as it discusses a proposed rule, you might be surprised to learn just how intense those debates can be. Lawyers and judges do not differ so much about background values and policies. They just give them different weight and disagree over which should prevail when they clash.

Now people living in the world outside the academy have a more pragmatic view of things. Michael Ignatieff was a Harvard political science professor before returning to his native Canada, getting elected to Parliament, and becoming a leader in the Liberal Party. So he was in a good position to understand how ideas (being a synonym for theory) worked differently in different environments when on August 5, 2007, he published a New York Times Magazine article, "Getting Iraq Wrong," in which he tried to understand his own mistake in initially supporting the war.

> The philosopher Isaiah Berlin once said that the trouble with academics and commentators is that they care more about whether ideas are interesting than whether they are true. Politicians live by ideas just as much as professional thinkers do, but they can't afford the luxury of entertaining ideas that are merely interesting. They have to work with the small number of ideas that happen to be true and the even smaller number that happen to be applicable to real life. In academic life, false ideas are merely false and useless ones can be fun to play with. In political life, false ideas can ruin the lives of millions and useless ones can waste precious resources. An intellectual's responsibility for his ideas is to follow their consequences wherever they may lead. A politician's responsibility is to master those consequences and prevent them from doing harm.[2]

What does this mean for legal ethics? All legal rules must be pragmatic because they tell people how to behave. Or else. And legal ethics rules must be pragmatic because they tell lawyers how to behave when helping other people behave. Or else. To paraphrase Ignatieff, then, we "can't afford the luxury of entertaining

---

2. The same thought appears elsewhere in Berlin's work. "In one of his most famous essays, Isaiah Berlin quotes a fragment from the Greek poet Archilochus: 'The fox knows many things, but the hedgehog knows one big thing' ('The Hedgehog and the Fox'). The contrast is a metaphor for the crucial distinction at the heart of Berlin's thought between monist and pluralist accounts of moral value. According to monism, a single value or narrow set of values overrides all others, while in the pluralist view human goods are multiple, conflicting, and incommensurable. Monism, Berlin believes, harbors political dangers that pluralism avoids. While the great authoritarian visions of politics have all rested on monist foundations, pluralism is naturally aligned with toleration, moderation, and liberalism." George Crowder, Hedgehog and Fox, 38 Australian J. Political Science 333 (2003). Another philosopher, Yogi Berra, is reputed to have expressed the same idea more concisely: "In theory there is no difference between theory and practice, but in practice there is." See http://www.brainyquote.com/quotes/authors/y/yogi_berra.html. I can be a hedgehog when the situation demands it, but at heart I'm a fox and this book is mostly a fox book. — ED.

ideas that are merely interesting." Or more precisely, we can, but we can't stop there. In addition to being "true," our ideas must lead to rules "that are applicable to real life."

So with this responsibility in mind, we can try to identify those ideas that best guide us to the right rules. And perhaps we can see connections that enable us to move toward a theory if not of everything, then at least of some things. You should do this as you work through the assigned reading. For example, should there be an exception to the lawyer's confidentiality duty to protect others from the client's illegal conduct? "Yes," you might answer, and give a reason. Then you have to say why your reason is valid. What larger purpose does it serve? What idea does it advance? What values might the exception undermine (client candor, perhaps)? The conversation can go on, receding into broader and broader generalizations. And always you have to be cognizant of the need for your rule to be "applicable to real life."

Let me propose several ideas or values that may guide our analysis of particular rules. They don't add up to an all-inclusive theory, but they should be useful, even if only to prompt a dialogue.

The Client Is the Center of the Universe, If Not the Whole Universe. The law and rules governing lawyers should aim to protect the rights and to honor the autonomy of clients in a complex legal world. To do so, the rules must allow lawyers to act for clients in any lawful manner that clients could act for themselves if they were legally trained. Protecting a client's autonomy requires an environment in which the client is encouraged to be candid and honest with his or her lawyer. Talking to your lawyer should be as safe as talking to yourself. The rules must therefore assure clients that lawyers are forbidden to do anything to betray their clients' confidence and trust or otherwise cause a client harm. In addition, lawyers must be devoted to achieving the goals they have been retained or appointed to pursue. They must accept and defer to their clients' objectives once they accept a matter. So long as the clients' means and ends are lawful, lawyers should have no qualms over whether they are fair or hurt others. This theme can explain much of the material in chapters 2, 3, and 7, among other places.

Lawyers and the Legal Profession Also Deserve Autonomy. Lawyers are not technicians robotically obligated to ignore the wrongness of a client's instructions. They are moral agents entitled to decline to be the instruments of injury to others that they may find unconscionable even if lawful. The lawyer's autonomy is not limited to declining to accept a matter he or she finds repugnant: It includes the right to refuse to use highly offensive means or to pursue highly offensive ends that may first appear only after the lawyer is employed. In short, while the client may be entitled to full autonomy while acting unaided, that freedom is in some (even if only a minor) degree circumscribed when the client seeks help within the legal system. Respecting the lawyer's autonomy also recognizes that law is a profession associated with the administration of justice and not merely a collection of highly trained operatives willing to suspend all moral judgment for a fee. Beyond autonomy in their relationships with clients, lawyers have both commercial and noncommercial speech interests that may be seen to clash with other values that the governors of the profession wish to preserve. These themes appear in some of the material in chapters 2, 7, 15, and 16, among other places in this text.

The Bad Client Problem.   Some clients are willing to use lawyers to commit frauds or crimes against others or against the administration of justice. Of course, lawyers cannot knowingly assist a client's fraud or crime. Rule 1.2(d). But a lawyer may learn only too late that his or her services are or were part of a larger criminal or fraudulent scheme. Bad clients are owed no professional concern or protection. The rules and laws governing lawyers must therefore permit, perhaps even require, lawyers to protect the victims of a client's ongoing illegal conduct and the system of justice itself, even if that harms the client. This theme appears in chapters 2, 7, 9, and 10, among other places.

The Tempted Lawyer Problem.   Lawyers may be tempted to abuse their client's trust for their own benefit or the benefit of other clients or third parties. Alas, some lawyers will succumb to that temptation, although most will not. If, however, the rules permit lawyers to represent a client when there is *significant risk* that the lawyer's own conflicting interests or the conflicting interests of others will compromise the lawyer's devotion to the client, clients may hesitate fully to trust their lawyers. Since client trust is crucial in enabling lawyers to pursue their clients' goals and protect the clients' autonomy, the rules and law governing lawyers should forbid lawyers (absent client consent) ever to occupy positions in which they are tempted to betray their clients, without regard to whether any particular lawyer would actually succumb to the temptation. This theme mainly appears in the material on conflicts of interest (chapters 5 and 6) and in chapter 14, among other places.

The Poor Lawyer Problem.   Not all lawyers are above average. Only half minus one are (the one being exactly average). Even those who are above average may perform below average on occasion. Any lawyer, wherever on the scale, may on occasion perform so far below average that the law and rules governing lawyers should provide a compensation system for clients who suffer because their lawyer has seriously messed up. Just as important, the rules and law should adopt prophylactic measures that aim to insure competence in the first instance, so that the amount of messing up is as little as possible. Further, not only clients may be hurt by a lawyer's professional failures. Third parties, often a client's victims, may also suffer. The law should create a compensation system for them, too. This theme appears in the material in chapters 9, 12, and 13, among other places.

The Justice and Fairness Model.   Lawyers are the intermediaries between the law on paper and its application to the real problems of actual clients. We cannot have the rule of law without lawyers, at least not in a modern society. No matter how beautiful the legal theory, it is useless without lawyers to implement it. The law has many influences, but at least two are *justice* and *fairness*. We may disagree on what justice or fairness requires abstractly or in a particular situation, but we agree that legal rules have an interest in both. Consequently, so should lawyers. In constructing rules that will govern the behavior of the profession charged to "bring law to the people," we should therefore take care to insure that the content of those rules — what they permit, forbid, and require — respects the law's ancient concern for justice and fairness. Or to put it another way, we do not want justice and fairness to be lost in translation — left on the cutting-room floor — in actual practice.

The Professional Conspiracy Theory. Why do we need legal ethics rules at all? Why aren't the same legal rules that govern other agents and fiduciaries sufficient? This theory, subversive to many and apostasy to some, posits that the rules exist mainly to protect the interests of lawyers above all others and to impede what, in their absence, would be legislative and popular control of the bar. True, the bar can no longer be so obvious about its economic self-interest as it was in the days of minimum fee schedules (a/k/a price fixing, see page 176), but that only means it has better learned how to wrap itself in the mantle of the "public interest." Look deeper and it turns out to be "lawyers' interest." Judges (just lawyers in robes) are co-conspirators with the bar. They prevent democratic control of legal services through their use of the inherent powers and separation of powers doctrines discussed below. Even if you think this argument is a bit extreme — which I'm not prejudging — it is certainly necessary to ask for each rule we study (a) whether the rule serves any useful purpose; and (b) whether that purpose is mostly or only useful to the bar.

The "In Service of Other Theories" Theory. Legal ethics does not need its own theory. There are already more than enough theories and theory makers. Instead, the proper content of any ethical rule should respond to the theories developed in other areas of legal and jurisprudential study. The rules, Zelig-like, should adapt themselves as appropriate to serve contract theory, adversary justice theory, criminal law theory, constitutional theory, and so on. Let the scholars in those fields do the heavy theory lifting. The ethics rules will implement the insights and values they propound.

Does Legal Ethics Have An Ideology?

As I am using the word here, an ideology is not the same thing as a theory. This question asks whether the rules are, or a particular rule is, consciously meant to favor certain political, economic, or other interest groups over others. Of course, any legal rule may do that, because rules draw lines and different groups may have different views about where the lines should be, the better to advance their interests. Employers v. employees. Manufacturers v. consumers. Landlords v. tenants. A legal rule may nonetheless properly reconcile the competing interests in the area of the particular rule. Favoring one interest or another is not necessarily bad. It's often inevitable. The result, however, may be a product of political influence.

But political influence should not color the rules that govern lawyers. If the objectives of these rules is to ensure client legal autonomy and to protect clients and victims of clients, among others, shouldn't economic and political interests be irrelevant to deciding the proper rule? Every client should be entitled to the full scope of legal autonomy, full protection against misbehaving lawyers, and so on. The law that the lawyer deciphers for the client may be influenced by interest-group politics. But the law and rules that govern how the lawyer behaves should not be.

I may sound naïve for saying this. I may be naïve. But I don't see ideology lurking behind the legal ethics rules in the sense of an effort to favor one interest group over another. At least, ideology is not a strong presence. Which is not to deny that every rule strikes a balance or that someone cannot say that the balance is in the wrong place. And it is not to deny that balances sometimes are in the wrong place. Much of what we do academically is try to show where that imbalance occurs. But I see that as a contest over theory (or ideas, or values) and not over interest group competition in the narrow sense. You should feel free to disagree with me, and I suppose I would acknowledge some exceptions.

Normative and Empirical Arguments

I should say a final word about the two ways to argue about ethics rules (or probably anything else). We can defend or criticize a rule as right or wrong from the perspective of values. We can say, for example, that confidentiality is usually right because it gives the client a "space" in which to confer fully with and confide candidly in her lawyer, who can then best advise her. That maximizes the client's autonomy within the law, and individual autonomy is an important value. But notice an empirical assumption behind that claim. It is that clients will in fact be more forthcoming if the rules promise confidentiality. We may intuitively accept the accuracy of that assumption, but it is nonetheless an assumption about how people will, in fact, behave. The same empirical question arises when we discuss exceptions that allow or require a lawyer to reveal a client's confidence. While arguments for or against an exception may invoke values such as autonomy, they will also make empirical assumptions about the effect of the exception on client candor and the lawyer's work.

Now, here's a fact that I have always found remarkable. Even though arguments for or against many rules cite how they will affect the behavior of clients, lawyers, and others—although the behavior they are said to encourage or discourage is sometimes the main justification for or against many rules—rarely if ever do we test our empirical assumptions. Sometimes, the assumptions are so intuitively persuasive that lack of testing may not matter. But at other times, the assumptions can be quite debatable (and are debated), and yet the inquiry goes no further, perhaps because testing assumptions is often difficult or even impossible. Or perhaps we are silently making a calculation about the degree of harm any choice risks. For example, let's say we realize that we can't *know* the empirical effect of choosing rule X over rule Y. Both choices have upsides and downsides. One consideration in our choice may be the gravity of the comparative downside risks. With imperfect information, we evaluate and compare worst-case scenarios.

As you study the rules governing lawyers, therefore, you should ask not only what values a particular rule protects (or fails to protect), you should also be sure to identify and articulate the assumptions you may be making about how the rule will likely affect behavior. Do you have a high level of confidence in the accuracy of your assumptions? How important are they to your argument?

Who Makes the Rules?

So much for the metaquestions, at least for now. Let's turn to some practical ones. Asking who makes the rules is a good place to start.

The Constitution guides us here as elsewhere. Most obvious will be the First and Sixth Amendments. The First Amendment appears in the material on lawyer advertising and solicitation (chapter 16), lay participation in law offices, especially public interest offices (chapter 14), and the rights of lawyers to criticize judges or to comment on pending cases (chapter 15). The Sixth Amendment guarantee of the effective assistance of counsel in criminal cases appears in chapter 5's discussion of defense lawyer conflicts, chapter 7's treatment of the ethical duties of lawyers whose clients or witnesses lie (or plan to lie) under oath, and chapter 13's consideration of rules intended to protect the quality of legal services.

The Fifth Amendment's "takings" clause has surfaced in connection with state plans that require lawyers to put certain escrow funds (money belonging to clients or others that the lawyer is holding for a brief time) into interest-bearing accounts, with the interest going to the state to fund legal services for populations in need. See chapter 4. Also prominent is the Privileges and Immunities Clause in Article IV, which has been cited to invalidate laws impeding the ability of lawyers resident in one state to practice in another. See chapter 12. Due process rights restrict judges (chapter 11) and the operation of lawyer disciplinary bodies (chapter 13).

Many states have an "integrated bar," meaning that state bar association membership is mandatory and state law makes the bar a part of the apparatus for governing the profession. The bar may then be called upon to propose, interpret, or enforce rules. Mandatory bar membership means mandatory dues, which has led to litigation by lawyers who claim their First Amendment rights are violated when the state bar spends "their" dues on causes with which they disagree. States with mandatory bar membership include California, Florida, Oregon, Washington, and Wisconsin.

More prevalent sources of rules regulating lawyers are statutes; procedural and evidentiary (for instance, privilege) rules; the common law (especially agency, tort, and contract law, and the law of fiduciary duty); court rules; and state constitutions. State high courts often rely on their own state constitutions to assume responsibility for promulgating rules governing admission to practice and the conduct of attorneys. Sometimes state courts cite affirmative language in the state constitution, sometimes they rely on implications from separation-of-powers principles, and sometimes they speak about the courts' "inherent constitutional power" to regulate the profession. Sometimes, however, courts are not so clear about their source of authority. What they mostly are quite clear about is that courts rule.

Codes of conduct adopted by courts are by far the most important and most frequently debated source of rules governing lawyers. These are discussed shortly. First, though, a further word about the respective roles of judges and lawmakers.

Courts vs. Legislators. The inherent powers doctrine and specific or general constitutional language have been cited not only to support judicial rulemaking but also to invalidate direct legislative efforts to regulate the admission or conduct of lawyers, even when these legislative actions do not contradict any judicial ones. This has been called "negative" inherent power. Not only do we get to make the rules, the courts are saying, if and when we choose to do so, but you lawmakers do *not* get to make them, regardless of what we do or don't do.

The idea here is that the power to regulate the bar belongs to the courts almost exclusively. One effect of the negative inherent powers doctrine is to inhibit direct popular attempts (via legislation) to control the conduct of lawyers. When coupled with judicial deference to the bar's self-regulation, the negative inherent powers doctrine may result in precious little government oversight. Sometimes, however, courts do uphold (or perhaps the word is "tolerate") the regulatory efforts of legislators while taking pains to stress their own supremacy.

An example of the inherent powers doctrine is State ex rel. Fiedler v. Wisconsin Senate, 454 N.W.2d 770 (Wis. 1990), which struck down legislation that imposed a continuing legal education requirement on attorneys who wished to be appointed as guardians ad litem. The court held that "once an attorney has been determined to have met the legislative and judicial threshold requirements and is admitted to practice law, he or she is subject to the judiciary's inherent and exclusive authority to regulate the practice of law." Irwin v. Surdyk's Liquor, 599 N.W.2d 132 (Minn. 1999), held that statutorily imposed limitations on attorney's fee awards violated separation of powers. The Pennsylvania high court, citing its exclusive authority to regulate law practice, held that a state law that required lobbyists to register and report certain information and that prohibited certain conduct by lobbyists (e.g., charging fees contingent on success or lying) was unconstitutional as applied to lawyers who lobby. Gmerek v. State Ethics Commission, 807 A.2d 812 (Pa. 2002) (3-3 opinion affirming lower court). Even where the legislature's goal is to protect clients as consumers against exploitation, jealous courts may disallow it. Preston v. Stoops, 2008 Westlaw 2287217 (Ark. 2008) (refusing to apply deceptive trade practices law to out-of-state lawyers because "any action by the General Assembly to control the practice of law would be a violation of the separation-of-powers doctrine"). In Beyers v. Richmond, 937 A.2d 1082 (Pa. 2007), three justices held that a state's consumer protection law could not apply to lawyers under the state constitution; two justices concurred on the ground that the law was inapplicable as a matter of statutory construction (making the constitutional analysis unnecessary); and two justices dissented. The law was one of general applicability and did not purport to regulate attorneys in particular. Further, the alleged misconduct concerned the business, not the legal work, of the law firm. *Beyers* collects cases nationwide.

Some courts are more tolerant of legislative activity. How do we explain the difference? Crowe v. Tull, 126 P.3d 196 (Colo. 2006), held that the state's consumer protection law could be used to sue lawyers for false advertising. The court, while emphasizing its "inherent and plenary powers . . . to regulate . . . the practice of law," wrote that "some overlap between judicial rulemaking and legislative policy is constitutionally permissible as long as the overlap does not create a substantial conflict." Newton v. Cox, 878 S.W.2d 105 (Tenn. 1994), upheld legislation that limited attorney's fees in medical malpractice cases. The statute, an exercise of "the legislature's police powers, intended to protect the public," did not "directly conflict with the [state] Supreme Court's authority to regulate the practice of law." The court distinguished "situations where the legislative enactment is in direct conflict with and totally abrogates the Court's authority with regard to the practice of law." Chambers v. Stengel, 37 S.W.3d 741 (Ky. 2001), allowed criminal sanctions against attorneys who solicit accident or disaster victims within 30 days of the event causing injury. Even though the court has the power to regulate Kentucky lawyers, the legislature's police power permits "Kentucky to protect its citizens from practices deemed offensive by both in-state and out-of-state attorneys."

Unauthorized practice of law (chapter 12) is a prime area in which judges and lawmakers clash. Lawmakers may authorize "nonlawyers" to perform a particular "legal" service. Such provisions have economic consequences for lawyers and consumers. Do you see why? If such an effort is challenged, a court may invalidate it on the ground that the specified service constitutes "the practice of law" (a broad and fluid term), for which the court may insist that it alone can license practitioners. See, e.g., Cleveland Bar Assn. v. Picklo, 772 N.E.2d 1187 (Ohio 2002) (because conduct of landlord's agent in filing cases in housing court was the practice of law, authorizing statute held unconstitutional).

Ethics Rules.   Codes of ethics, under various names, and cases construing them, are the main source of rules governing the behavior of lawyers. Without doubt, the dominant influence in promulgating such codes has been the American Bar Association (ABA). Some may question the wisdom of allowing those who will be regulated to write the regulations. As we shall see, this skepticism has occasionally proved justified, but less so today because lawyers from diverse practice settings and different perspectives participate in developing the rules. Still, as a rule, only lawyers participate; rarely do clients.

Proponents of the practice argue that self-regulation is the hallmark of a profession. (For the profession's own reaffirmation of this position, see the Preamble to the Model Rules of Professional Conduct.) This loops us into a debate about professionalism: If lawyers are losing professional status because of "creeping commercialism," as some argue, do they also lose the right of self-regulation, assuming they should enjoy it in the first place? Asked another way: What is it about law that makes it a "profession" and thereby justifies allowing lawyers to have so significant a role in regulating their monopoly on the practice of law? Answers to these questions turn on our definition of "profession," a matter to which we presently turn.

How much power, however, do lawyers really have? The ABA is a private organization with no right to impose its rules on anyone. That is why its Code of Professional Responsibility and its Rules of Professional Conduct are both preceded by the word "Model." Before a rule in either document can be more than a model — that is, before it can actually govern a lawyer's behavior — a court must adopt it. Courts, however, have often deferred to the ABA's decisions as modified by proposals from state bar associations. Serious judicial scrutiny has often been the exception, not the rule. To some extent, that is changing, more in some states than in others. The latest ABA model, the Model Rules of Professional Conduct (written in 1983, but amended several times, most recently and extensively in 2002 and 2003) has been accompanied by substantial professional and even popular debate. Alerted, perhaps, by this debate, some courts have rejected a "rubber stamp" role and have exercised greater oversight before adopting the new ABA standards for their states, though the extent of that oversight has varied appreciably. High courts in California, Florida, Massachusetts, the District of Columbia, and New Jersey are among those active in

Court must adopt rule before it can govern

governing their bars, including deciding the content of their ethics rules. Despite these examples, no one should underestimate the influence of local lawyers. The bar is still very much a self-governing institution, and it is likely to remain so indefinitely.

The ABA's first effort at codifying ethical rules saw the adoption in 1908 of the Canons of Professional Ethics, which remained in effect — if of diminishing relevance — for 62 years.[3] Effective in 1970, the ABA (and soon thereafter all states, in some form) adopted the Code of Professional Responsibility (hereafter often referred to simply as the Code or Model Code). The Code is divided into nine Canons, numerous Ethical Considerations (ECs), which are said to be "aspirational," and many Disciplinary Rules (DRs). The courts in some states, like New York, adopted only the Disciplinary Rules.

The Code's excessive ambiguity and its gaps soon became apparent. In 1977, the ABA inaugurated a commission to prepare a new set of rules. That commission soon became known as the Kutak Commission, after Robert J. Kutak, an energetic and visionary lawyer from Omaha, Nebraska, who chaired the commission until his untimely death in early 1983. Meanwhile, perhaps because so many lawyers were implicated in Watergate and because the number of practicing lawyers was rising so rapidly, professional and popular interest in legal ethics increased dramatically. Consequently, the Kutak Commission's work prompted extensive discussion inside and outside bar associations. After much debate and several drafts, the ABA House of Delegates adopted the Model Rules of Professional Conduct (the Rules or Model Rules) on August 2, 1983. Whereas the Code was divided into Canons, ECs, and DRs, the Model Rules assume a "Restatement" format with black letter rules followed by comments. Each comment, according to the Scope section, "explains and illustrates the meaning and purpose of the Rule." They are "intended as guides to interpretation, but the text of each Rule is authoritative." Elsewhere, the Scope section tells us that comments "do not add obligations to the Rules but provide guidance for practicing in compliance with the Rules."

Whereas state adoption of the Model Code had been fairly quick, adoption of the Model Rules was slow. As of late 2008, though, 47 states and the District of Columbia had adopted the Model Rules, although with much variation. New Jersey was first in 1984.

New York continued to follow the Code until 2009, but added language lifted from the Model Rules. In 2007, following a five-year study the New York State Bar Association proposed a modified version of the Model Rules. In December 2008, the courts did adopt a new set of rules. Most of it tracks the old Code, though in restatement format. The bar's recommendations were largely rejected. The most dramatic change is a lawyer's heightened duty to prevent fraud on a tribunal. See page 392. Maine also still adheres to the Code but may be moving toward the Model Rules. Finally, California has long marched to its own drummer. California's Rules of Professional Conduct borrows modestly from the ABA

---

3. Were there legal ethics in the prior century? See Norman Spaulding, The Myth of Civil Republicanism: Interrogating the Ideology of Antebellum Legal Ethics, 71 Fordham L. Rev. 1397 (2003) (arguing that "the morally activist concept of lawyering so often said to prevail among nineteeth-century civic republican legal elites is more mythical than real"); Russell Pearce, Rediscovering the Republican Origins of the Legal Ethics Codes, 6 Geo. J. Legal Ethics 241 (1992).

Model Rules, but much of it contains provisions unique to that state. A state bar committee in California has been working on proposed revisions that, if adopted, will bring the state's rules closer to the ABA model.

The Kutak Commission proposed several drafts of the Model Rules between 1977 and August 1983. Occasionally, you will see cites to and excerpts from one of the publicly released drafts, which are dated January 30, 1980, May 30, 1981, and June 30, 1982. I will refer to them especially when the substance of a proposed rule differs significantly from the corresponding rule finally adopted by the ABA in 1983 or where there is no corresponding rule adopted by the ABA.[4]

One Size Fits (Almost) All.   As you study the codes and rules of ethics, consider that they apply to all lawyers without regard to practice setting or nature of client. A lawyer in suburban California who does house closings, wills, and like work for individuals is governed by the same rules as the California lawyer who works in Paris on international transactions and is a partner in a 1,500-lawyer firm the clients of which are global companies on the Fortune 500 list. The Model Rules do differentiate here and there. There are rules aimed at trial lawyers, a rule for prosecutors, and a rule aimed at corporate lawyers. There is also the suggestion that when lawyers have to get a client's informed consent (e.g., to get consent to a conflict), less need be explained to a "sophisticated" client. But these are exceptions. Mostly the Model Rules do not explicitly recognize different practice settings or the nature of the clients. That may have made sense decades ago, but does it make sense today? On the other hand, is there any way to avoid it? Should we draft different documents for lawyers in different kinds of practices? Is that even feasible?

Ethics Rules v. The Borderless Market for Legal Services: A Paradox. We interrupt this story to recognize a remarkable fact. The ethics rules for lawyers vary between modestly and significantly from place to place (depending on the rule and the place). There is greater dissimilarity today than during the era of the Model Code. No two states have identical rules. We have moved toward increased idiosyncrasy. Yet the American legal profession is more mobile now than ever. Lawyers freely practice across state lines, both physically and virtually, i.e., via e-mail, fax, and telephone. Practicing across state lines could not be easier. The laws of each state are immediately available to lawyers anywhere on desktop computers. Federal and international laws are identical everywhere. How can we reconcile the disparities among state legal ethics rules with the fact that, increasingly, lawyers (and not just large firm lawyers) view the entire nation, or at least their region of the country, as the relevant market for their services, especially if they specialize in a particular legal service?

---

4. For a discussion of the role and possible motives of the ABA in preparing and adopting ethics codes, see Richard Abel, Why Does the ABA Promulgate Ethical Rules?, 59 Tex. L. Rev. 639 (1981); Deborah Rhode, Why the ABA Bothers: A Functional Perspective on Professional Codes, 59 Tex. L. Rev. 689 (1981); Marvin Frankel, Why Does Professor Abel Work at a Useless Task?, 59 Tex. L. Rev. 723 (1981). For analyses of the interests at work in the Model Code and Model Rules, see, respectively, Thomas Morgan, The Evolving Concept of Professional Responsibility, 90 Harv. L. Rev. 702 (1977), and Stephen Gillers, What We Talked About When We Talked About Ethics: A Critical View of the Model Rules, 46 Ohio St. L.J. 243 (1985). Ted Schneyer reviews the six-year debate over the Model Rules from a political perspective in Professionalism as Bar Politics: The Making of the Model Rules of Professional Conduct, 14 Law & Soc. Inquiry 677 (1989).

The answer is we can't. This disjuncture between an expanding national bar and different local rules has created "cracks" in the regulatory edifice, which will concern us several times in this book, most notably in chapter 12B ("Transient Lawyers and Multijurisdictional Practice"). One consequence has been a choice-of-rule rule for when a lawyer's work crosses borders. See Model Rule 8.5.

The Ethics 2000 Commission.   In 1997, ABA President Jerome Shestack appointed a commission to study the Model Rules and recommend amendments. The chair was Chief Justice E. Norman Veasey of Delaware. Its Reporters were Nancy Moore (Boston University) and Carl Pierce (University of Tennessee). Although its official name was "The Commission on Evaluation of the Rules of Professional Conduct," it came to be known as the Ethics 2000 Commission (or E2K) because it was charged to report in the year 2000. It did issue a report in November 2000, but then made significant changes. The ABA House of Delegates began debating the commission's recommendations at its August 2001 convention and continued through 2002. The House of Delegates (which has 539 members) adopted nearly all of the Ethics 2000 Commission's recommendations. One that failed would have required written retainer agreements in most cases (discussed in chapter 4). Another would have allowed law firms to use screens to avoid some disqualifying conflicts (chapters 5 and 6). The House also rejected the commission's proposals to expand exceptions to a lawyer's duty of confidentiality (chapter 2). However, as next discussed, those exceptions and another were adopted a year later under the threat of federal intervention.

The Task Force on Corporate Responsibility.   In July 2002, as part of the Sarbanes-Oxley Act, which responded to a wave of corporate scandals (e.g., Enron, Tyco, Worldcom) that alarmed many, Congress passed and President Bush signed legislation that, among many other things, required the SEC to adopt certain rules governing lawyers appearing and practicing before it and authorized the agency to adopt additional rules as it might choose. This was a cataclysmic event in the history of the regulation of the bar because it gave explicit authority to (and to some extent required) a federal agency to make rules governing the practice of lawyers, in particular lawyers in an important and lucrative area of work. Whatever rules the Securities and Exchange Commission adopted would affect the lives of many professionals and their clients. (We discuss this development further in chapter 10.) More threatening, other federal agencies might seek the same authority. The ABA president quickly appointed a Task Force, headed by James H. Cheek III, of Tennessee, and charged it to propose rules and policies responsive to the corporate scandals. Undoubtedly, this was in part a defensive effort to show the SEC that the profession could react appropriately and thereby to discourage rules broader than the congressional mandate required. The effort did not entirely succeed although it did lead to significant agency deference to self-regulation. The federal threat also led the ABA to accept the two exceptions to lawyer confidentiality it had rejected just a year earlier. These are addressed in chapter 2B2. The ABA also accepted the Task Force's recommendation to amend Rule 1.13, which describes duties of lawyers for organizations, to permit those lawyers to go outside the organization (that is, "whistleblow") when the unlawful conduct of officials poses a likely threat of serious harm to the client. See chapter 10C.

Ethics Rules as Authority.   Different jurisdictions accord the Code and Rules varying degrees of respect. The New York Court of Appeals, for example, has said that the Code does not have "the status of decisional or statutory law." In re Weinstock, 351 N.E.2d 647 (N.Y. 1976). Nor is the court "constrained to read the rules literally or effectuate the intent of the drafters." On the other hand, the court will look to the rules "as guidelines to be applied with due regard for the broad range of interests at stake." People v. Herr, 658 N.E.2d 1032 (N.Y. 1995). Compare In re Vrdolyak, 560 N.E.2d 840 (Ill. 1990) ("Code operates with the force of law"). Federal courts often rely on a state's Code or Rule provisions, although it is sometimes said that there is no obligation to do so. "The ethical standards imposed upon attorneys in federal court are a matter of federal law." Bell Atlantic Corp. v. Bolger, 2 F.3d 1304 (3d Cir. 1993). "Federal courts may adopt state or ABA rules as their ethical standards, but whether and how these rules are to be applied are questions of federal law." In re American Airlines, Inc., 972 F.2d 605 (5th Cir. 1992).

Other Authorities.   Beyond the Code or Rules as adopted in particular jurisdictions and construed by judges, the ethics framework includes interpretations of these documents by bar association ethics committees. Most state and many local bar associations have ethics committees, composed of their members, and so does the ABA. A lawyer may write (or in an emergency sometimes telephone) for advice about prospective conduct. For example, a lawyer may be inclined to accept a new client but fear that conflict rules forbid it. He can ask an ethics committee for an advisory opinion. Compliance with such an opinion demonstrates a lawyer's good faith, although the opinions generally are not binding on a disciplinary committee or court. Important (that is, nonroutine) ethics opinions are published as guidelines for other lawyers and for whatever persuasive force (ranging from none to considerable) they may have with judges in future cases. Published opinions omit identifying information. Many bar groups, including the ABA, do not even await a lawyer's query before choosing to write on important new issues. As such, their work takes on the character of advisory opinions on broad questions meant to guide lawyers and courts. The ABA's opinions are particularly influential in the courts because its ethics committee is interpreting the organization's own widely copied rules. The ABA opinions and many state bar opinions are available on Lexis and Westlaw, and the state and local opinions are generally available on the bar association's site.

In addition to the sources listed here, ethics researchers may consult law review literature, where articles on professional regulation are appearing with greater frequency, and various books, treatises, manuals, and reporters. The Georgetown Journal of Legal Ethics, inspired by the late Father Robert Drinan, began publication in 1987 and has become essential reading for anyone working in this field. The multivolume Lawyers' Manual on Professional Conduct, published by the American Bar Association and the Bureau of National Affairs, is an exceptional resource for research in the area. Not only does the Manual monitor court decisions and other developments, it also provides summaries of important ethics opinions (and for ABA opinions, the full text).

In 1986 the American Law Institute undertook the massive job of producing a Restatement of the Law Governing Lawyers. Charles Wolfram of Cornell Law School, the Reporter, and associate Reporters John Leubsdorf, Rutgers

University Law School, Thomas Morgan, George Washington University National Law Center, and (from 1989 to 1993) Linda Mullenix, University of Texas Law School, produced many drafts toward the creation of a document that proposes to restate in black letter format the legal and ethical rules that govern the American legal profession. The Restatement was completed in 1999, and a two-volume set was published a year later. You will see it cited throughout this book.

Examining "the diverse and sometimes conflicting responsibilities of the modern-day lawyer," a Development Note in the Harvard Law Review looked at lawyers' responsibilities (including under state ethics codes) to clients and third parties, to the public, and to the courts. It then examined "lawyers' responses to these numerous responsibilities," especially efforts to shift or limit financial exposure. Note, Lawyers' Responsibilities and Lawyers' Responses, 107 Harv. L. Rev. 1547 (1994). See also Part IV ("Lawyer Conduct and Corporate Misconduct") in Note, Corporations and Society, 117 Harv. L. Rev. 2227 (2004).

Real Ethics. Are we forgetting something? Even using shorthand, the subject is called legal *ethics.* Do legal ethics have anything to do with real ethics — the kind that moral philosophers study in the tradition of Plato, Kant, and Mill? Yes and no. One interesting fact is that the title of the model ABA document has moved further and further away from ethics, as such, and toward pronouncements that are rather lawlike. Whereas the original document had "Professional Ethics" in its title, the next version opted for "Professional Responsibility," and that title has now yielded to "Professional Conduct." But "ethics" lives on. Appeals to ethics let the bar proclaim its allegiance to ancient ideals, though no effort has been made to ask real ethicists their views. (Someday, probably at the end of my career, I will attend a conference on legal ethics with a button reading "WWAS" — What Would Aristotle Say?) In recent decades, however, real ethicists have turned to the "ethics" of lawyers and held them up to the standards of moral philosophy. Richard Wasserstrom's pathbreaking article, Lawyers as Professionals: Some Moral Issues, 5 Hum. Rts. 1 (1975), was one of the first.

This attention has encouraged legal academics to join in turning the spotlight of moral philosophy on the behavior of practicing lawyers. David Luban's work, Lawyers and Justice: An Ethical Study (1988), is a prime example. Susan Kupfer's focus is the "ethical autonomy" of the lawyer as she seeks to "sketch a theory of ethical practice that would inform how a lawyer might retain and utilize moral initiatives in her practice." In doing so, she draws on "parallel recent developments in postmodern thought and in political theory as to the intersection of the individual's development of an authentic self and the community's reflection of larger goals." Susan Kupfer, Authentic Legal Practice, 10 Geo. J. Legal Ethics 33 (1996). Invaluable here, too, is Deborah Rhode's critique in Ethical Perspectives on Legal Practice, 37 Stan. L. Rev. 589 (1985). In Ethical Discretion in Lawyering, 101 Harv. L. Rev. 1083 (1988), Professor William Simon argues that as a "professional duty of reflective judgment," lawyers "should have ethical discretion to refuse to assist in the pursuit of legally permissible courses of action and in the assertion of potentially enforceable legal claims."

So far there has been little cross-fertilization, as a *practical* matter, between the philosophical and the professional enterprises. Undoubtedly, many lawyers would like to keep it that way. Moral philosophers may teach at law schools and influence law teachers, but they have not yet been invited to join the profession's ethics-writing committees. And although hospitals recognize the position of medical ethicist, so far no law firm has created a parallel position for legal ethicists versed in moral philosophy. So while the philosophers are not going to go away and are in fact becoming more influential in the academy, the force of their influence on the courts and the practicing bar remains to be seen.

What Is Professionalism?

In the mid-1980s, the word "professionalism" began to appear with some frequency in bar publications and to be heard increasingly at bar meetings large and small. The American Bar Association and some local bar groups formed committees on professionalism (or committees on the profession) to study the topic and write reports about it. Many meetings were held; many reports were written, most of them saying the same things. In 1986, the ABA's Commission on Professionalism issued its report, titled ". . . in the spirit of public service": A Blueprint for the Rekindling of Lawyer Professionalism, which is reprinted at 112 F.R.D. 243 (1986). The report offers dozens of solutions to correct the perception "that the Bar might be moving away from the principles of professionalism." In defining "professionalism," the commission quoted Roscoe Pound's 1953 definition of "profession":

> The term refers to a group . . . pursuing a learned art as a common calling in the spirit of public service — no less a public service because it may incidentally be a means of livelihood. Pursuit of the learned art in the spirit of a public service is the primary purpose.[5]

Today, we would strike "incidentally." The commission also quoted a definition for "profession" framed by Professor Eliot Freidson, a sociologist and commission member:

1. That its practice requires substantial intellectual training and the use of complex judgments,
2. That since clients cannot adequately evaluate the quality of the service, they must trust those they consult,
3. That the client's trust presupposes that the practitioner's self-interest is overbalanced by devotion to serving both the client's interest and the public good, and
4. That the occupation is self-regulating — that is, organized in such a way as to assure the public and the courts that its members are competent, do not violate their client's trust, and transcend their own self-interest.[6]

5. Roscoe Pound, The Lawyer from Antiquity to Modern Times 5 (1953).

6. For critiques of the commission's work, see Nancy Moore, Professionalism Reconsidered, 1987 Am. B. Found. Res. J. 773; Ronald Rotunda, Lawyers and Professionalism: A Commentary on the Report of the American Bar Association Commission on Professionalism, 18 Loy. U. Chi. L.J. 1149 (1987).

These definitions share a theme: A professional subordinates self-interest and private gain to the interests of clients or to the public good generally. Now, obviously, subordination must be a matter of degree or else professionals would be expected to work without regard to a client's or patient's ability to pay. Nothing so radical has been suggested. (In fact, the bar has long resisted mandatory pro bono requirements. See chapter 4F.) On the contrary, professionalism committees are quick to recognize the economic pressures on lawyers and their need to earn a living. Some forthrightly acknowledge that the practice of law shares many of the attributes of a business. The search seems to be for the proper balance between professionalism and business. Certain trends are said to take the profession too far in the wrong direction. We are warned against "overcommercialization."

No one can say for sure how it came about that so many lawyers in so many bar associations decided, seemingly simultaneously, to spend so many hours at bar dinners debating what it means to be a professional and drafting codes of professionalism for others to put on their shelves. Your guess is as good as mine, but since I'm writing this and you're not, I'll offer two thoughts: First, the advent of lawyer advertising, following the *Bates* decision protecting this activity in 1977 (see chapter 16A), inspired (if that's the right word) many offensive marketing schemes, which, coupled with pervasive, if tamer, efforts at self-promotion, conveyed the impression that lawyers were absolutely *consumed* with the goal of making money. Professionalism might then be seen as an antidote to this apparent fixation. Second, as the number of lawyers in the nation dramatically increased relative to its nonlawyer population (from 1 in every 625 persons in 1960 to less than half that ratio by century's end), a need was felt to remind lawyers that they were members of an elite club, or if (alas) the club was no longer quite so elite, at least it behooved lawyers to behave as though it were. Whatever. Professionalism is now a permanent resident of the legal world. You can find talk of it wherever lawyers congregate.

It is too soon to say what effect the idea of professionalism will have on rules regulating the practice of law. Several possibilities exist. The professionalism theme may be viewed as something of a public relations campaign through which lawyers reaffirm — to themselves at least and perhaps to the nation — their special status in American society. This is at least part of it, as anyone reading the visionary reports of bar association professionalism committees should quickly glean.

More substantively, professionalism may represent an effort to improve the behavior of the bar other than through rules whose violation carries sanctions. We see several indications of this. For example, in August 1988 the ABA House of Delegates adopted a Creed of Professionalism and a Pledge of Professionalism, though the former carried the disclaimer that "nothing in such a creed shall be deemed to . . . alter existing standards of conduct against which lawyer negligence might be judged or become a basis for the imposition of civil liability of any kind." The creed contains 33 numbered paragraphs describing a lawyer's responsibility toward clients, opposing parties and counsel, tribunals, and the system of justice. Much of it overlaps provisions of the Model Rules ("I will refrain from utilizing delaying tactics"). Other provisions are hortatory, with a tinge of religiosity ("my responsibilities as a lawyer include a devotion to the public good").

Finally, the concept of professionalism may actually come to influence both the content of rules regulating the conduct of lawyers and the way judges decide cases. For example, argument about whether law is a business or a profession has been prominent in the debate over whether law firms should be permitted to operate nonlaw businesses and have nonlawyer partners. See chapter 14. (I use the word "nonlawyer" with a certain self-consciousness. With some accuracy, it has been labeled a "lawyer chauvinist" word. Members of no other profession so describe everyone else. Have you ever heard of a nondentist or a nonarchitect?) The same theme appears in Supreme Court decisions on the constitutionality of state rules that limit ways in which lawyers may market their services. See chapter 16.

The ABA's Commission on Professionalism concluded: "All segments of the Bar should resist the temptation to make the acquisition of wealth a principal goal of law practice." But exactly what does that mean? And how should this caution influence support or opposition to particular proposals? For example, should lawyer advertising be opposed because it makes lawyers too conscious of the business aspects of practicing law, a reason Justice O'Connor found persuasive in her Shapero v. Kentucky Bar Assn. dissent (chapter 16B)? Or should lawyer advertising be supported because it tends, as the Federal Trade Commission concluded, to reduce the price of routine legal services?

Beyond debates about legal advertising and lawyer-owned businesses, a third trend that to many signals professionalism's decline is a supposed increase in lawyer incivility—also labeled "hardball," "Rambo," or "scorched earth" tactics—especially in litigation. Panel discussions, indeed entire conferences, on civility and incivility became as common in the 1980s and 1990s as red suspenders on male trial lawyers. A Seventh Circuit committee, headed by Federal District Judge Marvin E. Aspen, produced a study of lawyer civility. The Final Report of the Committee on Civility of the Seventh Federal Judicial Circuit, reprinted at 143 F.R.D. 441 (1992). Amy Mashburn explores the relationship between civility codes and professional hierarchy. Among other things, she considers "whether civility codes reflect unconscious desires to impose a reactionary and authoritarian conformity upon a rapidly diversifying profession and to resist redistributions of power to those who have been historically excluded from the practice of law and denied access to legal services." Amy Mashburn, Professionalism as Class Ideology: Civility Codes and Bar Hierarchy, 28 Val. U. L. Rev. 657 (1994).

Class-based or not, the "civility and professionalism" campaign has been influential. Even lawyers too young to remember whether the particular Camelot ever existed may yet be heard to invoke that kinder, gentler period when courtesy was king and lawyers treated each other like, well, professionals. Bar chatter today is spiced with anecdotes of other lawyers' (usually an adversary's) monstrous behavior. Meanwhile, some seek to turn the perceived decline to advantage by proudly (and loudly) proclaiming their readiness to "go right up to the line" for their clients. Yes, sir! Right up to the bloody line! This presumes, of course, that the *line*, like the one down the center of a two-lane road, is in all matters conspicuous, so that lawyers can always know when they've crossed it. Much of this book is meant to tell you that if ever there were such a time, it has long since passed and will never return. RIP.

FURTHER READING

A comprehensive effort to articulate a vision of professionalism comes from former Dean Anthony Kronman of Yale Law School. In his book, The Lost Lawyer (1993), Dean Kronman urges a return to the "ideal" of the "lawyer-statesman." He argues that this "ideal is now dying in the American legal profession. As it does, lawyers will find it harder to believe their work provides intrinsic fulfillment of any kind. . . . The result is a growing sense, among lawyers generally, that their yearning to be engaged in some lifelong endeavor that has value in its own right can no longer be satisfied in their professional work."

Kronman spends the first part of his book "explaining, in new but simple terms, the timeless value of the virtue that [the ideal of the lawyer-statesman] honors and the crucial role this virtue plays in the practice of law." The balance of the book describes "the intellectual and institutional forces that are now arrayed against the ideal of the lawyer-statesman and that together have caused its decline." Among these are movements in legal thought that share "an anti-prudentialist bias," the explosive growth of American law firms, and the "bureaucratization of our courts."

Professor Deborah Rhode of Stanford Law School has published In the Interests of Justice (2000). Professor Rhode takes on the length and breadth of the legal profession, from the education of lawyers, to advocacy structures, to the maldistribution of legal services and methodologies of lawyer regulation. "The central problem facing the American legal profession," she explains, "is its own unwillingness to come to terms with what the problems are. At issue are competing values and concerns. Yet bar commentary on professionalism tends to paper over two central conflicts: the tensions between lawyers' economic and non-economic interests, and the tensions between professional and public interests. Money is, of course, at the root of both conflicts." She calls on lawyers "to accept personal moral responsibility for the consequences of their professional acts," for "equitable access to legal services and adequate choices in the services available," and for "public accountability for professional regulation. . . . All too often, bar ethical codes and enforcement committees have resolved conflicts between professional and public interests in favor of those doing the resolving."

The third book-length effort to develop a theory of legal ethics is William Simon's volume, The Practice of Justice: A Theory of Lawyers' Ethics (1998). Simon demonstrates what he sees as the weaknesses in what he calls the "Dominant View" of legal ethics, the view that imposes on lawyers the duty, or at least the authority, to pursue the client's goals with undiluted zeal. Simon prefers a theory of legal ethics that he calls the Contextual View, which posits that "the lawyer should take such actions as, considering the relevant circumstances of a particular case, seem likely to promote justice."

There continues to be a bull market in articles and books on professionalism, or some phase of it, and on the relationship between legal ethics and morality. The explanation might lie in the fact that these topics permit — may even demand — the kind of interdisciplinary examination that the legal academy relishes. Writing on professionalism, an author can incorporate in one place lessons from legal ethics, moral philosophy, history, economics, and even the sociology of work. In addition to other works cited throughout the book, Russell Pearce's reaction is skepticism over the utility of continuing with the "Professional Paradigm" in the face of the obvious trend toward a "Business Paradigm." Professor Pearce does not suggest that law practice go wholly unregulated, subject only to market forces, but he does urge a middle ground that he believes would generate more competition and improve the quality of the product. Russell Pearce, The Professional Paradigm Shift: Why Discarding Professional Ideology Will Improve the Conduct and Reputation of the Bar, 70 N.Y.U. L. Rev. 1229 (1995). Looking at professionalism from another angle is Milton Regan, Jr., in Law Firms, Competition Penalties, and the Values of Professionalism, 13 Geo. J. Legal Ethics 1 (1999). Professor Regan uses the late-twentieth-century trend of greater competition among law firms and greater mobility of lawyers between firms to analyze the effect on professionalism of the rules that forbid law firms to impose "competition penalties" against lawyers who depart to compete in other firms. Professor Regan argues that, contrary to what the profession seems to assume is a salutary prohibition against these penalties, in fact they "may create space for nurturance of a distinctive firm culture that promotes the non-economic values traditionally included under the banner of professionalism."

On the interplay between legal ethics and moral theory, Professor Katherine Kruse "focuses attention on a subject that has been largely missing from the debate among legal ethicists: the challenge of moral pluralism." She offers a "moral conflict of interest" analysis to "cure the deficiencies in both traditional and social justice models of lawyering." Lawyers, Justice, and the Challenge of Moral Pluralism, 90 Minnesota L. Rev. 389 (2005). Bradley Wendel tackles the morality questions by looking at the Department of Justice's "torture memos" in Legal Ethics and the Separation of Law and Morals, 91 Cornell L. Rev. 67 (2005).

Using the "torture memos," Enron, and the "Catholic Church's ongoing sex abuse crisis," Robert Vischer examines the "various normative theories that have been proffered by academics and adhered to by the profession" and offers "some preliminary paths by which to address [the] fundamental disconnect between moral perspective and the normative theories." Legal Advice as Moral Perspective, 19 Geo. J. Legal Ethics 225 (2006).

Finally, as the bar celebrated the document's centenary, there has of late been renewed interest in the 1908 Canons of Ethics, proving once again that everything old becomes new again. Happy 100, Canons, despite your faults. James Altman "attempts to place the Canons in their particular historical context and to understand some of the meaning they had for those who promulgated or adopted them." James Altman, Considering the A.B.A.'s 1908 Canons of Ethics, 71 Fordham L. Rev. 2395 (2003). Or could it be that the good old days had better regulations? Benjamin Barton seems to think so. He endorses a return to the "moral, ethical, and practical guidance on how to practice law" that the Canons once provided to the bar. He argues that the 1970 Code of Professional Responsibility undercut this "unified statement" by separating "general considerations from the mandatory minimums," and that the Model Rules "eliminated the broad, philosophical standards" entirely, turning the governing document "into a quasi-criminal set of rules." Benjamin Barton, The ABA, The Rules, and Professionalism: The Mechanics of Self-Defeat and a Call for a Return to the Ethical, Moral and Practical Approach of the Canons, 83 N.C.L. Rev. 411 (2005).

The ABA threw a party for the Canons' centenary, with papers and panels but no cake. The papers, by Judith Maute, Deborah Rhode, Irma Russell, Ted Schneyer, Laurel Terry, Robert Vischer, and others are collected in the November 2008 edition of The Professional Lawyer (Art Garwin, ed.)

Part One

THE ATTORNEY-CLIENT RELATIONSHIP

II

Defining the Attorney-Client Relationship

- *Who Is a Client?*
- *A Lawyer's Duties to Clients*
- *Who Makes Which Decisions About the Work?*

In the beginning is the client. But also before the beginning and after the end. Which is another way of saying that many rules studied here may apply even before a person formally becomes a client (even if he or she never does become a client) and may continue even after the work is done and lawyer and client have gone their separate ways.

Lawyers love to quote Henry Brougham, the great British barrister and Lord Chancellor, who said that "an advocate, in the discharge of his duty, knows but one person in all the world, and that person is his client."[1] You can see how clarifying, how professionally liberating, that idea can be. One person. In all the world. But like all grand statements, it's not entirely true. Lawyers also have obligations to courts, adversaries, the public, partners, and associates. Brougham's reference to "one person" may be good public relations, but it's a bit over the top. Lawyers have interests of their own, as well, which may clash with those of clients. Still, fealty to clients (and its limits) is the primary focus of the ethical and legal rules governing lawyers, and it must therefore be ours. Whether these responsibilities, in addition to being more numerous, should always be viewed as more important than avoiding harm to others or the demands of "justice" or the "public interest" — and if so, when — are questions for debate. Indeed, debate is unavoidable.

The debate is more likely to occur in law schools and perhaps bar committees than in law offices. In the tumult of daily practice, lawyers don't have much time for the Big Questions. Many lawyers would generally agree with a veteran Connecticut trial lawyer's comment to me when I asked about the bar's duty to the public interest: "I serve the public interest by fighting for the private interests of each of my clients, one at a time," he said, and vehemently, too. He obviously had no truck with my highfalutin' notions. Is he right? Lord Brougham would

1. Trial of Queen Caroline 8 (J. Nightingale ed., 1821).

probably say yes. Rejecting any qualifiers, Brougham argued that "hazards and costs to other persons" are of no concern to the lawyer, who "must not regard the alarm, the torments, the destruction which he may bring upon others. . . . [H]e must go on reckless of the consequences, though it should be his unhappy fate to involve his country in confusion."[2] No ambiguity there. Is that what legal ethics rules (should) require, tolerate, or encourage?

Well, yes and no. Lawyers have a tendency to describe their commitment to their clients with the kind of fervor generally associated with religious zealots, Fourth of July orators, or deans at alumni events. If nothing else, it plays well; but, to be fair, the passion is truly felt. Passion, however, is neither a useful tool for analysis nor a reliable guide to professional conduct. We do have rules, after all, and some of them subordinate pursuit of a client's goals to other values. Sometimes, in fact, the clash is not between a client's interests and those other values but is instead a conflict between the interests of two (or more) current clients or between current and former clients. But when and who wins these contests? That's a question this book will try to help you answer while recognizing that there is and always has been much disagreement.

This chapter introduces the main attributes of the attorney-client relationship. What you study here is the foundation for much that follows. We will examine the lawyer's duties of competence, confidentiality (including the attorney-client privilege), loyalty, and diligence; the lawyer's status as an agent for and fiduciary toward clients; the lawyer's duty to keep a client informed about the client's matter; the allocation between client and lawyer of authority to choose the goals the lawyer will pursue and the means for reaching them; and the rules that determine how the relationship, once formed, ends.

In fairness, though, we should say a final word about Lord Brougham (who has an encore at page 355). The Lord made his comments while representing a client, and not just any client but the Queen of England, against a criminal charge of adultery. So it is possible to view his warning as a tactical effort to scare the opposition by threatening to go after the king. If so, it worked.[3]

A. IS THERE A CLIENT HERE?

A threshold question that recurs throughout this book is: What makes someone a client? That question is answered by case law, not by the Rules. But much can turn on the answer, such as whether a lawyer has a conflict of interest that restricts his or her practice and the practice of office colleagues, whether a lawyer is liable in malpractice or subject to discipline, and whether communications with the lawyer are confidential or privileged. For lovers of ambiguity, the question (is *X* a client) sometimes lacks an easy answer. Lawyers do love ambiguity, and you can see why. Ambiguity creates contests, requiring the services of

---

2. Id.
3. For a riveting account of the trial and of Lord Brougham's prowess as a lawyer, see Jane Robins, *The Trial of Queen Caroline* (Free Press 2006).

lawyers. Much of what lawyers do, especially in litigation, is find ambiguity, at least when apparent clarity disserves their clients. In transactional matters, lawyers avoid ambiguities that may harm their clients, but not those that a client may later exploit to advantage. But lawyers do *not* love ambiguity that creates dilemmas for lawyers, not when guessing wrong can be costly. Live with it. Lawyers, like others whose professional or commercial lives are governed by complex regulatory systems, operate in a risk environment where the answer to the question "May I do that?" will often be "Maybe. Maybe not. How risk-averse are you?"

The vast majority of lawyer-client relationships are still formed the old-fashioned way. By agreement, which can be implied.

> An attorney-client relationship is formed when: (1) a person manifests to a lawyer the person's intent that the lawyer provide legal services for the person; and . . . (b) the lawyer fails to manifest lack of consent to do so, and the lawyer knows or reasonably should know that the person reasonably relies on the lawyer to provide the services.

[handwritten: Definition of Atty-Client]

Attorney Grievance Comm'n of Maryland v. Kreamer, 946 A.2d 500 (2008). Court assignment is another common route to a professional relationship. But that's not the end of it.

"The client is no longer simply the person who walks into a law office," Judge Arthur Sprecher presciently wrote more than three decades ago in Westinghouse Electric Corp. v. Kerr-McGee Corp., 580 F.2d 1311 (7th Cir. 1978), capturing in a short, understated sentence an emerging trend whose reality has since become commonplace. So, for example, in Togstad v. Vesely, Otto, Miller & Keefe (page 707), a lawyer was held to have a professional relationship with Mrs. Togstad for purposes of malpractice liability although he *declined* to accept her case. Mr. Togstad was also a client although he and the lawyer had apparently never met. In Williams v. Ely, 668 N.E.2d 799 (Mass. 1996), an intermediary formed a professional relationship between a law firm and two people that the firm's lawyers had never met: The firm gave advice to *A*, which as the firm knew would be relayed to *B* and *C*. The firm filed papers for *B* and *C* and eventually sent them a bill. And, as we shall see in the material on conflicts of interest (pages 297 and 321), companies that are members of trade groups may be deemed clients of lawyers who represent those groups, at least for certain purposes.

Money need not change hands to create a client-lawyer relationship. A lawyer appointed by a court to represent an indigent criminal defendant has a professional relationship with the defendant and will generally be liable in malpractice for errors (see Ferri v. Ackerman, page 746). It is of no moment that lawyer and client do not get along (see Morris v. Slappy, page 820) or that they disagree on strategy (see Jones v. Barnes, page 89).

Even though a client-lawyer relationship can arise without a payment, the fact of payment is pretty good evidence of a relationship. A lawyer would be hard-pressed to deny a person's claim that he or she was the lawyer's client in the face of a bill and a canceled check. But it would not be impossible. As we shall see (page 231), a lawyer may be paid by one person to represent another, in which case the second person, not the first, is the lawyer's client. See Model Rules 1.8(f) and 5.4(c). See also In re Grand Jury Subpoena (Reyes-Requena), 926 F.2d 1423 (5th Cir. 1991), holding that the identity of a person who pays a lawyer's fee to represent another is not protected by the attorney-client privilege unless the lawyer can show that the fee payer was also meant to be a client of the lawyer and that the payer's identity was part of a confidential communication.

Courts are alert to what a person claiming to be a client might reasonably have believed under the circumstances, especially if the person has given the lawyer confidential information because the lawyer was performing a legal service that would benefit that person among others. In Analytica, Inc. v. NPD Research, Inc., (see page 310), a company wanted to give an employee stock as a reward for good service. The company gave financial information to a law firm that the employee hired for tax advice on the transaction. When the firm later sued the company for antitrust violations, it was in a position to use the company's own financial information against it. The firm was disqualified.

An attorney client relationship can arise via a law firm's website. Barton v. United States District Court, 410 F.3d 1104 (9th Cir. 2005) (protecting as privileged a potential client's internet communication with a law firm). A lawyer who gives advice over the phone on a 900 telephone number (where the caller is charged a fee depending on the length of the call) forms a client-lawyer relationship with the caller. Utah Opinion 96-12.

In certain situations conducive to misunderstanding, the Model Rules expressly require that lawyers clarify a possible misimpression. See Rules 1.13(f) and 4.3. Similarly, when a lawyer considers a representation to have ended, she should inform the client that she no longer is a client if there is a reasonable chance that the client may believe the representation is continuing. People v. Bennett, 810 P.2d 661 (Colo. 1991) (relationship is ongoing unless and until the client understands, or reasonably should understand, that he can no longer depend on it).

Duties in the professional relationship are, as we shall see, based in part on the law of agency. Even when a client-lawyer relationship is established, it almost always has a finite scope, as do principal-agent relationships generally. For example, in an antitrust case the Brobeck firm was retained to file a certiorari petition for Telex. Brobeck, Phleger & Harrison v. Telex Corp. (page 144). Brobeck had no right or duty to advise Telex on a commercial lease. The Telex retainer agreement was quite specific, but often the contours of the relationship will not be as clear. If a lawyer is retained to bring a negligence claim following a car crash, she has no responsibility for the client's employment contract. But must the lawyer protect the client's no-fault insurance benefits arising from the crash, even though that service was never mentioned? The client may look at the matter holistically, while the lawyer may define the retainer by reference to a particular service. So the client thinks, "This lawyer will help me get the money I'm owed because of this accident," while the lawyer thinks, "I'm retained only to sue the other driver for damages." Once again, courts will expect the lawyer to be sensitive to, and to clarify, any ambiguity. (That obligation is lessened if the client is sophisticated or is dealing with the lawyer through other lawyers, as in the *Telex* case.)

The conventional image of the client-lawyer relationship posits two people who have agreed that one will provide a defined service to the other for a fee. However, no formalism is necessary to create the relationship, nor must the participants be limited to two. (Sometimes, however, a lawyer must put the agreement in writing. See page 160.) There may be several or many lawyers and several or many clients. Common interest arrangements, where multiple lawyers and their clients collaborate, perhaps against a common foe, may create relationships with attributes of the lawyer-client relationship between one lawyer and the client of another lawyer (see page 282). Nor must the client be a person. Corporations, trade associations, estates, and governments may all be clients. Lawyers must still be people, of course. Whether the lawyers practice in a partnership, professional corporation, or legal aid office, one rule that has not changed is that flesh-and-blood professionals (as well, perhaps, as their colleagues, firms, and employers; see page 721) will be responsible for their failures.

Another type of "client" is the class, a collection of ordinary clients that is truly greater than the sum of its parts. Class-action lawyers have duties to class members whose names they may never know. "Beyond their ethical obligations to their clients, class attorneys, purporting to represent a class, also owe the entire class a fiduciary duty once the class complaint is filed." In re General Motors Corp. Pick-Up Truck Fuel Tank Prod. Liab. Litig., 55 F.3d 768 (3d Cir. 1995). Classes have pushed the boundaries of several lawyer regulatory concepts, especially conflicts rules and agency principles, nearly beyond the capacity of the traditional categories to accommodate. The bigger the class, the more daunting may be the conceptual challenge. See pages 287 and 328.

At some point, the distinction between a lawyer and a class client may begin to dissolve entirely because the lawyer may be the only one with a financial interest in the outcome of the litigation. See Deposit Guar. Natl. Bank v. Roper, 445 U.S. 326 (1980) ("For better or worse, the financial incentive that class actions offer to the legal profession is a natural outgrowth of the increasing reliance on the 'private attorney general' for the vindication of legal rights; obviously this development has been facilitated by [Fed. R. Civ. P.] 23."). In *Deposit Guaranty*, lawyers successfully appealed the denial of class action status and the dismissal of the case as moot. The named plaintiffs had nothing to gain from reinstatement of the case because their individual claims were satisfied; but the lawyers could look forward to a sizeable court-ordered fee from any class recovery.

Some ways remain in which client-lawyer relationships cannot be created. In United States v. Weinstein, 511 F.2d 622 (2d Cir. 1975), the district court judge, on his own initiative, appointed counsel to represent 23 fugitive defendants who had been indicted under the selective service (draft) laws. The judge ordered the government to produce the files of these defendants so that appointed counsel could determine whether motions might be made to dismiss the indictments. The Second Circuit told the judge to vacate his order, concluding that he had no power to create a client-lawyer relationship for a fugitive defendant. Any action taken by the lawyer "without the defendant's knowledge or consent could not bind the fugitive defendant." In Cooper v. Salomon Bros., Inc., 1 F.3d 82 (2d Cir. 1993), an attorney was denied compensation for work that benefited the defendant where the defendant never requested the work and no attorney-client relationship was shown. Lynch v. Deaconess Medical Center, 776 P.2d 681 (Wash. 1989), held that a hospital was not the client of a lawyer simply because it benefited from the attorney's work for a client who owed the hospital money. And perhaps surprising to some, confiding about your legal problems to a friend who happens to be a lawyer will not by itself create an attorney-client relationship. People v. Gionis, 892 P.2d 1199 (Cal. 1995).

FURTHER READING

Given the secrecy that surrounds attorney-client relationships, inevitably much of our knowledge about what goes on there is anecdotal. Empirical studies are rare. An oft-cited study reported that personal injury lawyers get better results when they let their clients participate in decisions. Douglas Rosenthal, Lawyer and Client: Who's in Charge? (1974). Lisa Lerman was able to pierce the profession's secrecy by promising lawyers anonymity, and her careful and disturbing study, descriptively titled Lying to Clients, can be found at 138 U. Pa. L. Rev. 659 (1990); responses from Carrie Menkel-Meadow, Frederick Miller, and Edmund Spaeth follow it. A third empirical report, by Austin Sarat and William Felstiner, titled Law and Social Relations: Vocabularies of Motive in Lawyer/Client Interaction, 22 Law & Soc. Rev. 737 (1988), analyzes 115 conferences between lawyers and matrimonial clients. The authors grapple with the different orientations of the lawyers and their clients and the effect on the exercise of professional authority. Professors Sarat and Felstiner continue their study of power in the professional relationship in Enactments of Power: Negotiating Reality and Responsibility in Lawyer-Client Interactions, 77 Cornell L. Rev. 1447 (1992).

The profession is still struggling to identify how and when professional relationships may form in cyberspace and the (possibly abbreviated) duties of lawyers who meet prospective clients there. Shedding much light on these issues and certain to be influential as cyberspace relationships mature is Catherine Lanctot, Attorney-Client Relationships in Cyberspace: The Peril and the Promise, 49 Duke L.J. 147 (1999).

B. WHAT DO LAWYERS OWE CLIENTS?

1. Competence

> About half of the practice of a decent lawyer is telling would-be clients that they are damned fools and should stop.[4]
>
> — Elihu Root, U.S. Secretary of State (1905-1909)

The very first rule in the Model Rules requires lawyers to provide clients with "competent" representation, defined to require "the legal knowledge, skill, thoroughness and preparation reasonably necessary for the representation." Rule 1.1. Incompetence has many parents: ignorance, inexperience, neglect, lack of time. Lawyers are warned against assuming more work than they can

---

4. Quoted, inter alia, in Amstar Corp. v. Envirotech Corp., 730 F.2d 1476 (Fed. Cir. 1984); MCI, LLC v. Patriot Engineering & Environmental, Inc., 487 F.Supp.2d 1029 (S.D. Ind. 2007); and Waton v. Maier, 827 P.2d 311 (Wash. App. 1992). I love this quote and use it a lot. The message is that sometimes it is wiser to tell a client to "forget about it" than to figure out how to do what the client wants. Of course, many clients don't want to hear that message and many lawyers don't want to deliver it because it means turning away business. That's no excuse.

competently handle. This applies both to subordinate lawyers, who get assignments from bosses, and to the bosses as well. See ABA Opinion 06-441.

Some states are more specific. New Hampshire, for example, says that "at a minimum" a lawyer should "gather sufficient facts," "formulate the material issues raised," "develop a strategy, in collaboration with the client," and "undertake actions . . . in a timely and effective manner." N.H. Rule 1.1.

How is this duty enforced? While incompetence may lead to discipline (chapter 13D), it rarely does absent egregious error or a pattern of neglect. Incompetence is often the basis for malpractice liability (chapter 13A), assuming the client suffers damages, or for an "ineffective assistance of counsel" claim under the Sixth Amendment (chapter 13E). Lawyers who hold themselves out as specialists will often be subject to a higher standard of care. See page 713. And, of course, if suspicions about a lawyer's competence persist, market forces should deter new clients. But that assumes knowledgeable consumers and available information. Sophisticated buyers of legal services, like large companies that retain lawyers with the aid of lawyers, can be expected to screen out incompetence. But how about individuals who use a lawyer two or three times in a lifetime?

I should add here that even great lawyers make errors of judgment. An error (which may appear clearer in retrospect) does not necessarily equal incompetence. Nor is a lawyer a guarantor of the result the client desires unless she agrees otherwise. (Whew!) In the malpractice area, the lawyer's performance is weighed against the skills of other lawyers in the jurisdiction. No jurisdiction claims a perfect bar.

One final thought about competence: We purport to test for it before an applicant is admitted to the bar (the dreaded bar exam), but, absent a further credentialing system for specialists, no state tests for competence again. Face it: The bar exam doesn't really establish competence to practice law; rather, it tests the intellectual capacity to learn how to be a competent lawyer. Should we have periodic examinations thereafter to confirm our predictions that newly minted lawyers have indeed attained, and that more seasoned lawyers have continued to maintain, acceptable skills? The duty of competence is further discussed at page 685.

2.   *Confidentiality*

"The Case of the Innocent Lifer"

In March 2008, CBS News correspondent Bob Simon reported this story on *60 Minutes*.

> Alton Logan was convicted of killing a security guard at a McDonald's in Chicago in 1982. Police arrested him after a tip and got three eyewitnesses to identify him. Logan, his mother and brother all testified he was at home asleep when the murder occurred. But a jury found him guilty of first degree murder. Logan, who maintains he didn't commit the murder, thought they were "crazy" when he was arrested for the crime.

Attorneys Dale Coventry and Jamie Kunz knew Logan had good reason to think that, because they knew he was innocent. And they knew that because their client, Andrew Wilson, whom they were defending for killing two policemen, confessed to them that he had also killed the security guard at McDonald's — the crime Logan was charged with committing.

"We got information that Wilson was the guy and not Alton Logan. So we went over to the jail immediately almost and said, 'Is that true? Was that you?' And he said, 'Yep it was me,' " Kunz recalled. "He just about hugged himself and smiled. I mean he was kind of gleeful about it. It was a very strange response," Kunz said, recalling how Wilson had reacted.

"How did you interpret that response?" Simon asked.

"That it was true and that he was tickled pink," Kunz said.

Wilson authorized the lawyers to reveal his guilt only after he died. He died 26 years later. Under the Model Rules, what options did the lawyers have? Would it make any difference if Logan were on death row? (His jury split 10 to 2 in favor of execution. Unanimity was required so he received a life sentence.) Would it make any difference if Wilson could be sentenced to death for the McDonald's murder? Whatever may be the result under Rule 1.6, what should a jurisdiction's rule permit on these facts? Is your answer different depending on whether the lawyer's knowledge of Wilson's guilt is based on his answer to their question or their own investigation while representing him?

Would you support the following exception to confidentiality, proposed by some in the ABA's Criminal Justice Section: "A lawyer may reveal information relating to the representation of a deceased client to the extent the lawyer reasonably believes necessary to prevent or rectify the wrongful conviction of another." And if this provision existed in Illinois at the time, would Wilson's lawyers have had to advise him of it before asking about the McDonald's murder?

"My Client Is HIV Positive"

"A year ago, I represented this woman, 'Anna,' on a small matter in probate court that's now over. She has a six-year-old, whose father is gone, maybe dead. Couple of days ago Anna asked me to defend her live-in boyfriend ('Ken'), who was arrested in a barroom fight. I interviewed Ken in jail. He has a misdemeanor conviction from four years ago for drug possession and an assault arrest last year, but nothing else. He has a job. The bar fight was just fists, but the other guy is pretty banged up. I should be able to get Ken out on low bail, which Anna says she can make. When I met Ken in jail, I said I needed to know some things about him to persuade the judge he's a good bail risk and make his situation, you know, sympathetic. He told me some stuff and also said he was HIV positive, but he said, 'Mr. Noonan, you can't tell the judge if Anna might find out because I don't want her to know.' This guy is having sex with the mother of a six-year-old without telling her his condition. He saw I was surprised and said he took precautions. Frankly, he doesn't strike me as the careful type. Look, I want to warn Anna. The way I see it, she's also my client and she's posting the bail and paying my fee. And it sure would be something she'd want to know. What can I do?"

"All's Not Well"

Ben Mackey is a lawyer in a summer and winter resort town about 120 miles from a large city. It is a place many city people go to buy second homes, and about half of Ben's practice consists of representing buyers or sellers of these homes. A buyer or seller will call him after reaching an oral agreement. The Winkler family called Ben in May to represent them in the sale of their home. Ben knows the family because he had represented Donny Winkler four years ago when Donny, then 17, drove the family SUV through a neighbor's backyard and into the swimming pool, a mishap that made the front page of the local weekly with a full-color picture.

The Winklers bought their home 15 years ago, when their children were small, and they made extensive improvements. Theirs is one of the pricier homes in the area. The main house is a five-bedroom, three-and-a-half bath, center-stair colonial. The Winklers added a Jacuzzi and hot tub. They built a tennis court, a swimming pool, a small guest house, and an underground sprinkler system that feeds a large garden and flower bed. The asking price was $2.4 million. The Houghtons offered $2.1 million, and after some back and forth they agreed to a purchase price of $2.2 million. Before putting the house on the market, the Winklers had had it inspected top to bottom by Copeland Engineering, which wrote a report. The Winklers e-mailed the report to the Houghtons with a "cc" to Ben. Ben gave a copy to Amy Trout, the Houghton's lawyer.

Ben negotiated the non-financial terms of the contract of sale with Amy and represented the Winklers at the closing.

Several days after the closing, Ben went to a July Fourth barbecue at Todd Canby's house. There, he ran into Brenda Lesher, the Copeland engineer who did the inspection. Brenda asked if "the well problem caused any issues on the Winkler sale." Ben asked what she meant. "I mean what kind of price reduction did the Houghtons want? They've got to start digging for a new well right away. I'm sure they didn't know that when they made their offer."

Ben said he recalled that Brenda's report said nothing about a well problem. After an awkward pause, Brenda shook her head. "The property was in excellent shape except for the well," she said. "It's running dry, and even if it weren't, it's way too small for the property with all of the Winkler's improvements — pool, guest house, sprinkler system. In a few months, it'll be useless. It's going to cost a pretty penny to find another water source. They'll have to dig very deep, once they figure out where to dig."

The next day Brenda sent Ben a copy of the Copeland report. It identified the well problem that Brenda had described at the barbecue. Ben's copy did not. Which meant that the copy he gave Amy did not and the copy the Winklers gave the Houghtons did not. Ben's copy did not indicate any omission of text or gaps in the pagination.

Ben called Brenda and asked what it would cost to dig a new well. "Depends how lucky you are in where you choose to dig. If you get it with the first hole or not. They'll find water eventually. The only questions are when and how deep they have to go. But I'd say for this property, they're looking at $70,000 give or take. They may need two wells and some fancy engineering. Could go over a hundred. I've seen it. The longer they wait, the worse it'll be." Ben asked why.

He should try to correct it or at least send this new info to the lawyer / purchaser

"First off, Ben, depending on several factors I mention in the report, their pipes may burst during the winter. That can cause a lot of damage inside the house. Second, and aside from that, you can't dig after October. Ground's too cold. They've got to start now or wait until May. And May and June, after the thaw, those are the big well digging months, so there's no saying they'll get someone to do it right away. No, they'd be advised to start this month."

Ben asks us what he can and should do now?

PEREZ v. KIRK & CARRIGAN
822 S.W.2d 261 (Tex. Ct. App. 1991)

DORSEY, JUSTICE.

Ruben Perez appeals a summary judgment rendered against him on his causes of action against the law firm of Kirk & Carrigan, and against Dana Kirk and Steve Carrigan individually (henceforth all three will be collectively referred to as "Kirk & Carrigan"). We reverse the summary judgment and remand this case for trial.

The present suit arises from a school bus accident on September 21, 1989, in Alton, Texas. Ruben Perez was employed by Valley Coca-Cola Bottling Company as a truck driver. On the morning of the accident, Perez attempted to stop his truck at a stop sign along his route, but the truck's brakes failed to stop the truck, which collided with the school bus. The loaded bus was knocked into a pond and 21 children died. Perez suffered injuries from the collision and was taken to a local hospital to be treated.

The day after the accident, Kirk & Carrigan, lawyers who had been hired to represent Valley Coca-Cola Bottling Company, visited Perez in the hospital for the purpose of taking his statement. Perez claims that the lawyers told him they were his lawyers too and that anything he told them would be kept confidential. With this understanding, Perez gave them a sworn statement concerning the accident. However, after taking Perez' statement, Kirk & Carrigan had no further contact with him. Instead, Kirk & Carrigan made arrangements for criminal defense attorney Joseph Connors to represent Perez. Connors was paid by National Union Fire Insurance Company which covered both Valley Coca-Cola and Perez for liability in connection with the accident.

Some time after Connors began representing Perez, Kirk & Carrigan, without telling either Perez or Connors, turned Perez' statement over to the Hildalgo County District Attorney's Office. Kirk & Carrigan contend that Perez' statement was provided in a good faith attempt to fully comply with a request of the district attorney's office and under threat of subpoena if they did not voluntarily comply. Partly on the basis of this statement, the district attorney was able to obtain a grand jury indictment of Perez for involuntary manslaughter for his actions in connection with the accident. . . .

By his sole point of error, Perez complains simply that the trial court erred in granting Kirk & Carrigan's motion for summary judgment. . . .

With regard to Perez' cause of action for breach of the fiduciary duty of good faith and fair dealing, Kirk & Carrigan contend that no attorney-client relationship existed and no fiduciary duty arose, because Perez never sought legal advice from them.

An agreement to form an attorney-client relationship may be implied from the conduct of the parties. Moreover, the relationship does not depend upon the payment of a fee, but may exist as a result of rendering services gratuitously.[4]

In the present case, viewing the summary judgment evidence in the light most favorable to Perez, Kirk & Carrigan told him that, in addition to representing Valley Coca-Cola, they were also Perez' lawyers and that they were going to help him. Perez did not challenge this assertion, and he cooperated with the lawyers in giving his statement to them, even though he did not offer, nor was he asked, to pay the lawyers' fees. We hold that this was sufficient to imply the creation of an attorney-client relationship at the time Perez gave his statement to Kirk & Carrigan.

[margin note: sufficient behavior to create an atty/client relationship]

The existence of this relationship encouraged Perez to trust Kirk & Carrigan and gave rise to a corresponding duty on the part of the attorneys not to violate this position of trust. Accordingly, the relation between attorney and client is highly fiduciary in nature, and their dealings with each other are subject to the same scrutiny as a transaction between trustee and beneficiary. Specifically, the relationship between attorney and client has been described as one of uberrima fides, which means, "most abundant good faith," requiring absolute and perfect candor, openness and honesty, and the absence of any concealment or deception. In addition, because of the openness and candor within this relationship, certain communications between attorney and client are privileged from disclosure in either civil or criminal proceedings under the provisions of Tex. R. Civ. Evid. 503 and Tex. R. Crim. Evid. 503, respectively.[5]

There is evidence that Kirk & Carrigan represented to Perez that his statement would be kept confidential. Later, however, without telling either Perez or his subsequently-retained criminal defense attorney, Kirk & Carrigan voluntarily disclosed Perez' statement to the district attorney. Perez asserts in the present suit that this course of conduct amounted, among other things, to a breach of fiduciary duty.

[margin note: Claim: Breach of fiduciary duty]

Kirk & Carrigan seek to avoid this claim of breach, on the ground that the attorney-client privilege did not apply to the present statement, because unnecessary third parties were present at the time it was given. However, whether or not the Rule 503 attorney-client privilege extended to Perez' statement, Kirk & Carrigan initially obtained the statement from Perez on the understanding that it would be kept confidential. Thus, regardless of whether from an evidentiary standpoint the privilege attached, Kirk & Carrigan breached their fiduciary duty to Perez either by wrongfully disclosing a privileged statement or by wrongfully representing that an unprivileged statement would be kept confidential. Either characterization shows a clear lack of honesty toward, and a deception of, Perez by his own attorneys regarding the degree of confidentiality with which they intended to treat the statement. . . .

[margin note: Holding — Breach]

4. An attorney's fiduciary responsibilities may arise even during preliminary consultations regarding the attorney's possible retention if the attorney enters into discussion of the client's legal problems with a view toward undertaking representation.

5. Disclosure of confidential communications by an attorney, whether privileged or not under the rules of evidence, is generally prohibited by the disciplinary rules governing attorneys' conduct in Texas. In addition, the general rule is that confidential information received during the course of any fiduciary relationship may not be used or disclosed to the detriment of the one from whom the information is obtained.

In addition, however, even assuming a breach of fiduciary duty, Kirk & Carrigan also contend that summary judgment may be sustained on the ground that Perez could show no damages resulting from the breach. Kirk & Carrigan contend that their dissemination of Perez' statement could not have caused him any damages in the way of emotional distress, because the statement merely revealed Perez' own version of what happened. We do not agree. Mental anguish consists of the emotional response of the plaintiff caused by the tortfeasor's conduct. It includes, among other things, the mental sensation of pain resulting from public humiliation.

Regardless of the fact that Perez himself made the present statement, he did not necessarily intend it to be a public response as Kirk & Carrigan contend, but only a private and confidential discussion with his attorneys. Perez alleged that the publicity caused by his indictment, resulting from the revelation of the statement to the district attorney in breach of that confidentiality, caused him to suffer emotional distress and mental anguish. We hold that Perez has made a valid claim for such damages.

Perez was eventually tried on 21 counts of involuntary manslaughter. He was acquitted on all counts after less than four hours of deliberation. Coca-Cola paid victims and survivors of the accident $133 million in settlement. The bus company, which had been criticized for windows that were difficult to open and because the bus had only one emergency means of escape, paid an additional $23 million. Dallas Morning News, May 6, 1993, at 1A.

It didn't matter that Kirk & Carrigan had only one meeting with Perez before Connors took over. The attorney-client privilege and the duty of confidentiality protect information gained from a potential client even if no retention ensues. The privilege "applies to all confidential communications made to an attorney during preliminary discussions of the prospective professional employment, as well as those made during the course of any professional relationship resulting from such discussions." Hooser v. Superior Court, 101 Cal. Rptr. 2d 341 (Ct. App. 2000); Restatement §15. Why are the rules so generous? Why protect *potential* clients at all?

While civil damage claims against lawyers for improper release of a client's confidential information are unusual, the doctrinal basis for them is clear. Elkind claimed that Bennett, his former lawyer, had revealed his confidential information, costing him his job. If so, the court held, that would be a breach of fiduciary duty and malpractice (as well as a violation of Rule 1.6). Elkind v. Bennett, 958 So.2d 1088 (Fla. App. 2007). Further, it didn't matter that the alleged revelation occurred after the lawyer's work ended because the confidentiality duty has no time limit.

Bye, a lawyer, had represented Thiery in a personal injury action. Before the matter ended, Bye asked Thiery if his nurse-investigator could use Thiery's medical records to teach a class at a local community college. Bye said Thiery would be paid $500 and that all identifying information would be removed (or "redacted"). Thiery agreed. Thiery then claimed that Bye had failed to remove some identifying information and sued for malpractice. Citing Rule 1.6, the agreement, and agency rules (see page 68), the court reversed summary judgment for Bye. Bye had an obligation to maintain Thiery's confidential information during and after the relationship. Nor did Thiery need an expert witness to prove her case. "A layperson would have little difficulty understanding the duty Bye accepted in his letter to Thiery or determining whether Bye's failure to assure the redaction was completed was a breach of his obligation to his client. We have concluded as a matter of law that Bye owed a duty to maintain the confidentiality of Thiery's records." Thiery v. Bye, 597 N.W.2d 449 (Wis. Ct. App. 1999).

Privileged and Ethically Protected Information: What's The Difference?

These two legal categories are quite distinct but they are easily confused because they both have protection of information (and sometimes the same information) as their objectives. They have different legal pedigrees, however, and create different rights and duties.

Rules 1.6, 1.8(b), and 1.9(c) define a category of confidential client information gained from the client *or from others* in the course of representing the client, which, absent exception (discussed below), a lawyer may never reveal unless doing so benefits the client. Sealed Party v. Sealed Party, 2006 Westlaw 1207732 (S.D. Texas 2006) (Atlas, J.) (collecting cases that hold that a lawyer's duty of confidentiality even extends to information in the public record). Even without these rules, restrictions would exist in some form because lawyers are agents and all agents have confidentiality obligations. See page 75.

The law of evidence, on the other hand, creates a privilege, but only for communications between a lawyer (or his agent) and a client (or agents of a client). The privilege is a shield. It allows lawyer and client to refuse to reveal their communication despite a subpoena without being held in contempt of court. But the two must treat their communication confidentially. No privilege will protect lawyer-client communications if a stranger is present during it. Lynch v. Hamrick, 968 So.2d 11 (Ala. 2007) (no privilege for communications at lawyer-client meeting in presence of client's adult daughter).

A subpoena can reach information that is confidential but not privileged. In re Original Grand Jury Investigation, 733 N.E.2d 1135 (Ohio 2000) (incriminating letter discovered by lawyer's investigator subject to grand jury subpoena because it is a "secret" but not privileged under Ohio rules). If the same lawyer had *voluntarily* revealed or used privileged or other ethically protected information he might be guilty of a disciplinary violation and subject to civil liability for breach of fiduciary duty or malpractice, unless an exception applied.

Unfortunately, but understandably, the word "privileged" is sometimes loosely and confusingly used to refer to the broader category of information protected by rules like Rule 1.6. To complicate matters further, courts have recognized that in criminal cases the evidentiary privilege enjoys Sixth Amendment protection in order to protect the right to counsel. People v. Johnson, 999 P.2d 825 (Colo. 2000); Neku v. United States, 620 A.2d 259 (D.C. 1993). The vocabulary in this area is not uniform. We will generally refer to information protected by the rules of ethics as ethically protected or confidential information (the Code called this information "secrets") and information protected under the rules of evidence as "privileged information" (the Code called this information "confidences"). Compare DR 4-101(A) of the Code with Rule 1.6(a) of the Model Rules.

Whatever the labels, it is important to realize that the two bodies of rules have different sources and define overlapping but not congruent categories of information. Confidentiality duties come from the professional conduct codes and the law of agency and fiduciary duty. Privilege comes from the law of evidence, which is usually statutory. Much information that is ethically protected will not be within the attorney-client privilege because the source of the information was not the client or its agents. (The information may be protected under the work-product doctrine, however.) On the other hand, privileged communications will also be ethically protected. Think of the two categories as concentric circles. One category is "lesser included" within the other. The inner (smaller) circle contains privileged information only. The outer circle comprises the inner circle and all other information "relating to the representation of a client," from any source.

A partner at a major U.S. firm was publicly censured after he gave a court pleading to a Business Week reporter who requested it. The partner, who was not assigned to the case, did not realize that the pleading was filed under seal. Even if the pleading were not under seal, however, it constituted a client confidence. "[R]espondent's failure to take adequate precautions to safeguard confidential materials of a client, even if considered unintentional, was careless conduct that reflects adversely on his fitness to practice law" within the meaning of DR 1-102(A)(7). In re Holley, 729 N.Y.S.2d 128 (1st Dept. 2001) (case of "first impression"). See also In re Goebel, 703 N.E.2d 1045 (Ind. 1998) (lawyer reprimanded for revealing address of one client to another client); In re Pressly, 628 A.2d 927 (Vt. 1993) (public reprimand of lawyer for former wife who, despite her contrary instruction, revealed to former husband's lawyer the wife's suspicion that husband was abusing their daughter during visitation).

Misuse of confidential information can also be a crime. United States v. O'Hagan, 521 U.S. 642 (1997), upheld the securities fraud conviction of a law firm partner who used nonpublic information of a firm client to purchase options in the target of the client's expected tender offer.

Like *Perez*, other cases also distinguish between privileged and confidential information. In Brennan's, Inc. v. Brennan's Restaurants, Inc., 590 F.2d 168 (5th Cir. 1979), the court resisted an effort to incorporate an exception to the privilege as an exception to the ethical duty. The court wrote:

> But the ethical duty is broader than the evidentiary privilege: "This ethical precept, unlike the evidentiary privilege, exists without regard to the nature or source of information or the fact that others share the knowledge." "A lawyer should not use information acquired in the course of the representation of a client to the disadvantage of the client. . . ." Information so acquired is sheltered from use by the attorney against his client by virtue of the existence of the attorney-client relationship. This is true without regard to whether someone else may be privy to it. The obligation of an attorney not to misuse information acquired in the course of representation serves to vindicate the trust and reliance that clients place in their attorneys.

Relying on *Brennan's*, X Corp. v. Doe, 805 F. Supp. 1298 (E.D. Va. 1992), aff'd, 17 F.3d 1435 (4th Cir. 1994), draws the same distinction. In one unusual case, the West Virginia high court publicly reprimanded the state attorney general, in part for revealing a state agency's confidential information to a third person. Lawyer Disciplinary Board v. McGraw, 461 S.E.2d 850 (W. Va. 1995).

At this point, if you haven't already done so, read Model Rule 1.6 to see the balance the ABA has struck between confidentiality and exceptions to it. Many jurisdictions subscribe to this balance, but many others do not. They either expand or contract the exceptions. And while the ABA's Rule 1.6 exceptions are all permissive ("may"), in some places some of them (like Rule 1.6(b)(1)) are mandatory ("shall"). (Another ABA exception, in Rule 3.3, dealing with candor to tribunals, is mandatory. See chapter 7C.)

Policies Behind Privilege and Confidentiality Rules

What purposes do privilege and the confidentiality rules serve? Two are often mentioned. The first is empirical. They will encourage the client to trust her lawyer and to be forthcoming with information (and sources of information) that the lawyer may need to represent her. This will allow the lawyer to do a better job. The trouble with the empirical argument is that it is based on an intuition — or some would say common sense — about how people will behave. But we have no rigorous test of this intuition. Will clients really conceal information from or lie to lawyers absent protection for information? Will they do so knowing that an ignorant lawyer is likely to be a less effective lawyer? And how does the empirical assumption fare when we also consider that information is not absolutely protected, that various exceptions permit or require lawyers to reveal client confidences?

A further problem with the empirical argument is that it does not work for communications with unrelated third parties, at least not those the lawyer discovers on her own. For example, an eyewitness to a construction site accident, who was just walking by, will not be less or more forthcoming depending on the lawyer's confidentiality duty to her client.

The second reason offered to support significant protection for client information is normative. Regardless of the effect on a client's willingness to be candid or the quality of the lawyer's work if lawyers are not informed, lawyers should respect a client's confidences just because it is right to do so. It respects the client's autonomy. The client should be in control of information about her legal matter (and therefore her life), the normative argument holds, except as she explicitly or implicitly delegates that control to enable the lawyer to protect her interests. Conversely, the lawyer, who is asking for the client's trust, should not be permitted then to exploit the client's confidences to his own or another person's advantage, and certainly not if doing so harms the client.

But how high should we elevate the client's interests? What if keeping mum will result in harm to others? The harm can be physical or financial. The lawyer may have provided unwitting assistance to the harmful conduct. The conduct may be illegal, fraudulent, even criminal. When should a lawyer be allowed, or even required, to "blow the whistle" on a client to protect others? Take another look at Rule 1.6(b). The confidentiality duty has six exceptions. Only the exception in paragraph (b)(5) appeared in its present form (as paragraph (b)(2)) when the Rules were first adopted in 1983. Paragraph (b)(1) was added in 2002. Previously, paragraph (b)(1) permitted a lawyer to reveal confidential information only if a *client* was likely to commit a *criminal* act likely to result in *imminent* death or substantial bodily harm. The three italicized words are now gone. Anticipation of death or serious physical harm will permit disclosure of confidences even if the client is not the cause, the harm is not imminent, and the conduct is not criminal. (For example, elimination of "criminal" and "imminent" may enable a lawyer to reveal potential harm from a dangerous consumer product.)

The remaining exceptions were added in 2003. Of particular interest are paragraphs (b)(2) and (b)(3). For 20 years, the ABA refused to adopt an exception for financial crimes and frauds, although some states did so. In 2003, partly as a result of a series of corporate scandals, the ABA relented, if barely. By small majorities in the House of Delegates, the ABA adopted these exceptions and another one, in Rule 1.13, for organizational clients. See page 64 and chapter 10C.

It is over the confidentiality exceptions that state rules especially diverge and lawyers most fiercely disagree. It is not practical to list all jurisdictional variations, but the differences can be seen by comparing the rules in three states with each other and with Model Rule 1.6. New Jersey and Florida may be least protective of client confidences; California most protective. Rule 1.6 is in the middle. New Jersey *requires* a lawyer to reveal confidential information "to the proper authorities . . . to prevent a client from committing a criminal, illegal, or fraudulent act . . . likely to result in death or substantial bodily harm or substantial injury to the financial interest or property of another." Florida *requires* a lawyer to reveal information the lawyer believes "necessary (1) to prevent a client from committing a crime or (2) to prevent death or substantial bodily harm to another." By contrast, for a long time California ethics rules had no confidentiality provision. Instead, a state law, §6068(e) of the California Business and Professions Code, said that a lawyer must "maintain inviolate the confidence, and at every peril to himself or herself to preserve the secrets, of his or her client." Until 2003, this law had no exception at all, leading the San Diego Bar Association to conclude that a lawyer could not even warn the intended victim of an armed client's imminent homicide. San Diego Op. 1990-1. Yes, you read that right. In 2003, the California legislature created a narrow exception to the statute, which permits but does not require disclosure "to the extent that the attorney reasonably believes the disclosure is necessary to prevent a criminal act that the attorney reasonably believes is likely to result in death of, or substantial bodily harm to, an individual." Then in 2004, a confidentiality rule (Rule 3-100), with the same single exception, was added to the state's Rules of Professional Conduct.

Exceptions to confidentiality and privilege are further discussed at page 53.

Finally, though rarely offered as a justification for confidentiality rules, is the bar's sense of professional identity. Go to a bar committee meeting where the rules are debated. It is apparent that many lawyers view the existence of these rules as closely tied to how they see themselves as professionals. And this is true even of lawyers who have never had to deal with the rules or their exceptions in their personal practice and probably never will. Our lips are sealed.

B. What Do Lawyers Owe Clients?

Entity Clients

"Slip and Fall"

Edith Walton, shopping in Tracy's Department Store, slipped in the third floor timepiece department and broke her hip. She sued, alleging that the floor was excessively waxed. Under store policy, whenever someone is injured in the store, the General Counsel's office will oversee an investigation. A half-hour after the fall, Jeanne Parr, an assistant GC, asked Mike Todd in security to investigate. Todd interviewed (a) Max Burkow, head of maintenance; (b) Tim Morse, who last waxed the floor; (c) Tina Sandstrom, a salesperson in men's furnishings who was returning from a break; (d) Rex McCormick, a buyer in the rug department who, though off work that day, had come to do personal shopping; (e) Delia Corcoran, Burkow's predecessor as head of maintenance, since retired, who established the store's standards and procedures for floor waxing a year ago; (f) Ed Rivera, president of the company that supplies wax to Tracy's; and (g) Angie Kuhl, who was at Tracy's buying a watch for her father. Only Sandstrom, McCormick, and Kuhl saw Walton fall. Todd wrote up the interviews and gave his memos to Parr. Cora Lundquist, Walton's lawyer, noticed the deposition of each of the seven people Todd interviewed. She asked Burkow about maintenance procedures. She asked Morse about procedures in waxing floors generally and on this occasion. She asked Corcoran about the floor waxing standards and procedures she established. She asked Rivera about the instructions his company may have given Tracy's on the use of the wax. She asked the others what they remembered of the incident. Each witness had some memory failure. Lundquist demanded production of Todd's memos, and Parr asserted attorney-client privilege. Is she right?

As Rule 1.13 and its comment make clear, a lawyer has the same confidentiality duties under Rule 1.6 whether the client is a biological person or an entity like a corporation, a labor union, the government, or a partnership. (Lawyers for companies and other entities confront distinct problems as well, which we discuss in chapter 10.) Harder questions emerge when we turn to privilege, which also protects communications between an entity client and counsel. Upjohn Co. v. United States, 449 U.S. 383 (1981). This is true whether the lawyer is an employee of the entity or an outside lawyer. Rossi v. Blue Cross & Blue Shield, 540 N.E.2d 703 (N.Y. 1989). One debated question, addressed here, is this: Since companies can't speak — only their agents and employees (sometimes collectively called "constituents") can do so — whose communications with company counsel are privileged? A related question is: Does the privilege belong only to the company, so it alone can choose to waive or assert it; or does it also belong to the constituent who communicates with counsel? The answer, discussed in chapter 10, is that the company alone controls the privilege, except for those unusual instances where the constituent and company are deemed co-clients. Because a constituent may not appreciate the distinction, Rule 1.13(f) may require a caution.

In thinking about the proper breadth for the corporate attorney-client privilege, recall the two justifications, for the privilege (as well as the duty of confidentiality): to encourage candor and to protect client autonomy. Are these reasons equally valid when the client is a fictional entity and the source of the information is not the client and has no power to claim or waive the privilege?

Obviously, the larger the group of constituents whose communications with counsel will be deemed to be privileged, the greater a company's ability to keep information secret. So while disguised as a seemingly technical question of privilege, this issue has broad policy implications because the extent of corporate secrecy does. One test, the least protective of entity clients (and let's talk about companies here), says that the privilege protects only communications with those who actually run the company. This is the "control group" test. A more protective test focuses not on the identity of the person with whom the lawyer communicates, but on the subject of the communication. The "subject matter" test looks at the nature and purpose of the information imparted to the lawyer, not merely the identity of the source. So communications with the mailroom intern can be privileged.

In *Upjohn*, management had reason to believe that some of the company's subsidiaries may have made payments to foreign government officials that were illegal under federal law. Attorneys for the company sent a questionnaire to employees worldwide seeking "detailed information concerning such payments." The attorneys also conducted interviews. The Internal Revenue Service subpoenaed the answers to the questionnaires and the records of the interviews. Upjohn resisted this subpoena, citing the attorney-client privilege and the work-product doctrine. Only the former concerns us here. Remember, whereas *Perez* introduced us to the operation of confidentiality rules that limit what information a lawyer may *voluntarily* reveal about a client, the next two cases focus on privilege and the government's power (or lack of it) to *force* a lawyer to reveal information his client wants to conceal.

Under Fed. R. Evid. Rule 501, federal courts are authorized to define the scope of evidentiary privileges by reference to common law principles. The Sixth Circuit, applying a "control group" test, held that the privilege did not apply to "communications . . . by officers and agents not responsible for directing Upjohn's actions in response to legal advice . . . for the simple reason that the communications were not the 'client's.'"

UPJOHN CO. v. UNITED STATES
449 U.S. 383 (1981)

REHNQUIST, JUSTICE . . .

The attorney-client privilege is the oldest of the privileges for confidential communications known to the common law. Its purpose is to encourage full and frank communication between attorneys and their clients and thereby promote broader public interests in the observance of law and administration of justice. The privilege recognizes that sound legal advice or advocacy serves public ends and that such advice or advocacy depends upon the lawyer's being fully informed by the client. . . .

The Court of Appeals, however, considered the application of the privilege in the corporate context to present a "different problem," since the client was an inanimate entity and "only the senior management, guiding and integrating the several operations, . . . can be said to possess an identity analogous to the corporation as a whole." . . .

Such a view, we think, overlooks the fact that the privilege exists to protect not only the giving of professional advice to those who can act on it but also the giving of information to the lawyer to enable him to give sound and informed advice. The first step in the resolution of any legal problem is ascertaining the factual background and sifting through the facts with an eye to the legally relevant. . . .

In the case of the individual client the provider of information and the person who acts on the lawyer's advice are one and the same. In the corporate context, however, it will frequently be employees beyond the control group as defined by the court below— "officers and agents . . . responsible for directing [the company's] actions in response to legal advice" — who will possess the information needed by the corporation's lawyers. Middle-level — and indeed lower-level — employees can, by actions within the scope of their employment, embroil the corporation in serious legal difficulties, and it is only natural that these employees would have the relevant information needed by corporate counsel if he is adequately to advise the client with respect to such actual or potential difficulties. . . .

The control group test adopted by the court below thus frustrates the very purpose of the privilege by discouraging the communication of relevant information by employees of the client to attorneys seeking to render legal advice to the client corporation. The attorney's advice will also frequently be more significant to noncontrol group members than to those who officially sanction the advice, and the control group test makes it more difficult to convey full and frank legal advice to the employees who will put into effect the client corporation's policy.

The narrow scope given the attorney-client privilege by the court below not only makes it difficult for corporate attorneys to formulate sound advice when their client is faced with a specific legal problem but also threatens to limit the valuable efforts of corporate counsel to ensure their client's compliance with the law. In light of the vast and complicated array of regulatory legislation confronting the modern corporation, corporations, unlike most individuals, "constantly go to lawyers to find out how to obey the law." . . . [2] The test adopted by the court below is difficult to apply in practice, though no abstractly formulated and unvarying "test" will necessarily enable courts to decide questions such as this with mathematical precision. But if the purpose of the attorney-client privilege is to be served, the attorney and client must be able to predict with some degree of certainty whether particular discussions will be protected. An uncertain privilege, or one which purports to be certain but results in widely varying applications by the courts, is little better than no privilege at all. The very

---

2. The Government argues that the risk of civil or criminal liability suffices to ensure that corporations will seek legal advice in the absence of the protection of the privilege. This response ignores the fact that the depth and quality of any investigations to ensure compliance with the law would suffer, even were they undertaken. The response also proves too much, since it applies to all communications covered by the privilege: an individual trying to comply with the law or faced with a legal problem also has strong incentive to disclose information to his lawyer, yet the common law has recognized the value of the privilege in further facilitating communications.

terms of the test adopted by the court below suggest the unpredictability of its application. The test restricts the availability of the privilege to those officers who play a "substantial role" in deciding and directing a corporation's legal response. Disparate decisions in cases applying this test illustrate its unpredictability. Compare, e.g., Hogan v. Zletz, 43 F.R.D. 308, 315-316 (N.D. Okla. 1967), aff'd in part sub nom. Natta v. Hogan, 392 F.2d 686 (CA 10 1968) (control group includes managers and assistant managers of patent division and research and development department), with Congoleum Industries, Inc. v. GAF Corp., 49 F.R.D. 82, 83-85 (E.D. Pa. 1969), aff'd, 478 F.2d 1398 (CA3 1973) (control group includes only division and corporate vice presidents, and not two directors of research and vice president for production and research). The communications at issue were made by Upjohn employees to counsel for Upjohn acting as such, at the direction of corporate superiors in order to secure legal advice from counsel. . . . Information, not available from upper-echelon management, was needed to supply a basis for legal advice concerning compliance with securities and tax laws, foreign laws, currency regulations, duties to shareholders, and potential litigation in each of these areas. The communications concerned matters within the scope of the employees' corporate duties, and the employees themselves were sufficiently aware that they were being questioned in order that the corporation could obtain legal advice. . . .

The Court of Appeals declined to extend the attorney-client privilege beyond the limits of the control group test for fear that doing so would entail severe burdens on discovery and create a broad "zone of silence" over corporate affairs. Application of the attorney-client privilege to communications such as those involved here, however, puts the adversary in no worse position than if the communications had never taken place. The privilege only protects disclosure of communications; it does not protect disclosure of the underlying facts by those who communicated with the attorney:

> [T]he protection of the privilege extends only to *communications* and not to facts. A fact is one thing and a communication concerning that fact is an entirely different thing. The client cannot be compelled to answer the question, "What did you say or write to the attorney?" but may not refuse to disclose any relevant fact within his knowledge merely because he incorporated a statement of such fact into his communication to his attorney.

Here the Government was free to question the employees who communicated with [inside] and outside counsel. Upjohn has provided the IRS with a list of such employees, and the IRS has already interviewed some 25 of them. While it would probably be more convenient for the Government to secure the results of petitioner's internal investigation by simply subpoenaing the questionnaires and notes taken by petitioner's attorneys, such considerations of convenience do not overcome the policies served by the attorney-client privilege. . . .

Needless to say, we decide only the case before us, and do not undertake to draft a set of rules which should govern challenges to investigatory subpoenas. Any such approach would violate the spirit of Federal Rule of Evidence 501. While such a "case-by-case" basis may to some slight extent undermine desirable certainty in the boundaries of the attorney-client privilege, it obeys the spirit of the Rules. At the same time we conclude that the narrow "control group test" sanctioned by the Court of Appeals in this case cannot, consistent with "the principles of the common law as . . . interpreted . . . in the light of reason and experience," govern the development of the law in this area.

[Chief Justice Burger concurred in part and concurred in the judgment.]

[handwritten: Rejects the control group test]

Upjohn construed the privilege under federal law. States are free to define the scope of privileges under state law. Even federal judges must apply state privileges when a case in federal court is governed by state law. Fed. R. Evid. 501. Some states, including California and Illinois, have rejected the broad *Upjohn* definition of the corporate privilege, opting for a narrower test. Following is one state supreme court's effort to grapple with the multiple policies underlying this debate. Justice Martone identifies a test somewhere between the "control group" and a "broad . . . subject matter test." Does it make sense to you? In deciding, think about the interests involved, including those of the bar, clients, and adversaries, and how particular solutions advance or frustrate these. Even though, as discussed hereafter, *Samaritan Foundation* is no longer Arizona law in *civil* cases (although it is in criminal ones), its different approach is worth studying for the way it balances policies behind the privilege against the justice system's interest in avoiding excessive secrecy and discovering the truth.

SAMARITAN FOUNDATION v. GOODFARB
176 Ariz. 497, 862 P.2d 870 (1993)

MARTONE JUSTICE. . . .

I. BACKGROUND

A child's heart stopped during surgery at the Phoenix Children's Hospital in the Good Samaritan Regional Medical Center in 1988. A Good Samaritan lawyer investigated the incident and directed a nurse paralegal to interview three nurses and a scrub technician who were present during the surgery. Each of these Samaritan employees signed a form agreeing to accept legal representation from Samaritan's legal department. The paralegal summarized the interviews in memoranda that she then submitted to corporate counsel.

The child and her parents brought an action against Phoenix Children's Hospital and the physicians who participated in the surgery, alleging that the cardiac arrest and resulting impairment were caused by the defendants' medical negligence. When deposed two years later, the four Samaritan employees were unable to remember what happened in the operating room. Having learned of the existence of the interview summaries through discovery, plaintiffs sought their production. Samaritan, a non-party, and Phoenix Children's Hospital resisted, arguing that the interview summaries were protected by the attorney-client privilege and the work product doctrine. . . .

II. ANALYSIS . . .

C. THE PRIVILEGE FOR COMMUNICATIONS IN THE
COURSE OF SEEKING LEGAL ADVICE

Client communications tend to fall into two categories: those initiated by the employee seeking legal advice and those made in response to an overture initiated by someone else in the corporation. It is universally accepted that communications directly initiated by an employee to corporate counsel seeking legal advice on behalf of the corporation are privileged. We agree that these kinds of communications by a corporate employee, regardless of position within the corporate hierarchy, are privileged. When a corporate employee or agent communicates with corporate counsel to secure or evaluate legal advice for the corporation, that agent or employee is, by definition, acting on behalf of the corporation and not in an individual capacity. These kinds of communications are at the heart of the attorney-client relationship. And it is plain that these communications can occur at any level of the chain of command. At one end of the spectrum is the chief executive officer seeking advice from corporate counsel on the antitrust implications of corporate behavior, even if the behavior is not his. At the other end, the driver of a corporate truck may run into corporate counsel's office seeking advice about an accident. In either case, the privilege applies because the employee is seeking legal advice concerning that employee's duties (the chief executive officer) or behavior (the driver) on behalf of the corporation. As to these kinds of legal communications, including the communication of facts, we hold that all communications made in confidence to counsel in which the communicating employee is directly seeking legal advice are privileged.

D. THE PRIVILEGE FOR FACTUAL COMMUNICATIONS MADE
BY EMPLOYEES IN RESPONSE TO OVERTURES
BY SOMEONE ELSE IN THE CORPORATION

The real debate concerning the proper scope of the corporation's attorney-client privilege is its applicability to factual communications made in response to an overture initiated by someone else in the corporation. Unless there is some self-limiting feature, the breadth of corporate activity could transform what would be witness communications in any other context into client communications. In such an event, the costs of the privilege are potentially much greater when asserted by a corporation over the statements of its agents than when asserted by an individual over his or her own statements. But there is no countervailing benefit. The rationale of the privilege is that by assuring the individual client that his or her communications cannot be disclosed without consent, it encourages the client to be candid. But this only works if the communicator controls the privilege. In the corporate context, the privilege belongs to the corporation and not the person making the communication.

If an employee has exposed the corporation to liability, it seems less problematic to legitimize the corporation's control over the privileged nature of the employee's communications. After all, it is the action of this employee that is being imputed to the corporation. It is this employee's statements that are directly admissible against the corporation under Rule 801(d)(2)(D), Ariz. R. Evid. This employee's statements are also the most important in enabling corporate counsel to assess the corporation's legal exposure and formulate a legal response. And none of this has anything at all to do with whether the employee is a member of a control group. We must, therefore, always look at the relationship between the communicator and the incident giving rise to the legal matter, the nature of the communication and its context.

If the employee is not the one whose conduct gives rise to potential corporate liability, then it is fair to characterize the employee as a "witness" rather than as a client. The vice of the control group test is that it includes in the privilege the factual statements of control group employees even if they were mere witnesses to the events in question, while at the same time it fails to take into account the need to promote institutional candor with respect to factual communications of non-control group employees whose conduct has exposed the corporation to possible adverse legal consequences. The test is both overinclusive and under-inclusive. We, therefore, reject the control group test as unsatisfactory on its own terms.

Over and above its inadequacy as a theory to deal with the complex problems of the attorney-client privilege in the corporate context, there are other reasons to avoid the control group test. Our world is growing smaller. Corporate activity is increasingly global and almost always national. Although its outer limits are unclear, *Upjohn* at a minimum rejects the control group test as a rule of federal common law. We should minimize disparities between federal and state law when it comes to privilege. When clients seek legal advice, they do not expect that the privilege will exist for purposes of some claims but not others. Much litigation today consists of both state and federal claims, sometimes in the same action. Federal and state claims can be asserted simultaneously in federal and state forums. For example, there are frequently pendent state claims attached to federal question claims in the United States district courts. Similarly, there are frequently federal claims, such as actions under 42 U.S.C. §1983, joined with state law claims in state court. The adoption of the control group test would mean that some communications would be admissible as to one claim but not the other. It is hard to imagine a judge instructing a jury to consider a communication received in evidence as to one claim, and because of privilege, not the other.

But what of *Upjohn*? After rejecting the control group test as too narrow a definition of the attorney-client privilege, the Court went on to hold that the communications at issue there were privileged. It declined, however, to "lay down a broad rule or series of rules to govern all conceivable future questions in this area." Nevertheless, Samaritan argues that *Upjohn* adopted a broad version of the subject matter test, which includes within the privilege communications by all employees who speak at the direction of their corporate superiors to the corporation's lawyer regarding matters within the scope of their corporate duties in order to facilitate the formulation of legal advice for the corporation.

There is language in *Upjohn* to support Samaritan's argument. The Court noted that "[t]he communications concerned matters within the scope of the employees' corporate duties, and the employees themselves were sufficiently aware that they were being questioned in order that the corporation could obtain legal advice." From this, Samaritan argues that the privilege protects the employee communications at issue here because the nurses and scrub technician were carrying out their corporate duties while present in the operating room. Plaintiffs argue that the employees were merely witnesses to what happened.

We are of the view that a broad interpretation of the subject matter test, requiring only that the communication concerns factual information gained in the course of performing the speaker's corporate duties, is inadequate. The employee's connection to the liability-causing event is too attenuated to fit the classical model of what it means to be a client. Such a standard would only exclude from the privilege factual communications of employees whose knowledge was truly fortuitous. For example, under a broad formulation, the statement of a corporate officer who glances out the window and happens to see the corporation's truck negligently collide with another vehicle would not be privileged. However, the statement of a corporate employee who is present in the truck by virtue of his or her corporate duties but was not driving the truck or otherwise involved in causing the accident would be privileged. This is the construction urged by Samaritan and the various amici. We believe, however, that the latter person also should be considered a mere witness for purposes of the privilege. Although the employee's presence, and hence the employee's knowledge, is a function of his or her corporate employment, the employee bears no other connection to the incident. The employee did not cause it. His actions did not subject the corporation to possible liability. When this employee speaks, it is not about his or her own actions, but the actions of someone else — the driver.

We, therefore, reject a broad version of the subject matter test. We believe it is subject to a narrower interpretation, one more consistent with the concerns we have expressed. Many of the most often cited authorities suggest that we require that the employee's communication relate to the employee's own activities that are within the scope of his or her employment and are being attributed to the corporation.

We believe that a functional approach that focuses on the relationship between the communicator and the need for legal services is truer to the objective sought to be achieved by the attorney-client privilege. The California Supreme Court adopted this approach 30 years ago. We also believe that such an approach is closer to the holding of *Upjohn*, if not some of its language. . . .

We are not persuaded by the amici that, without a broader privilege, corporations will forego prompt post-accident investigations. By not extending the privilege, we place the corporate client on a par with the individual client asserting a privilege as to his or her own communications. This is the purpose of our functional approach. It is, in any event, in the interest of the corporation to be informed, and in most cases it will conclude that ignorance is too high a price to pay to avoid taking witness statements that are potentially discoverable. After all, even those statements have the more qualified protection afforded by the work product doctrine. We are not persuaded that a corporation will intentionally put itself in the position of being the last to know the facts when it is facing potential liability for the acts of its agents. Finally, under the privilege as we have defined it, the kind of communications most likely to be characterized as client statements will be privileged. . . .

We therefore hold that, where someone other than the employee initiates the communication, a factual communication by a corporate employee to corporate counsel is within the corporation's privilege if it concerns the employee's own conduct within the scope of his or her employment and is made to assist the lawyer in assessing or responding to the legal consequences of that conduct for the corporate client. This excludes from the privilege communications from those who, but for their status as officers, agents or employees, are witnesses. . . .

III. RESOLUTION

Applying our test to the facts of this case, we conclude that the statements made by the nurses and the scrub technician to Samaritan's counsel are not within Samaritan's attorney-client privilege. These employees were not seeking legal advice in confidence. The initial overture was made by others in the corporation. Although the employees were present during the operation, their actions did not subject Samaritan to potential liability. Their statements primarily concerned the events going on around them and the actions of the physicians whose alleged negligence caused the injuries. These statements were not gathered to assist Samaritan in assessing or responding to the legal consequences of the speaker's conduct, but to the consequences for the corporation of the physician's conduct. Thus, these Samaritan employees were witnesses to the event, and their statements are not within the attorney-client privilege.

The effort by corporate counsel to sign these employees as independent clients is itself an acknowledgment that the corporation was not satisfied that the employee statements were within the corporation's privilege. . . . Because the employees in this case did not perceive a need for legal advice, and because no attorney-client relationship was established, it is difficult to see what these forms intended to accomplish other than to silence the employees by shielding their communications in the cloak of the attorney-client privilege. . . .

A year after *Samaritan Foundation*, the Arizona Legislature overruled the decision. The legislature amended §12-2234 of the Arizona Revised Statutes to provide:

B. For purposes of subsection A [defining the attorney-client privilege], any communication is privileged between an attorney for a corporation, governmental entity, partnership, business, association or other similar entity or an employer and any employee, agent or member of the entity or employer regarding acts or omissions of or information obtained from the employee, agent or member if the communication is either:

1. For the purpose of providing legal advice to the entity or employer or to the employee, agent or member.
2. For the purpose of obtaining information in order to provide legal advice to the entity or employer or to the employee, agent or member.

C. The privilege defined in this section shall not be construed to allow the employee to be relieved of a duty to disclose the facts solely because they have been communicated to an attorney.

Despite this amendment, as stated, *Samaritan Foundation* remains good law in criminal cases, where the privilege is governed by a different statute from the one at issue in *Samaritan Foundation,* a civil case. Roman Catholic Diocese of Phoenix v. Superior Court, 62 P.3d 970 (Ariz. App. 2003) (enforcing grand jury subpoena served on the Diocese).

The Restatement's Position

Consider how the Restatement defines the privilege for entity clients. Section 73 uses the term "organizational client" and includes within that category corporations, unincorporated associations, partnerships, trusts, estates, sole proprietorships, and "other for-profit or not-for-profit organization[s]." The section would privilege communications that satisfy the other criteria for privilege if the communication is "between an agent of the organization" and a lawyer (or the lawyer's agent) and the communication "concerns a legal matter of interest to the organization." Contrary to *Samaritan Foundation,* the comment to §73 says it is irrelevant whether the lawyer or the employee initiates the communication. Is the Restatement's position the same as *Upjohn's,* or is it more protective or less protective of professional communications?

What's the Right Policy?

1. You have now seen five different ways of describing the attorney-client privilege when a client is an organization: the control group test; *Upjohn* (which the Arizona Supreme Court recognizes is susceptible to two readings); *Samaritan Foundation*; a statute overruling *Samaritan Foundation*; and the Restatement. Which says it best? In thinking about that question, you might try applying these tests to the facts in *Samaritan Foundation,* to the truck accident hypothetical in that case, and to "Slip and Fall," at page 39.

2. One of *Upjohn's* goals — predictability — is lost if states can do as they please. Often an organization will not know in advance whether a particular communication between a corporate employee or agent and its counsel will become an issue in state court or in a federal court under federal law. But states *can* do as they please. Should we have a single, national privilege? (This is a theoretical question only. While Congress may have the power to do that — I say *may* — it's hard to imagine that it ever would.)

3. One consequence of *Upjohn,* the Restatement test, and even of the narrower control group test, is that companies are encouraged to place investigations that may produce embarrassing information under the overarching authority of counsel, thereby increasing the chance of successfully claiming privilege for what the investigator uncovers, so long as the client can show that counsel's purpose was "to render legal advice or services to the client." Spectrum Sys. Intl. Corp. v. Chemical Bank, 581 N.E.2d 1055 (N.Y. 1991). The lawyer doesn't have to do all the interviews herself so long as she supervises the entire effort. Citing *Upjohn,* courts have even upheld claims of privilege for a lawyer's purely factual investigations.

"[C]lients often do retain lawyers to perform investigative work because they want the benefit of a lawyer's expertise and judgment. . . . [I]f a client retains an attorney to use her legal expertise to conduct an investigation, that lawyer is indeed performing legal work." In re Allen, 106 F.3d 582 (4th Cir. 1997) (also holding that the "analysis applied by the Supreme Court in *Upjohn* to determine which employees fall within the scope of the privilege applies equally to former employees" questioned about their work while employed). See also United States v. Rowe, 96 F.3d 1294 (9th Cir. 1996). *Upjohn* produced work for lawyers because only lawyers can bless the inquiry with the attorney-client privilege. But is that result good for society? At least one state high court has expressed reservations about the *Upjohn*-inspired use of lawyers to privilege investigations, not that it had any effect on the use of lawyers for the work. Payton v. New Jersey Turnpike Authority, 691 A.2d 321 (N.J. 1997), observed:

> A substantial number of sexual harassment lawsuits raise the issue of the employer's response to the employee's internal complaint. If the attorney-client privilege were to apply broadly to any internal investigation . . . regardless of the pendency of litigation or the provision of legal advice, then all employers would commission attorneys as investigators, thus defeating the paramount public interest in eradicating discrimination. . . .

4. *Upjohn* assumed that the "Government was free to question the employees who communicated with . . . counsel." Is this true? What about Rule 4.2, called the "no-contact" or "anticontact" rule, which generally forbids a lawyer to speak with an opposing lawyer's client (including certain agents of a corporate client) without the opposing lawyer's permission? Nor may a lawyer circumvent this rule by enlisting the aid of a nonlawyer. See, for example, Model Rule 8.4(a) and chapter 3A. Won't these ethics rules prevent government lawyers from interviewing (or supervising interviews of) the same employees? Or is the government exempt from these ethics rules because of its law enforcement responsibilities? We address that contentious issue further in the next chapter. Here, it is sufficient to stress that when the no-contact rule does apply — and it certainly binds lawyers representing private clients — won't it further magnify corporate secrecy by preventing an opposing lawyer from seeking informal interviews with a company's constituents?

5. *Upjohn* said that the control group test "frustrates the very purpose of the [attorney-client] privilege by discouraging the communication of relevant information by employees of the client corporation to attorneys seeking to render legal advice to the client." Is that empirical assumption true? How does the Court know? I can make a pretty good argument that company lawyers will remain as eager to speak to employees with relevant information, privilege or not, just as they would any witness. In either case, the conversation may at least enjoy the qualified work-product privilege. I can make an argument that corporate

employees will be equally forthcoming. What might happen if they are not? Or, if the Court is right and information will be lost if the privilege doesn't protect communications with corporate employees, then isn't it wrong to assume that the government will be able to get the same information through its own interviews? If without the privilege those employees would be less candid when speaking to their employer's *own* counsel, how candid will they be with the IRS? Or with lawyers for private parties? Here, too, we have to remember that the company owns the privilege. So the constituent has no guarantee of confidentiality. Quite the opposite. She knows her bosses, and possibly others, too (prosecutors?), will learn what she says.

6. In *Samaritan Foundation*, the adversary attempted to get the same information from the interviewed employees through depositions. Understand that the lawyer for their corporate employer would be sitting at the deposition. That's not an environment conducive to candor, is it? In any event, two years had elapsed between the incident and the deposition, and the employees professed memory loss. So, for the plaintiffs, it was either the interview notes (which might be used to refresh recollection) or nothing. If the attorney-client privilege protects the notes, the court won't balance the competing interests, and the plaintiffs will get nothing. If only the qualified work-product privilege applies, the court would have authority to order production of the notes, with counsel's mental impressions removed. If we apply the attorney-client privilege, we sacrifice some truth to the values underlying the privilege. If we don't, we may get more truth but purportedly at the expense of those values. Should those values get less consideration when the source of the communication is not the client but its agents and employees?

7. It was not always clear that the attorney-client privilege would protect communications between the agents of an entity client and its lawyers. See Radiant Burners, Inc. v. American Gas Assn., 207 F. Supp. 771 (N.D. Ill. 1962), rev'd, 320 F.2d 314 (7th Cir.), cert. denied, 375 U.S. 929 (1963). The privilege against self-incrimination does not protect corporations. See Hale v. Henkel, 201 U.S. 43 (1906). As a matter of social policy, was the decision to extend the attorney-client privilege to entities wise? In answering this question, consider whether we should treat small, family-owned corporations differently from General Motors. What if the client is a government agency? (Read on.) Or is it impossible to ask these questions without asking whether any attorney-client privilege is defensible in the first place?

Is There a Government Attorney-Client Privilege?

Much authority seems to suggest that the government, as an entity client, enjoys the same protection for conversations between its lawyers and its agents as *Upjohn* bestowed on corporations. Proposed Fed. R. Evid. 503 included, within the definition of those entitled to claim privilege, "a person, public officer or corporation, association, or other organization or entity, either public or private. . . ." Section 74 of the Restatement, titled Privilege for a Governmental Client, states: "Unless applicable law otherwise provides, the attorney-client privilege extends to a communication of a governmental organization. . . ."

Bill Clinton's legal woes changed the map, beginning with the Eighth Circuit's decision in In re Grand Jury Subpoena Duces Tecum, 112 F.3d 910 (8th Cir. 1997). Whitewater Independent Counsel Kenneth Starr had subpoenaed the notes White House lawyers took in conversations they had on two occasions with First Lady Hillary Rodham Clinton. Mrs. Clinton's personal lawyer, David Kendall, was also present at these meetings. At one of the meetings, Mrs. Clinton discussed her activities following the death of Deputy White House Counsel Vincent Foster. The second meeting — really a series of meetings — took place on the day that Mrs. Clinton testified under subpoena before a federal grand jury convened by Mr. Starr. A federal district judge in Arkansas had refused to enforce Mr. Starr's subpoena for the White House lawyers' notes of these meetings, but, in a 2-1 ruling, the Eighth Circuit reversed. The opinion was initially issued under seal, but after the White House elected to seek Supreme Court review, it was publicly released, and the case was restyled Office of the President v. Office of Independent Counsel. The Supreme Court denied certiorari on June 23, 1997, 521 U.S. 1105 (1997), and the White House delivered the lawyers' notes to Mr. Starr's office the same day.

The Eighth Circuit opinion assumed that the government enjoys attorney-client privilege in contests with other litigants. Nevertheless, the court held that no government attorney-client privilege could be asserted to avoid a federal prosecutor's grand jury subpoena. The court did not rely on the narrower ground that Mrs. Clinton, in any event, was not a representative of the White House, the alleged client:

> We believe the strong public interest in honest government and in exposing wrongdoing by public officials would be ill-served by recognition of a governmental attorney-client privilege applicable in criminal proceedings inquiring into the actions of public officials. We also believe that to allow *any part* of the federal government to use its in-house attorneys as a shield against the production of information relevant to a federal criminal investigation would represent a gross misuse of public assets. [Emphasis added.]

Although the Eighth Circuit opinion addressed a federal prosecutor's grand jury subpoena of an *executive* branch lawyer, the quoted language would apply to lawyers in all three branches ("any part").

One reason the court gave for affording a branch of the federal government, in this case the White House, less protection than *Upjohn* gave private companies is that the "actions of White House personnel, whatever their capacity, cannot expose the White House as an entity to criminal liability. . . . A corporation, in contrast, may be subject to both civil and criminal liability for the actions of its agents, and corporate attorneys therefore have a compelling interest in ferreting out any misconduct by employees. The White House simply has no such interest with respect to the actions of Mrs. Clinton." In other words, the White House could not assert privilege because, unlike a corporation, the White House could have no civil or criminal liability for the conduct of its agents or employees and therefore the privilege was not needed to enable the government lawyers to do their job of protecting their client.

The Eighth Circuit acknowledged that it was dealing with a question of first impression. Nevertheless, it applied its ruling retroactively. The dissenting judge would have recognized a qualified attorney-client privilege for government lawyers, subject to judicial balancing, and would have applied the ruling prospectively only.

The following year, another federal appellate court also refused to recognize a government attorney-client privilege. But now the stakes were even higher. The communications at issue were between President Clinton and Deputy White House Counsel Bruce Lindsey. Independent Counsel Starr had subpoenaed Lindsey to a federal grand jury. Was Lindsey required to reveal communications with Clinton despite assertion of privilege? The answer was yes: "When an executive branch attorney is called before a federal grand jury to give evidence about alleged crimes within the executive branch, reason and experience, duty, and tradition dictate that the attorney shall provide that evidence. With respect to investigations of federal criminal offenses . . . government attorneys stand in a far different position from members of the private bar. Their duty is not to defend clients against criminal charges and it is not to protect wrongdoers from public exposure." In re Lindsey, 158 F.3d 1263 (D.C. Cir. 1998).

Judge Tatel dissented in part. The majority opinion, he wrote, "nowhere accounts for the unique nature of the Presidency, its unique need for confidential legal advice, or the possible consequences of abrogating the attorney-client privilege for a President's ability to obtain such advice." Judge Tatel predicted that future presidents "will avoid confiding in their lawyers because they can never know whether the information they share, no matter how innocent, might some day become 'pertinent to possible criminal violations.' . . . As a result, Presidents may well shift their trust on all but the most routine legal matters from White House Counsel, who undertake to serve the Presidency, to private counsel who represent its occupant." These opinions leave the following questions open:

1. Do they apply as well to prosecutorial *trial* subpoenas?
2. If so, may a criminal defense lawyer also defeat a claim of government attorney-client privilege with a trial subpoena or discovery demand? Concluding that a court could defeat a government assertion of privilege in a criminal case after balancing the defendant's need for information against the government's need for confidentiality is United States v. Peitz, 2002 Westlaw 31101681 (N.D. Ill. 2002) (ruling against the defendant on facts before it).
3. Do the opinions extend to federal grand jury or trial subpoenas of communications between state or local officials and their government lawyers? Answering yes for a federal grand jury subpoena is In re A Witness Before the Special Grand Jury 2000-2, 288 F.3d 289 (7th Cir. 2002) ("Although we recognize the importance of federalism in general, we do not see its relevance to the present situation."). The grand jury investigating Illinois Governor George Ryan for his conduct as Illinois Secretary of State had subpoenaed Roger Bickel, Chief Legal Counsel to the

Secretary during Ryan's tenure. The court did not need to reach this question. Bickel's client was not Ryan but Illinois or the Secretary's office, and the current Secretary had waived any privilege. But the court chose to address the privilege question instead of waiver, and having found no privilege, it did not reach waiver. (Ryan was later indicted and convicted.)

The Eighth and D.C. Circuit opinions were bad news for President and Mrs. Clinton. In the end, though, they actually strengthened the Presidency. Do you see why? The Eighth Circuit granted authority to federal prosecutors to override claims of governmental attorney-client privilege in "any part" of the federal government. Except for the rare use of Independent Counsel, under a law that has expired, federal prosecutors work for the Justice Department, which is run by the Attorney General, who works for the President. Could the Justice Department of a Democratic President subpoena the government lawyer for a Republican House Speaker before a grand jury and ask about conversations with her client? It would seem so.

But remember that the Supreme Court denied review of the Eighth Circuit opinion, so the issue is not settled. And there is contrary authority. Explicitly rejecting the views of the D.C., 7th and 8th Circuits, In re Grand Jury Investigation, 399 F.3d 527 (2d Cir. 2005), upheld a claim of privilege, in connection with a federal grand jury investigation, for communications between a government lawyer and a former Connecticut governor.

> We believe that, if anything, the traditional rationale for the privilege applies with special force in the government context. It is crucial that government officials, who are expected to uphold and execute the law and who may face criminal prosecution for failing to do so, be encouraged to seek out and receive fully informed legal advice. Upholding the privilege furthers a culture in which consultation with government lawyers is accepted as a normal, desirable, and even indispensable part of conducting public business. Abrogating the privilege undermines that culture and thereby impairs the public interest.

The current governor had declined to waive the privilege. The court expressed no view on whether a later governor's waiver would be effective. The same court later upheld a claim of privilege when a *private litigant* sought to discover advice that a lawyer gave county officials on how a strip search policy could be framed consistent with the Fourth Amendment. In re County of Erie, 473 F.3d 413 (2d Cir. 2007).

Kathleen Clark has written more broadly about the confidentiality duties of government lawyers and to whom they are owed (including the example of the lawyer called "Deep Throat" who was the source for Woodward and Bernstein's *All the President's Men*). Government Lawyers and Confidentiality Norms, 85 Wash. L. Rev. 1033 (2007).

Exceptions to the Privilege or the Ethical Duty

"Under the law, your statements to me and the advice I give you are privileged and confidential. What that means is that anything you tell me or my staff will not go outside

this law office without your permission and only for your benefit. Under the law and my ethical obligations, no one can make us reveal our conversations and I will keep them completely confidential."

If you earned ten dollars each time a lawyer said something like this to a client, you'd soon be as rich as Bill Gates. (Well, not quite.) Sure, this assurance puts clients at ease and encourages candor. But it's wrong, wrong, wrong. In several circumstances, lawyers may reveal, or may even be required to reveal, information clients wish to protect. The following examples are among the important exceptions to (or exclusions from) either the privilege or the duty to maintain client confidences (or both).

Self-Defense and Legal Claims.   A lawyer "may reveal [confidential] information . . . to the extent the lawyer reasonably believes necessary . . . to establish a defense to a criminal charge or civil claim against the lawyer based upon conduct in which the client was involved, or to respond to allegations in any proceeding concerning the lawyer's representation of the client." Rule 1.6(b)(5). Rule 1.6 and several cases recognize that a lawyer's right of self-defense applies whether charges against the lawyer are made by the client or third parties. In a leading case, Meyerhofer v. Empire Fire & Marine Insurance Co., 497 F.2d 1190 (2d Cir. 1974), Goldberg had been an associate in a law firm when the firm handled a registration statement for a client. The firm rejected Goldberg's view that certain information omitted from the statement had to be revealed. Goldberg quit and gave the Securities and Exchange Commission detailed information about the episode in affidavit form, with supporting documents. Three months later Goldberg was named as one of a number of defendants in a civil action arising out of the registration statement. In a successful effort to extricate himself from the civil action, he gave information, including the SEC affidavit, to the plaintiff's lawyers. In ruling on a motion to disqualify the plaintiff's lawyers for receiving the information, the Second Circuit found Goldberg's conduct proper.

Goldberg had not provided information to the plaintiff's lawyers in order to enable them to bring the lawsuit. Goldberg was a victim, not an instigator. The complaint against Goldberg alleged violation of civil and criminal statutes and sought damages of more than $4 million.

> The cost in money of simply defending such an action might be very substantial. The damage to [Goldberg's] professional reputation which might be occasioned by the mere pendency of such a charge was an even greater cause for concern. Under these circumstances Goldberg had the right to make an appropriate disclosure with respect to his role in the public offering. Concomitantly, he had the right to support his version of the facts with suitable evidence.

See also People v. Robnett, 859 P.2d 872 (Colo. 1993) (rule's authority to reveal is not restricted to proceedings initiated by a former client); In re Robeson, 652 P.2d 336 (Or. 1982) (lawyer facing charge filed with disciplinary committee by third party may reveal client confidences).

Goldberg did not have to wait until the trial to defend himself. He was allowed to reveal the information at an early stage of the action. In fact, had Goldberg known in advance that he was about to be sued, he could probably have revealed the information even before the action was filed. In In re Friend, 411 F. Supp. 776 (S.D.N.Y. 1975), the court applied *Meyerhofer* where a lawyer and his former client were under criminal investigation. The lawyer wanted to provide the grand jury with documents that would tend to exonerate him but which the client claimed were privileged. The court granted the lawyer's motion, citing *Meyerhofer* and DR 4-101(C)(4). "Although, as yet, no formal accusation has been made against Mr. Friend, it would be senseless to require the stigma of an indictment to attach prior to allowing Mr. Friend to invoke the exception of DR 4-101(C)(4) in his own defense." Friend's luck eventually ran out. Both he and his corporate client were indicted. United States v. Amrep Corp., 418 F. Supp. 473 (S.D.N.Y. 1976). Comment [10] to Rule 1.6 likewise states that the self-defense exception "does not require the lawyer to await the commencement of an action or proceeding that charges . . . complicity [in client wrongdoing], so that the defense may be established by responding directly to a third party who has made such an assertion." Restatement §64 agrees.

The self-defense exception is circumscribed by a rule of reasonable necessity. A lawyer must have good reason to believe that revelation of the information is necessary to his or her self-protection. David Bryan had a romantic relationship with a current client (not a good idea and sometimes improper, see pages 717 and 784). After it ended and she had new counsel, Bryan revealed confidential information that "exceeded that which was reasonably necessary to defend against [the client's] allegations." Matter of Bryan, 61 P.3d 641 (Kan. 2003), publicly censured Bryan in a lengthy opinion that reads like the script of a bad soap opera. (Is that redundant?)

Equivalent self-defense exceptions have been recognized as exceptions to assertions of privilege. See Apex Municipal Fund v. N-Group Securities, 841 F. Supp. 1423 (S.D. Tex. 1993); In re National Mortgage Equity Corp., 120 F.R.D. 687 (C.D. Cal. 1988); First Fed. Sav. & Loan Assn. v. Oppenheim, Appel, Dixon & Co., 110 F.R.D. 557 (S.D.N.Y. 1986). Lawyers may also be able to use Rule 1.6(b)(5) to prove claims against their employers for retaliatory discharge or illegal discrimination. Kachmar v. SunGard Data Systems, Inc., 109 F.3d 173 (3d Cir. 1997). See also chapter 10B.

Collection of Fees.   Rule 1.6(b)(5) also permits lawyers to reveal confidential information to the extent necessary when they sue to collect fees.

Waiver.   Clients can waive confidentiality. Rules 1.6(a), 1.8(b), 1.9. The interesting waiver debates are about privilege. A client may waive the privilege. Waiver may be explicit or implicit. Waiver will be inferred when the client puts the confidential communication in issue in a litigation. For example, a defendant charged with transporting fraudulently obtained securities in interstate commerce claimed that his actions were taken in good faith reliance on counsel's advice. Consequently, the government was entitled to cross-examine him about a letter from counsel that might otherwise have been privileged. United States v. Miller, 600 F.2d 498 (5th Cir. 1979). Similarly, in United States v. Bilzerian, 926 F.2d 1285 (2d Cir. 1991), the court upheld a ruling that if a defendant in a securities fraud case were to testify to his "good faith" belief in the "lawfulness" of his conduct, he would thereby waive the privilege for communications from his former counsel tending to contradict him. This is about fairness. A client cannot selectively cite counsel's advice in defense and then deny its opponent access to other parts of that advice that undermine the defense. By contrast, in United States v. White, 887 F.2d 267 (D.C. Cir. 1989), privilege was not waived when a defendant, charged with conspiring to defraud the United States, merely denied criminal intent. "To be acquitted for lack of criminal intent, White did not need to introduce any evidence of communications to and from [counsel], and he did not do so." He simply put the government to its proof. See also In re County of Erie, 546 F.3d 222 (2d Cir. 2008) (in §1983 case, public officials' assertion of qualified immunity merely claims "that their actions were lawful" and does not waive privilege because it is not "a good faith or state of mind defense"); In re Lott, 424 F.3d 336 (6th Cir. 2005) (habeas petitioner's assertion of actual innocence does not waive attorney-client privilege).

Clients may waive the protection of the attorney-client privilege by revelation of all or part of a confidential communication. In In re Martin Marietta Corp., 856 F.2d 619 (4th Cir. 1988), Martin Marietta gave the U.S. attorney a Position Paper describing why it should not be indicted. Later, a former employee of Martin Marietta was indicted for fraud and sought to subpoena this information in his defense. The court held that "the Position Paper as well as the underlying details are no longer within the attorney-client privilege." In another case, a company that revealed its counsel's tax advice in an SEC filing lost the privilege "with respect to all documents which formed the basis for the advice, all documents considered by counsel in rendering that advice, and all reasonably contemporaneous documents reflecting discussions by counsel or others concerning that advice." But the privilege was not lost "with respect to other matters." In re Pioneer Hi-Bred International, Inc., 238 F.3d 1370 (Fed. Cir. 2001) (also holding that the privilege was lost for communications disclosed to expert witnesses).

In one factually unusual case, MIT lost its attorney-client privilege for documents subpoenaed by the IRS. The university had provided the same documents to the Department of Defense in connection with an audit of DOD contracts with the school. MIT argued that "disclosure to the [DOD] audit agency was not 'voluntary' because of the practical pressures and the legal constraints to which it was subject as a government contractor." Maybe so, Judge Boudin wrote, but "MIT chose to place itself in this position by becoming a government contractor. In short, MIT's disclosure to the audit agency resulted from its own voluntary choice, even if that choice was made at the time it became a defense contractor and subjected itself to the alleged obligation of disclosure." Consequently, privilege for the disclosed documents was waived. United States v. Massachusetts Institute of Technology, 129 F.3d 681 (1st Cir. 1997).

One circuit has recognized what it called "limited waiver" where a company shares privileged information with the SEC but then seeks to protect the same information in private litigation. Diversified Industries, Inc. v. Meredith, 572 F.2d 596 (8th Cir. 1978) (en banc) ("To hold otherwise may have the effect of thwarting the developing procedure of corporations to employ independent outside counsel to investigate and advise them in order to protect stockholders, potential stockholders and customers."). Other circuit courts have rejected this view on the ground that recognition of a limited waiver is not necessary to encourage communications with counsel — the goal of the privilege in the first place — and might be employed for manipulative or tactical reasons. United States v. Massachusetts Institute of Technology, supra, collects the cases. See also In re Qwest Communications Intern. Inc., 450 F.3d 1179 (10th Cir. 2006).

A middle position would, if followed, permit limited waiver if a government agency agrees to keep the information confidential. Does that make sense? The scope of privilege (and waiver) is a legal question for the courts. Parties cannot expand the privilege with a contract. In re Columbia/HCA Healthcare Corp. Billing Practices Litig., 293 F.3d 289 (6th Cir. 2002). Efforts have been made to amend the Federal Rules of Evidence to permit limited waiver when a client shares information with a government agency, but none has succeeded. And yet, if a company has done an internal investigation of the events that interest the government, wouldn't it be better to allow the company to share its findings with the government (saving it time and money) without thereby losing privilege in private litigations? Or instead, as courts have repeatedly held, does the company have incentive enough to share its findings with the government without offering the added incentive of a limited waiver doctrine?

Contrast the rejection of limited waiver with the holding in In re von Bulow, 828 F.2d 94 (2d Cir. 1987). Claus von Bulow was convicted of attempting to murder his wife, Martha, but the Rhode Island Supreme Court reversed, and, on retrial, he was acquitted. Alan Dershowitz of Harvard Law School, who had been von Bulow's appellate lawyer, then wrote a book about the case called *Reversal of Fortune: Inside the von Bulow Case.* (It later became a pretty good film.) Thereafter, in a civil action against Claus brought by Martha's children from a prior marriage, the plaintiffs "moved to compel discovery of certain discussions between [Claus] and his attorneys based on the alleged waiver of the attorney-client privilege with respect to those communications related in the book." The court held that publication of the book was a "waiver by von Bulow as to the particular matters *actually disclosed* in the book," but no waiver of undisclosed conversations on the same or related subjects. The result would be opposite if a client made selective disclosure of privileged information in court. The "fairness doctrine" would then "requir[e] production of the remainder." But the "fairness doctrine" does not apply when "the privilege-holder or his attorney has made extrajudicial disclosures, and those disclosures have not subsequently been placed at issue during litigation."

Privilege is not waived for communications between a lawyer or client and agents of either if the purpose of the communication is to enable the lawyer to render professional legal services. So, for example, information a client gives to a lawyer's support staff can retain its privileged status. Similarly, a lawyer may need to hire an expert in another field in order to be able to understand the client's problem. Communications between them for that purpose are protected. United States v. Alvarez, 519 F.2d 1036 (3d Cir. 1975) (therapist), United States v. Kovel, 296 F.2d 918 (2d Cir. 1961) (accountant). Compare Cavallaro v. United States, 284 F.3d 236 (1st Cir. 2002) ("'The involvement of the third party must be nearly indispensable or serve some specialized purpose in facilitating the attorney-client communications. Mere convenience is not sufficient.'"). *Cavallaro* sets the bar unduly high.

Agents of clients, especially companies (which can only respond through agents) may discuss the lawyer's advice in order to implement it. If so, the advice remains protected. Zurich American Ins. Co. v. Superior Court, 66 Cal. Rptr. 3d

(App. Ct. 2007). Here's how Verschoth v. Time Warner Inc., 2001 Westalw 286763 (S.D.N.Y. 2001) explained it:

> The attorney-client privilege "protects from disclosure communications among corporate employees that reflect advice rendered by counsel to the corporation." "This follows from the recognition that since the decision-making power of the corporate client is diffused among several employees, the dissemination of confidential communications to such persons does not defeat the privilege."
>
> However, the person to whom an executive relays legal advice must "share [ ] responsibility for the subject matter underlying the consultation" in order for the privilege to be preserved. Furthermore, the originator of the communication must have intended that it be kept confidential, and it may not be circulated beyond those employees with a need to know the information. . . .
>
> The "need to know" must be analyzed from two perspectives: (1) the role in the corporation of the employee or agent who receives the communication; and (2) the nature of the communication, that is, whether it necessarily incorporates legal advice. To the extent that the recipient of the information is a policymaker generally or is responsible for the specific subject matter at issue in a way that depends upon legal advice, then the communication is more likely privileged. For example, if an automobile manufacturer is attempting to remedy a design defect that has created legal liability, then the vice president for design is surely among those to whom confidential legal communications can be made. So, too, is the engineer who will actually redesign the defective part: he or she will necessarily have a dialogue with counsel so that the lawyers can understand the practical constraints and the engineer can comprehend the legal ones. By contrast, the autoworker on the assembly line has no need to be advised of the legal basis for a change in production even though it affects the worker's routine and thus is within his or her general area of responsibility. The worker, of course, must be told what new production procedure to implement, but has no need to know the legal background.

As a sign of the times, perhaps, the same doctrine has been cited to protect communications between counsel and public relations experts, whom litigants may wish to hire in high-profile cases. The very purpose of a public relations expert is to help decide what information to make public, which can be seen as inconsistent with the purpose of the privilege. On the other hand, lawyers are legitimately concerned with how the media treat prominent cases and may need help in responding to press reports. (Not only are lawyers generally unschooled in these issues, many assume incorrectly that they can spin any journalist.) Compare In re Copper Market Antitrust Litig., 200 F.R.D. 213 (S.D.N.Y. 2001) (upholding privilege for communications with public relations firm); with Calvin Klein Trademark Trust v. Wachner, 198 F.R.D. 53 (S.D.N.Y. 2000) (rejecting privilege for communications with same firm). Judge Kaplan sought to reconcile these cases in upholding privilege in In re Grand Jury Subpoenas, 265 F. Supp. 2d 321 (S.D.N.Y. 2003) ("Lawyers may need skilled advice as to whether and how possible statements to the press—ranging from 'no comment' to detailed factual presentations—likely would be reported in order to advise a client as to whether the making of particular statements would be in the client's legal interest.").

Issues of waiver also arise when a law firm or client accidentally reveals allegedly privileged information to an adversary. For example, a response to a discovery demand may inadvertently include privileged information. Or a legal secretary, intending to fax a privileged document to the client, may press the wrong button and send it to the adversary. Will these unintentional mistakes result in loss of the privilege for the documents mistakenly sent, or even more broadly? May the receiving lawyer, on recognizing the error, nevertheless read and use the mistakenly transmitted documents? This issue is discussed in chapter 3B.

Waiver and the Debate over DOJ Requests.   In a series of memoranda from successive Deputy Attorneys General, the Department of Justice has defined, then refined and refined again, whether and when a prosecutor investigating a company or other organization may condition favorable treatment (like a promise not to indict) on the company's agreement to waive attorney-client privilege and work-product protection. The bar has been, to say the least, intensely hostile to the proposition that a prosecutor may use waiver demands as leverage when the alternative for the company may be indictment and serious harm if not certain death (RIP Arthur Anderson). In other words, the compulsion is seen as just too great and the protections as too important. In addition, as we've just seen, waiver for the government will, in all circuits but the Eighth, constitute waiver to civil claimants. DOJ would be receptive to a statutory limited waiver authority, but waiver opponents actually oppose even that because its mere existence would make it easier for DOJ to demand a waiver.

As the Department sees it, a company's willingness to waive these protections demonstrates that it is truly repentant and cooperative. The information thereby revealed will enable DOJ to pursue other (the real) malefactors (generally current or former constituents of the company). If the company wants to escape indictment on the ground that it is now cooperating and will be a good corporate citizen, the argument runs, it should start by helping the government nail the bad guys. The bar responds that if companies can be induced (actually, forced) to waive privilege on threat of indictment, the company's lawyers will not get information from corporate constituents who fear that the lawyer is as a practical matter working for the prosecutor and clam up, making it harder to represent the company.

This book would have to be a newspaper to report on the (relatively) fast-developing events in the resolution of this standoff, but they may recently have come to a (temporary?) halt. Congress threatened legislation forbidding DOJ to request waivers or even to give credit to waivers voluntarily offered (assuming anything can be voluntary in the face of possible indictment). Especially hostile to DOJ's position was Senator Arlen Spector and (forgive the pun) the specter of Senator Spector's bill forced DOJ via Deputy Attorney General Mark Filip to back off the latest iteration of its waiver policy (written by former Deputy Attorney General Paul McNulty and called, therefore, the McNulty memorandum) and to issue a less aggressive one.

This it did in August 2008. The new policy mostly capitulates. No company is obligated or can be asked to waive privilege or work product protection, though like all other subjects of investigation, including individuals, they may choose to do so. Failure to waive cannot be used against a company. However, prosecutors may consider whether a company, like any other subject, has voluntarily revealed *facts*. As we've seen, although a client's *communication* may be privileged, the underlying facts usually are not. The "government's key measure of cooperation must remain the same as . . . for an individual. Has the party timely disclosed the relevant facts about the putative misconduct?," the new memo asks. If so, "the corporation may receive due credit for such cooperation, regardless of whether it chooses to waive privilege or work product protection in the process."

But there's a hitch even here that may extend the hostilities. The memorandum does not say that voluntary disclosure of privileged communications cannot be considered in evaluating the company's cooperation. So we have half of "don't ask, don't tell" — the "don't ask" part. The prosecutor and defense lawyer are sitting in a room. There are things the prosecutor cannot say. But the defense lawyer knows that waiving privilege may avoid indictment. Some lawyers have argued that prosecutors should not be able to credit even voluntary, unrequested waivers, presumably because nothing is voluntary in that environment. Do you agree? What's the contrary argument?

"To Comply With Other Law."   Even before Rule 1.6(b)(6) was added as an exception to the confidentiality duty in 2002, permitting lawyers to reveal confidential information "to comply with other law or a court order," many observers thought that exception was implicit. And despite Rule 1.6(b)'s use of the term "may," this exception would seem to be mandatory. If the law or a court requires disclosure, a lawyer cannot expect to set up an overriding confidentiality duty to avoid it.

The Crime-Fraud Exception to the Privilege.   Communications between clients and counsel are not privileged (although they may be ethically protected) when the client has consulted the lawyer in order to further a crime or fraud, regardless of whether the crime or fraud is accomplished and even though the lawyer is unaware of the client's purpose and does nothing to advance it. See United States v. Doe, 429 F.3d 450 (3d Cir. 2005); In re Grand Jury Proceedings, 87 F.3d 377 (9th Cir. 1996).

What's fraud?   The D.C. Circuit has held that the exception applies not only to traditional frauds but also to "other misconduct." In re Sealed Case, 754 F.2d 395 (D.C. Cir. 1985). In re Richard Roe, Inc., 168 F.3d 69 (2d Cir. 1999), found that in limited circumstances the manner of conducting litigation could constitute a crime or fraud that would defeat the privilege. "Thus, a client's directing an attorney to make large numbers of motions solely for purposes of delay would be discoverable. Similarly, where a party suborns perjury by a witness to bolster a claim or defense, communications or work product relating to that witness might also be discoverable." The victim of the intended fraud need not be a distinct individual or entity. American Tobacco Co. v. State, 697 So. 2d 1249 (Fla. App. 1997), rejected a claim of privilege for communications between tobacco companies and their counsel based on proof that the companies "hid from and misrepresented to the public the health risks of smoking and that their conduct constituted fraud on the public." See also State v. Philip Morris, Inc., 606 N.W.2d 676 (Minn. 2000) (fraud can be on consumers generally).

The exception "does not apply simply because privileged communications would provide an adversary with evidence of a crime or fraud. . . . Instead, the exception applies only when the court determines that the client communication . . . in question was itself in furtherance of the crime or fraud." In re Richard Roe, Inc., 68 F.3d 38 (2d Cir. 1995). In re Grand Jury Subpoena, 419 F.3d 329 (5th Cir. 2005), agrees. That makes sense. We might then say that there was never a true professional relationship to begin with and therefore no entitlement to the protection the privilege bestows.

The Third Circuit has ruled, in what it said "may be . . . an issue of first impression," that the crime-fraud exception to the privilege will apply when the focus of the investigation is the misconduct of the law firm rather than the client. In re Impounded Case (Law Firm), 879 F.2d 1211 (3d Cir. 1989). See also In re Sealed Case, 107 F.3d 46 (D.C. Cir. 1997) ("may be rare cases . . . in which the attorney's fraudulent or criminal intent defeats a claim of privilege even if the client is innocent"). Is that fair? Why should a well-intentioned client have her communications with counsel revealed over her objection because her lawyer was the bad apple? The First Circuit says the fraud must be the client's. In re Grand Jury Proceedings, 417 F.3d 318 (1st Cir. 2005).

Jane Doe was an executive of an organization that a grand jury was investigating. A subpoena required production of certain e-mails. The organization's counsel read the subpoena to Doe who did nothing to stop the routine destruction of e-mails, including e-mails covered by the subpoena, pursuant to an otherwise legitimate organizational policy. Was Doe's *inaction* "fraud" so that her communications with counsel were no longer privileged? On these unusual facts, the court said failure to intercept the policy was fraud. In re Grand Jury Investigation, 445 F.3d 266 (3rd Cir. 2006) ("If, with knowledge of the Government's interest in retrieving any remaining e-mails, Jane Doe continued to receive emails that were arguably responsive to the subpoena and failed to use her position as an executive of the Organization to direct that all e-mail deletions stop immediately, she may be viewed as furthering the obstruction of the grand jury's investigation or the obstruction of justice").

Applying the exception. Say Joe asserts the attorney-client privilege and Boe wants to contest the assertion on the ground of the crime-fraud exception. Must Boe actually prove a crime or fraud in order to discover the allegedly privileged information? Sometimes, the ultimate issue in the case within which the privilege question arises will be the very same alleged crime or fraud. Unless something is done, this can lead to a "chicken and egg" problem, in which a party has to prove her case in order to get the information needed to prove her case.

Courts have avoided this problem by establishing a second (lesser) burden of proof to invoke the crime-fraud exception. As the Second Circuit said in In re Grand Jury Subpoena Duces Tecum (Marc Rich & Co.), 731 F.2d 1032 (2d Cir. 1984):

> The crime or fraud need not have occurred for the exception to be applicable; it need only have been the objective of the client's communication. And the fraudulent nature of the objective need not be established definitively; there need only be presented a reasonable basis for believing that the objective

was fraudulent. . . . [The courts] require that a prudent person have a reasonable basis to suspect the perpetration or attempted perpetration of a crime or fraud, and that the communications were in furtherance thereof.

The First Circuit also says the the test is a "reasonable basis to believe." In re Grand Jury Proceedings, supra.

Napster created problems for both the music business and intellectual property law. It also led to litigation in the Ninth Circuit that has changed the rules on the crime-fraud exception in two ways, at least in the Ninth Circuit. The first way is to heighten the burden of proof before a court may require disclosure of privileged information in civil cases (as opposed to grand jury investigations). The party seeking the allegedly privileged information must prove the crime or fraud by a preponderance of the evidence. A "reasonable basis to believe" was deemed insufficiently respectful of the privilege. In re Napster, Inc. Copyright Lit., 479 F.3d 1078 (9th Cir. 2007). At first glance, this may seem unfair. The party seeking the communications may want them to prove the very same fraud by a preponderance of the evidence to a jury. Yet now it must first make the same proof to the trial judge. The *Napster* court acknowledged this problem but held that it wasn't really a problem because, as next described, the trial judge may be able to consider the content of the allegedly privileged information in chambers in deciding whether the fraud has been proved. So there's something of a bootstrap operation here, and it benefits the moving party. *Napster's* second change appears below.

In camera review.   The Supreme Court has told us that the trial court may review the allegedly privileged information in camera when deciding if the opponent of the privilege has met the burden of proving the crime-fraud exception, whether that is the lower burden in the Second and other Circuits or the higher burden *Napster* created in the Ninth Circuit. United States v. Zolin, 491 U.S. 554 (1989). Zolin, however, creates yet a different and easier burden of proof for an in camera review:

> Before engaging in in camera review to determine the applicability of the crime-fraud exception, "the judge should require a showing of a factual basis adequate to support a good faith belief by a reasonable person" . . . that in camera review of the materials may reveal evidence to establish the claim that the crime-fraud exception applies.

But what evidence may a trial judge consider in determining whether in camera review of the allegedly privileged information is justified? (This has now become a "chicken and egg and chicken and egg" problem, *et cetera.*) The *Zolin* Court wrote that "the threshold showing to obtain in camera review may be met by using any relevant evidence, lawfully obtained, that has not been adjudicated to be privileged." And if this threshold is met, what may the judge inspect? In re Grand Jury Subpoena 92-1 (SJ), 31 F.3d 826 (9th Cir. 1994), held that absent "a continuing cover-up . . . in camera review pursuant to the crime-fraud exception should be limited to documents generated before the completion of the alleged crime or fraud." For one meticulous guide through the complexities of *Zolin*, see Judge Kleinfeld's opinion in United States v. Chen,

99 F.3d 1495 (9th Cir. 1996), which also holds that premature use of the alleg-edly privileged information in conducting a *Zolin* analysis was harmless error.

Napster's second innovation shows up here, again only for civil cases. Let's review the bidding. Boe (remember Boe?) wanted to get Joe's communications with his lawyer, alleging that Joe had been using his lawyer to accomplish a crime or fraud. Boe has introduced nonprivileged evidence to meet the *Zolin* burden, and the judge has proceeded to pour over Joe's attorney-client communications in chambers. She must decide if Boe has satisfied whatever may be the circuit's requirement (preponderance or a reasonable basis to believe) for proving a fraud and denying Joe the benefit of the privilege. Before she rules, however, Joe pipes up. "Your, honor. Don't I get to introduce evidence to defeat Boe's claim of crime or fraud?" he complains. "Boe got to introduce his evidence. You need to consider mine. It's only fair." *Napster* agreed.

> We hold that in civil cases where outright disclosure is requested the party seeking to preserve the privilege has the right to introduce countervailing evidence. In so holding, we agree with the well-reasoned decision of Judge Aldisert for the Third Circuit in [Haines v. Liggett Group Inc., 975 F.2d 81 (3d Cir. 1992)]. That court wrote:
>
>> Deciding whether the crime-fraud exception applies is another matter [from deciding whether to conduct in camera review]. If the party seeking to apply the exception has made its initial [*Zolin*] showing, then a more formal procedure is required than that entitling plaintiff to in camera review. The importance of the privilege, as we have dis-cussed, as well as fundamental concepts of due process require that the party defending the privilege be given the opportunity to be heard, by evidence and argument, at the hearing seeking an excep-tion to the privilege.

The effect of confidentiality exceptions on privilege.   Jeffrey Purcell was a legal services lawyer in Boston. His client, Joseph Tyree, had been discharged as a maintenance worker at an apartment building and had been ordered to vacate his apartment. While Tyree was meeting with Purcell about his situation, he made threats to burn down the apartment building. Purcell told the police, who found incendiary materials in Tyree's home. When Tyree was indicted, Purcell was subpoenaed to testify. He challenged the subpoena, citing the privilege. Purcell acted properly in revealing Tyree's intention to commit a crime, the court said, but that act did not waive the privilege. The crime-fraud exception would only apply if Tyree had sought to use Purcell's assistance to commit a crime. As the court saw it, "an informed lawyer may be able to dissuade the client from improper future conduct and, if not, under the ethical rules may elect in the public interest to make a limited disclosure of the client's threatened conduct." But lawyers

> will be reluctant to come forward if they know that the information that they disclose may lead to adverse consequences to their clients. A practice of the use of such disclosures might prompt a lawyer to warn a client in advance that the disclosure of certain information may not be held confidential, thereby chil-ling free discourse between lawyer and client and reducing the prospect that the lawyer will learn of a serious threat to the well-being of others. To best promote the purposes of the attorney-client privilege, the crime-fraud

exception should apply only if the communication seeks assistance in or furtherance of future criminal conduct.

Purcell v. District Attorney for the Suffolk District, 676 N.E.2d 436 (Mass. 1997). Newman v. State, 863 A.2d 321 (Md. 2004), a case whose nearly incredible facts defy summary, follows *Purcell* over three dissents. While it makes sense to permit a lawyer to reveal confidences without thereby waiving the privilege, why was Tyree's threat within the privilege at all? The court stressed that Tyree did not seek Purcell's help in committing the arson. If he had, of course, the privilege would be lost for that reason alone. But the opposite does not follow — that because Tyree did *not* seek Purcell's aid in committing arson, the threat is privileged. Tyree did not make his threat in order to get legal advice. He wasn't asking whether it's legal to commit arson. Compare United States v. Alexander, 287 F.3d 811 (9th Cir. 2002) (lawyer for criminal defendant alerted authorities to client's threats of physical violence then asserted privilege when subpoenaed before grand jury to testify to the threats; *held* that threats were not privileged because not made "in order to obtain legal advice").

Future Crimes or Frauds.   Like the crime-fraud exception to the privilege, confidentiality rules may allow or require lawyers to reveal a client's criminal or fraudulent conduct in certain circumstances. But as mentioned earlier (page 37), the circumstances vary greatly among American jurisdictions. The Code extended a permissive authority when the client intended to commit a crime, any crime. DR 4-101(C)(3). Some states retain that provision. Rule 1.6(b)(1) permits lawyers to reveal confidences to prevent death or substantial bodily harm, whoever the actor and even if no crime is involved. For example, a lawyer may learn that a company (whether or not a client) has marketed a defective product that can cause death or injury (e.g., tires that explode at high speeds; cars that easily burst into flame on impact because of the location of their gas tanks). Other states and the Model Rules permit revelation of frauds if the lawyer's services have been used in their commission (unwittingly we would hope), and some states dispense with the last condition. A small number of states require lawyers to reveal confidential information to prevent serious violence or, in a few places, to prevent financial harm from fraud.

Rule 1.6(b)(3) deserves special attention. It permits a lawyer to reveal confidential information "to prevent, mitigate or rectify" substantial financial harm "that is reasonably certain to result or has resulted" from a client's "crime or fraud in furtherance of which the client has used the lawyer's services." What catches your eye here? The confidentiality exception created by this provision does not merely stop ongoing or prospective crimes or frauds, the usual situation and addressed in Rule 1.6(b)(2). Rather, it focuses on the harm from *concluded* conduct. And the authority to reveal is not limited to prevention of prospective or ongoing harm, but extends to disclosure to "mitigate or rectify" harm that has already occurred as a result of a concluded fraud. This retrospective inquiry greatly expands the scope of permissive authority.

Noisy Withdrawal.   Yet another infelicitous legal trope. The Model Rules introduced the concept (though not the term) in 1983, where it appeared in the comment to Rule 1.6. Today, it appears in Rules 1.2 comment [10] and 4.1

comment [3]. The idea is that when a lawyer must withdraw from representing a client because of criminal or fraudulent behavior, the lawyer may be allowed or, to avoid assisting the fraud under substantive law, legally obligated to alert others that she also retracts any oral or written representation the client may still be using for the illegal purpose and which may have been based on false information. The retraction is what makes the withdrawal "noisy." A noisy withdrawal is not actually a full-blown exception to confidentiality because the lawyer says only that she retracts something previously said or written. She does not say why. Rule 1.6(b)(2) and (b)(3) reduces the importance of noisy withdrawals, but because these two exceptions to confidentiality are permissive, and a noisy withdrawal may be mandatory because of substantive law, and because the two provisions are not identical in what they cover, the idea lives on. We postpone further discussion of noisy withdrawals to chapter 9.

Identity and Fees. The attorney-client privilege protects "confidential communications made for the purpose of obtaining legal advice." Vingelli v. United States, 992 F.2d 449 (2d Cir. 1993). It sometimes happens that prosecutors or civil adversaries will seek to learn a client's identity, the source of legal fees, the amount of the fees, and other information about the representation not involving "communications." Assertions of privilege in response to these efforts are generally unsuccessful. Clarke v. American Commerce National Bank, 974 F.2d 127 (9th Cir. 1992), rejected a claim of privilege for legal bills that contained information on the "identity of the client, the case name for which payment was made, the amount of the fee, and the general nature of the services performed." The IRS, investigating a lawyer and his firm, subpoenaed records from their bank. The court upheld the subpoena even though the records could also reveal client names and their financial information and lead to investigation of the clients as well. Reiserer v. United States, 479 F.3d 1160 (9th Cir. 2007).

One court has identified three "special-circumstance" exceptions to the general rule that client identity and fees are not privileged. "The legal advice exception protects client identity and fee information when there is a strong probability that disclosure would implicate the client in the very criminal activity for which legal advice was sought. The last link exception, as its name implies, prevents disclosure of client identity and fee information when it would incriminate the client by providing the last link in an existing chain of evidence. The confidential communications exception . . . protects client identity and fee information if, by revealing the information, the attorney would necessarily disclose confidential communications." United States v. Sindel, 53 F.3d 874 (8th Cir. 1995) (internal quotes omitted). However, other courts have been less charitable. The Second Circuit has rejected the "legal advice exception," holding that the privilege " 'encompass[es] only those confidential communications necessary to obtain informed legal advice.' " Gerald B. Lefcourt, P.C. v. United States, 125 F.3d 79 (2d Cir. 1997) (rejecting *Sindel* to this extent). The court added that "it is clear that there is no special circumstance in this circuit simply because the provision of client-identifying information could prejudice the client in the case for which legal fees are paid." Efforts to invoke one of these exceptions, usually fruitless, succeeded in Matter of Grand Jury Proceeding (Cherney), 898 F.2d 565 (7th Cir. 1990). Cherney was hired by *X* to represent

Hrvatin. The government unsuccessfully sought to compel Cherney to disclose the identity of *X.* The court held that

> privilege protects an unknown client's identity where its disclosure would reveal a client's motive for seeking legal advice. . . . [Here, *X*] sought legal advice concerning his involvement in the drug conspiracy. Disclosure of [*X*'s] identity would necessarily reveal the client's involvement in that crime and thus reveal his motive for seeking legal advice in the first place. . . . This is not the typical case where the government seeks disclosure of a known client's general fee structure, which is usually to determine whether the attorney was paid with illicit funds. In that scenario, revelation of the fee information would most likely serve to incriminate the fee payer, but would not risk exposure of a confidential communication.

Nine years later, the same circuit cited *Cherney* to privilege the identity of persons who had paid the fees of clients under investigation for gambling offenses. In re Subpoenaed Grand Jury Witness, 171 F.3d 511 (7th Cir. 1999). Acknowledging that the contours of the exceptions are vague, the court, after reviewing the lawyer's affidavit in camera, concluded that the identities of the persons paying his fees were privileged:

> [W]e are sure that disclosure of this information would identify a client of Hagen's who is potentially involved in targeted criminal activity which, on this record, would lead to revealing that client's motive to pay the legal bills for some of Hagen's other clients. And motive, we think, is protected by the attorney-client privilege.

Public Policy?   Courts occasionally suggest that the attorney-client privilege may sometimes have to give way to other values. The court wrote in Payton v. New Jersey Turnpike Authority, 691 A.2d 321 (N.J. 1997) (internal quotes omitted): "Moreover, the privilege, although important, is not sacrosanct. It may be pierced upon a showing of need, relevance and materiality, and the fact that the information could not be secured from any less intrusive source. That principle is especially appropriate in this case, where the powerful public interest in eliminating discrimination and sexual harassment is present and where defendant's claim to the privilege is tenuous at best." See also People v. Osorio, 549 N.E.2d 1183 (N.Y. 1989): "[E]ven if the technical requirements of the privilege are satisfied, it may, nonetheless, yield in a proper case where strong public policy requires disclosure." Still, it is rare to find a case in which public policy requires disclosure of privileged information.

Perhaps the most famous case to test the policies underlying the attorney-client privilege arose in Independent Counsel Kenneth Starr's effort to secure the testimony of the lawyer for Vincent Foster. (As we've seen, Starr's work has generated much law in this area.) Foster was the Deputy White House Counsel who committed suicide as the investigation of the Clintons' Whitewater deal escalated. Starr argued that because of the government's great need to learn what Foster told his lawyer, the privilege should give way. In a 6-3 opinion, the Supreme Court disagreed:

> Knowing that communications will remain confidential even after death encourages the client to communicate fully and frankly with counsel. While

the fear of disclosure and the consequent withholding of information from counsel may be reduced if disclosure is limited to posthumous disclosure in a criminal context, it seems unreasonable to assume that it vanishes altogether. Clients may be concerned about reputation, civil liability, or possible harm to friends or family. Posthumous disclosure of such communications may be as feared as disclosure during the client's lifetime.

Swidler & Berlin v. United States, 524 U.S. 399 (1998) (Rehnquist, C.J.). Dissenting for herself and for Justices Scalia and Thomas, Justice O'Connor wrote:

> Where the exoneration of an innocent criminal defendant or a compelling law enforcement interest is at stake, the harm of precluding critical evidence that is unavailable by any other means outweighs the potential disincentive to forthright communication. In my view, the cost of silence warrants a narrow exception to the rule that the attorney-client privilege survives the death of the client.

For other cases in which courts have rejected the argument that death ends the privilege, even in compelling circumstances, see Matter of John Doe Grand Jury Investigation, 562 N.E.2d 69 (Mass. 1990) (unsuccessful effort to question attorney for deceased husband suspected of murdering his wife in concert with one or more others as yet unidentified); People v. Knuckles, 650 N.E.2d 974 (Ill. 1995) (declining to adopt "a generalized public interest exception" to the attorney-client privilege). California has a different rule by statute: "When [Bing] Crosby died, his privilege transferred to his personal representative, i.e., the executor of his estate. But once Crosby's estate was finally distributed and his personal representative discharged, the privilege terminated because there was no longer any privilege holder statutorily authorized to assert it." HLC Properties, Ltd. v. Superior Court, 105 P.3d 560 (Cal. 2005).

Is There a Professional Relationship? Remember that in order for a communication to be ethically protected or to be privileged, there must be a client-lawyer relationship. The presence of a lawyer is a necessary but not a sufficient condition for that relationship. One case that caused quite a stir in the corporate lawyer community was Georgia-Pacific Corp. v. GAF Roofing Manufacturing Corp., 1996 Westlaw 29392 (S.D.N.Y. 1996). The court there denied privilege for the communications between an in-house lawyer and corporate officials. The lawyer had negotiated the environmental drafts of a business transaction. The lawyer's communications on the business issues were heavily intertwined with his advice on the legal ramifications of proposed terms. Balancing everything, the court held that the lawyer (Scott) "was acting in a business capacity."

> Since Mr. Scott negotiated the environmental terms of the Agreement, GP is entitled to know what environmental matters he determined would not be covered in the proposed agreement; the extent to which they were covered in the provisions he negotiated in the Agreement; and whether Scott advised GAF management of the degree to which his negotiations had left GAF protected and unprotected. Only by such testimony can it be determined whether GAF, as a matter of business judgment agreed to assume certain environmental risks when it entered the Agreement.

Short of limiting Scott's role to legal advice only, what could GAF have done to avoid this result?

In In re Grand Jury Investigation (Schroeder), 842 F.2d 1223 (11th Cir. 1987), an attorney-accountant prepared a client's tax returns and also gave him tax advice. Preparation of the returns was held not to be "legal advice within the scope of [the] privilege," although the tax advice was. Consequently, the attorney could be required to answer questions about the tax returns. A defendant's statements to an attorney-friend after the attorney said he would not represent the defendant are not privileged. People v. Gionis, 892 P.2d 1199 (Cal. 1995) ("a communication is not privileged, even though it may involve a legal matter, if it has no relation to any professional relationship of the attorney with the client").

Finally, of course, the purported client's communication must be with an attorney or at least someone the client reasonably believes to be an attorney. In United States v. Arthur Young & Co., 465 U.S. 805 (1984), the Court unanimously refused to recognize "a work-product immunity for an independent auditor's tax accrual workpapers." How can we square this result with *Upjohn*? Why should one profession (law) enjoy protection denied to another profession (accounting) when the two sell essentially the same kind of tax advice? After *Arthur Young*, Lloyd Cutler, a lawyer in Washington, D.C., said: "I think the reason why there are more confidentiality privileges for lawyers is the historic one that lawyers were around long before accountants. In areas where they are doing similar kinds of work, it doesn't make much sense to separate the two." N.Y. Times, Apr. 3, 1984, at D2. Ah, but in which direction should we make them even?

FURTHER READING

Issues of confidentiality reappear throughout this book. Students interested in a critique of the fundamental justification for confidentiality rules might begin by looking at Fred Zacharias's two-part study, Rethinking Confidentiality, 74 Iowa L. Rev. 351 (1989), and Rethinking Confidentiality II: Is Confidentiality Constitutional?, 75 Iowa L. Rev. 601 (1990). Nancy Moore has analyzed the values that inform the attorney-client privilege and compared the privilege in the physician-patient context. Nancy Moore, Limits to Attorney-Client Confidentiality: A "Philosophically Informed" and Comparative Approach to Legal and Medical Ethics, 36 Case W. Res. L. Rev. 177 (1985). Geoffrey Hazard has examined the attorney-client privilege in its historical context. Geoffrey Hazard, An Historical Perspective on the Attorney-Client Privilege, 66 Cal. L. Rev. 1061 (1978). See also Developments in the Law—Privileged Communication, 98 Harv. L. Rev. 1450 (1985).

3. Agency

Lawyers are their clients' agents. The law of agency therefore applies to the client-lawyer relationship. As attorneys, or agents, before the law (compared to attorneys in *fact*), lawyers have certain authority and certain duties within the scope of their agency (i.e., what they are retained to do). Agents are also fiduciaries. Restatement (Third) of Agency §1.01. In the next section, we shall discuss some of the *duties* imposed by agency and fiduciary status. Here we review the *authority* that lawyers have by virtue of being agents. Not surprisingly, it is an authority to act and speak for the client on the subject matter of the retainer. Acting for the client means that the lawyer's conduct will be attributable to the client even if the lawyer makes a negligent mistake or willfully misbehaves. In litigation, courts say that a "litigant chooses counsel at his peril." Boogaerts v. Bank of Bradley, 961 F.2d 765 (8th Cir. 1992). See also Link v. Wabash R.R. Co., 370 U.S. 626 (1962). (Is that disturbing? Isn't the same true for choosing doctors?) To make sure that the lawyer stays within the scope of work the client gives her, it is important to define so far as reasonably possible what the lawyer is retained to do. That definition may require revision as the representation proceeds. A second reason to define the scope of the lawyer's retainer is to protect the lawyer against a charge of neglect or malpractice. An ambiguous retainer might be construed to include services the lawyer never intended to perform. A client may interpret the lawyer's responsibility more expansively and allege neglect, or seek damages for malpractice, when the anticipated work is not performed. See page 79.

TAYLOR v. ILLINOIS
484 U.S. 400 (1988)

[Taylor's lawyer, in order to gain "a tactical advantage," willfully failed to reveal the identity of a prospective witness, Wormley, as required by Illinois discovery rules. The trial court refused to let Wormley testify. Taylor, who was not party to his lawyer's tactic, claimed a violation of his rights under the Sixth Amendment's Compulsory Process Clause. Following are excerpts from the majority opinion of Justice Stevens and the dissent of Justice Brennan (in which Justices Marshall and Blackmun joined).]

The argument that the client should not be held responsible for his lawyer's misconduct strikes at the heart of the attorney-client relationship. Although there are basic rights that the attorney cannot waive without the fully informed and publicly acknowledged consent of the client,[24] the lawyer has — and must have — full authority to manage the conduct of the trial. The adversary process could not function effectively if every tactical decision required client approval. Moreover, given the protections afforded by the attorney-client privilege and the fact that extreme cases may involve unscrupulous conduct by both the client and the lawyer, it would be highly impracticable to require an investigation into their relative responsibilities before applying the sanction of preclusion. In responding to discovery, the client has a duty to be candid and forthcoming with the lawyer, and when the lawyer responds, he or she speaks for the client. Putting to one side the exceptional cases in which counsel is ineffective, the client must accept the consequences of the lawyer's decision to forgo cross-examination, to decide not to put certain witnesses on the stand, or to decide not to disclose the identity of certain witnesses in advance of trial. In this case, petitioner has no

---

24. See, e.g., Brookhart v. Janis, 384 U.S. 1 (1966) (defendant's constitutional right to plead not guilty and to have a trial where he could confront and cross-examine adversary witness could not be waived by his counsel without defendant's consent); Doughty v. State, 470 N.E.2d 69 (Ind. 1984) (record must show "personal communication of the defendant to the court that he chooses to relinquish the right [to a jury trial]"); Cross v. United States, 117 U.S. App. D.C. 56, 325 F.2d 629 (1963) (waiver of right to be present during trial).

greater right to disavow his lawyer's decision to conceal Wormley's identity until after the trial had commenced than he has to disavow the decision to refrain from adducing testimony from the eyewitnesses who were identified in the Answer to Discovery. . . .

JUSTICE BRENNAN, dissenting.

Although we have sometimes held a defendant bound by tactical errors his attorney makes that fall short of ineffective assistance of counsel, we have not previously suggested that a client can be punished for an attorney's *misconduct*. There are fundamental differences between attorney misconduct and tactical errors. Tactical errors are products of a legitimate choice among tactical options. Such tactical decisions must be made within the adversary system, and the system requires attorneys to make them, operating under the presumption that the attorney will choose the course most likely to benefit the defendant. Although some of these decisions may later appear erroneous, penalizing attorneys for such miscalculations is generally an exercise in futility because the error is usually visible only in hindsight — at the time the tactical decision was made there was no obvious "incorrect" choice, and no prohibited one. . . .

The rationales for binding defendants to attorneys' routine tactical errors do not apply to attorney misconduct. An attorney is never faced with a legitimate choice that includes misconduct as an option. Although it may be that "[t]he adversary process could not function effectively if every tactical decision required client approval," that concern is irrelevant here because a client has no authority to approve misconduct. Further, misconduct is not visible only with hindsight, as are many tactical errors. Consequently, misconduct is amenable to direct punitive sanctions against attorneys as a deterrent that can prevent attorneys from systemically engaging in misconduct that would disrupt the trial process. There is no need to take steps that will inflict the punishment on the defendant . . .

Taylor held that preclusion will not always be an appropriate remedy. Other sanctions may suffice. But because the defense lawyer in *Taylor* acted wilfully and tactically, preclusion was allowed even if "prejudice to the prosecution could have been avoided" with a less harsh remedy. Compare Michigan v. Lucas, 500 U.S. 145 (1991) (reversing a holding that preclusion is *never* allowed when a defendant in a sexual abuse case who did not give required notice offers to prove a prior sexual relationship with the victim); and Noble v. Kelly, 246 F.3d 93 (2d Cir. 2001) (absent finding of willfulness in failure to notice alibi witness, preclusion of testimony violated Confrontation Clause).

S.E.C. v. McNULTY
137 F.3d 732 (2d Cir. 1998)

KEARSE, CIRCUIT JUDGE:

Defendant John M. Shanklin, against whom a default judgment was entered . . . for failure to answer the complaint filed by plaintiff Securities and

Exchange Commission ("SEC" or the "Commission"), challenges the order . . . denying his motion to vacate the default judgment. In denying the motion, the district court ruled that Shanklin had failed to show that the default was not willful and that he was not culpable, and had failed to proffer a meritorious defense to the SEC's claims. On appeal, Shanklin contends principally that the district court erred in imputing his attorney's [Fred Rucker's] neglect to him and in failing to resolve doubts as to the merits of Shanklin's defenses in his favor. Finding no merit in these contentions, we affirm.

I. Background

The present action was commenced against Shanklin and others, including defendant Robert J. McNulty, in connection with several corporations controlled by McNulty, which in 1988-1990 had raised $ 78 million through various public and private offerings of securities. According to the complaint, portions of these moneys were diverted to McNulty and other entities he controlled, an intended use that the defendants had fraudulently concealed. . . . The complaint alleged that company books and certain of the SEC filings misrepresented or falsely concealed material transactions, and that Shanklin knew, or recklessly failed to know, of those misrepresentations or concealments. . . .

II. Discussion . . .

A. Willfulness

The issue of willfulness in the present case comprises two questions: (1) whether Rucker's failure to file an answer to the complaint was the result of a shortcoming more culpable than negligence or even gross negligence, and (2) whether that shortcoming was appropriately attributed to Shanklin. The district court properly answered both questions in the affirmative.

We have interpreted "willfulness," in . . . the context of a default, to refer to conduct that is more than merely negligent or careless . . . the court may find a default to have been willful where the conduct of counsel or the litigant was egregious and was not satisfactorily explained. . . .

The district court's finding that Rucker's conduct was egregious is . . . amply supported. There can be no question on this record that the district court was correct in concluding that the neglect was not excusable and that the default was willful. Accordingly, we turn to the question of whether the willful default was permissibly attributed to Shanklin himself. . . .

Normally, the conduct of an attorney is imputed to his client, for allowing a party to evade "the consequences of the acts or omissions of his freely selected agent" "would be wholly inconsistent with our system of representative litigation, in which each party is deemed bound by the acts of his lawyer-agent." [Citing *Link.*] . . .

[In precedent we] affirmed the denial of the motion to vacate because the defendants, one of whom was "an experienced businessman," stated merely that the reason for counsel's failure was "unknown," and the defendants provided no evidence to suggest that they had ever made any efforts to determine that counsel was tending to the lawsuit. . . .

In the present case, the district court properly found that Shanklin had made no showing of diligence that would warrant relieving him of the default judgment. Though Shanklin's memorandum of law stated that "Shanklin, by his own conduct, has done everything in his power to *reverse the consequences* of Rucker's outrageous incompetence" (emphasis added), neither the memorandum nor his affidavit gave any indication that Shanklin had done anything whatever to prevent the default's occurrence. For example, although Shanklin stated in his affidavit that he had placed some 20 calls to Rucker in the wake of the default judgment, he did not suggest that he had discussed the case with Rucker at all from the time the case was commenced in October 1994 until the default was entered in September 1995, or that he had made any effort to reach Rucker during that nearly one-year period. Similarly, although Shanklin indicated in his affidavit that he believed Rucker was preparing a motion to vacate the default, in part because Rucker billed him for alleged services on such a motion, Shanklin did not state, suggest, or in any way intimate that he had received any bills from Rucker with respect to the lawsuit at any time prior to the default. Thus, the record reveals a party who by his own description is a sophisticated businessman, who after being sued by the SEC apparently did not talk to his attorney for nearly a year, and who apparently received no bills during that time to indicate that any attention was being given to his case. We see no basis on which to overturn the district court's conclusion that the willful default of Rucker should be imputed to Shanklin.

Binding the Client

Why couldn't Shankln assume that his lawyer was taking care of things? Must clients supervise their lawyers? What about Taylor, who was likely ignorant of the notice of alibi rule? Many are the circumstances in which a lawyer may bind a client. By hiring counsel, a client necessarily delegates authority to speak and act on a range of issues reasonably within the scope of the retainer. If the attorney acts improperly or negligently, the client may still be bound, but he may be able to sue the lawyer for damages. In litigation, as the previous two cases show, an attorney's default, even if inexcusable, may be laid to the client. As between the client and a third party, isn't that the correct resolution? In criminal cases too?

Cases disagree on whether a client can disavow a settlement after her lawyer has accepted one. Rule 1.2(a) and case law give the client the unqualified right to decide whether to settle a civil matter or enter a plea in a criminal matter. McKnight v. Dean, 270 F.3d 513 (7th Cir. 2001):

> We do not condone [attorney] Dean's actions in "forcing" McKnight to settle. If McKnight was pigheaded and wanted to tilt at windmills, that was his right. Dean didn't have to continue representing him in those circumstances, but he could not, whether to safeguard his fee or for any other reason, use deception to induce his client to settle against the client's will. The decision to settle is the client's alone.

Clients, however, may delegate authority to their lawyers to settle civil disputes ("get the most you can over two million"), although the client can revoke the authority before it is exercised. If a lawyer has such actual authority to settle (that is, express or implied by the client herself), no problem. The lawyer will have acted properly, and the client will be bound. See Pohl v. United Airlines, Inc., 213 F.3d 336 (7th Cir. 2000); Hallock v. State, 474 N.E.2d 1178 (N.Y. 1984). A few courts have held that lawyers have "inherent power" to settle in certain circumstances. "Inherent agency power" was described in §8A of the Restatement (Second) of Agency. It is a power that derives solely from the existence of the agency relationship for the protection of persons harmed by, or dealing with, a servant or other agent. See Koval v. Simon Telelect, Inc., 693 N.E.2d 1299 (Ind. 1998) (concluding that a lawyer has inherent power to settle in court, which includes alternate dispute resolution; client may withdraw the power by an explicit communication). Restatement (Third) of Agency dropped the term but that won't necessarily stop the courts from using it.

What happens if the lawyer settles without actual or inherent authority? The lawyer may still have *apparent* authority to settle, created because the client has said or done something that has led the other party to conclude reasonably, though mistakenly, that the lawyer has actual authority to settle. See United States v. International Brotherhood of Teamsters, 986 F.2d 15 (2d Cir. 1993) (finding both actual and apparent authority to settle civil contempt charges); Edwards v. Born, Inc., 792 F.2d 387 (3d Cir. 1986); Hallock v. State, supra. Some courts presume that an attorney who has appeared for a party has actual authority to settle. Anyone challenging that authority has the burden of proof. See In re Artha Management, Inc., 91 F.3d 326 (2d Cir. 1996). But see Luethke v. Suhr, 650 N.W.2d 220 (Neb. 2002) (lawyer may not settle without express authority; apparent authority recognized only "when a lawyer settles a claim . . . *in the presence of his or her client,* generally in open court, and the client remains silent regarding the terms of the settlement") (emphasis in original), Reutzel v. Douglas, 870 A.2d 787 (Pa. 2005) (actual authority needed). For a thorough analysis of American law — and the law of Canada, England, and Australia — on a lawyer's settlement authority, see Grace Giesel, Enforcement of Settlement Contracts: The Problem of the Attorney Agent, 12 Geo. J. Legal Ethics 543 (1999) (concluding that a presumption in favor "of an attorney's authority to settle is an excellent way to distinguish the attorney as a unique type of agent, and to lend value and recognition to the obligations and environment under which an attorney operates").

The cases are all over the map on this question. But it really boils down to a fundamental policy issue, doesn't it? When a lawyer without actual authority (express or implied in fact) settles, who takes the risk? If apparent authority is sufficient, or if the jurisdiction subscribes to the idea of inherent authority, the client is bound and must look to her lawyer if she wants to claim that he exceeded his authority. If the opposing party takes the risk because the lawyer needs actual authority and may not have it, it may insist that the client ratify the deal personally or that the lawyer produce proof of actual authority. Where do you think the risk ought to be?

A lawyer's authority can also bind a government. A trial court "relied upon [Assistant U.S. Attorney Gevers's] representations in imposing a non-Guidelines, non-mandatory sentence." The government later challenged the sentence without success. " 'An attorney cannot agree in open court with the judge's proposed course of conduct and then charge the court with error in following that course.' AUSA Gevers bound his principal and client, the

United States, to the position that the application of the Guidelines and a mandatory minimum sentence . . . was discretionary with the district court." United States v. Byerley, 46 F.3d 694 (7th Cir. 1995).

The Illinois Supreme Court divided 4-3 on whether a client was liable to a third party for its law firm's allegedly tortious conduct when attempting to enforce the client's judgment. The majority ruled that when a law firm exercises its independent professional judgment, it is in the role of an independent contractor, whose torts are not attributable to the client unless the client authorized the allegedly tortious acts or thereafter ratified them. Horwitz v. Holabird & Root, 816 N.E.2d 272 (Ill. 2004) (recognizing division of authority). South Carolina takes the opposite view. It rejected the independent contractor defense and held a client liable to its former opponent for the alleged dilatory tactics and deception of the client's retained lawyer. Koutsogiannis v. BB&T, 616 S.E.2d 425 (S.C. 2005).

Vicarious Admissions

A lawyer's statements may be the vicarious admissions of a client. A lawyer, as an agent, falls within the vicarious admission rules of the law of evidence. See, for example, Fed. R. Evid. 801(d)(2)(C) and (D) (statements are nonhearsay). These rules apply in litigation and in negotiations. For statements in negotiation, see United States v. Margiotta, 662 F.2d 131 (2d Cir. 1981) (statements by criminal suspect's attorney to persuade attorney general not to indict are vicarious admissions of suspect, but excluded because of immunity agreement), and Brown v. Hebb, 175 A. 602 (Md. 1934) (debt to doctor admitted when patient's lawyer responded to doctor's bill by offering a lesser amount "for the services rendered").*

For the operation of this principle in litigation, consider the unusual case of United States v. McKeon, 738 F.2d 26 (2d Cir. 1984), where the government wanted to introduce the opening statement of the defense lawyer in an earlier mistrial as a vicarious admission against the defendant on retrial. The opening statement revealed a theory of the case at odds with the theory the defendant was planning to present on retrial. (Do you see the evidentiary value there?) The Second Circuit held that whether a lawyer's prior trial statement may be used vicariously against his client at a new trial was dependent on a balancing test the court described. The prior statement must involve "an assertion of fact inconsistent with similar assertions in a subsequent trial." The inconsistency "should be clear and of a quality which obviates any need for the trier of fact to explore other events at the prior trial." The lawyer's statements must be "such as to be the equivalent of testimonial statements" by the client. "Some participatory role of the client must be evident, either directly or inferentially as when the argument is a direct assertion of fact which in all probability had to have been confirmed" by the client. Finally, the court must make a factual determination that the adversary's proposed inference from the inconsistency is fair and that there is no "innocent explanation" for it. The court then upheld use of the statement in the case before it. One consequence of this holding was that the lawyer had to be

---

* Statements made in the context of settlement discussions are often inadmissible as a matter of policy, whether made by the lawyer or the client. See Fed. R. Evid. 408.

disqualified from retrying the case because the defendant might now need to call him as a witness to explain his earlier statement. (See chapter 5C on the advocate-witness rule.) Likewise, but less dramatic, prior inconsistent *pleadings* authored by a lawyer can be used as substantive evidence or to impeach on cross-examination. Dugan v. EMS Helicopters, Inc., 915 F.2d 1428 (10th Cir. 1990).

Vicarious admissions may be used against the client in evidence, but they don't *bind* the client. That means that the client may try to disown them or even introduce contrary proof. However, some statements a lawyer makes in court can indeed bind the client. These are called *judicial admissions* and they occur when the statements are made in a case then on trial — in open court or in pleadings or other papers that have *not* been superseded. In McLhinney v. Lansdell Corp., 254 A.2d 177 (Md. 1969), the plaintiff's lawyer was relieved of having to introduce proof of the identity of the driver of the truck that hit the plaintiff's car because the defense lawyer's opening statement admitted that the truck was driven by the defendant's employee. Opening statements are not evidence, but assertions in them are "judicial admissions" and established as true for the purpose of trial. See also Oscanyan v. Arms Co., 103 U.S. 261 (1880); Purgess v. Sharrock, 33 F.3d 134 (2d Cir. 1994) (statement in memorandum of law or brief can be either evidentiary or binding judicial admission); DiLuglio v. Providence Auto Body, Inc., 755 A.2d 757 (R.I. 2000) (a judicial admission of a fact "removes that fact from the controversy, and obviates the need of one party to produce evidence concerning the fact [and] precludes the pleader who admitted the fact from challenging it. . . ."); United States v. McKeon, supra.

Procedural Defaults. In criminal cases, an attorney's failure to raise a defendant's constitutional rights in compliance with valid state procedures will generally prevent the defendant from asserting those rights collaterally in federal court unless she can prove "actual innocence." Coleman v. Thompson, 501 U.S. 722 (1991); Smith v. Murray, 477 U.S. 527 (1986); Murray v. Carrier, 477 U.S. 478 (1986). If, however, the error is so serious as to amount to the ineffective assistance of counsel, the client will not be bound. See, e.g., Kimmelman v. Morrison, 477 U.S. 365 (1986); Evitts v. Lucey, 469 U.S. 387 (1985). Standards for ineffective assistance claims are discussed in chapter 13E.

Confidentiality Duties in Agency Law

We have studied the rules that require lawyers to protect client confidences. But lawyers are also agents and have a parallel duty of confidentiality under agency law. Although the confidentiality rules for lawyers and agents are not identical (the degree of variance depends on the jurisdiction), there is wide overlap. You might wonder why, if agency law already imposes confidentiality duties, we need to include them in lawyer ethics codes as well. A good answer is that lawyers, as their clients' agents in the legal system, need (or at least benefit from) greater specificity to take account of the unique situations that lawyer-agents are likely to encounter. The ethics rules are indeed more focused than is the agency doctrine.

The Restatement (Third) of Agency §8.05 provides: "An agent has a duty . . . (2) not to use or communicate confidential information of the

principal for the agent's own purposes or those of a third party." Comment *c*
would seem to go beyond Rule 1.6 by requiring agents to protect a principal's
information even if it is not related to the purpose of the agency:

> An agent's relationship with a principal may result in the agent learning infor-
> mation about the principal's health, life history, and personal preferences that
> the agent should reasonably understand the principal expects the agent to
> keep confidential. An agent's duty of confidentiality extends to all such infor-
> mation concerning a principal even when it is not otherwise connected with
> the subject matter of the agency relationship.

See also ABKCO Music, Inc. v. Harrisongs Music, Ltd., 722 F.2d 988 (2d Cir.
1983), where the former manager of the Beatles was found to have used confidential information to compete with his former principal and thereby to have
violated his fiduciary obligations. "Both this Circuit and numerous New York
courts have held that an agent has a duty not to use confidential knowledge
acquired in his employment in competition with his principal." North Atlantic
Instruments, Inc. v. Haber, 188 F.3d 38 (2d Cir. 1999) (internal quotes omitted).

4. Fiduciary

A lawyer has a fiduciary relationship with his client. Lawyers must place
their clients' interests above their own in the area of the representation and
must treat their clients fairly. Words like "honor," "integrity," and "trust"
appear often in discussions of fiduciary duty. Loyalty and diligence are also
part of the equation and are the focus of the next section. When a lawyer's
interests or the interests of another client or a third person create a significant
risk to a lawyer's fiduciary obligations, we say the lawyer has a conflict of interest.
The lawyer must then not take up or must give up the matter, unless the conflict
can be cured with the client's informed consent. Conflicts are the subject of
chapters 5 and 6.

Lawyers are, in fact, not garden-variety fiduciaries. They are said to occupy a
"unique position of trust and confidence" toward clients. Milbank, Tweed,
Hadley & McCloy v. Boon, 13 F.3d 537 (2d Cir. 1994). The "unique fiduciary
reliance stemming from people hiring attorneys to exercise professional judgment on a client's behalf . . . is imbued with ultimate trust and confidence."
Matter of Cooperman, 633 N.E.2d 1069 (N.Y. 1994). The message is clear:
Some fiduciaries have higher obligations than other fiduciaries, and lawyers
have among the highest. The fiduciary duty is said to arise after the formation
of the attorney-client relationship. In re Marriage of Pagano, 607 N.E.2d 1242
(Ill. 1992). The *Pagano* court, quoting a century-old precedent, said that no
"confidential relation" exists either before "the attorney undertakes the business of the client" or in regard to

> dealings which take place after the relation has been dissolved. But the law
> watches with unusual jealousy over all transactions between the parties, which
> occur while the relation exists. [Consequently,] when an attorney, once
> retained, enters into a transaction with a client, it is presumed that the attorney
> exercised undue influence.

At least three reasons support imposing fiduciary obligations on a lawyer after the professional relationship is established. First, the client will presumably have begun to depend on the attorney's integrity, fairness, superior knowledge, and judgment, putting aside the usual caution when dealing with others on important matters. Second, the attorney may have acquired information about the client that gives the attorney an unfair advantage in dealings with the client. Finally, many clients will not be in a position where they are free to change attorneys, but rather will be financially or psychologically dependent on the attorney's continued representation. In short, during (and possibly even after) a representation, the client is vulnerable to the attorney's overreaching. We rely on the lawyer's professional obligation of utmost solicitude for the client's interest, even as against the lawyer's own interests, to prevent exploitation. The lawyer's fiduciary obligation applies to a fee agreement reached after the attorney-client relationship has been entered. See page 224.

The demands of a lawyer's fiduciary duty will be defined throughout much of this book, especially in this chapter and in the material on conflicts of interest and malpractice. But let's pause for a moment to observe a few examples.

In Benson v. State Bar, 531 P.2d 1081 (Cal. 1975), the attorney borrowed money from a current client. The attorney "was heavily in debt, and insolvent, at the time he approached [the client] for these loans." In return for the loans, he gave the client unsecured promissory notes. In disbarring the lawyer, the court said:

> Furthermore, given the fiduciary nature of petitioner's relationship with [the client], it can be fairly inferred that his suggestion of an unsecured promissory note met with her approval because she trusted his judgment. The gravamen of the charge is abuse of that trust, and regardless of petitioner's contention that he never specifically recommended the unsecured loans to [the client], it is undisputed that in soliciting them he failed to reveal the extent of his pre-existing indebtedness and financial distress.

James Smith, an attorney, was under investigation for drug use. He offered to cooperate with Colorado police as an undercover informant. He secretly recorded a telephone conversation with a former client in which he asked the former client to sell him cocaine. He then met with the former client wearing a body microphone. The recorded conversations were ultimately used to convict the former client of three felony charges. The Colorado Supreme Court held that although Smith

> no longer represented the [former client], the conduct in all probability would not have occurred had [Smith] not relied upon the trust and confidence placed in him by the [former client] as a result of the recently completed attorney-client relationship between the two. The undisclosed use of a recording device necessarily involves elements of deception and trickery which do not comport with the high standards of candor and fairness to which all attorneys are bound.

For these and other offenses, Smith was suspended for two years. People v. Smith, 778 P.2d 685 (Colo. 1989). For a refusal to suppress tape recordings when offered against the client on similar facts, see United States v. Heinz, 983 F.2d 609 (5th Cir. 1993).

Lerner, a lawyer, was a member of both the board of a cooperative apartment building and its legal committee. Lerner recommended that the co-op retain a particular law firm to challenge its real estate taxes. He allegedly failed, however, to tell the board that the firm was going to split its fee with Lerner and his firm. The board sued for Lerner's portion of the fee plus other damages. The court held that these facts established a claim for breach of fiduciary duty and fraudulent concealment. "Client knowledge of a joint representation agreement between lawyers is the sine qua non of its ethical validity. . . . Here, where claims of self-dealing and divided loyalty are presented, a fiduciary may be required to disgorge any ill-gotten gain even where the plaintiff has sustained no direct economic loss." Excelsior 57th Corp. v. Lerner, 553 N.Y.S.2d 763 (1st Dept. 1990).

A lawyer who goes into secret competition with his own client, or assists another of the client's fiduciaries in doing so, may be liable to the client in a civil action. In Avianca, Inc. v. Corriea, 705 F. Supp. 666 (D.D.C. 1989), the lawyer had secretly helped an officer of the lawyer's corporate client compete with the client in violation of that officer's fiduciary duty. In David Welch Co. v. Erskine & Tulley, 250 Cal. Rptr. 339 (Ct. App. 1988), the defendant law firm became the competitor of a client, a collection business, after receiving confidential information from the client about that business. See also Tri-Growth Centre City, Ltd. v. Silldorf, Burdman, Duignan & Eisenberg, 265 Cal. Rptr. 330 (Ct. App. 1989) (allegation that lawyer used confidential information to usurp client's business opportunity).

For a good discussion of fiduciary duty under agency law, see Restatement (Third) of Agency §1.01, comment *e*.

5. Loyalty and Diligence

The duties of loyalty and diligence may be considered together, since they somewhat overlap. The duty of loyalty (a subset of fiduciary duty) requires the lawyer to pursue, and to be free to pursue, the client's objectives unfettered by conflicting responsibilities or interests. The duties of loyalty and confidentiality form the basis of the conflict-of-interest rules discussed in chapters 5 and 6. As we shall see, loyalty survives the termination of the attorney-client relationship and prevents a lawyer from acting "adversely" to a former client in matters "substantially related" to the former representation. The requirement of diligence imposes on the lawyer an obligation to pursue the client's interests without undue delay. Divided loyalties may undermine the lawyer's ability to be diligent in pursuit of the client's interests as well as threaten the lawyer's fiduciary position. An undivided loyalty will not, however, assure diligence. Lawyers have been known to procrastinate. (It's true.)

The 1908 Canons of Professional Ethics provided, in Canon 15, as follows:

The lawyer owes "entire devotion to the interest of the client, warm zeal in the maintenance and defense of his rights and the exertion of his utmost learning and ability," to the end that nothing be taken or be withheld from him, save by the rules of law, legally applied.

The Code stated in Canon 7 that "[a] lawyer should represent a client zealously within the bounds of the law." But EC 7-17 makes clear that the duty of loyalty applies only to the lawyer's professional relationship. Rule 1.2(b) emphasizes that a "lawyer's representation of a client . . . does not constitute an endorsement of the client's political, economic, social or moral views or activities."

Close readers may notice that whereas the Code gave the duty to "zealously" represent a client the status of a canon (canonization is one notch below getting carved on Mount Rushmore), the Rules relegate the root of the same word ("zeal") to the *comment* to Rule 1.3 (on diligence), qualify it with a prepositional phrase, and immediately temper it with "however," to wit: "A lawyer must also act with commitment and dedication to the interests of the client and with zeal in advocacy upon the client's behalf. A lawyer is not bound, however, to press for every advantage that might be realized for a client." What do you make of this? Some — let's call them the members of the Lord Brougham Club — see in it a dilution of the lawyer's role as gladiator for the client ("knows but one person in all the world").

The Rules say that "[a] lawyer shall act with reasonable diligence and promptness in representing a client." Rule 1.3. One of the most frequent grounds for complaints to disciplinary committees is failure to pursue a client's interests. (This failure generally goes hand in hand with the related failure, discussed below, to keep the client informed about the status of a matter.) Sometimes the failure to act diligently will actually prejudice a client's rights, as when a lawyer permits a statute of limitations to expire. If so, the client will have a malpractice claim against the lawyer. If not, the lawyer may still be disciplined. In re Brown, 967 So.2d 482 (La. 2007). In an astonishing example of a lack of diligence, a California lawyer was ordered to show cause why he should not be held in contempt where he had asked for, and received, 19 extensions of time from the state supreme court to file a brief on behalf of a capital defendant, but had failed to file the brief. The court found that the lawyer "had the ability to comply" with its orders and that the failure was therefore willful. He was sentenced to five days in jail. In re Young, 892 P.2d 148 (Cal. 1995).

6. The Duty to Inform and Advise

NICHOLS v. KELLER
15 Cal. App. 4th 1672, 19 Cal. Rptr. 2d 601 (1993)

[Nichols was injured on the job. He hired attorneys Fulfer and Keller, who pursued a workers' compensation claim against Nichols' employer. They did not advise Nichols that he might also have civil tort claims against third parties. Nichols learned of this possibility only after the statute of limitations had run out on those claims. He sued the lawyers for malpractice. The trial court granted summary judgment for the defendants.]

A significant area of exposure for the workers' compensation attorney concerns that attorney's responsibility for counseling regarding a potential third-party action. One of an attorney's basic functions is to advise. Liability can exist because the attorney failed to provide advice. Not only should an attorney furnish advice when requested, but he or she should also volunteer opinions when necessary to further the client's objectives. The attorney need not advise and caution of every possible alternative, but only of those that may result in adverse consequences if not considered. Generally speaking, a workers' compensation attorney should be able to limit the retention to the compensation claim if the client is cautioned (1) there may be other remedies which the attorney will not investigate and (2) other counsel should be consulted on such matters. However, even when a retention is expressly limited, the attorney may still have a duty to alert the client to legal problems which are reasonably apparent, even though they fall outside the scope of the retention. The rationale is that, as between the lay client and the attorney, the latter is more qualified to recognize and analyze the client's legal needs. The attorney need not represent the client on such matters. Nevertheless, the attorney should inform the client of the limitations of the attorney's representation and of the possible need for other counsel. . . .

In the context of personal injury consultations between lawyer and layperson, it is reasonably foreseeable the latter will offer a selective or incomplete recitation of the facts underlying the claim; request legal assistance by employing such everyday terms as "workers' compensation," "disability," and "unemployment"; and rely upon the consulting lawyer to describe the array of legal remedies available, alert the layperson to any apparent legal problems, and, if appropriate, indicate limitations on the retention of counsel and the need for other counsel. In the event the lawyer fails to so advise the layperson, it is also reasonably foreseeable the layperson will fail to ask relevant questions regarding the existence of other remedies and be deprived of relief through a combination of ignorance and lack or failure of understanding. And, if counsel elects to limit or prescribe his representation of the client, i.e., to a workers' compensation claim only without reference or regard to any third party or collateral claims which the client might pursue if adequately advised, then counsel must make such limitations in representation very clear to his client. Thus, a lawyer who signs an application for adjudication of a workers' compensation claim and a lawyer who accepts a referral to prosecute the claim owe the claimant a duty of care to advise on available remedies, including third-party actions.

[Reversed.]

A law firm, representing a class, recovered about $90 million on the ground that the defendant had failed to pay overtime as required by the Labor Code. Two members of the class then brought a class action against the law firm for failure to assert an additional basis for overtime liability under the state's Unfair Competition Law. That law, they claimed, would have permitted recovery for an extra year of unpaid overtime. The law firm pointed out that the class certification in the underlying action specified only the Labor Code. It argued that the "obligations of class counsel under a class certification order should be analogized to the obligations that an attorney assumes under a retainer agreement" and be read no more broadly. The court agreed but concluded that the analogy worked to the firm's disadvantage. Janik v. Rudy, Exelrod & Zeiff, 14 Cal. Rptr. 3d 751 (Ct. App. 2004). After citing *Nichols v. Keller*, the court wrote:

> If prudence dictates that a claim beyond the scope of the retention agreement be pursued, the client can then consider whether to expand the retention or

pursue the additional claim in some other manner. In the context of a class action, both the representative plaintiffs and the absent class members similarly are entitled to assume that their attorneys will consider and bring to the attention of at least the class representatives additional or greater claims that may exist arising out of the circumstances underlying the certified claims that class members will be unable to raise if not asserted in the pending action.

Contrast AmBase Corp. v. Davis Polk & Wardwell, 866 N.E.2d 1033 (NY 2007). When the IRS assessed a $21 million tax liability against AmBase, it hired Davis Polk to contest the claim. The firm was completely successful. The liability was rejected. In the "No Good Deed Goes Unpunished" Department, AmBase then sued Davis Polk for malpractice because, it alleged, Davis Polk had failed to advise it that apart from its challenge to the amount of the IRS claim, it had a separate argument that its former parent, not it, was primarily liable for any taxes in any event. As a result, AmBase claimed that it was led to believe that it had to maintain a large loss reserve on its books during the litigation, which in turn cost it business opportunities. The question, then, was whether the law firm, hired to challenge the amount of the tax also had to challenge the IRS's claim that AmBase was the primary responsible party. The court rejected AmBase's claim, focusing on the language of the retainer agreement.

> The plain language of the retainer agreement indicates that Davis Polk was retained to litigate the amount of tax liability and not to determine whether the tax liability could be allocated to another entity. Thus, the issue whether plaintiff was primarily or secondarily liable for the subject tax liability was outside the scope of its representation. As such, defendants exercised the ordinary reasonable skill and knowledge commonly possessed by a member of the legal profession when they focused their efforts on the controversy between AmBase and the IRS—the subject of the retainer agreement—resulting in a most favorable outcome, which was publicly praised by AmBase principals.

The court also rejected AmBase's theory of damages.

Why didn't Davis Polk have a duty to advise that the IRS may have targeted the wrong taxpayer? True, the retainer agreement said only that the firm was hired to challenge the tax, but AmBase claimed that the firm had been given the document that would have alerted it to the second theory as well, yet "never fully reviewed" it. That omission was the basis for the malpractice claim, which the court rejected.

Can this decision be reconciled with the other opinions above? One explanation is that the client was sophisticated and could be expected to understand the scope of the retainer. What if the client were an unsophisticated individual who had received a deficiency notice from the IRS, brought it to counsel, and signed the same retainer agreement? Should the court rule the same way?

Robert S. Caine*
A LAWYER'S VIEW OF BEING A LITIGANT
Letter, New York Law Journal, May 16, 1994, at 2

It's different being a litigant than a lawyer. I know. I am both. As a litigant, you're often subjected to indignities and lack of consideration by lawyers and judges.

Try calling your attorney to obtain information you deem important, and experience responses from his receptionist or secretary, such as, "He's in court," "He's on vacation this week," "He's in a deposition," "He's out to lunch," "He's at a closing," "He's moving today," "He's on the phone," "He's in conference," or "He's on trial." You strongly infer from her/his statements that the lawyer is actually in the office. Call back later and receive the same responses. And try the next day, the day after that, and the day after that — all without success.

Experience for yourself the ultimate callback from your lawyer, such as, "I'm just a single practitioner," "I was moving," "I was involved in so-and-so's campaign," "You're driving me crazy leaving all those messages," "That's the system," "I was very busy with priority matters," "I was in court all day," or "I had nothing to tell you." Hear your lawyer tell you that the judge went on vacation without deciding your critical matter, when the judge could have decided it quickly and properly in your favor. Or, a judge who routinely grants — or denies — stays without properly considering the papers. Or, a judge who is rude to or short-tempered with lawyers or litigants.

Then, too, listen carefully as your lawyer tells you that it's not his fault, as he tried to get the other lawyer on the telephone but he wasn't in; that he has called the other lawyer 10 times without success; that the other lawyer called him back yesterday, just after he left the office, and the other lawyer's not in now. One of the lawyers is at fault.

Hear that your "million dollar deal" is being held up by telephone tag and failure of your lawyer to attend to your matter because he had more pressing affairs to take care of. And you're paying for that telephone tag! (What ever happened to making telephone conference call appointments, like business people do?)

There's something wrong with us lawyers — and judges, too — when we can't realize the harm we're doing to our clients and to the public, the heartache and frustration and pain we cause to others because we fail to attend civilly and promptly to the needs of others for communication. If we can't take care of a client properly, which includes communication with the client, we shouldn't accept the retainer. No excuses are acceptable, except honest illness, death or other *real* emergencies. In other businesses, if you don't deliver properly and courteously, you don't get paid or you lose the customer, or both. Why don't we at a minimum tell our secretaries or paralegals to call the client, explain what the delay is, determine what the client's concerns are, and give and receive messages? And if judges don't have the will to deal more slowly and carefully with some people than others, they should step aside in favor of others who can and will. Speed and numbers of cases are not all the public wants and deserves.

---

* Robert S. Caine is a member of the New York bar.

Whether we like it or not, clients become captives of a lawyer-oriented system from which they cannot extricate themselves. Clients can't just hang up in disgust and take their matters to the next lawyer in the Yellow Pages. It doesn't work like that. Many know it and play upon it.

Trust me. If we don't clean up our act, someone's going to do it for us, and we will deserve what happens. Be careful, lest an overhaul kills our goose and our golden egg.

The Client's Right to Know

A lawyer representing a plaintiff in a personal injury action did not relay a $90,000 settlement offer. He considered it too skimpy. The case went to trial. The jury was even more skimpy. It found for the defendant. The client thereafter learned of the settlement offer and sued the lawyer. The client testified that he would have accepted the offer (of course), and the jury believed him. On appeal, the court said it "need not decide . . . whether a lawyer has an obligation to transmit a patently unreasonable offer to his client" because the jury could reasonably have decided that competent counsel would have presented the $90,000 offer. Moores v. Greenberg, 834 F.2d 1105 (1st Cir. 1987). The lawyer in First National Bank v. Lowrey, 872 N.E.2d 447 (Ill. App. 2007), had to make good on $1 million after he failed to convey the settlement offer and then lost at trial. Rizzo v. Haines, 555 A.2d 58 (Pa. 1989), held that a lawyer has a duty to communicate settlement offers to a client, that failure to do so is malpractice, and that expert testimony was not necessary to establish the lawyer's negligence. Compare the criminal analogue, plea bargains. Cottle v. State, 733 So. 2d 963 (Fla. 1999), held that defense attorneys have a duty to inform clients of plea bargain offers. Failure to do so justifies postconviction relief. The accused need not prove that the "trial court would have actually accepted the plea arrangement offered by the state but not conveyed to the defendant."

In the course of a representation, a lawyer is likely to learn a great deal of information bearing on the client's matter. How much of it must she share? The answer cannot be "all" because a lot of the information will be technical or trivial. Time is also a factor. Yet the answer cannot be "none" because the lawyer is the client's agent on the matter. It is the client who must live with the result. So where do we draw the line? This issue slides into the autonomy question next discussed, but some introduction is in order.

Take a look at Rules 1.2(a) and 1.4. Rule 1.2(a) tells us that in civil matters, whether to settle is a decision for the client, and in criminal matters, the client has the right to decide whether to testify, whether to accept a plea and whether to waive a jury trial. Ordinarily, a lawyer is impliedly authorized to choose the means (strategies, legal theories) he will employ to achieve the client's goals. Those are the easy questions. But comment [2] to Rule 1.2 and Rule 1.4 ("Communication") recognize that clients have an interest in participating in questions of strategy too, and in any event have an interest in knowing what the lawyer intends to do and why. Good lawyers, conscious of maintaining positive client relations, will respond to these interests without being asked. On top of all else, failure to communicate may lead to discipline even if the client's legal interests are unaffected. In re Shaughnessy, 467 N.W.2d 620 (Minn. 1991) (failures to communicate are "intensely frustrating to the client, reflect adversely on the bar, and are destructive of public confidence in the legal profession"). Rule 1.4, significantly expanded in 2002, accordingly requires communication even on decisions that the lawyer has authority to make.

The conflict-of-interest rules are also a repository of duties to inform. Take a look at Rules 1.7, 1.8(a), 1.8(f), 1.8(g), and 1.9. These all contemplate that a lawyer will inform a client of a conflict of interest, possibly as a prelude to the lawyer's effort to obtain consent "after consultation." The Terminology tells us that "consult" or "consultation" requires "communication of information reasonably sufficient to permit the client to appreciate the significance of the matter in question."

FURTHER READING

The subject of the attorney's duty to inform, and the twin issue of the client's right of informed consent, have attracted academic attention. Mark Spiegel, Lawyering and Client Decisionmaking: Informed Consent and the Legal Profession, 128 U. Pa. L. Rev. 41 (1979); Gary Munneke & Theresa Loscalzo, The Lawyer's Duty to Keep Clients Informed: Establishing a Standard of Care in Professional Liability Actions, 9 Pace L. Rev. 391 (1989); and Cornelius Peck, A New Tort Liability for Lack of Informed Consent in Legal Matters, 44 La. L. Rev. 1289 (1984).

"In a Box"

"My name is Martin Chin. I do general corporate work in Seattle. One of my partners, Sally Zagott, represents Jennie Marsh, an independent investor. Marsh wants to do a joint venture with a half dozen others, including Endicott Press. Marsh and the others would put up a total of about $20 million. Endicott will manage the venture, which has something to do with online publishing. Although Sally is taking the lead here, I met with Marsh twice and I'm helping Sally with some of the corporate issues. The venture is still in negotiation but close to closure.

"Last week, one of my clients, Font & Blue, a stationery wholesaler, got a visit from an investigator from the state Attorney General's office. She told Mort Green, the F&B president, that the AG was looking into a possible kickback scheme aimed at getting business from state officials. The investigator described the transactions under investigation. Mort said he could not say anything without advice of counsel. Then he called me. In addition to F&B, Endicott and a few others were parties to the transactions. From what Mort told me, F&B and Endicott are both subjects of the investigation. F&B is not involved in the Marsh deal, but of course Endicott is. This is the kind of information we would give Marsh if permitted to do so. It might cause her to abandon the investment.

"My questions are:

1. May we tell Marsh what I learned about Endicott without mentioning F&B? We'd just say something like 'we have good reason to believe that the state is investigating certain of Endicott's financial transactions.'

Or we could say 'We don't think you should do this deal, Jennie, but we can't say why.'

2.   Alternatively, can we get consent from F&B to tell Marsh?

3.   If we tell Marsh nothing, may we continue to represent her on the deal anyway?

4.   What if I just never tell Sally? Will that free Sally to represent Marsh? After all, if we withdraw from Marsh, no other lawyer will know about Endicott either."

"What Are The Odds?"

On the very day I was working on this part of the book, I had an e-mail discussion with a senior lawyer at a prominent U.S. firm. It raises the following question, which I present as a hypothetical.

Imagine that a client has developed a business plan. It is a novel plan and will face risks under various regulatory schemes. Much can be done to minimize the risks but not eliminate them. If the venture is ever challenged (and it might not be), a court might find a problem. Or maybe not.

The novelty of the plan makes prediction difficult. Also, the more the client has to do to minimize regulatory risk, the less financially attractive the plan will be. Starting up the business will cost many millions of dollars.

The lawyer gives the client a list of ten things it could do (let's call them precautions) to reduce risk. But each one will also reduce likely profitability, although to varying degrees. The client, quite sophisticated, can predict the effect of each precaution on profitability, but it doesn't know the extent to which each precaution will reduce legal risk (or the extent to which absence of the precaution will increase legal risk), and this is obviously important to its choices.

Because the most important question for the client is cost/benefit, it gives the lawyer ten different business models, each of which incorporates some of the precautions the lawyer has identified. The client then asks the lawyer to estimate degree of legal risk for each business model.

The lawyer is willing to do that only to the extent of saying that the legal risk is "low," "moderate," or "high," or, perhaps, in a close case "low/moderate" or "moderate/high." The client wants greater specificity. What percentages do "low," "moderate," and "high" cover? How is the lawyer using those words? Perhaps what the lawyer considers a high risk is one that the client's investors (being sophisticated business people) are willing to accept if they can know a little more about what the lawyer means.

What should the lawyer do? In my e-mail discussion, I suggested that the lawyer might give a percentage range for each word. For example, "low" means less than a 20-percent chance that the plan will violate the regulations; "moderate" means a 30- to 45-percent chance of violation; and so on. I got the following reply: "I routinely tell clients that I will not handicap risk with percentages. No matter how carefully a lawyer may try to avoid it with cautionary language, from the client's perspective the effort takes on an appearance of precision that is never warranted. In the end it is more misleading than helpful."

What do you think? Is this information the client has a right to have? Isn't it paying for the lawyer's judgment? Can the lawyer use words like "low," "moderate," and "high" and refuse to further define them? Or is the client better off not succumbing to the illusion that legal predictions can be presented with near arithmetical precision? Is the lawyer legitimately worried that greater specificity increases the *lawyer's* risk of malpractice?

C. AUTONOMY OF ATTORNEYS AND CLIENTS

Lawyers as professionals and as agents of their clients exercise judgment and make decisions to help achieve their clients' objectives through the law. Clients delegate authority to their lawyers and therewith some of their autonomy. The ends/means distinction only roughly allocates those decisions that properly belong to the lawyer and those that belong to the client. See Rule 1.2 comment [2]. Often, though, the distinction works. For example, criminal clients must decide whether to plead guilty, and civil clients must decide whether to settle (although that power may be delegated). On the other hand, a defendant will have no complaint if his lawyer stipulates to the easily provable fact that the banks he allegedly robbed were federally insured. Poole v. United States, 832 F.2d 561 (11th Cir. 1987). Between these examples may lie uncertainty.

Several questions confront us in deciding how we allocate authority within the professional relationship. Should medicine's informed-consent standard guide us, or are the two professions too dissimilar? Clients can delegate some authority to their lawyers (e.g., to settle). Should they also have the right to insist on more authority than whatever rule we develop might allow? What will it do to professionalism if lawyers are required to get client approval of too many "means" decisions or are required to abide by an instruction that the lawyer deems imprudent? After all, the lawyer was retained because he is an expert on means—legal means. The freedom to choose those means is important to the lawyer's professional satisfaction and the quality of his work for the client. If pushed too far, lawyers will turn into bureaucrats, scribes, or mouthpieces.

Still, some means decisions are not all that complicated, especially if a lawyer is willing to explain a few technical points. Some strategies raise important moral or financial issues for the client. Many clients are sophisticated about the subject that forms the basis of the legal representation. In litigation or negotiation, the client may be better able to take the measure of a known opponent. Further, it is the client, not the lawyer, who will have to live with the result. In an oft-told, possibly apocryphal story, a lawyer represented a client in a serious criminal trial that resulted in conviction. "What do we do now?" the anxious client asked after the jury announced the verdict. "We? Now?" replied the lawyer with a shrug. "Now, I go back to my office and you go to prison."

These considerations argue for fluidity in the allocation of authority. Fluidity, however, has its limits. At times a decision will have to be made although the client and lawyer disagree, in which case we need a rule that tells us whose decision it is. And even before we reach that point, we must recognize that lawyers make dozens of decisions weekly (perhaps hundreds during a trial).

They cannot consult on all of them. They need to know which decisions can safely (that is, without risk of discipline or malpractice liability) be made without consultation.

We have been talking about what standard the legal or ethical rules should adopt. That standard may define the minimum, but it is not the only reference. Can't a lawyer consult with, or defer to, a client more than the rules demand? Consultation can lead to a better result. It also makes sense from the perspective of good client relations. It shows the client that the lawyer has been thinking about the case, has concern for the client's point of view, and has respect for the client's intelligence. In settlements, many lawyers believe that a client who is consulted is more likely to be satisfied with a result than a client who is simply presented with the same result and told to take it or leave it. One empirical study, by Professor Ann Southworth, looked at client and lawyer decision-making in civil rights and poverty law practices in Chicago. Professor Southworth's interviews with 69 lawyers found significant variety in degrees of paternalism and deference to clients, in part depending on the lawyers' practice settings (such as legal services, law school clinic, advocacy organization) and the nature of their work (such as civil rights litigation, business advice). Ann Southworth, Lawyer-Client Decisionmaking in Civil Rights and Poverty Practice: An Empirical Study of Lawyers' Norms, 9 Geo. J. Legal Ethics 1101 (1996).

1.   The Lawyer's Autonomy

"Ms. Niceperson"

"I have an urgent problem. I am representing a family-owned company in a $15 million litigation that, if fully successful, could force it into bankruptcy. However, the claims are imaginative or hard to prove, and the more likely result will be a settlement my client can live with, though not happily.

"The plaintiff is represented by a nice fellow I know in town, Gary Larsen. We have been adversaries now and again. He has always been a decent opponent. Gary was a senior associate at Rendell Wyatt. A few years ago, he and three other Rendell lawyers started a litigation boutique. They're doing quite well. Many of the larger firms, including mine, refer matters to Gary's firm.

"The case is now on remand from an appellate decision giving us most of what we asked for on a motion to dismiss. But Gary has a right to file an amended complaint for which he has already had one stipulated extension. He called me this morning from out of town to ask for a second extension. His papers are due in three days. He explained that his father, who is retired, has had a stroke, and he had to fly out to help his mother last night, making it impossible to complete his amended complaint, which is sitting on his desk in draft form. He said he'd send over the written stipulation when he got back to town early next week.

"I quickly agreed. But a half-hour later I recalled that my agreement is insufficient under our rules because Gary has already had one extension. What Gary may have forgotten in the turmoil of his situation, is that given the procedural posture of the case, he needs a court order and good cause to get a further extension. My stipulation will not do. And his motion for a second extension has to be filed before the deadline. Of course, he *has* good cause. I would not oppose his request, but he must ask within the next three days.

"Furthermore, it's jurisdictional. If he doesn't file his amended complaint in the next three days and has not moved for an order granting him a second extension by then, the court must dismiss because it will have no jurisdiction. If Gary knew all this, one of his partners would finish the draft and file it.

"My questions are: Am I free now to warn Gary? If I do nothing, the time will pass, and he's out of court. Do I have to tell my client? If my client tells me to take no further action, do I have any choice?

"I'm a nice person. Sure, I'm able to take advantage of another lawyer's mistakes, or what I assume are mistakes, just as they do mine, but this seems of a different order. I asked one of my partners what to do, and he said to do nothing and let the chips fall where they may. Our client avoids a $15 million judgment. But Gary's firm gets sued for malpractice. My partner asked if I would alert an opponent who failed to assert an obvious defense when responding to a complaint. Of course not. But isn't that different? Failing to assert what we might think is 'an obvious defense' can actually have a tactical motive of which we are unaware. This error cannot be tactical. What should I do?"

"I Don't Plea Bargain"

"Professor Gillers asked me to write this after I told him about my practice at a bar meeting. I said I would on two conditions — my identity remains confidential and he doesn't change a word.

"First, some background. I'm a criminal defense lawyer with 30 years of experience. This is why I went to law school and this is all I ever wanted to do. If I could try cases five days a week, I'd be in heaven. I love to be 'on.' I hate the pretrial garbage that civil litigators spend their life having to deal with. I'm not a litigator. I'm a trial lawyer. I try cases. I do white collar, blue collar, no collar, starched collar, you name it. And I'm very successful. And respected in a sort of begrudging way. Juries trust me. Articles have been written about me in the law and popular press. I practice alone.

"If I told you my name, you'd probably recognize it although I'll never be one of those talking head on the cable shows. I hate those shows. Bunch of 'formers' second-guessing real working lawyers. Maybe you don't like me already just from what I've said so far. That's all right. If you ever got busted for something serious in this state, or anywhere in the U.S. actually, and you could afford me, I'd be among the top five lawyers on your list.

"Now this is what I'm asked to tell you. I don't plea bargain. I try cases. My practice is as close as you can get in the U.S. to a British barrister. I've reached the stage of my career where I can give myself that gift. If a client comes to me, I make it all very clear. 'If you want someone to cut a deal for you, it's not me,' I say. I am definitely *not* saying that everyone should go to trial. Many defendants absolutely should not go to trial. They'll get slaughtered. If one of those people comes to me, and it's clear at the outset that the guy has to plead, I send him elsewhere. If not, I'll take the case.

"If a client, fully informed about who I am and what I do and don't do, hires me and later the D.A. or U.S. attorney suggests a deal, I tell my client the government wants to deal. If the client wants to negotiate, he can find another lawyer, and I'll even give referrals. He makes a deal, fine. I go on to the next case. If not, not. If while I'm working on a matter, it becomes clear that my client should consider a deal, I advise him to hire someone to open negotiations. If nothing comes of it, I'm around for the trial.

"In fact, and this is another fact that seemed to interest Gillers, some clients come to me *because* I don't bargain. They want to go to trial. They tell me, 'If the government offers a deal or invites negotiation, don't even tell me. I'm not interested in pleading to anything or providing information to convict someone else.' Am I supposed to turn down those clients? Far as I'm concerned, they're my dream.

"So those are the terms on which a client can hire me. I spell them out with great clarity. Gillers, whom I've known quite a while and basically respect, even though he's a little naïve, questioned whether I could have this policy. He meant ethically. He's been living in his head too long, no offense. (Steve: Let's see if you take out that line!) I work in the real world."

Does this lawyer have a problem? Does his policy violate ethical rules?

JONES v. BARNES
463 U.S. 745 (1983)

CHIEF JUSTICE BURGER delivered the opinion of the Court.

We granted certiorari to consider whether defense counsel assigned to prosecute an appeal from a criminal conviction has a constitutional duty to raise every nonfrivolous issue requested by the defendant.

I

In 1976, Richard Butts was robbed at knifepoint by four men in the lobby of an apartment building; he was badly beaten and his watch and money were taken. Butts informed a Housing Authority Detective that he recognized one of his assailants as a person known to him as "Froggy," and gave a physical description of the person to the detective. The following day the detective arrested respondent David Barnes, who is known as "Froggy." . . .

The Appellate Division of the Supreme Court of New York, Second Department, assigned Michael Melinger to represent respondent on appeal [of an assault conviction]. Respondent sent Melinger a letter listing several claims that he felt should be raised. Included were claims that Butts' identification testimony should have been suppressed, that the trial judge improperly excluded psychiatric evidence, and that respondent's trial counsel was ineffective. Respondent also enclosed a copy of a pro se brief he had written.

In a return letter, Melinger accepted some but rejected most of the suggested claims, stating that they would not aid respondent in obtaining a new trial and that they could not be raised on appeal because they were not based on evidence in the record. Melinger then listed seven potential claims of error that he was considering including in his brief, and invited respondent's "reflections and suggestions" with regard to those seven issues. The record does not reveal any response to this letter.

Melinger's brief to the Appellate Division concentrated on three of the seven points he had raised in his letter to respondent: improper exclusion of psychiatric evidence, failure to suppress Butts' identification testimony, and improper cross-examination of respondent by the trial judge. In addition, Melinger submitted respondent's own pro se brief. Thereafter, respondent filed two more pro se briefs, raising three more of the seven issues Melinger had identified.

At oral argument, Melinger argued the three points presented in his own brief, but not the arguments raised in the pro se briefs. [The court affirmed the conviction.]

[The Second Circuit, relying on Anders v. California, 386 U.S. 738 (1967), page 446, granted Barnes's habeas corpus petition on the ground that he had a Sixth Amendment right to have his lawyer raise all nonfrivolous issues on appeal. The Second Circuit also held that Barnes did not have to demonstrate a likelihood of success on these issues. One judge dissented.]

II

In announcing a new per se rule that appellate counsel must raise every nonfrivolous issue requested by the client, the Court of Appeals relied primarily upon Anders v. California, supra. There is, of course, no constitutional right to an appeal, but in Griffin v. Illinois, 351 U.S. 12, 18 (1955), and Douglas v. California, 372 U.S. 353 (1963), the Court held that if an appeal is open to those who can pay for it, an appeal must be provided for an indigent. It is also recognized that the accused has the ultimate authority to make certain fundamental decisions regarding the case, as to whether to plead guilty, waive a jury, testify in his or her own behalf, or take an appeal. In addition, we have held that, with some limitations, a defendant may elect to act as his or her own advocate, Faretta v. California, 422 U.S. 806 (1975). Neither *Anders* nor any other decision of this Court suggests, however, that the indigent defendant has a constitutional right to compel appointed counsel to press nonfrivolous points requested by the client, if counsel, as a matter of professional judgment, decides not to present those points.

This Court, in holding that a State must provide counsel for an indigent appellant on his first appeal as of right, recognized the superior ability of trained counsel in the "examination into the record, research of the law, and marshalling of arguments on [the appellant's] behalf." Yet by promulgating a per se rule that the client, not the professional advocate, must be allowed to decide what issues are to be pressed, the Court of Appeals seriously undermines the ability of counsel to present the client's case in accord with counsel's professional evaluation.

Experienced advocates since time beyond memory have emphasized the importance of winnowing out weaker arguments on appeal and focusing on one central issue if possible, or at most on a few key issues. Justice Jackson, after observing appellate advocates for many years, stated:

> One of the first tests of a discriminating advocate is to select the question, or questions, that he will present orally. Legal contentions, like the currency, depreciate through over-issue. The mind of an appellate judge is habitually receptive to the suggestion that a lower court committed an error. But

receptiveness declines as the number of assigned errors increases. Multiplicity hints at lack of confidence in any one. . . . [E]xperience on the bench convinces me that multiplying assignments of error will dilute and weaken a good case and will not save a bad one. [Jackson, Advocacy Before the Supreme Court, 25 Temple L.Q. 115, 119 (1951).]

Justice Jackson's observation echoes the advice of countless advocates before him and since. . . .

There can hardly be any question about the importance of having the appellate advocate examine the record with a view to selecting the most promising issues for review. This has assumed a greater importance in an era when oral argument is strictly limited in most courts — often to as little as 15 minutes — and when page limits on briefs are widely imposed. Even in a court that imposes no time or page limits, however, the new per se rule laid down by the Court of Appeals is contrary to all experience and logic. A brief that raises every colorable issue runs the risk of burying good arguments — those that, in the words of the great advocate John W. Davis, "go for the jugular" — in a verbal mound made up of strong and weak contentions.

This Court's decision in *Anders*, far from giving support to the new per se rule announced by the Court of Appeals, is to the contrary. *Anders* recognized that the role of the advocate "requires that he support his client's appeal to the best of his ability." Here the appointed counsel did just that. For judges to second-guess reasonable professional judgments and impose on appointed counsel a duty to raise every "colorable" claim suggested by a client would disserve the very goal of vigorous and effective advocacy that underlies *Anders*. Nothing in the Constitution or our interpretation of that document requires such a standard.[7]

The judgment of the Court of Appeals is accordingly reversed.

[Justice Blackmun, concurring in the judgment, thought that "as an *ethical* matter, an attorney should argue on appeal all nonfrivolous claims upon which his client insists." However, Justice Blackmun did not believe that his view on the "ideal allocation of decision-making authority between client and lawyer necessarily assumes constitutional status." The client's "remedy, of course, is a writ of habeas corpus."]

JUSTICE BRENNAN, with whom JUSTICE MARSHALL joins, dissenting. . . .

I believe the right to "the assistance of counsel" carries with it a right, personal to the defendant, to [decide which nonfrivolous issues should be raised on appeal] against the advice of counsel if he chooses.

If all the Sixth Amendment protected was the State's interest in substantial justice, it would not include such a right. However, in Faretta v. California, we decisively rejected that view of the Constitution. . . . *Faretta* establishes that the

7. The only question presented by this case is whether a criminal defendant has a constitutional right to have appellate counsel raise every nonfrivolous issue that the defendant requests. The availability of federal habeas corpus to review claims that counsel declined to raise is not before us, and we have no occasion to decide whether counsel's refusal to raise requested claims would constitute "cause" for a petitioner's default within the meaning of Wainwright v. Sykes, 433 U.S. 72 (1977). See also Engle v. Isaac, 456 U.S. 107 (1982).

right to counsel is more than a right to have one's case presented competently and effectively. It is predicated on the view that the function of counsel under the Sixth Amendment is to protect the dignity and autonomy of a person on trial by *assisting* him in making choices that are his to make, not to make choices for him, although counsel may be better able to decide which tactics will be most effective for the defendant.

Anders v. California also reflects that view. Even when appointed counsel believes an appeal has no merit, he must furnish his client a brief covering all arguable grounds for appeal so that the client may "raise any points that he chooses."

The right to counsel as *Faretta* and *Anders* conceive it is not an all-or-nothing right, under which a defendant must choose between forgoing the assistance of counsel altogether or relinquishing control over every aspect of his case beyond its most basic structure (i.e., how to plead, whether to present a defense, whether to appeal). A defendant's interest in his case clearly extends to other matters. . . .

It is no secret that indigent clients often mistrust the lawyers appointed to represent them. There are many reasons for this, some perhaps unavoidable even under perfect conditions — differences in education, disposition, and socio-economic class — and some that should (but may not always) be zealously avoided. A lawyer and his client do not always have the same interests. Even with paying clients, a lawyer may have a strong interest in having judges and prosecutors think well of him, and, if he is working for a flat fee — a common arrangement for criminal defense attorneys — or if his fees for court appointments are lower than he would receive for other work, he has an obvious financial incentive to conclude cases on his criminal docket swiftly. Good lawyers undoubtedly recognize these temptations and resist them, and they endeavor to convince their clients that they will. It would be naive, however, to suggest that they always succeed in either task. A constitutional rule that encourages lawyers to disregard their clients' wishes without compelling need can only exacerbate the clients' suspicion of their lawyers. As in *Faretta*, to force a lawyer's *decisions* on a defendant "can only lead him to believe that the law conspires against him." In the end, what the Court hopes to gain in effectiveness of appellate representation by the rule it imposes today may well be lost to decreased effectiveness in other areas of representation. . . .

Finally, today's ruling denigrates the values of individual autonomy and dignity central to many constitutional rights, especially those Fifth and Sixth Amendment rights that come into play in the criminal process. Certainly a person's life changes when he is charged with a crime and brought to trial. He must, if he harbors any hope of success, defend himself on terms — often technical and hard to understand — that are the State's, not his own. As a practical matter, the assistance of counsel is necessary to that defense. Yet, until his conviction becomes final and he has had an opportunity to appeal, any restrictions on individual autonomy and dignity should be limited to the minimum necessary to vindicate the State's interest in a speedy, effective prosecution. The role of the defense lawyer should be above all to function as the instrument and defender of the client's autonomy and dignity in all phases of the criminal process. . . .

The Court subtly but unmistakably adopts a different conception of the defense lawyer's role — he need do nothing beyond what the State, not his client, considers most important. In many ways, having a lawyer becomes one of the many indignities visited upon someone who has the ill fortune to run afoul of the criminal justice system. . . .

The Scope of the Lawyer's Autonomy

Since Barnes's points were not frivolous and he is the one who will do the time if the appeal fails, perhaps you think Melinger should have deferred. Barnes is an adult. He deserves to be able to make important decisions in his life that affect only him. But would you say the same thing if Barnes for whatever reason had instructed Melinger not to include what Melinger, based on decades of experience, believed to be Barnes's strongest argument? Should Melinger be able to override him?

Barnes apparently did not protest Melinger's decision to exclude Barnes's appeal point from Melinger's brief and instead to submit them under Barnes's name pro se. Why didn't the Court find that the absence of protest equaled acquiescence and waiver of any claim?

In footnote 7, the court takes no position on whether counsel's failure to raise his client's arguments would constitute "cause" for any default in a subsequent collateral attack on the state conviction. Without citing *Jones*, the Eighth Circuit addressed a prisoner's constitutional claim in a collateral attack on his state conviction where the prisoner's lawyer in state postconviction proceedings refused to raise the claim (the earliest time it could have been raised) despite the prisoner's request that he do so. The prisoner, "in an effort to save the issue, attempted to file a pro se supplemental brief" with the state supreme court, but his motion to do so was denied. While recognizing that an appellate lawyer need not raise "every issue appearing in the record," and that in fact "it could be bad lawyering to do so," the court held that the client "is and always remains the master of his cause. Here, Clemmons did the only thing he could do: He tried to bring the issue to the attention of the Missouri Supreme Court himself." Consequently, the court held that there was no procedural default on the claim and that its "merits are now open for decision on federal habeas corpus." Clemmons v. Delo, 124 F.3d 944 (8th Cir. 1997).

Jones v. Barnes held that there was no Sixth Amendment right to instruct counsel on issues to raise on appeal. The Court saw this result as consistent with the right, established in Faretta v. California, to self-representation at trial. Could a defendant then reject appellate counsel, represent himself, and raise whatever issues he wishes? In Martinez v. Court of Appeal of California, 528 U.S. 152 (2000), without citing *Jones* but in accord with it, the Court said no. Neither the Sixth Amendment nor the Due Process Clause entitles a convicted defendant to self-representation on appeal.

The Constitution aside, Justice Blackmun believes the lawyer acted unethically. Do you agree? What if the lawyer thought it clear beyond doubt that inclusion of the client's nonfrivolous claims would undermine the effectiveness of the brief? What if the lawyer would be professionally embarrassed to assert them? In the final paragraph of his dissent, Justice Brennan went on to write that a client's choices "should be respected unless they would require lawyers to violate their consciences, the law, or their duties to the court." Would Justice Brennan approve if Melinger were conscientiously opposed to including the client's arguments in the appeal brief?

Jones concerned a matter of strategy. The Rules allow for lawyer autonomy in several additional ways. Rule 3.3(a)(3) permits a lawyer to decline to offer evidence (other than the testimony of a criminal defendant) that the lawyer "reasonably believes is false." A lawyer has discretion to "limit the scope" of a representation if the client consents and the limitation is "reasonable under the circumstances." Rule 1.2(c). The question is whether the limitation will impede competent representation. It would, for example, be reasonable to counsel a client on the legality of a business strategy with the understanding that the lawyer will not represent the client in the implementation of that strategy. On the other hand, it would be unreasonable to accept the defense of a criminal case on the understanding that the lawyer will not do any investigation or make any pretrial motions. We are told further that a lawyer's representation of a client on a matter does not "constitute an endorsement of the client's political, economic, social or moral views or activities." Rule 1.2(b). What is a statement like that doing in an ethics code? This is not a rule that tells lawyers to act or refrain from acting in a particular way. It is not a rule that can be violated. It's not a rule at all. Why is it there?

In Ethical Discretion in Lawyering, 101 Harv. L. Rev. 1083 (1988), Professor William Simon argues that "[l]awyers should have ethical discretion to refuse to assist in the pursuit of legally permissible courses of action and in the assertion of potentially enforceable legal claims." In exercising this discretion, he writes, a basic consideration of the lawyer "should be whether assisting the client would further justice." Professor Simon would apparently permit lawyers to exercise this discretion not only in choosing whether to accept a client, as they now may, but also in deciding how to represent the client. What do you think about that?

Fred Zacharias urges lawyers to exercise greater independence in their representations of clients. He argues that lawyers have failed to accept the moral authority that the ethics codes in fact recognize, and he proposes solutions to counteract that failure. Fred Zacharias, Reconciling Professionalism and Client Interests, 36 Wm. & Mary L. Rev. 1303 (1995). In the same vein is Susan Kupfer's article, Authentic Legal Practices, 10 Geo. J. Legal Ethics 33 (1996). See also Stephen Gillers, Can a Good Lawyer Be a Bad Person?, 2 J. Inst. Study of Legal Ethics 131 (1999), which posits a series of hypotheticals and asks whether the lawyers who populate them can fairly be subject to moral criticism for their behavior. See generally on these issues Rodney Uphoff & Peter Wood, The Allocation of Decisionmaking Between Defense Counsel and Criminal Defendant: An Empirical Study of Attorney-Client Decisionmaking, 47 U. Kan. L. Rev. 1 (1998).

A lawyer who disagrees with a client, or who feels that professional autonomy is unduly limited, may be able to withdraw from the representation. See page 104. Indeed, the threat of withdrawal gives the lawyer great leverage to get her way, doesn't it?

2. The Client's Autonomy

"Memorandum from General Counsel: Diversity in Staffing"

"As you know, women, minorities, and gay men and lesbians remain seriously underrepresented among senior associates and partners of major U.S. law firms. The firms we hire often fall way short of the diversity we have on our own staff. The General Counsel's office of Foogleplex, in consultation with the Board of Directors, is therefore considering the following policy. We give tens of millions of dollars worth of work to outside firms, most of them large firms. We are prepared to say that we expect that minorities, women, and gay men and lesbians must be significant members of the teams doing our work. Obviously, we can expect more from larger firms than from smaller ones. But we will ask the firms to tell us the race, ethnicity, sex (if not obvious from the name), and sexual orientation (if "out") of every lawyer who works on our matters, and whether or not they are partners. We will also ask for the same breakdown for all of the firm's lawyers. We will take diversity or lack of it into consideration when we decide on future retentions. We will ask firms to update this information yearly. We won't have a quota. We respect staffing needs. We don't expect every case to have a minority, a woman, etc., but we do expect diversity among the lawyers handling our matters across the run of cases. Before we announce this policy, the General Counsel wishes to have your advice and suggestions."

"I'd Rather Die"

"I represent Malcolm Voss, who as you probably know is on death row for two convenience store homicides eight years ago when he was 19. Voss has had his execution delayed four times, twice when it was only hours away. He's been living in a 7-by-8-foot cell since his conviction. Gets out an hour a day to exercise alone in a yard with 22-foot-high brick walls. Voss has always maintained his innocence to me. I got his case when the Death Penalty Project at the Lawyers' Human Rights Committee asked me to take it. Voss had very poor representation at trial—an appointed lawyer who did almost no investigation, hardly talked with Voss before the trial, and introduced almost no evidence in mitigation at the penalty phase.

"We've been through the state and federal systems on ineffectiveness claims, but no luck. The courts say the trial lawyer had adopted a 'low profile' strategy so he wasn't ineffective. That's a very generous assessment. I keep looking for new claims, but it gets harder and harder to get the courts to accept habeas petitions. Voss is now scheduled to be executed in five weeks. I've been putting a petition together that makes some new arguments based on recent case law and some additional facts I've been able to uncover, including serious improprieties by the state crime lab chemist who testified against Voss on DNA identification. I don't know if the courts will hear me, but this is the best chance we've ever had, not only to upset the sentence but also to get a new trial. You don't have to believe me, but just accept the fact that I believe this guy is innocent. He's no angel but he's not a murderer. I've represented other death row inmates for the Project, and I knew very well what I was dealing with.

"A month ago, I went to see Voss to tell him about my discoveries and show him some papers in draft. He said he didn't want to file. 'Let's get it over with, Emily,' he said. 'I can't take this life any more. I'd rather be dead than live on death row. Or even spend the rest of my life in this stink-hole prison.' I let it pass and kept working on the papers, but each time I went back to see him or talked to him on the phone, he was adamant. He even wrote me a letter saying I was not to file any more papers. I told him I had a problem with his position. He said he would discharge me as his lawyer if that made my problem easier. I'm telling you this because I don't know what to do next."

"Accept the Offer"

"I do matrimonial work. Aside from custody issues, I have one main objective for my client: money. Look, I don't mean to be crass, but after 26 years at this business, I know that the one thing my clients always regret if they regret anything is that they didn't get enough (usually if they're women) or they agreed to pay too much (men). Whatever they think at the time, if there's disappointment later (and there may not be), it's about money. Take that on faith because it's true.

"The client I wanted to ask you about is someone I'll call Chloe, who was married to Russell for 12 years and then fell out of love or decided she was never in it and married too young. She told Russell she wanted a divorce. It hit him hard and he's still reeling. He thought they had a great marriage. He'd take her back in a heartbeat. I've seen this before. Usually, the spouse leaving has a lover, but I'm certain that's not true here. She just wants her life back while she's still fairly young.

"Chloe and Russell have two children, aged two and five. Before the older one was born, Chloe taught third grade, but she has since stayed home to raise them. She's 33, and Russell is 37.

"Anyway, Russell, who's an investment banker, made a low-ball offer, in the ballpark for first offers but low in light of his income and earning prospects and obviously an invitation for a counteroffer. It's what I would do if I had Russell. I presented the offer to Chloe because I'm supposed to and told her not to be offended that it's so low, because first offers are low and this one isn't any lower than most. What she said next blew me away. 'Greg, I want you to take it.' She doesn't want to negotiate, not even if she assumes — as I told her based on my experience she should — that I can get another $350,000 (about 30 percent more) on the property division and half again as much (another $50,000) yearly on the support, with escalators, for her and the children. Chloe will have custody. I could do this with one phone call to Russell's lawyer, and Chloe would still be getting too little by 20 percent at least. I told her this.

"Chloe said she feels bad enough about what she's doing to Russell; she feels that his offer is an amount she can live with, and she doesn't want to bargain or do anything to create further ill feeling. She says Russell is a good person and will do right by her and the children even if he doesn't have to. I've been back to her several times, but she insists. I'm certain that she's going to regret it within a year, when it'll be too late. Her quality of life will change dramatically while his will increase.

"I've had this happen to me before — women who want little or nothing, men who want to give away the store, both operating from guilt — but always I've been able to talk them out of it. Don't get me wrong. I'm no bomber. I understand and often advise taking less or giving more for the sake of harmony. These people have to cooperate over the kids for another twenty years. Okay. So you don't push for every nickel. But this would be a catastrophe for Chloe. She'll regret it within the year. What should I do?"

OLFE v. GORDON
93 Wis. 2d 173, 286 N.W.2d 573 (1980)

[Olfe hired Gordon to handle the sale of her real property to Demman. She instructed Gordon that she was willing to take back a first mortgage but only a first mortgage. Gordon negotiated a contract that provided for a second mortgage. Gordon and his partner led Olfe to believe that it was a first mortgage. After the purchaser defaulted and the first mortgage was foreclosed, Olfe lost more than $25,000. The trial court dismissed the case because of the insufficiency of the evidence and "a lack of expert testimony relating to the standard of care required of attorneys in similar circumstances." On this point, the state supreme court wrote:]

Since Olfe did not present expert testimony to establish the standard of care and a departure from that standard, we must determine whether Gordon's actions fall within the exception to the rule requiring expert testimony. Olfe's first two allegations, that Gordon failed to provide in the offer to purchase that Olfe's security interest would be a first mortgage and that he failed to draft or cause to be drafted a mortgage that would be senior to any other Demman would obtain on the premises of sale, are contentions that Gordon is liable for damages caused by his negligent disregard of Olfe's instructions. The legal theory on which these allegations are premised is well established:

It has generally been recognized that an attorney may be liable for all losses caused by his failure to follow with reasonable promptness and care the explicit instructions of his client. Moreover, an attorney's honest belief that the instructions were not in the best interests of his client provides no defense to a suit for malpractice. [Footnotes omitted.] Note, Attorney Malpractice, 63 Colum. L. Rev. 1292, 1302 (1963).

The attorney-client relationship in such contexts is one of agent to principal, and as an agent the attorney "must act in conformity with his authority and instructions and is responsible to his principal if he violates this duty." While actions for disregard of instructions can be based upon fiduciary and contractual principles, the principal's cause of action for an agent's breach of duty may also lie in tort. "[I]f a paid agent does something wrongful, either knowing it to be wrong, or acting negligently, the principal may have either an action of tort or an action of contract." Restatement (Second) of Agency, sec. 401, Comment *a*, 238 (1958). See also [precedent], where this court stated, "It is elementary that a principal has a cause of action sounding in tort against his agent when the latter violates a duty that he owes to the former." Expert testimony is not required to show that the agent (attorney) has violated his duty. [Reversed.]

The Scope of the Client's Autonomy

Here's a riddle: Gordon failed to follow Olfe's instructions. Melinger refused to follow Barnes's instructions. Barnes lost, and Olfe won. Why? Was it simply because one action depended on the Sixth Amendment and the other was in malpractice? Olfe's employment of Gordon did not authorize him to make the decision he did in the face of her contrary instruction. The court finds Gordon's conduct improper. Not only did Olfe not have to present expert evidence on the issue, she won as a matter of law. If Olfe had said nothing about security, could Gordon then have elected to accept a second mortgage without talking to Olfe? Or would he have had to ask for direction? Is this decision a "means" or an "end?" Does it matter?

With autonomy comes responsibility, at least in New York. Petrovich, charged with the murder of his parents, rejected his lawyer's advice that the jury be given the choice of convicting him of manslaughter should it find that he acted under extreme emotional disturbance. Petrovich wanted the jury to have but three choices: guilty of murder, not guilty, and not guilty by reason of insanity. (Do you see why?) Guess which the jury chose. On appeal of his murder conviction, Petrovich argued that the decision belonged to his lawyer, not to him, and that the trial judge should not have allowed his choice to prevail. The court was unimpressed: "Defendant was attempting to minimize the risk of conviction. . . . [H]is decision did not implicate a matter of trial strategy or tactics. . . . [D]efendant perceived that charging the jury on both murder . . . and manslaughter . . . provided two opportunities for the jury to convict, and he calculated that eliminating consideration of manslaughter increased his chance for an acquittal. . . . That defendant now questions the wisdom of his decision cannot relieve him of the consequences of his request." People v. Petrovich, 664 N.E.2d 503 (N.Y. 1996). Reaching the exact opposite conclusion and granting a new trial is Arko v. People, 185 P.3d 555 (Colo. 2008). The defense lawyer wanted the trial judge to instruct on lesser included offenses. The defendant did not, and the judge listened to the defendant. On appeal from his conviction, the defendant argued that the trial judge should have heeded counsel instead. The court agreed. The "decision to request a lesser offense instruction is strategic and tactical in nature, and is therefore reserved for defense counsel."

If Jones v. Barnes was rightly decided, is *Petrovich* wrong? That is, if Barnes's autonomy did not entitle him to override Melinger's decision, why was Petrovich allowed to override his lawyer? Shouldn't the autonomy issue be resolved the same way whether the issue is what arguments to make on appeal or what lesser included offense options to offer the jury?

One decision that certainly does belong to an accused is whether to testify. "When a defendant asserts that he desires to exercise his constitutional right to testify truthfully, counsel's duty is to inform the defendant why he believes this course will be unwise or dangerous. If a defendant insists on testifying, however irrational that insistence might be from a tactical viewpoint, counsel must accede." United States v. Mullins, 315 F.3d 449 (5th Cir. 2002). Reconsider

Jones v. Barnes (page 89). If a criminal defendant has the right to testify, plead guilty, or waive a jury even over counsel's contrary strategic advice, and even if the decision is "irrational," why couldn't Jones require his lawyer to make non-frivolous appeal arguments even though the lawyer believed it was strategically unwise to do so? Why couldn't Arko make the call on a lesser included offense charge? Even if a distinction is tenable as a matter of text and history, does it make sense as a matter of policy and logic?

As Olfe v. Gordon proves, autonomy questions need not arise in litigation. The plaintiff in Nicolet Instrument Corp. v. Lindquist & Vennum, 34 F.3d 453 (7th Cir. 1994), had sold its subsidiary for $22 million, but the law firm that negotiated the sale for the plaintiff did not also negotiate to have the buyer assume liability for the subsidiary's lease obligations. The seller was a guarantor on the lease, and when the subsidiary defaulted, the seller had to pay the landlord $2.6 million. The seller sued its former law firm, alleging that it had instructed the firm to protect it against contingent liability on the lease but that the firm was "negligen[t] in having failed to make any effort" to do so. The court observed that the "failure to obey a client's lawful instructions in a negotiation is an unusual form of legal malpractice, but the defendants do not deny that it is an actionable form." The court recognized that the plaintiff might have a hard time establishing causation. See chapter 13(B)(2).

Autonomy questions are a bit more complicated when the law is unsettled. Justice Holmes said that law is what judges do in fact. Lawyers are hired to make these predictions. When they err, the doctrine of judgmental immunity may protect them from liability. That doctrine holds that a lawyer's "judgment or recommendation on an unsettled point of law is immune from suit" even if it turns out wrong, so long as it is reasonable. Wood v. McGrath, North, Mullin & Kratz, 589 N.W.2d 103 (Neb. 1999). In other words, lawyers are not guarantors. But if the law is unsettled, is a lawyer free to proceed on one view of how it will develop without informing her client of its unsettled state? In *Wood*, the plaintiff claimed that the defendant law firm failed to advise her that the law was unsettled on whether certain property would be deemed part of a marital estate. As a result, she said, she settled for less than her legal share. The firm claimed that its judgment that the property was not part of the estate was reasonable. The court rejected this defense. The question was not whether the firm's view was reasonable, but the client's right to weigh the unsettled law in making her decisions. "The decision to settle a controversy is the client's. . . . The attorney's responsibilities to the client may not be satisfied . . . by unilaterally deciding the issue. Where there are reasonable alternatives, the attorney should inform the client that the issue is uncertain, unsettled or debatable and allow the client to make the decision."

Majority-Rule Settlements and Client Autonomy.   While we're on the subject of settlement and client autonomy, consider this paradox. Say a lawyer represents 50 clients, all with the same claim in a nonclass action against a common opponent, maybe a company, maybe a government entity. The lawyer anticipates that any settlement offer the defendant makes will be conditioned on acceptance by all clients. The lawyer does not relish the prospect of trying to secure unanimity. She also recognizes that if unanimity is needed, an opportunistic client will be able to use the leverage of his veto power to get disproportionately more for himself. So the lawyer prepares a retainer agreement that says that all clients will be bound if two-thirds of the clients approve. She requires that all clients agree to this after taking time to mull it over and consult other counsel should they wish to do so. Is it binding? Can each client give explicit authority to settle to a super-majority (or just a majority) of the co-clients? One would think so, since a client can delegate that authority to settle to counsel or indeed any other agent.

But courts, citing Rule 1.8(g) on aggregate settlements (read the rule), say the promise is not binding. In New Jersey, a lawyer cannot even ask clients for such an agreement. The state supreme court so held in a case of first impression in that state, collecting abundant primary and secondary authorities. Tax Authority, Inc. v. Jackson Hewitt, Inc., 898 A.2d 512 (N.J. 2006) (citing among other sources: Howard M. Erichson, A Typology of Aggregate Settlements, 80 Notre Dame L. Rev. 1769, 1809 (2005); Nancy J. Moore, The Case Against Changing the Aggregate Settlement Rule in Mass Tort Lawsuits, 41 S. Tex. L. Rev. 149, 165 (1999); Charles Silver & Lynn A. Baker, Mass Lawsuits and the Aggregate Settlement Rule, 32 Wake Forest L. Rev. 733, 763 (1997)).

One might timidly ask in the face of so much contrary case law and secondary authority whether this rule actually harms rather than protects client autonomy. The New Jersey case had 154 plaintiffs (all franchisees) against a franchisor. Each had a monetary claim but the size of the claims differed. Their lawyer secured an aggregate monetary settlement and devised a formula for dividing the sum. The entire package was presented to the plaintiffs, all of whom had previously pledged to accept majority rule. Eventually, all but 18 plaintiffs accepted the settlement.

These were sophisticated clients. Doesn't the court decision, by forbidding lawyers to seek majority-rule settlement agreement in multiclient matters, actually restrict client autonomy? It will make it less attractive for lawyers to accept such matters, since it will be harder to "get to yes." It also reduces the probability of settlement, which courts otherwise favor. (The defendant wants to buy peace, not half-peace.) What business does the state have telling people how they may delegate authority to resolve their claims? Or am I missing something? Can the clients achieve the same result by contracting among themselves without the lawyer's participation? If so, what have we achieved?

About my analogy to the rule allowing a client to delegate settlement authority to counsel: It's not a perfect fit. The client can always withdraw that authority before it is exercised. A "majority rule" arrangement only works if the commitment is irrevocable. Does that affect your view of the issue?

Clients with Diminished Capacity

The allocation of decision-making authority is difficult enough when a client is competent. When a client suffers from diminished capacity because of a physical or mental disability, or because the client is a minor, the issue becomes even harder. Read Rule 1.14. Justice Pollock relied on it in Matter of M.R., 638 A.2d 1274 (N.J. 1994). M.R. was "a mildly- to moderately-retarded twenty-one-year-old woman with Down's Syndrome." Her parents were divorced. She had been living with her mother since 1979. Her father had visitation rights at his home. M.R. "expressed a desire to move from her mother's to her father's home." In order to prevent that move, M.R.'s mother filed a guardianship proceeding. The "trial court appointed Paul G. Hunczak, Esq. to act as M.R.'s attorney." On appeal, Justice Pollock held that M.R.'s mother had the burden of proving by clear and convincing evidence that M.R. was not competent to choose to live with her father. Since the trial court had placed the burden of proof on M.R.'s father, the case was remanded. The court then turned to the role of M.R.'s lawyer:

> M.R.'s father contends that the hearing was unfair because M.R.'s appointed counsel did not zealously advocate her stated preference to live with him. That contention raises the question whether the role of appointed counsel for an incompetent is zealously to advocate the incompetent's position or simply to inform the court of counsel's perception of the incompetent's best interests.
>
> The Rule pertaining to the duties of appointed counsel in guardianship proceedings provides:
>
>> Counsel shall be responsible to meet with the alleged incompetent; to make inquiry of persons having knowledge of the alleged incompetent's circumstances, his or her physical and mental state and his or her estate; and to file, in lieu of an Answer, a written report of findings and recommendations to the court at least three days prior to the hearing. [R. 4:86-4(b).]
>
> Consistent with that Rule, Mr. Hunczak interviewed M.R., her mother, and her father. His written report to the court concluded that M.R. was competent and that the court should give "considerable weight" to her choice to live with her father. After M.R.'s interview in chambers, however, Mr. Hunczak concluded that "less weight should be afforded to her choice to live with [her father]" than he had originally indicated and that either household would serve M.R.'s best interests.
>
> Mr. Hunczak's written report complied with Rule 4:86-4(b). Nonetheless his change of position after the hearing draws our attention to the proper role of an attorney for an incompetent under that Rule. . . .

The court then quoted statutory law and Rule 1.14. It distinguished between a guardian ad litem and counsel. Counsel "is a zealous advocate for the wishes of the client. The guardian ad litem evaluates for himself or herself what is in the best interests of his or her client-ward and then represent[s] the client-ward in accordance with that judgment." The court continued:

> Ordinarily, an attorney should "abide by [the] client's decisions concerning the objectives of representation," RPC 1.2(a), and "act with reasonable diligence . . . in representing [the] client," RPC 1.3. The attorney's role is not to determine whether the client is competent to make a decision, but to advocate the decision that the client makes. That role, however, does not extend to advocating decisions that are patently absurd or that pose an undue risk of harm to the client.
>
> An adversarial role for the attorney recognizes that even if the client's incompetency is uncontested, the client may want to contest other issues, such as the identity of the guardian or, as here, the client's place of residence. With proper advice and assistance, the developmentally-disabled client may be

able to participate in such a decision. From this perspective, the role of an attorney for a developmentally-disabled person is like that of an attorney representing any other client.

Advocacy that is diluted by excessive concern for the client's best interests would raise troubling questions for attorneys in an adversarial system. An attorney proceeds without well-defined standards if he or she forsakes a client's instructions for the attorney's perception of the client's best interests. Further, "if counsel has already concluded that his client needs 'help,' " he is more likely to provide only procedural formality, rather than vigorous representation. Finally, the attorney who undertakes to act according to a best-interest standard may be forced to make decisions concerning the client's mental capacity that the attorney is unqualified to make.

In the related context of civil commitment proceedings, other jurisdictions have mandated that counsel zealously protect the wishes of the proposed ward. . . .

Until such time as we amend Rule 4:86, we offer the following guidelines to assist the attorney for an incompetent. First, a declaration of incompetency does not deprive a developmentally-disabled person of the right to make all decisions. The primary duty of the attorney for such a person is to protect that person's rights, including the right to make decisions on specific matters. Generally, the attorney should advocate any decision made by the developmentally-disabled person. On perceiving a conflict between that person's preferences and best interests, the attorney may inform the court of the possible need for a guardian ad litem.

FURTHER READING

The issue of the autonomy of lawyers and clients has won increased attention since the sixth edition of this casebook. Stephen Pepper posits that by making "the law accessible to the client," lawyers may "facilitate injustice." Although a lawyer's "primary job is providing access to the law," Professor Pepper argues that when "the gap between law and justice is significant, it ought to be part of the lawyer's ethical responsibility to clarify to the client that he or she has a moral choice in the matter. The lawyer ought to be held responsible for ensuring that the client knows there is, in the lawyer's opinion, a gap between law and justice, and that it is the client . . . who is primarily responsible for injustice if it occurs." Pepper, Lawyers' Ethics in the Gap Between Law and Justice, 40 S. Tex. L. Rev. 181 (1999). Professor Zacharias criticizes ethical "provisions limiting client autonomy" and identifies those provisions that fail "to tailor" their limitations "to their justifications." Fred Zacharias, Limits on Client Autonomy in Legal Ethics Regulation, 81 B.U. L. Rev. 199 (2001).

Susan Martyn has proposed a statute to define a right of informed consent, and to provide damages for its violation, in Informed Consent in the Practice of Law, 48 Geo. Wash. L. Rev. 307 (1980). A cause of action is established if a client proves that a lawyer "failed to disclose reasonably foreseeable choices of action in a manner permitting the client to make a knowledgeable evaluation of the legal consequences of the choices." The client, who also has to prove proximate cause and damages, can waive the protection of the statute. David Luban addresses the issue of client autonomy in his article, Paternalism and the Legal Profession, 1981 Wis. L. Rev. 454. Professor Luban poses several detailed hypotheticals, each of which he answers after a philosophical inquiry into the bases for paternalism.

D. TERMINATING THE RELATIONSHIP

The Rules describe the circumstances under which lawyers may withdraw from a representation. Case law describes the client's authority to discharge a lawyer.

1. *Termination by the Client*

Clients, it is said, may fire their lawyers for any reason or no reason. Carlson v. Nopal Lines, 460 F.2d 1209 (5th Cir. 1972). One court has held that a client may even fire a retained lawyer because he wants to be represented by a lawyer of a different race. Giaimo & Vreeburg v. Smith, 599 N.Y.S.2d 841 (2d Dept. 1993) (construing state and federal civil rights laws).

On the other hand, laws that protect employees against discrimination or retaliatory discharge may also protect *employed* lawyers. An employed lawyer may be able to invoke the Rule 1.6(b)(5) exception to confidentiality to prove such a case. Kachmar v. SunGard Data Systems, Inc., 109 F.3d 173 (3d Cir. 1997); Tranello v. Frey, 962 F.2d 244 (2d Cir. 1992); Plessinger v. Castleman and Haskell, 838 F. Supp. 448 (N.D. Cal. 1993). See also chapter 10B.

In an unusual case, a *retained* lawyer, alleging that he was discharged because of his religion (Jewish), brought an action under 42 U.S.C. §1981, which guarantees "[a]ll persons . . . the same right . . . to make and enforce contracts . . . as is enjoyed by white citizens." The defendants moved for summary judgment, citing the "strong public policy supporting the right of a client to discharge an attorney at any time, despite contractual provisions to the contrary." Judge Martin found "direct evidence that plaintiff was discharged because he was 'a New York Jew.' If this is in fact what happened, the public policy embodied in §1981 clearly requires that plaintiff be provided with a remedy." Mass v. McClenahan, 893 F. Supp. 225 (S.D.N.Y. 1995).

Indigent criminal defendants may not fire the lawyers who have been appointed to represent them, although they may ask the court to assign a new lawyer or may choose to represent themselves. Recall the Brennan dissent in Jones v. Barnes (page 91). Even a litigant with a retained lawyer may not be permitted to fire counsel close to or during trial. By then, the interests of others — the courts and the opponent — in not delaying trial will be given substantial weight. Courts also suspect that efforts to fire counsel close to trial are sometimes indirect efforts to force delay. When a matter is in litigation, a lawyer must also comply with the withdrawal requirements of the particular tribunal. Rule 1.16(c).

When a client fires a lawyer, the client may still be liable to the lawyer for fees earned up to the time of termination. Much depends on the law of the particular jurisdiction. Whether the client is liable (and for how much) may depend on whether the termination was for cause (that is, whether the lawyer did something to justify the client's decision). The amount of any liability will depend on the reason for the termination, the contract between the parties, if there is one, and whether the lawyer was working on a contingency basis.

When a professional relationship ends, whether terminated by the lawyer or by the client or simply at the end of the matter, the client is "presumptive[ly]" entitled to the lawyer's "entire file on the represented matter." However, "narrow exceptions" will entitle the lawyer to keep "firm documents intended for internal law office review and use." Sage Realty Corp. v. Proskauer Rose Goetz & Mendelsohn, L.L.P., 689 N.E.2d 879 (N.Y. 1997) (presenting this as the majority view, collecting cases, and acknowledging that a valid lien may supersede the client's right to the file). Iowa Supreme Court Disciplinary Bd. v. Gottschalk, 729 N.W.2d 812 (Iowa 2007) holds that the client is presumptively entitled to the entire file. Lippe v. Bairnco Corp., 1998 Westlaw 901741 (S.D.N.Y. 1998), citing *Sage Realty*, denied a former client "internal law office documents" other than timesheets, which had to be provided. Swift, Currie, McGhee & Hiers v. Henry, 581 S.E.2d 37 (Ga. 2003), followed *Sage Realty*, which it said was the majority view, but also held that a firm might "refuse discovery . . . where disclosure would violate an attorney's duty to a third party [or] where the document assesses the client himself or includes 'tentative preliminary impressions of the legal or factual issues . . . ' " (quoting *Sage Realty*).

Why shouldn't the client get the whole file? After all, wasn't it created for him and at his expense? For further reading, see Fred Zacharias, Who Owns Work Product?, 2006 Ill. L. Rev. 127 (2006).

2. Termination by the Lawyer

The lawyer's right to terminate a professional relationship is circumscribed by Rule 1.16, which tells us when a lawyer may or must withdraw. Leaving a client without a good reason can be characterized as abandonment, which is disloyal and has consequences. Consider Augustson v. Linea Aerea Nacional-Chile S.A., 76 F.3d 658 (5th Cir. 1996). Plaintiff's law firm requested and received permission to withdraw after plaintiff rejected a settlement offer against the firm's advice. The case arose out of an air crash, and other clients of the law firm had accepted the offer. With new counsel, the plaintiff secured a substantially higher settlement. The firm then sought a fee for its work. In Texas, whose law applied, as elsewhere, a lawyer who abandons a client loses all right to compensation. The firm cited the court's permission to withdraw as proof that it had not abandoned the client, but the Fifth Circuit rejected this argument. The decision whether to settle belonged to the client, not the law firm. The withdrawal was an abandonment. Permission to withdraw merely reflected the lower court's evaluation of what was in the "best interests of the client," not a determination that the firm acted correctly. See also Faro v. Romani, 641 So. 2d 69 (Fla. 1994) (when a lawyer working on a contingent fee matter withdraws without justification, he forfeits his entire fee in the matter); Bell & Marra v. Sullivan, 6 P.3d 965 (Mont. 2000) (same).

Both the Code and the Rules recognize permissive withdrawal for what might be called "professional" reasons. Rule 1.16(b)(2) permits withdrawal if the client "persists in a course of action involving the lawyer's services that the lawyer reasonably believes is criminal or fraudulent." Where a law firm withdrew because it had good reason to believe that its client intended to commit perjury, it did not give up its right to unpaid fees. A Sealed Case, 890 F.2d 15 (7th Cir. 1989). Rule 1.16(b)(4) permits withdrawal if the client "insists upon taking action that the lawyer considers repugnant or with which the lawyer has a fundamental disagreement."

These authorities not only allow the lawyer to get out of the representation, they allow the lawyer to *threaten* to get out (subject to court approval if the matter is in litigation). Further, a lawyer may withdraw for the reasons cited even if the withdrawal will have a "material adverse effect on the interests of the client." Rule 1.16(b)(1). You can imagine then that the threat to withdraw can work wonders with a recalcitrant client. What does *that* do to client autonomy?

We will see several circumstances in which lawyers have a duty to withdraw, whether from litigation (page 389) or from negotiation (page 508), because of the misconduct or anticipated misconduct of their clients.

As stated, lawyers who wish to withdraw from a litigation may need the court's permission. To get it, they may need to rely on client confidences. Although the opposing parties are entitled to notice of a request to withdraw, In re Gonzalez, 773 A.2d 1026 (D.C. 2001), held that lawyers should not include client confidences in motion papers served on adversaries, but instead in a sealed document submitted in camera. *Gonzalez* informally admonished a lawyer who failed to do that.

3. Termination by Drift

Some representations end for reasons other than lawyers' or clients' choosing to end them. Some, probably most, end because the work ends. But does the end of the work necessarily mean the end of the professional relationship? The answer can be important. If the relationship is not over, the lawyer may have a duty to continue to protect the client's legal interests. Lama Holding Co. v. Shearman & Sterling, 758 F. Supp. 159 (S.D.N.Y. 1991) (denying motion to dismiss malpractice claim where following completion of work, firm allegedly failed to advise client of relevant tax law changes after promising to do so); Barnes v. Turner, 606 S.E.2d 849 (Ga. 2004) (lawyer would have a continuing duty to renew client's security interest five years after representation ended if lawyer failed to advise client of need for renewal at the end of five years). Duties under conflict rules (see chapters 5 and 6) are also greater when a client is current rather than former. In Jones v. Rabanco, Ltd., 2006 U.S. Dist. LEXIS 53766 (W.D. Wash. 2006), a particularly extreme decision, a firm that had not done work for a client for more than three years was deemed still to be its current counsel because (a) it stored many files from the matter; (b) it had not marked the matter closed in its own records; and (c) it was listed on settlement documents from the matter to receive a copy of any notice to the client. Consequently, it was disqualified.

Episodic clients. Lawyers might believe that a client is no longer a client if they are doing no work for the client at the moment and haven't for quite a while. This is not necessarily true. Courts recognize what we might call an "episodic client." For example, a firm may have done work for a client two or three times a year for the past few years, creating a reasonable client expectation that the professional relationship continues during the intervals. Say I ask you, "Who's your dentist?" You might answer "Dr. Goodsmile," even if you haven't seen her in eight months, because that's whom you go to if your teeth need care. She's your dentist. Clients feel the same way about lawyers. Obviously, this is a question of fact that looks at the frequency with which the client has called on the firm and over what period of time. International Business Machines Corp. v. Levin, 579 F.2d 271 (3d Cir. 1978) ("Although CBM had no specific assignment from IBM on hand on the day the antitrust complaint was filed . . . the pattern of repeated retainers, both before and after the filing of the complaint, supports the finding of a continuous relationship"); S.W.S. Financial Fund A v. Salomon Bros., Inc., 790 F. Supp. 1392 (N.D. Ill. 1992) ("once established, a lawyer-client relationship does not terminate easily," quoting the comment to Rule 1.3); Oxford Systems, Inc. v. CellPro, Inc., 45 F. Supp. 2d 1055 (W.D. Wash. 1999) (Perkins Coie, which represented Becton intermittently from 1985 to May 1997, deemed still to represent Becton in April 1998 though no matters were pending).

Given the consequences, it makes good sense to clarify the situation where the status of the relationship is ambiguous. Some firms send a "termination letter," explaining that "our representation of you is now concluded." But many firms reject doing that for business reasons. What might those be?

III

Protecting the Attorney-Client Relationship Against Invasion

- *The No-Contact Rule*
- *A Special Rule for Law Enforcement?*
- *Improper Acquisition of Confidential Information*

The pervasive theme of this chapter is the legal ethics equivalent of espionage.

Ethics rules and case law protect the client-lawyer relationship against spies, at least when the spies are other lawyers. That shouldn't come as a surprise given the many ways that the rules seek to protect clients from their own lawyers. If we're going to hammer home the importance of a lawyer's fealty to a client, we should expect rules to prevent any interference with that duty from other lawyers. Exhibit One here is Rule 4.2. (The Code equivalent was DR 7-104(A)(1).) It forbids a lawyer to communicate with another lawyer's client under certain circumstances. This "no-contact" (or "anti-contact") rule, examined in Part A, is the subject of much debate in both the civil and criminal arenas. Prohibited contact, however, is not the only way in which an outsider may intercept confidential communications or otherwise undermine a client-lawyer relationship. Some other ways, and the responses to them, are discussed in Part B.

Before moving to this material, we should identify other rules whose purpose or effect, directly or indirectly, is to protect the client-lawyer relationship against improper influence or interference. The attorney-client privilege (chapter 2) protects communications between client and lawyer from the reach of a subpoena. Rule 1.7(a)(2) forbids a lawyer to represent a client if "there is a significant risk" the representation will be "materially limited" by the interests of other clients, the lawyer, or third persons (chapter 5). Rules 1.8(f) and 5.4(c) permit lawyers to accept payment from one person to represent another person, but caution the lawyer against letting the payer intrude on the professional relationship. Rule 1.13 reminds lawyers for organizations that their client is the entity, not its managers or other constituents, and imposes certain duties on lawyers to protect the client even from its constituents (chapter 10). Rule 1.17 protects the client's interests in the professional relationship when a lawyer sells her practice. Rule 5.4 restricts lay managerial authority over, or financial interests in, law firms to avoid exposure to the corrupting influence of non-lawyers.

(This is discussed in chapter 14. I know that sounds funny, maybe even paranoid, but it's a real anxiety lawyers have or claim to have.) Rule 5.6, which prohibits certain agreements that limit a lawyer's right to practice, purports to ensure that *potential* clients are not frustrated in their choice of counsel.

A. COMMUNICATING WITH ANOTHER LAWYER'S CLIENTS

Rule 4.2 says that "[i]n representing a client, a lawyer shall not communicate about the subject of the representation with a person the lawyer knows to be represented by another lawyer in the matter, unless the lawyer has the consent of the other lawyer or is authorized to do so by law or court order." DR 7-104(A)(1) was substantially identical but used "party" instead of "person," as did Rule 4.2 before a 1995 amendment. Nevertheless, courts construed the term "party" to include represented persons who were not parties to a litigation, such as witnesses and parties to a negotiation. Iowa Supreme Court Attorney Disciplinary Board v. Box, 715 N.W.2d 758 (Iowa 2006); Monceret v. Board of Professional Responsibility, 29 S.W.3d 455 (Tenn. 2000). See also ABA Opinion 95-396. This prohibition applies only under certain very specific conditions:

- The communication must occur while the lawyer is "representing a client" on the matter. A lawyer who is not acting in a representative capacity is not foreclosed by this rule from talking to another lawyer's client about the matter on which the other lawyer is representing the client. A client who is dissatisfied with a lawyer's performance can therefore shop for a new lawyer without fear that other lawyers will not speak with her. Iowa Supreme Court Bd. of Prof. Ethics & Conduct v. Herrera, 626 N.W.2d 107 (Iowa 2001). Does Rule 4.2 apply to a client who happens to be an attorney, whether proceeding pro se or with counsel? Authorities are divided. Concluding that Rule 4.2 applies are In re Haley, 126 P.3d 1262 (Wash. 2006); and Runsvold v. Idaho State Bar, 925 P.2d 1118 (Idaho 1996). Holding it does not apply is Pinsky v. Statewide Grievance Comm., 578 A.2d 1075 (Conn. 1990); Restatement §99.
- The communicating lawyer must know that the person with whom she is communicating is represented by another lawyer on the subject of the communication. Comment [8] to Rule 4.2 warns that knowledge "may be inferred from the circumstances" and that a "lawyer cannot evade the requirement . . . by closing eyes to the obvious." Gaylard v. Homemakers of Montgomery, Inc., 675 So. 2d 363 (Ala. 1996), held that a lawyer who, before filing suit, called an employee of a nursing home in which his client was injured did not "know" that the home had retained counsel in the matter. Is that conclusion consistent with the comment [8]? If the nursing home were owned by a large company with a general counsel's office of 100 lawyers, should knowledge be inferred? See Oklahoma Bar Assn. v. Harper, 995 P.2d 1143 (Okla. 2000) ("explicit language of the rule requires actual knowledge of the representation on the matter of the

subject of the communication"); Jorgensen v. Taco Bell Corp., 58 Cal. Rptr. 2d 178 (Ct. App. 1996) (answering no to this question under the California version of the rule). But cf. State v. Miller, 600 N.W.2d 457 (Minn. 1999). In *Miller*, the court suppressed the statements of a defendant that were elicited after prosecutors "knew or at least had clear reason to know" that the defendant, a target of the investigation, "was represented by counsel." The court also "imputed" one government lawyer's knowledge to a prosecutor. But the issue arose on the defendant's motion to suppress, not in the context of lawyer discipline. In any event, even if a person is not known to have counsel, the lawyer must be conscious of the requirements that Rule 4.3 imposes when lawyers speak with unrepresented persons.

- Members of an uncertified class are not represented by counsel so the lawyers on either side of the matter may contact them. ABA Opinion 07-455.
- The communicating lawyer is only forbidden to communicate about the "subject" of the representation. She may communicate about anything else. See Rule 4.2 comment [4].
- The prohibition does not apply if the other lawyer consents to the communication or if it is "authorized . . . by law or a court order." Several courts have held that a represented client may not waive the protection of this rule without counsel's consent. State v. Miller, supra, states that the "right belongs to the party's attorney, not the party, and the party cannot waive the application of the no-contact rule — only the party's attorney can approve the direct contact and only the party's attorney can waive the attorney's right to be present during a communication between the attorney's client and opposing counsel." Monceret v. Board of Professional Responsibility, supra, and In re Capper, 757 N.E.2d 138 (Ind. 2001) agree. What if the opposing client says she has fired her lawyer? Compare In re Users System Services, Inc., 22 S.W.3d 331 (Tex. 1999) (no violation where opposing client provided lawyer with a letter stating that he was "no longer represented by any attorney in this matter," notwithstanding that his attorney had not yet withdrawn and was still counsel of record; lawyer had no duty to call opposing counsel to confirm that the representation had ended), with *Box*, supra: When a client claims to have discharged her lawyer, the opposing lawyer was required "at the very least, to verify the status of [the] representation by a simple telephone call." Does it seem overly protective to deny represented clients the right to waive the protection of this rule without permission from their lawyers unless they are prepared to fire their lawyers? Or is that prohibition justified on the ground that unsophisticated clients need the advice of counsel in deciding whether to waive the advice of counsel?
- Forbidden is "communication." Videotaping employees of an opposing company "going about their activities in what those employees believe is the normal course" is allowed. Hill v. Shell Oil Co., 209 F. Supp. 2d 876 (N.D. Ill. 2002). Here, the plaintiffs claimed that certain gas stations required African-American customers to pay for gas before pumping it while allowing others to pay after pumping. The plaintiffs, with the aid of counsel, videotaped the attendants to gather proof of their claim. The

court also held that merely asking the employees whether a pump was prepay did not (rise to the level of communication protected" by the Rule. See also the discussion of testers at page 119.

- A violation occurs if a lawyer engages in forbidden communication through a third party, such as an investigator or even the lawyer's own client. Rule 8.4(a). Even a negligent failure to prevent improper contact might trip up a lawyer. In In re Industrial Gas Antitrust Litigation, 1986 Westlaw 1846 (N.D. Ill. 1986), vacated, 1986 Westlaw 68509, a lawyer was sanctioned for negligently failing to instruct an investigator not to speak with managerial employees of the opponent. The court relied on the supervisory duties of Rule 5.3(b) for its conclusion that a negligent, not merely a knowing, failure to supervise was forbidden. The court thereafter vacated its holding after concluding that, as a matter of fact, the lawyer was not negligent.

- Clients are free to talk to each other. Lawyers are not obligated to discourage that effort. In fact, it will sometimes be useful. Clients may be able to get past a problem when the lawyers could not. But the authorities are unclear on the extent to which a lawyer may assist a client in communicating with other clients. Can she tell the client what strategy to pursue, what information to try to learn, how to respond to anticipated questions or proposals? Can she continue to give this advice in the intervals between client-client conversations? Rule 4.2, comment [4] says only that "a lawyer is not prohibited from advising a client concerning a communication that the client is legally entitled to make." But "advising" is not a precise term; nor is "assisting" in Restatement §99(2) (rule "does not prohibit the lawyer from assisting the client in otherwise proper communication by the lawyer's client with a represented nonclient").

What interests does this rule protect? Here are several. The rule prevents a lawyer from

- getting a damaging admission from the opposing client;
- learning a fact or getting a document she would not learn or get if counsel were present to protect the opposing client;
- settling or winning a concession in the matter or learning the client's true position in negotiation;
- learning the client's strategy or gaining information protected by the attorney-client privilege or the work-product doctrine;
- weakening the opposing client's resolve by casting doubt on the strength of his position; and
- disparaging the opposing lawyer to the client.

Of the countervailing values, the most significant arise when the opposing client is an organization (a company, a government body) and the contact is with an employee or official who is not literally the opposing client. Then, the competing interests are in informal and inexpensive access to information — interviews rather than formal discovery in the (inhibiting?) presence of the adversary's lawyer; the interest in facilitating compliance with rules (like Fed. R. Civ. P. 11) that obligate lawyers to conduct factual investigations *before* filing complaints or other court papers; and the interest of law enforcement in solving crimes or preventing them.

1. Civil Matters

"Slip and Fall Redux"

"Slip and Fall," page 39, asked you to determine whether memoranda from the interviews Mike Todd, Tracy's investigator, had with various witnesses were subject to the attorney-client privilege. Cora Lundquist, the plaintiff's lawyer, would like to seek informal interviews with Todd and the individuals whom Todd interviewed. Can she do so consistent with the "no-contact" rule? Can Jeanne Parr, Tracy's lawyer, instruct those individuals not to talk to Lundquist?

Application of the rule presents little or no problem in civil cases and transactions when the adverse party is a represented biological person. Then it is straightforward. See Inorganic Coatings, Inc. v. Falberg, 926 F. Supp. 517 (E.D. Pa. 1995) (plaintiff's lawyer disqualified after he accepted a telephone call from a represented defendant); Papanicolaou v. Chase Manhattan Bank, 720 F. Supp. 1080 (S.D.N.Y. 1989) (bank's entire law firm disqualified after partner at firm had an unauthorized conversation with plaintiff about the merits of the case). Fulco v. Continental Cablevision, Inc., 789 F. Supp. 45 (D. Mass. 1992), ruled that all members of a certified class were clients of class counsel for purposes of the no-contact rule. But members of a putative class are not. ABA Opinion 07-445.

The story is different if another party is a corporation, the government, a partnership, or any other legal entity. Take corporations. Recall *Upjohn* (page 40). The Court assumed that the government would be able to speak to the same employees as did Upjohn's general counsel. The underlying information was not privileged, the Court said; only the communications to counsel were privileged. But would Rule 4.2 prohibit government lawyers from contacting Upjohn's current or former employees without consent? *Upjohn* was a criminal investigation, where policy considerations may (or may not) differ (see part A2). How would the Court's assumption fare in a civil matter?

NIESIG v. TEAM I
76 N.Y.2d 363, 558 N.E.2d 1030, 559 N.Y.S.2d 493 (1990)

KAYE, JUDGE.

Plaintiff in this personal injury litigation, wishing to have his counsel privately interview a corporate defendant's employees who witnessed the accident, puts before us a question that has generated wide interest: are the employees of a corporate party also considered "parties" under Disciplinary Rule 7-104(A)(1) of the Code of Professional Responsibility, which prohibits a lawyer from communicating directly with a "party" known to have counsel in the matter?[1] ...

As alleged in the complaint, plaintiff was injured when he fell from scaffolding at a building construction site. At the time of the accident he was employed by DeTrae Enterprises, Inc.; defendant J. M. Frederick was the general contractor, and defendant Team I the property owner. Plaintiff thereafter commenced a damages action against defendants, asserting two causes of action centering on Labor Law §240, and defendants brought a third-party action against DeTrae.

Plaintiff moved for permission to have his counsel conduct ex parte interviews of all DeTrae employees who were on the site at the time of the accident, arguing that these witnesses to the event were neither managerial nor controlling employees and could not therefore be considered "personal synonyms for DeTrae." DeTrae opposed the application, asserting that the disciplinary rule barred unapproved contact by plaintiff's lawyer with any of its employees. ...

The Appellate Division concluded, for theoretical as well as practical reasons, that current employees of a corporate defendant in litigation "are presumptively within the scope of the representation afforded by the attorneys who appeared [in the litigation] on behalf of that corporation." ...

In the main we disagree with the Appellate Division's conclusions. However, because we agree with the holding that DR 7-104(A)(1) applies only to current employees, not to former employees, we modify rather than reverse its order, and grant plaintiff's motion to allow the interviews. ...

The difficulty is not in whether DR 7-104(A)(1) applies to corporations. It unquestionably covers corporate parties, who are as much served by the rule's fundamental principles of fairness as individual parties. But the rule does not define "party," and its reach in this context is unclear. In litigation only the entity, not its employee, is the actual named party; on the other hand, corporations act solely through natural persons, and unless some employees are also considered parties, corporations are effectively read out of the rule. The issue therefore distills to *which* corporate employees should be deemed parties for purposes of DR 7-104(A)(1), and that choice is one of policy. The broader the definition of "party" in the interests of fairness to the corporation, the greater the cost in terms of foreclosing vital informal access to facts.

The many courts, bar associations and commentators that have balanced the competing considerations have evolved various tests, each claiming some adherents, each with some imperfection. At one extreme is the blanket rule adopted by the Appellate Division and urged by defendants, and at the other is the "control group" test—both of which we reject. The first is too broad and the second too narrow.

Defendants' principal argument for the blanket rule—correlating the corporate "party" and all of its employees—rests on Upjohn v. United States. As the Supreme Court recognized, a corporation's attorney-client privilege includes communications with low- and midlevel employees; defendants

---

1. Employees individually named as parties in the litigation, and employees individually represented by counsel, are not within the ambit of the question presented by this appeal. Nor, obviously, are direct interviews on consent of counsel, or those authorized by law, or communications by the client himself (unless instigated by counsel).

argue that the existence of an attorney-client privilege also signifies an attorney-client relationship for purposes of DR 7-104(A)(1).

Upjohn, however, addresses an entirely different subject, with policy objectives that have little relation to the question whether a corporate employee should be considered a "party" for purposes of the disciplinary rule. First, the privilege applies only to *confidential communications* with counsel, it does not immunize the underlying factual information — which is in issue here — from disclosure to an adversary. Second, the attorney-client privilege serves the societal objective of encouraging open communication between client and counsel, a benefit not present in denying informal access to factual information. Thus, a corporate employee who may be a "client" for purposes of the attorney-client privilege is not necessarily a "party" for purposes of DR 7-104(A)(1).

The single indisputable advantage of a blanket preclusion — as with every absolute rule — is that it is clear. No lawyer need ever risk disqualification or discipline because of uncertainty as to which employees are covered by the rule and which not. The problem, however, is that a ban of this nature exacts a high price in terms of other values, and is unnecessary to achieve the objectives of DR 7-104(A)(1).

Most significantly, the Appellate Division's blanket rule closes off avenues of informal discovery of information that may serve both the litigants and the entire justice system by uncovering relevant facts, thus promoting the expeditious resolution of disputes. Foreclosing all direct, informal interviews of employees of the corporate party unnecessarily sacrifices the long-recognized potential value of such sessions. "A lawyer talks to a witness to ascertain what, if any, information the witness may have relevant to his theory of the case, and to explore the witness' knowledge, memory and opinion — frequently in light of information counsel may have developed from other sources. This is part of an attorney's so-called work product." Costly formal depositions that may deter litigants with limited resources, or even somewhat less formal and costly interviews attended by adversary counsel, are no substitute for such off-the-record private efforts to learn and assemble, rather than perpetuate, information.

Nor, in our view, is it necessary to shield all employees from informal interviews in order to safeguard the corporation's interest. Informal encounters between a lawyer and an employee-witness are not — as a blanket ban assumes — invariably calculated to elicit unwitting admissions; they serve long-recognized values in the litigation process. Moreover, the corporate party has significant protection at hand. It has possession of its own information and unique access to its documents and employees; the corporation's lawyer thus has the earliest and best opportunity to gather the facts, to elicit information from employees, and to counsel and prepare them so that they will not make the feared improvident disclosures that engendered the rule. . . .

We are not persuaded, however, that the "control group" test — defining "party" to include only the most senior management exercising substantial control over the corporation — achieves [the proper "balance"]. Unquestionably, that narrow (though still uncertain) definition of corporate "party" better serves the policy of promoting open access to relevant information. But that test gives insufficient regard to the principles motivating DR 7-104(A)(1), and wholly overlooks the fact that corporate employees other than senior management also can bind the corporation. The "control group" test all but "nullifies the benefits of the disciplinary rule to corporations." Given the practical and theoretical problems posed by the "control group" test, it is hardly surprising that few courts or bar associations have ever embraced it.

By the same token, we find unsatisfactory several of the proposed intermediate tests, because they give too little guidance, or otherwise seem unworkable. In this category are the case-by-case balancing test and a test that defines "party" to mean corporate employees only when they are interviewed about matters within the scope of their employment. The latter approach is based on Rule 801(d)(2)(D) of the Federal Rules of Evidence, a hearsay exception for statements concerning matters within the scope of employment, which is different from the New York State rule.

Definition of "party"/ client

The test that best balances the competing interests, and incorporates the most desirable elements of the other approaches, is one that defines "party" to include corporate employees whose acts or omissions in the matter under inquiry are binding on the corporation (in effect, the corporation's "alter egos") or imputed to the corporation for purposes of its liability, or employees implementing the advice of counsel. All other employees may be interviewed informally.

Unlike a blanket ban or a "control group" test, this solution is specifically targeted at the problem addressed by DR 7-104(A)(1). The potential unfair advantage of extracting concessions and admissions from those who will bind the corporation is negated when employees with "speaking authority" for the corporation, and employees who are so closely identified with the interests of the corporate party as to be indistinguishable from it, are deemed "parties" for purposes of DR 7-104(A)(1). Concern for the protection of the attorney-client privilege prompts us also to include in the definition of "party" the corporate employees responsible for actually effectuating the advice of counsel in the matter. . . .

Apart from striking the correct balance, this test should also become relatively clear in application. It is rooted in developed concepts of the law of evidence and the law of agency, thereby minimizing the uncertainty facing lawyers about to embark on employee interviews. A similar test, moreover, is the one overwhelmingly adopted by courts and bar associations throughout the country, whose long practical experience persuades us that — in day-to-day operation — it is workable.[6]

. . . Today's decision resolves the present controversy by allowing ex parte interviews with nonmanagerial witnesses employed by a corporate defendant; even in that limited context, we recognize that there are undoubtedly questions not raised by the parties that will yet have to be answered. Defendants' assertions that ex parte interviews should not be permitted because of the dangers of overreaching, moreover, impel us to add the cautionary note that, while we have not been called upon to consider questions relating to the actual conduct

---

6. Given the nationwide experience with the test we now adopt, we find no basis for the assertion made in the concurrence that the test will unnecessarily curtail informal fact gathering or itself generate litigation. Above all, our test is decidedly different from the Appellate Division's blanket ban; in this very case, for example, we are reversing the Appellate Division's prohibition and permitting interviews of employee-witnesses to an accident, which would not be allowed under a blanket ban. In order to put to rest any possible confusion, we make clear that the definition of "party" we adopt for the purposes of DR 7-104(A)(1) is not derived from the Official Comment to ABA Model Rule 4.2.

of such interviews, it is of course assumed that attorneys would make their identity and interest known to interviewees and comport themselves ethically. . . .

[Judge Bellacosa, concurring, would have adopted the "control group" test and viewed the majority's test to be "similar" to language in the comment to Rule 4.2.]

How Large the Circle of Secrecy?

Does it surprise you to learn that amicus briefs supporting the plaintiff in *Niesig* were filed by the Committee on Civil Rights of the New York City Bar Association, the NAACP Legal Defense Fund, a teachers' union, the New York State Attorney General, and a civil service employees' union? What common interest could this diverse group possibly have?

Niesig has been a highly influential decision nationwide. It takes a bit of unpacking to see how. Before *Niesig* (and to a lesser extent after it), some courts prohibited communication on any subject within a current employee's scope of employment. This is because certain evidentiary rules, like Fed. R. Evid. 801(d)(2)(D), will admit these statements against the company as vicarious admissions. In this view, the rule on vicarious admissions turns the employee into the client for purposes of the no-contact rule. Weeks v. Independent School District No. I89, 230 F.3d 1201 (10th Cir. 2000) (using Fed. R. Evid. 801(d)(2)(D) as "guidance in determining whether an employee has such speaking authority, although it can offer only assistance by analogy because it addresses a different issue: hearsay, rather than ethical rules"). *Niesig* did not use the broad vicarious admission rule to define the scope of the no-contact rule because New York's vicarious admission rule follows common law and is quite narrow. Only statements of agents actually authorized to speak for a principal are admissible against the principal. Is it wise policy to use the vicarious admission rule to define the no-contact rule? The two rules were developed to advance different policies. Using a broad vicarious admission rule (like the federal one) to "wag" the no-contact rule will forbid many contacts, foster corporate secrecy, and frustrate inexpensive discovery.

The Restatement's position is to ignore the vicarious admission rule and permit contact with an adverse entity's agents or employees even if their statements will be admissible against the entity. The Restatement adopts this policy in order to facilitate candid and informal access to information, which can also be seen as the common motive of the *Niesig* amici. See §100 and Comments *b* and *e*. But the Restatement forbids contact with entity agents who direct counsel, who have the power to "compromise or settle the matter," whose conduct "may be imputed to the organization for purposes of civil or criminal liability," or whose statements would bind the organization. (A statement "binds" a litigant in the rare circumstance when applicable law forbids the litigant to challenge its accuracy. See page 72). Though differently worded, these are essentially the *Niesig* categories.

Niesig and the Restatement have influenced even those jurisdictions whose vicarious admission rules for corporate agents are as broad as the federal rule.

See, e.g., EEOC v. Hoya, 2007 Westlaw 1875834 (3d Cir. 2007) (lawyer contacted administrative assistant at defendant company; Pennsylvania hearsay exception same as federal one); Messing, Rudavsky & Weliky, P.C. v. President and Fellows of Harvard College, 764 N.E.2d 825 (Mass. 2002). The *Niesig* influence *is* particularly remarkable because until 2002, Rule 4.2's comments said the rule did encompass agents or employees whose statements would be an "admission on the part of the organization." Some of those jurisdictions, including Massachusetts, had this language in their rules when they chose to follow *Niesig* instead. But courts are divided. Some still adhere to a test that forbids contact with agents or employees whose statements, under evidence rules, are admissible against their principals. Midwest Motor Sports v. Arctic Cat Sales, Inc., 347 F.3d 693 (8th Cir. 2003).

A company's lawyers are not without remedies to discourage employees and agents from cooperating with an opponent. Rule 3.4(f) permits an entity lawyer to request (but not require) its employees and agents to "refrain from voluntarily giving relevant information to another party" so long as the "lawyer reasonably believes that [that] person's interests will not be adversely affected." One solution is not available. The "[r]ule does not contemplate that a lawyer representing the entity can invoke the rule's prohibition to cover all employees of the entity, by asserting a blanket representation of all of them. So, for example, if in-house counsel for the *XYZ* corporation announces that no one may talk to any *XYZ* employee without obtaining in-house counsel's permission, the communicating lawyer is not barred from communicating with all employees." ABA Opinion 95-396.

Niesig and much other authority hold that the rule does not prohibit contact with *former* employees, regardless of their former status, so long as they are not represented by their own counsel. Fair enough, but be careful what you ask about. A lawyer must not seek "to elicit privileged or confidential information from an opponent's former employee." Muriel Siebert & Co., Inc. v. Intuit, Inc., 868 N.E.2d 208 (N.Y. 2007) (collecting cases). The ABA agrees. "Rule 4.2 does not prohibit contacts with former officers or employees of a represented corporation, even if they were in one of the categories with which communication was prohibited while they were employed," according to ABA Opinion 95-396. But Opinion 91-359 warns that "the potentially-communicating adversary attorney must be careful not to seek to induce the former employee to violate the privilege attached to attorney-client communications." See also Rule 4.2 comment [7]. That's what happened in MMR/Wallace Power & Industrial, Inc. v. Thames Associates, 764 F. Supp. 712 (D. Conn. 1991). Judge Burns held that the "spirit of the ethical norms . . . if not the letter . . . precludes an attorney from acquiring, inadvertently or otherwise, confidential or privileged information about his adversary's litigation strategy." She disqualified a defense firm that had obtained just such information from a former employee who had been part of the plaintiff's litigation team.

Judge Kaye in *Niesig* assumed that lawyers will reveal their "identity and interest" when interviewing former employees. Another court has specifically listed Rules 4.1, 4.3, and 4.4 as applicable to the interviews, adding: "Further counsel must also be careful to avoid violating applicable privileges or matters subject to appropriate confidences or protections." Clark v. Beverly Health and Rehabilitation Services, Inc., 797 N.E.2d 905 (Mass. 2003), citing "abundance of authority." One authority is Restatement §102, which says that even when communication is permitted, lawyers must not seek "information that the lawyer reasonably should know the nonclient may not reveal without violating a duty of confidentiality to another imposed by law." The comment identifies privileges and fiduciary duties as the source of such law. See also *Muriel Siebert*, supra: Attorneys "properly advised [employee] of their representation and interest in the litigation, and directed [him] to avoid disclosing privileged or confidential information." But how was the nonlawyer employee to know what that might be? Is the safeguard of a warning an illusion?

Sometimes a lawyer opposing a company, unable to get anywhere with the company's outside lawyers, will want to speak to someone from the company's internal office of general counsel. May she bypass outside counsel and go directly to the in-house lawyer? On one hand, this is a direct contact with an employee of the opposing client without permission. On the other hand, the contact is with a *lawyer*, who presumably does not need the rule's protection. Bar associations that have addressed the issue come down in favor of permitting contact with inside counsel unless specifically instructed otherwise. ABA Opinion 06-443; D.C. Opinion 331 (2005).

When the Government is the Adversary

Does the no-contact rule require as broad a definition of "party" or "person" when the attorney's adversary is a government body? In Note, DR 7-104 of the Code of Professional Responsibility Applied to the Government "Party," 61 Minn. L. Rev. 1007 (1977), the author discussed the issue at some length and concluded as follows:

It is submitted that the rule should be narrowly construed when contact with the government is sought. A government "party" under the rule should be defined as any official who has the authority to bind the government in a matter that could be litigated. No restrictions should apply to communication with other government employees, except that the attorney be required to disclose his identity and the nature of his representation. Finally, DR 7-104 should be triggered only when a matter has been turned over to the government agency's legal counsel. This interpretation of the rule best accommodates the conflicting considerations that exist when the interests of the government as a party are adverse to those of a member of the public it is charged to serve.

California's rule contains the following sentence: "This rule shall not prohibit [c]ommunications with a public officer, board, committee, or body." Rule 2-100(C)(1). The New York State Bar Association, in its Opinion 404 (1975), concluded that an attorney may speak with dissenting members of a board of education without first obtaining the permission of the attorney for the board:

The overriding public interest compels that an opportunity be afforded to the public and their authorized representatives to obtain the views of, and pertinent facts from, public officials representing them. Minority members of a public body should not, for purposes of DR 7-104(A)(1), be considered adverse parties to their constituents whom they were selected to represent.

The comment to Model Rule 4.2 speaks obliquely to the relationship between the rule's prohibition and entity clients, governmental or otherwise. As one example of legal authorization justifying an exception to the rule, the comment cites "communications by a lawyer on behalf of a client who is exercising a constitutional or other legal right to communicate with the government." Restatement §101 significantly limits the protection of the anticontact rule when the government is a party. Except in a "negotiation or litigation . . . of a specific claim . . . against a governmental agency or against a governmental officer in the officer's official capacity," the prohibition does not apply. Requiring contact with the government to go through the government's lawyer as a general rule would "compromise the public interest in facilitating direct communication between representatives of citizens and government officials. . . ." Comment *b*. ABA Opinion 97-408 goes even further. It permits contact with officials "who have authority to take or to recommend action in the matter, provided that the sole purpose of the lawyer's communication is to address a policy issue, including settling the controversy." The lawyer must, however, "give government counsel reasonable advance notice of his intent to communicate with such officials, to afford an opportunity for consultation between government counsel and the officials on the advisability of their entertaining the communication." The no-contact rule continues to apply where the official lacks the described authority or if the lawyer's goal is simply to "develop evidence" or learn information that would be useful in the matter.

Several courts have refused to prohibit counsel from speaking with the non-managerial employees of a government opponent outside opposing counsel's presence. Carter-Herman v. City of Philadelphia, 897 F. Supp. 899 (E.D. Pa. 1995) (in civil rights action against city police department, the court allowed plaintiff's counsel to contact persons below rank of lieutenant, but required that the interviewee be told the purpose of the contact and his or her right to refuse the interview and to have counsel present); Brown v. State of Oregon Department of Corrections, 173 F.R.D. 265 (D. Or. 1997) (following *Carter-Herman* in an action against a public entity, court permits contact with current nonmanagerial employees of entity and all former employees of entity so long as interviewer gives the same warnings); Rivera v. Rowland, 1996 Westlaw 753941 (Conn. Super. Ct. 1996) (in action against the state in which the plaintiff class alleged the state's failure to provide effective counsel for indigent criminal defendants, court refused request to prevent plaintiff's counsel from speaking with assistant public defenders, but court required that interviewers provide an appropriate warning to interviewees and not solicit the defendants' privileged information).

Criminal cases present the most common example of a situation in which the government is the opposing party. Who is the prosecutor's client? The answer is that the client is the state or "the People," not the prosecutor's witnesses, not the arresting officers, and not even the victim. Defense counsel are free to attempt to speak to unrepresented witnesses, including the victim, who may, of course, refuse the interview. See Stearnes v. Clinton, 780 S.W.2d 216 (Tex. Crim. App. 1989) (mandamus issued against trial judge who disqualified appointed counsel after counsel had attempted to interview the state's witnesses without permission of the prosecutor).

Testers

You work for a public interest law firm that brings housing discrimination cases. You've settled a dispute with a private builder, but you hear rumors that the builder is continuing to discriminate. You want to send "testers" to negotiate for the purchase of a home. A "tester" is someone who pretends to be what she is not. One of your testers will be white and the other will be a member of a minority group. Their financial and employment circumstances will be the same. Your goal is to learn whether the white tester is treated differently from the minority tester. You know that the developer is represented by a lawyer on this matter. May you use testers? Indeed, this question goes beyond the no-contact rule because lawyers are also forbidden to engage in "deceit" or "mis-representation," personally or "through the acts of another." Rule 8.4(a), (d). Sending in a tester is one example of what has come to be known as "pretext-ing," or developing a false pretext to get information, and because pretexting relies on deceit, it may be improper whether or not the source of the informa-tion is known to have counsel on the matter. Two cases that would be beyond belief if they weren't true — and may be beyond belief anyway — are the disbar-ment opinions in In re Crossen, 880 N.E.2d 352 (Mass. 2008) and In re Curry, 880 N.E.2d 388 (Mass. 2008). Two lawyers (one a former high-ranking assistant U.S. attorney and partner in a large law firm) implemented an elaborate ruse against a judge's law clerk to learn information they hoped to use (unsuccess-fully as it turns out) to challenge the judge's opinion.

The use of testers is often an appealing strategy. A common situation is where a lawyer for a manufacturer believes that a seller is "passing off" someone else's product as having been made by her client. If you look only at the text of the no-contact rule, it would seem that the lawyer may not use a tester to speak to the employees of the seller if she knows that the seller has a lawyer on the subject. On the other hand, the tester ordinarily does no more than pretend to be a member of the buying public seeking only information that the seller freely offers to anyone. So the kinds of abuses that the no-contact rule is meant to prevent are absent.

That was the conclusion of Judge Shira Scheindlin in Gidatex, S.r.L. v. Campaniello Imports, Ltd., 82 F. Supp. 2d 119 (S.D.N.Y. 1999) (collecting other authority). A law firm had sent testers to the business establishment of a wholesale company, which the firm believed was guilty of violating its client's trademark. Posing as interior decorators, they talked with the sales clerks and tape-recorded some of the conversations. The court addressed claims that this tactic violated both the no-contact rule and the rule forbidding lawyers to engage in misrepresentation. Rule 8.4(c). It wrote that

> hiring investigators to pose as consumers is an accepted investigative tech-nique, not a misrepresentation. The policy interests behind forbidding mis-representations by attorneys are to protect parties from being tricked into making statements in the absence of their counsel and to protect clients

from misrepresentations by their own attorneys. The presence of investigators posing as interior decorators did not cause the sales clerks to make any statements they otherwise would not have made. There is no evidence to indicate that the sales clerks were tricked or duped by the investigators' simple questions such as "is the quality the same?" or "so there is no place to get their furniture?" . . .

These ethical rules should not govern situations where a party is legitimately investigating potential unfair business practices by use of an undercover posing as a member of the general public engaging in ordinary business transactions with the target. To prevent this use of investigators might permit targets to freely engage in unfair business practices which are harmful to both trademark owners and consumers in general.

It was obviously important to the *Gidatex* court that the alleged wrongdoing was ongoing and that the testers did no more than elicit the very same answers that the sales clerks would give to any interior decorator. To reach the result it did, however, the court had to ignore the literal language of the disciplinary rule, whose prohibition, it acknowledged, may "technically" have been violated, and to focus instead on the absence of harm to the rule's underlying policies.

The *Gidatex* view of life is not universal. A local snowmobile dealer sued the manufacturer and another local dealer, claiming that the manufacturer violated state franchise law by terminating the plaintiff and making the other dealer the new franchisee. The manufacturer's lawyers hired an investigator to go to the plaintiff's showroom and, wearing a hidden tape recorder, elicit information from the dealer's salespeople that would support its trial position. The lawyers also sent the investigator to the new franchisee, where he spoke to and recorded its president (not just salespeople) to learn data about sales (which would bear on damages). Midwest Motor Sports v. Arctic Cat Sales, Inc., 347 F.3d 693 (8th Cir. 2003), held that this conduct violated Rule 4.2. The court stressed the availability of discovery to learn the same information. It is possible (if barely) to square this holding with *Gidatex*, where the lawyers were investigating ongoing violation of a court order (therefore contempt). In *Midwest*, the lawyers were using an undercover agent to gather evidence to be used at an upcoming trial in a pending case, which, they hoped, would support the client's decision to terminate the plaintiff's dealership.

FURTHER READING

Professor Ernest Lidge, in Government Civil Investigations and the Ethical Ban on Communicating with Represented Parties, 67 Ind. L.J. 549 (1992), explores the borderland between application of the no-contact rule in private litigation and its application in criminal investigation. Professor Lidge looks in particular at the application of the rule to government civil investigations, proposing a "test for determining whether a given communication is authorized by law," and, among other things, addressing the federalism issues raised when a government agency authorizes its lawyers to engage in conduct that may violate state ethics rules. For further discussion of this issue in a civil context, see John Leubsdorf, Communicating with Another Lawyer's Client: The Lawyer's Veto and the Client's Interests, 127 U. Pa. L. Rev. 683 (1979); Samuel Miller & Angelo

Calfo, Ex Parte Contact with Employees and Former Employees of a Corporate Adversary: Is It Ethical?, 42 Bus. Law. 1053 (1987); Comment, Ex Parte Communications with Corporate Parties: The Scope of the Limitations on Attorney Communications With One of Adverse Interest, 82 Nw. U. L. Rev. 1274 (1988) (authored by Jerome Krulewitch); Note, Ex Parte Communication and the Corporate Adversary: A New Approach, 66 N.Y.U. L. Rev. 1456 (1991) (authored by Stephen Sinaiko).

2. Criminal Matters

"The Case of the Cooperating Target"

United States Attorney Nell Werker is investigating commercial bribery by companies in the local building trades. Among the dozens of "persons of interest" are Letitia Wall and Mort Blakely, executives at Newton Construction, which is also under investigation. Wall is believed to be the ringleader. While the investigation is in progress, Blanche Menendez, a lawyer for Blakely, asks Werker for a meeting. At it, Blakely offers to cooperate with Werker's investigation in exchange for a deal. A week later, Werker offers to let Blakely plead to a 5-year felony count (he could have faced a 20-year count) with a promise that the government would recommend a sentence of not more than 18 months. In exchange, Blakely must have conversations with Wall while wearing a wire. Blakely must do the same with other Newton officers who are not under investigation (and do not have lawyers), but who, in Werker's view, have not been fully candid in the investigation of Wall and Newton. The purpose of the conversations will be to identify past bribes and ongoing efforts of concealment. She gives Blakely a week to decide whether to accept the deal. The next morning, coincidentally, Werker receives a letter from a lawyer stating that Wall has retained him in connection with the building trades investigation and reminding her of her obligations under Rule 4.2. And the same day she gets a letter from another lawyer, stating that Newton Construction has retained her for the same matter, reminding her of her Rule 4.2 obligations, and calling particular attention to comment [7]. May Werker nevertheless continue with her plan to use Blakely?

Rule 4.2 applies in both civil and criminal matters, as its comment recognizes. The Sixth Amendment right to counsel also applies in criminal cases and prohibits the state from questioning a defendant outside the presence of his counsel after "judicial proceedings have been initiated." Brewer v. Williams, 430 U.S. 387 (1977). See also Rothgery v. Gillespie County, 554 U.S. _____ (2008) ("a criminal defendant's initial appearance before a judicial officer, where he learns the charge against him and his liberty is subject to restriction, marks the start of adversary judicial proceedings that trigger attachment of the Sixth Amendment right to counsel"). But even where the Sixth Amendment right has not yet attached, what about the no-contact rule? What if a person is merely under investigation but nevertheless is known to the prosecutor to be represented by counsel in the matter? In the last two decades, this simple question has opened a fascinating and often heated debate, still ongoing, not only about ethics but also about federalism and separation of powers. Even if all of the issues were now resolved, which they are not, I would include this history for what it tells us about the intersection of legal ethics and constitutional law, and the right to counsel's protection versus society's interest in catching criminals.

Here are the two curtain raisers: Dobbs was suspected of extortion. He retained counsel. Nevertheless, an FBI agent interviewed him outside the presence of counsel, allegedly at the direction of the U.S. Attorney. Dobbs claimed that he was entitled to suppression of admissions made in the interview, citing DR 7-104(A)(1), the Code's version of Rule 4.2. The court in United States v. Dobbs, 711 F.2d 84 (8th Cir. 1983), responded:

> Assuming that this disciplinary rule is applicable in this case, it does not require government investigatory agencies to refrain from any contact with a criminal suspect because he or she previously had retained counsel. Although in some circumstances the conduct of a prosecutor and an investigator acting at the prosecutor's behest may implicate the ethical concerns addressed by DR 7-104(A)(1), in this case, [the FBI agent's] noncustodial interview of Dobbs prior to the initiation of judicial proceedings against [him] did not constitute an ethical breach.

Why not? Should the court have ruled that even if there was an ethical breach, discipline, not suppression, was the correct remedy?

United States v. Jamil, 707 F.2d 638 (2d Cir. 1983), also said that no ethical rule was violated where a government investigator made contact with a represented suspect but without the prosecutor's knowledge. It pointedly did not decide whether the rule would have been violated if the investigator had "been acting as the prosecutor's alter ego," nor did it decide "whether suppression would have been warranted *if* the disciplinary rule had been violated." A year later, United States v. Foley, 735 F.2d 45 (2d Cir. 1984), in affirming a conviction, was even more pointed.

> We think that this practice of routinely conducting pre-arraignment interviews raises serious constitutional questions, as well as ethical ones. The ethical problems surrounding this practice are especially vivid in this case, where the [Assistant U.S. Attorney], by interviewing Edler in spite of a specific request from Edler's soon-to-be appointed Legal Aid Attorney not to do so, contravened the principles of DR 7-104(A)(1), which prohibits a lawyer from communicating "with a party he knows to be represented by a lawyer" without the consent of the party's lawyer. . . .
>
> Our concern is enhanced by the fact, acknowledged at oral argument, that when a defendant is known to be represented by private counsel the government does not conduct a pre-arraignment interview. In effect, therefore, the practice is invoked only against a defendant who is poor and unrepresented.

A prosecutor's custodial pre-arraignment interview of an indigent suspect may be seen to support application of the no-contact rule and suppression even though, technically, the suspect does not yet have a lawyer. The lawyer's identity is nevertheless known: It will be the public defender, whose appointment awaits only a formal charge, an event entirely within the prosecutor's control. Furthermore, the custodial nature of the interview is conducive to the very tactical advantage that the no-contact rule aims to prevent. Nevertheless, until United States v. Hammad apparently no reported case had suppressed a suspect's statement obtained in violation of the no-contact rule and before attachment of the Sixth Amendment right to counsel. Some courts denied that the rule even applied to criminal investigations. Others found no violation.

Now comes Act One. Hammad's facts were not as sympathetic as Jamil's. Hammad had a *retained* lawyer, and his *non*-custodial statement was made not to a prosecutor but to a former accomplice who had secretly agreed to cooperate with the government. The rest of the story is in the opinion. But the opinion is only one act in a tale that was destined to command the attention of the ABA, all branches of the federal government, and state judiciaries.

UNITED STATES v. HAMMAD
858 F.2d 834 (2d Cir. 1988), cert. denied, 498 U.S. 871 (1990)

KAUFMAN, JUDGE.

On Nov. 30, 1985, the Hammad Department Store in Brooklyn, N.Y., caught fire under circumstances suggesting arson. The Bureau of Alcohol, Tobacco and Firearms was assigned to investigate in conjunction with the U.S. Attorney for the Eastern District of New York.

During the course of his investigation, an Assistant U.S. Attorney (AUSA) discovered that the store's owners, Taiseer and Eid Hammad, had been audited by the New York State Department of Social Services for Medicaid fraud. The audit revealed that the Hammad brothers had bilked Medicaid out of $400,000; they claimed reimbursement for special orthopedic footwear but supplied customers with ordinary, non-therapeutic shoes. Consequently, the department revoked the Hammads' eligibility for Medicaid reimbursement and demanded return of the $400,000 overpayment. The Hammads challenged the department's determination and submitted invoices purporting to document their sales of orthopedic shoes. The invoices were received from Wallace Goldstein of the Crystal Shoe Co., a supplier to the Hammads' store.

On Sept. 22, 1986, however, Goldstein informed the AUSA that he had provided the Hammads with false invoices. Government investigators, therefore, suspected the fire had been intended to destroy actual sales records, thereby concealing the fraudulent Medicaid claims. Goldstein agreed to cooperate with the government's investigation. Accordingly, the prosecutor directed Goldstein to arrange and record a meeting with the Hammads.

Some three weeks later, on Oct. 9, Goldstein telephoned the Hammads. He spoke briefly with Eid, who referred him to Taiseer. Goldstein falsely told Taiseer he had been subpoenaed to appear before the grand jury investigating the Hammads' Medicaid fraud. He added that the grand jury had requested records of Crystal's sales to the Hammad Department Store to compare them with the invoices the Hammads had submitted. Taiseer did not deny defrauding Medicaid, but instead urged Goldstein to conceal the fraud by lying to the grand jury and by refusing to produce Crystal's true sales records. He also questioned

Goldstein regarding the contents of his subpoena, which did not actually exist. Goldstein responded that he did not have the subpoena in his possession. He agreed to inquire further. One hour later, presumably after speaking with the AUSA, Goldstein telephoned Taiseer again and described the fictitious subpoena.

Goldstein and Hammad saw each other five days later. The meeting was recorded and videotaped. Goldstein showed Hammad a sham subpoena supplied by the prosecutor. The subpoena instructed Goldstein to appear before the grand jury and to provide any records reflecting shoe sales from Crystal to the Hammad Department Store. Hammad apparently accepted the subpoena as genuine because he spent much of the remainder of the meeting devising strategies for Goldstein to avoid compliance. The two held no further meetings.

On April 15, 1987, after considering the recordings, videotapes and other evidence, the grand jury returned a 45-count indictment against the Hammad brothers. . . .

Before trial, Taiseer Hammad moved to suppress the recordings and videotapes, alleging the prosecutor had violated DR 7-104(A)(1). . . .

Judge Glasser granted Taiseer's motion to suppress the recordings and videotapes. . . .

This circuit conclusively established the applicability of DR 7-104(A)(1) to criminal prosecutions in United States v. Jamil. . . .

The applicability of DR 7-104(A)(1) to the investigatory stages of a criminal prosecution presents a closer question. The government asserts the rule is coextensive with the Sixth Amendment, and hence, that it remains inoperative until the onset of adversarial proceedings. The appellee responds that several courts have enforced DR 7-104(A)(1) prior to attachment of Sixth Amendment protections. We find no principled basis in the rule to constrain its reach as the government proposes. . . . Nonetheless, we urge restraint in applying the rule to criminal investigations to avoid handcuffing law enforcement officers in their efforts to develop evidence. . . .

The government contends that a broad reading of DR 7-104(A)(1) would impede legitimate investigatory practices. In particular, the government fears career criminals with permanent "house counsel" could immunize themselves from infiltration by informants. We share this concern and would not interpret the disciplinary rule as precluding undercover investigations. Our task, accordingly, is imposing adequate safeguards without crippling law enforcement.

The principal question presented to us herein is: To what extent does DR 7-104(A)(1) restrict the use of informants by government prosecutors prior to indictment, but after a suspect has retained counsel in connection with the subject matter of a criminal investigation? In an attempt to avoid hampering legitimate criminal investigations by government prosecutors, Judge Glasser resolved this dilemma by limiting the rule's applicability "to instances in which a suspect has retained counsel specifically for representation in conjunction with the criminal matter in which he is held suspect, and the government has knowledge of that fact." Thus, he reasoned, the rule exempts the vast majority of cases where suspects are unaware they are being investigated.

While it may be true that this limitation will not unduly hamper the government's ability to conduct effective criminal investigations in a majority of instances, we nevertheless believe that it is unduly restrictive in that small but persistent number of cases where a career criminal has retained "house counsel" to represent him in connection with an ongoing fraud or criminal enterprise. This court has recognized that prosecutors have a responsibility to perform investigative as well as courtroom-related duties in criminal matters. . . . As we see it, under DR 7-104(A)(1), a prosecutor is "authorized by law" to employ legitimate investigative techniques in conducting or supervising criminal investigations, and the use of informants to gather evidence against a suspect will frequently fall within the ambit of such authorization.

Notwithstanding this holding, however, we recognize that in some instances a government prosecutor may overstep the already broad powers of his office, and in so doing, violate the ethical precepts of DR 7-104(A)(1). In the present case, the prosecutor issued a subpoena for the informant, not to secure his attendance before the grand jury, but to create a pretense that might help the informant elicit admissions from a represented suspect. Though we have no occasion to consider the use of this technique in relation to unrepresented suspects, we believe that use of the technique under the circumstances of this case contributed to the informant's becoming the alter ego of the prosecutor. Consequently, the informant was engaging in communications proscribed by DR 7-104(A)(1).[1] Therefore, we agree with Judge Glasser that the prosecution violated the disciplinary rule in this case.

Notwithstanding requests for a bright-line rule, we decline to list all possible situations that may violate DR 7-104(A)(1). This delineation is best accomplished by case-by-case adjudication, particularly when ethical standards are involved. As our holding above makes clear, however, the use of informants by government prosecutors in a pre-indictment, noncustodial situation, absent the type of misconduct that occurred in this case, will generally fall within the "authorized by law" exception to DR 7-104(A)(1) and therefore will not be subject to sanctions.

On appeal, the government also claims that even if there was a violation of the disciplinary rule, exclusion is inappropriate to remedy an ethical breach. We have not heretofore decided whether suppression is warranted for a DR 7-104(A)(1) violation. We now hold that, in light of the underlying purposes of the Professional Responsibility Code and the exclusionary rule, suppression may be ordered in the district court's discretion. . . . Judge Glasser apparently assumed . . . that suppression is a necessary consequence of a DR 7-104(A)(1) violation. Exclusion, however, is not required in every case. Here, the government should not have its case prejudiced by suppression of its evidence when the law was previously unsettled in this area. Therefore, in light of the prior uncertainty regarding the reach of DR 7-104(A)(1), an exclusionary remedy is inappropriate in this case.

---

1. See also ABA Standards Relating to the Administration of Criminal Justice, Standard 3-3.1(d) ("It is unprofessional conduct for a prosecutor to secure the attendance of persons for interviews by use of any communication which has the appearance or color of a subpoena or similar judicial process unless the prosecutor is authorized by law to do so.").

Ethics and Crime Fighting in a Federal System

Almost from the day it was written, *Hammad* has been on life support, but it is not dead yet. Other circuit courts have refused to follow *Hammad*. Cases are collected in United States v. Balter, 91 F.3d 427 (3d Cir. 1996). The Second Circuit has seriously weakened *Hammad.* In United States v. DeVillio, 983 F.2d 1185 (2d Cir. 1993), the government wired a co-defendant who elicited incriminating statements from the defendant *after* his Sixth Amendment rights had already attached. The court found no constitutional violation for unrelated reasons. Turning to the no-contact rule, it distinguished *Hammad* on the ground that the *Hammad* prosecutors used a fake subpoena. Why should that matter? Did *Hammad* depend on the fake subpoena? Later, in Grievance Committee v. Simels, 48 F.3d 640 (2d Cir. 1995), the court narrowly interpreted the words "party" and "matter" in the New York no-contact rule to reverse the discipline of a criminal defense lawyer who interviewed a represented person who was technically (or perhaps hypertechnically) not a "party" (but for practical purpose only a witness) in his client's "matter." (Today, Rule 4.2 uses the term "person," not "party," but the New York equivalent continues to use "party.") The court said that the Rule "should be construed narrowly in the interests of providing fair notice to those affected by the Rule and insuring vigorous advocacy not only by defense counsel, but by prosecutors as well."*

So? You may be wondering why it is even worthwhile to read *Hammad*. Good question. There are three answers. The first is that the *Hammad* saga is valuable historical background to an important question: Do prosecutors operate under different rules from other lawyers? The second reason is that the opinion has sparked a debate among lawyers and judges that raises basic questions about who regulates lawyers. The debates will be easier to understand with *Hammad* in mind. And third, *Hammad*, despite the cool reception it received in the ensuing decades, refuses internment in the Dead Cases Morgue. United States v. Talao, 222 F.3d 1133 (9th Cir. 2000) and State v. Miller, 600 N.W.2d 457 (Minn. 1999), cite it as good law. In *Miller*, a defendant's statements were suppressed based on a finding that prosecutors had violated the no-contact rule. See also State v. Clark, 738 N.W.2d 316 (Minn. 2007) (relying on *Miller*, holds that prosecutor violated Rule 4.2 by allowing the police to question a represented defendant who was in custody, notwithstanding that the accused consented to the interview [though his lawyer had not] and had waived his Sixth Amendment rights); United States v. Carona, 2008 Westlaw 1970218 (C.D. Cal. 2008) (following *Talao* and *Hammad*). So *Hammad's* relevance assured, let's go to the questions.

Hammad's Historical Background.   The opinion you just read is actually the fourth *Hammad* opinion. Count'em! Four. In the first, 846 F.2d 854 (2d Cir. 1988), the court said the government had violated the no-contact rule simply by sending Goldstein to talk to Hammad. The lower court's suppression order was reversed only because "the law was previously unsettled in this area." Alarmed by

---

* If you're interested in the lore of law (a/k/a gossip), you'll be interested to know that *Simels* was written by a district judge, sitting by designation, who was U.S. Attorney in Brooklyn when *Hammad* was decided and who was active in trying to persuade the court to back off on its opinion. This effort is discussed in the text following.

the opinion, all U.S. Attorneys in the Second Circuit petitioned for rehearing. The court denied one at 855 F.2d 36, but Judge Kaufman issued a brief "clarification" because of "some confusion as to the thrust of our opinion." You bet there was confusion. Hysteria might be more like it. Thereafter, possibly because a petition for rehearing en banc remained pending, the same panel issued a third opinion (now unavailable) that is substantially the same as the one you just read except for its description of the grand jury subpoena. The third opinion said that the subpoena was "counterfeit," "specious and contrived," and "an improper and illegitimate stratagem" and that the prosecutor was guilty of "egregious" misconduct. How could the conduct have been "egregious," given the court's statement in its first opinion that "the law was previously unsettled in this area"? That contradiction may explain why the final opinion, printed above, deleted all of the just quoted words, declined to rule generally on the use of sham subpoenas, and held only that the subpoena "under the circumstances of this case contributed to the informant's becoming the alter ego of the prosecutor." In other words, the court seemed all but to say that *Hammad* stood for itself. That freed Judge Kaufman from the embarrassment of en banc reversal. *Hammad* went from a bark to a whimper in a few short months.

If the story of *Hammad* stopped there, it would warrant but a footnote, if that. But it did not stop there. The Justice Department, the ABA, state judges and disciplinary bodies, and Congress, not to mention armies of law review contributors, all got into the act. The debate focused on two issues. First: To what extent does (or should) the no-contact rule restrain government lawyers engaged in criminal (or even civil) law enforcement? Second: When the law enforcers are federal lawyers, do state no-contact rules even apply? The Justice Department did not relish the prospect of having its lawyers nationwide bound by disparate state ethics rules (and not merely their no-contact rules) and subject to state discipline. So if *Hammad* was *Act One, Act Two* was the famous (or infamous) memorandum of June 8, 1989, in which Attorney General Dick Thornburgh emphatically rejected the notion that state ethics rules could restrict federal prosecutors. Compliance was voluntary only. The sole external limits on prosecutorial conduct were the Constitution and federal statutes. While the attorney general focused on the no-contact rule, in subsequent statements the Justice Department rejected application of other state ethics rules to federal prosecutors and even to other federal lawyers. The department suggested, if gingerly, that the separation-of-powers doctrine prevented federal judges from using ethical rules to restrict federal criminal investigations.*

Actions beget reactions. *Act Three*: Criminal defense lawyers and others protested the department's effort to "exempt" itself from rules that constrain all other lawyers. *Act Four*: At its February 1990 convention, the American Bar Association adopted a policy that Justice Department lawyers "may not be given blanket exemption from [the no-contact rule] as adopted in individual jurisdictions." The ABA also voted "to oppose any attempt by the Department of Justice unilaterally to exempt its lawyers from the professional conduct rules that

---

* Exercise of Federal Prosecutorial Authority in a Changing Legal Environment, Hearing Before the Subcommittee on Government Information, Justice and Agriculture of the House Committee on Government Operations, 101st Cong. 241 (1990) (statement of Edward S. Dennis, Jr.).

apply to all lawyers under applicable rules of the jurisdiction in which they practice." *Act Five*: The attorney general then declared that the ABA's position was, well, kind of treasonous, at least to the law enforcement mission. There's no other way to put it. In a press release during the ABA convention, Mr. Thornburgh declared war: "It is most unfortunate," he said, "that the ABA has lent *aid and comfort*" to the "tactics" of the "defense bar" in "attempting to use rules of professional conduct to stymie criminal investigations and prosecutions" (emphasis added). *Act Six*: In 1993, Janet Reno became Attorney General. In an effort to bring coherence, calm, and legal credibility to Thornburgh's over-the-top accusations and broad claims, Reno promulgated detailed rules in the Code of Federal Regulations to replace the Thornburgh memorandum.

The "Reno Rules," as they came to be known, were issued in August 1994. They permitted federal prosecutors and other federal lawyers enforcing certain civil statutes (like antitrust and civil rights laws) to contact represented parties or represented persons or, where the party or person was an entity, the employees or controlling individuals of the entity. A "represented party" was someone who had a lawyer and was a party in a current proceeding. A "represented person" was someone who had a lawyer but was not then named in a proceeding. Represented parties (or their controlling individuals) could not be approached on the subject of the representation unless an exception applied. One exception was for investigation of additional, different, or ongoing crimes or civil violations. The Reno Rules purported to supersede ethics rules in states in which federal lawyers worked or were admitted.

The theory behind the Reno Rules was that, once promulgated, the power they conferred would be "authorized by law" within the meaning of this exception to Rule 4.2. But to succeed, the Justice Department had to have the statutory authority to adopt the rules in the first place. It didn't. United States ex rel. O'Keefe v. McDonnell Douglas Corp., 132 F.3d 1252 (8th Cir. 1998), without addressing the merits of the rules themselves, concluded that the department did not have "valid statutory authority" to adopt them. The court wrote:

> Because we cannot reasonably conclude that the grants of authority in the statutory provisions cited by the government contemplate the issuance of anything resembling [the Reno Rules], we find this regulation to be invalid. Accordingly, we reject the government's argument that its ex parte contacts are "authorized by law" and therefore satisfy [Missouri's no-contact rule].

The Eighth Circuit's opinion was the first in a one-two punch that eviscerated any claim the Justice Department might have had to determine the legal ethics rules governing its own lawyers. *Any* legal ethics rules. The second punch came on October 21, 1998, when Congress passed what has come to be known as the "McDade Amendment." The lesson here is be careful whom you mess with or, in this case, whom you indict. Joseph McDade, a powerful Republican congressman from Pennsylvania, was acquitted in 1996 of federal conspiracy and racketeering charges. Enlightened by the unhappy experience of being a federal defendant, perhaps, McDade then sponsored a bill that added §530B to Title 28 of the United States Code. The section provides that lawyers for the federal government "shall be subject to State laws and rules, and local Federal court rules, governing attorneys in each State, where such attorney engages in that attorney's duties to the same extent and in the same manner as other attorneys in that State." The attorney general is directed to "make and amend rules . . . to assure compliance with this section." Those rules can be found at 28 C.F.R. Part 77. The key provision (§77.3) states:

> In all criminal investigations and prosecutions, in all civil investigations and litigation (affirmative and defensive), and in all civil law enforcement investigations and proceedings, attorneys for the government shall conform their conduct and activities to the state rules and laws, and federal local court rules, governing attorneys in each State where such attorney engages in that attorney's duties, to the same extent and in the same manner as other attorneys in that State, as these terms are defined in §77.2 of this part.

As befits a C.F.R. provision, nearly every phrase and noun in this sentence is defined.

But do not think that the passage of the McDade Amendment and the invalidation of the Reno Rules resolved all questions. Not for lawyers. Whether the governing rule is state or federal, whether promulgated by the executive, legislative, or judicial branches, the substantive question lives on: To what extent should the no-contact rule constrain government lawyers engaged in civil or criminal law enforcement?

Hammad tells us that the rule did not forbid a federal prosecutor to send Goldstein, Hammad's ally, to talk to Hammad. Goldstein had "flipped," though Hammad did not know it. Goldstein was wired and had a false grand jury subpoena. The prosecutor knew that Hammad had counsel. Hammad was not in custody, not indigent, and not charged. The sham subpoena tipped the balance. In fact, it was the only basis for the opinion after all the revisions. At least, that's how Judge Rambo read *Hammad* in United States v. Grass, 239 F. Supp. 2d 535 (M.D. Pa. 2003). She held that Rule 4.2 did not prevent a prosecutor from wiring a cooperating target and telling him the topics to cover in conversations with the defendants, who had counsel but were not in custody or yet indicted. The prosecutor's conduct was "authorized by law," she said. Further, unlike *Hammad*, Third Circuit precedent *did* allow use of a sham subpoena in criminal investigations. And for good measure, Judge Rambo added that suppression of the taped conversations would not have been an appropriate remedy for the alleged Rule 4.2 violation in any event.

***Hammad* Meets *Niesig*.**   Perhaps the greatest concern of people in law enforcement is when a lawyer for a corporation or other entity under investigation takes the position that the no-contact rule prevents government lawyers from questioning all corporate agents and employees. The lawyer makes no claim to represent employees personally, yet contends that her representation of the company prevents communication with its agents and employees on matters within the scope of their agency or employment? Think of this as *Hammad* meets *Niesig*. If the broad claim is credited, a lawyer for a large entity could frustrate the government's effort to gather information about possible wrongdoing through communications with any of its (perhaps thousands of) employees.

The court in United States v. Talao, supra, faced a situation in which government lawyers questioned the employee of a target company that they knew to be represented by Brose. But the employee, Ferrer, was not personally represented by Brose and in fact did not want Brose to represent her for reasons that will become apparent. Yet Brose claimed that by virtue of his representation of the company, the government could not informally question Ferrer on matters within the scope of her employment. The court cited *Hammad* as stating the "proper" rule. It also wrote that Brose's representation of the company restricted communications with (at least some) company employees. (Could Brose purport to represent *all* company employees, not personally but as employees? The ABA would not allow such "blanket" assertions. See page 116.) But here, the court said, the rule (Rule 2-100 in California) was not violated.

> Appellees maintain that application of Rule 2-100 is necessary here in order to protect the attorney-client relationship between the corporation and its counsel. We are keenly aware that assuring the proper functioning of the attorney-client relationship is an important rationale behind the rule. Again, however, like the attorney-client privilege, the prohibition against ex parte contacts protects that relationship at the expense of "the full and free discovery of the truth." For that reason, the attorney-client privilege "applies only where necessary to achieve its purpose." When a corporate employee/ witness comes forward to disclose attempts by the corporation's officers to coerce her to give false testimony, the prohibition against ex parte contacts does little to support an appropriate attorney-client relationship. Once the employee makes known her desire to give truthful information about potential criminal activity she has witnessed, a clear conflict of interest exists between the employee and the corporation. Under these circumstances, corporate counsel cannot continue to represent both the employee and the corporation. Indeed, Brose made clear in his testimony at the evidentiary hearing before the district court that if Ferrer had approached him with information adverse to the interests of the corporation he would have advised her that she should retain her own lawyer. Under these circumstances, because the corporation and the employee cannot share an attorney, ex parte contacts with the employee cannot be deemed to, in any way, affect the attorney-client relationship between the corporation and its counsel. In this setting, the corporation's interest, therefore, clearly does not provide the basis for application of the rule. The trial court erred in otherwise concluding.

Talao emphasized that Ferrer came forward. Were government lawyers precluded from contacting her in the first instance to see whether she wished to talk with them about her employer?

FURTHER READING

Pamela Karlan, Discrete and Relational Criminal Representation: The Changing Vision of the Right to Counsel, 105 Harv. L. Rev. 670 (1992). Viewing this debate through a wide lens, including federalism, are Roger Crampton & Lisa Udell, in State Ethics Rules and Federal Prosecutors: The Controversies Over the Anti-Contact and Subpoena Rules, 53 U. Pitt. L. Rev. 291 (1992). For a defense of the position that some deception by prosecutors in criminal investigations is acceptable, see William Stuntz, Lawyers, Deception, and Evidence Gathering, 79 Va. L.

Rev. 1903 (1993). The *Hammad* issue is thoroughly treated in Note, Prosecutorial Investigations and DR 7-104(A)(1), 89 Colum. L. Rev. 940 (1989) (authored by Marc Schwartz); and Alafair Burke examines these issues in light of the Reno Rules in Note, Reconciling Professional Ethics and Prosecutorial Power: The No-Contact Rule Debate, 46 Stan. L. Rev. 1635 (1994). Section 530B is analyzed, along with the broader question of the regulation of federal prosecutors, in Fred Zacharias & Bruce Green, The Uniqueness of Federal Prosecutors, 88 Geo. L.J. 207 (2000). See also Andrew Kaufman, Who Should Make the Rules Governing Conduct of Lawyers in Federal Matters?, 75 Tul. L. Rev. 149 (2000).

B. IMPROPER OR ACCIDENTAL ACQUISITION OF CONFIDENTIAL INFORMATION

"Something You Should Know"

"I got a call yesterday from a woman named Linda Yates. I didn't recognize her name but she told me she had formerly worked as a paralegal at Wentworth's, a company I am suing on behalf of a class. I told her I was sorry but I couldn't talk to her, but she said there was 'something you should know,' and I didn't hang up. She said that it was her job to work with Wentworth's outside counsel, Michner, Balken & Traub. She said Wentworth had not given me all the documents in our discovery demands. She said she no longer worked at Wentworth's but had some of the documents she claims were suppressed. Frankly, there were gaps in what MBT produced, and Wentworth's explanation for these gaps was rather lame. Yates said I could not reveal her name because she needed Wentworth's as a reference. She left her contact information, and I said I would get back to her.

"I don't know if she is telling me the truth. I don't know what to do. This may all be a setup. Or maybe she's telling the truth. I don't want to risk getting kicked off this case. I don't want to get documents I have no business seeing. But don't I have an obligation to get to the bottom of it?"

RICO v. MITSUBISHI MOTORS CORP.
42 Cal. 4th 807, 171 P.3d 1092, 68 Cal. Rptr.3d 758 (2007)

CORRIGAN, JUSTICE: . . .

Two Mitsubishi corporations (collectively, Mitsubishi or defendants), and the California Department of Transportation (Caltrans), were sued by various plaintiffs after a Mitsubishi Montero rolled over while being driven on a freeway. Subsequently, Mitsubishi representatives met with their lawyers, James Yukevich and Alexander Calfo, and two designated defense experts to discuss their litigation strategy and vulnerabilities. Mitsubishi's case manager, Jerome Rowley, also attended the meeting. Rowley and Yukevich had worked together over a few years. Yukevich asked Rowley to take notes at the meeting and indicated specific areas to be summarized. The trial court later found that Rowley, who had typed the notes on Yukevich's computer, had acted as Yukevich's paralegal. At the end of the six-hour session, Rowley returned the computer and never saw a printed version of the notes. Yukevich printed only one copy of the notes, which he later edited and annotated. Yukevich never intentionally showed the notes to anyone, and the court determined that the sole purpose of the document was to help Yukevich defend the case.

Less than two weeks after the strategy session, Yukevich deposed plaintiffs' expert witness, Anthony Sances, at the offices of plaintiffs' counsel, Raymond Johnson. Yukevich, court reporter Karen Kay, and Caltrans counsel Darin Flagg were told that Johnson and Sances would be late for the deposition. After waiting in the conference room for some time, Yukevich went to the restroom, leaving his briefcase, computer, and case file in the room. The printed document from the strategy session was in the case file. While Yukevich was away, Johnson and Sances arrived. Johnson asked Kay and Flagg to leave the conference room. Kay and Flagg's departure left only plaintiffs' representatives and counsel in the conference room. Yukevich returned to find Kay and Flagg standing outside. Yukevich waited approximately five minutes, then knocked and asked to retrieve his briefcase, computer, and file. After a brief delay, he was allowed to do so.

Somehow, Johnson acquired Yukevich's notes. Johnson maintained that they were accidentally given to him by the court reporter. Yukevich insisted that they were taken from his file while only Johnson and plaintiffs' team were in the conference room. As a result, Mitsubishi moved to disqualify plaintiffs' attorneys and experts. The trial court ordered an evidentiary hearing to determine how Johnson obtained the document.

The court reporter was deposed and denied any specific recollection of the Sances deposition. She could not testify what she had done with the deposition exhibits that night and could only relate her general practice. She said she generally collects exhibits and puts them in a plastic covering. She did not remember ever having given exhibits to an attorney. She also testified that she had never seen the document in question. If documents other than exhibits remain on a conference table, she leaves them there. The trial court found that the Sances deposition took place over approximately eight hours. It was a document-intense session and documents were placed on the conference table.

Another member of plaintiffs' legal team submitted a declaration supporting Johnson's assertion that he received the document from the reporter. The court ultimately concluded that the defense had failed to establish that Johnson had taken the notes from Yukevich's file. It thus ruled that Johnson came into the document's possession through inadvertence.

The court found the 12-page document was dated, but not otherwise labeled. It contained notations by Yukevich. Johnson admitted that he knew within a minute or two that the document related to defendants' case. He knew that Yukevich did not intend to produce it and that it would be a "powerful impeachment document." Nevertheless, Johnson made a copy of the document. He scrutinized and made his own notes on it. He gave copies to his co-counsel and his experts, all of whom studied the document. Johnson specifically discussed the contents of the document with each of his experts.

A week after he acquired Yukevich's notes, Johnson used them during the deposition of defense expert Geoffrey Germane. The notes purportedly indicate that the defense experts made statements at the strategy session that were inconsistent with their deposition testimony. Johnson used the document while questioning Germane, asking about Germane's participation in the strategy session.

Defense Counsel Calfo defended the Germane deposition. Yukevich did not attend. Calfo had never seen the document and was not given a copy during the deposition. When he asked about the document's source, Johnson vaguely replied that, "It was put in Dr. Sances' file." Calfo repeatedly objected to the "whole line of inquiry with respect to an unknown document." He specifically said that, "I don't even know where this exhibit came from." . . .

Only after the deposition did Johnson give a copy of the document to Calfo, who contacted Yukevich. When Yukevich realized that Johnson had his only copy of the strategy session notes and had used it at the deposition, he and Calfo wrote to Johnson demanding the return of all duplicates. The letter was faxed the day after Germane's deposition. The next day, defendants moved to disqualify plaintiffs' legal team and their experts on the ground that they had become privy to and had used Yukevich's work product. As a result, they complained, Johnson's unethical use of the notes and his revelation of them to co-counsel and their experts irremediably prejudiced defendants.

The trial court concluded that the notes were absolutely privileged by the work product rule.[1] The court also held that Johnson had acted unethically by examining the document more closely than was necessary to determine that its contents were confidential, by failing to notify Yukevich that he had a copy of the document, and by surreptitiously using it to gain maximum adversarial value from it. The court determined that Johnson's violation of the work product rule had prejudiced the defense and "the bell cannot be 'unrung' by use of in limine orders." Accordingly, the court ordered plaintiffs' attorneys and experts disqualified. . . .

ETHICAL DUTY OWED UPON RECEIPT OF ATTORNEY WORK PRODUCT

Because the document is work product we consider what ethical duty Johnson owed once he received it. Plaintiffs rely on *Aerojet-General Corp. v. Transport Indemnity Insurance* (1993) 18 Cal.App.4th 996 (*Aerojet*), to argue that because the document was inadvertently received, Johnson was dutybound to use the nonprivileged portions of it to his clients' advantage. . . .

A review of *Aerojet* demonstrates that it does not assist plaintiffs. Aerojet's insurance brokers had sent a package of materials to Aerojet's risk manager. The risk manager sent them on to Aerojet's attorney, DeVries. Among these documents was a memo from an attorney at an opposing law firm. It was never ascertained how opposing counsel's memo found its way into the package of documents. The memo revealed the existence of a witness whom DeVries ultimately deposed. When opposing counsel learned that DeVries had received the memo and thus discovered the witness, counsel sought sanctions. The trial court imposed monetary sanctions. . . . The Court of Appeal reversed the sanctions order.

---

1. The trial court also held that the document fell under the attorney-client privilege. The Court of Appeals held to the contrary. That issue is not before us and we express no view thereon.

The *Aerojet* court first noted that DeVries was free of any wrongdoing in his initial receipt of the document. The court also observed that the existence and identification of the witness was not privileged. "Nor can 'the identity and location of persons having knowledge of relevant facts' be concealed under the attorney work product rule. . . . [Citation.]" The defendants claimed no prejudice to their case as a result of the witness's disclosure. Indeed, they prevailed at trial. Because counsel was blameless in his acquisition of the document *and because* the information complained of was not privileged, DeVries was free to use it. Plaintiffs' reliance on *Aerojet* founders on the facts that distinguish it. Here, Yukevich's notes were absolutely protected by the work product rule. Thus, Johnson's reliance on *Aerojet* is unavailing, particularly in light of the clear standard set out in *State Fund.*

In [State *Comp. Ins. Fund v. WPS. Inc., 82 Cal. Rptr. 2d 799* (Cal. App. 1999)], the plaintiff sent the defendant's attorney (Telanoff) three boxes of documents that were identical to the documents provided during discovery. Inadvertently, the plaintiff also sent 273 pages of forms entitled, " 'Civil Litigation Claims Summary,' " marked as " '**Attorney-Client Communication/Attorney Work Product**,' " and with the warning, " '**Do Not Circulate or Duplicate**.' " In addition, "[t]he word '**Confidential**' [was] repeatedly printed around the perimeter of the first page of the form." When counsel discovered the mistake and demanded return of the documents, Telanoff refused. The trial court, relying on American Bar Association (ABA) Formal Ethics Opinion No. 92-368, imposed monetary sanctions.*

The Court of Appeal framed the issue as follows: "[W]hat is a lawyer to do when he or she receives through the inadvertence of opposing counsel documents plainly subject to the attorney-client privilege?" After determining that the documents were privileged and that inadvertent disclosure did not waive the privilege, the court discussed an attorney's obligation. The Court of Appeal disagreed that the ABA opinion should regulate Telanoff's conduct. The court noted that the ABA Model Rules of Professional Conduct on which the opinion was based "do not establish ethical standards in California, as they have not been adopted in California and have no legal force of their own. Likewise, the court held that an "ABA formal opinion does not establish an obligatory standard of conduct imposed on California lawyers." Thus, under the circumstances "Telanoff should not have been sanctioned for engaging in conduct which has been condemned by an ABA formal opinion, but which has not been condemned by any decision, statute or [r]ule of [p]rofessional [c]onduct applicable in this state."

The *State Fund* court went on to articulate the standard to be applied prospectively: "When a lawyer who receives materials that obviously appear to be subject to an attorney-client privilege or otherwise clearly appear to be confidential and privileged and where it is reasonably apparent that the materials were provided or made available through inadvertence, the lawyer receiving such materials should refrain from examining the materials any more than is essential to ascertain if the materials are privileged, and shall immediately notify the sender that he or she possesses material that appears to be privileged. The parties may then proceed to resolve the situation by agreement or may

---

* This ABA opinion was later withdrawn by ABA Opinion 06-440, following adoption of Model Rule 4.4(b), as discussed later in this chapter. The result in *Rico* would not have been affected by the development.–Ed.

resort to the court for guidance with the benefit of protective orders and other judicial intervention as may be justified." To ensure that its decision was clear in setting forth the applicable standard in these cases, the court explicitly stated that it "declared the standard governing the conduct of California lawyers" in such instances.

The existing *State Fund* rule is a fair and reasonable approach. The rule supports the work product doctrine, and is consistent with the state's policy to "[p]reserve the rights of attorneys to prepare cases for trial with that degree of privacy necessary to encourage them to prepare their cases thoroughly and to investigate not only the favorable but the unfavorable aspects of those cases" and to "[p]revent attorneys from taking undue advantage of their adversary's industry and efforts."

The *State Fund* rule also addresses the practical problem of inadvertent disclosure in the context of today's reality that document production may involve massive numbers of documents. A contrary holding could severely disrupt the discovery process. As amicus curiae the Product Liability Advisory Council, Inc., argues, "Even apart from the inadvertent disclosure problem, the party responding to a request for mass production must engage in a laborious, time consuming process. If the document producer is confronted with the additional prospect that any privileged documents inadvertently produced will become fair game for the opposition, the minute screening and re-screening that inevitably would follow not only would add enormously to that burden but would slow the pace of discovery to a degree sharply at odds with the general goal of expediting litigation."

Finally, we note that "[a]n attorney has an obligation not only to protect his client's interests but also to respect the legitimate interests of fellow members of the bar, the judiciary, and the administration of justice." The *State Fund* rule holds attorneys to a reasonable standard of professional conduct when confidential or privileged materials are inadvertently disclosed.

Here, it is true that Yukevich's notes were not so clearly flagged as confidential as were the forms in *State Fund*. But, as the Court of Appeal observed, "[T]he absence of prominent notations of confidentiality does not make them any less privileged." The *State Fund* rule is an objective standard. In applying the rule, courts must consider whether reasonably competent counsel, knowing the circumstances of the litigation, would have concluded the materials were privileged, how much review was reasonably necessary to draw that conclusion, and when counsel's examination should have ended.

The standard was properly and easily applied here. Johnson admitted that after a minute or two of review he realized the notes related to the case and that Yukevich did not intend to reveal them. Johnson's own admissions and subsequent conduct clearly demonstrate that he violated the *State Fund* rule. We note, however, that such admissions are not required for the application of the objective standard in evaluating an attorney's conduct.

DISQUALIFICATION OF COUNSEL AND EXPERTS

The court properly applied the *State Fund* rule and determined that Johnson violated it. The next question is whether disqualification was the proper remedy. . . .

The *State Fund* court held that " '[m]ere exposure' " to an adversary's confidences is insufficient, standing alone, to warrant an attorney's disqualification. The court counseled against a draconian rule that " '[could] nullify a party's right to representation by chosen counsel any time inadvertence or devious design put an adversary's confidences in an attorney's mailbox.' " However, the court, did not "rule out the possibility that in an appropriate case, disqualification might be justified if an attorney inadvertently receives confidential materials and fails to conduct himself or herself in the manner specified above, assuming other factors compel disqualification."

After reviewing the document, Johnson made copies and disseminated them to plaintiffs' experts and other attorneys. In affirming the disqualification order, the Court of Appeal stated, "The trial court settled on disqualification as the proper remedy because of the unmitigable damage caused by Johnson's dissemination and use of the document." Thus, "the record shows that Johnson not only failed to conduct himself as required under *State Fund,* but also acted unethically in making full use of the confidential document." The Court of Appeal properly concluded that such use of the document undermined the defense experts' opinions and placed defendants at a great disadvantage. Without disqualification of plaintiffs' counsel and their experts, the damage caused by Johnson's use and dissemination of the notes was irreversible. Under the circumstances presented in this case, the trial court did not abuse its discretion by ordering disqualification for violation of the *State Fund* rule. . . .

The prohibition on communications with another lawyer's client has, as one of its objectives, protection of attorney-client confidences. A lawyer may learn an opposing side's confidential information in other ways too. Courts have been protective here as well. In a case that received much attention in the legal and popular press, a New York appellate court, in two highly critical opinions, disqualified a prominent New York law firm in a surrogate's court litigation. The basis for the court's order was its conclusion that the firm had knowingly misused the state's discovery rules to obtain the opposing party's confidential information. In re Beiny, 517 N.Y.S.2d 474 (1st Dept. 1987); In re Beiny, 522 N.Y.S.2d 511 (1st Dept. 1987), appeal dismissed, 524 N.E.2d 879 (N.Y. 1988).

Another risk zone lies in talking to expert witnesses whom an opponent has also interviewed. Latham & Watkins spoke with a couple of accountants as prospective experts, even though the opposing law firm had previously interviewed the very same accountants and had told them its theory of the case. Latham argued that it had not elicited confidential information from the accountants. The court created a presumption otherwise and disqualified the firm because it could not rebut the presumption. Shadow Traffic Network v. Superior Court, 29 Cal. Rptr. 2d 693 (Ct. App. 1994). *Shadow Traffic* was distinguished in Western Digital Corp. v. Superior Court, 71 Cal. Rptr. 2d 179 (Ct. App. 1998). Irell & Manella was able to rebut the presumption that it had received an opposing law firm's confidential information from an expert. The opposing firm, Mayer Brown, had interviewed several potential experts at Hankin & Co., but did not hire them. Irell & Manella then interviewed and hired Carter, who had joined Hankin after the Mayer Brown interviews. Hankin screened Carter from the experts Mayer Brown had interviewed, meaning that Carter had no access to what the others had learned in the interviews. The court presumed that the Hankin experts had learned confidential information in the interviews, but the screen served to rebut the presumption that this information was shared with Carter. Of course, Mayer Brown's client would have to trust that Hankin would respect the screen. How could Mayer Brown have avoided this result? We talk further about how and when screens can rebut presumptions of shared confidences in law firms in chapter 6B.

Courts have dismissed claims where the litigant is a participant in the invasion of the opponent's confidential relationship. Joan Lipin brought a sexual harassment claim against her former employer and supervisor. During a pretrial proceeding, she surreptitiously read a confidential memorandum of the opposing party's law firm. "At a break, [she] slipped the documents into a Redweld file 'for her own protection.' . . ." When she told her lawyer what she had done, he first declined to look at the papers but then, after concluding "that any claim of privilege as to the documents had been lost as a result of [his opponent's] careless handling of them . . . he read through them." After the trial judge granted protective orders, with which the plaintiff only partly complied, the case was dismissed. The New York Court of Appeals affirmed the dismissal. Lipin v. Bender, 644 N.E.2d 1300 (N.Y. 1994). Chief Judge Kaye wrote:

> The trial court, and the Appellate Division, could hardly have been clearer in their conclusions, characterizing plaintiff's conduct — as well as that of her attorney — as "heinous" and "egregious," a threat to the attorney-client privilege, to the concept of civilized, orderly conduct among attorneys, and even to the rule of law. . . .
>
> Having deliberately taken the initial misstep of secretly reading what she recognized as attorneys' confidential documents, plaintiff was presented with several opportunities to purge herself and minimize prejudice to defendants. At each juncture, however, she chose the course of action that exacerbated the harm. . . .
>
> While the Appellate Division made plain that it would reach the same result whether or not the documents were actually privileged, in fact both courts agreed as to the protected nature of the documents. . . . Similarly lacking any basis in the record . . . is plaintiff's claim that defendants waived the privilege by leaving the documents on the hearing room table during argument.

Arthur Wisehart, Lipin's lawyer, was later suspended from practice for two years for this and other conduct. Matter of Wisehart, 721 N.Y.S.2d 356 (1st Dept. 2001).

A case for which I have a special category called "*What Were They Thinking?*," a question that makes a factual assumption, is In re Winkler, 834 N.E.2d 85 (Ind. 2005). Two prosecutors, Goode and Winkler, attended a deposition in connection with a criminal case. Apparently, depositions are allowed in criminal cases in Indiana. The court describes what happened next after the defendant and his lawyer left the room:

> Goode seized notes the defendant had written and shared with his attorney. Goode tore the notes from a legal pad that had been turned face down on a table before the defendant and his counsel left the room to confer.

Goode gave the notes to Winkler who concealed them by placing the notes among a stack of files she had before her on the table. Respondents wanted to use the notes as a handwriting exemplar to compare with other evidence in the case. When defendant and his counsel returned to the room neither respondent advised them that they had seized the notes. When counsel and the defendant began looking for the notes, Winkler went so far as to shuffle through her files as if looking for the notes. Only when defendant saw the edge of a yellow piece of paper protruding from Winkler's files, did she acknowledge having the notes and return them to defendant.

The court found violations of Rules 4.1(a), 4.4, and 8.4(c). Both prosecutors were suspended.

The problem here, as the *Rico* court recognized, is that modern technology has made it increasingly likely that even careful lawyers will slip up and provide privileged or other protected information to an opponent. Push the wrong button on a fax machine. Click "Reply All" on a screen. Include a privileged document among thousands of documents delivered (or electronically transmitted) in discovery. Forget to strip an electronic document of metadata (all that stuff you thought you had deleted and which does not appear on the screen but can be restored with a few mouse clicks). It can happen to anyone. And because it can happen to anyone, the impetus to develop a rule that will avoid inadvertent waiver has been strong.

In 2002, the ABA adopted Rule 4.4(b), which requires prompt notice to the opposing lawyer when a recipient "knows or reasonably should know that [a] document was inadvertently sent." The rule then leaves to substantive law whether the lawyer must comply with the opponent's instructions to return it. The new rule is discussed in ABA Opinion 05-437, which withdrew Opinion 92-368, cited in *Rico*. See also ABA Opinion 06-440. But even as modified, the new ABA rule would still forbid the lawyers' conduct there. Some local bar associations would require more than prompt notice to the opposing lawyer. NYC Opinion 03-04, for example, instructs lawyers to return or destroy the communication if requested or, in the alternative, to present any claim of waiver to court.

Let's say the privilege issue does go to court, with the recipient claiming waiver and the embarrassed opponent arguing that the material should be returned and the adversary instructed not to use anything she may have learned. What should the court do?

"Since I have for years taught the survey course on evidence at various of our local law schools and at continuing legal education programs, this is a matter to which I have given some thought," wrote Chief Judge Young in Amgen, Inc. v. Hoechst Marion Roussel, Inc., 190 F.R.D. 287 (D. Mass. 2000), which raised these very questions. Judge Young identified three approaches: Inadvertent disclosure never forfeits the privilege, it always does, and it sometimes does. He opted for sometimes:

> This approach empowers courts to consider a number of circumstances relating to the inadvertent production, including (1) the reasonableness of the precautions taken to prevent inadvertent disclosure, (2) the amount of time it took the producing party to recognize its error, (3) the scope of the production, (4) the extent of the inadvertent disclosure, and (5) the overriding

interest of fairness and justice. Thus, depending on the totality of these factors, the court may rule either that the inadvertent disclosure has effected a waiver of the privilege or that the privilege remains intact. . . .

A 2008 amendment to the Federal Rules of Evidence adds Rule 502. It seems to take the position that inadvertent disclosure never waives the privilege. It provides in part: "When made in a federal proceeding or to a federal office or agency, the disclosure does not operate as a waiver in a federal or state proceeding if: (1) the disclosure is inadvertent; (2) the holder of the privilege or protection took reasonable steps to prevent disclosure; and (3) the holder promptly took reasonable steps to rectify the error, including (if applicable) following Fed. R Civ. P. 26(b)(5)(B)."

The bar ethics opinions diverge in describing a recipient lawyer's responsibility when a document contains metadata. ABA Opinion 06-442 concludes that the recipient lawyer "generally" may review and use the metadata. It takes no position on whether the sending lawyer must be notified. N.Y. Opinion 749 (2001) concludes that even searching for metadata in a document is forbidden as dishonest and prejudicial to the administration of justice. D.C. Opinion 341 (2007) takes a middle view. It says that reviewing metadata in a document is unethical only if the lawyer "knows" that it was inadvertently sent. The D.C. opinion makes the important point that different rules apply when the metadata is contained in documents sought in discovery or via subpoena. Then, the receiving lawyer may have a right to it under rules of procedure, and obstruction of justice statutes may forbid the sending lawyer from stripping documents of metadata.

Trina Jones uses the debate over the "ethical obligations of recipients of inadvertently disclosed privileged information" as a context for discussing "the ways in which lawyers make ethical decisions and the factors that inform those decisions." Professor Jones argues in favor of moving away from "an over-reliance upon ethical rules promulgated by courts and bar associations [and] a belief that loyalty to one's client is the preeminent, if not the sole, consideration." She chooses inadvertent disclosure as her analytical context because "it presents a practical problem whose ethical dimensions have not been adequately explored"; "it concerns conduct that does not fall squarely within a rule of ethics and is an area where the law is unclear"; and it "involves two values that are central to the law of lawyering: confidentiality and zealous representation of client interests." Trina Jones, Inadvertent Disclosure of Privileged Information and the Law of Mistake: Using Substantive Legal Principles to Guide Ethical Decision Making, 48 Emory L.J. 1255 (1999).

IV

Lawyers, Money, and the Ethics of Legal Fees

There can be no equal justice where the kind of trial a man gets depends on the amount of money he has.

> —Justice Hugo Black, in Griffin v. Illinois, 351 U.S. 12 (1956)

Kent: This is nothing, Fool.
Fool: Then 'tis like the breath of an unfee'd lawyer, you gave me nothing for 't.

> —Shakespeare, *King Lear,* 1.04.128-130

A factory owner manufactured a product, any product, which required the use of a particular machine. The machine broke down and no one could fix it. Repairperson after repairperson tried and failed. The owner was frantic. Circumstances were reaching crisis proportions. Employees were threatening to quit because there was no payroll money; creditors were threatening bankruptcy because their bills were unpaid; and customers were threatening to take their business to competitors because no product was forthcoming.

The owner was on the brink of disaster. Just as all was about to be lost, a person walked into the factory and offered to fix the machine. "Please," cried the owner, "everything I have worked for my whole life is in jeopardy." The repairperson walked around the machine for just a few minutes and, then, with a nail clipper that one can buy off a cardboard display at most checkout counters, bent down and turned a screw. Lo and behold the machine started to work! All was saved. The employees were paid and did not quit; the creditors were paid and there was no bankruptcy; and the customers received their product and stayed with the company.

Now, the moment of truth. The repairperson sent the bill and it read: "Fixed the machine — $25,000." The owner called the repairperson and said "Do not get me wrong. I am eternally grateful, but would you please itemize your statement?" "Sure," was the response, "I will bring one right over." A short while later, the repairperson appeared before the owner and presented the itemized statement, which read: "Turned the screw in the machine, $50; knowing which screw to turn, $24,950."

—James Fox Miller, The Curse of the Legal Profession,
Florida Bar Journal, Feb. 1991, at 6*

- *Market Fees, Unethical Fees, and Contingent Fees*
- *Court Ordered Fees*
- *Pro Bono: Requirements and Expectations*

Legal services have value. Who pays? How much? What rules, if any, limit the nature and size of fees?

Most lawyers get paid by their clients. Lawyers in firms charge fees. Other lawyers, like those who work for corporations or government, are salaried. Fees, in turn, can be structured in many ways: a flat fee for a specified service, an hourly fee, a contingent fee, a minimum fee, a general or special retainer, or some combination of the these. Some law firms ask for a "performance fee," an additional payment for highly favorable results.

The client is usually the source of the fee, but not always. A lawyer may represent a client but be paid by someone else. One example is an insurance company that retains counsel to represent an insured. Another is when the state pays a lawyer to represent an indigent criminal defendant to comply with Gideon v. Wainwright, 372 U.S. 335 (1963). States may also pay for lawyers in civil matters. State-financed lawyers may work for an institutional law office (like a legal aid society), or they may be in private practice. The Legal Services Corporation, a federally funded, congressionally created entity, provides money for local legal services offices that represent legally indigent clients in civil matters.

In a market economy, where products and services are traded for money, people without money get less of those products and services. Yet, as the above quotation from Justice Black tells us, some services should not be left to market forces. In the last several decades, one of the most successful innovations to help fund legal services goes by the awkward name IOLTA. Its arrival was not without opposition.

Lawyers are required to hold a client's money in separate accounts, usually called escrow or special accounts. See page 774. These accounts often pay interest. Every state requires or permits lawyers whose clients do not direct otherwise to pool client money in a single account and to contribute the interest to a trust that is then used to fund legal help for individuals who cannot afford it. IOLA and IOLTA, acronyms for Interest On Lawyer (Trust) Accounts, are the terms used to describe these programs. But the Supreme Court held, 5-to-4, that interest on client funds in Texas's Mandatory IOLTA Program constituted client "property" within the meaning of the Fifth Amendment's takings clause, which threatened to kill the idea. But even if the interest was "property," left open was

---

* Mr. Miller writes that this story "was first told to me almost 25 years ago by the late Paul Anton, a lawyer's lawyer who was kind enough to help guide me when I hung up a shingle and started to learn what the *practice* of law was really about."

whether the program effected a "taking" of the property without "just compensation." Phillips v. Washington Legal Foundation, 524 U.S. 156 (1998). On remand, the district court found that no "taking" occurred; nor in any event were clients denied "just compensation" for use of their property. Washington Legal Foundation v. Texas Equal Access to Justice Foundation, 86 F. Supp. 2d 624 (W.D. Tex. 2000), rev'd, 270 F.3d 180 (5th Cir. 2001) (2-1), vacated and remanded, 538 U.S. 942 (2003). The Fifth Circuit found that a "taking" occurred even if the clients would have received zero interest because of the small sums of money involved. It remanded for an injunction. Judge Wiener, in dissent, concluded that "just compensation for zero is zero."

While a certiorari petition was pending, the Supreme Court decided Brown v. Legal Foundation of Washington, 538 U.S. 216 (2003). Justice Stevens cited "the overall, dramatic success of these programs in serving the compelling interest in providing legal services to literally millions of needy Americans." That success established the "public use" of the IOLTA programs within the meaning of the Fifth Amendment. The Court had already held that interest generated in IOLTA programs was property, and in *Brown* it assumed that the state's use of this money was a "taking" of the property. The Fifth Amendment therefore required "just compensation," which the Court said is "measured by the property owner's loss rather than the government's gain." The question, then, was whether clients suffered a loss.

Washington's program required lawyers "to deposit client funds in non-IOLTA accounts whenever those funds could generate net earnings for the client." Only if the client's funds were too small to generate net earnings did IOLTA apply. Justice Stevens cited an example from a dissenting opinion below: $2,000 held for two days in an account paying 5 percent would yield 55 cents interest. But the administrative cost of computing the interest and mailing a check to the client would be higher than 55 cents. "The fair market value of a right to receive $.55 by spending perhaps $5.00 to receive it would be nothing," he wrote. Justice Scalia dissented in an opinion in which Chief Justice Rehnquist and Justices Kennedy and Thomas joined. IOLTA survived, barely.

Sometimes a lawyer will be paid by a client's adversary. This may be by agreement, as when a person who obtains a mortgage pays the lender's lawyer, or when a statute authorizes a court to order one litigant to pay the fees of a prevailing adverse party. Fee-shifting statutes appear in civil liberties and civil rights cases and also in antitrust, copyright, and patent litigation, among other places.

Legal services need not be financed with the payment of money at all. Lawyers sometimes work pro bono publico ("for the public good"). When they do, it is the lawyer herself who "finances" the arrangement. Many lawyers do pro bono work voluntarily. Some have argued that lawyers should be required to perform pro bono work or contribute to legal services organizations. About 80 percent of the legal needs of the poor go unmet by some estimates.

Beyond the various ways of financing legal services are questions about the nature and amount of legal fees. How are they controlled? Most prominent are market forces of supply and demand. Ethical and legal rules, however, also constrain the nature and size of fees, at least at the extremes. It is not a wholly a laissez faire system. Should it be? Should courts or legislatures be able to deny a willing lawyer and a competent and informed client the right to determine the structure and amount of the lawyer's fee? At the very least, should the market alone determine the value of legal services to clients (the Fortune 500, say) sophisticated in evaluating legal work, who are free to shop around, and who often use their own employed lawyers to negotiate legal fees?

Once we identify the bounds on proper legal fees, the next task is to identify who receives the money. What limits are there on the division of fees among lawyers in a single firm? When may fees be divided among lawyers in different firms (as in referral fees or fee-sharing)? And what exactly do we mean by "firm" in the first place?

Last, these questions assume that all legal fees will go to lawyers. But must they? When, if ever, may nonlawyers or businesses other than law firms receive legal fees? These questions raise the issues of "unauthorized" law practice and of lay participation in law firms and the delivery of legal services, which we take up in chapters 12 and 14, respectively.

FURTHER READING

Lisa Lerman, who has written extensively and prominently on legal fees and especially about misconduct in billing, analyzed 16 cases of overbilling or other improprieties by lawyers in prominent firms. All resulted in professional discipline, mostly removal from the bar, and many resulted in criminal convictions and prison sentences. Professor Lerman's book-length study can be found at Blue-Chip Bilking: Regulation of Billing and Expense Fraud by Lawyers, 12 Geo. J. Legal Ethics 205 (1999). Two other law professors who have studied the historical factors leading to the introduction of hourly billing suggest that modern conditions are operating to encourage return to fixed-fee billing. George Shepherd & Morgan Cloud, Time and Money: Discovery Leads to Hourly Billing, 1999 U. Ill. L. Rev. 91 (1999).

A. THE ROLE OF THE MARKETPLACE

BROBECK, PHLEGER & HARRISON v. TELEX CORP.
602 F.2d 866 (9th Cir.), cert. denied, 444 U.S. 981 (1979)

PER CURIAM.

This is a diversity action in which the plaintiff, the San Francisco law firm of Brobeck, Phleger & Harrison ("Brobeck"), sued the Telex Corporation and Telex Computer Products, Inc. ("Telex") to recover $1,000,000 in attorney's fees. Telex had engaged Brobeck on a contingency fee basis to prepare a petition for certiorari after the Tenth Circuit reversed a $259.5 million judgment in Telex's favor against International Business Machines Corporation ("IBM") and affirmed an $18.5 million counterclaim judgment for IBM against Telex. Brobeck prepared and filed the petition, and after Telex entered a "wash settlement" with IBM in which both parties released their claims against the other, Brobeck sent Telex a bill for $1,000,000, that it claimed Telex owed it under their written contingency fee agreement. When Telex refused to pay,

Brobeck brought this action. Both parties filed motions for summary judgment. The district court granted Brobeck's motion, awarding Brobeck $1,000,000 plus interest. Telex now appeals. . . .

Having had reversed one of the largest antitrust judgments in history, Telex officials decided to press the Tenth Circuit's decision to the United States Supreme Court. To maximize Telex's chances for having its petition for certiorari granted, they decided to search for the best available lawyer. They compiled a list of the preeminent antitrust and Supreme Court lawyers in the country, and Roger Wheeler, Telex's Chairman of the Board, settled on Moses Lasky of the Brobeck firm as the best possibility. Wheeler and his assistant made preliminary phone calls to Lasky on February 3, 4, and 13, 1975 to determine whether Lasky was willing to prepare the petition for certiorari. Lasky stated he would be interested if he was able to rearrange his workload. When asked about a fee, Lasky stated that, although he would want a retainer, it was the policy of the Brobeck firm to determine fees after the services were performed. Wheeler, however, wanted an agreement fixing fees in advance and arranged for Lasky to meet in San Francisco on February 10th to discuss the matter further with Telex's president, Stephen Jatras, and Floyd Walker, its attorney in the IBM litigation.

[When the parties met, Telex officials wanted a contingent fee with a ceiling. Lasky said there should then be a floor. Drafts were exchanged and the following agreement was eventually signed.]

MEMORANDUM

1. Retainer of $25,000.00 to be paid. If Writ of Certiorari is denied and no settlement has been effected in excess of the Counterclaim, then the $25,000.00 retainer shall be the total fee paid; provided however, that

2. If the case should be settled before a Petition for Writ of Certiorari is actually filed with the Clerk of the Supreme Court, then the Brobeck firm would bill for its services to the date of settlement at an hourly rate of $125.00 per hour for the lawyers who have worked on the case; the total amount of such billing will be limited to not more than $100,000.00, against which the $25,000.00 retainer will be applied, but no portion of the retainer will be returned in any event.

3. Once a Petition for Writ of Certiorari has been filed with the Clerk of the United States Supreme Court then Brobeck will be entitled to the payment of an additional fee in the event of a recovery by Telex from IBM by way of settlement or judgment of its claims against IBM; and, such additional fee will be five percent (5%) of the first $100,000,000.00 gross of such recovery, undiminished by any recovery by IBM on its counterclaims or cross-claims. The maximum contingent fee to be paid is $5,000,000.00, provided that if recovery by Telex from IBM is less than $40,000,000.00 gross, the five percent (5%) shall be based on the net recovery, i.e., the recovery after deducting the credit to IBM by virtue of IBM's recovery on counterclaims or cross-claims, but the contingent fee shall not then be less than $1,000,000.00.

4. Once a Writ of Certiorari has been granted, then Brobeck will receive an additional $15,000.00 retainer to cover briefing and arguing in the Supreme Court.

5. Telex will pay, in addition to the fees stated, all of the costs incurred with respect to the prosecution of the case in the United States Supreme Court.

Jatras signed Lasky's proposed agreement, and on February 28 returned it to Lasky with a letter and a check for $25,000 as the agreed retainer. To "clarify" his thinking on the operation of the fee agreement, Jatras attached a set of hypothetical examples to the letter. This "attachment" stated the amount of the fee that would be paid to Brobeck assuming judgment or settlements in eight different amounts. In the first hypothetical, which assumed a settlement of $18.5 million and a counterclaim judgment of $18.5 million, Jatras listed a "net recovery" by Telex of "$0" and a Brobeck contingency fee of "$0."

Lasky received the letter and attachment on March 3. Later that same day he replied: "Your attachment of examples of our compensation in various contingencies is correct, it being understood that the first example is applicable only to a situation where the petition for certiorari has been denied, as stated in paragraph 1 of the memorandum."

No Telex official responded to Lasky's letter. . . .

On October 2 IBM officials became aware that the Supreme Court's decision on the petition was imminent. They contacted Telex and the parties agreed that IBM would release its counterclaim judgment against Telex in exchange for Telex's dismissal of its petition for certiorari. On October 3, at the request of Wheeler and Jatras, Lasky had the petition for certiorari withdrawn. Thereafter, he sent a bill to Telex for $1,000,000. When Telex refused to pay, Brobeck filed its complaint. On the basis of depositions and exhibits, the district court granted Brobeck's motion for summary judgment.

In a somewhat contradictory fashion, Telex contends on appeal that a number of genuine issues of fact exist with respect to Brobeck's motion for summary judgment but that none exists concerning its own motion. . . .

[The court dismissed the contention that Brobeck had been discharged by Telex, finding no facts to support that view. It credited Brobeck's interpretation of the contracts, which was unambiguous on its face. Extrinsic evidence also tended to confirm Brobeck's interpretation.]

Finally, Telex contends that the $1 million fee was so excessive as to render the contract unenforceable. Alternatively it argues that unconscionability depends on the contract's reasonableness, a question of fact that should be submitted to the jury.

Preliminarily, we note that whether a contract is fair or works an unconscionable hardship is determined with reference to the time when the contract was made and cannot be resolved by hindsight.

There is no dispute about the facts leading to Telex's engagement of the Brobeck firm. Telex was an enterprise threatened with bankruptcy. It had won one of the largest money judgments in history, but that judgment had been reversed in its entirety by the Tenth Circuit. In order to maximize its chances of gaining review by the United States Supreme Court, it sought to hire the most experienced and capable lawyer it could possibly find. After compiling a list of highly qualified lawyers, it settled on Lasky as the most able. Lasky was interested but wanted to bill Telex on an hourly basis. After Telex insisted on a contingent fee arrangement, Lasky made it clear that he would consent to such an arrangement only if he would receive a sizable contingent fee in the event of success.

In these circumstances, the contract between Telex and Brobeck was not so unconscionable that "no man in his senses and not under a delusion would make on the one hand, and as no honest and fair man would accept on the other." This is not a case where one party took advantage of another's ignorance, exerted superior bargaining power, or disguised unfair terms in small print. Rather, Telex, a multi-million [dollar] corporation, represented by able counsel, sought to secure the best attorney it could find to prepare its petition for certiorari, insisting on a contingent fee contract. Brobeck fulfilled its obligation to gain a stay of judgment and to prepare and file the petition for certiorari. Although the minimum fee was clearly high, Telex received substantial value from Brobeck's services. For, as Telex acknowledged, Brobeck's petition provided Telex with the leverage to secure a discharge of its counterclaim judgment, thereby saving it from possible bankruptcy in the event the Supreme Court denied its petition for certiorari. We conclude that such a contract was not unconscionable.

The judgment of the district court is affirmed.

Telex was in trouble. Moses Lasky was one of the nation's best antitrust litigators. The client had other lawyers to advise it on the fee negotiation with Lasky's firm. It's hard to imagine how a fee agreement could be more "arm's length" than this one. Further, Lasky's petition for certiorari did provide "leverage" for a settlement that eliminated the possibility of Telex's bankruptcy. We need not weep for Telex. The court refused to save the company from its own business judgment. Yet Telex must have been pretty mad. It hired other lawyers to fight the fee ($1 million 1975 equals about $4.1 million in 2009) all the way to the Supreme Court.

Even if our heart does not go out to Telex, we can question the court's standards for testing unconscionability. Are they the same standards the Massachusetts court applied in *Fordham*, the next principal case? Would they have led to a different result in *Fordham*?

The Ninth Circuit said that unconscionability "is determined with reference to the time when the contract was made and cannot be resolved by hindsight." Can that be true? Assume Susan Robins, a successful stock trader, receives a letter from an enforcement agency saying that she is the subject of a civil and criminal investigation. She goes right out and hires Claire Sparrow, the best defense lawyer in town for these matters. Sparrow's "minimum fee" is $50,000 if the matter is resolved without charges being filed. Assume that fee would be deemed reasonable at "the time when the contract was made" given Sparrow's prominence and the gravity of the threat to the client. Two days later, the government informs the trader that it has made a mistake. It has confused her with someone else. ("We meant Susan Dobins, not Susan Robins. So sorry. Have a nice day.") The lawyer has spent three hours on the case. Is the fee conscionable?

Telex's position on hindsight is unusual, especially in contingent fee matters, which *Telex* was in part. When the City of Detroit settled a police brutality complaint for $5.25 million within a month after the incident and three weeks after the complaint was filed, in part because of a public outcry over the event, the court refused to enforce an agreement for one-third of the recovery, a common contingent fee in personal injury cases. "Courts have broad authority to refuse to enforce contingent fee arrangements that award excessive fees." Green v. Nevers, 111 F.3d 1295 (6th Cir. 1997). King v. Fox, 851 N.E.2d 1184 (NY 2006) ("A contingent fee may be disallowed as between attorney and client in spite of [a] contingent fee retainer agreement, where the amount becomes large enough to be out of all proportion to the value of the professional services rendered"[internal quote omitted]). Should this authority extend to noncontingent fees too? That's what Rule 1.5(a) does, doesn't it? Contingency is but one factor in the assessment of reasonableness.

The Ninth Circuit, quoting California case law, wrote that Brobeck's fee was "not so unconscionable that 'no man in his senses and not under a delusion would make on the one hand, and as no honest and fair man would accept on the other.' " Does it necessarily follow that no fee to which a client like Telex might agree could possibly be unconscionable no matter how high? Shall we say that, by definition, when dealing with informed (and separately counseled?) clients, the market is (or should be) the only test? But if we do say that, why even have standards like those in Rule 1.5(a) for such clients? It can't be that the courts will enforce fees that disciplinary committees will punish, can it? So maybe the rule should simply duplicate the *Brobeck* test. *Brobeck* did not even cite California's then counterpart to Rule 1.5 (today it's Rule 4-200).

Time or Value (or Does Value = Time)?

If we omit personal injury cases, where contingent fees predominate, hourly billing is probably the most common way lawyers charge for their services and certainly time is the most common ingredient in determining a fee. Also common, in simple matters, are flat fees, which individual clients might prefer because "I know what it will cost me." A lawyer may offer a flat fee for a simple estate plan, a home purchase, or the defense of a misdemeanor. But flat fees are often hourly rates in disguise. A lawyer predicts how much time the work will require and multiplies by an hourly rate.

In the first decade of the twenty-first century, hourly rates for American lawyers range from around $100 to more than $1,000 for specialists in major cities (or at least New York). Much depends on geographical location, the lawyer's experience, the nature of the service, and the urgency of the client's need. At the same time, many clients (and some lawyers) are questioning the wisdom of hourly billing. In the words of James Fox Miller, past president of the Florida bar: "Hourly billing promotes inefficiency and penalizes productivity. Unfortunately, in some cases it promotes outright dishonesty." He instead believes that "a lawyer should be paid for what is done and not for how long it took to do it." James Fox Miller, The Curse of the Legal Profession, Fla. B.J., Feb. 1991, at 6. What Mr. Miller favors is sometimes called "value billing." He defends his position at length, beginning with the anecdote at the start of this chapter.*

---

* On value billing, see generally Elizabeth Kovachevich & Geri Waksler, The Legal Profession: Edging Closer to Death with Each Passing Hour, 20 Stetson L. Rev. 419 (1991). After gathering data

As the "value-billers" see it, a fee should not be fixed or formulaically determined in advance. Rather, at the conclusion of the matter, lawyer and client should sit down and evaluate what the lawyer has achieved for the client. If the achievement is substantial, it will support a fee higher than what the lawyer's hourly rate would yield. In theory, though it is not much discussed, if the work is poor, it should lead to a lower fee.

The "value billing" debate appears when courts award fees to prevailing parties under fee-shifting statutes. Courts routinely use a multiple of time and hourly rate to determine a fee. But sometimes this can result in a fee way in excess of the client's recovery, which in turn leads some critics to question the logic of the policy. In City of Riverside v. Rivera, 477 U.S. 561 (1986), two relatively young lawyers sued the City of Riverside, California, in federal court on behalf of eight Chicano individuals, alleging that Riverside police used unnecessary physical force in breaking up a party. At a 1980 trial, the lawyers recovered $33,350 in compensatory and punitive damages, of which $13,300 (or about $40,000 in 2009 dollars) was for federal civil rights violations. For winning this $13,300, they were awarded fees in excess of $245,000 (or about $750,000 in 2009 dollars) under 42 U.S.C. §1988. This is a federal fee-shifting statute that authorizes federal judges to award "reasonable" fees to parties who prevail on certain federal civil rights claims. Does that make you think the system has gone bonkers?

Justice Rehnquist seemed to think so. Dissenting from a 5-to-4 decision affirming the fee award, he made an argument that could well be cited by proponents of value billing anywhere. This is part of what he wrote:

> The analysis of whether the extraordinary number of hours put in by respondents' attorneys in this case was "reasonable" must be made in light of both the traditional billing practices in the profession, and the fundamental principle that the award of a "reasonable" attorney's fee under §1988 means a fee that would have been deemed reasonable if billed to affluent plaintiffs by their own attorneys. . . .
>
> Suppose that A offers to sell Blackacre to B for $10,000. It is commonly known and accepted that Blackacre has a fair market value of $10,000. B consults an attorney and requests a determination whether A can convey good title to Blackacre. The attorney writes an elaborate memorandum concluding that A's title to Blackacre is defective, and submits a bill to B for $25,000. B refuses to pay the bill, the attorney sues, and the parties stipulate that the attorney spent 200 hours researching the title issue because of an extraordinarily complex legal and factual situation, and that the prevailing rate at which the attorney billed, which was also a "reasonable" rate, was $125. Does anyone seriously think that a court should award the attorney the full $25,000 which he claims? Surely a court would start from the proposition that, unless special arrangements were made between the client and the attorney, a "reasonable" attorney's fee for researching the title to a piece of property worth $10,000 could not exceed the value of the property. Otherwise the client would have been far better off never going to an attorney in the first place, and simply

from 272 attorneys and 80 corporate counsel, Professor William Ross meticulously explores "the ethical aspects of time-based billing" and "whether various alternative forms of billing would encourage more ethical billing practices." William Ross, The Ethics of Hourly Billing by Attorneys, 44 Rutgers L. Rev. 1 (1991). See also The Honest Hour: The Ethics of Time-Based Billing by Attorneys (1996) by the same author.

giving *A* $10,000 for a worthless deed. The client thereby would have saved himself $15,000. . . .

The amount of damages which a jury is likely to award in a tort case is of course more difficult to predict than the amount it is likely to award in a contract case. But even in a tort case some measure of the kind of "billing judgment" previously described must be brought to bear in computing a "reasonable" attorney's fee. Again, a hypothetical example will illustrate the point. If, at the time respondents filed their lawsuit in 1976, there had been in the Central District of California a widely publicized survey of jury verdicts in this type of civil rights action which showed that successful plaintiffs recovered between $10,000 and $75,000 in damages, could it possibly be said that it would have been "reasonable" for respondents' attorneys to put in on the case hours which, when multiplied by the attorneys' prevailing hourly rate, would result in an attorney's fee of over $245,000? In the absence of such a survey, it might be more difficult for a plaintiff's attorney to accurately estimate the amount of damages likely to be recovered, but this does not absolve the attorney of the responsibility for making such an estimate and using it as a guide in the exercise of "billing judgment."

Reasonable as Justice Rehnquist's analysis is as a general observation, can you think why it should not apply in fee-shifting cases under civil rights and anti-discrimination laws? Is the "value" produced by a victory in these cases solely the benefit conferred upon the successful plaintiff? See Blanchard v. Bergeron, 489 U.S. 87 (1989) ("a civil rights plaintiff seeks to vindicate important civil and constitutional rights that cannot be valued solely in monetary terms") (citing *Rivera*).

But ignoring "billing judgment" in fee-shifting cases may skew incentives. Assume two cases. Prosecuting the first case through trial will require 500 hours from an attorney whose work is billed at $500 hourly. That's $250,000. Assume that damages, if the case is successful, will be $50,000, but the claim has an 80 percent chance of success. The discounted value of the case is $40,000 (80 percent of $50,000). That's not a case a client will likely finance. Conversely, assume the second case has a value of $2 million but only a 20 percent chance of success. It requires 800 hours of work by a lawyer who also bills at $500 hourly. The discounted value of the case is $400,000 (20 percent of $2 million). Again, a private client is unlikely to finance this litigation because the discounted recovery is equal to the projected fee (of $400,000). Should a court ignore these numbers and set fees based solely on hours reasonably worked times hourly rate (called the lodestar) after the lawyers win, respectively, $50,000 and $2 million? Or should a court give the second lawyer more than her lodestar because she took a greater risk and got a much larger recovery? You might be inclined to say she should get more. But if so, doesn't it follow that the first lawyer should get less, because her chance of recovery was high and the value she produced was modest? In other words, if we're going to ignore value and risk in compensating the first lawyer, don't we have to do the same for the second lawyer, in each case paying only for time? Or can we enhance but not reduce the lodestar based on risk? Does it matter if the cases don't seek to vindicate constitutional rights? See further on this issue in part E1 of this chapter.

We began by putting contingent fees to the side, but contingent fees are the quintessential example of value billing, aren't they? The lawyer says, "You win,

I win; you lose, I lose." In fact, the main difference between value billing and contingent fees is that the latter are determined by a formula, which lawyer and client agree to (almost always in writing) in advance. ("Lawyer gets one-third of client's net recovery.") So the risk of misunderstanding should be nearly nil. Yet even as the arguments for value billing have become more common, contingent fees (as we discuss further at page 168 below) have come under increasing criticism, especially in the editorial pages of the Wall Street Journal (but not only there). How do we explain that paradox?

B. UNETHICAL FEES

Rule 1.5(a) limits the size of attorney's fees. Brobeck's fee was enforced. The court, drawing on California precedent, said that the fee contract "was not so unconscionable that 'no man in his senses and not under a delusion would make on the one hand, and as no honest and fair man would accept on the other.' " Nor was it "a case where one party took advantage of another's ignorance, exerted superior bargaining power, or disguised unfair terms in small print." Are these the right tests? Actually, do they impose any limits at all, realistically speaking? They are not the standard of the Rules. Even today, California only forbids an "unconscionable" fee. Rule 4-200. Rule 1.5(a) requires a "reasonable" fee. (Can there be an unreasonable, conscionable fee?) Whatever the test, should it matter whether the issue arises in an action to collect fees (*Brobeck*) or in discipline (*Fordham*, below)?

"What Are You Worth?"

Scott Porgby, at age 45, is worth $25 billion, all earned as a money manager in his own San Francisco trading company. He is indicted for hiring two men to kill his partner, whose body is found one morning floating in Lake Tahoe. He goes to see Johnnie Scheck, acknowledged by all to be the best defense lawyer in the country for homicide cases. Scheck recently retired at age 57 and spends his time racing his sailboat and flying his Cessna. Scheck declines the case politely explaining that he has no interest in coming out of retirement. But Porgby persists. Finally, Porgby (out on bail) confronts Scheck sailing on San Francisco Bay. Scheck makes this offer, expecting it will get rid of Porgby. "I'll take the case through trial for 2 percent of your net worth, that's half a billion. Win or lose, of course."

Porgby asks Scheck what he would have charged if he were still in practice and Porgby were just "plain vanilla" rich.

"Ten million for me and then probably another five million for expenses and for the other lawyers I'd have to hire to help with research and whatnot. I heard tell that Jeffrey Skilling of Enron fame paid Daniel Petrocelli $40 million and owed him another $30 million before he got sentenced to 24 years," Scheck says. "Don't know if Petrocelli ever got the balance.

"But," Scheck adds, "I'm not in practice, and I don't especially like you. From all I've heard, you're not a nice guy whether or not you're a killer. And if I do this, I miss some important boat races and an eclipse of the sun off the Canaries, not to mention the two years it will take out of my retirement, which probably represents ten percent of my current life expectancy. I don't need it. I'll die rich as it is. So you have to interest me. Half a billion, I can start a foundation for stray dogs. Besides, how old are you?"

"Forty-five," Porgby says.

"There you go. If I win, you've got 25 more high-earning years at least. Anyway, you'll recoup my fee in a year or less, before we even get to trial. I understand you work miracles in the market, with consistent double digit returns."

"I do okay. But, um, what if you lose?"

"If I lose?" Scheck asks. "Well, I don't often lose, which is why you're here. But I have lost some and I could lose this one. It's possible. Well, what if I lose? What would you do with the money anyway? You can't spend it in prison. Besides, we'll get Alan Dershowitz to do the appeal. He sprung Von Bulow, you know."

"I don't like your sense of humor, Mr. Scheck," Porgby says.

"At my age and in my position, Scottie — can I call you Scottie? — I don't have to make you laugh. You called me. I didn't call you. Now, please move that monster boat of yours out of my way. A nice wind is coming up."

Porgby confers with other prominent homicide counsel, none of whom would charge more than $10 million for the work. After thinking about it for a few more days, he hires Scheck and is acquitted after a six week trial. Porgby then challenges the fee as unconscionable, illegal, and unethical. The evidence shows that Scheck worked full time on the case for 25 months, for a total of about 3,000 hours. So his recovery is more than $166,666 per hour. It is stipulated that the case was complicated and that Scheck did an excellent job. It is also stipulated that when Porgby hired Scheck, the case could have lasted between 20 and 30 months and required between 2,000 and 4,000 hours of work.

In arguing for Porgby, his lawyer says: "Imagine if Scheck were a great brain surgeon and Porgby needed a difficult operation to avoid profound disability. Dr. Scheck usually charged $500,000, but because of Porgby's wealth he demands $5 million. Would a court enforce that fee? We say no. Neither should it enforce this one. Professionals agree, in exchange for their monopoly power and state licenses, to limit their fees. Courts make certain they do. This fee is not reasonable."

Assume Rule 1.5 applies. Who wins?

MATTER OF LAURENCE S. FORDHAM*
423 Mass. 481, 668 N.E.2d 816 (1996), cert. denied, 519 U.S. 1149 (1997)

O'CONNOR, JUSTICE.

This is an appeal from the Board of Bar Overseers' (board's) dismissal of a petition for discipline filed by bar counsel against attorney Laurence S. Fordham.

---

* Matter of Fordham was decided under the Massachusetts version of DR 2-106, which is the same as the Model Code provision. Massachusetts has since adopted the format of the Model Rules of Professional Conduct. The factors in Model Rule 1.5(a) are the same in the Massachusetts version, but the state continues to forbid a "clearly excessive fee," whereas the Model Rules require that a "fee shall be reasonable." — ED.

[Timothy Clark, then 21, was charged with drunk driving (OUI). The police found "a partially full quart of vodka" in his car and he failed a sobriety and two breathalyzer tests.]

Subsequent to Timothy's arraignment, he and his father, Laurence Clark (Clark) consulted with three lawyers, who offered to represent Timothy for fees between $3,000 and $10,000. Shortly after the arrest, Clark went to Fordham's home to service an alarm system which he had installed several years before. While there, Clark discussed Timothy's arrest with Fordham's wife who invited Clark to discuss the case with Fordham. Fordham then met with Clark and Timothy.

At this meeting, Timothy described the incidents leading to his arrest and the charges against him. Fordham, whom the hearing committee described as a "very experienced senior trial attorney with impressive credentials," told Clark and Timothy that he had never represented a client in a driving while under the influence case or in any criminal matter, and he had never tried a case in the District Court. The hearing committee found that "Fordham explained that although he lacked experience in this area, he was a knowledgeable and hard-working attorney and that he believed he could competently represent Timothy. Fordham described himself as 'efficient and economic in the use of [his] time.' . . .

"Towards the end of the meeting, Fordham told the Clarks that he worked on [a] time charge basis and that he billed monthly. . . . In other words, Fordham would calculate the amount of hours he and others in the firm worked on a matter each month and multiply it by the respective hourly rates. He also told the Clarks that he would engage others in his firm to prepare the case. Clark had indicated that he would pay Timothy's legal fees." After the meeting, Clark hired Fordham to represent Timothy.

According to the hearing committee's findings, Fordham filed four pretrial motions on Timothy's behalf, two of which were allowed. One motion, entitled, "Motion in Limine to Suppress Results of Breathalyzer Tests," was based on the theory that, although two breathalyzer tests were exactly .02 apart, they were not "within" .02 of one another as the regulations require. The hearing committee characterized the motion and its rationale as "a creative, if not novel, approach to suppression of breathalyzer results." Although the original trial date was June 20, 1989, the trial, which was before a judge without jury, was held on October 10 and October 19, 1989. The judge found Timothy not guilty of driving while under the influence.

Fordham sent the following bills to Clark:

"1. April 19, 1989, $3,250 for services rendered in March, 1989.
"2. May 15, 1989, $9,850 for services rendered in April, 1989.
"3. June 19, 1989, $3,950 for services rendered in May, 1989.
"4. July 13, 1989, $13,300 for services rendered in June, 1989.
"5. October 13, 1989, $35,022.25 revised bill for services rendered from March 19 to June 30, 1989.
"6. November 7, 1989, $15,000 for services rendered from July 1, 1989 to October 19, 1989."

The bills totaled $50,022.25, reflecting 227 hours of billed time, 153 hours of which were expended by Fordham and seventy-four of which were his associates' time. . . .

Bar counsel and Fordham have stipulated that all the work billed by Fordham was actually done and that Fordham and his associates spent the time they claim to have spent. They also have stipulated that Fordham acted conscientiously, diligently, and in good faith in representing Timothy and in his billing in this case. . . .

In concluding that Fordham did not charge a clearly excessive fee, the board adopted, with limited exception, the hearing committee's report. The board's and the hearing committee's reasons for dismissing the petition are as follows: Bar counsel and Fordham stipulated that Fordham acted conscientiously, diligently, and in good faith in his representation of the client and his billing on the case. Although Fordham lacked experience in criminal law, he is a "seasoned and well-respected civil lawyer." The more than 200 hours spent preparing the OUI case were necessary, "in part to educate [Fordham] in the relevant substantive law and court procedures," because he had never tried an OUI case or appeared in the District Court. The board noted that "[a]lthough none of the experts who testified at the disciplinary hearing had ever heard of a fee in excess of $15,000 for a first-offense OUI case, the hearing committee found that [Clark] had entered into the transaction with open eyes after interviewing other lawyers with more experience in such matters." The board also thought significant that Clark "later acquiesced, despite mild expressions of concern, in [Fordham's] billing practices." Moreover, the Clarks specifically instructed Fordham that they would not consider a guilty plea by Timothy. Rather they were interested only in pursuing the case to trial. Finally, Timothy obtained the result he sought: an acquittal. . . .

Four witnesses testified before the hearing committee as experts on OUI cases. One of the experts, testifying on behalf of bar counsel, opined that "the amount of time spent in this case is clearly excessive." He testified that there were no unusual circumstances in the OUI charge against Timothy and that it was a "standard operating under the influence case." . . .

A second expert, testifying on behalf of bar counsel, expressed his belief that the issues presented in this case were not particularly difficult, nor novel, and that "[t]he degree of skill required to defend a case such as this . . . was not that high." He did recognize, however, that the theory that Fordham utilized to suppress the breathalyzer tests was impressive and one of which he had previously never heard. Nonetheless, the witness concluded that "clearly there is no way that [he] could justify these kind of hours to do this kind of work." . . .

An expert called by Fordham testified that the facts of Timothy's case presented a challenge and that without the suppression of the breathalyzer test results it would have been "an almost impossible situation in terms of prevailing on the trier of fact." He further stated that, based on the particulars in Timothy's case, he believed that Fordham's hours were not excessive and, in fact, he, the witness, would have spent a comparable amount of time. The witness later admitted, however, that within the past five years, the OUI cases which he had brought to trial required no more than a total of forty billed hours, which encompassed all preparation and court appearances. He explained that, although he had not charged more than forty hours to prepare an OUI case, in comparison to Fordham's more than 200 expended hours, Fordham nonetheless had spent a reasonable number of hours on the case in light of the continuance and the subsequent need to reprepare, as well as the "very ingenious" breathalyzer suppression argument, and the Clarks' insistence on trial. In addition, the witness testified that, although the field sobriety test, breathalyzer tests, and the presence of a half-empty liquor bottle in the car placed Fordham at a serious disadvantage in being able to prevail on the OUI charge, those circumstances were not unusual and in fact agreed that they were "[n]ormal circumstances."

The fourth expert witness, called by Fordham, testified that she believed the case was "extremely tough" and that the breathalyzer suppression theory was novel. She testified that, although the time and labor consumed on the case was more than usual in defending an OUI charge, the hours were not excessive. They were not excessive, she explained, because the case was particularly difficult due to the "stakes [and] the evidence." She conceded, however, that legal issues in defending OUI charges are "pretty standard" and that the issues presented in this case were not unusual. . . .

In considering whether a fee is "clearly excessive" within the meaning of S.J.C. Rule 3:07, DR 2-106(B), the first factor to be considered pursuant to that rule is "the novelty and difficulty of the questions involved, and the skill requisite to perform the legal service properly." DR 2-106(B)(1). That standard is similar to the familiar standard of reasonableness traditionally applied in civil fee disputes. . . . Based on the testimony of the four experts, the number of hours devoted to Timothy's OUI case by Fordham and his associates was substantially in excess of the hours that a prudent experienced lawyer would have spent. According to the evidence, the number of hours spent was several times the amount of time any of the witnesses had ever spent on a similar case. We are not unmindful of the novel and successful motion to suppress the breathalyzer test results, but that effort cannot justify a $50,000 fee in a type of case in which the usual fee is less than one-third of that amount.

The board determined that "[b]ecause [Fordham] had never tried an OUI case or appeared in the district court, [Fordham] spent over 200 hours preparing the case, in part to educate himself in the relevant substantive law and court procedures." Fordham's inexperience in criminal defense work and OUI cases in particular cannot justify the extraordinarily high fee. It cannot be that an inexperienced lawyer is entitled to charge three or four times as much as an experienced lawyer for the same service. A client "should not be expected to pay for the education of a lawyer when he spends excessive amounts of time on tasks which, with reasonable experience, become matters of routine." [Citation omitted.] "While the licensing of a lawyer is evidence that he has met the standards then prevailing for admission to the bar, a lawyer generally should not accept employment in any area of the law in which he is not qualified. However, he may accept such employment if in good faith he expects to become qualified through study and investigation, as long as such preparation would not result in unreasonable delay or expense to his client." [Citing EC 6-3.] Although the ethical considerations set forth in the ABA Code of Professional Responsibility and Canons of Judicial Ethics are not binding, they nonetheless serve as a guiding principle.

DR 2-106(B) provides that the third factor to be considered in ascertaining the reasonableness of a fee is its comparability to "[t]he fee customarily charged in the locality for similar legal services." The hearing committee made no finding as to the comparability of Fordham's fee with the fees customarily charged in the locality for similar services. However, one of bar counsel's expert witnesses testified that he had never heard of a fee in excess of $15,000 to defend a first OUI charge, and the customary flat fee in an OUI case, including trial, "runs from $1,000 to $7,500." Bar counsel's other expert testified that he had never heard of a fee in excess of $10,000 for a bench trial. In his view, the customary charge for a case similar to Timothy's would vary between $1,500 and $5,000. One of Fordham's experts testified that she considered a $40,000 or $50,000 fee for defending an OUI charge "unusual and certainly higher by far than any I've ever seen before." The witness had never charged a fee of more than $3,500 for representing a client at a bench trial to defend a first offense OUI charge. She further testified that she believed an "average OUI in the bench session is two thousand [dollars] and sometimes less." . . .

Although finding that Fordham's fee was "much higher than the fee charged by many attorneys with more experience litigating driving under the influence cases," the hearing committee nevertheless determined that the fee charged by Fordham was not clearly excessive because Clark "went into the relationship with Fordham with open eyes," Fordham's fee fell within a "safe harbor," and Clark acquiesced in Fordham's fee by not strenuously objecting to his bills. The board accepted the hearing committee's analysis apart from the committee's reliance on the "safe harbor" rule.

The finding that Clark had entered into the fee agreement "with open eyes" was based on the finding that Clark hired Fordham after being fully apprised that he lacked any type of experience in defending an OUI charge and after interviewing other lawyers who were experts in defending OUI charges. Furthermore, the hearing committee and the board relied on testimony which revealed that the fee arrangement had been fully disclosed to Clark including the fact that Fordham "would have to become familiar with the law in that area." It is also significant, however, that the hearing committee found that "[d]espite Fordham's disclaimers concerning his experience, Clark did not appear to have understood in any real sense the implications of choosing Fordham to represent Timothy. Fordham did not give Clark any estimate of the total expected fee or the number of $200 hours that would be required." The express finding of the hearing committee that Clark "did not appear to have understood in any real sense the implications of choosing Fordham to represent Timothy" directly militates against the finding that Clark entered into the agreement "with open eyes."

That brings us to the hearing committee's finding that Fordham's fee fell within a "safe harbor." The hearing committee reasoned that as long as an agreement existed between a client and an attorney to bill a reasonable rate multiplied by the number of hours actually worked, the attorney's fee was within a "safe harbor" and thus protected from a challenge that the fee was clearly excessive. The board, however, in reviewing the hearing committee's decision, correctly rejected the notion "that a lawyer may always escape discipline with billings based on accurate time charges for work honestly performed."

The "safe harbor" formula would not be an appropriate rationale in this case because the amount of time Fordham spent to educate himself and represent

Timothy was clearly excessive despite his good faith and diligence. Disciplinary Rule 2-106(B)'s mandate that "[a] fee is clearly excessive when, after a review of the facts, a lawyer of ordinary prudence, experienced in the area of the law involved, would be left with a definite and firm conviction that the fee is substantially in excess of a reasonable fee," creates explicitly an objective standard by which attorneys' fees are to be judged. We are not persuaded by Fordham's argument that "unless it can be shown that the 'excessive' work for which the attorney has charged goes beyond mere matters of professional judgment and can be proven, either directly or by reasonable inference, to have involved dishonesty, bad faith or overreaching of the client, no case for discipline has been established." Disciplinary Rule 2-106 plainly does not require an inquiry into whether the clearly excessive fee was charged to the client under fraudulent circumstances, and we shall not write such a meaning into the disciplinary rule.

Finally, bar counsel challenges the hearing committee's finding that "if Clark objected to the numbers of hours being spent by Fordham, he could have spoken up with some force when he began receiving bills." Bar counsel notes, and we agree, that "[t]he test as stated in the DR 2-106(A) is whether the fee 'charged' is clearly excessive, not whether the fee is accepted as valid or acquiesced in by the client." Therefore, we conclude that the hearing committee and the board erred in not concluding that Fordham's fee was clearly excessive. . . .

[Fordham argued that imposition of discipline would deny him due process of law because "there is a dearth of case law in the commonwealth meting out discipline for an attorney's billing of a clearly excessive fee." The Court rejected this claim of lack of adequate notice. "The fact that this court has not previously had occasion to discipline an attorney in the circumstances of this case does not suggest that the imposition of discipline in this case offends due process."]

In charging a clearly excessive fee, Fordham departed substantially from the obligation of professional responsibility that he owed to his client. The ABA Model Standards for Imposing Lawyer Sanctions §7.3 (1992) endorses a public reprimand as the appropriate sanction for charging a clearly excessive fee. We deem such a sanction appropriate in this case. Accordingly, a judgment is to be entered in the county court imposing a public censure . . . .

In constant dollars, Moses Lasky earned a lot more per hour than Fordham. Fordham reached his agreement in 1989. Lasky was hired in 1975. In 1989 dollars, Lasky's fee would equal $2.3 million. Assuming Lasky and his firm spent as many as 150 hours on the certiorari petition (a generous assumption*), his hourly fee would be $15,333 in 1989 dollars. (In 2008 dollars, it would be about $26,000 hourly.) The client of each attorney knew the score. Fordham's client received monthly bills showing the accumulating fee. Yet Brobeck wins the civil dispute and Fordham loses the discipline case. How can that be? If the *Fordham* court had applied the *Brobeck* standard, would Fordham have won? It would seem so. Or did the results turn on the relative sophistication of the

---

* By comparison, the agreement required Telex to pay only $15,000 more for briefing and oral argument if certiorari were granted. But those tasks demand many multiples of the time required to write a petition for certiorari.

clients? Would Fordham have been exonerated had he explained that his fee could reach as high as $50,000? Compare King v. Fox, 851 N.E.2d 1184 (N.Y. 2006) ("Where a fully informed client with equal bargaining power knowingly and voluntarily affirms an existing fee arrangement that might otherwise be considered voidable as unconscionable, ratification can occur so long as the client has both a full understanding of the facts that made the agreement voidable and knowledge of his or her rights as a client"). Should it make a difference that Lasky was la crème de la crème for antitrust while Fordham was just a nice guy? Should it make a difference that Lasky's fee was partly contingent while Fordham's was not? Maybe. But Lasky did get a fixed $25,000 up front, win or lose. If again we assume the petition required 150 hours, that's $383 hourly in noncontingent 1989 dollars ($640 in 2008 dollars).

The hearing committee and the board refused discipline because the client entered the arrangement "with open eyes." The hearing committee said that Fordham enjoyed a "safe harbor" when he proceeded to do exactly what he told his client he would do. That's a market approach, isn't it? A willing buyer and a willing seller. No problem had the product been soybean oil. Then, no court would refuse to enforce the contract on the ground that the buyer had not "understood [it] in any real sense" or was not given an "estimate" of total cost. But apparently a contract that will be enforced in a commercial context may still be unethical when it is between lawyer and client. If we are looking for a guidepost in *Fordham*, it might be this: If a fee is likely to be completely out of line with what competing lawyers generally charge for the same service, then even if you think it's justified because of unusual factors (your special skill, the client's comfort level, complete disclosure), you had better go out of your way to explain everything in great detail, in writing, including worst-case scenarios, and insist that the client get independent counsel to advise on the fee. Even then, you can't be sure.

Imagine a replay of *Fordham*. Six months after the decision, a lawyer in exactly the same position as Mr. Fordham is approached by a client who wants exactly the same service. The lawyer makes complete disclosure. The client still wants to hire the lawyer. But now the lawyer has to factor in the risk of discipline and loss of fee. Either the lawyer takes the case and runs these risks, or she works for much less, or she doesn't take the case at all. The client protests that "I want to pay you whatever it will cost even if it's a lot more than I'd have to pay any other lawyer. I want you." To which the lawyer may respond: "It will take me 5X hours to do this job. A specialist will take X hours. Hours are all I have to sell. I can sell them to others for my current rate, but the state won't let me charge you my current rate for 5X hours. I'm not willing to eat the time."

Can you imagine a court saying to counsel for a large corporate client what the court said to Fordham? To counsel for the billionaire parents of a child charged with DUI? So what we may have here for people like Fordham's client is either excessive state paternalism or heightened consumer protection, or maybe both, depending on how you feel about state interference with private choices by consenting and informed adults.

For further discussion about legal fees in criminal cases, including an analysis of *Fordham*, see Gabriel Chin & Scott Wells, Can a Reasonable Doubt Have an Unreasonable Price? Limitations on Attorneys' Fees in Criminal Cases, 41 B.C. L. Rev. 1 (1999).

Courts May Reduce or Deny Unethical Fees

Discipline is not the only risk faced by lawyers who charge excessive or otherwise unethical fees. Courts may order a reduction of the fee or deny a fee altogether. In Kaplan v. Pavalon & Gifford, 12 F.3d 87 (7th Cir. 1993), a lawyer who failed to comply with the Illinois rule requiring a written agreement when unaffiliated lawyers share fees (see page 208) was denied any fee. In United States v. Strawser, 800 F.2d 704 (7th Cir. 1986), a trial lawyer whose former client was represented by appointed counsel on appeal was ordered to return more than half of his $47,500 trial fee to the U.S. Treasury, which was paying the appointed counsel. The excess was labeled "exorbitant and unreasonable." And in White v. McBride, 937 S.W.2d 796 (Tenn. 1996), the court refused to award a lawyer any fee (denying quantum meruit) after concluding that a one-third contingent fee on what was nearly a sure thing was unconscionable.

> A violation of DR 2-106 is an ethical transgression of a most flagrant sort as it goes directly to the heart of the fiduciary relationship that exists between attorney and client. To permit an attorney to fall back on the theory of quantum meruit when he unsuccessfully fails to collect a clearly excessive fee does absolutely nothing to promote ethical behavior. On the contrary, this interpretation would encourage attorneys to enter exorbitant fee contracts, secure that the safety net of quantum meruit is there in case of a subsequent fall.

When the fee agreement is reached or modified after the attorney-client relationship is formed, courts are especially strict in reviewing it for fairness. A lawyer for an estate who switched from an hourly to a contingent fee after he learned that the estate would recover substantial assets was suspended for six months. The renegotiated fee agreement violated Rule 1.8(a). Matter of Hefron, 771 N.E.2d 1157 (Ind. 2002). For an especially disturbing example of a postretainer fee agreement — signed while the client was in a hurry to catch a plane — see Mar Oil, S.A. v. Morrissey, 982 F.2d 830 (2d Cir. 1993) (lawyer "buried" critical fee information in papers he asked client to sign). See also Johnson v. Gudmundsson, 35 F.3d 1104 (7th Cir. 1994) (the presumption of undue influence exists when an attorney enters a transaction with a current client, but is not present before formation of the professional relationship or after it is dissolved); Spilker v. Hankin, 188 F.2d 35 (D.C. Cir. 1951). A fee agreement reached during the professional relationship can be analogized to any financial arrangement between lawyer and client and subject to Rule 1.8(a). After retainer, the client is presumed to be less free to go elsewhere, and the attorney is assumed to be in a significantly superior bargaining position. The client may have begun to rely on and confide in the attorney, especially in personal legal matters, with the result that the client is not as independent as he or she may have been before retainer. See also page 224.

Should a Lawyer be Required to Put Fee Agreements in Writing?

The January 1980 draft of the Model Rules proposed:

The basis or rate of a lawyer's fee shall be put in writing before the lawyer has rendered substantial services in the matter, except when (1) [a]n agreement as to the fees is implied by the fact that the lawyer's services are of the same general kind as previously rendered to and paid for by the client; or (2) [t]he services are rendered in an emergency where a writing is impracticable.

As finally adopted, Rule 1.5(b) simply says that the fee "shall be communicated to the client, preferably in writing, before or within a reasonable time after commencing the representation." The Ethics 2000 Commission said lawyers should be required to have a written fee agreement with some exceptions. The ABA rejected the idea. A contingent fee, however, "shall be in a writing." Rule 1.5(c). Do you think the change from the January 1980 draft to the Model Rules as finally adopted was salutary? How does it affect your answer to know that fees are often a basis for client complaints or bitterness? Why would a profession — which, if you recall, is supposed to put service and the public interest above the quest for wealth (see page 15) — refuse to require written fee agreements along the lines contemplated by the January 1980 draft of the Model Rules? Can you defend this omission? The New Jersey, Pennsylvania, and Washington, D.C., rules retain the draft's position where the lawyer has not regularly represented the client. See also Cal. Bus. & Prof. Code §6148 (writing generally required) and N.Y. Rule of Ct. part 1215 (same).

Inflating Bills

Donald Hess had a difficult client. He was a good client in one sense: He produced a lot of work. But he paid his bills very late. What's more, he insisted on a discount. Hess's firm orally agreed to give him a 15 percent discount, but only if he paid his bills on time. But the client continued to pay late. So, employing a kind of self-help and without telling the client, Hess began "inflating the bills to offset the discount for prompt payment." This went on for more than two years and involved hundreds of matters. Hess eventually told the client what he had done. The client was not sympathetic. The firm repaid the client more than $470,000. Hess was suspended for three years. Attorney Grievance Commission of Maryland v. Hess, 722 A.2d 905 (Md. 1999) (court cited other cases of inflated bills "where there was no offsetting purported discount" and where the lawyers were disbarred). See also Matter of Glesner, 606 N.W.2d 173 (Wis. 2000) (60-day suspension of lawyer who added false charges to two bills); Matter of Zaleon, 504 S.E.2d 702 (Ga. 1998) (six-month suspension for lawyer who charged clients disbursements in amounts more than actually expended). See also page 780 for other examples of sometimes prominent lawyers who faced severe discipline for defrauding clients or their own law firms.

Nonrefundable Fees and Liquidated Damage Clauses in Retainer Agreements

What do lawyers sell? Various services, of course, but what is the common denominator? Contingent fee lawyers sell results. Others sell time. When a retainer agreement provides for hourly rates but includes a provision for more in the event of a particular good outcome, the lawyer is selling both time and results. The value of a lawyer's time is determined by many factors, including those listed in Rule 1.5(a). Apart from time and results, do lawyers sell anything else? May lawyers get paid even when they spend no time on a matter and produce no results? Paid for doing nothing? That depends, doesn't it, on whether a lawyer can offer something of value even when she does nothing.

"Meet Sara Bennet"

Sara Bennet is an antitrust expert in a 700-lawyer firm. A major American corporation, let's call it Yooha, is negotiating to acquire iText, which makes PDAs and other fancy gadgets. The deal may or may not go through; if it does, regulators or competitors may or may not challenge it under antitrust laws. None of this will happen, if it happens at all, for three or four months. The company wants Sara to be available to advise it and possibly represent it if and when needed. Sara's hourly fee is $800, but apart from an initial meeting and review of some documents, which will take about five hours, there is nothing for Sara to do at the moment and there may never be anything for her to do.

Sara is not willing to accept the work under these circumstances. The way she sees it, by signing on she is selling something worth more than $4,000. First, she is promising Yooha availability on a moment's notice regardless of what might otherwise be going on in her personal or professional life. Second, Yooha will be able to use Sara's name and reputation to allay the concerns of iText and the investing public. Regulators or competitors who might be tempted to challenge the acquisition will also know that Sara and her team are prepared to defend it. Third, as we shall see in chapter 5, if Yooha becomes Sara's client, it will conflict all lawyers in her firm from *any* representation adverse to Yooha while it remains a client, which could last for a year or more, and from some matters even thereafter. Last, while Sara would be obligated to be available to Yooha, it would have no obligation to use her. In the event of a challenge, Yooha would be free to choose to hire someone else and tell Sara goodbye. Conflict rules (chapter 6) will forbid Sara's firm from representing anyone who may challenge the deal.

Sara figures that what she'd be giving up is worth more than five hours of billable time. How much more? She thinks about it and has a number in mind, or actually two numbers: for $10,000 she will promise availability. That's all it buys. Beyond that, she wants a guaranteed $24,000 as a minimum (nonrefundable) fee against the first 30 hours of Sara's time. If that is not acceptable to Yooha, or if lawyer ethics rules don't allow her strike this deal even if it is acceptable (and it turns out to be quite acceptable to Yooha, such is Sara's stature and

Yooha's interest), then Sara's position is clear. "Call me if and when you need me, and I'll see at that time if I'm available and interested."

The answer to Sara's dilemma might seem easy to you. It seems easy to me. What business does the state have to forbid this financial agreement? What value would that prohibition possibly protect? But my view was thrown into doubt as a result of dicta (but rather dogmatic dicta) in *Cooperman*, the next principal case. The language of *Cooperman* is vague and confusing (though still dogmatic), and the court's opinion seems unaware of the complexities of the legal marketplace as revealed in Sara Bennet's story or the cases following. *Cooperman* remains good law and has been cited in other cases even as they chipped away at *Cooperman*'s broad language. (And incidentally, far broader than was necessary to sanction Cooperman himself.) At bottom, the interesting issue common to these cases is this: Beyond time or results, what may lawyers ethically sell to a willing and knowledgeable buyer (and for how much)? If the buyer *is* willing and knowledgeable, and assuming full disclosure, does the state have any business interfering?

MATTER OF COOPERMAN
83 N.Y.2d 465, 633 N.E.2d 1069, 611 N.Y.S.2d 465 (1994)

BELLACOSA, JUDGE.

The issue in this appeal is whether the appellant attorney violated the Code of Professional Responsibility by repeatedly using special nonrefundable retainer fee agreements with his clients. Essentially, such arrangements are marked by the payment of a nonrefundable fee for specific services, in advance and irrespective of whether any professional services are actually rendered . . . .

I . . .

The first five charges derive from a written fee agreement to represent an individual in a criminal matter. It states: "My minimum fee for appearing for you in this matter is Fifteen Thousand ($15,000.00) Dollars. This fee is not refundable for any reason whatsoever once I file a notice of appearance on your behalf." One month after the agreement, the lawyer was discharged by the client and refused to refund any portion of the fee. . . .

Charges 6 through 10 refer to a written retainer agreement in connection with a probate proceeding. It states in pertinent part: "For the MINIMAL FEE and NON-REFUNDABLE amount of Five Thousand ($5,000.00) Dollars, I will act as your counsel." The agreement further provided: "This is the minimum fee no matter how much or how little work I do in this investigatory stage . . . and will remain the minimum fee and not refundable even if you decide prior to my completion of the investigation that you wish to discontinue the use of my services for any reason whatsoever." The client discharged Cooperman, who refused to provide the client with an itemized bill of services rendered or refund any portion of the fee, citing the unconditional nonrefundable fee agreement.

The last five charges relate to a fee agreement involving another criminal matter. It provides: "The MINIMUM FEE for Mr. Cooperman's representation . . . to any extent whatsoever is Ten Thousand ($10,000.00) Dollars. . . . The above amount is the MINIMUM FEE and will remain the minimum fee no matter how few court appearances are made. . . . The minimum fee will remain the same even if Mr. Cooperman is discharged." Two days after execution of the fee agreement, the client discharged Cooperman and demanded a refund. As with the other clients, he demurred. . . .

The particular analysis begins with a reflection on the nature of the attorney-client relationship. Sir Francis Bacon observed, "The greatest trust between [people] is the trust of giving counsel" (Bacon, Of Counsel, in The Essays of Francis Bacon, at 181 [1846]). This unique fiduciary reliance, stemming from people hiring attorneys to exercise professional judgment on a client's behalf — "giving counsel" — is imbued with ultimate trust and confidence. . . .

The Code of Professional Responsibility reflects this central ingredient by specifically mandating, without exception, that an attorney "shall not enter into an agreement for, charge, or collect an illegal or excessive fee" (DR 2-106[A]), and upon withdrawal from employment "shall refund promptly any part of a fee paid in advance that has not been earned" (DR 2-110[A][3]). . . .

The unqualified right to terminate the attorney-client relationship at any time has been assiduously protected by the courts. An attorney, however, is not left without recourse for unfair terminations lacking cause. If a client exercises the right to discharge an attorney after some services are performed but prior to the completion of the services for which the fee was agreed upon, the discharged attorney is entitled to recover compensation from the client measured by the fair and reasonable value of the completed services. We have recognized that permitting a discharged attorney "to recover the reasonable value of services rendered in quantum meruit, a principle inherently designed to prevent unjust enrichment, strikes the delicate balance between the need to deter clients from taking undue advantage of attorneys, on the one hand, and the public policy favoring the right of a client to terminate the attorney-client relationship without inhibition on the other."

Correspondingly and by cogent logic and extension of the governing precepts, we hold that the use of a special nonrefundable retainer fee agreement clashes with public policy because it inappropriately compromises the right to sever the fiduciary services relationship with the lawyer. Special nonrefundable retainer fee agreements diminish the core of the fiduciary relationship by substantially altering and economically chilling the client's unbridled prerogative to walk away from the lawyer. To answer that the client can technically still terminate misses the reality of the economic coercion that pervades such matters. If special nonrefundable retainers are allowed to flourish, clients would be relegated to hostage status in an unwanted fiduciary relationship — an utter anomaly. Such circumstances would impose a penalty on a client for daring to invoke a hollow right to discharge. The established prerogative which, by operation of law and policy, is deemed not a breach of contract is thus weakened. Instead of becoming responsible for fair value of actual services rendered, the firing client would lose the entire "nonrefundable" fee, no matter what legal services, if any, were rendered. This would be a shameful, not honorable, professional denouement. Cooperman even acknowledges that the essential purpose of the nonrefundable retainer was to prevent clients from firing the lawyer, a purpose which, as demonstrated, directly contravenes the Code and this State's settled public policy in this regard.

Nevertheless, Cooperman contends that special nonrefundable retainer fee agreements should not be treated as per se violations unless they are pegged to a "clearly excessive" fee. The argument is unavailing because the reasonableness of a particular nonrefundable fee cannot rescue an agreement that impedes the client's absolute right to walk away from the attorney. . . .

Our holding today makes the conduct of trading in special nonrefundable retainer fee agreements subject to appropriate professional discipline. Moreover, we intend no effect or disturbance with respect to other types of appropriate and ethical fee agreements (see Brickman and Cunningham, Nonrefundable Retainers Revisited, 72 N.C. L. Rev. 1, 6 [1993]). Minimum fee arrangements and general retainers that provide for fees, not laden with the nonrefundability impediment irrespective of any services, will continue to be valid and not subject in and of themselves to professional discipline. . . .

A Lawyer's Inventory

So the question of nonrefundable fees is inextricably bound up with the question of what a lawyer may ethically sell. Is Sara Bennet's fee proposal allowed in New York? Perhaps the answer depends on the definitions of "special retainer," "general retainer," and "minimum fee." The court offers a rather casual definition of "special retainer" in the second sentence of its opinion. "Minimum fee" is not defined, but Lester Brickman and Lawrence Cunningham, who are cited in *Cooperman*, later defined it as follows:

> Minimum fee agreements typically provide that a lawyer will work on an hourly or fixed fee basis to complete a particular task. For example, the agreement may provide that, although the task will likely require twenty hours of work, even if it is completed in fewer hours, the fee will still be the twenty hour fee. The agreement may also provide, however, that the fee can be more than the minimum fee if the task requires more hours or effort than contemplated. This kind of minimum fee also raises no inherent ethical objections. In such a case, the client's right to discharge the lawyer prior to completion of the service, with liability only in quantum meruit, is unimpaired.

Nonrefundable Retainers: A Response to Critics of the Absolute Ban, 64 U. Cin. L. Rev. 11 (1995). "General retainer" is not defined either, but the court cited an earlier Brickman and Cunningham article that says:

> [A] general retainer is an agreement between attorney and client in which the client agrees to pay a fixed sum to the attorney in exchange for the attorney's promise to be available to perform, at an agreed price, any legal services (which may be of any kind or of a specified kind) that arise during a specified period. Since the general retainer fee is given in exchange for availability, it is a charge

separate from fees incurred for services actually rendered. In other words, such fees are "earned when paid" because the payment is made for availability.*

Now can you answer Sara Bennet's questions. Perhaps the $10,000 is a "general retainer." But Sara is not offering to be available to perform "any legal services," not even "any" legal services "of a specified kind," but only legal services limited to a particular matter. Other courts define general retainers, sometimes called classic retainers, as money paid for availability alone. See, e.g., Dowling v. Chicago Options Assoc., Inc., 875 N.E.2d 1012 (Ill. 2007) (a classic retainer "is paid to secure the lawyer's availability during a specified period of time or for a specified matter"; it is "earned when paid and immediately becomes property of the lawyer, regardless of whether the lawyer ever actually performs any services for the client"). Barron v. Countryman, 432 F.3d 590 (5th Cir. 2005) (same). The additional $24,000 is a minimum fee. Is it legitimate? Yes, but according to Brickman & Cunningham, Sara must return it (less quantum meruit) if the client later fires her, which it might well do if it concludes her services are not required. In their view, unless Yooha can get the money back, we interfere with its right to change lawyers. What do you think?

We might say—we probably should say—that *Cooperman* and Sara Bennet's questions cry out for different analyses because of the vast discrepancy in the sophistication of the clients and the financial facts. Yet *Cooperman's* relied neither on the lack of sophistication of the client nor on the amount of the fees. The Oklahoma Supreme Court addressed the issue on facts closer to Sara's and showed a considerably keener appreciation of the underlying policies.

MCQUEEN, RAINS, & TRESCH LLP v. CITGO PETROLEUM CORP.
195 P.3d 35 (Okla. 2008)

WATT, J:

[When CITGO moved its corporate office to Houston from Tulsa, three in-house lawyers chose not to move and instead opened a law firm (MRT) in Tulsa. In a series of agreements, CITGO, through its general counsel, negotiated an arrangement under which the firm would handle specified work for CITGO for four years for a fixed annual fee and do other work according to a fee schedule. The agreement provided for liquidated damages in the event that CITGO chose to terminate the firm. CITGO did terminate the firm, which sued CITGO in federal court. The following opinion responds to certified questions from the federal court. CITGO argued that the liquidated damage provision interfered with its absolute right under Rule 1.16(a)(3) to discharge its lawyers. The court's opinion surveyed numerous opinions from other jurisdictions. These citations, but not the

---

* Responding to this article, Professor Steven Lubet concluded that "a blanket proscription" against nonrefundable fees "requires stronger justification than has yet been offered." Steven Lubet, The Rush to Remedies: Some Conceptual Questions About Nonrefundable Retainers, 73 N.C. L. Rev. 271 (1994). Brickman and Cunningham reply to their critics, including Lubet, in the U. Cin. L. Rev. article cited above.

court's characterization of their holdings, are omitted. While the court refers to the "unique facts" of this case ten times, its reasoning has broader application.]

The amended engagement agreement and the amended supplemental engagement agreements form the basis of the firm's federal suit against CITGO, filed on June 1, 2007, alleging that the client breached the three fixed-fee, fixed-term retainer agreements. These agreements contain virtually identical liquidated damages clauses providing:

> CITGO acknowledges that in reliance on this [Agreement], the Firm [MRT] has undertaken and continues to undertake costs and expenses to provide optimal legal representation to CITGO and acknowledges that a premature termination of this [Agreement] would result in losses and damages to the firm that may be impossible to quantify. Consequently, in the event CITGO terminates this [Agreement] prior to the end of the initial term, CITGO will pay the Firm, as liquidated damages, the lesser of all monthly installments for the Initial Term remaining under the contract or 12 months of installments, in lieu of other direct, indirect or consequential damages. Such liquidated damages will be due and payable within 30 days after termination of this [Agreement].

With approximately twenty-one months left in the contractual period or roughly halfway through the term of the contracts, on April 5, 2007, CITGO informed the firm that it was terminating the relationship created by the letter agreements. It is agreed that CITGO prematurely terminated the amended engagement agreement and the supplemental engagement agreements. Nevertheless, the parties dispute whether the termination was excusable. Although CITGO contends that the attorneys were discharged based on their inferior performance, the firm argues that the contracts were breached without cause. In filing the federal lawsuit, the firm did not seek recovery for services performed prior to its discharge. Rather, it claims that CITGO owes it termination payments required by the liquidated damages clauses contained in the various agreements.

Under the liquidated damages clauses, CITGO's premature termination of its attorney-client relationship with the firm requires it to pay up to twelve monthly installments of each fixed fee in lieu of other direct, indirect, or consequential damages. The liquidated damages sought exceed $ 4.6 million . . . .

Courts considering contractual relationships between attorneys and clients similar to the one presented here disagree as to whether the contracts should be enforced. In a majority of jurisdictions, the contracts have been determined to be unenforceable, leaving attorneys to recover damages in quantum meruit rather than under the provisions of the attorney fee contract. These cases generally turn on the fact that a non-refundable retainer compromises the client's absolute right to terminate the unique fiduciary-client relationship. Nevertheless, even in jurisdictions where such contracts are normally struck down as against public policy, an attorney may recover contractual fees if, in entering into such a contract, the attorney has changed positions or incurred expenses.

A significant number of courts uphold contracts containing either non-refundable fee or liquidated damages provisions executed between clients and their attorneys. Non-refundable retainer fees and other non-refundable provisions have been upheld where: the fees set out are reasonable; the contract is negotiated with a sophisticated client and the retainer agreement contains an agreement by the client to compensate the lawyer if the client terminates the

relationship; the contract is in writing with a clear statement of the consequences of the provision; or where the attorney, in entering the contract, has
changed positions or incurred expenses to meet the needs of the client. At least
one court has determined that non-refundable contractual provisions should be
enforced if the client's desire to have a particular attorney as a representative
necessitates an immediate commitment at the risk to the attorney of forgoing or
losing other potential business. Another acknowledges that fees paid to a lawyer
that the client has agreed are not refundable are not prohibited per se. . . .

The unique facts presented place the contracts at issue here squarely within the
ambit of jurisprudence from other states in which such non-refundable fee agreements have been found enforceable. Here, the client is a large corporation sophisticated both in the commercial and the legal environment and was represented by
its Vice President of Legal Affairs and General Counsel in contract negotiations.
There are no allegations that the terms of the liquidated damages provisions are
ambiguous. At a minimum, the firm altered its position to the extent that it
equipped an office and provided legal counsel in an out-of-state location. Further,
the liquidated damages provisions contain CITGO's express acknowledgment
that the firm further changed its position by undertaking costs and expenses to
meet the demands of the contractual relationship. Therefore, under the unique
facts presented, we determine that the contract at issue is not per se unenforceable under either our jurisprudence or the Rules of Professional Conduct.

[The court held that the liquidated damage clause should be upheld if it was
not a penalty. It would "not be considered a penalty if: 1) the injury caused by
the breach is difficult or impossible to estimate accurately; 2) the parties intend
to provide for damages rather than a penalty; and 3) the sum stipulated is a
reasonable pre-breach estimate of the probable loss."]

Ryan v. Butera Beausang Cohen & Brennan, 193 F.3d 210 (3d Cir. 1999),
upheld a nonrefundable $1 million fee that the plaintiff paid to the defendant
law firm to persuade it to participate in a nationwide network of attorneys to
represent the plaintiff in asbestos defense litigation. In addition to the $1 mil-
lion retainer, which was labeled "nonrefundable," the fee agreement between
the plaintiff and the law firm contemplated additional fixed-fee quarterly payments for organizational and legal services. Raymark (through its bankruptcy
trustee, Ryan) sued for repayment of the retainer after it terminated the relationship in only ten weeks. The district court granted summary judgment to the
law firm, and the Third Circuit affirmed. In words that would comfort Sara
Bennet, the trial court (as summarized on appeal)

held that instead of merely calculating the amount that Beausang had earned
on an hourly basis, it could consider benefits beyond those paid for "legal
services." Finding that the legal and organizational services were to be covered
by other payments, the court determined that the $1 million was a "carrot" or
"financial incentive" used to attract Beausang and was reasonable. The court
reasoned that Raymark had spent $1 million to buy the "opportunity" to use
Beausang's services at capped costs — analogizing this to an options contract,
where the option is worth something, though less than the fully-realized

opportunity. Thus, the court concluded that Beausang had earned the $1 million, despite working for only ten weeks, because Raymark paid the $1 million for access to Beausang's services on terms favorable to Raymark.

Sara Bennet would also be pleased with Matter of Sather, 3 P.3d 403 (Colo. 2000). The court wrote:

> Funds given by clients to attorneys as advance fees or retainers benefit attorneys and clients. Some forms of advance fees or retainers appropriately compensate an attorney when the fee is paid because the attorney makes commitments to the client that benefit the client immediately. Such an arrangement is termed a "general retainer" or "engagement retainer," and these retainers typically compensate an attorney for agreeing to take a case, which requires the attorney to commit his time to the client's case and causes the attorney to forego other potential employment opportunities as a result of time commitments or conflicts. Although an attorney usually earns an engagement retainer by agreeing to take the client's case, an attorney can also earn a fee charged as an engagement retainer by placing the client's work at the top of the attorney's priority list. Or the client may pay an engagement retainer merely to prevent the attorney from being available to represent an opposing party. In all of these instances, the attorney is providing some benefit to the client in exchange for the engagement retainer fee.

But what if Sara is a New York lawyer? Can she achieve her goals without risking her reputation? Or is that not possible in New York?*

C. CONTINGENT FEES

In a contingent fee agreement, a lawyer's fee depends on the occurrence or nonoccurrence of an event. Usually, the event is recovery of a sum of money, and the fee is a percentage of the recovery. This fee is most prevalent in personal injury or property damage actions, whether based in negligence or strict liability. But there are other possibilities. For example, a lawyer may agree that she will be entitled to a fee only if she achieves a particular result for a client (for example, a mortgage commitment). Or a lawyer may agree to a percentage of the amount of money he *saves* the client. Such "reverse" contingent fees have been approved. See ABA Opinion 93-373. Contingent fees are conceptually possible in all representations that have a definable objective, but they are generally forbidden in criminal and matrimonial cases (see page 171).

One of the most unusual (and most rewarding) contingent fees in U.S. history was the 1932 agreement between Greenbaum, Wolff & Ernst, a now defunct New York firm specializing in publishing and the First Amendment, and Random House, then a new publisher. Random House retained the firm to protect it from an obscenity prosecution after it secured the rights to publish James Joyce's *Ulysses* in the United States. A dozen years earlier, Margaret Anderson and Jane

---

* The new New York Rules forbid "nonrefundable" fees while allowing a "minimum fee," a term they do not define, and say nothing about special and general retainers.

Heap were convicted in New York state court of obscenity for including part of one chapter of *Ulysses* (then a work in progress) in The Little Review, their small circulation literary magazine. Random House could not afford Greenbaum's hourly rates (or, more accurately, the rates of its prominent partner Morris Ernst). So Ernst's fee included a royalty of 5 percent of the price of the trade edition of the book, 2 percent of any reprint edition, and 5 percent from book club sales, apparently for the duration of the copyright (it is still in copyright), although some sources say that it was only for the life of Ernst, who died in 1976. Either way, the deal would net a lot of money. Ernst won, of course, with a brilliant strategy. See generally Stephen Gillers, A Tendency to Deprave and Corrupt: The Transformation of American Obscenity Law from *Hicklin* to *Ulysses II,* 85 Wash. U. L.Rev. 215 (2007).

From the lawyer's perspective, the contingent fee will sometimes enable her to have a client when otherwise she would not, either because the client cannot afford a traditional fee or because the client is unwilling to invest money in his claim. Another advantage is the prospect of substantially greater compensation for the lawyer than she would earn with an hourly rate. Whether a contingent fee is more favorable to the lawyer than an hourly fee ordinarily depends on five factors. Try to list them before reading on.

Take your time.

All right. The factors are: the likelihood of the occurrence of the contingency, when it is likely to occur, the probable size of the recovery, the amount of work required, and the size of the lawyer's percentage. The first four factors require predictions, which in turn should influence the size of the lawyer's share, the fifth factor. (For example, the less likely the contingency is to occur, the greater the percentage the lawyer will want because of the greater risk of nonrecovery.) Lawyers are usually better able than clients to make these predictions. This capability puts clients at a disadvantage when negotiating the final factor (the amount of the percentage) and in deciding whether to opt for a contingent fee at all (assuming they can pay a regular fee).

Usually, the most important factor in evaluating a contingent fee is the likelihood that the contingency will occur. Usually, lawyers will not agree to a contingent fee unless there is a high probability of occurrence. If the contingency does not occur, the lawyer does not get paid (unless he has a "hybrid" fee as in *Telex*), although the client may be responsible for the lawyer's out-of-pocket costs. To compensate for this risk, a lawyer may be entitled to a contingent fee that would be unconscionably high if it were a guaranteed fee. See In re Brown & Williamson, 777 N.Y.S.2d 82 (1st Dep't 2004) (tobacco liability class action; reportedly an average of $13,000 hourly per lawyer regardless of experience); McKenzie Constr. v. Maynard, 823 F.2d 43 (3d Cir. 1987) (contingent fee that yields $790 an hour [about $1,430 in 2008 dollars] is not unreasonable, although 13 times the lawyer's usual hourly rate, given the favorable result).

From a client's perspective, a contingent fee gives a lawyer incentive. It is the most common example of "value billing" (see page 148). From the perspective of critics of contingent fees, however, the lawyer's financial interest in the client's recovery warps the lawyer's judgment and leads to frivolous litigation. See page 172. The rules recognize the conflict danger in a backhanded way. Rule 1.8(i) makes the contingent fee an exception to a general prohibition against a lawyer acquiring an interest in the client's claim.

Courts have been willing to exert greater control over contingent fee agreements, at least when they are used in personal injury cases, than over ordinary fee agreements. This can be explained by a series of factors: the perception that personal injury plaintiffs are relatively unsophisticated in the use of lawyers; historical abuses of contingency fees; the fact that a contingency agreement can fortuitously yield a lawyer a windfall; the unequal bargaining positions of attorney and client as a result of the lawyer's greater predictive ability described above; and, finally, the danger of conflicts of interest between lawyer and client, as suggested in the example below. See, Green v. Nevers, supra; King v. Fox, supra. Where one law firm represented clients before the Tax Court for a percentage of the difference between the amount the IRS had demanded and the amount the client actually paid, the court eventually refused to enforce a fee claim in excess of $4.8 million. The court held that it had the power to review the reasonableness of the contingent fee agreement as of the time it was made and also as of the time the eventual fee was "quantified" following the occurrence of the contingency. The fee here failed on both counts, but the court made it clear that a contingent percent that is reasonable when agreed to can turn out to be unreasonable when the results are in. Brown & Sturm v. Frederick Road Ltd. Partnership, 768 A.2d 62 (Md. App. 2001). See also Lawrence v. Miller, 2008 Westlaw 5055393 (N.Y. 2008) (same). IRS rules separately limit the use of contingent fees. 31 C.F.R. §10.

Contingent Fees and Conflicts of Interest

Can a lawyer's contingent fee agreement lead to a conflict of interest between what is good for the lawyer and what is good for the client? If so, what should we do about it? Remember that the client will be looking for advice to the very lawyer who may have the conflicting interest.

Assume Lawyer (L) estimates that a personal injury case is worth $600,000 to $750,000 in damages if the jury finds that the defendant was at fault. Assume a 25 percent chance that the jury will find the defendant blameless. Assume a contingent fee of one-third.

Scenario A: With 100 hours of work, L gets an offer of $330,000, yielding L a contingent fee of $110,000 or $1,100 hourly. The client would get $220,000.

Scenario B: If L puts in another 100 hours of work, experience tells him he could increase the offer to $420,000 closer to trial, yielding an hourly rate of $700 (a $140,000 fee divided by 200 hours). The client would get $280,000 instead of $220,000. That's much worse for L on an hourly basis, but better for the client (putting aside the longer wait).

Scenario C: To go to trial would increase the time requirement to a total of 400 hours (because trials are labor intensive) with a prospect of a fee of up to $250,000 if the client wins the $750,000 maximum, yielding an hourly rate of $625 ($250,000 / 400 hours). The client would get $500,000. If the client wins $600,000, the lawyer's hourly rate is $500. But there's a 25 percent chance the client will lose and the lawyer then gets nothing.

The Lesson: So while going to trial carries a risk of loss for both, the upside advantage to the client is significantly greater than for the lawyer. Or to put it another way, it will often be better for the lawyer, but not the client, to accept early offers and go on to the next matter because doing so maximizes hourly compensation without extra risk of losing the trial. True, these numbers "prove" the point only because I got to pick the numbers. It won't always play out this way. Perhaps most times it won't. But often it will, and when it does, you can see the dramatic fall off in the lawyer's rate, giving him incentive to encourage an early low settlement, even when that might not be in the client's interest.

Prohibitions on Contingent Fees in Criminal and Matrimonial Cases

The January 1980 draft of the Model Rules excluded contingent fees where they are "prohibited by law or the Rules of Professional Conduct." As adopted, the Model Rules forbid a contingent fee in a criminal case and impose substantial limits on contingent fees "in a domestic relations matter." Rule 1.5(d). Maryland also singles out "custody matters," and Washington adds "annulments." In some jurisdictions, if a lawyer charges an illegal contingent fee, she will be denied even quantum meruit compensation. In re Malec, 562 N.E.2d 1010 (Ill. App. 1990).

Why are contingent fees banned in matrimonial matters? Here are some reasons often advanced. (1) The state has an interest in seeing as much money stay with the family as possible (especially for nonworking spouses and children). (2) Since the law empowers the judge to order a wealthier spouse to pay the other spouse's counsel fees, the less wealthy spouse does not need a contingent fee to be able to attract a lawyer. (3) A contingent fee gives the lawyer a stake in the outcome that might lead to a recommendation of a course of action not in the client's best interests. For example, a fee contingent on divorce might prevent the lawyer from encouraging reconciliation. A fee that is a percentage of alimony might cause the lawyer to litigate a matter — with attendant acrimony — when settlement ought to be urged. Do these reasons persuade you? Is at least part of it a perception of unseemliness? Is that a valid reason to interfere with freedom of contract?

The rules of some jurisdictions, such as Washington, D.C., and California, have no prohibition on contingent fees in matrimonial matters. Courts, furthermore, sometimes allow a contingency factor to creep into matrimonial fee agreements. For example, Alexander v. Inman, 974 S.W.2d 689 (Tenn. 1998), upheld an agreement that provided for a fee of a "reasonable amount taking into consideration the time and labor required, the novelty and difficulty of the questions involved, the skill required to perform the services properly, the amount involved and results obtained. . . ." The agreement said that the law firm's fee could not exceed 15 percent of alimony and property recovered after trial (10 percent if after settlement), nor be less than $10,000 or the firm's time charges. The court collected various cases and concluded that the fee was not contingent within the meaning of the prohibition. "Payment itself is certain; only the exact amount of payment is uncertain. The percentage of the total award merely marks the upward limit for the fee to be charged, and it is not the sole basis for the fee." Do you agree that by using a percentage only as a ceiling on the final fee, which is computed hourly but includes a factor for "results obtained," the fee agreement honors the policies that underlie the rule? Or might the firm still be encouraged to act in a way that undermines those policies?

The reasons for prohibiting contingent fees in criminal cases are not hard to understand. A fee contingent on acquittal could, for example, prompt a lawyer to encourage the client to reject a favorable plea bargain and go to trial in order to give the lawyer a chance to secure the acquittal. It is also sometimes said that a contingent interest in a particular disposition of a criminal case could lead the lawyer to behave improperly (for example, to introduce false evidence) in order to achieve that disposition. But that argument proves too much, doesn't it? It could be made in non-criminal cases, too.

Every once in a while a convicted person will seek to have his conviction overturned on the ground that his lawyer had been working for a contingent fee. These efforts usually fail. The fact that contingent fees are banned in criminal matters because of the risk of disloyalty does not mean counsel actually misbehaved. Potential conflicts are usually not enough to prompt a reversal. See Winkler v. Keane, 7 F.3d 304 (2d Cir. 1993), People v. Winkler, 523 N.E.2d 485 (N.Y. 1988). See also the discussion of conflicts in criminal representation at page 241.

Should Contingent Fees be Outlawed or Further Regulated?

Contingent fees are quite controversial. For some reason (what might it be?), the division seems to fall along a left/right axis. Conservatives argue that the fees lead to frivolous litigation, which one expects liberals to oppose as well. Liberals argue that they give ordinary people access to the courts for legitimate claims, which one would also expect conservatives to support (the rule of law and all that). So what's this debate about?

In The Litigation Explosion (1991), Walter Olson (conservative) compares lawyers paid by contingent fee to "impresarios of the boxing arena, whose productions, in pain and ringside drama, have so much in common with those of the courtroom." He adds: "Entrepreneurs of litigation are middlemen not of commerce but of combat. They search out and sedulously promote chances for their fellow citizens to fight." Unlike boxers, however, the contestants in the contingency fee lawsuit don't enter "the ring of their own free will." Rather, plaintiffs are enticed or coerced into initiating lawsuits by the manipulation of unscrupulous lawyers who cannot resist the "countless temptations to exploit opponents and clients" to reap the benefits of a contingent fee.

Contingent fees are considered unethical in many professions, Olson writes. "[P]rofessional sports forbids athletes to bet on their games. . . . Likewise doctors have never been allowed to charge contingency fees — in effect to place bets with their patients on the success of their therapies. . . . Contingency fees tend to be disfavored in professions to whom the interests of others are helplessly entrusted, where misconduct is hard to monitor."

The client should be "master of his suit," Olson contends, providing the "impetus not only for the initial filing but for any major escalation of the battle."

Contingent fees, however, provide a "powerful incentive" for lawyers to go for the biggest award possible, even if this is not really what the client may want. (But earlier we saw three scenarios in which the lawyer might be eager to cash out early, even though that might not be in the client's interest.) Contingent fees encourage dishonesty, Olsen writes:

> The tradition of the English common law, the French and German civil law, and the Roman law all agree that it is unethical for lawyers to accept contingency fees. . . . [The British] explained that lawyers would no longer make their cases "with scrupulous fairness and integrity" [if contingency fees were allowed]. . . . America is the only major country that denies to the winner of a lawsuit the right to collect legal fees from the loser. In other countries, the promise of a fee recoupment from the opponent gives lawyers good reason to take on a solidly meritorious case for even a poor client.

What do you make of the fact that Olson segues from his opposition to contingent fees to his support of a "loser pays" rule? Under that rule, the winner of a litigation gets reasonable counsel fees from the loser. Olson and others cite England as a model because it has a "loser pays" rule and generally forbids contingent fees. Imagine a person seriously burned when an apparent defect in an electric tool causes it to overheat. Under Olson's proposals, the lawyer the person consults would have to charge her a fixed or hourly rate, win or lose, and tell her that she will have to pay the manufacturer's lawyer if she loses (but that it would have to pay her lawyer if she wins). Asked to estimate the chances of victory or settlement, the lawyer rightly says there can be no guarantees, but he thinks it's a good case and replies "70 percent, maybe better." How will these facts affect the client's decision to go to court? If she does proceed, how will they affect settlement negotiations? The client might be able to afford an hourly fee, but if she loses, she'll owe two fees. Her lawyer might warn her that the manufacturer will hire high-priced talent.

The prospect of prohibiting contingent fees is nil. But some voices have spoken in favor of limiting contingent fees. Rethinking Contingent Fees (Manhattan Inst. 1994), authored by law professors Lester Brickman and Jeffrey O'Connell and by Michael Horowitz, then of the Hudson Institute, offers a creative alternative. It deserves serious attention.

Consider that we permit contingent fees to be larger than what would constitute a reasonable hourly fee because if the contingency does not occur, the lawyer will go unpaid. But most personal injury cases — certainly most that lawyers are willing to accept — have some value. The defendant will likely pay something. Why should the plaintiff's lawyer get a full contingent fee for "recovering" this amount? She need not do anything (or hardly anything) to secure it. We just have to figure out what that sum is.

The following rule is based on a 1996 California voter referendum that failed by less than two percentage points and which was inspired by the Brickman-O'Connell-Horowitz proposal.

> A plaintiff 's lawyer in individual (*i.e.*, non-class) tort cases must make a settlement demand within 60 days of being retained. The defendant may respond with an offer. If it does not, this rule is inapplicable. If the defendant does

make an offer and it is accepted, the contingent fee is limited to 15 percent of the settlement. If the offer is not accepted, the contingent fee for any ultimate recovery, by settlement or trial, is 15 percent of the amount of the rejected offer and the lawyer's usual percentage for any excess.

Here's an example. Green is injured by *XYZ* Corp.'s truck. He hires Smith to represent him. Smith demands $300,000. *XYZ* immediately offers to settle for $100,000. If Green accepts, Smith's fee is limited to $15,000 under the proposal. If Green rejects the offer and Smith later gets Green $250,000 in trial or settlement, Smith's fee is limited to 15 percent of the first $100,000 ($15,000) and her usual contingent rate for the excess ($150,000). So if that rate is one-third, Smith's gross fee would be $65,000 instead of $83,333 (a third of the total). And here's the icing: The difference goes to Green, not *XYZ*.

Proponents of this rule argue that it will encourage early settlement because plaintiffs will have to pay a lower "lawyer tax" on the defendant's early settlement offer. Eighty-five cents of every dollar offered will go to the injured plaintiff, making a deal more likely. Since Smith did not take a significant risk in eliciting the early offer and would not have done much work to get it, she has no fair claim to a one-third contingent fee on this amount.

Trial lawyers vigorously opposed the California proposal. Is that because of greed, or is it unwise policy?* If you view the situation through the eyes of a lawyer engaged in Smith's line of work, self-interest may cause you to reject the proposal. But if we say that rules governing legal fees should be fair to clients, that they don't exist to enrich lawyers, and if we forget for a minute that we are or will soon be lawyers, can we defend giving to Smith (and taking from Green) a third of the money that *XYZ* was willing to pay early on (perhaps even before Green hired Smith)?

Here's another curious fact: In a truly competitive market, we would expect some plaintiffs' lawyers to offer to charge a lower percentage of any early offer *XYZ* makes in order to attract Green's business. After all, that amount is probably the minimum the case is worth. While this sort of competition may happen occasionally, it doesn't happen often. A personal injury plaintiff is likely to discover that, absent unusual facts, all lawyers in a jurisdiction quote the very same percentage. No one will lower the fee to get the business. Why not? Is there some reason to distrust the market for legal services, at least in the world of contingency fees? What's your best argument against the proposal?

---

* Following publication of the Brickman-O'Connell-Horowitz study, a group of lawyers, including the study's authors, asked the ABA to address the propriety of charging a "standard" contingency percentage fee in cases where there was no real risk of nonrecovery. ABA Opinion 94-389 was the response, and it endorsed the status quo. (Surprise!) Professor Brickman's article critiquing the ABA Opinion ("disingenuous" is among the kinder words he has for it) can be found at Lester Brickman, ABA Regulation of Contingency Fees: Money Talks, Ethics Walks, 65 Fordham L. Rev. 247 (1996).

"Petra Bento's Hybrid Fee Agreement"

Our client is Petra Bento, a successful personal injury lawyer, most of whose work is on contingency. Before she takes a case, she evaluates the likelihood of recovery, the amount of work she'll need to do, and the amount she can expect in settlement or at trial. The usual factors. Most of the time, things work out well. A few years ago, though, a client settled for a rather low offer, against her advice, as the client had a right to do. Petra says the case was worth conservatively $250,000, but the client took $54,000 on the eve of trial. Petra walked away with $18,000 for a lot of work. Same thing happened a year later.

Petra's memo seeking our advice says: "What I want to do to protect myself is quote a contingent fee of one-third, but add a condition. If the client settles against my advice for an amount that nets me less than $300 hourly, I get my hourly rate. So let's say in that $250,000 case, I had put in 100 hours to get to trial. My fee would be $30,000 instead of $18,000. My position is that if the client decides to end her case (and my investment along with it) in a fire sale, I ought to have a right to get my hourly. It's like the client changed our deal out from under me.

"As you may know, our state follows a rule that is common in many places. It says that a contingency fee client (like any other) can discharge her lawyer for any reason. If so, the lawyer can seek quantum meruit from the client, meaning the lawyer gets a reasonable hourly rate. Or the lawyer can instead agree to take a percentage of the successor lawyer's contingent fee, like a third of his third. He gets to choose. See Cohen v. Grainger, Tesoriero & Bell, 622 N.E.2d 288 (N.Y. 1993). In effect, I'd be making the same election but under different circumstances."

Let's discuss this at our next firm meeting.

FURTHER READING

Pamela Karlan has questioned the wisdom of a continuing ban on contingent fees in criminal cases. She offers examples of cases "in which certain forms of partially contingent fees might be particularly worthwhile," including white-collar cases with sophisticated clients. Pamela Karlan, Contingent Fees and Criminal Cases, 93 Colum. L. Rev. 595 (1993). Lester Brickman has written critically of the contingent fee regime. See Lester Brickman, Contingent Fees Without Contingencies: *Hamlet* Without the Prince of Denmark?, 37 UCLA L. Rev. 29 (1989). Elihu Inselbuch, Contingent Fees and Tort Reform: A Reassessment and Reality Check, 64 Law & Contemp. Probs. 175 (2001), reviews criticisms of the contingent fee "and offers alternatives . . . on how to address the problems" cited by its critics.

D. MINIMUM FEE SCHEDULES

Canon 12 of the 1908 Canons of Ethics stated that it was "proper" for a lawyer determining his fee "to consider a schedule of minimum fees adopted by a Bar

Association, but no lawyer should permit himself to be controlled thereby or to follow it as his sole guide in determining the amount of his fee." Some disciplinary authorities considered it unprofessional for a lawyer consistently to charge less than the minimum fee schedule. In their view, doing so led to price competition, which was seen as inconsistent with a learned profession. Of course, enforcement of minimum fee schedules through threat of discipline could be viewed less charitably—as a form of price fixing in violation of the antitrust laws. That was the position presented to the Supreme Court in the following case, which dramatically reveals the effect of a fee schedule on the cost of a routine legal service.

GOLDFARB v. VIRGINIA STATE BAR
421 U.S. 773 (1975)

CHIEF JUSTICE BURGER delivered the opinion of the Court. . . .

I

In 1971 petitioners, husband and wife, contracted to buy a home in Fairfax County, Va. The financing agency required them to secure title insurance; this required a title examination, and only a member of the Virginia State Bar could legally perform that service. Petitioners therefore contacted a lawyer who quoted them the precise fee suggested in a minimum-fee schedule published by respondent Fairfax County Bar Association; the lawyer told them that it was his policy to keep his charges in line with the minimum-fee schedule which provided for a fee of 1% of the value of the property involved. Petitioners then tried to find a lawyer who would examine the title for less than the fee fixed by the schedule. They sent letters to 36 other Fairfax County lawyers requesting their fees. Nineteen replied, and none indicated that he would charge less than the rate fixed by the schedule; several stated that they knew of no attorney who would do so. . . .

Because petitioners could not find a lawyer willing to charge a fee lower than the schedule dictated, they had their title examined by the lawyer they had first contacted. They then brought this class action against the State Bar and the County Bar alleging that the operation of the minimum-fee schedule, as applied to fees for legal services relating to residential real estate transactions, constitutes price fixing in violation of §1 of the Sherman Act. Petitioners sought both injunctive relief and damages. . . .

II

Our inquiry can be divided into four steps: did respondents engage in price fixing? If so, are their activities in interstate commerce or do they affect interstate commerce? If so, are the activities exempt from the Sherman Act because they involve a "learned profession"? If not, are the activities "state action" . . . and therefore exempt from the Sherman Act?

A . . .

A purely advisory fee schedule issued to provide guidelines, or an exchange of price information without a showing of an actual restraint on trade, would present us with a different question. The record here, however, reveals a situation quite different from what would occur under a purely advisory fee schedule. Here a fixed, rigid price floor arose from respondents' activities: every lawyer who responded to petitioners' inquiries adhered to the fee schedule, and no lawyer asked for additional information in order to set an individualized fee. The price information disseminated did not concern past standards, but rather minimum fees to be charged in future transactions, and those minimum rates were increased over time. The fee schedule was enforced through the prospect of professional discipline from the State Bar, and the desire of attorneys to comply with announced professional norms; the motivation to conform was reinforced by the assurance that other lawyers would not compete by underbidding. . . .

Moreover, in terms of restraining competition and harming consumers like petitioners, the price-fixing activities found here are unusually damaging. A title examination is indispensable in the process of financing a real estate purchase, and since only an attorney licensed to practice in Virginia may legally examine a title, consumers could not turn to alternative sources for the necessary service. All attorneys, of course, were practicing under the constraint of the fee schedule. . . .

B

[The Court concluded that the services at issue affected interstate commerce and were therefore within the ambit of the antitrust laws.]

C . . .

In arguing that learned professions are not "trade or commerce" the County Bar seeks a total exclusion from antitrust regulation. Whether state regulation is active or dormant, real or theoretical, lawyers would be able to adopt anticompetitive practices with impunity. We cannot find support for the proposition that Congress intended any such sweeping exclusion. The nature of an occupation, standing alone, does not provide sanctuary from the Sherman Act, nor is the public-service aspect of professional practice controlling in determining whether §1 includes professions. Congress intended to strike as broadly as it could in §1 of the Sherman Act, and to read into it so wide an exemption as that urged on us would be at odds with that purpose. . . .

In the modern world it cannot be denied that the activities of lawyers play an important part in commercial intercourse, and that anticompetitive activities by lawyers may exert a restraint on commerce.

D

In Parker v. Brown, 317 U.S. 341 (1943), the Court held that an anticompetitive marketing program which "derived its authority and its efficacy from the legislative command of the state" was not a violation of the Sherman Act because the Act was intended to regulate private practices and not to prohibit a

State from imposing a restraint as an act of government. Respondent State Bar and respondent County Bar both seek to avail themselves of this so-called state-action exemption. . . .

The threshold inquiry in determining if an anticompetitive activity is state action of the type the Sherman Act was not meant to proscribe is whether the activity is required by the State acting as sovereign. Here we need not inquire further into the state-action question because it cannot fairly be said that the State of Virginia through its Supreme Court Rules required the anticompetitive activities of either respondent. Respondents have pointed to no Virginia statute requiring their activities; state law simply does not refer to fees, leaving regulation of the profession to the Virginia Supreme Court; although the Supreme Court's ethical codes mention advisory fee schedules they do not direct either respondent to supply them, or require the type of price floor which arose from respondents' activities. Although the State Bar apparently has been granted the power to issue ethical opinions, there is no indication in this record that the Virginia Supreme Court approves the opinions. Respondents' arguments, at most, constitute the contention that their activities complemented the objective of the ethical codes. In our view that is not state action for Sherman Act purposes. It is not enough that, as the County Bar puts it, anticompetitive conduct is "prompted" by state action; rather, anticompetitive activities must be compelled by direction of the State acting as a sovereign. . . .

III

We recognize that the States have a compelling interest in the practice of professions within their boundaries, and that as part of their power to protect the public health, safety, and other valid interests they have broad power to establish standards for licensing practitioners and regulating the practice of professions. We also recognize that in some instances the State may decide that "forms of competition usual in the business world may be demoralizing to the ethical standards of a profession." The interest of the States in regulating lawyers is especially great since lawyers are essential to the primary governmental function of administering justice, and have historically been "officers of the courts." In holding that certain anticompetitive conduct by lawyers is within the reach of the Sherman Act we intend no diminution of the authority of the State to regulate its professions. . . .

Reversed and remanded.

JUSTICE POWELL took no part in the consideration or decision of this case.

Antitrust and Legal Ethics

The *Goldfarb* holding has had modest influence on other regulatory efforts by the bar. *Goldfarb* and the lawyer advertising cases (see chapter 16), operating in tandem, have introduced the price competition that some in the pre-*Goldfarb* bar feared. Now, not only may lawyers undersell the competition, they may announce their lower fees to the entire community.

Government has also used the antitrust laws against lawyers, not only against the organized bar. In FTC v. Superior Court Trial Lawyers Assn., 493 U.S. 411

(1990), lawyers who regularly accepted court appointments to represent indigent defendants in the District of Columbia agreed to refuse new cases until hourly rates were increased to $35. It worked: The District raised its rates. But then the FTC filed a complaint against the lawyers, charging a "conspiracy to fix prices and to conduct a boycott." The Court upheld the charge. It rejected the claim that the First Amendment protected their conduct as "politically motivated": "[A] clear objective of the boycott [was] to economically advantage the participants."

Attempts to use the antitrust laws to challenge other bar regulatory efforts have been unsuccessful. In Bates v. State Bar of Arizona, 433 U.S. 350 (1977), page 915, the Court rejected the claim that Arizona's prohibition on legal advertising violated the Sherman Act. The Court concluded that "the challenged restraint is the affirmative command of the Arizona Supreme Court. . . . That court is the ultimate body wielding the State's power over the practice of law, and, thus, the restraint is 'compelled by direction of the State acting as a sovereign.'" Consequently, the action was shielded from the antitrust laws under Parker v. Brown, 317 U.S. 341 (1943). The Court went on to hold the restrictions unconstitutional under the First Amendment.

E.   COURT-AWARDED FEES

1.   *What's the Right Amount?*

Fee-Shifting Cases.   With the advent of fee-shifting statutes in civil rights and environmental cases, and the concomitant growth of class actions, courts must often decide the size of the fee that must be paid to a successful plaintiffs' counsel by the defendant or from the fund recovered for the class. This trend has engendered a cottage industry of judicial opinions and law review articles that seek to identify how fees should be determined. Obviously, to the extent that courts are more generous, more lawyers will accept and bring class actions or cases under fee-shifting statutes. And the less, the less. The Supreme Court has often been sharply divided on these questions.

In federal fee-shifting cases, the Supreme Court has created a strong presumption in favor of the "lodestar," which it defines as "the number of hours reasonably expended on the litigation multiplied by a reasonable hourly rate." Hensley v. Eckerhart, 461 U.S. 424 (1983). *Hensley* added that judges should exclude hours that were not reasonably expended. As discussed above (page 149), the result can yield a fee far above the client's recovery. At the same time, the Supreme Court has refused to permit percentage fee enhancements exceeding the lodestar based on results, rejecting arguments that the lodestar does not adequately compensate lawyers for the contingent risk that a case will fail and the lawyers will get nothing. City of Burlington v. Dague, 505 U.S. 557 (1992). This may be seen as the flip side of ignoring market forces when computing the lodestar by giving lawyers a lot for winning meager sums. Recall the two hypotheticals on page 150. Do plaintiffs' lawyers want to have it both ways? Justice Scalia wrote for the Court that to "engraft this [enhancement] feature onto the lodestar model would be to concoct a hybrid scheme that resorts to the contingent-fee model to increase a fee award but not to reduce it." That's right, isn't it? Contingency fee lawyers get paid a percentage of the recovery if they win, which may yield more or less than their lodestar. Fee-shifting lawyers get their lodestar if they win, which may far exceed the recovery and therefore any percentage of it.

However, lawyers representing individual plaintiffs in fee-shifting cases are not restricted to the amount a court may award. They can have fee agreements with their clients that yield more. Venegas v. Mitchell, 495 U.S. 82 (1990). Nor will such an agreement put a ceiling on the amount the court may later award, although it is a factor the court can weigh. Blanchard v. Bergeron, 489 U.S. 87 (1989). In both cases, the Court was unanimous.

Class Actions.   Where lawyers representing a class win a judgment or a settlement that yields a common fund, courts are empowered to award attorney's fees, which are subtracted from the fund. (Of course, if the underlying claim provides for fee shifting, courts will order the loser to pay, as discussed above.) The options for determining class fees are greater than in fee-shifting cases. Courts may apply the lodestar approach, or they may award a percentage of the recovered amount. Of course, unlike fee-shifting, the fee is going to be less than the recovery because it is paid *from* the recovery. If the court uses a lodestar, it may also award a "risk multiplier," which increases the fee by multiplying the lodestar by a number greater than one. A risk multiplier compensates for risk of loss or for particularly skillful work. Some circuit courts have insisted on use of the percentage method. See Swedish Hospital Corp. v. Shalala, 1 F.3d 1261 (D.C. Cir. 1993). Others leave it to the discretion of the trial judge. See Goldberger v. Integrated Resources, Inc., 209 F.3d 43 (2d Cir. 2000) (recognizing that two circuits require the percentage method but holding, along with six other circuits, that district courts have discretion to use either the lodestar or the percentage method so long as the fee awarded is "reasonable"; counsel had sought 25 percent of a $54 million settlement in a securities class action, but the trial judge, who was affirmed on appeal, awarded a lodestar of only $2.1 million, amounting to 4 percent of the recovery). In Florin v. Nationsbank of Ga., N.A., 34 F.3d 560 (7th Cir. 1994), appeal after remand, 60 F.3d 1245 (7th Cir. 1995), the court acknowledged the circuit's general preference for use of the percentage method but left "the decision as to which method is the most efficient and suitable to this case up to the district court." On remand, the district court used the lodestar approach with a "risk multiplier" of 1.01. Do you think counsel viewed that as an insult? They appealed. The circuit court found the district court's risk multiplier erroneous. It awarded counsel the 1.53 risk multiplier requested, which yielded a fee of about 18.5 percent of the settlement fund.

"Those Fees Are Outrageous"

"If someone ever publishes a Guinness Book of Records for legal absurdities, *Rivera* (page 149) should win first place. Can you imagine giving the young lawyers in that case nearly a quarter-million dollars for recovering $13,300 on their federal claim? That's more than $750,000 in 2009 dollars for recovering

1983
42 USC 1988

$40,000. And that includes 45 hours for time spent sitting around a hotel room and nearly 200 hours on a single pretrial order. This at a time when cities around the country were starving for funds for desperate social problems. If they can get this kind of money for $13,300, why not for winning $5,000 or $1,000? Where's the limit? Make no mistake about it. This is taxpayer money, money that could otherwise go to making life easier or safer or less costly for the body politic. I entirely agree that we want to encourage lawyers to accept civil rights cases. But I disagree that awards like this are needed to do that. The market should have some relevance in deciding the fee. Is there any doubt that if the award were, say, half as large, lawyers would still be willing to bring those cases? The test should be the lowest fee that the court concludes will motivate skilled lawyers to take similar cases, not a ridiculous windfall for two wet-behind-the-ears beginners. Don't you agree?"

$1,000/hr → is this reasonable?

2.   Settlement Conditioned on Fee Waiver

The next case has long been controversial in the public interest legal community. Civil rights lawyers hate it. Defendants (especially government entities) love it. But love it or hate it, it is quite clear that the ruling gives defendants in fee-shifting cases a potent weapon to limit the amount of legal fees they must pay when the parties settle.

EVANS v. JEFF D.
475 U.S. 717 (1986)

JUSTICE STEVENS delivered the opinion of the Court . . . .

I

[In August 1980 the Idaho Legal Aid Society filed a class action challenging "the educational programs and the healthcare services" available to "children who suffer from emotional and mental handicaps." The Society quickly settled the educational claims, waiving its legal fees, but the healthcare claims remained. In March 1983, a week before trial, the defendants "offered virtually all of the injunctive relief [the class] had sought in their complaint." But the settlement offer "included a provision for a waiver . . . of any claim to fees for costs," including those under §1988. Charles Johnson, the Legal Aid attorney, "determined that his ethical obligations to his clients mandated acceptance of the proposal. The parties conditioned the waiver on approval by the District Court."

The district court denied Johnson's motion for fees, but the Ninth Circuit reversed, holding that "the strong federal policy embodied in the Fees Act normally requires an award of fees to prevailing plaintiffs in civil rights actions, including those who have prevailed through settlement." When "attorney's fees are negotiated as part of a class action settlement, a conflict frequently exists between the class lawyers' interest in compensation and the class members' interest in relief." The court therefore "disapproved simultaneous negotiation of settlements and attorney's fees" absent "unusual circumstances," which were not present here. The Supreme Court granted review.]

II

The disagreement between the parties and amici as to what exactly is at issue in this case makes it appropriate to put certain aspects of the case to one side in order to state precisely the question that the case does present.

To begin with, the Court of Appeals' decision rested on an erroneous view of the District Court's power to approve settlements in class actions. Rule 23(e) wisely requires court approval of the terms of any settlement of a class action, but the power to approve or reject a settlement negotiated by the parties before trial does not authorize the court to require the parties to accept a settlement to which they have not agreed. Although changed circumstances may justify a court-ordered modification of a consent decree over the objections of a party after the decree has been entered, and the District Court might have advised petitioners and respondents that it would not approve their proposal unless one or more of its provisions was deleted or modified, Rule 23(e) does not give the court the power, in advance of trial, to modify a proposed consent decree and order its acceptance over either party's objection. The options available to the District Court were essentially the same as those available to respondents: it could have accepted the proposed settlement; it could have rejected the proposal and postponed the trial to see if a different settlement could be achieved; or it could have decided to try the case. The District Court could not enforce the settlement on the merits and award attorney's fees any more than it could, in a situation in which the attorney had negotiated a large fee at the expense of the plaintiff class, preserve the fee award and order greater relief on the merits. The question we must decide, therefore, is whether the District Court had a duty to reject the proposed settlement because it included a waiver of statutorily authorized attorney's fees.

That duty, whether it takes the form of a general prophylactic rule or arises out of the special circumstances of this case, derives ultimately from the Fees Act rather than from the strictures of professional ethics. Although respondents contend that Johnson, as counsel for the class, was faced with an "ethical dilemma" when petitioners offered him relief greater than that which he could reasonably have expected to obtain for his clients at trial (if only he would stipulate to a waiver of the statutory fee award), and although we recognize Johnson's conflicting interests between pursuing relief for the class and a fee for the Idaho Legal Aid Society, we do not believe that the "dilemma" was an "ethical" one in the sense that Johnson had to choose between conflicting duties under the prevailing norms of professional conduct. Plainly, Johnson had no *ethical* obligation to seek a statutory fee award. His ethical duty was to serve his clients loyally and competently. Since the proposal to settle the merits was more favorable than the probable outcome of the trial, Johnson's decision to recommend acceptance was consistent with the highest standards of our profession. The District Court, therefore, correctly concluded that approval of the settlement involved no breach of ethics in this case.

The defect, if any, in the negotiated fee waiver must be traced not to the rules of ethics but to the Fees Act. Following this tack, respondents argue that the statute must be construed to forbid a fee waiver that is the product of "coercion." They submit that a "coercive waiver" results when the defendant in a civil rights action (1) offers a settlement on the merits of equal or greater value than that which plaintiffs could reasonably expect to achieve at trial but (2) conditions the offer on a waiver of plaintiffs' statutory eligibility for attorney's fees. Such an offer, they claim, exploits the ethical obligation of plaintiffs' counsel to recommend settlement in order to avoid defendant's statutory liability for its opponents' fees and costs.

The question this case presents, then, is whether the Fees Act requires a district court to disapprove a stipulation seeking to settle a civil rights class action under Rule 23 when the offered relief equals or exceeds the probable outcome at trial but is expressly conditioned on waiver of statutory eligibility for attorney's fees. For reasons set out below, we are not persuaded that Congress has commanded that all such settlements must be rejected by the District Court. Moreover, on the facts of record in this case, we are satisfied that the District Court did not abuse its discretion by approving the fee waiver.

III

The text of the Fees Act provides no support for the proposition that Congress intended to ban all fee waivers offered in connection with substantial relief on the merits. On the contrary, the language of the Act, as well as its legislative history, indicates that Congress bestowed on the "prevailing *party*" (generally plaintiffs) a statutory eligibility for a discretionary award of attorney's fees in specified civil rights actions. It did not prevent the party from waiving this eligibility any more than it legislated against assignment of this right to an attorney, such as effectively occurred here. Instead, Congress enacted the fee-shifting provision as "an integral part of the remedies necessary to obtain" compliance with civil rights laws, to further the same general purpose — promotion of respect for civil rights — that led it to provide damages and injunctive relief. The statute and its legislative history nowhere suggest that Congress intended to forbid *all* waivers of attorney's fees — even those insisted upon by a civil rights plaintiff in exchange for some other relief to which he is indisputably not entitled[20] — any more than it intended to bar a concession on damages to secure broader injunctive relief. Thus, while it is undoubtedly true that Congress expected fee-shifting to attract competent counsel to represent citizens deprived of their civil rights, it neither bestowed fee awards upon attorneys nor rendered them nonwaivable or nonnegotiable; instead, it added them to the arsenal of remedies available to combat violations of civil rights, a goal not invariably inconsistent with conditioning settlement on the merits on a waiver of statutory attorney's fees.

In fact, we believe that a general proscription against negotiated waiver of attorney's fees in exchange for a settlement on the merits would itself impede

---

20. Judge Wald has described the use of attorney's fees as a "bargaining chip" useful to plaintiffs as well as defendants.

vindication of civil rights, at least in some cases, by reducing the attractiveness of settlement. . . .

Most defendants are unlikely to settle unless the cost of the predicted judgment, discounted by its probability, plus the transaction costs of further litigation, are greater than the cost of the settlement package. If fee waivers cannot be negotiated, the settlement package must either contain an attorney's fee component of potentially large and typically uncertain magnitude, or else the parties must agree to have the fee fixed by the court. Although either of these alternatives may well be acceptable in many cases, there surely is a significant number in which neither alternative will be as satisfactory as a decision to try the entire case.[23]

The adverse impact of removing attorney's fees and costs from bargaining might be tolerable if the uncertainty introduced into settlement negotiations were small. But it is not. The defendants' potential liability for fees in this kind of litigation can be as significant as, and sometimes even more significant than, their potential liability on the merits. . . .

The unpredictability of attorney's fees may be just as important as their magnitude when a defendant is striving to fix its liability. . . . Among other considerations, the district court must determine what hours were reasonably expended on what claims, whether that expenditure was reasonable in light of the success obtained, and what is an appropriate hourly rate for the services rendered. Some District Courts have also considered whether a "multiplier" or other adjustment is appropriate. . . .

It is therefore not implausible to anticipate that parties to a significant number of civil rights cases will refuse to settle if liability for attorney's fees remains open, thereby forcing more cases to trial, unnecessarily burdening the judicial system, and disserving civil rights litigants. Respondents' own waiver of attorney's fees and costs to obtain settlement of their educational claims is eloquent testimony to the utility of fee waivers in vindicating civil rights claims.[29] We conclude, therefore, that it is not necessary to construe the Fees Act as embodying a general rule prohibiting settlements conditioned on the waiver of fees in order to be faithful to the purposes of that Act.[30]

---

23. It is unrealistic to assume that the defendant's offer on the merits would be unchanged by redaction of the provision waiving fees. If it were, the defendant's incentive to settle would be diminished because of the risk that attorney's fees, when added to the original merits offer, will exceed the discounted value of the expected judgment plus litigation costs. If, as is more likely, the defendant lowered the value of its offer on the merits to provide a cushion against the possibility of a large fee award, the defendant's offer on the merits will in many cases be less than the amount to which the plaintiff feels himself entitled, thereby inclining him to reject the settlement. Of course, to the extent that the merits offer is somewhere between these two extremes the incentive of both sides to settle is dampened, albeit to a lesser degree with respect to each party.

29. Respondents implicitly acknowledge a defendant's need to fix his total liability when they suggest that the parties to a civil rights action should "exchange information" regarding plaintiff's attorney's fees. If this exchange is confined to time records and customary billing rates, the information provides an insufficient basis for forecasting the fee award for the reasons stated above. If the "exchange" is more in the nature of an "assurance" that attorney's fees will not exceed a specified amount, the rule against waiving fees to obtain a favorable settlement on the merits is to that extent breached. . . .

30. The Court is unanimous in concluding that the Fees Act should not be interpreted to prohibit all simultaneous negotiations of a defendant's liability on the merits and his liability for his opponent's attorney's fees. We agree that when the parties find such negotiations conducive

IV

The question remains whether the District Court abused its discretion in this case by approving a settlement which included a complete fee waiver. . . .

The Court of Appeals, respondents, and various amici supporting their position . . . suggest that the court's authority to pass on settlements, typically invoked to ensure fair treatment of class members, must be exercised in accordance with the Fees Act to promote the availability of attorneys in civil rights cases. Specifically, respondents assert that the State of Idaho could not pass a valid statute precluding the payment of attorney's fees in settlements of civil rights cases to which the Fees Act applies. From this they reason that the Fees Act must equally preclude the adoption of a uniform statewide policy that serves the same end, and accordingly contend that a consistent practice of insisting on a fee waiver as a condition of settlement in civil rights litigation is in conflict with the federal statute authorizing fees for prevailing parties, including those who prevail by way of settlement. Remarkably, there seems little disagreement on these points. Petitioners and the amici who support them never suggest that the district court is obligated to place its stamp of approval on every settlement in which the plaintiffs' attorneys have agreed to a fee waiver. The Solicitor General, for example, has suggested that a fee waiver need not be approved when the defendant had "no realistic defense on the merits," . . . or if the waiver was part of a "vindictive effort . . . to teach counsel that they had better not bring such cases."

We find it unnecessary to evaluate this argument, however, because the record in this case does not indicate that Idaho has adopted such a statute, policy, or practice. Nor does the record support the narrower proposition that petitioners' request to waive fees was a vindictive effort to deter attorneys from representing plaintiffs in civil rights suits against Idaho. It is true that a fee waiver was requested and obtained as a part of the early settlement of the education claims, but we do not understand respondents to be challenging that waiver . . . and they have not offered to prove that the petitioners' tactics in this case merely implemented a routine state policy designed to frustrate the objectives of the Fees Act. Our own examination of the record reveals no such policy.

In light of the record, respondents must—to sustain the judgment in their favor—confront the District Court's finding that the extensive structural relief they obtained constituted an adequate quid pro quo for their waiver of attorney's fees. The Court of Appeals did not overturn this finding. Indeed, even that court did not suggest that the option of rejecting the entire settlement and

---

to settlement, the public interest, as well as that of the parties, is served by simultaneous negotiations. This reasoning applies not only to individual civil rights actions, but to civil rights class actions as well. Although the dissent would allow simultaneous negotiations, it would require that "whatever fee the parties agree to" be "found by the court to be a 'reasonable' one under the Fees Act." The dissent's proposal is imaginative, but not very practical. Of the 10,757 "other civil rights" cases filed in federal court last year—most of which were §1983 actions for which §1988 authorizes an award of fees—only 111 sought class relief. Assuming that of the approximately 99% of these civil rights actions that are not class actions, a further 90% would settle rather than go to trial, the dissent's proposal would require district courts to evaluate the reasonableness of fee agreements in several thousand civil rights cases annually while they make that determination in slightly over 100 civil rights class actions now. Moreover, if this novel procedure really is necessary to carry out the purposes of the Fees Act, presumably it should be applied to all cases arising under federal statutes that provide for fee-shifting.

requiring the parties either to try the case or to attempt to negotiate a different settlement would have served the interests of justice. Only by making the unsupported assumption that the respondent class was entitled to retain the favorable portions of the settlement while rejecting the fee waiver could the Court of Appeals conclude that the District Court had acted unwisely.

What the outcome of this settlement illustrates is that the Fees Act has given the victims of civil rights violations a powerful weapon that improves their ability to employ counsel, to obtain access to the courts, and thereafter to vindicate their rights by means of settlement or trial. For aught that appears, it was the "coercive" effect of respondents' statutory right to seek a fee award that motivated petitioners' exceptionally generous offer. Whether this weapon might be even more powerful if fee waivers were prohibited in cases like this is another question,[34] but it is in any event a question that Congress is best equipped to answer. Thus far, the Legislature has not commanded that fees be paid whenever a case is settled. Unless it issues such a command, we shall rely primarily on the sound discretion of the district courts to appraise the reasonableness of particular class-action settlements on a case-by-case basis, in the light of all the relevant circumstances. In this case, the District Court did not abuse its discretion in upholding a fee waiver which secured broad injunctive relief, relief greater than that which plaintiffs could reasonably have expected to achieve at trial.

The judgment of the Court of Appeals is reversed.

JUSTICE BRENNAN, with whom JUSTICE MARSHALL and JUSTICE BLACKMUN join, dissenting. . . .

III

A

Permitting plaintiffs to negotiate fee waivers in exchange for relief on the merits actually raises two related but distinct questions. First, is it permissible under the Fees Act to negotiate a settlement of attorney's fees simultaneously with the merits? Second, can the "reasonable attorney's fee" guaranteed in the Act be waived? As a matter of logic, either of these practices may be permitted without also permitting the other. For instance, one could require bifurcated settlement negotiations of merits and fees but allow plaintiffs to waive their fee claims during that phase of the negotiations. Alternatively, one could permit simultaneous negotiation of fees and merits but prohibit the plaintiff from waiving statutory fees. This latter possibility exists because there is a *range* of "reasonable attorney's fees" consistent with the Fees Act in any given case.

More importantly, since simultaneous negotiation and waiver may have different effects on the congressional policy of encouraging counsel to accept

---

34. We are cognizant of the possibility that decisions by individual clients to bargain away fee awards may, in the aggregate and in the long run, diminish lawyers' expectations of statutory fees in civil rights cases. If this occurred, the pool of lawyers willing to represent plaintiffs in such cases might shrink, constricting the "effective access to the judicial process" for persons with civil rights grievances which the Fees Act was intended to provide. That the "tyranny of small decisions" may operate in this fashion is not to say that there is any reason or documentation to support such a concern at the present time. Comment on this issue is therefore premature at this juncture. We believe, however, that as a practical matter the likelihood of this circumstance arising is remote.

civil rights cases, each practice must be analyzed independently to determine whether or not it is consistent with the Fees Act. Unfortunately, the Court overlooks the logical independence of simultaneous negotiation and waiver and assumes that there cannot be one without the other. As a result, the Court's discussion conflates the different effects of these practices, and its opinion is of little use in coming to a fair resolution of this case. An independent examination leads me to conclude: (1) that plaintiffs should not be permitted to waive the "reasonable fee" provided by the Fees Act; but (2) that parties may undertake to negotiate their fee claims simultaneously with the merits so long as whatever fee the parties agree to is found by the court to be a "reasonable" one under the Fees Act.

B

1

It seems obvious that allowing defendants in civil rights cases to condition settlement of the merits on a waiver of statutory attorney's fees will diminish lawyers' expectations of receiving fees and decrease the willingness of lawyers to accept civil rights cases. Even the Court acknowledges "the possibility that decisions by individual clients to bargain away fee awards may, in the aggregate and in the long run, diminish lawyers' expectations of statutory fees in civil rights cases." The Court tells us, however, that "[c]omment on this issue" is "premature at this juncture" because there is not yet supporting "documentation." The Court then goes on anyway to observe that "as a practical matter the likelihood of this circumstance arising is remote."

I must say that I find the Court's assertions somewhat difficult to understand. . . . [Pre-Act] experience surely provides an indication of the immediate hardship suffered by civil rights claimants whenever there is a reduction in the availability of attorney's fee awards.[7] Moreover, numerous courts and commentators have recognized that permitting fee waivers creates disincentives for lawyers to take civil rights cases and thus makes it more difficult for civil rights plaintiffs to obtain legal assistance.

But it does not require a sociological study to see that permitting fee waivers will make it more difficult for civil rights plaintiffs to obtain legal assistance. It requires only common sense. Assume that a civil rights defendant makes a settlement offer that includes a demand for waiver of statutory attorney's fees. The decision whether to accept or reject the offer is the plaintiff's alone, and the lawyer must abide by the plaintiff's decision. As a formal matter, of course, the statutory fee belongs to the plaintiff and thus technically the decision to waive entails a sacrifice only by the plaintiff. As a practical matter, however, waiver affects only the lawyer. Because "a vast majority of the victims of civil rights violations" have no resources to pay attorney's fees, lawyers cannot hope to recover fees from the plaintiff and must depend entirely on the Fees Act

7. It is especially important to keep in mind the fragile nature of the civil rights bar. Even when attorney's fees are awarded, they do not approach the large sums which can be earned in ordinary commercial litigation. It is therefore cost inefficient for private practitioners to devote much time to civil rights cases. Consequently, there are very few civil rights practitioners, and most of these devote only a small part of their time to such cases.

for compensation.[10] The plaintiff thus has no real stake in the statutory fee and is unaffected by its waiver. Consequently, plaintiffs will readily agree to waive fees if this will help them to obtain other relief they desire.[11] . . .

Of course, from the lawyer's standpoint, things could scarcely have turned out worse. He or she invested considerable time and effort in the case, won, and has exactly nothing to show for it. Is the Court really serious in suggesting that it takes a study to prove that this lawyer will be reluctant when, the following week, another civil rights plaintiff enters his office and asks for representation? Does it truly require that somebody conduct a test to see that legal aid services, having invested scarce resources on a case, will feel the pinch when they do not recover a statutory fee?

And, of course, once fee waivers are permitted, defendants will seek them as a matter of course, since this is a logical way to minimize liability. Indeed, defense counsel would be remiss *not* to demand that the plaintiff waive statutory attorney's fees. A lawyer who proposes to have his client pay more than is necessary to end litigation has failed to fulfill his fundamental duty zealously to represent the best interests of his client. Because waiver of fees does not affect the plaintiff, a settlement offer is not made less attractive to the plaintiff if it includes a demand that statutory fees be waived. Thus, in the future, we must expect settlement offers routinely to contain demands for waivers of statutory fees.[12]

The cumulative effect this practice will have on the civil rights bar is evident. It does not denigrate the high ideals that motivate many civil rights practitioners to recognize that lawyers are in the business of practicing law, and that, like other business people, they are and must be concerned with earning a living. The conclusion that permitting fee waivers will seriously impair the ability of civil rights plaintiffs to obtain legal assistance is embarrassingly obvious.

Because making it more difficult for civil rights plaintiffs to obtain legal assistance is precisely the opposite of what Congress sought to achieve by enacting the Fees Act, fee waivers should be prohibited. We have on numerous prior occasions held that "a statutory right conferred on a private party, but affecting the public interest, may not be waived or released if such waiver or release contravenes the statutory policy." This is simply straightforward application of

10. Nor can attorneys protect themselves by requiring plaintiffs to sign contingency agreements or retainers at the outset of the representation. Amici legal aid societies inform us that they are prohibited by statute, court rule, or Internal Revenue Service regulation from entering into fee agreements with their clients. Moreover, even if such agreements could be negotiated, the possibility of obtaining protection through contingency fee arrangements is unavailable in the very large proportion of civil rights cases which, like this case, seek only injunctive relief. . . .

11. This result is virtually inevitable in class action suits where, even if the class representative feels sympathy for the lawyer's plight, the obligation to represent the interests of absent class members precludes altruistic sacrifice. In class action suits on behalf of incompetents, like this one, it is the lawyer himself who must agree to sacrifice his own interests for those of the class he represents.

12. The Solicitor General's suggestion that we can prohibit waivers sought as part of a "vindictive effort" to teach lawyers not to bring civil rights cases, a point that the Court finds unnecessary to consider, is thus irrelevant. Defendants will seek such waivers in every case simply as a matter of sound bargaining. Indeed, the Solicitor General's brief suggests that this will be the bargaining posture of the United States in the future.

the well-established principle that an agreement which is contrary to public policy is void and unenforceable.[14]

2

This all seems so obvious that it is puzzling that the Court reaches a different result. The Court's rationale is that, unless fee waivers are permitted, "parties to a significant number of civil rights cases will refuse to settle. . . ." This is a wholly inadequate justification for the Court's result.

First, the effect of prohibiting fee waivers on settlement offers is just not an important concern in the context of the Fees Act. I agree with the Court that encouraging settlements is desirable policy. But it is *judicially* created policy, applicable to litigation of any kind and having no special force in the context of civil rights cases. The *congressional* policy underlying the Fees Act is, as I have argued throughout, to create incentives for lawyers to devote time to civil rights cases by making it economically feasible for them to do so. As explained above, permitting fee waivers significantly undercuts this policy. Thus, even if prohibiting fee waivers does discourage some settlements, a *judicial* policy favoring settlement cannot possibly take precedence over this express *congressional* policy. We must implement Congress' agenda, not our own. . . .

Second, even assuming that settlement practices are relevant, the Court greatly exaggerates the effect that prohibiting fee waivers will have on defendants' willingness to make settlement offers. This is largely due to the Court's failure to distinguish the fee waiver issue from the issue of simultaneous negotiation of fees and merits claims. The Court's discussion mixes concerns over a defendant's reluctance to settle because total liability remains uncertain with reluctance to settle because the cost of settling is too high. However, it is a prohibition on simultaneous negotiation, not a prohibition on fee waivers, that makes it difficult for the defendant to ascertain his total liability at the time he agrees to settle the merits. Thus, while prohibiting fee waivers may deter settlement offers simply because requiring the defendant to pay a "reasonable attorney's fee" increases the total cost of settlement, this is a separate issue altogether, and the Court's numerous arguments about why defendants will not settle unless they can determine their total liability at the time of settlement are simply beside the point.[17] With respect to a prohibition on fee waivers (and again merely assuming that effects on settlement are relevant), the sole question to be asked is whether the increased cost of settlement packages will prevent enough settlement offers to be a dispositive factor in this case.

The Court asserts, without factual support, that requiring defendants to pay statutory fee awards will prevent a "significant number" of settlements. . . . I believe that the Court overstates the extent to which prohibiting fee waivers will deter defendants from making settlement offers. Because the parties can

14. To be sure, prohibiting fee waivers will require federal courts to make a determination they would not have to make if fees could be waived. However, this additional chore will not impose a significant burden. . . .

17. For the reasons stated in Part III-C [omitted], I would permit simultaneous negotiation of fees and merits. The parties could agree upon a reasonable fee which would be subject to judicial approval under the Fees Act. Any settlement on the merits could be made contingent upon such approval. By permitting defendants to ascertain their total liability prior to settling, this approach fully alleviates the Court's concerns in this regard.

negotiate a fee (or a range of fees) that is not unduly high and condition their settlement on the court's approval of this fee, the magnitude of a defendant's liability for fees in the settlement context need be neither uncertain nor particularly great. Against this, the defendant must weigh the risk of a nonnegotiated fee to be fixed by the court after a trial; as the Court reminds us, fee awards in *this* context may be very uncertain and, potentially, of very great magnitude. . . .

All of which is not to deny that prohibiting fee waivers will deter some settlements; any increase in the costs of settling will have this effect. However, by exaggerating the size and the importance of fee awards, and by ignoring the options available to the parties in settlement negotiations, the Court makes predictions that are inflated. . . .

IV

Although today's decision will undoubtedly impair the effectiveness of the private enforcement scheme Congress established for civil rights legislation, I do not believe that it will bring about the total disappearance of "private attorneys general." It is to be hoped that Congress will repair this Court's mistake. In the meantime, other avenues of relief are available. The Court's decision in no way limits the power of state and local bar associations to regulate the ethical conduct of lawyers. Indeed, several Bar Associations have already declared it unethical for defense counsel to seek fee waivers. Such efforts are to be commended and, it is to be hoped, will be followed by other state and local organizations concerned with respecting the intent of Congress and with protecting civil rights.

In addition, it may be that civil rights attorneys can obtain agreements from their clients not to waive attorney's fees.[20] Such agreements simply replicate the private market for legal services (in which attorneys are not ordinarily required to contribute to their client's recovery),[21] and thus will enable civil rights practitioners to make it economically feasible — as Congress hoped — to expend time and effort litigating civil rights claims. . . .

QUESTIONS ABOUT EVANS V. JEFF D.

1. By saying the fee belongs to the client, has Justice Stevens put the immediate interests of an individual plaintiff over the interests of civil rights plaintiffs generally in being able to attract competent counsel? Well, yes, he has because the decision will affect the willingness of lawyers to take these cases. You may be out of luck if the defendant offers your client all she wants but only if she waives your fee. Indeed, the majority acknowledges that a "tyranny of small

---

20. Since Congress has not sought to regulate ethical concerns either in the Fees Act or elsewhere, the legality of such [agreements] is purely a matter of local law.

21. One of the more peculiar aspects of the Court's interpretation of the Fees Act is that it permits defendants to require plaintiff's counsel to contribute his compensation to satisfying the plaintiff's claims. In ordinary civil litigation, no defendant would make — or sell to his adversary — a settlement offer conditioned upon the plaintiff's convincing his attorney to contribute to the plaintiff's recovery. Yet today's decision creates a situation in which plaintiff's attorneys in civil rights cases are required to do just that. . . .

decisions" could operate to shrink the pool of available civil rights lawyers but finds no "reason or documentation to support such a concern at the present time." See note 34. When then? The California Supreme Court has rejected *Evans* for fee shifting under that state's Fair Employment and Housing Act. Absent contrary agreement, it held that the fee belongs to the lawyer. Flannery v. Prentice, 28 P.3d 860 (Cal. 2001). But the anti-*Evans* view is not without problems. By saying that the fee belongs to the lawyer, the court gives the lawyer the power to veto a settlement the client finds attractive unless the opponent is willing to disaggregate the client's recovery from the fee and negotiate or try the two separately. Consider the alternatives: the claims of client and lawyer are discussed concurrently; the claims of one are resolved (or tentatively resolved) before negotiating the claims of the other.

2. Would you support an ethical rule that prohibited simultaneous negotiation of the merits and counsel fees in actions in which statutory law allows counsel fees to the prevailing plaintiff? Could such a requirement "overrule" *Evans*? How would you respond to the arguments of the defense bar acknowledged in note 29 of *Evans*? What about forbidding offers conditioned on fee waivers? In 1988, the Board of Governors of the California State Bar recommended that the State Supreme Court adopt the following amendment to the state's ethics code:

> A member shall not make or present a settlement offer in any case involving a request by the opposing party for attorney's fees pursuant to private attorney general statutes which is conditioned on opposing counsel waiving all or substantially all fees. This rule does not preclude a member from making or presenting an offer of a lump sum to settle all claims including attorney's fees.

What do you think of this solution? The State Supreme Court rejected it. Efforts to overturn *Evans* have also been made in Congress. One version, part of an attempt to overturn a number of Supreme Court decisions in the civil rights area, would have amended the Civil Rights Act of 1964 to provide as follows:

> No consent order or judgment settling a claim under this title shall be entered, and no stipulation of dismissal of a claim under this title shall be effective, unless the parties or their counsel attest to the court that a waiver of all or substantially all attorney's fees was not compelled as a condition of the settlement.

How would this language actually work? Assume a defense lawyer says: "I will give your clients the relief they request, but you have to accept a waiver of substantially all of your fees. However, I will not make this offer if you feel that you are compelled to accept that waiver as a condition of this settlement. Get back to me."

3. After *Evans*, may a plaintiff's lawyer require a plaintiff irrevocably to agree not to waive or negotiate counsel fees until a settlement is

reached on the merits — that is, where the client waives recourse to the "powerful weapon" described in the penultimate paragraph of the majority opinion? What about Rule 1.2(a), which gives clients the right to decide whether to settle? Can the client assign her fee rights to the lawyer? Pony v. County of Los Angeles, 433 F.3d 1138 (9th Cir. 2006) (California law forbids an irrevocable assignment). Of course, this strategy may not in any event aid legal aid offices that are prohibited from entering fee agreements with clients. See note 10 of the dissent.

4. *Evans* was a class action; settlement required judicial approval. What happens when an attorney is representing an individual plaintiff in a case subject to a fee-shifting statute? See the post-*Evans* decision in Freeman v. B&B Associates, 790 F.2d 145 (D.C. Cir. 1986) (following *Evans*, holding that attorney has no right to a statutory fee where client waives one).

5. Justice Brennan would allow simultaneous negotiation of the fee and the merits, with the entire package contingent on the judge's approval of the fee. In this way, the defendant knows its full obligation before it finally commits to the package. Justice Brennan would apply his rule in class and nonclass actions. Why does the majority reject this solution, which is already the rule in class actions and which seems to accommodate all interests? See note 30. Do you agree with Justice Brennan? Think about how the Brennan rule would work in practice. What considerations would inform the trial judge's decision whether to approve the fee? Could the judge reject a fee as too high or too low even if it were acceptable to all parties? Jones v. Amalgamated Warbasse Houses, Inc., 721 F.2d 881 (2d Cir. 1983) (judge could properly reduce agreed fee in class action civil rights case even though no one objected and even though the reduction would not benefit the plaintiff class, which sought only injunctive relief); Weinberger v. Great Northern Nekoosa Corp., 925 F.2d 518 (1st Cir. 1999) (citing *Jones* to support "scrutiny" of counsel fees in class actions). It looks like the courts here fear a sweetheart deal between lawyer and opponent. After *Evans*, are courts expected to guard against class action fees that may be too high but have no duty to inquire about fees that seem too low or are waived altogether?

6. Prior to *Evans*, the New York City Bar Association, in Opinion 1980-94, decided that it would be unethical for a defendant to make an offer of settlement in "public interest" cases conditioned on the plaintiff's agreement to waive his or her counsel fee. The opinion, which was withdrawn after *Evans*, relied mainly on the fact that such an offer could create a conflict of interest between the plaintiff's attorney and her client. Justice Stevens (page 182 supra) rejected this explanation: Because an attorney's duty is to urge whatever is best for her client, regardless of her own interests, there can be no "ethical dilemma." The New York City opinion would have required delay in negotiation of the fee until resolution of the merits, but plaintiff's

counsel would have been free to give the defense lawyer information (hourly rates, hours spent) that would enable her to predict the fee. No member of the Court accepted that solution. Why not? See note 29. But consider this: Justice Stevens in note 29 and the text assumed that information on the plaintiff's lawyer's hourly rate and time would be insufficient to enable the defendant to predict the eventual fee award. This was so because of the possibility of a "multiplier." Yet six years later, in City of Burlington v. Dague, supra, the Court rejected multipliers in fee-shifting cases. So now the plaintiff's lawyer's lodestar tells the defendant what the maximum fee is almost certain to be. Should we therefore reconsider the solution of forbidding simultaneous negotiation of the claim and the fee while allowing counsel to reveal his lodestar? Some judicial decisions have disallowed simultaneous negotiation of counsel fees and settlement in some circumstances. Ramirez v. Sturdevant, 26 Cal. Rptr. 2d 554 (Ct. App. 1994); Coleman v. Fiore Bros., Inc., 552 A.2d 141 (N.J. 1989) (forbidding simultaneous negotiation in public interest cases but permitting it in nonclass actions brought by private lawyer).

3. Who May Receive Court-Ordered Fees?

Lawyers, of course. But many lawyers who are eligible for fee awards are salaried employees of nonprofit organizations such as the ACLU or the Environmental Defense Fund. If a court awards a fee for their work, may their employers get it, assuming the client agrees? The employer may not be authorized to practice law. That raises unauthorized practice and fee-splitting questions and, more broadly, questions about who (or what) can be a law firm. After some uncertainty, the dominant view now is that a non-profit employer may get court-awarded legal fees. Rule 5.4(a)(4). This issue is further explored in chapter 14.

FURTHER READING

Court-awarded counsel fees have tax implications. They are income to the successful plaintiff. But as Laura Sager and Stephen Cohen explain, it is possible that a successful plaintiff with a low recovery and a high counsel fee will have an after-tax loss despite winning the case. In part, this is because of the operation of the alternative minimum tax. See Laura Sager & Stephen Cohen, How the Income Tax Undermines Civil Rights Law, 73 S. Cal. L. Rev. 1075 (2000). Commissioner of Internal Revenue v. Banks, 125 S. Ct. 826 (2005), held that an attorney's fee award is income to the client. However, legislation, previously passed, prospectively ameliorates the harshness of that result in a broad range of discrimination cases.

Note, Fee As the Wind Blows: Waivers of Attorney's Fees in Individual Civil Rights Actions Since Evans v. Jeff D., 102 Harv. L. Rev. 1278 (1989), says that "lower courts have indicated an unwillingness to bridle defendants' use of conditional fee waivers in settlement negotiations in individual civil rights actions," as distinguished from class actions. The author "argues that district courts should be receptive to attorneys' challenges to fee waivers in individual civil rights actions" and suggests a way to reintroduce "a mechanism for judicial oversight of the negotiating process while remaining faithful to *Evans*' construction of the Fees Act."

F. MANDATORY PRO BONO PLANS

"Should We Adopt Mandatory Pro Bono?"

The Chief Justice of your state's supreme court appoints you to chair a committee to study whether the court should adopt a mandatory pro bono requirement for lawyers in the state. Everything is on the table. Should the court require lawyers to do pro bono work? If not, should it follow the Florida and Illinois scheme? Florida's plan encourages (but does not mandate) a specified number of hours of pro bono work and requires lawyers to report their hours (and how they were spent) in records open to the public. If the committee does recommend mandatory pro bono, or the Florida plan, how should the court define "pro bono" work? How many hours should be required (or expected) annually? May a lawyer satisfy the requirement with a cash payment? May a firm satisfy the requirement cumulatively or should the obligation be personal to each lawyer?

In addition, as it happens, the dean of the law school from which you graduated has asked you and a few other alumni to advise her on whether the school should establish a pro bono work requirement for graduation. If so, again, subsidiary questions include the required number of hours and the definition of "pro bono." A quick search reveals that the great majority of American law schools do not now have a pro bono graduation requirement. How does this affect your view? For example, is competition for students a legitimate consideration? Would adoption of an obligation improve, harm, or have no effect on enrollment? The dean gives you the text of the requirement at Florida State University College of Law as one example of a pro bono requirement:

> To obtain a degree, a student must satisfy the law school's pro bono requirement. To satisfy this requirement, students must do a minimum of 20 hours of civil pro bono legal work during their second or third year of law school. Pro bono legal work is defined as "work on behalf of indigent individuals or other uncompensated legal work in conjunction with an individual lawyer, law firm or organization on behalf of a disadvantaged minority, the victims of racial, sexual, or other forms of discrimination, those denied human and civil rights, or other work on behalf of the public interest. Work on behalf of the public interest means legal work that is designed to present a position on behalf of the public at large on matters of public interest. . . ." Public interest work does not include the direct representation of litigants in actions between private persons, corporations, or other representations of litigants in which the financial interests at stake would warrant representation from private legal sources. The Office of Student Affairs has the responsibility for determining whether a student has satisfied the pro bono requirement. There is a mandatory pro

bono orientation that covers all aspects of this requirement. The orientation is available online and must be completed before students may receive pro bono credit.

And you discover this from the website of the University of Pennsylvania Law School:

> Faculty guidelines stipulate that all law students complete 35 hours of approved public service work during the academic year in their 2nd and 3rd years of attendance, for a total of 70 hours.
>
> Public service work is broadly defined and encompasses unpaid legal work: In the public sector (i.e., governmental and quasi-governmental entities); In public interest or pro bono organizations, or any other non-profit group (other than trade associations), regardless of the political priorities of the organization; With private practitioners or firms where the work is performed at no cost or at a reduced fee on behalf of underrepresented clients.
>
> The work must be professional, non-clerical law-related work and carried on under the supervision of an attorney or faculty member. In exceptional cases, the Public Interest Committee, which oversees the requirement, may approve other arrangements.

What are your recommendations to the chief justice and the dean?

In the 1980 Kutak Commission draft, Rule 8.1 provided as follows:

> A lawyer shall render public interest legal service. A lawyer may discharge this responsibility by service in activities for improving the law, the legal system or the legal profession, or by providing professional services to persons of limited means or to public service groups or organizations. A lawyer shall make an annual report concerning such service to appropriate regulatory authority.

As finally adopted by the ABA, Rule 6.1 was aspirational. The word "shall" was changed to "should." Rule 6.1, among other changes, also stated that its purpose could be satisfied "by financial support to organizations that provide legal services to persons of limited means."

In 1993, the ABA substantially rewrote Rule 6.1 (and its comment). The rule is still aspirational, but it specifies the number of hours — 50 — that a lawyer should render to pro bono publico legal services each year. The rule also identifies in greater detail the ways in which this time might be spent, ranging from aid to "persons of limited means" to "participation in activities for improving the law, the legal system or the legal profession." Does that mean serving on a bar association committee? The rule also encourages lawyers to "voluntarily contribute financial support to organizations that provide legal services to persons of limited means." In 2002, the ABA accepted the Ethics 2000 Commission's recommendation to add the first sentence of Rule 6.1, strengthening its aspirational force but keeping it aspirational.

Adoption of Rule 6.1 did not end the debate over mandatory pro bono rules. Several local courts have them. See Symposium, Mandatory Pro Bono, 19

Hofstra L. Rev. 739 (1991); Debra Burke, George Mechling & James Pearce, Mandatory Pro Bono: Cui Bono?, 25 Stetson L. Rev. 983 (1996). It looked for a while as though the Supreme Court might address the constitutional and other issues these plans raise when, in Mallard v. United States Dist. Court, 490 U.S. 296 (1989), an attorney challenged his assignment to represent an indigent prisoner. The Court, however, held that the statute under which the lower court had assigned the lawyer, 28 U.S.C. §1915(d), did not authorize the assignment. The Court declined to say whether the lower court had "inherent authority to require lawyers to serve," because the issue had not been considered below. Four Justices dissented in an opinion by Justice Stevens. The lower court's plan for "representation for indigent litigants was in operation when petitioner became a member of that court's bar," Justice Stevens wrote. "When a court has established a fair and detailed procedure for the assignment of counsel to indigent litigants, a formal request to a lawyer by the court pursuant to that procedure is tantamount to a command."

Distinguishing *Mallard*, the Eighth Circuit held that Title VII of the 1964 Civil Rights Act empowered a trial court to appoint lawyers to represent poor persons who allege employment discrimination. Scott v. Tyson Foods, Inc., 943 F.2d 17 (8th Cir. 1991). The Ninth Circuit upheld an Arizona scheme that authorized trial judges to require lawyers to serve as arbitrators two days a year with minimal compensation. It relied on circuit precedent upholding the power of trial judges to require lawyers to represent indigent litigants. Scheehle v. Justices of the Supreme Court of Arizona, 508 F.3d 887 (9th Cir. 2007).

Florida and Illinois and a few other states have adopted detailed voluntary pro bono plans, which, however, require lawyers to report their pro bono activities. In Florida, lawyers may satisfy this voluntary provision each year by giving "twenty hours of pro bono legal service to the poor annually or contribute $350 to a legal aid organization." The annual report is mandatory and available to the public. Two judges dissented from the reporting requirements. Two other judges would have made the obligation mandatory. In re Amendments to Rules Regulating the Florida Bar, 630 So. 2d 501 (Fla. 1993), and 598 So. 2d 41 (Fla. 1992). In In re Amendments to Rule 4-6.1 of the Rules Regulating the Florida Bar, 696 So. 2d 734 (Fla. 1997), the court retained the mandatory reporting requirements in response to an effort to delete them. A federal challenge to the Florida scheme on due process grounds failed in Schwarz v. Kogan, 132 F.3d 1387 (11th Cir. 1998). Among other arguments, plaintiffs claimed that the mandatory reporting obligation converted the aspirational goals of the Rule into a mandatory obligation because "private lawyers are implicitly coerced into satisfying the Rule's aspirations in order to preserve their professional 'honor' and ability to climb the professional and political ladder." In response, the court held that "even assuming that the reporting requirement may have some implicit coercive effect, and thereby motivates otherwise reluctant lawyers to honor their professional responsibility, this result justifiably furthers the Rule's legitimate purpose."

For a near-encyclopedic study of the rise and "institutionalization" of pro bono in American law practice, including the ways pro bono work is organized and the "systemic consequences" of the pro bono "architecture," see Scott Cummings, The Politics of Pro Bono, 52 U.C.L.A. L. Rev. 1 (2004).

Deborah L. Rhode
CULTURES OF COMMITMENT: PRO BONO
FOR LAWYERS AND LAW STUDENTS
67 Fordham L. Rev. 2415 (1999) . . .

A wide gap remains between the rhetoric and reality of America's commitment to equal justice. Studies of low-income groups find that over three-quarters of their legal needs remain unmet. Studies cutting across income groups estimate that individuals do not obtain lawyers' help for between thirty to forty percent of their personal legal needs. Moreover, these legal needs studies do not include many collective problems where attorneys' services are often crucial, such as environmental risks or consumer product safety. The bar's response to inadequate access alternates between confession and avoidance. Some lawyers simply deny the data. Unburdened by factual support, they insist that no worthy cause goes unassisted, thanks to voluntary pro bono efforts, legal-aid programs, and contingent fee representation. A more common approach is to acknowledge the problem of unmet needs but to deny that mandatory pro bono service is the solution. In one representative survey, about sixty percent of California attorneys believed that poor people's access to legal assistance would continue to decline, but an equal number opposed minimum pro bono requirements.

Opponents raise both moral and practical objections. As a matter of principle, some lawyers insist that compulsory charity is a contradiction in terms. From their perspective, requiring service would undermine its moral significance and compromise altruistic commitments.

There are several problems with this claim, beginning with its assumption that pro bono service is "charity." As the preceding discussion suggested, pro bono work is not simply a philanthropic exercise; it is also a professional responsibility. Moreover, in the small number of jurisdictions where courts now appoint lawyers to provide uncompensated representation, no evidence indicates that voluntary assistance has declined as a result. Nor is it self-evident that most lawyers who currently make public-service contributions would cease to do so simply because others were required to join them. As to lawyers who do not volunteer but claim that required service would lack moral value, David Luban has it right: "You can't appeal to the moral significance of a gift you have no intention of giving."

Opponents' other moral objection to mandatory pro bono contributions involves the infringement of lawyers' own rights. From critics' vantage, conscripting attorneys undermines the fundamental rights of due process and just compensation; it is a form of "latent fascism" and "involuntary servitude."

The legal basis for such objections is unconvincing. A well-established line of precedent holds that Thirteenth Amendment prohibitions extend only to physical restraint or a threat of legal confinement. They do not apply if individuals may choose freedom at a price. Since sanctions for refusing pro bono work would not include incarceration, most courts have rejected involuntary servitude challenges.

Leading decisions have also dismissed objections based on the takings clause. Their reasoning is that "the Fifth Amendment does not require that the Government pay for the performance of a public duty [if] it is already owed." As long as the required amount of service is not unreasonable, takings claims generally have failed. Although the Supreme Court has never ruled directly on the scope of judicial authority to compel uncompensated legal assistance, its dicta and summary dismissal of one challenge suggest that such authority is constitutional.

Not only are lawyers' takings and involuntary-servitude objections unpersuasive as a legal matter, they are unconvincing as a moral claim. Requiring the equivalent of an hour a week of uncompensated assistance hardly seems like slavery. Michael Millemann puts the point directly:

> It is surprising—surprising is a polite word—to hear some of the most wealthy, unregulated, and successful entrepreneurs in the modern economic world invoke the amendment that abolished slavery to justify their refusal to provide a little legal help to those, who in today's society, are most like the freed slaves.

The stronger arguments against pro bono obligations involve pragmatic rather than moral concerns. Many opponents who support such obligations in principle worry that they would prove ineffective in practice. A threshold problem involves defining the services that would satisfy a pro bono requirement. If the definition is broad, and encompasses any charitable work for a nonprofit organization or needy individual, then experience suggests that poor people will not be the major beneficiaries. Most lawyers have targeted their pro bono efforts at friends, relatives, or matters designed to attract or accommodate paying clients. A loosely defined requirement is likely to assist predominately middle-class individuals and organizations such as hospitals, museums, and churches. By contrast, limiting a pro bono requirement to low-income clients who have been given preferred status in the ABA's current rule would exclude many crucial public-interest contributions, such as work for environmental, women's rights, or civil rights organizations. Any compromise effort to permit some but not all charitable groups to qualify for pro bono credit would bump up against charges of political bias.

A related objection to mandatory pro bono requirements is that lawyers who lack expertise or motivation to serve under-represented groups will not provide cost-effective assistance. In opponents' view, having corporate lawyers dabble in poverty cases will provide unduly expensive, often incompetent services. The performance of attorneys required to accept uncompensated appointments in criminal cases does not inspire confidence that unwillingly conscripted practitioners would provide acceptable representation. Critics also worry that some lawyers' inexperience and insensitivity in dealing with low-income clients will compromise the objectives that pro bono requirements seek to advance.

Requiring all attorneys to contribute minimal services of largely unverifiable quality cannot begin to satisfy this nation's unmet legal needs. Worse still, opponents argue, token responses to unequal access may deflect public attention from the fundamental problems that remain and from more productive ways of addressing them. Preferable strategies might include simplification of legal procedures, expanded subsidies for poverty law programs, and elimination of the professional monopoly over routine legal services.

Those arguments have considerable force, but they are not as conclusive as critics often assume. It is certainly true that some practitioners lack the skills and motivation necessary to serve those most in need of assistance. As Michael Millemann notes, however, the current alternative is scarcely preferable:

> Assume that after four years of college, three years of law school, and varying periods of law practice, some lawyers are "incompetent" to help the poor. . . . All this despairing assumption tells us is that the poor are far less competent to represent themselves, and do not have the readily available access to attaining competency that lawyers have. . . .

Moreover, mandatory pro bono programs could address concerns of cost-effectiveness through various strategies. One option is to allow lawyers to buy out of their required service by making a specified financial contribution to a legal-aid program. Another possibility is to give credit for time spent in training. Many voluntary pro bono projects have effectively equipped participants to provide limited poverty-law services through relatively brief educational work-shops, coupled with well-designed manuals and accessible backup assistance.

A final objection to pro bono requirements involves the costs of enforcing them. Opponents often worry about the "Burgeoning Bureaucratic Boondog-gle" that they assume would be necessary to monitor compliance. Even with a substantial expenditure of resources, it would be extremely difficult to verify the amount of time that practitioners reported for pro bono work or the quality of assistance that they provided.

Supporters of mandatory pro bono programs have responded with low-cost enforcement proposals that would rely heavily on the honor system. In the absence of experience with such proposals, their effectiveness is difficult to assess. There is, however, a strong argument for attempting to impose pro bono requirements even if they cannot be fully enforced. At the very least, such requirements would support lawyers who want to participate in public-interest projects but work in organizations that have failed to provide adequate resources or credit for these efforts. Many of the nation's most profitable law firms and leading corporate employers fall into that category. They could readily afford a greater pro bono commitment and a formal requirement might nudge them in that direction. As to lawyers who have no interest in public-interest work, a rule that allowed financial contributions to substitute for direct service could materially assist underfunded legal-aid organizations.

Jonathan R. Macey
MANDATORY PRO BONO: COMFORT FOR THE
POOR OR WELFARE FOR THE RICH?
77 Cornell L. Rev. 1115 (1992) . . .

The reason lawyers ought not to be obliged to help the poor — indeed the reason forcing lawyers to serve the poor is odious and unethical — is that we can make both lawyers *and* the poor better off by abandoning mandatory pro bono and providing the poor with lump sum transfers of cash. In other words, if the rationale for mandatory pro bono is to help the poor, then it is a peculiarly bad way to provide assistance. Alternatively, mandatory pro bono may really be designed to serve some other purpose besides helping the poor. In fact, I will argue that the real effect of a mandatory pro bono system will be to transfer wealth from solo practitioners and lawyers in small- and medium-sized firms to lawyers in large firms.

I Mandatory Pro Bono and the Poor

Contrary to popular belief, mandatory pro bono will not help the poor. To understand why this is so, one must first understand that the real reason why the poor do not presently consume more legal services is because they are rational. Given their limited wealth, the poor simply would rather spend their money on other things. In other words, legal services are very, very low on a poor person's shopping list. Food is higher. Shelter is higher. Clothing is higher. And even after all of those expenses are covered, lawyers should not be surprised to learn that a poor person might choose to allocate his resources in ways other than hiring a lawyer—like buying a car or obtaining an education.

The low demand for lawyers' services by the poor and the middle class provides strong evidence that most people regard legal services as an expendable luxury rather than as a necessity:

> Except for a narrow range of property-related matters—conveyances, wills, and marital separations—the middle class makes just about as little use of legal services as those who literally cannot afford them. Even prepaid legal insurance plans have proved surprisingly unpopular. Why? Because people do not want to give up what they would have to in order to buy a little more of our lawyer justice, except when the expected benefit is worth the cost. People's priorities are different.[5]

In other words, poor people do not hire lawyers because they use their limited resources to buy things that they value more than legal services.

Given a choice between $2500 in cash and twenty billable hours of legal services provided by a partner at a Wall Street law firm (valued at around $10,000), most people—middle class or poor—would take the $2500 in cash. . . .

Ironically, the increased consumption of legal services by the poor may actually harm the indigent rather than help them. For example, among the primary justifications for a regime of mandatory pro bono is that poor people need representation in landlord-tenant and matrimonial disputes.

Lawyers forced to do pro bono work will spend much of their time representing people involved in matrimonial disputes who are unable or unwilling to pay for legal representation. People getting divorced may decline to hire lawyers to represent them for a variety of reasons. The most plausible explanation for the failure of indigent people to hire lawyers in matrimonial disputes is that there are not enough assets in the matrimonial estate to justify the expense. A recent study by Marsha Garrison shows that 31 percent of divorcing couples in New York State had a net worth of less than $5000 and 18 percent of divorcing

---

5. John A. Humbach, *Serving the Public Interest: An Overstated Objective*, 65 A.B.A. J. 564, 564565 (1979).

couples had a *negative* net worth. . . . With the possible exception of matrimonial work, lawsuits against landlords are expected to occupy the lion's share of the time that lawyers compelled to provide legal services for the poor would spend on mandatory pro bono. If more marginal lawsuits are brought against landlords because lawyers need something to do to fulfill their mandatory pro bono obligations, the landlords' costs of providing housing to the indigent inevitably will go up. As the cost of providing housing goes up, rents will increase, and the supply of housing for the poor will go down. The benefit that some poor people derive from having representation in landlord-tenant disputes must be weighed against the increased costs to tenants that will result from a regime of mandatory pro bono in which lawsuits are brought against landlords regardless of whether the expected benefits to the tenants outweigh the costs of the suit.[7]

Litigation often produces benefits for plaintiffs and for society as a whole because individuals who expect to pay damages for the harm they cause have an incentive to reduce their harmful activities. But pro bono litigation is different. When clients must incur costs to hire a lawyer, they will only bring lawsuits when the expected benefits from litigation outweigh the costs of bringing suit, including the costs of hiring a lawyer. In the case of pro bono lawyering, however, the cost of mounting litigation is reduced to zero, and clients will pursue litigation that produces little or no benefits. . . .

II   MANDATORY PRO BONO AND TRANSFERS OF WEALTH WITHIN
THE LEGAL PROFESSION . . .

Mandatory pro bono programs will help large law firms by increasing the demand for lawyers to defend suits brought under such programs. Lawyers forced to bring cases on behalf of poor people will usually be bringing them against defendants who must pay to hire lawyers to defend those suits. In other words, mandatory pro bono programs artificially expand society's demand for paid legal services. In particular, the demand for the services of lawyers at large firms who specialize in representing defendants will increase. As one commentator presciently has observed, "[W]henever clients who cannot pay get more legal services, clients who can pay need more legal services. This results in new business for the bar."[12]

A mandatory pro bono requirement will increase the demand for lawyers in large law firms in other, subtler ways. First, under the New York plan, lawyers at large law firms could credit the excess pro bono hours of some lawyers in the firm to meet the obligation of other lawyers in the firm. This flexibility will benefit large firms far more than small firms, because large firms can more easily afford to hire lawyers to specialize in pro bono work. In large firms the pro bono activities of these lawyers can be amortized over a large number of lawyers. In addition, at any given time, large firms predictably will have excess capacity in certain practice areas and no room for additional work in others. These large firms can ameliorate this problem by shifting the burden of pro bono work onto the shoulders of the lawyers with extra time in their schedules.

7. Humbach, supra note 5, at 566.
12. Humbach, supra note 5, at 566.

This is a luxury that smaller, more specialized firms lack because all of the lawyers in such firms are likely to have slack times and busy times simultaneously.

Even if lawyers in large law firms were prohibited from assigning the burden of their pro bono obligations to other, more junior lawyers in the firm, satisfying the burdens of a mandatory pro bono obligation would still be easier for a large firm. Suppose, for example, that a solo practitioner is scheduled to make a court appearance on a particular day for a pro bono client. During that day the solo practitioner will be unable to represent any of his paying clients. By contrast, a large law firm simply can reassign personnel (many of whom will have expertise in the relevant area of law) to handle the work of the absent lawyer. . . .

Mandatory pro bono programs also benefit large firms at the expense of smaller firms because under some pro bono plans, large firms can fulfill their obligations by doing work for foundations and other low-pay/high-prestige clients that such firms normally represent. Similarly, unlike small firms and solo practitioners, large firms can use mandatory pro bono programs as vehicles for training associates because younger lawyers working for large firms that deal almost exclusively with very high stakes legal issues understandably do not get as much courtroom experience or contact with paying clients as lawyers at smaller firms that litigate smaller stakes issues.

III   THE GOOD OLD DAYS: THE LEGAL PROFESSION AS SOMETIME MONOPOLY

A final argument in favor of mandatory pro bono is that lawyers are professionals, and as such, their license to practice law comes with certain societal obligations. In less prosaic terms, the licensing requirements of the bar have created barriers to entry that permit lawyers to earn super-competitive profits. According to this argument, lawyers are under an obligation to perform legal services for the poor in order to compensate society for the social losses associated with their monopoly position. Since the legal profession's monopoly allows it to charge above-market prices, this monopoly status permits lawyers to transfer wealth from the rest of society to themselves. Mandatory pro bono requirements merely effectuate a retransfer back to society of this initial wealth transfer. But this argument is completely flawed.

If at any time in history the legal profession was a monopoly, it is not any longer. If one hundred years ago lawyers erected barriers to entry that enabled them to obtain monopoly profits, those were short-term gains that are not presently being enjoyed by members of the profession. This is because nonlawyers, observing the economic rents earned by a cartelized legal profession, would begin expending the resources and developing the human capital necessary to enter the profession and obtain these rents. Thus any gains from cartelizing the legal profession were lost long ago by competition from new entrants. . . .

Thus, as with most regulations, lawyer licensing requirements, once in place, create an incentive for the people subject to those requirements to lobby for keeping them in place even after the abnormal returns from the entry restrictions have disappeared. The point is not that licensing requirements for lawyers should be maintained, but rather that lawyers currently in practice are earning only normal — not super-competitive — returns on their investments in human capital. Consequently, the presence of entry restrictions in the form of state bar licensing rules does not justify imposing a mandatory pro bono requirement on lawyers currently in practice. . . .

Dennis Jacobs
PRO BONO FOR FUN AND PROFIT
http://www.fed-soc.org/publications/pubid.1178/pub_detail.asp

[Dennis Jacobs, Chief Judge of the Second Circuit Court of Appeals, gave a speech to the Rochester chapter of the Federalist Society on October 6, 2008. It was entitled "Pro Bono for Fun and Profit," and it caused quite a stir. Judge Jacobs supports the pro bono work of lawyers. He emphasized as examples "wills for the sick, corporate work for non-profit schools and hospitals, and the representation of pro se litigants whose claims have likely merit." He added help "to assist aliens who are working their way through our immigration system." But he criticized "public interest litigation," which he called "policy work." His criticism was based in part on the fact that such litigation seeks to achieve political goals best left to the political branches, not the courts. While that criticism is not new, what was new (at least to me) was his assertion of the way that, and the reasons why, the bench and bar have cooperated to resist challenges to their alleged usurpation of political power. Here is an excerpt from his speech.]

When I started talking I said that I would be articulating some views that you don't hear from judges, and I said that I would explain why this occasion — on which a judge says a single word critical of public interest litigation — is so rare. The fact is, most judges are very grateful for public interest and impact litigation. Cases in which the lawyers can and do make an impact are (by the same token) cases in which the judges can make an impact; and impacts are exercises of influence and power. Judges have little impetus to question or complain when activist lawyers identify a high-visibility issue, search out a client that has at least a nominal interest, and present for adjudication questions of consequence that expand judicial power and influence over hotly debated issues. If the question is sufficiently important, influential and conspicuous, it matters little to many judges whether the plaintiff has any palpable injury sufficient to support standing or even whether there is a client at all behind the litigation, as opposed to lawyers with a cause whose preparation for suit involves (in addition to research and drafting) the finding of a client — as a sort of technical requirement (like getting a person over 18 years old to serve the summons).

Similarly, you will hear no criticism of public interest litigation or impact litigation at the bar associations, and I submit that is for essentially the same reason. When matters of public importance are brought within the ambit of the court system, lawyers as well as judges are empowered. True, we have an adversary system, but the adversary system is staffed on every side by lawyers. There is a neutral judge, but judges are lawyers too; and it is hard for a judge to avoid an insidious bias in favor of assuming that all things important need to be contested by the workings of the legal profession, and decided by the judiciary.

In the courtroom, advocates advocate, and judges rule, but lawyers as a profession encounter no competitors for influence and power. In the solution of political, social, moral and policy questions, everyone else is subordinated: public officials, the voters, the rate-payers, the clergy, the teachers and principals, the wardens, the military and the police. The lawyers and judges become the only active players, and everything that matters — the nature of the proceedings, how the issues are presented, what arguments and facts may be considered, the allowable patterns of analysis — are all decided and implemented by legal professionals and the legal profession, and dominated and ordered by what we think of proudly as the legal mind.

Great harm can be done when the legal profession uses pro bono litigation to promote political ends and to advance the interests and powers of the legal profession and the judicial branch of our governments. Constitutionally necessary principles are eroded: the requirement of a case or controversy; the requirement of standing. Democracy itself is impaired: The people are distanced from their government; the priorities people vote for are re-ordered; the fisc is opened. These things are done by judges who are unelected (or designated in arcane ways), at the behest of a tiny group of ferociously active lawyers making arguments that the public (being busy about the other needs of family and work) cannot be expected to study or understand.

And, on those rare occasions when our competitors protest, when elected officials and the public contend that the courts and legal profession have gone too far and have arrogated to themselves powers that belong to other branches of government, to other professions or other callings, or that would benefit from other modes of thinking (such as morals or faith), the Bar forms a cordon around the judiciary and declares that any harsh or effective criticism is an attack on judicial independence.

G. WHO GETS THE MONEY?

When a sole practitioner gets paid, there's not much trouble deciding who gets the money. Many lawyers, however, practice in firms whose sizes range from two to more than two thousand lawyers. These firms must decide how to divide their profits. Sometimes lawyers affiliate to handle a single case. Or one lawyer may refer a matter to another lawyer. As we shall see, ethics codes have traditionally restricted fee-sharing among lawyers who are not in the same firm. (Lawyers have been forbidden to share legal fees with laypersons under almost all circumstances. See chapter 14.) The restrictions against splitting fees outside a firm make it important to be able to identify a "firm.".

Dividing Money (or Clients) Within a Firm

The last two decades have seen marked growth in the number of consultants, books, and articles dedicated to the elusive art of "law office management." Among management issues is how to divide a firm's profits fairly and with as little resentment as possible. For our purposes it is worth noting that the rules generally do not limit how profits are divided within a firm. (One notable exception is reflected in Rule 1.11, which allows a firm to screen a former government lawyer who is personally disqualified from working on a matter by virtue of her government service. But the lawyer must be "apportioned no part of the fee" from the work.) As a practical matter, many firms tend to reward the same contributions. Partnership shares are divided according to formulas that recognize partners who bring in more clients (or whose clients pay higher fees) and partners who bill more hours. (As used here, "partner" includes shareholders in limited liability professional corporations.) Seniority (years at the firm or since law school graduation) often carries independent weight. For a partner to benefit from bringing in a client, she need not work on the client's matter. In fact, law firm partners commonly known as "rainmakers" may be handsomely rewarded merely for bringing clients to the firm and keeping them happy, though they may actually do (or be capable of doing) little legal work. I once asked a friend at a firm that represented famous people in the entertainment world — a temperamental group to be sure — what the very successful top lawyer did. I never saw him do any work when I visited the firm. He was drinking tea or sherry or he was "out" somewhere unspecified. "He sends flowers," my friend said. "He knows when to send flowers and he knows what flowers to send. He knows how to order wine. He knows how to listen and show concern."

Not all firms work this way. A small number of (generally older) firms divide profits based solely on length of service in the firm or membership in the bar. Law firms in the first category ("eat what you kill" firms) are said to encourage competition and individual success along with the interests of the firm as an entity. But those firms may see more defections if a partner believes he will be able to keep more of what he "kills" at another home. The firms in the second category encourage behavior that benefits the firm as an entity and the partners derivatively but encounter freeriders.

Partners also make money from associate time. One rule of thumb is that associate time is billed at an hourly rate that, when multiplied by the number of hours the associate is expected to bill yearly, will yield three times the associate's salary and benefits. Assuming that one-third of an associate's billings is spent to support the associate (space, secretary) and one-third for salary and benefits, this leaves one-third of annual billings for the firm. If a firm has a partner-to-associate ratio of 1:2, which is common, each partner on average earns the equivalent of double an associate's salary from associate work, above and beyond what the partner may earn for his own work. (Some argue that this "pyramid" structure encourages overstaffing and unnecessary work. Some clients have grown skeptical. Articles on "value billing" often make this point.) The nice rate of return on associate labor is one that the private market might be willing to undersell. Since, however, nonlawyers cannot invest in law firms, Rule 5.4(b) and (d), only lawyers may profit from the sale of the legal work of other lawyers. The result may be an increase in the cost of legal services. Can the increase be justified by a need to protect lawyers' "professional independence of judgment," as the comment to Rule 5.4 suggests? See chapter 14.

Generalization beyond this point is risky and not helpful. Firms differ greatly, both from other firms and over time. As partners develop or lose significant practices, their bargaining power within their firms may rise or fall, leading to major readjustments in partnership shares. Sometimes, and increasingly since the 1980s, the result may be defection of a valuable partner to another firm that promises more generous rewards and more power to direct the firm or, when a career is going south, a request to pack up and leave or accept sharply reduced compensation.

Partnership agreements generally define the future firm income to which a departing partner is entitled and the terms for payment. Why should a departing partner be entitled to any income that arrives after he leaves? Good question. Payment of fees lags behind the work done to earn the fee, so the firm will receive fees after a partner departs for work she or others did before she left. AR/WIP is the abbreviation here. It stands for accounts receivable and work in progress. A partnership may, of course, deny a departing partner any share in this forthcoming money as part of the partnership agreement. Or the firm may recognize the partner's interest, as most do. Because it will ordinarily be complicated and time-consuming to do a full accounting every time a partner leaves, firms use a formula for determining post-departure payments. The formula may look at the firm's average partnership profits for the last three years (i.e., the pie that got divided up after expenses) and multiply the result by the departing partner's partnership share.

Rule 5.6 prevents partnerships from restricting the post-departure work of lawyers. The rules forbid outright bans on competition, but they also forbid reducing or denying entitlement to a contractual payout because of the lawyer's post-departure competition, which is seen as an *indirect* restriction on practice. The purported justification for the rule is that such a restriction "not only limits [a lawyer's] professional autonomy but also limits the freedom of clients to choose a lawyer." Rule 5.6 comment. The rule does not forbid partnership agreements that deny all departing partners *any* share in future income, notwithstanding the autonomy consequences to the lawyer, so long as payment is not conditioned on noncompetition. Think of it as an equal protection rule for lawyers. The partnership agreement must be competition neutral. An exception permits noncompete obligations when they are a condition for receiving retirement payments. Do you understand the reason for the exception? What social good is encouraged? Donnelly v. Brown, Winick, Graves, Gross, Baskerville, Schoenebaum & Walker, P.L.C., 599 N.W.2d 677 (Iowa 1999) (upholding a retirement plan that required "ten years of service and sixty years of age or twenty-five years of service" and conditioned payment on noncompetition); Schoonmaker v. Cummings and Lockwood of Connecticut, P.C., 747 A.2d 1017 (Conn. 2000) (firm need not "require the absolute cessation of practice as a condition of retirement under the retirement benefits exception of the rule").

Is Rule 5.6 realistic given the rapid increase in lawyer mobility among firms? Sometimes many partners in a particular practice field may leave for a competing firm all at once. That can really dent a firm's profitability until it can rebuild. Don't law firms have a valid interest in protecting their financial integrity with reasonable rules restricting the payout to former partners while those partners are continuing to receive money from their former firms, especially if the firm expects to be able to rely on the work to generate the revenue for the payout? Alternatively, should a partnership be permitted to be more generous with postdeparture payments to those who enter government or other public interest or public service jobs, which generally pay much less than firm partnerships, even though such a provision would not be competition neutral because it treats lawyers who go into competitive private practice less favorably?

These questions have stirred a robust debate in state appellate courts. The majority view would permit firms to deny postdeparture compensation to everyone (equally), but would forbid firms to treat departing partners who enter competitive practice less favorably than those who do not. In other words, all or nothing. Pierce v. Morrison Mahoney LLP, 897 N.E. 2d 562 (Mass. 2008); Cohen v. Lord, Day & Lord, 550 N.E.2d 410 (N.Y. 1989). Compare Pettingell v. Morrison, Mahoney & Miller, 687 N.E.2d 1237 (Mass. 1997) (forfeiture of compensation because of postdeparture competition declared void where "the firm has not presented evidence . . . that the plaintiffs' departures have caused, or have seriously threatened to cause, any harm to the firm or its continuing partners"); Eisentstein v. David G. Conlin, P.C., 827 N.E.2d 686 (Mass. 2005) (rejecting nonretirement provision that required departing partner to pay firm 15 percent of income from certain clients partner continued to represent; firm offered no evidence that provision was needed in order to protect its interests); Hackett v. Milbank, Tweed, Hadley & McCloy, 654 N.E.2d 95 (N.Y. 1995). *Hackett* upheld an arbitrator's conclusion that a firm could ethically reduce a partner's postdeparture compensation "dollar-for-
dollar to the extent that the withdrawing partner's annual earned income, from any source, exceeds $100,000." This provision was competition neutral.

A deferential minority view that cites the economic realities of modern law firm practice is revealed in Howard v. Babcock, 863 P.2d 150 (Cal. 1993) ("An agreement that assesses a reasonable cost against a partner who chooses to compete with his or her former partners does not restrict the practice of law. Rather, it attaches an economic consequence to a departing partner's unrestricted choice to pursue a particular kind of practice"); Fearnow v. Ridenour, Swenson, Cleere & Evans, P.C., 138 P.3d 723 (Ariz. 2006) (after thorough review of case law from other jurisdictions, and with no Arizona precedent, court finds *Howard* "compelling" and remands for determination of reasonableness of provision).

Do not confuse division of fees within a firm with division of clients. When a lawyer leaves a firm, it is the client's decision, not the firm's or the lawyer's, whether to leave as well. The single "exception" to this rule, if it can be called that, is the provision for the sale of a law practice. See Rule 1.17, which allows a lawyer or firm to sell a practice subject to notice to the clients of their rights to retain other counsel. Other restrictions also apply.

Because principals in a firm owe fiduciary duties to each other and associates have fiduciary duties to the firm, a lawyer who has chosen to leave must proceed cautiously:

At one end of the spectrum . . . taking steps to locate alternative space and affiliations would not violate a partner's fiduciary duties. . . . As a matter of ethics, departing partners have been permitted to inform firm clients with whom they have a prior professional relationship about their impending with-drawal and new practice, and to remind the client of its freedom to retain counsel of its choice. . . .

At the other end of the spectrum, secretly attempting to lure firm clients (even those the partner has brought into the firm and personally represented) to the new association, lying to clients about their rights with respect to the choice of counsel, lying to partners about plans to leave, and abandoning the firm on short notice (taking clients and files) would not be consistent with a partner's fiduciary duties.

Graubard Mollen Dannett & Horowitz v. Moskovitz, 653 N.E.2d 1179 (N.Y. 1995). See also Dowd & Dowd, Ltd. v. Gleason, 693 N.E.2d 358 (Ill. 1998) (surreptitious predeparture solicitation of a firm's clients may constitute breach of fiduciary duty and tortious interference with prospective economic advantage); Prince, Yeates & Geldzahler v. Young, 94 P.3d 179 (Utah 2004) (associate who secretly competed with his firm breached his fiduciary duty and must disgorge fees he earned); Johnson v. Brewer & Pritchard, P.C., 73 S.W.3d 193 (Texas 2002) (associate has fiduciary duty not to profit personally by referring potential clients to other lawyers but absent agreement can do so without personal benefit); Reeves v. Hanlon, 95 P.3d 513 (Cal. 2004) (firm lawyers who secretly solicit firm employees when planning a competitive practice and who misuse firm's client list violate fiduciary duty to firm and state trade secrets act); ABA Opinion 99-414 ("departing lawyer is prohibited by ethical rules, and may be prohibited by other law, from making in-person contact prior to her departure with clients with whom she has no family or client-lawyer relationship"). *Eisenstein*, supra, found no violation of fiduciary duty when former partners showed their new firm the former firm's partnership agreement and client list and services performed because the agreement did not prohibit this conduct.

Division of Fees Outside Firms

Two or more lawyers who are not formally affiliated in a firm may nevertheless work together on many matters. One lawyer may refer a client to another lawyer because the first lawyer is not skilled in the client's problem or has an inadequate support staff, or because the client needs a lawyer in a jurisdiction in which the first lawyer is not admitted. Sometimes the referring lawyer will want to work on the referred matter with the receiving lawyer, and sometimes the referring lawyer will be happy never to hear about the matter again. Despite the absence of restrictions on how fees are divided *within* firms — even to the point that a lawyer may be generously rewarded for bringing to the firm a client on whose matter the lawyer does no work at all — the Rules constrain fee divisions by lawyers who are not in the same firm. How can this difference be explained?

Canon 34 of the 1908 Canons prohibited a division of fees among lawyers unless "based upon a division of service or responsibility." Notice that Canon 34 used the conjunction "or," so two lawyers were permitted to divide a legal fee so long as they both worked on the matter or so long as they were both responsible for the matter.

The Code changed this rule to require, among other things, that the fee division be "made in proportion to the services performed and responsibility assumed by each" lawyer. DR 2-107(A)(2). The use of the conjunction "and" was taken to mean that it was not enough merely to accept "responsibility" for the other lawyer's work. Both lawyers had to work on the case and the fee division had to be "in proportion" to their work. See, e.g., In re Diamond, 368 A.2d 353 (N.J. 1976); Palmer v. Breyfogle, 535 P.2d 955 (Kan. 1975).

The Model Rules partly return to the standard set by the Canons. Rule 1.5(e) allows a division of fee "in proportion to the services performed by each lawyer or [if] each lawyer assumes joint responsibility for the representation." The client must agree after being told each lawyer's share, and the agreement must be confirmed in writing. The total fee must be reasonable. Possibly, as well, each lawyer's share of the fee must be "reasonable" within the meaning of Rule 1.5(a).

Courts will sometimes refuse to enforce a fee-sharing agreement if it does not substantially comply with Rule 1.5(e) in the jurisdiction. Christensen v. Eggen, 577 N.W.2d 221 (Minn. 1998); Post v. Bregman, 707 A.2d 806 (Md. 1998). That means the referring lawyer does not get paid, yet both lawyers will have violated the rule. Why should the receiving lawyer get a windfall when he or she is equally culpable? Compare Ballow Brested O'Brien & Rusin P.C. v. Logan, 435 F.3d 235 (2d Cir. 2006) ("We also note our agreement with [New York precedent's] recognition that 'it ill becomes [the parties seeking to avoid paying the fee], who are also bound by the Code of Professional Responsibility, to seek to avoid on "ethical" grounds the obligations of an agreement to which they freely assented and from which they reaped the benefits.' "). Perhaps the amount of the fee that the referring lawyer would have received had the agreement complied with the rule should instead be given to the client. See Post v. Bregman, supra (Chasanow, J., dissenting) ("Isn't allowing Post to keep more of the fee than he can prove he earned at least as unethical as allowing Bregman to recover more of the fee than he can prove he earned?"). Some courts will allow the referring lawyer quantum meruit. Huskinson & Brown, LLP v. Wolf, 84 P.3d 379 (Cal. 2004) (plaintiff awarded $5,000 quantum meruit instead of more than $18,000 claimed). That's some compensation, but quantum meruit is only available if the referring lawyer worked on the case and, in any event, is likely to yield much less than the fee division would have allowed.

What is a Law Firm?

Because law firms can divide the profit pie virtually any way they like without disciplinary risk or judicial control, it can sometimes be attractive to be able to claim status as a firm, even if only for the passing moment. Rule 7.5(d) permits lawyers to "state or imply that they practice in a partnership or other organization only when that is the fact." This rule has two ostensible purposes. It prevents lawyers from giving clients the misimpression that the lawyers have a formal professional relationship when they do not. It also prevents lawyers from circumventing limitations on fee sharing with an unaffiliated lawyer.

Part Two

CONFLICTS OF INTEREST

V

Concurrent Conflicts of Interest

Motions to disqualify opposing counsel are viewed with disfavor because they impinge on a party's right to employ the counsel of its choice. Additionally, the drastic remedy of disqualification is subject to strict scrutiny because of the strong potential to stall and derail the proceedings, redounding to the strategic advantage of one party over another. Hence, the moving party bears the heavy burden in proving the facts required for disqualification.

> —Judge Chin in First Interregional Advisors Corp. v.
> Wolff, 956 F. Supp. 480, 489 (S.D.N.Y. 1997)

One of the Court's duties and responsibilities is to ensure that attorneys who appear before it preserve the public's confidence in the judicial system. . . . Thus, when the Court must make a disqualification determination upon difficult facts, it does not weigh the circumstances with hair-splitting nicety but . . . with a view of preventing the appearance of impropriety, it is to resolve all doubts in favor of disqualification.

> —Judge Williams in Buckley v. Airshield Corp. 908 F. Supp. 299
> (D.Md. 1995)

There are no conflicts above $5 million.

> —Famous American lawyer (circa 1984)

No man can serve two masters: for either he will hate the one, and love the other; or else he will hold to the one, and despise the other. Ye cannot serve God and mammon.

> —Matthew 6:24, King James Bible, often quoted by
> plaintiffs' lawyers in action against law firms for
> conflicts of interest

- *Lawyer-Client Conflicts*
- *Client-Client Conflicts: Civil and Criminal Matters*
- *Civil Liability for Conflicts*
- *Advocate-Witness Rule*

Conflicts are a minefield for lawyers and law offices. Often, no litmus test exists for deciding if a particular representation violates conflict rules. Judgment is necessary. The risk of mistakes creates a bit of anxiety, because the sanctions for a finding of conflict, summarized below, can be unpleasant. So why don't lawyers just resolve doubts in favor of rejecting the possibly conflicting matter? Because conflict rules are business killers. They say, in effect, "Sorry, friend. We know you really want that new client or that new matter. We know it will be great for your career, make your name, put you on the road to fame and fortune. But no way." This isn't a message lawyers want to hear, so they are understandably tempted to resolve doubts *against* finding a conflict and hope for the best. Hope is not a good way to run a law practice.

On top of it all, as the two court quotes above reveal, judges vary greatly in their interpretation of the conflict doctrine. Judge Chin, following circuit precedent, is disinclined to see a disqualifying conflict. His assumption is contrary. But Judge Williams's test is opposite. Indeed, you can sometimes find this inconsistency in the same opinion, as when a judge writes that a party alleging a conflict bears a "heavy burden" but "doubts are to be resolved in favor of disqualification." In re Cendant Corp. Sec. Lit. 124 F. Supp. 2d 235 (D.N.J. 2000). Say what?

A Typology of Conflicts

Conflicts come in many shapes and sizes. The next few pages offer a general introduction to give you a road map for the balance of this chapter and chapter 6.

Definition and Context.   Despite the variety of conflicts, and their dependency on the facts of each matter, a general definition is possible. Here is the one in Restatement §121: "A conflict of interest is involved if there is a *substantial* risk that the lawyer's representation of the client would be *materially and adversely* affected by the lawyer's own interests or by the *lawyer's duties* to another current client, a former client, or a third person." (Italics added.) The devil here is in the detail. The sentence tries as hard as it can to capture the degree of *risk* that other interests *may* interfere with a lawyer's commitment to her client's cause. The client is entitled to an undistracted lawyer, one with no incentives inconsistent with her duties to the client. Note that the sentence does not say that a finding of conflict depends on a conclusion that the lawyer *will* disserve the client, only that sometimes the risk that she will do is too great. (Later, we will see that often a client can give informed consent to a conflict.) There's something rather biblical about this. We're trying to quantify temptation. So how much risk is too much? Good question. Welcome to conflicts. It depends, doesn't it, on how we define "substantial," "materially," and "adversely." Critical, too, is what we recognize to be a "lawyer's duties."

The same can be said about three words in Rule 1.7(a)(2). That rule says that a current client conflict exists if "there is a *significant* risk that the representation of one or more clients will be *materially* limited by the lawyer's *responsibilities* to another client, a former client or a third person or by a personal interest of the lawyer." (Italics added.) This imprecision means lawyers must make predictions on imperfect doctrinal information. (Since the need to predict often arises at the start of a representation, the facts may be unclear, too.) If the question is close, lawyers must then assess their tolerance for risk. As the third quote at the start of this chapter suggests, as a matter of human nature, that tolerance may increase with the size of the expected fee.

Lawyers aren't the only ones who labor under conflict rules. Lawyers are their clients' agents, and all agents have duties to avoid situations that do or could present conflicts between the interests of their principals and those of others or their own. Even if there were no lawyer ethics codes, lawyers would be subject to conflict rules under the law of agency and the law of fiduciary duty. (Recall from chapter 2 that all agents are fiduciaries.) Lawyer ethics rules happen to provide greater specificity for the operation of conflict rules as they apply to the work of lawyers, but the law of agency and fiduciary duty are not displaced.

In this chapter we review varieties of concurrent conflicts — conflicting interests a lawyer may have at the same time that he or she is representing a client. In chapter 6, we turn to successive conflicts. We distinguish between these shortly, but as should be apparent, one difference between the two types of conflict is *temporal*. Ethics rules apprehend different risks to client interests depending on whether a person is now a client (i.e., current) or once was a client (i.e., former). Although each kind of conflict presents risks to both loyalty and confidentiality, a lawyer has stronger loyalty obligations to a current client than to a former client, as we shall see.

Conflict-of-interest dilemmas may arise in any practice and can take many forms. They may confront lawyers who have many clients and lawyers with only one client. They arise in private practice, in corporate law departments, in criminal defense and prosecutorial offices, in public interest practice, and in government agencies. It would be a rare lawyer who never had need to measure her contemplated conduct against the conflict-of-interest rules. Some lawyers confront conflict questions often. Large law firms confront them weekly. And not only must a lawyer be cognizant of conflicts in her own work. She must also take heed of the conflicts of her office colleagues and of opposing lawyers.

Conflict issues present some of the most complex problems in the area of legal ethics. What's more, their complexity is increasing. Because conflict questions are often highly fact-specific, they don't easily lend themselves to generalization. Law firms use increasingly sophisticated methods, often relying on specially designed computer programs, to avoid conflicts. Avoiding them is crucial. A lawyer caught in a conflict faces a number of unhappy possibilities. Discipline is one, although disciplinary authorities seem to recognize that the technical nature of many (but by no means all) conflicts often makes them inappropriate candidates for professional sanctions. Conflicts can also lead to disqualification from a representation, with attendant embarrassment and cost; delay of a client's cause; negative publicity; fee forfeiture (chapter 13B); and civil liability (page 289). In the rare case, failure to reveal a conflict can result in a criminal conviction. United States v. Gellene, 182 F.3d 578 (7th Cir. 1999) (upholding perjury conviction of large law firm partner whose sworn declaration and oral testimony to bankruptcy court failed to reveal firm's representation of clients with conflicting interests).

As if all this were not daunting enough, it could easily escape your attention (until now) that most conflicts rules do not contain a mens rea requirement:

They are absolute liability rules. Think about that. A lawyer may violate them unintentionally through lack of awareness, or even believing, erroneously but in good faith, that she was acting properly. A major exception concerns *imputed* conflicts — a conflict that arises only because the conflict of a colleague in a firm is imputed to other lawyers in that firm. Rule 1.10(a) forbids a lawyer "knowingly" to accept certain work that a conflicted colleague would have to decline. Without such knowledge, the lawyer is spared discipline, but her firm still risks disqualification and civil liability based on the conflict.

To have a conflict, a lawyer must have a client, or at least a person or an entity that a court is prepared to treat as a client for conflict purposes. The more clients a lawyer has, the greater the risk of conflict. The more office colleagues with their own clients, the greater the risk of imputed conflicts. As we saw in chapter 2 (and shall see again), whether a client-lawyer relationship exists is not always clear. For example, a member of a trade association represented by a law firm may not be a traditional client of the firm but may be deemed a client for conflicts of interest analysis. See page 297.

The following pages introduce some of the ideas that will recur in chapters 5 and 6. These pages are dense and introduce the issues any conflicts regime must address. The purpose right now is to ask the questions that chapters 5 and 6 will then answer. The goal is to give you an aerial snapshot of the terrain and get you thinking. Thereafter, we begin our study at ground level with concurrent conflicts of interest. You might want to come back to this "flyover" summary at the end of your study of conflicts, as a way of reviewing the highlights of what you learned.

First: Current Client Conflicts. Let us more fully distinguish between concurrent and successive conflicts of interest. In a concurrent conflict situation, the lawyer may find her loyalties divided between two or more current clients, that is, clients she is then representing. For example, a lawyer for co-defendants in a civil or criminal case may find that one wants to blame the other. Or the prosecutor may tell a lawyer that she is prepared to offer one of two criminal clients a generous plea bargain in exchange for testimony against the other client. A lawyer representing two parties wishing to enter into a contract may find that he cannot draft a clause one way or another way without disadvantaging one of his two clients.

In these situations helping one client in a matter will hurt a second client in that very same matter. But the conflict may also be less focused. May a lawyer represent Joe against Delia if the lawyer also happens to represent Delia on a distinct and entirely unrelated matter? May a lawyer who does products liability defense for a company that manufactures consumer products represent a person who wants to sue a subsidiary of the company for breach of an employment contract? May a lawyer who represents a city's Hilton Hotel in labor negotiations with its unions also represent the city's Sheraton in labor negotiations with its unions?

Concurrent conflicts need not be between or among current clients. The lawyer may have personal interests that pose a loyalty threat. May a lawyer whose spouse has a big stock investment in a corporation represent a plaintiff wishing to sue the corporation for a great sum? May a lawyer represent a person who wishes to challenge the legality of a tax regulation that happens to benefit the lawyer or her law partners?

These examples all raise issues about the lawyer's ability to be loyal and, to a lesser extent, about danger to client confidences. Comment [1] to Rule 1.7 uses the word "loyalty."

Second: Former Client Conflicts.   The term "successive conflicts" may sound like a self-contradiction at first. Do you really have duties to former clients once you have finished the work? Yes. Maybe even long after. Consider a lawyer representing client *A* in defending the legality of a patent. The lawyer is successful. Later the lawyer is retained by client *B* to sue client *A* on the ground that the very same patent has been used to violate antitrust laws. At the time client *B* enters the picture, what is the lawyer's obligation to his now former client *A*? Shall we say that the duty of loyalty continues after the end of the representation and that it prevents the lawyer from doing anything to undermine the value of the patent rights he has won for *A*? Whatever our answer, there is a further problem. The lawyer will likely have gained confidential information in the course of the representation of client *A*. If the lawyer reveals or uses this information on *B*'s behalf, he may violate Rule 1.9(c). May the lawyer represent client *B* without using the information? You know, just put it out of your mind. Is that even possible? On the other hand, if client *B* seeks to sue former (patent) client *A* for violation of the provisions of a lease, is there any problem? Should we then say that, because the nature of the representation is wholly different from the patent work that the lawyer once did for *A*, the lawyer may proceed to sue former client *A* without disloyalty or danger to confidences? Or should we have a flat prohibition against ever suing persons or entities with whom a lawyer once had a professional relationship? (We don't have a flat prohibition. Imagine what that would do to the availability of counsel of choice.)

The Model Rules speak to successive conflicts in private law offices in Rule 1.9.

Third: Imputed Conflicts.   If we conclude that a lawyer is prevented from representing a client because of a concurrent conflict (either with the interests of another client or with the interests of the lawyer or of others close to her) or a former client conflict, shall we nevertheless permit another lawyer with whom the first lawyer is affiliated to accept the representation? In other words, shall we *impute* the conflicted lawyer's status to his or her partners, associates, or office colleagues? Matters become more complicated if the first lawyer had represented her former client while in a different law office and has since changed firms (what we sometimes call a *lateral* lawyer). Should the conflict *travel* with the lateral lawyer to her new firm? Should conflicts *ever* be imputed? When? In some jurisdictions, law offices can sometimes avoid the imputation of a lateral lawyer's conflict by screening the conflicted lawyer. The Code provisions dealing with imputed conflicts are DRs 5-101(B), 5-102, and 5-105(D). The Model Rules cover the issue at Rules 1.10, 1.11, 1.12, and 3.7.

Fourth: Government-Lawyer Conflicts.   Lawyers who work for government and move to the private sector or who leave the private sector to work for government introduce us to a phenomenon sometimes labeled "the revolving door." Consider the lawyer who leaves government for private practice. Should he personally be treated exactly like the lateral lawyer who leaves one private firm to join another? Shall the new firms of each lawyer be treated exactly the same with regard to the lateral lawyer's imputed conflicts? Take a lawyer who works for the Justice Department investigating antitrust violations in the automobile industry. He spends two years looking into *QRS* Motors. Eventually he leaves government and joins a firm. At the firm, may he represent a competitor of *QRS* that wants to sue *QRS* for the same antitrust violations? If he may not do so, may the firm do so? Alternatively, if *QRS* comes to the firm seeking representation when it is charged with the antitrust violations (by the government or a competitor), may the former government lawyer defend *QRS*? May the firm do so after screening the former government lawyer? As we'll see, conflict rules have traditionally been more generous toward allowing firms to screen former government lawyers than lateral lawyers from other private practice situations. This difference aims to encourage lawyers to go to work for government without fear that they will find it hard to get a job after they leave. See Rule 1.11.

Fifth: Lawyer-Witness Conflicts.   A problem arises when a lawyer for a client in a litigation will or should be a witness, called either by the client or the opposing side. See Rule 3.7. This so-called advocate-witness rule seeks to avoid a conflict between the lawyer's interest in being an advocate and the interest of the client, the adversary, or the system of justice in having the lawyer testify. As a rule, a lawyer cannot occupy both roles.

Sixth: Organizational Lawyer Conflicts.   Conflicts can arise when a lawyer represents an entity but deals with the entity through its officers and employees. For example, a lawyer for a corporation works with its agents, such as board members, the president, the financial officers, and nonmanagerial employees. Conflicts can develop if the lawyer is deemed to represent both the entity and its agents if their interests happen to diverge. The entity need not be a corporation. It may also be a labor union, a trade association, a partnership, or a government agency. When companies are all part of the same corporate family, can representation of one of the members of that family be deemed, for conflict purposes at least, representation of another company in the same family? The answer is sometimes, as we see in chapter 10.

Seventh: Conflicts in Conflict Rules.   Conflict rules vary significantly among American jurisdictions. Further, federal trial courts may, but need not, apply the conflict rules of the states in which they sit. The Fifth Circuit has held that "[m]otions to disqualify are substantive motions. Therefore, they are decided under federal law. When reviewing the disqualification of an attorney, we must consider the motion governed by the ethical rules announced by the national profession in the light of the public interest and the litigant's rights." The court would look to "norms embodied in the Model Rules and the Model Code" as well as state rules. FDIC v. United States Fire Ins. Co., 50 F.3d 1304 (5th Cir. 1995) (internal quotes omitted). See also Cole v. Ruidoso Municipal Schools, 43 F.3d 1373 (10th Cir. 1994). When a dispute touches more than one jurisdiction and their conflicts rules differ, a court must decide which rules will apply. White Consol. Indus., Inc. v. Island Kitchens, Inc., 884 F. Supp. 176 (E.D. Pa. 1995) (Pennsylvania choice-of-law rules dictated use of New York conflict rules by federal court in Philadelphia). Model Rule 8.5 also provides guidance in identifying which jurisdiction's rules apply.

Eighth: Conflicts as Default Rules.   Last, despite all the ink and energy that has gone into fashioning and interpreting the conflict rules, it turns out (surprise!) that lawyers and clients may displace nearly all of them if the client gives *informed consent*. The rules are mostly default rules. They are what you get if you say nothing. Rules 1.7 through 1.12 recognize client consent to what they would otherwise forbid. (The consent may have to be written or confirmed in writing and must be informed, as we shall see in this and the next chapter.) But the door swings both ways. A client might demand *more* protection against conflicts than the rules offer. Why would lawyers agree to a greater restriction on their professional autonomy? Answer: Money and business. A client may have a lot of business to bestow and a firm, in return for (or in expectation of) that business, might be willing to accept a greater restriction on its practice. (Would a firm, offered a big piece of Microsoft's legal work, agree not to represent Apple on anything? Of course.)

The Competing Interests

The conflict rules and how we interpret them carry substantial — I'm tempted to say *profound* but it sounds too grandiose — public policy implications. As you think about the issues raised in this and the next chapter, remember that these rules, especially those dealing with client-client conflicts, will have a significant effect on the nature and growth of a lawyer's and a firm's practice. The broader the rules and the greater the number of matters that a lawyer or the lawyer's firm will be forbidden to accept, the greater the number of clients who will be denied counsel of choice, and the greater the disincentive for lawyers to specialize in a narrow area of the law or the problems of a specific industry (because the client base will be smaller). Conflict rules also induce firms to venture beyond their traditional jurisdiction in search of new clients who do not present conflicts. This partly explains why some U.S. firms went national in the 1970s and 1980s and then global in the ensuing decades.

The narrower the rules, on the other hand, the less protection they will afford clients, who may suffer (or believe they will suffer) from a breach of confidentiality or an act of disloyalty. If clients begin to fear the loyalty of their lawyers or the confidentiality of their communications, we risk weakening the trust on which the relationship depends, even if it turns out there was no need to worry.

Complicating all of this is the fact that the conflict rules may be abused for strategic advantage. A person who wants to deny a particular firm's expertise to a anticipated future adversary might retain the firm with that goal in mind. The broader the scope of the eventual disqualification, the easier it will be to use the rules in this tactical way. For an approach to these and other policy issues from an economic perspective, see Jonathan Macey & Geoffrey Miller,

An Economic Analysis of Conflict of Interest Regulation, 82 Iowa L. Rev. 965 (1997).

A. CLIENT-LAWYER CONFLICTS

1. *Business Interests*

"Lawyer. Realtor. Any Problem?"

"Dear Ethics Advisory Committee:
     "I request an opinion on the following facts. Can I do what I plan to do and if so, under what circumstances? I used to be a real-estate broker. I made good money. But the real- estate market slowed during a credit crunch, and I was only five years out of college, so I went to law school. For the last six years I've had a general practice, but as you might predict most of my work has been representing buyers and sellers of real property, mainly single-family homes. Anyway, my law practice has hit some speed bumps, probably because of all the city lawyers moving up here and hanging a shingle. Meanwhile, the real-estate market has picked up again, and the realtors are just raking it in. I did a closing yesterday where my fee was $4,600, and the broker's commission was $30,000. Can you believe it?
     "I still have my real-estate license so I figure why not do some broker-ing along with the lawyering. I can do both for the same client. Say a seller hires me as a broker and I find a buyer, I could then be the lawyer for the seller as well. Way I see it, we all have the same goal. Sell the house. Before I went ahead, I wanted to get your advice.

"Melanie Winterbottom"

"My Opponent's Firm is an Occasional Client."

"We're a twelve-lawyer litigation boutique. We each have a specialty. Mine is intellectual property. I represent Kyle Abernathy in a case against Mogul Press. Kyle says Mogul is infringing on a registered trade name. Yesterday, I got Mogul's answer to our complaint. Its lawyer is Rich Bello. Bello is a partner at a good firm in town, Petersen, Esher & Zell (PEZ). From time to time, PEZ gets sued for malpractice. We all do nowadays. Lawyers are convenient targets. For five years or so, my partner Nola Krinksy, whose specialty is lawyer malpractice, has done the defense work for Bello's firm, although we're not handling any cases for it now. Two or three claims will come in each year. Most go nowhere or settle for small sums. Maybe one in three ends up in court. Anyway, I'm a little uncom-fortable with the situation, and I asked Nola about it. Bello's firm is, or has been, our client. Nola pointed out that none of the work we've done for PEZ has anything to do with Kyle's trade-name claim, and we've never had a case for PEZ involving intellectual property. True. Does that make it all fine, or is there a conflict here that I should be thinking about?"

MATTER OF NEVILLE
147 Ariz. 106, 708 P.2d 1297 (1985)

FELDMAN, JUSTICE.

[Attorney Neville represented Bly in other real estate matters. Bly was "a licensed real estate broker" and "a knowledgeable and sophisticated real estate investor." Neville purchased options in certain of Bly's properties. Thereafter, Neville, Bly, and a third party entered into a contract, drafted by Neville, under which the Bly property in which Neville had an option would go to the third party, the third party's property would go to Neville, and Neville would give Bly a promissory note. "Bly created the substantive terms [for these transfers], and respondent [Neville] accepted these terms with no negotiation." The court considered whether Neville violated DR 5-104(A), the Code equivalent to Rule 1.8(a), since adopted in Arizona.]

A. WAS BLY RESPONDENT'S "CLIENT"? . . .

We think it quite likely that Bly was told or at least knew that respondent, the buyer, was not also undertaking to act as Bly's attorney [in these real estate transactions].

However, Bly's knowledge does not resolve the question of whether respondent was engaged in a business transaction in which his interests were adverse to those of his "client." The rule does not expressly limit its applicability to situations in which the lawyer represents the client in the very transaction in which their interests differ. We believe that the rule should not be so limited for several reasons. First, the rule is grounded in the fiduciary duty owed by an attorney to his client. That duty continues beyond the completion of any particular matter which the attorney undertakes for the client. The fiduciary duty arises when the attorney-client relationship is established and continues until it is abandoned. Abandonment is found when the lawyer's influence over the client has dissipated. Thus, DR 5-104 is applicable "as long as the influence arising from an attorney-client relationship continues." Second, the policy expressed by DR 5-104 is based on the realization that those who consider themselves clients come to depend upon the confidentiality and fairness arising from their relationships with their attorneys. They do not take a transactional approach to these relationships, turning their confidence on and off at the end of each transaction. Clients can be expected to assume that one whom they have come to look upon as "their lawyer" will protect them or, at least, not harm them. A lawyer's analytical training may permit expansion or limitation of professional obligations as circumstances warrant, but clients are usually neither required nor trained to make so careful an analysis. In any event, the profession prefers that its clients continue to repose confidence in their lawyers even after the immediate case has been finished, partly, no doubt, in the expectation that when the next case arises the clients will return. A third objective served by the rule is the hope that clients will obtain full disclosure on which to base their decision in all transactions. This objective is not served by a narrow, transactional application of the rule to situations in which the attorney is formally acting as counsel for the client.

We hold, therefore, that application of DR 5-104(A) is not limited to those situations in which the lawyer is acting as counsel in the very transaction in which his interests are adverse to his client. It applies also to transactions in which, although the lawyer is not formally in an attorney-client relationship with the adverse party, it may fairly be said that because of other transactions an ordinary person would look to the lawyer as a protector rather than as an adversary. The provisions of DR 5-104(A) apply so long as the client may reasonably feel that he is dealing with a person whose advice and counsel should be given weight and respect, rather than as one whose words must be taken with that grain of salt that the law expects from people dealing with those who are not fiduciaries. We recognize that we paint broadly, that lawyers are provided no bright line by which to determine when they can act as ordinary business people in relation to the interests of those whom they have represented in the past or whom they represent on other matters at the present. No doubt, we make it more difficult for lawyers to deal adversely with past and present clients. We believe that this result conforms to the obligation of the profession and is in the public interest.

It is appropriate to note at this point that the evidence does not permit a finding that respondent intended to defraud his client. We do not believe this to be of consequence. The rule contains no words which limit its applicability to cases where scienter is shown. The rule is not intended to deter and punish actual fraud alone. Other rules (see, e.g., DR 4-101(B)) proscribe fraudulent conduct damaging the client. The objectives of DR 5-104 are served by holding that the rule is applicable even in situations in which the attorney did not intend to defraud or act with improper motives.

B.   Did Bly Expect Respondent to Exercise his Professional Judgment for Bly's Protection?

The resolution of this question is substantially controlled by the determination of the existence of the attorney-client relationship. It is natural and proper for a client with a longstanding business relationship with a lawyer to feel that the lawyer is to be trusted, will not act unfairly, and will protect him against danger. This is true even though he knows that the lawyer is not representing him in the particular transaction and the lawyer is drawing papers for the use of both parties. We believe the [State Bar] Committee's findings on this point are well supported by the record.

C.   Did Respondent Make Full Disclosure and Obtain Bly's Knowing & Voluntary Consent?

We assume that respondent actually did tell Bly — or Bly realized — that respondent was not acting as Bly's attorney in the transaction in question, and that Bly should get independent counsel. Is this the "full disclosure" required by the rule? We think not. The words "I am not representing you in this matter" may convey a great deal to another lawyer, but their full legal import will escape most laymen. The lay person may realize that the lawyer is not representing him and that he will not have to pay for legal services, but he may not recognize that he is in a situation where he must protect himself from his own lawyer. Justifiably, he may continue to repose confidence in the person who usually acts as "his lawyer" and feel that he can be trusted to do nothing unfair or harmful. In short, the confidence which lawyers wish to engender in their clients may still exist and the consequent influence may extend to the transaction. We believe, therefore, that the requirement of "full disclosure" means much more than advising the client that he is not being represented in the particular transaction.

Thus, even accepting respondent's version of the disclosure, he failed to make full disclosure as required by the Disciplinary Rule. We adopt the view of the cases which hold that full disclosure requires not only that the lawyer make proper disclosure of nonrepresentation, but that he also must disclose every circumstance and fact "which the client should know to make an intelligent decision concerning the wisdom of entering the agreement." The rule is strict. The lawyer must give the client that information which he would have been obliged to give if he had been counsel rather than interested party, and the transaction must be as beneficial to the client as it would have been had the client been dealing with a stranger rather than with his lawyer. Thus, "full disclosure" requires not only a full explanation of the divergence in interest between the lawyer and the client and an explanation about the need to seek independent legal advice, but also "a detailed explanation of the risks and disadvantages to the client which flow from the agreement." The "consent" after "full disclosure" required by DR 5-104(A) must be the client's consent, after full explanation, to all terms that are either advantageous to the lawyer or disadvantageous to the client.

We believe . . . the agreement drawn by respondent contained terms that were, to say the least, disadvantageous to Bly. These should have been called to his attention, explained and removed from the agreement unless Bly had some reason for wanting the terms to be included. [The court here outlines provisions of Neville's promissory note and the terms for its repayment, which the court concludes "no respectable practitioner would have allowed a seller to accept."]

We believe that respondent should have called such problems to Bly's attention and should have explained why they were adverse to Bly's interests. Respondent argues, however, that the terms of the transaction were set by Bly and that he should not be subject to discipline for mere acquiescence. We disagree. First, although Bly may have outlined the transaction (including the concept of precomputed interest, payment of principal on sale and the like), respondent drafted the actual agreement between himself and a client with whom he had an ongoing relationship; he was obligated to be fair to and protect his client. The client had no duty to foresee all the dangers inherent in the deal which he had outlined. Respondent's fiduciary duty required that he take no advantage except with his client's "consent" after "full disclosure." . . .

Respondent is censured.

A Lawyer's Financial Interests

Let's make a convenient distinction. First, a lawyer's financial deal with a current client is subject to the substantive and procedural requirements of Rule 1.8(a), intended to protect the client. Second, a lawyer may have business or financial interests with others that create a personal conflict with the interests of a client within the meaning of Rule 1.7(a)(2). *Neville* is analyzed as within the former category, a deal with a current client. In which category are the two problems above? Read on.

Deals with Clients.   Suspicion of business deals between attorneys and clients, reflected in Rule 1.8(a) and DR 5-104(A), is a product of the same factors that lead courts to scrutinize post-retainer fee agreements (see page 159), also addressed here. After payment of a retainer, the client and attorney have a fiduciary relationship. The client will probably have come to depend on the attorney and to assume that the attorney is protecting the client's interest. The attorney may have had access to client confidences that give the attorney an advantage. In short, clients are not likely to see postretainer deals as being at "arm's length," and neither are the courts. Rule 1.8(a) duties may continue even after the conclusion of the matter for which the lawyer was hired. Matter of Timpone, 804 N.E.2d 560 (Ill. 2004) (lawyer represented client in home sale, then borrowed money from proceeds after the sale).

The importance of this rule was dramatically, and painfully, illustrated in Passante v. McWilliam, 62 Cal. Rptr. 2d 298 (Ct. App. 1997), where a lawyer accepted 3 percent of a client company's stock in exchange for helping the company raise funds at a difficult time. The company then prospered wildly (it made baseball cards with holograms), and the lawyer's 3 percent eventually came to be worth $33 million. But the company balked at delivering the stock. A jury found for the lawyer, but the trial court granted the company a judgment notwithstanding the verdict because the lawyer "had violated his ethical duty" in accepting the stock without complying with California's equivalent to Rule 1.8(a). The appellate court recognized that the company "had a clear moral obligation to honor its promise," but affirmed.

Neville deciphered the Code provision on attorney-client business deals. The language of Rule 1.8(a) is even more demanding. The rule's requirements, for example, apply whenever lawyers "knowingly acquire an ownership, possessory, security or other pecuniary interest adverse to a client." That specifically includes taking a security interest in a client's property, which lawyers sometimes do to protect their fee. ABA Opinion 427 (2002). And the rule is broad enough to encompass fee agreements entered after creation of the professional relationship. Holding that it does so are Valley/50th Ave., L.L.C. v. Stewart, 153 P.3d 186 (Wash. 2007) ("A fee agreement between a lawyer and a client, revised after the relationship has been established on terms more favorable to the lawyer than originally agreed upon may be void or voidable unless the attorney shows that the contract was fair and reasonable, free from undue influence, and made after a fair and full disclosure of the facts on which it is predicated.") and Matter of Hefron, 771 N.E.2d 1157 (Ind. 2002). But see Renouf & Polivy v. Multicultural Broadcasting, Inc., 1994 Westlaw 499060 (D.D.C. 1994) (despite "compelling arguments," Rule 1.8(a) inapplicable to contingent agreement entered during the representation).

Like many provisions of the Code and Rules, these provisions reflect (although they may not be congruent with) the law of fiduciary duty. In Greene v. Greene, 436 N.E.2d 496 (N.Y. 1982), the defendant lawyers drafted a trust agreement for the plaintiff. The agreement granted the lawyers certain advantages, including the right to 10 percent of "profits from the sale of trust assets." Later, the plaintiff challenged the agreement, and the court held that her allegation stated a cause of action. The court relied exclusively on fiduciary duty law. It wrote:

> An attorney is not prohibited from entering into a contract with a client. He must do so, of course, with respect to his retainer for legal services. And, although it is not advisable, an attorney may also contract with a client with respect to matters not involving legal services, or in addition to legal services. Thus a contract between an attorney and his client is not voidable at the will of the client.
>
> However, the relationship between an attorney and his client is a fiduciary one and the attorney cannot take advantage of his superior knowledge and position. The basic rule, as stated in an early case, is that
>
>> an attorney who seeks to avail himself of a contract made with his client, is bound to establish affirmatively that it was made by the client with full knowledge of all the material circumstances known to the attorney, and was in every respect free from fraud on his part, or misconception on the part of the client, and that a reasonable use was made by the attorney of the confidence reposed in him.
>
> Under this rule it is not necessary for the client to show that the agreement was obtained by fraud or undue influence on the part of the attorney, although, of course, that would make the agreement unenforceable if it were proven. Even in the absence of such misconduct the agreement may be invalid if it appears that the attorney "got the better of the bargain," unless he can show that the client was fully aware of the consequences and that there was no exploitation of the client's confidence in the attorney.
>
> In the case now before us the plaintiff alleges, in her complaint and motion papers, that the defendants took unfair advantage of the attorney-client relationship by purporting to create a trust for her, which in fact granted them powers greater than they would be entitled to have as fiduciaries and relieved them of normal fiduciary liability. She has stated under oath that she did not understand the terms or the effect of the agreement. If proven these allegations should be sufficient to entitle the plaintiff to rescission of the agreement unless the defendants can convincingly show that she was fully and fairly informed of the consequences of the agreement and the special advantages it gave to them.

A breach of fiduciary duty or a violation of Rule 1.8(a) may entitle the client to void the agreement with its lawyer. Liggett v. Young, 877 N.E.2d 178 (Ind. 2007) (under fiduciary duty law, "[t]ransactions between an attorney and client are presumed to be fraudulent, so that the attorney has the burden of proving the fairness and honesty thereof"). See also DiLuglio v. Providence Auto Body, Inc., 755 A.2d 757 (R.I. 2000) (where an attorney's investment in a close corporation fails to comply with Rule 1.8(a), the "self-interested transaction will be voidable at the election of the close-corporate client within a reasonable time after the client learns or should have learned of the material facts — even if the transaction is economically fair to all concerned"). In *Neville*, client Bly's sophistication in real-estate matters did not help Neville. Other courts agree. Schlanger sued Flaton, his former lawyer, to void a contract between them. "Flaton attempts to excuse his conduct by claiming that he made such disclosure as was appropriate to a sophisticated businessman in Schlanger's position. Yet, in [precedent] this Court rejected this sort of reasoning when it observed that 'the [Code] places the burden upon counsel, irrespective of the sophistication of the client, to obtain his consent after full disclosure before entering into a business transaction . . . where the differing interests of counsel and the client may interfere with the exercise of professional judgment for the client's protection.' " Schlanger v. Flaton, 631 N.Y.S.2d 293 (1st Dept. 1995). *Valley/50th Ave.*, supra, also rejects a defense based on a client's alleged sophistication. As does the comment to Rule 1.8, the court exempts "standard commercial transactions"; so, for example, it would not be presumptively fraudulent for a lawyer to take a mortgage from a bank that was his client.

Interests Adverse to Clients.   So far we have addressed financial dealings between lawyers and current clients. But a lawyer's financial interests may arise other than in deals with clients and either before or during the professional relationship. These interests can create conflicts under Rule 1.7(a)(2).

Roland St. Louis, a very successful Florida lawyer, was disbarred because while representing claimants against DuPont for crop losses allegedly caused by use of the fungicide Benlate (resulting in settlements of nearly $59 million), his firm accepted more than $6 million to represent DuPont. The Court explained the misconduct this way:

> St. Louis knowingly entered into the engagement agreement with DuPont, forming a lawyer-client relationship with DuPont while still representing the Benlate clients. The record reveals that St. Louis even pressured some of his Benlate clients to accept DuPont's settlement offer. He informed clients that he would cease representing them unless they accepted the settlement, although he refused to inform those clients of the settlement details. In addition, St. Louis decided not to inform his clients about his decision to represent DuPont, the very decision he made while negotiating their cases against DuPont. Thus, the record demonstrates that through his actions St. Louis had divided loyalties, and that his divided loyalties could have adversely affected his Benlate clients. . . . [T]he record also demonstrates that St. Louis did not consult with or receive the consent of the Benlate clients before he entered into the engagement agreement. In fact, St. Louis went to great efforts to keep the engagement agreement secret from his Benlate clients.

The Florida Bar v. St. Louis, 967 So.2d 108 (Fla. 2007). In a similar case, Mark Hager, a tenured law professor, ran afoul of D.C. ethics rules, including its version of Rule 1.7. Hager and another lawyer, Traficonte, represented a potential consumer class against Warner-Lambert. They charged that the company violated federal law because the label on its head lice shampoo, Nix, and its advertising, claimed that Nix eradicated head lice when in fact "a Nix-resistant strain of lice had evolved." The potential class representatives were two health-care professionals whose goal was to force the company to change its label and ads. Hager and Traficonte negotiated for this goal, but they also negotiated for a $225,000 legal fee to be paid to them by the company. Hager did not tell his clients about the fee.

The court suspended Hager for one year. Hager "faced a classic conflict of interest — his interest in maximizing his fee versus his clients' interest in maximizing the amount paid to them." Before Hager could simultaneously negotiate for a fee from the adverse party, "what was needed, and what was conspicuously lacking here, was client consent." Matter of Hager, 812 A.2d 904 (D.C. 2002). Hager argued that the clients got everything they wanted from Warner-Lambert so what was the big deal if he got a secret fee? What was the big deal?

Compared to Charles Hausmann, St. Louis and Hager got off easy. Hausmann was a personal injury lawyer in Wisconsin. He worked on contingency of about one-third of the client's recovery prior to deduction of the expenses of litigation. He referred certain clients to Scott Rise, a chiropractor. Payments to Rise came from the client's portion of the settlements, which was appropriate. But Rise secretly gave Hausmann twenty percent of the fees from the referral. So, in effect, because of that extra twenty percent, Hausmann got more than a third of the recovery, notwithstanding his fee agreement.

Stop for a second. What interest did Hausmann have that was in conflict with the interests of his clients?

Hausmann and Rise were convicted of conspiracy to commit mail and wire fraud. United States v. Hausmann, 345 F.3d 952 (7th Cir. 2003). The theory behind Hausmann's conviction was simple. He used the mails to deprive his clients of his honest services in violation of his fiduciary duty.

> Appellants contend that Rise's third-party payments were not kickbacks, but rather constituted the legitimate spending of income derived from use of fees to which Rise was legally entitled. They maintain that Hausmann's clients had no right to the settlement funds paid to Rise nor, consequently, to the allocation of twenty percent of those funds to expenditures designated by Hausmann. In this sense, reason Appellants, no harm resulted to Hausmann's clients, who were deprived of nothing to which they were entitled. This reasoning ignores the reality that Hausmann deprived his clients of their right to know the truth about his compensation: In addition to one third of any settlement proceeds he negotiated on their behalf, every dollar of Rise's effective twenty percent fee discount went to Hausmann's benefit. Insofar as Hausmann misrepresented this compensation, that discount should have inured to the benefit of his clients. It is of no consequence, despite Appellants' arguments to the contrary, that Rise's fees (absent his discount) were competitive, or that clients received the same net benefit as they would have absent the kickback scheme. The scheme itself converted Hausmann's representations to his clients into misrepresentations, and Hausmann illegally profited at the expense of his clients, who were entitled to his honest services as well as their contractually bargained-for portion of Rise's discount.

Does this mean that every conflict of interest (or breach of fiduciary duty) that deprives the client of honest services is mail fraud (if the mails are used)? The full implications of this prosecution remain to be seen.

2. Media Rights

Maybe what you really want to do is write novels, true-crime books, and scripts for movies and *Law & Order*. You figured that legal work would give you good plot lines (and besides you need to support yourself and repay college loans). Well, yes, there are great stories in the law. Every litigation is a potential short story, or even a long one. Many lawyers have tried their hand at popular culture and six or seven have been able handsomely to support themselves. Well, more than that, but not much more. Try it if you like, but keep in mind that there are limits on how you can use your legal work in your written work.

Rule 1.8(d) forbids lawyers to acquire publicity rights to a story based on the subject of the representation before its conclusion. Why should acquisition of media or publicity rights in a matter create a potential conflict between client and attorney? Consider a lawyer retained to represent a defendant in a case as celebrated as the murder trial of O. J. Simpson. Suppose the lawyer agrees that all or part of his fee will be the exclusive rights to the defendant's story, which the lawyer plans to write or to sell to the movies, but only after the case is over. If the case is truly over, and if the lawyer never uses or reveals confidential information where the rules forbid it, where is the conflict?

Clients who assign rights to their lawyers tend to be criminal defendants. The media are more interested in those cases. (When did you last read or see a blockbuster about a breach of contract?) If the defendant is convicted, she may seek to vacate the conviction on the ground that the lawyer's possession of the media rights created an impermissible conflict of interest leading to denial of the effective assistance of counsel guaranteed by the Sixth Amendment. Notice the overlap between the conflict rules and the constitutional guarantee. As we shall see later in this chapter, some but not all conflicts of interest can render counsel constitutionally ineffective. (And, of course, a lawyer may be ineffective even if he has no conflict.) Where a lawyer has taken media rights in a criminal defendant's story, courts say that, while the lawyer may have had a *potential* conflict of interest, this will be insufficient to bring relief unless the defendant can show that the conflict affected the lawyer's performance. (The lawyer is still subject to discipline.) Clients are usually unable to meet this burden of proof. United States v. Hearst, 638 F.2d 1190 (9th Cir. 1980) (Patty Hearst's bank robbery conviction; her lawyer was F. Lee Bailey). Of course, denying a client the right to "pay" a lawyer she could not otherwise afford with the publicity rights to her story can be seen as paternalistic — because it is. We're protecting the client from her own bad decision. But there is also another interest. The ethics rules operate from the assumption that the state's interest in conflict-free criminal representation may be superior to the client's interest in waiving a conflict in order to get a purportedly better lawyer.

But back to the threshold question. Where's the conflict? Here's a hint. The lawyer's media rights will, as a rule, be more valuable if there's a trial (whatever the verdict) than if the client takes a plea. Trials are dramatic. Guilty pleas are boring. So the lawyer's incentives are skewed in favor of going to trial.*

In one of those coincidences that never happen except that this time it did, the California Supreme Court decided two cases on the same day involving,

---

* Apart from the conflict, a lawyer who wants to use a client's matter as fodder for a book, fiction or not, must be conscious of his or her Rule 1.6 duty to protect the client's confidences even after the case is done. Nor could the lawyer cast the client in a bad light even without explicitly revealing confidential information, because the public will infer that the lawyer has a basis for the treatment.

respectively, a book and a movie. The book was self-published by a prosecutor, whom a defendant then sought to disqualify on the ground that the book was based on and tended to exploit her case. The defendant argued that the prosecutor's interest in promoting her book meant she could not make the sort of disinterested decisions that we want prosecutors to be able to make. While recognizing the potential for a problem on facts like these, the court rejected the claim after finding that the book wasn't really based on the defendant's case. Haraguchi v. Superior Court, 182 P.3d 579 (Cal. 2008). In the other case, a prosecutor helped a movie company make a film about an infamous murder case. He even opened his file to the filmmakers to improve accuracy. He helped because one of the defendants — a man whose name was Jesse James Hollywood, honest — was a fugitive, and the prosecutor, who received no compensation for helping, figured that the film might lead to Hollywood's capture. As it happened, Hollywood was captured in Brazil before the movie came out and soon moved to disqualify the prosecutor. The court declined, finding that nothing the prosecutor did could be seen to compromise his objectivity. Hollywood v. Superior Court, 182 P.3d 590 (Cal. 2008). By the way, the film is *Alpha Dogs*.

3.   Financial Assistance and Proprietary Interests

Mary O'Meara is injured in a car crash. She loses her waitress job. She has medical bills. She faces eviction when her small savings run out. She has to eat. Mary has a lawyer who says, conservatively, that her claim is worth a million dollars given her injuries, and maybe a lot more. It will take two years or so to settle, longer if the case goes to trial. If the defendant's insurance company gets wind of Mary's financial plight, it may seek to delay as long as possible. Mary can't wait. She'll soon be living on the street. Mary's lawyer doesn't think that would be good for the case, and there are also the humanitarian concerns. Mary's lawyer is confident that Mary will have a substantial recovery. So he wants to lend her $1,000 monthly to help her get by, no interest; she'll pay him back out of the proceeds. He figures the total loan will be a pittance compared to his investment of time and one-third contingent fee. And the loan pales next to the money he's advancing for expert witnesses, court reporters, and investigators, not to mention direct office expenses. Any problem?

Contingent fees (page 168) give a lawyer a direct interest in the client's cause, yet they are permitted (though regulated), often on the ground that less wealthy clients would not otherwise be able to afford to retain a lawyer. Other provisions of the Rules, however, place strict limits on the ability of a lawyer to have other kinds of direct or indirect interests in a client's case. Why is that?

Consider court costs and other litigation expenses, which can be high. May a lawyer advance these? Must the client repay them? Rule 1.8(e) permits the lawyer to make repayment contingent on the outcome of the matter and does away with repayment entirely if the client is indigent. But the Model Rules forbid a lawyer to advance more than court costs and the expenses of litigation. Rule 1.8(e) excludes living and medical expenses. Connecticut Opinion 1990-3 declares that there is no "humanitarian exception" to the prohibition against advancing living expenses. Even small sums are forbidden. But see Florida Bar v. Taylor,

648 So. 2d 1190 (Fla. 1994) (recognizing humanitarian exception where lawyer gave client $200 for "basic necessities" with no expectation of repayment). Early drafts of the Model Rules would have permitted lawyers to advance "reasonable and necessary medical and living expenses, the repayment of which may be contingent on the outcome of the matter." Rule 1.8(e) (May 1981 draft).

In In re Brown, 692 P.2d 107 (Or. 1984), a lawyer was suspended from practice. One of the charges upheld against him was that he advanced $361 to a client, an accident victim, for living expenses in violation of DR 5-103(B). By so doing, he allegedly acquired a forbidden interest in the subject matter of the litigation. What is going on here? What risks did Brown's loan create that are not already present when lawyers work for a contingent fee or when they advance the expenses of litigation, both of which are permitted? The Oklahoma Supreme Court has rejected a constitutional challenge to the rule. It suspended a lawyer for 60 days for advancing a $1,200 loan to a workers' compensation client whose home had been destroyed by fire. The court said that the rule's purpose was to prevent clients from "selecting a lawyer based on improper factors" and avoid "conflicts of interests, including compromising a lawyer's independent judgment in the case." State v. Smolen, 17 P.3d 456 (Okla. 2000).

Do these reasons persuade you? Why is there an absolute ban in Rule 1.8(e) on "financial assistance to a client in connection with pending or contemplated litigation," but *no ban at all* if the client's matter is not litigation? Perhaps we see here a vestige of the historical hostility to litigation, which also informed opposition to lawyer advertising (see chapter 16) and efforts to inhibit public interest groups and unions from recourse to courts to vindicate rights (chapter 14).

Permitting lawyers to advance living costs would enable poorer plaintiffs to endure the procedural (and time-consuming) maneuvers of wealthy defendants, who might use delay to win a favorable settlement. The Rules, as we shall see (page 434), are halfhearted about discouraging dilatory tactics, which are hard to prevent in any event. How, then, can they properly deny the frequent victims of those tactics the remedy of borrowing from their lawyers in order to persevere? It must be that the risks of even small loans are large. But what are they?

Maryland follows Oklahoma in Attorney Grievance Commission v. Kandel, 563 A.2d 387 (Md. 1989). A lawyer was publicly reprimanded for giving a client money to travel to a medical treatment facility. The court wrote that the rule

> is directed at avoiding the acquisition of an interest in litigation through financial assistance to a client. An important public policy interest is to avoid unfair competition among lawyers on the basis of their expenditures to clients. Clients should not be influenced to seek representation based on the ease with which monies can be obtained, in the form of advancements, from certain law firms or attorneys.

What do you think of this reason? We don't want lawyers using offers of support in order to get cases. We don't want clients choosing their lawyers based on who'll pay more of their rent. Why not? We have no problem if clients choose lawyers based on whose fees are lower. So what's the difference?

California and a few other states address the question differently. California Rule 4-210(A) states that a lawyer may not "pay or agree to pay . . . the personal or business expenses of a prospective or existing client, except that this rule shall not prohibit [a lawyer after] employment, from lending money to the client upon the client's promise in writing to repay such loan."

The District of Columbia's rule is even more permissive. It allows a lawyer to "pay or otherwise provide . . . financial assistance which is reasonably necessary to permit the client to institute or maintain" a case. D.C. Rule 1.8(d)(2). The comment to the rule says the permission is limited to expenses that are "strictly necessary to sustain the client during" the matter in order "to avoid situations in which a client is compelled by exigent financial circumstances to settle a claim on unfavorable terms. . . ." In his article surveying American jurisdictions, Professor John Sahl quotes D.C. bar counsel's comments that the rule has been in place for a "long time and has not produced any official complaints." John Sahl, Helping Clients With Living Expenses: "No Good Deed Goes Unpunished," 13 Professional Lawyer 1 (2002).

In an enlightened opinion, the Mississippi Supreme Court looked favorably on a lawyer's application to pay the monthly premium ($401.39) for an injured client's medical insurance, which she would otherwise lose because her injuries prevented her from working. The court held that Rule 1.8(e) did not categorically forbid the payment and remanded to the state bar ethics committee for further review in light of the court's analysis. Application of G.M., 797 So.2d 931 (Miss. 2001). By the way, it was smart of Mr. G.M. to apply for permission, wasn't it?

4.   Fee-Payer Interests

Lawyers may sometimes get paid by one person to represent another person. Liability insurance policies generally obligate the insurer to defend the insured if a claim that is made against the insured is wholly or partly within the policy's coverage. See page 300. Or a company might provide counsel for its employees if alleged wrongdoing is within the scope of employment. A person may pay a relative's lawyer. Rules 1.8(f) and 5.4(c) permit these payments under certain circumstances. The client must consent to the arrangement; the payer must not interfere with the lawyer's "independence of professional judgment or with the client-lawyer relationship," and the lawyer must protect the client's confidences. Whether or not the fee payer is a client of the lawyer along with the person for whom the lawyer performs the service, the lawyer should be aware, and make the fee payer aware, that the fact and amount of the payment will not likely be privileged. (See page 65.)

Sometimes this "triangular" relationship can create conflicts between the interests of the payer and the person for whom services are being rendered. In Wood v. Georgia, 450 U.S. 261 (1981), the petitioners were sentenced to jail after failing to pay fines imposed following their convictions for distributing obscene materials. The petitioners' lawyer was hired and paid by their employer. Although certiorari had been granted to review the constitutionality of incarcerating persons unable to pay a fine, the Court declined to pass on this issue after it became apparent that the employer's interest in litigating the constitutional question may have conflicted with the defendants' interests in avoiding assessment of the huge fines required to preserve it. The Court said:

> Courts and commentators have recognized the inherent dangers that arise when a criminal defendant is represented by a lawyer hired and paid by a third party, particularly when the third party is the operator of the alleged criminal enterprise. One risk is that the lawyer will prevent his client from obtaining leniency by preventing the client from offering testimony against his former employer or from taking other actions contrary to the employer's interest. Another kind of risk is present where, as here, the party paying the fees may have had a long-range interest in establishing a legal precedent and could do so only if the interests of the defendants themselves were sacrificed. . . .

The Court vacated the conviction and remanded for determination of whether a conflict of interest "actually existed." The Second Circuit relied on *Wood* in Amiel v. United States, 209 F.3d 195 (2d Cir. 2000), in ordering an evidentiary hearing on the petitioner's motion to vacate her sentence. Amiel, along with her mother and her aunt, had been convicted of mail fraud. Each had separate counsel, but her mother paid for Amiel's lawyer. In her petition, Amiel alleged that her lawyer advised Amiel

> not to testify, even though testifying was in [her] best interests, because doing so would inculpate [her] mother whom counsel sought to protect. If these facts were established at a factual hearing, they would entitle [Amiel] to relief on the ground that trial counsel abdicated his duty of loyalty by permitting a third party who paid his fees to influence his professional judgment in representing [her].

In another case, lawyers representing Vone, who was facing drug charges, had a policy against representing clients who wanted to cooperate with the government by providing information against others in exchange for leniency. The court found that it was "a reasonable possibility" that the individuals who had hired the defense lawyers to represent Vone were her accomplices and that they had "sought out the [lawyers] and paid their fees for the very reason that under their established policy, the [lawyers] would influence Vone to not implicate the accomplices." Do you see why that's a problem? The court wrote that the "convergence of the non-cooperation policy and the reasonable possibility that attorneys' fees were being paid by accomplices, impermissibly conflicted with the independence of the respondents' professional judgment," establishing a violation of Rules 1.7(b) and 1.8(f). The lawyers were suspended for 30 days. Matter of Maternowski, 674 N.E.2d 1287 (Ind. 1996).

5. *Related Lawyers, Significant Others, and Friends*

GELLMAN V. HILAL
159 Misc. 2d 1085, 607 N.Y.S.2d 853 (Sup. Ct. 1994)

STANLEY L. SKLAR, JUSTICE.

[This was a medical malpractice case. The plaintiff was represented by Bogaty, whose wife, Brody, previously represented the defendants (two doctors and a hospital) in another malpractice action the subject of which was the same medical procedure challenged in the current action. The defendants, Brody's former clients, moved to disqualify Bogaty, her husband, in the current action.]

Defendants argue that if Brody divulges her knowledge to Bogaty, defendants will be prejudiced; moreover, as Bogaty's wife, Brody has a financial incentive to aid Bogaty in the prosecution of the instant suit since any contingent fee he earns would likely benefit the Brody-Bogaty marital household. Defendants also allege a danger of inadvertent disclosure in the ordinary course of spousal intimacy of daily life in a shared household.

The most relevant [New York] disciplinary rule addressing the propriety of attorney-spouses representing opponents is 9-101(D) [patterned after Rule 1.8(i)]:

> A lawyer related to another lawyer as parent, child, sibling or spouse shall not represent in any matter a client whose interests differ from those of another party to the matter who the lawyer knows is represented by the other lawyer unless the client consents to the representation after full disclosure and the lawyer concludes that the lawyer can adequately represent the interests of the client.

[The court questioned whether the prior action presented a conflict with the current action, but then went on to discuss imputation of conflicts among spouses.]

In the context of attorney-spouses working for opposing law firms, plaintiff has asserted and defendants have conceded that there is no per se rule of disqualification based on marital status. See ABA Formal Opinion 340 (Sept. 23, 1993); Blumenfeld v. Borenstein, 247 Ga. 406, 276 S.E.2d 607. The ABA Standing Committee on Ethics and Professional Responsibility reasoned that:

> [a] lawyer whose husband or wife is also a lawyer must, like every other lawyer, obey all disciplinary rules, for the disciplinary rules apply to all lawyers without distinction to marital status. We cannot assume that a lawyer who is married to another lawyer necessarily will violate any particular disciplinary rule, such as those that protect a client's confidences, that proscribe neglect of a client's interest, and that forbid representation of differing interests.

Thus, while Brody might have a financial incentive in seeing her husband bring home a contingency fee by winning his client's lawsuit, to act on that incentive by divulging to him confidences she may have gained from the defendants would violate serious ethical and statutory rules against such conduct, and could injure her reputation and her interest in her license and impede her ability to advance her career.

The ABA also noted that:

> the relationship of husband and wife is so close that the possibility of an inadvertent breach of a confidence or the unavoidable receipt of information concerning the client by the spouse other than the one who represents the client (for example, information contained in a telephoned message left for the lawyer at home) is substantial.

However, the danger of inadvertent revelation of confidences was not considered fatal; rather, attorney-spouses were cautioned to adhere carefully to ethical guidelines set forth in the Canons, Ethical Considerations, and Disciplinary Rules. In the present case Bogaty asserts that neither he nor Brody maintains an office at home, that their files are not available to each other and that, as lawyers who have made careers working on opposite sides of medical malpractice litigation, they have spent their shared personal lives together without endangering professional confidences. Indeed, Bogaty claims that prior to the commencement of this action he was unaware that his wife had ever represented Hilal. . . .

Accordingly, defendants' motion for an order disqualifying plaintiff 's attorney is denied.

Private and Public Lives

In Non-Punitive Segregation Inmates of Holmesburg Prison v. Kelly, 589 F.Supp. 1330 (E.D.N.Y. Pa. 1984), Judge Pollak wrote:

> Advertent disclosures of a client's confidences and secrets by an attorney to his or her spouse would violate DR 4-101(B) [requiring lawyers to protect a client's confidences] whether or not the attorney's spouse also practiced law. However, without more, a court should not presume that such advertent disclosures have occurred merely from the fact of the marriage relationship. "We cannot assume that a lawyer who is married to another lawyer necessarily will violate any particular disciplinary rule, such as those that protect a client's confidences, that proscribe neglect of a client's interest, and that forbid representation of differing interests." [ABA 340.] Lawyers have many close relationships of which marriage is only one. Just as a court will not presume that lawyers will disclose confidences to their close friends, courts will not presume that lawyers will disclose confidences to their spouses. . . .
>
> [If] courts regularly disqualified attorneys and their law firms from representing clients with interests adverse to clients represented by the attorneys' spouses' law firms, courts would effectively preclude married lawyers from practicing in the same communities as their spouses.

The Model Rules once allowed lawyers who are related as "parent, child, sibling or spouse" to represent direct adversaries only if the clients consent after consultation. (Former Rule 1.8(i).) The Ethics 2000 Commission deleted the provision (although it remains in many states) and left resolution of "relationship" issues to the generic standard in Rule 1.7(a).

California Rule 3-320 requires a lawyer to reveal if "another party's lawyer" is a close relative of the lawyer, lives with her, or has "an intimate personal relationship with" her. Does this last provision go too far? It would seem to require a lawyer to tell a client if he or she is intimate with the opposing lawyer, even if intermittently. What if it's a same-sex relationship? Is the lawyer required to reveal his sexual orientation to the client? In People v. Jackson, 213 Cal. Rptr. 521 (Ct. App. 1985), decided before the California rule was adopted, the (heterosexual) defense lawyer and prosecutor had been dating for eight months before the start of the trial and continued dating during the trial. Neither the defendant nor the judge was informed. The court reversed the conviction on the ground that the defendant had been denied the effective assistance of counsel under the state constitution. It did not address the ethical issue.

A lawyer's intimate relationship with persons other than the opposing lawyer may also create conflicts. People v. Singer, 275 Cal. Rptr. 911 (Ct. App. 1990), vacated a murder conviction where defense counsel had failed to disclose his affair with the defendant's wife. The affair "introduced deception and duplicity to the advocate-client relationship, which by definition must be grounded in trust and fidelity." But Hernandez v. State, 750 So. 2d 50 (Fla. App. 1999) (en banc) (6-4), refused to vacate a conviction where it came to light that the defense lawyer had a sexual relationship with the client's wife during the trial. The defendant had not shown "that the asserted conflict had an adverse effect upon the lawyer's performance." Four judges dissented in an opinion that somehow seems better to capture the subtleties of human nature, especially when it comes to sex:

> Sex is at the top of the list of compelling emotional forces. It propelled Quinon into a conflict of interest with Hernandez with the precise effect on his representation being unknown and unknowable. Would Quinon, whose character may otherwise be sterling, hold back a bit at trial, or change his strategy, in order to assure Hernandez' unavailability to his wife — leaving Quinon a clear field? Those who know Quinon may not think it likely or even possible, but countless examples exist of betrayals of duty for sexual favors to the surprise of the betrayer's friends and family. I would point out only one, known to all of us: King David's betrayal of his loyal officer, Uriah, the Hittite, who was slain on King David's orders so that King David could possess Bathsheba. The difference between King David's deadly action, and a trial counsel's deliberate weakening of the client's case, lies not only in degree, but most important here, also in the likelihood of discovery. Obviously King David's action became supremely public. A trial counsel's surreptitious actions done in order to continue his sexual betrayal are not readily hunted down. . . . Requiring proof by a defendant that his attorney not only cuckolded him, but reduced his trial performance, leaves that defendant with an impossible task, and thus no remedy.

6.   A Lawyer's Legal Exposure

"The Client Says We Messed Up"

"We're a huge firm. We do a lot of transactional work. I'm the managing partner, which, as the saying goes, is like being the only hydrant in the dog pound. Sorry. I've had a bad day.

"Anyway, we are representing a big wholesaler, Marginex, in the purchase of a smaller company's assets. The general counsel of Marginex, a guy I know well professionally, called me yesterday and said he thinks we messed up in some aspect of our work on the deal. I didn't quite follow his explanation since it's not my area. Then the conversation went something like this:

> "'Are you firing us, Bill?,' I asked.
> "'No, because we're past the middle of the transaction and it will hurt us, maybe a lot, to lose counsel in the middle. We need you to finish it.'
> "'So are you saying you're going to sue us when it's over?'
> "'Betty, look, we might,' he says. 'Nothing personal. But it depends. We'll consult counsel. I'm just giving you a heads up. A courtesy.'

"My question to you is may we ethically continue to represent Marginex on this deal? Is there a conflict? Do we need a waiver? Of course, we need to do an internal investigation right away to see if there's a problem. I could ask our in-house GC to do it (like all big firms, we have one now). Or I can ask the outside firm that handles our liability claims, Gabbé & Minter. What's your advice?"

How would you describe any conflict Betty's firm may be facing? What, in other words, are the possibly inconsistent incentives? Consider whether the following cases, which admittedly arise in criminal representation, help you answer these questions.

Government of Virgin Islands v. Zepp, 748 F.2d 125 (3d Cir. 1984), reversed a conviction for possession of cocaine and destruction of evidence. The defense lawyer was alone with the defendant on the premises where the cocaine was allegedly present and then flushed down a toilet. Defense counsel agreed to stipulate that he had not flushed anything down the toilet. Why would he do that? How did the stipulation, which was read to the jury, harm the client? The court held that because the lawyer was "potentially liable for aiding and abetting or encouraging the destruction of evidence" and, in any event, "could have faced severe disciplinary consequences," he had an actual conflict of interest that denied Zepp her Fifth and Sixth Amendment rights. The stipulation further denied Zepp her right of cross-examination. Do you see why? For other cases in which a lawyer's legal exposure required disqualification, sometimes over client objection, see United States v. Reeves, 892 F.2d 1223 (5th Cir. 1990); United States v. Jones, 381 F.3d 114 (2d Cir. 2004); Matter of Kern, 555 N.E.2d 479 (Ind. 1990) (lawyer must withdraw when client is offered immunity to testify against lawyer).

Can a false accusation against counsel create a conflict? What do you think of the Second Circuit's reasoning on the facts of United States v. Fulton, 5 F.3d 605 (2d Cir. 1993)? Lawyer X was representing Fulton, who was charged with a drug-importation conspiracy. X was cross-examining Lateju, an alleged co-conspirator who had agreed to cooperate with the government. Interrupting Lateju's cross-examination, the government told the trial judge in an ex parte communication that Lateju had "weeks ago called up the DEA agent" and told him that X had received a portion of a different (earlier) heroin shipment. (Why did the government wait so long?) What should the trial judge have done? What he did was inform X and Fulton of the government's information, giving Fulton the option of changing lawyers or waiving cross-examination of Lateju. (Why should Fulton have had to waive cross-examination?) Fulton chose the second option. The Second Circuit held that X had a nonwaivable conflict for which the defendant did not have to show prejudice. The existence of the conflict rendered X's representation constitutionally ineffective. Here's why:

> When a government witness alleges that the defendant's counsel engaged in criminal conduct related to the charges for which the defendant is on trial, it creates one of two actual conflicts. First, if the allegations are true . . . the attorney may fear that a spirited defense could uncover convincing evidence of the attorney's guilt or provoke the government into action against the attorney. Moreover, the attorney is not in a position to give unbiased advice to the

client about such matters as whether or not to testify or to plead guilty and cooperate since such testimony or cooperation from the defendant may unearth evidence against the attorney.

Second, even if the attorney is demonstrably innocent and the government witness's allegations are plainly false, the defense is impaired because vital cross-examination becomes unavailable to the defendant. Ordinarily, a witness's blatantly false allegations provide a rich source for cross-examination designed to cast doubt on the witness's credibility; but, when the allegations are against the defendant's attorney, this source cannot be tapped. An attorney cannot act both as advocate for his client and a witness on his client's behalf. And, in questioning a witness concerning his allegations against the attorney, the attorney effectively becomes an unsworn witness.

In rejecting the waiver, the court wrote:

> Where a government witness implicates defense counsel in a related crime, the resultant conflict so permeates the defense that no meaningful waiver can be obtained. In such a case, we must assume that counsel's fear of, and desire to avoid, criminal charges, or even the reputational damage from an unfounded but ostensibly plausible accusation, will affect virtually every aspect of his or her representation of the defendant.

This result was good for Fulton. He'll get a new trial. But is it fair to defendants generally? Hereafter, whenever an informant implicates defense counsel, the defendant will lose her lawyer of choice, without the option of waiving the conflict. The Second Circuit did recognize one exception: If the trial court could "definitively rule out the possibility that the allegations are true, a meaningful waiver is possible since the falsely accused attorney is conflicted only to the extent that she cannot cross-examine the witness regarding the false allegations." How often will trial judges be able to make such definitive rulings? In any event, is it paternalistic to refuse to allow defendants in Fulton's position to waive the conflict? What other interests are we protecting? See Wheat v. United States at page 253. Issues surrounding criminal defense lawyer conflicts are further explored in Part B1 of this chapter.

And here's something else Betty should think about. An internal investigation to check out the client's accusation would seem obligatory. But for whose benefit? Should we say that there is now a conflict between client Marginex and Betty's firm, as a client of its inside GC, with the result that the firm loses privilege for its internal investigation? Asset Funding Group, LLC v. Adams & Reese, LLP, 2008 Westlaw 4948835 (E.D. La. 2008), is one of a number of cases, not all consistent, that answers yes. What if the firm hired Gabbé & Minter to do the work instead?

7.   *Gender, Religion, Race*

"Karen Horowitz's Dilemma"

Karen Horowitz: "I'm a 30-year-old fifth-year litigation associate at a large midwestern law firm. I went to law school at Berkeley, clerked for a Ninth Circuit judge, then started at my current firm. Because it is relevant to what I'm about to raise, you also have to know that I'm Jewish. I'm married and have two kids. My husband's a chemist.

"I have learned a lot at my job. I have always been treated with respect and courtesy. I work with all the litigation partners. That is not to say I like everyone here equally, but that's another matter.

"Two years ago I began working on a very complicated civil case, brought by a certain southern state in state court, arising out of an alleged violation of state banking laws. The defendant is a bank holding company that our firm represents on many matters. I worked on the pleadings, discovery, evidentiary issues, motions to dismiss and for partial summary judgment, and on a challenge on federal preemption grounds to the constitutionality of the statute under which our client is charged. We won some, and we lost some.

"The case is about to go to trial in a particular county of the state that is not, to put it mildly, known for its enlightened attitudes — religious, gender, or racial. Some say it's a county that has not yet finished fighting the Civil War. There is some not insubstantial anti-Semitism and antiblack sentiment among the population.

"Last week Blair Thomas, the head of our litigation department, told me that I would not be going down as part of the defense team. The reason: They think a Jewish woman lawyer on the defense team will prejudice the jury against our client. I was told that the client concurred in this judgment. They said it was bad enough that some of the lawyers are Northerners — we also have local counsel — we couldn't afford to complicate matters by bringing me into the courtroom. I must say, Blair was quite candid. He could have made some excuse — they needed me elsewhere, for instance. I appreciate that, I guess. He said I was a valuable associate whose work was appreciated and would be recognized at bonus time and with other important assignments. But the firm had a responsibility to its client, which came first.

"Well, I think the firm has a responsibility to me too, and that's a responsibility not to exclude me from an important case — on which I've already been working for two years — because of my gender or religion. If clients don't like it, the firm shouldn't represent them. It used to be that businesses justified discrimination against this group or that by pointing to their customers. 'It's not us,' they'd say, 'we're not prejudiced. But our customers won't work with you-name-it, so what can we do?' Or, 'We can hire you, but we can't let you interact with the clientele.'

"Well, if you ask me, this is no different. The firm tells me it's not prejudiced, even its clients aren't prejudiced, it says, but someone else is and so my career gets sidetracked.

"I don't know what I'm going to do about this. I don't know what I can do. But I don't buy the 'our client comes first' explanation."

J. Blair Thomas: "I know how Karen feels. It stinks. No question about it. We would never tolerate such treatment here for any other reason but this one — our responsibility to our client. Make no mistake about it. It's not the firm that wants to exclude Karen, or even the client, which has worked with Karen on this matter and other matters for years. But we can't ignore where we're trying this case. The demographics of this county are astonishing. Most of the jurors will be fundamentalist rednecks, and the judge isn't much better. If these people don't belong to some hate group or supremacist organization, they probably have at least one friend who does.

"Also, this case can cost our client between $20 million and $30 million if it goes the wrong way. Look what happened to Texaco before a local jury in Texas. They had to settle for $3 billion. I think Karen has to be reasonable. The fact is, there are situations—other cases, other states—where we'd *want* her in the courtroom because we'd expect to do better if we had a woman or a Jewish lawyer on our team. The same goes for members of other groups—racial, religious, you name it. Some cases, I want a minority right up there. Other cases, I want a woman. Other cases, I want a younger lawyer or an older lawyer, depending. Gosh, there are some courtrooms a client would have to be crazy to send in an obvious Yankee WASP like me. This courtroom is a good example. I'm not going either.

"A good lawyer structures his or her trial team to appeal to the jury, or at least not to alienate it. You know it's the same thing when a firm hires local counsel. Those guys down there don't do anything but sit around, smile at the jurors, and talk in the local idiom a couple of minutes a day. Why do we—why does anyone—hire them? And we all do. It's not because they know the law. It's to curry favor with the locals.

"The judge and jury are going to decide this case. We have to appeal to them whether we like their biases or not. I find those biases repulsive. But I don't count. I'm a lawyer with a client who is at serious risk. My client is my only concern, whether it's a bank or a death-row inmate. Karen has to understand that. Her day will come in other matters. Her career hasn't been sidetracked at all. No one blames her for not being able to continue on this case, and no decision is going to be made based on her religion or the fact that she's a gal or anything else except the quality of her work."

How Roger Baldwin Picked a Lawyer

Is Karen putting her own professional interest ahead of the interest of her client? Is her "problem" a "conflict" within the meaning of ethics rules? At the very least, isn't it disturbing that Blair—and I admit I stacked the deck against him a bit in how I wrote his part of the dialogue—might be right (I say "might be"), because, despite our efforts to eradicate bias on the basis of religion, race, gender, and other attributes, it might still be legitimate, even advisable, to take these into consideration in making trial assignments like the one here? Why is that?

I used to discuss this problem at bar events. My law school even hired actors to record the parts of Blair and Karen on videotape. Let me share two stories from audiences that saw the tape. At a Chicago event, a lawyer in the audience said he represents plaintiffs injured in motorcycle accidents. (Yes, I know, but it *is* an age of specialization after all). The defendant was a manufacturer of motorcycles. On the first day of jury selection, an older Korean-American woman was chosen. The next day, the defense lawyer showed up with a male Korean-American associate at counsel's table. This associate (and the lawyer telling the story said he assumed it was an associate, not a file clerk or an actor) had never appeared in any of the pretrial work in the case, nor was his name on any of the papers for the two years the case had been pending. The lawyer believed that defense counsel brought him in just to sit at counsel table across from the Korean-American woman. If so, do you have any problem with that? Is there anything that can be done about it, even if you do?

I heard my second story from a lawyer in the audience at an event in the South. His regional firm included an obviously Jewish name. The firm tries cases all over the south. He said that opposing lawyers, especially in smaller communities, routinely emphasized the firm's full name before juries, taking pains to pause over and stress the Jewish name. The firm had considered changing its name, but chose not to do so.

Consider the perspective of Roger Baldwin, founder of the American Civil Liberties Union, an organization committed to eradication of bias. (This information comes to us in a portrait of Baldwin by Peggy Lamson.*) Baldwin was arrested in a labor demonstration in Patterson, New Jersey, in the fall of 1924. Citing a 1796 statute, the indictment charged that Baldwin "unlawfully, riotously and tumultuously did make and utter great and loud noises and threatenings" with the intent to "commit assault and battery upon the police officers and . . . to break, injure, damage and destroy and wreck the city hall." Baldwin was convicted by the trial judge and sentenced to six months in jail. A New York lawyer, Samuel Untermyer, "volunteered to take the case on appeal to the New Jersey Supreme Court," and "Roger and his ACLU colleagues accepted with gratitude." But after a delay of nearly two years, the conviction was affirmed.

One more possible appeal remained, to the Court of Errors, the highest tribunal in the state. At this point Roger and all the ACLU lawyers came to a conclusion that Mr. Untermyer would have to be replaced. "They all said, including our Jewish lawyers, that a New Yorker, a rich Jew like Untermyer, would certainly get licked pleading before the Court of Errors in New Jersey."

Lamson then pursued the issue with Baldwin:

"Does that mean you can't conceive of a situation in which a black lawyer would defend, let's say, a Mormon who was prevented from holding a public meeting?"

"No, I can't conceive of such a situation."

"Then do you think Mr. Redding [an ACLU cooperating lawyer] or any other black lawyer would be less effective in such a case *just because* he was black?"

"Yes, of course, that's what I think. He'd be less effective unless he was extraordinarily good. Because he'd have to be extraordinarily good to overcome a jury's prejudice."

"Whereas a white lawyer would just have to be average good, is that it?"

"Not necessarily," Roger said calmly. "It depends on the prejudice. For instance, we wouldn't use a New York lawyer in Alabama, and we wouldn't use a southern lawyer, particularly one with a strong accent, in a northern court. In New Jersey we all decided not to use a Jewish lawyer when we knew prejudice against him existed. And you have to remember that because of that

* Peggy Lamson, Roger Baldwin, Founder of the American Civil Liberties Union: A Portrait 160-162 (1976).

tactic we won the Patterson, New Jersey, case, which was far more of a victory than just keeping me out of jail."

"I realize that, Roger, but still—"

"If the original judgment had stood in New Jersey," Roger broke in, now pressing his advantage, "it would have meant that men could go to jail for doing something which the Constitution clearly says they have a perfect right to do—peaceably to assemble and petition for redress of grievance."

Is this ancient history? School District of Abington Township v. Schempp, 374 U.S. 203 (1963), was an important Supreme Court opinion on the constitutionality of school prayer. Ellory Schempp was a high school student in Abington Township, a Philadelphia suburb. In 1957 he wrote to the ACLU's Philadelphia chapter. As a Unitarian, he wrote, he felt uncomfortable when the Lord's Prayer and the Bible were read each day in school. Bernard Wolfman, a young partner at a Philadelphia firm and a member of the ACLU, interviewed Ellory and urged the ACLU to take the case. It agreed. But as Judge Louis Pollak writes in a memorial to Henry Sawyer, Wolfman (now a Harvard law professor) did not argue the case. Instead, the work fell to Sawyer, then a young partner at another Philadelphia firm.

> The Board's decision to provide counsel for the Schempps, however, did not mean that Wolfman would be that counsel. Wolfman decided that for him, as a Jew, to represent the Schempps in a challenge to Bible reading and recitation of the Lord's Prayer merely would add unnecessary and probably detrimental baggage to what clearly would be a controversial and, in many quarters, an unpopular course.

Louis Pollak, Lawyer Sawyer, 148 U. Pa. L. Rev. 25 (1999).

B. CLIENT-CLIENT CONFLICTS

1. Criminal Cases (Defense Lawyers)

"Murder One, Murder Two"

Andy Simon is retained to represent Tommy "Pinball" Dash and Malcolm "Reb" Snyder in a murder case arising out of an alleged turf battle between two gangs, both engaged in drug sales in a section of Culver City. Dash is 51. Snyder is 23. Dash allegedly ran one gang's drug trade and has three prior felony convictions. Snyder has no record. The indictment charges that Snyder, claiming to be interested in a major purchase, lured Vincent "Little Man" Mallen (who got his nickname because he weighed over 300 pounds and was 6 feet 4 inches tall) to a vacant lot, where Dash shot him. The indictment charges murder one, which carries a life sentence without parole. Dash and Snyder tell Simon they were 180 miles away in Dorchester when Mallen was shot. They produce alibi witnesses whose credibility Simon seriously doubts, but he can't say that the alibi is certainly false.

The prosecutor, Tina Rand, offers to accept a plea to murder two, which carries a sentence of life with parole eligibility after 20 years. Dash figures whether he's convicted of murder one or murder two, he'll never get out of prison given his record, even if he lives 20 years, which he doubts he will. So he wants to go to trial and take his chances. Snyder wants to take the plea, but not if he has to testify against Dash. While maintaining his alibi to Simon, Snyder (whom Simon thinks is a little slow) also implies that Dash only wanted to scare Mallen.

Simon tells Rand that Snyder wants to accept the deal but only if he doesn't have to testify against Dash and that Dash insists on going to trial.

"It's both or nothing," Rand says. "I'm only offering the deal if it frees resources. If Dash doesn't plead, I've got to try it anyway so I'll try them both. I don't need Snyder's testimony anyway."

"But this way you get one sure conviction."

"My proof on Snyder, as you know, is stronger than my proof on Dash. I've got two separate eyewitnesses who saw Snyder with Mallen near the murder scene an hour before the time of death. He wasn't in Dorchester."

"A lot can happen in an hour, Tina."

"Snyder is history, Andy. His best chance is, because of his age, the jury convicts him of murder two as a lesser included. So I get that anyway."

"Snyder better get another lawyer," Simon says. "I think I've got a conflict."

"Snyder can get ten lawyers. The story ends the same way. Nothing more anyone can do for him. If Dash goes to trial, Snyder goes to trial, and you're telling me Dash is going to trial. Snyder is too. That's my final offer, and it stays open only until Tuesday noon."

Simon relates his conversation with Rand to his clients, but Dash is adamant about going to trial, which both do. Neither testifies. The jury convicts both of murder one. A new lawyer for Snyder then seeks a reversal on the ground that Simon had a conflict that deprived Snyder of his Sixth Amendment right to the effective assistance of counsel. Did Simon have a conflict? Did it amount to a denial of Snyder's Sixth Amendment right?

"Did Officer Schwarz Get the Effective Assistance of Counsel?"

One of the most famous cases featuring a defense lawyer's concurrent client (and personal) conflict (at least for us who work in the area) arose from the brutal police station assault on Brooklyn resident Abner Louima in 1997. Several officers, including Justin Volpe, Charles Schwarz, and Thomas Wiese, were jointly tried in 1999. Before the case went to the jury, Volpe pled guilty and received a 30-year sentence. An open question was whether Volpe acted alone or whether, as Louima and other witnesses testified, a second officer was present in the bathroom during the assault. The government claimed that Schwarz was the second officer, and the jury convicted him of conspiracy to violate Louima's civil rights and of violating them. On appeal, Schwarz claimed that Stephen Worth, his lawyer, had a conflict that rendered him ineffective. United States v. Schwarz, 283 F.3d 76 (2d Cir. 2002). Here are the salient facts. How would you rule (which need not be the way the court ruled)?

- Worth and his firm had a $10 million contract with the PBA, the police union, to represent it, including in all civil matters. The PBA could terminate the contract on 30 days' notice. It was up for renewal in 2000.

- Louima had a suit pending against the PBA and its president, charging that they "participated in a conspiracy to injure Louima and cover it up." Neither Worth nor his firm represented the defendants in that civil action.
- The government introduced proof from Louima and others tending to prove that Schwarz was the second officer in the bathroom.
- Worth had some proof that a second officer was in the bathroom with Volpe and that it was Wiese, not Schwarz. Among the proof was that Volpe, at his guilty plea, said that there was a second officer in the bathroom with him and that it was not Schwarz. Also, Wiese and Schwarz look alike. Worth had no relationship with Wiese.
- Worth argued to the jury that Volpe acted alone. That is, he chose not to accept the government's claim that another officer was in the bathroom.
- At a pretrial hearing, Schwarz acknowledged and waived all conflicts on the record, after being advised by independent counsel provided by the court. That counsel told the court that "he had advised Schwarz of all these conflicts and believed Schwarz understood them." The judge accepted the waiver and permitted Worth to continue to represent Schwarz.

How would you articulate the conflict from Schwarz's point of view. (Try a sentence in the "On one hand, Worth was required to [*fill in the blank*], but on the other hand he [*fill in the blank*]." If you were on the circuit court, what weight would you give (a) Schwarz's informed waiver; (b) the effect of a reversal on the (un)willingness of future trial judges to defer to a defendant's informed decision to proceed with conflicted counsel of choice?

Issues of concurrent conflicts between clients in criminal representation arise when a single lawyer represents two or more defendants or persons under investigation. Representation can occur during the investigation of the matter (including before the grand jury), in plea negotiations, at trial, or on appeal. Sometimes two partners will each represent one of two defendants. Burger v. Kemp, 483 U.S. 776 (1987) (assumes partners are one lawyer for conflicts purposes). The conflicts issue may be raised, among other ways, if the defendants (or one of them) are convicted and challenge the lawyer's performance as constitutionally ineffective.

The conflicts issue arises in an inverted way when a defendant wants to hire a lawyer and the judge refuses to allow it (usually in response to an objection from the prosecution) on the ground that the lawyer has a disqualifying conflict. The defendant may be fully prepared to waive any conflict and argue that denying him his chosen lawyer violates his Sixth Amendment right to counsel of choice. In turn, the prosecutor may argue that because of the conflict the lawyer cannot ethically represent the defendant or offer constitutionally effective representation. "She's a walking Sixth Amendment violation, your Honor. You can't always get what you want." Why is that the prosecutor's business?

Because these issues are intertwined with the Sixth Amendment guarantee, the question whether counsel faced a conflict of interest is only part of a court's analysis. Another issue is the kind of harm a defendant must show to win relief from a conviction if the defense lawyer was constitutionally conflicted. Must the accused prove that the conflict somehow affected the lawyer's performance? Must the accused also prove that she would not have been convicted but for the lawyer's performance? Will the fact of a conflict ever be sufficient in and of itself to warrant relief? In addition to the constitutional and ethical questions that swirl around this problem, Rule 44(c) of the Federal Rules of Criminal Procedure applies in federal criminal trials. Adopted in 1979, it is set out in relevant part in Wheat v. United States (page 253) and in note 10 of the next case.

CUYLER v. SULLIVAN
446 U.S. 335 (1980)

JUSTICE POWELL delivered the opinion of the Court.

The question presented is whether a state prisoner may obtain a federal writ of habeas corpus by showing that his retained defense counsel represented potentially conflicting interests.

I

Respondent John Sullivan was indicted with Gregory Carchidi and Anthony DiPasquale for the first-degree murders of John Gorey and Rita Janda. . . .

Two privately retained lawyers, G. Fred DiBona and A. Charles Peruto, represented all three defendants throughout the state proceedings that followed the indictment. Sullivan had different counsel at the medical examiner's inquest, but he thereafter accepted representation from the two lawyers retained by his codefendants because he could not afford to pay his own lawyer. At no time did Sullivan or his lawyers object to the multiple representation. Sullivan was the first defendant to come to trial. The evidence against him was entirely circumstantial, consisting primarily of [a Mr.] McGrath's testimony. At the close of the Commonwealth's case, the defense rested without presenting any evidence. The jury found Sullivan guilty and fixed his penalty at life imprisonment. Sullivan's posttrial motions failed, and the Pennsylvania Supreme Court affirmed his conviction by an equally divided vote. Sullivan's codefendants, Carchidi and DiPasquale, were acquitted at separate trials. . . .

DiBona and Peruto had different recollections of their roles at the trials of the three defendants. DiBona testified that he and Peruto had been "associate counsel" at each trial. Peruto recalled that he had been chief counsel for Carchidi and DiPasquale, but that he merely had assisted DiBona in Sullivan's trial. DiBona and Peruto also gave conflicting accounts of the decision to rest Sullivan's defense. DiBona said he had encouraged Sullivan to testify even though the Commonwealth had presented a very weak case. Peruto remembered that he had not "wanted the defense to go on because I thought we would only be exposing the defense witnesses for the other two trials that were coming up." Sullivan testified that he had deferred to his lawyers' decision not to present evidence for the defense. But other testimony suggested that Sullivan preferred not to take the stand because cross-examination might have disclosed an extra-marital affair. Finally, Carchidi claimed he would have appeared at Sullivan's trial to rebut McGrath's testimony about Carchidi's statement at the time of the murders. . . .

[Sullivan sought release in habeas corpus. The Third Circuit ruled in his favor and the state petitioned for certiorari.]

IV

We come at last to Sullivan's claim that he was denied the effective assistance of counsel guaranteed by the Sixth Amendment because his lawyers had a conflict of interest. The claim raises two issues expressly reserved in Holloway v. Arkansas, [435 U.S. 475, 483-484 (1978)]. The first is whether a state trial judge must inquire into the propriety of multiple representation even though no party lodges an objection. The second is whether the mere possibility of a conflict of interest warrants the conclusion that the defendant was deprived of his right to counsel.

A

In *Holloway*, a single public defender represented three defendants at the same trial. The trial court refused to consider the appointment of separate counsel despite the defense lawyer's timely and repeated assertions that the interests of his clients conflicted. This Court recognized that a lawyer forced to represent codefendants whose interests conflict cannot provide the adequate legal assistance required by the Sixth Amendment. Given the trial court's failure to respond to timely objections, however, the Court did not consider whether the alleged conflict actually existed. It simply held that the trial court's error unconstitutionally endangered the right to counsel.

Holloway requires state trial courts to investigate timely objections to multiple representation. But nothing in our precedents suggests that the Sixth Amendment requires state courts themselves to initiate inquiries into the propriety of multiple representation in every case.[10] Defense counsel have an ethical obligation to avoid conflicting representations and to advise the court promptly when a conflict of interest arises during the course of trial.[11] Absent special circumstances, therefore, trial courts may assume either that multiple representation entails no conflict or that the lawyer and his clients knowingly accept such risk of conflict as may exist. . . .

Nothing in the circumstances of this case indicates that the trial court had a duty to inquire whether there was a conflict of interest. . . .

10. In certain cases, proposed Federal Rule of Criminal Procedure 44(c) provides that the federal district courts "shall promptly inquire with respect to . . . joint representation and shall personally advise each defendant of his right to the effective assistance of counsel, including separate representation." See also ABA Project on Standards for Criminal Justice, Function of the Trial Judge §3.4(b) (App. Draft 1972).

11. ABA Code of Professional Responsibility, DR 5-105, EC 5-15 (1976); ABA Project on Standards for Criminal Justice, Defense Function §3.5(b) (App. Draft 1971).

B

Holloway reaffirmed that multiple representation does not violate the Sixth Amendment unless it gives rise to a conflict of interest. Since a possible conflict inheres in almost every instance of multiple representation, a defendant who objects to multiple representation must have the opportunity to show that potential conflicts impermissibly imperil his right to a fair trial. But unless the trial court fails to afford such an opportunity, a reviewing court cannot presume that the possibility for conflict has resulted in ineffective assistance of counsel. Such a presumption would preclude multiple representation even in cases where " '[a] common defense . . . gives strength against a common attack.' " Glasser v. United States, 315 U.S. 60, 92 (1942) (Frankfurter, J., dissenting).

In order to establish a violation of the Sixth Amendment, a defendant who raised no objection at trial must demonstrate that an actual conflict of interest adversely affected his lawyer's performance. In Glasser v. United States, for example, the record showed that defense counsel failed to cross-examine a prosecution witness whose testimony linked Glasser with the crime and failed to resist the presentation of arguably inadmissible evidence. The Court found that both omissions resulted from counsel's desire to diminish the jury's perception of a codefendant's guilt. Indeed, the evidence of counsel's "struggle to serve two masters could not seriously be doubted." Since this actual conflict of interest impaired Glasser's defense, the Court reversed his conviction.

Dukes v. Warden, 406 U.S. 250 (1972), presented a contrasting situation. Dukes pleaded guilty on the advice of two lawyers, one of whom also represented Dukes' codefendants on an unrelated charge. Dukes later learned that this lawyer had sought leniency for the codefendants by arguing that their cooperation with the police induced Dukes to plead guilty. Dukes argued in this Court that his lawyer's conflict of interest had infected his plea. We found " 'nothing in the record . . . which would indicate that the alleged conflict resulted in ineffective assistance of counsel and did in fact render the plea in question involuntary and unintelligent.' " Since Dukes did not identify an actual lapse in representation, we affirmed the denial of habeas corpus relief.

Glasser established that unconstitutional multiple representation is never harmless error. Once the Court concluded that Glasser's lawyer had an actual conflict of interest, it refused "to indulge in nice calculations as to the amount of prejudice" attributable to the conflict. The conflict itself demonstrated a denial of the "right to have the effective assistance of counsel." Thus, a defendant who shows that a conflict of interest actually affected the adequacy of his representation need not demonstrate prejudice in order to obtain relief. But until a defendant shows that his counsel actively represented conflicting interests, he has not established the constitutional predicate for his claim of ineffective assistance.

C

The Court of Appeals granted Sullivan relief because he had shown that the multiple representation in this case involved a possible conflict of interest. We hold that the possibility of conflict is insufficient to impugn a criminal conviction. In order to demonstrate a violation of his Sixth Amendment rights, a defendant must establish that an actual conflict of interest adversely affected his lawyer's performance. Sullivan believes he should prevail even under this standard. He emphasizes Peruto's admission that the decision to rest Sullivan's defense reflected a reluctance to expose witnesses who later might have testified for the other defendants. The petitioner, on the other hand, points to DiBona's contrary testimony and to evidence that Sullivan himself wished to avoid taking the stand. Since the Court of Appeals did not weigh these conflicting contentions under the proper legal standard, its judgment is vacated and the case is remanded for further proceedings consistent with this opinion.

So ordered.

Justice Brennan, concurring [in part and in the result]. . . .

"[A] possible conflict inheres in almost every instance of multiple representation." Therefore, upon discovery of joint representation, the duty of the trial court is to ensure that the defendants have not unwittingly given up their constitutional right to effective counsel. This is necessary since it is usually the case that defendants will not know what their rights are or how to raise them. This is surely true of the defendant who may not be receiving the effective assistance of counsel as a result of conflicting duties owed to other defendants. Therefore, the trial court cannot safely assume that silence indicates a knowledgeable choice to proceed jointly. The court must at least affirmatively advise the defendants that joint representation creates potential hazards which the defendants should consider before proceeding with the representation.

Had the trial record in the present case shown that respondent made a knowing and intelligent choice of joint representation, I could accept the Court's standard for a postconviction determination as to whether respondent in fact was denied effective assistance. Where it is clear that a defendant has voluntarily chosen to proceed with joint representation, it is fair, if he later alleges ineffective assistance growing out of a conflict, to require that he demonstrate "that a conflict of interest actually affected the adequacy of his representation." Here, however, where there is no evidence that the court advised respondent about the potential for conflict or that respondent made a knowing and intelligent choice to forgo his right to separate counsel, I believe that respondent, who has shown a significant possibility of conflict, is entitled to a presumption that his representation in fact suffered. Therefore, I would remand the case to allow the petitioners an opportunity to rebut this presumption by demonstrating that respondent's representation was not actually affected by the possibility of conflict.

Justice Marshall, concurring in part and dissenting in part. . . .

I believe . . . that whenever two or more defendants are represented by the same attorney the trial judge must make a preliminary determination that the joint representation is the product of the defendants' informed choice. I therefore agree with Mr. Justice Brennan that the trial court has a duty to inquire whether there is multiple representation, to warn defendants of the possible risks of such representation, and to ascertain that the representation is the result of the defendants' informed choice.

I dissent from the Court's formulation of the proper standard for determining whether multiple representation has violated the defendant's right to the effective assistance of counsel. The Court holds that in the absence of an objection at trial, the defendant must show "that an actual conflict of interest adversely affected his lawyer's performance." If the Court's holding would require a defendant to demonstrate that his attorney's trial performance differed from what it would have been if the defendant had been the attorney's only client, I believe it is inconsistent with our previous cases. Such a test is not only unduly harsh, but incurably speculative as well. The appropriate question under the Sixth Amendment is whether an actual, relevant conflict of interests existed during the proceedings. If it did, the conviction must be reversed. Since such a conflict was present in this case, I would affirm the judgment of the Court of Appeals. . . .

Turning Conflicts into Sixth Amendment Claims After *Cuyler*

Cuyler was decided before Strickland v. Washington, which stated the test for determining ineffective assistance of counsel (see page 811). That test asks whether counsel's performance "was reasonable considering all the circumstances." If not, the "defendant must show that there is a reasonable probability that, but for counsel's unprofessional errors, the result of the proceeding would have been different." In Burger v. Kemp, 483 U.S. 776 (1987), the Court made it clear that the burden on the defendant who claims ineffective assistance of counsel based on a conflict is less demanding than for defendants asserting other kinds of ineffectiveness. While the fact of an actual conflict will not generally result in automatic reversal of a conviction, neither must the defendant prove *Strickland*-type prejudice:

> We have never held that the possibility of prejudice that "inheres in almost every instance of multiple representation" justifies the adoption of an inflexible rule that would presume prejudice in all such cases. [Citing *Cuyler*.] Instead, we presume prejudice "only if the defendant demonstrates that counsel 'actively represented conflicting interests' and that 'an actual conflict of interest adversely affected his lawyer's performance.'" [Citing *Strickland* quoting *Cuyler*.]

Sullivan's travels continued for three more years. Ultimately, the Third Circuit affirmed a judgment finding ineffective assistance of counsel. Counsel's conflict led him to fail to call Carchidi, one of his other clients who was awaiting trial. The court quoted lawyer Peruto, who helpfully explained the failure to call Carchidi this way:

> "Carchidi took the position of, hey, don't hurt me. If it's going to help John, yes, I'm willing to help John; but not if it's going to hurt me. So on the one hand I have to listen to John Sullivan, on the other hand I have to listen to Carchidi." [Sullivan v. Cuyler, 723 F.2d 1077 (3d Cir. 1983).]

Pennsylvania made a kind of proximate cause argument: If Carchidi had had separate counsel, that counsel would have advised him to assert his privilege against self-incrimination and not testify. Same result. Consequently, Sullivan was not prejudiced. The court responded: "But, as we noted earlier, a defendant need not demonstrate actual prejudice to make out a violation of his sixth amendment rights where he has already established an actual conflict of interest adversely affecting counsel's performance." What was the adverse effect on performance? The inability even to try to get Carchidi to testify because of a duty to Carchidi?

Here are two more examples of convicted defendants who have relied on a *Cuyler-Strickland* analysis to win relief. The facts in the first case show just how convoluted conflict analysis can be. James McConico was charged with killing Ricky Morton, his wife's brother. He hired Fred Pickard to represent him. Morton had a life insurance policy. Brenda McConico, James's wife and Ricky's sister, was a partial beneficiary. Brenda hired Pickard to recover the insurance proceeds. James's defense was self-defense. This defense required Pickard to argue that Morton was the aggressor, but the insurance policy had an exclusion clause that would have denied coverage if Morton was the aggressor. *(Aha moment here!)* Brenda testified for the prosecution, against her husband, that her brother had not been the aggressor. The court concluded that Pickard had an actual conflict of interest between his obligation to defend James and his obligation to help Brenda get the insurance money. Further, the conflict "had some adverse effect on counsel's performance," including his less than vigorous cross-examination of Brenda. James did not have to "show that the result of the trial would have been different without the conflict of interest." McConico v. State, 919 F.2d 1543 (11th Cir. 1990).

Goldenhersh represented Griffin and Smith in their joint trial for murder. The defense was alibi, which was weak, given eyewitnesses who placed both men at the scene of the crime. However, Griffin had a separate defense — that although he was present at the scene, he was an innocent bystander. Obviously, a single lawyer could not assert both defenses for Griffin. Goldenhersh chose alibi. The Seventh Circuit, affirming a grant of habeas corpus, held that Goldenhersh had an actual conflict:

> In the face of the uncontradicted evidence placing Smith at the scene during the shootings, Griffin's testifying to an alibi which involved Smith could do nothing but damage his own case. . . . There was only the slimmest chance, if any, that a jury would believe the alibi in the face of the consistent eyewitness testimony placing Griffin and Smith at the scene of the murders. On the other hand, an attorney representing only Griffin could have impeached the identifications of Griffin as a shooter by exploiting obvious inconsistencies in testimony. The joint representation prevented Mr. Goldenhersh from exploiting the disparity in strength of the respective prosecution cases against Griffin and Smith.

Griffin v. McVicar, 84 F.3d 880 (7th Cir. 1996). See also Boykin v. Webb, 541 F.3d 638 (6th Cir. 2008) ("Where, as here, the facts at trial show that a defendant's best defense is to point the finger at his co-defendant, it almost goes without saying that the two co-defendants cannot be represented by the same trial counsel"); People v. Hernandez, 896 N.E.2d 297 (Ill. 2008) ("per se conflict", requiring automatic reversal, for a lawyer to represent defendant on charge of solicitation to murder *X* while the same lawyer represented *X* on an unrelated criminal charge, notwithstanding that *X* was a fugitive and counsel had had no contact with him for more than two years).

Holloway Error

Holloway v. Arkansas, 435 U.S. 475 (1978), is a dramatic opinion because it can lead to reversal of a conviction without the need to show any harm at all or any effect on counsel's performance. The trial court had appointed a public defender to represent three defendants in the same trial. The lawyer repeatedly requested separate counsel, citing conflicts of interest, but the trial judge refused to consider the request. The Supreme Court held that the trial court's failure to investigate the alleged conflicts required reversal without any need to demonstrate prejudice. Why would the Court adopt this generous remedy? Look at it systemically. If the trial judge ignores defense lawyer's motion, it will create posttrial headaches on appeal and in collateral attacks. Far better to resolve the conflict question before any harm is done. An automatic reversal rule encourages trial judges to do so, because they are now warned that their work trying the case, in the event of conviction, will be for naught if they do not. Viewed this way, *Holloway*'s remedy is not so much for the benefit of the defendant (who gets a windfall) as it is meant to insure systemic efficiency.

Relying on language in Wood v. Georgia, 450 U.S. 261 (1981), discussed at page 231, some lower courts then applied *Holloway*'s automatic reversal rule even where the defense lawyer did not call the possibility of conflict to the court's attention, so long as the trial judge knew or should have known of its existence. See, e.g., Armienti v. United States, 234 F.3d 820 (2d Cir. 2000) (where "court is sufficiently apprised of even the possibility of a conflict of interest, the court . . . has" an inquiry obligation). The Supreme Court put a stop to that view in Mickens v. Taylor, 535 U.S. 162 (2002) (5-4), and in dicta the Court cast doubt on the breadth of *Sullivan* itself.

Mickens was charged with killing Hall. Saunders had been representing Hall on an unrelated charge at the time of his death. Four days after a trial judge relieved Saunders from representing the now dead Hall, she appointed Saunders to represent Mickens for allegedly killing his former client. Mickens was convicted and sentenced to death. The first time Mickens learned that Saunders had been Hall's lawyer was when his postconviction counsel inspected Hall's court file years later. (Hall was a juvenile and the file was under seal, but a clerk mistakenly gave it to Mickens's counsel.)

Mickens argued that the trial judge's failure to inquire into Saunders's conflict warranted automatic reversal under *Holloway* because she knew or should have known about the conflict. After all, the same judge relieved Saunders from representing Hall and then appointed him for Mickens. But Justice Scalia's opinion for the Court held that *Holloway* did not apply. The automatic reversal rule operates "only where defense counsel is forced to represent codefendants over his timely objection, unless the trial court has determined that there is no conflict." It didn't matter what the trial judge may actually have known. The defense lawyer made no objection, so *Holloway* did not apply. End of story. As a result, Mickens had to satisfy the *Sullivan* test by proving that the conflict affected Saunders's performance. The Fourth Circuit had rejected a Cuyler v. Sullivan claim and certiorari was not granted to review that decision. The dissents argued either that *Holloway* did apply or that Saunders's performance was actually affected within the meaning of *Cuyler* because Saunders's continuing confidentiality obligations to Hall would prevent him from using what he knew about Hall to defend Mickens, either at the guilt phase of his capital trial or at the penalty phase. Mickens was sentenced to death and executed.

The dramatic upshot of *Mickens's* treatment of *Holloway* can be seen in Campbell v. Rice, 302 F.3d 892 (9th Cir. 2002). The prosecutor informed the trial judge that his office was then prosecuting the defense lawyer, McCann, on unrelated charges. (Do you see why that would create a conflict?) The trial judge asked McCann whether she wished "to make any statement at this time." She did not. The judge then "determined there is no conflict of interest." Before *Mickens* was decided, the Ninth Circuit found this to be *Holloway* error. The judge knew of the conflict and didn't follow the *Holloway* script. After *Mickens,* the court withdrew its opinion and held that Campbell did not establish *Holloway* error (which would obviate the need to show harm) because the defense lawyer did not press the conflict with the court. Why didn't she, do you imagine? Wasn't her failure to do so itself a product of her conflict?

Beyond limiting *Holloway,* the *Mickens* Court (in dicta) questioned whether the *Cuyler* test for ineffectiveness (more generous to defendants than is the *Strickland* test) should even apply to someone in Mickens's position. The lawyers in *Cuyler* had a conflict between *current* clients. Saunders's conflict was between his duty of confidentiality to Hall, a *former* client, and his duty to Mickens, a current client. The Court pointedly left open the possibility that the stricter *Strickland* test might govern conflicts that are not current client conflicts. Why should that be? *Cuyler* is premised on the difficulty of predicting how the case would have turned out with an unconflicted lawyer where the conflict is shown actually to have affected the lawyer's performance. *Cuyler* says, in effect, that once we know that a lawyer's conflict adversely affected how he or she tried the case, we really aren't in a position to judge whether a different lawyer's different strategy would have made a difference. Given this rationale, what would be the intellectual justification for distinguishing among conflicts? A former client conflict or, indeed, a current *lawyer*-client conflict, can be as debilitating to a lawyer's performance as a conflict between two current clients and prediction of how the case would have ended with an unconflicted lawyer equally suppositional. Or is a current client conflict somehow more worrisome? Eventually, the Supreme Court will have to decide whether to turn its *Mickens's* dicta into a holding. Some lower courts have treated the dicta as no more than dicta. See United States v. Infante, 404 F.3d 376 (5th Cir. 2005). But other courts have taken it more seriously. See Schwab v. Crosby, 451 F.3d 1308 (11th Cir. 2006) (postconviction analysis); People v. Rundle, 180 P.3d 224 (Cal. 2008) (lawyer-client conflict). Whatever the federal rule, state courts may offer defendants greater protection against conflicted counsel under their state constitutions, as was true in *Rundle.* See also People v. Cottle, 946 A.2d 550 (N.J. 2008) (prejudice presumed where lawyer under indictment in same county as case he was defending).

Disqualification of Defense Counsel

The *Cuyler* question arises after trial and conviction. Its test is retrospective. Did defense counsel labor under a conflict that affected her performance? In a different way, the question can also arise prospectively: Will the defense lawyer's alleged (or as in *Holloway,* asserted) conflict lead to ineffectiveness? A judge and prosecutor cannot (certainly should not) relish having a trial if the convicted defendant may be able to mount a successful *Cuyler* challenge. But isn't it awfully hard to predict in advance whether a conflict will adversely affect a lawyer's performance? Yes, it's hard; but sometimes the likelihood of an effect on performance is high enough to warrant a prospective remedy. Now a new constitutional right comes into the picture. Faced with a prosecutorial motion (or a judge's decision) to disqualify an allegedly conflicted defense lawyer before trial, the defendant may respond that he's quite willing to waive the conflict, thereby removing the possibility of a *Cuyler* ineffectiveness challenge later. Consequently, the argument goes, disqualification will needlessly violate his Sixth Amendment right to counsel of choice.

"Murder at the Ballgame"

Shari LaGuardia was found murdered in a toilet stall during the seventh inning stretch at an afternoon ballgame at Reynoso Park. A 30-pound piece of scrap metal was dropped forcefully on her head from the adjacent stall. The police were called and began questioning patrons who might have seen Shari or others go into the bathroom.

Shari was estranged from her husband Pete, whose threats of harm had caused Shari to get an order of protection four months earlier. Pete had a criminal record and was at the time of Shari's death facing charges for breaking into vending machines. Pete denied any culpability in Shari's death. Asked for an alibi, Pete said he slept days because he worked the midnight to 8 a.m. shift at a factory. The police confirmed that Pete worked that shift, but no one could support Pete's claim that he was asleep at home when Shari was killed because he lived alone. No forensic or other evidence pointed to Pete. No one at the game saw Pete or his car there. Pete claimed that he had not seen Shari nor gone near her home or workplace since she got the order of protection and that he was over her. "I'm not saying I'm sorry the bitch is dead," he told one detective. "But I didn't kill her."

Working with tape from video surveillance cameras, a partial shoe print on the floor of the bathroom, and the results of interviews, the police arrested Juan Potero, a short-order cook at Reynoso Park. The police theorized that Potero's motive was to steal LaGuardia's pocketbook but he panicked and fled when he realized that instead of stunning Shari, he might have killed her. Potero maintained his innocence, but some of the answers he gave the police were (in their view) either inconsistent or contradicted by other information the police unearthed. No one could connect Potero with the scrap metal that killed LaGuardia, but Potero was an avid weight lifter.

Potero was indicted for murdering Shari LaGuardia in the course of an attempted robbery. The D.A. announced that she would seek the death penalty. Potero's family and friends put up the money to hire Lydia Hinajosa, whose resume included eight years as an assistant district attorney in the city (the last three as head of the homicide bureau), followed by 12 years defending serious felonies.

Two months after Lydia noted her appearance and filed her first set of discovery motions, the prosecutor, Paul Chen, moved to disqualify her, citing the fact that one of Lydia's partners, Virgil Pajyk, then represented Pete LaGuardia on the current vending machine charges and had represented Pete in three prior assault cases, two against women he met in bars.

"What's that got to do with anything?" an angry Lydia asked Paul when she received the motion.

"It means your defenses are limited by one. You can't argue that Pete did it in order to give the jury a reasonable doubt. You can't even consider that strategy."

"Pete's not the killer, Paul. You don't think he's the killer. I don't think he's the killer. Why would anyone even want to consider that strategy?"

"Oh, come on, Lydia. It doesn't matter what we think. You can't get the jury to wonder maybe we got the wrong guy. You can't even argue that. And you've got the evidence to do it: Pete threatened Shari in the past; she had to get an order of protection; he's strong and could easily lift and toss a 30-pound weight; he has no confirmed alibi; he works in factories with a lot of junk metal around. When informed of her death, he showed no regret. Maybe the judge would let you introduce evidence of violent temper. It's an obvious ploy. That's why the police considered him a serious suspect in the first place."

"It would be the dumbest defense in the world to blame Pete when no one can place him or his car at the park. You showed Pete's picture to everyone, probably including the team mascot. He's not on the video. He had no contact with Shari in four months. No calls. No visits. The lab guys can't say if the scrap metal that killed LaGuardia came from Pete's factory. A Pete-did-it defense would be so transparent. I mean it's like saying look how pathetic we are. You're trying to knock me out because I can't do — assuming you're even right that I can't — what I wouldn't do anyway, and no competent defense lawyer we know would do. Besides, I've got a lot better than that."

"Like what?"

"Screw you, Paul. You'll find out in court."

"But not from you. I don't want to win this case and then have to beat back a *Cuyler* challenge."

"Potero will waive that crap now. In writing. Under oath. It's so stupid."

"If the judge lets him waive."

Chen's motion seeks to disqualify Lydia and her firm. What do you think?

WHEAT v. UNITED STATES
486 U.S. 153 (1988)

CHIEF JUSTICE REHNQUIST delivered the opinion of the Court.

The issue in this case is whether the District Court erred in declining petitioner's waiver of his right to conflict-free counsel and by refusing to permit petitioner's proposed substitution of attorneys.

I

Petitioner Mark Wheat, along with numerous codefendants, was charged with participating in a far-flung drug distribution conspiracy. Over a period of several years, many thousands of pounds of marijuana were transported from Mexico and other locations to southern California. Petitioner acted primarily as an intermediary in the distribution ring; he received and stored large shipments of marijuana at his home, then distributed the marijuana to customers in the region.

Also charged in the conspiracy were Juvenal Gomez-Barajas and Javier Bravo, who were represented in their criminal proceedings by attorney Eugene Iredale. Gomez-Barajas was tried first and was acquitted on drug charges overlapping with those against petitioner. To avoid a second trial on other charges, however, Gomez-Barajas offered to plead guilty to tax evasion and illegal importation of merchandise. At the commencement of petitioner's trial, the District Court had not accepted the plea; Gomez-Barajas was thus free to withdraw his guilty plea and proceed to trial.

Bravo, evidently a lesser player in the conspiracy, decided to forgo trial and plead guilty to one count of transporting approximately 2400 pounds of marijuana from Los Angeles to a residence controlled by Victor Vidal. At the conclusion of Bravo's guilty plea proceedings on August 22, 1985, Iredale notified the District Court that he had been contacted by petitioner and had been asked to try petitioner's case as well. In response, the Government registered substantial concern about the possibility of conflict in the representation. After entertaining some initial discussion of the substitution of counsel, the District Court instructed the parties to present more detailed arguments the following Monday, just one day before the scheduled start of petitioner's trial.

At the Monday hearing, the Government objected to petitioner's proposed substitution on the ground that Iredale's representation of Gomez-Barajas and Bravo created a serious conflict of interest. The Government's position was premised on two possible conflicts. First, the District Court had not yet accepted the plea and sentencing arrangement negotiated between Gomez-Barajas and the Government; in the event that arrangement were rejected by the court, Gomez-Barajas would be free to withdraw the plea and stand trial. He would then be faced with the prospect of representation by Iredale, who in the meantime would have acted as petitioner's attorney. Petitioner, through his participation in the drug distribution scheme, was familiar with the sources and size of Gomez-Barajas' income, and was thus likely to be called as a witness for the Government at any subsequent trial of Gomez-Barajas. This scenario would pose a conflict of interest for Iredale, who would be prevented from cross-examining petitioner and thereby from effectively representing Gomez-Barajas.

Second, and of more immediate concern, Iredale's representation of Bravo would directly affect his ability to act as counsel for petitioner. The Government believed that a portion of the marijuana delivered by Bravo to Vidal's residence eventually was transferred to petitioner. In this regard, the Government contacted Iredale and asked that Bravo be made available as a witness to testify against petitioner, and agreed in exchange to modify its position at the time of Bravo's sentencing. In the likely event that Bravo were called to testify, Iredale's position in representing both men would become untenable, for ethical proscriptions would forbid him to cross-examine Bravo in any meaningful way. By failing to do so, he would also fail to provide petitioner with effective assistance of counsel. Thus, because of Iredale's prior representation of Gomez-Barajas and Bravo and the potential for serious conflict of interest, the Government urged the District Court to reject the substitution of attorneys.

In response, petitioner emphasized his right to have counsel of his own choosing and the willingness of Gomez-Barajas, Bravo, and petitioner to waive the right to conflict-free counsel. Petitioner argued that the circumstances posited by the Government that would create a conflict for Iredale were highly speculative and bore no connection to the true relationship between the co-conspirators. If called to testify, Bravo would simply say that he did not know petitioner and had no dealings with him; no attempt by Iredale to impeach Bravo would be necessary. Further, in the unlikely event that Gomez-Barajas went to trial on the charges of tax evasion and illegal importation, petitioner's lack of involvement in those alleged crimes made his appearance as a witness highly improbable. Finally, and most importantly, all three defendants agreed to allow Iredale to represent petitioner and to waive any future claims of conflict of interest. In petitioner's view, the Government was manufacturing implausible conflicts in an attempt to disqualify Iredale, who had already proved extremely effective in representing Gomez-Barajas and Bravo.

After hearing argument from each side, the District Court noted that it was unfortunate that petitioner had not suggested the substitution sooner, rather than two court days before the commencement of trial. The court then ruled:

> [B]ased upon the representation of the Government in [its] memorandum that the Court really has no choice at this point other than to find that an irreconcilable conflict of interest exists, I don't think it can be waived, and accordingly, Mr. Wheat's request to substitute Mr. Iredale in as attorney of record is denied.

Petitioner proceeded to trial with his original counsel and was convicted. . . .

II

The Sixth Amendment to the Constitution guarantees that "[i]n all criminal prosecutions, the accused shall enjoy the right . . . to have the Assistance of Counsel for his defence." . . .

The Sixth Amendment right to choose one's own counsel is circumscribed in several important respects. Regardless of his persuasive powers, an advocate who is not a member of the bar may not represent clients (other than himself) in court.[3] Similarly, a defendant may not insist on representation by an attorney he cannot afford or who for other reasons declines to represent the defendant. Nor may a defendant insist on the counsel of an attorney who has a previous or ongoing relationship with an opposing party, even when the opposing party is the Government. The question raised in this case is the extent to which a criminal defendant's right under the Sixth Amendment to his chosen attorney is qualified by the fact that the attorney has represented other defendants charged in the same criminal conspiracy. In previous cases, we have recognized that multiple representation of criminal defendants engenders special dangers of which a court must be aware. . . .

---

3. Our holding in Faretta v. California, 422 U.S. 806 (1975), that a criminal defendant has a Sixth Amendment right to represent *himself* if he voluntarily elects to do so, does not encompass the right to choose any advocate if the defendant wishes to be represented by counsel.

Petitioner insists that the provision of waivers by all affected defendants cures any problems created by the multiple representation. But no such flat rule can be deduced from the Sixth Amendment presumption in favor of counsel of choice. Federal courts have an independent interest in ensuring that criminal trials are conducted within the ethical standards of the profession and that legal proceedings appear fair to all who observe them. Both the American Bar Association's Model Code of Professional Responsibility and its Model Rules of Professional Conduct, as well as the rules of the California Bar Association (which governed the attorneys in this case), impose limitations on multiple representation of clients. Not only the interest of a criminal defendant but the institutional interest in the rendition of just verdicts in criminal cases may be jeopardized by unregulated multiple representation.

For this reason, the Federal Rules of Criminal Procedure direct trial judges to investigate specially cases involving joint representation. In pertinent part, Rule 44(c) provides:

> The court shall promptly inquire with respect to such joint representation and shall personally advise each defendant of his right to the effective assistance of counsel, including separate representation. Unless it appears that there is good cause to believe no conflict of interest is likely to arise, the court shall take such measures as may be appropriate to protect each defendant's right to counsel.

Although Rule 44(c) does not specify what particular measures may be taken by a district court, one option suggested by the Notes of the Advisory Committee is an order by the court that the defendants be separately represented in subsequent proceedings in the case. . . .

To be sure, this need to investigate potential conflicts arises in part from the legitimate wish of district courts that their judgments remain intact on appeal. As the Court of Appeals accurately pointed out, trial courts confronted with multiple representations face the prospect of being "whipsawed" by assertions of error no matter which way they rule. If a district court agrees to the multiple representation, and the advocacy of counsel is thereafter impaired as a result, the defendant may well claim that he did not receive effective assistance. On the other hand, a district court's refusal to accede to the multiple representation may result in a challenge such as petitioner's in this case. Nor does a waiver by the defendant necessarily solve the problem, for we note, without passing judgment on, the apparent willingness of Courts of Appeals to entertain ineffective-assistance claims from defendants who have specifically waived the right to conflict-free counsel.

Thus, where a court justifiably finds an actual conflict of interest, there can be no doubt that it may decline a proffer of waiver, and insist that defendants be separately represented. . . .

Unfortunately for all concerned, a district court must pass on the issue of whether or not to allow a waiver of a conflict of interest by a criminal defendant not with the wisdom of hindsight after the trial has taken place, but in the murkier pretrial context when relationships between parties are seen through a glass, darkly. The likelihood and dimensions of nascent conflicts of interest are notoriously hard to predict, even for those thoroughly familiar with criminal trials. It is a rare attorney who will be fortunate enough to learn the entire truth from his own client, much less be fully apprised before trial of what each of the Government's witnesses will say on the stand. A few bits of unforeseen testimony or a single previously unknown or unnoticed document may significantly shift the relationship between multiple defendants. These imponderables are difficult enough for a lawyer to assess, and even more difficult to convey by way of explanation to a criminal defendant untutored in the niceties of legal ethics. Nor is it amiss to observe that the willingness of an attorney to obtain such waivers from his clients may bear an inverse relation to the care with which he conveys all the necessary information to them.

For these reasons we think the District Court must be allowed substantial latitude in refusing waivers of conflicts of interest not only in those rare cases where an actual conflict may be demonstrated before trial, but in the more common cases where a potential for conflict exists which may or may not burgeon into an actual conflict as the trial progresses. In the circumstances of this case, with the motion for substitution of counsel made so close to the time of trial, the District Court relied on instinct and judgment based on experience in making its decision. We do not think it can be said that the court exceeded the broad latitude which must be accorded it in making this decision. Petitioner of course rightly points out that the Government may seek to "manufacture" a conflict in order to prevent a defendant from having a particularly able defense counsel at his side; but trial courts are undoubtedly aware of this possibility, and must take it into consideration along with all of the other factors which inform this sort of a decision.

Here the District Court was confronted not simply with an attorney who wished to represent two coequal defendants in a straightforward criminal prosecution; rather, Iredale proposed to defend three conspirators of varying stature in a complex drug distribution scheme. The Government intended to call Bravo as a witness for the prosecution at petitioner's trial.[4] The Government might readily have tied certain deliveries of marijuana by Bravo to petitioner, necessitating vigorous cross-examination of Bravo by petitioner's counsel. Iredale, because of his prior representation of Bravo, would have been unable ethically to provide that cross-examination.

Iredale had also represented Gomez-Barajas, one of the alleged kingpins of the distribution ring, and had succeeded in obtaining a verdict of acquittal for him. Gomez-Barajas had agreed with the Government to plead guilty to other charges, but the District Court had not yet accepted the plea arrangement. If the agreement were rejected, petitioner's probable testimony at the resulting trial of Gomez-Barajas would create an ethical dilemma for Iredale from which one or the other of his clients would likely suffer.

Viewing the situation as it did before trial, we hold that the District Court's refusal to permit the substitution of counsel in this case was within its discretion and did not violate petitioner's Sixth Amendment rights. Other district courts might have reached differing or opposite conclusions with equal justification, but that does not mean that one conclusion was "right" and the other "wrong." The District Court must recognize a presumption in favor of petitioner's counsel of choice, but that presumption may be overcome not only by a demonstration

---

4. Bravo was in fact called as a witness at petitioner's trial. His testimony was elicited to demonstrate the transportation of drugs that the prosecution hoped to link to petitioner.

of actual conflict but by a showing of a serious potential for conflict. The evaluation of the facts and circumstances of each case under this standard must be left primarily to the informed judgment of the trial court.

The judgment of the Court of Appeals is accordingly affirmed.

JUSTICE MARSHALL, with whom JUSTICE BRENNAN joins, dissenting. . . .

The Court's resolution of the instant case flows from its deferential approach to the District Court's denial of petitioner's motion to add or substitute counsel; absent deference, a decision upholding the District Court's ruling would be inconceivable. Indeed, I believe that even under the Court's deferential standard, reversal is in order. . . .

At the time of petitioner's trial, Iredale's representation of Gomez-Barajas was effectively completed. As the Court notes, Iredale had obtained an acquittal for Gomez-Barajas on charges relating to a conspiracy to distribute marijuana. Iredale also had negotiated an agreement with the Government under which Gomez-Barajas would plead guilty to charges of tax evasion and illegal importation of merchandise, although the trial court had not yet accepted this plea arrangement. Gomez-Barajas was not scheduled to appear as a witness at petitioner's trial; thus, Iredale's conduct of that trial would not require him to question his former client. The only possible conflict this Court can divine from Iredale's representation of both petitioner and Gomez-Barajas rests on the premise that the trial court would reject the negotiated plea agreement and that Gomez-Barajas then would decide to go to trial. In this event, the Court tells us, "petitioner's probable testimony at the resulting trial of Gomez-Barajas would create an ethical dilemma for Iredale."

This argument rests on speculation of the most dubious kind. The Court offers no reason to think that the trial court would have rejected Gomez-Barajas' plea agreement; neither did the Government posit any such reason in its argument or brief before this Court. The most likely occurrence at the time petitioner moved to retain Iredale as his defense counsel was that the trial court would accept Gomez-Barajas' plea agreement, as the court in fact later did. Moreover, even if Gomez-Barajas had gone to trial, petitioner probably would not have testified. The record contains no indication that petitioner had any involvement in or information about crimes for which Gomez-Barajas might yet have stood trial. The only alleged connection between petitioner and Gomez-Barajas sprang from the conspiracy to distribute marijuana, and a jury already had acquitted Gomez-Barajas of that charge. It is therefore disingenuous to say that representation of both petitioner and Gomez-Barajas posed a serious potential for a conflict of interest.

Similarly, Iredale's prior representation of Bravo was not a cause for concern. The Court notes that the prosecution intended to call Bravo to the stand at petitioner's trial and asserts that Bravo's testimony could well have "necessitat[ed] vigorous cross-examination . . . by petitioner's counsel." The facts, however, belie the claim that Bravo's anticipated testimony created a serious potential for conflict. Contrary to the Court's inference, Bravo could not have testified about petitioner's involvement in the alleged marijuana distribution scheme. As all parties were aware at the time, Bravo did not know and could not identify petitioner; indeed, prior to the commencement of legal proceedings, the two men never had heard of each other. Bravo's eventual testimony at petitioner's trial related to a shipment of marijuana in which petitioner was not involved; the testimony contained not a single reference to petitioner.

Petitioner's counsel did not cross-examine Bravo, and neither petitioner's counsel nor the prosecutor mentioned Bravo's testimony in closing argument. All of these developments were predictable when the District Court ruled on petitioner's request that Iredale serve as trial counsel; the contours of Bravo's testimony were clear at that time. Given the insignificance of this testimony to any matter that petitioner's counsel would dispute, the proposed joint representation of petitioner and Bravo did not threaten a conflict of interest.[3]

Moreover, even assuming that Bravo's testimony might have "necessitat[ed] vigorous cross-examination," the District Court could have insured against the possibility of any conflict of interest without wholly depriving petitioner of his constitutional right to the counsel of his choice. Petitioner's motion requested that Iredale either be substituted for petitioner's current counsel or be added to petitioner's defense team. Had the District Court allowed the addition of Iredale and then ordered that he take no part in the cross-examination of Bravo, any possibility of a conflict would have been removed. Especially in light of the availability of this precautionary measure, the notion that Iredale's prior representation of Bravo might well have caused a conflict of interest at petitioner's trial is nothing short of ludicrous. . . .

JUSTICE STEVENS, with whom JUSTICE BLACKMUN joins, dissenting. . . .

As Justice Marshall demonstrates, the Court exaggerates the significance of the potential conflict. Of greater importance, the Court gives inadequate weight to the informed and voluntary character of the clients' waiver of their right to conflict-free representation. Particularly, the Court virtually ignores the fact that additional counsel representing petitioner had provided him with sound advice concerning the wisdom of a waiver and would have remained available during the trial to assist in the defense. Thus, this is not a case in which the District Judge faced the question whether one counsel should be substituted for another; rather the question before him was whether petitioner should be permitted to have *additional* counsel of his choice. I agree with Justice Marshall that the answer to that question is perfectly clear.

Accordingly, although I agree with the Court's premise that district judges must be afforded wide latitude in passing on motions of this kind,* in this case it is abundantly clear to me that the District Judge abused his discretion and

---

3. The very insignificance of Bravo's testimony, combined with the timing of the prosecutor's decision to call Bravo as a witness, raises a serious concern that the prosecutor attempted to manufacture a conflict in this case. The prosecutor's decision to use Bravo as a witness was an 11th-hour development. Throughout the course of plea negotiations with Bravo, the prosecutor never had suggested that Bravo testify at petitioner's trial. At Bravo's guilty-plea proceedings, when Iredale notified the District Court of petitioner's substitution motion, the prosecutor conceded that he had made no plans to call Bravo as a witness. Only after the prosecutor learned of the substitution motion and decided to oppose it did he arrange for Bravo's testimony by agreeing to recommend to the trial court a reduction in Bravo's sentence. Especially in light of the scarce value of Bravo's testimony, this prosecutorial behavior very plausibly may be viewed as a maneuver to prevent Iredale from representing petitioner at trial. Iredale had proved to be a formidable adversary; he previously had gained an acquittal for the alleged kingpin of the marijuana distribution scheme. . . .

* In my view, deference to the trial judge is appropriate in light of his or her greater familiarity with such factors as the ability of the defendant knowingly and voluntarily to waive a potential conflict (including the possibility that a co-defendant may be exerting undue influence over the defendant), the character of the lawyers, the particular facts of the case, and the availability of alternative counsel of a like caliber.

deprived this petitioner of a constitutional right of such fundamental character that reversal is required.

Wheat's Harvest

Compare the burden of proof the court imposed on Sullivan before he could vacate his conviction with the burden that *Wheat* required a prosecutor to meet in order to disqualify defense counsel. Why is the second burden so much lower than the first?

Wheat has provided fertile ground for prosecutors asking judges to disqualify defense lawyers.

The lawyer in United States v. Moscony, 927 F.2d 742 (3d Cir. 1991), had represented multiple targets of an investigation, including the defendant and three of his employees. After the defendant was indicted, the government successfully moved to disqualify the lawyer on the ground that the three employees would be prosecution witnesses. The defendant was not allowed to waive cross-examination of the employees because the waiver would have resulted in ineffective assistance of counsel. The trial judge had "an institutional interest in protecting the truth-seeking function of the proceedings," as well as an interest in "protecting a fairly-rendered verdict from trial tactics that may be designed to generate issues on appeal."

In his trial for murdering Carl Watson, John Loyal was represented by William Cucco, a public defender. Sharonda Posey, who was with Loyal when Watson was shot, told the police that Loyal did it. But before she was called to testify at trial, she announced that she had falsely implicated Loyal because the police had threatened her. The state planned to call her anyway and then introduce her statement under a hearsay rule exception. Cucco planned to argue that Posey's statement to the police was unreliable.

On the morning that Posey was scheduled to testify, the prosecutor discovered that Cucco, as a public defender, had represented Posey more than two years earlier on a drug charge. The charge resulted in a guilty plea. Neither Cucco nor Posey recalled the representation, which appears to have lasted less than two months, and both Loyal and Posey were willing to waive any conflict. The prosecutor initially moved for a mistrial and disqualification of Cucco, but then withdrew the motion. The trial judge declared a mistrial and disqualified Cucco anyway. The New Jersey Supreme Court affirmed. State v. Loyal, 753 A.2d 1073 (N.J. 2000). It cited *Wheat* and a New Jersey rule prohibiting lawyers from engaging in conduct that creates the "appearance of impropriety." This phrase appears in the Code of Professional Responsibility (see page 326), but has been deleted from the Model Rules and the rules in the great majority of American jurisdictions. The *Loyal* court wrote:

> The trial court correctly found that Cucco's representation of defendant created an unacceptable appearance of impropriety. The trial court reasoned that Cucco may have obtained confidential information during his prior representation of Posey that he could now use to impeach her credibility on cross-examination. We note that Posey's prior conviction was drug-related and that defendant Loyal was charged with a murder that occurred during a drug transaction. Additionally, because of their prior relationship, the trial court

may have been concerned that Cucco would cross-examine Posey less vigorously at the expense of defendant's interests. Moreover, Posey's decision to recant her statement implicating defendant enhanced the trial court's concerns. The prosecutor had contended that the jury would have to be notified of Cucco's prior representation of Posey in order to assess the proper weight to be given to both Posey's testimony and her statement to police. Both Posey's interest and defendant's interest may have been disserved by counsel's prior relationship with Posey.

Additionally, the public interest would have been disserved by Cucco's continued representation of defendant. The trial court noted that an independent observer might believe that "something is fishy" when a witness who was previously represented by defendant's counsel recants a prior statement that identified defendant as the shooter. . . .

In the context of this prosecution for a drug-related murder and other offenses, we are convinced that an appearance of impropriety existed where defendant's counsel previously had represented on drug charges a material recanting State's witness. Cucco's and Posey's failure to recall that prior representation or to recognize each other prior to trial is of no consequence.

Unless courts carefully evaluate government claims of defense lawyer conflicts, defendants may lose their chosen counsel even though the purported conflict is highly improbable. Also, we cannot entirely reject the danger that the government will use the *Wheat* rationale to remove a formidable opponent. The First Circuit called United States v. Lanoue, 137 F.3d 656 (1st Cir. 1998), a case whose facts "may well reach the outer limits of 'potential conflict.' " Does it exceed those limits? Lanoue and Cole had been tried for various firearm and other crimes. Cole was acquitted. Lanoue was convicted on some counts, but his conviction was reversed and a new trial ordered. At the first trial, Thomas Briody represented both defendants. At the second trial, he appeared for Lanoue.

The government told the district court that it might call Cole as a witness to testify on whether Lanoue possessed a firearm on December 23, 1993 [the day of his arrest] and that a conflict of interest could arise if Briody had to cross-examine Cole. Both Cole and Briody waived any right to conflict-free representation, and Cole submitted an affidavit that he did not know that Lanoue possessed a firearm on the day of his arrest and had no knowledge concerning whether Lanoue possessed a firearm at any time prior to his arrest. The government offered no reason, other than the possibility that Cole might have known of the firearm, for calling him as a witness.

With barely any analysis, the court of appeals affirmed the disqualification as within the district judge's discretion. "If the attorney is allowed to continue and the conflict does arise then the defendant may not receive the representation to which he is entitled, resulting in an ineffective assistance of counsel appeal." Should this sort of conjecture be sufficient to deny counsel of choice?

Criminal Case Disqualification and the "Automatic Reversal" Debate

Flanagan v. United States, 465 U.S. 259 (1984), unanimously held that pretrial orders disqualifying criminal defense counsel are not subject to immediate appeal under 28 U.S.C. §1291. If defense counsel is disqualified and review is not otherwise available (as through a certified question or mandamus), the defendant will have to proceed with another lawyer. If the defendant is convicted, he will be able to raise the disqualification order on appeal from the judgment of conviction. If the appellate court finds that the order was in error, should it reverse automatically? Or should the defendant have to show that the lawyer he got was constitutionally ineffective under *Strickland*? If he does have to satisfy *Strickland*, then the erroneous disqualification order is irrelevant, isn't it? Maybe there's a middle position. Perhaps the defendant need only show that the lawyer he lost was more skilled than the one he got and could have (would have?) won? (But how in the world does one prove that?)

Lower courts struggled with these questions and reached different conclusions. Then in 2006, the Supreme Court ended the debate. In a 5-4 decision, it said that an erroneous denial of counsel of choice warrants automatic reversal, even if the defendant can show no other trial error. The defendant was represented by a California lawyer who was admitted to the federal court in Missouri pro hac vice. The trial judge erroneously concluded that the lawyer had violated the no-contact rule and revoked his admission. After conviction, the government agreed that the trial judge was mistaken but argued that there was no harm because the trial was fair anyway. Justice Scalia responded that the Sixth Amendment "commands, not that a trial be fair, but that a particular guarantee of fairness be provided — to wit, that the accused be defended by the counsel he believes to be best. 'The Constitution guarantees a fair trial through the Due Process Clauses, but it defines the basic elements of a fair trial largely through the several provisions of the Sixth Amendment, including the Counsel Clause.' [Quoting *Strickland*.] In sum, the right at stake here is the right to counsel of choice, not the right to a fair trial; and that right was violated because the deprivation of counsel was erroneous. No additional showing of prejudice is required to make the violation 'complete.'" United States v. Gonzalez-Lopez, 548 U.S. 140 (2006).

We have been discussing issues that may arise when a criminal defense lawyer (or her firm) represents two or more defendants or subjects of investigation. Comparable issues may arise when two or more lawyers represent two or more litigants (civil or criminal) who, because of their common interest, wish to cooperate in the position they will take toward the same opponent. Will conversations between the lawyer for one client and the client of another lawyer be privileged? Who can waive any privilege that does apply? What confidentiality duties does one lawyer have to the common interest client of another lawyer? Because these questions can arise in both civil and criminal cases, or even in transactional matters, we flag them here but postpone discussion to the material on concurrent civil conflicts at page 282.

FURTHER READING

Bruce Green reviews Supreme Court decisions on defense counsel conflicts before *Wheat* and argues that *Wheat* "ignores the more sophisticated aspects of the Court's earlier jurisprudence, including . . . the relative importance of client autonomy and the sanctity of the attorney-client relationship." Professor

Green says the Court unfairly assumes that defense lawyers will not comply with their professional responsibilities. He concludes that trial judges need "further guidance in cases in which defense counsel has a potential conflict of interest," and he proposes "a framework" for the exercise of judicial discretion in such cases. Bruce Green, "Through a Glass, Darkly": How the Court Sees Motions to Disqualify Criminal Defense Lawyers, 89 Colum. L. Rev. 1201 (1989). The Illinois Supreme Court has sought to impose order on the labels used to describe criminal conflicts. See People v. Holmes, 565 N.E.2d 950 (Ill. 1990), and People v. Spreitzer, 525 N.E.2d 30 (Ill. 1988), which attempt to come to grips with such terms as "per se conflict," "potential conflict," "possible conflict," "actual conflict," "prejudice," and "actual prejudice."

2.   Criminal Cases (Prosecutors)

"Contributions to Justice"

"I've been the elected D.A. in Clarendon County for 14 years. Last time I ran, I had no opposition. I run a nonpolitical office. I hire on merit and that's also how I make my prosecutorial decisions. The county seat is Ralston, where I have my office. It's a city of about 100,000, about a quarter of the population of the county. A lot of what I do is management, not law. I have 17 assistant prosecutors responsible for trying cases. We're stretched. Our budget, which we get from the state, is inadequate for the job I'd like to do. I don't think there's a D.A. in my state (or maybe any other) who doesn't say the same. But we do our best.

"One of the biggest employers in the county is Extant Technologies, which makes computer chips and other components. Extant came into the county about a dozen years ago, starting small, but it grew as the demand for computers grew. It pays good salaries and augments the tax base, so all in all it's been a real blessing.

"Two months ago, Sally Hendricks, who's a partner at a Ralston firm and a lawyer for Extant, made an appointment to see me because, she said, Extant believed that certain former employees had stolen secret technology. Our penal law was amended a half dozen years ago to cover such things. Sally gave me a four-inch-thick file, the product of her firm's investigation. Tell you the truth, this is not what we're used to dealing with. It's not fingerprints, ballistics, and lineups.

"I tried to read the file but I didn't understand the half of it. A couple of my assistants, the younger ones, understood more than I did. But not a lot more. The bottom line is we haven't got the resources to prosecute this case. We don't have the money to hire the experts who can help us understand what happened and conduct an investigation or the experts to testify if it goes to trial. The people Extant suspects do have the money and expertise and they'd run rings around us.

"I had another meeting with Sally and told her just that. She said Extant realized this might be so and was prepared to do one of two things. It would make its personnel available to walk us through the technology and testify at trial. Or it would give us a budget to hire any qualified experts we chose to do the same. Extant was quite concerned that failure to prosecute would only invite additional thefts. Of course, I understand that.

"'Aren't you in effect looking to privatize the prosecutorial function?' I asked Sally. I've known her a long time. She used to work for me.

"'No, Wyatt,' she said, 'not at all. You'll make all the decisions — whatever kind of help Extant gives you — whether to charge at all, what to charge, whether to offer a plea. We'll just provide the knowledge base. We don't want you to reject this case because you don't understand the technology or can't afford the experts. Those would be the wrong reasons.' I said I'd get back.

"That brings me to my questions. I have four unless you can think of others. First, is there any ethical reason why I cannot accept Extant's offer? Second, if I do accept it, is one option preferable to the other? Third, is there anything I should do by way of an understanding to eliminate any ethical concerns there might be for either option? And fourth, even if I can ethically accept their money or help from their people, as a matter of the policy of my office, is this something I should not do?"

"A Reasonable Doubt"

At 2 A.M. on a Sunday morning in June, Patsy Prasad was robbed and assaulted while on her way home from a college party. The incident left a half-inch scar on her chin. She stayed calm enough to study the face of her assailant, though it was dark and the entire incident took less than a minute. A passerby saw the face of the assailant under a street lamp as he ran off. The police discover a footprint in the mud a half block away in the direction the assailant fled.

Following days of looking at mug shots, Prasad and the passerby, Arturo Mendez, independently pick the same photo from a book of mug shots, and then each separately identifies the same man in a lineup. The man is Morris Charles. A search of his home produces a pair of sneakers with caked mud and a footprint that is "consistent with" the one found near the scene of the robbery, according to the police lab. Prasad says she is "totally sure he's the guy who hurt me," and Mendez is "very sure."

Charles, who is 23, has two misdemeanor convictions for street crime, one of which was the result of a plea bargain to a felony charge. Charles makes no statement at his arrest, but Asher McEvoy, his appointed lawyer, later asserts an alibi defense. Charles claims he was miles away drinking with friends at the time of the robbery.

The case is assigned to Viveka Montrose, an assistant D.A. with six years of experience trying felony cases. Montrose believes she has a strong case. She believes she will successfully cross-examine Charles's three alibi witnesses. Two of them were vague when questioned by the police and in fact contradicted each other on some details. One of the witnesses is distantly related to Charles, and all three are his friends. And Charles had said nothing about an alibi when first questioned at his home before his arrest. Also, Prasad has been highly cooperative, which has not always been Montrose's experience with victims, especially as cases drag on.

At trial, Montrose's case begins to fall apart. Mendez is now only "kinda sure" when he identifies Charles in court. On cross, McEvoy gets Mendez to admit "it could have been someone else but I don't think so. I mean it was dark." Prasad gets confused on cross-examination and has to correct herself on some details. McEvoy spends a half hour reviewing the precise number and types of drinks Prasad had at her party and whether she is an experienced drinker (not very). Charles and his three alibi witnesses testify more credibly than expected despite some inconsistencies. A manager of the company that made Charles's sneakers testifies that more than six hundred pairs were sold in the county in the prior two years.

As the evidence draws to a close after six days of trial, Montrose begins to question Charles's guilt. In fact, she thinks it is likely that he is factually innocent. She can't be sure of that, of course, but she realizes that she has a reasonable doubt. If she were on the jury, she would vote to acquit. She's also sure that if she had had her current view of the evidence before indicting Charles, she would have recommended that her office not do so. At the same time, Montrose believes her evidence can readily support a finding of guilt beyond a reasonable doubt if the jury accepts it.

Prasad, however, has no doubt at all. "I remember him like it was yesterday," she tells Montrose after Charles testifies. "This is the guy that cut me. You did a really good cross. The jury didn't believe him either. I watched their faces. He'll do it again if he's not locked up."

Montrose takes her concerns to her boss, Burton Morgenstern, the elected D.A. Summations are scheduled for the following Monday after Montrose calls one rebuttal witness on the footprint evidence. What should Montrose do? What can she do? What if Montrose wants to drop the case and Morgenstern instructs her to continue? What if anything at this stage does Montrose or the prosecutor's office owe to Prasad? Charles? Society?

A prosecutor may have a conflict, concurrent or successive, for the same variety of reasons as any other lawyer. We saw (at page 234) one possible conflict in People v. Jackson, where the prosecutor and the defense lawyer were dating. See also State ex rel. Burns v. Richards, 248 S.W.3d 603 (Mo. 2008) (prosecutor who as public defender once represented defendant on drug charge cannot later prosecute him on a drug charge); In re Ockrassa, 799 P.2d 1350 (Ariz. 1990) (prosecutor suspended for 90 days after using defendant's prior convictions to enhance sentence, where prosecutor, as a public defender, had been defendant's lawyer in the prior cases).

YOUNG v. UNITED STATES EX REL. VUITTON ET FILS S.A.
481 U.S. 787 (1987)

[Vuitton, a leather goods manufacturer, had settled a trademark dispute with the defendants. The settlement enjoined the defendants from further trademark violations. When the defendants violated the injunction, Vuitton's counsel secured an order to show cause why the defendants should not be held in contempt. Vuitton's counsel were appointed special prosecutors and won a conviction. The Supreme Court upheld the district court's power to appoint private counsel to prosecute a contempt charge. It then considered whether Vuitton's counsel could be appointed. Part III-A of Justice Brennan's opinion for the Court follows.]

In Berger v. United States, 295 U.S. 78, 88 (1935), this Court declared:

> The United States Attorney is the representative not of an ordinary party to a controversy, but of a sovereignty whose obligation to govern impartially is as compelling as its obligation to govern at all; and whose interest, therefore, in a criminal prosecution is not that it shall win a case, but that justice shall be done. As such, he is in a peculiar and very definite sense the servant of the law, the twofold aim of which is that guilt shall not escape nor innocence suffer.

This distinctive role of the prosecutor is expressed in Ethical Consideration (EC) 7-13 of Canon 7 of the American Bar Association (ABA) Model Code of Professional Responsibility (1982): "The responsibility of a public prosecutor differs from that of the usual advocate; his duty is to seek justice, not merely to convict."

Because of this unique responsibility, federal prosecutors are prohibited from representing the Government in any matter in which they, their family, or their business associates have any interest. 18 U.S.C. §208(a). Furthermore, the Justice Department has applied to its attorneys the ABA Model Code of Professional Responsibility, 28 C.F.R. §45.735-1(b) (1986), which contains numerous provisions relating to conflicts of interest. The concern that representation of other clients may compromise the prosecutor's pursuit of the Government's interest rests on recognition that a prosecutor would owe an ethical duty to those other clients. "Indeed, it is the highest claim on the most noble advocate which causes the problem — fidelity, unquestioned, continuing fidelity to the client."

Private attorneys appointed to prosecute a criminal contempt action represent the United States, not the party that is the beneficiary of the court order allegedly violated. . . . The prosecutor is appointed solely to pursue the public interest in vindication of the court's authority. A private attorney appointed to prosecute a criminal contempt therefore certainly should be as disinterested as a public prosecutor who undertakes such a prosecution.

If a Justice Department attorney pursued a contempt prosecution for violation of an injunction benefitting any client of that attorney involved in the underlying civil litigation, that attorney would be open to a charge of committing a felony under §208(a). Furthermore, such conduct would violate the ABA ethical provisions, since the attorney could not discharge the obligation of undivided loyalty to both clients where both have a direct interest. The Government's interest is in dispassionate assessment of the propriety of criminal charges for affronts to the Judiciary. The private party's interest is in obtaining the benefits of the court's order. While these concerns sometimes may be congruent, sometimes they may not. A prosecutor may be tempted to bring a tenuously supported prosecution if such a course promises financial or legal rewards for the private client. Conversely, a prosecutor may be tempted to abandon a meritorious prosecution if a settlement providing benefits to the private client is conditioned on a recommendation against criminal charges.

Regardless of whether the appointment of private counsel in this case resulted in any prosecutorial impropriety (an issue on which we express no opinion), that appointment illustrates the *potential* for private interest to influence the discharge of public duty. Vuitton's California litigation had culminated in a permanent injunction and consent decree in favor of Vuitton against petitioner Young relating to various trademark infringement activities. This decree contained a liquidated damages provision of $750,000 for violation of the injunction. The prospect of such a damages award had the potential to influence whether Young was selected as a target of investigation, whether he might be offered a plea bargain, or whether he might be offered immunity in return for his testimony. In addition, Bainton [Vuitton's lawyer] was the defendant in a defamation action filed by Klayminc [one of the petitioners] arising out of Bainton's involvement in the litigation resulting in the injunction whose violation was at issue in this case. This created the possibility that the investigation of Klayminc might be shaped in part by a desire to obtain information useful in the defense of the defamation suit. Furthermore, Vuitton had various civil claims pending against some of the petitioners. These claims theoretically could have created temptation to use the criminal investigation to gather information of use in those suits, and could have served as bargaining leverage in obtaining pleas in the criminal prosecution. In short, as will generally be the case, the appointment of counsel for an interested party to bring the contempt prosecution in this case at a minimum created *opportunities* for conflicts to arise, and created at least the *appearance* of impropriety.

As should be apparent, the fact that the judge makes the initial decision that a contempt prosecution should proceed is not sufficient to quell concern that prosecution by an interested party may be influenced by improper motives. A prosecutor exercises considerable discretion in matters such as the determination of which persons should be targets of investigation, what methods of investigation should be used, what information will be sought as evidence, which persons should be charged with what offenses, which persons should be utilized as witnesses, whether to enter into plea bargains and the terms on which they will be established, and whether any individuals should be granted immunity. These decisions, critical to the conduct of a prosecution, are all made outside the supervision of the court. . . .

The use of this Court's supervisory authority has played a prominent role in ensuring that contempt proceedings are conducted in a manner consistent with basic notions of fairness. The exercise of supervisory authority is especially appropriate in the determination of the procedures to be employed by courts to enforce their orders, a subject that directly concerns the functioning of the Judiciary. We rely today on that authority to hold that counsel for a party that is the beneficiary of a court order may not be appointed as prosecutor in a contempt action alleging a violation of that order. . . .

Prosecutors Avec Deux Chapeaux

May prosecutors wear two hats?

The Court was fractured in *Young*. Although the printed excerpt represents that seven Justices chose to rely on the Court's supervisory powers, only four

(Brennan, Marshall, Blackmun, and Stevens) agreed that "harmless-error analysis is inappropriate in reviewing the appointment of an interested prosecutor in a case such as this." Justice Blackmun would also have held that due process forbids appointment of any "interested party's counsel" to prosecute for criminal contempt. Justice Scalia, using a separation-of-powers analysis, concluded that the appointment of a private prosecutor was not an exercise of the "judicial power of the United States" within the meaning of Article III, §§1, 2 of the Constitution. "Since that is the only grant of power that has been advanced as authorizing these appointments, they were void."

Justice Powell, joined by the Chief Justice and Justice O'Connor, agreed that where "a private prosecutor . . . also represents an interested party, the possibility that his prosecutorial judgment will be compromised is significant," warranting an "exercise of this Court's supervisory powers to hold [such an appointment] improper." He disagreed, however, with the plurality's harmless-error conclusion and would have remanded the case to determine whether the error was harmless. Justice White, who "would also prefer" that district judges not appoint interested private prosecutors but discerned no constitutional or other error in doing so, would have affirmed. State courts have embraced harmless error analysis. Pabst v. State, 192 P.3d 630 (Kan. 2008) (conflict harmless where lawyer hired by victim assisted prosecutor while also representing victim in civil case).

Not all courts see a problem when a lawyer for a private party prosecutes an opposing client for contempt. Wilson v. Wilson, 984 S.W.2d 898 (Tenn. 1998), allowed a husband's lawyer in a divorce case to prosecute the wife for violating a court order. The wife faced a maximum fine of $50 and a maximum term of imprisonment of ten days. The court distinguished *Young* because "unlike the private attorneys appointed as special prosecutors in *Young*, private attorneys prosecuting criminal contempt actions in Tennessee are not ordinarily clothed with all the powers of a public prosecutor."

> The risk that a defendant's liberty interest will be erroneously deprived by the current practice which allows a litigant's private attorney to prosecute contempt is slight because it is the trial judge, not the private attorney, who actually decides whether a contempt action may proceed. . . . Contempt proceedings often arise in domestic relations cases in state courts. However, unlike the federal system, there is no fund in Tennessee from which to compensate private counsel appointed to prosecute criminal contempt actions. It is unrealistic to expect district attorneys to prosecute contempt actions arising from alleged violations of civil court orders. . . . Were we to hold that due process precludes a litigant's private attorney from prosecuting contempt proceedings, many citizens would be deprived of the benefits to which they already have been adjudged entitled by state courts and many state court orders would remain unenforced.

The court rejected the allegation that private counsel would have a conflict of interest.

> In a contempt proceeding alleging a violation of a court order . . . the interest of the private litigant coincides with the interest of the court. The common goal is to force compliance with the court order. Although the motivational reasons may differ, the interest is the same. The private lawyer is

ethically obligated to exercise his or her independent professional judgment to protect the common interest. . . . The trial court obviously will realize when the attorney representing the beneficiary of the court order in the underlying civil litigation is also the attorney filing the application to institute contempt. The trial court will be in a position to carefully scrutinize the application. The judicial oversight . . . virtually eliminates any danger that contempt actions will proceed if instituted for improper motives or without regard to the interests of justice.

Two years before *Young*, the California Supreme Court faced a similar situation. A city seeking to rid itself of stores selling explicit sexual material passed a nuisance statute aimed at closing them. The city then retained Clancy, a private lawyer, to bring civil abatement proceedings. His fee was to be $60 hourly if he was successful in closing an establishment, but $30 hourly if he was not. The court disqualified Clancy. It applied the "heightened ethical requirements" that bind government lawyers despite a claim that Clancy was an independent contractor. It then held that the arrangement was "antithetical to the standard of neutrality" required of government lawyers. "When a government attorney has a personal interest in the litigation, the neutrality so essential to the system is violated." The court did not forbid employment of private counsel for contingent fees in all matters, but it stressed the close relationship between civil abatement proceedings and criminal prosecutions. People ex rel. Clancy v. Superior Court, 705 P.2d 347 (Cal. 1985). Clancy had personally drafted the civil abatement ordinance (as well as a previous ordinance that had been declared unconstitutional). He was associated with an organization called "Committee for Decency Through Law." After the court ruling, could the city properly hire Clancy to handle all civil abatement proceedings for a fixed hourly fee?

In State v. Culbreath, 30 S.W.3d 309 (Tenn. 2000), the court dismissed indictments for obscenity because the underlying investigation and eventual charges were the work of a private lawyer (Parrish) who was assisting prosecutorial authorities but who was paid by a private citizen's group. The court wrote that

> Parrish had an actual conflict of interest under the circumstances of this case. He was privately compensated by a special interest group and thus owed a duty of loyalty to that group; at the same time, he was serving in the role of public prosecutor and owed the duty of loyalty attendant to that office. Moreover, because Parrish was compensated on an hourly basis, the reality is that he acquired a direct financial interest in the duration and scope of the ongoing prosecution. In short, the dual role was such that Parrish could not exercise his independent professional judgment free of "compromising influences and loyalties." [Citing EC 5-1.]

Justice Stewart Pollock's description of the dangers when a private prosecutor also represents a civil claimant against the same defendant reveals the practice as extremely dubious indeed. In State v. Storm, 661 A.2d 790 (N.J. 1995), he wrote:

> Representation of the complainant in a related civil action could invest the prosecutor with a monetary interest in the outcome of the matter. That risk

is particularly high if the prosecutor has agreed to receive a contingent fee in the civil action. Even in the absence of actual conflict, the appointment as prosecutor of an attorney for an interested party creates the appearance of impropriety. . . . Conflicting interests, moreover, can undermine a prosecutor's impartiality. The loss of impartiality can affect the prosecutor's assessment of probable cause to proceed; the disclosure of exculpatory evidence; and the willingness to plea bargain. . . . In addition, private prosecutions pose the risk that the complainant will use [the criminal proceeding] to harass the defendant or to obtain an advantage in a related civil action.

In *Storm*, the court disqualified the lawyer for the civil claimant from acting as private prosecutor of the defendant, but it did not categorically forbid the practice. The Pennsylvania Supreme Court reversed a conviction for vehicular homicide where the district attorney's private law firm sued the defendant civilly on behalf of the victim's estate while the criminal prosecution was pending in the district attorney's office. The court said the prosecutor had "an actual conflict of interest" and that the defendant "need not prove actual prejudice." Commonwealth v. Eskridge, 604 A.2d 700 (Pa. 1992). See also State v. Ross, 829 S.W.2d 948 (Mo. 1992) (conviction reversed where lawyers at private firm defending client in civil assault case were part-time prosecutors in office prosecuting client for the same assault). This is the converse of *Eskridge*. Part-time prosecutors were *defending* Ross in the civil case while office colleagues prosecuted him in the criminal case arising from the same facts. The state might have a problem with that, but why should Ross?

In *Young*, an interested party's private counsel was appointed to prosecute a contempt case. May the court appoint a government lawyer whose agency has an interest in the underlying proceeding? The Federal Trade Commission obtained a temporary restraining order against Godfree and others, which Godfree allegedly violated. The court appointed FTC attorneys to act as special prosecutors in the ensuing contempt proceeding. Godfree was convicted and appealed. *Young* was not controlling. The FTC, as an independent agency, was not "the equivalent of a private party." Although the court rejected a "per se bar to the participation of government lawyers in contempt prosecutions, we recognize that under certain circumstances a government attorney may lack the impartiality and appearance of impartiality that our system of justice demands of its prosecutors." In resolving this issue, the court cited two factors that increased the likelihood of a disinterested prosecution: The U.S. Attorney's office participated in the contempt prosecution, and the FTC attorneys handling the contempt prosecution were not the same as those who participated in the underlying civil suit. FTC v. American Natl. Cellular, 868 F.2d 315 (9th Cir. 1989). In United States v. Terry, 17 F.3d 575 (2d Cir. 1994), a contempt citation against an abortion rights protestor was upheld over a claim that the district court should not have appointed the New York State Attorney General to prosecute. The Attorney General had also brought a civil action in which he was seeking to enjoin Terry's allegedly illegal activities during an abortion protest. The court closely analyzed the competing influences on the Attorney General's independence and concluded that they did not create an actual or apparent conflict.

3. Civil Cases

"Will You Represent Us Both?"

"As the Supreme Court has made it harder to bring Title VII actions for employment discrimination, and harder for plaintiffs' lawyers to collect counsel fees, my colleagues and I have gotten more requests for help. We work at the Deadwood Fair Employment Resource Center. The other day two guys, Miguel Nunez and William Joseph — who are Hispanic and African-American, respectively — came in to see me. They were both passed over for a supervisory promotion. Instead, their employer, Beware Industries, a manufacturer of security devices, gave the job to a white guy with substantially less seniority. Miguel and Bill believe they were the victims of discrimination based on their national origin and race. They have pretty much the same qualifications, training, and experience. 'Sheila,' they told me, 'we went to five or six lawyers, but we can't afford to pay, and the lawyers are afraid they won't get a big enough fee from the court.' No one else at Beware is in Miguel and William's position. There's certainly no class action here. I'm not sure we can take on another case right now, but even if we can, I'm not sure whether or how we could represent both of them. Whoever we don't represent will not get a lawyer. What's your advice?"

"They're On the Same Page"

"I have a solo practice in a small city. I do work for small companies. Tax. Corporate. Employment. Basil, my partner, is a T&E guy. Together we're Masuda & Simonetti. I'm Penelope Masuda. I'm called Penlo (not Penny, please).

"One thing I really enjoy is startups, a young person usually with an idea and a lot of energy and determination but not so much money. They want advice — how to get started, should they incorporate, taxes, negotiate a lease, raise capital, trade name. I love this. They really believe in themselves, figure they'll be the next Bill Gates, whatever. I try to help, don't charge a whole lot. I figure if they survive, and many do, I have a good client. And they use me for other work and eventually they hire Basil to plan their estate. So all in all it's a good business plan, don't you think?

"Yesterday, I read an article in the state bar journal about conflicts. Written by some law professor who probably never had a client. But it got me nervous. Some of the startups are two, three, four people. The professor says this sort of thing can be rife with conflicts and a minefield for malpractice. And meanwhile, a day earlier, some new clients come in, three nice people who want to start a partnership that will run birthday parties for children. One's a magician. One's a baker and makes the birthday cake with the children. One does a thing with puppets I'm not too clear about. And they each play a musical instrument. They hope eventually to hire others and offer different packages.

"They've divided the responsibility. The magician said she is going to put up most of the money. The baker has most of the contacts because he has been baking for children's parties for eight years. The puppeteer, she is going to handle the management.

"Way I see it, my clients are all on the same page. They all want this business to thrive. I don't see the conflict. What do you think?"

"May We Do Both Cases?"

"Our Chicago office has been asked to represent some landowners who want to file a federal action challenging the constitutionality of a Wisconsin law that regulates the use of their land in a way that, they say, amounts to a taking. We'd be seeking to invalidate the law under the Fourteenth Amendment and the state constitution. The case will eventually be resolved in the Seventh Circuit or maybe higher.

"Meanwhile, a partner in our Los Angeles office is a member of an organization, Pacific United Respiratory Alliance (PURA), that wants him to file a brief for it as amicus on the side of the county in a federal action brought by some developers. The developers are challenging a county law that restricts the use of their property. PURA doesn't think the county lawyers, good as they are, are as familiar as our partner with this specialized field, and they're right.

"Now the two laws are very similar but not identical. It's possible that one is valid and the other is not, or that neither is valid, or that both are. It's possible that either is invalid under the respective state constitutions. But the validity of either may well turn on an interpretation of the Fourteenth Amendment with the answer the same for both laws. So in one case we will be arguing for a federal constitutional construction that is inconsistent with our argument in the other case.

"My question is, may we take both cases? Do we need consent? Is there anything else you need to know?"

FIANDACA v. CUNNINGHAM*
827 F.2d 825 (1st Cir. 1987)

COFFIN, JUDGE.

This opinion discusses ... a class action brought by twenty-three female prison inmates sentenced to the custody of the warden of the New Hampshire State Prison. The suit challenges the state of New Hampshire's failure to establish a facility for the incarceration of female inmates with programs and services equivalent to those provided to male inmates at the state prison. After a bench trial on the merits, the district court held that the state had violated plaintiffs' right to equal protection of the laws and ordered the construction of a permanent in-state facility for plaintiffs no later than July 1, 1989. It also required the state to provide a temporary facility for plaintiffs on or before November 1, 1987, but prohibited the state from establishing this facility on the grounds of the Laconia State School and Training Center ("Laconia State

---

* Using the text of the current version of Rule 1.7, was NHLA's conflict under Rule 1.7(a)(1) or a(2)? (At the time of the decision, the rule had a different numbering system.)

School" or "LSS"), New Hampshire's lone institution for the care and treatment of mentally retarded citizens. . . .

Michael Cunningham, warden of the New Hampshire State Prison, and various executive branch officials responsible for the operation of the New Hampshire Department of Corrections ("state") . . . challenge the district court's refusal to disqualify plaintiffs' class counsel, New Hampshire Legal Assistance ("NHLA"), due to an unresolvable conflict of interest. See N.H. Rules of Professional Conduct, Rule 1.7(b). They also seek to overturn that portion of the district court's decision barring the establishment of an interim facility for female inmates at LSS, arguing that this prohibition is unsupported either by relevant factual findings, see Fed. R. Civ. P. 52(a), or by evidence contained in the record. . . .

This case began in June, 1983, when plaintiffs' appellate counsel, Bertram Astles, filed a complaint on behalf of several female inmates sentenced to the custody of the state prison warden and incarcerated at the Rockingham County House of Corrections. NHLA subsequently became co-counsel for plaintiffs and filed an amended complaint expanding the plaintiff class to include all female inmates who are or will be incarcerated in the custody of the warden. In the years that followed, NHLA assumed the role of lead counsel for the class, engaging in extensive discovery and performing all other legal tasks through the completion of the trial before the district court. Among other things, NHLA attorneys and their trial expert, Dr. Edyth Flynn, twice toured and examined potential facilities at which to house plaintiffs, including buildings at the Laconia State School, the New Hampshire Hospital in Concord, and the Youth Development Center in Manchester. . . .

The state extended a second offer of judgment to plaintiffs on October 21, 1986. This offer proposed to establish an in-state facility for the incarceration of female inmates at an existing state building by June 1, 1987. Although the formal offer of judgment did not specify a particular location for this facility, the state informed NHLA that it planned to use the Speare Cottage at the Laconia State School. NHLA, which also represented the plaintiff class in the ongoing *Garrity* litigation, rejected the offer on November 10, stating in part that "plaintiffs do not want to agree to an offer which is against the stated interests of the plaintiffs in the *Garrity* class."* The state countered by moving immediately for the disqualification of NHLA as class counsel in the case at bar due to the unresolvable conflict of interest inherent in NHLA's representation of two classes with directly adverse interests. The court, despite recognizing that a conflict of interest probably existed, denied the state's motion on November 20 because NHLA's disqualification would further delay the trial of an important matter that had been pending for over three years. It began to try the case four days later.

[After trial and before decision, the parties reached a tentative settlement that provided for incarceration of female inmates at the Laconia State School. NHLA then "moved to withdraw as class co-counsel . . . and attorney Astles signed the settlement agreement on plaintiffs' behalf. The state, however, refused to sign the agreement." Thereafter, plaintiffs withdrew their consent in light of the state's refusal to sign. The trial judge then issued a decision which

---

* The plaintiffs in the *Garrity* class were challenging conditions at the Laconia State School. Their counsel was NHLA, which was also co-counsel to the plaintiffs in the present action. The *Garrity* plaintiffs opposed the use of Speare Cottage to incarcerate female inmates — ED.

found that "the conditions of confinement, programs, and services available to New Hampshire female prisoners are not on par with the conditions, programs, and services afforded male inmates." He ordered the state to build a permanent facility that "shall not be located at the Laconia State School or its environs."]

As noted above, the state challenges the district court's decision on two independent grounds. First, it claims that the court should have disqualified NHLA as plaintiffs' class counsel prior to the commencement of the trial. Second, it contends that the court's proscription of the use of a site at the Laconia State School is unsupported either by relevant findings of fact or by evidence contained in the record. Because we find in favor of the state on its first claim and remand for a new trial on the issue of an appropriate remedy, we confine ourselves to an analysis of the disqualification issue.

A. Refusal to Disqualify for Conflict of Interest

The state's first argument is that the district court erred in permitting NHLA to represent the plaintiff class at trial after its conflict of interest had become apparent. As we recognized in Kevlik v. Goldstein, 724 F.2d 844 (1st Cir. 1984), a district court is vested with broad power and responsibility to supervise the professional conduct of the attorneys appearing before it. It follows from this premise that "[w]e will not disturb the district court's finding unless there is no reasonable basis for the court's determination." Id. We must determine, therefore, whether the court's denial of the state's disqualification motion amounts to an abuse of discretion in this instance.

The state's theory is that NHLA faced an unresolvable conflict because the interests of two of its clients were directly adverse after the state extended its second offer of judgment on October 21, 1986. [The court quoted N.H. Rule 1.7 and its comment.] In this case, it is the state's contention that the court should have disqualified NHLA as class counsel pursuant to Rule 1.7 because . . . NHLA's representation of the plaintiff class in this litigation was materially limited by its responsibilities to the *Garrity* class.

We find considerable merit in this argument. The state's offer to establish a facility for the incarceration of female inmates at the Laconia State School, and to use its "best efforts" to make such a facility available for occupancy by June 1, 1987, presented plaintiffs with a legitimate opportunity to settle a protracted legal dispute on highly favorable terms. As class counsel, NHLA owed plaintiffs a duty of undivided loyalty: it was obligated to present the offer to plaintiffs, to explain its costs and benefits, and to ensure that the offer received full and fair consideration by the members of the class. Beyond all else, NHLA had an ethical duty to prevent its loyalties to other clients from coloring its representation of the plaintiffs in this action and from infringing upon the exercise of its professional judgment and responsibilities.[4]

---

4. The fact that the conflict arose due to the nature of the state's settlement offer, rather than due to the subject matter of the litigation or the parties involved, does not render the ethical implications of NHLA's multiple representation any less troublesome. Among other things, courts have a duty to "ensur[e] that at all stages of litigation . . . counsel are as a general rule available to advise each client as to the particular, individualized benefits or costs of a proposed settlement." Smith v. City of New York, 611 F. Supp. 1080, 1090 (S.D.N.Y. 1985).

NHLA, however, also represents the residents of the Laconia State School who are members of the plaintiff class in *Garrity*. Quite understandably, this group vehemently opposes the idea of establishing a correctional facility for female inmates anywhere on the grounds of LSS. As counsel for the *Garrity* class, NHLA had an ethical duty to advance the interests of the class to the fullest possible extent and to oppose any settlement of the instant case that would compromise those interests. In short, the combination of clients and circumstances placed NHLA in the untenable position of being simultaneously obligated to represent vigorously the interests of two conflicting clients. It is inconceivable that NHLA, or any other counsel, could have properly performed the role of "advocate" for both plaintiffs and the *Garrity* class, regardless of its good faith or high intentions. Indeed, this is precisely the sort of situation that Rule 1.7 is designed to prevent.

Plaintiffs argue on appeal that there really was no conflict of interest for NHLA because the state's second offer of judgment was unlikely to lead to a completed settlement for reasons other than NHLA's loyalties to the *Garrity* class. We acknowledge that the record contains strong indications that settlement would not have occurred even if plaintiffs had been represented by another counsel. . . . The question, however, is not whether the state's second offer of judgment would have resulted in a settlement had plaintiffs' counsel not been encumbered by a conflict of interest. Rather, the inquiry we must make is whether plaintiffs' counsel was able to represent the plaintiff class unaffected by divided loyalties, or as stated in Rule 1.7(b), whether NHLA could have reasonably believed that its representation would not be adversely affected by the conflict. Our review of the record and the history of this litigation — especially NHLA's response to the state's second offer, in which it stated that "plaintiffs do not want to agree to an offer which is against the stated interests of plaintiffs in the *Garrity* case" — persuade us that NHLA's representation of plaintiffs could not escape the adverse effects of NHLA's loyalties to the *Garrity* class. . . .

Absent some evidence of *true* necessity, we will not permit a meritorious disqualification motion to be denied in the interest of expediency unless it can be shown that the movant strategically sought disqualification in an effort to advance some improper purpose. Thus, the state's motivation in bringing the motion is not irrelevant; as we recognized in *Kevlik*, "disqualification motions can be tactical in nature, designed to harass opposing counsel." However, the mere fact that the state moved for NHLA's disqualification just prior to the commencement of the trial is not, without more, cause for denying its motion. There is simply no evidence to support plaintiffs' suggestion that the state "created" the conflict by intentionally offering plaintiffs a building at LSS in an effort "to dodge the bullet again" with regard to its "failure to provide in-state housing for the plaintiff class." We do not believe, therefore, that the state's second offer of judgment and subsequent disqualification motion were intended to harass plaintiffs. Rather, our reading of the record indicates that a more benign scenario is more probable: the state made a good faith attempt to accommodate plaintiffs by offering to establish a correctional facility in an existing building at the Laconia State School and, once NHLA's conflict of interest with regard to this offer became apparent, the state moved for NHLA's disqualification to preserve this settlement option.

As we are unable to identify a reasoned basis for the district court's denial of the state's pre-trial motion to disqualify NHLA from serving as plaintiffs' class counsel, we hold that its order amounts to an abuse of discretion and must be reversed.

B.   PROPER REMEDY

In light of the district court's error in ignoring NHLA's conflict of interest, we believe it necessary to remand the case for further proceedings. We must consider a further question, however: must the district court now start from scratch in resolving this dispute? The state argues that the court's failure to disqualify NHLA is plain reversible error, and therefore requires the court to try the matter anew. We subscribe to the view, however, that merely "conducting [a] trial with counsel that should have been disqualified does not 'indelibl[y] stamp or taint' the proceedings." With this in mind, we look to the actual adverse effects caused by the court's error in refusing to disqualify NHLA as class counsel to determine the nature of the proceedings on remand.

We do not doubt that NHLA's conflict of interest potentially influenced the course of the proceedings in at least one regard: NHLA could not fairly advocate the remedial option — namely, the alternative of settling for a site at the Laconia State School — offered by the state prior to trial. The conflict, therefore, had the potential to ensure that the case would go to trial, a route the state likely wished to avoid by achieving an acceptable settlement. Nevertheless, we do not see how a trial on the merits could have been avoided given the manner in which the case developed below. Judge Loughlin stated on the record that he would not approve a settlement infringing on the rights of LSS residents, and under Rule 23(e), any settlement of this class action required his approval to be effective. It seems to us, therefore, that even if some other counsel had advised plaintiffs to accept the state's offer for a building at LSS, a trial on the merits would have been inevitable. . . .

The situation is different, however, with respect to the remedy designed by the district court. We believe that it would be inappropriate to permit the court's remedial order — which includes a specific prohibition on the use of LSS — to stand in light of the court's refusal to disqualify NHLA. The ban on the use of buildings located on the grounds of LSS is exactly the sort of remedy preferred by NHLA's other clients, the members of the *Garrity* class, and therefore has at least the appearance of having been tainted by NHLA's conflict of interest. Consequently, we hold that the district court's remedial order must be vacated and the case remanded for a new trial on the issue of the proper remedy for this constitutional deprivation. . . .

Imputed Conflicts

Assume NHLA had more than one lawyer on staff. Why couldn't one of them represent the *Garrity* class while the other represented the plaintiffs in *Fiandaca*? Or assume (surely counterfactually) that NHLA had 100 lawyers in five different cities. Wouldn't it then be plausible to screen the *Garrity* team from professional contact with the *Fiandaca* team so that neither team had anything to do with the other and had no access to the files of the other? Why didn't the court consider this solution? Why didn't the lawyers suggest it?

With some exceptions, mainly in the areas of government law offices, former government lawyers, and successive representations, both the Code and the Rules impute client conflicts among all affiliated lawyers. See Rule 1.10(a). When Ted Wells moved from his New Jersey law firm to Paul Weiss, the court ordered him to give up representation of his client Ernst & Young because Paul Weiss was then representing a former official of Ernst's litigation opponent, who was likely to be a key witness against Ernst. The former official was not a party to the case, but Wells would need to cross-examine her and attempt to undermine her credibility, which would be deemed legally adverse and disloyal. The court declined to recognize screening as an effective antidote to the concurrent conflict, which it imputed firmwide. In re Cendant Corp. Securities Litig., 124 F. Supp. 2d 235 (D.N.J. 2000).

Lawyers are affiliated for imputation purposes if they work in the same office, regardless of their title. In a private firm, partners and associates impute conflicts to each other. Lawyers with titles like "Senior Counsel," "Special Counsel," and "Of Counsel" are all deemed part of the same firm for conflicts purposes. All are presumed to have a significant relationship with their firm. See, e.g., People v. Speedee Oil Change Systems, Inc., 980 P.2d 371 (Cal. 1999). See also Rule 1.10(a) and comment [1]. But see Hempstead Video, Inc. v. Valley Stream, 409 F.3d 127 (2nd Cir. 2005) (imputation from lawyers in an "of counsel" status is not automatic). The term "of counsel" is used to describe many different kinds of affiliations. Traditionally, it meant a close, ongoing professional relationship where a lawyer is affiliated with a firm but not a partner or associate. Occasionally, two law firms will promote their "affiliation" while retaining their independent legal status. Mustang Enterprises v. Plug-in Storage Systems, Inc., 874 F. Supp. 881 (N.D. Ill. 1995), held that two firms that publicly promoted their affiliated status would be deemed a single firm and conflicts would be imputed between them. ABA Opinion 94-388 likewise concludes that two firms, though practicing under different names, may be deemed one firm for conflict purposes if they promote themselves as "affiliated" or "associated."

Sometimes law firms affiliate for a single matter, creating a "joint defense" or "common interest" arrangement (see page 282) because it works to the advantage of their joint or multiple clients. But then let's say that one of the firms is disqualified because of a conflict arising out of work for an opposing party. Is its conflict imputed to the other lawyers in the common interest arrangement? No. Courts will not conclusively presume that the confidential information that required the disqualification of one firm was passed to other firms in the common interest arrangement. The other firms will have an opportunity to prove they received no such information. Essex Chemical Corp. v. Hartford Accident and Indemnity Co., 993 F. Supp. 241 (D.N.J. 1998); In re Terminix International Co. L.P., 736 So. 2d 1092 (Ala. 1998); In re American Home Products Corp., 985 S.W.2d 68 (Tex. 1998) (elaborate discussion of how presumptions operate between co-counsel).

Some courts have refused to impute conflicts within a public defender's office on the assumption that the relationship of public defenders to their office is not the same as the relationship between a private lawyer to her firm. See People v. Miller, 404 N.E.2d 199 (Ill. 1980) ("Rather than applying a per se rule, thereby disqualifying an entire public defender's office whenever one of its members is confronted with a conflict, a case-by-case inquiry is contemplated whereby it is determined whether any facts peculiar to the case preclude the representation of competing interests by separate members of the public defender's office."). What do you think of this result? The public defender's office is being allowed to represent clients whose inconsistent interests would forbid joint representation by a single private firm. Wyoming conclusively presumes prejudice whenever two criminal defendants are represented by lawyers from the same firm, a rather powerful rule, but it will not do so for a public defender's office. Among its reasons: A public defender's office, unlike a private firm, will have no reason to favor one client over another; the lawyers themselves have no financial incentive to prefer one client over another; indigent clients are likely to get better counsel from the defender than from appointed counsel; and "[p]aying outside counsel . . . would, no doubt, be quite an expense for the taxpayers of the state." Asch v. State, 62 P.3d 945 (Wyo. 2003). What do you make of this last reason? Is the court saying ethics must bow to fiscal concerns? If a goal of conflict rules is to encourage client trust and confidence, what difference should it make that the public defenders (presumably) have no financial interest in their cases?

Imputation has its limits. Rule 1.10(a), which imputes Rule 1.7 and Rule 1.9 conflicts firmwide, was amended in 2002 to exclude imputation when one lawyer's conflict is based on her personal interest if, in addition, there is no "significant risk" that the representation will be "materially" limited. So if a lawyer is conscientiously opposed to representing tobacco companies or hospitals that provide abortion services, for example, other firm lawyers may still do so. But if a lawyer powerful in the firm has a large personal investment in a company that is adverse to a firm client and could not personally represent that client because of her financial interests, her conflict might be imputed to other firm lawyers.

Standing to Object

Another interesting aspect of *Fiandaca* is that the conflicts issue was raised by the defendant state officials, not either of the NHLA clients. Since conflict rules mean to protect clients, why did the court let the adversary raise the matter? And once the matter was raised, why didn't the court check with NHLA's clients to see if *they* objected to the conflict? One reason for the First Circuit's view of standing in *Fiandaca* may be the fact that the NHLA clients, a class under some disability in each case, were not viewed as freely able to assert their rights. Another explanation may be the public interest in the correct resolution of the litigation, especially given the nature of these cases. Recall that courts let the government raise the issue of criminal defense lawyer conflicts and will disqualify counsel even if all clients are prepared to consent. However, neither of these narrow explanations for allowing the state in *Fiandaca* to assert the conflict may fully explain it. The First Circuit has generally recognized nonclient standing to raise an opposing lawyer's conflict. Kevlik v. Goldstein, cited in *Fiandaca* at page 274.

The First Circuit's generous standing rule is predicated on the assumption that it is the duty of every lawyer to call a court's attention to another lawyer's violation of conflict rules. But the First Circuit is in a minority here. Some courts suggest that only a client or former client has standing to complain. In re Yarn Processing Patent Validity Litig., 530 F.2d 83 (5th Cir. 1976). Dawson v. City of Bartlesville, 901 F. Supp. 314 (N.D. Okla. 1995), severely limits a nonclient's standing to seek disqualification after collecting and rejecting cases broadly recognizing such standing.

A third group of cases seems to take an inevitable middle position. In In re Appeal of Infotechnology, 582 A.2d 215 (Del. 1990), the defendant complained that the firm representing plaintiff would likely need to cross-examine one of its own clients, which, however, was not a party to the litigation. That client did not itself make formal objection. The court ruled that nonclients do not ordinarily have standing to assert an opposing lawyer's conflict. Drawing on the comment to Rule 1.7, the court held that a nonclient would have standing only if "he or she can demonstrate that the opposing counsel's conflict somehow prejudiced *his* or *her* rights. The nonclient litigant does not have standing to merely enforce a technical violation of the Rules." The burden of proof was on the nonclient to show by clear and convincing evidence that a conflict existed and that it would "prejudice the fairness of the proceedings." See also Colyer v. Smith, 50 F. Supp. 2d 966 (C.D. Cal. 1999) (relying on *Infotechnology* and Article III standing requirements in federal court to hold that the moving party "must establish a personal stake in the motion to disqualify" and emphasizing, as a policy matter, that the "standing requirement protects against the strategic exploitation of the rules of ethics long disfavored by the Courts").

May a Lawyer Act Adversely to a Client on an Unrelated Matter?

The conflict in *Fiandaca* lay in the perceived inability of NHLA to advise the class about the wisdom of using the Laconia State School as a site for female prisoners. Independent judgment was compromised because NHLA also represented residents of the Laconia School. The clients' interests were inconsistent on a question *related* to the representation of each client—namely, the use of the school. Now, of course, it may be that the clients' interests were not inconsistent at all, that it was actually in the best interest of neither class to use the school as a site for female prisoners. Or maybe it was in the interest of one class but not the other (the prisoners but not the students). NHLA was required to give each class its best judgment on this question, but the court did not believe it was positioned to do so. The court did not have confidence that NHLA's advice to the *Fiandaca* class would be unaffected by its duty (and sense of duty) to the *Garrity* class.

Now consider these alternatives:

Lewis Calderon is suing Micro Used Autos for breach of warranty. Barry Schmidt represents neither party. But Schmidt is doing Calderon's estate plan, and Schmidt's partner, Delia Mickeljohn, is handling a zoning matter for Micro. Any problem? The same firm represents two clients on *unrelated* matters, and those two clients happen to be adversaries in a third matter where the firm represents neither one. The answer is that there is no problem because the work Schmidt and Mickeljohn are doing will not threaten the confidences of either client in the matter in which they are adverse, nor will the work justify a sense of betrayal in either client, at least not one we are prepared to honor. Fremont Indemnity Co. v. Fremont General Corp., 49 Cal. Rptr.3d 82 (App. Ct. 2006).

Now suppose instead that Schmidt agrees to represent Calderon on the breach of warranty claim against Micro while Mickeljohn is handling Micro's zoning problem. Assume that, unlike *Fiandaca,* the two matters — the warranty claim and the zoning matter — are unrelated, which for this purpose means nothing the lawyers do or learn in either matter can have any bearing on the other matter. Are the representations allowed without informed consent from both Micro and Calderon? The conflict with Micro is governed by Rule 1.7(a)(1), and the conflict with Calderon by Rule 1.7(a)(2). Do you see why the difference? What valid interests of each client does Rule 1.7 protect? See Rule 1.7 comment [6].

In Cinema 5, Ltd. v. Cinerama, Inc., 528 F.2d 1384 (2d Cir. 1976), as seminal a case in the modern world of legal ethics as you are ever going to find (it helps to be among the first), an order disqualifying the plaintiff's lawyer was affirmed because his partner was representing the defendant in another *(unrelated)* litigation. The court wrote:

> Whether such adverse representation, without more, requires disqualification in every case, is a matter we need not now decide. We do hold, however, that the "substantial relationship" test [page 314] does not set a sufficiently high standard by which the necessity for disqualification should be determined. That test may properly be applied only where the representation of a former client has been terminated and the parameters of such relationship have been fixed. Where the relationship is a continuing one, adverse representation is prima facie improper, and the attorney must be prepared to show, at the very least, that there will be no actual or *apparent* conflict in loyalties or diminution in the vigor of his representation. We think that appellants have failed to meet this heavy burden. . . .

In IBM v. Levin, 579 F.2d 271 (3d Cir. 1978), another early and prominent case, the law firm CBM represented Levin in an antitrust action against IBM. Before and during the prosecution of that action, certain partners at CBM, not involved in the antitrust action, were representing IBM on various unrelated matters (labor disputes, a replevin action, and the like). IBM moved to disqualify CBM from representing Levin in the antitrust action. CBM argued that DR 5-105 (the precursor to Rule 1.7) did not foreclose the representation since "no effect adverse to IBM resulted from CBM's concurrent representation . . . and no adverse effect on CBM's exercise of its independent professional judgment on behalf of IBM was likely to result." The court, rejecting this argument, concluded that it is "likely that some 'adverse effect' on an attorney's exercise of his independent judgment on behalf of a client may result from the attorney's adversary posture toward that client in another legal matter." CBM argued that nevertheless it ought not be disqualified because disqualification was "too harsh a sanction," especially in light of the lower court's finding that "CBM did not obtain any information which would aid it in the prosecution of the antitrust suit against IBM." But the court wrote:

> The plaintiffs' interest in retaining counsel of its choice and the lack of prejudice to IBM resulting from CBM's violation of professional ethics are not the only factors to be considered in this disqualification proceeding. An attorney who fails to observe his obligation of undivided loyalty to his client injures his profession and demeans it in the eyes of the public. The maintenance of the integrity of the legal profession and its high standing in the community are important additional factors to be considered in determining the appropriate sanction for a Code violation. The maintenance of public confidence in the propriety of the conduct of those associated with the administration of justice is so important a consideration that we have held that a court may disqualify an attorney for failing to avoid even the appearance of impropriety.

Cinema 5 and IBM v. Levin are frequently cited. Yet are you able, from the excerpts, to identify the precise client interests we protect by prohibiting a lawyer from acting adversely to a current firm client on a matter unrelated to the representation of that client? By definition, because the matters are unrelated, no confidential information is at risk. Because of imputation of client conflicts throughout a firm, the prohibition against unrelated adverse representation has significant consequences to a law firm's ability to accept a matter, so we should have good reasons for imposing it. What goals does it advance? *Cinema 5* speaks of the "diminution in the vigor of [the lawyer's] representation." Imagine that you are representing Client *A* against *B* (it can be a litigation or a hard-fought negotiation). You or another lawyer in your firm represents *B* on an unrelated matter. If *B* is a significant client of the firm, perhaps you will compromise the ardor with which you pursue *A*'s matter. You don't want to offend *B* and lose its business. But let's say *B* is not a significant client or *A* is willing to consent to the conflict. (As we see later, page 293, consent can cure many conflicts.) What then? *B* also has a concern that the rule respects. *B* may find it rather difficult to trust in and confide to the very law firm that is also representing its opponent. *B*'s discomfort is something the rules aim to prevent.

Some have argued that the prohibition against concurrent unrelated conflicts is too harsh, especially given the size of some modern law firms. Imagine a firm with 15 worldwide offices and 1,500 lawyers. On behalf of a longstanding client, a lawyer in the firm's Chicago office is asked to accept a matter adverse to Company *X*. A conflicts check reveals that a partner in the Hong Kong office is currently handling an unrelated corporate matter for Company *X*. This is the only work Company *X* has ever given to the law firm and, relatively speaking, it is "very small potatoes." Yet the status of Company *X* as a current client of the firm will prevent the Chicago partner from accepting a matter adverse to it unless Company *X* consents. Imagine that Company *X* is a large worldwide entity. Do the policies behind the prohibition on adverse unrelated representation really apply here? Surely not as forcefully as they would if all the clients were individuals or small companies. But how can the rule distinguish between clients based on their size and sophistication? On the other hand, under the current rule, large companies can tactically exploit a near-absolute prohibition on concurrent adverse representation. Do you see how? Should the tactic concern us?

Perhaps one argument in favor of the current rule is that it can readily be displaced by agreement. The firm may ask Company X, before accepting its "small potatoes" business, to give its consent to adverse representation on unrelated matters. Many large firms do just that. Advance consents are sometimes permitted. (See page 295.) Of course, the opposite is also true. If the "default" rule instead *permitted* unrelated adverse representations unless the client and the law firm agreed otherwise, then a client like Company X could insist on a stricter rule as a condition of giving the firm its business. In fact, that happens today anyway. When they have the market clout to do so, some big clients with a lot of legal business to throw around insist on stricter conflict rules than are contained in the jurisdiction's default rules.

The usual remedy when a lawyer acts adversely to a current client, even on an unrelated matter, is disqualification, although discipline and civil liability are also possible. A civil action will be for malpractice or breach of fiduciary duty. See chapter 13A. While disqualification, as in *Fiandaca*, is fairly common, it is not inevitable. Research Corporation Technologies, Inc. v. Hewlett-Packard Co., 936 F. Supp. 697 (D. Ariz. 1996), shows why disqualification should not be automatic. Hewlett-Packard had previously been a client of MW&E. Then, between March 28 and April 3, 1996, MW&E gave Hewlett-Packard tax advice. The advice took three hours. As it happens, on April 1, MW&E had merged with another law firm then representing the plaintiff against Hewlett-Packard. So for three days (April 1 to April 3), the firm, as merged, was both counseling Hewlett-Packard on a tax matter and suing it. The court found a violation of Rule 1.7, but declined to disqualify MW&E, given the absence of any threat to client confidences and only a minor breach of the client's expectation of loyalty. Under a more permissive version of Rule 1.7 in effect until 2002 and still the rule many places, some courts have declined to hold a particular adverse representation improper where the lawyers were able to represent the two clients "with equal vigor, without conflict of loyalties, and without using confidential information to the detriment of either client." SST Castings, Inc. v. Amana Appliances, Inc., 250 F. Supp. 2d 863 (S.D. Ohio 2002).

Confidentiality and Privilege in Multiple Client Representations

Because the lessons are alike in both civil and criminal matters, we postponed this discussion in the material on criminal defense lawyer conflicts (page 262). The questions are easy to state and the problems are easy to understand, but judicial responses have varied, and the subject suffers from a certain analytical and linguistic inconsistency. Regardless, these are not merely theoretical issues. They arise often, so it is important to recognize them when they do, even if the answers may require some research in the jurisdiction in which you practice. Also, like so much else in the fields of confidentiality and conflicts, you can often save yourself and your clients a lot of grief with a little planning and an explicit (preferably written) agreement.

Joint Representations.   Start with what may be the most common situation. Two criminal defendants (or subjects of an investigation that may lead to a charge) decide to hire the same lawyer. If there is no conflict in their interests, or if they can and do consent to any conflict that may exist, they may have a couple of good reasons to hire one lawyer: First, it can save money, and, second, it enables them to adopt a unified strategy. As Justice Powell wrote in Cuyler v. Sullivan, quoting Justice Frankfurter, "a common defense . . . gives strength against a common attack."

Of course, these considerations are not limited to criminal defendants or subjects of investigation. They can apply equally well to clients who are or can anticipate becoming civil litigants, whether as plaintiffs or defendants. Efficiency and cost may also encourage employment of a single lawyer in transactional matters. Think of two individuals who want to start a business. They have similar goals and they will not likely want to pay two lawyers, one for each of them, even though their interests may not be identical.

The general rule is that communications between one common lawyer and the two clients in these situations retain their privileged status so long as the communications would have been privileged in the first place. The fact that the communications between client *A* and the lawyer are shared with client *B* (who may be present at the time or informed later) will not sacrifice the privilege, as it would if a stranger had access to the communication, because, very simply, client *B* is not a stranger. See generally Restatement §75. However, in the event of a dispute between the two clients, neither client will be able to assert privilege for communications with the common lawyer. See, for example, FDIC v. Ogden Corp., 202 F.3d 454 (1st Cir. 2000); Garner v. Wolfinbarger, 430 F.2d 1093 (5th Cir. 1970); proposed Rule 503(d)(5), Fed.R. Evid. See also Restatement §75(2), which further concludes, without authority, but sensibly, that the joint clients can agree that communications will continue to enjoy privilege even in the event of a later dispute between them.

The *Eureka* Exception.   Eureka Inv. Corp. v. Chicago Title Ins. Co., 743 F.2d 932 (D.C. Cir. 1984), carved out an exception to the principle that joint clients cannot assert privilege in a later dispute between them. As described and invoked by the Third Circuit in In re Teleglobe Communications Corp., 493 F.3d 345 (3d Cir. 2007), this exception applies when the common lawyer should not have accepted or continued the joint representation in the first place, because of a conflict between the joint clients:

> The Restatement's conflicts rules provide that when a joint attorney sees the co-clients' interests diverging to an unacceptable degree, the proper course is to end the joint representation. (Citing §121 cmts. e(1)-(2)). As [*Eureka* noted], courts are presented with a difficult problem when a joint attorney fails to do that and instead continues representing both clients when their interests become adverse. In this situation, the black-letter law is that when an attorney (improperly) represents two clients whose interests are adverse, the communications are privileged against each other notwithstanding the lawyer's misconduct.

The context of the *Eureka* case was the joint representation of an insured and insurer. Over the course of the litigation, the parties began to disagree. The insured, a developer trying to effect a condo conversion, wanted to settle in order to get its conversion plans back on track. The title insurer, on the other hand, wanted to continue opposing liability and would not agree to within-policy-limits settlement terms. Having decided that the insurer's refusal to settle was tortious, the insured entered into a unilateral settlement with its adversaries and promptly sued the insurer for indemnification and consequential damages. The trouble was that the insured continued to use the joint attorneys throughout the process, relying on their advice in deciding to enter into a unilateral settlement and to sue the insurer. Thus, upon filing its action, the insurer sought discovery of the insured's communications with the joint attorneys in the hope that those communications would support the affirmative defense of non-cooperation. The insurer argued that because those communications were generated during the attorneys' joint representation of the parties on the claim against the insured, they were discoverable in an action between the joint clients.

The Court rejected the insurer's argument, holding instead that "[t]he policy behind [the co-client privilege] — to encourage openness and cooperation between joint clients — does not apply to matters known at the time of communication not to be in the common interest of the attorney's two clients." It emphasized that both the insured and the joint attorneys thought that they had begun a separate, individual representation of the insured on the insurance bad-faith claim that was distinct from the underlying liability action, calling these understandings "crucial." Noting the attorneys' potential ethical violations, the Court concluded that they were of no moment: "[C]ounsel's failure to avoid a conflict of interest should not deprive the client of the privilege. The privilege, being the client's, should not be defeated solely because the attorney's conduct was ethically questionable."

The Common Interest Rule.   Let us now alter the example and imagine that our two clients decide to hire separate counsel. They still have some general interests in common, but perhaps the interests are not identical and a single lawyer would need a conflict waiver, which one or both of them are unwilling to give. Or perhaps their interests diverge too much, so that a conflict waiver would not suffice. Maybe one or both wants to protect confidentiality and privilege, even as against the other client. Or it may simply be a matter of personal preference. If we are prepared to afford the protection of the privilege when two clients hire the same lawyer, will they now have to sacrifice that protection for information they share, even if all other facts remain unchanged? In other words, if client *A* authorizes her lawyer to share some of what she says with the lawyer for client *B* in order to advance their common goal, will she lose the privilege for that information as against the common opponent?

No. If we were to say that a client loses the privilege by sharing her privileged information with the lawyer for another client with a common interest, we would be exacting a rather high price for the decision to hire separate counsel. We would also discourage cooperation. This seems a little harsh. On the other hand, we must remember that the privilege, for all its virtues, limits access to information. If we extend the protection of the privilege too far when multiple lawyers represent multiple clients, we may create a very large zone of secrecy. We have been talking about two lawyers and two clients. But what if there are 20 lawyers and 20 clients? Where's the stopping place?

The issue of privilege in multiple-lawyer situations arises most often in criminal matters, which explains why the courts began to talk about a "joint defense privilege" when holding that otherwise privileged information will not lose that status if two or more defense lawyers for two or more defendants (or suspects) exchange the information. But it should not matter whether the two clients are criminal defendants or plaintiffs or defendants in civil matters. So perhaps a better phrase is "joint litigant privilege." That term, however, would seem to limit the doctrine to litigation. Clients may also have legitimate confidentiality interests when cooperating in transactional matters. What then about using the term "common interest privilege," a phrase that extends the concept to nonlitigation matters?

But that phrase still uses the word "privilege." We are not really discussing a privilege as such, are we, but rather an exception to the rule that an existing privilege is waived when a lawyer-client communication is shared with a third party. Other clients who have a common interest (and their lawyers) should not be viewed as third parties within the meaning of the waiver rule. So in the end the best term may be the "common interest rule." That is the conclusion and reasoning of United States v. Schwimmer, 892 F.2d 237 (2d Cir. 1989), among other cases. It is also the term in proposed Rule 503(b)(3), Fed. R. Evid. *Teleglobe*, supra, uses the term "community of interest privilege" and traces its history, but as we see, it is not a privilege. Rather, the rule avoids loss of privilege for communications between lawyers or between any client and any lawyer in the common interest arrangement. Communications between the clients (absent a lawyer) are not privileged, which is why the lawyers should tell their clients not to discuss the matter among themselves. *Teleglobe*, supra.

The common interest rule applies in pending or impending litigations. In re Santa Fe International Corp., 272 F.3d 705 (5th Cir. 2001) ("in this circuit . . . there must be a palpable threat of litigation at the time of the communication, rather than a mere awareness that one's questionable conduct might some day result in litigation"). Some courts have held that it can also apply in transactional matters. United States v. BDO Seidman, LLP, 492 F.3d 806 (9th Cir. 2007); Hanover Ins. Co. v. Rapo & Jepsen Ins. Services, 870 N.E.2d 1105 (Mass. 2007). In re Regents of the University of California, 101 F.3d 1386 (Fed. Cir. 1996), recognized that the legal interest between the owner of a patent and a prospective exclusive licensee was sufficient to privilege the communications between the owner and the licensee's counsel. See also Restatement §76(1) ("If two or more clients with a common interest in a litigated or a nonlitigated matter are represented by separate lawyers and they agree to exchange information concerning the matter, a communication of any such client that otherwise qualifies as privileged . . . that relates to the matter is privileged as against third persons. . . ."); OXY Resources California LLC v. Superior Court, 9 Cal. Rptr. 3d 621 (Ct. App. 2004) (recognizes privilege for two companies that negotiated a property swap).

Transactional matters are often less focused, more open-ended, than litigations, with a greater (almost an endless) variety of interests, so one danger of applying the rule freely there is excessive secrecy. Perhaps for this reason some courts have required that parties to a transactional matter have "identical" legal interests that are not "solely commercial." Duplan Corp. v. Deering Milliken, Inc., 397 F. Supp. 1146 (D.S.C. 1974). In re Regents of the University of California, supra, was more lenient. It accepted "substantially identical" legal interests intermingled with commercial ones. *Hanover Ins.*, supra, following the

Restatement, requires only "a sufficiently similar interest" and an effort "to promote it" by sharing privileged communications. A written agreement containing the terms of the common interest arrangement is not necessarily required to enjoy the benefits of the rule, though it will often be advisable. Wilson P. Abraham Construction Corp. v. Armco Steel Corp., 559 F.2d 250 (5th Cir. 1977). In United States v. Weissman, 195 F.3d 96 (2d Cir. 1999), a client lost his claim of privilege because his lawyer failed to clearly establish that a meeting with counsel for another party would be subject to the common interest rule. A written agreement before the meeting would have changed the result.

Some Other Issues.   What should a lawyer do if one of two joint clients gives her information about the joint matter but instructs her not to tell the other client? The lawyer may be trapped between her duty of confidentiality and her duty to inform. Authorities diverge on which duty is superior. Compare Restatement §60 comment *l*; Johnson v. Superior Court, 45 Cal. Rptr. 2d 312 (Ct. App. 1995) (both upholding the duty or power to inform); with ABA Opinion 08-450 (2008) (a poorly drafted analysis that seems to suggest that the duty of confidentiality is superior to the duty to inform and that the lawyer must withdraw). The Restatement has the better position, doesn't it? By hiring a single lawyer, the clients should expect that the lawyer may share all information relevant to the lawyer's work with each of them. In any event, the lawyer can and should avoid the problem by making clear in the retainer agreement that information from either client may be shared with the other client. A. v. B., 726 A.2d 924 (N.J. 1999) ("an attorney, on commencing joint representation of co-clients, should agree explicitly with the clients on the sharing of confidential information. . . . Such a prior agreement will clarify the expectations of the clients and the lawyer and diminish the need for future litigation"). Giving this warning at the outset may also smoke out conflict situations that argue against the joint representation.

A second repetitive issue concerns waiver. Does either (or any) joint client, or either (or any) of the clients in a common interest arrangement, have the right to waive the protection for otherwise privileged information? The law is in a bit of a muddle here. When one lawyer represents two or more clients, California purports to resolve this issue by statute. Section 912(b) of the California Evidence Code provides that when "two or more persons are joint holders of a privilege . . . a waiver of the right of a particular joint holder of the privilege to claim the privilege does not affect the right of another joint holder to claim the privilege." The Restatement gives co-clients or clients in a "common-interest arrangement" the right to waive the privilege only for their own communications to counsel, absent contrary agreement. See §§75 and 76. If a document contains communications from two or more co-clients or members of the common interest arrangement, waiver is effective only if all the clients agree, unless a nonwaiving client's communications "can be redacted." Section 75 comment *e*; §76 comment *g*.

A final important question, which arises only in a common interest arrangement, asks what, if any, duties Lawyer *A* owes to client *B*? Remember, we are assuming that client *B* is the client of Lawyer *B*, not of Lawyer *A*, so the gamut of duties that lawyers owe clients would seem to be inapplicable. But absent agreement to the contrary, the common interest arrangement may give Lawyer *A* a *fiduciary* duty to client *B*. That duty may prevent Lawyer *A* from using client *B*'s information to client *B*'s disadvantage. GTE North Inc. v. Apache Products Co., 914 F. Supp. 1575 (N.D. Ill. 1996); National Medical Enterprises, Inc. v. Godbey, 924 S.W.2d 123 (Tex. 1996); Restatement §132 comment *g*. In a criminal case, the Ninth Circuit went further and held that a "joint defense agreement established an implied attorney-client relationship" between a lawyer for one defendant and the co-defendant. As a result, when the co-defendant pled guilty and appeared as a prosecution witness against the lawyer's client, the lawyer's motion to withdraw to avoid cross-examining the co-defendant should have been granted. United States v. Henke, 222 F.3d 633 (9th Cir. 2000). Reading *Henke* narrowly is United States v. Stepney, 246 F. Supp. 2d 1069 (N.D. Cal. 2003) (*Henke* says only that the lawyers had a duty of confidentiality to the cooperating co-defendant, which in that case worked to preclude cross-examination, but not that they had a duty of loyalty to the codefendant). Reaching a result contrary to *Henke* is United States v. Almeida, 341 F.3d 1318 (11th Cir. 2003) (when one party to a common interest arrangement decides to cooperate and testifies against the others, he waives protection of the privilege for his communications with lawyers for the other parties). In re Gabapentin Pat. Lit., 407 F.Supp.2d 607 (D.N.J. 2005), held that a joint defense agreement created fiduciary and attorney-client relationships between each lawyer and each client. Do you think courts should find attorney-client relationships — with all the duties that entails — when the parties to the agreement, represented by counsel, did not choose to so stipulate? In any event, these opinions make it imperative that lawyers address the issue explicitly at the outset in the common interest agreement, rather than leave it to a court to apply a default rule.

FURTHER READING

A meticulous analysis of the complex and subtle issues arising when two or more lawyers cooperate in the representation of multiple clients can be found in Howard Erichson, Informal Aggregation: Procedural and Ethical Implications of Coordination Among Counsel in Related Lawsuits, 50 Duke L.J. 381 (2000).

Class Conflicts

Conflicts within a class can occur concurrently or successively. Successive conflicts are discussed at page 328. Rule 23(a)(4) requires courts, as a condition of class certification, to find that the named class members "will fairly and adequately protect the interests of the class." In one of the largest class actions to reach the Supreme Court, Amchem Products, Inc. v. Windsor, 521 U.S. 591 (1997), the Court held that this requirement was unsatisfied when the purported settlement class (that is, a class certified solely for the purpose of settling the matter), as well as the named plaintiffs, consisted both of persons who had already manifested injuries from asbestos exposure and also those who had been exposed to asbestos but had not yet become ill. The two groups had different interests. "Most saliently, for the currently injured, the critical goal is generous immediate payments. That goal tugs against the interest of exposure-only plaintiffs in ensuring an ample, inflation-protected fund for the future." Furthermore, there was "diversity within each category." Permitting each named class member to represent the entire class of asbestos claimants was therefore improper. Although the Court was addressing inconsistent interests between class representatives and class members, its identification of a conflict necessarily means that any lawyer purporting to represent all of the diverse subclasses would also have a conflict.

Class actions also create potential conflicts between the interests of class counsel in settlement and the attendant court-awarded fees, on the one hand, and the interest in the class in maximum recovery on the other. Since in many class actions no single class member may have a substantial enough interest in an eventual recovery to invest the time needed to police counsels' decisions, the lawyers as a practical matter make the decisions that traditionally belong to the client. While a court must ultimately approve a settlement and fee request, no one may be available to challenge either, especially if the fee comes from the settlement fund, not from the defendant. These problems are parsed by Susan Koniak and George Cohen in Under Cloak of Settlement, 82 Va. L. Rev. 1051 (1996).

Appealability of Civil Disqualification Orders

An order granting or denying a motion to disqualify civil counsel is not subject to immediate appeal as of right in federal court. Richardson-Merrell, Inc. v. Koller, 472 U.S. 424 (1985) (disqualification order); Firestone Tire & Rubber Co. v. Risjord, 449 U.S. 368 (1981) (refusal to disqualify). The Ninth Circuit has refused to entertain an appeal by permission (under 28 U.S.C. §1292(b)) from a refusal to disqualify counsel because to do so "would greatly enhance [the] usefulness [of such motions] as a tactical ploy." Shurance v. Planning Control Intl., 839 F.2d 1347 (9th Cir. 1988). Mandamus remains a possible route to review a disqualification order, but the scope of review on mandamus is narrow. Matter of Sandahl, 980 F.2d 1118 (7th Cir. 1992).

FURTHER READING

For the rules that should apply when a law firm takes a legal position in one matter that is contrary to the position taken on behalf of a current or former client in another and unrelated matter, see John Dzienkowski, Positional Conflicts of Interest, 71 Tex. L. Rev. 457 (1993). Nathan Crystal examines two approaches the courts take in analyzing unrelated-matter conflicts and offers a "new framework" that, among other things, evaluates disqualification and damages as alternative remedies. Nathan Crystal, Disqualification of Counsel for Unrelated Matter Conflicts of Interest, 4 Geo. J. Legal Ethics 273 (1990). Thomas Morgan argues that the proposition that a lawyer can never take a position directly adverse to a client does not correctly interpret Rule 1.7(a) and is not the right rule in any event. Thomas Morgan, Suing a Current Client, 9 Geo. J. Legal Ethics 1157 (1996). Brian Redding agrees with Professor Morgan that the "current application of the Rule causes real problems . . . and that those problems cry out for attention," but he differs on the "most practical . . . remedy." Brian Redding, Suing a Current Client: A Response to Professor Morgan, 10 Geo. J. Legal Ethics 487 (1997).

Malpractice Based on Conflicts

Sometimes the remedy for a conflict of interest will be disqualification, as in *Fiandaca*. Sometimes it will be discipline, as in Iowa Supreme Court Attorney Discipline Board v. Clauss, 711 N.W.2d 1 (Iowa 2006) (attorney suspended six months for representing creditor against debtor while representing debtor on unrelated matter); Matter of Twohey, 727 N.E.2d 1028 (Ill. 2000) (lawyer suspended for six months for advising one client to invest in the business of another client and representing multiple clients in a single matter without full disclosure and consent). Conflicts can also lead to malpractice liability and fee forfeiture. These remedies are not mutually exclusive. We discuss malpractice and fee forfeiture more extensively in chapter 13A, but here, as a coming attraction, we view civil liability through the conflicts prism. The conflict in Simpson v. James occurred not in litigation but in transactional representation. (I mention that because people in my line of work are continuously amazed when transactional lawyers insist that conflicts are for litigators, not for them.) As you read this opinion, ask yourself: What did Ed Oliver and David James do wrong? Whatever it was, how did it cause Sheila Simpson to lose money? What, if anything, could the lawyers have done to protect themselves?

SIMPSON V. JAMES
903 F.2d 372 (5th Cir. 1990)

WISDOM, CIRCUIT JUDGE.

This appeal concerns a malpractice suit brought by the sellers of corporate assets against the partners of a law firm that represented both the buyers and the sellers in the transaction. The plaintiffs alleged two incidents of negligence on the part of the attorneys: the handling of the original sale and the subsequent restructuring of the buyers' note in favor of the plaintiffs. After a jury trial, the court rendered judgment in favor of the plaintiffs, awarding the sellers $100,000 for each act of negligence. We affirm.

STATEMENT OF THE CASE

The plaintiffs, Sheila Simpson and Lovie and Morelle Jones, were the sole stockholders in H.P. Enterprises Corporation. The business of H.P. Enterprises was operating and franchising catfish restaurants. Sheila Simpson's late husband, Buck Simpson, handled most of the business affairs of the corporation until his death. Mrs. Simpson then took over operation of the company, but she later decided to sell the corporation to devote more time to her children.

Mrs. Simpson turned to Ed Oliver for help in selling the corporation. Since 1968, Oliver practiced in Texarkana, Texas, with the firm now known as Keeney,

Anderson & James. He had represented Mr. Simpson for many years in matters relating to H.P. Enterprises and in personal matters. In November 1983 a group of investors approached Oliver to inquire into purchasing H.P. Enterprises. Oliver formed a corporation for the investors, Tide Creek, and drew up the legal documents to transfer the assets of H.P. Enterprises to Tide Creek. Oliver was the sole source of legal advice for both parties.

The price agreed upon was $500,000, of which $100,000 was paid at the execution of the sale. As security for the sellers, Oliver provided for a lien on the stock of Tide Creek, personal guarantees of the buyers on the corporation's $400,000 note to the sellers, and certain restrictions on operation of the business. The sale took place on November 18, 1983. After the transaction, Mr. Oliver's firm continued to represent Mrs. Simpson in estate and tax matters. During this time, all of her business records were kept at the firm's office.

Thereafter, two significant events occurred. In April 1984 a fire destroyed Tide Creek's commissary, which contained its inventory. David James, a partner in Oliver's firm, represented Tide Creek in recovering over $200,000 in insurance proceeds. In October 1984, Oliver left the firm to practice in Houston. The firm was renamed Keeney, Anderson & James. An associate in the firm, Fred Norton, took over tax and estate work for Mrs. Simpson.

Under the original terms of the sale arranged by Oliver, a $200,000 note by Tide Creek in favor of the plaintiffs became due on November 18, 1984. Tide Creek did not meet this obligation. On January 29, 1985, the plaintiffs visited David James at his office. James told them that Tide Creek was having financial difficulties, and that the company could pay them only $50,000 at that time. James restructured the note between the parties. At that meeting, Mrs. Simpson asked James what he would do if her interests and those of Tide Creek diverged. James replied: "We would have to support you."

In the Fall of 1985, Mrs. Simpson became concerned when she heard rumors of Tide Creek's impending bankruptcy. She called Fred Norton, an associate at the firm, and Norton arranged a meeting for her with David James. James advised Mrs. Simpson that her interests were in conflict with those of Tide Creek. He told her that she should find another lawyer to represent her; James was representing Tide Creek.

The plaintiffs received their last payment from Tide Creek on October 1, 1985. Tide Creek then filed for bankruptcy. The plaintiffs filed a claim in bankruptcy court, but received nothing. Their efforts to enforce the personal guarantees proved fruitless; the guarantors filed for personal bankruptcy.

Mrs. Simpson filed suit against the three partners of Keeney, Anderson & James on January 16, 1987. The suit alleged that acts of negligence by Oliver and James proximately damaged the plaintiffs. The plaintiffs alleged that the defendants had a conflict of interest that prevented them from acting in the plaintiffs' best interests. The jury found that Ed Oliver was negligent in his representation of Mrs. Simpson and the Joneses and awarded them $100,000 damages. It also found David James liable for negligence for his role in restructuring the delinquent note and awarded $100,000 damages to Simpson. . . .

In Texas, an attorney malpractice claim is based on negligence. A plaintiff in a malpractice action must prove four elements to recover: that 1) the defendant owed a duty to the plaintiff; 2) the defendant breached that duty; 3) the breach proximately caused the plaintiff injury; and 4) damages resulted. The defendants challenge the existence of a number of these elements.

A. ATTORNEY-CLIENT RELATIONSHIP: JAMES AND SIMPSON

The defendants argue that no attorney-client relationship existed between David James and Sheila Simpson, and consequently, James owed no duty to her that could form the basis of malpractice liability. . . .

The evidence adduced at trial indicated that Ed Oliver represented the plaintiffs' business interests in H.P. Enterprises before and at the time of the sale of its assets to Tide Creek. After Oliver left, the firm represented Mrs. Simpson in tax and estate matters and continued to maintain all of her business records. Mrs. Simpson testified that on January 29, 1985, at the time the note was restructured, and on a subsequent occasion, James encouraged her about Tide Creek's future economic viability. She added that she relied on those assurances. Significantly, Simpson stated that James advised her that she was entering into a good deal in agreeing to the restructuring. At the same meeting, James assured Simpson that he would stand by her in the event of a conflict of interest between Simpson and Tide Creek. James stated that at no time did Mrs. Simpson specifically ask him to represent her interests against Tide Creek. He testified that he never gave any advice to Mrs. Simpson and never charged her for his time. Nevertheless, the evidence was sufficient for a reasonable jury to conclude that an attorney-client relationship existed, as manifested through the parties' conduct.

B. NEGLIGENCE

Under Texas law, an attorney "is held to the standard of care which would be exercised by a reasonably prudent attorney." This is not a result-oriented analysis; an attorney will not be liable for undesirable effects of a decision that was reasonable at the time it was made.

The plaintiffs alleged negligent acts that arose out of the defendants' conflicts of interest in representing both sides of a transaction. Liability may not be premised solely on the fact that an attorney represented both buyer and seller; after full disclosure by the attorney, it may be proper in some circumstances for an attorney to represent both sides in a real estate transaction.

Both sides in this case presented expert testimony on the propriety of Oliver's representing both the plaintiffs and the investors from Tide Creek. Of course, in case of conflicting expert testimony, the jury is entitled to make credibility determinations and to believe the witness it considers more trustworthy. Although the defense maintains that Oliver merely reduced a settled agreement to writing, the plaintiffs presented evidence suggesting that Oliver negotiated the sale price for the assets of H.P. Enterprises and determined the "mechanics" of the sale. Moreover, the plaintiffs' expert witness, John Ament, testified that Oliver did not adequately protect Simpson against the possibility that Tide Creek would fail financially. For example, he stated that instead of a lien on Tide Creek stock, Oliver should have provided for a lien on the assets. Oliver also might have named the plaintiffs as beneficiaries of insurance policies. Ament added that the interests of plaintiffs and buyers varied significantly from the beginning. Although the evidence of Oliver's negligence is not overwhelming, we are not persuaded that the jury's conclusion is unreasonable.

David James prepared the instrument whereby Tide Creek's note in favor of Simpson and Jones was restructured. Simpson argues that James did not disclose Tide Creek's desperate financial condition, did not explain other options to her, and did not pursue over $200,000 insurance money for her benefit. The plaintiffs' expert also testified that it was improper for James to represent parties with such divergent interests: a creditor seeking recovery and a debtor in default. We believe that this evidence is sufficient to uphold the jury's finding of negligence.

C.   WHETHER ATTORNEY NEGLIGENCE PROXIMATELY CAUSED THE PLAINTIFFS' DAMAGES

The plaintiffs have the burden to prove that but for the defendants' negligence, they would have recovered the payments due. The jury found that Oliver and James, by their individual acts of negligence, each caused the plaintiffs $100,000 damages. We review the record to determine whether the plaintiffs proved that amount of damages.

It is apparent that proper conduct on the part of Oliver could have averted the loss of at least $100,000. The plaintiff's expert accountant testified that the sellers of the corporate assets were not adequately protected. Protection could have been provided by a lien on the conveyed assets or by naming the plaintiffs as beneficiaries of property insurance. The evidence is sufficient on this issue.

Whether the plaintiffs proved damages as a result of James's conduct is a closer question. The plaintiff's expert accountant testified that as of March 1985, Tide Creek had combined equity of over $368,000. His estimate was based on internal corporation figures that were not verified. Had the plaintiffs foreclosed on Tide Creek, however, they would have taken it back with over $477,000 in worthless accounts receivable. Moreover, it is undisputed that as of September 30, 1985, Tide Creek had equity of −$483,427.

However, the plaintiffs presented evidence that James was involved in recovering over $200,000 in insurance proceeds after a fire destroyed the restaurant's commissary. As argued by the plaintiff and admitted by the defendants' expert witness, James could have seized the insurance proceeds to satisfy the delinquent note. Perhaps because of a conflict of interest, James did not mention this possibility to the plaintiffs. We conclude that the plaintiffs proved damages caused by James.

What Did Oliver and James Do Wrong?

What was the basis for Oliver's malpractice? For James's malpractice? If the two had acted differently, Simpson and the Joneses *might* have been protected even after the purchasers declared bankruptcy. Fine. But then what does the alleged conflict of interest have to do with it? Wouldn't any lawyer who failed in the same way, assuming the failure was negligent, be liable, conflict or no conflict? Could it possibly be that the conflict transformed a *non*negligent act into an actionable one?

Or perhaps the conflict just made the negligence clearer. After all, Oliver and James seem to have had dual loyalties. Perhaps these prevented them from seeking maximum protection for the plaintiffs or giving better advice. In this view, the conflict had forensic (that is, courtroom) value by making it easier for the plaintiffs to persuade the jury that the lawyers should pay. Without the conflict, Oliver and James could easily have argued that they got the best economic deal possible for their client. Indeed, without the conflict, they would not likely have been sued at all or could have won a dispositive motion. Negotiation means compromise. The conflict allowed Simpson to argue that divided loyalties prevented her lawyers from getting her a better deal. The more they got for her, the worse it would have been for their other clients. Since, as a practical matter, we can't know for sure whether an independent lawyer could have better protected her, Simpson would in effect be urging the jury to resolve doubts in her favor.

It is not hard to see how appealing that argument would be to a lay jury. Yet Oliver, at least, insisted on the buyers' personal guarantees, which suggests that he had no qualms about offending them. May *they* now sue on the ground that an unconflicted lawyer would have protected them against promises that ultimately forced them into bankruptcy? It seems that anything the lawyers might have done to favor one side would necessarily disfavor the other side, creating a potential ground for malpractice claims from either (or both!). A zero-sum game for the clients becomes a lose-lose situation for their common lawyer. Or is that the point?

Let's not leave the issue of proximate cause quite yet. Simpson sought to prove that she would have had a better deal absent the conflict. See Viner v. Sweet, 70 P.3d 1046 (Cal. 2003), set out at page 729. Are you satisfied that she carried that burden? It's not really possible to tell from the opinion, is it, but the jury thought so. Compare McCann v. Davis, Malm & D'Agostine, 669 N.E.2d 1077 (Mass.1996), a strikingly similar case where the plaintiff failed to prove proximate cause. One half-owner of a company's stock sold it to the other half-owner. The same law firm represented both. The purchase price was to be paid across 20 years. The buyer made a few payments, but then a creditor foreclosed on the corporate property, and the buyer went bankrupt. The seller lost nearly everything and sued the firm. The court found the dual representation improper, but it upheld a jury verdict for the firm. Even if security had been demanded, the buyer had no security to post. So the conflict, a breach of fiduciary duty, did not proximately cause the loss. The court does not discuss whether independent counsel might have advised the plaintiff to keep his stock, perhaps because the court assumes he would have ended up in the same position even if he had. The "better deal/no deal" aspect of proximate cause is discussed in connection with Viner v. Sweet.

Consent and Waiver

"What Kind of Consent?"

Return to "They're On the Same Page," page 271. Penlo asks you for advice on how to get appropriate consent from her three clients. What do you advise?

> I agree to the doctrine urged at the bar, as to the delicacy of the relation
> of client and attorney, and the duty of a full, frank, and free disclosure by
> the latter of every circumstance, which may be presumed to be material,
> not merely to the interests, but to the fair exercise of the judgment, of the client.
> —Justice Story in Williams v. Reed, 29 F. Cas. 1386, 1390 (No. 17,733)
> (C.C.D. Me. 1824), quoted by Justice Stevens, dissenting, in Mickens v. Georgia,
> 535 U.S. 162 (2002).

What about James and Oliver? Would their troubles have been over if they had gotten appropriate consents? Rule 1.7 and the other conflict rules let clients consent to work that would otherwise be forbidden. (But not all work. See Rule 1.7(b).) Courts and the rules require lawyers to explain the conflict to a client before accepting consent. Rule 1.7 requires "informed consent" that is "confirmed in writing." Both phrases are defined. The Restatement and numerous courts recognize that a client's sophistication is a significant consideration in determining whether its consent to a conflict is adequate. See Restatement §122 and comment.

A lawyer at a large Canadian law firm, Gowling Lafleur Henderson ("Gowlings"), represented CenTra in its effort to win regulatory permission to build a second bridge between Detroit and Windsor, Canada ("the Bridge Plan"). Simultaneously, Estrin, another Gowlings lawyer, was representing Windsor in its effort to stop the bridge. (How did that get past the firm's conflicts committee? Or am I making an assumption?) CenTra eventually learned of the conflict and sued Gowlings and Estrin for breach of contract, breach of fiduciary duty, and malpractice, including a charge that Estrin may have used CenTra's confidential information against CenTra, which Estrin denied. Centra v. Estrin, 538 F.3d 402 (6th Cir. 2008). Among other things, Gowlings claimed that CenTra had implicitly consented to the conflict because it continued to use Gowlings even though Gowlings also represented Windsor against CenTra on a related but distinct matter ("the Site Plan"). Relying in part on professional conduct rules to identify the firm's legal duties (see chapter 13B), the court wrote:

> According to Gowlings, because CenTra had notice of a general conflict, Cen-Tra's continued retention of Gowlings as its counsel served as implicit consent to future conflicts of interest that would include Gowlings's work on behalf of Windsor to oppose the Bridge Plan while simultaneously assisting CenTra in arranging for funding for the Bridge Plan.
>
> A client's knowledge that his law firm has, on previous occasions, represented parties that opposed the client in different matters does not provide an adequate foundation for informed consent with respect to a current simultaneous representation of two adverse clients with opposing interests in a specific dispute. Gowlings does not claim that it provided to CenTra more specific information regarding the current conflict on which informed consent could have been based, because Gowlings itself admits that it was not aware until 2006 of the conflict with respect to the Bridge Plan. . . .
>
> If the vague and general information that CenTra possessed regarding prior, different conflicts was enough, then the client would bear the burden of identifying and understanding the full scope of any conflict of interest. It is not the client, however, to whom the various codes of conduct have given this responsibility; "[t]he affirmative duty here rests not with [the clients] but with [the law firm] and its attorneys." . . .

In the cases that have found implied consent, the reviewing court has found it clear that the impliedly consenting party was fully aware of the conflict and, armed with that knowledge, that party still took actions that are consistent only with consent.

Back to Oliver and James. Think about what the lawyers could have asked Simpson or the buyers to consent to. The multiple representation? The omission of a security interest in the assets? Supervening loyalty to the buyers or sellers? Malpractice? See Rule 1.8(h)(1) (no on malpractice, unless the client is independently represented); Van Kirk v. Miller, 869 N.E.2d 534 (Ind. 2007) (where lawyer represented both buyer and seller of business, court emphasizes that "by holding that Van Kirk knowingly signed the conflict waiver, we are *not* holding that he was not entitled to competent, diligent representation," which the court goes on to hold Miller provided).

If Oliver and James failed to protect Simpson as a competent lawyer would, it should not matter that Simpson may have given informed consent to the dual representation. But we can appreciate that proof of informed consent could have changed the dynamics in the courtroom and put Oliver and James in a somewhat better light. Indeed, there might never have been a trial.

As mentioned earlier (page 282), clients may consent to conflicts in advance of their occurrence. Of course, a blanket prospective consent can hardly be fully "informed" because the parties cannot then know what the future will hold. ABA Opinion 93-372 took the position that some specificity ("potential opposing party," "nature of the likely matter") is probably required and that if and when a conflict does arise, the lawyer must then make the independent judgment required by Rule 1.7 that "the representation will not be adversely affected." As rewritten in 2002, the comment to Rule 1.7 now recognizes that a blanket advance consent can stand up if the "client is an experienced user of the legal services involved and is reasonably informed regarding the risk that a conflict may arise . . . particularly if . . . the client is independently represented by other counsel in giving consent and the consent is limited to future conflicts unrelated to the subject of the representation." In light of the new comment, Opinion 93-372 was withdrawn in ABA Opinion 05-436. Why "unrelated?"

The Restatement also calibrates the need for specificity by looking to the sophistication of the client. "Client consent to conflicts that might arise in the future is subject to special scrutiny, particularly if the consent is general. A client's open-ended agreement to consent to all conflicts normally should be ineffective unless the client possesses sophistication in the matter in question and has had the opportunity to receive independent legal advice about the consent." §122 comment *d*. One court has held that consent to future "adverse" representation is insufficient to alert the client to the prospect that its lawyers can oppose it in litigation. Worldspan L.P. v. Sabre Group Holdings, Inc., 5 F. Supp. 2d 1356 (N.D. Ga. 1998). Another court has reached the opposite conclusion where the particular adverse litigation was implicit in the circumstances. Zador Corp. v. Kwan, 37 Cal. Rptr. 2d 754 (Ct. App. 1995).

In another case involving the same law firm (Heller Ehrman), an advance consent was upheld because the identity of the possible litigation opponent was specified although no litigation was then anticipated. Visa U.S.A., Inc. v. First Data Corp., 241 F. Supp. 2d 1100 (N.D. Cal. 2003). Fisons Corp. v. Atochem North

America, Inc., 1990 Westlaw 180551 (S.D.N.Y. 1990), accepted a new client's advance consent where it specifically named the possible litigation opponent and the events that might give rise to the claim, but in dicta the court said that the consent would not have sufficed to allow the lawyer to charge the client with fraud. An advance waiver will not be effective, however, if the circumstances have changed. The lawyer must go back to the client and get "a second, more specific waiver." Concat LP v. Unilever, PLC, 350 F.Supp.2d 796 (N.D. Cal. 2004).

Analyzing some of the cases cited here, and others, Richard Painter proposes amendments to ethics rules to allow for binding advance conflict waivers under described conditions that are intended to protect the interests of the client. Richard Painter, Advance Waiver of Conflicts, 13 Geo. J. Legal Ethics 289 (2000). Taking a profoundly skeptical view of prospective waivers is Lawrence Fox, All's O.K. Between Consenting Adults: Enlightened Rule on Privacy, Obscene Rule on Ethics, 29 Hofstra L. Rev. 701 (2001).

Consent should be distinguished from waiver and estoppel. Consent contemplates the client's conscious, informed agreement. A client who has not consented may nevertheless waive a conflict depending on such factors as "(1) the length of the delay in bringing the motion to disqualify, (2) when the movant learned of the conflict, (3) whether the movant was represented by counsel during the delay, (4) why the delay occurred, and (5) whether disqualification would result in prejudice to the non-moving party." The court will also investigate "whether the motion was delayed for tactical reasons." Alexander v. Primerica Holdings, Inc., 822 F. Supp. 1099 (D.N.J. 1993). Despite these technical distinctions, "waiver" is often used interchangeably with "consent," including inevitably in this book.

Is There a Client-Lawyer Relationship?

Defendant James said he had no professional relationship with Simpson and therefore owed her no duty. This defense is often asserted in malpractice actions and usually fails. See *Togstad* at page 707 and *Analytica* at page 310. As we have recognized throughout this book, whether a client-lawyer relationship exists will not always be evident and may depend on why we are asking. The answer will sometimes surprise you. Was there a client-lawyer relationship in the following three cases?

1.   Dorothy Loughman owned 50 acres of land. The Monongahela Railroad offered $50,000 for her land. She rejected the offer. The railroad threatened to take less than all the land in eminent domain proceedings, leaving an undesirable parcel. Loughman telephoned Ewing Pollock, an attorney she had known for 42 years and who had represented her and her family on occasion. Loughman did not know that Pollock was then doing work for Monongahela. She "explained the situation, and Pollock told her not to worry because Monongahela would be fair. He also told her she did not need an attorney to negotiate" with the railroad's agent. The single telephone call created an attorney-client relationship:

> [Loughman called Pollock] to seek his legal advice. He accepted this offer and readily gave advice. That Pollock previously represented her

only furthers this conclusion. When Pollock told her that Monongahela would be fair without knowing what price had been offered,
and when he failed to tell her [that Monongahela was his client
and that a second client was dependent on the railroad's acquisition
of the land to ship coal], Pollock failed to exercise ordinary skill
and knowledge. Since Loughman testified that she agreed to sell
only after she had consulted with Pollock, his advice and representations proximately caused her lost profits. Therefore the district
court erred by failing to uphold the jury verdict on malpractice.
Hughes v. Consol-Pennsylvania Coal Co., 945 F.2d 594 (3d Cir.
1991).

2. In Glueck v. Jonathan Logan, Inc., 653 F.2d 746 (2d Cir. 1981), the
plaintiff, a former executive of the defendant, alleged breach without
cause of an employment contract. The firm representing him also conducted collective bargaining for a trade association of which the
defendant was a member. The court characterized the case as one in
which "an adverse party is only a vicarious client." Consequently, disqualification would only be ordered if "the subject matter of [the] suit is
sufficiently related to the scope of the matters on which [the] firm represents [the] association as to create a realistic risk either that the plaintiff
will not be represented with vigor or that unfair advantage will be taken of
the defendant." Here the trial court could properly have identified such a
risk. "[T]he issue of whether Logan had cause to terminate Glueck might
well arise in the course of collective bargaining discussions conducted by
[Glueck's law firm for the trade association]." Furthermore, the law firm
might, "in preparing for collective bargaining sessions . . . learn of
Logan's policies or past practices bearing on the subject of Glueck's
termination."

3. Morgan Lewis & Bockius had agreed to represent the plaintiff in connection with possible securities actions against various entities and persons as
might be disclosed by the investigation Morgan Lewis would undertake.
Morgan Lewis was aware that the investigation could unearth accusations
against its current client, Arthur Andersen & Co., which it eventually did.
Morgan Lewis sued other entities on behalf of the plaintiff. In these cases,
co-counsel was Robert Meister, of a different firm. When it became clear
that the plaintiff also had a claim against Andersen, Meister's firm was
selected (it is unclear exactly by whom) to assert it. Nevertheless, Morgan
Lewis's files and associates were used to assist Meister. In moving to disqualify Meister, the defendant called him the "understudy" of Morgan
Lewis, and the court agreed. In effect, Morgan Lewis was suing its own
client:

> The truism that the firm of Morgan Lewis would have been dis-
> qualified [under Canon 5] from suing Andersen because it was Ander-
> sen's counsel, is of little comfort to Andersen which now finds itself
> embroiled in litigation resulting from Morgan Lewis's extensive inves-
> tigation of the natural resource assets scheme. And Robert Meister is
> the extension of Morgan Lewis's continuing involvement in the

underlying action for, as we have earlier stated, Morgan Lewis was instrumental in the choice of Meister and his firm . . . to bring the suit and helpful to Meister in advancing the suit even if, as claimed by Meister, that help was of small significance.

The court separately cited Morgan Lewis's use of Andersen's confidences:

> The impropriety of Meister's continued representation of the Fund appears with even greater clarity in the context of Canon 4's admonition that an attorney must not disclose the confidences of his client. . . . In undertaking the background investigation, and in segregating the papers which were, in part, ultimately used against Andersen, Morgan Lewis was applying its privileged knowledge with respect to Andersen. For, as Judge Stewart found, Morgan Lewis was privy to Andersen's practices and procedures, and had access to internal papers. It is inevitable that Meister, who dealt closely with Morgan Lewis throughout this entire period, was afforded the opportunity to benefit from this privileged information with regard to Andersen. Fund of Funds, Ltd. v. Arthur Andersen & Co., 567 F.2d 225 (2d Cir. 1977).

Subsequent cases have emphasized that Meister was not merely a lawyer in a co-counsel relationship with Morgan Lewis; he was the beneficiary of its legal work and client files. Because Morgan Lewis could not do that work to the direct detriment of its client Arthur Andersen, neither could it do so indirectly through Meister. In Sumitomo Corp. v. J.P. Morgan & Co., 2000 Westlaw 145747 (S.D.N.Y. 2000), Paul Weiss was representing the plaintiff against J.P. Morgan while a firm it recommended, Kronish Lieb, was representing the same plaintiff against Chase Manhattan Bank, a Paul Weiss client. The cases arose out of the same series of events and were eventually consolidated. Yet the court declined to view Kronish Lieb as a Paul Weiss "understudy." It distinguished *Fund of Funds* as "a case where the disqualified law firm had been substantially assisted in suing the defendant. . . . Chase argued that Paul Weiss is in a position similar to Morgan Lewis. . . . However, here, Paul Weiss' assistance to Kronish Lieb has been minimal and does not rise to the level of that found in *Fund of Funds*."

FURTHER READING

Using hypotheticals, Russell Pearce analyzes how the conflict rules may affect lawyers who represent families. Professor Pearce urges a "new legal ethic for representing families," which he calls the "Optional Family Representation." It would "permit representation of family members as a group even where actual or potential risks to individual interests would prohibit joint or intermediation representation under established doctrine." Russell Pearce, Family Values and Legal Ethics: Competing Approaches to Conflicts in Representing Spouses, 62 Fordham L. Rev. 1253 (1994). On the idea of the "vicarious" client, a person or entity a court will treat as a client at least for conflict purposes as in *Glueck*, see Virtual Clients: An Idea in Search of a Theory (with Limits), 42 Valp. L. Rev. 797 (2008) (Tabor Lecture). Using interviews with law firm coordinators and others, Norman Spaulding tackles positional conflicts in pro bono work in The Prophet and the Bureaucrat: Positional Conflicts in Service Pro Bono Publico, 50 Stan. L. Rev. 1395 (1998) ("the specter of positional conflicts . . . has a very real effect on lawyers' autonomy in selecting pro bono work and thus a dramatic impact on the distribution of public interest legal services"). See also Developments in the Law—Conflicts of Interest in the Legal Profession, 94 Harv. L. Rev. 1244, 1292-1315 (1981).

Many of the problems that arise throughout this chapter can be avoided entirely if we prohibit joint representation. Should we adopt a rule that says that no lawyer may represent more than one client in the same matter? Making the bold argument that we should is Debra Lyn Bassett, Three's a Crowd: A Proposal to Abolish Joint Representation, 32 Rutgers L.J. 387 (2001) ("Joint representation necessarily divides an attorney's loyalties, and the requirement of informed consent provides merely illusory protection to clients."). Professor Bassett, who would apply her rule to both criminal cases and civil representations (and not only to those in court), concludes that the benefits of joint representation—for example, easier cooperation among clients and sharing of costs—are far outweighed by the risks of disloyalty.

4.   The Insurance Triangle

"The Insurer Would Want to Know"

"Our partner, Brett Welcome, called me about an ethics problem. She was hired by POM Insurance to defend a case against its insured, a law firm, whose acronym is RIO. RIO is being sued for negligence by Spindlecraft, its former client, a maker of hobby materials. Also named is RIO's partner, Meredith Tipton. Spindlecraft claims that Tipton messed up on a public offering, which then failed, and seeks $40 million, which is within the limits of RIO's policy with POM. Brett appeared for both defendants.

"In complying with our electronic discovery obligations, an associate came across two RIO e-mails that imply that Tipton didn't just mess up but practically sabotaged the case because Spindlecraft's success would have been economically harmful to one of her other clients. Brett isn't sure that this is true, but she says the implication is strong and Spindlecraft would certainly urge it. Brett hasn't yet confronted Tipton.

"POM's policy does not cover intentional wrongdoing or punitive damages. Spindlecraft's complaint does not allege intentional wrongdoing or seek punitive damages. But if Spindlecraft got a whiff of intentional wrongdoing, it might amend the complaint. Then again, it might not. Why not? Because then it would not be able to reach the insurance policy. RIO is an LLP, which means if there's no coverage, Spindlecraft must look to Tipton and the firm's own assets for any judgment. A settlement predicated on RIO's negligence, however, will be paid by POM.

"Brett wants to know what to do. So do I. Should she confront Tipton? Should she tell the insurance company? Should or must she tell RIO's management committee? May she try to persuade the insurer to settle using the $40 million as a benchmark without telling it about her discovery? Is there anything else we should be thinking about?"

PUBLIC SERVICE MUTUAL INSURANCE CO. V. GOLDFARB

53 N.Y.2d 392, 425 N.E.2d 810, 442 N.Y.S.2d 422 (1981)

JASEN, JUDGE.

The question before us is whether a policy of professional liability insurance issued by plaintiff affords coverage to a dentist in a civil suit commenced by a former patient grounded upon an act of sexual abuse alleged to have occurred in the course of dental treatment.

Plaintiff Public Service Mutual Insurance Company, a multi-line insurer, issued a "Dentist's Professional Liability Policy" to the Dental Society of the State of New York. Defendant, Saul Goldfarb, a member of the society, obtained coverage under that policy. Defendant Jacqueline P. Schwartz is a former patient of Dr. Goldfarb who received dental treatment from him on May 23, 1977. She claims that in the course of receiving such treatment, she was sexually abused by Dr. Goldfarb. This claim, which is the subject of a pending civil suit, also formed the basis of professional disciplinary proceedings against Dr. Goldfarb and resulted in a criminal conviction of the crime of sexual abuse in the third degree. In this declaratory judgment action, plaintiff has asked the court to determine whether its policy of insurance provides coverage for the civil claim seeking compensatory and punitive damages. . . .

On this appeal, plaintiff argues that its policy of insurance was not intended by the parties to provide coverage against a claim of sexual abuse. . . . It is further argued that even if, as a contractual matter, coverage exists, it should not be enforced in this case because the public policy of this State does not allow contractual indemnification for civil liability which arises out of the commission of a crime.

Defendant argues that the broad language of the insurance policy in issue specifically provides coverage for a claim of sexual abuse in the course of dental treatment. . . . He further argues that where, as here, the policy explicitly provides coverage, such protection should not be denied upon public policy grounds. . . .

[T]he insurance policy in issue was intended by the parties to provide coverage for liability arising out of the acts complained of by defendant Schwartz. The policy specifically states that the insurer will

> pay on behalf of the Insured named in this certificate all sums, including punitive damages, which the Named Insured shall become obligated to pay by reason of the liability imposed upon him by law for damages because of injury resulting from professional dental services rendered . . . and resulting from any claim or suit based upon . . . [m]alpractice, error, negligence or mistake, assault, slander, libel [or] undue familiarity.

This language clearly indicates an intent on the part of the insurer to pay both compensatory and punitive damages arising out of unlawful or inappropriate physical contact which occurs during the course of dental treatment. Defendant Schwartz claims that such contact occurred. Hence, as a purely contractual matter absent any consideration of public policy, a claim within the stated coverage has been made and the insurer is obligated to defend the suit.

Whether indemnity will ultimately be required, however, cannot be determined at this stage of the proceeding. It is possible, of course, that the trier of fact could find that unlawful contact with defendant Schwartz occurred, but that it did not occur in the course of professional dental services. In this event, defendant Schwartz could recover from defendant Goldfarb, but he, in turn, could not seek contractual indemnity from his insurer because the policy imposes liability upon the insurer only for "injury resulting from professional dental services rendered." This being so, any determination as to whether the insurer must indemnify Dr. Goldfarb must await a trial of defendant Schwartz' claim, at which time a special verdict should be obtained on the issue of whether or not the acts complained of occurred in the course of professional dental treatment.

Having determined that plaintiff has contractually obligated itself at least to defend Dr. Goldfarb against the claim in issue, we must now address the question whether the public policy of this State precludes insurance coverage for a claim of sexual abuse in the course of dental treatment. Plaintiff notes that defendant was convicted of the crime of sexual abuse in the third degree and argues that, as a matter of public policy, he may not be indemnified for any civil liability arising out of this criminal act. We disagree. The mere fact that an act may have penal consequences does not necessarily mean that insurance coverage for civil liability arising from the same act is precluded by public policy. Whether such coverage is permissible depends upon whether the insured, in committing his criminal act, intended to cause injury. One who intentionally injures another may not be indemnified for any civil liability thus incurred. However, one whose intentional act causes an unintended injury may be so indemnified.

In this case, the complaint against Dr. Goldfarb alleges both intentional acts which caused unintended injury, seeking compensatory damages therefor and intentional causation of injury, seeking compensatory and punitive damages therefor. To the extent that defendant Schwartz' complaint can be construed as a claim for injuries unintentionally caused by Dr. Goldfarb, he may seek indemnity from his insurer for that claim. Thus, the insurer would be obligated to pay any judgment against Dr. Goldfarb for compensatory damages only, assuming, of course, that the trier of fact determined, in a special verdict, that such unintended injury occurred in the course of dental treatment.*

Under no circumstances, however, can the insurer be compelled to indemnify Dr. Goldfarb for punitive damages. Such damages are, as the name implies, a punishment for intentional wrongdoing. As we have only recently noted, to allow insurance coverage for such damages "is totally to defeat the purpose of punitive damages." . . .

Furthermore, if a finding that defendant Goldfarb *intended to injure* defendant Schwartz is made in a special verdict, he would be precluded from seeking

---

* Doubts have been raised on whether this conclusion — that intentional conduct causing unintentional damages can be covered by insurance consistent with public policy — remains good law in New York. Dodge v. Legion Insurance Co., 102 F. Supp. 2d 144 (S.D.N.Y. 2000) (claim against psychiatrist for improper sexual conduct toward patient). The holding has been rejected elsewhere. Worcester Insurance Co. v. Fells Acres Day School, Inc., 558 N.E.2d 958 (Mass. 1990). However, the wisdom of the holding is irrelevant to the analysis of the conflicts question. — ED.

indemnity from his insurer for either compensatory or punitive damages flowing from this intentional causation of *injury*. This is so because to allow such indemnity would be to violate the "fundamental principle that no one shall be permitted to take advantage of his own wrong." . . .

We note also that although the insurer need not indemnify Dr. Goldfarb for any liability for punitive damages, it must, nonetheless, defend him in the pending lawsuit because a claim within the stated coverage has been made. Moreover, inasmuch as the insurer's interest in defending the lawsuit is in conflict with the defendant's interest — the insurer being liable only upon some of the grounds for recovery asserted and not upon others — defendant Goldfarb is entitled to defense by an attorney of his own choosing, whose reasonable fee is to be paid by the insurer.*

In sum, we hold that plaintiff is obligated to defend Dr. Goldfarb in the lawsuit commenced by defendant Schwartz and to provide independent counsel for the defense, to be chosen by Dr. Goldfarb. At this stage of the litigation, however, it is impossible to determine whether any indemnity for any compensatory damages which ultimately may be assessed against Dr. Goldfarb will be required, for such a determination can only be made after the trier of fact in the Schwartz action has rendered its special verdict. . . .

Client Identity and the Obligation to Defend

Two questions have significant, often determinative, influence in analyzing insurance defense work. The first is client identity. Who is the client: the insurer, the insured, or both? Second, what does it mean to say that the insurer's obligation to defend is broader than the obligation to indemnify?

The first question will likely be of only academic interest if the entire claim against the insured is covered by the insurance. Then, the insurer and the insured have congruent interests and may have the same lawyer. Nevertheless, that won't always be so, and there is a diversity of opinion on whether the lawyer represents the insured alone or the insurer, too. Charles Silver, Does Insurance Defense Counsel Represent the Company or the Insured?, 72 Tex. L. Rev. 1583 (1994). Finley v. Home Insurance Co., 975 P.2d 1145 (Haw. 1998), says "the modern view" is that "the sole client of the attorney is the insured," citing and quoting Douglas Richmond, Walking a Tightrope: The Tripartite Relationship Between Insurer, Insured, and Insurance Defense Counsel, 73 Neb. L. Rev. 265 (1994).

* That is not to say that a conflict of interest requiring retention of separate counsel will arise in every case where multiple claims are made. Independent counsel is only necessary in cases where the defense attorney's duty to the insured would require that he defeat liability on any ground and his duty to the insurer would require that he defeat liability only upon grounds which would render the insurer liable. When such a conflict is apparent, the insured must be free to choose his own counsel whose reasonable fee is to be paid by the insurer. On the other hand, where multiple claims present no conflict — for example, where the insurance contract provides liability coverage only for personal injuries and the claim against the insured seeks recovery for property damage as well as for personal injuries — no threat of divided loyalty is present and there is no need for the retention of separate counsel. This is so because in such a situation the question of insurance coverage is not intertwined with the question of the insured's liability.

But another view, which probably considers itself to be just as modern, thank you, says that the insurer is also a client. Sometimes the insured is referred to as the "primary" client, which would make the insurer a "secondary" client. Exactly how these imprecise terms affect the lawyer's duties is unclear. See Nevada Yellow Cab Corp. v. Eighth Judicial District Court, 152 P.3d 737 (Nev. 2007) (insured was the "primary" client, but insurer was also a client if there is no conflict). The Nevada court, citing cases from six jurisdictions, called this the "majority rule." As a result, the lawyer in *Nevada Yellow Cab* could not, after the liability trial, represent the insured against the insurer for bad faith refusal to settle the claim against the insured. Doing so violated the rule (studied in chapter 6) against acting adversely to a former client (the insurer) on a substantially related matter.

Abundant authority on the "who is the client" question can be found in Restatement §134, comment *f* and the Reporter's Notes to that comment. The Restatement takes no position on the question, probably because the ALI was too divided, leaving it instead to the facts of each case.

This brings us to the second question. What happens when the interests of the insurer and insured do, in fact, conflict, so that the same lawyer could not represent both, not even in Nevada? What does it mean, as in *Goldfarb*, to say that an insurer's obligation to defend its insured in court is "broader" than its obligation to indemnify the insured in the event the insured has to pay?

As stated, no conflict arises if the complaint against the insured alleges conduct squarely within the policy and seeks damages below the policy limit. Nor does a problem arise if the complaint alleges conduct entirely outside the language of the policy. But where the complaint alleges conduct and injuries that may fall both within and outside the policy, depending on what the judge or jury decide are the facts, the interests of the insurer and the insured may diverge. This is so because, as *Goldfarb* put it, "the question of insurance coverage is [then] intertwined with the question of the insured's liability." We will eventually learn whether the insured is covered, because the jury will tell us the facts that answer that question in a "special verdict." But by then the defense costs will have been expended. Even though the jury's verdict may mean that the insurance company does not have to pay the judgment, so long as the complaint contained theories of recovery that, if successful, would have required payment, the insured will be the beneficiary of the insurer's (broader) duty to defend by fronting the costs of defense. The plaintiff can eliminate that duty to defend merely by asserting only those theories of recovery that are not within the policy. Why might it choose *not* to do that? Indeed, why might it choose only to assert claims within the policy?

Another way the interests of the insured and insurer may diverge, even if the complaint alleges conduct within the policy's coverage, is if the insured violated some term of the policy thereby canceling or suspending it and freeing the insurer from responsibility. This is called a coverage dispute. For example, a landlord's fire insurance policy may stipulate that the insured will keep a designated number of extinguishers of certain capacity on the premises, failing which the policy will be suspended. After a fire negligently set by the landlord's employee, the tenants sue for their losses. The insurer may challenge coverage because of the lack of extinguishers, notwithstanding that the complaint alleges conduct (negligence) within the terms of the policy. Obviously, the interests of insured and insurer conflict.

Now we consider some really interesting strategy moves. What will happen at the impending trial of Schwartz v. Goldfarb? Consider the three interests: Goldfarb has an interest in (1) avoiding liability for compensatory or punitive damages or (2) limiting his liability to compensatory damages for nonintentional injuries. Do you see why (2) is the fallback position? Schwartz has an interest in (3) establishing liability for compensatory and punitive damages. Would she prefer that the compensatory damages be based on intentional injuries or nonintentional injuries? Schwartz will need to know the extent to which she can get punitive damages for intentional injuries, Goldfarb's insurance coverage, and Goldfarb's net worth. The insurance company doesn't much care about punitive damages since it won't have to pay them in New York under any circumstances. With regard to compensatory damages, it prefers that these be based on intentional injuries. Doesn't this mean that the insurance company, in addition to hiring a lawyer to defend Goldfarb, must have the right to participate in Schwartz v. Goldfarb through its own counsel to protect its interests? The same lawyer cannot represent Goldfarb and the insurer on these facts.

The leading California case on insurance-related conflicts is San Diego Navy Fed. Credit Union v. Cumis Ins. Socy., Inc., 208 Cal. Rptr. 494 (Ct. App. 1984), which attempted to describe when an insured was entitled to separate counsel. Three years after the *Cumis* decision (which gave birth to the term "*Cumis* counsel"), California adopted §2860 of the Civil Code, whose focus is the obligation of an insurance company when a conflict of interest requires independent counsel for the insured. It states that "when an insurer reserves its rights on a given issue and the outcome of that coverage issue can be controlled by counsel first retained by the insurer for the defense of the claim, a conflict of interest may exist." The statute also provides that if independent counsel is appointed, both that lawyer and the insurer's lawyer "shall be allowed to participate in all aspects of the litigation." What do you think the legislature meant by the phrase "can be controlled?"

The law also states that "[n]o conflict of interest shall be deemed to exist as to allegations of punitive damages or be deemed to exist solely because an insured is sued for an amount in excess of the insurance policy limits." Can that be right? What should a lawyer appointed by the insurer do if a plaintiff, who has sued an insured for more than the policy limits and also for uninsured punitive damages, offers to settle for the policy limits and the insured tells the lawyer that he wants to accept? Sure he does; he won't have to pay. May the lawyer act as an advocate for the insured in describing the risks of going to trial? Or is the lawyer limited to an objective assessment of those risks?

Goldfarb and the California statute both assume that when independent counsel is required, the insured may select him or her. But why does the insured get to choose the lawyer? Despite the coverage dispute, the insurance company may eventually have to pay any judgment or settlement. Why shouldn't it be able to select an independent lawyer whose competence it trusts? Or should we assume that anyone it picks will have (or be seen to have) supervening loyalty to it (a possible source of more work). The Model Rules allow a third person to pay a lawyer to represent a client so long as the lawyer does not allow the fee payer to interfere with the professional relationship. Rule 1.8(f). Why deny the insurance company the power to make the selection? Finley v. Home Insurance Co., supra, held that the insurer did have the right to choose independent counsel. Any risk that the chosen lawyer would favor the insurer over the client was diminished by the insured's remedies for such misconduct. These included: "(1) an action against the attorney for professional malpractice; (2) an action against the insurer for bad faith conduct; and (3) estoppel of the insurer to deny indemnification." The court found these remedies "adequate to deter unethical conduct on the behalf of the insurer and retained counsel." By contrast, *Goldfarb* said the insured gets "an attorney of his own choosing."

C. THE ADVOCATE-WITNESS RULE

A special conflict confronts attorneys who are or ought to be called as witnesses in a litigation in which they represent one of the parties. It may be that the attorney ought to be a witness for the party she represents. Or for an opposing party. Model Rule 3.7 does not distinguish between testimony for or against a client. Unless one of the narrow exceptions applies, it simply prohibits lawyers from acting "as advocate at a trial [if] the lawyer is likely to be a necessary witness." FDIC v. United States Fire Insurance Co., 50 F.3d 1304 (5th Cir. 1995) (thorough review of application of Rule 3.7). Notice the several limitations the quoted words imply. The disqualification runs only to advocacy at trial, not to pretrial work. A lawyer will not be disqualified under the rule simply because his testimony would be "relevant" or even "highly useful." Macheca Transp. Co. v. Philadelphia Indem. Co, 463 F.3d 827 (8th Cir. 2006).

Rule 3.7(a) disqualifies the lawyer personally but not her firm. Only in the limited circumstance described in Rule 3.7(b) will imputation arise. Rule 3.7(b) allows officemates of the disqualified lawyer to act as advocates "unless precluded from doing so by Rule 1.7 or Rule 1.9." In other words, the conflict must run deeper than the reasons underlying the advocate-witness rule (hereafter discussed) in order to trigger imputation. Can you think of an example in which the entire firm of a lawyer-witness should be disqualified? What if in *P* v. *D*, *D* calls *W*, a partner in the firm representing *P*? *W*'s testimony is expected to be highly damaging to *P*'s case. What will *P*'s trial lawyer wish to do if free to do it?

Policies Behind the Advocate-Witness Rule

The policies are several, somewhat overlapping, and somewhat inconsistent.

First, it is said that the jury may accord the lawyer's testimony too much weight because of her "special knowledge of [the] case." MacArthur v. Bank of N.Y., 524 F. Supp. 1205 (S.D.N.Y. 1981). (Unless indicated otherwise, subsequent quotes are from *MacArthur*.) Of course, this argument is overinclusive. Even if the lawyer-witness is not also the trial lawyer, the jury may learn about her "special knowledge" in the course of the testimony.

Second, it is said that professional courtesy may handicap the opposing lawyer on cross-examination. But why is this any more true if the lawyer-witness is also an advocate than if she is merely a witness? Anyway, does anyone really believe professional courtesy will turn a cross-examiner into Miss Manners?

Third, it is said that "the bar is ill-served when an attorney's veracity becomes an issue in a case; lay observers especially might speculate whether counsel has compromised his integrity on the stand in order to prevail in the litigation." If that is true, then perhaps we should retain the imputed disqualification rule because the lawyer-witness will have an obvious interest in the outcome even if someone else in her firm is representing a party.

Fourth, the jury might not distinguish between the lawyer's role as witness and the lawyer's role as advocate. As a result it may "accord testimonial weight to his closing arguments." In addition, in summation the lawyer will be in a position to say to the jury, "As I told you when I testified. . . ." Can you reconcile the concern that the jury might give undue weight to the lawyer's argument with the concern that the lawyer may appear to have "compromised his integrity on the stand in order to prevail in the litigation"? Is the advocate-witness more or less credible?

MacArthur was a jury trial. Do the reasons supporting the advocate-witness rule apply at judge trials? The rule itself makes no distinction, but some cases do. See, e.g., Keoseian v. Von Kaulbach, 707 F. Supp. 150 (S.D.N.Y. 1989) (in judge trial, "there is no fear . . . that the appearance of a lawyer as a witness will confuse lay people").

A client whose lawyer has testimony favorable to the client may wish to keep the lawyer and waive the testimony. Too bad. As the *MacArthur* court explained:

> Nor may the client waive the rule's protection by promising not to call the attorney as a witness. The ostensible paternalism of disregarding such waivers is justified by the circumstances in which the problem arises. The client will generally be reluctant to forego the assistance of familiar counsel or to incur the expense and inconvenience of retaining another lawyer. The most serious breaches of the rule, in which an attorney has become intimately involved in the subject matter of the dispute, will often be the very situations in which withdrawal is most burdensome. Moreover, the party will generally be guided in its decision by the very attorney whose continued representation is at issue. At the same time, the attorney will be reluctant to jeopardize good relations with the client and may — against his better judgment — defer to the client's desire for representation.

When the rule is mandatory, it "requires that the court be able to disqualify counsel sua sponte when the need arises." In *MacArthur* the judge disqualified an entire law firm in the middle of trial. In Lamborn v. Dittmer, 873 F.2d 522 (2d Cir. 1989), a judgment for $30 million was reversed where the trial judge had erroneously refused to let the defendant call the plaintiff's lawyer as a witness. The proper remedy was disqualification of the lawyer, who would then be a witness.

Not all courts agree that the rule should be mandatory. Since other concurrent conflict rules may be waived, within limits, why not this one?

In both civil and criminal cases, courts have recognized the client's right to consent to forgo his lawyer's testimony in order to keep the lawyer as an advocate. United States v. Kliti, 156 F.3d 150 (2d Cir. 1998) (reversing conviction where a trial court failed to determine whether defendant knowingly consented to forgo counsel's testimony and remanded for a hearing consistent with the trial court's discretion under Wheat v. United States (page 253) to reject a conflict waiver); Nolte v. Pearson, 133 F.R.D. 585 (D. Neb. 1990) (rejecting *MacArthur*'s "ostensible paternalism").

The Advocate-Witness Rule in Criminal Cases

The rule has been used to to disqualify defense counsel, notwithstanding that the defendant is willing to waive counsel's testimony in order to keep her as the advocate. See United States v. Arrington, 867 F.2d 122 (2d Cir. 1989); Gonzalez v. State, 117 S.W.3d 831 (Texas 2003) (5-4 decision upholding disqualification of defense lawyer on state's motion despite defendant's waiver of counsel's purportedly favorable testimony, citing *Wheat*).

Perhaps the best known application of the advocate-witness rule is the disqualification of Bruce Cutler as mob boss John Gotti's lawyer in United States v. Locascio, 6 F.3d 924 (2d Cir. 1993). The trial judge's disqualification order was upheld because, among other reasons, Cutler's voice was recorded on secret tapes the government planned to use at trial.

> The government was legitimately concerned that, when Cutler argued before the jury for a particular interpretation of the tapes, his interpretation would be given added credibility due to his presence in the room when the statements were made. This would have given Gotti an unfair advantage, since Cutler would not have had to take an oath in presenting his interpretation, but could merely frame it in the form of legal argument.

In addition, as part of the government's proof of a tax fraud count, it planned to introduce proof of Gotti's statements referring to Cutler's acceptance of fees "under the table." The court said that if Cutler had been allowed to argue "Gotti's defense to that count, he would not only have had a conflict of interest [do you see why?], but he would have been arguing as to events in which he was allegedly involved."

Does the rule apply to prosecutors? According to an en banc decision of the Seventh Circuit, the rule not only applies to prosecutors, but in an apparent case of first impression, the court held that it applies in a suppression hearing before a judge without a jury. Although the court found the rule inapplicable in the case before it for other reasons, it quoted an ABA criminal justice standard:

> The prosecutor should avoid interviewing a prospective witness except in the presence of a third person unless the prosecutor is prepared to forego impeachment of a witness by the prosecutor's own testimony as to what the witness stated in an interview or to seek leave to withdraw from the case in order to present his impeaching testimony.

United States v. Johnston, 690 F.2d 638 (7th Cir. 1982) (en banc). The *Johnston* court cited United States v. Birdman, 602 F.2d 547 (3d Cir. 1979), on the reasons for applying the advocate-witness rule to prosecutors:

> First, the rule eliminates the risk that a testifying prosecutor will not be a fully objective witness given his position as an advocate for the government. Second, there is fear that the prestige or prominence of a government prosecutor's office will artificially enhance his credibility as a witness. Third, the performance of dual roles by a prosecutor might create confusion on the part of the trier of fact as to whether the prosecutor is speaking in the capacity of an advocate or of a witness, thus raising the possibility of the trier according testimonial credit to the prosecutor's closing argument. Fourth, the rule reflects a broader concern for public confidence in the administration of justice, and implements the maxim that "justice must satisfy the appearance of justice." This concern is especially significant where the testifying attorney represents the prosecuting arm of the federal government.
>
> In addition to the policies articulated in *Birdman*, there is at least one other consequence deserving of consideration, particularly by United States Attorneys. United States Attorneys are expected to adhere to the highest standards of professional behavior and to be worthy of public trust and confidence. Nevertheless, the United States Attorney who becomes both witness and advocate runs the risk of impeachment or otherwise being found not credible by the district judge. That would be an unfortunate situation for government counsel which could impair not only continuation as an effective advocate in the case, but could also produce lingering adverse aftereffects.

VI

Successive Conflicts of Interest

- *Former-Client Conflicts*
- *Imputation of Lateral Lawyer Conflicts*
- *Former Government Lawyers: The Revolving Door*

A. PRIVATE PRACTICE

"Divorce and Default"

In 2005, Clarissa Rasmussen represented Patrick Roth in a divorce from his wife, Leila, after a 28-year marriage. Representation took 11 months, during which time Clarissa negotiated with Leila's lawyer over the economic terms of the divorce. Their three children were grown and quite self-sufficient, so there were no custody or child support issues. Leila had not worked outside the home for 24 years, while Pat had built a substantial business, Slipshod, Inc., a maker of casual footwear. Slipshod was a closely held corporation. Pat was its president and majority shareholder. Eight investors, all but one employees of the company, had small stock interests. Pat and Leila signed a separation agreement dividing their property, giving Leila a five percent equity interest in Slipshod and providing for lifetime support payments.

In September 2008, Slipshod was having trouble meeting its payments to Wumco Bank on its line of revolving credit. After several months, Wumco sent Pat Roth a letter threatening to invoke the acceleration clause of the credit agreement, which would obligate Slipshod to pay the outstanding balance immediately, something Slipshod could not do. The inevitable result would be bankruptcy.

Roth alleged duress and other actionable conduct that violated Wumco's lender obligations to Slipshod. He requested a meeting with his counsel, Lincoln Grey, present. On the meeting date, Wumco appeared with its counsel, Kevin DeVries. The negotiating session was not productive, but the parties planned a second meeting a week later. When they exchanged business cards, Pat realized for the first time that Kevin was a partner in the same firm as Clarissa Rasmussen, his former divorce lawyer. Lincoln then wrote to Kevin, asserting that neither Kevin nor anyone from his firm could represent Wumco in the negotiations with Slipshod because the firm previously represented Pat in the divorce. Kevin replied:

> The Roths were divorced more than two years ago. That was purely a personal law issue. It was between Patrick and Leila Roth. The current financial matter is between Wumco Bank, my client, and Slipshod, Inc., two different parties. Not only are the parties different, but the issues are different, the areas of law are different, our professional duties are different. There is no conflict.

Who is right?

"Do I Still Owe the Record Store?"

Jane Lopez has developed a practice representing retail startups in New York City. She has represented dozens of restaurants, bakeries, shoe stores, you name it. Jane is retained by Bill Tallman to help him with the legal work required to open a store that will specialize in the folk music of indigenous peoples, mostly in third world countries. Lopez incorporates the store, negotiates and reviews the terms of the lease, works out credit financing arrangements with banks and suppliers, and helps Tallman get a registered trade name for the store. She successfully petitions the city to rezone Tallman's street to permit retailers to place merchandise bins on the sidewalk in front of their stores. Six months after Lopez's work is done and she has billed the store for her services and been paid:

1. May she represent Tallman's landlord in an action to evict Tallman for breach of his lease? The landlord claims that music from speakers in the store is producing "excessive noise," affecting the "quiet enjoyment" of the building's other commercial and residential tenants, in violation of a lease term forbidding "excessive noise" affecting "quiet enjoyment."
2. May she represent a community group in an effort to repeal the rezoning? The community group claims that the rezoning has resulted in narrowed sidewalk space up and down the block. Not only do the retail bins occupy sidewalk space, but in addition shoppers congregate around them, resulting in congestion that has forced some pedestrians into the gutter and has made navigation a challenge for people with disabilities. Meanwhile, Tallman's bins have produced significant sales of merchandise in the bins and also in the store.
3. May she represent Cassandra Dundee, who wants to hire Lopez to help her open a store with the same specialty across the street from Tallman's store?

ANALYTICA, INC. v. NPD RESEARCH, INC.
708 F.2d 1263 (7th Cir. 1983)

POSNER, JUDGE.

Two law firms, Schwartz & Freeman and Pressman and Hartunian, appeal from orders disqualifying them from representing Analytica, Inc. in an antitrust suit against NPD, Inc. . . .

[Malec was an employee of NPD between 1972 and 1977. Malec had two shares, or 10 percent, of NPD's stock. During the course of his employment, his two co-owners wished to give him an additional two shares of stock as compensation for his services. They told him to find "a lawyer who would structure the transaction in the least costly way." Malec hired Richard Fine, a partner in Schwartz & Freeman, and Fine devised a plan for the transfer of the stock. Since Malec had to pay income tax on the stock, it was necessary to evaluate it. NPD gave Fine information on its financial condition, sales trends, and management, after which Fine fixed a value for the stock, which the corporation adopted. NPD paid Fine's bill for the services. Eventually, Malec and his wife, who was also employed at NPD, left their jobs. Mrs. Malec thereafter incorporated Analytica to compete with NPD in the market-research business.

In October 1977, several months after the Malecs had left NPD, Analytica retained Schwartz & Freeman to represent it in connection with its claim of anticompetitive behavior against NPD. After complaints to the Federal Trade Commission proved unavailing, Analytica authorized Schwartz & Freeman to hire Pressman and Hartunian as trial counsel. An antitrust suit was brought against NPD in 1979. The defendant moved to disqualify both of the plaintiff's law firms. The district judge disqualified both firms and ordered Schwartz & Freeman to pay NPD $25,000 for resisting the disqualification motion. Both firms appealed but the Pressman firm's appeal was judged moot.]

For rather obvious reasons a lawyer is prohibited from using confidential information that he has obtained from a client against that client on behalf of another one. But this prohibition has not seemed enough by itself to make clients feel secure about reposing confidences in lawyers, so a further prohibition has evolved: a lawyer may not represent an adversary of his former client if the subject matter of the two representations is "substantially related," which means: if the lawyer could have obtained confidential information in the first representation that would have been relevant in the second. It is irrelevant whether he actually obtained such information and used it against his former client, or whether—if the lawyer is a firm rather than an individual practitioner—different people in the firm handled the two matters and scrupulously avoided discussing them.

There is an exception for the case where a member or associate of a law firm (or government legal department) changes jobs, and later he or his new firm is retained by an adversary of a client of his former firm. In such a case, even if there is a substantial relationship between the two matters, the lawyer can avoid disqualification by showing that effective measures were taken to prevent confidences from being received by whichever lawyers in the new firm are handling the new matter.* The exception is inapplicable here; the firm itself changed sides.

Schwartz & Freeman's Mr. Fine not only had access to but received confidential financial and operating data of NPD in 1976 and early 1977 when he was putting together the deal to transfer stock to Mr. Malec. Within a few months,

---

* This is a reference to the utility of screening against imputed disqualification where a conflicted lawyer changes firms and her new firm wants to avoid disqualification. Authorities are divided on whether screening can prevent imputation. See page 336. Screening would, in any event, be inadequate here because of the next sentence in Judge Posner's opinion. — ED.

Schwartz & Freeman popped up as counsel to an adversary of NPD's before the FTC, and in that proceeding and later in the antitrust lawsuit advanced contentions to which the data Fine received might have been relevant. Those data concerned NPD's profitability, sales prospects, and general market strength — all matters potentially germane to both the liability and damage phases of an antitrust suit charging NPD with monopolization. The two representations are thus substantially related, even though we do not know whether any of the information Fine received would be useful in Analytica's lawsuit (it might just duplicate information in Malec's possession, but we do not know his role in Analytica's suit), or if so whether he conveyed any of it to his partners and associates who were actually handling the suit. If the "substantial relationship" test applies, however, "it is not appropriate for the court to inquire into whether actual confidences were disclosed," unless the exception noted above for cases where the law firm itself did not switch sides is applicable, as it is not here. . . .

Schwartz & Freeman argues, it is true, that Malec rather than NPD retained it to structure the stock transfer, but this is both erroneous and irrelevant. NPD's three co-owners retained Schwartz & Freeman to work out a deal beneficial to all of them. All agreed that Mr. Malec should be given two more shares of the stock; the only question was the cheapest way of doing it; the right answer would benefit them all. Cf. Coase, The Problem of Social Cost, 3 J. Law & Econ. 1 (1960). The principals saw no need to be represented by separate lawyers, each pushing for a bigger slice of a fixed pie and a fee for getting it. Not only did NPD rather than Malec pay Schwartz & Freeman's bills (and there is no proof that it had a practice of paying its officers' legal expenses), but neither NPD nor the co-owners were represented by counsel other than Schwartz & Freeman. Though Millman, an accountant for NPD, did have a law degree and did do some work on the stock-transfer plan, he was not acting as the co-owners' or NPD's lawyer in a negotiation in which Fine was acting as Malec's lawyer. As is common in closely held corporations, Fine was counsel to the firm, as well as to all of its principals, for the transaction. If the position taken by Schwartz & Freeman prevailed, a corporation that used only one lawyer to counsel it on matters of shareholder compensation would run the risk of the lawyer's later being deemed to have represented a single shareholder rather than the whole firm, and the corporation would lose the protection of the lawyer-client relationship. Schwartz & Freeman's position thus could force up the legal expenses of owners of closely held corporations.

But it does not even matter whether NPD or Malec was the client. In Westinghouse's antitrust suit against Kerr-McGee and other uranium producers, Kerr-McGee moved to disqualify Westinghouse's counsel, Kirkland & Ellis, because of a project that the law firm had done for the American Petroleum Institute, of which Kerr-McGee was a member, on competition in the energy industries. Kirkland & Ellis's client had been the Institute rather than Kerr-McGee but we held that this did not matter; what mattered was that Kerr-McGee had furnished confidential information to Kirkland & Ellis in connection with the law firm's work for the Institute. Westinghouse Elec. Corp. v. Kerr-McGee Corp., [580 F.2d 1311 (7th Cir.), cert. denied, 439 U.S. 955 (1978)]. As in this case, it was not shown that the information had actually been used in the antitrust litigation. The work for the Institute had been done almost entirely by Kirkland & Ellis's Washington office, the antitrust litigation was being handled in the

Chicago office, and Kirkland & Ellis is a big firm. The connection between the representation of a trade association of which Kerr-McGee happened to be a member and the representation of its adversary thus was rather tenuous; one may doubt whether Kerr-McGee really thought its confidences had been abused by Kirkland & Ellis. If there is any aspect of the Kerr-McGee decision that is subject to criticism, it is this. The present case is a much stronger one for disqualification. If NPD did not retain Schwartz & Freeman — though we think it did — still it supplied Schwartz & Freeman with just the kind of confidential data that it would have furnished a lawyer that it had retained; and it had a right not to see Schwartz & Freeman reappear within months on the opposite side of a litigation to which that data might be highly pertinent.

We acknowledge the growing dissatisfaction, illustrated by Lindgren, Toward a New Standard of Attorney Disqualification, 1982 Am. Bar Foundation Research J. 419, with the use of disqualification as a remedy for unethical conduct by lawyers. The dissatisfaction is based partly on the effect of disqualification proceedings in delaying the underlying litigation and partly on a sense that current conflict of interest standards, in legal representation as in government employment, are too stringent, particularly as applied to large law firms — though there is no indication that Schwartz & Freeman is a large firm. But we cannot find any authority for withholding the remedy in a case like this, even if we assume contrary to fact that Schwartz & Freeman is as large as Kirkland & Ellis. NPD thought Schwartz & Freeman was its counsel and supplied it without reserve with the sort of data — data about profits and sales and marketing plans — that play a key role in a monopolization suit — and lo and behold, within months Schwartz & Freeman had been hired by a competitor of NPD's to try to get the Federal Trade Commission to sue NPD; and later that competitor, still represented by Schwartz & Freeman, brought its own suit against NPD. We doubt that anyone would argue that Schwartz & Freeman could resist disqualification if it were still representing NPD, even if no confidences were revealed, and we do not think that an interval of a few months ought to make a critical difference.

The "substantial relationship" test has its problems, but conducting a factual inquiry in every case into whether confidences had actually been revealed would not be a satisfactory alternative, particularly in a case such as this where the issue is not just whether they have been revealed but also whether they will be revealed during a pending litigation. Apart from the difficulty of taking evidence on the question without compromising the confidences themselves, the only witnesses would be the very lawyers whose firm was sought to be disqualified (unlike a case where the issue is what confidences a lawyer received while at a former law firm), and their interest not only in retaining a client but in denying a serious breach of professional ethics might outweigh any felt obligation to "come clean." While "appearance of impropriety" as a principle of professional ethics invites and maybe has undergone uncritical expansion because of its vague and open-ended character, in this case it has meaning and weight. For a law firm to represent one client today, and the client's adversary tomorrow in a closely related matter, creates an unsavory appearance of conflict of interest that is difficult to dispel in the eyes of the lay public — or for that matter the bench and bar — by filing of affidavits, difficult to verify objectively, denying that improper communication has taken place or will take place between the lawyers in the firm handling the two sides. Clients will not repose confidences in lawyers whom they distrust and will not trust firms that switch sides as nimbly as Schwartz & Freeman.

[The court affirmed the disqualification and the $25,000 payment. Judge Coffey dissented on the ground that the presumption of shared confidential information should not be irrebuttable.]

The "Substantial Relationship" Test

Did you catch Schwartz & Freeman's argument that NPD was never its client? We saw this tactic (unsuccessfully) employed in Simpson v. James (page 289) and will again in *Togstad* (page 707). Notice the court's two reasons for quickly disposing of this formal argument: Forcing NPD and Malec to hire separate counsel would have been inefficient (costly); and NPD gave the law firm confidential information to enable the firm to perform a legal service from which NPD would directly benefit. So for conflict purposes at least, there was a professional relationship. The first reason may be true, but economic prudence does not establish an attorney-client relationship, does it? The second reason is essential to the opinion.

The modern articulation of the substantial relationship test, preserved in Rule 1.9(a) of the Model Rules and Restatement §132, is generally credited to Judge Edward Weinfeld's opinion in T.C. Theatre Corp. v. Warner Bros. Pictures, Inc., 113 F. Supp. 265 (S.D.N.Y. 1953). Judge Weinfeld was considered among the best federal trial judges in the nation during his decades on the bench (1950-1988), He wrote:

> [W]here any substantial relationship can be shown between the subject matter of a former representation and that of a subsequent adverse representation, the latter will be prohibited. . . .
>
> [T]he former client need show no more than that the matters embraced within the pending suit wherein his former attorney appears on behalf of his adversary are substantially related to the matters or cause of action wherein the attorney previously represented him, the former client. The Court will assume that during the course of the former representation confidences were disclosed to the attorney bearing on the subject matter of the representation.

Despite Judge Weinfeld's deserved status as the father of the substantial relationship test in its present form, several courts have noted its roots in the law of fiduciary duty and agency. In re American Airlines, Inc., 972 F.2d 605 (5th Cir. 1992) (Higginbotham, J.); Maritrans GP Inc. v. Pepper, Hamilton & Scheetz, 602 A.2d 1277 (Pa. 1992).

The test aims to tell *when* a lawyer may not be adverse to a former client. The answer is not *never*. "Certainly, a client does not own a lawyer for all time. In appropriate circumstances our rules allow lawyers to take positions adverse to former clients and even to bring suit against them." Matter of Carey, 89 S.W.3d 477 (Mo. 2002). And that is pretty much the question: When are circumstances appropriate? In *Analytica,* Judge Posner wrote that the lawyer will be disqualified if the "subject matter of the two representations is 'substantially related,'" and then immediately stated this to mean: "if the lawyer *could* have obtained confidential information in the first representation that would have been relevant in the second." Emphasis added. That's the correct inquiry, isn't it? It's not the kind of legal advice the lawyer rendered in the two matters but the information she "could have obtained."

Why did Judge Posner write "could have obtained" and not "did obtain"? Why not ask whether it is really true, not merely whether it could be true, that a lawyer has relevant confidential information?

Asking whether the *two matters* are related *in substance* is a proxy (or substitute) for having the court actually inspect the information from the prior matter. Actual inspection by the court is rejected for three reasons. First, requiring the former client to reveal to the court the very information it wants to protect seems somehow inconsistent with the client's legitimate wish to keep the information confidential. (Notwithstanding, some courts have permitted former clients who wish to do so to submit information to the judge ex parte as a way of bolstering their claim of conflict. See Decora, Inc. v. DW Wallcovering, 901 F. Supp. 161 (S.D.N.Y. 1995).) Second, as we see below, while protection of confidential information is the dominant objective of the rule, the prohibition against subsequent adverse representation also protects a second interest, namely loyalty to the former client even when we can be sure that no information is threatened. Third, it would require impossible amounts of time for courts actually to inspect the files in prior representations. In short, we must have a proxy, because there is no other way to do it.

Asking if the first and second matters are the "same or substantially related" is the proxy. The word "same" presents no problem. A lawyer who switches from representing the plaintiff to the defendant in a litigation has changed sides in the *same* matter. So, too, a lawyer who switches sides at a negotiation. But that rarely happens. It would be so obvious. The real policy questions reside in the words "substantially related." When are two matters substantially related? Much is at stake here. The more broadly we define the term, the greater the scope of disqualification and interference with the subsequent client's choice of counsel. Remember, too, that the lawyer's conflict will be imputed to all of her office colleagues. Rule 1.10(a). So a lot rides on this from the point of view of law firms and client choice. But if we define the test to demand too close a connection between the prior and later matters, we risk undermining trust in the professional relationship. Clients will soon realize that lawyers may later appear opposed to them in matters that, to the clients at least, will look very much like side switching in (nearly) the same matter.

As if these facts alone do not make the policy choices difficult, we have to be cognizant of the risk of error. Because the test is a proxy, it can offer only an approximation of what is true, although we hope a very good one. Under any definition of the test, we will get some false negatives (i.e., where the test *mistakenly* reveals no threat to confidential information) and false positives (where the test *mistakenly* identifies a threat that does not exist).

The danger of false positives emphasizes another aspect of the test. The answer it yields is conclusive. The law firm can't say "but, judge, please, we can prove we don't know anything that would help us here if you would just give us the chance." Firms don't get the chance. If the former client can show that the new (adverse) matter is substantially related to the former matter (using language like the language in *Analytica* or some variation), the court will conclusively presume that the lawyer gained confidential information in the prior matter relevant to the new one and available to be used to injure the former client. (This presumption is tautological, isn't it? If the two matters are truly substantially *related*, then we would expect a lawyer to have information *relevant* to the second matter. That may explain why Judge Posner segued from the term "substantially related" to a definition that focused on a threat to confidences.)

With that background, the question remains: When should we say two matters are "substantially related"? In *Analytica*, the answer was pretty clear. From its prior tax work, Schwartz & Freeman would likely have received a great deal of financial information about NPD. An antitrust action also delves into a company's financial information. The two matters were therefore substantially related. The common denominator was the financial information. Disqualification protected NPD against the danger of adverse use of its confidences. End of story.

Could Schwartz & Freeman have argued that "even if we assume that we have financial information, we promise, promise, promise not to use it?" No, not even if it were a firm of 2,000 lawyers. For one thing, the promise is impossible to police as a practical matter. For another, we don't ask clients to accept such a promise on faith (unless they want to do so via consent).

How do you decide the problems at the start of this chapter, or the ones in part B, all of which require us to define the breadth of "substantial relationship" and to answer some other questions about the test?

Can "Playbook" Create a Substantial Relationship?

A lawyer formerly employed (or retained) by Company *X* represented it in (say) employment matters, but has since resigned (or all matters have concluded). Can she now accept a client who wishes to sue *X* on an employment matter, so long as she has never represented *X* in the particular dispute? The suit is certainly "adverse" to *X*, but is it "substantially related" to the matters in which the lawyer previously represented *X*? The facts will be different, won't they? Another way to put this question is: Can a matter be "substantially related" to *an area of law* in which the lawyer previously represented the client? Paragraph [2] of the comment to Rule 1.9 suggests that the lawyer may accept the new matter: "[A] lawyer who recurrently handled a type of problem for a former client is not precluded from later representing another client in a wholly distinct problem of that type even though the subsequent representation involves a position adverse to the prior client." On the other hand, the lawyer is benefited by knowing *X*'s strategy in employment cases. What's more, she has other deep background information — about *X*'s employment policies generally, its settlement positions, even how it organizes its files — which gives the lawyer a leg up in discovery. So maybe she should be disqualified. On the third [sic] hand, if the representation of *X* in a single Title VII case, or even several, can thereafter disable the lawyer from ever suing *X* in that area of law, isn't *X* well positioned to monopolize competent lawyers long after the professional relationship has ended? It might even make its retention decisions with that strategy partly in mind.

Courts have recognized that a lawyer may have a conflict based on significant familiarity with the operations and strategies of a former client even when the subsequent adverse matter involves different facts and is otherwise unrelated to matters the lawyer had handled for the former client. This is sometimes called "playbook" knowledge, and some cases have ruled that it can be enough to create a substantial relationship, depending on its scope. The cases are hard to reconcile, and there aren't all that many of them. But the issue is important because to the extent we recognize playbook as adequate to conflict a firm, we expand the potential reach of the substantial relationship test beyond *matter-specific* facts and thus sideline more firms. Which is not to say we shouldn't do it, only that we should be aware of what we're doing.

Sometimes the decision is painfully easy. Chrysler sued two really imprudent lawyers who, while working as associates at their former firm, "did a significant amount of work on several 'class action' lawsuits. After leaving the firm, the two attorneys formed their own firm and agreed to serve as plaintiff's counsel in a putative class action against Chrysler albeit involving an alleged defect different from the defects claimed to exist in the cases on which they had worked while at their former firm. Claiming that the conduct of the attorneys was not only unethical but also tortious, Chrysler filed the instant suit." The court, in denying the lawyers' summary judgment motion wrote that

> a reasonable juror could find or not find that defendants breached their duty of loyalty to Chrysler. The undisputed facts in this case show that Carey and Danis elected to prosecute a class action product liability lawsuit against Chrysler within a year after leaving a firm where they had performed significant work defending Chrysler in product liability class actions. Given their intimate familiarity with Chrysler's approach to vehicular defect class actions, a reasonable juror could find that it was a breach of loyalty for them to turn around and bring such a lawsuit against Chrysler.

Chrysler Corp. v. Carey, 5 F.Supp. 2d 1023 (E.D. Mo. 1998). This was obviously a compelling situation for the playbook theory. It is difficult — no, impossible — to defend the conduct of these lawyers. The court also struck the defendants' pleadings and defaulted them on the issue of liability as a sanction for their discovery abuse. An appeal of that decision lost. Chrysler Corp. v. Carey, 186 F.3d 1016 (8th Cir. 1999).

Other courts have also disqualified counsel based on possession of significant playbook information. Frazoni v. Hart Schaffner Marx, 726 N.E.2d 719 (Ill. App. 2000) ("Stein's involvement in defending hundreds of discrimination claims against HC and its subsidiaries and in setting the company's human resources policies is sufficient to compel disqualification here"). See also Webb v. E.I. DuPont de Nemours & Co., Inc., 811 F. Supp. 158 (D.Del. 1992) (lawyer disqualified from bringing suit for ERISA benefits where he was responsible for ERISA matters for three years prior to retirement from defendant); Ullrich v. Hearst Corp., 809 F. Supp. 229 (S.D.N.Y. 1992) (disqualification of plaintiff's lawyer in employment discrimination case where lawyer had represented defendant in employment discrimination matters for 20 years). ABA Opinion 99-415 discusses the circumstances under which a former in-house lawyer for an organization may be disqualified from adverse representation.

These cases are easy to defend because the lawyers' involvement with the former client was prolonged and intimate in the very area of the later adverse matter. But how far should the concept go? A lawyer can learn an awful lot about a client's playbook and internal operations from a single matter. Will that exclude the lawyer and her firm from later opposing the lawyer in a distinct matter of the same type?

The Loyalty Duty to Former Clients
(*or* It's Not Only About Confidences)

Analytica used the substantial relationship test as a proxy for determining whether confidences from a prior matter would be relevant in a later matter. A proxy is used so that the former client need not reveal the very confidences it wishes to protect and because the court doesn't have time or resources to delve any deeper. But confidentiality is not the only goal of successive conflict rules. Though much less prominent, another value the rule protects is loyalty to a former client as a way to encourage clients to repose trust in their lawyers during the professional relationship. The rule forbids lawyers to switch sides and oppose a client even if no confidential information is at risk. Trone v. Smith, 621 F.2d 994 (9th Cir. 1980), which early on identified this interest, held:

> Both the lawyer and the client should expect that the lawyer will use every skill, expend every energy, and tap every legitimate resource in the exercise of independent professional judgment on behalf of the client and in undertaking representation on the client's behalf. That professional commitment is not furthered, but endangered, if the possibility exists that the lawyer will change sides later in a substantially related matter. Both the fact and the appearance of total professional commitment are endangered by adverse representation in related cases. From this standpoint it matters not whether confidences were in fact imparted to the lawyer by the client. The substantial relationship between the two representations is itself sufficient to disqualify.

The notion that loyalty to a former client survives the termination of the relationship is carried over in Model Rule 1.9 and its comment. Notice that the text of Rule 1.9 does not depend on the existence of confidential information. The word "confidential" or variants of it do not appear in the text of the rule. Even if no such information is at risk, a subsequent adverse representation on a substantially related matter is forbidden. Sullivan County Regional Refuse Disposal District v. Town of Acworth, 686 A.2d 755 (N.H. 1996) ("even in the absence of any confidences, an attorney owes a duty of loyalty to a former client that prevents that attorney from attacking, or interpreting, work she performed, or supervised, for the former client"). See also the oft-cited decision in Brennan's, Inc. v. Brennan's Restaurants, Inc., 590 F.2d 168 (5th Cir. 1979), discussed in chapter 2B.

To make this clear, let's play a little mind game. It's a mind game because it would never happen. (I hope.) AB gets a $10 million judgment against XY. XY then hires famed lawyer Daniel Webster Darrow to appeal to the state's intermediate appellate court. It says, "Darrow, all we want you to do is argue that the statute under which AB got its judgment violates the state constitution. Pure question of law. All you need to know in order to do that is the trial record, a public document. You don't need anything from us. Just win." Darrow wins and charges a bundle. Darrow never got confidential information. Can AB now hire Darrow to represent *it* in a further appeal to the state's highest court in an effort to reinstate the judgment? No. Why not? Because it would be disloyal to XY, which paid Darrow to achieve one specific objective: reverse the judgment. Darrow cannot take money from AB to undo precisely what XY paid him to do. (Nor would he, of course.) Confidential information doesn't enter the equation.

Loyalty to former clients arises in a more complicated way, too. Assume attorney Blue jointly represents clients Brown and Grey in connection with a business deal between them and others. After a falling out, Brown hires Blue to sue Grey. When Grey protests, Brown and Blue respond that Grey could have had no expectation that information she gave Blue would be secret from Brown. They cite the exception to the attorney-client privilege for joint representations. See page 283. Maybe they point out that the three had agreed that Blue would share all confidential information with both of them. Should this argument defeat Grey's effort to disqualify Blue? Or can Grey argue that it's not about confidences? Rather, she claims, a loyalty obligation independently forbids her former lawyer to turn on her in the area of representation. Courts have held that the duty of loyalty is sufficient all by itself to prohibit the second (adverse) representation, even with no confidential information at risk. Attorney Grievance Comm'n of Maryland v. Siskind, 930 A.2d 328 (Md. 2007) ("We are of the opinion that when Respondent filed a suit sounding in contract against a former client, an entity he created, over a business transaction he helped construct by creating the relevant documents now central to the contract suit, he effectively changed sides") (citing *Brennan's*).

Despite the prevalence of this view, two prominent older cases have been read, possibly overread, to go the other way. They are Allegaert v. Perot, 565 F.2d 246 (2d Cir. 1977) (construing New York Code), and Christensen v. United States District Court, 844 F.2d 694 (9th Cir. 1988). However, in both cases unusual facts should have alerted the former client to anticipate that the lawyer would side with the other client in the event of a dispute. The Restatement, citing *Allegaert,* introduces the idea of an "accommodation" client — one who, under the circumstances, would have "understood and impliedly consented to the lawyer's continuing to represent the regular client in the matter." Restatement §132 comment *i.* See In re Rite Aid Corp. Securities Litig., 139 F. Supp. 2d 649 (E.D. Pa. 2001) (relying on Restatement's concept of accommodation client to reject disqualification). But see Universal City Studios, Inc. v. Reimerdes, 98 F. Supp. 2d 449 (S.D.N.Y. 2000) (rejecting the concept on the facts before the court).

Allegaert and *Christensen* should be read narrowly for a second (perhaps dispositive) reason. *Allegaert,* which arose under the old Code, specifically declined to analyze whether the lawyer's duty of loyalty prevented the subsequent adverse representation because this argument was not made. Similarly, *Christensen* was based solely on the confidentiality provisions of the California Rules, not loyalty duties. The California Rules have since been rewritten and the loyalty and confidentiality provisions combined. In re Jaeger, 213 B.R. 578 (C.D. Cal. 1997).

Other courts that have rejected a broad reading of these cases, although not necessarily by name, include In re American Airlines, Inc., 972 F.2d 605 (5th Cir. 1992) (applying "federal" ethics standards); Western Continental Operating Co. v. Natural Gas Corp., 261 Cal. Rptr. 100 (Ct. App. 1989); and Casco Northern

Bank v. JBI Associates, Ltd., 667 A.2d 856 (Me. 1995) ("*Allegaert* rule . . . has been strongly criticized in several jurisdictions and we decline to adopt it"). Even lower courts within the Second Circuit have distinguished *Allegaert* or read it narrowly. Prisco v. Westgate Entertainment, Inc., 799 F. Supp. 266 (D. Conn. 1992) (pointing out that Connecticut's Rule 1.9 is broader than the New York Code provision construed in *Allegaert*); Universal City Studios, Inc. v. Reimerdes, supra. The court in *Western Continental* wrote:

> In the first instance, we are not concerned in this case with discovery of allegedly privileged communications. Instead, the pertinent issue is the propriety of an attorney's representation adverse to a former client. Our courts have distinguished the rule against representing conflicting interests from the attorney-client evidentiary privilege noting that the former is broader than the latter. "The evidentiary privilege and the ethical duty not to disclose confidences both arise from the need to encourage clients to disclose all possibly pertinent information to their attorneys, and both protect only the confidential information disclosed. The duty not to represent conflicting interests . . . is an outgrowth of the attorney-client relationship itself, which is confidential, or fiduciary, in a broader sense. Not only do clients at times disclose confidential information to their attorneys; they also repose confidence in them. The privilege is bottomed only on the first of these attributes, the conflicting-interests rule, on both."

The Consequences of Disqualification

Analytica and Rule 1.10(a) impute a lawyer's former-client conflict to all other lawyers in his office. (Rule 1.18 allows for an exception in the case of potential clients.) Mr. Fine's disqualification in *Analytica* was imputed to his entire firm. It is not knowledge as such, but the conflicted status, that the rule conclusively imputes.

When a lawyer or firm is disqualified, the client will have to hire new counsel, who will want to receive the disqualified firm's files. The opposing party might object on the ground that this gives the new firm the benefit of the suspect work. Nevertheless, absent an identifiably tainted item, the courts have been disposed to allow turnover to successor counsel. First Wis. Mortgage Trust v. First Wis. Corp., 584 F.2d 201 (7th Cir. 1978) (en banc); IBM v. Levin, 579 F.2d 271 (3d Cir. 1978). The Texas Supreme Court has created a "rebuttable presumption that the work product contains confidential information. . . . The current client can rebut the presumption by demonstrating that there is not a substantial likelihood that the desired items of work product contain or reflect confidential information." If the trial judge cannot determine from an inventory of the contents of the file whether an item is tainted, she may "consider conducting an in camera inspection." In re George, 28 S.W.3d 511 (Tex. 2000). In Fund of Funds, Ltd. v. Arthur Andersen & Co., 567 F.2d 225 (2d Cir. 1977), the court declined to follow disqualification with dismissal of the complaint or suppression of facts or documents. Ackerman v. National Property Analysts, Inc., 887 F. Supp. 510 (S.D.N.Y. 1993), dismissed an action without prejudice where the disqualified plaintiffs' lawyer, who formerly represented the defendants, had used the defendants' confidences to bring the action.

Malpractice Based on Successive Conflicts

A law firm that acts adversely to a former client in violation of the substantial relationship test will subject itself to liability for breach of fiduciary duty. At the very least, the conduct will violate the lawyer's continuing duty of loyalty, Sargent v. Buckley, 697 A.2d 1272 (Me. 1997), and, to the extent that the lawyer has revealed or used the former client's confidential information, the conduct will also violate her obligation to protect this information. Id. Of course, in a civil action, the client will have to prove damages. Damron v. Herzog, 67 F.3d 211 (9th Cir. 1995); Griffith v. Taylor, 937 P.2d 297 (Alaska 1997). A law firm was sued for substantial damages in Spur Products Corp. v. Stoel Rives LLP, 122 P.3d 300 (Idaho 2005). The plaintiff, a former client, alleged that the firm had revealed its confidential information to one of the firm's own lawyers. By agreement, that lawyer was supposed to have been screened from the plaintiff's case because he had formerly represented its opponent on a substantially related matter. The complaint also alleged that the law firm never informed the client of the breach of confidentiality. The trial court granted summary judgment for the firm after declining to allow the plaintiff to amend the complaint. Reversing, the state supreme court ruled that plaintiff's amended complaint, which alleged that the firm's breach had caused it to lose the chance to arbitrate the underlying dispute, stated a malpractice claim.

Who is a Former Client?

We encountered the client identity issue in the prior chapter. It is a question that often arises in the conflicts world because without a client there cannot be a conflict. In the area of successive conflicts, the issue is more complex, because not only must we ask whether a person or entity was a *client* for conflict purposes (the subject of this discussion), but if so, whether the client is a *former* or still current (the subject of the next discussion). Ponder the following variations:

1. In *Analytica*, the company that provided the information was either the client of the firm or treated as a client because it had provided "just the kind of confidential data that it would have furnished a lawyer that it had retained."
2. In the *Westinghouse* case, cited in *Analytica*, Kerr-McGee was not a formal client of Kirkland & Ellis, but it had given the firm relevant confidential information so that the firm could perform certain work for a trade association of which Kerr-McGee was a member. (See also *Glueck* at page 297.)
3. In Trinity Ambulance Service, Inc. v. G. & L. Ambulance Services, Inc., 578 F. Supp. 1280 (D. Conn. 1984), one of two plaintiffs in an antitrust action realigned as a defendant. While a plaintiff, however, its counsel had participated in joint strategy sessions with the other plaintiff and its counsel. The court disqualified the attorney for the realigned defendant after concluding that before the realignment the remaining plaintiff had divulged confidences in the belief that it was "approaching the attorney in a professional capacity with the intent to secure legal advice." See also Nemours Found. v. Gilbane, Aetna, Fed. Ins. Co., 632 F. Supp. 418 (D. Del. 1986).

4. A corporate attorney secured a patent. The inventor was a corporate employee. The patent was issued in the name of the corporation, which then assigned it to Medtronic. The attorney later represented a third party in an effort to invalidate the patent. Medtronic and the inventor moved for disqualification. The court rejected the motion. The lawyer had no professional relationship with the inventor, but only with his employer. Further, assignment of the patent did not mean that the lawyer's responsibilities to the assignor were now owed to the assignee. Telectronics Proprietary, Ltd. v. Medtronic, Inc., 836 F.2d 1332 (Fed. Cir. 1988). For a similar case, see Quaker Oats Co. v. Uni-Pak Film Systems, Inc., 683 F. Supp. 1186 (N.D. Ill. 1987).

5. First Boston retained Fried, Frank to assist it after Dart hired First Boston to advise Dart regarding a financial acquisition. Dart agreed to pay Fried, Frank's bills. Dart also had its own legal counsel at the time. Fried, Frank received permission from Dart's counsel to communicate directly with Dart. Thereafter, Fried, Frank represented a plaintiff in a factually related action against Dart. Dart moved to disqualify the firm. Among other things, the court had to decide whether Fried, Frank had had a client-lawyer relationship with Dart. It held that there was a relationship on three grounds: There was a traditional professional relationship by implication arising out of the fact that Dart provided information and Fried, Frank did legal work based on it; First Boston as Dart's agent had created a client-lawyer relationship between Dart and Fried, Frank; and, using the *Westinghouse* standard, Dart consulted with Fried, Frank on the assumption that the firm would exercise "the same professional judgment and . . . display the same loyalty as [its] own attorneys." Jack Eckerd Corp. v. Dart Group Corp., 621 F. Supp. 725 (D. Del. 1985).

6. A preliminary interview can create an attorney-client relationship. A professional relationship was established when someone wrote to a lawyer requesting an appointment and then had two or three telephone conversations with the lawyer in which legal issues were discussed. The lawyer was never retained, and the two never met. Bays v. Theran, 639 N.E.2d 720 (Mass. 1994). ABA Opinion 90-358 concludes that a firm can avoid a disqualifying conflict despite a preliminary interview if it limits receipt of information, seeks a waiver of confidentiality, or (if a local rule permits) screens the lawyer who conducted the interview. The Ethics 2000 Commission proposed and the ABA adopted just such a rule — Rule 1.18 — which allows a firm to avoid imputation arising from a preliminary interview that does not lead to retention by screening the firm lawyer who conducted the interview. Screening is addressed later in this chapter.

Like a Hot Potato

A client who wishes to disqualify a lawyer would prefer to be a current client, while the lawyer would prefer to say that the client is a former client if ever a client at all. You know why, right?

Imagine this situation. Smith Knight, a law firm, represents Corkskroo Ltd. on one small matter that will come to completion in the next six months. One day

Smith Knight receives a visit from Marie Shelton. Shelton has a claim against Cork-skroo for $50 million and wants the firm to take it. Assume Shelton's claim is factually unrelated to the matter the firm currently handles for Corkskroo. If Shelton had come in six months later, the representation of Corkskroo would have ended, and the firm could have accepted the factually unrelated claim. (P.S.: That's why it's better for the firm if the client is former, not current.) But Shelton wants to file her claim now. She doesn't want to wait. Maybe the limitations period will run.

Smith Knight may not accept Shelton's case and sue Corkskroo, while continuing to represent Corkskroo on unrelated matters, may it? How nice if Corkskroo could be made to just disappear (zap!) a little ahead of time. So Smith Knight "fires" Corkskroo (by withdrawing), returns all files, waits a week, and then accepts Shelton's retainer. Corkskroo moves to disqualify the firm, which defends by arguing that Corkskroo, as a (now) *former* client, can only disqualify it on a substantially related adverse matter, which Shelton's claim is not. Further, the firm argues, Corkskroo suffered not one penny's worth of injury. The matter was simple and a new firm (which Smith Knight offered to assist, free of charge no less) was able to get up to speed in two seconds flat.

Stop here.

What should Corkskroo argue? Assuming that Corkskroo has not suffered even a penny's worthy of injury, what interest might Corkskroo have (if any) that the court should be asked to protect and how should it do so?

Or shall we say that the court should balance the interests of Corkskroo against those of the law firm to accept a new case and of Marie Shelton to counsel of choice?

In Unified Sewerage Agency v. Jelco, Inc., 646 F.2d 1339 (9th Cir. 1981), Judge Alfred Goodwin wrote in a footnote that law firms could not escape the stricter current-client conflict rules simply by withdrawing from a representation and converting a current client into a former one. Why not? If the second matter is truly unrelated, who is hurt? Certainly the "former" client (unlike Corkskroo) may encounter some additional expense in bringing new counsel up to speed, but assume the former firm is prepared to absorb that expense.

The *Jelco* footnote honors a client's interest in uninterrupted representation to the conclusion of a matter. While a law firm may withdraw from a current representation, it may do so only for the reasons listed in Rule 1.16. The law firm's own economic interests have generally not been deemed an acceptable reason for dropping the client (despite some ambiguity in Rule 1.16(b)(1) and (b)(6)). This ruling does not balance at all. Corkskroo's interest in continuity is supreme.

The *Jelco* footnote acquired a trite but lasting metaphor in Picker International, Inc. v. Varian Associates, Inc., 670 F. Supp. 1363 (N.D. Ohio 1987), aff'd, 869 F.2d 578 (Fed. Cir. 1989). There, the district judge determined that Jones Day (Get it? Smith Knight? Jones Day?) had dropped one client "like a hot potato" in order to be free to continue with the representation of another client. (Okay, it's a simile, not a metaphor.) Was this characterization fair? The facts in *Picker* are a little more complicated than those in the Smith Knight hypothetical. Jones Day, which had been Picker's law firm since 1911, was representing Picker in an action against Varian in Ohio federal court. It came to pass that Jones Day, which is huge, had an opportunity to acquire MH&S, a boutique patent law firm in Chicago. Unfortunately, MH&S was then representing Varian on patent matters unrelated to Picker v. Varian. If the acquisition came off, Jones Day would find itself litigating against a current client, which is forbidden without consent. MH&S asked Varian to consent, explaining that the *Picker* litigation was factually unrelated to the patent matters, so there was no threat to Varian's confidences. And MH&S offered to screen the Chicago lawyers working on Varian's patent matters from the Jones Day lawyers in Cleveland working on the *Picker* litigation. Varian refused to consent, but Jones Day acquired MH&S anyway. A few days before it did, MH&S purported to withdraw as Varian's counsel.

Varian moved to disqualify Jones Day in the *Picker* litigation. Citing the *Jelco* footnote, Varian claimed protection as a current client despite MH&S's purported withdrawal. Judge Ann Aldrich agreed: "A firm may not drop a client like a hot potato, especially if it is in order to keep happy a far more lucrative client." MH&S's effort to "fire" Varian was rejected, Varian was deemed a current client of Jones Day (in its post-acquisition incarnation), and the rule prohibiting suits against current clients applied.

Should Jones Day's interest in acquiring MH&S (and MH&S's interest in being acquired) have been given more respect than the interest of the imaginary Smith Knight in dropping one client to sue it on behalf of another client? In this different setting, should the court have balanced the reasonableness of Varian's refusal to consent? After all, clients do behave strategically. It's not hard to imagine lawyers for a client in Varian's position advising Varian to refuse to consent not because the client is at any risk, or even because it really cares, but because refusal may create leverage for a favorable settlement. In thinking about these questions, consider the following variations on the "hot potato" problem and try to reconcile the holdings (it can be done, honest).

1. A law firm represents client *A* and client *B* on unrelated matters. Long-time client *A* then asks the firm to appear adverse to (more recent) client *B* on a matter unrelated to the representation of *B*. The firm seeks to withdraw from *B* so that it can represent *A*. May it? No. See Stratagem Dev. Corp. v. Heron Intl. N.V., 756 F. Supp. 789 (S.D.N.Y. 1991); Truck Ins. Exch. v. Fireman's Fund Ins. Co., 8 Cal. Rptr. 2d 228 (Ct. App. 1992). This is like the Smith Knight hypothetical except that the new adverse matter is for a current, not a new, client. Still, no.

2. A law firm represents *D* in litigation against its insurer to determine the insurer's liability to *D*. The law firm also represents another insurance company, FIGA, in unrelated matters. When *D*'s insurer fails, FIGA becomes the successor in interest to the failed insurer by operation of state law. The law firm now wants to withdraw from representing FIGA so that it may continue to represent *D* against FIGA. May it? Yes, if it acts "immediately." See Florida Ins. Guar. Assn. v. Carey Canada, Inc., 749 F. Supp. 255 (S.D. Fla. 1990).

3. A firm represents *P* against *D* when either (a) *D* acquires *T*, another client of the law firm, or (b) *T* acquires *D*. The firm wants to continue to represent *P*. May the firm withdraw from representing *T*? Yes. See Gould, Inc. v. Mitsui Mining & Smelting Co., 738 F. Supp. 1121 (N.D. Ohio 1990); Pennwalt Corp. v. Plough, Inc., 85 F.R.D. 264 (D. Del. 1980). Here, as in the prior paragraph, the conflict arose because of what others, not the law firm, did. Still, the firm is in a conflict situation. It has to get consent or get out of one of the representations. Should the firm be allowed to withdraw from

representing *P* instead of *T* on these facts? In Installation Software Technologies, Inc. v. Wise Solutions, Inc., 2004 Westlaw 524829 (N.D. Ill. 2004), Baker & McKenzie was representing the plaintiff when Altiris, another client on an unrelated matter, acquired defendant Wise. The plaintiff but not Altiris was willing to consent to the conflict. Baker asked the court to let it withdraw from representing the plaintiff or "other relief that [the] court deems appropriate." Whether Baker really wanted to withdraw is unclear. Perhaps the motion was a clever way for the firm to surface its dilemma and get a judicial ruling that would insulate it from liability when it withdrew from one client or the other. If so, it worked. After "balancing all of the equitable factors," including the plaintiff's investment in and reliance on Baker, the court sensibly refused to let Baker withdraw from representing the plaintiff. If "Altiris remains steadfast in its decision not to consent to the concurrent conflict of interest by written waiver, Baker will need to take the appropriate measures to cure the conflict, which will mean withdrawal of its representation of Altiris."

4. A law firm represents client One episodically for 13 years, but has had no matter with client One for over a year when client Two asks to retain the firm to sue client One. May it? Is client One a current or former client? Current. Oxford Systems, Inc. v. CellPro, Inc., 45 F. Supp. 2d 1055 (W.D. Wash. 1999). See also the cases (page 105) finding an attorney-client relationship during lulls in intermittent representations.

The situations described in paragraphs 2 and 3 have acquired a name, nearly as sonorous as *hot potato*. They are called "thrust upon conflicts." The conflicts in those situations are not the fault of the law firm. The firm did not fail in its policing duty. Rather, the conflicts arose because of client mergers or acquisitions (paragraph 3) or through operation of law (paragraph 2). The conflict was therefore "thrust upon" a well-behaving and conscientious firm . . . If the firm then has to drop one of its clients to escape the conflict, whether "like a hot potato" or some other well cooked vegetable, it is only doing what the rules require and should not be penalized. And so is born the "thrust upon" exception to the "hot potato" rule. Let's hope that's the end of the tired tropes.

Do you see how a prospective litigant can exploit the "hot potato" rule to conflict good law firms? Is there anything a law firm can do to protect itself and the other clients who may depend upon it? How about an advance consent from an incoming client that it will either agree to the conflict or let the firm withdraw, and not invoke the "hot potato" rule, in the event of adversity with a longstanding firm client? ABA Opinion 93-372 concludes that appropriately detailed advance consents can be proper. Courts can be skeptical. Celgene Corp. v. KV Pharmaceutical Co., 2008 Westlaw 2937415 (D.N.J. 2008), is an arguably indefensible rejection of a sophisticated client's detailed and counseled advance consent because law firm did not identify the disadvantages of and alternatives to giving it. See also page 295 for more balanced opinions.

In *Picker*, Jones Day was disqualified from representing Picker, not Varian. Assuming the conflict could not continue, who should choose which client remains? In Estates Theatres, Inc. v. Columbia Pictures Industries, 345 F. Supp. 93 (S.D.N.Y. 1972), Judge Weinfeld said it was the court, not the law firm. On appeal in *Picker*, the Federal Circuit agreed: "To allow the merged firm to pick and choose which clients will survive the merger would violate the duty of undivided loyalty that the firms owe each of their clients under DR 5-105." The court then affirmed the trial court's determination that Picker, not Varian, should lose its counsel. Jones Day could have anticipated the conflict months before the merger. Had it "withdrawn [from Picker] when it knew that the conflict was unavoidable," the district judge wrote, "new counsel could, by now, have become well acquainted with the case." But that was also true for MH&S and Varian. Why should Picker lose its counsel?

Both the district and circuit courts in *Picker* recognized that disqualification of either party's counsel would injure that party "through no fault of its own." Why then didn't the court undo Jones Day's acquisition of MH&S instead? That would have imposed the penalty on the two law firms, which both courts concluded *were* at fault. (Did Jones Day have a conflict in opposing the disqualification motion because it had no interest in arguing for that remedy?) Alternatively, will Picker now have a malpractice action against Jones Day for entering into a merger that forced it to lose its lawyers "through no fault of its own?"

In Kinzenbaw v. Case, LLC, 2004 Westlaw 1146462 (N.D. Iowa 2004), Perkins Coie found itself in a position much like Jones Day's, with one difference. Although Perkins's merger with another firm created a current client conflict — it found itself representing the plaintiffs as a result of the merger, but it was also representing Case, the defendant, on unrelated matters — the firm did not identify the problem for 17 months because of a recordkeeping snafu. It then withdrew from representing Case. The court held that Perkins violated the conflict rules but "[a]fter balancing all of the interests involved," the court rejected disqualification because it would "create an enormous burden on [plaintiffs], a completely innocent third party." Trial was only four months away. Was that the right balance? Perkins had been representing Case from 1996 to 2004. The merger that made Perkins counsel for plaintiffs against Case occurred in late 2002. Who will make Case whole?

For a *Jelco* variation, where a law firm removed a conflict by "firing" a lawyer, not a client, see page 339.

Standing and Waiver

As we saw, concurrent conflicts may sometimes be waived (page 293). Successive conflicts may always be waived. Rule 1.9(a). Why the difference? Given this distinction, should nonclients ever have standing to seek disqualification in successive conflict situations? Some courts have said yes because of the court's interest in ethical conduct. See Tessier v. Plastic Surgery Specialists, Inc., 731 F. Supp. 724 (E.D. Va. 1990) (collecting cases). Others have said no because the rule is meant to protect the former client, not a stranger. In re Yarn Processing Patent Validity Litig., 530 F.2d 83 (5th Cir. 1976). See also *Infotechnology* at page 279.

The Appearance of Impropriety

Neither the Canons of Professional Ethics nor the Code of Professional Responsibility contained a direct equivalent to Rule 1.9(a). Courts fashioned one, relying on the duty of loyalty, the duty of confidentiality, and, under Canon 9 of the Code, the direction to "avoid even the appearance of professional impropriety." Pretty soon the appearance-of-impropriety standard became over-used and the object of criticism, not least of all because of its unpredictability. In re Ainsworth, 614 P.2d 1127 (Or. 1980), held that appearance could not be an independent basis for discipline. The Second Circuit in Board of Education v. Nyquist, 590 F.2d 1241 (2d Cir. 1979), deemed it "too slender a reed" on which to base disqualification. The Eighth Circuit called it an "eye of the beholder" test. Fred Weber, Inc. v. Shell Oil Co., 566 F.2d 602 (8th Cir. 1977), overruled on jurisdictional grounds, 612 F.2d 377 (8th Cir. 1980). The Restatement and the Model Rules do not employ it. Courts continue to bury it. Arkansas Valley State Bank v. Phillips, 171 P.3d 899 (Okla. 2007) (rejecting the "appearance" test and also rejecting rule under which "any doubt about the appearance of the pro-priety of an attorney's actions must be resolved in favor of disqualification").

Judicial resort to the "appearance of impropriety" test bespoke the Code's inadequacy as a document on which to build a mature jurisprudence of legal ethics. The greater (if not entirely sufficient) specificity of the Model Rules permits a level of analysis that the Code did not. In fact, one could say that the growth of legal ethics as a discipline within which it is possible to "do" law is a product of the profession's greater effort first to identify underlying policies and values, without resort to nebulous phrases like "appearance of impropriety," and then to articulate rules that capture those goals and values in language as clear as the enterprise permits.

One *could* say that — in fact, I just did say it, and I'd say it again if asked — but one must then quickly caution against dismissing the "appearance" test altogether. First, tens of thousands of (now aging) lawyers and judges have grown up with "appearance of impropriety" etched in their consciousness. (Some lawyers actually call it the "smell test" (yuck) as in, "It doesn't pass the smell test." How's that for critical thinking?) Second, some courts, as in Rosman v. Shapiro, 653 F. Supp. 1441 (S.D.N.Y. 1987), may for a time continue to rely on the "appearance of impropriety" in disqualifying a lawyer. Third, even states that have adopted the Model Rules may continue to look to appearances. In First American Carriers, Inc. v. Kroger Co., 787 S.W.2d 669 (Ark. 1990), the court wrote: "The fact that [the test] is not in the Model Rules does not mean that lawyers no longer have to avoid the appearance of impropriety." The North Dakota Supreme Court agrees. "Although the new Rules do not use the language, the 'appearance of impropriety' standard has not been wholly abandoned in spirit." Heringer v. Haskell, 536 N.W.2d 362 (N.D. 1995). In spirit? How exactly does a lawyer make professional decisions or advise a client based on spirit?

Anyway, it is worth remembering that appearances may still count, depending on where you are. But, that said, as older generations of lawyers and judges retire to their golf carts and elder hostels, replaced by others who have come of age with the appearance-free Model Rules and casebooks whose authors are as dismissive as I am about the value of an appearance test to evaluate a private lawyer's conduct, we may soon see the concept fade away in most U.S. jurisdictions.

But not for everyone. The "appearance of impropriety" standard will con-tinue to have a role in evaluating the conduct of public officials — government lawyers and judges — because the public's perception of the fair administration of justice is almost as important (some would say as important) as its reality.

Conflicts in Class Actions

The application of traditional successive disqualification doctrine to class actions can work great hardship, sometimes for little gain. (Application of conflict rules to current class clients is discussed at page 287.) The Second Circuit had to confront this problem in In re "Agent Orange" Product Liability Litigation, 800 F.2d 14 (2d Cir. 1986), after class counsel switched from representing class members supporting a settlement to those opposing it. See also Bash v. Firstmark Standard Life Ins. Co., 861 F.2d 159 (7th Cir. 1988); Lazy Oil Co. v. Witco Corp., 166 F.3d 581 (3d Cir. 1999). Rejecting disqualification in *Agent Orange,* Judge Kearse wrote:

> Class action litigation presents additional problems that must be considered in determining whether or not to disqualify an attorney who has represented the class and who seeks to represent thereafter only a portion of the class. See generally [In re Corn Derivatives Antitrust Litig., 748 F.2d 157, 162-165 (3d Cir. 1984)] (Adams, J., concurring). These problems are created by, inter alia, the facts that there are, by definition, numerous class members and that there is often no clear allocation of the decision-making responsibility between the attorney and his clients. Further, though there will be common questions affecting the claims of the class members, it is not unusual for their interests, especially at the relief stage, to diverge. Such a divergence presents special problems because the class attorney's duty does not run just to the plaintiffs named in the caption of the case; it runs to all of the members of the class. . . .
>
> Automatic application of the traditional principles governing disqualification of attorneys on grounds of conflict of interest would seemingly dictate that whenever a rift arises in the class, with one branch favoring a settlement or a course of action that another branch resists, the attorney who has represented the class should withdraw entirely and take no position. Were he to take a position, either favoring or opposing the proposed course of action, he would be opposing the interests of some of his former clients in the very matter in which he has represented them.
>
> Nonetheless, as Judge Adams noted in his concurring opinion in *Corn Derivatives,* although automatic disqualification might "promote the salutary ends of confidentiality and loyalty, it would have a serious adverse effect on class actions." When many individuals have modest claims against a single entity or group of entities, the class action may be the only practical means of vindicating their rights, since otherwise the expenses of litigation could exceed the value of the claim. In such class actions, often only the attorneys who have represented the class, rather than any of the class members themselves, have substantial familiarity with the prior proceedings, the fruits of discovery, the actual potential of the litigation. And when an action has continued over the course of many years, the prospect of having those most familiar with its course and status be automatically disqualified whenever class members have conflicting interests would substantially diminish the efficacy of class actions as a method of dispute resolution. This is so both because the quality of the information available to the court would likely be impaired and because even if a class member were familiar with all the prior proceedings, the amount of his stake in the litigation might well make it unattractive for him to participate actively, either on his own or through new counsel. . . .
>
> Thus, we conclude that the traditional rules that have been developed in the course of attorneys' representation of the interests of clients outside of the

class action context should not be mechanically applied to the problems that arise in the settlement of class action litigation. . . .

B. IMPUTED DISQUALIFICATION AND MIGRATORY LAWYERS

"You Don't Know Anything" ⊁

Sherry Lakoff was an associate at Penbauer Rich, Ivanhoe, & Mora (PRIM) for three years and eight months following law school. PRIM, based in Chicago, represented AxiMartin Carburetor (which made other auto parts too) as outside counsel on transactional and litigation matters, sometimes working with Axi-Martin's three inside lawyers. Lakoff worked on the litigation side, and she helped the partners defend AxiMartin in a mix of matters, including breach of contract, breach of warranty, and tort cases. Occasionally, AxiMartin got involved in employment issues, including union issues, and ERISA, labor law, OSHA, and overtime claims. Lakoff worked on some of these. AxiMartin was twice sued for age discrimination while Lakoff was at PRIM, and she worked on both suits, which settled. After leaving PRIM, Lakoff went to another Chicago firm, Cross, Cudlup & Charles. CCC, as it was known, styled itself a "litigation boutique," which so far as Lakoff could tell, only meant that it was small (nine lawyers counting Lakoff), and that is exactly why she chose it.

Two years after Lakoff went to CCC, she was asked to assist Cudlup on a sex discrimination case against AxiMartin to be filed in federal court in the Northern District of Illinois. This was a new case. Ariana Stile, the plaintiff, joined AxiMartin *after* Lakoff left PRIM. Stile claimed that AxiMartin constructively discharged her because the other mechanical engineers, all men, were complaining about working with a woman and because she objected to what she considered sexist comments and conduct.

"Can I do this?" Lakoff asked Cudlup. "I mean I used to work at PRIM defending AxiMartin, including in two age discrimination cases. PRIM will probably defend this one, too."

"You didn't work on this case," Cudlup said. "You never worked on a sex discrimination case. What do you know about it or the company's defenses? You don't know anything. No rule says you can never sue a former client. Also, we've been told that PRIM won't even be representing the defendant here."

May Lakoff work on Stile v. AxiMartin? If not, or if it is unclear, can CCC take the case and avoid disqualification by excluding Lakoff from having anything to do with it?

"Can We Hire Taylor Monk?" ⊬

Kane, Grossman & Russo (KGR) handles the products liability defense work for Admiral Industries, a nationwide manufacturer of consumer products. The firm has 800 lawyers, about two-thirds of them associates. Admiral is the defendant in some forty lawsuits nationwide, brought by consumers who have alleged that they suffered injuries as a result of malfunctions in various Admiral products. Taylor Monk graduated from UCLA Law School in 2006, passed the New York bar, and has since been working as an associate at Horton, Israel & Pinto (HIP), a plaintiff's firm in Buffalo, New York, where her partner, a physician, was doing an ophthalmology residency. She is now about to join the faculty at Weill Cornell Medical School in Manhattan, where KGR has an office. Monk writes to the firm about employment.

Before Monk is hired, KGR's conflicts committee does a check, as it does for all lateral hires. It discovers that KGR is currently handling one case against HIP: Crickett v. Admiral, pending in federal court in Buffalo based on diversity jurisdiction. The Cricketts seek damages for an injury to their son Jimmy, from the use of an Admiral toaster oven. When asked, Monk tells KGR that her only work on *Cricket* was a legal memo on punitive damages and federal pre-emption issues, and research on industry wiring standards, for a total of 24 hours. The committee also learns that HIP is part of a national consortium of ten law firms representing plaintiffs with toaster-oven claims. The group discusses strategies and shares legal research and information from investigations and laboratory tests pursuant to a common-interest agreement (see pages 284-286). Monk has occasionally attended the group's discussions but only to take notes. KGR is eager to hire Monk, depending on whether it will be able to avoid disqualification based on Monk's conflicts. The conflicts committee asks your advice under the New York rule in *Kassis* (page 337).

In *Analytica* (page 310) the "firm itself changed sides." What happens when a conflicted lawyer who is subject to disqualification at one firm moves to a second firm? That person is generally called a lateral lawyer, or "a lateral" for short. To what extent is a lateral's status "contagious"? That is, is the lawyer's new firm saddled with the conflicts she had at her former firm? To the extent the answer is yes, we impinge on career mobility. It will be harder for the lateral to be a lateral. Firms may be wary about hiring her if her mere presence may be a business-killer. While a firm may be willing to accept that risk to attract seasoned lawyers with established reputations and a healthy client base, younger lawyers tend to have neither. On the other hand, to the extent that we say that the lateral can be screened to avoid imputation, do we risk abuse of confidential information and distrust of lawyers? Whatever the answer, we must also identify the status of the firm left behind. When a personally conflicted lawyer leaves a firm, does the lawyer take his conflict with her, so that the former firm is now free to do what it would not have been permitted to do had the lawyer remained?

It is possible to argue that a disqualifying conflict ought *not* be imputed as a matter of course even where, as in *Analytica*, the firm itself changes sides. For example, if several lawyers in a large firm once represented client *A*, the firm might argue that different lawyers in the firm could subsequently (or, indeed, concurrently) represent client *B* against client *A*, even on a substantially related matter, so long as each group of lawyers (and their relevant files) are screened from the other group. As we have seen, however, efforts to avoid imputed disqualification within a single firm have not been successful. Rule 1.10(a), like case law, operates from the "premise that a firm of lawyers is essentially one lawyer for purposes of the rules governing loyalty to the client, or from the premise that each lawyer is vicariously bound by the obligation of loyalty owed by each lawyer with whom the lawyer is associated." Rule 1.10, comment [2].

When a conflicted lawyer changes firms, the considerations differ. First, we should ask why the lateral lawyer was conflicted in the first place. Was it because of work she *personally* did at the former firm? Or was the conflict merely imputed to the lawyer because of the work of a colleague at that firm? If the latter, perhaps on departure the conflict should evaporate, since imputation of it depended on her being at the former firm, and she no longer is. Second, even if the conflict is personal (not imputed), should we tolerate screening at the new firm to facilitate career mobility? It would mean trusting, and asking clients to trust, lawyers. Will they?

The next opinion, decided by the same court that decided *Analytica*, which it cites in note 3, permits firms to screen lateral lawyers. Be aware, however, that the Seventh Circuit is still in the minority in its willingness to permit a screen. A report of an ABA committee in 2009 counted 24 jurisdictions whose ethics rules permit screening, at least in some circumstances. It may well be that during the life of this eighth edition of this book, a majority of U.S. jurisdictions will accept screening of lateral lawyers. When first adopted, the Model Rules did not permit screening lateral lawyers (other than former government lawyers, see part C below). The Ethics 2000 Commission recommended a change. But the ABA House of Delegates rejected the recommendation (one of its very few rejections). Nonetheless, courts nationwide have increasingly allowed screening, at least sometimes, so the ABA Model Rule on the question was less and less reflective of the situation on the ground, not a good thing for a purported *model* document. Then, in February 2009, the ABA House of Delegates voted 226-191 to permit lateral lawyer screening without need for client consent. New Rule 1.10 requires, among other safeguards, that "certifications of compliance . . . with the screening procedures [be] provided to the former client by the screened lawyer and by a partner of the firm, at reasonable intervals upon the former client's written request and upon termination of the screening procedures." This requirement mirrors those in the Oregon, Massachusetts, and Washington State rules discussed below.

By the way, the following opinion ignores two conflict issues suggested by the facts of the case. These are identified after the case. As you read through it, see if you can figure out what they are. Perhaps plaintiff's lawyer didn't argue them. But wouldn't you?

CROMLEY v. BOARD OF EDUCATION
17 F.3d 1059 (7th Cir.), Cert. Denied, 513 U.S. 816 (1994)

RIPPLE, CIRCUIT JUDGE.

Marcella Ann Cromley, a high school teacher, brought an action under 42 U.S.C. §1983. She claimed that she had been denied various administrative positions because she had exercised her right to free speech as guaranteed by the First Amendment and made applicable to the states by the Fourteenth Amendment. The district court granted summary judgment to the defendants Board of Education of Lockport Township High School District 205 and its superintendent, assistant superintendent, principal, and one teacher (the "defendants"). It also denied Ms. Cromley's motion to disqualify defendants' attorneys. She now appeals the judgment of the district court. For the reasons that follow, we affirm.

[Cromley alleged that the defendants "had retaliated against her because she had complained to [a state agency] about the sexual misconduct of [a co-worker], a complaint which she asserted was protected speech." After two years of pretrial litigation, Cromley's attorney, Larry Weiner, accepted a partnership in the Scariano law firm, which was representing the defendants. Weiner withdrew as Cromley's lawyer. The district court denied Cromley's motion to disqualify the Scariano firm.]

The approach taken by this circuit for determining whether an attorney should be disqualified is a three-step analysis.

> First, we must determine whether a substantial relationship exists between the subject matter of the prior and present representations. If we conclude a substantial relationship does exist, we must next ascertain whether the presumption of shared confidences with respect to the prior representation has been rebutted. If we conclude this presumption has not been rebutted, we must then determine whether the presumption of shared confidences has been rebutted with respect to the present representation. Failure to rebut this presumption would also make the disqualification proper.

Schiessle v. Stephens, 717 F.2d 417, 420 (7th Cir. 1983).

The "substantial relationship" test is easily met in this case. It is undisputed that the subject matter under scrutiny both before and after Mr. Weiner changed law firms was the litigation brought by Ms. Cromley against the School Board. The only change made was attorney Weiner's shift from the firm of Schwartz & Freeman, the firm representing Ms. Cromley, to . . . the firm representing the School Board. Because Mr. Weiner's representation of Ms. Cromley before he moved to the Scariano firm is substantially related to his new firm's relationship to the School Board, a "presumption of shared confidences" arises:

> Implicit in a finding of substantial relationship is a presumption that particular individuals in a law firm freely share their clients' confidences with one another. . . . [However, we have] recognized that the presumption that an attorney has knowledge of the confidences and secrets of his firm's clients is rebuttable.

> As a first step in deciding whether that presumption has been rebutted, "we must determine whether the attorney whose change of employment created the disqualification issue was actually privy to any confidential information his prior law firm received from the party now seeking disqualification of his present firm."[3] The rebuttal can be established either by proof that "the attorney in question had no knowledge of the information, confidences

_____

3. In Analytica, Inc. v. NPD Research Inc., 708 F.2d 1263 (7th Cir. 1983), this court held that the presumption of shared confidences was irrebuttable when an entire law firm changed sides. We acknowledged in *Analytica*, however, that a lawyer who changes jobs and moves to a firm retained by an adversary "can avoid disqualification by showing that effective measures were taken to prevent confidences from being received by whichever lawyers in the new firm are handling the new matter." In the case now before us, one attorney changed employment from the firm representing the plaintiff to a firm representing the defendants. This circumstance falls within the exception recognized in *Analytica*; therefore our analysis does not conflict with that decision.

and/or secrets related by the client in the prior representation," or by proof that screening procedures were timely employed in the new law firm to prevent the disclosure of information and secrets. Uncontroverted affidavits are sufficient rebuttal evidence.

Because Mr. Weiner, Ms. Cromley's attorney for two years, clearly had confidential information from his client when he moved to the firm representing the defendant School Board, we must focus on whether the Scariano law firm that Mr. Weiner later joined has demonstrated that it had established an effective screening procedure to block the disclosure of Ms. Cromley's confidences within the "new" firm. "[T]he presumption of shared confidences should be rebutted by demonstrating that 'specific institutional mechanisms' (e.g., 'Chinese Walls') had been implemented to effectively insulate against any flow of confidential information from the 'infected' attorney to any other member of his present firm."

The types of institutional mechanisms that have been determined to protect successfully the confidentiality of the attorney-client relationship include: (1) instructions, given to all members of the new firm, of the attorney's recusal and of the ban on exchange of information; (2) prohibited access to the files and other information on the case; (3) locked case files with keys distributed to a select few; (4) secret codes necessary to access pertinent information on electronic hardware; and (5) prohibited sharing in the fees derived from such litigation. Moreover, the screening devices must be employed "as soon as the 'disqualifying event occurred.'" Other factors have been considered helpful in determining whether adequate protection of the former client's confidences has been achieved: the size of the law firm, its structural divisions, the "screened" attorney's position in the firm, the likelihood of contact between the "screened" attorney and one representing another party, and the fact that a law firm's and lawyer's most valuable asset is "their reputations for honesty and integrity, along with competence." In addition, the attorneys in question must have affirmed these screening devices under oath. The district court must find that the internal safeguards applied indeed did shield effectively the "tainted attorney."

In this case, the defendants have rebutted the presumption of shared confidences by describing the timely establishment of a screening process. When Mr. Weiner joined the firm he was denied access to the relevant files, which were located in a different office, under the control of David Kula, the partner handling the case. Mr. Weiner and all employees of the firm were admonished not to discuss any aspect of the case, and all were subject to discipline. In addition, Mr. Weiner was not allowed to share in the fees derived from this case. The defendants also submitted the affidavit of David Kula, the attorney representing them. In that sworn statement, Mr. Kula stated that, as soon as he was informed that his law firm was discussing with Mr. Weiner the possibility of Mr. Weiner's joining the law firm, he and Mr. Weiner "agreed that absolutely nothing of a substantive nature regarding the instant lawsuit would occur" until decisions were made and the clients were made aware of them. The affidavit describes the procedures that were put in effect from December 15, 1989, the date that Mr. Weiner joined the firm. Mr. Weiner's new office was in Scariano's downtown Chicago building, and Mr. Kula's office was located in the firm's Chicago Heights office; each came to the other office only for specific business. Mr. Kula maintained the files for this case in his private office. When it implemented specific screening procedures, the firm required all members and employees of the firm to read and sign the memorandum describing the internal rules. Mr. Kula affirmed that "all of the admonitions of the screening memo have been adhered to by all attorneys and all support staff employed by this firm." We conclude, as did the district court, that the Scariano law firm successfully rebutted the presumption of shared confidences by proving that the screening procedures were timely employed and fully implemented.

Nevertheless, Ms. Cromley contends that a per se rule of disqualification is needed in this case: This court should require the withdrawal both of her former attorney and of the Scariano law firm he joined while representing her. Even if "specific institutional mechanisms" are in place, she insists, they cannot go far enough "to maintain public confidence in the legal profession."

We cannot agree with this contention. In the first place, the presumption of shared confidences has been found to be irrebuttable only when an entire law firm changes sides, and not when one attorney changes sides. Moreover, this court [has] recognized that, although the court's duty is "to safeguard the sacrosanct privacy of the attorney-client relationship," it must also be recognized that "disqualification, as a prophylactic device for protecting the attorney-client relationship, is a drastic measure which courts should hesitate to impose except when absolutely necessary." Thus, in deciding the appropriate safeguards necessary in the case of attorney disqualification, we must balance the respective interests of the parties and the public. We hold that the measures employed by the Scariano law firm sufficiently screened Ms. Cromley's former counsel from the School Board's present counsel. . . .

Why Didn't the *Cromley* Court Inquire . . . ?

Before we unpack the two presumptions in lateral lawyer conflict analysis, our main reason for reading *Cromley*, let's detour to the two arguments the court did not address. Weiner had been representing Cromley for two years, as her main lawyer, when he informed her that he was leaving Schwartz & Freeman (the same firm that figured in *Analytica*) to join the opposing law firm. What issues does that fact suggest to you?

1. Why didn't the *Cromley* court address whether it was proper for Weiner to negotiate his partnership with the Scariano firm while he was representing Cromley *against* the Scariano firm's clients? For a time at least Weiner was both Cromley's advocate against the Scariano firm and negotiating with the firm for his own interests. Do you see *potential* for abuse or disloyalty there? The court recounts an affidavit from Kula, the Scariano attorney opposing Weiner. It "stated that, as soon as [Kula] was informed that his law firm was discussing with Mr. Weiner the possibility of Mr. Weiner's joining the law firm, he and Mr. Weiner 'agreed that absolutely nothing of a substantive nature regarding the instant lawsuit would occur' until decisions were made and the clients were made aware of them." So the lawyers realized that there was an issue, but is the remedy sufficient? Was a standstill agreement in Cromley's interest or the lawyers' interest? And was *she* told about the negotiations or that her matter was on ice?

ABA Opinion 96-400 concludes that once a lawyer's negotiations with an opposing law firm reach a critical stage, which can happen in a single conversation, the lawyer must obtain client consent. The opinion also concludes that the opposing firm may need the consent of *its* client as well. Can you explain why? What was the risk to Cromley's opponent? Stanley v. Richmond, 41 Cal. Rptr. 2d 768 (Ct. App. 1995), holds that it is a triable issue of fact whether a lawyer breached fiduciary duty by negotiating to join a law firm while also negotiating against that firm over her divorce client's property settlement. Kala v. Aluminum Smelting & Refining Co., Inc., 688 N.E.2d 258 (Ohio 1998), disqualified the defendant's law firm after the plaintiff's lawyer joined the firm during the litigation. The court wrote that nothing the new firm "could have done would have had any effect on Kala's perception that his personal attorney had abandoned him with all of his shared confidences and joined the firm representing his adversary while the case was still pending. No steps of any kind could possibly replace the trust and confidence that Kala had in his attorney or in the legal system if such representation is permitted."

2. Why didn't the *Cromley* court ask whether it was proper for Weiner to drop a client in the middle of a representation in order to further his own career? Did Weiner's obligations to Cromley require him to put her interests in uninterrupted and diligent representation above his own professional and financial interest in becoming a partner at the Scariano firm? Weiner's situation resembles the facts in some "hot potato" cases (page 322), including Picker v. Varian itself. Is Weiner's wish for a professional realignment any different from Jones Day's desire to acquire MH&S? If anything, Cromley is in a worse position than Varian. She lost her lawyer, who now works for the opposing firm. Varian could have kept its lawyer with consent. And we may assume that Cromley, a schoolteacher, had even less power than Varian in finding new counsel. But the court assumes Weiner had an absolute right to walk away from Cromley, his client of two years, without regard to the harm to her, so long as he was screened. It certainly says nothing about her interest in avoiding the "hot potato" fate.

Well, it's always possible that no one raised these issues and courts, as we know, respond to arguments. They don't generally suggest them.

Presumptions in Imputed Disqualification

But let that pass. Consider this diagram.

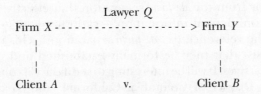

The diagram schematically depicts the *Cromley* facts. Firm *X* has represented Client *A*. Lawyer *Q* has worked at Firm *X* as a partner or an associate. *Q* moves to Firm *Y*. When *Q* changes firms, Client *A* is in the middle of a litigation against

Client *B*, represented by Firm *Y*. In *Cromley*, (lateral) Lawyer *Q* (i.e., Weiner) was the lawyer who was personally working on Client *A*'s (Ms. Cromley's) matter when he joined Firm *Y* (Scariano). That won't always be true. Sometimes the lateral lawyer will have had nothing to do with the matter, won't even know about it.

The *Cromley* issues can also arise in other ways. For example, the matter need not be a litigation, although it usually is. Firm *Y* may not be handling the same or a substantially related matter when Lawyer *Q* joins it, but it may get one later. In *Cromley*, for example, another firm might have been representing the Board of Education when Weiner joined Scariano, but a month later the Board might have decided to hire the Scariano firm instead. This temporal difference should not matter to the analysis of lateral lawyer conflicts. The fundamental question is the same: Will the lateral lawyer's new firm be disqualified by virtue of his presence? Does it depend on whether the lateral lawyer worked on the matter at his former firm?

The Seventh Circuit holds that Client *A* can object if (1) Firm *X*'s representation of Client *A* was on a matter that has a "substantial relationship" to (or is the same as) Firm *Y*'s representation of Client *B*; *and* (2) Lawyer *Q* shared confidences of *A* on the matter while at Firm *X* (this will almost always happen by working on *A*'s matter); *and* (3) the other lawyers at Firm *Y* have received (or are likely to receive) those confidences from *Q* after he arrives there.

The Seventh Circuit creates rebuttable presumptions that (2) and (3) are true. While there is general agreement that the first presumption (identified in (2)) should be rebuttable — meaning that Lawyer *Q* should have the chance to prove that he has no confidential information about the matter — if it is not rebutted, much authority disagrees with the Seventh Circuit's willingness to permit the use of screening mechanisms to rebut the second presumption (identified in (3)). Let us inspect the differences between the two presumptions and the relative merits of rebuttability for each.

First, as stated, the profession and the courts disagree over whether the presumption in step (3) should be rebuttable. Whereas a slim majority of jurisdictions reject rebuttability, Restatement §124 would allow it if, in addition to screening, the information at risk "is not likely to be significant" in the second matter.* Illinois, Massachusetts, Michigan, Oregon, and Pennsylvania, among other jurisdictions, permit lateral screening in their ethics rules. As of February 2009, Model Rule 1.10 does, too.

The Second Circuit has signaled its willingness to permit screening on the right facts, a decision that should be influential in the tug of war over this issue. Hempstead Video, Inc. v. Incorporated Village of Valley Stream, 409 F.3d 127 (2d Cir. 2005) ("We see no reason why, in appropriate cases and on convincing facts, isolation — whether it results from the intentional construction of a 'Chinese Wall,' or from the *de facto* separation that effectively protects against any sharing of confidential information — cannot adequately protect against taint"). Notice the reference to "*de facto* separation." This is new. Courts that allow screens insist that they be formally established and in place when the conflicted lawyer arrives. It will be interesting to see if the Circuit's alternate remedy catches on. The District of Columbia, California, and Texas are among the

---

* In fact, the Restatement goes even further. It would sometimes allow screening in successive conflict situations even when no lawyer has changed firms, but rather the firm itself has changed sides.

jurisdictions that either reject or make no allowance for screening in their rules. NewYork, like the Restatement, has opted for a middle position between never and always. Case law has recognized screening when the lateral lawyer's information is "unlikely to be significant or material." Kassis v. Teachers' Ins. & Annuity Assn., 717 N.E.2d 674 (N.Y. 1999). The new New York Rules, like the predecessor Code, do not provide for screening lateral lawyers from private practice. Still, *Kassis* is likely to survive.

What is the justification for allowing the presumptions in step (2) to be rebutted but not the one in step (3)? It should be possible for the migrating lawyer in the first instance persuasively to establish *lack* of knowledge of a client's confidential information without the client running the risk of having its confidential information revealed. This is because the lawyer's proof will generally be by way of billing records showing, and the lawyer's affidavit stating, that the lawyer did not work on any matter for the particular client.

In one unusual case, however, the court rejected a lawyer's claim that he acquired no confidential information about a case at his prior firm. Wolf, the lawyer, worked in the six-lawyer satellite office of a large firm (Steptoe). Four colleagues worked on the case, including two lawyers whose individual offices were on either side of Wolf's office, and the lawyers commonly "met to discuss" their cases. "In light of the office schematic and dynamics associated with Wolf's former law firm, we find it highly likely that [he] would have been exposed to discussions regarding Steptoe's representation of Bucklew," even if Wolf did not work on the case. Cosenza v. Hill, 607 S.E.2d 811 (W. Va. 2004) (also finding that situation created an "appearance of impropriety"). But most lawyers who are affiliated with even moderate-sized law firms and corporate law offices will never learn all the confidential information possessed by their offices. If a presumption that they do is conclusive, lawyer mobility between firms will be severely constrained, an effect especially damaging to lawyers at the start of their careers.

Silver Chrysler Plymouth, Inc. v. Chrysler Motors Corp., 518 F.2d 751 (2d Cir. 1975), is an early and influential decision that nicely illustrates this point.* The plaintiff was represented by a small firm, one of whose partners, Schreiber, formerly worked as an associate at Kelley Drye, which represented Chrysler. Kelley Drye sought to disqualify Schreiber's firm because Schreiber, while an associate at Kelley Drye, had had access to confidential information regarding Chrysler. The Second Circuit rejected this effort:

> It is unquestionably true that in the course of their work at large law firms, associates are entrusted with the confidences of some of their clients. But it would be absurd to conclude that immediately upon their entry on duty they become the recipients of knowledge as to the names of all the firm's clients, the contents of all files relating to such clients, and all confidential disclosures by client officers or employees to any lawyer in the firm. Obviously such legal osmosis does not occur. . . .
>
> Fulfilling the purpose of the disqualification remedy . . . does not require such a blanket approach. . . . Thus, while this Circuit has recognized that an inference may arise that an attorney formerly associated with a firm himself received confidential information transmitted by a client to the firm, that

---

* *Silver Chrysler*, like other interlocutory appeals of disqualification motions, has been overruled on the issue of appellate jurisdiction. See page 288. That hasn't diminished its influence.

inference is a rebuttable one. . . . The importance of not unnecessarily constricting the careers of lawyers who started their practice of law at large firms simply on the basis of their former association underscores the significance of [not making "the standard of proof for rebuttal unattainably high"].

The court concluded that Schreiber had rebutted any presumption that he had obtained substantially related confidential information about Chrysler while at Kelley Drye. Today, under the Model Rules, we would say that Schreiber's imputed conflict would have ended on leaving Kelley Drye, freeing him and his new firm to oppose Chrysler. Rule 1.9(b) and comments [4] and [5].

Why is the step (3) presumption irrebuttable? A lawyer who, in a prior affiliation, acquired confidential information about a client will be tempted, it is argued, to share it with new colleagues. Screens will not assure clients that their confidences will be protected. Rather, the temptation to violate the screen will be (or clients will see them to be) too powerful. Consequently, in jurisdictions that reject screening, the entire firm will be disqualified from representing a client whose interests are materially adverse to those of the opposing client about whom a lateral lawyer has acquired relevant confidences at his former firm. One commentator described the justification for irrebuttability as follows:

> From the moment an attorney has reason to expect that he will represent a client in a matter to which the confidences and secrets of one of his present affiliate's [i.e., firm colleague's] former clients may be relevant, he has a significant incentive . . . to elicit such information deliberately from his colleague. Although the fellow lawyer need not knowingly cooperate in the sharing of information (seemingly innocuous questioning or casual examination of relevant files will suffice), he may have appreciable incentive and opportunity to do so. The fact of affiliation alone is generally enough to guarantee that there will be economic, sentimental, and hegemonic ties between the associated lawyers sufficient to induce an affiliate's cooperation with his colleague. Although such ties might exist even between former affiliates, the probability that an attorney will feel free to request his affiliate's sub rosa assistance and that the affiliate will oblige is plainly greater when the lawyers are presently affiliated. It is this risk of deliberate sharing, customarily disregarded in the case of former affiliates, that is the distinctive danger of present affiliation.*

Are you persuaded that the second presumption should be irrebuttable? Look at it from the lawyer's point of view. If it is irrebuttable, firms will not hire lawyers who have worked elsewhere (however incidentally) on matters that present a conflict with a current representation of the firm. But that's not all. Even though the firm can check its current client inventory against the new lawyer's experience to make sure that by hiring him it will not thereby conflict itself out of a matter, what about the future? The new lawyer's experience expands the orbit of future disqualification. His prior work becomes, presto, the new firm's prior work for conflict purposes. The danger of imputed disqualification will be especially high in smaller communities or in specialized areas of practice where the client population is smaller.

---

* Harvard Conflicts Note, page 299, at 1361-1363.

But look at it from the client's point of view. A client may find itself opposed by a law firm one lawyer of which has relevant confidential information about the client gained in a prior affiliation. Maybe that lawyer knows everything about the former client's case. Can a client be comfortable that a purported screen will be honored? How can the client know? Should the profession ask clients to "trust us"? What then about the middle ground adopted in the Restatement and in New York, which permits screens so long as the lawyer's knowledge is not "material" or "significant" (or words to that effect)? We all love a good compromise, but how practical is this one? Think about the hiring partner in "Can We Hire Taylor Monk?" above. Her goal is to figure out if KGR will be able to avoid disqualification by invoking the New York rule on screening. (Colorado, Minnesota, and other states have the same compromise.) She must estimate whether Taylor's knowledge is significant or material. How does she decide? If unsure, what will she do? Remember, Taylor has a duty of confidentiality to her clients. In other jurisdictions, where screening is expansively allowed (as in *Cromley*), the new firm doesn't face this dilemma. If the situation is unclear, it can avoid any risk simply by creating a screen. Paul Tremblay has addressed these issues and offers proposals to resolve them in Migrating Lawyers and the Ethics of Conflict Checking, 19 Geo. J. Legal Ethics 489 (2006).

Removing Conflicts from a Former Firm

The Model Rules and case law also speak to the situation where a lawyer terminates an association with a firm and the firm then wishes to represent a new client whose interests are materially adverse to those of a former client represented by the formerly associated lawyer while at the firm. Rule 1.10(b) permits the firm to represent the new client, even if the matter is the same or substantially related to the one in which the formerly associated lawyer represented the former client, so long as the firm can show that no lawyer remaining in the firm has protected information that could be used to the disadvantage of the former client. Thus, just as a disqualified lawyer who comes to a firm with certain confidential information may "infect" every lawyer there if screening is not allowed or not implemented, when a disqualified lawyer departs, the entire firm may be "cured" of the imputed disqualification.

Here is a story to tell the next time someone proclaims that law is a profession, not a business. Client *ABC* asks its longtime firm to represent it in an action against *XYZ*. But it happens that *XYZ* is a client of the firm on an unrelated matter. We know from *Picker*, page 323, that the firm cannot simply drop *XYZ* "like a hot potato" and accept the representation of *ABC*. But it also happens that all of *XYZ*'s matters have been handled by a particular partner at the firm — call him James Polk — who joined the firm laterally a few years earlier, bringing *XYZ* with him. *XYZ* is devoted to Polk and the feeling is reciprocal. May the firm fire Polk, correctly predicting that *XYZ* will choose to leave with him, and thereby free itself to accept *ABC*'s matter? The firm can then argue that it is not dropping *XYZ* "like a hot potato." Rather, *XYZ* would be leaving of its own accord after the firm dropped Polk like a hot potato. You probably find this tactic too clever for words. Yet in Hartford Accident & Indemnity Co. v. R.J.R. Nabisco, Inc., 721 F. Supp. 534 (S.D.N.Y. 1989), it worked. LeBoeuf, Lamb sued R.J.R. on behalf of Hartford while its partner Wood was representing Reynolds, an R.J.R. subsidiary.

LeBoeuf then "fired" Wood, and Reynolds left with him. R.J.R. moved to disqualify LeBoeuf from representing Hartford. Judge Walker held that R.J.R. was a LeBoeuf client via parent Reynolds because the parent controlled the subsidiary's litigation. (See page 555 on this issue.) But he rejected R.J.R.'s conflict argument because here it was the lawyer, not the client, who got tossed. The client had not been denied its "longtime counsel."

Is Judge Walker's distinction persuasive? Judge Patel reached a contrary result, despite the departure of the firm lawyer whose presence created a conflict, because a concurrent violation "occurred at the time the complaint was filed, and . . . cannot be cured [by the lawyer's] resignation from [the firm]." Teradyne, Inc. v. Hewlett-Packard Co., 1991 Westlaw 239940 (N.D. Cal. 1991). But there was a period of overlap in Judge Walker's case too.

Rebutting the Second Presumption

Cromley well describes the sort of "institutional mechanisms" or screens that will satisfy those courts that allow rebuttal of the *second* presumption (step (3) above). The Model Rules also define "screening" in Rule 1.0(k): " 'Screened' denotes the isolation of a lawyer from any participation in a matter through the timely imposition of procedures within a firm that are reasonably adequate under the circumstances to protect information that the isolated lawyer is obligated to protect under these Rules or other law."

Look at the precautions the Scariano firm took to prevent exchange of information between Weiner and its lawyers opposing Cromley. Of course, the client can never know for sure. Even lawyers, it has been rumored, have been known to succumb to temptation. That's why many courts still do not allow screening of lateral lawyers. Courts that do allow screens tend to be rather demanding in exchange. In one remarkable case, an Illinois appellate court removed Winston & Strawn from a matter in which the firm had put much time (and billed much money) because, *in medias res*, it hired an associate who had done a small amount of work on the opposite side of the matter. (Poor soul who conducted that conflicts check! Imagine having to explain it to the client.) The firm did build a screen but, alas, not until several weeks after the new lawyer's arrival. The court would not let the firm show that nothing untoward had occurred in the interval. The missing screen made the second presumption conclusive. SK Handtool Corp. v. Dresser Indus., 619 N.E.2d 1282 (Ill. App. 1993). Accord, Cobb Publishing, Inc. v. Hearst Corp., 891 F. Supp. 388 (E.D. Mich. 1995) (disqualification when new firm waited two weeks before screening lateral lawyer who had worked on opposite side of matter notwithstanding absence of any evidence that lawyer had disclosed confidences to a new firm).

Oregon permits screening but adds a novel precaution to enhance confidence that the screen will be respected. The Oregon rule requires the "personally disqualified lawyer" to give his or her former firm an affidavit attesting that he or she "will not participate in any manner in the matter or the representation and will not discuss the matter or the representation with any other firm member." In addition, if requested, the personally disqualified lawyer must submit a further affidavit once the matter is over, "describing the lawyer's actual compliance with these undertakings." Finally, a member of the lawyer's new firm must also provide the first affidavit and, if asked, the second as well. Do you think these procedures are adequate to satisfy the former client of the personally disqualified lawyer? Oregon Rule 1.10(c). Washington State rule 1.10(e) and Massachusetts Rule 1.10(d) provide safeguards similar to the Oregon rule. Massachusetts further authorizes the former client to seek judicial review of a screen and "supervision" of its effectiveness. Michigan requires the new firm to give the court "written notice . . . to enable it to ascertain compliance." A firm that forgot to do that was booted off a case notwithstanding that it had erected a screen. National Union Fire Ins. Co. of Pittsburgh, Pa. v. Alticor, Inc., 472 F.3d 436 (6th Cir. 2007).

Even in jurisdictions that do not allow screening, a client may always consent to one and clients often do, especially to facilitate job mobility of younger lawyers, at least where the client is not threatened by what the lateral lawyer knows. Perhaps this is because their law firms encourage consent, knowing that some day they may need the same favor.

Nonlawyer Conflicts

Question: Who is more trustworthy, a lawyer or her paralegal? Don't answer that.

Lateral lawyers are the usual but not the only inspiration for the presumption of shared confidences. Paralegals, summer associates, and secretaries can carry information too, although some courts are then more likely to tolerate screens. Compare Hayes v. Central States Orthopedic Specialists, Inc., 51 P.3d 562 (Okla. 2002), and In re American Home Products Corp., 985 S.W.2d 68 (Tex. 1998) (permitting nonlawyers to be screened), with the view that equates support staff with lawyers and forbids screening of a secretary who had access to confidential information of an adverse client at a prior law firm. Zimmerman v. Mahaska Bottling Co., 19 P.3d 784 (Kan. 2001). Does it seem anomalous to trust secretaries or paralegals and then to forbid screening of lawyers?

Some jurisdictions will apply the successive conflict rules to summer associates. See, e.g., Actel Corp. v. Quicklogic Corp., 1996 Westlaw 297045 (N.D. Cal. 1996). Uh oh. You know what that means, don't you? The work you do at a firm during a summer job may diminish your allure to a different firm after graduation. It all depends. At the very least, it means that you should keep track of the matters you work on. A careful permanent employer will want to learn whatever the jurisdiction's confidentiality rules let you tell it.* The Model Rules allow screening of support personnel and former summer associates. Rule 1.10 comment [4].

---

* Law firms perceive the risk. One of my students received an offer from a western firm that contained the following footnote: "This offer assumes that you have not previously been involved in any representation that gives rise to a conflict at [the firm] or, alternatively, that any ethical conflict arising from your prior representation will be waived." The student was told that if he accepted the offer, he would have to "fill out a tedious form describing your previous legal work." Is the firm asking for confidential information?

Reflections on the Term "Chinese Wall"

The term "Chinese Wall," as a metaphor for the ethical screen required to avoid imputation of conflicts (assuming the jurisdiction allows it), began to appear in judicial opinions in the mid-1970s and has been ubiquitous ever since. A computer search shows Fund of Funds, Ltd. v. Arthur Andersen & Co., 435 F. Supp. 84 (S.D.N.Y. 1977), to contain the first such use. Although the term has been questioned informally, judicial criticism is rare. Concurring in Peat, Marwick, Mitchell & Co. v. Superior Court, 245 Cal. Rptr. 873 (Ct. App. 1988), Judge Low wrote:

> The enthusiasm for handy phrases of verbal shorthand is understandable. Occasionally, however, lawyers and judges use a term which is singularly inappropriate. "Chinese Wall" is one such piece of legal flotsam which should be emphatically abandoned. The term has an ethnic focus which many would consider a subtle form of linguistic discrimination. Certainly, the continued use of the term would be insensitive to the ethnic identity of the many persons of Chinese descent. Modern courts should not perpetuate the biases which creep into language from outmoded, and more primitive, ways of thought.
>
> It may be sobering to recall that little more than a century ago our own Supreme Court held that persons of Chinese ancestry could not testify in court against a person of Caucasian descent. In People v. Hall (1854) 4 Cal. 399, 404, the court, speaking through Chief Justice Hugh C. Murray declared that "[t]he same rule which would admit them to testify, would admit them to all the equal rights of citizenship, and we might soon see them at the polls, in the jury box, upon the bench, and in our legislative halls." . . .
>
> Aside from this discriminatory flavor, the term "Chinese Wall" is being used to describe a barrier of silence and secrecy. The barrier itself may work to further the cause of ethics in litigation; but the term ascribed to that barrier will necessarily be associated with constraints on the freedom of open communication. To employ in this context the image of the Great Wall of China, one of the magnificent wonders of the world and a structure of great beauty, is particularly inappropriate. One can imagine the response to the negative use of the images of the Eiffel Tower, the Great Pyramid of Cheops, or the Colossus of Rhodes.
>
> Finally, "Chinese Wall" is not even an architecturally accurate metaphor for the barrier to communication created to preserve confidentiality. Such a barrier functions as a hermetic seal to prevent two-way communication between two groups. The Great Wall of China, on the other hand, was only a one-way barrier. It was built to keep outsiders out — not to keep insiders in.

FURTHER READING

Charles Wolfram, Former Client Conflicts, 10 Geo. J. Leg. Ethics 677 (1977); Steven Goldberg, The Former Client's Disqualification Gambit: A Bad Move in Pursuit of an Ethical Anomaly, 72 Minn. L. Rev. 227 (1987); Howard Liebman, The Changing Law of Disqualification: The Role of Presumption and Policy, 73 Nw. U.L. Rev. 996 (1979); Martin Lipton & Robert Mazur, The Chinese Wall Solution to the Conflict Problems of Securities Firms, 50 N.Y.U. L. Rev. 459 (1975); Comment, The Chinese Wall Defense to Law-Firm Disqualification, 128 U. Pa. L. Rev. 677 (1980).

C. GOVERNMENT SERVICE

"Investigating Landlords"

After the local press reports abuses by landlords in the city—charging excessive rents, failure to provide services, and the like—the City Attorney and the City Council hire Cynthia Chen from private practice as a Special Assistant City Attorney to conduct an investigation and recommend legislation. Chen, who is an expert on the state's housing laws, uses subpoena power to conduct a six-month investigation, followed by three months of hearings before a city council committee. After the hearings Chen spends two months refining legislation that would give tenants treble-damage claims against landlords who violate certain provisions of the new law. The legislation passes. Chen then returns to private practice. Six months later, may either Chen or others at her law firm represent (1) a tenant suing a landlord under the statute, or (2) a landlord sued under the statute? In either instance, does it matter whether the particular landlord was a subject of Chen's investigation and if so, how?

Government lawyers are confronted by many of the same problems that corporate and other entity lawyers face. We encountered the privilege issue in chapter 2 (page 50). Others are raised in chapter 10. The problem of identifying the client is especially acute for government lawyers. Consider an attorney who works in the northeast regional office of a bureau of a federal agency in a department of the executive branch. Does the lawyer owe her loyalty to the head of that regional office, the regional office as an entity, the bureau of the agency, the head of that bureau, the agency as a whole, the head of that agency, the department, the president, or the entire federal government? These intriguing questions are unanswerable in the abstract—that is, without having a context from which they arise. Recall the litigation over whether the president, in response to a federal grand jury subpoena, could claim privilege for communications with White House counsel (page 52). In that context, neither the president nor the White House could invoke the client's traditional prerogative of asserting privilege. It didn't belong to them.

In one important way, the rules governing government lawyers vary from those that apply in private practice. You have surely heard about the "revolving door" that leads in and out of government service. Toil in the vineyards of public service, acquire know-how and know-who in a lucrative field, then trade on this knowledge in the private market. The prospect of attractive postgovernment employment makes the official tour of duty appealing to many, even if the pay is (much) lower than they can earn in private practice. Nothing wrong with that. It is, in fact, a good thing, isn't it? It enables government to attract talent without paying through the roof, and, at least in part, it avoids an encrusted, permanent governing class.

Still, many rules limit the postdeparture conduct of government employees (whether or not they are lawyers). Some of these are in federal and state statutes. Some of these laws carry criminal sanctions. For lawyers, restrictions also appear in the Rules, which are written so that it does not matter whether the lawyer's government work was as a lawyer or assistant secretary of commerce. Rule 1.11. The Code provision was DR 9-101(B). You can look at this issue as a type of successive conflict when the lawyer's former employer was a government entity.

One prominent example of a government lawyer who "revolved" to represent a private client in violation of Rule 1.11 is Abraham Sofaer. Sofaer, a former federal judge, was later legal adviser to the State Department. Still later, he went into private practice, where he briefly represented Libya in connection with criminal and civil issues arising out of the bombing of Pan Am Flight 103 over Lockerbie, Scotland. Unfortunately for him, while at the State Department, Sofaer had participated in the government's investigation of Libya's role in the bombing. After a hearing, disciplinary panels

> concluded that respondent had violated [Rule 1.11(a)] by undertaking to represent the government of Libya in connection with criminal and civil disputes and litigation arising from the 1988 bombing of Pan American Flight 103 over Lockerbie, Scotland, after respondent, while serving as Legal Advisor in the United States Department of State, took part personally and substantially in the government's investigation of the bombing and in related diplomatic and legal activities.

The court sustained these findings. In re Sofaer, 728 A.2d 625 (D.C. App. 1999).

The revolving door revolves in the opposite direction, too, imposing limits on government lawyers (and sometimes others in government office) because of their earlier private work. Rule 1.11(d), discussed below.

For those of you who will start your careers as law clerks, take heed of Monument Builders of Pennsylvania, Inc. v. Catholic Cemeteries Assn., 190 F.R.D. 164 (E.D. Pa. 1999), citing Pa. Rule 1.12(a), whose focus is the conduct of former judges and law clerks and federal court rules governing law clerks. The court held that a former law clerk to a federal judge could not represent a private client in a matter on which she worked as a law clerk. As a clerk, the lawyer had assisted on an antitrust class action. She then proposed to represent a client on a claim alleging breach of the agreement settling the action. But her conflict was not imputed to her firm.

If the government were no different from any other former client, Rules 1.9 and 1.10 would define the limits on postgovernment work. Why do we need a special rule for government lawyers who change jobs? What broader or different issues does their postdeparture (or prearrival) employment raise? Rule 1.10(d) specifically excludes the use of private lawyer imputation rules for government lawyers, referring instead to the different resolution in Rule 1.11.

ARMSTRONG v. McALPIN
625 F.2d 433 (2d Cir. 1980) (en banc), vacated on other grounds, 449 U.S. 1106 (1981)

[Altman, while a lawyer at the SEC, supervised an investigation and litigation against certain of the defendants, including McAlpin. The SEC litigation alleged that McAlpin and others had looted millions of dollars from the Capital Growth companies. McAlpin and other defendants defaulted, and the trial judge appointed Armstrong as receiver of the Capital Growth companies.

[Armstrong was charged with recovering all misappropriated property. With the trial judge's permission, he retained the law firm of Barrett Smith, of which he was a partner. When it appeared that Barrett Smith had a conflict of interest, the law firm of Gordon Hurwitz was substituted as counsel. Prior to the substitution, Altman ended a nine-year tenure with the SEC and became associated with Gordon Hurwitz. In the last three years of his tenure, Altman was assistant director of the SEC's Enforcement Division, with responsibility over numerous cases including the Capital Growth investigation and litigation. Although Altman "was not involved on a daily basis, he was generally aware of the facts of the case and the status of the litigation. . . . Altman's name appeared on the SEC complaint, although he did not sign it."

[Gordon Hurwitz and Armstrong concluded that Altman "should not participate in the Gordon firm's representation of the receiver, but that the firm would not be disqualified if Altman was properly screened from the case." Thereafter Gordon Hurwitz "asked the SEC if it had any objection to the retention, and was advised in writing that it did not, so long as Altman was screened from participation." After Armstrong began this action, McAlpin and others moved to disqualify Gordon Hurwitz. The trial judge (Werker) denied the disqualification, but a panel of the Second Circuit reversed. The case was then reargued to the court en banc. Following is a portion of the opinion of Judge Feinberg joined by four of the other eight judges on the court.

[Judge Feinberg first held that the denial of disqualification was not immediately appealable, but nevertheless concluded that there were "strong reasons in the unusual context of this case to reach the merits of the appeal rather than to dismiss it." (Ultimately the Supreme Court vacated the Second Circuit's decision in *Armstrong* on the ground of nonappealability, but the case remains influential.)]

[The trial judge] noted that Altman was concededly disqualified from participating in the litigation under Disciplinary Rule 9-101(B). . . . That Rule prohibits an attorney's private employment in any matter in which he has had substantial responsibility during prior public employment. The judge then considered the effect of Disciplinary Rule 5-105(D), which deals with disqualification of an entire law firm if one lawyer in the firm is disqualified. . . . The ABA, in its Formal Opinion No. 342, had recognized that "[p]ast government employment creates an unusual situation in which an inflexible application of D.R. 5-105(D) would actually thwart the policy considerations underlying D.R. 9-101(B)," and concluded that, absent an appearance of significant impropriety, a government agency could waive Rule 5-105(D), if adequate screening procedures effectively isolated the former government lawyer from those members of his firm handling the matter. . . .

Judge Werker then carefully examined the screening of Altman by the Gordon firm. . . .

Under all the circumstances, the district judge concluded that "the proper screening of Altman rather than disqualification of the Gordon firm is the solution to the present dispute." . . . On appeal . . . a panel of this court reversed the order of the district court, apparently on the ground that disqualification was required "as a prophylactic measure to guard against misuse of authority by government lawyers."

[Amicus briefs from the United States and former government lawyers warned that refusal to recognize screening could reduce the allure of government service. Prospective private employers will be reluctant to hire former government lawyers because "hiring them may result in the disqualification of an entire firm in a possibly wide range of cases."]

Not only is the panel decision possibly of great practical importance, the ethical issues it addresses are also complex and are currently being hotly contested by various groups. . . .

We do not believe that it is necessary or appropriate for this court to enter fully into the fray, as the panel opinion did. Indeed, the current uncertainty over what is "ethical" underscores for us the wisdom, when considering such issues, of adopting a restrained approach that focuses primarily on preserving the integrity of the trial process. . . .

We believe that this approach is dispositive here and requires our affirmance of the ruling of the district court. It is apparent from a close reading of Judge Werker's opinion that he saw no threat of taint of the trial by the Gordon firm's continued representation of the receiver. Nor did the panel opinion in this case challenge that view. Although appellants assert that the trial will be tainted by the use of information from Altman, we see no basis on the record before us for overruling the district court's rejection of that claim. [Using the analysis in Board of Education v. Nyquist, 590 F.2d 1241 (2d Cir. 1979)], there is certainly no reason to fear any lack of "vigor" by the Gordon firm in representing the receiver; this is not a case where a law firm, by use of a "Chinese wall," is attempting to justify representation of conflicting interests at the same time. Nor is the Gordon firm "potentially in a position to use privileged information" obtained through prior representation of the other side. And finally, the receiver will not be making unfair use of information obtained by Altman as a government official, since the SEC files were turned over to the receiver long before he retained the Gordon firm and Altman has been entirely screened from all participation in the case, to the satisfaction of the district court and the SEC.[24] Nor is there any reason to believe that the receiver retained the Gordon firm because Altman was connected with it or that Altman had anything to do with the retention. If anything, the presence of Altman as an associate at that time was a problem, not a benefit, for the Gordon firm, as the district court, the receiver and the Gordon firm all apparently recognized.

Thus, because the district court justifiably held that the Gordon firm's representation of the receiver posed no threat to the integrity of the trial process, disqualification of the firm can only be based on the possible appearance of impropriety stemming from Altman's association with the firm. However, as previously noted, reasonable minds may and do differ on the ethical propriety of screening in this context. But there can be no doubt that disqualification of

---

24. The case therefore is entirely distinguishable from General Motors Corp. v. City of New York, 501 F.2d 639 (2d Cir. 1974), where an attorney who had substantial responsibility over antitrust litigation against General Motors Corporation while he was employed by the Antitrust Division of the Justice Department later accepted employment as plaintiff's attorney in a private antitrust action against the same defendant for substantially the same conduct.

the Gordon firm will have serious consequences for this litigation; separating the receiver from his counsel at this late date will seriously delay and impede, and perhaps altogether thwart, his attempt to obtain redress for defendant's alleged frauds. Under the circumstances, the possible "appearance of impropriety is simply too slender a reed on which to rest a disqualification order . . . particularly . . . where . . . the appearance of impropriety is not very clear." Thus, we need not resolve the ethical propriety of the screening procedure used here at this time as long as the district court justifiably regarded it as effective in isolating Altman from the litigation.

We recognize that a rule that concentrates on the threat of taint fails to correct all possible ethical conflicts. In adopting this approach, we do not denigrate the importance of ethical conduct by attorneys practicing in this courthouse or elsewhere, and we applaud the efforts of the organized bar to educate its members as to their ethical obligations. However, absent a threat of taint to the trial, we continue to believe that possible ethical conflicts surfacing during a litigation are generally better addressed by the "comprehensive disciplinary machinery" of the state and federal bar, or possibly by legislation.[27] While there may be unusual situations where the "appearance of impropriety" alone is sufficient to warrant disqualification, we are satisfied that this is not such a case. Nor do we believe . . . that a failure to disqualify the Gordon firm based on the possible appearance of impropriety will contribute to the "public skepticism about lawyers." While sensitive to the integrity of the bar, the public is also rightly concerned about the fairness and efficiency of the judicial process. We believe those concerns would be disserved by an order of disqualification in a case such as this, where no threat of taint exists and where appellants' motion to disqualify opposing counsel has successfully crippled the efforts of a receiver, appointed at the request of a public agency, to obtain redress for alleged serious frauds on the investing public. Thus, rather than heightened public skepticism, we believe that the restrained approach this court has adopted towards attempts to disqualify opposing counsel on ethical grounds avoids unnecessary and unseemly delay and reinforces public confidence in the fairness of the judicial process.

Accordingly, we vacate the panel opinion in this case and affirm the judgment of the district court.

[Two other judges concurred with the majority on the merits but disagreed on the appealability issue. Another judge would have dismissed the appeal for lack of jurisdiction. A final judge agreed with the majority on the appealability issue but disagreed on the merits.]

The Revolving Door in the Model Rules

In *Armstrong* the successive conflict risks were not the traditional ones that arise when a lawyer opposes a former client on a substantially related matter because the Gordon firm was not opposing Altman's former client. The concern here is different. Would the Gordon firm and its client, Armstrong as receiver,

---

27. Cf. 18 U.S.C. §207.

benefit from information Altman learned at the SEC? We don't want lawyers to be able to exploit any information they may have learned while working for government for the benefit of their private clients. Yet we also encourage people to enter government service by emphasizing that they will acquire knowledge and experience they can later use. How do we reconcile these positions? The following discussion tries to identify the line dividing "good" and "bad" use of government experience.

Could Altman, the former SEC lawyer in *Armstrong*, personally have represented the receiver? The firm offered to screen him, but did it have to? In General Motors Corp. v. City of New York, 501 F.2d 639 (2d Cir. 1974), distinguished in note 24 of *Armstrong*, New York City brought an antitrust action against GM charging monopolization in the manufacture and sale of city buses. The city was represented by private counsel, George Reycraft, who had previously worked for the Antitrust Division of the Department of Justice. In that job, Reycraft had substantial involvement in an action the United States brought against GM for monopolizing the manufacture and sale of buses. Resisting GM's motion to disqualify Reycraft, the city argued that he had not "switched sides" but was continuing to represent a government entity, although a different one and as a private practitioner, against the same defendant, GM. I always found that a clever and appealing argument. But the Second Circuit did not. It wrote:

> We believe, moreover, that this is as it should be for there lurks great potential for lucrative returns in following into private practice the course already charted with the aid of governmental resources. And, with such a large contingent fee at stake, we could hardly accept "pro bono publico" as a proper characterization of Reycraft's work, simply because the keeper of the purse is the City of New York. . . .

The court, applying a literal reading of DR 9-101(B), did not want former government lawyers and their private clients to profit from information gained in their government employment. It did not credit the city's argument that disqualification would "chill the ardor for Government service by rendering worthless the experience gained in Government employ."

The Model Rules *partly* reject *General Motors*. Rule 1.11(a) would allow a lawyer to represent a private "client in connection with a matter in which the lawyer participated personally and substantially as a public officer or employee" so long as the "appropriate government agency gives its informed consent." State v. Romero, 578 N.E.2d 673 (Ind. 1991) (former prosecutor disqualified from defending accused where he had consulted on case while a prosecutor and current prosecutor did not consent). Furthermore, Rule 1.11(a) is not limited to the situation where the lawyer remains on the same "side," as the city unsuccessfully claimed that Reycraft had because he was still working for government, just a different one and in private practice. With consent, Rule 1.11(a) would permit the lawyer to represent the other "side" on the very matter on which he had worked while in public office — for example, *for* GM in New York City's case against it.

Is the agency consent provision objectionable on the ground that those responsible for giving the consent have a personal interest in saying yes, given their own expectations after leaving government service? Should we fear that government lawyers will identify a work agenda based on their expectations of future private employment and the likelihood of consent? New Jersey's Rule 1.11 does not allow the government to consent to allow its former lawyers to represent clients "in connection with a matter (1) in which the lawyer participated personally and substantially as a public officer or employee, or (2) for which the lawyer had substantial responsibility as a public officer or employee." Iowa also forbids waiver of this conflict. Sorci v. Iowa Dist. Ct. for Polk County, 671 N.W.2d 482 (Iowa 2003).

There is one instance in which the Model Rules would not allow the government to consent to private representation after leaving government and that instance is present in the GM case. This is where the lawyer has "confidential government information" about a person that could be used in the representation of a private client whose interests are adverse to that person. Reycraft was in that position. He had "confidential government information" about GM that he would have been able to use to benefit the city, GM's adversary. We are here concerned with "confidential *government* information," a term to be distinguished from "confidential information." Compare Rule 1.6 with Rule 1.11(c). Rule 1.11 contemplates that while in government service a lawyer may gain information about individuals to which only the government has access or which is particularly within the power of the government to compel. Think tax returns, trade secrets, and grand jury testimony. The Rules prevent a private client from hiring a former government lawyer in order to exploit such information about an opponent. (The information can be exploited even if the lawyer does not reveal it.)

If the former government lawyer cannot get the consent contemplated by Rule 1.11, or is disqualified because she possesses "confidential government information" under Rule 1.11(c), the Rules still permit her firm to accept the representation so long as the lawyer is screened and receives no portion of the fee. (In case of a Rule 1.11(a) screen, "written notice" must go to the appropriate agency.) No permission need be obtained from the government to use a screening device. You should recognize the policy reasons for tolerating screening in this situation, although the Rules have so far rejected it for lateral private lawyers.

The Model Rules also speak to a lawyer's responsibility when moving from private practice to government employment. See Rule 1.11(d). A government lawyer is disqualified under this rule as well as under Rule 1.9(a) from participating "in a matter in which the lawyer participated personally and substantially while in private practice or nongovernmental employment." Reaves v. State, 574 So. 2d 105 (Fla. 1991), reversed a murder conviction and death sentence where the prosecutor had previously represented the defendant in a prosecution involving similar issues. The court said it would allow screening in future cases but that, absent adequate screening, a trial court may be required "to disqualify the entire state attorney's office." In United States v. Caggiano, 660 F.2d 184 (6th Cir. 1981), the court refused to disqualify the entire U.S. Attorney's Office on the retrial of a matter even though a new assistant prosecutor (not assigned to the matter) had represented the accused during his first trial. See also United States v. Goot, 894 F.2d 231 (7th Cir. 1990), where the court accepted a screen of the newly appointed U.S. Attorney.

But some courts are less tolerant of screens when the government office at issue is the prosecutor and the conflicted lawyer is a high official in the office. In State v. Tippecanoe County Court, 432 N.E.2d 1377 (Ind. 1982), the entire prosecutorial office was disqualified because the chief prosecutor had represented the accused as a public defender on substantially related matters. People v. Shinkle, 415 N.E.2d 909 (N.Y. 1980) ("fact that the attorney who had initially represented defendant and participated actively in the preparation of his defense was chief assistant in the office of the prosecutor in the months preceding and during the defendant's trial inescapably gave both defendant and the public the unmistakable appearance of impropriety and created the continuing opportunity for abuse of confidences entrusted to the attorney during the months of his active representation of defendant").

Consider, too, City and County of San Francisco v. Cobra Solutions, Inc., 135 P.3d 20 (Cal. 2006). A lawyer for Cobra Solutions was elected city attorney. Thereafter, the city sued the company for civil fraud. The court held that screening the city attorney would not avoid imputation of his conflict to other lawyers in the office. He was head of the office, with power to hire and fire those directly below him. "Public perception that a city attorney and his deputies might be influenced by the city attorney's previous representations of the client, at the expense of the best interests of the city, would insidiously undermine public confidence in the integrity of municipal government and its city attorney's office." Elsewhere, the court stressed that the city attorney knew the company's "confidential information." What concerned the court? That the public might think the city attorney's subordinates will favor Cobra, their boss's former client, given his power over them? Or that Cobra had reason to fear that the city attorney would share its secrets with the lawyers handling the prosecution? If the concern is the threat to confidential information, doesn't that mean screening will be equally ineffective when the new lawyer in the office is not the boss but the lowest line assistant? Indeed, a line assistant may be even more susceptible to importuning given his lowly status. Of course, it was Cobra that made the disqualification motion. So either it was worried about its confidential information or it took advantage of an opportunity to stymie the prosecution by disqualifying the office. Or both.

Many jurisdictions have statutes controlling the postdeparture work of government employees, including lawyers. In the federal system, 18 U.S.C. §207 imposes certain postdeparture restrictions on former government employees. These include permanent restrictions on certain work and two-year restrictions and one-year restrictions on a variety of activities before the employee's former department or agency. The duration of the disability depends on the nature of the employee's work and his or her status. Violation of the section is a crime.

Part Three

SPECIAL LAWYER ROLES

VII

Ethics in Advocacy

Bassanio: So may the outward shows be least themselves—
The world is still deceiv'd with ornament.
In law, what plea so tainted and corrupt
But, being season'd with a gracious voice,
Obscures the show of evil? In religion,
What damn'd error but some sober brow
Will bless it, and approve it with a text,
Hiding the grossness with fair ornament?
—Shakespeare, *The Merchant of Venice,* 3.02.73-80

And yet, while we should never prosecute the innocent, we need not have scruples against undertaking on occasion the defence of a guilty person, provided he be not infamously depraved and wicked. For people expect it; custom sanctions it; humanity also accepts it. It is always the business of the judge in a trial to find out the truth; it is sometimes the business of the advocate to maintain what is plausible, even if it be not strictly true, though I should not venture to say this, especially in an ethical treatise, if it were not also the position of Panaetius, that strictest of Stoics. Then, too, briefs for the defence are most likely to bring glory and popularity to the pleader, and all the more so, if ever it falls to him to lend his aid to one who seems to be oppressed and persecuted by the influence of someone in power. This I have done on many other occasions; and once in particular, in my younger days, I defended Sextus Roscius of Ameria against the power of Lucius Sulla when he was acting the tyrant. The speech is published, as you know.

—Cicero, *De Officiis*

I said there was a society of men among us, bred up from their youth in the art of proving by words multiplied for the purpose, that white is black, and black is white, according as they are paid. To this society all the rest of the people are slaves.

—Jonathan Swift

The only real lawyers are trial lawyers, and trial lawyers try cases to juries.
—Clarence Darrow

353

- *Client Perjury and Related Dilemmas*
- *Legitimate Advocacy that Frustrates Truth*
- *Hardball, Incivility, Biased Conduct*

The role of the courtroom advocate probably raises more controversial ethical and moral issues, for both the public and the bar, than any other part of a lawyer's work. Popular culture's appetite for tales about trial lawyers is seemingly bottomless. Why is that? In this chapter we look at a panoply of issues that confront trial lawyers and litigators (the latter being lawyers whose cases rarely go to trial), both civil and criminal. In chapter 8 we look at some special issues in litigation. First is the ethical duty of lawyers who come into possession or control of real evidence. Real evidence includes such disparate items as weapons used in the commission of a crime, fruits of a crime, contraband (e.g., drugs or counterfeit money), and such ordinary items as documents, clothing, parts of machines, and photographs that have evidentiary value because they tend to prove or disprove a material fact in a civil or criminal case. Mostly, the issues concern the obligations of defense counsel in criminal cases, but not only in such cases. Chapter 8 takes up a few questions specific to criminal prosecutors, as well.

But back to the threshold question: What is it about the role society assigns to trial lawyers, a/k/a advocates, that makes them and their professional dilemmas fascinating?

Many people think of the advocate as amoral, and many advocates will accept this characterization. Amoral, but not immoral, they will insist, because the moral thing is to remain true to your assigned role. The immoral thing is to betray that role. In the advocate's world, the justice system defines their role, and whatever result the process reaches is justice by definition. If a particular result seems unjust when looked at from outside the process, possibly even to the lawyer who achieved it, why, that's the concern of the judges, legislators, and rule makers, and perhaps of the philosophers, but not of the advocate. The advocate just does her job, one case at a time, a field laborer in the vineyards of the process.

An advocate may concede that she means to win all or as much as possible for her client, regardless of who is "right." The advocate may deny that it is possible to talk about "right" in the conventional sense. (That will not, however, prevent the advocate from trying to get as much mileage as possible from conventional notions of "right" and "wrong," "good" and "bad," or "fair" and "unfair.") The advocate may see herself as the agent for her client in a highly structured, artificial combat system called litigation, a system the client may only barely understand but that can play havoc with the client's life. In this system, as the advocate knows, you are "right" if you win; you don't necessarily win because you are right.

The advocate views her job as to use all available legal and ethical means to achieve her client's goal, subject only to her client's willingness and ability to pay the cost, which includes the advocate's fee, if any. It matters not that a particular strategy might encourage the "wrong" result, because in advocacy just as there is no "right," there is no "wrong," except by reference to how the court rules. As Johnson is said to have told Boswell (page 361), "[Y]ou do not know [a cause] to be good or bad till the judge determines it." So far as the advocate is concerned, the loser is wrong by definition.

The advocate adopts this perspective only after she has been retained by a client. She may, of course, reflect on the rightness of a client's matter *before* accepting it and decline cases she finds repugnant. Lawyers have personal autonomy, too. Or do they? Some lawyers — law firm associates, employed corporate lawyers, lawyers in government and public defender offices — may have little choice. They do what they are assigned. Enlightened offices will allow for some conscientious objection, but there must be a limit.

Let's say a lawyer accepts a repugnant case. Professionally, she must forget her personal views. Once she has taken an assignment, she acts as though the client's cause were her own. Trial lawyers delight in quoting Lord Brougham (1778-1868), who was the lawyer for Queen Caroline in her criminal trial for adultery. Brougham apparently had some evidence that would embarrass the King, but would he use it to defend the Queen? Brougham let it be known not only that he would use it, but he felt bound to do so. As quoted in the introduction to chapter 2, Brougham told the judges: "[A]n advocate, in the discharge of his duty, knows but one person in all the world, and that person is his client." He then added, lest there be any doubt about his intentions, that the "hazards and costs to other persons" are of no concern to the advocate, that the advocate "must not regard the alarm, the torments, the destruction which he may bring upon others. . . . [H]e must go on reckless of the consequences, though it should be his unhappy fate to involve his country in confusion." Whew!

For many people outside the legal community, Lord Brougham's attitude is offensive. Popular suspicion of this conduct encourages cynicism about lawyers, especially criminal defense lawyers, and often leads to that ancient question: "How can you defend a guilty person?" For the advocate, that question is utter nonsense. Guilt is a legal conclusion. By definition no one can be guilty until declared so after a due process trial with the assistance of counsel, if desired. If the question is rephrased as "How can you defend someone who did it?" the advocate will invoke her historical role in the Anglo-American criminal justice system and patiently explain that the system could not work as envisioned unless she or another lawyer performed in accordance with it. To many members of the public, this sounds like "lawyer talk" or dissembling. To lawyers it is a sacred truth that holds us together as a civilized people.

The public may also find it duplicitous once it realizes that, despite the advocate's effort to defend herself by appealing to some systemic good, her motives are often financial. ("She wouldn't do it if she weren't getting paid, and she'd probably work for the first one to hire her.") The public may also wonder how lawyers can separate their professional and personal lives. How can you be one person at your work and someone completely different with friends and family? For many lawyers, the greater risk is *not* that they will be unable to adopt the advocate's mask at work, but that they will be unable to remove it at home. "Oh, stop acting like a lawyer, would you? You're not in court now." That sort of thing. Maybe this explains why, as some claim to have noticed, lawyers tend to marry lawyers.

Things get more complicated when the focus shifts from the (perhaps) morally dubious, if nonetheless legal, goals of the advocate's client, goals she is helping him achieve, to the means the advocate chooses to help the client reach those goals. Those means, though legal and ethical, may appear unfair to the public. It is even easier to blame the advocate for unfair *means* than for questionable goals because, while clients choose the goals, chapter 2 taught us that lawyers ordinarily choose the means and have the specialized knowledge required to implement them.

But just as the words "right" and "wrong" do not have the same meaning in the advocate's world, neither does the word "unfair" retain its conventional meaning. For lawyers, any strategy that the rules permit the advocate to employ in order to prevail is fair by definition. An example is when a well-funded client prolongs a litigation with creative but valid procedural motions, thereby forcing a needy plaintiff to compromise for much less than the value of his claim. Another example is when a lawyer knowingly humiliates a truthful witness through vigorous but legitimate cross-examination.

What rules should a justice system adopt to govern the behavior of a lawyer when acting as an advocate? Answers to this question have filled libraries. To answer it, we need a satisfactory theory of justice. Common law nations need a satisfactory theory of adversary justice. Adversary justice is seen as the best way both to discover truth and honor individual autonomy. (Those goals will sometimes clash. The attorney-client privilege honors autonomy but may defeat truth.) We honor autonomy by giving litigants a good deal of control over their cases before a mostly passive judge and jury. Maybe these Anglo-American assumptions are right. Maybe not. Who knows? To some extent, they must be explained historically and taken on faith. The precepts are not immutable, of course. Rules do change.

A civilized society can be built around other postulates, and many are. But this is a book about legal ethics in the United States. So the rules must be viewed against the backdrop of the adversary system.

We must next remember that theories, however beautiful, are not self-executing. Law professors do not always acknowledge that fact. That's fine. Their job is to be brilliant, not necessarily practical. But theories are just the start. (See the quote from Michael Ignatieff in chapter 1.) Theories must accommodate a political and historical tradition. They must take account of human frailty and institutional incompetence. They must evaluate how wealth or lack of it will distort the operation of the theory. An imperfect system of justice might be as close to the "most perfect" system of justice that a society's traditions and institutions are capable of at the time. Or not. In measuring a nation's system of justice, therefore, we also take the political measure of the nation.

The rule of unintended consequences intrudes here as elsewhere. Since we are dealing with a system of great complexity, with many participants in different roles and serving a diverse society, we must be aware that any changes we might make in one place to advance a perceived good can prove to have harmful effects elsewhere in the system, effects we cannot fully anticipate. This is not an argument against change, only an argument for caution. For similar reasons, lawyers may not act outside their role to achieve what they perceive as "justice" in the particular situation (although the popular culture loves to play with that narrative). Lacking omniscience, they may be wrong about what justice requires and actually work injustice as a result. Beyond that, the system operates on the assumption that across the vast run of cases, justice will be best served when lawyers stick to the job that they have been assigned and that they have taken an oath to perform — serving clients — and equally important, when clients can be assured that they will.

Finally, once again, we must examine our own biases as (imminent) members of the legal profession. Are our choices influenced by self-advantage? Do we, for example, favor rules that promote or at least tolerate more disputing (or that make resolution of disputes more complicated) because knowledge about disputing is a large part of a lawyer's inventory of services? We should try to look at the issues without regard to our professional affiliations or indeed our particular position in society.

We begin this chapter with selections from the vast literature defending and criticizing the adversary system in the United States. It is not possible to provide a representative survey or even to develop fully the views of the few authors included here. I can, however, give you a feel for the debate from four highly articulate authors. In turn, you should be able to begin to form your own conclusions as you assess the particular practices described in the succeeding material.

FURTHER READING

For further background reading, see Arthur Isak Applbaum, Ethics for Adversaries: The Morality of Roles in Public and Professional Life (1999); W. Bradley Wendel, Professional Roles and Moral Agency, 89 Geo. L.J. 667 (2001) (reviewing Applbaum); David Luban, Lawyers and Justice: An Ethical Study (1988); Stephen Bundy & Einer Elhauge, Do Lawyers Improve the Adversary System? A General Theory of Litigation Advice and Its Regulation, 79 Cal. L. Rev. 315 (1991) (using "rational actor analysis" to examine the "considerations that determine the informational effects and social value of litigation advice"); Charles Fried's classic defense of adversary justice in The Lawyer as Friend: The Moral Foundations of the Lawyer-Client Relation, 85 Yale L.J. 1060 (1976); Stephen Gillers, Can a Good Lawyer Be a Bad Person?, 84 Mich. L. Rev. 1011 (1986), revised at 2 J. Inst. Study of Legal Ethics 131 (1999); Kevin McMunigal, Are Prosecutorial Ethics Standards Different?, 68 Fordham L. Rev. 1453 (2000) (criticizing the general and ambiguous language with which ethics doctrine often characterizes the "different" or "dual" role of prosecutors and arguing for greater "guidance on when prosecutors should seek justice by adopting a cooperative stance and when they should seek it by adopting an adversarial stance"); David Barnhizer, The Virtue of Ordered Conflict: A Defense of the Adversary System, 79 Neb. L. Rev. 657 (2000) (with citations to Hobbes, Locke, and other social philosophers, Barnhizer concludes that the "adversary system is the primary mechanism for ensuring the authoritative mediation and resolution of disputes. . . . The only potentially legitimate buffer against abuses of power [and interest group competition] is to provide articulate and strong professional voices for all the competing interests"); and Stephen Pepper's challenging discussion in The Lawyer's Amoral Ethical Role: A Defense, a Problem, and Some Possibilities, 1986 Am. B. Found. Res. J. 613 (with responses in the same volume from Professors Luban and Andrew Kaufman and a rejoinder from Professor Pepper).

For a view of the lawyer's role that goes beyond advocacy, see Richard Wasserstrom's path-breaking article, Lawyers as Professionals: Some Moral Issues, 5 Hum. Rts. 1 (1975).

Should answers to questions raised here differ when a lawyer litigates civil matters for the government? Catherine Lanctot contrasts a lawyer's traditional duty of adversarial zeal with the government lawyer's special duty "to seek justice." EC 7-14. "This double standard," she writes, "furnishes much of the ethical tension inherent in the role of the government lawyer." After framing the issues with three hypotheticals, Professor Lanctot develops and seeks to clarify them in The Duty of Zealous Advocacy and the Ethics of the Federal Government Lawyer: The Three Hardest Questions, 64 S. Cal. L. Rev. 951 (1991).

A.   FOUR VIEWS OF ADVERSARY JUSTICE

Simon Rifkind was a district judge in the Southern District of New York from 1941 to 1950, when he joined Paul, Weiss, Rifkind, Wharton & Garrison (as it was then renamed). Marvin Frankel, formerly a Columbia law professor, was a judge on the same court (1965-1978) and then a partner in Kramer, Levin, Naftalis & Frankel. Robert Post is a law professor at Yale Law School. Anthony Trollope (1815-82) needs no introduction.

Anthony Trollope
ORLEY FARM*

[Moulder, a traveling salesman, purportedly worldly wise, is explaining to his brother-in-law, John Kennerby, what Kennerby should expect when he testifies as a witness at an impending criminal trial.]

'All right,' said Moulder. 'And now, John, I'll just tell you what it is. You've no more chance of being allowed to speak freely there than — than — than — no more than if you was in church. What are them fellows paid for if you're to say whatever you pleases out in your own way?'

'He only wants to say the truth, M.,' said Mrs. Moulder, who probably knew less than her husband of the general usages of courts of law.

'Truth be —— ,' said Moulder.

'Mr. Moulder!' said Mrs. Smiley. 'There's ladies by, if you'll please to remember.'

'To hear such nonsense sets one past oneself,' continued he; 'as if all those lawyers were brought together there — the cleverest and sharpest fellows in the kingdom, mind you — to listen to a man like John here telling his own story in his own way. You'll have to tell your story in their way; that is, in two different ways. There'll be one fellow 'll make you tell it his way first, and another fellow 'll make you tell it again in his way afterwards; and it's odds but what the first 'll be at you again after that, till you won't know whether you stand on your heels or your head.'

* Oxford Univ. Press edition, book 2, pages 212-213 (2000).

'That can't be right,' said Mrs. Moulder.

'And why can't it be right?' said Moulder. 'They're paid for it; it's their duties; just as it's my duty to sell Hubbles and Grease's sugar. It's not for me to say the sugar's bad, or the samples not equal to the last. My duty is to sell, and I sell; — and it's their duty to get a verdict.'

'But the truth, Moulder——!' said Kennerby.

'Gammon!' said Moulder. 'Begging your pardon, Mrs. Smiley, for making use of the expression. Look you here, John, if you're paid to bring a man off not guilty, won't you bring him off if you can? I've been at trials times upon times, and listened till I've wished from the bottom of my heart that I'd been brought up a barrister. Not that I think much of myself, and I mean of course with education and all that accordingly. It's beautiful to hear them. You'll see a little fellow in a wig, and he'll get up; and there'll be a man in the box before him, — some swell dressed up to his eyes, who thinks no end of strong beer of himself; and in about ten minutes he'll be as flabby as wet paper, and he'll say — on his oath, mind you, — just anything that that fellow wants him to say. That's power, mind you, and I call it beautiful.'

'But it aint justice,' said Mrs. Smiley.

'Why not? I say it is justice. You can have it if you choose to pay for it, and so can I. If I buy a greatcoat against the winter, and you go out at night without having one, is it injustice because you're perished by the cold while I'm as warm as a toast. I say it's a grand thing to live in a country where one can buy a greatcoat.'

Rifkind and Frankel: Defender and Critic

Simon H. Rifkind
THE LAWYER'S ROLE AND RESPONSIBILITY IN MODERN SOCIETY
30 The Record 534, 535-545 (1975)

When I was first admitted to the bar, I was formally authorized to act as an attorney-at-law. The concept of attorneyship, of course, includes agency. An agent must have a principal; so must an attorney have a client. The lawyer's role and responsibility as attorney comes into being only when he is a member of a client-attorney, symbiotic team.

Once he becomes a member of such a team then, in the United States and in other countries having a common law tradition, he works in an environment called the adversary system and engages in maneuvers called the adversary process.

Awareness of this fact is crucial to the understanding of the attorney's duty and responsibility. Failure to grasp the significance of the adversary system has given rise to much misunderstanding, both within and without the bar, and has, I suggest, led to some unproductive developments.

In an actual lawsuit, the operation of the adversary process becomes fully visible even to the uninitiated. As a matter of history and habit, we accept unquestioningly the bizarre arrangement by which the State hires one lawyer to prosecute a citizen for an alleged crime, another to defend him and a third to decide between them. A visitor from Mars might inquire, "Why not hire one to ascertain the truth?"

But it is not only for litigated matters that the adversary system constitutes the living ambience. Consensual arrangements may become the subject of litigation; the draftsman must, to the best of his ability, anticipate the vicissitudes his writing will experience during its voyage in the adversary process. Every will prepared in the privacy of a law office may be contested, every advice given may be challenged, every opinion given must be formulated in the light of the possibility of attack upon its validity and its subjection to the adversary process and judicial arbitrament.

Both the prospect of litigation and its actuality impose great restraint upon the attorney and challenge his learning, his wisdom and his capacity to prophesy. It also relieves him of much responsibility. In the course of his advocacy, he may urge propositions of which he is less than certain, because the lawyer is not the final arbiter. The final judgment will emerge out of the contest. In the collision of the two opposing forces, out of the cross-exposure by each of his adversary's weakness and out of the need to discover and articulate one's own virtues and advantages, in the fire of that antagonism a more refined truth is smeltered and a better judgment is filtered.

The adversary process is thus seen as a form of organized and institutionalized confrontation. Because organized confrontations also occur in many forms of sport, some have seized upon the superficial similarity to downgrade the adversary process as socially trivial. This condemnation would be appropriate if the object of the adversary process were to select the more skillful lawyer, as it is, for instance, to select the better boxer or tennis player. In the courtroom contest, the judge does not award prizes for skill. He uses the adversary process for illumination. And it is, I believe, the teaching of experience that the incentives generated by the adversary system do, indeed, tend to bring about a more thorough search for and evaluation of both the facts and the law. . . .

From some of my philosophically oriented brethren I hear murmurs that the Anglo-American reliance on the adversary process may have exceeded the limits of its utility and that re-examination is now in order. Re-examination of a major premise is always in order. Most logical errors are imbedded in major premises uncritically accepted. I have no doubt that to the logician, the adversary process will present many flaws. The inequality of resources between the contestants, the disparity in talent, are but two of many. But I should recall the sage words of the Yankee from Olympus, "The life of the law has not been logic; it has been experience."

Experience tells me that the adversary system has been good for liberty, good for peaceful progress and good enough to have the public accept that system's capacity to resolve controversies and, generally, to acquiesce in the results.

And it has also accomplished something else. It has tended to reward most highly those lawyers who are best suited to the adversary process. In consequence, such lawyers have established the norms of performance. Anyone who has worked with lawyers around the globe knows that those brought up in the Anglo-American tradition of the adversary process devote themselves more comprehensively, more passionately, to the solution of their clients' problems than the lawyers reared under any other system.

Recent events surrounding the whole epoch called Watergate have caused an unflattering light to shine upon quite a number of lawyers. Some laymen have suggested that the very function the attorney presumes to discharge involves a conflict of interest between his duty to his client and his duty to society.

Those who have voiced such views have not taken account of the operation of the adversary process. The utility of that process is that it relieves the lawyer of the need, or indeed the right, to be his client's judge and thereby frees him to be the more effective advocate and champion. Since the same is true of his adversary, it should follow that the judge who will decide will be aided by greater illumination than otherwise would be available.

Lord MacMillan in his famous address on the ethics of advocacy delivered in 1916 quotes this exchange:

Boswell: But what do you think of supporting a cause which you know to be bad?
Johnson: Sir, you do not know it to be good or bad till the judge determines it.
     You are to state facts clearly; so that your *thinking,* or what you call *knowing,* a
     cause to be bad must be from reasoning, must be from supposing your
     arguments to be weak and inconclusive. But, sir, that is not enough.
     An argument which does not convince yourself may convince the judge to
     whom you urge it; and if it does convince him, why then, sir, you are wrong
     and he is right. It is his business to judge; and you are not to be confident in
     your opinion that a cause is bad, but to say all you can for your client, and
     then hear the judge's opinion.

Of course the process I have described is subject to human frailty. Sometimes the poorer cause prevails. That is a price worth paying for the long-range benefits of the system. It is comparable to the price we are willing to pay for democracy in the acceptance of the mistakes of the majority. We pay a price for the jury system. We pay these in return for values which we believe exceed the costs.

Even when the poorer cause prevails at the end of the adversary process, it is not necessarily a total loss. Sometimes it flags an error in the law. Sometimes it stokes the fires of reform and produces corrective legislative action.

What I have said thus far would have sounded orthodox twenty years ago. Today I think it is radical doctrine. It is radical because it rejects the notion which has gained considerable ground at the bar and very widespread allegiance on the campus that the lawyer should not be client-oriented but cause oriented. . . .

In the Cardozo lecture delivered last December at the Association of the Bar of the City of New York, Judge Marvin Frankel, a superb scholar and unusually gifted judge, spoke of the search for truth in the litigational world which he explored. On innumerable occasions I have heard judges, presiding at a trial, express an impatient desire to get at the truth or pronounce the generalization that the object of a trial was the ascertainment of the truth.

In general terms, truth commands a very high respect in our society. No one can be heard to challenge judges when they pay homage to truth.

With some trepidation I should like to tender the suggestion that in actual practice the ascertainment of the truth is not necessarily the target of the trial, that values other than truth frequently take precedence, and that, indeed, courtroom truth is a unique species of the genus truth, and that it is not necessarily congruent with objective or absolute truth, whatever that may be.

When I once casually expressed this notion to a group of laymen, they expressed shock and dismay as if I were a monk uttering some unutterable heresy to a Tenth Century congregation of bishops. But that reaction has not deterred me. On reflection, I have framed the hypothesis that courtroom truth is one of several varieties of truth and I have discovered that, consciously or unconsciously, the practicing trial lawyer behaves in a way compatible with that hypothesis. I have also formulated the conclusion that the object of a trial is not the ascertainment of truth but the resolution of a controversy by the principled application of the rules of the game. In a civilized society these rules should be designed to favor the just resolution of controversy; and in a progressive society they should change as the perception of justice evolves in response to greater ethical sophistication.

When the author of the Song of Solomon says, "I am the rose of Sharon and the lily of the valleys," no one believes that he is speaking of horticultural specimens. Nor is he suspected of suborning perjury when he causes a maiden to avow to her lover, "I have compared thee, o my love, to a company of horses in Pharaoh's chariots." Manifestly, a poet's perception of the truth is different from that of a speaker of prose. So, too, I believe, the courtroom has developed its own version of truth.

The reception of information in most court proceedings is conducted through a complex filtering process. The filtering is designed in large measure to exclude information which is suspect or which experience has adjudged generally untrustworthy. In addition, there are baffles which exclude information, without reference to its truthbearing quality. These exclusions have been established to serve policies and to recognize values totally unrelated to truth.

It seems inescapable to me that the so-called truth which the trier of the facts, judge or jury, will discover at the end of the trial may, likely will, differ materially from the truth it might have found had no such barriers to information been in place. I make no assessment whether, measured by some standard not yet invented, such truth is of higher or lesser quality than courtroom truth. All I assert is that it may very well, and likely will, be different.

A few specific illustrations may help to flesh out the proposition I am asserting.

1. *The burden of proof:* By rule of law, we assign the burden of proof to one or the other of the courtroom contestants on every issue to be resolved. If the bearer of the burden fails to discharge it, the issue goes against him. Certainly, no such rule is observed in scientific research. Science has the advantage that it may leave issues unresolved in the interest of truth, but trials are primarily concerned with the resolution of controversies, the search for truth being merely one of the tools for the accomplishment of that purpose.

2. *Competence:* Courts have excluded and still exclude vast bodies of information as incompetent. For example, in some jurisdictions a wife may not give testimony against her husband except in limited circumstances, although she is the bearer of information both relevant and material.

3. *Privileged possessors of both relevant and material information:* Clergymen, lawyers, doctors, Congressmen and, in some jurisdictions, news reporters are either forbidden to disclose or permitted to withhold that which they

had learned in confidence. This exclusion is not occasioned by the suspect quality of the information. This exclusion serves societal policies which presumably are regarded as superior to truth. They rest upon a pragmatic need for such confidential exchanges. To this category may be added executive privilege, the ambassador's privilege, the Speech or Debate privilege, the informer's privilege, the privilege with respect to offers of compromise, and others.

4. *Exclusions responsive to the commands of the Fifth and Fourth Amendments to the Constitution of the United States:* These have no such pragmatic underpinning. They are nourished by profound philosophical appraisals of man's need for a zone of such deep privacy that no one may penetrate it.

5. *Exclusionary rules founded on so-called experience of lack of trustworthiness:* These include the hearsay rule, the parol evidence rule, the deadman's statute, the statute of frauds.

6. *Exclusionary rules founded on the apprehension that the information will carry more persuasion than is warranted:* An example is the rule prohibiting a prosecutor from offering during his direct case proof of prior convictions.

It seems to me that were trials exposed to information utterly unfiltered by rules of the kind I have mentioned, the truth they would reveal would frequently be different from the truth presently ascertained. If I had to hazard a guess I would assert that the quality of our justice would suffer grievously were trials exposed to such unrestricted information.

Having over the years entertained these reflections, I have freed myself of the necessity of uttering the litany that the object of trials is to ascertain the truth and I have come to embrace the perhaps less exalted but more viable proposition that the office of a trial is to resolve a controversy.

This perception has more than academic significance. It affects the day to day work of the practicing trial lawyer. I have seen lawyers struggling like a butterfly beating its wings against an enveloping net when they find themselves caught in a contest between what they "know" of an event and the version of that event which emerges from the witness stand. Only the latter is the operative scenario. The effective lawyer must learn to deal with it even as an artist accommodates himself to the limitations of his pigments or the playwright to the time frame of one evening on the stage.

Marvin E. Frankel
PARTISAN JUSTICE
Pages 11-19 (1980)

Our leading religions may teach about loving our neighbors, about the expectancies of the meek, and about forbearance, gentleness, and other fond virtues. In our arena for secular justice, however, we enthrone combat as a paramount good. The "adversary system," as we call it, is not merely borne as a supposedly necessary evil. It is cherished as an ideal of constitutional proportions, not only because it embodies the fundamental right to be heard, but because it is thought (often) to be the best assurance of truth and sound results. Decisions of the Supreme Court give repeated voice to this concept. We are taught to presume as a vital premise the belief that "partisan advocacy on both sides," according to rules often countenancing partial truths and concealment, will best assure the discovery of truth in the end. We are not so much as slightly rocked in this assumption by the fact that other seekers after truth have not emulated us. Ours is, after all, a special world of special cases. Even we who made and run that world would fear for our lives if physicians, disagreeing about the cause of our chest pains, sought to resolve the issue by our forms of interrogation, badgering, and other forensics. But for the defendant whose life is at stake — and for the public concerned whether the defendant is a homicidal menace — this is thought to be the most perfect form of inquiry. We live, at any rate, as if we believe this.

Like any sweeping proposition, the claim that our adversary process is best for truth seeking has qualifications and limits recognized by its staunchest proponents. While it would not be essential, we have again the high authority of Supreme Court pronouncements noting that lawyers in the process are often expected, with all propriety, to help block or conceal rather than pursue the truth. These endeavors are commonly justified in the service of interests that outweigh truth finding — interests in privacy, personal dignity, security, autonomy, and other cherished values. The problem of how to weigh the competing values is, obviously, at the heart of the concerns to be addressed in these chapters. Nobody doubts that there are ends of diverse kinds, at diverse times and places, more worthy than the accurate discovery or statement of facts; that there are even occasions, not easily defined with unanimity, when a lie is to be preferred. One way to state the thesis of this book is to say, recognizing the complex relativities of life, that the American version of the adversary process places too low a value on truth telling; that we have allowed ourselves too often to sacrifice truth to other values that are inferior, or even illusory. But the elaboration of the position is best postponed until after we have described how the process works and how its actors perform.

The quality of private initiative and private control is, in its degree, the hallmark of the American judicial process. While the administration of justice is designated as the public's business and the decision-makers are public people (whether full-time judges or the lay judges who sit in jury boxes), the process is initiated, shaped, and managed by the private contestants in civil matters and by the government and non-government lawyer-contestants in criminal matters. The deciders, though commissioned to discover the truth, are passive recipients, not active explorers. They take what they are given. They consider the questions raised by counsel, rarely any others. Issues not joined are not resolved, though they might have led to wiser, fairer dispositions than those reached. The parties, almost always the lawyers or those under their direction, investigate the facts, interview possible witnesses, consult potential experts to find opinions most agreeable to their causes, decide what will be told and what will not be told. The judges and jurors almost never make inquiries on their own, and are not staffed or otherwise equipped to do so. The reconstructions of the past to be given in the courtroom are likely to be the sharply divergent stories told by partisans, divergent from each other and from the actual events supposed to be portrayed. If history can never reproduce the past with total fidelity, one wonders often whether we could not miss by margins much narrower than those marked in courtrooms. . . .

The system rests, we must always remember, on the assumption that we can accurately re-create the facts so that our rules of law, democratically evolved, will work just results. If the rule is that the signer of the note must pay, it works acceptably only if we correctly identify the signer. If we fail to make the identification, or, worse yet, falsely identify one who really did not sign, the result will be an injustice. It is no answer that some of our laws are no good. Nobody who thinks the society good enough to preserve, and improve, argues seriously that the cure for bad laws is feckless decisions about facts.

The simple point to be stressed, here and throughout, is that many of us trained in the learned profession of the law spend much of our time subverting the law by blocking the way to the truth. The subversion is not for the most part viewed as a pathology; rather, if somewhat paradoxically, it follows from the assigned roles of counsel in the very system of law which thus finds its purposes thwarted.

The games we play about fact finding are, of course, an old story and an old source of professional worry and efforts toward reform. During the last half century or so, much has been done through rules of "discovery" to cut down on concealment and surprises at trial. The idea is to allow demands for information before trial and to require responses from the adverse party. The device has on the whole worked substantial improvements. Predictably, however, it has been turned — and twisted — to adversary uses. Lawyers react characteristically by demanding as much as possible and giving as little as possible. What is not demanded is not given. It remains as true as ever that if a lawyer fails to ask the right question, the adversary will cheerfully refrain from disclosing what might be vital or decisive information. The discovery process itself, with rules that frequently are (or are made to be) intricate and abstruse, becomes the occasion for expensive contests, producing libraries full of opinions. Where the object always is to beat every plowshare into a sword, the discovery procedure is employed variously as weaponry. A powerful litigant in a complex case may impose costly, even crushing, burdens by demands for files, pretrial testimony of witnesses, and other forms of discovery. An approximately converse ploy has also been evolved to make the procedure a morass rather than the revelatory blessing it was meant to be. A litigant may contrive to dump truckloads of [unsorted] files on the party demanding discovery, hoping, often not in vain, that the searcher will be so exhausted that the damaging items will be overlooked or never reached.

The key point at every stage, which will bear recalling from time to time, is that the single uniformity is always adversariness. There are other goods, but the greatest is winning. There are other evils, but scarcely any worse than losing. Every step of the process, and any attempt to reform it, must be viewed in this light until or unless the adversary ethic comes to be changed or subordinated. The lawyer's response to a tax is how to avoid or minimize its impact on the client. Every law is probed for its loopholes — unless the lawyer has done the job in advance by being placed strategically to sew them in during the legislative process. Every idea for improved procedures must be imaginatively pretested to foresee its evolving shapes under the fires of adversary zeal.

Because the route of a lawsuit is marked by a running battle all the way, the outcome is nothing like the assuredly right result imagined in our dream that "justice will out." In that dream, neither eloquence nor lawyers' techniques nor cunning has much place. The person who is "right" should win. But that is very far from assured in the kind of contest we've been considering. When skill and trickery are so much involved, it must inevitably happen that the respective qualities of the professional champions will make a decisive difference. Where sheer power and endurance may count, the relative resources of clients become vital. Describing the tendency of the enterprise as the major forces propel it, two students of the American legal system were led to conclude: "In an ideal adversary system, the less skillful antagonist is expected to lose, which under the laissez-faire notion is the proper outcome."

If that is, fortunately, an exaggeration, it describes a probability high and uncertain enough to be harrowing. One of the nation's greatest judges, Learned Hand, paid grim tribute to the uncertainty in a famous utterance: "I must say that, as a litigant, I should dread a lawsuit beyond almost anything else short of sickness and of death." Hand's distinguished colleague for a number of years, Jerome Frank [once] focused . . . on the utter chanciness of factual determinations as the main reason why lawsuits are gambles too often and routes to justice more seldom than they should be.

The Advocate as Performance Artist

> *Q* (to a successful trial lawyer):   What is the single most important quality
> for success as a trial lawyer?
> *A:*   Sincerity. There are other qualities, too, of course, and sincerity alone is
> not enough. But sincerity is number one. If you don't feel it, you have to
> be able to fake it. I'm telling you the truth even if you don't want to hear it.

Clinton realized that the new medium permitted a much more sophisticated level of communication with voters, by playing intimate scenes before the camera as if the camera weren't there. He understood that the camera rewarded the evocation of a different kind of sincerity in politics. It transmitted more than words; it transmitted performances, and the performances it transmitted most effectively were all about seduction. The right words and the right nonverbal signals — the way in which a politician stood, sat, listened, laughed, smiled, frowned — combined to create a message that overrode the content of the words alone. If a politician was good at this, he could create not only a political reality out of perception, but also several conflicting realities at the same time . . . so that each member of his audience saw and heard what he wanted to see and hear. It was possible to speak even on a subject that aroused sharp division . . . and have people on opposing sides perceive the speaker to be one of them.

Bill Clinton was beyond good at this new political performance art.

— Michael Kelly, The President's Past, The New York
Times Magazine, July 31, 1994, at 27

Sarah Palin is many things — somber is not one of them. There's something about her delivery that suggests she's almost always having fun. You know how they call Joe Biden the happy warrior? Palin has a similar quality — the ability to attack without seeming angry. Some of that is the smile on her face and the evident humor in her voice, as Sheila Tate, Nancy Reagan's former press secretary, points out.

But there's a lot more at work. It starts with the way Palin's delivery allows her to leap through the camera into your living room. Perhaps in part because of her background as a television reporter and beauty pageant competitor, she seems to understand how the camera works.

"What she knows is that the camera is a thief," says Republican strategist Ron Bonjean, who has worked for former House speaker Dennis Hastert and former Senate majority leader Trent Lott, among others. "The camera will steal your emotions and make you flat, and what she's doing is over-emphasizing her emotions, over-emphasizing her delivery, in order to get that realness across to the camera."

The realness is what her fans talk about — that she's like them, that she doesn't seem contrived. "We feel like she talks like we do," says Susan Geary, a Richmond retiree who attended a McCain-Palin rally in Fairfax last month. "Like she's sitting in your kitchen." . . .

"That's been her bread and butter for 20 years, from the day she sat down in front of the TV cameras to do her sportscasting," says Anchorage-based pollster Ivan Moore. "Her success in her political career has been based on being able to project this enormously friendly, enormously appealing physical presence — and, some people would argue, use it to conceal this very much more ruthless and nakedly political character."

— Libby Copeland, Shooting from the Hip, With a Smile to Boot,
Washington Post, October 1, 2008

Judge Rifkind uses artistic imagery to explain the role of the advocate and the meaning of truth in the adversary system. Professor Robert Post has attempted to explain popular ambivalence toward lawyers, especially advocates, by reference to their status as performers. They are in the business of presenting a "self" that is not their actual self, while persuading their audience otherwise. An excerpt from Professor Post's article follows.

Robert C. Post
ON THE POPULAR IMAGE OF THE LAWYER:
REFLECTIONS IN A DARK GLASS
75 Cal. L. Rev. 379 (1987)

The most striking aspect of the image of the lawyer in popular culture is the intense hostility with which it is invested. Lawyers, to be sure, may have more than their fair share of common moral shortcomings. But they do not as individuals seem so very different from the rest of the population as to justify the special level of animosity that the profession seems to arouse in the general public. One thinks, for example, of the present genre of what has come to be called "lawyer jokes." For instance:

Question: What is the difference between a dead lawyer in the road and a dead skunk?
Answer: There are skid marks by the skunk.

Or:

Question: Why did the research scientist substitute lawyers for rats in his lab-
    oratory experiments?
Answer: Lawyers breed more rapidly, scientists become less attached to them,
    and there are some things rats just won't do.

Lawyer bashing is of course nothing new. The genre goes back a long way.
St. Luke says in the New Testament: "Woe unto you also, ye lawyers! for ye lade
men with burdens grievous to be borne. . . ."[1] Every lawyer or legal academic
carries as a particularly heavy part of her cultural training the usual and vicious
swipes at lawyers, from Shakespeare's "let's kill all the lawyers,"[2] to Sir Thomas
More's exclusion of lawyers from his Utopia because they are "a sort of people,
whose profession it is to disguise matters."[3] The nineteenth-century readers and
spellers of American school children often contained a game called "the
Colonists," which ranked various occupations.
    Farming, of course, always stood at the head of the list. The attitude toward
lawyers was contained in the following quatrain:

> To fit up a village with tackle for tillage
> Jack Carter he took to the saw.
> To pluck and to pillage, the same little village
> Tim Gordon he took to the law.[4]

The question, then, is what accounts for this pervasive and intense hostility.
A recent poll conducted by The National Law Journal asked people what most
closely represented their view of the most negative aspect of lawyers. By far the
largest proportion, 32%, disapproved of lawyers because "[t]hey are too interested in money."[5] While that may well (for all I know) be a correct characterization of lawyers, it is hardly a unique one: Avarice does not seem to distinguish
lawyers from businessmen or architects or doctors. But the second and third
reasons for thinking ill of lawyers were different. They were that lawyers "manipulate the legal system without any concern for right or wrong" (22%), and that
they "file too many unnecessary lawsuits" (20%).[6]

---

1. Luke 11:46.
    2. W. Shakespeare, Henry VI, pt. II, act 4, sc. 2, 1.68. Because the character who actually makes
this remark is so very unsavory, it is by no means clear that Shakespeare meant the line to carry the
opprobrious meaning for which it is cited in popular literature.
    3. T. More, Utopia 128 (G. Burnet trans. 1821) (1516). For pure venomous hatred, however, it is
hard to match Coleridge's lesser known lines:

> He saw a Lawyer killing a Viper
> On a dunghill hard by his own stable;
> And the Devil smiled, for it put him in mind
> Of Cain and his brother Abel.

S. T. Coleridge, The Devil's Thoughts, in Complete Poetical Works 320 (1912).
    4. Quoted in R. M. Elson, Guardians of Tradition: American Schoolbooks of the Nineteenth
Century 26 (1964).
    5. What America Really Thinks About Lawyers, Natl. L.J., Aug. 18, 1986, at S-3.
    6. Id.

These are reasons to dislike lawyers that are specific to the legal profession. What is fascinating about these reasons, however, is that when The National Law Journal asked the public what were the most positive aspects of lawyers, far and away the most popular responses were that their "first priority is to their clients" (38%), and that they "know how to cut through bureaucratic red tape" (31%).[7] In other words, lawyers are applauded for following their clients' wishes and bending the rules to satisfy those wishes; and they are at the very same time condemned for using the legal system to satisfy their clients' desires by bringing lawsuits at their clients' behest and using the legal system to get what their clients want, rather than to uphold the right and denounce the wrong. . . .

We owe especially to the sociologist Erving Goffman the insight that the self in modern society can be understood not as something of substance that actually exists, but rather as a series of performances. The character attributed by others to an individual is the result of these performances. Goffman tells us:

> In our society the character one performs and one's self are somewhat equated, and this self-as-character is usually seen as something housed within the body of its possessor. . . . I suggest that this view is . . . a bad analysis of the presentation. In this [book] the performed self was seen as some kind of image, usually creditable, which the individual on stage and in character effectively attempts to induce others to hold in regard to him. While this image is entertained *concerning* the individual, so that a self is imputed to him, this self does not derive from its possessor, but from the whole scene of his action, being generated by that attribute of local events which renders them interpretable by witnesses.[29]

It is of immense importance for us as a society, however, to deny this insight. We get queasy when we view the personality of others to be constituted merely by a series of staged performances.[30] Sartre makes a similar point in his famous analysis in Being and Nothingness:

> A grocer who dreams is offensive to the buyer, because such a grocer is not wholly a grocer. Society demands that he limit himself to his function as a grocer, just as the soldier at attention makes himself into a soldier-thing with a direct regard which does not see at all. . . . There are indeed many precautions to imprison a man in what he is, as if we lived in perpetual fear that he might escape from it, that he might break away and suddenly elude his condition.[31]

This perpetual fear of the self escaping its concrete and given substance is in some measure behind the centuries of abuse and loathing that the premodern era poured onto actors,[32] for actors are the living embodiment of the performing, protean self. Jean-Jacques Rousseau, for example, thought actors

7. Id.
29. E. Goffman, The Presentation of Self in Everyday Life 252 (1959).
30. For a criticism of "the 'dramaturgic approach' to social experience," see Messinger, Life as Theater: Some Notes on the Dramaturgic Approach to Social Reality, 25 Sociometry 98 (1962).
31. J. Sartre, Being and Nothingness 59 (H. Barnes trans. 1956).
32. "[I]n every country their profession is one that dishonors, . . . [t]hose who exercise it, excommunicated or not, are everywhere despised. . . ." J. Rousseau, Politics and the Arts: Letter to M. D'Alembert on the Theatre 76 (A. Bloom trans. 1960) (1758).

"dishonorable" because the talent of the actor lies in "the art of counterfeiting himself, of putting on another character than his own, of appearing different than he is, . . . of forgetting his own place by dint of taking another's."[33] Rousseau contrasted the actor to the orator:

> When the orator appears in public, it is to speak and not to show himself off; he represents only himself; he fills only his own role, speaks only in his own name, says, or ought to say, only what he thinks; the man and his role being the same, he is in his place; he is in the situation of any citizen who fulfills the functions of his estate. But an actor on the stage, displaying other sentiments than his own, saying only what he is made to say, often representing a chimerical being, annihilates himself, as it were, and is lost in his hero.[34]

Actors, however, lie directly: we all know that Olivier is only pretending to be King Lear, and that it is just a performance. But consider, in this light, the trial lawyer making a summary to the jury. In that case we know both (1) that the lawyer must be representing the interests of his client, so that his speech does not sincerely represent his "personal" views; and (2) that if the lawyer distinguishes between his personal views and those of his client, his client will suffer, so that the lawyer can perform his job only if he "appears" to be and in fact convinces us that he is sincere. Unlike the actor, then, the lawyer's job requires that he totally conceal his performance. And he must do this about issues of public importance, where the integrity of the self as a constituted member of the community is most at stake. To paraphrase Rousseau, the lawyer must convince us that he is an orator, exercising his highest function as a citizen, when in reality he is simply a secret actor, "lost" in the identity of his client.

This is extraordinarily disturbing. And so in popular culture we say of the lawyer, as the old adage goes, "A good lawyer must be a great liar."[35] Or we say, with Jonathan Swift, that lawyers are a "society of men . . . bred up from their youth in the art of proving by words multiplied for the purpose, that white is black and black is white, according as they are paid."[36]

These hostile characterizations of the lawyer put her at a distance, as though her performances were something specially devious and different from the rest of us. If our acceptance of the acting profession demonstrates that we have come to acknowledge that role-playing is an integral aspect of modern experience, our excoriation of lawyers illustrates that this acceptance has definite limits. The performances of the lawyer are hidden, and hence they obliterate the distinction between the performing self and the true or innate self. But in this the lawyer is merely representative of the concealed performances we must all undertake

---

33. J. Rousseau, supra note 32, at 79. In language that is often today applied directly to lawyers, Rousseau condemned the actor's profession as

> a trade in which he performs for money, submits himself to the disgrace and the affronts that others buy the right to give him, and puts his person publicly on sale. I beg every sincere man to tell if he does not feel in the depths of his soul that there is something servile and base in this traffic of oneself.

Id. . . .

34. J. Rousseau, supra note 32, at 80-81.
35. The Facts on File Dictionary of Proverbs (R. Ferguson ed. 1983), at 139.
36. J. Swift, Gulliver's Travels 295 (P. Dixon & J. Chalker eds. 1967) (1726).

every day. We would like to believe that we are the master of our many roles, rather than the reverse, but the persistent and unsettling example of the lawyer will not let us rest easy in this belief. If Goffman is correct, and if we are in fact constituted by our performances, the intensity of the animosity we bear toward lawyers may come precisely from the fact that they are so very threatening to our need to believe that we possess stable and coherent selves.

Analyzed in this way, the special hatred that popular culture holds for the lawyer can be an illuminating resource for understanding cultural contradictions of the deepest and most profound kind. The lawyer is the public and unavoidable embodiment of the tension we all experience between the desire for an embracing and common community and the urge toward individual independence and self-assertion; between the need for a stable, coherent, and sincerely presented self and the fragmented and disassociated roles we are forced to play in the theater of modern life. In popular imagery the lawyer is held to strict account for the discrepancy between our aspirations and our realities. But this discrepancy is not the lawyer's alone, and once we understand this we may also come to see that in popular culture the lawyer is so much our enemy, because his failings are so much our own.

"Which System Is Better?"

A nation has recently deposed a longtime dictator and is doing the groundwork to become a constitutional democracy with an independent judiciary and bar. In constructing a civil litigation system, the leaders of the new nation are considering adversarial and cooperative models. No local precedents exist from which the leaders can work. The economy of the nation is undeveloped but it has abundant natural resources, many ports and tourist attractions, and a highly motivated population with an educated elite that has returned from exile. The leaders hope to move rapidly toward a market economy. How would you advise them to choose between the two following models? To what extent are you influenced by your current and anticipated status?

Under the adversarial system, it is a lawyer's responsibility to win (or get the best possible settlement) regardless of the merits of his client's case, so long as the lawyer does nothing illegal or unethical. A client's chance of winning is improved if the client has more information than the adversary. Information may be factual or legal. Factual information is obtained by hiring investigators and experts (economists, scientists, and the like). Legal information is secured by hiring smart lawyers able to engage in extensive research and capable of making novel arguments using their excellent persuasive skills. If the factual or legal investigations produce information that is damaging to the client's matter, the client will generally have no obligation to reveal this information to the adversary or the judge. In fact, the lawyer will have an obligation not to do so. Hiring investigators, experts, and smart lawyers costs money, sometimes large amounts of money. Therefore, other things being equal, the more money a client has, the greater the likelihood that he will win, or at least be able to force a settlement more generous than he would have obtained if he did not have all the information.

In the cooperative legal system, on the other hand, lawyers for both sides are responsible for pooling all information about a dispute in an effort to determine what really happened. All reports from investigators and experts must be shared. Lawyers are also responsible for sharing their legal research, favorable or unfavorable. While no client and no lawyer is obligated to search for facts or find cases useful to his opponent, if in preparing his case a lawyer happens to come upon such facts or cases, he must reveal them. There is no work product protection for facts, although there is for a lawyer's thought processes. In effect, the facts in each lawyer's file belong to his or her opponent. The attorney-client privilege remains to the extent that lawyers and clients may not be forced to reveal their communications. Lawyers would always be free to argue different inferences from the facts, to challenge the credibility of any witness, to argue different facts when supported by evidence, and to argue different theories of what the law is (or should be). The supporters of the cooperative system argue that (a) it will provide greater accuracy in fact finding, (b) it will reduce unfairness due to disparities in wealth, and (c) it will lead to swifter and cheaper resolution of civil disputes.

B. ARE LAWYERS EVER MORALLY ACCOUNTABLE FOR THEIR CLIENTS?

Model Rule 1.2(b) states: "A lawyer's representation of a client, including representation by appointment, does not constitute an endorsement of the client's political, economic, social or moral views or activities." What is a sentence like that doing in a legal ethics document? It's not a rule one can violate, is it? (The Code has no equivalent.) Well, it's there, so what does it mean? Does it mean I may not (ought not?) publicly criticize a lawyer because of the clients she has chosen to represent, perhaps over a lifetime? Let's say the lawyer's clients have routinely been large-quantity drug conspirators, organized crime defendants, purveyors of porn, brutal dictators, tobacco companies in products liability cases, or manufacturers of Saturday Night Specials. Or what about the lawyers who for years after Brown v. Board of Education and other high court cases helped state and local governments avoid integration of schools and places of public accommodation? Was their help immoral, even if ethical? Many lawyers would say that making any moral judgments about other lawyers because of the identity or goals of their clients or the nature of their work will impede the availability of counsel, including counsel for political dissidents, minorities, and others most in need of the law's protection. So think what you want privately, but don't criticize publicly. Are they right? Here's one representation that spilled into public debate.

Cravath Represents Credit Suisse

Under the headline "N.Y. Law Firm to Advise Swiss Bank Accused of Laundering Nazi Loot," the Washington Post (February 28, 1997, at A3) reported that Cravath Swaine & Moore had agreed — over objection from some partners and associates — to represent Credit Suisse, described by a U.S. official as "the most frequent violator" of rules against laundering plundered Nazi gold. Cravath had agreed to advise the bank in its negotiations of the claims of Holocaust victims (or their families) that they were the owners of the looted wealth. The Washington, D.C., firm Wilmer, Cutler & Pickering had earlier agreed to represent Credit Suisse and two other Swiss banks in litigation brought by the same claimants. The Post cited government findings that Credit Suisse had accepted German gold bars and had provided Germans with "millions of Swiss francs, which allowed Adolf Hitler to finance his war machine."

The internal Cravath memo protesting the decision to represent Credit Suisse said in part:

> It is our conviction that one cannot represent Credit Suisse in its role as bankers to those who committed genocide and do the justice we are all obliged to do to the victims and survivors of the slaughter. The two are simply incompatible.
>
> It seems implausible that Cravath could both serve Credit Suisse and bring about a fair and honorable resolution for those who suffered at the hands of the Nazis and their collaborators. We suspect, even with the best intentions, Credit Suisse's interest may be too closely connected with containing the financial consequences of scandal for justice to be served by our representation of them.

The Cravath story drew many reactions from the bar, including comparisons to Abraham Sofaer's representation of Libya's Moammar Gadhafi (page 344). Saundra Torry quoted Harvey Pitt, then at Fried, Frank, Harris, Shriver & Jacobson, as seeing "a huge difference between [representing] Credit Suisse and Moammar Gadhafi. The essential difference is that [Credit Suisse] is an upstanding financial institution whose general policy is to comply with all the rules and laws applicable. If it makes a mistake, it is entitled to a defense. But if someone is deliberately assassinating people . . . they don't earn the same entitlement to legal representation." Saundra Torry, When the Sins of the Client Are Visited on the Firm, Washington Post, March 3, 1997, at F7. The following Op-Ed article, written by a prominent Washington lawyer, takes a different view.

Ronald Goldfarb
LAWYERS SHOULD BE JUDGED BY THE
CLIENTS THEY KEEP
Washington Post, April 6, 1997, at C3

Recently, 12 lawyers at Cravath, Swaine & Moore, a prestigious New York law firm, protested their employer's decision to represent Credit Suisse in its dispute with the families of Holocaust victims. In their memo to the firm's managing partners, the lawyers pleaded that representing the Swiss bank would add their firm's "imprimatur" and legitimacy to a client that profited from laundering Nazi loot under egregious circumstances, and concealed its collaboration.

The Cravath partners reached a consensus that the client was now trying to do the right thing — and that the firm was just providing neutral advice. Someone had to defend the bank.

The case raises interesting questions about which ideals lawyers should answer to. It is an article of faith among many lawyers that their professional obligation is to represent all clients, regardless of the charges against them. A lawyer's reputation should not be associated with his client's conduct, the argument goes. Forty states, including the District of Columbia, have adopted the standard from the Model Rules of Professional Conduct that states that "a lawyer's representation of a client . . . does not constitute an endorsement of the client's political, economic, social or moral views or activities." Professionals should simply provide their services, the argument goes, and not judge their clients: Would a doctor refuse to treat a sick sinner?

But is there no more to be said about attorneys who spend their careers representing murdering drug dealers or manufacturers of deadly products, making oodles of money in the process? Is this money grubbing or selfless professionalism?

Lawyers do have choices, and we should not set aside our moral scruples when we go to work. Private lawyers have refused and dismissed clients over ethical differences. We should sit in judgment of those who walk into our offices — or be prepared to be judged by the company we keep.

In a television debate with a group of successful Washington lawyers, I questioned the mantra that since every person is entitled to representation, attorneys should not be judged by the clients they represent. One of the lawyers told me that, given my views, I should have gone to medical school.

Consider an alternative point of view. I agree that every client is entitled to a lawyer, but not necessarily to me or to any particular lawyer. If we lawyers do not want to be classified with our clients, by what standard should we be defined? We do what we want, and thus should be defined by what we do.

According to the Model Rules, no lawyer must take any case, except those assigned by a court. When the court orders them to do so, lawyers must represent even the most unpopular defendants (unless the client or cause is so "repugnant" as to impair the lawyer-client relationship). I have a friend whose career with the federal public defenders' office has included defending some despicable terrorists. People like him are carrying out the principled constitutional mandate that all defendants must have professional representation. So too are groups like the ACLU, which represents issues more so than the people who raise them.

But taking non-mandated cases is always at a lawyer's discretion. If lawyers can say "no" because the fee is insufficient, they can say no because the position they are asked to take is repugnant, to use a word from the Model Rules. So a lawyer who accepts such a case should be prepared to take, along with the fee, the heat that may come with it.

Under our adversary system, lawyers zealously assert their client's interest and challenge their adversaries in order that the truth may emerge. But does it? When I observe an insurance company lawyer harassing a rape victim in a deposition, or a mob lawyer intimidating a witness, or an attorney aggressively advancing his corporate client's anti-environmental or anti-public health interests, or a white-collar defense lawyer using the media to sell his client's phony position,

I understand why my profession evokes widespread condemnation. Like the medical profession's fiat "do no harm," shouldn't lawyers be ethically bound to do no injustice? How, the Cravath 12 asked, can the firm do all that the adversary system requires on their client's behalf, and not do an injustice to their client's adversaries, who in this case happen to be Holocaust victims?

Lawyers can't have it both ways, representing plundering companies for a living and not taking on their coloration, or representing scuzzy clients and avoiding public cynicism for doing so. It is not unfair to associate lawyers with their clients. This is particularly so when they are the attorneys for only one kind of client, such as a drug company that fought to keep deleterious drugs on the market, or when they represent someone who is intimately associated with a morally despicable cause, such as the Ku Klux Klan. What is the responsibility of those tobacco company lawyers who, knowing what they must have known about their clients' conduct, nonetheless fought off attempts at government regulation and poured daunting resources into thwarting private litigation? I would argue that they are as responsible as the companies they represent, if not more so.

Many lawyers claim that in representing an unpopular client or position, they are performing a constitutional or professional duty worthy of praise, not scorn. Some lawyers may be interested in issues only, but I can't help wondering why so many poor clients don't have lawyers and so many rich scoundrels do; superstar lawyers rarely seem to be available for poor clients. There is self-justification — or just plain hypocrisy — going on here in the name of ethics.

If American lawyers had to represent all comers, as is the case elsewhere, they could argue that they should not be judged according to their clients. Since that is not the situation in the United States, lawyers have to face an inherent conflict between their duty to their clients and their obligations to society.

Credit Suisse has the right to seek representation. Cravath has the right to represent anyone it chooses and to be paid well for its work. But whoever does Credit Suisse's bidding is, as the conscientious dissenters at Cravath complained, serving as the agent of bankers who abetted genocidal murderers. In doing so, the lawyers inevitably help justify and minimize the consequences from the reprehensible acts in question.

All lawyers, including those at Cravath, also have the right to say no. What would happen to justice if all the lawyers said no in cases involving important moral issues?

Imagine.

Cravath was advising Credit Suisse in negotiation with families of Holocaust victims. Wilmer Cutler was representing Credit Suisse in court against the same group. Do the different roles make a difference in moral culpability? The term "adversary system excuse" has appeared — sometimes earnestly and sometimes dismissively — to describe the immunity from moral criticism that litigators claim for themselves. Are the moral tests we apply to litigators different from those we apply in transactional matters (assuming we make moral judgments at all)? If so, why? Or if you would prefer a different context, consider lawyers for tobacco companies. One group defended class actions in which former smokers (or their estates) sought damages for tobacco-related illnesses. Another group helped with all of the mundane transactional work required to market any consumer product. Let's assume that none of the lawyers violated any ethical or legal rule. Can we morally criticize the lawyers in either of these groups? Does it matter if, when they did their work, they (a) knew or (b) had good reason to believe that smoking causes death? Are both sets of lawyers immune to moral criticism (at least from other lawyers) precisely because they were acting as lawyers, in the role our justice system assigns, and we should therefore defend them so as to encourage the bar to accept the representation of unpopular clients? Would you extend the same immunity to other professionals who helped bring the product to market, say the creative teams that designed print (and, until the ban, electronic) advertisements that portrayed smoking as sophisticated, glamorous and sexy?

Daniel Markovits explores questions like these in Adversary Advocacy and the Authority of Adjudication, 75 Fordham L. Rev. 1367 (2006). Professor Markovits writes:

> I shall argue that partisan client-centered rather than impartial justice-centered lawyers are necessary for the legitimacy of adjudication (and indeed for the broader practices of applying general laws to particular cases). And although I shall not seek to establish the precise metes and bounds of the partisanship that legitimacy requires lawyers to display — or to ask how the positive law of lawyering stands with respect to the argument that I develop — it will be apparent that the required partisanship is substantial. . . .
>
> [The] case for partisanship will be stronger as lawyers' activities move nearer to addressing externally imposed resolutions of their clients' claims — because this is when the legitimacy of such resolutions is most insistently in need of a defense. Litigation, of course, represents the central example of such a case, but other activities, even those at some distance from litigation, also implicate the authority of the state's mechanisms for applying law to resolve disputes.

C.   TRUTH AND CONFIDENCES

Truth loves open dealing.

— Queen Katherine to Cardinal Wolsey in Shakespeare, *Henry VIII*, 3.01.39

A lawyer will do anything to win a case, sometimes he will even tell the truth.

— Patrick Murray, British actor

"Out Carousing With Mikey"

"I'm sorry to disturb you with this e-mail on July Fourth, but my friend Slade, who used to work with you, Slade Catterson, said 'Tanya, your problem is beyond my casual knowledge of the ethics rules.' Given the dangers in guessing wrong, he told me to e-mail you. I would have waited until Monday, but I think I have to act quickly. Or anyway make a decision.

"Anyway, I'm defending a man named Carlo on a manslaughter charge. He's indigent and I'm court appointed. The whole case comes down to identity. The crime took place at two in the morning last August 4 on a street corner. Poor lighting. There are two eye-witnesses, one of whom had had a lot to drink. Both picked out Carlo in a lineup. Nothing else connects Carlo with the victim. They were strangers. All in all a weak case. No DNA, no prints. The state's theory is that it was a robbery gone wrong. The victim resisted, the robber hit him a few times, the victim fell and banged his head on a steel pipe in the street.

"Carlo says it wasn't him; he was carousing with his friend Mikey miles away. He can't say exactly where this carousing put them at two in the morning. They had four six-packs between them and were sitting in the park, then they went over to the docks, then they walked around the financial district, just getting drunk. It was a warm night.

"So of course I talked to Mikey, who's got a demeanor you associate with a punch drunk ex-boxer, which he is. Not very bright. Not even a little bright. But very sweet. He does odd jobs. Cutting grass. Chopping wood. He has some injury from the first Gulf war that seems to have made concentration a bit of a challenge. Mostly, he lives on disability.

"This was not an easy conversation, getting Mikey to focus. He keeps losing the thread. But he says he and Carlo hang together a lot, buy beer, get drunk, vomit, buy more beer. They're friends from the service. He says they were doing that August 4, the morning of the crime, actually from late on the third until daylight on the fourth. Basically he confirms Carlo's story — the beer, the park, the docks.

"I put Carlo on the stand to testify to how he was out carousing with Mikey. Of course, it helps greatly to confirm a defendant's story, so I also called Mikey, who is, as I say, a sweet guy, very credible, open, a ready smile. He supports Carlo's testimony and, to my amazement, he does well on cross. This was two days ago, and I rested yesterday morning. The state has some rebuttal after the July Fourth weekend. Then we'll sum up. We had off yesterday afternoon, and when I get to my office, there's Mikey.

"This is where I have my problem. He says it wasn't August 3-4 when he and Carlo went carousing. He thought it was because 'after Carlo reminded me when it was, I remembered when it was.' I have no doubt he testified to what he believed was the truth.

"So why now all of a sudden does he not believe it was true? Yesterday, July 3, he called his sister who lives in Fort Wayne to wish his niece a happy birthday, and his sister says he's got the wrong month. Her birthday is not July 3 but August 3 and doesn't he remember because last year he came to her sweet sixteen in Fort Wayne, which is 700 miles from here, and he gave her an iPod. Suddenly, he does remember and realizes that he must have gone carousing with Carlo a different night last August. Or maybe July. Or maybe September. He's really mixed up now.

"One of the things about Mikey is he's a pack rat. He saves everything. He pulls out his bus ticket stub and receipt showing a roundtrip to Fort Wayne last August 3, returning August 5. And the iPod receipt. And an ATM receipt for $20 from a bank in Fort Wayne dated August 5 so he could buy lunch for the trip. I confirmed that Mikey's debit card was used for each transaction. He feels really bad about this, he says, and thought he should tell me. He hasn't told anyone else. So don't I now know that Mikey's testimony is false and that Carlo lied? I don't know what to do but I'm hoping you do."

What should a lawyer do if he learns, through a confidential communication, that a client has committed or is in the process of committing a fraud on the court, personally or through others? Perhaps the lawyer has actually been used as the unwitting instrument of this fraud. Of course, if the fraud is still (even partly) prospective, the lawyer cannot legally or ethically aid it, Rule 1.2(d), and may be guilty as an accessory if he does. Chapter 2 showed us that outside litigation, a lawyer may have the authority, or in some jurisdictions an obligation, to reveal a future crime or fraud or even a concluded one if the harm can be prevented or remedied, at least where the lawyer has provided unwitting help (see page 64).

In litigation, the authority to reveal the misdeeds of a client committed while the lawyer was representing the client has also been the subject of much debate. The attention we pay this issue is surely disproportionate to the frequency with which lawyers know about such conduct. Why do we spend the time? Perhaps because the issue raises fundamental questions about what it means to be an American lawyer. Paradoxically, lawyers feel they have a lot riding on the answers — professional identity itself — even if it is unlikely that any lawyer will actually encounter the dilemma.

Several variables should be noted. The issue may arise in transactional work, discussed again in chapter 9, or litigation, discussed here. A litigation may be civil or criminal. The fraud may come in the form of a false document that the lawyer has unwittingly introduced in evidence. Or it may come via client perjury or the perjury of a witness for the client, who lies with or without the client's connivance. The lie may come on direct or cross-examination. Where the client is an organization, it can commit fraud on a court only through its agents, who (as we further discuss in chapter 10) are not ordinarily the lawyer's clients. Last, a trial lawyer may learn that his client or witness made a false statement believing it to be true. That will not be perjury but Rule 3.3(a)(3) may require correction.

Despite these variables, the paradigmatic example of fraud on a court has been the perjury of a criminal defendant. This is seen to present the hardest case, in large part because the criminal defendant has a constitutional right to testify in his own defense, even if his lawyer believes it would be tactically foolish, although of course the defendant has no right to lie under oath. Given the stakes, if we resolve the criminal defendant's perjury in favor of revelation, do we thereby solve all the "easier" cases?

What should a lawyer do when she knows that a client plans to lie on the witness stand? Or when after the client testifies the lawyer first learns, perhaps from the client, that he has already lied? Or when the lawyer has called the client to testify and is then surprised when the client lies without warning, whether on direct or cross? Should these three situations — anticipated perjury, completed perjury, and surprise perjury — be treated alike? Should it matter whether the case is still on trial when the lawyer learns of the perjury? Whether it is on appeal?

The specter of a perjurious *criminal* defendant requires us to address not only the ethical issue, but also the Sixth Amendment right to the effective assistance of counsel. Does this right impose separate duties on defense counsel *not* to reveal client perjury? If it does, a state ethics rule could not override those.

Stated most broadly, then, the debate is over whether a lawyer's duties of confidentiality and loyalty to a client should be superior to any duty the lawyer would otherwise have to prevent or correct a fraud on the court, or whether instead the lawyer as an "officer of the court" should have a duty to prevent or correct such a fraud notwithstanding that doing so will reveal a client's confidences and perhaps subject a criminal defendant to further prosecution and longer incarceration and a civil litigant to a devastating loss and a perjury charge.

Legislative History of the Code

The legal profession has been debating these questions for decades, and given the division of opinion, it will likely continue to do so for decades to come. The 1908 Canons of Professional Ethics and the 1970 Code of Professional Responsibility both treated confidentiality and loyalty as more important than a duty to correct perjury. The Model Rules (reflecting the majority view) reversed that priority, at least in part, including in criminal cases (although some jurisdictions, including Massachusetts, Washington, D.C., and Washington State, retained the former priority in their versions of the rules). While most of this history is described in the following selections, to preserve institutional memory (remember what Santayana said about forgetting history), we add some background, including one piece of Code legerdemain and a brief backdrop to the Model Rules provision.

In DR 7-102(B)(1), the Code provided that if a lawyer has "receive[d] information clearly establishing that [a] client has, in the course of the representation, perpetrated a fraud upon a . . . tribunal" and the client refuses to correct it, the lawyer "shall reveal the fraud to the affected . . . tribunal, except when the information is protected as a privileged communication." As originally adopted, the provision did not have the "except" clause. That was added in 1974 to make it clear that the lawyer's duty was subordinate to the duty to maintain the confidences and secrets of a client. The Code defines "confidences" as information protected by the attorney-client privilege, while "secrets" includes most other information gained in the professional relationship (not only from the client or its agents). Unfortunately, the 1974 amendment except clause referred only to "privileged" communications. This would seem to suggest that the lawyer's duty under DR 7-102(B)(1) is not "excepted" if the lawyer knows of the client's fraud through a "secret" as opposed to a "confidence." (By contrast, the New York version of the same "except" clause eliminated the lawyer's duty to correct client fraud on a tribunal if the lawyer's knowledge is *either* a secret *or* a confidence.)

To the rescue, ABA Opinion 341 (1975) conveniently, if disingenuously, interpreted the words "privileged communication" in DR 7-102(B)(1) to include both secrets and confidences. In reaching this odd construction, which contradicts the definitions of DR 4-101(A), the opinion said that its "interpretation does not wipe out DR 7-102(B)." Oh, really? Can you imagine a realistic situation in which a lawyer might acquire information that a client has committed a fraud on a tribunal "in the course of the representation" where the information would *not* have been gained in the professional relationship? A majority of jurisdictions rejected the 1974 amendment. Even more reject it today because they have the Model Rules.

Legislative History of the Rules

Rule 3.3 was intensely debated on its way to ABA adoption. Earlier versions were significantly broader and would have changed the architecture of the adversary system significantly. For example, the January 1980 draft (where what would become Rule 3.3 appeared as Rule 3.1) said in part:

RULE 3.1   Candor Toward Tribunal

A lawyer shall be candid toward a tribunal. . . .

(b)   Except as provided in paragraph (f), if a lawyer discovers that evidence or testimony presented by the lawyer is false, the lawyer shall disclose that fact and take suitable measures to rectify the consequences, even if doing so requires disclosure of a confidence of the client or disclosure that the client is implicated in the falsification. . . .

(d)   Except as provided in paragraph (f), a lawyer shall disclose a fact known to the lawyer even if the fact is adverse, when disclosure: . . .

    (2)   is necessary to correct a manifest misapprehension resulting from a previous representation the lawyer has made to the tribunal.

Paragraph (f) concerns lawyers for defendants in criminal cases.

Rule 3.3 as finally adopted in 1983 continued unchanged until 2002, when the E2K commission rewrote it. Here is the current rule showing important changes from the rule as originally adopted:

(a) A lawyer shall not knowingly:

    (1) make a false statement of material fact or law to a tribunal <u>or fail to correct a false statement of material fact or law previously made to the tribunal by the lawyer</u>;

    ~~(2) fail to disclose a material fact to a tribunal when disclosure is necessary to avoid assisting a criminal or fraudulent act by the client;~~

    ~~(3)~~ (2) fail to disclose to the tribunal legal authority in the controlling jurisdiction known to the lawyer to be directly adverse to the position of the client and not disclosed by opposing counsel; or

    ~~(4)~~ (3) offer evidence that the lawyer knows to be false. If a lawyer, the lawyer's client, or a witness called by the lawyer, has offered material evidence and the lawyer comes to know of its falsity, the lawyer shall take reasonable remedial measures, including, if necessary, disclosure to the tribunal. A lawyer may refuse to offer evidence, other than the testimony of a defendant in a criminal matter, that the lawyer reasonably believes is false.

(b) <u>A lawyer who represents a client in an adjudicative proceeding and who knows that a person intends to engage, is engaging or has engaged in criminal</u>

or fraudulent conduct related to the proceeding shall take reasonable remedial measures, including, if necessary, disclosure to the tribunal.

~~(b)~~(c) The duties stated in ~~paragraph~~ paragraphs (a) and (b) continue to
the conclusion of the proceeding, and apply even if compliance requires disclosure of information otherwise protected by Rule 1.6.

~~(c) A lawyer may refuse to offer evidence that the lawyer reasonably believes
is false.~~

(d) In an ex parte proceeding, a lawyer shall inform the tribunal of all
material facts known to the lawyer that will enable the tribunal to make an
informed decision, whether or not the facts are adverse.

Now back to that overhanging question. When the rules were adopted in
1983, uncertainty existed over whether a criminal defense lawyer who alerts
(or threatens to alert) the judge that a client will commit or has committed
perjury thereby renders ineffective assistance of counsel under the Sixth
Amendment. A unanimous Supreme Court responded to that uncertainty as
a matter of constitutional law in 1986, but the answer, as we shall see, has simply
sparked more questions.

NIX v. WHITESIDE
475 U.S. 157 (1986)

CHIEF JUSTICE BURGER delivered the opinion of the Court.

We granted certiorari to decide whether the Sixth Amendment right of a
criminal defendant to assistance of counsel is violated when an attorney refuses
to cooperate with the defendant in presenting perjured testimony at his trial.[1]

I

A

Whiteside was convicted of second-degree murder by a jury verdict which was
affirmed by the Iowa courts. The killing took place on February 8, 1977, in Cedar
Rapids, Iowa. Whiteside and two others went to one Calvin Love's apartment late
that night, seeking marihuana. Love was in bed when Whiteside and his companions arrived; an argument between Whiteside and Love over the marihuana
ensued. At one point, Love directed his girlfriend to get his "piece," and at

---

1. Although courts universally condemn an attorney's assisting in presenting perjury, Courts of
Appeals have taken varying approaches on how to deal with a client's insistence on presenting
perjured testimony. The Seventh Circuit, for example, has held that an attorney's refusal to call the
defendant as a witness did not render the conviction constitutionally infirm where the refusal to call
the defendant was based on the attorney's belief that the defendant would commit perjury. United
States v. Curtis, 742 F.2d 1070 (C.A.7 1984). The Third Circuit found a violation of the Sixth
Amendment where the attorney could not state any basis for her belief that the defendant's
proposed alibi testimony was perjured. United States ex rel. Wilcox v. Johnson, 555 F.2d 115
(C.A.3 1977). See also Lowery v. Cardwell, 575 F.2d 727 (C.A.9 1978) (withdrawal request in the
middle of a bench trial, immediately following defendant's testimony).

another point got up, then returned to his bed. According to Whiteside's testimony, Love then started to reach under his pillow and moved toward Whiteside. Whiteside stabbed Love in the chest, inflicting a fatal wound. Whiteside was charged with murder, and when counsel was appointed he objected to the lawyer initially appointed, claiming that he felt uncomfortable with a lawyer who had formerly been a prosecutor. Gary L. Robinson was then appointed and immediately began an investigation. Whiteside gave him a statement that he had stabbed Love as the latter "was pulling a pistol from underneath the pillow on the bed." Upon questioning by Robinson, however, Whiteside indicated that he had not actually seen a gun, but that he was convinced that Love had a gun. No pistol was found on the premises; shortly after the police search following the stabbing, which had revealed no weapon, the victim's family had removed all of the victim's possessions from the apartment. Robinson interviewed Whiteside's companions who were present during the stabbing and none had seen a gun during the incident. Robinson advised Whiteside that the existence of a gun was not necessary to establish the claim of self defense, and that only a reasonable belief that the victim had a gun nearby was necessary even though no gun was actually present.

Until shortly before trial, Whiteside consistently stated to Robinson that he had not actually seen a gun, but that he was convinced that Love had a gun in his hand. About a week before trial, during preparation for direct examination, Whiteside for the first time told Robinson and his associate Donna Paulsen that he had seen something "metallic" in Love's hand. When asked about this, Whiteside responded that "[I]n Howard Cook's case there was a gun. If I don't say I saw a gun, I'm dead." Robinson told Whiteside that such testimony would be perjury and repeated that it was not necessary to prove that a gun was available but only that Whiteside reasonably believed that he was in danger. On Whiteside's insisting that he would testify that he saw "something metallic" Robinson told him, according to Robinson's testimony,

> [W]e could not allow him to [testify falsely] because that would be perjury, and as officers of the court we would be suborning perjury if we allowed him to do it. . . . I advised him that if he did do that it would be my duty to advise the Court of what he was doing and that I felt he was committing perjury; also, that I probably would be allowed to attempt to impeach that particular testimony.

Robinson also indicated he would seek to withdraw from the representation if Whiteside insisted on committing perjury.[2]

Whiteside testified in his own defense at trial and stated that he "knew" that Love had a gun and that he believed Love was reaching for a gun and he had acted swiftly in self defense. On cross examination, he admitted that he had not actually seen a gun in Love's hand. Robinson presented evidence that Love had been seen with a sawed-off shotgun on other occasions, that the police search of

---

2. Whiteside's version of the events at this pretrial meeting is considerably more cryptic:

Q. And as you went over the questions, did the two of you come into conflict with regard to whether or not there was a weapon?

A. I couldn't — I couldn't say a conflict. But I got the impression at one time that maybe if I didn't go along with — with what was happening, that it was no gun being involved, maybe that he will pull out of my trial. . . .

the apartment may have been careless, and that the victim's family had removed everything from the apartment shortly after the crime. Robinson presented this evidence to show a basis for Whiteside's asserted fear that Love had a gun.

The jury returned a verdict of second-degree murder and Whiteside moved for a new trial, claiming that he had been deprived of a fair trial by Robinson's admonitions not to state that he saw a gun or "something metallic." The trial court held a hearing, heard testimony by Whiteside and Robinson, and denied the motion. The trial court made specific findings that the facts were as related by Robinson.

[The Iowa Supreme Court affirmed, holding that Robinson's actions were not only "permissible, but were required." The Eighth Circuit directed that Whiteside be granted a writ of habeas corpus.]

II

A

The right of an accused to testify in his defense is of relatively recent origin. Until the latter part of the preceding century, criminal defendants in this country, as at common law, were considered to be disqualified from giving sworn testimony at their own trial by reason of their interest as a party to the case. . . .

By the end of the nineteenth century, however, the disqualification was finally abolished by statute in most states and in the federal courts. Although this Court has never explicitly held that a criminal defendant has a due process right to testify in his own behalf, cases in several Circuits have so held and the right has long been assumed. We have also suggested that such a right exists as a corollary to the Fifth Amendment privilege against compelled testimony.

B

In Strickland v. Washington, [466 U.S. 668 (1984)], we held that to obtain relief by way of federal habeas corpus on a claim of a deprivation of effective assistance of counsel under the Sixth Amendment, the movant must establish both serious attorney error and prejudice. To show such error, it must be established that the assistance rendered by counsel was constitutionally deficient in that "counsel made errors so serious that counsel was not functioning as 'counsel' guaranteed the defendant by the Sixth Amendment." To show prejudice, it must be established that the claimed lapses in counsel's performance rendered the trial unfair so as to "undermine confidence in the outcome" of the trial.

In *Strickland*, we acknowledged that the Sixth Amendment does not require any particular response by counsel to a problem that may arise. Rather, the Sixth Amendment inquiry is into whether the attorney's conduct was "reasonably effective." To counteract the natural tendency to fault an unsuccessful defense, a court reviewing a claim of ineffective assistance must "indulge a strong presumption that counsel's conduct falls within the wide range of reasonable professional assistance." In giving shape to the perimeters of this range of reasonable professional assistance, *Strickland* mandates that "[p]revailing norms of practice as reflected in American Bar Association Standards and the like . . . are guides to determining what is reasonable, but they are only guides."

Under the *Strickland* standard, breach of an ethical standard does not necessarily make out a denial of the Sixth Amendment guarantee of assistance of counsel. When examining attorney conduct, a court must be careful not to narrow the wide range of conduct acceptable under the Sixth Amendment so restrictively as to constitutionalize particular standards of professional conduct and thereby intrude into the state's proper authority to define and apply the standards of professional conduct applicable to those it admits to practice in its courts. In some future case challenging attorney conduct in the course of a state court trial, we may need to define with greater precision the weight to be given to recognized canons of ethics, the standards established by the State in statutes or professional codes, and the Sixth Amendment, in defining the proper scope and limits on that conduct. Here we need not face that question, since virtually all of the sources speak with one voice.

C

We turn next to the question presented: the definition of the range of "reasonable professional" responses to a criminal defendant client who informs counsel that he will perjure himself on the stand. We must determine whether, in this setting, Robinson's conduct fell within the wide range of professional responses to threatened client perjury acceptable under the Sixth Amendment.

In *Strickland*, we recognized counsel's duty of loyalty and his "overarching duty to advocate the defendant's cause." Plainly, that duty is limited to legitimate, lawful conduct compatible with the very nature of a trial as a search for truth. Although counsel must take all reasonable lawful means to attain the objectives of the client, counsel is precluded from taking steps or in any way assisting the client in presenting false evidence or otherwise violating the law. This principle has consistently been recognized in most unequivocal terms by expositors of the norms of professional conduct since the first Canons of Professional Ethics were adopted by the American Bar Association in 1908. The 1908 Canon 32 provided that

> No client, corporate or individual, however powerful, nor any cause, civil or political, however important, is entitled to receive nor should any lawyer render any service or advice involving disloyalty to the law whose ministers we are, or disrespect of the judicial office, which we are bound to uphold, or corruption of any person or persons exercising a public office or private trust, or deception or betrayal of the public. . . . He must . . . observe and advise his client to observe the statute law. . . .

Of course, this Canon did no more than articulate centuries of accepted standards of conduct. Similarly, Canon 37, adopted in 1928, explicitly acknowledges as an exception to the attorney's duty of confidentiality a client's announced intention to commit a crime:

> The announced intention of a client to commit a crime is not included within the confidences which [the attorney] is bound to respect.

These principles have been carried through to contemporary codifications of an attorney's professional responsibility. . . . Both the Model Code of

Professional Responsibility and the Model Rules of Professional Conduct also adopt the specific exception from the attorney-client privilege for disclosure of perjury that his client intends to commit or has committed. DR 4-101(C)(3) (intention of client to commit a crime); Rule 3.3 (lawyer has duty to disclose falsity of evidence even if disclosure compromises client confidences). Indeed, both the Model Code and the Model Rules do not merely *authorize* disclosure by counsel of client perjury; they *require* such disclosure. See Rule 3.3(a)(4); DR 7-102(B)(1); Committee on Professional Ethics and Conduct of Iowa State Bar Association v. Crary, 245 N.W.2d 298 (Iowa 1976).* . . .

It is universally agreed that at a minimum the attorney's first duty when confronted with a proposal for perjurious testimony is to attempt to dissuade the client from the unlawful course of conduct. Wolfram, Client Perjury, 50 S. Cal. L. Rev. 809, 846 (1977). A statement directly in point is found in the Commentary to [Rule 3.3] under the heading "False Evidence." . . . The Commentary . . . also suggests that an attorney's revelation of his client's perjury to the court is a professionally responsible and acceptable response to the conduct of a client who has actually given perjured testimony. Similarly, the Model Rules and the Commentary, as well as the Code of Professional Responsibility adopted in Iowa expressly permit withdrawal from representation as an appropriate response of an attorney when the client threatens to commit perjury. Withdrawal of counsel when this situation arises at trial gives rise to many difficult questions including possible mistrial and claims of double jeopardy.[6]

The essence of the brief amicus of the American Bar Association reviewing practices long accepted by ethical lawyers, is that under no circumstance may a lawyer either advocate or passively tolerate a client's giving false testimony. This, of course, is consistent with the governance of trial conduct in what we have long called "a search for truth." The suggestion sometimes made that "a lawyer must believe his client not judge him" in no sense means a lawyer can honorably be a party to or in any way give aid to presenting known perjury.

---

* Has the Chief Justice accurately described the duty imposed by DR 7-102(B)(1) in light of ABA Opinion 341 (1975)? See page 379. — Ed.

6. In the evolution of the contemporary standards promulgated by the American Bar Association, an early draft reflects a compromise suggesting that when the disclosure of intended perjury is made during the course of trial, when withdrawal of counsel would raise difficult questions of a mistrial holding, counsel had the option to let the defendant take the stand but decline to affirmatively assist the presentation of perjury by traditional direct examination. Instead, counsel would stand mute while the defendant undertook to present the false version in narrative form in his own words unaided by any direct examination. This conduct was thought to be a signal at least to the presiding judge that the attorney considered the testimony to be false and was seeking to disassociate himself from that course. Additionally, counsel would not be permitted to discuss the known false testimony in closing arguments. Sec ABA Standards for Criminal Justice, 4-7.7 (2d ed. 1980). Most courts treating the subject rejected this approach and insisted on a more rigorous standard, see, e.g., United States v. Curtis, 742 F.2d 1070 (C.A.7 1984); McKissick v. United States, 379 F.2d 754 (C.A.5 1967), aff'd after remand, 398 F.2d 342 (C.A.5 1968); Dodd v. Florida Bar, 118 So. 2d 17, 19 (Fla. 1960). The Eighth Circuit in this case and the Ninth Circuit have expressed approval of the "free narrative" standards. Whiteside v. Scurr, 744 F.2d 1323, 1331 (C.A.8 1984); Lowery v. Cardwell, 575 F.2d 727 (C.A.9 1978).

The Rule finally promulgated in the current Model Rules of Professional Conduct rejects any participation or passive role whatever by counsel in allowing perjury to be presented without challenge.

D

Considering Robinson's representation of respondent in light of these accepted norms of professional conduct, we discern no failure to adhere to reasonable professional standards that would in any sense make out a deprivation of the Sixth Amendment right to counsel. Whether Robinson's conduct is seen as a successful attempt to dissuade his client from committing the crime of perjury, or whether seen as a "threat" to withdraw from representation and disclose the illegal scheme, Robinson's representation of Whiteside falls well within accepted standards of professional conduct and the range of reasonable professional conduct acceptable under *Strickland*. . . .

The Court of Appeals' holding that Robinson's "action deprived [Whiteside] of due process and effective assistance of counsel" is not supported by the record since Robinson's action, at most, deprived Whiteside of his contemplated perjury. Nothing counsel did in any way undermined Whiteside's claim that he believed the victim was reaching for a gun. Similarly, the record gives no support for holding that Robinson's action "also impermissibly compromised [Whiteside's] right to testify in his own defense by conditioning continued representation . . . and confidentiality upon [Whiteside's] *restricted* testimony." The record in fact shows the contrary: (a) that Whiteside did testify, and (b) he was "restricted" or restrained only from testifying falsely and was aided by Robinson in developing the basis for the fear that Love was reaching for a gun. Robinson divulged no client communications until he was compelled to do so in response to Whiteside's post-trial challenge to the quality of his performance. We see this as a case in which the attorney successfully dissuaded the client from committing the crime of perjury.

Paradoxically, even while accepting the conclusion of the Iowa trial court that Whiteside's proposed testimony would have been a criminal act, the Court of Appeals held that Robinson's efforts to persuade Whiteside not to commit that crime were improper; *first*, as forcing an impermissible choice between the right to counsel and the right to testify; and *second*, as compromising client confidences because of Robinson's threat to disclose the contemplated perjury. . . .

Robinson's admonitions to his client can in no sense be said to have forced respondent into an *impermissible* choice between his right to counsel and his right to testify as he proposed for there was no *permissible* choice to testify falsely. For defense counsel to take steps to persuade a criminal defendant to testify truthfully, or to withdraw, deprives the defendant of neither his right to counsel nor the right to testify truthfully. . . . When an accused proposes to resort to perjury or to produce false evidence, one consequence is the risk of withdrawal of counsel.

On this record, the accused enjoyed continued representation within the bounds of reasonable professional conduct and did in fact exercise his right to testify; at most he was denied the right to have the assistance of counsel in the presentation of false testimony. Similarly, we can discern no breach of professional duly in Robinson's admonition to respondent that he would disclose respondent's perjury to the court. The crime of perjury in this setting is indistinguishable in substance from the crime of threatening or tampering with a witness or a juror. A defendant who informed his counsel that he was arranging to bribe or threaten witnesses or members of the jury would have no "right" to insist on counsel's assistance or silence. Counsel would not be limited to advising against that conduct. . . .

E

We hold that, as a matter of law, counsel's conduct complained of here cannot establish the prejudice required for relief under the second strand of the *Strickland* inquiry. Although a defendant need not establish that the attorney's deficient performance more likely than not altered the outcome in order to establish prejudice under *Strickland,* a defendant must show "that there is a reasonable probability that, but for counsel's unprofessional errors, the result of the proceeding would have been different." According to *Strickland,* "[a] reasonable probability is a probability sufficient to undermine confidence in the outcome." The *Strickland* Court noted that the "benchmark" of an ineffective assistance claim is the fairness of the adversary proceeding, and that in judging prejudice and the likelihood of a different outcome, "[a] defendant has no entitlement to the luck of a lawless decisionmaker."

Whether he was persuaded or compelled to desist from perjury, Whiteside has no valid claim that confidence in the result of his trial has been diminished by his desisting from the contemplated perjury. Even if we were to assume that the jury might have believed his perjury, it does not follow that Whiteside was prejudiced. . . .

Whiteside's attorney treated Whiteside's proposed perjury in accord with professional standards, and since Whiteside's truthful testimony could not have prejudiced the result of his trial, the Court of Appeals was in error to direct the issuance of a writ of habeas corpus and must be reversed.

Reversed.

JUSTICE BLACKMUN, with whom JUSTICE BRENNAN, JUSTICE MARSHALL, and JUSTICE STEVENS join, concurring in the judgment.

How a defense attorney ought to act when faced with a client who intends to commit perjury at trial has long been a controversial issue. But I do not believe that a federal habeas corpus case challenging a state criminal conviction is an appropriate vehicle for attempting to resolve this thorny problem. When a defendant argues that he was denied effective assistance of counsel because his lawyer dissuaded him from committing perjury, the only question properly presented to this Court is whether the lawyer's actions deprived the defendant of the fair trial which the Sixth Amendment is meant to guarantee. Since I believe that the respondent in this case suffered no injury justifying federal habeas relief, I concur in the Court's judgment. . . .

II . . .

B

The Court approaches this case as if the performance-and-prejudice standard requires us in every case to determine "the perimeters of [the] range of reasonable professional assistance" . . . but Strickland v. Washington explicitly contemplates a different course:

Although we have discussed the performance component of an ineffectiveness claim prior to the prejudice component, there is no reason for a court deciding an ineffective assistance claim to approach the inquiry in the same order or even to address both components of the inquiry if the defendant makes an insufficient showing on one. . . .

In this case, respondent has failed to show any legally cognizable prejudice. Nor, as is discussed below, is this a case in which prejudice should be presumed.

The touchstone of a claim of prejudice is an allegation that counsel's behavior did something "to deprive the defendant of a fair trial, a trial whose result is reliable." The only effect Robinson's threat had on Whiteside's trial is that Whiteside did not testify, falsely, that he saw a gun in Love's hand. Thus, this Court must ask whether its confidence in the outcome of Whiteside's trial is in any way undermined by the knowledge that he refrained from presenting false testimony. . . .

C

In light of respondent's failure to show any cognizable prejudice, I see no need to "grade counsel's performance." Strickland v. Washington. The only federal issue in this case is whether Robinson's behavior deprived Whiteside of the effective assistance of counsel; it is not whether Robinson's behavior conformed to any particular code of legal ethics.

Whether an attorney's response to what he sees as a client's plan to commit perjury violates a defendant's Sixth Amendment rights may depend on many factors: how certain the attorney is that the proposed testimony is false, the stage of the proceedings at which the attorney discovers the plan, or the ways in which the attorney may be able to dissuade his client, to name just three. The complex interaction of factors, which is likely to vary from case to case, makes inappropriate a blanket rule that defense attorneys must reveal, or threaten to reveal, a client's anticipated perjury to the court. Except in the rarest of cases, attorneys who adopt "the role of the judge or jury to determine the facts," United States ex rel. Wilcox v. Johnson, 555 F.2d 115, 122 (C.A.3 1977), pose a danger of depriving their clients of the zealous and loyal advocacy required by the Sixth Amendment.[8]

I therefore am troubled by the Court's implicit adoption of a set of standards of professional responsibility for attorneys in state criminal proceedings. The States, of course, do have a compelling interest in the integrity of their criminal trials that can justify regulating the length to which an attorney may go in seeking his client's acquittal. But the American Bar Association's implicit suggestion in its brief amicus curiae that the Court find that the Association's Model Rules of Professional Conduct should govern an attorney's responsibilities is

---

8. A comparison of this case with *Wilcox* is illustrative. Here, Robinson testified in detail to the factors that led him to conclude that respondent's assertion he had seen a gun was false. The Iowa Supreme Court found "good cause" and "strong support" for Robinson's conclusion. Moreover, Robinson gave credence to those parts of Whiteside's account which, although he found them implausible and unsubstantiated, were not clearly false. . . . By contrast, in *Wilcox*, where defense counsel actually informed the judge that she believed her client intended to lie and where her threat to withdraw in the middle of the trial led the defendant not to take the stand at all, the Court of Appeals found "no evidence on the record of this case indicating that Mr. Wilcox intended to perjure himself," and characterized counsel's beliefs as "private conjectures about the guilt or innocence of [her] client."

addressed to the wrong audience. It is for the States to decide how attorneys should conduct themselves in state criminal proceedings, and this Court's responsibility extends only to ensuring that the restrictions a State enacts do not infringe a defendant's federal constitutional rights. . . .

JUSTICE STEVENS, concurring in the judgment.

Justice Holmes taught us that a word is but the skin of a living thought. A "fact" may also have a life of its own. From the perspective of an appellate judge, after a case has been tried and the evidence has been sifted by another judge, a particular fact may be as clear and certain as a piece of crystal or a small diamond. A trial lawyer, however, must often deal with mixtures of sand and clay. Even a pebble that seems clear enough at first glance may take on a different hue in a handful of gravel.

As we view this case, it appears perfectly clear that respondent intended to commit perjury, that his lawyer knew it, and that the lawyer had a duty — both to the court and to his client, for perjured testimony can ruin an otherwise meritorious case — to take extreme measures to prevent the perjury from occurring. The lawyer was successful and, from our unanimous and remote perspective, it is now pellucidly clear that the client suffered no "legally cognizable prejudice."

Nevertheless, beneath the surface of this case there are areas of uncertainty that cannot be resolved today. A lawyer's certainty that a change in his client's recollection is a harbinger of intended perjury — as well as judicial review of such apparent certainty — should be tempered by the realization that, after reflection, the most honest witness may recall (or sincerely believe he recalls) details that he previously overlooked. Similarly, the posttrial review of a lawyer's pre-trial threat to expose perjury that had not yet been committed — and, indeed, may have been prevented by the threat — is by no means the same as review of the way in which such a threat may actually have been carried out. Thus, one can be convinced — as I am — that this lawyer's actions were a proper way to provide his client with effective representation without confronting the much more difficult questions of what a lawyer must, should, or may do after his client has given testimony that the lawyer does not believe. The answer to such questions may well be colored by the particular circumstances attending the actual event and its aftermath.

Because Justice Blackmun has preserved such questions for another day, and because I do not understand him to imply any adverse criticism of this lawyer's representation of his client, I join his opinion concurring in the judgment.

After *Nix*, What?

The Best Ethical Solution.   *Nix* may have answered some constitutional questions, and Rule 3.3 may answer some ethical ones, but questions remain, including questions about the answers. Both the Court and the ABA have rejected narrative as a solution (see note 6 in *Nix*), but state courts are free to adopt it anyway. Both before and after *Nix*, a few courts have invoked narrative as the best solution when a criminal defendant wishes to testify and her lawyer knows (or thinks he knows) that she will lie. (How certain should the lawyer

be? We discuss that below.) One thorough treatment of this subject appears in
People v. Johnson, 72 Cal. Rptr. 2d 805 (Ct. App. 1998). The court first identified several other possible solutions:

1. "Full Cooperation with Presenting Defendant's Testimony even when
   Defendant Intends to Commit Perjury." The court rejected this view, finding that no tribunal has ever endorsed it and concluding that it could result
   in disciplinary action. It would also be subornation of perjury.
2. "Persuading the Client Not to Commit Perjury." The court said that
   "when it succeeds," this was the "ideal solution," but does not tell a
   lawyer what to do should his client insist on testifying falsely.
3. "Withdrawal From Representation." "This approach, while it protects
   the attorney's interest in not presenting perjured testimony, does not
   solve the problem. The court may deny the motion to withdraw. Even
   if the motion to withdraw is granted, the problem remains." The next
   lawyer may have the same dilemma or the client may deceive the next
   lawyer about his intentions.
4. "Disclosure to the Court." This approach "has been criticized because it
   compromises the attorney's ethical duty to keep client communications
   confidential. . . . Additionally, until the defendant actually takes the
   stand and testifies falsely, there is always a chance the defendant will
   change his mind and testify truthfully. . . . Disclosure before the
   defendant testifies could result in a mini-trial on the perjury issue. . . ."
5. "Refusing to Permit the Defendant to Testify." "Preclusion of the testimony as a solution has been criticized because it essentially substitutes
   defense counsel for the jury as the judge of witness credibility. . . .
   Further, a determination of whether the defendant will commit perjury
   may result in a mini-trial, with the attorney essentially 'testifying' against
   the defendant. Finally, this approach, while safeguarding the attorney's
   ethical obligations not to participate in presenting perjured testimony,
   results in a complete denial of the defendant's right to testify."
6. "The Narrative Approach Represents the Best Accommodation of the
   Competing Interests."

The court gave the following reasons for this conclusion:

> None of the approaches to a client's stated intention to commit perjury is
> perfect. Of the various approaches, we believe the narrative approach repre-
> sents the best accommodation of the competing interests of the defendant's
> right to testify and the attorney's obligation not to participate in the presen-
> tation of perjured testimony since it allows the defendant to tell the jury, in his
> own words, his version of what occurred, a right which has been described as
> fundamental, and allows the attorney to play a passive role. . . .
>
> We disagree with those commentators who have found the narrative
> approach necessarily communicates to the jury that defense counsel believes
> the defendant is lying. As was pointed out in [precedent] the jury may surmise
> the "defendant desired to testify unhampered by the traditional question and
> answer format." Because the defendant in a criminal trial is not situated the
> same as other witnesses, it would not be illogical for a jury to assume that
> special rules apply to his testimony, including a right to testify in a narrative

fashion. We do not believe the possibility of a negative inference the defendant is lying should preclude the use of the narrative approach since the alternative would be worse, i.e., the attorney's active participation in presenting the perjured testimony or exclusion of the defendant's testimony, neither of which strikes a balance between the competing interests involved.

The danger that the defendant may testify falsely is mitigated by the fact that the defendant is subject to impeachment and can be cross-examined just like any other witness. The jury is no less capable of assessing the defendant's credibility than it is of any other witness. As the Supreme Court stated in *Rock v. Arkansas*: "Like the truthfulness of other witnesses, the defendant's veracity, which was the concern behind the original common-law rule, can be tested adequately by cross-examination." Further, to preclude the defendant's testimony entirely based on a possibility that defendant may lie, deprives the jury of making that assessment and may deprive the jury of hearing other, nonperjurious evidence to which the defendant would have testified about had he been given the opportunity. In utilizing the narrative approach, the jury has the benefit of hearing the defendant's version.

The narrative approach also avoids having a pre-perjury hearing, a mini-trial on whether the defendant might commit perjury if called to the stand; a hearing which could result in the attorney testifying against the client and which would require the court to be able to see into the future and determine that an individual who has stated only an intention to testify falsely (at least as according to his attorney) will actually testify falsely once on the witness stand.

The narrative approach may or may not be the best option, but the court's exuberance is excessive. Even if narrative does not "necessarily" telegraph that the defendant may be lying, it certainly creates a significant risk of doing so. So will the lawyer's failure to argue the narrative in summation. "What of it?" we may respond. "Why worry about a lying defendant?" But if the defendant is lying, *Nix* tells us he has no right to testify at all (at least not about the lies), so why give him half a loaf (a narrative) when he's entitled to no loaf at all? On the other hand, if the lawyer does not *know* that the defendant is lying, he's entitled to a full loaf, not half. The court rejects the solution of not letting the defendant testify because that substitutes the lawyer "for the jury as the judge of witness credibility." But the lawyer must make that very credibility determination before invoking the narrative approach. Last, the court says that a narrative avoids a "mini-trial" to determine whether in fact the lawyer really does "know" that the defendant will lie. But does it? What should a court do when a client, whose lawyer wishes to invoke narrative because he thinks he knows his client will lie, insists that his testimony will be true and protests that a narrative will deny him his constitutional right to testify with the "effective" assistance of counsel? Does the court just accept the lawyer's word for it or do we get that mini-trial anyway?

Or maybe the defendant doesn't get a right to be heard before the lawyer and the judge agree that the lawyer will proceed in a narrative fashion and ignore the narrative testimony in summation, notwithstanding the harmful consequences to the defendant. That can't possible be true, can it? No right to be heard? In People v. Andrades, 828 N.E.2d 599 (N.Y. 2005), a client planned to testify at a suppression hearing where the judge would be the factfinder. The court held that the defendant did not have a constitutional right to be present when his lawyer told the judge that because of an ethical problem the lawyer would have to use narrative. The Court of Appeals said "a colloquy of this nature involves procedural matters at which a defendant can offer no meaningful input." No meaningful "input" on the accuracy of the lawyer's claim about the defendant's own intentions?

Massachusetts and Wisconsin both opt for narrative where a criminal defendant will testify falsely and neither requires a mini-trial on the issue during the trial, although one might be required later if the defendant challenges his conviction. But the standard for "knowledge" in Wisconsin is quite high, though not in Massachusetts. Commonwealth v. Mitchell, 781 N.E.2d 1237 (Mass. 2003) (where during trial defense lawyer had "firm factual basis" to believe client would lie, narrative approach properly invoked after notice to judge and without need for a hearing). State v. McDowell, 681 N.W.2d 500 (Wis. 2004) ("Absent the most extraordinary circumstances, [the defense lawyer's] knowledge must be based on the client's expressed admission of intent to testify untruthfully." It "must be unambiguous and directly made to the attorney."). Other cases approving use of the narrative solution include People v. DePallo, 754 N.E.2d 751 (N.Y. 2001); Commonwealth v. Jermyn, 620 A.2d 1128 (Pa. 1993); and Shockley v. State, 565 A.2d 1373 (Del. 1989). People v. Andrades, supra, rejected the claim that the strategy signaled that the client would lie. Indeed, the court went further. It said that because the New York Code permits lawyers to reveal a client's intention to commit a crime, the lawyer could have told the judge explicitly that the client would lie under oath. What am I missing here? There is no right to lie under oath, so why go through this charade? Why let the defendant testify at all? Yet the court stressed the defendant's constitutional right to testify. (As of April 2009, new New York Rule 3.3, reversing priorities, requires a lawyer to correct false evidence or fraud on a tribunal even if that means revealing a client's confidences.

When a defense lawyer does employ narrative, may the prosecutor ask the jury to draw inferences of guilt from the lawyer's failure to argue the defendant's testimony? State v. Long, 714 P.2d 465 (Ariz. Ct. App. 1986), sensibly holds no: "We find this effort to make affirmative evidence of guilt out of defense counsel's ethical behavior to be prejudicial error."

Addressing problems with the narrative solution is Professor L. Timothy Perrin, The Perplexing Problem of Client Perjury, 76 Fordham L. Rev. 1707 (2007) (part of a symposium on ethics and evidence). Professor Perrin writes:

> Narrative testimony is certainly no panacea, but are there viable alternatives? Two very basic principles should guide lawyers, courts, and drafters of the ethics rules in addressing this ethical dilemma. The first principle is that lawyers should not be required to participate, even passively, in the presentation of evidence that they know is false. To do otherwise undermines the truth-seeking purpose of the trial. As recognized by the 2002 draft of the Model Rules, the defense lawyer's position as an officer of the court means that he must be able to exercise control over false evidence.
>
> The second principle, which is a matter of procedural necessity, is that defendants must have some opportunity to be heard before the court decides to exclude their allegedly false testimony. This is a fundamental aspect of due process and comports with the process followed in deciding preliminary questions of fact under [Rule 104(a) of the Federal Rules of Evidence]. Here, of course, is where things turn particularly perplexing. The defendant and the defendant's lawyer are placed in the position of opposing each other before the trial judge. The defense lawyer must reveal communications from the client and must argue against the defendant's expressed desire to testify.

The "cure" of attempting to adjudicate the defendant's right to testify may be worse than the disease, though the disease is nothing less than an affront to the system's search for the truth.

The Epistemology Problem.   *Nix* moved the focus of the inquiry back a few squares. While we continue to debate defense counsel's obligations when a defendant testifies falsely or intends to do so, what has suddenly become of prime importance is how the defense lawyer *knows* that the defendant is lying. All agree that a defense lawyer does not act improperly merely by calling a witness (defendant or not) who the lawyer merely *believes* is going to lie. In United States v. Midgett, 342 F.3d 321 (4th Cir. 2003), the court held that a defendant was denied his constitutional right to testify. "Defense counsel's mere belief, albeit a strong one supported by other evidence, was not a sufficient basis to refuse Midgett's need for assistance in presenting his own testimony." And see People v. Riel, 998 P.2d 969 (Cal. 2000):

> Although attorneys may not present evidence they know to be false or assist in perpetrating known frauds on the court, they may ethically present evidence that they suspect, but do not personally know, is false. Criminal defense attorneys sometimes have to present evidence that is incredible and that, not being naive, they might personally disbelieve. Presenting incredible evidence may raise difficult tactical decisions — if counsel finds evidence incredible the fact finder may also — but, as long as counsel has no specific undisclosed factual knowledge of its falsity, it does not raise an ethical problem.

When does a lawyer *know* that testimony is false? In *Nix,* Justice Stevens recognized that the Supreme Court was in the relatively luxurious position of being able to assume that the defendant planned to lie. But a trial lawyer may face ambiguous facts. In Commonwealth v. Mitchell, supra, the Massachusetts court identified various tests that courts have used in deciding when a lawyer's level of confidence is the equivalent of knowledge: "good cause to believe," "compelling support," "knowledge beyond a reasonable doubt," "firm factual basis," "good-faith determination," and "actual knowledge." The court adopts "firm factual basis," which Wisconsin rejected as inadequate. State v. McDowell, supra (knowledge will almost always require the client's unambiguous statement to counsel that he will lie). Thinking you know your client intends to lie, when you don't, will make a motion to withdraw based on what you think you know, but don't really, improper. State v. Jones, 923 P.2d 560 (Mont. 1996) (lawyer also revealed client confidence in support of his motion).

Can it be said that lawyers never "know" anything, or otherwise they would be witnesses? Even when a client confesses, the lawyer doesn't truly *know* that the client is telling the truth, in this view. The client may be delusional or protecting someone. Is this a fair response to the *Nix* problem? Or is it too cute? May lawyers rightfully use the concept of knowledge in their ethics code and then claim that knowledge can never exist (at least not for lawyers, trained as they are as professional skeptics)? My vote: too cute.

Avoiding Knowledge.   Assuming knowledge can exist, is it ethical for a lawyer to avoid getting it? Without knowledge, a lawyer might be able to do certain things helpful to a client (for example, call a witness or introduce a document) that the lawyer could not do if she "knew" that the testimony or evidence was false. A lawyer might avoid knowledge by not doing an investigation, by not even asking for the client's story. But then the lawyer would find it rather difficult to represent the client competently. Indeed, intentional ignorance would be certain malpractice and, in criminal cases, ineffective assistance of counsel. Maybe it's possible to learn the facts but not "know" them. This is not a riddle. Consider the following solution attributed to one prominent lawyer (though others also claim credit for it and innumerable defense lawyers will admit to a similar strategy — off the record):

> I never ask the client what it is that he contends are the facts from his point of view in the initial interview . . . [in order to avoid being] compromised [in deciding whether to put him on the witness stand]. The thing to do is to ask him what he suspects the other side might claim.

And on November 29, 1994, Harvard law professor Alan Dershowitz said this on the *Charlie Rose Show:* "I never ask a client whether he did it or not. I don't want the client to feel that he has to start his relationship with me by lying." Pretty clever, isn't it? Is there anything wrong with it?

Is there anything wrong, alternatively, with telling a client the elements of a defense before asking the client to relate the facts of the alleged crime? Is that just another way to avoid knowledge?

"The Lecture"

Before there was John Grisham, before Scott Turow, before Philip Margolin, there was Robert Traver. Traver, a pseudonym for a former Michigan Supreme Court justice, wrote *Anatomy of a Murder* (1958). It is slower paced than modern courtroom dramas, but it does an astonishing job of capturing the detail of law practice and the intellectual content of the law, at least the law of homicide and insanity. Few lawyer movies are its equal in this regard.

Paul Biegler, a former prosecutor and now a defense lawyer, is retained to represent Lt. Frederic Manion, who is charged with murdering Barney Quill. Quill raped Manion's wife in a bar. Manion went to the bar and shot Quill about an hour after he learned of the attack. The most discussed scene in the book (at least for lawyers) occurs when Biegler visits Manion in jail and gives him what Biegler calls "The Lecture." Biegler starts by describing the defenses to a murder charge. "For all the elaborate hemorrhage of words in the law books about the legal defenses to murder, there are only about three basic defenses: one, that it didn't happen but was instead a suicide or accident or what not; two, that whether it happened or not, you didn't do it, such as alibi, mistaken identity, and so forth; and three, that even if it happened and you did it, your action was legally justified or excusable."

"Where do I fit in that rosy picture?" Manion asks.

"Since a whole barroom full of people saw you shoot down Barney Quill in apparent cold blood, you scarcely fit in the first two classes of defenses. I'm afraid we needn't waste time on those."

Biegler then explains that justification would not work either because Manion did not shoot Quill in the act, but an hour later. Biegler then lists and dismisses other defenses, including intoxication. The Lecture then continues:

"Then finally there's the defense of insanity." I paused and spoke abruptly, airily: "Well, that just about winds it up." I arose as though making ready to leave.

"Tell me more."

"There is no more." I slowly paced up and down the room.

"I mean about this insanity."

"Oh, insanity," I said, elaborately surprised. It was like luring a trained seal with a herring. "Well, insanity, where proven, is a complete defense to murder. It does not legally justify the killing, like self-defense, say, but rather excuses it." The lecturer was hitting his stride. He was also on the home stretch. "Our law requires that a punishable killing — in fact, any crime — must be committed by a sapient human being, one capable, as the law insists, of distinguishing between right and wrong. If a man is insane, legally insane, the act of homicide may still be murder but the law excuses the perpetrator. . . . So the man who successfully invokes the defense of insanity is taking a calculated risk. . . ."

I paused and knocked out my pipe. The Lecture was about over. The rest was up to the student. The Lieutenant looked out the window. . . . I sat very still. Then he looked at me.

"Maybe," he said, "maybe I was insane."

Very casually: "Maybe you were insane when?" I said. . . .

"You know what I mean. When I shot Barney Quill."

Thoughtfully: "Hm. . . . Why do you say that?"

"Well, I can't really say," he went on slowly. "I — I guess I blacked out. I can't remember a thing after I saw him standing behind the bar that night until I got back to my trailer."

"You mean — you mean you don't remember shooting him?" I shook my head in wonderment.

"Yes, that's what I mean."

"You don't even remember driving home?"

"No."

"You don't even remember threatening Barney's bartender when he followed you outside after the shooting — as the newspaper says you did?" I paused and held my breath. "You don't remember telling him, 'Do you want some, too, Buster?'"

The smoldering dark eyes flickered ever so little. "No, not a thing."

"My, my," I said, blinking my eyes, contemplating the wonder of it all. "Maybe you've got something there."

The Lecture was over; I had told my man the law; and now he had told me things that might possibly invoke the defense of insanity. It had all been done with mirrors. Or rather with padded hammers. . . .

Did Biegler act ethically? Was there any legitimate reason for this exercise other than to steer Manion toward telling Biegler the story he needed to hear in order to mount the only plausible defense? Why didn't Biegler simply ask Manion if he had blacked out? *Video tip*: The book was made into a film (Otto Preminger, director). Try to see it. Like the book, it is a classic in the genre called trial movies. Jimmy Stewart plays Biegler. Ben Gazzara plays Manion. Lee Remick plays Mrs. Manion and steals every scene she's in. (Catch the one in which Biegler interviews her and she sprawls seductively across the couch.) Most important, watch the "lecture" scene carefully. Notice Stewart's body language and phrasing in response to Gazzara's questions and statements. Notice his use of silences. It's all done to impart a meaning that a transcript would not convey. Furthermore, the dialogue is better. See if your answers to the questions posed above change at all.*

Giving the Problem to the Judge.   We've mostly been considering what a lawyer should do where the perjury is prospective. But what if it is concluded? The lawyer has called the witness in good faith and, either during the testimony or after it, comes to know (remember that knowledge is the trigger here) that she lied. Rule 3.3(a) will require the lawyer to remedy the situation even if that means revealing a client confidence. It's mandatory.

Let's examine what might happen when the lawyer follows Rule 3.3. What does the judge do? Imagine a lawyer informing a judge that a criminal defendant has lied on the stand. How might the judge respond? What if the client denies the lawyer's allegation, assuming he even gets the chance (see *Andrades*, supra)? If the judge instructs the jury to ignore the testimony, isn't there a risk that the lawyer will turn out *not* to have "known" that the testimony was false (even though the lawyer truly believed he knew)? Compare the *Wilcox* case in note 8 of Justice Blackmun's opinion in *Nix*. One possibility is to have the judge do nothing and to leave the credibility issue to the jury. (As judges and trial lawyers often say: "The jury is the lie detector in the courtroom.") But if *that's* the solution, why should we require defense counsel to reveal the suspected perjury in the first place? Just to insulate herself against any suspicion of complicity?

Consider the following segment from the former television series *L.A. Law.* I thought the show was the first attempt on television to present legal ethics issues seriously and in all their complexity. See Stephen Gillers, Taking *L.A. Law* More Seriously, 98 Yale L.J. 1607 (1989).

Michael Kuzak represents a man named Sears, who is accused of leaving the scene of an accident. The car belongs to Sears's aunt, whom Kuzak calls as a witness to explain, truthfully, how others may have gained access to it. In the middle of her highly credible testimony, and to Kuzak's surprise, the aunt volunteers (and the judge lets her proceed in monologue) that she and Sears were at the beach when the accident occurred. Kuzak knows (as a result of a prior discussion with Sears) that the alibi is false and the witness is lying at the request of her nephew. He asks to speak with the judge alone in chambers, then moves to withdraw. (*L.A. Law* had a lot of ex parte contacts for dramatic purposes. Good as the show was on legal ethics issues, it still had to pull an audience.) The judge

---

* **Trivia note:** The man who plays the judge in the movie is Joseph Welch, a partner at Hale and Dorr in Boston. Welch had been the lawyer for the Army in the 1954 Army-McCarthy hearings. His question to Senator McCarthy ("Have you no sense of decency, sir? At long last, have you left no sense of decency?") marked the beginning of the end for the senator's career, in the view of many. You can see it all in the riveting documentary *Point of Order*. How Welch went from the Senate chamber to Hollywood, I do not know.

denies the motion after a discussion that might have enlightened the Supreme Court in Nix v. Whiteside:

Judge: What's to prevent him [the defendant] from playing the same time- and money-wasting game with his next lawyer and the one after that? No, Mr. Kuzak, withdrawing is not the answer to your dilemma. The answer is to let the system work. You do your job, let the D.A. do her job, and the jury will do their job of sorting out the truth, the falsity, of the testimony.

Kuzak: That's a comforting homily, Your Honor. But you know as well as I that Sears will be acquitted. That sweet little old lady had the jury eating out of the palm of her hand. . . .

Judge: Witnesses lie on the stand every day, Mr. Kuzak. You want to debate the ethical conundrum, we'll have dinner after this thing is over. In the meantime, let's just do our jobs.

Noble Kuzak, confused and distraught, returns to court, tries to resume questioning, cannot, announces that he withdraws from the case, and is jailed for contempt. The judge tells the defendant to get a new lawyer and return for a new trial. What has been gained? Who was right?

Life follows Hollywood. In United States v. Litchfield, 959 F.2d 1514 (10th Cir. 1992), a jury had convicted the defendant of conspiracy, mail and wire fraud, and other crimes. In an ex parte conversation, defense counsel had advised the trial judge that the defendant wished to testify but that counsel worried that the testimony he would elicit "would include untruths." The judge had responded:

> Well, you're not in a position that seems to me to decide — not in the best position, let's put it that way, to decide what is true and not true. Certainly, there may be things that he testifies to that are contradictory. Nor am I in a good position even based upon what I've heard from you because I don't hear a declaration from you that I believe that my client will speak untruthfully or that a fraud will be perpetrated upon the Court, and so I'm not making up my mind or making any decision in that regard and would prefer to let the jury listen to the evidence, weigh it and arrive at its own conclusions.

Astonishing, isn't it, the similarity between what the television and the "real" judges said? Do you think the real judge saw the TV judge? In the real case, the defendant testified and was convicted. The Tenth Circuit affirmed.

Return for a moment to the *L.A. Law* episode. Maybe Kuzak isn't the boy scout he pretends to be. Consider: Kuzak called the aunt to testify that the key to the car was on a nail in her accessible garage. That was true. This testimony would then have allowed Kuzak to argue to the jury that someone else might have been driving the car at the time of the accident. If Kuzak knew that Sears was the actual driver, which the entire episode assumes he did, was it proper for him to employ this strategy? The testimony he meant to elicit was true, but he knew that the inference he wished to argue from it was false. Wasn't Kuzak prepared to distort the truth indirectly rather than directly? And is that a difference on which the rules of ethics should turn? (See page 420.)

Ethics, Lies, and Rule 26

In civil matters, a lawyer is perhaps most likely to encounter perjury or fraud on a court during pretrial discovery. ABA Opinion 93-376, applying Rule 3.3, concludes that revelation "may prove to be the only reasonable remedial measure in the client fraud situations most likely to be encountered in pretrial proceedings," including discovery. This is because even a conspicuous withdrawal at that time may not be adequate to correct the fraud, as the rule requires. United States v. Shaffer Equipment Co., 11 F.3d 450 (4th Cir. 1993), contains a meticulous Rule 3.3 analysis that faults government lawyers for failing to reveal a government witness's deposition perjury.

The 1993, 2000, and 2007 amendments to the Federal Rules of Civil Procedure, especially when coupled with Rule 3.3, will further encourage revelation or correction of discovery misstatements, possibly at the expense of confidentiality. Rule 26(a)(1) now states that "a party must, without awaiting a discovery request, provide to other parties" certain information including (A) the "name" of persons with "discoverable information . . . that the disclosing party may use to support its claims or defenses" and (B) a "copy" or "description" of "all documents, electronically stored information, and tangible things" in the party's control "that it may use to support its claims or defenses." In addition, "a party" who has made a disclosure under Rule 26(a), or who has "responded to an interrogatory, request for production, or request for admission," must "supplement or correct its disclosure . . . if the party learns that in some material respect the disclosure or response is incomplete or incorrect, and if the additional or corrective information has not otherwise been made known to the other parties. . . ." Rule 26(e)(1).

Some observers criticized these rules when they first appeared in 1993, on the ground that they would require lawyers to reveal privileged information and that they are inconsistent with adversarial litigation. One of these observers was Justice Scalia, who dissented from the Court's decision to transmit certain of the new rules to Congress. On the Rule 26 changes, Justice Scalia, joined by Justices Souter and Thomas, wrote:

> The proposed new regime does not fit comfortably within the American judicial system, which relies on adversarial litigation to develop the facts before a neutral decisionmaker. By placing upon lawyers the obligation to disclose information damaging to their clients — on their own initiative, and in a context where the lines between what must be disclosed and what need not be disclosed are not clear but require the exercise of considerable judgment — the new Rule would place intolerable strain upon lawyers' ethical duty to represent their clients and not to assist the opposing side. Requiring a lawyer to make a judgment as to what information is "relevant to disputed facts" plainly requires him to use his professional skills in the service of the adversary.

Isn't that view now eclipsed by Rule 3.3, which imposes remedial duties on lawyers even at the expense of revealing "information damaging to their clients"? To put it another way, as envisioned by the Rules, the American system of civil litigation is really a *modified* adversarial system, where lawyers have duties to the tribunal that are superior to the "ethical duty to represent their clients."

Robert Bennett's Letter to Judge Susan Webber Wright

Bennett was President Clinton's lawyer in Paula Jones's sexual harassment lawsuit against Clinton. Clinton was deposed in this action in Washington, D.C., on January 17, 1998. Judge Wright presided at the deposition. Lawyers for Jones asked many pointed questions about Clinton's relationship with Monica Lewinsky. As we now know, the lawyers had obtained information about that relationship from Linda Tripp, who had gotten her information from Lewinsky (recording the conversations without Lewinsky's knowledge). Prior to the deposition, Lewinsky had submitted an affidavit denying "a sexual relationship with the President." Bennett, unaware that Clinton and Lewinsky did have a sexual relationship, introduced Lewinsky's affidavit at the deposition. Later, under grant of immunity, Lewinsky testified to a federal grand jury that she and Clinton had a sexual relationship. Bennett is a Washington, D.C., lawyer but was admitted pro hac vice to the federal court in Arkansas, where the *Jones* case was pending. The federal court's rules incorporated the Arkansas professional conduct rules. The Arkansas rules included Model Rule 3.3. That rule, in turn, required Bennett to rectify material false evidence he may have unwittingly introduced. This Bennett did in the following letter:

Dear Judge Wright,
As you are aware, Ms. Monica Lewinsky submitted an affidavit dated January 7, 1998, in the above-captioned case in support of her motion to quash the subpoena for her testimony. This affidavit was made part of the record of President Clinton's deposition on Jan. 17, 1998.
It has recently been made public in the Starr Report that Ms. Lewinsky testified before a federal grand jury in August 1998 that portions of her affidavit were misleading and not true. Therefore, pursuant to our professional responsibility, we wanted to advise you that the Court should not rely on Ms. Lewinsky's affidavit or remarks of counsel characterizing that affidavit.

Very truly yours,
Bob Bennett

This letter may go down as the most famous Rule 3.3 rectification ever.
We will further explore legal ethics issues in or arising from Jones v. Clinton at page 404. Jones v. Clinton and the impeachment and Senate trial of President Clinton, of course, raised many more ethical questions for lawyers than those that arose in the course of the president's deposition. Deborah Rhode examines the "competing personal, political, and professional interests of the Independent Counsel and some of the attorneys for Paula Jones and Monica Lewinsky . . . the conflicting roles and responsibilities that confronted the President's lawyers: conflicts between their client's political and legal needs, and conflicts between their own obligations to their client's defense and to the justice system [and] ethical conflicts in the exercise of prosecutorial power[s] [including] the scope and confidentiality of the Independent Counsel's investigation, the treatment of witnesses, the referral of charges to Congress, and the management of the Senate trial." Deborah Rhode, Conflicts of Commitment: Legal Ethics in the Impeachment Context, 52 Stan. L. Rev. 269 (2000).

FURTHER READING

Monroe Freedman's Provocative Argument and Criticism Thereof.
The article that first identified the multiple ethical dilemmas presented when a criminal defense lawyer's client commits or intends to commit perjury, and which has been a continuing source of discussion ever since, is Monroe Freedman, Professional Responsibility of the Criminal Defense Lawyer: The Three Hardest Questions, 64 Mich. L. Rev. 1469 (1966). Professor Freedman's analysis of *Nix* can be found in Client Confidences and Client Perjury: Some Unanswered Questions, 136 U. Pa. L. Rev. 1939 (1988). Elaboration of Professor Freedman's position appears in his book, co-authored with Abbe Smith, entitled Understanding Lawyers' Ethics. The articles and book argue that if a criminal defense lawyer cannot dissuade a client from testifying falsely, then the best solution is to allow the lawyer to call the client, question him in the usual way, and argue the testimony. The lawyer would not be allowed to prepare the client for the testimony. This authority would extend only to the criminal defendant as a witness. No court has ever accepted this argument, but it has sparked a good deal of debate and surely finds some support among the bar. The Freedman position is analyzed and criticized in Stephen Gillers, Monroe Freedman's Solution to the Criminal Defense Lawyer's Trilemma Is Wrong as a Matter of Policy and Constitutional Law, 34 Hofstra Law Review 821 (2006), and Professor Freedman has in turn criticized the critic in Monroe Freedman, Getting Honest About Client Perjury, 21 Geo. J. Legal Ethics 133 (2008). So far the critic has not had a chance to respond to the criticism of his criticism but he has placed it on his overly long to-do list.

See also Brent Appel, The Limited Impact of Nix v. Whiteside on Attorney-Client Relations, 136 U. Pa. L. Rev. 1913 (1988). Mr. Appel argues that *Nix* was a narrower decision than subsequent courts have assumed, that it permits the states "broad leeway to determine their own solutions" to the client perjury problem, and that the decision will "rarely [have] a direct impact on criminal defense attorneys and their clients."

Summary: Variables in Analyzing Issues Concerning Witness Perjury

1. Timing
   a. Prospective perjury
   b. Surprise perjury
   c. Concluded perjury
2. Nature of the case
   a. Criminal
      i. The defendant as witness
      ii. Other witnesses
   b. Civil (court, other adjudicative tribunal)
3. Lawyers' state of mind
   a. Knowledge
   b. Reasonable belief

4. Remedies
    a. Remonstrate with client
    b. Reveal to tribunal
    c. Withdraw if allowed
    d. Let criminal defendant testify in narrative and refrain from arguing in summation
    e. Refuse to call client (prospective perjury)
    f. Let criminal defendant testify, question client, argue testimony
5. Legal considerations
    a. Text of jurisdiction's rule
    b. Constitutional right of criminal defendants to testify and to assistance of counsel
    c. Client autonomy
    d. Duty of confidentiality
    e. Duty of competence
    f. Criminal law prohibitions against suborning perjury (and like crimes)

D. FOSTERING FALSITY OR ADVANCING TRUTH?

Here we discover a variety of strategies that a lawyer may employ in civil or criminal cases, often quite properly, sometimes not, to increase the chances of victory, at the risk (or even with the intention) of misleading the judge or jury. A trial, we learn, may be a search for truth, but the path has many roadblocks. Some of these are doctrinal and aim to serve other values deemed more important than an accurate verdict. In this category are the attorney-client and other privileges, suppression of evidence illegally obtained, and the criminal law standard of proof beyond a reasonable doubt. Other roadblocks are the tactics and strategies of lawyers, whose job description requires them to pursue only those truths that benefit their clients and wherever possible to try to exclude or discredit those truths that do not. (We omit prosecutors from this description. They are a special case, as later explained in this and the next chapter.) And as we discover, truth has a different meaning for lawyers (at least when acting as lawyers) than for other varieties of humankind. This may be one reason people don't trust lawyers. For lawyers, a statement can be true so long as she can conceive of any set of circumstances or interpretations, no matter how far-fetched, under which it could (possibly, possibly) be true. Bill Clinton tried that in the material that follows. The problem is that judges might not be quite so willing to go as far, assuming they learn about it. If the wordplay occurs in discovery, which it often does, the judge may not learn. And if the judge does find out, what's the worst that can happen? She rejects your highly imaginative interpretation, and you have to reveal the information. So perhaps this is nothing more than a question of risk v. gain. Sometimes, however, the worst that can happen is a hefty sanction. For an extreme example of a law firm's fancy dancing to avoid discovery obligations and the financial penalty it and the client had to pay, see Washington State Physicians Insurance Exchange & Assn. v. Fisons Corp., 858 P.2d 1054 (Wash. 1993).

1. *Literal Truth*

If we are going to give lawyers certain duties that turn on the truth or falsity of information, we might be expected to know what we mean by "true" and "false." Linguists and philosophers of language would tell us that this is actually more complicated than might first appear. Harvard linguist Steven Pinker wrote, in discussing President Clinton's (mis)use of language: "When the shampoo bottle says, 'Lather, rinse, repeat,' we don't spend the rest of our lives in the shower; we infer that it means 'repeat once.'" Listening Between the Lines, New York Times, Oct. 3, 1998 at 17. He adds that "Conversation requires cooperation." But litigation operates from the postulate that lawyers should be as uncooperative as possible. I recall as a young lawyer — this was before e-mail and faxes — that a witness was asked whether there was any "correspondence" between him and Jack on a particular subject during a particular month. No, said he. It transpired, however, that there was a telegram, a very relevant telegram at that. The witness had decided, probably instructed by counsel, that "correspondence" meant letters and the term did not include a telegram. Now, you can look at this as really clever. But if your best friend or your mother asked the same question and you said no on the same theory, they would probably call it a lie. Quite right, too. But "true" and "false" have a somewhat different meaning in litigation than in everyday life. Just how slippery can a lawyer be and not cross "the line" that trial lawyers proudly proclaim they will "go right up to" for their clients?

a. The Parable of Billy

His parents come home before dinner and find eight-year-old Billy in the kitchen and crumbs around the cookie jar. "Are you eating the cookies?" his mother asks. "No," says Billy with a straight face. When Billy later admits that he did in fact enjoy a cookie, his parents lecture him about lying. "I didn't lie," he insists. "First, I only ate one cookie, and you said 'cookies.' Second, when you asked '*Are* you eating the cookies,' I had already finished. You should have asked 'Did you eat one or more cookies?'" Was Billy's answer false? Does it depend on what the meaning of "are" is and whether the plural includes the singular?

b. The Romance of Annie and Bill

Billy grew up and called himself Bill. He went to law school (naturally), where he met Annie. A romance began, and they talked about moving in together after graduation. One Sunday afternoon, three months into their relationship, Annie had to stay home to write a paper. Bill went out around 6 o'clock for a dinner of pizza and Ben & Jerry's chocolate fudge brownie ice cream, taking his MPRE review along for some quick studying. Wouldn't you know it, but who should he run into but Jana, a classmate. Sweet Jana. One thing led to another and then another, a walk in the park, a cappuccino, a beer, another beer, and Bill wound up at Jana's place, where they watched reruns of *Law and Order,* and by then it was very late. Very. Too late for Bill to go home, although home was only two blocks away. So Bill spent the night and part of the morning. The next day, Annie and Bill had the following conversation:

Annie: Did you go out last night?
Bill: I ran out for some ice cream and pizza.
Annie: I tried calling.
Bill: I didn't hear the phone. It might have been while I was out.
Annie: It was after eleven.
Bill: Oh, I must have been in the shower. ("Not a lie," Bill thinks. "I *was* in the shower, just not mine.")
Annie: What did you do?
Bill: Watched *Law and Order* and went to bed. ("Well, that's also true," thinks Bill. "This is pretty easy.")

A week later Annie discovers Jana's legal ethics casebook under Bill's couch. Bill confesses all and begs forgiveness. "You lied to me," Annie says.

"I didn't lie," Bill replies. ("It's like the cookies," he thinks.) "Everything I said was true. You didn't ask the right questions. If you had asked the right questions, I would have admitted it." Seeing Annie's (sweet Annie's) incredulous expression, Bill adds, then regrets adding, "We're in law school, not divinity school, right?"

Did Bill lie?*

c. The Two Boys and the Butcher

Professor Richard Underwood has written an amusing and disturbing (both!) article recounting the various ways in which lawyers, through argument and otherwise, properly and improperly might seek to avoid fact and logic in their presentations to juries. Richard Underwood, Logic and the Common Law Trial, 18 Am. J. Trial Advoc. 151 (1994). Professor Underwood reports this fifteenth-century fable, "The Two Boys and the Butcher," from a Florentine manuscript:

> Two young boys went to buy meat at a butcher's shop. Seeing that the butcher was busy helping a customer, one of the boys grabbed a piece of beef and stuffed it down the shirt of the other. The butcher, having finished serving the customer, came over to where the boys were standing and immediately noticed that some beef was missing. He accused the boys of theft, but the one who had taken it said that he didn't have it, and the one who had it said that he hadn't taken it. The butcher understood their trickery and warned them: "You may think that you can get away with this bit of double talk here, but the gods won't be deceived by sophistry." The moral of the fable is: Sometimes lying and telling the literal truth can amount to the same thing.**

---

* Bill becomes a successful lawyer and reappears in this story later on.
** Id., quoting the Medici Aesop (Adele Westbrook ed. & Bernard McTigue trans., 1989).

With citations to the philosopher H. P. Grice and others, Professor Underwood concludes that the boys lied to the butcher. "The philosopher-logician would explain it this way. The butcher was operating in the atmosphere of the humdrum, everyday life of the town. In theoretical terms, day to day, cooperative activity takes for granted certain conversational rules. . . . For better or worse, however, the conversational rules down at the courthouse are at least a little bit different."

d. In the Matter of William Jefferson Clinton

Bill (formerly Billy) did *not* go on to be president of the United States. But another Bill did. As you may recall (or maybe not), President Clinton was deposed on Saturday, January 17, 1998, in Paula Jones's sexual harassment claim against him. The deposition occurred in Washington, D.C., but the action had been filed in federal court in Arkansas. Judge Susan Webber Wright flew up and was present at the deposition. President Clinton was represented by Robert Bennett of Skadden Arps. Hours before the deposition, Jones's lawyers had received information from Linda Tripp about Clinton's intimate sexual relationship with Monica Lewinsky. Many of the deposition questions focused on that relationship, which Bill, I mean Clinton, emphatically denied. The lawyers had a degree of detail that probably surprised the president and Bennett. At one point in the deposition, Mr. Bennett referred to an affidavit filed by Lewinsky in which she denied a sexual relationship with the president. (Recall from page 399 Bennett's letter to Judge Wright withdrawing this reference.)

Seven months later, on August 17, 1998, after Lewinsky had testified before a grand jury and admitted a sexual relationship with the president and after physical evidence (the stained blue dress) made it impossible for Clinton to continue to deny one, Clinton was himself questioned before the grand jury.

Q: [by prosecutor, quoting statement that Bennett had made at Clinton's deposition]: "Counsel is fully aware that Ms. Lewinsky has filed an affidavit saying that there *is* absolutely no sex of any kind in any manner, shape or form, with President Clinton." (Emphasis added.)

That statement is made by your attorney in front of Judge Susan Webber Wright, correct?

A: That's correct.

Q: That statement is a completely false statement. Whether or not Mr. Bennett knew of your relationship with Ms. Lewinsky, the statement that there *was* "no sex of any kind in any manner, shape or form, with President Clinton," was an utterly false statement. Is that correct? (Emphasis added.)

A: It depends on what the meaning of the word "is" is. If the — if he — if "is" means is and never has been that is not — that is one thing. If it means there is none, that was a completely true statement.

Is (was) the president right?*

Two subjects before the grand jury were whether the president lied when he denied having had "sexual relations" with Lewinsky and whether he lied when he denied being "alone" with her in the White House. "Sexual relations" was given an NC-17 definition to encompass any act you might imagine. Here is the colloquy on the second issue. First, testimony from the deposition:

Q: At any time were you and Monica Lewinsky together alone in the Oval Office?

A: I don't recall. But as I said, when she worked at the legislative affairs office, they always had somebody there on the weekends. I typically worked some on the weekends. . . .

Q: So I understand, your testimony is that it was possible then, that you were alone with her, but you have no specific recollection of that ever happening?

A: Yes, that's correct. It's possible that she, in, while she was working there, brought something to me and that at the time she brought it to me, she was the only person there. That's possible.

Q: At any time have you and Monica Lewinsky ever been alone together in any room in the White House?

A: I think I testified to that earlier. I think that there is a, it is—I have no specific recollection. . . .

Q: At any time were you and Monica Lewinsky alone in the hallway between the Oval Office and this kitchen area?

A: I don't believe so, unless we were walking back to the dining room with the pizza. I just don't remember. I don't believe we were alone in the hallway, no.

Eight months later, the president began his grand jury testimony with this statement: "When I was alone with Ms. Lewinsky on certain occasions in early 1996, and once in early 1997, I engaged in conduct that was wrong." The prosecutor then asked:

Q: Let me ask you, Mr. President, you indicate in your statement that you were alone with Ms. Lewinsky. Is that right?

A: Yes, sir.

Q: How many times were you alone with Ms. Lewinsky?

A: Let me begin with the correct answer—I don't know for sure. . . .

Q: You were alone with her on December 28th, 1997?

A: Yes, sir. I was.

Q: Do you agree with me that the [January 17, 1998, deposition] statement "I was never alone with her" is incorrect? You were alone with Monica Lewinsky, weren't you?

* Clinton might have cited Shakespeare in his defense. In *As You Like It*, 4.3.20-29, Rosalind is complaining to her cousin Celia that Orlando, whom she loves, has missed their appointment.

Rosalind: But why did he swear he would come this morning, and comes not?
Celia: Nay, certainly there is no truth to him.
Rosalind: Do you think so? . . . Not true in love?
Celia: Yes, when he is in, but I think he is not in.
Rosalind: You have heard him swear downright he was.
Celia: "Was" is not "is."

A: Well, again, it depends on how you define "alone." Yes, we were alone
       from time to time, even during 1997, even when there was absolutely
       no improper conduct occurring. Yes, that is accurate.

       But there were also a lot of times when, even though no one could see us,
       the doors were open to the halls, on both sides of the halls, people could
       hear. The Navy stewards could come in and out at will, if they were around.
       Other things could be happening. So, there were a lot of times when we
       were alone, but I never really thought we were.

Did the president lie at the deposition? Were his answers false? On his last day
in office, Clinton settled all possible criminal and bar disciplinary charges against
him by accepting a five-year suspension of his Arkansas bar license (as of late 2008
he had not requested readmission) and by making certain admissions. He admitted that he had given false answers under oath, but he insisted that he did not lie.
Huh? The president's exceptionally talented lawyer, David Kendall of Williams &
Connolly, maintained that it was never the president's intention to give false
answers, but some of his answers turned out to be false despite his intentions.
(Is your head spinning?) Here's what both Kendall and Clinton said:

Clinton: I tried to walk a fine line between acting lawfully and testifying falsely,
             but I now recognize that I did not fully accomplish this goal and that certain
             of my responses to questions about Ms. Lewinsky were false.
Kendall: Reasonable people may conclude he crossed over that line he was
             trying to walk, and walking that line was plainly a dangerous and risky
             exercise. But when it comes to stating now what the president's intent
             was then in the deposition, all he can in conscience do is say what he
             told the earlier grand jury: he *tried* to avoid testifying falsely. When it
             comes to what his subjective motivation was, what the president actually
             believed . . . all he can do is to state what that was.

For his part, the president acknowledged that his answers violated Rule
8.4(d), which forbids "conduct that is prejudicial to the administration of justice." This rule does not require intent. The president did not admit to violating
Rule 8.4(c), which forbids "conduct involving dishonesty, fraud, deceit or misrepresentation." Is that tenable? Consider Office of Disciplinary Counsel v.
Anonymous Attorney A, 714 A.2d 402 (Pa. 1998) (violation of Rule 8.4(c)
requires "knowingly made" misrepresentation or "recklessness," defined as
"deliberate closing of one's eyes to facts that one had a duty to see or stating
as fact, things of which one was ignorant"). Here is the content of the document
the president signed, which accepts greater blame than his public statement
quoted above:

    Mr. Clinton admits . . . that . . . he knowingly gave evasive and misleading
    answers . . . concerning his relationship with Ms. Lewinsky, in an attempt to
    conceal from plaintiff Jones's lawyers the true facts [and] that by knowingly
    giving evasive and misleading answers . . . he engaged in conduct that is
    prejudicial to the administration of justice in that his discovery responses
    interfered with the conduct of the Jones case by causing the court and counsel
    for the parties to expend unnecessary time, effort, and resources. . . .

e. The Law of Perjury

If a statement is literally true, is it therefore not a lie? Billy's statement to his parents and Bill's answers to Annie's questions were literally true. Clinton claimed his answers were literally true if you were willing to indulge in a strained interpretation. Were any of these statements nevertheless false? Were they lies? Whatever your answer in the context of familial and romantic relationships, law is a parallel universe with its own interpretive standards and tests for meaning.

Consider Bronston v. United States, 409 U.S. 352 (1973). The defendant was convicted of perjury. A company of which he was sole owner had filed a petition under the Bankruptcy Act. At a hearing, Bronston testified under oath as follows:

Q: Do you have any bank accounts in Swiss banks, Mr. Bronston?
A: No, sir.
Q: Have you ever?
A: The company had an account there for about six months, in Zurich.
Q: Have you any nominees who have bank accounts in Swiss banks?
A: No, sir.
Q: Have you ever?
A: No sir.

At the time of the questioning, Bronston did not have a Swiss bank account in his own name, but he had previously had one. Did Bronston lie? (Reread the dialogue.) The Supreme Court unanimously reversed the conviction. Bronston's answer (the second one above) was "true and complete on its face." It did not matter that Bronston may have intended to evade and mislead. Protection against misleading answers lay in effective cross-examination.

> It is the responsibility of the lawyer to probe; testimonial interrogation, and cross-examination in particular, is a probing, prying, pressing form of inquiry. If a witness evades, it is the lawyer's responsibility to recognize the evasion and to bring the witness back to the mark, to flush out the whole truth with the tools of adversary examination.

Perjury is a willfully false statement, under oath, regarding facts material to the hearing. If Bronston's lawyer had coached him to give literally truthful but evasive and misleading answers (but not untruthful ones) — including perhaps the very answer he gave to the second question — would the lawyer have acted unethically, even if Bronston would not thereby have committed perjury? Remember that Rule 3.3 uses the word "false." Can an answer be false for purposes of that rule but not perjurious? Of course. "False" is broader than "fraud" and "fraudulent," words used in Rules 1.2(d), 1.6(b), and 4.1(b). And Rule 8.4(c) forbids deceit, dishonesty, and misrepresentation. Can a statement be any of these even if not perjury? Even if not false? The reach of ethical rules is not limited by criminal law definitions. Perhaps President Clinton could not be prosecuted for perjury (but read on), but he did confess to violating Arkansas ethical rules.

In Matter of Shorter, 570 A.2d 760 (D.C. 1990), the court disbarred Shorter, who (among other things) had given "technically true" answers to IRS agents who were trying to locate his assets. Although the agents asked about many asset categories (bank accounts, cars), they did not ask about Shorer's law partnership interest, and he didn't volunteer. The court "decline[d] to describe [Shorter's] . . . parsimonious dissemination of information as either fraudulent, deceitful, or misrepresentative" within the meaning of the predecessor to Rule 8.4(c). But it ruled that the answers "evince[d] a lack of integrity and straightforwardness and [were] therefore dishonest. . . . As long as the IRS did not ask just the right questions, respondent was prepared to deprive it of the right answers. This conduct was of a dishonest character" and unethical.

Lawyers love *Bronston*. Let's face it. It seems to defend language games intended to hide harmful but true information. Before you get too comfortable with the license it appears to extend, remember lawyer Shorter. Your client may go free but you may lose your bar card if you help him frame overly precise answers. And consider, too, United States v. DeZarn, 157 F.3d 1042 (6th Cir. 1998), which reads *Bronston* narrowly and tells us that your client might not go free but rather to prison. *DeZarn* was decided just as the Clinton impeachment debate got underway. Lawyers don't love *DeZarn*. Withdrawn. Lawyers *hate DeZarn*.

The Inspector General of the Army was investigating whether contributions to a Kentucky gubernatorial campaign improperly influenced subsequent appointments to the Kentucky National Guard. The suspected fundraising had allegedly occurred at a 1990 party held at the home of Billy Wellman, a former Guard officer. Sixty people, including the candidate, the then current Lieutenant Governor, had attended this party, which had been billed as a "Preakness Party." The investigation of the 1990 party was headline news in Kentucky. Various witnesses were questioned under oath. Robert DeZarn was one of them. Following are some of the questions and answers:

Q: Okay. In 1991, and I recognize this is in the period that you were retired, he [Wellman] held the Preakness Party at his home. Were you aware of that?
A: Yes.
Q: Did you attend?
A: Yes.
Q: Okay. Sir, was that a political fundraising activity?
A: Absolutely not.
Q: Okay. Did then Lieutenant Governor Jones, was he in attendance at the party?
A: I knew he was invited. I don't remember if he made an appearance or not.

As you can see, the questioner misspoke. He said "1991," not 1990. DeZarn was indicted for perjury. The government proved that DeZarn had attended a 1990 political fundraiser at Wellman's home. The jury convicted him. On appeal, DeZarn argued that because Wellman had a dinner party during the Preakness in 1991, which was not a fundraiser but could be characterized as a "Preakness Party," his answer was literally true and therefore not perjury. He relied on Bronston v. United States, which Clinton's lawyers also cited during his impeachment hearings and trial.

The Sixth Circuit affirmed DeZarn's conviction. It distinguished *Bronston* on the ground that Bronston gave literally true answers that were "nonresponsive," thereby alerting the questioner and permitting the questioner to pursue the line of inquiry further. By contrast, Judge Rosen wrote, DeZarn gave responsive and "categorical answers to questions" in order to mislead.

> [A] perjury inquiry which focuses only upon the precision of the question and ignores what the Defendant knew about the subject matter of the question at the time it was asked, misses the very point of perjury: that is, the Defendant's intent to testify falsely and, thereby, mislead his interrogators. Such a limited inquiry would not only undermine the perjury laws, it would undermine the rule of law as a whole. . . .

Wellman's 1991 dinner party was a small affair with only three couples. Although it was held during the Preakness, the government claimed that, as DeZarn knew, it was not *the* Preakness Party cited in the deposition question. The Court upheld the jury's finding that DeZarn knew that the questioner misspoke.

> Even if the questioning was not perfectly precise, the context in which the questions were asked made the object of the questioning clear and, more importantly, it is clear that DeZarn knew exactly the party to which Colonel Tripp [the questioner] was referring. The evidence at trial clearly established that Billy Wellman held only one Preakness Party and that was in 1990. No Preakness Party was held in 1991.

So *DeZarn* stands for the proposition (which surprises and discomforts many lawyers) that a responsive answer that, viewed narrowly and out of context, has a fair claim to being literally true, may nevertheless, viewed in the larger context, be perjurious because of the state of mind of the witness when giving his literally true answer. Now imagine that before DeZarn has a chance to answer the fatal question, a break is called. In the hallway, DeZarn tells his lawyer, "He said 1991. How can we use that?" Wouldn't the lawyer be guilty of suborning perjury and behaving unethically if he advised DeZarn to give the literally truthful answer he did?

f. The Law of Contempt

We have seen that in deciding whether a literally true statement might be considered "false," or otherwise forbidden, we must evaluate it both under the law of perjury and under legal ethics rules. Discovery rules and the law of contempt also count. Clinton was never prosecuted for perjury. He has now settled any such charge. But Judge Wright, who presided at his deposition, cited the president for civil contempt. She relied solely on his testimony denying that he was ever "alone" with Monica Lewinsky in the White House and his denial of "sexual relations" with Lewinsky.

> Simply put, the President's deposition testimony regarding whether he had ever been alone with Ms. Lewinsky was intentionally false, and his statements regarding whether he had ever engaged in sexual relations with Ms. Lewinsky likewise were intentionally false, notwithstanding tortured definitions and interpretations of the term "sexual relations." . . .

In sum, the record leaves no doubt that the President violated this
Court's discovery Orders regarding disclosure of information deemed by
this Court to be relevant to plaintiff's lawsuit. The Court therefore adjudges
the President to be in civil contempt of court pursuant to Fed. R. Civ.
P. 37(b)(2).

Jones v. Clinton, 36 F. Supp. 2d 1118 (E.D. Ark. 1999). Judge Wright subsequently ordered the president to pay Jones's lawyers $89,484.05 to compensate
them for their fees and expenses arising out of the president's civil contempt of
court. She also ordered the president to pay the court $1,202.00 for its expenses
in attending the deposition at which he gave false testimony. Jones v. Clinton,
57 F. Supp. 2d 719 (E.D. Ark. 1999). The president chose not to appeal (most
wisely, because the Eighth Circuit had displayed a sharp hostility to his arguments during the Whitewater investigation).

"Did You Communicate with Cassie?"

Bill (formerly Billy) and Annie broke up. Jana dumped him. He married
Natasha Jung, a psychiatrist, who warned him that she could read his mind,
which he believed. He joined a litigation boutique. He started to earn a lot of
money. He exuded charm and sincerity. Juries loved him.

One day Bill was retained by a man I'll call Pierre Monnier — to protect his
real identity. (That's a joke. This whole tale is made up. Well, that's not entirely
true either. The essence of the story did happen to me when I was a baby lawyer.
I've never forgotten it. See page 402.) Angela Barnes had sued Pierre for fraud in
a complicated real estate deal. She demanded damages of $10 million. The case
turned on whether Pierre knew the poor financial condition of a company called
Bamboozle Equities when he entered the deal with Angela (knowing falsity
being an element of fraud). Pierre denied knowing about Bamboozle. There
was circumstantial evidence that he did know, but it was ambiguous and so far
there was no direct evidence. Lucia Beach, the lawyer for Angela, had reason to
believe that Pierre had learned about Bamboozle's finances directly from Cassandra Beaumont (whereabouts unknown) in November 2008. The following
transcript is from Pierre's deposition in May 2009:

Q: Do you know Cassandra Beaumont?
A: Yes, Cassie. I know Cassie.
Q: In November 2008, did you speak with her?
A: No.
Q: Did you receive e-mail or text messages from Cassie?
A: Many times.
Q: In November 2008.
A: No.
Q: Have you reviewed all of your e-mails and text messages for that month as a
basis for your answer?
A: Yes. You know we did. You got a court order for a forensic IT guy to go
through the hard drive on the office computer, laptop, and iPhone I was
using at the time.

Q: Did you in any way communicate with Cassandra Beaumont in November 2008?
A: I did not communicate with Cassie in November 2008.
Q: And prior to November 2008 when did you last communicate with Cassie?
A: To the best of my recollection, the last time I talked with Cassie was when she called from Prague to wish me a happy birthday.
Q: When was that?
A: June 6, 2008.

A few days later, Lucia reduced her settlement offer from $6 million to $3 million. Bill said he'd confer with Pierre and get back to her. At their meeting, Pierre said, "Bill, you know, Lucia never asked if I had heard from Cassie in November 2008."

"What do you mean," Bill asked, puzzled.

"She asked about e-mails and whether I spoke with her."

"Or communicated with her."

"Right."

"And you said no."

"Right, and that's true."

"Okay. I'm glad to hear it."

"But I did hear from her."

Bill sat down. "You did hear from her," he repeated.

"She left a voicemail. I didn't communicate with her. She communicated with me. We never talked."

Bill said nothing.

"You told me not to volunteer."

"Where is the voicemail now?"

"Deleted."

"Did she say anything about the financial condition of Bamboozle on the voicemail?"

"Not really."

"Not really."

"I mean Lucia would probably see it in a different light. But no, not really."

Bill said nothing.

"You told me to just answer the question, listen to the question and just answer it."

Bill said nothing. He thought about the cookies. He thought of sweet Annie (again). He thought of his legal ethics teacher whose name he forgot and whose classes he mostly missed and he wondered if he could call for advice. (Yes, Bill, you can.) He thought about the outstanding settlement offer. He thought maybe he should have gone into politics.

What are Bill's options now?

2.   *Cross-Examining the Truthful Witness*

Max Steuer was a renowned criminal defense lawyer in New York City in the early 1900s, at the pinnacle of the criminal defense bar. He represented the defendants in the criminal case arising out of the infamous Triangle Shirtwaist

Company fire, described below. Daniel Kornstein's article praises Steuer's skills in that case. A response to the article follows. If you want to learn more about the legendary Max Steuer, read the relevant chapter in Francis Wellman's classic book on cross-examination, cited in Kornstein's article.

Daniel J. Kornstein
A TRAGIC FIRE — A GREAT CROSS-EXAMINATION
New York Law Journal, Mar. 28, 1986, at 2

We remember events for different reasons. For example, March 25 was the seventy-fifth anniversary of the terrible Triangle Shirtwaist Fire, which killed 146 sweatshop workers, mostly young immigrant women barred by locked doors from escaping the blaze in their New York City factory. The fire in 1911 stands as a turning point in the history of labor because it led to significant labor reforms in workplace health and safety laws. Important as those reforms are, however, they are not the only reason for lawyers to remember the Triangle Shirtwaist Fire.

Lawyers should remember the fire for another reason, unmentioned in the anniversary accounts. Lawyers should remember it because it was the subject of one of the all-time great cross-examinations in American courtroom history.

The memorable cross-examination grew out of the criminal case that followed the fire. Within a month after the fire, the government indicted the two owners of the Triangle Shirtwaist Company on manslaughter charges. The indictment was based on a New York State law providing that factory doors "shall be so constructed as to open outwardly, where practicable, and shall not be locked, bolted or fastened during working hours." For their defense counsel, the proprietors chose Max D. Steuer.

It was a good choice, for Max D. Steuer is still a courtroom legend. In the early part of this century, he was perhaps the leading trial lawyer in New York City. Realist and idealist, shrewd and comprehensive of the ways of men, Steuer built a reputation as a superb master of trial tactics. "No one at the New York Bar," wrote Francis L. Wellman, author of The Art of Cross-Examination, "knows more about the way to conduct a trial from an artistic standpoint than Mr. Steuer." Wellman includes Steuer's performance in the Triangle Shirtwaist Fire case in the section of his book called "Cross-Examination of the Perjured Witness."

Steuer had to bring to bear all of his considerable skills in the Triangle Fire criminal case. The tragedy had, understandably, aroused public opinion against his clients. The undisputed facts — locked doors forcing scores of women, clothes and hair ablaze, to leap from windows to their deaths — made the defendants' prospects bleak. Surely this was a case that would result in convictions. But the zealous prosecutor overplayed his hand and did not count on Steuer's ability.

The trial lasted several weeks. Just before it rested, the prosecution called a final witness to supply a missing piece of crucial evidence. This final witness was supposed to testify that Rose Schwartz, one of the fire's victims named in the indictment, was in fact the same person who lost her life in the fire. Up to that point in the trial, the testimony had uniformly been that the bodies discovered in the building were so charred that identification was impossible.

The prosecution had built suspense. It had kept its final witness in Philadelphia, beyond reach of defense counsel who knew neither her identity nor her location. There, the prosecutor and his staff met with her several times in preparation for her testimony. When the government's final witness appeared, everyone in the courtroom felt that something important was about to happen. They were not disappointed.

First, the key witness testified to preliminary details. She said that she had been an employee at the factory and was there when the fire broke out and that she knew Rose Schwartz. Then the prosecutor asked her: "Now tell everything that you saw and did on the ninth floor of those premises from the time the fire broke out." The response was heartrending.

The witness told how she first saw the flames. She described how the girls scattered from one floor and ran to another. She testified that many of them ran to the windows and began to jump out and that she herself had decided to follow their example.

While at the window ready to jump, the witness said she looked around the room in a last-ditch effort to escape. She then saw Rose Schwartz, the witness said, with both hands on the knob of the door desperately turning and pushing, but the door would not give.

Watching Rose, the witness was mesmerized. She saw the flames envelop Rose's hands, saw her fall to the floor and then saw her once more struggle to her feet, again grab the knob of the door and turn it one way and then another, pull and then push, but the door would not give. Once more the flames enveloped Rose and again she had to withdraw her hands from the door knob and she fell to the floor; the flames were now coming very close to the witness; she turned once more toward the door and there for the third time, was Rose Schwartz, on her knees, screaming and praying, with both hands on the door knob, turning it first one way, then the other, and pulling and pushing, but the door would not give, and finally she was completely covered by the flames, and fell to the floor within a foot of the door. At the end of her direct testimony, tears ran down the cheeks of the jurors.

Steuer began his cross-examination slowly. He spent the first half hour on preliminaries. At the end of the half hour, using the exact words employed by the prosecutor, he asked the witness to state all she did herself and all that she saw done on the ninth floor from the moment she first saw the fire.

There was something odd about the witness's answer. She started her narrative with exactly the same word that she had used when telling her story the first time. She went on in precisely the same words that she had used when answering the same question put to her by the prosecutor.

Steuer changed the subject for a while and asked the witness to describe what happened for the third time. The witness again started with the same word and continued to narrate the story in precisely the same words that she had used twice before. The only difference was that this time she omitted one word. Steuer asked her if she had omitted a word, naming the word.

Her lips began to move and start the narrative to herself all over again, and when she reached the position where that word belonged she said: "Yes, I made a mistake; I left that word out." [*Question:*] "But otherwise your answer was correct?" She again began to move her lips, obviously reciting to herself what she had previously said, and then said, "Yes, otherwise my answer is correct."

When Steuer asked her the same question a third time, the prosecutor objected but was overruled. After twenty minutes on other subjects, Steuer asked, for the fourth time: "Will you please tell the jury what you saw and what you did after you first observed any sign of the flames?"

She started with the same word, and continued her narrative, but again left out one word, this time a different word. Asked whether she had not now omitted a word, naming it, she went through the same lip performance and replied that she had, and upon being asked to place the word where it belonged, she proceeded to do so.

Neither Steuer nor the prosecutor had any further questions of that witness. The tears in the jury box had dried. The situation had entirely changed. The witness had not hurt, but had very materially helped, the defense; she had succeeded in casting grave suspicion on the testimony of many of the girls who had previously testified; her carefully prepared story had aroused the suspicion of the jury regarding the entire case of the prosecution.

The jury acquitted the two defendants. Historians say the acquittal was due to the trial judge's narrow charge to the jury. But Steuer's brilliant cross-examination of the People's star witness must have had more than a little to do with the result.

Steuer's performance vividly illustrated an unorthodox style of cross-examination. Normally we are told not to ask an opposing witness to repeat harmful testimony on cross-examination. The usual reason is that such repetition only reinforces the original bad impact of such testimony. But Steuer found a proper occasion for breaking this rule and compelling a witness to repeat on cross-examination every detail of the story given on direct. The constant repetition of the story showed a carefully prepared recital, rather than a spontaneous recollection of actual events.

So let us remember the Triangle Shirtwaist Fire and celebrate the labor reforms it engendered. But let us also recall the cross-examination that exploded perjured testimony about that tragedy. And let us celebrate the importance of cross-examination — what Wigmore once called the "greatest engine ever developed for the discovery of truth."

Ann Ruben & Emily Ruben
LETTER TO THE EDITOR
New York Law Journal, Apr. 14, 1986, at 2

In 1911, one hundred forty-six sweatshop workers, mostly young immigrant women, were incinerated as a result of the sweatshop's owners' efforts to ensure maximization of profit. When fire broke out at the Triangle Shirtwaist Factory, workers were unable to escape because the owners had bolted exits shut. The men charged with responsibility were acquitted after trial.

Daniel Kornstein's eulogy of Max Steuer's role in this acquittal underscores the moral vacuum in which many lawyers operate. Kornstein asks us to "celebrate" Max Steuer's cross-examination of Kate Alterman, one of the young immigrant women who managed to survive the fire. We cannot.

Mr. Kornstein's facile assumption that this young woman's testimony was perjured leads him to extol the virtues of Steuer's cross-examination. Mr. Kornstein exhibits all of the narrow-mindedness of the men (judge, jury, and lawyers) who exonerated those responsible for the results of this tragic fire. He fails even to consider the very obvious and likely possibility that the testimony was not perjured. To equate Kate Alterman's possibly rehearsed testimony with premeditated dishonesty represents an enormous leap of faith and completely ignores the socioeconomic and historic context of that testimony. The women who testified at the trial spoke little English. Approximately half of them spoke no English at all, and many of those who did were illiterate. (A. Steuer, Max D. Steuer Trial Lawyer, Random House, NY [1950], p.86.) They had barely survived a traumatic fire in which many of their friends and co-workers had burned to death. The notorious conditions under which they had worked in this country provided no basis for them to believe that their own words could sway the power structure the legal system represented. Unfortunately, the judge's narrow jury instructions, Steuer's technique, and the jury results underscored the power-lessness of young immigrant women.

Mr. Kornstein has used the anniversary of the Triangle Shirtwaist Factory Fire to applaud the technique of Max Steuer and to belittle the courage of women like Kate Alterman who came forward to testify. It would be more appropriate for lawyers to remember those who lost their lives in the fire and to explore ways to combat the oppressive working conditions that still exist throughout this country.

In response to the letter from Ann Ruben and Emily Ruben, Daniel Kornstein has written:

The Rubens movingly make telling points that, in retrospect, I wish I had expressly taken into consideration. First, they are absolutely correct in saying that I neglected to distinguish between outright perjury and overly rehearsed, overly memorized but essentially truthful testimony. I should have drawn that distinction, and I regret not having done so. But even that distinction in no way lessens Steuer's tactical achievement in neutralizing and offsetting the natural sympathy the jury must have had for the witness. For, in light of the obvious coaching, the fact remains that we simply do not know if the witness's testimony was or was not truthful and accurate.

Second, as the Rubens point out, the class struggle aspects of the cross-examination and the whole trial are obvious. But that economic overhang is not the end of the story. Unless we have come to the point where representing unpopular clients (such as sweatshop owners, landlords, large corporations, defendants accused of heinous crimes, or persons with controversial political, social, or moral beliefs) is itself unethical, I do not see how Steuer overstepped his professional responsibility. We have not yet so abandoned the presumption of innocence of the adversary process, so that we know who will win or lose a trial before the evidence is in.

The Rubens rightly press for a closer moral study of Steuer's trial tactics and their impact on the trial outcome. That is quite different from broadside attacks on the "power structure the legal system represented." It may be that, in some cosmic sense, the wrong side prevailed in the Triangle Shirtwaist factory case; but it was not because Steuer did anything inappropriate. He did precisely what he should have done — and what any good lawyer should have done. I don't think Steuer acted irresponsibly or in a "moral vacuum" by cross-examining the witness as he did. He took advantage of an adversary's blunder, which happens all the time.

Is Kornstein right? If he is right, is the system that permitted his strategy wrong? Does your answer change if you assume that Steuer had incontrovertible proof (i.e., he knew) that Kate Alterman was telling the precise truth? Would your answer change if Steuer had instead been the prosecutor and had employed the same tactic in cross-examination of a defense witness? Would it matter what prosecutor Steuer knew when he cross-examined?

3.   Appeals to Bias

Earlier we asked whether a law firm could staff a case — decide to include or exclude particular lawyers — based on race, sex, or ethnicity to appeal to or avoid presumed jury bias (page 237). What about lawyers who try to exploit jury bias in their argument by calling attention to the status or origins of the opposing lawyer or client assuming, as will almost always be true, that these facts are irrelevant? On occasion, appellate courts have reversed verdicts because an advocate, in questioning a witness or in summation, has explicitly or implicitly invited the jury to base its decision on race, religion, national origin, or similar considerations. The rules of many jurisdictions forbid lawyers to exhibit bias in their professional activities. See page 792. In addition, the ABA Code of Judicial Conduct obligates judges to require "lawyers in proceedings before the judge to refrain from manifesting bias or prejudice, or engaging in harassment, based upon attributes including but not limited to race, sex, gender, religion, national origin, ethnicity, disability, age, sexual orientation, marital status, socioeconomic status, or political affiliation, against parties, witnesses, lawyers, or others." The prohibition does "not preclude . . . lawyers from making legitimate reference to the listed factors or similar factors, when they are relevant to an issue in a proceeding." Rule 2.3(C) and (D).

In LeBlanc v. American Honda Motor Co., Inc. 688 A.2d 556 (N.H. 1997), the plaintiff sued Honda for defective design and failure to warn of alleged product defects in the Honda Odyssey. Honda lost. On appeal, it cited certain comments by plaintiff's counsel, Martina. The court wrote:

> The defendant points to several statements made by Martina as grounds for reversal. The first, directed at Honda's vehicle design expert, focused on the color scheme of the Odyssey. Martina asked the expert if he knew the color of the Japanese flag. After Honda objected, Martina explained that he was curious about how the machine's color happened to be designed. The court decided to give Martina "some latitude." Martina then questioned the expert

about whether the expert had ever wondered why the Odyssey is "red, white and blue, the color of the American flag."

The second series of statements highlighted by Honda occurred during the plaintiff's closing argument:

> What's this case about? It's not about Honda making great automobiles or Sony making good Walkmans. But also it's not about Pearl Harbor or the Japanese prime minister saying Americans are lazy and stupid. . . . What this case is about is not American xenophobia; it's about corporate greed.

Counsel for Honda again objected and, at a bench conference, moved for a mistrial. At the bench conference, Martina explained that he was certain that the fact that the defendant is a foreign corporation had entered the minds of the jurors, and he was trying to tell them that that was irrelevant to the case. The court denied the motion for a mistrial but warned Martina: "I am, however, Mr. Martina, cautioning you that there's a limit to how far argument can go, and I think you're right at the wall on it. So please back away from it and focus on the issues in the case." The court did not strike the remarks or issue a curative instruction to the jury.

At the conclusion of the trial, the court instructed the jury:

> I try to be fair and impartial, just as you are required to be. . . . You must decide the case only on the basis of the evidence and the law as I give it to you. You should keep in mind that all parties, whether an individual or a corporation, are equal before the law. . . .

And again:

> [Y]ou should decide this case without passion, without prejudice, and without sympathy. It is your highest duty as officers of this court to conscientiously determine a fair and just result in this case.

A plurality of the New Hampshire Supreme Court rejected a rule that would make "appeals to racial bias per se incurable." The court then went on to conclude that although "when viewed in isolation and outside of the context of the trial, [the remarks] may not seem to be so 'explicit and brazen' as to warrant the severe remedy of reversal," under "the circumstances of this case, we conclude that Martina's remarks, 'calculated as they were to encourage the jury to make a decision based on . . . bias rather than reason and the presented evidence, were so prejudicial as to require a new trial.' " One judge would have adopted a per se rule of reversal. Two judges dissented.

Kevin Pappas hurt himself skiing in Vermont. Pappas lived in New Jersey. He brought a federal diversity action in Vermont against the company that managed the property on which he had injured himself. Pappas lost and appealed, citing the following summation:

Defendants' Counsel: . . . There's no question there's a legitimate injury here. And we didn't even ask Dr. Abrams any question, and that's why. We do not dispute that, yes, there was an injury here. But isn't what they're really asking is that they can come up from New Jersey—

Plaintiff's Counsel: Objection. . . .

The Court: Objection overruled. You may proceed.

Defendants' Counsel: — if they can come up here from New Jersey to Vermont to
enjoy what we experience every year, for those of us who are here originally
for most of our lives, for most of us who come here for our own reasons, for
the rest of the time that we're here, and without a care in the world for their
own safety when they encounter what we, ourselves do not take for granted,
and they can injure themselves, and they can sit back and say, "Well, yes. I'm
on long-term disability, and I sit around and I watch golf on TV, but I'd like
you to retire me. Retire me now. Pay me now what I would get or what
I claim I would get until I work for age 65."

The Second Circuit described what happened next:

> Later in the same summation, counsel for defendant continued, "Would we
> go to New Jersey and walk on a tugboat without looking where we were going?"
> In its charge the trial judge simply cautioned the jury that arguments and
> questions of counsel were not evidence. After three hours of deliberation,
> the jury reached a verdict in favor of the defendants.

The court reversed. After quoting James Madison and John Marshall on the
reasons for diversity jurisdiction, Judge Cardamone, citing Rule 3.4(e) and DR
7-106(C)(1), wrote:

> Defense counsel's summation in the case at bar amply demonstrates that
> these fears, though expressed some two hundred years ago, unfortunately
> retain validity, at least insofar as they are based on the belief that some attor-
> neys may attempt to bring improper influences to bear upon a jury. There is no
> doubt whatever that appeals to the regional bias of a jury are completely out of
> place in a federal courtroom. Appeals tending to create feelings of hostility
> against out-of-state parties are so plainly repugnant that the Supreme Court
> long ago stated their condemnation "require[d] no comment." This sort of
> argument improperly distracts the jury from its sworn duty to hand down a just
> verdict based on the evidence presented to it. . . .
>   The combination of the overruled objection, the absence of a curative
> instruction, and the giving of only the standard jury charge regarding argu-
> ments of counsel "could only have left [the jury] with the impression that they
> might properly be influenced by [the improper argument] in rendering their
> verdict, and thus its prejudicial effect was enhanced."

Pappas v. Middle Earth Condominium Assn., 963 F.2d 534 (2d Cir. 1992).
   Apparently, though, lawyers believe that it pays to appeal to regional or class
bias. As reported in the American Lawyer, when the Greenberg, Traurig law firm
was sued in a Texas state court for securities fraud and other claims, a plaintiff's
lawyer referred to the firm on occasion as "Goldberg" and to one of its lawyers,
whose name was Kirshenberg, as "Kirshenbaum," which the firm claimed was
meant to emphasize its Jewish roots. Although the trial judge instructed the
plaintiff's lawyer not to use the word "Yankee," the lawyer then referred to
the firm's lawyers as "privileged," "Park Avenue," "Manhattan" lawyers who
attended "private schools" and wore "$3,000 suits," "$500 shoes," and "silk
stockings." Plaintiff's lawyers rejected the accuracy of the inferences Greenberg
drew. "Instead of looking at their conduct," one said, "they resort to saying this

is a Jewish thing. Oh, come on." The same lawyer said that the references to private schools and Park Avenue were meant only to point out that the Greenberg lawyers should know better. The jury returned a verdict against Greenberg for $25 million. Nathan Koppel, "Home Court Advantage," American Lawyer (May 2002) at 67. On appeal, some of the plaintiffs' claims were reversed and dismissed and others reversed and remanded for assorted legal reasons. The court made no mention of the allegedly biased comments. Greenberg Traurig of New York, P.C. v. Moody, 161 S.W.3d 56 (Tex. Civ. App. 2004). We know from *Pappas* that this sort of thing would not be tolerated in the Second Circuit.

An aside: When I asked a Houston lawyer about this case, he said. "You're from New York. You can't understand Texas. Let me tell you about Texas. I'm from East Texas. A client would have to be nuts to hire me to try a case in West Texas, where I might just as well be from Mars. Same thing the other way around." How sad.

4. The Boundaries of Proper Argument

> And yet as [Mr. Furnival] sat down [after his summation] he knew that [his client] had been guilty! To his ear her guilt had never been confessed; but yet he knew that it was so, and, knowing that, he had been able to speak as though her innocence were a thing of course. That those witnesses [against her] had spoken truth he also knew, and yet he had been able to hold them up to the execration of all around them as though they had committed the worst of crimes from the foulest of motives! And more than this, stranger than this, worse than this, — when the legal world knew — as the legal world soon did know — that all this had been so, the legal world found no fault with Mr. Furnival, conceiving that he had done his duty by his client in a manner becoming an English barrister and an English gentleman.
>
> —Anthony Trollope, *Orley Farm*

Improper Argument

The plaintiffs asserted antitrust and tortious interference claims. The jury awarded $38 million in compensatory and $200 million in punitive damages. The district judge granted the defendant's motion for judgment n.o.v. or, in the alternative, a new trial. Fineman v. Armstrong World Indus., 774 F. Supp. 225 (D.N.J. 1991) and 774 F. Supp. 266 (D.N.J. 1991). The Third Circuit reversed the judgment n.o.v. but affirmed the grant of a new trial. Fineman v. Armstrong World Indus., 980 F.2d 171 (3d Cir. 1992). One of the bases for the grant of a new trial, affirmed by the circuit court, was misconduct of the plaintiffs' counsel in his argument to the jury. Both courts cited Rule 3.4(e). Before the new trial, the defendant moved to disqualify the plaintiffs' counsel based on the finding of misconduct. The district judge denied the motion but required that the plaintiffs' counsel have co-counsel at the retrial who must be "prepared to assume primary responsibility for the conduct of these proceedings should [original counsel] be removed or restricted in his participation, either permanently or temporarily." Fineman v. Armstrong World Indus., 1993 Westlaw 414752

(D.N.J.). Following is the district court's description of the plaintiffs' counsel's conduct that formed the basis of the grant of the motion for a new trial.*

> Mr. Kramer, during the course of his closing arguments in particular, repeatedly testified as to his own truthfulness and trustworthiness, although of course he was not a witness. His testimony on summation included supplying "facts" not in the record about what he knew, didn't know, found out, etc. He also expressed his opinion, on countless occasions, that Armstrong concealed information and lied during the course of the trial. Furthermore, Mr. Kramer repeatedly referred to a crime and to a conspiracy in which Armstrong supposedly engaged despite the fact that this Court directed a verdict in Armstrong's favor as to plaintiffs' civil conspiracy claims and there are, of course, no criminal claims involved in this civil lawsuit. References to crimes and criminals (often comparing witnesses to such celebrated figures as Jack Palance) undoubtedly persuaded the jury to fictionalize the claims herein and act out of a sense of drama rather than reality. . . .
>
> Perhaps the most troubling to this Court is the unadorned, disparaging attack upon defense counsel throughout Mr. Kramer's closing argument. . . .
>
> Mr. Kramer even went so far, in a particularly egregious example of misconduct, as to infer that one defense attorney either counseled a witness to lie (as was suggested by the language he used), or engaged in sexual misconduct with a witness (as was suggested by his tone and the innuendo inherent in his statements):
>
>> [Referring to defense witness Alan Abrahamson]: Look, when he got up here on the witness stand after spending 22 hours with Edith Payne [a defense lawyer], hold [sic] up in a conference room God knows what he was doing for 22 hours for three hours of testimony? . . .
>>
>> That's perjury. He's admitting it. I cannot believe my ears. I really cannot. This is the same Alan Abrahamson, yeah, Ms. Payne's in the room. She's in the second row. There, flower dress. She spent 22 hours held up in a conference with Alan Abrahamson. . . .
>>
>> But I mean, if you're going to tell the truth, why do you have to be terrified? Why do you have to spend 22 hours preparing if all you're going to do is get up there, tell it the way it is, as they say, right?
>>
>> Do you need 22 hours to prepare? To do what? I know what they did. You know what they did. I don't have to tell you what they did during those 22 hours.**

Arguing for False Inferences

"The Eyewitness" (Part I)

"My name is Guy White and I am a criminal defense lawyer. My client is charged with robbing the First Federal Bank. He has confessed his guilt to me, and I have no doubt he is telling me the truth because we have successfully

---

* The plaintiffs ultimately had separate counsel on retrial and lost. N.Y. Times, Aug. 22, 1994, at D2, col. 1.

** Mr. Kramer, who had received 38 sanctions, criticisms, and other forms of professional discipline over an 11-year period, was ultimately disbarred. Matter of Kramer, 677 N.Y.S.2d 576 (1st Dept. 1998).

suppressed a detailed confession to the police and the bank money seized in an unlawful search of his home. But he was wearing a ski mask at the time, so no one at the bank will be able to identify him. However, after he left the bank, he ran into the metro station and removed his ski mask. The prosecutor has a witness who will accurately testify that she saw a man remove a ski mask while running down the station steps. The witness will identify my client as that man. I have evidence that two years ago this witness pled guilty to lying on a loan application. Can I use this evidence to impeach her and then argue to the jury that she is lying now even though I know she is telling the truth?

"I have a second question. I have a witness who will testify that my client was in a Burger King five blocks from the bank ten minutes before the robbery. In fact, he *was* there at that time. You can get to the bank in ten minutes if you move quickly, but it's not easy. Can I call my witness, elicit her testimony, then argue that the jury should have a reasonable doubt of my client's guilt based on the difficulty of covering the five blocks in ten minutes?"

"The Eyewitness" (Part II)

"My name is Charlotte Darling. I am a prosecutor. I am about to try a case in which a man is charged with armed robbery of the First Federal Bank. We know he is guilty because he confessed and his confession led us to the gun and stolen money, but the confession and the money and gun were then suppressed. So we are going to trial. The defense has an eyewitness who can place the defendant in a Burger King five blocks away about ten minutes before the robbery. We believe the witness is correct. For one thing, the defendant told us the same thing in his suppressed confession. It is further corroborated by the time-stamped tape from a video camera in the Burger King, which shows a person who looks like the defendant leaving the Burger King ten minutes before the robbery. The picture is blurry so I can argue that it is not the defendant.

"Now, even with the defendant in the Burger King ten minutes before the robbery, he could still have done it. However, he would have had to move quickly in heavy pedestrian traffic. I am worried that the defense lawyer will use his witness to argue reasonable doubt, even though he knows his client did it. That's why I want the jury to reject the evidence that he was in the Burger King in the first place. So may I impeach the credibility of the witness with a two-year old conviction for lying on a bank loan application and argue to the jury that she is lying now? May I then argue to the jury that it should find that the person shown on the blurry videotape is not the defendant? I myself believe it is the defendant and have no reason to think otherwise."

A lawyer may argue for false inferences in two ways. One of them is pretty simple to deal with; the other is harder, at least for some observers. The easy one first: A lawyer who asks the jury to draw an inference from the evidence when the evidence does not rationally support that inference may be in violation of Rule 3.4(e). When a prosecutor does it, it may deny the defendant a fair trial. So in Hopson v. Riverbay Corp., 190 F.R.D. 114 (S.D.N.Y. 1999), the court granted the plaintiff a new trial when the defense lawyer, in an otherwise routine civil rights case, misstated the record to the jury in her summation. (The court found other professional misconduct as well.) And in United States v. Wilson, 135 F.3d 291 (4th Cir. 1998), the court held that the defendant was denied a fair trial on criminal conspiracy charges when the prosecutor argued to the jury that the evidence showed that the defendant committed murder when he shot at a moving car, when at most the evidence showed that his "gunfire hit the car, or perhaps that a shot struck the driver, [but the evidence was] not enough to suggest that the driver *died* as a result of any gunshot from [the defendant]."

Putting aside these easy cases, let us consider a lawyer's choices when faced with harmful evidence, assuming he cannot persuade the judge to exclude it. First, the lawyer may try to discredit the evidence through impeachment devices, which are calculated to encourage the jury to believe that a witness is mistaken or lying or that a document is false. Second, if the evidence is ambiguous, the lawyer can ask the jury to draw the inference most favorable to his client. These strategies can be used concurrently. Earlier we considered the ethics of impeaching a truthful witness (as accomplished by Max Steuer). Now we ask another question. May a lawyer ask a jury to draw an inference she knows is false as long as the evidence rationally supports it? We know that lawyers may not knowingly introduce false evidence. Doesn't it follow then, sensibly if not ineluctably, that a lawyer may not ask a jury to infer the truth of a false fact, a fact that ethics and criminal law forbid the lawyer to introduce through testimony or documentary evidence?

William H. Fortune, Richard H. Underwood & Edward J. Imwinkelried
MODERN LITIGATION AND PROFESSIONAL RESPONSIBILITY HANDBOOK
Pages 468-470 (2d ed. 2001)

After arguing the credibility of witnesses, the attorney argues the inferences to be drawn from the witnesses' testimony. [A prior section] pointed out that as a general proposition during summation the lawyer may not mention favorable testimony that he knows to be perjurious. This section deals with a closely related problem. Suppose, on the one hand, that the testimony is truthful, or at least that the lawyer does not "know" that the testimony is perjurious. On the other hand, the testimony is logically relevant to support an inference that the lawyer knows to be false. May the lawyer use the testimony to construct an argument for that inference? As in [a prior section], discussing the cross-examination of truthful witnesses, the answer turns on the identity of the lawyer's client.

The answer is "yes" if the client is a criminal accused. So long as he does not rely on perjurious testimony, a criminal defense attorney can argue for a false inference. The criminal defense attorney may attack the prosecution's version of the facts, even when he knows that the version is true. Suppose, for example, that the accused has confided in her lawyer that she, the accused, was present at the crime scene. However, although the police found some latents at the scene, none of the latents matches the accused's fingerprints. The defense counsel could ethically argue that the examiner's testimony shows that the accused was not even at the crime scene. In Johns v. Smyth,[3] a federal judge held that a defense lawyer must argue a false inference that is fairly supported by the evidence. *Johns* was a homicide case in which the prosecution introduced the defendant's confession; the confession admitted the killing, but claimed provocation. The defendant did not testify. Apparently, the defendant had told his attorney that the claim of provocation was false, and the attorney did not argue provocation to mitigate the offense. The federal court granted a writ of habeas corpus because the lawyer had allowed his conscience to trump his duty to the defendant. The court held that the lawyer was obligated to take advantage of the favorable, but false, aspects of the confession introduced by the prosecutor.

The answer is "no" when the client is the prosecuting sovereign. The prosecutor may not argue for a false inference, even if the admissible evidence in the record would support the inference.[5] Prosecution Function Standard 3-5.8(a) states that the prosecutor may not "mislead the jury as to the inferences it may draw."

The answer is unclear when the client is a civil litigant. Leading authorities argue that it is unethical for a civil lawyer to knowingly argue for a false inference, and the Code and the Model Rules proscribe false statements of fact. However, there is no language comparable to Prosecution Function Standard 3-5.8(a), forbidding arguments for "mislead[ing] . . . inferences."

U.S. v. Crawford.   In 2004, on parole, Crawford was legally stopped and searched in New York City when he was discovered on the street late at night in violation of his parole conditions. The court describes what happened:

> The officers then began to search Crawford, and in his pocket they discovered a tin containing a small amount of marijuana. The officers placed Crawford under arrest for possessing marijuana and violating his curfew. At that point, one officer began to search a black gym bag that Crawford had with him. That search was interrupted, however, when Crawford began to flee and the searching officer dropped the bag to chase after him. The bag was picked up by another officer and was later searched when the officers arrived at the police precinct station. The search revealed a .45 caliber semi-automatic pistol and a box containing fifteen rounds of ammunition. . . .
>
> Crawford testified in the defense case. He stated that he was arrested for violating his curfew, but denied resisting arrest. He testified that at his arrest

---

3. 176 F. Supp. 949 (E.D. Va. 1959).

5. United States v. Latimer, 511 F.2d 498 (10th Cir. 1975), provides an excellent example of the different responsibilities of the prosecutor and defense counsel. In a trial for bank robbery, there was testimony that a surveillance camera was activated, but no reference was made to any photographs obtained. In closing, the defense counsel alluded to this gap in the record and suggested that the reason no photographs were introduced was that the photographs would show that the accused was not the robber. The truth of the matter was that the surveillance camera had malfunctioned, and that there were no photographs. To rebut the false inference, the prosecutor informed the jury of the malfunction; the appellate court reversed because the prosecutor had gone outside the record. It was improper for the prosecutor to do so, even to rebut a false inference. (The prosecutor should have moved to reopen the case for the purpose of adducing the admissible evidence needed to rebut the false inference.)

the officers searched his bag and his person and found nothing. He denied possessing a gun or marijuana. In closing argument, his counsel emphasized that the gun was not found at the scene of the arrest, that no fingerprints were taken to match the gun to Crawford, and that no testimony was presented concerning a trace report.

The sole factual question for the jury was: Was the gun in the bag that Crawford was carrying or did the police frame him? The government did do a "trace report" on the gun, which identified the chain of title, and it had given a copy of the report to defense counsel before trial. The report showed that the gun was last legally purchased in 1996. The government said it would introduce the report but then did not do so because, it claimed, of an oversight. It may not have seemed all that important to the factual question either.

But the jury seemed to think otherwise. During the second day of deliberation, the jury asked: "Why wasn't the gun traced to the original owner?" The district judge then allowed the government to reopen the case and call a witness who introduced the trace report and who also testified that the defense counsel had been given a copy of it. This obviously hurt counsel's credibility with the jury given that his summation used the absence of a trace report to punch holes in the prosecutor's proof. When the defense lawyer objected, the trial judge said: "You've left an erroneous impression with the jury. They picked up on it and I don't know why it can't be corrected. It's one thing to put the government to its burden of proof. It's another to play games here."

Crawford was convicted and appealed. Did the defense lawyer "play games" by asking the jury to draw a negative inference against the government and find a reasonable doubt from the apparent failure to introduce a trace report when he knew that in fact the government had done a report, which he himself had chosen not to introduce? What should the Second Circuit do? (Read on.)

The Subin-Mitchell Debate

Professor Harry Subin has envisioned a role for criminal defense lawyers that is sharply less adversarial than the present conception. He would forbid defense lawyers to present "a false case" using the techniques described below. The right to present a defense, he argues, is "not absolute." Witness the prohibition on the use of perjured testimony. Professor Subin criticizes "the utterly arbitrary line we have drawn" between the use of perjured testimony (disallowed) and the presentation of a "false case" (allowed).

After Professor Subin's article appeared, John Mitchell, an experienced criminal defense lawyer whose previous work Professor Subin had cited, challenged Subin's conception with a fact pattern and the argument he would make to the jury based on it. Subin then replied to Mitchell's critique. Excerpts from all three articles follow.*

---

* See Harry Subin, The Criminal Lawyer's "Different Mission": Reflections on the "Right" to Present a False Case, 1 Geo. J. Legal Ethics 125, 146-150 (1987); John Mitchell, Reasonable Doubts Are Where You Find Them: A Response to Professor Subin's Position on the Criminal Lawyer's

Subin.   The question is not, however, whether a "guilty" person has a right to a defense, but what kind of defense can be advanced on behalf of anyone, whether known to be guilty or not, or even if known to be innocent. Here what the defense attorney knows should be crucial to what he or she does.

It may help to explain this position by positing the defense function as consisting of two separate roles, usually intertwined but theoretically distinct. One enlists the attorney as the "monitor" of the state's case, whose task it is to assure that a conviction is based on an adequate amount of competent and admissible evidence. The lawyer as monitor is a kind of quality inspector, with no responsibility for developing a different product, if you will, to "sell" to the jury. The other attorney role involves the attorney as the client's "advocate," whose task is to present that different product by undermining the state's version of the facts or presenting a competing version sufficient at least to establish a reasonable doubt about the defendant's guilt. The monitor's role is to assure that the state has the facts to support a conviction. The advocate attempts to demonstrate that the state's evidence is not fact at all. Where, as in most cases, the facts are in doubt, or where the state's case is believed or known to be based upon mistaken perceptions or lies, the defense attorney quite properly plays both roles. Having monitored the state's case and found it factually and legally sound, however, should he or she be permitted to act as advocate and attempt to undermine it? I submit that the answer to that is no, and that the defendant's rights in cases of this kind extend only as far as the monitoring role takes the attorney. The right in question, to have the state prove guilt beyond a reasonable doubt, can be vindicated if the attorney is limited to good faith challenges to the state's case; to persuading the jury that there are legitimate reasons to doubt the state's evidence. It may on occasion be more effective for the attorney to use his or her imagination to create doubts; but surely there cannot be a right to gain an acquittal whenever the imagination of one's attorney is good enough to produce one. . . .

I propose a system in which the defense attorney would operate not with the right to assert defenses known to be untrue, but under the following rule:

> It shall be improper for an attorney who knows beyond a reasonable doubt the truth of a fact established in the state's case to attempt to refute that fact through the introduction of evidence, impeachment of evidence, or argument.

In the face of this rule, the attorney who knew there were no facts to contest would be limited to the "monitoring" role. Assuming that a defendant . . . wanted to assert his right to contest the evidence against him, the attorney would work to assure that all of the elements of the crime were proven beyond a reasonable doubt, on the basis of the competent and admissible evidence. This would include enforcing the defendant's rights to have privileged or illegally

"Different Mission," 1 Geo. J. Legal Ethics 339, 343-346 (1987); Harry Subin, Is This Lie Necessary? Further Reflections on the Right to Present a False Defense, 1 Geo. J. Legal Ethics 689, 691-692 (1988).

obtained evidence excluded: The goal sought here is not the elimination of all rules that result in the suppression of truth, but only those not supported by sound policy. It would also be appropriate for the attorney to argue to the jury that the available evidence is not sufficient to sustain the burden of proof. It would not, however, be proper for the attorney to use any of the presently available devices to refute testimony known to be truthful. I wish to make clear, however, that this rule would not prevent the attorney from challenging *inaccurate* testimony, even though the attorney knew that the defendant was guilty. Again, the truth-seeking goal is not applicable when a valid policy reason exists for ignoring it. Forcing the state to prove its case is such a reason. . . .

Mitchell.   [I]magine I am defending a young woman accused of shoplifting a star one places on top of Christmas trees. I interview the store manager and find that he stopped my client when he saw her walk straight through the store, star in hand, and out the door. When he stopped her and asked why she had taken the star without paying, she made no reply and burst into tears. He was then about to take her inside to the security office when an employee called out, "There's a fire!" The manager rushed inside and dealt with a small blaze in the camera section. Five minutes later he came out to find my client sitting where he left her. He then took her back to the security room and asked if she would be willing to empty her pockets so that he could see if she had taken anything else. Without a word, she complied. She had a few items not belonging to the store and a ten-dollar bill. The star was priced at $1.79.

In an interview with my client, she admitted trying to steal the star: "It was so pretty, and would have looked so nice on the tree. I would have bought it, but I also wanted to make a special Christmas dinner for Mama and didn't have enough money to do both. I've been saving for that dinner and I know it will make her so happy. But that star. . . . I could just see the look in Mama's eyes if she saw that lovely thing on our tree."

At trial, the manager tells the same story he told me, except he *leaves out* the part about her waiting during the fire and having a ten-dollar bill. If I bring out these two facts on cross-examination and argue for an acquittal based upon my client's "accidentally" walking out of the store with the star, surely Professor Subin will accuse me of raising a "false defense." I have brought out testimony, not itself false, to accredit a false theory and have argued to the jury based on this act. But I am not really arguing a false theory in Professor Subin's sense.

My defense is not that the defendant accidentally walked out, but rather that the prosecution cannot prove the element of intent to permanently deprive beyond a reasonable doubt. Through this theory, I am raising "doubt" in the prosecution's case and therefore questioning the legitimacy of the government's lawsuit for control over the defendant. In my effort to carry out this legal theory, I will *not assert* that facts known by me to be true are false or those known to be false are true. As a defense attorney, I do not have to prove what *in fact* happened. That is an advantage in the process I would not willingly give up. Under our constitutional system, I do not need to try to convince the factfinder about the truth of any factual propositions. I need only try to convince the fact-finder that the prosecution has not met its burden. Again, I will not argue that particular facts are true or false. Thus, in this case I will not claim that my client walked out of the store with innocent intent (a fact which I know is false); rather, I will argue:

> The prosecution claims my client stole an ornament for a Christmas tree. The prosecution further claims that when my client walked out of the store she intended to keep it without paying. Now, maybe she did. None of us were there. On the other hand, she had $10.00 in her pocket, which was plenty of money with which to pay for the ornament without the risk of getting caught stealing. Also, she didn't try to conceal what she was doing. She walked right out of the store holding it in her hand. Most of us have come close to innocently doing the same thing. So, maybe she didn't. But then she cried the minute she was stopped. She might have been feeling guilty. So, maybe she did. On the other hand, she might just have been scared when she realized what had happened. After all, she didn't run away when she was left alone even though she knew the manager was going to be occupied with a fire inside. So, maybe she didn't. The point is that, looking at all the evidence, you're left with "maybe she intended to steal, maybe she didn't." But, you knew that before the first witness was even sworn. The prosecution has the burden, and simply can't carry any burden, let alone "beyond a reasonable doubt," with a maybe she did, maybe she didn't case. . . .

Is this a "false defense" for Professor Subin? Admittedly, I am trying to raise a doubt by persuading the jury to appreciate "possibilities" other than my client's guilt. Perhaps Professor Subin would say it is "false" because I know the possibilities are untrue. But if that is so, Professor Subin will have taken a leap from defining "false defense" as the assertion that true things are false and false things are true, for I am doing neither of those things here. The fact that one cannot know how Subin will reach this "pure" reasonable doubt case only reinforces my initial statement that Professor Subin's categories are imprecise.

Another perspective from which to look at the function of a defense attorney involves understanding that function in the context of the nature of evidence at trial. Professor Subin speaks of facts and the impropriety of trying to make "true facts" look false and "false facts" look true. But in a trial there are no such things as facts. There is only information, lack of information, and chains of inferences therefrom. In the courtroom there will be no crime, no store, no young girl with a star in her hand. All there will be is a collection of witnesses who are strangers to the jury, giving information which may include physical evidence and documents. For example, most people would acknowledge the existence of eyewitness identifications; however, in an evidentiary sense they do not exist. Rather, a particular person with particular perceptual abilities and motives and biases will recount an observation made under particular circumstances and will utter particular words on the witness stand (e.g., "That's the man"). From this mass of information, the prosecution will argue, in story form, in favor of the inference that the defendant is their man (e.g., "The victim was on her way home, when . . ."). The defense will not then argue that the defendant is the wrong man in a *factual sense,* but instead will attack the persuasiveness of the criminal inference and resulting story (e.g., "The sun was in the witness's eyes; she was on drugs").

In our shoplifting example, the prosecution will elicit that the defendant burst into tears when stopped by the manager. From this information will run a chain of inferences: defendant burst into tears; people without a guilty conscience would explain their innocence, not cry; defendant has a guilty conscience; her guilty conscience is likely motivated by having committed a theft. Conversely, if the defense brings out that the manager was shaking a lead pipe in his hand when he stopped the defendant, defense counsel is *not asserting* that defendant did not have a guilty conscience when stopped. Counsel is merely *weakening* the persuasiveness of the prosecution's inference by raising the "possibility" that she was crying not from guilt, but from fear. By raising such "possibilities," the defense is making arguments against the ability of the prosecution's inferences to meet their burden of "beyond a reasonable doubt." The defense is not arguing what are true or false facts (i.e., that the tears were from fear as opposed to guilt). Whatever Professor Subin cares to call it, this commentary on the prosecution's case, complete with raising possibilities which weaken the persuasiveness of central inferences in that case, is in no ethical sense a "false case." "False case" is plainly a misnomer. In a system where factual guilt is not at issue, Professor Subin's "falsehoods" are, in fact, "reasonable doubts."

Subin. [Subin notes Mitchell's statement that he will not "claim that my client walked out of the store with innocent intent (a fact which I know is false)," but will instead make what Mitchell calls a "pure" reasonable doubt argument.]

I applaud this apparent concession that presenting a false defense might be ethically wrong. (Why else would Mitchell go to the trouble of making the argument?) I believe, moreover, that if defense attorneys were required to give this kind of closing argument in "reasonable doubt" cases, it would help to reconcile the goals of assuring a truthful verdict and putting the state to its proof. Mitchell's presentation is, however, flawed in two respects. In the first place, the closing argument which he offers, with its intimations that the defense theory is not dependent upon the facts, is much more forthright than those which most attorneys would give. What they would actually say would be more cryptic with respect to what the jury should conclude about the truth, something like:

> The prosecution claims that my client walked out of the store intending not to pay. I ask you, members of the jury, why would this young lady, with $10.00 in her pocket, steal a $1.79 Christmas tree ornament? Isn't it more likely that in the hustle and bustle of Christmas shopping she saw the ornament, focused for a second on the beautiful Christmas tree she was decorating, picked it up and then forgot she had it when she left the store? At the very least, don't you believe that possibility creates a reasonable doubt about whether she intended to steal the ornament?

Moreover, even if Mitchell's sanitized closing was given, it still is designed to persuade the jury of the existence of facts he knows not to be true: here, that the woman in fact left the store accidentally (i.e., "maybe she did (leave accidentally). None of us was there."). That is not a lie, but it certainly creates a false impression, which amounts to the same thing.

Consider another example of "not arguing what are true or false facts" which Mitchell draws from his hypothetical: the woman bursts into tears after being caught stealing the ornament. The lawyer knows that she did so as a result of her guilty conscience. The store manager, however, was shaking a lead pipe in his hand when he stopped the woman. Mitchell says that if he brings out that fact, he is not "asserting" that the defendant did not have a guilty conscience; he is merely "weakening the persuasiveness of the prosecutor's inferences." It is perfectly clear, however, that he is attempting to do this by suggesting to the jury that this woman was in fact frightened by this lead pipe. Mitchell would, moreover, make this argument even if his client swore to him that she never even *saw* the lead pipe.

QUESTIONS

1. Who wins this debate? Mitchell, you say? Then how do you answer Subin's argument that it is "utterly arbitrary" to draw the line at perjurious testimony while permitting a "false case"? If the latter is acceptable, why not the former? If the former is unacceptable, why do we permit the latter? False is false in the search for truth.

2. Subin believes that defense lawyers would give a different summation from what Mitchell sets out. Mitchell himself says that his "defense is not that the defendant accidentally walked out, but rather that the prosecution cannot prove the element of intent to permanently deprive beyond a reasonable doubt." Is there anything wrong with the summation Subin describes? He seems to think that his alternate summation undermines Mitchell's position.

3. Does Mitchell concede more than he must? Using Mitchell's hypothetical, could the defense lawyer ask the jury to find as a fact that his client did not knowingly take the ornament? That the defendant's tears were caused by the lead pipe? Could he make these arguments even though he knew both were false? He would not, of course, state his own belief. He would frame the argument by identifying inferences (with phrases like "I submit" or "I ask you to find") that support a reasonable doubt.

4. Remember Kuzak from *L.A. Law?* (Page 396) He put the defendant's aunt on the stand to establish that others had access to the car involved in the hit and run. That was true. But Kuzak knew that his client did it. Presumably, from this true testimony, Kuzak planned to argue for a reasonable doubt. Any problem?

5. Do any of your answers change if the lawyer arguing for the false inference is a prosecutor? A government lawyer in a civil case? See United States v. Blueford, 312 F.3d 962 (9th Cir. 2002) (prosecutor may urge inferences she "believes in good faith might be true," but "decidedly improper . . . to propound inferences [she] has very strong reasons to doubt . . ."). If that is so, isn't the government at a serious disadvantage before the jury? Alternatively, if the public learns that defense lawyers, but not prosecutors or other government lawyers, can argue for false inferences, won't that knowledge undermine the credibility of lawyers arguing against the government?

6. Maybe you think that juries will not know that prosecutors (and other government lawyers) have greater duties of candor than other lawyers or what those duties are. You are undoubtedly right. (Did you know the

differences before law school?) How can we accept juror ignorance? Why not include these differences in the jury instructions? After all, if we are asking citizens to participate in a solemn public event, don't they have a right to know the rules governing that event?

7. Remember Crawford, whose story preceded the Subin-Mitchell debate? The Second Circuit reversed his conviction and remanded for a new trial. Most of the opinion concerns standards for reopening a case following the start of deliberations. But the court also addressed the legitimacy of defense counsel's argument. Recall that he had asked the jury to draw a negative inference from the government's apparent failure to introduce a gun-trace report, even though he knew the government had in fact done one because he had it. The appellate court said: "Crawford's counsel could have reasonably concluded that the government had either made a strategic decision to withhold [the] report, or that it had simply done a poor job in presenting its evidence. In either event, it was appropriate for Crawford's counsel to highlight that omission in his summation." Reopening the case was error, especially as the government was also permitted to prove that defense counsel had the report. "The implication that Crawford [who had testified] and Crawford's counsel lied to the jury was very likely to have undermined Crawford's defense." United States v. Crawford, 533 F.3d 133 (2d Cir. 2008).

8. Whenever we discuss the Subin-Mitchell debate in class, Subin gets creamed (to put it gently, as he does among lawyers), and I do my best to defend him, a former colleague after all. But he does have a point somewhere in there, doesn't he? We can't just react intuitively to his argument. I suspect that Subin would fare better in a college philosophy class or in a discussion among clergy. Let me make it a little harder for Professor Mitchell. Mitchell's argument is based on his claim that the defense lawyer is merely exposing a reasonable doubt about the state's proof of the client's mental state: Was the conduct intentional or accidental? This argument benefits from the fact that the state has the burden of proof regarding mental state. But what if the defense lawyer is seeking to establish an affirmative defense, say self-defense, where the defendant has the burden of proof in some jurisdictions? Does Mitchell run into trouble when he is no longer suggesting why the jury should doubt the state's proof, but is instead introducing true evidence and then asking the jury affirmatively to infer that a false fact is true?

You ask, would I please make this a little more concrete? All right. Try this problem.

"Maxwell's Silver Handle .38"

Calvin is charged with murdering Maxwell in a city park by shooting him. Next to Maxwell's body is a silver-handled .38. Calvin admitted to Otto, his lawyer, that he shot Maxwell because Maxwell was encroaching on his drug territory. Calvin was unaware that Maxwell was even carrying a gun. Calvin was also unaware that the day before he shot Maxwell, Maxwell had told Porky and Juvie that he was going to "snuff" Calvin because Calvin was interfering with Maxwell's drug business. And Maxwell showed Porky and Juvie his silver-handled .38 to make it clear he had the means to do it. But Calvin shot Maxwell before Maxwell ever had a chance to carry out his threat. Only after Calvin shot him did Maxwell reach for his gun, but he collapsed before he could fire back, which is how the .38 wound up next to his body.

In the jurisdiction, self-defense is an affirmative defense, which means Calvin must prove it by a preponderance of the evidence. Otto wants to argue that Calvin shot Maxwell to defend himself against Maxwell's use of deadly force. Can Otto call Porky and Juvie to testify to what Maxwell said and to identify the gun Maxwell showed them, and then argue that the jury should find as a fact that Maxwell was the initial aggressor, thereby hoping to prove self-defense? Calvin can't testify because he has a record from here to the Grand Canyon.

FURTHER READING

Rosemary Nidiry has examined excesses in defense and prosecutorial summations in criminal cases. She argues that although "high levels of combativeness potentially threaten the effectiveness and legitimacy of trials . . . critics have largely ignored excess in closing argument." After describing the relevant rules and ethical standards and problems with their enforcement, Ms. Nidiry offers examples of excessive closing arguments and proposes remedies. Note, Restraining Adversarial Excess in Closing Argument, 96 Colum. L. Rev. 1299 (1996).

E.   FRIVOLOUS POSITIONS AND ABUSIVE TACTICS

Judicial sanctions for various forms of bad behavior are a subject you probably studied in Civil Procedure. Or at least you studied Rule 11 of the Federal Rules of Civil Procedure. While these sanctions get due attention, less noticed are the occasional actions against lawyers for abuse of process and malicious prosecution, which seem to be experiencing an uptick of late. A few examples, including a $10 million punitive damage judgment in Montana against a major U.S. firm, appear at page 765.

Court-imposed sanctions for frivolous claims or defenses and abusive tactics have increased dramatically in the last three decades. Judges and commentators disagree on the wisdom of these sanctions generally and in particular cases; they also disagree on the many subissues that a sanctions regime must resolve. But there is one thing on which they cannot disagree: Rule 11 is a force to be reckoned with.

The modern Rule 11 was born in 1983. The Supreme Court construed it in Business Guides, Inc. v. Chromatic Communications Ent., 498 U.S. 533 (1991); Cooter & Gell v. Hartmarx Corp., 496 U.S. 384 (1990); and Pavelic & LeFlore v. Marvel Entertainment Group, 493 U.S. 120 (1989). *Cooter & Gell* held (1) that a judge could impose Rule 11 sanctions notwithstanding that the plaintiff had voluntarily dismissed its complaint; (2) that the scope of review on appeal should be for an abuse of discretion; and (3) that Rule 11 did not authorize attorney's fees on appeal. *Pavelic & LeFlore* held that only the signer of the offending court paper could be sanctioned, not the entire firm or other lawyers working on the matter. *Business Guides* upheld Rule 11 sanctions against a *client* who had signed an offending paper (an application for a restraining order).

In 1993, Rule 11 was again amended, becoming both narrower and broader, but mostly narrower. The new rule overturns *Pavelic & LeFlore*, clarifies *Business Guides*, and partly overturns the first holding of *Cooter & Gell*. It would be sensible at this point to read the entire rule. Essentially, a lawyer's signature on a pleading, written motion, or other paper certifies, among other things, that "to the best of [his or her] knowledge, information, and belief, formed after an inquiry reasonable under the circumstances" —

(1) it is not being presented for any improper purpose, such as to harass or to cause unnecessary delay or needless increase in the cost of litigation;

(2) the claims, defenses, and other legal contentions therein are warranted by existing law or by a nonfrivolous argument for the extension, modification, or reversal of existing law or the establishment of new law;

(3) the allegations and other factual contentions have evidentiary support or, if specifically so identified, are likely to have evidentiary support after a reasonable opportunity for further investigation or discovery; and

(4) the denials of factual contentions are warranted on the evidence or, if specifically so identified, are reasonably based on a lack of information or belief.

Sanctions must be "limited to what suffices to deter repetition of such conduct or comparable conduct [including by others]." When a motion for sanctions is made by a party, the rule now has a safe-harbor provision that gives the opposing party three weeks to withdraw the offending document before the motion can be decided. A court cannot award a monetary sanction against a party who has voluntarily dismissed or settled claims before the court issues its order to show cause. Sanctions may include an order to pay a penalty into court, "nonmonetary directives," and, if imposed after motion, an order to pay attorney's fees and "other expenses directly resulting from the violation." A party (as opposed to a lawyer) who signs a document is not subject to a monetary sanction for violation of paragraph (2). (Do you see why?) Absent "exceptional circumstances, a law firm shall be held jointly responsible for violations committed by its partners, associates, and employees."

You should know that although Rule 11 gets most of the attention, it is not the only source of judicial sanctioning power at the federal level. (Furthermore, many states have their own sanctioning provisions.) Other provisions in a federal judge's arsenal include: 28 U.S.C. §1927, which says that any "attorney or other person . . . who so multiplies the proceedings in any case unreasonably and vexatiously may be required" to pay costs and attorney's fees "reasonably incurred because of such conduct"; Rules 16, 26, and 37 of the Federal Rules of Civil Procedure, which permit sanctions for discovery abuse and other misconduct in civil litigation; and Rule 38 of the Federal Rules of Appellate Procedure, which permits "damages and single or double costs to the appellee" if "an appeal is frivolous." My favorite §1927 case in this edition is Riddle & Assoc. P.C., 414 F.3d 832 (7th Cir. 2005), whose facts might best be described as "Lawyer Gone Wild." The case defies easy summary. Suffice it to say that a lawyer's baseless and threatening letters in response to plaintiff's effort to collect on his client's $100 bounced check eventually led to a federal action and counterclaim and to sanctions against the lawyer of $18,037.22 to the plaintiff and a remand for determination of hefty additional sanctions to be paid to the plaintiff's law firm.

Courts also have inherent power to award counsel fees and expenses if an opposing lawyer has acted in bad faith, vexatiously, wantonly, or for oppressive reasons. This power is not displaced by Rule 11 or other provisions of the federal rules. Chambers v. NASCO, Inc., 501 U.S. 32 (1991), affirmed a district judge's award of nearly $1 million against a plaintiff for bad-faith litigation. The sum represented the entire amount of the defendant's litigation costs over a three-year period. See also Fink v. Gomez, 239 F.3d 989 (9th Cir. 2001) (court has inherent power to sanction a lawyer who recklessly misstates the law or facts and does so for an improper purpose, "such as an attempt to influence or manipulate proceedings in one case in order to gain tactical advantage in another case").

The scope of these various rules and authorities varies. Some require subjective bad faith, while others use an objective standard; some are only available on appeal, while others are for the trial court. There is also much overlap. By far, however, it is Rule 11 that has received the most attention, some of it highly critical, even caustic. One early but startling discovery was that only a few judges accounted for a disproportionate number of Rule 11 sanctions. According to Professor Grosberg (and other investigators), in the first two years of the revised rule's operation (1983 to 1985), three federal judges (out of 684) "wrote 14.2 percent of the opinions in which the rule was cited and 12.2 percent of the opinions in which sanctions were imposed." Lawrence Grosberg, Illusion and Reality in Regulating Lawyer Performance: Rethinking Rule 11, 32 Vill. L. Rev. 575 (1987).

Rule 11 and related sanctions alarm lawyers for several reasons. For most, having a judge find that they engaged in frivolous or vexatious conduct, no matter how modest the sanction, is disturbing. The court's opinion may appear in the case reports, on line, or in the popular or legal press. Client relations may suffer if sanctions are jointly imposed on the lawyer and client, if the sanction undermines the client's cause, or if it requires additional legal expense beyond the sanction itself. In addition, a sanction may be sizeable. Avirgan v. Hull, 932 F.2d 1572 (11th Cir. 1991) (affirming Rule 11 sanctions of more than $1 million); Brandt v. Schal Associates, Inc., 960 F.2d 640 (7th Cir. 1992) (affirming sanction of $443,000 where unsuccessful RICO claim required defendant to pay for 3,000 hours of lawyer and paralegal time in a four-year period).

F. DILATORY TACTICS

WASHINGTON MONTHLY
September 1979, at 10

[A lawyer who once practiced with a large Washington, D.C., firm told the editor-in-chief of the Washington Monthly that] a major corporate client came to his firm with an antitrust problem. The firm's advice was that the problem was hopeless in the sense that the client was ultimately doomed to lose. But the case could be stretched out for as long as ten years. Would the client be prepared to pay the $500,000 to $1,000,000 in annual legal fees that delay would require? Of course. Here is a client who knows he's wrong and whose law firm knows he's wrong. Yet they are both willing to make the government spend millions over ten years to win a case that they know it deserves to win now.

It is often charged that lawyers use delay as a pressure tactic to win or favorably settle lawsuits. Here, we consider the ethics of delay and other "indirect" strategies for gaining legal advantage. "Indirect" strategies refer to conduct whose primary purpose is to avoid a contest on "the merits" of a dispute through concentration on collateral issues.

Marian Small is injured in a car accident. She sues the other driver, who is defended by a lawyer retained by the driver's insurer. Small is in need of a quick recovery. She has no real savings and sick leave will only cover three weeks' pay. Her medical bills, only a portion of which are insured, are mounting, as are other incidental expenses. She asks her lawyer for a loan. Although he is willing to make one because he anticipates a recovery from which she will be able to repay him, he may not. Model Rule 1.8(e). (See page 229.)

Small senses a subtle pressure from her lawyer to be receptive to a settlement. Her lawyer, after all, is working under a contingent fee arrangement. Delay in settlement increases his uncompensated time in the case. On the other hand, quick settlement, even for less than the case may be "worth," will yield the lawyer a *certain* fee (perhaps at an effective hourly rate higher than the fee he'd get *if* he wins the trial, see page 170) and free up time for other cases. Also, it's certain. He might lose the trial.

Small's lawyer tells her that if the matter goes to trial and she wins, she will be entitled to prejudgment interest on the amount of the recovery, but the interest rate allowed in Small's state is only 4 percent, at a time when the prime rate is 6 percent. Consequently, the lawyer explains, from the insurance company's point of view, it may literally "pay" to delay settlement as long as possible since the company will be able to invest the money at a substantially greater return than it will have to pay in prejudgment interest. Small asks whether the company is under pressure to settle because of the legal costs it incurs in continuing to litigate. Small's lawyer explains that the company is handling the litigation in-house, through a salaried lawyer, and so its costs are comparatively low and are, in any event, tax deductible. (And tax deductions aside, the company buys legal work "in bulk," which allows it to keep costs down even when it retains outside lawyers.)

Small's lawyer also tells her that the state court in which her case is pending has a lengthy civil trial calendar so that even when the case is ready for trial, it may take an extra year to get into a courtroom.

The insurance company's lawyer is aware of all these pressures on Small and of the ways in which pretrial maneuvers in discovery will, along with the systemic delay, postpone Small's recovery. She does her best to put off judgment day as long as possible by, among other things, insisting on every procedural right the state's rules offer a litigant.

Is any of this conduct by the insurance company's lawyer unethical? Is it the insurance company's fault that the system is backed up? Doesn't the company have a right to take advantage of all procedural and discovery devices that may (however slightly) increase its chances at trial, even though these take a lot of time and time works to the disadvantage of the plaintiff? After all, the insurance company is not a charitable organization. It has a responsibility to conserve its assets. In making a settlement offer early in a litigation, isn't it well within propriety for the insurer to factor in the plaintiff's need for funds and the effect of the prospect of delay on the plaintiff's willingness to settle? If so, isn't the company's lawyer entitled to assist it? Are there *any* limits? Compare Sussman v. Bank of Israel, 56 F.3d 450 (2d Cir. 1995) (nonfrivolous complaint cannot be punished even if lawyer has improper purpose, but using valid claim to generate adverse publicity is in any event not improper).

Close on the heels of Rule 11 is the issue of delay for improper purposes. Delay for such purposes may not only violate Rule 11, it may also be unethical. Indeed, some of the language of Model Rules 3.1 and 4.4 echoes language in Rule 11 and may even be broader. (Rule 4.4 requires that a tactic serve a "substantial purpose.") At first blush, Rule 3.2 appears to go beyond Rule 11. It says that "[a] lawyer shall make reasonable efforts to expedite litigation consistent with the interests of the client." Do the last seven words make the rule meaningless? If delay is in the client's interest, the lawyer has no duty to expedite. If delay is not in the client's interest, the lawyer has a duty to expedite because of the duty of diligence owed the client (Model Rule 1.3). The comment to Model Rule 3.2 seems beside the point. Where the rule speaks about expediting litigation, the comment talks about the impropriety of dilatory tactics. But can't a lawyer refrain from the latter without pursuing the former? How is your interpretation of the rule influenced by the fact that a draft of the rule referred to the client's "legitimate interests"? The adjective was left out. In the end, the Rules do not seem to forbid the behavior of Marian Small's opponent.

G. HARDBALL AND INCIVILITY

"Hardball" is a late addition to the bar's lexicon and the debate about its behavior. Along with ancillary businesses (page 852) and marketing (chapter 16), the use of "hardball" tactics in litigation and elsewhere is seen to betoken a decline in professionalism. The opposite of "hardball," apparently, is not "softball," but "civility." Committees and commissions nationwide have called for a "return" to civility, the assumption being that it was a place lawyers once dwelled. See the Final Report of the Committee on Civility of the Seventh Federal Judicial Circuit, reprinted at 143 F.R.D. 441 (1992).

The *Mullaney* opinion below imposes monetary sanctions for rather uncivil gender-biased conduct at a civil deposition. Racist comments, though more rare today, are not unknown. See Thomas v. Tenneco Packaging Co., 293 F.3d 1306 (11th Cir. 2002) (lawyer censured for filing documents "strewn with generalizations and conclusory comments that paint opposing counsel as a racist bigot and thus impugn his character").

Behavior need not be sexist or racist to suffer judicial criticism. In Paramount Communications, Inc. v. QVC Network, Inc., 637 A.2d 34 (Del. 1994), the court chastised famed Texas lawyer Joe Jamail for the manner in which he defended a deposition, held in Texas but incident to a Delaware court contest for control of Paramount. One example of Jamail's deposition statements: "Don't 'Joe' me, asshole. You can ask some questions, but get off of that. I'm tired of you. You could gag a maggot off a meat wagon." (The meaning of the last comment has always escaped me. It must be a Texas thing.) Jamail was not a member of the Delaware bar, so the court invited him to explain his conduct. Jamail responded: "I'd rather have a nose on my ass than go to Delaware for any reason." Tex. Law., Feb. 14, 1994, at 11. (If Jamail appears rather independent, recall that he was the lawyer who got a $10 billion judgment against Texaco for his client Pennzoil and ultimately settled for $3 billion. Did I mention that he was working on contingency?)

A similar example of incivility is revealed in Carroll v. The Jaques Admiralty Law Firm, P.C., 110 F.3d 290 (5th Cir. 1997). Jaques was a lawyer whose firm had been sued by a former client. He appealed a sanction of $7,000 imposed on him for his behavior as a witness at a videotaped deposition. Among his comments were: "Where the fuck is this idiot going?"; "Get off my back you slimy son-of-a-bitch"; and, after opposing counsel terminated the deposition, "Fuck you, you son-of-a-bitch." The court said Jaques's conduct was not excused by the fact that he was "tired, hypoglycemic, and feeling put-upon by repetitive and, in his view, irrelevant questioning."

Incivility can be toward the court as well as counsel. In my "What Got Into Them?" file (further revealed at page 891) is Taboda v. Daly Seven, Inc., 636 S.E.2d 889 (Va. 2006). After losing an appeal, lawyer Barnhill's petition to rehear "described this Court's opinion as 'irrational and discriminatory' and 'irrational at its core.' He wrote that 'George Orwell's fertile imagination could not supply a clearer distortion of the plain meaning of language to reach such an absurd result.'" (He didn't invoke Kafka.) For reasons that escape me, Barnhill included the following line: "'[I]f you attack the King, kill the King; otherwise the King will kill you.'" Obviously, Barnhill was very angry. He probably broke RULE NUMBER ONE, which says: NEVER SEND ANYTHING YOU WROTE WHEN YOU WERE VERY ANGRY. When the court told Barnhill to show why he should not be sanctioned, he sensibly hired a lawyer and expressed "his apology and sincere regret." The episode was aberrational. He would not file any more briefs until another lawyer reviewed them. The court, however, said the conduct was "very serious" and suspended Barnhill's right to practice before it for one year.

I could fill quite a few of this book's pages with examples of male lawyers behaving badly toward female lawyers, witnesses, opposing clients, and even their own clients. For other examples of highly offensive sexist behavior see page 792. Why does this happen? Possibilities include (a) it's strategic — the aggressors believe that it will rattle the women; (b) it's instinctive — this is just the way they treat women, nothing personal; (c) it's generational — the offenders are mainly older lawyers for whom women professionals are unnerving or a threat of some kind; (d) it's a product of confusion — the offenders don't know how to talk to women as equals; (e)? What do you think may have been the explanation in the next case?

MULLANEY v. AUDE
126 Md. App. 639, 730 A.2d 759 (Ct. Spec. App. 1999)

Adkins, Judge.

This case involves the adversarial use of gender bias in the discovery process. James L. Mullaney, Esq., and Allan E. Harris, Esq., appellants, appeal from the imposition . . . of attorneys' fees incurred in obtaining a protective order against them. . . .

Facts and Procedural Background

Betty Sue Aude, appellee, brought a tort action for fraud, negligence, intentional infliction of emotional distress, and battery against Mr. Mullaney, alleging that he infected her with genital herpes. Susan R. Green, Esq., and Gary S. Bernstein, Esq., represented Ms. Aude. Mr. Mullaney was represented by Mr. Harris and Benjamin Lipsitz, Esq. After a trial, the jury found that Mr. Mullaney negligently infected Ms. Aude with genital herpes, but that Ms. Aude was contributorily negligent. Accordingly, judgment was entered in favor of Mr. Mullaney on December 10, 1996.

Appellants' Deposition Conduct

During the course of pre-trial discovery, Ms. Aude was deposed. At the deposition, she was asked about a document that she failed to bring with her. As Ms. Aude was leaving the room to retrieve that document, Mr. Harris remarked that she was going to meet "[a]nother boyfriend" at the car. Ms. Green and Mr. Bernstein quickly told Mr. Harris that his comment was in poor taste and asked him to refrain from making further derogatory comments. The following ensued:

Mr. Mullaney: It's going to be a fun trial.
Mr. Harris: It must have been in poor taste if Miss Green says it was in poor taste. It must have really been in poor taste.
Ms. Green: You got a problem with me?
Mr. Harris: No, I don't have any problem with you, babe.

Ms. Green: Babe? You called me babe? What generation are you from?
Mr. Harris: At least I didn't call you a bimbo.
Mr. Lipsitz: Cut it out.
Ms. Green: The committee will enjoy hearing about that.
Mr. Bernstein: Alan, you ought to stay out of the gutter. . . .

Appellants next contend that Mr. Harris's comments to Ms. Green at Ms. Aude's deposition were not sexist behavior or disruptive to the discovery process. We unequivocally reject this assertion, and with this decision hope to make it crystal clear how this Court views the exhibition of gender bias by lawyers in the litigation process.

A.   STRATEGIC NAME CALLING AND BIAS

The absence of civility and respect exhibited by lawyers towards one another has been for years the subject of significant concern for bar and bench leaders. In the words of Judge Paul L. Friedman of the United States District Court for the District of Columbia:

> Although the "modern age" of the legal profession has witnessed progress in opening its doors wider to women and minorities and others who were previously excluded, this age has also opened its doors to the "Rambo litigator" which has spawned a generation of lawyers, too many of whom think they are more effective when they are more abrasive. . . .

Some attorneys engage in actively undermining another attorney's case by using gender. . . . Mr. Harris's behavior with respect to Ms. Aude and her counsel at the deposition was a crass attempt to gain an unfair advantage through the use of demeaning language, a blatant example of "sexual [deposition] tactics." With respect to the effect on the profession, we think Judge Waldron stated it well when he said: "These actions . . . have no place in our system of justice and when attorneys engage in such actions they do not merely reflect on their own lack of professionalism but they disgrace the entire legal profession and the system of justice that provides a stage for such oppressive actors."

Appellants refused to acknowledge, in their brief or at oral argument, that it was derogatory for Mr. Harris to address Ms. Green as "babe," during a deposition. They unblushingly ask this Court to construe Mr. Harris's use of the term "babe" as a term of endearment because it is "a nickname for 'Babe' Ruth, a towering athletic figure and an American folk hero, and 'Babe' Didrickson, an outstanding and multi-talented female athlete. . . ." They contend that the term "indicates approval, [and] is a sign of approbation." Thus, they say, Mr. Harris's "calling someone 'babe' would to him not in any way be a derogatory act, but would at least imply a commendatory opinion of the person so addressed." We find this argument singularly unpersuasive. If Ms. Green, when up to bat at the annual Bar Association softball tournament, hit a home run, and in that context Mr. Harris chose to call her "Babe," this argument *might* be plausible. In the context of this case, however, we can only characterize the argument as disingenuous.

Lest there by any doubt about Mr. Harris's intended meaning when he addressed Ms. Green as "babe," we need look no further than the transcript of the deposition. When Ms. Green asked him to refrain from the use of that term, Mr. Harris responded: "At least I didn't call you a bimbo." To our knowledge, neither Babe Ruth nor Babe Didrickson was endearingly addressed as "bimbo."

Let us move from common sense to the dictionary. The term "babe" is defined as:

1. a baby or child. 2. an innocent or inexperienced person. 3. (*usually cap.*) *Southern U.S.* (used, often before the surname, as a familiar name for a boy or man, esp. the youngest of a family). 4. *Slang.* a. *Sometimes Disparaging and Offensive.* a girl or woman, esp. an attractive one. b. (*sometimes cap.*) an affectionate or familiar term of address (sometimes offensive when used to [address] strangers, causal acquaintances, subordinates, etc., esp. by a male to a female).

The Random House Dictionary of the English Language, at 148 (2d ed. unabridged 1987). The term "bimbo" is defined as: "1. a foolish, stupid, or inept person. 2. a man or fellow, often a disreputable or contemptible one. 3. *a disreputable woman; tramp; whore.*" *Id.* at 208. When used to address another attorney in the context of a discovery deposition or court proceeding, all of the dictionary definitions of the word "babe" are gender biased and derogatory.[5] To explain further why this conduct is objectionable, we briefly review the study of gender bias in the court system. In 1987, former Chief Judge Robert Murphy appointed a Special Joint Committee on Gender Bias in the Courts, which resulted in the 1989 Report of the Special Joint Committee on Gender Bias in the Courts prepared after extensive public hearings and research. The Committee reported that "[f]emale attorneys feel demeaned when they are addressed informally . . . such as 'hon,' 'dear,' 'baby doll,' 'honey,' and 'sweetheart.' " Professor Karen Czapanskiy of the University of Maryland School of Law aptly explained the nature of the problem presented when she quoted the words of an attorney who reported in a gender bias study from New Jersey:

I have . . . observed the use of a demeaning term of pseudo endearment to belittle and undermine the professionalism of a female attorney. Such terms are used by both . . . judges and attorneys, to single out a female attorney and set her on a lower plateau. Rather than a direct attack on the legal issue or the argument advanced, the demeaning term is used to dismiss the female attorney's position or relegate it to a lesser status. . . .

If Mr. Harris, by the use of such tactics, can evoke in Ms. Green any emotional response that puts her off-balance, makes her defensive, makes her feel inadequate, or just plain angry and distracted, he has succeeded with his strategy. In so doing, he likely has interfered with the discovery process. While strategy and

---

5. The southern colloquial use of "babe" preceding a boy's surname (as in "Babe Jones") to refer to the youngest male of a family, is clearly not applicable to the usage in this case.

tactics are part of litigation, and throwing your adversary off-balance may well be a legitimate tactic, it is not legitimate to do so by the use of gender-based insults.

Mr. Harris defends his action by including in the record copies of advertisements in which Ms. Green held herself out to be a "hardball" attorney. At oral argument, counsel suggested that if she advertises herself as "hardball" she should expect some "rough and tumble"[7] experiences during the course of litigation. This incident, he posits, was simply that. Mr. Harris and his counsel widely miss the mark with this argument. There is no doubt that with our adversarial system of justice, lawyers who choose to litigate must withstand pressure, adversity, and the strategic maneuvers of their opponent. Fortunately, however, we have long passed the era when bias relating to sex, race, religion, or other specified groups is considered acceptable as a litigation strategy. The Maryland Code of Judicial Conduct mandates that "[a] judge shall require lawyers in proceedings before the judge to refrain from manifesting, by words or conduct, bias or prejudice based upon race, sex, religion, national origin, disability, age, sexual orientation or socioeconomic status, against parties, witnesses, counsel or others."*

We think that the trial court, in finding that Mr. Harris's conduct exhibited gender bias in a deposition, acted in a manner consistent with the directives of this Canon. . . .

The imposition of sanctions under these circumstances reinforces the commitment of the judicial system to impartiality. "Whether it is men or women who experience the burden of bias . . . the public has an interest because the judicial system has failed to adhere to the highest standards of fairness and impartiality." This concept was well stated by the Supreme Court of New York when it was presented with a request for sanctions relating to gender-biased insulting remarks[8] made to counsel during depositions:

> Seeking sanctions from this court is not a display of an inability to overlook obnoxious conduct, but an indication of a commitment to basic concepts of justice and respect for the mores of the profession of law. The movant has turned to the court to give force to a basic professional tenet.

Principe v. Assay Partners, 154 Misc. 2d 702, 586 N.Y.S.2d 182, 186 (1992). . . .

Susan Green's half-page Yellow Pages ad had the word "HARDBALL" across the top in bold capital letters about an inch high.

---

7. The term "rough and tumble" is a paraphrase of the words used by counsel at argument.
* Today, the ABA's Code of Judicial Conduct is broader. See Rule 2.3(C) and (D), quoted at page 416 above. — ED.
8. A male attorney made the following comments to an opposing female attorney during a deposition:
"I don't have to talk to you, little lady";
"Tell that little mouse over there to pipe down";
"What do you know, young girl";
"Be quiet, little girl";
"Go away, little girl."

H. MISSTATING FACTS, PRECEDENT, OR THE RECORD

Whatever tolerance courts may have when lawyers engage in the artful use of language with each other, expectations are higher when lawyers talk to judges. Justice Department lawyer Mikki Graves Walser learned that lesson the hard way. Her experience is especially instructive because although her omissions were far from egregious, the court was not inclined to accept fine distinctions.

The Court of International Trade had given Walser a deadline of May 5 to file a summary judgment motion in a customs case. On May 4, not having started work on the motion, she requested an extension. On May 10, the court denied the extension and ordered her to file the motion "forthwith." She filed it May 22. The court struck it as untimely. The government moved for reconsideration. Its argument, which Walser wrote, claimed that the delay from May 10 to May 22 was "forthwith" as case law had construed that word. Walser cited or quoted several sources. For two of them, she omitted language from her quotations. First, in the body of her memo, she wrote the following:

> See City of New York v. McAllister Brothers, Inc., 278 F.2d 708, 710 (" 'Forthwith' means immediately, without delay, *or as soon as the object may be* accomplished by reasonable exertion") (emphasis added).

She omitted the following additional sentence in the court's opinion:

> The Supreme Court has said of the word that "in matters of practice and pleading it is usually construed, and sometimes defined by rule of court, as within twenty-four hours."

Next, in a footnote, Walser wrote:

> While we did not review the Supreme Court's decision in Henderson v. United States, 517 U.S. 654, 680, in interpreting the meaning of "forthwith," it is noteworthy that in his dissenting opinion, Justice Thomas, with whom The Chief Justice and Justice O'Connor joined, citing Amella v. United Northern Trust Co., 732 F.2d 711, 713 (C.A. 1984), stated that "[a]lthough we have never undertaken to define 'forthwith' . . . , *it is clear that the term 'connotes action which is immediate, without delay, prompt, and with reasonable dispatch.'* "

The ellipsis replaced the italicized words from the opinion:

> "Although we have never undertaken to define 'forthwith' *as it is used in the SAA* [Suits in Admiralty Act], it is clear that the term 'connotes action which is immediate, without delay, prompt, and with reasonable dispatch.' "

Walser did not reveal that the emphasis in the footnote was hers, not the court's. Both opinions from which Walser quoted cited to a 1900 Supreme Court case that supported language she omitted, but Walser also omitted the cite.

The lower court issued a Rule 11 reprimand in an unpublished opinion. The Federal Circuit affirmed.

The effect of Walser's editing of this material and ignoring the [1900] Supreme Court decision that dealt with the issue — a decision that seriously weakened her argument — was to give the Court of International Trade a misleading impression of the state of the law on the point. She eliminated material that indicated that her delay in filing the motion for reconsideration had not met the court's requirement that she file "forthwith," and presented the remaining material in a way that overstated the basis for her claim that a "forthwith" filing requirement meant she could take whatever time would be reasonable in the circumstances. This distortion of the law was inconsistent with and violated the standards of Rule 11.

Precision Specialty Metals, Inc. v. United States, 315 F.3d 1346 (Fed. Cir. 2003).

Contrast what Walser did with what Michael Fletcher did. Matter of Fletcher, 424 F.3d 783 (8th Cir. 2005). Fletcher was found to have "selectively quot[ed] deposition testimony in a way that grossly mischaracteriz[ed] deponents' statements," and he was suspended for three years. Ms. Walser's transgression, though serious, pales next to Fletcher's deceptions. She might have thought it was all part of the adversary system: Make the best argument you can, and let your opponent bring your omissions to the attention of the court if it chooses. What the court's reaction tells us, however, is that it is not the same adversary system when you're talking to the judge as when you are talking to the opposing lawyer.

In re Curl, 803 F.2d 1004 (9th Cir. 1986), ordered a lawyer to show cause why he should not be disciplined. In an earlier appeal, the lawyer had mischaracterized a Mexican court's judgment, resulting in a meritless appeal, double costs, and attorney's fees against the lawyer's client. The court accepted the lawyer's claim that his mischaracterization was negligent, not intentional. Nevertheless, it publicly admonished him and cautioned that it would be prepared "to sanction future negligence with substantial monetary fines, suspensions, or disbarment."* In the course of his opinion, Judge Noonan quoted the following passage from Chief Justice Vanderbilt's decision in In re Greenberg, 104 A.2d 46 (N.J. 1954), with regard to a lawyer's duty when he or she tries to persuade the court of inferences:

> [A lawyer] may assert any inferences from the facts of the case that seem to him arguable, but he cannot present his inferences from the facts as if they were the very facts themselves. When he is indulging, as he has every right to do, in inferences or reasoning from the facts, he must say so — there are many words in the English language fitted to express this process of inference — and to be effective he should state the facts in the record from which he is making his inferences. A fortiori, if, as here, there are no facts on which to predicate a statement or from which he may reason or argue, he makes such false statement of facts or false inferences from such non-existing facts at his peril. The failure of his adversary to discover his mistake here or below is no excuse for what may turn out to be an imposition on the court, even if it can be attributed merely to carelessness and lack of thoroughness in the preparation of the appeal.

The New Mexico Supreme Court censured a lawyer who by omitting a couple of sentences from a trial court transcript created the false impression that he had

---

* *Curl* has been overruled insofar as it allowed Rule 11 sanctions on appeal. Partington v. Gedan, 923 F.2d 686 (9th Cir. 1991) (en banc).

clearly preserved an objection when the record was actually ambiguous. "That is not advocacy; it is deceit." Matter of Richards, 943 P.2d 1032 (N.M. 1997). See also Montgomery v. City of Chicago, 763 F. Supp. 301 (N.D. Ill. 1991): "We are gravely concerned with . . . counsel's failure to point out this plainly relevant fact, one that would appear to directly contradict [the client's] implicit assertion. Selective omission of such relevant and apparently contradictory information exceeds the bounds of zealous advocacy."

Several provisions of the Rules forbid lawyers to make false statements of fact or law. Rule 3.3(a)(1) provides that a lawyer "shall not knowingly make a false statement of fact or law to a tribunal." United States v. Williams, 952 F.2d 418 (D.C. Cir. 1991), relied on Rule 3.3 in issuing a public reprimand to a prosecutor for making five misstatements of material fact in the government's brief. The prosecutor was either "irresponsibly careless [or] deliberately misleading." The prosecutor had a duty to "assert facts only if, after a reasonably diligent inquiry, he believes those facts to be true." Rule 4.1(a) contains a prohibition against making "a false statement of material fact or law to a third person." And Rule 8.4(c) forbids a lawyer to "engage in conduct involving dishonesty, fraud, deceit or misrepresentation."

The lawyer's duty not to knowingly misstate fact or law can have consequences in addition to discipline. United States v. Thoreen, 653 F.2d 1332 (9th Cir. 1981) (contempt to place a person resembling defendant at counsel table in order to produce a misidentification); State v. Simac, 641 N.E.2d 416 (Ill. 1994) (same).

I. THE OBLIGATION TO REVEAL ADVERSE LEGAL AUTHORITY

Read Model Rule 3.3(a)(2). The January 1980 draft of the Model Rules contained the following provision (3.1(c)), which was eventually deleted: "If a lawyer discovers that the tribunal has not been apprised of legal authority known to the lawyer that would probably have a substantial effect on the determination of a material issue, the lawyer shall advise the tribunal of that authority." The difference in the obligation imposed by the Code and the Model Rules, on the one hand, and the January 1980 draft proposal, on the other, is clear, isn't it? What is the justification for the narrow duty adopted by the Code and Model Rules? A lawyer's silence is sometimes defended by reference to the client's superior interest in confidentiality. But where the subject is legal authority, it's hard to claim that the information is a client confidence. What then is the countervailing consideration?

MATTER OF THONERT
733 N.E.2d 932 (Ind. 2000)

PER CURIAM . . .

[R]espondent represented a client charged with operating a motor vehicle while intoxicated. Prior to the client's initial hearing and before the client met with or hired the respondent, the client was advised by videotape of his rights. He pleaded guilty to the charge, and the matter was set for sentencing hearing. Prior to that hearing, the client met with the respondent to discuss the possibility of withdrawing his guilty plea. During their meeting, the respondent told the client [about the 1989 *Snowe* case, decided by the intermediate Indiana appellate court] in which the respondent had prevailed on appeal for the defendant. . . .

Snowe . . . held that a trial court judge cannot rely solely on displaying a videotape advisement of rights, but instead must also determine whether the defendant knows of and understands his rights, the nature of the charge or charges against him, the full import of the rights waiver in his guilty plea, and the sentencing possibilities for the charges against him.

At the client's initial hearing, it was established that he had viewed the videotape, that the videotape advised him of his rights and the sentencing possibilities under the charges filed against him, that he understood the charge against him and his rights as explained in the videotape, and that he voluntarily waived those rights and pleaded guilty. On May 30, 1996, the respondent entered an appearance on behalf of the client and filed a motion to withdraw the guilty plea. The trial court denied the motion without hearing. The respondent appealed that ruling, alleging that his client had a right to withdraw the plea because, due to the absence of counsel at the time he entered it and the fact that the record did not reflect that the trial court properly examined the client as to waiver of his rights, the client had not made it knowingly, intelligently, or voluntarily. The respondent further argued that the client had a right to a hearing on his motion to withdraw the plea.

The respondent represented the defendant [in the 1995 *Fletcher* case decided by the Indiana Supreme Court]. In that case, this Court addressed the questions that the respondent raised in his client's case. The ruling in *Fletcher* was adverse to the arguments that the respondent offered on appeal of his [client in this] case. The respondent had served as counsel of record for defendant *Fletcher* in the appeal before this Court. This Court's ruling in *Fletcher* was issued on May 1, 1995, over one year before the respondent filed his appeal on behalf of the [current] client. In his appellate brief filed on behalf of the client, the respondent failed to cite to *Fletcher* or argue that its holding was not controlling authority in the client's case. The respondent also failed to argue that the holding in *Fletcher* should be changed or extended. Although he advised his client [of *Snowe*] he failed to advise him of *Fletcher* or explain any impact *Fletcher* might have on his case. Opposing counsel had not previously disclosed *Fletcher* to the Court of Appeals.

Indiana Professional Conduct Rule 3.3(a)(3) provides that a lawyer shall not knowingly fail to disclose to a tribunal legal authority in the controlling jurisdiction known to the lawyer to be directly adverse to the position of the client and not disclosed by opposing counsel. The concept underlying this requirement of disclosure is that legal argument is a discussion seeking to determine the legal premises properly applicable to the case. . . . [W]e find that the respondent violated the rule by failing to disclose *Fletcher* to the Court of Appeals. . . .

Professional Conduct Rule 1.4(b) provides that a lawyer shall explain a matter to the extent reasonably necessary to permit a client to make informed decisions regarding a representation. . . . By failing to advise his client of a ruling in the controlling jurisdiction that was adverse to the legal arguments contemplated for his client's case on appeal, and instead choosing only to advise the client of an earlier appellate decision favorable to his position, the respondent effectively divested his client of the opportunity to assess intelligently the legal environment in which his case would be argued and to make informed decisions regarding whether to go forward with it. Accordingly, we find that the respondent violated Prof. Cond. R. 1.4(b). . . .

The parties agree that the respondent should be publicly reprimanded for his misconduct. We agree. . . .

Willie Massey said he was sleeping in an abandoned building when a police dog attacked him, causing serious injury, even though Massey did not resist. Massey sued for violation of his civil rights. The judge granted summary judgment against the plaintiff on his federal claims. Thereafter, plaintiff's counsel called the court's attention to a Fourth Circuit case, Kopf v. Wing, which "clearly mandates denial of" defendants' summary judgment motion. As it happens, the same county was a defendant in *Kopf* as in Massey's case, and "at least one attorney for [the county] in *Kopf* . . . was an individual . . . still in the County Attorney's office." After concluding that *Kopf* "could hardly have been a run-of-the-mill case in Prince George's County's experience," Judge Messitte drew the "regrettable inference . . . that defense counsel in the instant case may in fact have deliberately failed to disclose to the Court directly controlling authority from this Circuit." The court ordered the defense lawyers to explain their failure to cite *Kopf*. Massey v. Prince George's County, 907 F. Supp. 138 (D. Md. 1995).

In a later opinion, Judge Messitte addressed the defense lawyers' explanations. He rejected the argument that *Kopf* could be factually distinguished. A "judge might disagree. . . . In this District, whenever a case from the Fourth Circuit comes anywhere close to being relevant to a disputed issue, the better part of wisdom is to cite it and attempt to distinguish it." The court then considered the argument that the lawyer handling the *Massey* case "did not know about the *Kopf* case. That, of course, may well be true, but the question is, ought he to have known?" The court answered "yes," citing Rules 1.1 and 1.3. The court also rejected the defense of senior attorneys in the County Attorney's Office, who argued that they were "not involved in the *Kopf* case (despite the presence of their name on the brief) or were not actively involved in the present case." Lawyers who sign a brief "have an obligation to know what it is that they are signing," citing Rule 11(b)(1). "Moreover, Senior County Attorneys ought to be supervising the pleadings of more junior assistants. . . . It should never happen that an excessive force case in which Prince George's County itself was a defendant, which went to the Fourth Circuit, and is carried in the Federal Reporter is not pervasively known throughout the County Attorney's Office." However, the court declined to impose sanctions. Massey v. Prince George's County, 918 F. Supp. 905 (D. Md. 1996).

Is There an Obligation to Reveal That Your Client Has No Case?

The question posed here may sound foolish. After all, if a client has no case, the lawyer shouldn't have accepted it. Furthermore, if the lawyer discovers the client has no case after accepting it, she must withdraw. Rules 1.16(a), 3.1. Ratliff v. Stewart, 508 F.3d 225 (5th Cir. 2007) (monetary sanction where lawyers sued the wrong doctor, then delayed a year before dismissing complaint). What if the lawyer is court-appointed to represent a criminal defendant? At trial, the lawyer can rightfully put the government to its burden of proving guilt beyond a reasonable doubt. Rule 3.1. How about on the defendant's appeal following conviction? Aren't appeals different because they require some affirmative steps by the appellant's lawyer, some claim of error in or before the trial? If there is no error, the lawyer can't make one up. Yet if the lawyer has been appointed to handle the appeal, neither can he ignore the case. He must tell the appellate court something.

In Anders v. California, 386 U.S. 738 (1967), the Court held that a court-appointed lawyer, who moved to withdraw after concluding that an indigent defendant had no grounds for appeal, should accompany his motion with a "brief referring to anything in the record that might arguably support the appeal." Smith v. Robbins, 528 U.S. 259 (2000), held that the quoted language was not a constitutionally obligatory procedure and that states could use other procedures to protect the Sixth Amendment right to counsel. But states are free to continue to mandate the briefing requirements, and New York has done so. People v. Stokes, 744 N.E.2d 1153 (N.Y. 2001).

Wisconsin, by contrast, requires a lawyer seeking to withdraw on the ground that an issue on appeal has no merit to include a "discussion of why the issue lacks merit." In McCoy v. Court of Appeals, 486 U.S. 429 (1988), the Court interpreted this duty to mean that lawyers must not only "cite the principal cases and statutes and the facts in the record that support the conclusion that the appeal is meritless," but must also include "a brief statement of why these citations lead the attorney to believe the appeal lacks merit." In effect, the lawyer would have to make a legal argument against the client. The Court saw the first duty as consistent with Rule 3.3(a). But it was the second duty—requiring counsel to "assert the basis for [the] conclusion" that the appeal is frivolous— that the accused especially contested. Upholding it, the Court wrote:

> To satisfy federal constitutional concerns, an appellate court faces two inter-related tasks as it rules on counsel's motion to withdraw. First, it must satisfy itself that the attorney has provided the client with a diligent and thorough search of the record for any arguable claim that might support the client's appeal. Second, it must determine whether counsel has correctly concluded that the appeal is frivolous. Because the mere statement of such a conclusion by counsel in *Anders* was insufficient to allow the court to make the required determinations, we held that the attorney was required to submit for the

court's consideration references to anything in the record that might arguably support the appeal. Wisconsin's Rule merely requires that the attorney go one step further. Instead of relying on an unexplained assumption that the attorney has discovered law or facts that completely refute the arguments identified in the brief, the Wisconsin court requires additional evidence of counsel's diligence. This requirement furthers the same interests that are served by the minimum requirements of *Anders*. Because counsel may discover previously unrecognized aspects of the law in the process of preparing a written explanation for his or her conclusion, the discussion requirement provides an additional safeguard against mistaken conclusions by counsel that the strongest arguments he or she can find are frivolous. Just like the references to favorable aspects of the record required by *Anders*, the discussion requirement may forestall some motions to withdraw and will assist the court in passing on the soundness of the lawyer's conclusion that the appeal is frivolous.

The rule does not place counsel in the role of amicus curiae. In *Anders* petitioner argued that California's rule allowing counsel to withdraw on the basis of a conclusory statement that the appeal was meritless posed the danger that some counsel might seek to withdraw not because they thought the appeal frivolous but because, seeing themselves as friends of the court, they thought after weighing the probability of success against the time burdens on the court and the attorney if full arguments were presented that it would be best not to pursue the appeal. We agreed that the California rule might improperly encourage counsel to consider the burden on the court in determining whether to prosecute an appeal. Wisconsin's Rule requiring the attorney to outline why the appeal is frivolous obviously does not pose this danger.

Justice Brennan's dissent was joined by Justices Marshall and Blackmun. The dissenters could find no "state interest that demands so drastic a departure from defense counsel's 'overarching duty' to advocate 'the undivided interests of his client.'" The dissenters stressed that only indigent clients with appointed counsel suffer the consequences of the state rule. Justice Kennedy did not participate.

VIII

Special Issues in Litigation

- *Real Evidence and Criminal Law*
- *Real Evidence and Privilege*
- *Real Evidence and Ethics*
- *Dilemmas for Prosecutors*

A. REAL AND ELECTRONIC EVIDENCE

"Reliable Sources Say" ✳

"I'm general counsel of a Fortune 500 drug company, Flash Pharma. We are one of four companies that account for 82 percent of the market for drugs that slow memory loss in the elderly. We recently moved from third to second in market share. This morning's Wall Street Journal has a story by a veteran reporter who covers our industry. It says that according to unnamed "reliable sources in the Justice Department," the department has begun an investigation of "possible price fixing" for these memory drugs and expects to convene a grand jury in the near future. This is the first I've heard of it. I have no reason to believe there has been any price fixing by Flash. Quite the contrary—we're under pressure to undercut the prices of our competitors.

"I mulled over what if anything I should do by way of document preservation and investigation. Under our document retention and destruction policy, our system automatically deletes most (but not all) e-mail messages and other electronic documents older than 120 to 210 days (depending on various criteria) unless the author or recipient saves a particular e-mail or document in a permanent file or flags it for retention. And of course documents don't have to be electronic, and electronic documents may have been printed and saved. Every quarter, to conserve costly space, managers in our various departments urge employees to review hard-copy files and shred anything obsolete. There are probably hard-copy and electronic documents in our files that may have some connection to this investigation. Beyond that, not all documents are on our system. Our executives and scientists, our lawyers as well, do work at home on their personal computers or company-owned laptops.

449

"Like many corporate counsel, I am all too familiar with the prosecution and conviction of Arthur Andersen and with the apparently heightened responsibility of lawyers with regard to e-discovery. But what, if anything, am I supposed to do based on this article to protect Flash and myself?"*

"Vanity Ink"

Serita Akalitis, a criminal defense lawyer in New Calais, has presented this problem to the ethics committee of our bar association:

"I represent a man — let's call him Chester — in a tax fraud prosecution. Chester is CFO of and a major shareholder in a local company. The government claims that, in order to save on taxes in a corporate matter, Chester backdated certain documents to make it appear that a particular obligation arose two months earlier. Chester was arrested and released on his own recognizance. We don't challenge the claim of backdating — we don't have to — Chester simply denies that he was the one who did it. In discovery, the government had to provide certain information about its case, including copies of the backdated forms. I also inspected the originals in the courthouse. The handwriting on the forms is not adequate to allow experts to say anything more than that it is 'consistent with' Chester's handwriting.

"There's some other evidence against Chester, evidence of motive, ambiguous statements to colleagues that could be seen as inculpatory. Basically, the government will make out enough of a case to get to the jury, but Chester never had a problem with the law before and will be a good witness. I will also call a few prominent business people who will testify to Chester's reputation for honesty. I think I can raise more than a reasonable doubt.

"One of the oddities of this case is that the ink used in the backdating is a very unusual purple ink. I've never seen it before. It's not quite purple, not quite violet. Actually, it turns out that words like 'purple' and 'violet' don't really mean anything in the world of color. Color charts identify colors by letters and numbers. Marketing people then play around with the nomenclature. Colors are named after fruits ('plum'), vegetables ('avocado'), and natural objects ('stone'). This was all new to me and more than you need to know. What you need to know is that the color of the ink used for the backdating was quite unusual, perhaps unique. The government could not find a match. If it had, it would have been required to tell us in discovery. In all likelihood, the ink was designed to specification. As I've learned, it is possible to order customized ink colors. Vanity ink.

"The trial is in three weeks. Yesterday, Chester came by to give me the list and c.v.'s of his character witnesses and discuss a few things. He was leaving for a business trip in Seattle in a few hours (his bail conditions allow it), and I asked

---

* "Reliable Sources Say," written long ago, turns out to be not quite as hypothetical as one, including yours truly, might have supposed. Herewith the start of a page one Wall St. Journal article that appeared on September 23, 2008, years after the first appearance of this problem: "Federal prosecutors have opened separate criminal probes into possible price-fixing by major egg producers and California tomato processors, the latest in a series of U.S. investigations of alleged collusion in food and agriculture. The investigations, which have not been previously reported. . . ." The GC of Flash Pharma could just as well be the GC of The Tomato Factory, Ltd.

him for contact information. He wrote the name of his hotel on his business card. This morning, I discovered that he forgot his pen. You know the rest of the story. The ink in the pen is the precise color ink used on the backdated forms. I checked. The pen cartridge, which I examined, contains a customized ink mix and contains the name of the specialty company in Portugal that offers this product. Chester travels to Portugal for business. And I also now have his business card with his contact information in his handwriting in the same color ink. What should I do with the card and pen?"

Lawyers who represent clients in civil or criminal cases may come into possession of what the law of evidence calls "real evidence," essentially a document or object that may have relevance to a pending or impending case. Or perhaps the lawyer does not come into possession of the item but knows that the client has it. Consider these variations:

- The client shows up at his lawyer's office. "I shot a guy," he says, then takes a gun and the victim's wallet from his pocket and puts them on the lawyer's desk.
- In preparing for an anticipated (but not yet filed) civil action against or by her client, a lawyer discovers potentially damaging notes on the company's computer.
- A man charged with murder tells his appointed lawyer that he has committed three other murders as well. The victims have been reported as "missing." The client directs the lawyer to the bodies in shallow graves in the woods. The lawyer, incredulous, checks and finds the bodies.
- A church tells its lawyer that an employee has found images of child pornography on a laptop computer owned by the church but used by its 72-year-old choirmaster, who has worked at the church for 28 years. The choirmaster has confessed to downloading the pictures. The church fired him but does not want to report him to the authorities. It is a crime knowingly to possess child pornography.

What may or must the lawyers in each of these situations do with regard to the gun and wallet, the computer notes, the bodies, and the laptop? Do *Ryder*, below, and the other authorities in this chapter tell us?

Let us distinguish among at least four factual situations. *First*, generally applicable in civil cases, is the situation in which the client comes to the lawyer because there is the prospect of a lawsuit against it or one that it wants to bring. Or perhaps the action has already started. The lawyer realizes that there are documents in the client's file that can be used against the client. But either the action has not yet begun or, if it has begun, no request for those documents has been served. May the lawyer tell the client to destroy the documents? May the lawyer say nothing? Must the lawyer tell the client not to destroy the documents? May the lawyer tell the client the legal implications of the documents, expecting that this information will result in their destruction? Of course, the lawyer may wish to preserve the documents. They may not be so harmful, and their destruction, if or when the fact of it is revealed in discovery and at trial, may raise an inference that the documents were even more damaging than they truly are.

The *second* situation generally concerns evidence in criminal cases. In this situation the criminal defendant gives the lawyer physical evidence of the crime. For example, the defendant may show up at the lawyer's office with the unlicensed gun used to kill the victim, with the heroin that was smuggled into the country, with the fruits of the robbery, and so on. The gun, the heroin, the robbery proceeds, are all in themselves contraband, illegal to possess. What is the lawyer's responsibility? Does your answer change if the client shows up with evidence that is not in itself illegal to possess? For example, in a forgery prosecution, the client brings the lawyer the pen used to create the forged instrument. The pen itself is lawfully owned, but it was used in connection with a crime and will help prove responsibility. Or the client delivers a written plan for the crime. The plan, in the client's handwriting, proves his guilt, but like the pen, and unlike the unlicensed gun, its mere possession is not illegal.

A *third* situation, somewhat blending into the second, is where the client reveals the existence of physical evidence of a crime. The client doesn't bring the evidence with him, but tells the lawyer where it can be found. May the lawyer inspect or remove the evidence? Must the lawyer do so? Whether or not the lawyer does so, must the lawyer turn the evidence over to the authorities or inform them of its location?

Yet a *fourth* possibility is where evidence of the crime comes into the possession of the lawyer through the conduct of a third person who is not the lawyer's client, but is perhaps a friend or relative of the client.

Possibly the most famous (and surely the most consequential) example of "real" evidence is the case of the White House tapes. These were secret recordings that President Richard Nixon made in the Oval Office. The tapes became an issue during investigations of the burglary of the Democratic National Headquarters in Washington's Watergate Hotel prior to the 1972 presidential election. In July 1973, White House aide Alex Butterfield was first to reveal the existence of the tapes in response to a question from the Senate Watergate Committee chaired by Senator Sam Ervin of North Carolina. In the next few days, before the Committee subpoenaed the tapes, Nixon and his advisers discussed whether they could lawfully destroy them. That discussion will concern us presently. Imagine being a lawyer who had to give that advice. Could Nixon have lawfully destroyed the tapes? Could a lawyer tell him he could?

As it happened, the tapes were not destroyed, and eventually a federal district court in Washington, D.C., subpoenaed the tapes upon motion of a special prosecutor investigating the burglary. Nixon challenged the subpoena but the Supreme Court upheld it in United States v. Nixon, 418 U.S. 683 (1974). Transcripts of the tapes were released on August 5, 1974. The president announced his resignation August 8, effective August 9, 1974. Nixon had recorded his own criminal conduct. He was never prosecuted because Gerald Ford, his successor, pardoned him.

Doctrinally, real evidence questions occupy at least four untidy and interconnected categories. *First* are the ethical obligations of a lawyer when dealing with real evidence. What are the disciplinary risks, depending on what the lawyer does or does not do with the evidence? *Second* are obligations under the criminal law, especially obstruction of justice statutes (by whatever name). Violation of these can lead to prosecution. As we will see, at the federal level, the reach of these laws is surprisingly broad and was broadened further by Sarbanes-Oxley legislation passed in the wake of the U.S. corporate scandals of the 1990s and the ensuing decade. *Third* is the interplay between real evidence and the attorney-client privilege. To what extent can lawyers legitimately claim that their knowledge or possession of real evidence — or even the evidence itself — is privileged? *Fourth,* of late, are the discovery obligations of lawyers actively to assure the preservation and production of electronic documents when a litigation involving a client is pending or anticipated. The key word is "actively." While the parties have discovery obligations for all sorts of items, the courts seem to have carved out heightened duties with regard to electronic documents. These categories are untidy because their boundaries are fuzzy — a situation can implicate two or all of them — and because their requirements are not entirely clear. Let's take them seriatim.

Real Evidence and Legal Ethics

In re Ryder, though a bit old now, remains an ideal introduction to the ethical duties of lawyers who come into (or take) possession of real evidence.

IN RE RYDER
263 F. Supp. 360 (E.D. Va. 1967)

PER CURIAM.

This proceeding was instituted to determine whether Richard R. Ryder should be removed from the roll of attorneys qualified to practice before this court. Ryder was admitted to this bar in 1953. He formerly served five years as an Assistant United States Attorney. He has an active trial practice, including both civil and criminal cases. . . .

On August 24, 1966, a man armed with a sawed-off shotgun robbed the Varina Branch of the Bank of Virginia of $7,583. Included in the currency taken were $10 bills known as "bait money," the serial numbers of which had been recorded.

On August 26, 1966, Charles Richard Cook rented safety deposit box 14 at a branch of the Richmond National Bank. Later in the day Cook was interviewed at his home by agents of the Federal Bureau of Investigation, who obtained $348 from him. Cook telephoned Ryder, who had represented him in civil litigation. Ryder came to the house and advised the agents that he represented Cook. He said that if Cook were not to be placed under arrest, he intended to take him to his office for an interview. The agents left. Cook insisted to Ryder that he had not robbed the bank. He told Ryder that he had won the money, which the agents had taken from him, in a crap game. At this time Ryder believed Cook.

Later that afternoon Ryder telephoned one of the agents and asked whether any of the bills obtained from Cook had been identified as a part of the money taken in the bank robbery. The agent told him that some bills had been identified. Ryder made inquiries about the number of bills taken and their denominations. The agent declined to give him specific information but indicated that several of the bills were recorded as bait money.

The next morning, Saturday, August 27, 1966, Ryder conferred with Cook again. He urged Cook to tell the truth, and Cook answered that a man, whose name he would not divulge, offered him $500 on the day of the robbery to put a package in a bank lockbox. Ryder did not believe this story. Ryder told Cook that if the government could trace the money in the box to him, it would be almost conclusive evidence of his guilt. He knew that Cook was under surveillance and he suspected that Cook might try to dispose of the money.

That afternoon Ryder telephoned a former officer of the Richmond Bar Association to discuss his course of action. He had known this attorney for many years and respected his judgment. The lawyer was at home and had no library available to him when Ryder telephoned. In their casual conversation Ryder told what he knew about the case, omitting names. He explained that he thought he would take the money from Cook's safety deposit box and place it in a box in his own name. This, he believed, would prevent Cook from attempting to dispose of the money. The lawyers thought that eventually F.B.I. agents would locate the money and that since it was in Ryder's possession, he could claim a privilege and thus effectively exclude it from evidence. This would prevent the government from linking Ryder's client with the bait money and would also destroy any presumption of guilt that might exist arising out of the client's exclusive possession of the evidence.

Ryder testified:

> I had sense enough to know, one, at that time that apparently the F.B.I. did have the serial numbers on the bills. I had sense enough to know, from many, many years of experience in this court and in working with the F.B.I. and, in fact, in directing the F.B.I. on some occasions, to know that eventually the bank — that the F.B.I. would find that money if I left that money in the bank. There was no doubt in my mind that eventually they would find it. The only thing I could think of to do was to get the money out of Mr. Cook's possession. . . . The idea was that I assumed that if anybody tried to go into a safety deposit box in my name, the bank officials would notify me and that I would get an opportunity to come in this court and argue a question of whether or not they could use that money as evidence.

The lawyers discussed and rejected alternatives, including having a third party get the money. At the conclusion of the conversation Ryder was advised, "Don't do it surreptitiously and to be sure that you let your client know that it is going back to the rightful owners."

On Monday morning Ryder asked Cook to come by his office. He prepared a power of attorney, which Cook signed. . . .

Ryder did not follow the advice he had received on Saturday. He did not let his client know the money was going back to the rightful owners. He testified about his omission:

> I prepared it myself and told Mr. Cook to sign it. In the power of attorney, I did not specifically say that Mr. Cook authorized me to deliver that money to the appropriate authorities at any time because for a number of reasons. One, in representing a man under these circumstances, you've got to keep the man's

confidence, but I also put in that power of attorney that Mr. Cook authorized me to dispose of that money as I saw fit, and the reason for that being that I was going to turn the money over to the proper authorities at whatever time I deemed that it wouldn't hurt Mr. Cook.

Ryder took the power of attorney which Cook had signed to the Richmond National Bank. He rented box 13 in his name with his office address, presented the power of attorney, entered Cook's box, took both boxes into a booth, where he found a bag of money and a sawed-off shotgun in Cook's box. The box also contained miscellaneous items which are not pertinent to this proceeding. He transferred the contents of Cook's box to his own and returned the boxes to the vault. He left the bank, and neither he nor Cook returned. . . .

The same day Ryder also talked with other prominent persons in Richmond — a judge of a court of record and an attorney for the Commonwealth. Again, he stated that what he intended to say was confidential. He related the circumstances and was advised that a lawyer could not receive the property and if he had received it he could not retain possession of it.

On September 7, 1966, Cook was indicted for robbing the Varina Branch of the Bank of Virginia. A bench warrant was issued and the next day Ryder represented Cook at a bond hearing. Cook was identified as the robber by employees of the bank. He was released on bond. Cook was arraigned on a plea of not guilty on September 9, 1966.

On September 12, 1966, F.B.I. agents procured search warrants for Cook's and Ryder's safety deposit boxes in the Richmond National Bank. They found Cook's box empty. In Ryder's box they discovered $5,920 of the $7,583 taken in the bank robbery and the sawed-off shotgun used in the robbery.

On September 23, 1966, Ryder filed a motion to suppress the money obtained from Cook by the agents on August 26, 1966. The motion did not involve items taken from Ryder's safety deposit box. The motion came on to be heard October 6, 1966. Ryder called Cook as a witness for examination on matters limited to the motion to suppress. The court called to Ryder's attention papers pertaining to the search of the safety deposit boxes. Ryder moved for a continuance, stating that he intended to file a motion with respect to the seizure of the contents of the lockbox.

On October 14, 1966, the three judges of this court removed Ryder as an attorney for Cook; suspended him from practice before the court until further order; referred the matter to the United States Attorney, who was requested to file charges within five days; set the matter for hearing November 11, 1966; and granted Ryder leave to move for vacation or modification of its order pending hearing. . . .

At the outset, we reject the suggestion that Ryder did not know the money which he transferred from Cook's box to his was stolen. We find that on August 29 when Ryder opened Cook's box and saw a bag of money and a sawed-off shotgun, he then knew Cook was involved in the bank robbery and that the money was stolen. The evidence clearly establishes this. Ryder knew that the man who had robbed the bank used a sawed-off shotgun. He disbelieved Cook's story about the source of the money in the lockbox. He knew that some of the bills in Cook's possession were bait money. . . .

We also find that Ryder was not motivated solely by certain expectation the government would discover the contents of his lockbox. He believed discovery was probable. In this event he intended to argue to the court that the contents of his box could not be revealed, and even if the contents were identified, his possession made the stolen money and the shotgun inadmissible against his client. He also recognized that discovery was not inevitable. His intention in this event, we find, was to assist Cook by keeping the stolen money and the shotgun concealed in his lockbox until after the trial. His conversations, and the secrecy he enjoined, immediately after he put the money and the gun in his box, show that he realized the government might not find the property.

We accept his statement that he intended eventually to return the money to its rightful owner, but we pause to say that no attorney should ever place himself in such a position. Matters involving the possible termination of an attorney-client relationship, or possible subsequent proceedings in the event of an acquittal, are too delicate to permit such a practice.

We reject the argument that Ryder's conduct was no more than the exercise of the attorney-client privilege. The fact that Cook had not been arrested or indicted at the time Ryder took possession of the gun and money is immaterial. Cook was Ryder's client and was entitled to the protection of the lawyer-client privilege.

Regardless of Cook's status, however, Ryder's conduct was not encompassed by the attorney-client privilege. . . .

It was Ryder, not his client, who took the initiative in transferring the incriminating possession of the stolen money and the shotgun from Cook. Ryder's conduct went far beyond the receipt and retention of a confidential communication from his client. Counsel for Ryder conceded, at the time of argument, that the acts of Ryder were not within the attorney-client privilege. . . .

The money in Cook's box belonged to the Bank of Virginia. The law did not authorize Cook to conceal this money or withhold it from the bank. His larceny was a continuing offense. Cook had no title or property interest in the money that he lawfully could pass to Ryder. . . .

No canon of ethics or law permitted Ryder to conceal from the Bank of Virginia its money to gain his client's acquittal.

Cook's possession of the sawed-off shotgun was illegal. 26 U.S.C. §5851. Ryder could not lawfully receive the gun from Cook to assist Cook to avoid conviction of robbery. Cook had never mentioned the shotgun to Ryder. When Ryder discovered it in Cook's box, he took possession of it to hinder the government in the prosecution of its case, and he intended not to reveal it pending trial unless the government discovered it and a court compelled its production. No statute or canon of ethics authorized Ryder to take possession of the gun for this purpose. . . .

In helping Cook to conceal the shotgun and stolen money, Ryder acted without the bounds of law. He allowed the office of attorney to be used in violation of law. The scheme which he devised was a deceptive, legalistic subterfuge — rightfully denounced by the canon as chicane. . . .

There is much to be said, however, for mitigation of the discipline to be imposed. Ryder intended to return the bank's money after his client was tried. He consulted reputable persons before and after he placed the property in his lockbox, although he did not precisely follow their advice. Were it not for these facts, we would deem proper his permanent exclusion from practice before this court. In view of the mitigating circumstances, he will be suspended from practice in this court for eighteen months effective October 14, 1966. . . .

The Fourth Circuit affirmed Ryder's suspension in In re Ryder, 381 F.2d 713 (4th Cir. 1967). In some ways, *Ryder* is an easy case. The money and gun were illegal for Ryder to possess. The money belonged to the bank. It was stolen property. Possessing the sawed-off shotgun was also crime. While these facts aggravated Ryder's transgression, they were unnecessary to the opinion. Ryder could not lawfully, and therefore could not ethically, conceal this evidence from the authorities in any event. Ryder had no duty to help the prosecutor, but neither could he hinder it by moving the evidence to his lockbox, where discovery was less likely. We return to these issues with People v. Meredith below, where a lawyer also removed evidence, but in rather different circumstances.

The Model Rule that specifically addresses a lawyer's responsibility for real evidence is entirely unhelpful as a guide to conduct. Rule 3.4(a) simply forbids a lawyer "unlawfully [to] alter, destroy or conceal a document or other material having potential evidentiary value." Nor can a lawyer assist another person in doing so. In other words, it depends on the criminal law. Drafts of the rule didn't simply punt to the criminal law.

RULE 2.5   Alteration or Destruction of Evidence

A lawyer shall not advise a client to alter or destroy a document or other material when the lawyer reasonably should know that the material is relevant to a pending proceeding or one that is clearly foreseeable.

RULE 3.2   Fairness to an Opposing Party and Counsel

(b) A lawyer shall not:
    (1) improperly obstruct another party's access to evidence, destroy, falsify or conceal evidence, or use illegal methods of obtaining evidence. . . .

So our next stop on this journey must be the criminal law.

Real Evidence and Criminal Law

It turns out that the criminal law on this issue can be pretty demanding. State statutes on obstruction of justice (or like crimes) vary, so let's look at the federal criminal code. Its provisions are broad and overlapping. The smallest attempt at interference with the work of the courts or enforcement agencies can lead to years, even decades, in prison, even if the effort fails.

We return to Richard Nixon and the White House tapes that ultimately led to his downfall, but which he never attempted to destroy. Could Nixon have legally destroyed the tapes? Could his lawyers have advised him to do so? Did they? Therein lies a tale.

Mr. Nixon thought he could destroy the tapes. He told the New York Times (April 6, 1984) that one reason for his failure to do so was bad advice "from well-intentioned lawyers who had sort of the cockeyed notion that I would be destroying evidence," even though no subpoena had been served for the tapes' production. Who were those lawyers with cockeyed notions?

In a Times op-ed (August 18, 1988), journalist Henry Brandon quoted the late Edward Bennett Williams (of Williams & Connolly fame) as saying in 1985: "Nixon had no obligation to make or keep the tapes and could have argued that his motive in destroying them was to prevent secret exchanges with other heads of government from being compromised." Really? Could Williams have given Nixon this advice if protecting secrets was *never* Nixon's motive? Isn't Williams inventing a false story? May a lawyer advise a client to lie if the lie isn't a crime or fraud? It would seem so. If the lie is not criminal or fraudulent, and if the advice doesn't aid a crime or fraud, then, so far as I can tell, the advice is allowed. We may not like lies, but it is rumored across the land that, on occasion, many people, including politicians of all persuasions, have found lying to be a convenient way to get out of a sticky situation.

But back to 1973: Who were the cockeyed lawyers with the well-intentioned notions (or was it the other way around)? Brandon goes on to tell us. Nixon had received advice contrary to Williams's advice from his legal counsel and Washington wise man, Leonard Garment. Garment advised that destruction of the tapes would be a crime. Although a subpoena had not been served, all knew it would be. Destroying the tapes in the face of that knowledge would then constitute obstruction of justice, in Garment's view. In 1985, Brandon related Williams's different perspective to Garment, who defended himself by citing a "1956 decision by the Federal District Court in New York City," discussed below, which held that the crime of obstruction of justice can occur even though no subpoena has yet been served. Later, according to Brandon, even Garment conceded that Williams's pragmatic advice "was probably right and that Nixon could have got away with the destruction of the tapes." That, of course, means Nixon would have served out his term, which in turn means that a lot of national politics would likely have played out very differently. Would Gerald Ford or Jimmy Carter have become president in 1976? Would John Paul Stevens, appointed by Ford in 1975, have made it to the Supreme Court? The "what if" game can go on endlessly.

In his autobiography, Crazy Rhythm (1997), Leonard Garment reflects on his legal advice to the president. He writes (pp.280-281):

> Among Watergate revisionists it is conventional wisdom that the failure to destroy the tapes was the event, or nonevent, that led to the destruction of the Nixon presidency. If the tapes had been burned, they say, in the Rose Garden on national television or by shoveling them secretly into a furnace and announcing it afterward, the president would have survived. I have come to think that as a practical matter, *as opposed to a legal one,* they are probably right.
>
> In 1973 I was still relatively new to presidential politics and did not really know how strong the pull of the presidency was, at least then. Nixon, in particular, had come to symbolize the kind of protective experience and personal strength that to the vast majority of citizens were of the greatest importance. Without the tapes, Nixon would still have faced the investigative

batterings of Ervin, Rodino, Cox, and their myriad helpers. But he would have had more than a fighting chance. He would have been spared the constant repetition of grotesque White House conversations, the endless public embarrassment of missing or allegedly erased tapes, the March 21 tape that prosecutors considered criminal, and eventually the June 23 "smoking gun" tape, actually only faintly "smoking" but against which a demoralized White House and an enfeebled president could no longer defend because even his oldest and staunchest political comrades were now saying, "Enough."

The tapes did most of this damage. It's hard to argue with defeat, so I confess error. If I had foreseen the future, I would probably have stood with Fred Buzhardt [Nixon's special counsel] and said something like: The tapes will kill you. Now you alone must decide what to do with them. If you destroy them, disassociate your staff from the decision and its implementation. Just do it: You'll have plenty of volunteer helpers.

If he had done something like this, would I have quit? Almost certainly not. But if I had given him this advice, would it have changed Nixon's ultimate decision? Almost certainly not. . . .

Nixon clearly did not want to destroy his tapes. He was intensely occupied, as most serious leaders are, by symbols of his place in history. The tapes were among those symbols, historically unique presidential memoirs and matchless evidence of the "real" positions participants took, particularly Kissinger and Nixon himself, during the historic meetings of Nixon's presidency. They were also financially priceless. [Emphasis added.]

If Leonard Garment thought it would have been illegal to destroy the tapes, could he nevertheless have given the president the advice Williams advocated and which he now says he should have offered?

The 1956 case Mr. Garment had in mind was United States v. Solow, 138 F. Supp. 812 (S.D.N.Y. 1956), which refused to dismiss the indictment of a man who allegedly destroyed documents he knew were wanted by a sitting grand jury, even though neither the man nor the documents were yet under subpoena. The defendant was charged under 18 U.S.C. §1503, which applies when a person obstructs a *pending* court or grand jury proceeding. Today, the obstruction statutes have exponentially expanded. No pending proceeding is needed under some of them. And redundancy reigns. The same act can be obstruction under multiple statutes that provide for varying periods of incarceration from five to twenty years. Further, the list of synonyms used to describe how obstruction can occur (alters, conceals, destroys, mutilates, impedes) suggests that the drafters worked from a thesaurus, not a law book.

Obstruction and related laws have been headlined in recent years in the prosecutions of Big Five accounting firm Arthur Andersen for wholesale destruction of documents in anticipation of and during an SEC investigation; of investment banker Frank Quattrone of Credit Suisse for sending one e-mail urging deletion of files during an SEC investigation (following reversal of a conviction, he was acquitted); and of Martha Stewart, convicted for attempting to conceal stock trades allegedly made on inside information. (The underlying trades were probably not criminal, which makes the point, a paradox for many, that a person can be guilty of obstructing the investigation of an innocent act.) Arthur Andersen was convicted, but a unanimous Supreme Court reversed the conviction because of errors in the judge's jury charge (see below). Arthur

Andersen LLP v. United States, 544 U.S. 696 (2005). Although the evidence could easily have supported conviction, the government did not retry Andersen because its fate (corporate death) was sealed the day it was indicted, following the precedent of the Red Queen in *Alice in Wonderland:* "Sentence first, trial after."

Here's just one example of the breadth of the obstruction statutes, taken from 18 U.S.C. §1512, which was adopted in 1982 and amended several times. Paragraph (b) was used in the prosecution of Arthur Andersen and Frank Quattrone. Paragraph (c) was added by the Sarbanes-Oxley Act in 2002 in response to a wave of corporate scandals.

(b) Whoever . . . corruptly persuades another person, or attempts to do so, or engages in misleading conduct toward another person, with intent to —
    (2) cause or induce any person to —
        (B) alter, destroy, mutilate, or conceal an object with intent to impair the object's integrity or availability for use in an official proceeding . . . shall be fined under this title or imprisoned not more than 10 years, or both.
(c) Whoever corruptly —
    (1) alters, destroys, mutilates, or conceals a record, document, or other object, or attempts to do so, with the intent to impair the object's integrity or availability for use in an official proceeding; or
    (2) otherwise obstructs, influences, or impedes any official proceeding, or attempts to do so, shall be fined under this title or imprisoned not more than 20 years, or both.

Appreciate the reach of these provisions. Paragraph (b) makes it a crime for one person to "corruptly persuade" another person (or to attempt to do so) to act as described. This is sometimes called witness tampering. Paragraph (c) makes it a crime for the first person to do similar acts personally. Then, just in case paragraph (c)(1) is insufficiently broad to catch all obstructionist conduct, (c)(2) is added as a catchall. An "official proceeding" need not be pending or even impending for this section to apply, §1512(f)(1), so long as the defendant "expected a grand jury investigation and/or trial in the foreseeable future." United States v. Frankhauser, 80 F.3d 641 (1st Cir. 1996). And the term "official proceeding" includes not only court cases but also congressional hearings and "proceedings before a Federal Government agency which is authorized by law." §1515(a)(1).* But what if the destroyed or altered item would have been inadmissible at trial because, for example, of a privilege or as irrelevant? It does not matter. It's still obstruction. §1512(f)(2). So depending on your state of mind, asking one person to shred one document or to delete one e-mail, or doing either yourself, can send you to prison for 10 or 20 years, even if the person refuses or your own efforts fail. Powerful stuff.

Arthur Andersen's conviction under paragraph (b)(2)(B) was based on the claim that four company officers, including a lawyer (!), had "corruptly persuaded" unsuspecting support staff to destroy vast quantities of documents

---

* United States v. Ramos, 537 F.3d 439 (5th Cir. 2008) (distinguishing cases), concluded that the reference to agency proceedings implied a "formal convocation of the agency," and did not cover an internal agency investigation in its preliminary stages.

relating to its representation of Enron. (Well-established rules expose a company to liability for the crimes of its agents.) The conviction was reversed in part because the jury instructions relieved the government from proving conscious wrong-doing. "Only persons conscious of wrongdoing can be said to 'knowingly . . . corruptly persuad[e],' " the Court wrote.

The temptation to destroy or to have someone else destroy a document that may be harmful in court can be rather strong, especially if (one thinks) it's the only copy and the consequences of losing a court case are dire. Destruction is private. Who's looking? And documents can be destroyed without a trace — shredded, burned, sent to the bottom of the ocean. But, of course, often copies of the document surface, especially if it is was composed on a computer.

Today, at least, §1512 would forbid a lawyer to advise Nixon to destroy the tapes for the purpose of keeping them from a foreseeable grand jury, court, or legislative proceeding, even before the tapes had been subpoenaed. Lawyers are not immune to obstruction charges arising out of the representation of a client. United States v. Kellington, 217 F.3d 1084 (9th Cir. 2000), and United States v. Kloess, 251 F.3d 941 (11th Cir. 2001), were both §1512 prosecutions of lawyers. Both appeals — one from a conviction, which the court reversed and remanded; the other from dismissal of an indictment, which the court reinstated — construed §1515(c). That section creates a safe harbor for lawyers who "provid[e] lawful, bona fide, legal representation services in connection with or anticipation of an official proceeding."

United States v. Philip Russell. Perhaps the prosecution of Attorney Philip Russell is the most disturbing example of a lawyer charged under the federal obstruction laws. Even though Russell's case had nothing to with corporate malfeasance, he was prosecuted under the two obstruction sections added by Sarbanes-Oxley to address the U.S. corporate scandals. 18 U.S.C. §§1512(c) and 1519. Russell represented a church in Greenwich, Connecticut. A church employee discovered pictures of child pornography on the laptop computer of the long-time church choirmaster. The computer belonged to the church. Church officials confronted the choirmaster, who confessed. The officials called Russell. Russell asked if the church wished to report the choirmaster to the authorities. It did not. It preferred simply to fire him. Russell knew that the church and its officials would not be criminally liable for the choirmaster's conduct, of which they were unaware, but he also knew that, going forward, their knowing possession of child pornography would be a crime. Yet the church did not want to report the choirmaster.

What would you do? Destroy the porn? Ignore the client and alert the FBI? Tell the client that continued possession of the pictures was a crime and that destruction might be a crime as well, but refuse to say more? And by the way, whatever your answer, the same situation can happen in a company or a law firm.

Russell destroyed the laptop hard drive. Unfortunately for him, the U.S. Attorney's office in Connecticut was already investigating the choirmaster and asked Russell to deliver the laptop. After Russell revealed that he had destroyed the hard drive, he was indicted under statutes that carry 20-year prison terms. These statutes require, among other things, that destruction have been for purpose of keeping the evidence from a "foreseeable" official proceeding. Russell claimed that he did not foresee a proceeding because the church was not going to report the choirmaster. He didn't know about the independent investigation, he said.

But facing up to 20 years in prison, Russell eventually pled guilty to misprision of a felony, which is itself a felony. He got community service and home confinement for six months. The crime of misprision of a felony is defined in 18 U.S.C. §4: "Whoever, having knowledge of the actual commission of a felony cognizable by a court of the United States, conceals and does not as soon as possible make known the same to some judge or other person in civil or military authority under the United States, shall be fined under this title or imprisoned not more than three years, or both." Russell was later suspended from practice for six months, which shows that Connecticut judges did not share the U.S. Attorney's view of the seriousness of his conduct. The choirmaster pled guilty.

Now, let's return to "Reliable Sources Say," the problem at the top of this chapter. What should the company's general counsel do on reading the Journal article? What should he worry about? We return to this fact pattern again after the discussion of e-discovery below.

Real Evidence and the Attorney-Client Privilege

Meredith is a law teacher's dream opinion. If it weren't a famous case in this field, it would be a great exam question. It forces hard policy choices. Did the court choose correctly?

PEOPLE v. MEREDITH
29 Cal. 3d 682, 631 P.2d 46, 175 Cal. Rptr. 612 (1981)

TOBRINER, JUSTICE.

Defendants Frank Earl Scott and Michael Meredith appeal from convictions for the first degree murder and first degree robbery of David Wade. Meredith's conviction rests on eyewitness testimony that he shot and killed Wade. Scott's conviction, however, depends on the theory that Scott conspired with Meredith and a third defendant, Jacqueline Otis, to bring about the killing and robbery. To support the theory of conspiracy the prosecution sought to show the place where the victim's wallet was found, and, in the course of the case this piece of evidence became crucial. The admissibility of that evidence comprises the principal issue on this appeal.

At trial the prosecution called Stephen Frick, who testified that he observed the victim's partially burnt wallet in a trash can behind Scott's residence. Scott's trial counsel then adduced that Frick served as a defense investigator. Scott himself had told his former counsel that he had taken the victim's wallet, divided the money with Meredith, attempted to burn the wallet, and finally put it in the trash can. At counsel's request, Frick then retrieved the wallet from the trash can. Counsel examined the wallet and then turned it over to the police.

The defense acknowledges that the wallet itself was properly admitted into evidence. The prosecution in turn acknowledges that the attorney-client privilege protected the conversations between Scott, his former counsel, and counsel's investigator. Indeed the prosecution did not attempt to introduce those conversations at trial. The issue before us, consequently, focuses upon a narrow point: whether under the circumstances of this case Frick's observation of the *location* of the wallet, the product of a privileged communication, finds protection under the attorney-client privilege.

This issue, one of first impression in California, presents the court with competing policy considerations. On the one hand, to deny protection to observations arising from confidential communications might chill free and open communication between attorney and client and might also inhibit counsel's investigation of his client's case. On the other hand, we cannot extend the attorney-client privilege so far that it renders evidence immune from discovery and admission merely because the defense seizes it first. . . .

On the night of April 3, 1976, Wade (the victim) and Jacqueline Otis, a friend of the defendants, entered a club known as Rich Jimmy's. Defendant Scott remained outside by a shoeshine stand. A few minutes later codefendant Meredith arrived outside the club. He told Scott he planned to rob Wade, and asked Scott to go into the club, find Jacqueline Otis, and ask her to get Wade to go out to Wade's car parked outside the club.

In the meantime, Wade and Otis had left the club and walked to a liquor store to get some beer. Returning from the store, they left the beer in a bag by Wade's car and reentered the club. Scott then entered the club also and, according to the testimony of Laurie Ann Sam (a friend of Scott's who was already in the club), Scott asked Otis to get Wade to go back out to his car so Meredith could "knock him in the head."

When Wade and Otis did go out to the car, Meredith attacked Wade from behind. After a brief struggle, two shots were fired; Wade fell, and Meredith, witnessed by Scott and Sam, ran from the scene.

Scott went over to the body and, assuming Wade was dead, picked up the bag containing the beer and hid it behind a fence. Scott later returned, retrieved the bag, and took it home where Otis and Meredith joined him.

We now recount the evidence relating to Wade's wallet, basing our account primarily on the testimony of James Schenk, Scott's first appointed attorney. Schenk visited Scott in jail more than a month after the crime occurred and solicited information about the murder, stressing that he had to be fully acquainted with the facts to avoid being "sandbagged" by the prosecution during the trial. In response, Scott gave Schenk the same information that he had related earlier to the police. In addition, however, Scott told Schenk something Scott had not revealed to the police: that he had seen a wallet, as well as the paper bag, on the ground near Wade. Scott said that he picked up the wallet, put it in the paper bag, and placed both behind a parking lot fence. He also said that he later retrieved the bag, took it home, found $100 in the wallet and divided it with Meredith, and then tried to burn the wallet in his kitchen sink. He took the partially burned wallet, Scott told Schenk, placed it in a plastic bag, and threw it in a burn barrel behind his house.

Schenk, without further consulting Scott, retained Investigator Stephen Frick and sent Frick to find the wallet. Frick found it in the location described by Scott and brought it to Schenk. After examining the wallet and determining that it contained credit cards with Wade's name, Schenk turned the wallet and its contents over to Detective Payne, investigating officer in the case. Schenk told Payne only that, to the best of his knowledge, the wallet had belonged to Wade.

The prosecution subpoenaed Attorney Schenk and Investigator Frick to testify at the preliminary hearing. When questioned at that hearing, Schenk said that he received the wallet from Frick but refused to answer further questions on the ground that he learned about the wallet through a privileged communication. Eventually, however, the magistrate threatened Schenk with contempt if he did not respond "yes" or "no" when asked whether his contact with his client led to disclosure of the wallet's location. Schenk then replied "yes," and revealed on further questioning that this contact was the sole source of his information as to the wallet's location.

At the preliminary hearing Frick, the investigator who found the wallet, was then questioned by the district attorney. Over objections by counsel, Frick testified that he found the wallet in a garbage can behind Scott's residence.

Prior to trial, a third attorney, Hamilton Hintz, was appointed for Scott. Hintz unsuccessfully sought an in limine ruling that the wallet of the murder victim was inadmissible and that the attorney-client privilege precluded the admission of testimony concerning the wallet by Schenk or Frick.

At trial Frick, called by the prosecution, identified the wallet and testified that he found it in a garbage can behind Scott's residence. On cross-examination by Hintz, Scott's counsel, Frick further testified that he was an investigator hired by Scott's first attorney, Schenk, and that he had searched the garbage can at Schenk's request. Hintz later called Schenk as a witness: Schenk testified that he told Frick to search for the wallet immediately after Schenk finished talking to Scott. Schenk also stated that Frick brought him the wallet on the following day; after examining its contents Schenk delivered the wallet to the police. Scott then took the stand and testified to the information about the wallet that he had disclosed to Schenk.

The jury found both Scott and Meredith guilty of first degree murder and first degree robbery. It further found that Meredith, but not Scott, was armed with a deadly weapon. Both defendants appeal from their convictions.

Defendant Scott concedes, and we agree, that the wallet itself was admissible in evidence. Scott maintains, however, that Evidence Code section 954 bars the testimony of the investigator concerning the location of the wallet. We consider, first, whether the California attorney-client privilege codified in that section extends to observations which are the product of privileged communications.

[The court concluded that California law protected as privileged the defendant's statements to his lawyer regarding the location of the wallet. Furthermore, the information retained its protection even though the lawyer disclosed the substance of the communication to the investigator, since the purpose of this disclosure was to aid in the representation.]

The statutes codifying the attorney-client privilege do not, however, indicate whether that privilege protects facts viewed and observed as a direct result of confidential communication. To resolve that issue, we turn first to the policies which underlie the attorney-client privilege, and then to the cases which apply those policies to observations arising from a protected communication.

The fundamental purpose of the attorney-client privilege is, of course, to encourage full and open communication between client and attorney. "Adequate legal representation in the ascertainment and enforcement of rights or the prosecution or defense of litigation compels a full disclosure of the facts by the client to his attorney. . . . Given the privilege, a client may make such a disclosure without fear that his attorney may be forced to reveal the information confided to him."

In the criminal context, as we have recently observed, these policies assume particular significance:

> "As a practical matter, if the client knows that damaging information could more readily be obtained from the attorney following disclosure than from himself in the absence of disclosure, the client would be reluctant to confide in his lawyer and it would be difficult to obtain fully informed legal advice." . . . Thus, if an accused is to derive the full benefits of his right to counsel, he must have the assurance of confidentiality and privacy of communication with his attorney.

Judicial decisions have recognized that the implementation of these important policies may require that the privilege extend not only to the initial communication between client and attorney but also to any information which the attorney or his investigator may subsequently acquire as a direct result of that communication. In a venerable decision involving facts analogous to those in the instant case, the Supreme Court of West Virginia held that the trial court erred in admitting an attorney's testimony as to the location of a pistol which he had discovered as the result of a privileged communication from his client. That the attorney had observed the pistol, the court pointed out, did not nullify the privilege:

> All that the said attorney knew about this pistol, or where it was to be found, he knew only from the communications which had been made to him by his client confidentially and professionally, as counsel in this case. And it ought, therefore, to have been entirely excluded from the jury. It may be, that in this particular case this evidence tended to the promotion of right and justice, but as was well said in Pearce v. Pearce, 11 Jar. 52, in page 55, and 2 De Gex & Smale 25-27: "Truth like all other good things may be loved unwisely, may be pursued too keenly, may cost too much."

State of West Virginia v. Douglass, 20 W. Va. 770, 783 (1882). . . .

More recent decisions reach similar conclusions. In State v. Olwell, 64 Wash. 2d 828, 394 P.2d 681 (1964), the court reviewed contempt charges against an attorney who refused to produce a knife he obtained from his client. The court first observed that "[t]o be protected as a privileged communication . . . the securing of the knife . . . must have been the *direct result of information* given to Mr. Olwell by his client." (Emphasis added.) The court concluded that defense counsel, after examining the physical evidence, should deliver it to the prosecution, but should not reveal the source of the evidence: "[b]y thus allowing the prosecution to recover such evidence, the public interest is served, and by refusing the prosecution an opportunity to disclose the source of the evidence, the client's privilege is preserved and a balance reached between these conflicting interests." (See also Anderson v. State (Fla. Dist. Ct. App.) 297 So. 2d 871.)

Finally, we note the decisions of the New York courts in People v. Belge (N.Y. Sup. Ct. 1975) 83 Misc. 2d 186, 372 N.Y.S.2d 798, affirmed in People v. Belge

(N.Y. App. Div. 1975) 50 A.D.2d 1088, 376 N.Y.S.2d 771. Defendant, charged with one murder, revealed to counsel that he had committed three others. Counsel, following defendant's directions, located one of the bodies. Counsel did not reveal the location of the body until trial, 10 months later, when he exposed the other murders to support an insanity defense.

Counsel was then indicted for violating two sections of the New York Public Health Law for failing to report the existence of the body to proper authorities in order that they could give it a decent burial. The trial court dismissed the indictment; the appellate division affirmed, holding that the attorney-client privilege shielded counsel from prosecution for actions which would otherwise violate the Public Health Law.[5]

The foregoing decisions demonstrate that the attorney-client privilege is not strictly limited to communications, but extends to protect observations made as a consequence of protected communications. We turn therefore to the question whether that privilege encompasses a case in which the defense, by removing or altering evidence, interferes with the prosecution's opportunity to discover that evidence.[7]

In some of the cases extending the privilege to observations arising from protected communications the defense counsel had obtained the evidence from his client or in some other fashion removed it from its original location (State v. Olwell, supra, 394 P.2d 681; Anderson v. State, supra, 297 So. 2d 871); in others the attorney did not remove or alter the evidence (People v. Belge, supra). None of the decisions, however, confronts directly the question whether such removal or alteration should affect the defendant's right to assert the attorney-client privilege as a bar to testimony concerning the original location or condition of the evidence.

When defense counsel alters or removes physical evidence, he necessarily deprives the prosecution of the opportunity to observe that evidence in its original condition or location. As the amicus Appellate Committee of the California District Attorneys Association points out, to bar admission of testimony concerning the original condition and location of the evidence in such a

---

5. In each of the cases discussed in text, a crucial element in the court's analysis is that the attorney's observations were the direct product of information communicated to him by his client. Two decisions, People v. Lee, 3 Cal. App. 3d 514, 83 Cal. Rptr. 715 (1970), and Morrell v. State, 575 P.2d 1200 (Alaska 1978), held that an attorney must not only turn over evidence given him by *third parties*, but also testify as to the source of that evidence. Both decisions emphasized that the attorney-client privilege was inapplicable because the third party was not acting as an agent of the attorney or the client.

7. We agree with the parties' suggestion that an attorney in Schenk's position often may best fulfill conflicting obligations to preserve the confidentiality of client confidences, investigate his case, and act as an officer of the court if he does not remove evidence located as the result of a privileged communication. We must recognize, however, that in some cases an examination of evidence may reveal information critical to the defense of a client accused of crime. If the usefulness of the evidence cannot be gauged without taking possession of it, as, for example, when a ballistics or fingerprint test is required, the attorney may properly take it for a reasonable time before turning it over to the prosecution. (*Olwell*, supra, 394 P.2d, pp.684-685.) Similarly, in the present case the defense counsel could not be certain the burnt wallet belonged in fact to the victim: in taking the wallet to examine it for identification, he violated no ethical duty to his client or to the prosecution. (See generally, Legal Ethics and the Destruction of Evidence, 88 Yale L.J. 1665 (1979).)

case permits the defense in effect to "destroy" critical information; it is as if, he explains, the wallet in this case bore a tag bearing the words "located in the trash can by Scott's residence," and the defense, by taking the wallet, destroyed this tag. To extend the attorney-client privilege to a case in which the defense removed evidence might encourage defense counsel to race the police to seize critical evidence. (See In re Ryder, 263 F. Supp. 360, 369 (E.D. Va. 1967); Comment, The Right of a Criminal Defense Attorney to Withhold Physical Evidence Received From His Client, 38 U. Chi. L. Rev. 211, 227-228 (1970).)

We therefore conclude that courts must craft an exception to the protection extended by the attorney-client privilege in cases in which counsel has removed or altered evidence. Indeed, at oral argument defense counsel acknowledged that such an exception might be necessary in a case in which the police would have inevitably discovered the evidence in its original location if counsel had not removed it. Counsel argued, however, that the attorney-client privilege should protect observations of evidence, despite subsequent defense removal, unless the prosecution could prove that the police probably would have eventually discovered the evidence in the original site.

We have seriously considered counsel's proposal, but have concluded that a test based upon the probability of eventual discovery is unworkably speculative. Evidence turns up not only because the police deliberately search for it, but also because it comes to the attention of policemen or bystanders engaged in other business. In the present case, for example, the wallet might have been found by the trash collector. Moreover, once physical evidence (the wallet) is turned over to the police, they will obviously stop looking for it; to ask where, how long, and how carefully they would have looked is obviously to compel speculation as to theoretical future conduct of the police.

We therefore conclude that whenever defense counsel removes or alters evidence, the statutory privilege does not bar revelation of the original location or condition of the evidence in question.[8] We thus view the defense decision to remove evidence as a tactical choice. If defense counsel leaves the evidence where he discovers it, his observations derived from privileged communications are insulated from revelation. If, however, counsel chooses to remove evidence to examine or test it, the original location and condition of that evidence lose the protection of the privilege. Applying this analysis to the present case, we hold that the trial court did not err in admitting the investigator's testimony concerning the location of the wallet. . . .

---

8. In offering the evidence, the prosecution should present the information in a manner which avoids revealing the content of attorney-client communications or the original source of the information. In the present case, for example, the prosecutor simply asked Frick where he found the wallet; he did not identify Frick as a defense investigator or trace the discovery of the wallet to an attorney-client communication.

In other circumstances, when it is not possible to elicit such testimony without identifying the witness as the defendant's attorney or investigator, the defendant may be willing to enter a stipulation which will simply inform the jury as to the relevant location or condition of the evidence in question. When such a stipulation is proffered, the prosecution should not be permitted to reject the stipulation in the hope that by requiring defense counsel personally to testify to such facts, the jury might infer that counsel learned those facts from defendant. (Cf. People v. Hall, 28 Cal. 3d 143, 152, 167 Cal. Rptr. 844, 616 P.2d 826 (1980).)

The Turnover Duty (But How Broad?)

Attorney Schenk gave the wallet to the police. Did he have to? At least where the evidence is a fruit or instrumentality of a crime, illegal in itself to possess, a lawyer cannot keep the evidence. That's one lesson of In re Ryder, at page 453. Reaching the same result as *Meredith* is United States v. Hunter, 1995 Westlaw 12513 (N.D. Ill. 1995).

A lawyer can escape the turnover obligation simply by not taking possession of the item. The lawyer has no obligation to reveal its location. Wemark v. State, 602 N.W.2d 810 (Iowa 1999). Of course, sometimes a defense lawyer will want to take possession of an item for tactical reasons. "If the defense lawyer does not take possession of the instrument of the crime, there can be no opportunity to have it examined for any evidence that may be critical to the defense. Thus, the particular facts of a case may justify disclosing the location of the instrument of a crime even if disclosure is not legally required and the information is legally protected." Id.

Where the client gives counsel something as ordinary as a telephone bill, must she turn it over? Perhaps the telephone bill can form a link in a chain of evidence tending to prove criminality. Still, it is not the stolen loot or the weapon. It is not the sort of thing that's illegal to possess. A telephone bill was precisely the issue in Matter of Grand Jury Subpoenas, 959 F.2d 1158 (2d Cir. 1992). The bill had been subpoenaed from the client's lawyer in connection with an investigation of the client. (The client had delivered it to his lawyer.) The court held that no privilege protected such a document, which a law firm must therefore produce in response to a subpoena. Did the firm have a duty to produce the bill even without the subpoena? Professor Reitz's research produced no case in which the duty to produce has been applied to documentary evidence of a white-collar crime. See Kevin Reitz, Clients, Lawyers, and the Fifth Amendment: The Need for a Projected Privilege, 1991 Duke L.J. 572 (proposing, too, "a new investigative tool" to reach evidence in law offices without the need for a physical search). Of course, altering or destroying the phone bill may be obstruction. But what about putting the phone bill in a safe place in the lawyer's office? It would not be much of a stretch for a prosecutor to argue that a lawyer who did this has concealed evidence, no less than Ryder did by putting the evidence in his lockbox, because the government would be unable to discover the phone bill in a search of the client's files. If (unlike in the actual case) the government does not know that the lawyer has been retained, it cannot subpoena the phone bill from the lawyer. As of 1991, as Professor Reitz concluded in his study, no such charge had been made against a lawyer. I know of no such charge since then.

Meredith cites the decision of the Alaska Supreme Court in Morrell v. State. See note 5. The facts of that case are intriguing and its holding ambiguous. Stephen Cline, a public defender, was appointed to represent Clayton Morrell, who was charged with kidnapping. While Morrell was in prison, his friend, John Wagner, used his car and residence with his permission. Wagner discovered a plan for the kidnapping in Morrell's car written in Morrell's handwriting. He gave the plan to Cline. Cline unsuccessfully attempted to return it to Wagner and then, after seeking ethics advice, gave the plan to the prosecutor, who used it to convict Morrell. Morrell claimed that Cline's conduct violated Morrell's Sixth

Amendment right to the effective assistance of counsel. The obstruction-of-justice statute in Alaska made it a crime for a person to willfully destroy, alter, or conceal evidence of a crime "which is being sought for production during an investigation, inquiry or trial, with the intent to prevent the evidence from being discovered or produced." Remember, the question for the court was whether Cline's representation was constitutionally ineffective. At one point, the court concluded that Cline "would have been obligated to see that the evidence reached the prosecutor in this case even if he had obtained the evidence from Morrell," not from a third party. That's a remarkable statement. Was Cline obligated to take the evidence from his client and hand it over? At another point, the court says only that Cline could "reasonably have concluded" that he was required to "reveal the existence of the evidence." Those are two very different conclusions, aren't they? In any event, whichever is correct, the court found that Cline's conduct did not make his representation ineffective where the source was not his client, but a third person. See also People v. Sanchez, 30 Cal. Rptr. 2d 111 (Ct. App. 1994) (lawyer who received incriminating documents in client's own handwriting from another lawyer, who had received them from the client's sister, acted properly when he gave them to the court, which gave them to the prosecutor).

An attorney may assert the attorney-client privilege in resisting a summons to produce documents that were delivered to him by his client, *if* the documents would have been privileged while in the client's possession. In Fisher v. United States, 425 U.S. 391 (1976), the issue was whether an attorney had to produce certain tax workpapers delivered by the client. The client claimed that the papers would have enjoyed Fifth Amendment immunity from subpoena while in the client's possession and retained that protection despite delivery to counsel. The Court agreed with the major premise but concluded on the facts before it that the Fifth Amendment did not apply.

Moving Pictures

In his review of Lawrence Schiller's *American Tragedy*, a book on the prosecution of O. J. Simpson for murdering his ex-wife Nicole Brown Simpson and her friend Ronald Goldman, Jeffrey Rosen calls defense lawyer Johnnie Cochran "an applied critical race theorist" and writes that Cochran "insisted from the beginning that the facts of the Simpson case were less important to the defense than the social meaning that might be attached to the protagonists." Schiller quotes Cochran as saying: "Our theory was based not only on the facts before us but also on what our experience suggested to us about their meaning." Jeffrey Rosen, The Bloods and the Crits, The New Republic, Dec. 9, 1996, p.27. Rosen continues:

So how, precisely, did Cochran construct a story that transformed a wealthy shill for white corporations into an oppressed tribune of the underclass? Among other things, by interior decoration. Perhaps the most shameful of Cochran's many shameful exercises in racial storytelling was his redecoration of Simpson's home, in preparation for the look-see visit of the black jurors. All day on Saturday, according to Schiller, members of the defense team were hard at work "establishing O. J.'s African-American identity." The lawyers found Simpson's walls lined with pictures of white people: girlfriends, celebrities, corporate sponsors. "The faces were overwhelmingly white," Schiller notes. "That's not the way to please a jury dominated by African-American women." On Cochran's orders, "[t]he white women on the walls have to go, and the black people have to come in." Down went a nude portrait of Paula Barbieri that had been hanging near the fireplace, and up went pictures of Simpson's family — "his black family," in Cochran's words. Kardashian had the photographs enlarged at Kinko's, and nicely framed. "The jurors won't notice that they are color photocopies," Schiller notes cheerfully.

But homey Xeroxed pictures of Simpson and his mother weren't enough for Cochran. As Schiller reports: "Cochran wants something depicting African-American history. 'What about that framed poster from my office of the little girl trying to get to school?' he asks. Johnnie means Norman Rockwell's famous 1963 painting, *The Problem We All Live With,* in which a black grade school girl walks to school surrounded by federal marshals." And so Cochran's framed picture was hung at the top of the stairs, where the jury couldn't miss it as they trooped up to Simpson's bedroom. "Everyone," Schiller reports, "is pleased."

The prosecutors seem to have been outmaneuvered here. In her book, Marcia Clark, the lead prosecutor, recounts that the state had argued against a visit to Simpson's house, which was not the crime scene. But the defense insisted on it, since the jury was going to inspect the home of Nicole Brown Simpson. Plus, some trial evidence had been discovered in Simpson's home (remember the bloody socks?). Before the jury entered, the lawyers did a walk-through, and Clark saw the changes for the first time. "I'd gotten no farther than the foyer when I realized something was very wrong here. . . . [T]he most dramatic transformation was that collection of photographs. The Wall of Fat Cats had been cleansed of Caucasians. Gone were the golfing buddies and shots of Nicole in Aspen. Every single shot contained a black face. Simpson's mother, his sister, their husbands, their kids. Upstairs there was even a Norman Rockwell reproduction. . . . But the piece de resistance was the master bedroom. On the mantel above the fireplace sat books on philosophy and religion. On the nightstand, next to a Holy Bible, stood a photo of defendant's mother, Eunice." Marcia Clark, *Without A Doubt* 302 (1997).

Did the defense lawyers act ethically? Did they tamper with evidence? Rosen teaches at George Washington University Law School, so we can expect a greater understanding of the issues from him than we might from nonlawyer book reviewers. (Who can stop us?) Is his criticism fair? Separately, did Judge Lance Ito rule properly in allowing the visit to Simpson's home over the state's objection? Did he let the defense get away with unfair even if ethical tactics? Or were the tactics fair by definition if ethical?

Does the Source Matter?

In *Meredith,* would Scott's lawyer have had to reveal the source of the wallet if the source had been Scott himself, not his "burn barrel"? Analytically the answer would seem to be yes. By removing the wallet from Scott, the lawyer would have made it impossible for the authorities to seize it from the defendant, a more likely subject of a search. And as with the burn barrel, the evidentiary value of the wallet depended on its location. On the other hand, *Meredith* cited *Olwell*, which on those facts would not allow the prosecutor to elicit the client as the source of the incriminating evidence. In People v. Nash, 341 N.W.2d 439 (Mich. 1983), a divided court concluded that *Olwell* was correct, but a minority read *Meredith* to require revelation of the source of the incriminating evidence even when the source is the client directly. Siding with the *Nash* majority is Hitch v. Pima County Superior Court, 708 P.2d 72 (Ariz. 1985). The "venerable" West Virginia opinion cited by *Meredith* at page 465 held that the prosecutor could inform the jury that the alleged murder weapon, a gun, had been found in the possession of the defendant's lawyer, but the privilege protected any communications between lawyer and client on the subject. "The simple fact, that the identical pistol produced before the jury was found in the possession, at a certain time, of the prisoner's counsel is all that the commonwealth has a right to prove in reference to the finding of this pistol." State v. Douglass, 20 W. Va. 770 (1882). If the rule should be the same regardless of source, what should it be? In a jurisdiction that subscribed to the *Nash* minority view, what should a lawyer do when a client brings incriminating evidence to the lawyer's office? What if the evidence is a semi-automatic weapon, money from a bank robbery, or as in the prosecution of Philip Russell, child pornography?

A Lawyer's E-Discovery Obligations

What is it about electronic documents that has led courts to give lawyers heightened duties to insure their preservation in civil discovery? Of course, lawyers have always had oversight responsibility for discovery. But the rules here seem different. Judge Shira Schiendlin's *Zubulake* opinions (pronounced with four syllables, the last of which is pronounced with a long e), while not the first to tackle the problem of e-discovery, have been highly influential. Here is an excerpt from the fifth of five opinions on the issue. The case is otherwise unremarkable, an ordinary discrimination case. For our purposes, what is important is that Judge Schiendlin explicitly imposed duties on lawyers, not just litigants, and with a level of specificity about how lawyers must behave that goes far beyond what was needed to decide the discovery and sanction motions before her. Notice how often in the excerpt that follows the court refers to counsel's obligations, not those of the parties.

ZUBULAKE v. UBS WARBURG LLC
229 F.R.D. 422 (S.D.N.Y. 2004).

SCHIENDLIN, J. . . .

Once a party reasonably anticipates litigation, it must suspend its routine document retention/destruction policy and put in place a "litigation hold" to ensure the preservation of relevant documents. As a general rule, that litigation hold does not apply to inaccessible backup tapes (*e.g.*, those typically maintained solely for the purpose of disaster recovery), which may continue to be recycled on the schedule set forth in the company's policy. On the other hand, if backup tapes are accessible (*i.e.*, actively used for information retrieval), then such tapes *would* likely be subject to the litigation hold. ...

A party's discovery obligations do not end with the implementation of a "litigation hold" — to the contrary, that's only the beginning. Counsel must oversee compliance with the litigation hold, monitoring the party's efforts to retain and produce the relevant documents. Proper communication between a party and her lawyer will ensure (1) that all relevant information (or at least all sources of relevant information) is discovered, (2) that relevant information is retained on a continuing basis; and (3) that relevant non-privileged material is produced to the opposing party.

1.   Counsel's Duty to Locate Relevant Information

Once a "litigation hold" is in place, a party and her counsel must make certain that all sources of potentially relevant information are identified and placed "on hold," to the extent required in *Zubulake IV*. To do this, counsel must become fully familiar with her client's document retention policies, as well as the client's data retention architecture. This will invariably involve speaking with information technology personnel, who can explain system-wide backup procedures and the actual (as opposed to theoretical) implementation of the firm's recycling policy. It will also involve communicating with the "key players" in the litigation, in order to understand how they stored information. In this case, for example, some UBS employees created separate computer files pertaining to Zubulake, while others printed out relevant e-mails and retained them in hard copy only. Unless counsel interviews each employee, it is impossible to determine whether all potential sources of information have been inspected. A brief conversation with counsel, for example, might have revealed that Tong maintained "archive" copies of e-mails concerning Zubulake, and that "archive" meant a separate on-line computer file, not a backup tape. Had that conversation taken place, Zubulake might have had relevant e-mails from that file two years ago.

To the extent that it may not be feasible for counsel to speak with every key player, given the size of a company or the scope of the lawsuit, counsel must be more creative. It may be possible to run a system-wide keyword search; counsel could then preserve a copy of each "hit." Although this sounds burdensome, it need not be. Counsel does not have to review these documents, only see that they are retained. For example, counsel could create a broad list of search terms, run a search for a limited time frame, and then segregate responsive documents. When the opposing party propounds its document requests, the parties could negotiate a list of search terms to be used in identifying responsive documents, and counsel would only be obliged to review documents that came up as "hits" on the second, more restrictive search. The initial broad cut merely guarantees that relevant documents are not lost.

In short, it is *not* sufficient to notify all employees of a litigation hold and expect that the party will then retain and produce all relevant information. Counsel must take affirmative steps to monitor compliance so that all sources of discoverable information are identified and searched. This is not to say that counsel will necessarily succeed in locating all such sources, or that the later discovery of new sources is evidence of a lack of effort. But counsel and client must take *some reasonable steps* to see that sources of relevant information are located.

2. Counsel's Continuing Duty to Ensure Preservation

Once a party and her counsel have identified all of the sources of potentially relevant information, they are under a duty to retain that information (as per *Zubulake IV*) and to produce information responsive to the opposing party's requests. Rule 26 creates a "duty to supplement" those responses. Although the Rule 26 duty to supplement is nominally the party's, it really falls on counsel. As the Advisory Committee explains,

> Although the party signs the answers, it is his lawyer who understands their significance and bears the responsibility to bring answers up to date. In a complex case all sorts of information reaches the party, who little understands its bearing on answers previously given to interrogatories. In practice, therefore, the lawyer under a continuing burden must periodically recheck all interrogatories and canvass all new information.

To ameliorate this burden, the Rules impose a continuing duty to supplement responses to discovery requests *only* when "a party[,] or more frequently his lawyer, obtains actual knowledge that a prior response is incorrect. This exception does not impose a duty to check the accuracy of prior responses, but it prevents knowing concealment by a party or attorney."

The *continuing* duty to supplement disclosures strongly suggests that parties also have a duty to make sure that discoverable information is not lost. Indeed, the notion of a "duty to preserve" connotes an ongoing obligation. Obviously, if information is lost or destroyed, it has not been preserved.

The tricky question is what that continuing duty entails. What must a lawyer do to make certain that relevant information — especially electronic information — is being retained? Is it sufficient if she periodically re-sends her initial "litigation hold" instructions? What if she communicates with the party's information technology personnel? Must she make occasional on-site inspections?

Above all, the requirement must be reasonable. A lawyer cannot be obliged to monitor her client like a parent watching a child. At some point, the client must bear responsibility for a failure to preserve. At the same time, counsel is more conscious of the contours of the preservation obligation; a party cannot reasonably be trusted to receive the "litigation hold" instruction once and to fully comply with it without the active supervision of counsel.

There are thus a number of steps that counsel should take to ensure compliance with the preservation obligation. While these precautions may not be enough (or may be too much) in some cases, they are designed to promote the continued preservation of potentially relevant information in the typical case.

First, counsel must issue a "litigation hold" at the outset of litigation or whenever litigation is reasonably anticipated. The litigation hold should be periodically re-issued so that new employees are aware of it, and so that it is fresh in the minds of all employees.

Second, counsel should communicate directly with the "key players" in the litigation, *i.e.,* the people identified in a party's initial disclosure and any subsequent supplementation thereto. Because these "key players" are the "employees likely to have relevant information," it is particularly important that the preservation duty be communicated clearly to them. As with the litigation hold, the key players should be periodically reminded that the preservation duty is still in place.

Finally, counsel should instruct all employees to produce electronic copies of their relevant active files. Counsel must also make sure that all backup media which the party is required to retain is identified and stored in a safe place. In cases involving a small number of relevant backup tapes, counsel might be advised to take physical possession of backup tapes. In other cases, it might make sense for relevant backup tapes to be segregated and placed in storage. Regardless of what particular arrangement counsel chooses to employ, the point is to separate relevant backup tapes from others. One of the primary reasons that electronic data is lost is ineffective communication with information technology personnel. By taking possession of, or otherwise safeguarding, all potentially relevant backup tapes, counsel eliminates the possibility that such tapes will be inadvertently recycled. . . .

Has the court exceeded its powers in producing a code of conduct for lawyers rather than simply describing the parties' duties and leaving it to their lawyers to decide how best to insure those duties are honored? Be that as it may, the *Zubulake* rules are likely here to stay, and lawyers who do not want to incur the wrath of the trial judge must attend to them. In fact, amendments to the Federal Rules of Civil Procedure, while less explicit, echo some of *Zubulake*'s directives. Now go back to the problem at the start of this chapter. The lawyer for Flash Pharma must recognize the possibility of consumer class action suits. How does the *Zubulake* excerpt affect your advice?

FURTHER READING

Two articles with analysis about the destruction of documents at Arthur Andersen and the facts in the ensuing prosecution for obstruction of justice are Kathleen Brickey, Andersen's Fall From Grace, 81 Wash. U. L.Q. 917 (2003); and Note, Nancy Temple's Duty: Professional Responsibility and the *Arthur Andersen* Verdict, 18 Geo. J. Legal Ethics 261 (2004) (authored by KC Goyer).

B.   SOME ISSUES CONCERNING PROSECUTORS

A great deal has been written about how prosecutors should make decisions and the rules that should channel those decisions. Of course, the Constitution is dominant here, but its requirements are mostly stated at a high level of generality. Do we need greater specificity? Rule 3.8 focuses on prosecutors and, as amended in 2008, even gives prosecutors certain duties to help free those who may be wrongly convicted. At the same time, prosecutors have enormous power — to decide whom to investigate and charge, to pick the charges, to offer plea bargains or to withhold them — that are largely beyond review. Oh, yes, and there is the trial, of course. To be sure, a trial is where a prosecutor's charging decision will be tested. Judges and juries will examine the prosecutor's work under the rules of evidence and will subject it to a proof beyond a reasonable doubt standard and other legal safeguards meant to insure fairness and to avoid convicting the innocent. But the vast majority of cases are resolved without trial, and at trial a prosecutor ordinarily has resources that far exceed those of most defendants.

Perhaps the most famous recent case of prosecutorial misconduct — maybe the most famous in all American history — is now known as the "Duke Lacrosse Case." In it, North Carolina prosecutor Mike Nifong went completely off the rails — morally, ethically, legally, you name it — causing serious harm to the innocent suspects, Duke University students, notwithstanding their eventual vindication. Stuart Taylor and KC Johnson offer a full account of this sorry tale in their book *Until Proven Innocent* (2007). Robert Mosteller focuses on an important legal aspect of the investigation of the lacrosse team members — the false identifications — and concludes that the "case shows once again the need for concrete rules," not mere "guidelines for identification procedures." Professor Mosteller argues for greater exclusion of out-of-court identifications that significantly violate these procedures. The Duke Lacrosse Case, Innocence, and False Identification: A Fundamental Failure to "Do Justice," 76 Fordham L. Rev. 1337 (2007). Bruce Green and Fred Zacharias also favor greater specificity in the rules governing prosecutors beyond the imprecise admonition of neutrality in making decisions. Prosecutorial Neutrality, 2004 Wisc. L. Rev. 837 (2004) ("prosecutors should make decisions based on articulable principles or subprinciples that command broad public acceptance").

Professor R. Michael Cassidy, by contrast, argues for the importance of character, not only rules, to guide prosecutorial decisions. In Character and Context: What Virtue Theory Can Teach Us About a Prosecutor's Ethical Duty to "Seek Justice," 82 Notre Dame L. Rev. 635 (2006), he writes: "Any attempt to regulate how prosecutors should 'act' in certain highly contextualized and nuanced situations by developing more specific normative rules is unworkable. Prosecutorial discretion would be better constrained in these areas by focusing on what type of character traits prosecutors should possess or strive to acquire. Only after we answer the critical preliminary question of who we want our public prosecutors to 'be' can we possibly hope to discern what we expect our prosecutors to 'do.' "

1.   *Public Comments That Deny a Fair Trial*

Ethics rules (see chapter 15) forbid lawyers to make a public statement "that will have a substantial likelihood of materially prejudicing" the trial in their matters. NY DR 7-107(A), Rule 3.6(a). The facts of the following case are as dramatic as the miscarriage of justice they describe. The prosecution of Oliver Jovanovic became worldwide news. The publicity was especially prominent in

VIII.   Special Issues in Litigation

New York City, where the alleged crime took place. The notoriety depended in part on the identity of Jovanovic and the alleged victim — respectively a doctoral candidate at Columbia University and a Barnard undergraduate. In part, too, interest in the case flowed from the fact that they met via the internet in 1996, when online dating and social networking were still new phenomena. The extreme nature of the alleged acts (labeled "cybersex torture" by the tabloids) also helped keep the story on the front page. Linda Fairstein, a high-ranking assistant district attorney, had a national reputation as a sex crimes prosecutor, having been instrumental in establishing (and then heading) the sex crimes unit of the Manhattan D.A.'s office. (She has since retired to write best-selling crime novels.) Finally, the judge, Paul Crotty, had been corporation counsel for New York City, which makes his treatment of the issue of the city's liability especially interesting.

After his vindication, Jovanovic sued Fairstein, New York City, and Milton Bonilla, the arresting officer. We are not concerned here with Bonilla, but his name naturally figures in the story. The defendants moved to dismiss the complaint on the pleadings. This is Judge Crotty's ruling. If you were the city's lawyer, would you advise your client to settle? For how much? If you were Jovanovic's lawyer, how strong a case would you think you have? How much would you take to settle?

JOVANOVIC v. CITY OF NEW YORK
2006 U.S. Dist. LEXIS 59165 (S.D.N.Y. 2006)

PAUL A. CROTTY, J.: . . . [1]

On November 27, 1996, Jamie Ruzcek ("Ruzcek"), a twenty-year-old Barnard student, reported to Bonilla that she had been sexually assaulted by Jovanovic, a thirty-year-old doctoral candidate at Columbia University, with whom she had corresponded by e-mail prior to the alleged incident. Ruzcek told Bonilla that Jovanovic had assaulted her for twenty hours, starting on the night of November 22, 1996, and continuing through the day of November 23, 1996. Ruzcek provided a detailed and graphic statement of the incident, in which she alleged — among other heinous acts — that Jovanovic had hogtied her for nearly twenty hours, violently raped and sodomized her, struck her repeatedly with a club, severely burned her with candle wax, and repeatedly gagged her with a variety of materials.

The physical evidence did not match Ruzcek's assertions. A comprehensive gynecological examination of Ruzcek on November 27, 1996, found no bleeding, teeth marks, bruises, scratches, swelling, redness, or burn marks, all of which would be expected if Ruzcek's account were true. Further, there was no forensic evidence to support Ruzcek's claims. No traces of Jovanovic's DNA were found on the victim, her clothing, or any of the undergarments she wore on the night of the alleged assault. No blood was found on any of the victim's clothes, no ligature marks upon her body, and no abrasions about her mouth. Hair and fiber tests showed no signs of a violent struggle or sexual assault.

---

1. The background information is taken directly from the complaint, which for the purposes of this motion, must be accepted as true.

Ruzcek's allegations were questionable in other ways as well. She had given contradictory accounts of the alleged assault to Bonilla, "changing critical facts every time she recounted the event." She waited four full days before seeking medical treatment, "despite her claims that she experienced profuse bleeding, severe burns and intense pain." Moreover, Ruzcek had "a history of making false sexual accusations, and in fact, had falsely accused her own father and uncle of sexual molestation," and a week before filing her own complaint against Jovanovic, Ruzcek had encouraged an acquaintance to file a false rape complaint against a New York University student.

Despite the gravity of Ruzcek's allegations, Bonilla waited a full nine days before attempting to question Jovanovic. It is unclear whether Bonilla conducted any additional investigation during this nine-day period. On December 5, 1996, Bonilla went to Jovanovic's apartment and, without providing any explanation, ordered Jovanovic to accompany him to the precinct house for interrogation. When Jovanovic requested an attorney, Bonilla placed him under arrest, charging him with Rape, Sodomy, and Unlawful Imprisonment.

Later that same day, Bonilla and several other police officers returned to Jovanovic's apartment, searching for the items allegedly used in the assault; but no such items were ever recovered from Plaintiff or his apartment. During the search, two separate investigative teams took photographs of Jovanovic's apartment—photographs that revealed none of the items described by the alleged victim.

After searching Jovanovic's apartment, Bonilla prepared police reports containing false and misleading information regarding Jovanovic's arrest and the evidence allegedly collected at Jovanovic's apartment, which he then forwarded to the New York County District Attorney's Office. He told prosecutors that he had observed incriminating evidence in Plaintiff's apartment, and that Jovanovic had "conspired to obstruct the police at the time of the search, and had destroyed incriminating evidence prior to the search," claims he knew to be false. Bonilla repeated these false and misleading claims before the grand jury, the trial judge, and the petit jury.

On December 6, 1996, Jovanovic was arraigned in the New York County Criminal Court. Fairstein, the Chief of the Sex Crimes Unit of the New York County District Attorney's Office, personally appeared as the sole representative of that office. Following the arraignment, Fairstein made "highly inflammatory and prejudicial remarks about Jovanovic to the press." Fairstein was quoted as saying: "He terrorized this young woman to the point that she was too frightened to call the authorities until weeks after it happened"; "He tied her to a chair, undressed her, and tortured her with sex toys and other objects for almost a full day"; "[H]e tortured and sexually abused the woman, burning her with candle wax, biting her, sexually assaulting her and threatening to dismember her as Jeffrey Dahmer, the serial killer, had done with his victims"; He "tied the woman's legs to a chair and gagged her before sexually torturing her"; "[H]e was so prepared for this and carried it off so smoothly"; "We believe this was not the first time he did something like this"; and "We believe there are other victims."

Fairstein's comments made the headlines of every local newspaper. For instance, one New York Post cover page featured a full page picture of Jovanovic and read, "Prosecutor: Cyber fiend struck before" and "HOW MANY MORE VICTIMS?" Fairstein "repeatedly emphasized to the press that this was her office's 'first internet-related sex prosecution' and that the case represented a 'whole new entry in the acquaintance-rape category.' " Throughout the proceedings, Fairstein continued to provide highly damaging leaks to the press, "including but not limited to, releasing select portions of the e-mail correspondence between [Plaintiff] and [the alleged victim] which further demonized [P]laintiff."

Coverage of the case in the press was so extensive that trial witnesses were influenced by it. "One material witness, Mary Jo Parlier Chambers, testified about critical 'facts' that she had actually learned from reading a newspaper article." These alleged "facts" were addressed by both parties during summations, and became "the subject of a read-back requested by the jury during their deliberations." At least three other material witnesses gave testimony tainted by the pre-trial publicity.

On April 15, 1998, the jury convicted Jovanovic of Kidnapping in the First Degree, three counts of Sexual Abuse in the First Degree, Assault in the Second Degree, and Assault in the Third Degree. Plaintiff was then sentenced to a term of 15 years to life in prison. He served more than 20 months in prison. The Appellate Division reversed Plaintiff's conviction on December 21, 1999, finding that the trial judge improperly hampered the defendant's ability to present a defense by erroneously invoking the rape-shield law, thereby denying the jury access to key evidence in the case.

Anticipating a second trial, the prosecution offered Jovanovic several plea deals. The prosecution offered Jovanovic a deal wherein Jovanovic could avoid serving any further time in prison, if he would plead guilty to a single felony charge. Maintaining his innocence, Jovanovic refused. The prosecution then offered Jovanovic a promise of no further prison time, if he would plead guilty to a single, nonsexual, misdemeanor charge. Again, Jovanovic refused, maintained his innocence, and insisted on a trial. On November 1, 2001, the prosecution moved to dismiss all charges against Jovanovic. The motion was granted and all charges were dismissed, with prejudice.

As a result of his arrest and prosecution, Jovanovic suffered damage both to his career and to his reputation. Prior to his arrest, Jovanovic had completed his research and written his thesis for a Ph.D. in Microbiology. As a result of his arrest on December 5, 1996, however, he was prevented from defending his thesis as scheduled on December 20, 1996. Consequently, Jovanovic was prevented from obtaining his Ph.D. for over five years, thereby losing five years of wages as a computational biologist.[3]

Plaintiff also suffered physical and emotional injury. While incarcerated at Rikers Island and later at state prisons, Jovanovic was repeatedly strip-searched and humiliated. Further, Plaintiff was repeatedly threatened and attacked by fellow inmates. On one occasion, an inmate stabbed him in the neck and slashed his throat, as a result of which Jovanovic almost died. . . .

III.   CLAIM AGAINST ASSISTANT DISTRICT ATTORNEY LINDA FAIRSTEIN

Plaintiff pleads only one cause of action against Assistant District Attorney Fairstein. He claims that Fairstein's extrajudicial statements to the press were so

---

3. On May 7, 2002, Plaintiff defended his thesis and earned his Ph.D. with distinction from Columbia University, receiving "departmental honors for outstanding and innovative work."

inflammatory and prejudicial that they denied Plaintiff his constitutionally protected right to a fair trial. Defendants seek to dismiss this claim on multiple
grounds. First, as with the claims against Bonilla, Defendants argue that the
fair trial claim against Fairstein is barred by the applicable statute of limitations.
Second, Defendants claim that Plaintiff fails to adequately plead a claim for
denial of a fair trial against Fairstein. Finally, Defendants argue that Fairstein
is protected from suit by the doctrines of absolute and qualified immunity.

A.   [THE COURT REJECTED A STATUTE OF LIMITATIONS ARGUMENT.]

B.   MERITS OF THE CLAIM

1.   The sufficiency of the complaint

To prevail upon a claim for denial of a fair trial due to prejudicial publicity,
a plaintiff must establish three elements: (1) that there were improper leaks;
(2) that the plaintiff had in fact been denied a fair trial; and (3) that other
remedies (e.g., voir dire, peremptory challenges, and challenges for cause)
were not available, or were used to no avail, to alleviate the effects of the
leaks. See Powers v. Coe, 728 F.2d 97, 105-06 (2d Cir. 1984). Defendants
urge that Plaintiff failed to plead the third element, namely, that the
procedural safeguards of voir dire and peremptory challenges were unavailable
or used to no avail. Defendants rely on Powers, but they misunderstand its
teaching. In Powers, which also dealt with a motion to dismiss prior to discovery, the Second Circuit actually refused to dismiss the plaintiff's denial of a fair
trial claim. In so doing, the court explained: "Powers is entitled to the opportunity to show that his constitutional right to a fair trial was violated by the
alleged leaks." The court emphasized, however, that "its holding in no way
diminishes the burden that the plaintiff must meet in order to prove his
allegations," and its decision did "not foreclose, on appropriate papers, summary judgment." Id. at 105-06 (emphasis added).

Furthermore, the plaintiff in Powers never explicitly alleged in his complaint
that pre-trial remedies were of no avail, and still the Second Circuit refused to
dismiss his claim. The Powers court did not cite any allegations from Powers's
complaint regarding the unavailability or the failure of voir dire and other
procedural safeguards. Rather, the court merely recited Powers's allegations
that the Chief State's Attorney leaked grand jury information to the press "maliciously and in bad faith in order to prejudice public opinion against [Powers],
deprive [Powers] of his right to an unbiased jury and a fair trial." The court
found these allegations sufficient to withstand a motion to dismiss. Thus, in
articulating the third prong, the Powers court appears to have set the stage
for a motion for summary judgment, while making it clear that such particularity
is not necessary at the pleading stage. See id. Thus, if anything, Powers
suggests — rather strongly — that Defendants' motion be denied.

Defendants' reliance on Schiavone Construction Co. v. Merola, 678 F.Supp.
64 (S.D.N.Y. 1988), is equally misguided. In Schiavone, the District Attorney
made all of his prejudicial statements before the trial began, and the court
determined that voir dire and peremptory challenges sufficiently purged the
jury of the prejudicial effects of such statements. Further, the court dismissed

the plaintiff's fair trial claim largely because the trial jury had acquitted the plaintiff, thereby creating a strong presumption that the jury was unbiased. Considering the trial jury's verdict in Schiavone, any allegation that the jury had been irremediably prejudiced would have been — beyond doubt — impossible for the plaintiff to prove.

Jovanovic's case is easily distinguished from Schiavone. Here, Plaintiff alleges that Fairstein, unlike the District Attorney in Schiavone, continued to make extrajudicial statements to the press throughout the criminal proceedings. Plaintiff's complaint suggests that this steady stream of "leaks" eliminated the safeguards of voir dire and peremptory challenge. Fairstein's own statements to the Media Studies Journal support such an inference, most notably her comments about the effects of publicity on a jury:

> The period of greatest impact is pretrial because that could be anywhere from three months to a year. Depending on the coverage, people can become immersed in reading about the case. And from this reading-and-listening public come the people who sit on our juries. After the trial has begun, the jurors are given a rule — that they don't read or listen to media accounts of the case. Most people try hard to comply. But it's almost impossible with the highest-profile cases for it to really happen.
>
> When a case like [Robert] Chambers, the [Central Park] jogger, the subway bomber or the [first] World Trade Center bomber is on trial in New York — and it is literally a page A1 headline — our jurors are coming to work on the subway and the bus . . . I mean you can't sit on a train and not see what's there. . . . And you deal with a jury pool that is just saturated with that kind of information. You hope that you get jurors who are telling you the truth, that they can set aside what they've heard and just listen to the evidence in the courtroom. In the end, both sides use the press to great advantage before you get anywhere near the trial stage.

Further, while the plaintiff in Schiavone was acquitted at trial, Jovanovic was convicted. Thus, unlike the court in Schiavone, this Court cannot say with certainty that the jury lacked all bias in Jovanovic's trial. Taking Plaintiff's allegations as true, there remains a possibility that, after discovery, Jovanovic may be able to prove his claim. Accordingly, the Court will not dismiss Plaintiff's claim against Fairstein.

2.   Absolute immunity

Defendants next contend that Plaintiff's claim against Fairstein is barred by the doctrine of absolute immunity. It is a well-established legal principle that "a state prosecuting attorney, acting within the scope of her duties in initiating and prosecuting a criminal prosecution, is immune from a civil suit for damages under §1983." But absolute immunity only "attaches to the official prosecutorial function"; activities that fall outside the scope of initiating and continuing a prosecution are not entitled to absolute immunity. In light of this distinction, the Second Circuit made clear that "only qualified good faith immunity is available where a prosecutor distributes extraneous statements to the press designed to gain unfair advantage at trial." Fairstein made a number of statements to members of the press outside of the courtroom, in a manner that can reasonably be described as beyond the scope of her official duties as prosecutor.[5] As such, Fairstein does not have absolute immunity against Plaintiff's denial of fair trial claim.

3. Qualified immunity

Defendants argue that, even if Fairstein is not entitled to absolute immunity, she is still entitled to qualified immunity. The Court does not agree. The constitutional right to a fair trial, free from the taint of prejudice occasioned by a prosecutor's extrajudicial statements to the press, was clearly established at the time that Fairstein allegedly made extrajudicial statements to the press in 1996. See Powers, 728 F.2d at 105 (recognizing the constitutional right to a fair trial, free from the bias occasioned by a prosecutor's prejudicial, extrajudicial statements to press); Schiavone, 678 F. Supp. at 65 (finding, in 1988, that qualified immunity did not justify dismissal of a fair trial claim based on extrajudicial statements to the press by a prosecutor). A reasonable prosecutor would have known that Plaintiff's constitutional right to a fair trial might be violated by making a continuing stream of prejudicial extrajudicial statements. Further, Fairstein's comments to the Media Studies Journal imply that she fully understood the damaging effects of pre-trial publicity. Accordingly, to the extent that Fairstein actually committed the acts as alleged by Plaintiff, qualified immunity will not protect her from suit.

IV. CLAIMS AGAINST THE CITY OF NEW YORK

In Monell v. Dep't. of Soc. Servs. of the City of New York, 436 U.S. 658 (1978), the Supreme Court expressly held that local governments and their agencies may be sued as "persons" under §1983. Municipalities are not insurers or guarantors, however, and they are not liable on a theory of respondeat superior for the acts of their employees. See Walker v. City of New York, 974 F.2d 293, 296 (2d Cir. 1992). Municipalities are liable only for their own misdeeds, that is, "when execution of a government's policy or custom, whether made by its lawmakers or by those whose edicts or acts may fairly be said to represent official policy, inflicts the injury that the government as an entity is responsible under §1983." Monell, 436 U.S. at 694.

To ensure that a municipality is not held liable solely for the actions of its employees, a plaintiff must plead a municipal policy or custom that leads to the constitutional deprivation. Board of County Comm'rs v. Brown, 520 U.S. 397 (1997). The complaint does not allege an official policy, but rather a municipal "custom," which does not require official sanction. "[A]n act performed pursuant to a 'custom' that has not been formally approved by an appropriate decisionmaker may fairly subject a municipality to liability on the theory that the relevant practice is so widespread as to have the force of law." To prevail on this theory, plaintiff must prove that the custom is a widespread and permanent

---

5. To the extent that Defendants argue that Plaintiff fails to establish that the alleged statements were made outside the courtroom, defendant imposes a higher burden on Plaintiff than permitted on a motion to dismiss. Plaintiff alleges in his complaint that Fairstein made statements to the press outside of the arraignment or trial proceedings. Plaintiff provides quotes. These allegations are more than sufficient to withstand Defendants' motion to dismiss.

practice, such that it is "so severe as to constitute 'gross negligence' or 'deliberate indifference' to a plaintiff's rights."

Plaintiff alleges that the City had a custom or practice of permitting prosecutors to make extrajudicial statements to the press in high profile cases. Specifically, he alleges that the assistant district attorneys in the Sex Crimes Unit of the District Attorney's Office, when working on high-profile cases, routinely maligned the accused to the press, releasing information about defendants' prior arrest histories or criminal records and stating that the suspects had engaged in similar conduct before, even though there was no evidence to support such statements. In addition, Plaintiff alleges a municipal custom or policy of allowing New York Police Department officials to leak information to the press by making "off-the-record statements" that contained otherwise non-public information. Finally, Plaintiff alleges a deliberate indifference by the City to the training and supervision of Assistant District Attorneys, which was so widespread and severe that it led to a "practice" of prosecuting innocent citizens for crimes they did not commit. To support all of these allegations, Plaintiff points to other high-profile trials, such as the "Central Park Jogger" case, the "Preppie Murder" case against Robert Chambers, the sexual abuse case against Dr. Patrick Griffin, and the internet sexual assault case against Paul Krauth.

The Court must reject at this time the argument that Jovanovic's allegations are insufficient to establish municipal liability. Plaintiff alleges multiple policies or customs by the City and directly explains how they impacted his trial. He points to other cases in which similar conduct was carried out by City employees and he names specific policymaking officials that were involved in the allegedly violative conduct. While Plaintiff's allegations are vague, the Court finds they are sufficient to withstand Defendants' motion for judgment on the pleadings.

QUESTIONS ABOUT JOVANOVIC

1. Did Fairstein's comments really deny Jovanovic a fair trial? Does it matter how long before the trial the comments were made? Would it matter if the defendants can show that defense counsel was impugning the character of Jamie Ruzcek at the same time?

2. The opinion focuses on the third element of what Jovanovic must prove — that other remedies like voir dire and peremptory challenges would not have worked to protect his right to a fair trial. The court concludes that the pleading adequately alleges this element but at trial Jovanovic would have to prove that he was in fact denied a fair trial and that these other remedies were insufficient to protect him. How does he do that? The fact that he was convicted does not mean the trial was unfair. An innocent person can be convicted in a fair trial (as we know from some of the DNA exonerations) because a trial is art, not science. How can Jovanovic prove that it is more likely than not that Fairstein's public

comments caused an unfair trial? Who will be the witnesses? Psychologists? What about the fact that Fairstein's comments influenced the testimony of the People's witnesses?

3. A prosecutor enjoys absolute immunity "in initiating and prosecuting a criminal prosecution." Footnote 5 implies that Fairstein would be immunized if any of the alleged statements were made in court before trial, for example at arraignment or in argument on a motion. Yet the media would be there as well and can report whatever she may have said. So what is gained? If the extrajudicial statement prejudiced Jovanovic, wouldn't the same statements if made in court do so as well? Is absolute immunity too much to grant prosecutors, given the potential for opportunistic behavior — take care to make the inflammatory statements in court or court papers — and the harm it can cause?

4. What do you make of the chronology? It's telling isn't it, and raises a separate concern. An intermediate appellate court reversed Jovanovic's conviction on December 21, 1999. He was then released on bail. The New York Court of Appeals denied review in July 2000. The D.A. then offered Jovanovic a felony plea without jail time. No dice. Well, then, how about a misdemeanor with no jail time? Still no. Jovanovic wanted to establish his innocence at a trial. The People blinked first. The prosecution moved to dismiss the indictment in November 2001.

   What was going on here? The eventual decision to dismiss pretty clearly reveals that the prosecution knew it had no case. It would lose a retrial abysmally. Yet the indictment was left hanging over Jovanovic from July 2000 until November 2001. Is that defensible? Didn't the People have a duty, once the Court of Appeals rejected its appeal, to dismiss immediately? Why did it use the threat of a new trial — and a possible return to prison — to leverage a "no-prison time" plea bargain? Is it because a conviction, even for a misdemeanor, would have made it difficult, pehaps impossible, for Jovanovic to sue the city, the officer, or the prosecutor for violation of his constitutional rights? Is that a legitimate reason?

5. Why is the city liable for Fairstein's statements? Let's assume she did make the statements, which seems not to be in doubt. How could it be that a sophisticated prosecutorial office like the Manhattan D.A.'s office, and an experienced prosecutor like Fairstein, would let this happen? Some of the statements seem to exceed the bounds of what Rule 3.6 (and the New York equivalent) allow, don't they? Here's one possible (and worrisome) answer to my questions. Perhaps it never occurred to anyone that the statements were a problem. Perhaps the culture of the office had (d)evolved to a point where no one paid the issue much mind. If so, that explains why the city faces liability. Under §1983, the city cannot be liable on a vicarious liability theory. Fairstein's conduct has to be a policy or custom of the city itself, which means it must have been approved, through action or failure to train, by a person high enough to make city policy or establish a custom. That person might be someone at Fairstein's level and it would certainly be the District Attorney himself. So the lesson is that the city could have protected itself (or the D.A.'s office could have protected the city) by insuring that assistant prosecutors follow the ethical rules they swear to uphold.

A similar lesson appears in Goldstein v. City of Long Beach, 481 F.3d 1170 (9th Cir. 2007). Here the issue was not the city's liability, but the liability of the leaders of the office. The court denied absolute immunity to the elected D.A. and his deputy for their "alleged failure to develop a policy of sharing information regarding jailhouse informants within [their office] . . . to provide adequate training and supervision" on the duty to turn over exculpatory information. As a result, Goldstein was wrongfully convicted and imprisoned for 24 years. The defendants' appeal was argued in the Supreme Court in November 2008. For a case that resulted in the largest settlement for a wrongful conviction in New York's history ($5 million), see Ramos v. City of New York, 729 N.Y.S.2d 678 (1st Dep't. 2001) (District Attorney's failure to train or discipline assistants despite repeated failures to provide exculpatory evidence can establish city policy through deliberate indifference). Joel Rudin, the lawyer who represented Ramos, later won a $3.5 million settlement from the City based on prosecutorial misconduct that resulted in an innocent man's incarceration for 12 years. Jim Dwyer, Prosecutor Misconduct, At a Cost of $3.5 Million, New York Times, Oct. 22, 2008. For the fascinating background on the *Ramos* case, and how Rudin proved that the failure of Ramos's prosecutor to turn over exculpatory information was not an individual lapse but a city policy, see Stephen Gillers, "In the Pink Room," in Law Stories: Legal Ethics (Foundation Press 2006) (reprinted in the TriQuarterly Review, Spring 2006).

2. *Ethical Issues in Making the Charging Decision*

Rule 3.8(a) requires a prosecutor to "refrain from prosecuting a charge that the prosecutor knows is not supported by probable cause." That's not much of a rule. First of all, who could possibly argue with it? Prosecutors can't prosecute people who are legally innocent even if they think the target is factually guilty. What else is new? Second, why would a prosecutor waste resources prosecuting someone likely to be acquitted or whose conviction is likely to be overturned? I suppose one reason might be that the charge itself will shake loose cooperation in the probe of someone else or will force a plea bargain because the defendant, who doesn't know what proof the prosecutor may or may not have, doesn't want to risk a higher conviction. But Rule 3.8(a) does not recognize those motives as legitimate. Third, the rule applies only when the prosecutor "knows" the charges are not supported by probable cause. It would seem practically impossible to prove a violation of the rule. Sure, charges may turn out to lack probable cause (there are directed verdicts of acquittal, after all) but that doesn't mean the prosecutor knew it. You would need a smoking-gun confession, which is highly improbable. So why do I bring this up?

The ethical issue here is not whether, before proceeding, the prosecutor must have probable cause to charge or, as some would have it, whether she has evidence sufficient to support a finding of proof beyond a reasonable doubt (which is perhaps a higher burden). Let's say she has that proof. Then, she may charge or not, and if she charges, she may be able to select from a menu of statutes. Since no rule constrains her behavior, the choices truly are ethical in the common meaning of the word. When should a prosecutor refrain from charging under the harshest statute (the one carrying the longest sentence), even though she could do so, and instead use a statute with a lower sentence?

Remember lawyer Philip Russell (page 461). The prosecutor could have indicted Russell for misprision of a felony, the crime to which he eventually pled guilty and which carries a maximum of three years in prison. Instead, he was indicted on two statutes carrying 20-year prison terms. Assume the facts available to the government could support conviction of the 20-year crimes. So the U.S. Attorney's office in Connecticut violated no rule. But can it be criticized for using the 20-year statutes? Is it appropriate to use the harshest possible charge because the prosecutor figures that the defendant, facing a long prison term, will be more amenable to a plea bargain?

Before we go further, a little advice from the ABA. ABA Criminal Justice Standard 3.39 provides in part:

(b) The prosecutor is not obliged to present all charges which the evidence might support. The prosecutor may in some circumstances and for good cause consistent with the public interest decline to prosecute, notwithstanding that sufficient evidence may exist which would support a conviction. Illustrative of the factors which the prosecutor may properly consider in exercising his or her discretion are:

(i) the prosecutor's reasonable doubt that the accused is in fact guilty;

(ii) the extent of the harm caused by the offense;

(iii) the disproportion of the authorized punishment in relation to the particular offense or the offender;

(iv) possible improper motives of a complainant;

(v) reluctance of the victim to testify;

(vi) cooperation of the accused in the apprehension or conviction of others; and

(vii) availability and likelihood of prosecution by another jurisdiction. . . .

(f) The prosecutor should not bring or seek charges greater in number or degree than can reasonably be supported with evidence at trial or than are necessary to fairly reflect the gravity of the offense.

Now what do you think of the charging decision in the Russell case?

The following problem offers a more complicated set of facts. As they say, any resemblance to persons living or dead is purely coincidental.

"People v. Anita Winslow"

The County of Skyler, Montana, is a community of 21,300 people. Skyler is the name of both the county and the county seat. The major industries are ranching and farming. It gets a bit of tourism, mostly people on their way to Yellowstone or Grand Teton National Park. It's a typical rural Western town in just about every way, including one way it would have preferred not to be. In the last five years, methamphetamine has come to Skyler.

Sheriff Baxter Lovell and D.A. Sue Kochin have had to learn about the drug. What they have learned is that meth can be manufactured in a person's backyard from relatively inexpensive, over-the-counter ingredients such as

Pseudoephedrine — a common cold medicine. According to the Center for Disease Control:

> As a central nervous system stimulant, meth directly affects the brain and the spinal cord by interfering with the normal release and uptake of neurotransmitters (chemicals that nerve and brain cells produce to communicate with each other). Dopamine is the primary neurotransmitter affected by methamphetamine, but norepinephrine and epinephrine are also affected. The use of meth causes the release of large quantities of neurotransmitters. The neurotransmitters, in turn, cause increased heart rate and blood pressure levels and produce sensations of pleasure, self-confidence, energy, and alertness. They also suppress the appetite and enhance sexual arousal. Users may report sleeplessness, talkativeness, teeth grinding, increased body temperature, and compulsive behavior, such as skin picking. Long-term use can cause physical symptoms (decayed teeth, weight loss, skin lesions, stroke, and heart attack) as well as mental symptoms (paranoia, hallucinations, anxiety, and irritability) and behavioral symptoms (aggressiveness, violence, and isolation). The long-term use of meth can lead to reduced levels of dopamine and other neurotransmitters, making the user crave methamphetamine to raise dopamine levels. Because bingeing on the drug depletes neurotransmitter stores, coming down from the high is often described as a "crash," which includes a phase of depression. Additional doses of methamphetamine are often used to alleviate these negative feelings. This cycle can lead to addiction, which can be very difficult to overcome.

Early on, Lovell and Kochin had to deal with small meth factories, family operations, in the more rural parts of Skyler County. They thought they had put an end to it. But lately they learned that quantities of meth are coming through Montana from the east for sale on the Pacific coast. Some of it is sold in Skyler. They haven't been able to stop this distribution or trace its sources. They have only witnessed the effects of the drug. The victims of the epidemic include infants and children whose parents neglect them, whole families when a meth user withdraws savings or pawns valuables, and targets of criminal activity, sometimes violent, aimed at getting money to buy meth. Skyler is not the only Montana community afflicted with a meth influx. Lovell and Kochin are part of a group of police officers and prosecutors from around the state who are trying to contain it.

Anita Winslow is the daughter of a single mother. Her father deserted the family when she was three. Her mother works two jobs to support the family, which also includes Anita's younger brother Andy. Anita is 17 and a high school senior.

Lovell has been trying to make a controlled purchase of meth for some time in an effort to get information about distributors. But the users he finds have no helpful information about anyone higher up, not even their suppliers, who are rarely the same person from buy to buy. Over Thanksgiving weekend, Lovell gets lucky. One of his undercover deputies has arranged a controlled buy in the parking lot of a big box store. At dusk, a car pulls up and Anita Winslow gets out of the passenger side and walks over to the undercover's car with a paper bag; she passes it through the window and receives in return $1,000 in marked money. Lovell, in the backup team, recognizes Anita. The bag contains meth. The backup team planned to follow Anita and whoever was driving the car (identified as a male in his late 20s but his face was obscured by a wide-brimmed hat and sunglasses). The driver apparently suspected a setup and sped away. The police gave chase but lost him. They check the license plate of the car, which turns out to have been stolen in Minnesota and is found abandoned at the edge of town and wiped clean of prints.

Anita is arrested. The case against her is strong. The entire event was video-taped, and when Anita handed the bag to the undercover she made statements (recorded) showing that she knew the contents.

Lovell's investigation (mainly interviews with Anita's friends and her diary entries) reveals that Anita had been using meth for six months. She told friends that meth helped you lose weight, although no one in her family or her school thought she had any extra weight to lose. Lovell's investigation also reveals that Anita and the man driving the car may have been romantically involved for three months.

Anita is released to the custody of her mother but required to wear an ankle bracelet. A lawyer, Beth Wooten, is appointed to represent her. Two days before her next court appearance, Anita tries to board an interstate bus in violation of her bail conditions. Alerted by the ankle bracelet, police follow for a while, but fearful of losing her, take her into custody and remand her. Kochin tells Wooten that she's prepared to overlook the flight attempt and to prosecute Anita on the lowest-grade drug felony, which is the only charge currently pending. In light of Anita's age, conviction will permit a diversionary sentence of treatment and eventual expungement of the conviction. But as part of the deal, Anita has to plead guilty to the charge. She also has to tell Kochin everything she knows about her source and testify against him and others if needed.

Anita repeatedly refuses to talk to either Kochin or even Wooten. Wooten tells her that absent a deal, the quantity of the meth Anita sold would permit Kochin to prosecute under the top felony drug charge, which carries a mandatory sentence of 20 years to life. The judge won't have a choice, and while Anita would likely get out in 20 years, at age 37, there would be no guarantee. Wooten explains in great and unpleasant detail the conditions of confinement at the women's prison in Billings, which is a six-hour drive from her home. Her family will not be able to afford the time or money to visit more than three or four times a year. Wooten brings Anita's mother, brother, pastor, and best friend to the local jail to try to persuade Anita to cooperate, but Anita is adamant. At one point, she blurts out, "He loves me and will wait for me." This strikes the others as delusional, but, as Wooten knows, that is not the same as being incompetent to stand trial.

Kochin, Lew Tan, her senior deputy, Cody Miller, Montana's criminal justice coordinator, and Tom Whitehorse, the first assistant attorney general, meet to decide what to do. All have been working on the meth problem in the state, which, since Anita's arrest, has grown worse. A week earlier the police found three children under age five in a trailer park, all dehydrated and hungry, neglected by their parents, who were passed out in another trailer nearby. One child later died. It was the second death of a child in the state due to meth abuse. Many other children have suffered serious medical problems.

Whitehorse wants Kochin to charge Anita as an adult with the highest drug felony plus conspiracy and to seek consecutive sentences, which can lead to a mandatory minimum of 27½ years. "Conviction is certain," he says, "given the tapes and the mood in the county. She'll come around pretty fast after that. You can then ask the court to vacate the convictions. I realize it's out of our hands at that point. It's up to the court based on our recommendation."

"What if she doesn't budge?" Miller asks. "Her life will be ruined."

Whitehorse says, "How about the children who are suffering in this epidemic? I include the teenage users in that category, as well as the children of parents who are too strung out to take care of them. Aren't their lives ruined? We owe all of them to try to turn her. We don't owe Anita Winslow anything if she won't help us."

"Maybe whatever she knows won't help us anyway," Tan says. "The guy driving knows we got her, and he's going to cover his tracks. We don't even know if she knows who he is. Really is."

"We're only asking her to tell us what she does know," Kochin says. "She knows what the driver looks like. Things he might have said over three months that could give us a clue. We do know that in this period Anita disappeared several times and then lied to her mother about where she was. A Greyhound driver remembers her going to Yakima about two months ago. She was absent from school three days. DEA says that Yakima is a major distribution point for Portland, Eugene, Seattle, and Spokane. Big college markets. Maybe she was meeting her boyfriend. Maybe she met others. For all we know, she was carrying. Why else would a 17-year-old spend three days in Yakima?"

"She doesn't know what her life will be like at Billings," Whitehorse says. "She may think he'll get her out. What's that called? Magical thinking. After all, he loves her, right? She has no father, no male attention, not popular with boys. The only way we're going to turn her is if she gives up those delusions, and Billings is where that can happen. Fast." He pauses and looks at Miller. "Or not. And if not, as I say, we don't owe her anything."

They're silent for a minute, then Tan says, "You know if she were just a user who had no idea where the stuff came from, we would never send her away, or maybe for six months to clean her out. Sometimes we don't even prosecute if the child — and really she is a child — stays out of trouble for a year. I know why you want to treat her differently. But is that a valid reason?"

"If it could prevent dead or abused babies, it is. It's compelling," Whitehorse says. "If we can catch the bastards who are spreading this stuff in the state. This is the first possible break we've had. Sue, I realize it's your call. You're the elected D.A. The attorney general will support whatever you decide."

What should Kochin do?

"CONVICTION OR COMPENSATION"

Roseanna Lash, 41, was a film actress. She never played the lead, but she did get a lot of supporting roles because she had talent, a terrific singing voice, and the ability to play four instruments well. She was often cast as the sympathetic friend in whose company the leading man could find platonic comfort as he struggled with (a) his troubled career; (b) his family life; (c) his lack of a family life; (d) catching the bad guys; (e) his secret past, or (f) all of the above. Roseanna earned about $100,000 plus yearly. Roseanna's husband earned less than half her salary as a high-school Latin teacher. They have three school-age children.

Roseanna, riding her bike in Santa Monica, is hit by a drunk driver. The accident leaves her in a wheelchair for life. Her acting career is over.

The driver is George Paladin, an investment adviser. George admits to being seriously inebriated and is charged with vehicular assault and related felonies. His lawyer, Senta MacIntosh, tells the prosecutor, Dudley Washington, that George will entertain any plea bargain that helps reduce prison time. Dudley and his colleagues believe, consistent with other vehicular assault cases, that George should get a 30-month sentence, and they are prepared to offer that deal, which Senta says George will accept.

Then Senta tells Dudley that George has an umbrella insurance policy that will pay for any negligent harm he causes up to $5 million. However, the policy has an exclusion clause if the injury is caused during the commission of a crime. If George pleads to a felony or even a misdemeanor, the policy is inoperative. On the other hand, if he pleads to a traffic violation, which carries a maximum 15-day sentence, the policy will pay. Senta tells Dudley that George is prepared to plead to a violation and to state under oath at the plea that he had four martinis immediately before getting into his car and was unaware he was going the wrong way down a one-way street when he hit Roseanna. This would leave no doubt that Roseanna will be able to establish George's liability and, given her injuries, collect the entire value of the policy.

What should Dudley do? Are there any other facts you would like to know?

3. Throwing a Case (in the Interests of Justice?)

On June 23, 2008, the New York Times published a story by Benjamin Weiser that lit up the law blogs and garnered much discussion, especially among lawyers. Its subject was a Manhattan prosecutor who, contrary to instructions, stepped out of his adversary role and helped his opponents win. In colloquial terms, he threw the case. He claimed he did it to correct a grave injustice. Some lawyers and law teachers supported him. Some did not. Here's the full Times story, followed by excerpts from the ensuing blog discussions and D.A. Robert Morgenthau's response in letters to the Times and to me.

Benjamin Weiser
**DOUBTING CASE, A PROSECUTOR HELPED THE
DEFENSE***
New York Times, June 23, 2008

The Manhattan district attorney, Robert M. Morgenthau, had a problem. The murder convictions of two men in one of his office's big cases — the 1990 shooting of a bouncer outside the Palladium nightclub — had been called into question by a stream of new evidence.

So the office decided on a re-examination, led by a 21-year veteran assistant, Daniel L. Bibb.

Mr. Bibb spent nearly two years reinvestigating the killing and reported back: He believed that the two imprisoned men were not guilty, and that their convictions should be dropped. Yet top officials told him, he said, to go into a court hearing and defend the case anyway. He did, and in 2005 he lost.

But in a recent interview, Mr. Bibb made a startling admission: He threw the case. Unwilling to do what his bosses ordered, he said, he deliberately helped the other side win.

He tracked down hard-to-find or reluctant witnesses who pointed to other suspects and prepared them to testify for the defense. He talked strategy with defense lawyers. And when they veered from his coaching, he cornered them in the hallway and corrected them.

"I did the best I could," he said. "To lose."

Today, the two men are free. At the end of the hearing, which stretched over six weeks, his superiors agreed to ask a judge to drop the conviction of one, Olmedo Hidalgo. The judge granted a new trial to the other, David Lemus, who was acquitted in December.

Mr. Bibb, 53, who said it was painful to remain in the office, resigned in 2006 and is trying to build a new career as a defense lawyer in Manhattan — with some difficulty, friends say, in a profession where success can hang on the ability to cut deals with prosecutors.

Mr. Morgenthau's office would not comment on Mr. Bibb's claims. Daniel J. Castleman, chief assistant district attorney, would say only: "Nobody in this office is ever required to prosecute someone they believe is innocent. That was true then, as it is now. That being the case, no useful purpose would be served in engaging in a debate with a former staff member." The office has said it had good reason to believe that the two men were guilty.

Yet whatever the facts of the murder, the dispute offers an unusual glimpse of a prosecutor weighing the demands of conscience against his obligation to his office, and the extraordinary measures he took to settle that conflict in his own mind.

"I was angry," Mr. Bibb said, "that I was being put in a position to defend convictions that I didn't believe in."

The case also reveals a rare public challenge to one of the nation's most powerful district attorneys from within his office. As the hearing unfolded in 2005, Mr. Morgenthau, running for re-election, was sharply criticized by an opponent who said he had prosecuted the wrong men.

By then, the Palladium case had become one of the most troubled in the city's recent history, stirred up every few years by fresh evidence, heralded in newspaper and television reports, that pointed to other suspects.

It is not as if Mr. Morgenthau has refused to admit mistakes. In 2002, in spectacular fashion, his office recommended dismissing the convictions of five men in the attack on a jogger in Central Park, after its reinvestigation showed that another man had acted alone. "It's my decision," Mr. Morgenthau said then. "The buck stops here."

In fact, the prosecutor who led that inquiry, Nancy E. Ryan, was Mr. Bibb's supervisor in the Palladium case — though Mr. Bibb would not detail his conversations with her or other superiors, saying they were privileged.

Defense lawyers confirmed that Mr. Bibb helped them, though he never explicitly stated his intentions. Some praised his efforts to see that justice was done. Others involved in the case suggested he did a disservice to both sides — shirking his duty as an assistant district attorney, and prolonging an injustice by not quitting the case, or the office.

And some blame Mr. Bibb's superiors. Steven M. Cohen, a former federal prosecutor who pushed Mr. Morgenthau's office to reinvestigate, said that while Mr. Bibb should have refused to present the case, his bosses should not have pressed him.

"If Bibb is to be believed, he was essentially asked to choose between his conscience and his job," Mr. Cohen said. "Whether he made the right choice is irrelevant; that he was asked to make that choice is chilling."

At 6-foot-6, Mr. Bibb looks every inch the lawman, with a square jaw, a gravelly voice and a negotiating style that lawyers describe as brutally honest. He joined the district attorney's office right out of Seton Hall Law School in 1982 and went on to handle some of its major murder cases and cold-case investigations.

The Palladium case certainly looked open and shut in 1992, when Mr. Lemus and Mr. Hidalgo were sentenced to 25 years to life. Several bouncers identified them as the men they scuffled with outside the East Village nightclub. Mr. Lemus's ex-girlfriend said he claimed to have shot a bouncer there.

But the next decade brought a string of nagging contradictions. A former member of a Bronx drug gang confessed that he and a friend had done the shooting. That spurred new examinations by the district attorney's office, federal prosecutors, defense lawyers, the police, and the press.

When Mr. Morgenthau's office was asked to take another look, Mr. Bibb said, his supervisors gave him carte blanche. "It really was, leave no stone unturned," he said.

Over 21 months, starting in 2003, he and two detectives conducted more than 50 interviews in more than a dozen states, ferreting out witnesses the police had somehow missed or ignored.

Mr. Bibb said he shared his growing doubts with his superiors. And at a meeting in early 2005, he recalled, after defense lawyers won court approval for a hearing into the new evidence, he urged that the convictions be set aside. "I made what I considered to be my strongest pitch," he said.

Instead, he said, he was ordered to go to the hearing, present the government's case and let a judge decide — a strategy that violated his sense of a prosecutor's duty.

"I had always been taught that we made the decisions, that we made the tough calls, that we didn't take things and throw them up against the wall" for a judge or jury to sort out, he said. "If the evidence doesn't convince me, then I'm never going to be able to convince a jury."

Still, Mr. Bibb said, he worried that if he did not take the case, another prosecutor would — and possibly win.

Defense lawyers said he plunged in. In long phone conversations, he helped them sort through the new evidence he had gathered.

"If I make a mistake in my interpretation of what he said, he'll correct me," said Gordon Mehler, who represented Mr. Lemus. "If there's a piece of evidence that bears on another piece of evidence I'm talking about, he'll remind me of it. That's not something that a prosecutor typically does."

As the defense decided which witnesses to call, he again hunted them down — sometimes in prison or witness protection — and, when necessary, persuaded them to testify in State Supreme Court in Manhattan.

"I made sure all of their witnesses were going to testify in a manner that would have the greatest impact, certainly consistent with the truth," Mr. Bibb said. "I wasn't telling anybody to make anything up."

He told them what questions to expect, both from the defense and his own cross-examination — which he admitted felt "a little bit weird." Defense lawyers say they first met some of their witnesses on the day of testimony, outside the courtroom.

During breaks, Mr. Bibb confronted the lawyers when he felt they were not asking the right questions. "Don't you understand?" one lawyer recalled him saying. "I'm your best friend in that courtroom."

Cross-examining the witnesses, Mr. Bibb took pains not to damage their credibility. Facing a former gang member who had pleaded guilty to six murders, he asked only a few perfunctory questions about the man's record.

Daniel J. Horwitz, the other defense lawyer, said the help was invaluable. "Did Dan play a useful role in making sure that justice prevailed in that courtroom? The answer is unequivocally yes."

When the testimony was over, Mr. Bibb said he made one last appeal to his superiors to drop the convictions. They agreed to do so for Mr. Hidalgo, but not for Mr. Lemus — who was still implicated by "strong evidence," the office said at the time.

"I said, 'I'm done,'" Mr. Bibb recalled. "I wanted nothing to do with it."

Another prosecutor made final written arguments, and in October 2005, Justice Roger S. Hayes ordered the new trial for Mr. Lemus. Demoralized by the case, Mr. Bibb resigned a few months later.

A close friend, Robert Mooney, a New York City police detective, said that if not for the Palladium case, Mr. Bibb "would have spent his entire professional life at the prosecutor's office.

"He's brokenhearted that he's not doing this anymore."

In a brief interview after he quit, Mr. Bibb defended Mr. Morgenthau against criticism that the case had been mishandled. "There was never any evil intent on the part of the D.A.'s office," Mr. Bibb said then.

But around the same time, he distanced himself from the office's decisions in remarks to "Dateline NBC." He said that during the hearing, he already believed the two men were not guilty, but proceeded because he had a client to represent: Mr. Morgenthau.

"He was aware of what was going on," Mr. Bibb told the interviewer. "The decision to go to a hearing was not made in my presence."

As for Mr. Bibb's new revelation that he helped the defense, lawyers and others are divided.

Stephen Gillers, a legal ethics professor at the New York University School of Law, said he believed that Mr. Bibb had violated his obligation to his client, and could conceivably face action by a disciplinary panel. "He's entitled to his conscience, but his conscience does not entitle him to subvert his client's case," Mr. Gillers said. "It entitles him to withdraw from the case, or quit if he can't."

On the other hand, he added, Mr. Morgenthau could have defused any conflict by assigning another prosecutor.

John Schwartz, a former detective who worked to exonerate the convicted men, said Mr. Bibb did them no favor by continuing in the case. "He effectively took part in keeping two innocent men in prison an additional year at least, for not going with what he felt was the truth," Mr. Schwartz said.

But Mr. Mehler, the defense lawyer, said Mr. Bibb acted honorably. While lawyers on both sides must advocate for their clients, he said, "a prosecutor has an additional duty to search out the truth.

"I say that he lived up to that."

Today, Mr. Bibb says he does not believe he crossed any line.

"I didn't work for the other side," he said. "I worked for what I thought was the right thing."

Okay. The article outs me. I can't pretend to be a neutral casebook author/editor whose only interest is in collecting material to shed light on a difficult issue. But am I right? Maybe not. Imagine my surprise when, sitting in a taxi after a 19 hour flight from the U.S. to Singapore, my Blackberry alerted me to the thoughtful and critical comments of Professor David Luban of Georgetown Law Center, posted on Balkinization, a blog mostly aimed at lawyers and law teachers. David, whom I have long known and admired (and still do), has a Ph.D. in philosophy and is a national expert on legal ethics, especially the intersection between ethics (as in moral reasoning) and ethics (as in legal). So I knew I needed to "rethink myself." Excerpts follow, as do excerpts from the reactions on the same site from Professor Martin Lederman (also of Georgetown) and John Steele, an internal ethics counsel to a law firm in California and a lecturer in legal ethics at the University of California (Berkeley) School of Law. I conclude with comments from Anthony Barkow, a former federal prosecutor in Manhattan and now director of the Center on Administration of Criminal Law and an adjunct clinical law professor at New York University School of Law. He posted on the website of the American Constitution Society. I end with the views of Bibb's boss, District Attorney Robert Morgenthau, in a letter to the editor of the Times and separately in a letter to me. I thank all of them for permission to republish and gratitude, too, to Ben Weiser for tackling this important story.

Reaction in the Blogosphere

From balkin.blogspot.com

David Luban

I have great admiration for Steve Gillers, but in this case I think he's wrong. Daniel Bibb deserves a medal, not a reprimand.

Before I explain why, let's see what the ethics case against Bibb might be. Imagine that a private lawyer representing a private client did the same thing: located truthful but adverse witnesses, revealed his cross-examination, coached the opposing lawyers. And suppose his client lost. The lawyer did it because he thought the other side was right. First, there is no question that the lawyer could be sued for malpractice. As for ethics violations, the lawyer could be charged with violating the requirement of competency; the requirement that the client, not the lawyer, sets the goals of the representation; the requirement of diligence; and the conflict of interest provision. Conceivably the lawyer could also be charged with using client confidences against the client's interests, if any of his conduct was based on confidential information from the client. In short, a mountain of ethics violations.

Presumably, the same could be said of a prosecutor (except for the confidentiality violation);* and New York's rules contain counterparts to all these ABA rules.

But there is a difference. Prosecutors aren't supposed to win at all costs. In a time-honored formula, their job is to seek justice, not victory. It's a mantra that appears in all the crucial ethics documents. Fred Zacharias, a noted ethics authority [at the University of San Diego Law School], thinks that the "justice" prosecutors seek "has two fairly limited prongs: (1) prosecutors should not prosecute unless they have a good faith belief that the defendant is guilty; and, (2) prosecutors must ensure that the basic elements of the adversary system exist at trial."

But what, after all, did Bibb do wrong? He persuaded witnesses to show up in court and testify (against the state). Think for a moment about the alternative. Bibb was charged with investigating the case, and he did a yeoman's job to locate the witnesses. Bibb "and two detectives conducted more than 50 interviews in more than a dozen states, ferreting out witnesses the police had somehow missed or ignored." Once he had these witnesses' evidence, he was under an obligation to turn it over to the defense.

The alternatives: don't investigate the case for fear you'll find out that the guys doing 25-years-to-life are innocent; or, having investigated it, don't turn over the exculpatory evidence to the defense, violating your constitutional and ethical obligations; or, having turned it over, put the defense to the difficulty of locating the witnesses and getting them to court — so, if they don't succeed, the truth stays buried. *That's* the ethical obligation of a public prosecutor? Admittedly, it's weirder to have the prosecutor remind the defense about how the evidence fits together, and weirder still to tell witnesses what you're planning to ask them on cross-examination. But how does that subvert criminal justice? How does that harm anybody or violate anyone's interests?

This is the real question.

Steve Gillers says that Bibb subverted his client's case. But who is his client? Bibb himself seems to think his client was Morgenthau, the DA, but that's a misunderstanding. Prosecutors work for their boss, they don't represent them. The court record says that a prosecutor's client is the "people" or "state" of New York. That doesn't help much, but it helps some. It helps us to focus on the question of why the people or state of New York have an interest in two innocent men serving long prison terms. For that matter, wouldn't the people or state be

---

* Is that right? Does Rule 1.6 not apply to prosecutors? — ED.

better served if the police couldn't close the books on the Palladium killings, given that the real killers are very likely still at large? The fact is that Bibb didn't harm any discernible interest of his client.

And don't think that Bibb's conduct is totally unusual. A former federal prosecutor tells me that prosecutors often throw cases at the grand jury stage, because they think the case stinks but they're under political pressure to take it to the grand jury. That's less conspicuous than Bibb throwing the case at the hearing, but morally it's hard to see the difference; and if my former prosecutor friend is right, it's how conscientious prosecutors operate. To "seek justice, not merely to convict" means that prosecutors aren't supposed to be the ruthless partisan warriors the adversary system presupposes. Bibb was in a tough spot — ordered, for whatever reason, to defend convictions that he thought were wrong. He became a conscientious objector on the battlefield. His way out was unusual enough to land him on the front page of the New York Times. But he did the right thing, and hopefully *that* isn't unusual.

John Steele

How do the [rules in Article 5 of the Model Rules] factor in your analysis? We know that a subordinate lawyer can ethically do things she thinks are unethical if it is in a course of conduct that represents a reasonable resolution of an arguable question.

Suppose, for example, a subordinate lawyer thinks that the evidence doesn't meet the high threshold a prosecutor should have before trying a defendant — but the supervisory lawyer disagrees. Suppose further that the subordinate lawyer recognizes that reasonable minds could differ on that question. Finally, suppose that the law legitimately provides that the supervisory lawyer is entrusted with the final decision about going to trial.

Should the subordinate lawyer accede to the supervisor's orders and try the case, ask to be moved to another case, resign from the organization, or secretly subvert the supervisor's orders while pretending to follow them?

The only answer I can't support is the last one. It's deceit on the supervisor, deceit on the organization, and deceit on the court.

David Luban

First, I think the [Article 5] rules don't much affect the answer. Rule 5.2 says that even if the subordinate lawyer thinks it's unethical to go forward, he or she doesn't violate the rules by acceding to the supervisor's reasonable judgment to the contrary. It in no way indicates that the subordinate has to go forward, only that the subordinate can't be disciplined for going forward. In any case, I don't think that what the superior (Morgenthau?) asked Bibb to do was unethical in the technical sense of the rules. As long as there was probable cause (a pretty low standard), it was okay to continue to prosecute the two men. There is no ethical rule that says that a lawyer should not prosecute a case in which the lawyer is convinced that the defendant is not guilty; perhaps there should be. But, absent that rule, I don't see any of the [Article 5] rules being engaged.

Your second set of points is really interesting. Let's assume that you're right, and Bibb's help to the defense was done secretly, without notifying his supervisor. In that case, there is no question that he was being deceitful to the supervisor, and presumably the organization. That is a conscience call — he stayed in the case because he thought that otherwise the organization would go ahead and try to keep two innocent men in prison, after he had spent 21 months trying to ascertain their innocence. Obviously, he must have thought that the organization was working a serious injustice, after he'd given his best nondeceitful shot at stopping it. The stakes were not trifling — 25 or more years of two men's lives. Bibb must have thought that in the balance of evils, the deceit was the lesser one. And I agree with him.

But, third, I don't see why you think this was a deceit on the court. Putting on honest witnesses (I'm assuming) to testify truthfully, with defense lawyers drawing legitimate connections between the evidence, and Bibb asking honest questions on cross (even if the witnesses knew what those questions would be) is NOT a deceit on the court. It's a trial that's closer to a search for truth than the alternative. Maybe you mean it's a deceit on the court because the court is assuming a real adversary hearing, and instead it's a bit of a charade. But it's a charade in an upside-down sense: it's the kind of trial that would have happened if the defense was better and more heavily resourced. In other words, it's a *better* adversarial trial than it would have been if Bibb hadn't helped the defense.

Martin Lederman

The prosecutor here was the elected Manhattan D.A., who chose to go ahead with the prosecution. Let's look at that actor for a second. You quote Zacharias as saying that "prosecutors should not prosecute unless they have a good faith belief that the defendant is guilty." If the D.A. only thought there was probable cause, and not proof beyond a reasonable doubt, then it was wrong to go forward with the prosecution: There might not be any *ethical* rule that says that a lawyer should not prosecute a case in which the lawyer is convinced that the defendant is not guilty, but it's unconstitutional: a denial of due process. One should not be urging a jury to make findings that you don't think the evidence supports, when you represent the state and the jury's verdict will result in such a radical restriction on liberty.

But let's assume, as we must here, that the D.A. was not persuaded by Bibb, and concluded that the defendant was guilty beyond a reasonable doubt.

At that point, Bibb is acting as an agent of the D.A. If he firmly believes his supervisor was wrong, Steele is correct that he can — perhaps should — ask to be removed from the case, or resign. If he thinks the D.A. is willfully acting unlawfully, perhaps he should even make a stink about [it] to the relevant authorities or in public.

But act as an unfaithful agent? This may not be an ethics violation — but it's a violation of one's contract with the principal, a violation of agency principles, and, as you concede, a fraud on the D.A.

None of which, of course, answers the moral question whether one should commit all of those wrongs in order to prevent what one sees as a miscarriage of justice. You appear to answer "yes." I'm pretty sure (but not certain) that I disagree.

Yes, one could imagine an egregious case in which Bibb is confident that the D.A. himself knows the defendant is innocent: Even then, my inclination would be to say that the proper thing to do is to resign and, perhaps, reveal the wrong-doing in an appropriate manner.

But Steele posited that "the subordinate lawyer recognizes that reasonable minds could differ on that question." If that's the premise, then why should Steele favor his own (sincerely held) views to those of his superior? Why is he so confident that his judgment is better? Shouldn't his presumption be that it's not, when to act otherwise would be to egregiously abuse his role of the D.A.'s agent?

All of which is to say that your description needs a richer account — perhaps outside the realm of legal ethics — for the complex dynamics of elected officials who must act through many folks who are supposed to be trusted agents of the principal. Bibb is not a lone wolf here: He is part of an organization acting on behalf of someone else. That complicates the picture, surely.

David Luban

My response to Marty:

Let's assume that Bibb was indeed being a faithless agent of his elected-official boss. My two claims were (1) that he, not the boss, was closer to the prosecutor's ethical ideals as expressed in the official documents and — more importantly (2) that being a faithless agent of the DA is a lesser moral wrong than keeping two innocent men in prison for decades. You say you don't agree with me on (2), but I don't really understand why.

Part of the problem is the gap between what the minimalist ethics rules require (don't prosecute without probable cause) and what the "seek justice not victory" ideal requires (don't prosecute someone you think is innocent even if you have probable cause — indeed, even if and especially if you are sure you can win a conviction or a plea agreement). Let's suppose that both Bibb and Morgenthau agree that the probable-cause standard is met (that's easy), so no rule would forbid them trying to defend the convictions. And, as you say, let's suppose that Bibb is convinced they're innocent, Morgenthau disagrees, and that Morgenthau's side of the argument is not unreasonable. You think the subordinate should not substitute his reasonable judgment for the boss's. (Because the boss is elected? Or would you say the same thing if the boss was a political appointee?) I think that the most that follows from the superior-subordinate relation is that Bibb should think hard about whether he might be wrong. He should not be cocksure. Maybe he's gotten too invested in his own earlier investigation and lost his objectivity. Maybe he's overlooked something in the evidence that Morgenthau noticed. I agree that he must consider these possibilities.

But if, after considering them, he remains convinced of the men's innocence, I think he cannot in good conscience try to keep them locked up, and if he thinks that resigning will simply allow the DA's office to proceed with a terrible injustice, conscientious disobedience is the morally praiseworthy path.

Take a far more extreme case. One of the heroes of WW II was the German lawyer Helmut James Moltke. (There's a magnificent volume of his letters to his wife, *Letters to Freya*, in English.) He worked in the German foreign office, and stayed in his job during the Third Reich in order to do what he could to mitigate the evils. (He also belonged to the anti-Hitler resistance who created the July 20 bomb plot; he was captured and executed in grisly fashion, maintaining his dignity and courage until the end.) Moltke managed to save lives — kind of a lawyerly Oscar Schindler, but without Schindler's other vices. Moltke was, in your terms, a faithless agent, but I can't bring myself to criticize his choice to stay in the foreign office rather than resigning. — Don't get me wrong: I am not trying to equate the NYC DA's office with the Third Reich! My point is that someone who stays in a job rather than resigning, and sabotages a real injustice that the office is doing (and does so, moreover, without harming anyone) has a lot to be said on their behalf. Calling them a "faithless agent" is true, but it is only one factor in the story.

John Steele

My assertion about the [Article 5] rules was not that the subordinate is required to proceed, but just that under my hypo no ethics violation occurs if she does proceed. At that point, the subordinate is left with the choice of being nondeceitful (my first three options) or resorting to deceit (the fourth option).

As you are aware, being deceitful is generally not an option under the rules (e.g., 8.3 & 8.4) and is deeply problematic even if one takes an external view.

From ACSblog.org

Anthony Barkow

The focus should not be on Bibb; it should be on the supervisors who Bibb says ordered him to defend the convictions after he concluded the defendants were wrongly convicted.

Bibb alleges that, despite his conclusion — based on his two-year investigation — that the men were innocent, he was ordered to argue in support of the convictions anyway, and let the judge decide what to do. If Bibb's allegations are true, those who gave those orders committed an abuse of prosecutorial power. A prosecutor cannot and should not seek or defend a conviction if the prosecutor does not believe the defendant is guilty. No supervisor should instruct or pressure a prosecutor to do otherwise.

Every prosecutor's office has layers of supervision. Supervisors ensure that office policy is followed, approve charging decisions, and make sure that line prosecutors are neither too zealous nor too willing to offer "sweetheart" deals. Regardless of one's role, all prosecutors — whether on the line, in the supervisory office, or elected or appointed — have the same fundamental obligation: to do justice. No one in the prosecutor's office should let concerns about professional advancement or office image affect decisions about right and wrong.

Bibb's allegations of inappropriate pressure by supervisors to proceed despite his belief that the men were innocent should be investigated by an impartial body. If Bibb's story is true, his supervisors should be ashamed of themselves. And they, not Bibb, should be subject to disciplinary action by the bar — and by voters.

Robert Morgenthau
LETTER TO THE EDITOR

"Doubting Case, City Prosecutor Aided Defense," About Daniel L. Bibb, a Former Assistant District Attorney, Requires a Response:

On Nov. 23, 1990, Marcus Peterson, an unarmed 23-year-old bouncer, was gunned down at the Palladium nightclub. Two men were arrested and charged with the crime, which involved a number of participants.

The case against the two was based on substantial evidence, including multiple eyewitness identifications and a confession made by one defendant to his girlfriend. In December 1992, a jury convicted both defendants, who were sentenced to 25 years to life in prison. Their convictions were upheld in postjudgment proceedings in both state and federal court.

When new evidence later came to light, my office willingly reopened the case. Mr. Bibb was assigned to investigate. The investigation was protracted, partly because of the passage of time since the murder, but also because of the reluctance, the criminal backgrounds, the conflicting statements, and the dishonesty of a number of witnesses.

With the concurrence of his supervisors, Mr. Bibb kept the defense informed of the progress of the investigation and of the information developed as matters proceeded.

Ultimately, we consented to a hearing at which the relevant evidence would be aired before a judge. Even at that juncture, the investigation was not complete, as additional facts and witnesses continued to be found.

Given his familiarity with the case, Mr. Bibb was a necessary participant in the hearing. A second, senior assistant district attorney was assigned to conduct the hearing with him. Their mission was to conduct a fact-finding proceeding, with witnesses under oath and subject to cross-examination, affording us the opportunity to resolve substantial issues involving the weight and credibility of the evidence. In fact, the hearing resulted in the development of important new evidence.

Mr. Bibb was never asked to prosecute someone he believed to be innocent. He was asked to participate in a fact-finding hearing essential to determine the position my office should take with respect to two murder convictions.

It was only after that hearing that we reached a final conclusion as to our position regarding each defendant.

Ultimately, at the recommendation of every other staff member involved in the case, we consented to set one conviction aside, and determined that the second defendant should be tried again. We reached that determination because we believed him to be guilty.

To the extent Mr. Bibb disagreed with those conclusions, he was neither asked nor required to defend them. He did not participate in the retrial.

As the district attorney of New York County since 1975, I stand for the truth, and have taught generations of my assistants to do the same. Mr. Bibb recognized that in his letter of resignation, in which he wrote, "I will also always remember the consummate professionalism of the office and its unyielding pursuit of justice."

Robert M. Morgenthau

In a letter to me dated August 28, 2008, permitting me to reprint his letter to the Times, Mr. Morgenthau took issue with part of my quote in the story:

[Y]ou suggest that I could have "defused" any conflict by assigning another prosecutor to the case — presumably to conduct the hearing without Mr. Bibb. That was not, however, a realistic alternative.

By the time it was clear that a hearing was necessary, Mr. Bibb had been the ADA in charge of the investigation for over two years. At that point he was the only attorney who had met and interviewed all the witnesses, and he had an unparalleled knowledge of the history of the case. I did assign a senior prosecutor to work with Mr. Bibb and to conduct the hearing in tandem with him; but to reassign the case at such a juncture would not have been possible. The transfer of knowledge and experience takes time, and could only have been accomplished at the cost of prolonged delay in the proceedings. That would have prejudiced both the People and the defense, and in any event, would not have been countenanced by the court.

QUESTIONS ABOUT THE BIBB STORY

1. Luban argues that prosecutors throw cases in less visible ways: "And don't think that Bibb's conduct is totally unusual. A former federal prosecutor tells me that prosecutors often throw cases at the grand jury stage, because they think the case stinks but they're under political pressure to take it to the grand jury." What do you think of this argument as a defense of Bibb?

2. What do you think of Luban's analogy to a "conscientious objector on the battlefield" and his reference to Helmut Moltke? Luban later conceded that the conscientious objector analogy was "a bad one" because disobeying orders on the battlefield can lead to loss of life. But delete the battlefield. Is the conscientious objector comparison helpful here? Is Moltke's example helpful?

3.   A colleague at NYU offered a defense of Bibb by comparing him to whistleblowers who reveal government or corporate wrongdoing (often without going public themselves). We tend to approve of whistleblowing. We see it as an antidote to excessive secrecy that conceals misconduct and potential harm to others. Is that analogy useful?

4.   D.A. Morgenthau's letter to me says that Bibb could not be excused from the new trial hearing because no one else had his knowledge of the facts (a knowledge he gained as a public employee, of course). So the idea that the solution to these problems is to relieve the conscientious objector from handling a matter — a solution that Mr. Morgenthau generally accepts — would not have worked in this unusual setting because of Bibb's extensive knowledge. Bibb's only option if he remained morally opposed to the People's position would have been to quit. What of it, we might say; it comes with the territory. Does it?

5.   Luban's main argument seems to be that in the end justice was done and that should be the measure of Bibb's conduct and of the success of the adversary system, which is, after all, intended to produce the truth. That's a powerful argument. Who can argue with justice and truth? Does that mean that the legitimacy of Bibb's conduct depends on whether he turned out to be right about the defendants' guilt? How does Luban know justice was done? All he knows is that one person was found not guilty and another person was not prosecuted a second time.

6.   Where is the stopping place on Luban's and Barkow's argument? Could any assistant conscientiously opposed to prosecution after a long investigation "throw the case" despite the contrary, reasonable views of (and instructions from) her bosses? What should the answer be on the facts of "A Reasonable Doubt" at page 264?

7.   The court disciplinary committee in Manhattan investigated Bibb's conduct after the Times story appeared and concluded that there was "no basis" for any discipline. New York Times, March 5, 2009. Do you agree?

IX

Negotiation and Transactional Matters

He recalled that his favorite professor, Leonard Leech, once told him that, just as a good airplane pilot should always be looking for places to land, so should a lawyer be looking for situations where large amounts of money were about to change hands.

"In every big transaction," said Leech, "there is a magic moment during which a man has surrendered treasure, and during which the man who is due to receive it has not yet done so. An alert lawyer will make that moment his own, possessing the treasure for a magic microsecond, taking a little of it, passing it on. If the man who is to receive the treasure is unused to wealth, has an inferiority complex and shapeless feelings of guilt, as most people do, the lawyer can often take as much as half the bundle, and still receive the recipient's blubbering thanks."

— Kurt Vonnegut, Jr., *God Bless You, Mr. Rosewater*

Discourage litigation. Persuade your neighbors to compromise whenever you can. As a peacemaker the lawyer has superior opportunity of being a good man. There will still be business enough.

— Abraham Lincoln

Man is an animal that makes bargains: no other animal does this — no dog exchanges bones with another.

— Adam Smith

- *Client Fraud in Transactions: A Lawyer's Options*
- *Exploiting an Opponent's Error*
- *Issues in Settlement Negotiations*
- *Dealing with Unrepresented Persons*

"The Bad Builder's Good Lawyer"

MEMORANDUM

> *To:*   New Business Committee
> *From:*   Roslyn Hariri

"We've been asked to take a new case. The clients are the Sonibels, who purchased a second home in the Fair Mountain development. You recall the ads a few years back: high-end homes on three acres, lots of amenities, lakefront, tennis courts, golf, hiking trails. It has 52 homes in all, and the Sonibels, an older couple approaching retirement, bought one of the most expensive nearly three years ago. Assume we can prove the following facts, though we'll have to make a separate determination of that. The question for the new business committee is whether the Sonibels have a case if the facts are true.

"The builder is a guy named Howard Kluny. He'd been a home-builder 30 years. He started Fair Mountain more than four years ago, after he bought the Gerontin farm from Sam's estate. Kluny's lawyer, Lucy McIntosh, works — or I guess I should say she had been working — in-house for Kluny for about six years when these events occurred. Before that she was a real-estate partner at Berbash Kastenberg. A true professional and a pleasure to deal with.

"Lucy's job included preparing or reviewing three documents: She wrote the master contract for the sales, which then became a form with the sales force filling in the blanks (price, home, financing, closing, etc.). She reviewed the promotional materials and approved them, including brochures and ads. And she filled out the forms and wrote the disclosure statements filed with state and county agencies, including the state Department of Real Estate Development (ST DRED). Each of these documents represented that all systems in the homes would be above code. In fact, given the prices (the Sonibels paid about $2.6 million), each document specified particular brands and qualities for appliances and materials. For the plumbing, the documents specified Arrow Point as the supplier, and the top of its line specifically, known as the A-X line. Lucy's name is on the contracts as Kluny's lawyer and she signed the ST DRED filings.

"Lucy also handled the negotiation of the legal terms of the contracts and went to the closings with the buyers' lawyers. Kluny or his sales chief negotiated the economic terms of the contract — price up to a point, whether Kluny would put in an extra window, a cook's oven, whatever. The Sonibels' lawyer and Lucy spent about an hour on a few small changes, not relevant here.

"Well, it seems that before the Sonibels showed up to buy, there was a strike at Arrow Point, and Kluny couldn't get what he needed. Meanwhile, he was paying the scheduled plumbers, but he had to suspend work on the homes that were ready for the plumbing installation. When houses are ready for the plumbers, there's not much else you can do. Or so I'm told. Kluny could have terminated the plumbing subcontracts for a penalty, and stopped the meter that way, but then he might not be able to get them back as soon as the strike ended. He needed to finish the houses so he could sell them. He needed to sell them to show his lender the purchase contracts before it would let him continue to draw down on his line of credit. So Kluny was being squeezed pretty bad. He waited for a while. But the strike showed no sign of ending, and he was looking at mounting bills, and maybe thinking about bankruptcy, if he couldn't finish the houses and get them to market. He tried to get equivalent quality elsewhere, but other builders had the same idea and not much was immediately available. Also Arrow Point is the top of the line, and he had promised A-X Arrow Point fixtures, which is partly why the homes were so costly.

"So Kluny ordered inferior plumbing but still up to code. It was the best he could get at the time but way inferior to what he promised. This stuff went into seven of the 52 houses before the strike ended. When I say 'into,' I mean into. In the walls, under the floors, in the ground. And these are really big houses.

"The next thing that happened was that Lucy learned by accident what Kluny had done. She learned this months after the strike had ended in casual conversation with one of the subcontractors. She questioned Kluny, who confessed but refused to rip out the marginal stuff and replace it with what he had promised. The seven homes were done or nearly done. One had since been sold and closed, three were in contract, and three were on the market. One of those in contract was the Sonibel house. Lucy suggested telling the buyers the situation and reducing the price, letting them out of the contract, buying back the house that had closed, or make some other concessions. Kluny, a crusty old guy, wouldn't do it. He said the pipes he put in were good enough. And they were buried in the walls and floor. No one would ever know.

"Lucy quit her job the next day. I imagine she got advice from someone. But she said nothing about the plumbing to anyone or to ST DRED. Probably based on advice that her information was confidential. Couple of months later, the Sonibels closed on their house. Kluny got a new lawyer to handle the work Lucy used to do, and I'm sure told him nothing about the plumbing.

"Fast forward about three years. Two months ago, the pipes in the Sonibel house burst while they were abroad celebrating their fortieth anniversary and — I'll spare you the details — the house is unlivable. They burst around midnight on Thursday, January 3. The guy who checks the house for them twice weekly had just been by and all seemed fine. He didn't come by again until Monday the seventh. It is going to cost north of $200,000 to rip out the plumbing, repair the damage, and put the house back in shape. But that's not all. The Sonibels had valuable artwork, rugs, antiques, and a carload of stuff with sentimental value. All destroyed or seriously damaged. And, of course, they can't use the house for up to a year (not much work can get done in the winter). So the damages could hit above a million apart from any punitives. They have insurance, but it won't cover most of the loss.

"The Sonibels want to sue everyone. So would I in their situation. Kluny, the real bad apple here, is unfortunately broke or claims he is. If we sue at all, we'll add him but I'm not sure what we'd get. That leaves Lucy

McIntosh, who has a malpractice policy and significant personal assets. It's a terrible situation. Lucy is a good lawyer. She did the right thing in quitting. But maybe she should have done more. Warned people, ST DRED. I don't know. I hope I'm never in this sort of situation. So far the other six homes with inferior plumbing haven't had a flood, and the buyers are now all on notice and maybe they'll sue Lucy and Kluny, too. Their homes are worth less. But they haven't had the Sonibels' property loss.

"We've already concluded that Kluny's conduct is fraud under state law. My questions are about Lucy. Was her quiet withdrawal without any warning unethical? Did she assist Kluny's fraud by her failure to warn? Could she have revealed what she learned? Should we add her to the complaint?"

"The Case of the Complex Formula"

"My name is Michelle LeBlanc, and I represent a man named Chester in a divorce from his wife Phoebe. The couple has no children, but they do have a substantial amount of property acquired during the marriage, including a valuable art and wine collection.

"Chester and Phoebe have decided how to divide their property, but we've had prolonged negotiations over how to evaluate the items each will receive and the amount of any payments that the recipient of a particular piece of property will have to make to the other spouse in exchange for his or her interest.

"Kate, Phoebe's lawyer, proposed a rather complex formula for making this evaluation. I spoke with Chester about it, and we asked Phoebe to send us a written proposal that applies the formula and identifies a bottom line. Then, we would decide whether or not the proposal was acceptable.

"Kate did that, and I got her materials yesterday. In going over them, I realized, after a fair amount of study, that she made an arithmetical mistake in applying the formula to certain pieces of the art collection that the couple had decided would go to Chester. As a result, Kate underestimated the amount that Chester should pay Phoebe for these pieces. The upshot is that when this error is factored into the final number, Chester (who's getting a majority of the pieces) will have to pay Phoebe $515,000. But if Kate had not made the error, her formula would require Chester to pay Phoebe $721,000. Now, as I said, Chester and I have never bought into the formula. And we would not accept the $721,000 figure in any event. But we like the lower number.

"My questions are these: Must or may I alert Kate to her error without consulting Chester, or is this a decision Chester has a right to make? (He doesn't even know about it yet.) Do I even have to tell Chester?

"Second, if I don't have to tell Kate, or can't tell her if Chester doesn't want me to, and I want to take advantage of her mistake, can I just write back and say, "We agree to the $515,000 payment from Chester to Phoebe"? I won't mention the formula. Then, to make it less likely that she'll discover the mistake, I'll prepare the draft agreement and include it with my reply, again omitting any mention of the formula. Can I do that?"

Negotiating is not an intrinsically legal service. Persons who are not members of the bar frequently negotiate for clients without fear that they are engaging in unauthorized law practice. Agents of various kinds — real estate, literary, business, sports, talent, theatrical — negotiate large deals for clients. Most are not lawyers and do not have to be, unless they also want to draft the client's contract.

Although not every negotiator is a lawyer, virtually every lawyer is, at one time or another, a negotiator. It is practically impossible to have a legal career without some need to negotiate. Some lawyers negotiate rarely, others do so daily. Litigators negotiate settlements and pleas probably a lot more frequently than they try cases. How is it that lawyers have so large a share of the negotiating market even though negotiation is not necessarily a legal service? The answer seems clear enough for litigators negotiating settlements of their cases. They negotiate against the backdrop of the risks at trial, whose assessment requires legal judgment. But what about in transactional matters?

In part the answer must be circumstantial. Many clients who need services that only lawyers can lawfully provide under unauthorized practice of law rules — such as contracts, preparing instruments for filing in real-estate transactions, or establishing security for a loan — also need negotiation assistance directly incident to their need for the legal service. So, for example, a lawyer who has developed an expertise in copyright law may be asked to assist in the negotiation of the movie rights; a lawyer who has developed a specialty in the legal issues surrounding franchising may be asked to negotiate both the economic terms of the franchise agreement. Clients often negotiate the legal and the economic terms of their relationship simultaneously, or nearly so. What will be the scope of the "right of first refusal" and how will it be phrased? What are the parties' notice obligations? Where, how, and under what law will disputes be resolved? To the extent that terms of an agreement are legal or must be preserved in enforceable language, it is lawyers who have the training required (and usually the exclusive right) to do the job, and it is lawyers who know the "default" provisions supplied by the background law (if nothing is said).

What rules constrain a lawyer in conducting negotiations for a client? Certainly the status of being a lawyer representing a client will not shield the lawyer from personal liability if the lawyer commits or assists the client in committing a crime or fraud or actionable conduct. See United States v. Cavin, 39 F.3d 1299 (5th Cir. 1994); and Petrillo v. Bachenberg, 655 A.2d 1354 (N.J. 1995) (negligent misrepresentation), set out in chapter 13C. The lawyer also risks discipline. Rule 1.2(d) says that a "lawyer shall not counsel a client to engage, or assist a client, in conduct that the lawyer knows is criminal or fraudulent. . . ." Courts have upheld claims against law firms for knowing assistance, including through negotiation, of a client's breach of fiduciary duty to a third person. Thornwood, Inc. v. Jenner & Block, 799 N.E.2d 756 (Ill. App. 2003). But see Reynolds v. Shrock, 142 P.3d 1062 (Or. 2006) (lawyer not liable for assisting client's breach of fiduciary duty to third person). In *Reynolds*, the lawyer performed legal services and gave advice that allegedly aided a breach of fiduciary duty to plaintiff, but this work did not include negotiation as in *Thornwood*. Should that make a difference? Katerina Lewinbuk, Let's Sue All the Lawyers: The Rise of Claims Against Lawyers for Aiding and Abetting a Client's Breach of Fiduciary Duty, 40 Ariz. St. L. J. 135 (2008), parses the cases and the history of these claims.

The scope of a lawyer's responsibility to third persons when negotiating for a client raises some daunting issues in "big ticket" transactional matters. The term "transactional," as applied to a lawyer's work, came increasingly into vogue between the first and seventh editions of this book, at about the time male Wall Street lawyers started to copy the Gordon Gekko look (you know, from the movie *Wall Street*, where all the money men wore suspenders, had slicked-back hair, rarely smiled, perfected intimidating stares, and rode in stretch limos). The term has no precise meaning. It's sometimes used to mean "not litigation." But mainly it is used to describe the work of lawyers who do deals, usually very big deals. I've never heard of a lawyer who does residential house closings calling herself a "transactional lawyer," although the term would fit. Maybe that's because the more zeros in the value of a deal, the greater the need for an impressive phrase. Whatever the definition, the nexus between transactional work and negotiation should be apparent. Agreements or transactions with others require some amount of negotiation, often a lot.

Conflict, loyalty, privilege, and confidentiality issues that confront lawyers generally are equally pertinent to lawyers who negotiate. These topics are covered in other chapters of the book and some reappear here, where we address an issue particular to lawyers who represent clients in negotiations with other persons or entities (or their lawyers). How far can you go? This issue raises legal as well as ethical questions. Because lawyers often represent clients in large money transactions, if the deal goes south and an opposing party suffers a large loss, the temptation to lay the legal blame on the other side's heavily insured law firm will be nearly irresistible, especially if everyone else is broke. How can a lawyer protect herself from liability to the adverse client while zealously representing her own client's side of the deal? (These questions are further explored in chapter 13C, whose subject is lawyer liability to nonclients.)

The "Bad Client" Questions.   This chapter will focus on three questions for the negotiating lawyer. The bad client problem is first.* It is one subject of Rule 4.1(b) and is raised in "The Bad Builder's Good Lawyer." The question weighs loyalty and confidentiality against the interest in avoiding or minimizing harm to innocent victims of a client's illegal conduct. Which interest prevails in the event of a clash? Compare Rule 4.1(b) with Rule 3.3. A lawyer may have to correct fraud on a tribunal under the circumstances described in Rule 3.3, even if that means revealing confidences protected by Rule 1.6, as we saw in chapter 7. However, a lawyer's mandated duty under Rule 4.1(b) to speak up if "necessary" to avoid assisting a client's crime or fraud disappears when "disclosure is prohibited by Rule 1.6." This is true even though the client's crime or fraud will be financially devastating to third parties, even if revelation can stop the crime or fraud before it is concluded, and even though the lawyer may have been the unwitting conduit of false information.

Of course, a lawyer who discovers that a client is perpetrating a fraud or a crime on another cannot assist the client and will probably have to withdraw from the representation. Rules 1.2(d), 1.16(a)(1). But if the lawyer withdraws

---

* The second subject might be called the dissembling lawyer problem; and the third topic asks when, if ever, a lawyer must correct, or at least not exploit, an opposing lawyer's mistake or ignorance.

without alerting the former client's intended victim before the fraud is accomplished or when the harm can be avoided or undone, isn't there a risk that the victim will later sue the lawyer for failure to warn (see the famous O.P.M. incident discussed in the note on noisy withdrawals, below)? While the lawyer may defend by pointing to his confidentiality duty, the courts may interpret the tort law more expansively and find liability. After all, can the lawyer be confident that a so-called ethics rule will be a defense to a legal claim? Maybe. Maybe not.

Furthermore, the confidentiality duty may turn out to be illusory because of the exceptions introduced by the 2003 amendments to Rules 1.6 and 1.13. Rule 1.6 confidentiality prevails (according to Rule 4.1(b)) only when disclosure is "prohibited" by that rule. But Rule 1.6(b) contains six exceptions that permit disclosure of confidences. For example, Rule 1.6(b)(2) at times permits a lawyer to reveal confidential information to prevent a client's crime or fraud that will cause substantial financial injury to a third person. Rule 1.6(b)(3) permits disclosure even if the fraud is done but the injury can still be prevented, mitigated, or rectified. Rule 1.6(b)(6) permits disclosure of confidences "to comply with other law," thereby clearly subordinating the ethical duty to legal ones. When these or other exceptions are applicable, the Rule 1.6 prohibition on disclosure dissolves like the Cheshire Cat, and the Rule 4.1 obligation to "disclose" to avoid assisting the crime or fraud is left standing without an exception. Rule 1.13(c), dealing with lawyers for entities, contains its own exception to confidentiality, discussed in chapter 10. See Rule 1.13 comment [6]. So, often, the mandate imposed in Rule 4.1, which says "shall . . . not fail to disclose," though nominally subordinate to confidentiality obligations, will in fact prevail because there is no confidentiality obligation.

The Noisy Withdrawal.   This is the place to say a word about noisy withdrawals, an idea that was once as novel as it was controversial, but which has become less prominent (but still relevant) in light of the exceptions to confidentiality in Rule 1.6(b)(2) and (b)(3) and Rule 1.13. (You can get a sense of the noisy withdrawal debates by reading the separate opinions in ABA Opinion 92-366.) Think of a noisy withdrawal as halfway between quietly slinking away when a lawyer discovers a client's fraudulent or criminal designs, on one hand, and invoking the authority of a confidentiality exception to warn the victim by revealing confidential information, on the other. But how can you go halfway? Long ago and far away. . . . Well, actually, in New York in the 1970s and 1980s, a law firm called Singer Hutner represented a company called O.P.M. Without the firm's knowledge, O.P.M. officers used fictitious collateral (forged equipment leases) as security for bank loans. Lots of money. Believing that the collateral existed, the law firm had prepared documents that aided the client in getting the loans and made certain representations to the banks. The lawyers eventually discovered the ruse and confronted the client's officers, who confessed.

The lawyers sought advice from a local law dean and a practicing lawyer who taught legal ethics. The advisers said that the lawyers' confidentiality duty prevented disclosure to the banks and that the firm should stop representing the client unless the client promised not to do it again. The client promised not to do it again. The firm continued to represent the client. But the promise was as real as the collateral that didn't exist. When the firm realized that the client was still up to no good, it withdrew. Quietly. The client went to a new lawyer. The new lawyer called the former lawyer, a friend from law school, to find out why he had let such an attractive client go (it paid its bills). The former lawyer said something vague about a breakdown in the relationship. Soon enough, the roof fell in, the floor collapsed, and the client went up in flames. O.P.M. officers were convicted and sent to prison. The joke went around that O.P.M. was an acronym for Other People's Money. If a single incident can be cited as having the greatest influence on the expansion of exceptions to confidentiality rules, it is this debacle.

But I'm getting ahead of the story. Next, came the lawsuits. The banks wanted their money. The client was down the tubes. So the banks sued Singer Hutner, which was insured, among others. The firm's insurance company paid up (purportedly $20 million), revealing its lack of confidence in a defense based on a duty of confidentiality. But that wasn't the end of it. Lawyers everywhere worried. What if it happened again? (To *us*?) How should lawyers reconcile the confidentiality duty with the strong desire not to be sitting on the wrong side of a multimillion-dollar lawsuit brought by a client's victims? The solution was the noisy withdrawal, which the ABA Rules originally described in a comment to Rule 1.6, but in 2002 reworded and moved to Rules 1.2 comment [10] and 4.1 comment [3]. The idea is simple. Of course, a lawyer must withdraw from a representation if he learns that a client is engaged in a crime or fraud. Rules 1.2(d), 1.16(a)(1). The O.P.M. lawyers eventually did that, but they got sued anyway. So now, the comments say, when lawyers withdraw, they can also "disaffirm an opinion, document, affirmation or the like" that they may have given to the client's victim. That's the noisy part. The option is not always discretionary. If under the substantive law of accessorial liability, the only way to avoid "assisting" the client's crime or fraud is by disaffirming a document that the client could continue to exploit, a *noisy* withdrawal is mandatory. The conversation with opposing counsel might go like this:

"Hi, Hildegard. I just wanted you to know I'm no longer representing Crooked and Sly."

"Sorry to hear it, Sherlock. I've enjoyed working with you and your associate Watson."

"And I have to tell you something else, Hil. Remember that letter I sent you last March 5, where I gave you certain information about the deal?"

"Sure do. Very useful."

"Well, I take it back. Don't rely on anything I said there for anything whatsoever."

"What? Why, Sherlock?"

"I can't say any more. Bye, Hil." Click.

Clever, right? The lawyer gets to wave a red flag that should tell any sentient opponent that the deal is rotten. He thereby may prevent the harm or at least exonerate himself from liability for it (or so it is hoped). But at the same time the lawyer never literally reveals the client's confidences. The ABA was certainly ambivalent about this compromise. It placed it in a comment, not in a Model Rule. (New York, home to O.P.M., went further and put its somewhat differently worded version of the concept in its disciplinary rules.) As stated, the amendments to Rules 1.6(b)(2), 1.6(b)(3), and 1.13(c) have diminished the need for noisy withdrawal authority, because these exceptions allow more. They allow full-blown revelation. But the noisy withdrawal alternative remains relevant in jurisdictions that have not adopted the amendments. And even in those that have, it offers a route less traumatic than revealing confidential information.

Court opinions dealing with these issues in the context of negotiation are sparse, but one example is Matter of Potts, 158 P.3d 418 (Mont. 2007) (in will contest lawyer failed to correct misimpression created by client's statement about the size of the estate).

Questions About the Lawyer's Own Statements.   We've been addressing a lawyer's authority or duty on learning that a client is committing a crime or fraud. But what about the lawyer? Client crimes and frauds aside, may a lawyer representing a client in negotiation say on behalf of the client anything the client (or a nonlawyer agent) might legally be entitled to do in the client's behalf? Or are there ethical, though not legal, limitations on a lawyer as a negotiator that do not constrain the statements of others who sell negotiating services? If so, how can these be justified? Because the lawyer carries the imprimatur of bar membership? Because the lawyer, in addition to negotiating a deal, has the power, which nonlawyers generally do not, to put the agreement into binding form? Of course, to the extent we impose greater restraints on lawyer-negotiators than on others, lawyers may be competitively disadvantaged in selling services that nonlawyers may also perform. On the other hand, lawyers' special knowledge (and the existence of the attorney-client privilege) give them a competitive advantage.

Rule 4.1(a) tells us that in representing a client a lawyer may not knowingly "make a false statement of material fact or law to a third person." This prohibition does not depend on whether the false statement assists (or is) a fraud or crime. Lawyers cannot speak falsely to a third person or at least not *materially* falsely. The prohibition sounds right, doesn't it? But what exactly *is* false? We saw in chapter 7 how the words "true" and "false" have different meanings in the part of Lawyerland called Litigation than they do in Real Life. How about in the part called Negotiation? In what category would you place the following statements? How do you defend your answers and how do you differentiate between those statements you would label "false" within the meaning of Rule 4.1 (even if not true in Real Life) and those you would not?

a. "My client won't take less than $200,000." In fact, the client has authorized the lawyer to accept half that amount.

b. "If you don't lower your price, my client will find a new supplier." The client has told the lawyer that no one else can supply the particular product.

c. "We have documentary proof of the claim." None exists.

d. "We have an eyewitness that will (identify)(exonerate) the accused." None exists.

e. "We are considering very serious charges." In fact, the prosecutor says this to encourage cooperation and has no intention of charging the accused.

f. "That benefit would cost the company $200 per employee." In fact, the company lawyer in a labor negotiation knows it will cost only $20.

A Right to Rely?   When lawyers do make false statements in negotiation and are later challenged, they often argue that the opposing lawyers had no right to rely on what they said, that the adversary system entitled them to lie or in any event it did not entitle the opposing lawyers to believe them, and that the solution is for opponents to do their own investigations. This is a kind of "all's fair in love and law" argument. I am pleased to say that the next opinion dealt with it as it deserved.

FIRE INSURANCE EXCHANGE v. BELL
643 N.E.2d 310 (Ind. 1994)

DICKSON, *Justice.*

The principal issue in this case is whether, and to what extent, a party who is represented by counsel has the right to rely on a representation by opposing counsel during settlement negotiations. In this interlocutory appeal, the defendant-appellants, Fire Insurance Exchange, Illinois Farmers Insurance Company, and Farmers Group, Inc., d/b/a Farmers Underwriters Association (Farmers); the law firm of Ice Miller Donadio & Ryan (Ice Miller); and Phillip R. Scaletta (Scaletta), a partner in Ice Miller, are appealing the trial court's denial of their motions for summary judgment. . . .

The factual allegations favoring the plaintiff as nonmoving party are as follows. On May 28, 1985, sixteen-month-old Jason Bell was severely burned in a fire at the Indianapolis home of Joseph Moore (Moore), Jason's grandfather. Gasoline had leaked onto the floor of Moore's utility room and was ignited by a water heater. The fire department cited Moore for the careless storage of gasoline. The carrier for Moore's homeowner's policy was Farmer's, whose claims manager was Dennis Shank (Shank) and whose attorney was Scaletta. Jason's mother, Ruby Bell (Bell), retained attorney Robert Collins to represent Jason regarding his claims for injuries sustained in the fire. Collins communicated with Scaletta and Shank on many occasions in an effort to obtain information regarding the insurance policy limits. By October, 1985, Farmers informed Scaletta that Moore's policy limits were $300,000. In February, 1986, Scaletta told Collins that he did not know the policy limits, even though Farmers had already provided Scaletta with this information. Collins claimed that Scaletta and Shank told him on separate occasions that Moore had a $100,000 policy limit. Scaletta confirmed his misrepresentation to Collins in a letter he wrote to Shank on February 14, 1986. When Jason's condition stabilized, Shank and Scaletta each represented to Collins that Farmers would pay the $100,000 policy limit. As a result of these conversations, Collins advised Bell to settle. The agreement was approved by the probate court, and after settling with Farmers, Bell filed a products liability action against the manufacturer of Moore's water heater. Through negotiations with the water heater company, Collins learned that Moore's homeowner's policy limits were actually $300,000. Collins informed Bell that he had been deceived and advised her to seek independent counsel to assert claims against Farmers and Ice Miller. Bell filed a complaint against the appellants, alleging among other claims the fraudulent misrepresentation of the insurance policy limits.

Ice Miller and Scaletta each contend that they were entitled to summary judgment because of the absence of the right to rely, a component of the reliance element required to prove fraud. They contend that Bell's attorney had, as a matter of law, no right to rely on the alleged misrepresentations because he was a trained professional involved in adversarial settlement negotiation and had access to the relevant facts. With respect to the claims of Farmers, we agree with the analysis of the Court of Appeals, including its discussion and application of [precedent] and its conclusion that whether Collins had the right to rely upon the alleged misrepresentations by Farmers is a question of fact for the jury to decide. . . .

With respect to the alleged misrepresentations of Scaletta and Ice Miller, however, we grant transfer to recognize a separate and more demanding standard. This Court has a particular constitutional responsibility with respect to the supervision of the practice of law. The reliability and trustworthiness of attorney representations constitute an important component of the efficient administration of justice. A lawyer's representations have long been accorded a particular expectation of honesty and trustworthiness.

Commitment to these values begins with the oath taken by every Indiana lawyer; it is formally embodied in rules of professional conduct, the violation of which may result in the imposition of severe sanctions; and it is repeatedly emphasized and reinforced by professional associations and organizations. The Indiana Oath of Attorneys includes the promise that a lawyer will employ "such means only as are consistent with truth." Indiana Professional Responsibility Rule 8.4 declares that it is professional misconduct for a lawyer to "engage in conduct involving dishonesty, fraud, deceit or misrepresentation." Numerous other sources of guidelines and standards for lawyer conduct emphasize this basic principle. The Preamble of the Standards for Professional Conduct within the Seventh Federal Judicial Circuit begins with the following statement:

> A lawyer's conduct should be characterized at all times by personal courtesy and professional integrity in the fullest sense of those terms. In fulfilling our duty to represent a client vigorously as lawyers, we will be mindful of our obligations to the administration of justice, which is a truth-seeking process designed to resolve human and societal problems in a rational, peaceful, and efficient manner. . . .

Ice Miller and Scaletta contend that the plaintiff's attorney "had no right to rely on the representations he claims because he had the means to ascertain relevant facts, was in an adverse position, was educated, sophisticated and not involved in any dominant-subordinate relationship." They further argue "that the relationship was adverse, the negotiations were protracted and that both sides were at all times represented by counsel," and emphasize that policy limits information was available to Bell's attorney from a variety of sources, including the rules of discovery.

We decline to require attorneys to burden unnecessarily the courts and litigation process with discovery to verify the truthfulness of material representations made by opposing counsel. The reliability of lawyers' representations is an integral component of the fair and efficient administration of justice. The law should promote lawyers' care in making statements that are accurate and trustworthy and should foster the reliance upon such statements by others.

We therefore reject the assertion of Ice Miller and Scaletta that Bell's attorney was, as a matter of law, not entitled to rely upon their representations. However, rather than finding this to be an issue of fact for determination at trial, as did our Court of Appeals, we hold that Bell's attorney's right to rely upon any material misrepresentations that may have been made by opposing counsel is established as a matter of law. The resolution of the questions of what representations were actually made and the extent of reliance thereon are, along with any other remaining elements of plaintiff's case, issues of fact which must be determined at trial. . . .

Federal law imposes like duties. A lawyer's material misstatements *or omissions* can support securities law liability. Thompson v. Paul, 547 F.3d 1055 (9th Cir. 2008) (with citations to other circuits). In *Bell,* a client sued the opposing client's lawyer for failure to reveal the scope of the insurance coverage. Another line of cases has upheld claims by lawyers against lawyers. They arise when a client sues his own lawyer for malpractice for failing to protect him from an opposing lawyer's misrepresentation and the first lawyer then seeks indemnification from the opposing lawyer for any damages she is required to pay. See, e.g., Hansen v. Anderson, Wilmarth & Van Der Maaten, 630 N.W.2d 818 (Iowa 2001):

> We hold that once a lawyer responds to a request for information in an arm's length transaction and undertakes to give that information, the lawyer has a duty to the lawyer requesting the information to give it truthfully. Such a duty is an independent one imposed for the benefit of a particular person or class of persons. We further hold that a breach of that duty supports a claim of equitable indemnity by the defrauded lawyer against the defrauding lawyer.

Legal Opinions.   In treating the "what is false?" issue, we must also differentiate fact from legal opinion. Rule 4.1(a) forbids a lawyer knowingly to misstate the law as well as fact. But what if a lawyer merely ventures an opinion about the law, which turns out to be wrong? The difference is this: Saying "the court held X" when you know that the court held not-X is false. But saying what you think the case will mean in analogous situations is an opinion, even if you recognize strong contrary arguments. A mistaken opinion, if negligent, may create malpractice liability to your own client. But lawyers have no malpractice exposure to opposing clients for a negligent legal opinion unless they have accepted that responsibility, as by writing an opinion letter. Actually, the situation is a bit more complicated. As we see from the next case, a legal opinion may create liability because of facts that the opinion implies if those facts are false.

HOYT PROPERTIES, INC. v.
PRODUCTION RESOURCES GROUP, L.L.C.
736 N.W.2d 313 (Minn. 2007)

[Hoyt Properties brought an eviction action against Production Research Group (PRG) and Entolo, its subsidiary. Hoyt settled with Entolo and released

PRG. Before he agreed to release PRG, Steve Hoyt, a lawyer who owned and operated the plaintiff, alleges that he had a conversation with PRG's lawyer in which he said "I don't know of any reason how we could pierce the [corporate] veil, do you?" Hoyt claims that PRG's lawyer replied "There isn't anything. PRG and Entolo are totally separate." Later, Hoyt learned that a complaint in another action alleged contradictory facts. He sought to rescind the settlement so he could go after PRG, claiming that PRG's lawyer's reply was a fraudulent misrepresentation. To succeed, Hoyt would have to prove that the reply was (a) knowingly (b) false and that (c) he had relied on it. PRG's position was that the statement was one of legal opinion, not fact, and therefore not false, and that in any event it was not knowingly false. PRG won in the trial court, lost in the intermediate appellate court, and appealed to the supreme court. The court discussed when a legal opinion can be actionable because of the facts it implies. It then addressed what it means to be knowingly false. The part of the opinion dealing with reliance is omitted. Notice the two legal theories the court cites in the fourth paragraph as sufficient to deny PRG summary judgment.]

PAGE, JUSTICE: . . .

Appellants assert that the representations PRG's attorney allegedly made were statements of the attorney's legal opinion only and thus were not actionable. Appellants argue that Steve Hoyt's question, "I don't know of any reason how we could pierce the veil, do you?," solicited the view of PRG's attorney regarding a legal claim, to which PRG's attorney responded with the legal opinion "There isn't anything." As to the second part of the alleged representation, "PRG and Entolo are totally separate," appellants argue that this was also a legal opinion, and that the word "separate" is a legal term of art that "does not describe a particular factual predicate in a piercing-the-veil case, but rather, a general legal conclusion that piercing is not warranted." Hoyt asserts that the representation that "There isn't anything" "implied that PRG's and Entolo's business operations justified [the attorney's] conclusion that there was not 'anything' to a good-faith piercing claim" and that the representation that "PRG and Entolo are totally separate" was a direct factual statement bolstering the assertion that there were no facts supporting a veil-piercing claim. Hoyt further asserts that Steve Hoyt had no knowledge of the facts underlying PRG's corporate relationship. . . .

Here, the question allegedly asked by Steve Hoyt was, "I don't know of any reason how we could pierce the veil, do you?" Hoyt alleges that the response was "There isn't anything." When viewed in the light most favorable to Hoyt, as is required under the summary judgment standard, the representation "There isn't anything" is a representation that no facts exist that would support a piercing claim against PRG — for example, no facts indicating that Entolo did not maintain corporate formalities. Even if we assume, as appellants argue, that the alleged statement made by PRG's attorney was an expression of his legal opinion, that representation implies that the attorney was aware of facts supporting that opinion, namely, that there were no facts to support a claim to pierce the corporate veil. Because the representation was not an expression of pure legal opinion (for example, "I do not think someone could pierce the veil but I am not sure"), but rather a statement implying that facts existed that supported a legal opinion, we conclude that the representation is actionable.

We conclude that the second alleged representation, "PRG and Entolo are totally separate," is also actionable. Again viewed in the light most favorable to

Hoyt, the second representation constitutes a direct factual assertion that the relationship between PRG and Entolo is such that no facts exist that would allow the corporate veil to be pierced; for example, that no facts existed that would demonstrate that Entolo was a facade for PRG's own dealings. As such, it is the kind of representation that we have traditionally held to be actionable.

Having determined that the representations are actionable, we must next determine whether they create a genuine issue for trial. We have explained that, in order for the representation to be fraudulent, it must be "made with knowledge of the falsity of the representation or made as of the party's own knowledge without knowing whether it was true or false." For the purposes of summary judgment, we must determine whether PRG's attorney either: (1) knew of some facts that would support a piercing claim such that his representations to the effect that there were no facts supporting a piercing claim were knowingly false; or (2) made the representations without knowing whether there were facts that would support a piercing claim.

Appellants assert that the representations allegedly made by PRG's attorney were not false, much less knowingly false. Hoyt alleges that they were known or should have been known to be false when made. At this stage of the proceedings, the record as to whether the representations were knowingly false when made consists solely of the parties' assertions. Accordingly, the only way for the district court to have concluded that the representations were not knowingly false was to have weighed the evidence and assessed the credibility of the parties. Weighing the evidence and assessing credibility on summary judgment is error. Absent evidence in the record establishing, as a matter of law, that the representations were not knowingly false when made, we conclude that there is a genuine issue of material fact for trial on that issue.

The record is sufficient for us to conclude that there are also genuine issues of material fact for trial as to whether PRG's attorney made the representations at issue without knowing whether they were true or false. In his deposition, the attorney admitted that before he made the representations at issue he "knew what was contained in" the complaint brought by the third party. The complaint alleges a number of facts that, if true, would support the conclusion that PRG and Entolo did not maintain corporate formalities and that PRG would, therefore, be susceptible to a piercing claim. In his deposition, PRG's attorney also admitted that when he made the alleged representations at issue he had not yet formed an opinion, one way or the other, about the facts alleged in the complaint. Given these admissions, a finder of fact could conclude that when PRG's attorney responded to Steve Hoyt's question he did not know whether his representations were true. As such, there is a genuine issue of material fact for trial as to whether he made the representations "without knowing whether [they were] true or false."

Ausherman v. Bank of America Corp., 212 F. Supp.2d 435 (D.Md. 2002), refers a lawyer for discipline based on a false statement in the context of a settlement negotiation. The lawyer argued that his lie was merely settlement "bluster." No dice. The case is mainly of interest because the magistrate judge wrote an extended and thoughtful analysis of Rule 4.1, pulling together much of the case law and secondary authority, including this definition of the words "material fact":

> While the term "material" is not defined in Rule 4.1 or its commentary, it is not a difficult concept to comprehend. A fact is material to a negotiation if it reasonably may be viewed as important to a fair understanding of what is being given up and, in return, gained by the settlement. While the legal journals engage in some hand-wringing about the vagueness of this aspect of Rule 4.1, in reality, it seldom is a difficult task to determine whether a fact is material to a particular negotiation. In cases of real doubt, disciplinary committees and ultimately the courts will decide.*

Questions About the Failure to Correct the Opponent's Mistake. Finally, assume that the client has said nothing false, nor has the lawyer. What if the opposing party is just laboring under an error of fact that neither the client nor the lawyer induced? A lawyer realizes that her opponent has made this error. Can the lawyer take advantage of it? Isn't that what negotiation is all about — an imbalance in skill and knowledge that makes it possible for one side to gain the advantage, whether because of its own industry or because the other side is sloppy? The fittest shall get the best deal. Fair enough. But should a lawyer have any duty to correct a misunderstanding or mistaken belief that neither the lawyer nor his or her client created?

Maybe the answer depends on the nature of the mistake. Easiest is where the opposing party in a negotiation undervalues the property it is prepared to sell. It doesn't know about a planned commercial development next door that will double the value of the property. The buyer's diligence has uncovered this fact. We would all agree that the buyer's lawyer can (indeed must) keep silent. But how about "The Case of the Complex Formula," at the start of this chapter? Or those in the following opinion and note cases? Or in the "Ms. Niceperson" problem at page 87? Can you reconcile them? Remember that comment [1] to Rule 4.1 contains this foreboding warning: "Misrepresentations can also occur by . . . omissions that are the equivalent of affirmative false statements." So don't go thinking that silence = immunity.

VIRZI v. GRAND TRUNK WAREHOUSE AND COLD STORAGE CO.
571 F. Supp. 507 (E.D. Mich. 1983)

GILMORE, DISTRICT JUDGE.

This case raises an important issue relating to the ethical obligation of an attorney to inform opposing counsel and the Court, prior to concluding

---

* The opinion quotes at length John W. Cooley, *Mediation Magic: Its Use and Abuse,* 29 Loyola U. Chi. L.J. 1, 42 (1997). Have you noticed that magistrate judges write rather long opinions that get deep into the legal doctrines before them? My theory is that they do so not because deciding the cases requires it, nor because they are underworked, but rather because it's a way to showcase their qualifications for promotion. Nothing wrong with that, and some fine magistrate judges have been appointed to the district courts.

a settlement, of the death of his client. For the reasons set forth in this opinion, the Court holds the attorney has an absolute ethical obligation to do so, and sets aside the settlement ordered in this matter.

I

This is a personal injury diversity action. Pursuant to the authority contained in Rule 32 of the Rules of the United States District Court for the Eastern District of Michigan, the case was referred to a mediation panel for mediation prior to the final pretrial conference.

On June 2, 1983, plaintiff's attorney prepared and filed a mediation statement for plaintiff with the mediation panel. Three days later, plaintiff died unexpectedly from causes unrelated to the lawsuit. On June 14, 1983, the case was mediated, and the mediation panel placed an evaluation of $35,000 on the case. At the time of the mediation hearing, plaintiff's attorney did not know that his client had died.[2]

Several days after the mediation hearing of June 14, plaintiff's attorney learned of his client's death. A personal representative was appointed by the probate court on June 24, 1983, to administer plaintiff's estate, although no suggestion of death was made in this Court, and the representative was not substituted as plaintiff.

On July 5, 1983, counsel for plaintiff and defendants appeared before this Court at a pretrial conference and, after negotiations, entered into a settlement of the lawsuit for the amount of the mediation award — $35,000. At no time, from the time plaintiff's attorney learned of the plaintiff's death until the agreement to settle the case for $35,000 at the pretrial conference, did plaintiff's attorney notify defendants' attorney or the Court of the death of the plaintiff.

After the settlement was agreed upon in chambers and placed upon the record, as both attorneys were walking out of chambers to the elevator together, plaintiff's attorney, for the first time, informed defendants' attorney that plaintiff had died. . . .

Defendants' counsel claims that his sole reason for recommending acceptance of the mediation award was that plaintiff would have made an excellent witness on his own behalf if the case had gone to trial. . . .

II

The sole issue in the case is whether plaintiff's attorney had an ethical duty to advise this Court and defendants' attorney, who was unaware of the death of plaintiff, that plaintiff had died a few weeks prior to the settlement agreement. . . .

[The court quoted from EC 7-27, DR 7-102(A)(3) and (5), and Michigan's versions of Rule 1.6, Rule 3.3(a)(1), (2), (4), and (6), and Rule 4.1.]

The Court also cannot rely on case law to define the parameters of these Rules as there is a paucity of case law on the subject. Nonetheless, the following decisions are helpful. In Spaulding v. Zimmerman, 263 Minn. 346, 116 N.W.2d 704 (1962), plaintiff was injured in an automobile accident. In addition to plaintiff's

---

2. It should be noted that attendance of clients is not generally required in mediation hearings.

physician and two specialists, a fourth physician examined plaintiff at the request of defendants. The defendants' physician found an aneurysm of the aorta, which escaped the notice of the other physicians, and he reported this condition to defendants' lawyers.

Without disclosing this condition to plaintiff or plaintiff's counsel, defendants settled the case. Two years later, plaintiff, at a subsequent physical examination, learned of the aneurysm and brought an action for additional damages against the same defendants. The trial judge vacated the earlier settlement, and his order vacating the settlement was affirmed on appeal.

The Minnesota Court found that there was no duty on defendants to voluntarily disclose this knowledge during the course of negotiations, when the parties were in an adversary relationship, but that a duty to disclose arose once the parties reached a settlement and sought the court's approval. It quoted with approval the language of the trial court:

> To hold that the concealment was not of such character as to result in a non-conscionable advantage over plaintiff's ignorance or mistake, would be to penalize innocence and incompetence and reward less than full performance of an officer of the Court's duty to make full disclosure to the Court when applying for approval in minor settlement proceedings.

The Minnesota Court held that defendants' knowing failure to disclose this condition opened the way for the court to later exercise its discretion in vacating the settlement.

In Toledo Bar Association v. Fell, 51 Ohio St. 2d 33, 364 N.E.2d 872 (1977), an attorney specializing in workman's compensation law, with knowledge of the long-established practice of the Ohio Industrial Commission to deny any claim for permanent total disability benefits upon notice of death of a claimant, deliberately withheld information concerning his client's death prior to a hearing on a motion concerning the claim in order to collect a fee. The Supreme Court of Ohio held that this action violated the Code of Professional Responsibility and justified an indefinite suspension from the practice of law. . . .

Here, plaintiff's attorney did not make a false statement regarding the death of plaintiff. He was never placed in a position to do so because during the two weeks of settlement negotiations defendants' attorney never thought to ask if plaintiff was still alive. Instead, in hopes of inducing settlement, plaintiff's attorney chose to not disclose plaintiff's death, as he was well aware that defendants believed that plaintiff would make an excellent witness on his own behalf if the case were to proceed to trial by jury. Here, unlike the factual information withheld in *Spaulding*, above, plaintiff's death was not caused by injuries related to the lawsuit, and did not have any effect on the fairness of the $35,000 mediation award. But the fact of plaintiff's death nevertheless would have had a significant bearing on defendants' willingness to settle.

Also, while a personal representative was appointed by the probate court for the deceased, plaintiff's attorney failed prior to settlement to make a suggestion of death in the record before this Court, or to move for substitution of parties in accordance with Rule 25 of the Federal Rules of Civil Procedure. By not informing the Court of plaintiff's death, or filing a motion to substitute parties, plaintiff's attorney led this Court to enter an order of settlement for a nonexistent party. Arguably, this settlement order may be rendered void by Rule 25 [which concerns substitution of parties, including in case of death]. . . .

There is no question that plaintiff's attorney owed a duty of candor to this Court, and such duty required a disclosure of the fact of the death of the client. Although it presents a more difficult judgment call, this Court is of the opinion that the same duty of candor and fairness required a disclosure to opposing counsel, even though counsel did not ask whether the client was still alive. Although each lawyer has a duty to contend, with zeal, for the rights of his client, he also owes an affirmative duty of candor and frankness to the Court and to opposing counsel when such a major event as the death of the plaintiff has taken place. . . .

For the foregoing reasons, the settlement will be set aside and the case reinstated on the docket for trial. Counsel may present an order.

What Does *Virzi* Stand For?

That a lawyer must always reveal the death of a client? The death of a client who is a party to the settlement of a litigation? All facts that may be important to the other side in a negotiation? Courts have consistently upheld discipline of lawyers who conceal the death of their litigation clients citing, as the court here did, ethics rules and the court's own procedural rules. See, e.g., Matter of Forrest, 730 A.2d 340 (N.J. 1999) (failure to reveal client's death violated Rule 3.4(a) and Rule 8.4(c) despite the absence of any affirmative statement that client was still alive). How would you resolve the following actual cases? Should the settlement be invalidated? Should the lawyer be disciplined?

1.   A pedestrian, injured when two cars collided, hired Addison to represent him. The client incurred hospital expenses of about $112,000. One driver had a policy of $100,000 and a second policy of $1 million. The other driver had a $50,000 policy. When Addison approached the hospital about releasing its lien on his client's claim, he became aware that the hospital was ignorant of the $1 million policy. He negotiated a release for $45,000 without revealing the information. Later, the hospital learned of the policy and tried to withdraw its release. See State v. Addison, 412 N.W.2d 855 (Neb. 1987) (lawyer had a duty to disclose the second policy under DR 1-102(A)(1) and (4); failure to correct hospital's mistaken impression was a violation of DR 7-102(A)(5)). These provisions forbid deceit, false statements, and fraud. Addison was merely silent. Is it possible that *Virzi* is correct but that *Addison* is wrong? The opinion is short on analysis, putting it gently.

2.   *A, B,* and *C* are in litigation with *X* and *Y*. Previously, all five were clients of lawyer *Q* in a litigation resulting in a money judgment against them. *X* and *Y* paid it. *Q* then took the steps necessary to preserve the ability of *X* and *Y* to collect their pro rata share from *A, B,* and *C*, who were unaware of what *Q* did. (Did *Q* act improperly?) Later, with new counsel ("Boris"), *X* and *Y* sued *A, B,* and *C* for contribution. The plaintiffs rejected the defendants' offer of a $12,000 settlement. The defendants

then deposed *Q,* who denied that he had done anything to help *X* and *Y.* Whether he did or did not was relevant to the merits of the claim. Then, right after the deposition, Boris discovered documentary evidence, unknown to the opponent, confirming *Q's* secret work for *X* and *Y.* Without revealing the document, Boris asked defense counsel if the $12,000 offer was still open. It was. They settled. Did Boris act improperly under the Model Rules? Should the court vacate the settlement? This outline is based on Kath v. Western Media, Inc., 684 P.2d 98 (Wyo. 1984): The court wrote that the "sole issue in this case is whether appellees' attorney had an ethical duty to advise the court and appellants' attorney" of the facts. "We hold that he had such a duty." The court cited *Virzi,* DR 7-102(A), and Rule 3.3. Why? Does the result depend on *Q's* false deposition answer? Why was there a duty to the court? There is no suggestion that Boris was aware of *Q's* false testimony until after the deposition.

3. Plaintiff alleged that the county failed to hire her in violation of a law protecting handicapped individuals. Eventually plaintiff was hired, and the case was tentatively settled for lost pay. Plaintiff's lawyer demanded the retroactive pay that plaintiff would have received had she been properly hired in the first place and submitted a written settlement offer designating the pay at level "C." The county accepted the offer. Plaintiff's lawyer then learned that plaintiff's starting salary would have been level "D," which is higher. When accepting the settlement, the county's lawyer did not know, but thought it likely, that plaintiff's counsel had mistakenly assumed that level "C" was the highest pay level possible. Should the court grant the motion to vacate the consent judgment based on the settlement? Did the county's lawyer have a duty to reveal the other lawyer's apparent error? Brown v. County of Genesee, 872 F.2d 169 (6th Cir. 1989), denied the motion to overturn the settlement, concluding that "absent some misrepresentation or fraudulent conduct, the appellant had no duty to advise the appellee of any . . . factual error, whether unknown or suspected. . . . We need only cite the well-settled rule that the mere nondisclosure to an adverse party and to the court of facts pertinent to a controversy before the court does not add up to 'fraud upon the court' for purposes of vacating a judgment. . . ." Is this decision consistent with *Addison, Kath* and *Virzi*? What does "mere" mean?

4. The next case was the basis for an episode of *The Practice* (aired October 7, 2001). A prosecutor negotiated a plea bargain with a defense lawyer although, as the prosecutor knew but the defense lawyer did not, the victim of the defendant's crime had since died of unrelated causes. After the defendant is sentenced, he learned of the victim's death, and his lawyer moved to vacate the conviction, claiming accurately that with the victim dead the state could not have proved its case. People v. Jones, 375 N.E.2d 41 (N.Y. 1978) (prosecutor had no affirmative duty to reveal the victim's death; record contained no proof of "affirmative misrepresentation"). Is it possible to reconcile this decision with *Virzi*?

Transactions with Unrepresented Persons

In the following opinion, the court relied on Florida's version of Rule 1.7 but did not cite its version of Rule 4.3, which seems more on point. Florida's rule (like the Model Rules) said that when a "lawyer knows or reasonably should know that [an] unrepresented person misunderstands the lawyer's role in [a] matter, the lawyer shall make reasonable efforts to correct the misunderstanding." Nonetheless, the case is helpful for an understanding of the ethical responsibilities of lawyers where the opposing party in a transaction (or otherwise) has no lawyer.

THE FLORIDA BAR v. BELLEVILLE
591 So. 2d 170 (Fla. 1991)

PER CURIAM.

We have this on complaint of The Florida Bar for review of a referee's report recommending that Walter J. Belleville, an attorney licensed in Florida, be found not guilty of alleged ethical violations. We have jurisdiction.

In the summer of 1988, Belleville was retained as counsel for Bradley M. Bloch. Bloch had entered into an agreement with James F. Cowan to purchase property owned by the latter. Cowan was an elderly man, eighty-three years of age, who had a third-grade education. While the evidence showed that Cowan had substantial prior experience in selling real estate when he was younger, neither party to this cause disputes that the various written documents alleged to constitute the agreement overwhelmingly favored the buyer, Mr. Bloch. Cowan, in fact, has subsequently disputed that he ever agreed to some of the terms embodied in these documents.

Although Cowan and Bloch had negotiated only for the sale of an apartment building, the documents stated that Cowan was selling both the apartment building *and his residence,* which was located across the street from the apartments. The referee specifically found that Cowan had no intention of selling his residence and did not know that it was included in the sale. The record substantially supports this finding, which accordingly must be accepted as fact by this Court.

It is unclear whether Belleville knowingly participated in his client's activities or merely followed the client's instructions without question. Whatever the case, Belleville drafted the relevant documents to include the legal description of Cowan's house in the instruments of sale. Cowan then apparently signed the documents without realizing he was transferring title to his house. No one at the closing explained the significance of the legal description to him. Belleville only sent a paralegal to the closing and did not attend it himself. In fact, he had never met Cowan to this point in time.

In exchange for the apartment and his residence, Cowan received only a promissory note, not a mortgage. The loan thus was unsecured. This note provided for ten percent interest amortized over twenty-five years. However, the first payment was deferred for four months with no apparent provision for interest to accumulate during this time, and the note by its own terms will become unenforceable upon Cowan's death. Finally, the documents called for

Cowan to pay the closing costs, which Bloch and Belleville construed as including Belleville's attorney fee of $652.

When Cowan received the promissory note and closing documents, he realized that their terms varied from the agreement he thought he had entered. Cowan contacted an attorney, who wrote a letter to Belleville explaining the points of disagreement. The next day, Bloch attempted to evict Cowan from his home.

The referee recommended no discipline based on his conclusion that Belleville owed no attorney-client obligation to Cowan. The Board of Governors of The Florida Bar voted to appeal this decision, and the Bar now seeks a thirty-day suspension. . . .

Based on the facts, we cannot accept the referee's recommendation about guilt and punishment. The referee's factual findings established that Cowan had negotiated to sell the apartment, that he did not intend to sell anything other than the apartment, and that he did not know that the documents of sale would result in the loss of his residence. It also is clear Belleville should have harbored suspicions about the documents he was preparing, because the documents established on their face a transaction so one-sided as to put Belleville on notice of the likelihood of their unconscionability.

When faced with this factual scenario, we believe an attorney is under an ethical obligation to do two things. First, the attorney must explain to the unrepresented opposing party the fact that the attorney is representing an adverse interest. Second, the attorney must explain the material terms of the documents that the attorney has drafted for the client so that the opposing party fully understands their actual effect.[2] When the transaction is as one-sided as that in the present case, counsel preparing the documents is under an ethical duty to make sure that an unrepresented party understands the possible detrimental effect of the transaction and the fact that the attorney's loyalty lies with the client alone.

We recognize that The Florida Bar relies on *The Florida Bar v. Teitelman*, 261 So.2d 140 (Fla. 1972). . . .

We do not believe *Teitelman* stands for the proposition that an agreement by one party to pay the other party's attorney's fee always makes the payor a client of the attorney, provided dual representation has not occurred and provided the payor either is represented by counsel or is given the warnings required in this opinion if the payor is relying on legal statements or documents prepared by the attorney for the client. However, *Teitelman does* stand for the proposition that an attorney must avoid the appearance of simultaneously representing adverse interests, especially where the opposing party may be unfairly induced to rely on the attorney's advice or skill in preparing legal documents. Here, Belleville breached that duty.

For the foregoing reasons, we adopt the referee's findings of fact but reject the recommendations regarding guilt and discipline. The violation Belleville committed is a serious one in light of the fact that he previously has been disciplined for an ethical violation.

---

2. We limit this holding to the facts of this case. We have no intent to mandate that an attorney who has prepared documents for a real estate closing always must be present at the closing to explain the documents to the respective parties.

Accordingly, we grant the request of The Florida Bar. Walter J. Belleville is hereby suspended from the practice of law for a period of thirty days. . . .

It is so ordered.

Belleville drafted the papers after his client and Cowan cut a deal. The court says Belleville had a duty to Cowan, whom he had never met, because by drafting the documents he created the "appearance" of representing both sides of the case. Belleville had to disabuse Cowan of any such assumption with the warning the court spelled out. But there is no suggestion that Belleville did anything to encourage Cowan to trust him or to think that Belleville was his lawyer, too. So the court is creating an affirmative obligation, not merely a duty to avoid misunderstanding. How far does this go? In note 2, the court "limit[s] this holding to the facts of this case." What does that mean? Is the case limited to real estate? What if a nephew asks his lawyer to draft a power of attorney to run from his elderly, unrepresented aunt to the nephew? Does the lawyer have to meet the aunt and make sure she understands what she's doing?

Negotiating with an Unrepresented and Dangerous Fugitive

After the police discovered a grisly and sadistic triple homicide, they made cell phone contact with William Neal, the killer, but they did not know where he was. Neal said he would not surrender without legal representation and mentioned the name of a public defender (PD) who had once represented him. Working with the police was Mark Pautler, the Chief Deputy District Attorney. Pautler tried to locate the lawyer Neal named but could not. Matter of Pautler, 47 P.3d 1175 (Colo. 2002), tells what happened next:

> When Neal again requested to speak to an attorney, Sheriff Moore told him that "the PD has just walked in," and that the PD's name was "Mark Palmer," a pseudonym Pautler had chosen for himself. Moore proceeded to brief "Palmer" on the events thus far, with Neal listening over the telephone. Moore then introduced Pautler to Neal as a PD. Pautler took the telephone and engaged Neal in conversation. Neal communicated to Pautler that he sought three guarantees from the sheriff's office before he would surrender: (1) that he would be isolated from other detainees, (2) that he could smoke cigarettes, and (3) that "his lawyer" would be present. To the latter request, Pautler answered, "Right, I'll be present."
>
> Neal also asked, "Now, um, at this point, I want to know, um, what my rights are — you feel my rights are right now." Pautler did not answer the question directly, but asked for clarification. Neal then indicated he sought assurance that the sheriff's office would honor the promises made. Pautler communicated to Neal that he believed the sheriff's department would keep him isolated as requested. Pautler did not explain to Neal any additional rights, nor did Neal request more information on the topic. In later conversations, it was clear that Neal believed "Mark Palmer" from the PD's office represented him.
>
> Neal eventually surrendered to law enforcement without incident. An officer involved in the arrest approached Pautler with the news that Neal

had asked whether his attorney was present. Pautler was at the scene but did not speak with Neal, although he asked the officer to tell Neal that the attorney was indeed present. Evidence at the hearing indicated that Neal was put into a holding cell by himself and received his requested cigarettes as well as a telephone call.

Pautler made no effort to correct his misrepresentations to Neal that evening, nor in the days following. James Aber, head of the Jefferson County Public Defender's office, eventually undertook Neal's defense. Aber only learned of the deception two weeks later when listening to the tapes of the conversation, whereupon he recognized Pautler's voice. Aber testified at Pautler's [disciplinary] trial that he was confused when Neal initially said that a Mark Palmer already represented him. Aber told the board that he had difficulty establishing a trusting relationship with the defendant after he told Neal that no Mark Palmer existed within the PD's office. Several months later Neal dismissed the PD's office and continued his case pro se, with advisory counsel appointed by the court. Ultimately, Neal was convicted of the murders and received the death penalty. The parties dispute whether Neal dismissed Aber out of the mistrust precipitated by Pautler's earlier deception.

Attorney Regulation Counsel charged Pautler with violating both Colo. RPC 8.4(c) and 4.3 of the Colorado Rules of Professional Conduct ("Rules"). The presiding disciplinary judge granted summary judgment against Pautler on Rule 8.4(c); the 4.3 charge went to a hearing board because the judge ruled that (1) whether Neal was represented, and (2) whether Pautler gave advice, were disputed questions of fact. The board subsequently found that Pautler violated Rule 4.3. With one dissent, the board set the sanction for both violations at three months suspension, with a stay granted during twelve months of probation. During that period, Pautler was to retake the MPRE, take twenty hours of CLE credits in ethics, have a supervisor present whenever he engaged in any activity implicating Colo. RPC 4.3, and pay the costs of the proceedings.

Pautler made the novel argument that his conduct was justified by the threat of imminent public harm. Indeed, on the phone with the police, Neal had made "references to his continued ability to kill." The court left open the possibility that an "imminent public harm" might justify violation of an ethics rule on the right facts. (One hopes so.) But here, the court wrote, Pautler had an alternative.

"He had telephone numbers and a telephone and could have called a PD." The court added that "nothing [Neal said on the phone] indicated that any specific person's safety was in imminent danger." On the Rule 8.3 charge, the court wrote that the

> rule targets precisely the conduct in which Pautler engaged. . . . Pautler deceived Neal and then took no steps to correct the misunderstanding either at the time of arrest or in the days following. Pautler's failure in this respect was an opportunity lost. Where he could have tempered the negative consequences resulting from the deception, he instead allowed them to linger.

So is it the lingering that made the difference? On Rule 4.3 as well?

Threatening Criminal Prosecution or Discipline

The Code said a lawyer could not threaten criminal prosecution in order to gain an advantage in a civil matter, as in: "If you don't pay us the ten grand, we're going to the feds." DR 7-105(A). The Rules intentionally omitted this provision. Was that a mistake? Will the law of extortion fill the gap in any event, which would mean that so long as the threat is not illegal, it's ethical (unless another rule is violated)? ABA Opinion 92-363 concluded that a lawyer can raise the possibility of criminal charges in negotiating a civil claim, so long as the civil and criminal matters are related and the lawyer does not claim an improper influence over the criminal process. If the law allows, the lawyer can also agree to refrain from presenting the criminal charges. State v. Worsham, 957 P.2d 549 (Okla. 1998), cites this opinion in declining to discipline a lawyer who said that, absent a settlement of her client's claims, the client "will contact the District Attorney concerning the filing of criminal charges."

Some states, although adopting the Rules, have retained the Code provision. The District of Columbia, expanding it, forbids a lawyer to "[s]eek or threaten to seek criminal charges or disciplinary charges solely to obtain an advantage in a civil matter." D.C. Rule 8.4(g). California Rule 5-100 forbids a lawyer to "threaten to present criminal, administrative, or disciplinary charges to obtain an advantage in a civil dispute." Although the Florida rules are silent on the matter, Florida Opinion 89-3 reads them to continue the prohibition. Florida Opinion 94-5 extends the restriction to threats of disciplinary action. In reasoning that is a bit of a stretch, the ABA has concluded that even though the Model Rules do not "expressly" forbid threatening to file a disciplinary charge against opposing counsel, "there will frequently be circumstances in which such a threat will violate Rule 8.3" or other rules. ABA Opinion 94-383.

Michigan Opinion RI-78 (1991), by contrast, concludes that elimination of DR 7-105(A) was intentional. As a result, in negotiating a claim a Michigan lawyer in good faith may refer to possible criminal liability, may advise a client to pursue criminal prosecution in order to advance a civil claim, and may have a client agree not to report criminal conduct as a condition of settling a civil claim. The opinion concludes that abusive or harassing conduct can still be addressed by the Rules. Of course, none of these opinions can determine whether particular conduct is, or is not, criminal.

FURTHER READING

Some practices on the legal ethics map have gone largely unexamined, perhaps because no constituency is powerful enough to bring them to notice. This is true for the many civil litigations—and the attendant settlement negotiations—between a represented party and a legally indigent party who acts pro se. An example is housing court, where landlords, with counsel, oppose unrepresented tenants. Other examples are family law and consumer cases. Rule 4.3 and DR 7-104(A)(2) impose certain limits, though not the same ones, on lawyers who speak with unrepresented persons. Russell Engler examines what really goes on when lawyers negotiate with unrepresented persons, using the New York City Housing Court as his primary (but not his only) empirical source.

He concludes that ethics rules are routinely ignored in these venues, and he makes detailed suggestions of ways to correct the problem, including professional discipline, new rules, court oversight, and provision of counsel. Russell Engler, Out of Sight and Out of Line: The Need for Regulation of Lawyers' Negotiations With Unrepresented Poor Persons, 85 Cal. L. Rev. 79 (1997).

Other works on negotiation include Professor Gerald Wetlaufer's attempt to define "lying" in the context of negotiation. He offers an ethical analysis of this conduct and a "taxonomy of distinctions, excuses, and justifications" that the profession advances for lying in negotiation. Gerald Wetlaufer, The Ethics of Lying in Negotiations, 75 Iowa L. Rev. 1219 (1990). See also Judge Alvin Rubin's well-known discussion of negotiation ethics in A Causerie on Lawyers' Ethics in Negotiation, 35 La. L. Rev. 577 (1975). While the Model Rules were under consideration, Professor James White closely examined the implications of several proposals, using hypotheticals and recommending appropriate resolutions. James White, Machiavelli and the Bar: Ethical Limitations on Lying in Negotiation, 1980 Am. B. Found. Res. J. 926.

X

Lawyers for Companies and Other Organizations

- *Client Identity*
- *Internal Corporate Investigations*
- *Confidentiality and Conflicts*
- *No Taking Sides*
- *Retaliatory Discharge*

Introduction: Caught in the Internal (Eternal?) Triangle, or "Who's Your Client?"

Lawyers for an organization—for example, a corporation, government, union, or limited or general partnership—can confront especially tough professional problems. (The material on confidentiality introduced some of them. See chapter 2B.) These problems often flow from the fact that while the lawyer's client is the organization, the lawyer must represent it through its officers and agents, who usually are not clients. The resulting triangular arrangement is different from the one confronting lawyers employed by an insurer to represent an insured. See page 299. (Do you see how? Try diagramming each arrangement.)

In a single sentence, Rule 1.13(a) attempts to define the relationships between lawyers, corporate constituents, and the company. Does it succeed? Drafts of this sentence had put it differently. They said that a lawyer represents an entity "as distinct from its" constituents. What is the difference between representing an entity "as distinct from" its constituents and representing it by "acting through" its constituents, as Rule 1.13(a) finally put it? I find the difference merely atmospheric. "Distinct" creates more of a separation between lawyers and constituents than some corporate lawyers wanted. But the fact remains that while a constituent may be the lawyer's boss, she is not the lawyer's client.

Many of the issues that arise when a lawyer represents a company* are the same as those that confront all lawyers: issues of loyalty, conflicts, client identity,

---

* We will talk here about companies because they are the most common organizational client aside from government.

confidentiality, and the duty not to aid a client's crimes and frauds. When a client is represented "through" others and is itself a legal fiction, however, these problems can become exponentially more complex. The situation is further complicated when a lawyer is employed, rather than retained, by the company-client. A single-client lawyer is in an especially vulnerable position, isn't she? Company management will have significant control over her professional life — her title, income, assignments, office space, expense account, promotion, and support staff. Put her in a small city with a mortgage and two children headed for college, and we can begin to see the threat to professional independence. Yet her job, of course, is to protect her client, even as against the bad behavior of the management that has so much control over her life. While such facts are supposed to be irrelevant to how the lawyer acts, realistically, they may be hard to ignore when faced with a duty to her client that the CEO suggests she overlook. ("Don't be such a Goody Two-Shoes. Learn how to play ball.") The suggestion doesn't have to be explicit. Retained lawyers can be more independent, but not very much so if the company is their biggest client, producing most of their income.

What should general counsel of a large corporation do if a high-ranking officer tells her the following:

1. He is about to implement a business decision that the lawyer believes is unwise but defensible.
2. He is about to implement a business decision that the lawyer is certain will result in a substantial loss for the corporation.
3. He is about to implement a business decision that the lawyer recognizes could be profitable but which she also believes may subject the company to civil antitrust liability.
4. He is about to implement a business decision that the lawyer recognizes could be profitable but which will certainly subject the company to substantial damages for fraud if discovered and may even be criminal.
5. He is about to take action that will personally benefit the officer at the expense of the company and will violate the officer's fiduciary obligation to the corporation.

In responding to each of these situations, how much guidance does Rule 1.13 provide? How, if at all, might the lawyer's answers change if, instead of an officer of the corporation, the board of directors authorized (or tolerated) the conduct? Would the responses differ if the conduct was concluded? When may or must the lawyer go outside the company to protect it?

These questions are not idle ones. Recent years have witnessed serious wrongdoing at Enron, WorldCom, Tyco, Arthur Andersen, Computer Associates, Adelphi, KPMG, and in the investment banking and insurance industries. As I write this chapter, the media tell me that the FBI has opened an investigation of AIG, Lehman Brothers, Fannie Mae, and Freddie Mac.

The Wall Street Journal reports (Dec. 15, 2008):

> German Engineering company Siemens AG and U.S. authorities are expected to settle a longstanding bribes-for-business investigation . . . with

a record $800 million fine — almost twenty times higher than the largest previous penalty under the U.S. Foreign Corrupt Practices Act.

Documents . . . allege corruption reaching the top echelons of Siemens management. The conglomerate allegedly spent more than $1 billion bribing government officials around the globe.

The Journal reports that the fine could have reached $2.7 billion but for "aggressive steps to ferret out corruption" after the "scandal erupted in 2006."

In the past, headlines told of fraud against customers by the Hertz Corporation, check kiting by E. F. Hutton, and Beech-Nut's effort to pass sugar water off as children's apple juice.* An SEC charge that a trader at Salomon Brothers, Inc., had entered false bids in Treasury auctions resulted in a consent decree sanctioning high Salomon officials, 1992 SEC LEXIS 2939 (Dec. 3, 1992), and hundreds of millions of dollars in settlements of class action and government claims. Andy Pasztor, Salomon Settlement, Wall St. J., July 27, 1994, at B10. Not all crimes are financial. In 1994, "after five years of denials, Con Edison admitted in court . . . that for four crucial days in 1989 it failed to tell Federal authorities that asbestos had been released into the air when a steam pipe exploded near Gramercy Park in Manhattan." Ronald Sullivan, Con Ed Admits to Conspiracy to Cover Up Asbestos in Blast, New York Times, Nov. 1, 1994, at A1.

Sotheby's, the auction house, pled guilty to a price-fixing conspiracy and agreed to pay a $45 million fine. Sotheby's and its main competitor, Christie's, also settled a class action lawsuit arising out of the same events for more than $500 million. New York Times, Feb. 5, 2001, at C5. Exxon Corporation paid $1 billion to settle criminal and civil charges arising out of the Exxon Valdez oil spill in Alaska. New York Times, Oct. 9, 1991, at A14. Royal Caribbean Cruises Ltd., the world's second-largest cruise line, agreed to pay an $18 million fine for dumping oil and hazardous chemicals in U.S. coastal waters. The company "pleaded guilty to 21 counts of polluting and lying about it and storing hazardous waste illegally. . . ." New York Times, July 22, 1999, at A10. Moody's Investors Service, Inc., pleaded guilty to one count of obstructing justice by destroying documents in 1996 while the Justice Department was investigating it for antitrust violations. Wall St. J., Apr. 11, 2001, at B8. Arthur Andersen and three of its partners paid a total of $7 million to settle SEC fraud charges in connection with their audits of Waste Management. Wall St. J., June 20, 2001, at A3.

A company is not the only one at risk of indictment. Officers and employees can also be charged, because, after all, no company can commit a crime without help from biological persons. High officials at some of the companies listed here have been sentenced to decades in federal and state prisons. Rarely — but not never — lawyers get indicted, too. One example is the demise of Jenkens & Gilchrist, once the largest law firm in Dallas, which was forced to close in the wake of Justice Department investigations of its tax shelter opinions. Dallas Morning News, Apr. 1, 2007.

* See, respectively, N.Y. Times 1/26/88; 5/3/85; 2/18/88, all at page A1.

Stanley Sporkin's Famous Questions

Perhaps the largest scandal in an earlier period — and one that continues to haunt this topic — was the failure of so many of America's savings and loan institutions in the 1980s and early 1990s. See Martin Mayer, The Greatest-Ever Bank Robbery (1990). Were lawyers privy to some of these shenanigans, as some have charged? Law firms were named, along with others, in civil actions arising out of the S&L crisis. See Steve France, Savings and Loan Lawyers, A.B.A.J., May 1991, at 52. In Lincoln Savings & Loan Assn. v. Wall, 743 F. Supp. 901 (D.D.C. 1990), Judge Stanley Sporkin upheld the decision of the federal Office of Thrift Supervision to assume control of Lincoln Savings and Loan, run by Charles Keating. Lincoln's collapse, which alone is estimated to have cost the government billions of dollars in federal deposit insurance, led Judge Sporkin (a former SEC enforcement official) to end his opinion with some rhetorical questions that have since become famous in legal circles. Indeed, they get dusted off and quoted in each successive scandal. Spokin wrote:

> Keating testified that he was so bent on doing the "right thing" that he surrounded himself with literally scores of accountants and lawyers to make sure all the transactions were legal. The questions that must be asked are:
>
> [1.]   Where were these professionals, a number of whom are now asserting their rights under the Fifth Amendment, when these clearly improper transactions were being consummated?
>
> [2.]   Why didn't any of them speak up or disassociate themselves from the transactions?
>
> [3.]   Where also were the outside accountants and attorneys when these transactions were effectuated?
>
> What is difficult to understand is that with all the professional talent involved (both accounting and legal), why at least one professional would not have blown the whistle to stop the overreaching that took place in this case.

We can let the accountants worry about themselves. But what were the responsibilities of Lincoln's lawyers, some of whom were later sued by the government, as successor in interest to Lincoln, and by bondholders of Lincoln's parent company? Several prominent law firms settled these claims for tens of millions of dollars. The district court decision rejecting law firm motions for summary judgment is In re American Continental Corporation/Lincoln Savings and Loan Securities Litigation, 794 F. Supp. 1424 (D. Ariz. 1992).

Let's face it. Lawyers are the canaries in the mine shaft of fraud and corruption (to use an infelicitous metaphor). In the highly regulated world of big U.S. companies (or foreign ones with interests in the United States), it is impossible to engage in any financial transaction much more complicated than changing a twenty without expert legal advice, usually from a team of lawyers, each with his or her own specialty. (Yes, I exaggerate, but only for effect and not by a whole lot.) When something in a company smells really fishy, the lawyers employed in its general counsel's office will be especially close to the action and will either know about or be on notice. Many regulators therefore see lawyers as an early warning system against corporate wrongdoing and expect them to protect their client (and uphold regulatory requirements) even at the expense of their bosses and perhaps their own employment security. That, in fact, is part of the explanation for the Sarbanes-Oxley legislation discussed below and for the 2003 amendments to Rules 1.6 and 1.13. Many lawyers and officers protest that while it is true that the company's counsel owes all to the company, "deputizing" them to be the eyes and ears of government, as they put it, will lead to less, not more compliance, because the company's officers may then exclude lawyers from learning about questionable behavior for fear that the lawyer will then have a duty or authority to turn them in. As a consequence, they argue, the lawyers will never learn about the behavior in time to stop it.

This is one of those arguments that seems impossible to resolve with empirical investigation, partly because the experiment would seem impossible to construct and partly because the opposing camps are unlikely to be persuaded anyway. But one must wonder: In this highly regulated environment, could corporate honchos exclude lawyers from their plans, even if they wished to do so?

Employed lawyers rarely get sued for failing to protect the client from management's transgressions because, very simply, the very same management would have to authorize the suit. But when management changes, or if the company goes into bankruptcy, or if shareholders bring a derivative claim, the situation could change. It happened in Matter of World Health Alternatives, Inc., 385 B.R. 576 (D.Del. 2008), where the trustee in bankruptcy sued various corporate officials, including Licastro, its general counsel (who was also an officer). Licastro moved to dismiss the malpractice claim against him. The court refused:

> An attorney must "act[ ] with a proper degree of skill, and with reasonable care and to the best of his knowledge." *Savings Bank v. Ward*, 100 U.S. 195, 198 (1880). The Complaint alleges "Licastro breached the applicable standard of care, for example, by not providing oversight and failing to provide advice that would have prevented the Company from submitting SEC filings that included material misrepresentation." Moreover, "Members of the Company's management including . . . Licastro became aware or should have been aware of the malfeasance and misdealing and discrepancies in the Company's revenue; however, no actions were taken consistent with their fiduciary duties to remedy or ameliorate the discrepancies until after [the dominant officer's] resignation." And, as a result of Licastro's alleged professional negligence, World Health suffered damages. I believe the Trustee has alleged sufficient facts for a cause of action and the motion should be denied as to this count.

In this chapter, we examine several perspectives on regulatory issues pertaining to corporate lawyers. In section A, we take up the rules on confidentiality, loyalty, and conflict as they operate in several different arenas. First, we look at a routine corporate acquisition (and in a later case, at a routine corporate formation). Then, we look at the same doctrines in a growing area of law practice, one that lawyers find quite rewarding professionally and financially — internal corporate investigations. We conclude section A with a look at the operation of these rules when a firm represents only one member of a corporate family. Section B tracks how the same doctrines play out when lawyers sue their corporate employers for discrimination or retaliatory discharge. Sections C turns to Sarbanes-Oxley's effect on lawyers for public companies and to the consequent 2003 Model

Rules amendments, which affect all organizational lawyers, whether their clients are public companies under SEC jurisdiction or not.

A. CONFLICTS AND CONFIDENTIALITY IN ENTITY REPRESENTATION

Change of Corporate Control

"I Never Worked For The Buyer"

"My firm is outside counsel for the Matterick family of companies. In addition to Matterick, Ltd., the parent, there are 10 to 15 wholly owned subsidiaries. The number changes because subs are bought and sold quarterly. Matterick and its subs are vintners, importers, exporters, and retailers of fine wines and liquors. Last year, Matterick sold one of its wholly owned subsidiaries, Vasco Castillian Wines, Inc., to Cortina Foods. My firm represented Vasco for the five years that Matterick owned it, and I represented Matterick on the sale. Matterick made certain warranties about Vasco's financial situation and about two vineyards it owns in Spain. Cortina now says that these warranties were false, and Cortina and Vasco (now owned by Cortina) has sued Matterick in court. When my partner appeared for Matterick, Vasco said we were disqualified from opposing it because it is my firm's former client. It says I represented it at the buy-sell negotiation, when it was still owned by Matterick. And it says, correctly, that my firm represented Vasco when it acquired the two vineyards from its former British owners three years ago. On the financials, Vasco claims that Matterick overstated Vasco's profit margins. On the vineyards, Vasco claims that one of the vineyards is actually smaller by 300 acres (out of 7,000 acres) than Matterick represented because of errors my firm made in the deed's description. Are we disqualified? As I see it, we're still on the same side — Matterick's side — and any work for Vasco was only on behalf of its parent, Matterick, when Matterick wholly owned it.

"Sincerely,
"Ellis McNeil"

The following opinion has appeared in all editions of this book since it was decided. The facts are a bit unusual and a bit complicated, even if the lessons remain universal. With each edition, I consider omitting it, but then I reread it and keep it because it so perfectly distills the nature of the corporate attorney-client relationship, in particular the corporate lawyer's loyalty and confidentiality duties and to whom they are owed. The fact that the context happens to be a merger and acquisition is an incidental benefit because the court is required to address the questions before it in connection with a change of control. One surprising lesson here is that some part of what lawyers owe clients can be sold along with the rest of the company (machinery, pencils, trademarks). "Duty of loyalty? Sure, we'll buy that. How much you want for it?" So it turns out that a lawyer's obligations are commodified. Or maybe that's not so surprising. See what you think. The case also permits a quick review of the former client conflict rules.

TEKNI-PLEX, INC. v. MEYNER & LANDIS
89 N.Y.2d 123, 674 N.E.2d 663, 651 N.Y.S.2d 954 (1996)

KAYE, CHIEF JUDGE.

Central to this appeal, involving a dispute over a corporate acquisition, are two questions. *First,* can long-time counsel for the seller company and its sole shareholder continue to represent the shareholder in the dispute with the buyer? And *second,* who controls the attorney-client privilege as to pre-merger communications? We conclude that counsel should step aside, and that the buyer controls the privilege as to some, but not all, of the pre-merger communications.

A.   FACTS

Tekni-Plex, Inc., incorporated under the laws of Delaware in 1967, manufactured and packaged products for the pharmaceutical and other industries. For nearly 20 years, from 1967 to 1986, Tekni-Plex had 18 shareholders and was managed by a five-member Board of Directors. Appellant Tom Y.C. Tang was both a director and a shareholder of the company.

In 1986, Tang became the sole shareholder of Tekni-Plex. From that time until the corporation's sale in 1994, Tang was also the president, chief executive officer and sole director of Tekni-Plex.

Appellant Meyner and Landis (M&L), a New Jersey law firm, was first retained as Tekni-Plex counsel in 1971. During the ensuing 23 years, M&L represented Tekni-Plex on various legal matters, including environmental compliance. As the record indicates, M&L in the mid-1980's assisted Tekni-Plex in securing an environmental permit for the operation of a laminator machine at its Somerville, New Jersey, plant. Similarly, the law firm apparently assisted the company in an investigation by the New Jersey Department of Environmental Protection into Tekni-Plex's compliance with environmental laws. Additionally, during this period M&L represented Tang individually on several personal matters.

In March 1994, Tang and Tekni-Plex entered into an Agreement and Plan of Merger (the Merger Agreement) with TP Acquisition Company (Acquisition), whereby Tang sold the company to Acquisition for $43 million. M&L represented both Tekni-Plex and Tang personally. The two instant lawsuits grow out of that transaction.

Acquisition was a shell corporation created by the purchasers solely for the acquisition of Tekni-Plex. Under the Merger Agreement, Tekni-Plex merged into Acquisition, with Acquisition the surviving corporation, and Tekni-Plex ceased its separate existence. Tekni-Plex conveyed to Acquisition all of its tangible and intangible assets, rights and liabilities. Acquisition in return paid Tang the purchase price "in complete liquidation of Tekni-Plex," and all of Tang's shares in Tekni-Plex—the only shares outstanding—were canceled.

The Merger Agreement contained representations and warranties by Tang concerning environmental matters, including that Tekni-Plex was in full compliance with all applicable environmental laws and possessed all requisite environmental permits. It further provided for indemnification of Acquisition by Tang for any losses incurred by Acquisition as the result of misrepresentation or breach of warranty by either Tang or Tekni-Plex. Acquisition, in turn, agreed to indemnify Tang and Tekni-Plex for any similar losses suffered by them.

Following the transaction, Acquisition changed its name to "Tekni-Plex, Inc." (new Tekni-Plex). In June 1994, new Tekni-Plex commenced an arbitration against Tang, alleging breach of representations and warranties contained in the Merger Agreement regarding the former Tekni-Plex's (old Tekni-Plex) compliance with environmental laws.

Among other things, new Tekni-Plex claimed that Tang falsely represented that a laminator machine at the Somerville facility did not emit volatile organic compounds (VOCs). New management, however, allegedly learned that the machine did indeed emit VOCs into the air. New Tekni-Plex further claimed that the permit for the laminator machine had been obtained on the false premise that it did not emit VOCs and that VOC emissions were therefore not authorized. New Tekni-Plex also contended that Tang and old Tekni-Plex had taken steps to conceal from Acquisition the emission of VOCs at the Somerville facility.

Tang retained M&L to represent him in the arbitration. New Tekni-Plex moved [in court for an] order against M&L (1) enjoining the law firm from representing Tang in any action against new Tekni-Plex, (2) enjoining M&L from disclosing to Tang any information obtained from old Tekni-Plex, and (3) ordering M&L to return to new Tekni-Plex all of the files in the law firm's possession concerning its prior legal representation of old Tekni-Plex. . . .

Supreme Court concluded that New York was the proper forum for resolution of the disqualification issue and that the arbitrator's conclusion that he did not have authority to decide the issue was proper. The court held that M&L should be disqualified from representing Tang in the arbitration. It further enjoined M&L from representing Tang in the arbitration, enjoined M&L from disclosing to Tang any information obtained from old Tekni-Plex, and directed M&L to return to new Tekni-Plex all of the files in M&L's possession concerning its prior representation of old Tekni-Plex. Finally, the court denied both cross motions to dismiss. The Appellate Division affirmed.

We agree with the courts below that, in the circumstances presented, M&L should be disqualified from representing Tang in the arbitration. As for confidential communications between old Tekni-Plex and M&L generated during the law firm's prior representation of the corporation on environmental compliance matters, authority to assert the attorney-client privilege passed to the corporation's successor management. Moreover, because the record fails to establish that M&L also represented Tang individually on these matters, the exception to the privilege for co-clients who subsequently become adversaries in litigation is inapplicable. Thus, the Appellate Division correctly concluded that M&L should be enjoined from disclosing the substance of these communications to Tang and directed the law firm to return the files relating to this representation to new Tekni-Plex.

New Tekni-Plex, however, does not control the attorney-client privilege with regard to discrete communications made by either old Tekni-Plex or Tang individually to M&L concerning the acquisition — a time when old Tekni-Plex and Tang were joined in an adversarial relationship to Acquisition. Consequently, new Tekni-Plex cannot assert the privilege in order to prevent M&L from disclosing the contents of such communications to Tang. Nor is new Tekni-Plex entitled to the law firm's confidential communications concerning its representation of old Tekni-Plex with regard to the acquisition.

B.   THE APPLICABLE ETHICS PRINCIPLES

[The Court discussed the successive conflict rules that are the subject of chapter 6.]

C.   DISQUALIFICATION OF COUNSEL

New Tekni-Plex, as the party seeking M&L's disqualification, thus has the burden of satisfying the three-pronged test for disqualification by establishing that (1) it assumed the role of M&L's "former client," (2) the matters involved in both representations are substantially related, and (3) the interests of M&L's present client Tang are materially adverse to the interests of the former client. We next consider each of these elements.

1.   IS NEW TEKNI-PLEX A "FORMER CLIENT" OF M&L?

It is undisputed that M&L represented old Tekni-Plex for over 20 years on a variety of legal matters. As counsel to the corporation, the law firm's duties of confidentiality and loyalty ran to old Tekni-Plex on these matters. Concomitantly, the attorney-client privilege attached to any confidential communications that took place between M&L and Tekni-Plex corporate actors in the course of this representation. The power to assert or waive the privilege, moreover, belonged to the management of old Tekni-Plex, to be exercised by its officers and directors.

Appellants (Tang and M&L) argue that the purchase of old Tekni-Plex by Acquisition did not transfer the corporation's attorney-client relationship to the newly formed entity. According to appellants, the transaction effected nothing more than a transfer of assets, with old Tekni-Plex expiring upon the merger, there being no "former client" still in existence. In support of this contention, appellants point out that, under the Merger Agreement, Acquisition was designated the surviving corporation, old Tekni-Plex explicitly ceased to exist and all of the outstanding shares of stock in old Tekni-Plex were liquidated. They further note that, for tax purposes, the transaction was deemed a sale of assets.

When ownership of a corporation changes hands, whether the attorney-client relationship transfers as well to the new owners turns on the practical consequences rather than the formalities of the particular transaction. In Commodity Futures Trading Commn. v. Weintraub, 471 U.S. 343 [1985], the Supreme Court held that power to exercise the attorney-client privilege of an insolvent corporation passed to the bankruptcy trustee, who assumed managerial responsibility for operating the debtor company's business. In reaching this conclusion, the Court noted with regard to solvent corporations that

> when control of a corporation passes to new management, the authority to assert and waive the corporation's attorney-client privilege passes as well. New managers installed as a result of a takeover, merger, loss of confidence by shareholders, or simply normal succession, may waive the attorney-client privilege with respect to communications made by former officers and directors.

Weintraub establishes that, where efforts are made to run the preexisting business entity and manage its affairs, successor management stands in the shoes of prior management and controls the attorney-client privilege with respect to matters concerning the company's operations. It follows that, under such circumstances, the prior attorney-client relationship continues with the newly formed entity.

By contrast, the mere transfer of assets with no attempt to continue the preexisting operation generally does not transfer the attorney-client relationship. . . .

Here, appellants emphasize that old Tekni-Plex merged into Acquisition and ceased to exist as a separate legal entity. That Acquisition, rather than old Tekni-Plex, was designated the surviving corporation, however, is not dispositive. Acquisition was a mere shell corporation, created solely for the purpose of acquiring old TekniPlex. Following the merger, the business of old Tekni-Plex remained unchanged, with the same products, clients, suppliers and nonmanagerial personnel. Indeed, under the Merger Agreement, new Tekni-Plex possessed all of the rights, privileges, liabilities and obligations of old Tekni-Plex, in addition to its assets. Certainly, new Tekni-Plex is entitled to access to any relevant pre-merger legal advice rendered to old Tekni-Plex that it might need to defend against these liabilities or pursue any of these rights.

As a practical matter, then, old Tekni-Plex did not die. To the contrary, the business operations of old Tekni-Plex continued under the new managers. Consequently, control of the attorney-client privilege with respect to any confidential communications between M&L and corporate actors of old Tekni-Plex concerning these operations passed to the management of new Tekni-Plex. An attorney-client relationship between M&L and new Tekni-Plex necessarily exists.

Thus, the first of the three prongs for disqualification is established: new Tekni-Plex is a "former client" of M&L.

2. IS THERE A SUBSTANTIAL RELATIONSHIP BETWEEN THE CURRENT AND FORMER REPRESENTATIONS?

[The court concluded that there was one, first, because the current dispute concerned the merger agreement on which the law firm had represented old Tekni-Plex; and, second, because the plaintiff was alleging misrepresentation in connection with the Somerville permit and environmental law compliance generally, where the firm had also represented the company.]

3.   ARE THE INTERESTS OF M&L'S PRESENT CLIENT MATERIALLY ADVERSE
TO THE INTERESTS OF ITS FORMER CLIENT?

The arbitration claims pit Acquisition's interest as purchaser against Tang's interest as the selling shareholder. Furthermore, the Merger Agreement provides that Tang is responsible for indemnifying Acquisition for any misrepresentation or breach of warranty made by either Tang or old Tekni-Plex. Plainly the parties contemplated a unity of interest between old Tekni-Plex and Tang should a dispute arise between the buyer and seller regarding the representations and warranties. Thus, to the extent the arbitration relates to the merger negotiations—as opposed to corporate operations—Tang and old Tekni-Plex remain on the same side of the table. The interest of M&L's former client old Tekni-Plex is aligned with the interest of the law firm's present client Tang—both in opposition to the buyer.

International Elecs. Corp. v. Flanzer, 527 F.2d 1288 (2d Cir.), relied on by appellants, supports this analysis. Like new Tekni-Plex, the plaintiffs in Flanzer acquired a corporation through a sale and merger transaction. They subsequently filed a complaint against the selling stockholders alleging that misrepresentations were made during the sale negotiations. Plaintiffs then moved to disqualify the selling stockholders' law firm because counsel for the acquired corporation and the selling stockholders during the acquisition had worked for that firm. The Second Circuit denied the motion to disqualify, explaining that the law firm's current client (the selling stockholders) was in a position adverse to the buyer, not the merged corporation:

> The law firm and the plaintiffs were on opposite sides of the negotiations which were conducted at arm's length. The plaintiffs' attack is now on the bona fides of the selling stockholders. These defendants—the selling stockholders—not the buyer, were the clients of the law firm. They have a right to defend themselves as adversaries. . . . The earlier relationship of the law firm to the merged corporation cannot be a source of disqualification in these circumstances, even though a former client is surely entitled to protection.

The dispute here, however, unlike Flanzer, goes beyond the merger negotiations. It also involves issues relating to the law firm's long-standing representation of the acquired corporation on matters arising out of the company's business operations—namely, M&L's separate representation of old Tekni-Plex prior to the merger on environmental compliance matters. Any environmental violations will negatively affect not only the purchasers but also the business interests of the merged corporation. In this regard, the interests of M&L's current client Tang are adverse to the interests that new Tekni-Plex assumed from old Tekni-Plex.

Indeed, M&L's earlier representation of old Tekni-Plex provided the firm with access to confidential information conveyed by old Tekni-Plex concerning the very environmental compliance matters at issue in the arbitration.

M&L's duty of confidentiality with respect to these communications passed to new Tekni-Plex; yet its current representation of Tang creates the potential for the law firm to use these confidences against new Tekni-Plex in the arbitration.

Under the circumstances, the appearance of impropriety is manifest and the potential conflict of interest apparent. M&L should therefore be disqualified from representing Tang in the arbitration.

D. CONFIDENTIAL COMMUNICATIONS

As a final matter, we must determine whether M&L was properly enjoined from revealing to Tang any confidential communications obtained from old Tekni-Plex and whether new Tekni-Plex owns the confidences created during the law firm's prior representation of old Tekni-Plex. For analytical purposes, the attorney-client communications must be separated into two categories: general business communications and those relating to the merger negotiations.

1. GENERAL BUSINESS COMMUNICATIONS

As explained above, the management of new Tekni-Plex continues the business operations of the pre-merger entity. Control of the attorney-client privilege with regard to confidential communications arising out of those operations — including any pre-merger communications between old Tekni-Plex and M&L relating to the company's environmental compliance — thus passed to the management of new Tekni-Plex. As a result, new Tekni-Plex now has the authority to assert the attorney-client privilege to preclude M&L from disclosing the contents of these confidential communications to Tang. Likewise, ownership of the law firm's files regarding its pre-merger representation of old Tekni-Plex on environmental compliance matters passed to the management of new Tekni-Plex. This conclusion comports with new Tekni-Plex's right to invoke the pre-merger attorney-client relationship should it have to prosecute or defend against third-party suits involving the assets, rights or liabilities that it assumed from old Tekni-Plex.

Appellants urge that because Tang and old Tekni-Plex were co-clients of M&L, none of the communications made by corporate actors to the law firm are confidential from Tang. Generally, where the same lawyer jointly represents two clients with respect to the same matter, the clients have no expectation that their confidences concerning the joint matter will remain secret from each other, and those confidential communications are not within the privilege in subsequent adverse proceedings between the co-clients. While M&L jointly represented Tang and old Tekni-Plex during the acquisition, with respect to the environmental compliance matters the record before us establishes only M&L's representation of the corporation.

We note that some courts have held that, in the case of a close corporation, corporate representation may be individual representation as well. Here, the record indicates that at least some of M&L's representation of old Tekni-Plex on the environmental matters at issue took place before Tang became the corporation's sole shareholder and manager. Whether corporate counsel also functioned as Tang's individual attorney on the environmental matters involved factual questions not addressed by the trial court or Appellate Division. In this particular case there is an insufficient record from which we can conclude that M&L jointly represented the corporation and Tang individually on matters other than the merger.

2. COMMUNICATIONS RELATING TO THE MERGER NEGOTIATIONS

As to the other category of attorney-client communications between old Tekni-Plex and M&L — those relating to the merger transaction — new Tekni-Plex did not succeed to old Tekni-Plex's right to control the attorney-client privilege. New Tekni-Plex's misrepresentation and breach of warranty claims do not derive from the rights it inherited from old Tekni-Plex but from the rights retained by the buyer, Acquisition, with respect to the transaction. Under the Merger Agreement, moreover, the rights of old Tekni-Plex with regard to disputes arising from the merger transaction remain independent from — and, indeed, adverse to — the rights of the buyer. During this dispute stemming from the merger transaction, then, new Tekni-Plex cannot both pursue the rights of the buyer (Acquisition) and simultaneously assume the attorney-client rights that the buyer's adversary (old Tekni-Plex) retained regarding the transaction.

This conclusion is especially compelling here, where at the time of the acquisition the seller corporation was solely owned and managed by one individual, Tang. "As corporate stock ownership is concentrated into fewer and fewer hands, the distinction between corporate entity and shareholders begins to blur" and "[i]n the case of a sole-owner corporation, they may merge." To allow new Tekni-Plex access to the confidences conveyed by the seller company to its counsel during the negotiations would, in the circumstances presented, be the equivalent of turning over to the buyer all of the privileged communications of the seller concerning the very transaction at issue. The parties here, moreover, recognized the community between the selling shareholder and his corporation and expressly provided that it be preserved in any subsequent dispute regarding the acquisition.

Indeed, to grant new Tekni-Plex control over the attorney-client privilege as to communications concerning the merger transaction would thwart, rather than promote, the purposes underlying the privilege. The attorney-client privilege encourages "full and frank communication between attorneys and their clients and thereby promote[s] broader public interests in the observance of law and administration of justice." Where the parties to a corporate acquisition agree that in any subsequent dispute arising out of the transaction the interests of the buyer will be pitted against the interests of the sold corporation, corporate actors should not have to worry that their privileged communications with counsel concerning the negotiations might be available to the buyer for use against the sold corporation in any ensuing litigation. Such concern would significantly chill attorney-client communication during the transaction.

Thus, while generally "parties who negotiate a corporate acquisition should expect that the privileges of the acquired corporation would be incidents of the sale," the agreement between the parties here contemplated that, in any dispute arising from the merger transaction, the rights of the acquired corporation, old Tekni-Plex, relating to the transaction would remain independent from and adverse to the rights of new Tekni-Plex. . . .

Internal Investigations

Because the issues in *Tekni-Plex* and those in the Fourth Circuit case following raise parallel, if not identical, issues, I am postponing the note material until after the following opinion, which arose out of an internal investigation at AOL. The lawyers conducting the investigation (eventually) gave interviewees what the court calls "*Upjohn* warnings," but which others have called "corporate *Miranda* warnings." The opinion is of interest to us because it addresses the attorney-client privilege in the corporate context. The company's officers make claims of joint representation, and one of them also claims the common interest doctrine. These are distinct ideas (see page 282). Recall that a joint representation is when one or several lawyers represent two or more clients in a single matter. In that situation, each lawyer is representing *all* the clients jointly. By contrast, a common interest arrangement arises when each of two or more lawyers (*A* and *B*, say) *separately* represents a client (client *A* and client *B*) on a matter of common interest between the clients. The Third Circuit took pains to make the doctrinal distinction in In re Teleglobe Communications Corp., 493 F.3d 345 (3d Cir. 2007), discussed when we turn to corporate family issues below. But the Fourth Circuit's less precise terminology is no big deal. What is a big deal for us is what it says in the paragraph beginning "We note, however . . . ," just before part III. The court describes the dangers to corporate counsel and their client if warnings to corporate constituents are inadequate, as was nearly true here.

IN RE GRAND JURY SUBPOENA
415 F.3d 333 (4th Cir. 2005)

WILSON, District Judge:
This is an appeal by three former employees of AOL Time Warner ("AOL") from the decision of the district court denying their motions to quash a grand jury subpoena for documents related to an internal investigation by AOL. Appellants argued in the district court that the subpoenaed documents were protected by the attorney-client privilege. Because the district court concluded that the privilege was AOL's alone and because AOL had expressly waived its privilege, the court denied the appellants' motion. We affirm.

I.

In March of 2001, AOL began an internal investigation into its relationship with PurchasePro, Inc. AOL retained the law firm of Wilmer, Cutler & Pickering ("Wilmer Cutler") to assist in the investigation. Over the next several months, AOL's general counsel and counsel from Wilmer Cutler (collectively referred to herein as "AOL's attorneys" or the "investigating attorneys") interviewed appellants, AOL employees Kent Wakeford, John Doe 1, and John Doe 2.

The investigating attorneys interviewed Wakeford, a manager in the company's Business Affairs division, on six occasions. At their third interview, and the first one in which Wilmer Cutler attorneys were present, Randall Boe, AOL's General Counsel, informed Wakeford, "We represent the company. These conversations are privileged, but the privilege belongs to the company and the company decides whether to waive it. If there is a conflict, the attorney-client privilege belongs to the company." Memoranda from that meeting also indicate that the attorneys explained to Wakeford that they represented AOL but that they "could" represent him as well, "as long as no conflict appeared." The attorneys interviewed Wakeford again three days later and, at the beginning of the interview, reiterated that they represented AOL, that the privilege belonged to AOL, and that Wakeford could retain personal counsel at company expense.

The investigating attorneys interviewed John Doe 1 three times. Before the first interview, Boe told him, "We represent the company. These conversations are privileged, but the privilege belongs to the company and the company decides whether to waive it. You are free to consult with your own lawyer at any time." Memoranda from that interview indicate that the attorneys also told him, "We can represent [you] until such time as there appears to be a conflict of interest, [but] . . . the attorney-client privilege belongs to AOL and AOL can decide whether to keep it or waive it." At the end of the interview, John Doe 1 asked if he needed personal counsel. A Wilmer Cutler attorney responded that he did not recommend it, but that he would tell the company not to be concerned if Doe retained counsel.

AOL's attorneys interviewed John Doe 2 twice and followed essentially the same protocol they had followed with the other appellants. They noted, "We represent AOL, and can represent [you] too if there is not a conflict." In addition, the attorneys told him that, "the attorney-client privilege is AOL's and AOL can choose to waive it."

In November, 2001, the Securities and Exchange Commission ("SEC") began to investigate AOL's relationship with PurchasePro. In December 2001, AOL and Wakeford, through counsel, entered into an oral "common interest agreement," which they memorialized in writing in January 2002. The attorneys acknowledged that, "representation of [their] respective clients raised issues of common interest to [their] respective clients and that the sharing of certain documents, information, . . . and communications with clients" would be mutually beneficial. As a result, the attorneys agreed to share access to information relating to their representation of Wakeford and AOL, noting that "the oral or written disclosure of Common Interest Materials . . . [would] not diminish in any way the confidentiality of such Materials and [would] not constitute a waiver of any applicable privilege."

Wakeford testified before the SEC on February 14, 2002, represented by his personal counsel. Laura Jehl, AOL's general counsel, and F. Whitten Peters of Williams & Connolly, whom AOL had retained in November 2001 in connection with the PurchasePro investigation, were also present, and both stated that they represented Wakeford "for purposes of [the] deposition." During the deposition, the SEC investigators questioned Wakeford about his discussions with AOL's attorneys. When Wakeford's attorney asserted the attorney-client privilege, the SEC investigators followed up with several questions to determine whether the privilege was applicable to the investigating attorneys' March-June 2001 interviews with Wakeford. Wakeford told them he believed, at the time of the interviews, that the investigating attorneys represented him and the company.

John Doe 1 testified before the SEC on February 27, 2002, represented by personal counsel. No representatives of AOL were present. When SEC investigators questioned Doe about the March-June 2001 internal investigation, his counsel asserted that the information was protected and directed Doe not to answer any questions about the internal investigation "in respect to the company's privilege." He stated that Doe's response could be considered a waiver of the privilege and that, "if the AOL lawyers were [present], they could make a judgment, with respect to the company's privilege, about whether or not the answer would constitute a waiver."

On February 26, 2004, a grand jury in the Eastern District of Virginia issued a subpoena commanding AOL to provide "written memoranda and other written records reflecting interviews conducted by attorneys for [AOL]" of the appellants between March 15 and June 30, 2001. While AOL agreed to waive the attorney-client privilege and produce the subpoenaed documents, counsel for the appellants moved to quash the subpoena on the grounds that each appellant had an individual attorney-client relationship with the investigating attorneys, that his interviews were individually privileged, and that he had not waived the privilege. Wakeford also claimed that the information he disclosed to the investigating attorneys was privileged under the common interest doctrine.

The district court denied John Doe 1's and John Doe 2's motions because it found they failed to prove they were clients of the investigating attorneys who interviewed them. The court based its conclusion on its findings that: (1) the investigating attorneys told them that they represented the company; (2) the investigating attorneys told them, "we *can* represent you," which is distinct from "we *do* represent you"; (3) they could not show that the investigating attorneys agreed to represent them; and (4) the investigating attorneys told them that the attorney-client privilege belonged to the company and the company could choose to waive it.

The court initially granted Wakeford's motion to quash because it found that his communications with the investigating attorneys were privileged under the common interest agreement between counsel for Wakeford and counsel for AOL. Following a motion for reconsideration, the court reversed its earlier ruling and held that the subpoenaed documents relating to Wakeford's interviews were not privileged because it found that Wakeford's common interest agreement with AOL postdated the March-June 2001 interviews. In addition, the court held that Wakeford failed to prove that he was a client of the investigating attorneys at the time the interviews took place. The court based its conclusion on its findings that: (1) none of the investigating attorneys understood that Wakeford was seeking personal legal advice; (2) the investigating attorneys did not provide any personal legal advice to him; and (3) the investigating attorneys believed they represented AOL and not Wakeford. This appeal followed.

II.

Appellants argue that because they believed that the investigating attorneys who conducted the interviews were representing them personally, their communications are privileged. However, we agree with the district court that essential touchstones for the formation of an attorney-client relationship between the investigating attorneys and the appellants were missing at the time of the interviews. There is no evidence of an objectively reasonable, mutual understanding that the appellants were seeking legal advice from the investigating attorneys or that the investigating attorneys were rendering personal legal advice. Nor, in light of the investigating attorneys' disclosure that they represented AOL and that the privilege and the right to waive it were AOL's alone, do we find investigating counsel's hypothetical pronouncement that they *could* represent appellants sufficient to establish the reasonable understanding that they *were* representing appellants. Accordingly, we find no fault with the district court's opinion that no individual attorney-client privilege attached to the appellants' communications with AOL's attorneys.

We apply a two-fold standard of review in this case. We give deference to the district court's determination of the underlying facts, and review those findings for clear error. . . .

The person seeking to invoke the attorney-client privilege must prove that he is a client or that he affirmatively sought to become a client. "The professional relationship . . . hinges upon the client's belief that he is consulting a lawyer in that capacity and his manifested intention to seek professional legal advice." An individual's subjective belief that he is represented is not alone sufficient to create an attorney-client relationship. . . . Rather, the putative client must show that his subjective belief that an attorney-client relationship existed was reasonable under the circumstances.

With these precepts in mind, we conclude that appellants could not have reasonably believed that the investigating attorneys represented them personally during the time frame covered by the subpoena. First, there is no evidence that the investigating attorneys told the appellants that they represented them, nor is there evidence that the appellants asked the investigating attorneys to represent them. To the contrary, there is evidence that the investigating attorneys relayed to Wakeford the company's offer to retain personal counsel for him at the company's expense, and that they told John Doe 1 that he was free to retain personal counsel. Second, there is no evidence that the appellants ever sought personal legal advice from the investigating attorneys, nor is there any evidence that the investigating attorneys rendered personal legal advice. Third, when the appellants spoke with the investigating attorneys, they were fully apprised that the information they were giving could be disclosed at the company's discretion. Under these circumstances, appellants could not have reasonably believed that the investigating attorneys represented them personally. Therefore, the district court's finding that appellants had no attorney-client relationship with the investigating attorneys is not clearly erroneous.

The appellants argue that the phrase "we *can* represent you as long as no conflict appears," manifested an agreement by the investigating attorneys to represent them. They claim that, "it is hard to imagine a more straightforward assurance of an attorney-client relationship than 'we can represent you.'" We disagree. As the district court noted, "we *can* represent you" is distinct from "we *do* represent you." If there was any evidence that the investigating attorneys had said, "we *do* represent you," then the outcome of this appeal might be different. Furthermore, the statement actually made, "we *can* represent you," must be interpreted within the context of the entire warning. The investigating attorneys' statements to the appellants, read in their entirety, demonstrate that the attorneys' loyalty was to the company. That loyalty was never implicitly or explicitly divided. In addition to noting at the outset that they had been retained to represent AOL, the investigating attorneys warned the appellants that the content of their communications during the interview "belonged" to AOL.

This protocol put the appellants on notice that, while their communications with the attorneys were considered confidential, the company could choose to reveal the content of those communications at any time, without the appellants' consent.

We note, however, that our opinion should not be read as an implicit acceptance of the watered-down "Upjohn warnings" the investigating attorneys gave the appellants. It is a potential legal and ethical mine field. Had the investigating attorneys, in fact, entered into an attorney-client relationship with appellants, as their statements to the appellants professed they could, they would not have been free to waive the appellants' privilege when a conflict arose. It should have seemed obvious that they could not have jettisoned one client in favor of another. Rather, they would have had to withdraw from all representation and to maintain all confidences. Indeed, the court would be hard pressed to identify how investigating counsel could robustly investigate and report to management or the board of directors of a publicly-traded corporation with the necessary candor if counsel were constrained by ethical obligations to individual employees. However, because we agree with the district court that the appellants never entered into an attorney-client relationship with the investigating attorneys, they averted these troubling issues.

III.

Wakeford also claims that the documents in question are protected by the joint defense privilege because of his common interest agreement with AOL. However, the district court found that no common interest agreement existed at the time of the interviews in March-June 2001. This finding was not clearly erroneous.

The joint defense privilege, an extension of the attorney-client privilege, protects communications between parties who share a common interest in litigation. The purpose of the privilege is to allow persons with a common interest to "communicate with their respective attorneys and with each other to more effectively prosecute or defend their claims." For the privilege to apply, the proponent must establish that the parties had "some common interest about a legal matter." An employee's cooperation in an internal investigation alone is not sufficient to establish a common interest; rather "some form of joint strategy is necessary." *United States v. Weissman*, 195 F.3d 96, 100 (2d Cir. 1999).

The district court found that "an agreement to share information pursuant to a common interest did not exist prior to December 2001." Uncontradicted affidavits submitted by counsel for AOL, including Randall Boe, who participated in the March-June 2001 interviews, support the court's finding. Boe stated that, at the time of the interviews, AOL had not entered into an agreement with Wakeford regarding their joint defense. There is no evidence showing that AOL and Wakeford were pursuing a common legal strategy before December 2001. During the March-June 2001 interviews, AOL was in the early stages of its internal investigation; there is no evidence that the investigating attorneys' interviews with Wakeford were for the purpose of formulating a joint defense. Indeed, the stated purpose of the interviews was to gather information regarding AOL's relationship with PurchasePro; it would have been difficult for AOL to know at that time whether its interests were consistent with or adverse to Wakeford's personal interests. The court's finding was therefore not clearly erroneous.

Because there is no evidence that Wakeford and AOL shared a common interest before December 2001, we find no error in the district court's conclusion that Wakeford had no joint defense privilege before that time. . . .

"Who's Your Client?" (Reprise)

The multiple interests in organizational representation often create client identity issues. To reduce confusion and avoid unfairness, Rule 1.13(f) directs a lawyer to "explain the identity of the client when the lawyer knows or reasonably should know that the organization's interests are adverse to those of the constituents with whom the lawyer is dealing." Compare Rule 4.3 ("Dealing with Unrepresented Person"). Rule 1.13(g) permits joint representation of an organization and its constituents subject to the concurrent conflict provisions of Rule 1.7.

In the unlikely event that at this point in the course and the book you continue to view client identity as a simple matter, *Tekni-Plex* should dispel the illusion. Understand that it was not an all-or-nothing choice for Chief Judge Kaye. She split M&L's confidentiality and loyalty duties between Tang and old Tekni-Plex, on one hand, and new Tekni-Plex on the other. Take a moment to identify which of these duties belonged to whom and what is likely to happen on remand. Following *Tekni-Plex* is Goodrich v. Goodrich, 960 A.2d 1275 (N.H. 2008) ("If . . . an entity acquires control of [a] corporation's business operations, rights and liabilities, it . . . also acquires authority over the attorney-client privilege")

In *Tekni-Plex*, problems arose when the corporate client was dissolved and reborn. Let us move to a time even before a company is formed. Say a dozen people, Drummond Walsh among them, ask a lawyer to form a corporation. They each provide the lawyer with financial information about themselves. Maybe this information will enable the lawyer to create an entity providing maximum tax benefits to the future shareholders. Prior to formation of the corporation, who are the lawyer's clients? It can only be the individual organizers. There is no entity yet (and may never be one).

Now, assume the corporation is formed. The lawyer remains and represents it. It comes to pass that a new client, Priscilla Arden, wishes to retain the lawyer's firm to sue one of the corporate organizers, Drummond. Assume that Priscilla's claim is substantially related to the work the lawyer did for the corporate organizers, including Drummond. It should seem pretty clear that Drummond, having been a client before the corporation was formed, is now a former client and can protest. At the very least, as in *Analytica* (page 310), Drummond can argue, client or not, that he gave the lawyer confidential information about himself in the expectation that it would be used only for his benefit. Right?

Wrong. At least wrong in Wisconsin, where Jesse v. Danforth, 485 N.W.2d 63 (Wis. 1992), held that once the corporation is created, it becomes the *only* client *retroactively*, displacing the corporate organizers, including poor Drummond, who become retroactive *non*clients. It's like when a disfavored former official got airbrushed out of one of those old Soviet-era photos. The court held that the "clear purpose" behind Rule 1.13 "was to enhance the corporate lawyer's ability to represent the best interests of the corporation without automatically having the additional and potentially conflicting burden of representing the corporation's constituents." So the court pronounced this rule:

> We thus provide the following guideline: where (1) a person retains a lawyer for the purpose of organizing an entity and (2) the lawyer's involvement with that person is directly related to that incorporation and (3) such entity is eventually incorporated, the entity rule applies retroactively such that the lawyer's pre-incorporation involvement with the person is deemed to be representation of the entity, not the person.
>
> In essence, the retroactive application of the entity rule simply gives the person who retained the lawyer the status of being a corporate constituent during the period before actual incorporation, as long as actual incorporation eventually occurred.
>
> This standard also applies to privileged communications under [Rule 1.6]. Thus, where the above standard is met, communications between the retroactive constituent and the corporation are protected under [Rule 1.6]. And, it is the corporate entity, not the retroactive constituent, that holds the privilege. This tracks the Comment to [Rule 1.13] which states in part: "When one of the constituents of an organizational client communicates with the organization's lawyer in that person's organizational capacity, the communication is protected by Rule 1.6."
>
> However, where the person who retained the lawyer provides information to the lawyer not directly related to the purpose of organizing an entity, then it is the person, not the corporation which holds the privilege for that communication.

Two of the corporate organizers pointed to the fact that in the course of the corporate formation, they had given the lawyer information about their "personal finances and their involvement in pending litigation," yet this was deemed insufficient to avoid the retroactivity rule because the information was "directly related to the purpose of organizing" the company and became the company's information once it was formed.

Won't this rule discourage full disclosure? Is it nevertheless justified by the broader policy the court identified? Must lawyers who counsel corporate organizers now warn them that, if the company is successfully formed, everything they tell the lawyer relevant to the work will become its, not their, confidences and that their status as clients will be erased as though it never existed? Is the Wisconsin court right?

So much for the beginning and end of corporate life. Let us now turn to confidentiality and loyalty duties in ongoing entities of various kinds, including during internal investigations.

Corporate Officers and Employees

Unless the facts suggest otherwise, corporate lawyers will be deemed to represent the entity and not its officers, directors, employees, or shareholders. In Commodity Futures Trading Commission v. Weintraub, 471 U.S. 343 (1985), a trustee for a bankrupt corporation waived attorney-client privilege for all communications between the company's former counsel and its former officers,

directors, and employees. Former management objected, but the Supreme
Court upheld the waiver: "[W]hen control of a corporation passes to new management, the authority to assert and waive the corporation's attorney-client
privilege passes as well." In bankruptcy, the Court wrote, "the actor whose duties
most closely resemble those of management should control the privilege." That
actor was the trustee. The Court could find no "policies underlying the bankruptcy laws" inconsistent with this conclusion.

A corporate officer or employee will enjoy a privilege along with the company
if he can establish that his communications with entity counsel were part of a
joint representation. Such efforts usually fail as they did in In re Grand Jury
Subpoena above. Consider In re Grand Jury Proceedings, 156 F.3d 1038 (10th
Cir. 1998), as common a fact pattern as you are likely to find in this area. A grand
jury was investigating the CEO of a hospital. It subpoenaed certain documents
from the hospital. The CEO intervened to prevent the hospital from delivering
the documents. He claimed that the hospital's lawyers were also his lawyers
and that the documents were privileged. The court relied on Matter of Bevill,
Bresler & Schulman Asset Mgmt. Corp., 805 F.2d 120 (3d Cir. 1986), to identify
the five-part burden for corporate officers who claim a personal privilege for
communications with corporate counsel:

> First, they must show they approached [counsel] for the purpose of seeking
> legal advice. Second, they must demonstrate that when they approached
> [counsel] they made it clear that they were seeking legal advice in their
> individual rather than in their representative capacities. Third, they must
> demonstrate that the [counsel] saw fit to communicate with them in their
> individual capacities, knowing that a possible conflict could arise. Fourth,
> they must prove that their conversations with [counsel] were confidential.
> And fifth, they must show that the substance of their conversations with
> [counsel] did not concern matters within the company or the general affairs
> of the company.

In the Tenth Circuit case, the claim failed because the CEO could not establish the fourth and fifth prongs of the *Bevill* test. Other circuits have been equally
skeptical of corporate officials' personal assertions of privilege even without
endorsing all elements of the *Bevill* test. United States v. International Brotherhood of Teamsters, 119 F.3d 210 (2d Cir. 1997), finds a union officer's "reasonable belief" insufficient to create a professional relationship with union counsel.
The officer must instead "make it clear to corporate counsel that he seeks legal
advice on personal matters." The burden will be hard to meet if the constituent
is sophisticated in dealing with counsel. United States v. Okun, 2008 Westlaw
2385253 (4th Cir. 2008) ("there could be no objectively reasonable basis for
Okun—a sophisticated businessman who, as the record reveals, had an
understanding of the nature of personal attorney-client relationships—to
have had a belief that Perkins was acting as his personal attorney"). A rare
case in which a company constituent was found to have a professional relationship with company counsel is United States v. Walters, 913 F.2d 388 (7th Cir.
1990) (professional relationship recognized where shareholder gave lawyers
"highly personal information about his activities" in an effort to learn whether
the company's contemplated acts were criminal).

Sometimes, as in the AOL case, high officials or the board of directors hire counsel specifically to do an internal investigation because of evidence of misconduct that could be attributed to the company and put it in legal jeopardy. See United States v. Aramony, 88 F.3d 1369 (4th Cir. 1996) (internal investigation of United Way leading to conviction of its president, among others). The lawyer may then do an internal investigation and report back to the board. In that investigation, the lawyer will talk to corporate constituents at all levels. If anything, courts are even more reluctant than usual to find attorney-client relationships between lawyers conducting internal investigations and corporate constituents. That's right, isn't it? Do you see why? Think of the conflicts that would immobilize any lawyer conducting an internal investigation for possible wrongdoing if the subjects of that investigation could legitimately claim to be the lawyer's clients along with the corporate employer. That may explain why courts are especially skeptical of privilege claims in these circumstances, although, once again, the investigating lawyer should be aware of obligations imposed by Rules 1.13(f) and 4.3. See also the "trigger" for warnings in D.C. Opinion 269 (1996) (requiring a lawyer conducting an internal investigation to advise a corporate constituent that he or she is not the lawyer's client when an actual conflict exists or when there "may be" adversity between the entity and the constituent).

A finding that a company lawyer also represented a company constituent on a common matter can create problems for the company if the two clients later take different positions in a matter, as the Fourth Circuit's AOL opinion takes pains to point out. The lawyer may have to withdraw from working for either client and his conflicts may be imputed to other lawyers in his office. Of course, sometimes the company may wish to have a single lawyer represent both it and a constituent. For example, imagine that a company and a corporate officer are both sued for fraud arising out of the same commercial transaction. Or a claim of employment discrimination may name both. Using a single lawyer will save money and facilitate coordination of the response. In deciding whether to do so, the company may weigh the gravity of the allegations and whether a conflict between the interests of the company and its constituent is likely to emerge. Are there precautions a company choosing this route may take? One prominent labor lawyer told me that his routine practice is to require the corporate constituent to sign an agreement acknowledging that the company was the "primary" client, that the representation of the officer was an "accommodation," that anything the officer told the lawyer could be shared with the company (but not the reverse), and that in the event of a disqualifying conflict the lawyer could continue to represent the company, even if it had claims against the officer, who would have to get new counsel. Will that kind of waiver stand up? It seems rather one-sided, especially when we realize that the officer will often find it costly to hire his own counsel. This is, of course, an advance consent. Its validity will depend on compliance with the jurisdiction's requirements for advance consents. See page 295.

Where it is not the company's intent to have its lawyer represent a corporate constituent, how might the lawyer avoid any implication that she does? Demanding that the constituent get his own lawyer (even paying for one) will do the trick. A lesser remedy is to give *Upjohn* warnings to all corporate employees whenever a lawyer has reason to believe that a conversation may produce information that the company may later wish to use, possibly adversely to the employee. (Does Rule 1.13(f) go this far?)

Upjohn warnings carry a price, don't they? If entity constituents realize that interviews with corporate counsel may return to haunt them, they will be circumspect about what they say, frustrating the company's efforts to get information and good advice. Actually, given the great reluctance of courts to find an attorney-client relationship between a company lawyer and a company constituent, isn't there an argument that the lawyer should warn the constituent only in the most ambiguous circumstance, so as not to inhibit full disclosure? This may not be nice to the constituent, but the lawyer represents the company, and the company may need the information. Let's make this a bit more concrete: What should a corporate lawyer do if Buddy, a midlevel officer with whom she has frequently worked, walks into her office and says, "I've got a little problem, Anne, and I need your help;" or Buddy says, "Anne, can we have a discussion, just between us?" Kathryn Tate focuses on one arena in which these problems arise — the pre-indictment phase of a criminal investigation. She makes "several proposals for clarifying and strengthening the Model Rules and their comments," with a view toward more clearly defining "an attorney's responsibilities to identify conflict of interest situations" and take appropriate action. Kathryn Tate, Lawyer Ethics and the Corporate Employee: Is the Employee Owed More Protection Than the Model Rules Provide?, 23 Ind. L. Rev. 1 (1990).

Common Interest Arrangements and Corporate Investigations.   In the Fourth Circuit's AOL case, Wakeford argued that his communications were privileged because of a common interest agreement. That could have worked *if* there really was such an agreement, but the court concluded that none was in place during the March-June interviews. The court cites United States v. Weissman, 195 F.3d 96 (2d Cir. 1999), where an indicted company officer also asserted a common interest privilege for a meeting among corporate counsel and the officer and his personal attorney. The problem was that no one bothered to say that the meeting was being held pursuant to a common interest agreement, much less to put the agreement in writing (highly advisable but not necessary) and to define its terms. The court was not prepared to infer an agreement from the circumstances.

So *now* what would you advise a midlevel officer to do when a company lawyer gives her *Upjohn* warnings? Not cooperate unless the company's lawyer agreed to represent her, too? Insist on having her own counsel and a common interest agreement that accorded her a privilege for anything she said? That might protect her, but if she did make either course a condition of cooperation, what might happen to her? Right. "You're fired." The company has a right to learn about matters within the scope of the officer's employment. Is this a perfect example of "between a rock and a hard place" if the officer has something to hide?

Partnerships

Client identity issues also arise when lawyers represent partnerships. Does the lawyer represent the partnership entity or the partners? Does it matter whether the partnership is limited or general? (Broadly speaking, limited partners are passive investors in the partnership business with no power to direct it.)

For general partnerships, most authorities take the position that the lawyer's client is the partnership as an entity, not the individual partners. ABA Opinion 91-361 interprets Rule 1.13 this way. In accord are Rhode Island Depositors Economic Protection Corp. v. Hayes, 64 F.3d 22 (1st Cir. 1995); and Johnson v. Superior Court, 45 Cal. Rptr. 2d 312 (Ct. App. 1995).

Imagine a partner of a general partnership in a jurisdiction that subscribes to the majority view. She asks the partnership lawyer for certain partnership information but is rebuffed because the information belongs to the client, the partnership, not the individual partners. Has she any recourse? Indeed she does. Even though she may not be the lawyer's client, as a partner she has a "right to access to information and communications concerning partnership business, including communications with attorneys who are retained to give advice concerning partnership business." Johnson v. Superior Court, supra. ABA Opinion 91-361 is in accord.

Because limited partners are essentially passive, the entity theory receives near-universal support for limited partnerships.

None of this means that a partnership lawyer cannot have a professional relationship with an individual partner, general or limited. She can, just as a corporate lawyer can represent a corporate constituent. It depends on the facts. The *Johnson* court told us that the factors to consider are the size of the partnership, the nature and scope of the attorney's engagement, the kind and extent of contacts between the attorney and the individual partners, the attorney's access to financial information relating to the individual partner's interests, and inferences about the partner's understanding drawn from the totality of the circumstances. See also Kilpatrick v. Wiley, Rein & Fielding, 37 P.3d 1130 (Utah 2001) (whether limited partners had attorney-client relationship with partnership counsel is a question of fact depending on "totality of the circumstances").

Privilege and Conflicts in Shareholder (and Other Fiduciary) Actions

The neat distinction between the corporate client and its constituents suffers a bit when one set of constituents challenges another set. In a shareholder derivative action, a group of shareholders may sue officers and directors or third parties, on the theory that the company has an unasserted claim against the defendants that the plaintiffs seek to vindicate. The corporation is named as a nominal defendant. May corporate counsel represent both the corporation and any officers and directors of the corporation who are named as defendants? See Harvard Conflicts Note, page 299, at 1339-1341:

> The possibility for conflict of interest here is universally recognized. Although early cases found joint representation permissible where no conflict of interest was obvious, the emerging rule is against dual representation in all derivative actions. Outside counsel must thus be retained to represent one of the defendants. The cases and ethics opinions differ on whether there must be separate

representation from the outset or merely from the time the corporation seeks to take an active role. Furthermore, this restriction on dual representation should not be waivable by consent in the usual way; the corporation should be presumptively incapable of giving valid consent.

In Messing v. FDI, Inc., 439 F. Supp. 776 (D.N.J. 1977), the court identified the "division of authority" on whether there can be joint representation of a corporation and its directors in a derivative action against both of them. The court also reviewed arguments that there may not be joint representation, at least where the director is charged with fraud on the corporation or where the corporation elects to take an active role in the litigation. Finally, the court noted the view of "commentators . . . that the corporation should *always* be separately represented in a derivative action." The court sided with the commentators:

> Irrespective of the nature of the charges against the directors — whether it be fraud or negligence — the interests of the two groups will almost always be diverse. Nor can we readily perceive the need for independent counsel turning upon the question whether the corporation has already elected to pursue an active or passive stance in the litigation, for that very election may have already been tainted by conflict.

Going not quite so far as *Messing*, the Third Circuit distinguished between disloyalty and mismanagement. The duty of loyalty "requires a director to act in good faith and in the honest belief that the action taken is in the corporation's best interests." That duty would be violated by "self-dealing, stealing, fraud, intentional misconduct, conflicts of interest, or usurpation of corporate opportunities." Mismanagement, by contrast, is a violation of the "duty of care." The court held that "except in patently frivolous cases," allegations of disloyalty require separate counsel. Alleged mismanagement does not. Where the "line is blurred between duties of care and loyalty, the better practice is to obtain separate counsel for individual and corporate defendants." Bell Atl. Corp. v. Bolger, 2 F.3d 1304 (3d Cir. 1993). Cases are collected in Musheno v. Gensemer, 897 F. Supp. 833 (M.D. Pa. 1995) (corporation must retain independent counsel where derivative claim, not "patently frivolous," alleges directorial fraud and willful misconduct).

For a case raising a similar problem in the context of union representation, see Yablonski v. United Mine Workers, 448 F.2d 1175 (D.C. Cir. 1971). Dissident mine workers, seeking an accounting from union officers, sued the officers and (nominally) the union itself under federal labor laws. The issues were, first, whether the union's outside counsel, Williams & Connolly, could represent both it and the officers (no) and second, whether, after the firm withdrew from representing the officers (whom the firm had represented on other matters), it could continue to represent the union (no again). Why not?

Another issue that arises in shareholder derivative actions, and elsewhere that a breach of fiduciary duty is charged, is whether the plaintiffs can require the corporation's lawyer to produce privileged information on the theory that they are suing to enforce a right of the corporation. The leading case, Garner v. Wolfinbarger, 430 F.2d 1093 (5th Cir. 1970), held that in such an action the shareholders should be permitted "to show cause" why the privilege "should

not be invoked in the particular instance." Among the factors to consider, said
the court, were the following (with brackets added for convenience):

> There are many indicia that may contribute to a decision of presence or
> absence of good cause, among them [1] the number of shareholders and
> the percentage of stock they represent; [2] the bona fides of the shareholders;
> [3] the nature of the shareholders' claim and whether it is obviously colorable;
> [4] the apparent necessity or desirability of the shareholders having the
> information and the availability of it from other sources; [5] whether, if the
> shareholders' claim is of wrongful action by the corporation, it is of action
> criminal, or illegal but not criminal, or of doubtful legality; [6] whether the
> communication related to past or to prospective actions; [7] whether the com-
> munication is of advice concerning the litigation itself; [8] the extent to which
> the communication is identified versus the extent to which the shareholders are
> blindly fishing; [9] the risk of revelation of trade secrets or other information in
> whose confidentiality the corporation has an interest for independent reasons.

The *Garner* rationale has been extended to nonderivative shareholder actions
against corporate directors and officers, Panter v. Marshall Field & Co., 80 F.R.D.
718 (N.D. Ill. 1978); to actions in which the plaintiffs bought their stock only
after the alleged corporate misrepresentation, In re Bairnco Corp. Sec. Litig.,
148 F.R.D. 91 (S.D.N.Y. 1993); and to actions in which the plaintiffs charge the
defendant with breach of a fiduciary duty, Helt v. Metropolitan Dist. Commn.,
113 F.R.D. 7 (D. Conn. 1986) (rejecting defendant's claim of privilege in a
beneficiary's action against a pension fund trustee). The Fifth Circuit has
applied *Garner* to reject a claim of privilege where the plaintiffs, participants
in an Employee Stock Ownership Plan (ESOP), sued Occidental Petroleum
Corp. "as plan beneficiaries on behalf of the plan." Although the plaintiffs
were not themselves shareholders in Occidental, the ESOP was a shareholder.
The plaintiffs were allowed to assert the ESOP's *Garner* argument to defeat
Occidental's claim of privilege. In re Occidental Petroleum Corp., 217 F.3d
293 (5th Cir. 2000).

Weintraub (page 548) strengthens *Garner*, doesn't it, because it recognizes that
a company's privilege is controlled by its current management, who may choose
to reveal communications between former officers and corporate counsel. It's
just one further step, then, to say that the ultimate beneficiaries of the lawyer's
work, in this case shareholders, may be allowed to override even current management's claim of privilege using the *Garner* criteria.

Members of Corporate Families

One company may be the "parent" of other companies. It may, in fact, have
dozens or hundreds of "children," called subsidiaries, which it owns directly or
through other subsidiaries. Two companies may be co-subsidiaries of a parent,
in which case they are sometimes called "sister corporations," not "brother
corporations" or even "sibling corporations." I don't know the reason for
this nomenclature. Representation of a member of a corporate family generates
issues in the area of conflicts doctrine and also for the attorney-client privilege.
At bottom, these issues raise the same question, which in essence is this: When a

corporate lawyer does work for one member of a corporate family, what duties, if any, does she assume to other members of the corporate family? The answer to this question can have profound effect on the work of corporate lawyers.

Corporate Family Conflicts. Many corporate families are remarkably large (and their membership may change monthly). For example, in Reuben H. Donnelly Corp. v. Sprint Publishing and Advertising, Inc., 1996 Westlaw 99902 (N.D. Ill. 1996), Sprint sought to disqualify Jones Day from representing the plaintiff because Jones Day represented a Sprint affiliate, although not the defendant itself. Sprint argued that Jones Day was, in effect, suing its own client because representation of the affiliate made other family members clients of the firm. The court rejected the motion, noting that Sprint had "over 250 subsidiaries and affiliated entities," while Jones Day had "1098 attorneys spread over 20 world-wide offices." But if the representation of one company does not by itself automatically translate into a professional relationship with all separately incorporated affiliates in the same corporate family, does it ever do so?

ABA Opinion 95-390 concluded that the representation of one company will make its corporate affiliate a client only under limited circumstances. Certainly if the law firm and the client agree that affiliates of the client will be deemed clients of the law firm, that will suffice. Beyond agreement, which may be implicit, an affiliate of a client may be deemed a client if the two companies operate as alter egos; if the two companies have integrated operations and management; if the same in-house legal staff handles legal matters for both the affiliate and the client; or if representation of the client has provided the law firm with confidential information about the affiliate that would be relevant in any matter adverse to the affiliate. For a thorough discussion of the issues here and other authorities, see Morrison Knudsen Corp. v. Hancock, Rothert & Bunshoft, 81 Cal. Rptr. 2d 425 (Ct. App. 1999).

A court disqualified the law firm LeBoeuf Lamb from suing Gerling, which was a subsidiary of Gerling AG, because LeBoeuf was simultaneously representing GGRCA, another Gerling AG subsidiary. Travelers Indemnity Co. v. Gerling Global Reinsurance Corp., 2000 Westlaw 1159260 (S.D.N.Y. 2000). Applying the New York Code, the court wrote:

> In this action, the nature of the relationship between LeBoeuf and Gerling is predicated upon the relationship between Gerling and GGRCA. It is true that Gerling and GGRCA are separately incorporated entities. Indeed, if Travelers was seeking to impute liability between the two companies, Gerling would no doubt rely on the protection of the corporate veil. However, there is considerable overlap between the two companies, especially within their corporate structures, and this sways the Court to grant Gerling's motion. For example, the companies are engaged in very similar businesses while sharing the same chairman, president, chief operating officer, chief financial officer, and chief actuary. Further, the companies share office space, payroll and human resource departments, and corporate services. They even share the same computer networks and systems, travel agents, mail services, credit card issuers, and annual employee gatherings.
>
> With such overlap, LeBoeuf's representation of GGRCA while concurrently advocating against Gerling raises the specter of divided loyalty. One could imagine an endless number of scenarios. For example, LeBoeuf attorneys

will no doubt continue to advise GGRCA management regarding ongoing litigation, while at the same time other LeBoeuf attorneys may be preparing to depose these same individuals, in their capacity as Gerling management, for the prosecution of this case. Speculation aside, it is the mere risk of divided loyalty that the Court is concerned with, not only ethical scenarios that can be readily envisioned at this juncture. The purpose of Canon 5 is to protect a client not only from outright and egregious examples of divided loyalty, but also the subtle and indefinable impact that it might have on an attorney's representation.

Dorsey & Whitney got tossed off a case against defendant "WAII," a second-tier, wholly owned subsidiary of Wyeth, because the firm then represented a division of Wyeth Pharmaceuticals, which was another second-tier Wyeth subsidiary. Discotrade Ltd. v. Wyeth-Ayerst International, Inc., 200 F.Supp.2d 355 (S.D.N.Y. 2002). Judge Buchwald wrote that

> WAII and Pharmaceuticals share the same board of directors as well as several senior officers, including their President. . . . The two corporations also inter-act intimately, for example by using the same computer network, e-mail sys-tem, travel department, and health benefit plan. In short, WAII and Pharmaceuticals do not view each other as strangers, but more like members of the Wyeth family. Our conclusion is reinforced by the practical aspects of their relationship, including their common "Wyeth" letterhead, common "Wyeth" business cards, and common "Wyeth" e-mail addresses. WAII has met their burden of demonstrating that its relationship with Pharmaceuticals is so close that a conflict exists.

Over dissent, the ABA Opinion attempted to put one issue to rest, but it has resurfaced in the Restatement of Law Governing Lawyers, and the courts are not likely to accept the ABA resolution in all situations. That resolution can have significant consequences when law firms represent a member of a corporate family. Suppose a firm represents Parent in several matters. It is then retained to bring a claim against Subsidiary. Assume the claim is factually unrelated to any work the firm does for Parent. And assume that none of the tests in the ABA Opinion would make Subsidiary the client of the firm. But what if the action against Subsidiary involves a great deal of money? Perhaps it could put Subsidiary out of business. That in turn may cause Parent substantial harm. Should the fact that the action could have a serious financial effect on the firm's client prevent the firm from acting adversely to nonclient Subsidiary? On the one hand, much that a law firm may do for one client can have harmful economic consequences to another client, yet ordinarily that alone will not create a conflict situation. Firms may even represent economic competitors. See Rule 1.7 comment [6]. But the situation is different when a lawsuit against a client's affiliate could cause the client substantial financial injury. Then, the harm is more direct than helping a client's competitor better perform in the marketplace.

The ABA Opinion concluded that economic adversity, standing alone, would not create a conflict. But the Restatement of Law Governing Lawyers appears to disagree. Section 121 comment *d* states the general rule that when a lawyer represents Corporation *A*, the company "is ordinarily the lawyer's client; neither individual officers of Corporation *A* nor other corporations in which

Corporation *A* has an ownership interest, that hold an ownership interest in Corporation *A*, or in which a major shareholder in Corporation *A* has an ownership interest, are thereby considered to be the lawyer's client." So far, so good. But the comment then goes on to say that in some situations this will not be true, such as "where financial loss or benefit to the nonclient person or entity will have a direct, adverse impact on the client." The comment then gives this example:

> Lawyer represents Corporation *A* in local real-estate transactions. Lawyer has been asked to represent Plaintiff in a products-liability action against Corporation *B* claiming substantial damages. Corporation *B* is a wholly owned subsidiary of Corporation *A*; any judgment obtained against Corporation *B* will have a material adverse impact on the value of Corporation *B*'s assets and on the value of the assets of Corporation *A*. Just as Lawyer could not file suit against Corporation *A* on behalf of another client, even in a matter unrelated to the subject of Lawyer's representation of Corporation *A* (see §128, Comment *e*), Lawyer may not represent Plaintiff in the suit against Corporation *B* without the consent of both Plaintiff and Corporation *A* under the limitations and conditions provided in §122.

In JP Morgan Chase Bank v. Liberty Mutual Insurance Co., 189 F. Supp. 2d 20 (S.D.N.Y. 2002), Judge Rakoff cited a potentially huge economic impact, among other factors, in disqualifying Davis Polk from pursuing a $183 million claim against Federal, 95 percent of which was owned by Chubb, a firm client. Federal accounted for some 90 percent of Chubb's business.

But wait a minute. We began by asking when the representation of one corporate family member means another member is also client, at least for conflict purposes. And we identified various tests. When, however, the courts (or the Restatement) do not allow a firm to act adversely to a client's subsidiary because victory can economically harm the *parent*, the subsidiary does not thereby become a client. The firm owes it nothing. Rather, the action is seen as disloyal to the parent.

Privilege Issues in the Corporate Family.   Contained here are several issues of great importance to lawyers for corporate parents and an opinion that goes beyond the facts of the case before the court to offer a sort of Michelin Guide for the perplexed.

Teleglobe was a wholly owned subsidiary of Bell Canada (BCE). The in-house lawyers for BCE did work for both companies. It is common and efficient to centralize the general counsel's work for all entities in a corporate family. Probably, a parent's in-house lawyers don't think a whole lot about who the client is or isn't when their work addresses legal issues for a wholly owned subsidiary because the parent has the power to make all decisions for companies it wholly owns. "When one company wholly owns another, the directors of the parent and the subsidiary are obligated to manage the affairs of the subsidiary in the best interests only of the parent and its shareholders." Aviall, Inc. v. Ryder Systems Inc., 913 F.Supp. 826 (S.D.N.Y. 1996).* That means the parent controls the

---

* *Aviall* found no fiduciary duty to the subsidiary "even when the parent company announces a proposed spin-off of the subsidiary." On that point, *Teleglobe* seems to disagree. The court wrote: "It is inevitable that on occasion parents and subsidiaries will see their interests diverge, particularly in

subsidiary's attorney-client privilege and also the lawyer's duties of loyalty and confidentiality. The interests appear entirely congruent and usually are because the subsidiary's role in life is merely to please the parent. But the congruence can end when the parent is planning to sell the subsidiary or spin it off as an independent company or, as in *Teleglobe*, when the subsidiary becomes insolvent or in the zone of insolvency. Then what? As Judge Ambro put it in In re Teleglobe Communications Corp., 493 F.3d 345 (3d Cir. 2007) (internal citations are omitted):

> Delaware courts have recognized that parents and their wholly owned subsidiaries have the same interests because all of the duties owed to the subsidiaries flow back up to the parent. "[I]n a parent and wholly-owned subsidiary context, the directors of the subsidiary are obligated only to manage the affairs of the subsidiary in the best interests of the parent and its shareholders." While we normally assume that a corporation's primary interest is in maximizing its economic value, the only interest of a wholly owned subsidiary is in serving its parent. That doing so may not always involve maximizing the subsidiary's economic value is of little concern. If the subsidiary is not wholly owned, however, in the interest of protecting minority shareholders we revert to requiring that whoever controls the subsidiary seek to maximize its economic value with requisite care and loyalty. Similarly, if the subsidiary is insolvent, we require the same in the interest of protecting the subsidiary's creditors. "[T]he creditors of an *insolvent* corporation have standing to maintain derivative claims against directors on behalf of the corporation for breaches of fiduciary duties. The corporation's insolvency makes the creditors the principal constituency injured by any fiduciary breaches that diminish the firm's value. Therefore, equitable considerations give creditors standing to pursue derivative claims against the directors of an insolvent corporation. Individual creditors of an insolvent corporation have the same incentive to pursue valid derivative claims on its behalf that shareholders have when the corporation is solvent."

In *Teleglobe* itself, there came a time when BCE decided to spin off the subsidiary (and stop giving it money) but BCE's in-house lawyers allegedly continued to represent the soon-to-be spun off subsidiary on the details of the spin-off transaction. After the spin off, Teleglobe and *its* wholly owned subsidiaries (called "the Debtors" in the court's opinion) both landed in bankruptcy court in Canada and the Debtors also filed for bankruptcy in Delaware. The Debtors then sued BCE for breach of contract and fiduciary duty and on other theories. In the lawsuit, the Debtors claimed that because BCE's in-house lawyers had jointly represented both BCE and Teleglobe on the spin-off, Teleglobe (and therefore the Debtors) were entitled to BCE's privileged communications with its in-house counsel on the subject of the joint representation.

---

spin-off, sale, and insolvency situations. When this happens, it is wise for the parent to secure for the subsidiary outside representation. Maintaining a joint representation for the spin-off transaction too long risks the outcome [in precedent] in which parent companies were forced to turn over documents to their former subsidiaries in adverse litigation — not to mention the attorneys' potential for running afoul of conflict rules."

The Debtors also claimed that they were entitled to privileged information from BCE's *outside* lawyers, although these lawyers did not jointly represent Teleglobe, on the theory that the work of the outside lawyers had been "funneled" to the inside lawyers who were then obligated to share the information with their joint client Teleglobe. As we know, under an exception, joint clients cannot assert privilege in the event of later adversity between them. See page 283.

This claim (and its success in the district court) caused no small measure of alarm among lawyers for parents who routinely also do work for subsidiaries. The Association of Corporate Counsel (ACC) filed an amicus brief for BCE. The lower court's ruling seemed ominously to portend that corporate parents who let their lawyers do work for their subsidiaries would lose control of their attorney-client privilege if the interests of parent and subsidiary later became adverse. That was not a risk a parent would want to run. But neither would it want to hire separate counsel for each of its subsidiaries in order to protect its own privilege. The Third Circuit reversed and remanded for more fact finding, but in doing so, it endorsed four principles. BCE won the appeal, but the victory was not total.

First, the court held that if indeed a parent's counsel represented both the parent and the subsidiary, then the joint client exception to the privilege would apply and the subsidiary would be entitled to use the privileged information against the parent if the two became adverse. The court rejected a request to create a different "default" rule in the context of corporate family representations. (It's a "default" rule if the joint clients can contract around it.) Said the court:

> In the context of a joint attorney representing a parent and its solvent wholly owned subsidiary, BCE's argument that we should flip the normal default rule (that all information shared in the course of a joint representation is not privileged in subsequent adverse litigation between the former joint clients) has some appeal, as it probably is more in line with the typical parent company's intent. But because parent-subsidiary relationships often change, having opposite default rules for wholly owned, solvent subsidiaries, and not-wholly owned or insolvent subsidiaries, seems unwieldy. In the course of a joint representation, a subsidiary could go from being wholly owned and solvent to majority-owned or insolvent (or both). Under those circumstances, it is not clear which default rule BCE would have us apply. Because of the need for clarity and certainty in privilege law, creating multiple, ever-shifting default rules would be unwise. Simply following the default rule against information shielding creates simpler, and more predictable, ground rules.*

Second, the court reminded the parties, the lower court, and indeed the world, that a parent has a strong and legitimate interest in having its lawyers

---

* In addition, the court held that the Debtors would not be entitled to the privileged information from a joint representation in any event unless they were also clients of BCE's lawyers (a question to be decided on remand). Their claim to a sort of derivative entitlement based on their status as wholly owned subsidiaries of Teleglobe was rejected.

(especially inside lawyers) jointly represent its subsidiaries where their interests are aligned. Who can disagree with that!

> We agree with ACC that a rule forcing parent companies to choose between relinquishing the privilege on one hand and relinquishing any control over their subsidiaries makes little sense. If the parent chooses to forgo the use of its in-house counsel on an important transaction, then it loses the advisors that know the most about its legal health. If it chooses to cut off its subsidiary, then it risks liability when the subsidiary and parent do not operate in tandem. Putting that choice in the context of this case, it appears that BCE spent some four months deciding what to do with Teleglobe. Over the course of Project X ["a comprehensive reassessment of BCE's plans for Teleglobe"], it considered a variety of options that did not involve abandoning Teleglobe. Moreover, during this time it was still responsible for reviewing Teleglobe's public filings. Thus for BCE's in-house counsel to cut Teleglobe off would have been an expensive and risky proposition. Similarly, given that BCE was in the process of making a very serious business decision with important legal implications, to deprive it of its in-house counsel simply so that those attorneys could continue to advise Teleglobe on other matters seems overly harsh.
>
> To prevent this outcome, it is important for in-house counsel in the first instance to be clear about the scope of parent-subsidiary joint representations. By properly defining the scope, they can leave themselves free to counsel the parent *alone* on the substance and ramifications of important transactions without risking giving up the privilege in subsequent adverse litigation.

Third, the court wrote that the fact that the work of the parent's counsel concerns the subsidiary or requires dealing with or getting information from it does not mean that the subsidiary is *necessarily* a client as well. In fact, the court implies that the parent's counsel can avoid that conclusion by agreement.

> "[I]t is permissible (subject, of course, to conflict rules) for attorneys and clients to limit the scope of a joint representation in a sophisticated manner; nothing requires construing the scope of a joint representation more broadly than the parties to it intend." . . .
>
> In sum, in-house counsel have available numerous means to protect a parent company's privilege. By taking care not to begin joint representations except when necessary, to limit the scope of joint representations, and seasonably to [retain] separate counsel on matters in which subsidiaries are adverse to the parent, in-house counsel can maintain sufficient control over the parent's privileged communications.

Finally, the court invoked what it called "the *Eureka* principle" (discussed at page 283) to avoid loss of BCE's privilege based on the allegation that its in-house counsel jointly represented both BCE and Teleglobe. "The guiding principle of *Eureka* is that when an attorney errs by continuing to represent two clients despite their conflicts, the clients — who reasonably expect their communications to be secret — are not penalized by losing their privilege. Indeed, *Eureka* is merely one in a line of cases that hold that communications outside the scope of the joint representation or common interest remain privileged." In other words, BCE would not have to pay through loss of its privilege for the lawyer's "bad judgment" in continuing to represent Teleglobe after a conflict arose between its interests and those of BCE.

Closely Held Entities

Rule 1.13(a)'s distinctions work less well when the entity is small. Does it make sense to say that counsel to a corporation whose officers, directors, and shareholders total only three people "represents the organization acting through its duly authorized constituents"? Often it will make sense. If one of the three is found stealing from the company, we won't have much trouble if the corporate lawyer sues him. Or if a shareholder has sued the company, its lawyer will be allowed to defend it. Bobbitt v. Victorian House, Inc., 545 F. Supp. 1124 (N.D. III. 1982) (company counsel can defend dissolution and accounting action brought by 50-percent shareholder against company and other shareholder). By contrast, where one shareholder is seeking to get control over the company or is planning to start a competing business, the company's lawyer had better remain neutral. The following instructive opinion was delivered in open court on June 6, 1994, following a bench trial before Judge Roush of the Fairfax County (Virginia) Circuit Court. Afterward, the parties settled with no appeal.

Here's what you should know for background. Murphy & Demory was a corporation with a three-person board and two co-owners, Admiral Murphy and Mr. Demory. Its business was lobbying, and its law firm was Pillsbury, Madison & Sutro. The company sued Admiral Murphy, Pillsbury, and certain Pillsbury lawyers. Essentially, it charged that Murphy, aided by Pillsbury, attempted either to take control of the company (ousting Demory) or to start a competing company, even though he owed fiduciary duties to the plaintiff corporation. Judge Roush found against Murphy and then proceeded to consider the claim against Pillsbury. Note her findings on the firm's failure to heed the warnings of junior associates (some of which were discovered in e-mail) and her criticism of the firm's procedures for monitoring compliance with ethics rules.*

MURPHY & DEMORY, LTD., ET AL. v. ADMIRAL DANIEL J. MURPHY, U.S.N. (RET.), ET AL.

Circuit Court of Fairfax County (Virginia) Chancery No. 128219, June 6, 1994

ROUSH, JUDGE. . . .

On count VI of the bill of complaint, Murphy & Demory alleges a cause of action against the Defendants [Pillsbury], Deanne Siemer, and Keith Mendelson, for legal malpractice. I will refer to those Defendants collectively as the Pillsbury Defendants. All parties agree that the law of the District of Columbia applies. . . .

---

* The reporter's transcript has been reparagraphed for easier reading. Bracketed numbers are added.

In rendering my decision on count VI, I've considered and carefully reviewed the Rules of Professional Conduct of the District of Columbia . . . as well as the testimony of the Plaintiff 's expert witness, Mr. David Epstein.

I find Murphy & Demory has proven by a preponderance of the evidence that the Pillsbury Defendants have committed legal malpractice [1] by violating the standard of care for attorneys practicing in the District of Columbia; [2] by accepting representation of Admiral Murphy in his efforts either to take control of Murphy & Demory or to form, prior to his resignation from Murphy & Demory, a new corporation to compete with Murphy & Demory, [as a result of which] the exercise of their professional judgment on behalf of the corporation would likely be adversely affected; [3] by simultaneously representing Admiral Murphy in matters adverse to their client, Murphy & Demory, without disclosing to the corporation or to Admiral Murphy the fact of the dual representation in obtaining the corporation's consent of such representation; [4] by meeting with the director of the corporation, Margot Bester, for the purpose of enlisting her support in Admiral Murphy's plans to take over control of the corporation; [5] by inducing or attempting to induce employees of Murphy & Demory to resign from Murphy & Demory and to join Murphy & Associates and by assisting Murphy & Demory employees in drafting their letters of resignation from the company; [6] by generally assisting Admiral Murphy in his plans to either take control of Murphy & Demory or to divert business from Murphy & Demory in favor of his new competing company, Murphy & Associates, while at the same time representing Murphy & Demory without the corporation's consent to the dual representation after full disclosure of all material facts; [7] by drafting the restructuring or takeover proposal for Admiral Murphy; [8] by drafting letters for Murphy & Demory clients to send, terminating their relationship with Murphy & Demory and directing that their files be transferred to Murphy & Associates; [9] by assisting Admiral Murphy while still counsel to Murphy & Demory in preparing his remarks to be delivered to the Murphy & Demory employees on August 30, 1992, in which, among other things, Admiral Murphy in effect invited employees to join him in his new company if the board of Murphy & Demory did not accede to his demands for control of the corporation; [10] by calling and/or attending meetings with Mr. Demory and other Murphy & Demory employees in the Pillsbury Defendants' capacity as the corporation's counsel; [11] in using confidential information obtained at such meetings for the benefit of Admiral Murphy; [12] by failing to disclose to Murphy & Demory material information known to the Pillsbury Defendants that might affect how the board of directors of Murphy & Demory might act; [13] by filing on behalf of Murphy & Demory a lawsuit seeking judicial dissolution of their by-then former client, Murphy & Demory, based in part on the confidential information obtained from Murphy & Demory employees during the course of their representation of Murphy & Demory.

The Pillsbury Defendants ignored the warnings of junior associates at the law firm that the dual representation of Admiral Murphy was rife with conflicts of interest and the matters on which they were advising the Admiral entailed possible breaches of fiduciary duty and use of corporate opportunities.

I was struck and disturbed by the fact that every inquiry by an associate into the propriety of the firm's actions was referred back to Ms. Siemer for resolution. Clearly, Pillsbury, Madison & Sutro's internal mechanisms for resolution of ethical issues are seriously deficient. The partner in charge of the client relationship affected by the issue, who is least likely to be objective, is the ultimate arbiter of whether the firm has a conflict of interest. I found Ms. Siemer's testimony to lack credibility when she stated that she wrestled with the ethical issues posed by the joint representation of Murphy & Demory and Admiral Murphy and concluded that there was no conflict because both clients had an identical interest in ensuring that Admiral Murphy had the best information possible as to what his options were, even if one option was to divert business from Murphy & Demory and let the company wither. As Mr. Epstein aptly noted in his expert testimony, Murphy & Demory had no interest in Admiral Murphy's knowledge of how to undermine the company.

I find that Ms. Siemer willfully ignored the District of Columbia Rules of Professional Conduct with which she was well familiar, having written a treatise on legal ethics. I find that Pillsbury, Madison & Sutro is equally responsible for Ms. Siemer's lapses in this regard, particularly because in the face of warning bells from the associates, the firm allowed Ms. Siemer to be the final determiner of whether the firm had a conflict of interest.

Although I'm not unsympathetic to Mr. Mendelson's difficult position at the time of most of the activities complained of, I find that he too was equally responsible for the legal malpractice. Simply put, Mr. Mendelson was senior enough that he should have put a stop to the undisclosed dual representation of Admiral Murphy and Murphy & Demory by disclosing the conflict to Admiral Murphy and Murphy & Demory's board in obtaining their consent, or failing that, by withdrawing from the representation. . . .

I find that as a direct and proximate result of the Pillsbury Defendants' legal malpractice, Murphy & Demory suffered compensatory damages in the amount of $500,000. . . .

William Granewich was a shareholder in a closely held Oregon corporation. He sued the other two shareholders, Harding and Alexander-Hergert, claiming that they breached their fiduciary duties to him by "depriving plaintiff of his position as a director, of the value of his shares of stock, of his further employment with and compensation from FFG (the company), and of the benefits of participating in the corporate affairs of FFG." Granewich also named the company's outside counsel as defendants, charging that they knowingly assisted the other shareholders in violating fiduciary duties to him. Although there was no Oregon law directly on point, the state supreme court concluded that the legal authorities were "virtually . . . unanimous in expressing the proposition that one who knowingly aids another in the breach of a fiduciary duty is liable to the one harmed thereby. That principle readily extends to lawyers." Granewich v. Harding, 985 P.2d 788 (Or. 1999). Reinstating the complaint against the lawyers, the court wrote:

> The complaint alleges that the lawyers entered into an agreement with Harding and Alexander-Hergert to take such actions as may be necessary to squeeze plaintiff out of FFG and to deprive plaintiff of the value of his FFG stock, objectives that are alleged to be in breach of Harding's and Alexander-Hergert's

fiduciary duties to plaintiff as majority shareholders and directors. . . . In addition, the amended complaint alleges that the lawyers knew that the object to be accomplished was the breach of [these] duties . . . that the lawyers provided substantial assistance to them in their efforts in that regard, and that plaintiff was damaged as a result.

The court backed away from the breadth of its holding in Reynolds v. Schrock, 142 P.3d 1062 (Or. 2006). It explained that in *Granewich* the lawyer had assisted a breach of fiduciary duty *while he represented the company.* In *Reynolds,* by contrast, the lawyer's client was an individual, who allegedly breached a fiduciary duty to another person with the lawyer's advice.

Taking sides in fights for control can also create civil liability for lawyers who represent partnerships. Griva v. Davison, 637 A.2d 830 (D.C. 1994) (summary judgment denied where partnership's lawyer was sued for allegedly taking sides between feuding partners). Yet another entity of sorts is the joint venture. Whereas partnerships and corporations are usually treated as entity clients in their own right, at least one federal judge has held that each member of a joint venture has an attorney-client relationship with the venture's lawyer. Al-Yusr Townsend & Bottum Co. v. United Mid East Co., 1995 Westlaw 592548 (E.D. Pa. 1995) (relying on authority reaching same conclusion for unincorporated associations).

FURTHER READING

Lawrence Mitchell has grappled with the special problems of lawyers for closely held corporations in Professional Responsibility and the Close Corporation: Toward a Realistic Ethic, 74 Cornell L. Rev. 466 (1989). Using a hypothetical and analyzing conflicts in entity representation from three perspectives (favoring one of them) is William Simon, Whom (or What) Does the Organization's Lawyer Represent?: An Anatomy of Intraclient Conflict, 91 Cal. L. Rev. 57 (2003).

B. RETALIATORY DISCHARGE AND WHISTLEBLOWING

"Contraindications"

Lauren Sinder: If you could give me a brief professional history. . . .

Dan Worzek: Graduated from law school in '96. Masters in Public Health in '93. Associate at Goodman Dubnick Shaw & Hosada to '99, counseling health care providers. HMOs, hospitals, professional medical corporations. I went in house at Lifecare in '99 as an assistant GC. I'm now one of eight associate GCs, under one of the two deputy GCs. We have, I guess, about 85 in-house lawyers worldwide, 50 in the U.S. Is that coffee over there?

Sinder: Help yourself.

Worzek: Well, that's it. I'm closing in on 40, wife teaches science in the community college, two girls, three and six. We were thinking about a third until this happened. Um. We live in Marbury. We moved two years ago, for schools. And to be closer to work. That's it really. Just a midcareer lawyer doing an ordinary job.

Sinder. Then what?

Worzek: Four months ago, the deputy GC I report to, Roswell Killington, asked me to look into an inquiry we received from lawyers for Providencia Hospital. The hospital had administered one of our patented pain medicines, Amulex, to an elderly patient, who died. The patient's family hired a lawyer to look into it. The hospital's lawyer was asking about Amulex.

Sinder. This is a prescription medicine.

Worzek: Yes, and, uh, rather expensive, too. The research and marketing cost a lot. But it's a big seller.

Sinder. What did you turn up?

Worzek: Contraindications that were not in the advisories to doctors. That's not uncommon. We don't have to give the doctors or the public everything. It's a question of judgment. We don't include stuff that's statistically unreliable, as I understand it. You can't say everything, no matter how anecdotal or conjectural.

Sinder. How did you learn about these conjectures?

Worzek: I interviewed the researchers who did the tests.

Sinder: Did you have anything to do with bringing Alumex to market?

Worzek: It's Amulex. We spend a lot of money on these names. I imagine it's meant to sound like amulet. You know, a magic pill. No, I had nothing to do with it. I don't do the FDA, patent office, or marketing stuff as a rule and didn't on Amulex.

Sinder. What did you do with the information?

Worzek: I was going to write a report for Ros. But in checking e-mail archives on the drugs I found these [*hands file*]. Lab people expressing qualms. One you'll see from Dr. Dykstra, head of research, says Amulex might present cardiovascular hazards for some patients. Another e-mail from someone I don't know urges continued testing. I also looked at the paperwork we gave the FDA. It implies greater thoroughness than I was finding and none of the reservations.

Sinder. What do you mean "it implies"?

Worzek: Most anyone reading it would assume we had collected more data than we actually did and were more confident than we actually were.

Sinder. You were saying about Killington.

Worzek: Instead, I told him orally what I found and my suspicions. He asked my advice and I said, you know, the product is still out there. A big seller. Our ticker price is up 27 percent this year because of Amulex sales. Still, you know. So I said we had to tell Providencia and the FDA and change the advisories. He said he'd take care of it.

Sinder. Did he?

Worzek: Couple of weeks later, I asked him. He said Serena had decided we had nothing to hide; we did all the process right, so we weren't going public.

Sinder. Serena?

Worzek: Van Camp. The GC. So I said if we have nothing to hide, why have we decided not to go public? Yeah, that was snotty, I know.

Sinder. Then?

Worzek: At a monthly meeting of the associates with Ros and Serena a few weeks later, I raised it again. Serena said they had consulted counsel and concluded we were acting properly. She was pretty curt. We've never been buddies. It's civil but not warm. That was two months ago. Since then, I've been, I mean I don't think I'm imagining, I've been kept out of the loop on important things, and I haven't been given anything new to work on except routine stuff. Last week, Ros told me that the company was doing cost cutting and I couldn't go to the annual meeting of our professional group in Denver. But six other associate GCs are going and a few assistants.

Sinder: You think you're being squeezed out?

Worzek: Yeah, I do. That's what I think. I like my job. I have a new house and two little kids. I'm midcareer. I'm also worried, frankly, about professional and financial liability for myself. Plaintiffs' lawyers could go after individuals, too. I've seen it happen. And what about my duty to my client? I mean this could blow up. Millions of people take Amulex. So that's why I'm here. You're the ethics expert. What's your advice?

More than 40 jurisdictions recognize a retaliatory discharge claim for employees. The contours of the claim vary, but essentially it affords tort recovery when an employee is discharged for insisting on compliance with or the protection of an important public policy or legal obligation. Examples of such policies include reporting serious criminal conduct; applying for workers' compensation; and a refusal to commit perjury. Some jurisdictions recognize, in addition or instead, a right to sue for breach of implied contract on the same facts. A contract claim is not as powerful a tort claim because the plaintiff will have to persuade the court to infer a contract term (either as a matter of fact or law), and then to find that it was breached, and because contract damages are ordinarily not as generous as tort damages. No punitives. Only economic harm.

The last several decades have seen rapid growth in the number of lawyers employed by corporations and other entities. Inevitably the question has arisen: Do these lawyers enjoy the same rights that other corporate employees have to sue for retaliatory discharge or breach of implied contract? Or are they left out just because they're lawyers and stand in a different relationship to the employer-client than does management, even the CEO?

Balla v. Gambro, Inc., cited in *Crews*, the next principal case, was the first opinion clearly raising this issue to reach a state supreme court. And a compelling case it was. Balla told his employer that its imminent marketing of defective kidney dialysis machines violated FDA regulations. He was fired. The next day he reported the (now former) employer's plan to the FDA, and the FDA intervened. Balla sued for retaliatory discharge. The Illinois Supreme Court, although recognizing that a nonlawyer employee in Illinois would have a retaliatory claim on the identical facts, denied one to Balla only because he was a lawyer. Shocked? I was.

Two sidelights from *Balla* are worth noting. Illinois's version of Rule 1.6 (unlike the Model Rule) *required* Balla to report the defective machines. Should that fact have helped Balla establish his claim or made it harder? The second sidelight, seemingly odd but perhaps not after a moment's reflection, is this: The leading professional group that promotes the interests of house counsel (that is, lawyers *employed* by corporations and other entities) is the Association of Corporate Counsel (ACC), formerly the American Corporate Counsel Association (ACCA). ACC filed an amicus brief in *Balla*. Whom did it support? Gambro, the employer, or Balla, the lawyer? Gambro. How can you explain that? *Hint:* With whom do the members of ACC compete? *Second hint:* What might house counsel fear will happen if they, but not outside counsel, can bring retaliatory discharge claims?

After *Balla*, and despite some contemporaneous countervailing authority, few observers expected a bull market in retaliatory discharge claims for employed lawyers. Then, in the summer of 1993, an intermediate California court decided a retaliatory discharge case favorably to the lawyer, and the state supreme court granted review. It's probably an exaggeration, but not by much, to say that if the California Supreme Court had agreed with *Balla*, retaliatory discharge claims for lawyers would have been set back a generation or two. But California recognized the claim without dissent. General Dynamics Corp. v. Superior Court, 876 P.2d 487 (Cal. 1994). Years later, I asked a member of the court if the issue had been divisive. He expressed surprise and said not at all; the justices all agreed immediately. Other state high court decisions recognizing lawyer retaliatory discharge claims soon followed, including this incisive one from Tennessee, which summarizes many of them, including *General Dynamics*. A big issue for all of these cases has been how to reconcile the lawyer's claim with protection of the client's confidences.

CREWS v. BUCKMAN LABORATORIES INTERNATIONAL, INC.
78 S.W.3d 852 (Tenn. 2002)

WILLIAM M. BARKER, J.

The sole issue in this case is whether an in-house lawyer can bring a common-law claim for retaliatory discharge when she was terminated for reporting that her employer's general counsel was engaged in the unauthorized practice of law. The trial court dismissed the plaintiff's complaint for failure to state a claim, and the dismissal was affirmed by the Court of Appeals. We hold that in-house counsel may bring a common-law action for retaliatory discharge resulting from counsel's compliance with a provision of the Code of Professional Responsibility that represents a clear and definitive statement of public policy. Accordingly, the judgment of the Court of Appeals is reversed, and this case is remanded for further proceedings.

FACTUAL BACKGROUND . . .

According to the allegations of the complaint, the plaintiff was hired by Buckman in 1995 as associate general counsel in its legal department, and while working in this capacity, she reported to Buckman's General Counsel, Ms. Katherine Buckman Davis. Sometime in 1996, the plaintiff discovered that Ms. Davis, who "held herself out as a licensed attorney," did not possess a license to practice law in the State of Tennessee. The plaintiff became concerned that Ms. Davis was engaged in the unauthorized practice of law, and she discussed her suspicions with a member of Buckman's Board of Directors.[1]

Ms. Davis eventually took and passed the bar exam, but the plaintiff learned some time later that Ms. Davis had yet to complete the requirements for licensure by taking the Multi-State Professional Responsibility Examination. The plaintiff informed Buckman officials of the continuing problem, and she advised them on how best to proceed. On June 17, 1999, Ms. Davis allegedly entered the plaintiff's office, yelling that she was frustrated with the plaintiff's actions. The plaintiff responded that she also was frustrated with the situation, to which Ms. Davis remarked that "maybe [the plaintiff] should just leave." The plaintiff declined to leave, and she later received a below-average raise for the first time during her tenure at Buckman, despite having been told earlier by Ms. Davis that she was "doing a good job in position of Associate Counsel."

In August, the plaintiff sought legal advice concerning her ethical obligations, and based on this advice, she informed the Board of Law Examiners of Ms. Davis's situation. The Board later issued a show-cause order asking Ms. Davis to clarify certain facts in her bar application. Upon receipt of the order, Ms. Davis demanded to know from the plaintiff what information the Board possessed in its application file. The plaintiff stated that she knew nothing of the file, and she told Ms. Davis that her actions were threatening and inappropriate. Ms. Davis then apologized, but she immediately proceeded to schedule the plaintiff's performance review.

The plaintiff then informed Mr. Buckman and the Vice President of Human Resources that "the situation [had become] untenable and that she could not function under those circumstances." They agreed that the plaintiff should be immediately transferred to a position away from Ms. Davis's supervision and that she should eventually leave the company altogether within six to nine months. However, while the plaintiff was "in the midst of working out the new arrangement," Ms. Davis informed her that her services would no longer be needed. More specifically, Ms. Davis told her that "since [the plaintiff] had given her notice of resignation, it was logically best to end the Plaintiff's association with Buckman." Although the plaintiff denied that she had resigned, her computer was confiscated; she was placed on personal leave; and she was given a notice of termination.

On April 10, 2000, the plaintiff filed suit against Buckman in the Shelby County Circuit Court, alleging a common-law action for retaliatory discharge in violation of public policy. . . .

IN-HOUSE COUNCEL AND THE TORT OF RETALIATORY DISCHARGE

Tennessee has long adhered to the employment-at-will doctrine in employment relationships not established or formalized by a contract for a definite

---

1. This Director then requested an opinion from the Board of Professional Responsibility based on a hypothetical scenario mirroring the situation at Buckman. The Board replied that a person without a Tennessee law license may not be employed as general counsel in this state and that the failure to have such a license constitutes the unauthorized practice of law.

term. Under this "employment at will" doctrine, both the employer and the employee are generally permitted, with certain exceptions, to terminate the employment relationship "at any time for good cause, bad cause, or no cause." This relationship recognizes (1) that employers should be free to make their own business judgments without undue court interference, and (2) that employees may "refuse to work for a [person] or company" and "may exercise [their rights] in the same way, to the same extent, for the same cause or want of cause as the employer." Indeed, this Court has noted that an employer's " 'ability to make and act upon independent assessments of an employee's abilities and job performance as well as business needs is essential to the free-enterprise system.' "

However, an employer's ability to discharge at-will employees was significantly tempered by our recognition in Clanton v. Cain-Sloan Co., 677 S.W. 2d 441 (Tenn. 1984), of a cause of action for retaliatory discharge. Since that time, we have further recognized that an at-will employee "generally may not be discharged for attempting to exercise a statutory or constitutional right, or for any other reason which violates a clear public policy which is evidenced by an unambiguous constitutional, statutory, or regulatory provision." Therefore, in contrast to the purposes typically justifying the employment-at-will doctrine, an action for retaliatory discharge recognizes "that, in limited circumstances, certain well-defined, unambiguous principles of public policy confer upon employees implicit rights which must not be circumscribed or chilled by the potential of termination."

This Court has not previously addressed the issue of whether a lawyer may pursue a claim of retaliatory discharge against a former employer. At least initially, we must recognize that this cause differs significantly from the usual retaliatory discharge case involving non-lawyer employees. When the discharged employee served as in-house counsel, the issue demands an inquiry into the corporation's expectations as the lawyer's sole employer and client, the lawyer's ethical obligations to the corporation, and the interest of the lawyer — in her character as an employee — in having protections available to other employees seeking redress of legal harm. Therefore, because this issue is one of first impression in this state, it is perhaps helpful to examine how other jurisdictions have addressed it.

Decisions of Other States Relating to Discharge in Violation of Public Policy

Several jurisdictions have grappled with how to balance the competing interests involved in these types of cases. Although the rationales often differed, most of the earlier cases on this subject held that a lawyer could not bring a retaliatory discharge action based upon the lawyer's adherence to his or her ethical duties. [The court cites out of state cases.] This line of cases culminated in Balla v. Gambro, Inc., 584 N.E.2d 104 (1991), in which the Illinois Supreme Court reviewed the other cases and set forth several rationales why in-house counsel should not be permitted to assert an action for retaliatory discharge. These rationales included (1) that because "[i]n-house counsel do not have a choice of whether to follow their ethical obligations as attorneys licensed to practice law," id. at 109, lawyers do not need an action for retaliatory discharge to encourage them to abide by their ethical duties; and (2) that recognizing such an action would affect the foundation of trust in attorney-client relationships, which would then make employers "naturally hesitant to rely upon in-house counsel for advice regarding [the employer's] potentially questionable conduct."

In more recent years, however, other states have permitted a lawyer, under limited circumstances, to pursue a claim of retaliatory discharge based upon termination in violation of public policy. The principal case permitting such an action is General Dynamics Corp. v. Rose, 876 P.2d 487 (1994), in which the California Supreme Court rejected the views held by *Balla* and others and established an analytical framework permitting a lawyer to sue for retaliatory discharge. According to this framework, a lawyer is generally permitted to assert a retaliatory discharge action if the lawyer is discharged for following a mandatory ethical duty or engaging in conduct that would give rise to an action by a non-lawyer employee. However, the *General Dynamics* Court cautioned that the lawyer bringing the action could not rely upon confidential information to establish the claim and that any unsuccessful lawyer breaching his or her duty of confidentiality was subject to disciplinary sanctions.

Following California's lead, the Supreme Judicial Court of Massachusetts has also permitted in-house counsel to assert a limited retaliatory discharge action. In GTE Products Corp. v. Stewart, 653 N.E.2d 161 (1995), the court questioned why the employee's status as an attorney should preclude an action: "It thus seems bizarre that a lawyer employee, who has affirmative duties concerning the administration of justice, should be denied redress for discharge resulting from trying to carry out those very duties." Id. at 166 (internal quotation marks and citation omitted). However, while the *Stewart* Court permitted a limited retaliatory discharge action based upon a lawyer's refusal to violate "explicit and unequivocal statutory or ethical norms," it also restricted the scope of such an action to that in which "the claim can be proved without any violation of the attorney's obligation to respect client confidences and secrets."

Finally, and most recently, the Montana Supreme Court also held that inhouse counsel should be permitted to bring retaliatory discharge actions when necessary to protect public policy. In Burkhart v. Semitool, Inc., 5 P.3d 1031 (2000), the court discussed the rationales in favor of adopting such an action and noted that while clients have a right to discharge counsel at any time and for any reason, this right does not necessarily apply to in-house counsel. Instead, the court reasoned that "by making his or her attorney an employee, [the employer] has avoided the traditional attorney-client relationship and granted the attorney protections that do not apply to independent contractors, but do apply to employees. . . ." Moreover, unlike the previous cases recognizing such an action, the *Burkhart* Court permitted lawyers to disclose the employer's confidential information to the extent necessary to establish a retaliatory discharge claim. Id. at 1041 (relying upon Montana Rule of Professional Conduct 1.6(b)(2) adopted from the ABA's Model Rules of Professional Conduct).

REJECTION OF THE RATIONALES ADVANCED BY *BALLA* AND OTHER CASES

Considering these two general approaches to retaliatory discharge actions based upon termination in violation of public policy, we generally agree with the approaches taken by the courts in *General Dynamics, Stewart,* and *Burkhart.* The very purpose of recognizing an employee's action for retaliatory discharge in violation of public policy is to encourage the employee to protect the public interest, and it seems anomalous to protect only non-lawyer employees under these circumstances. Indeed, as cases in similar contexts show, in-house counsel do not generally forfeit employment protections provided to other employees merely because of their status or duties as a lawyer.[2]

Moreover, we must reject the rationales typically set forth by *Balla* and the Court of Appeals in this case to generally deny lawyers the ability to pursue retaliatory discharge actions. *Balla*'s principal rationale was that recognition of a retaliatory discharge action was not necessary to protect the public interest so long as lawyers were required to follow a code of ethics. Indeed, relying on *Balla,* the intermediate court in this case specifically concluded that statutory and ethical proscriptions are sufficient to protect the public policy against the unauthorized practice of law and that in-house counsel do not need incentives, by way of a cause of action for retaliatory discharge, to comply with the Disciplinary Rules.

We respectfully disagree that the public interest is adequately served in this context without permitting in-house counsel to sue for retaliatory discharge. It is true that counsel in this case was under a mandatory duty to not aid a non-lawyer in the unauthorized practice of law, see Tenn. Sup. Ct. R. 8, DR 3-101(A), and the intermediate court was also correct that lawyers do not have the option of disregarding the commandments of the Disciplinary Rules.[3] This is not to say, however, that lawyers can never *choose* to violate mandatory ethical duties, as evidenced by the number of sanctions, some more severe than others, imposed upon lawyers by this Court and the Board of Professional Responsibility for such violations.

Ultimately, sole reliance on the mere presence of the ethical rules to protect important public policies gives too little weight to the actual presence of economic pressures designed to tempt in-house counsel into subordinating ethical standards to corporate misconduct. Unlike lawyers possessing a multiple client base, in-house counsel are dependent upon only *one* client for their livelihood. As the *General Dynamics* Court acknowledged,

> the economic fate of in-house attorneys is tied directly to a single employer, at whose sufferance they serve. Thus, from an economic standpoint, the dependence of in-house counsel is indistinguishable from that of other corporate managers or senior executives who also owe their livelihoods, career goals and satisfaction to a single organizational employer.

The pressure to conform to corporate misconduct at the expense of one's entire livelihood, therefore, presents some risk that ethical standards could be

---

2. For example, courts have permitted in-house lawyers to sue for age and race discrimination in violation of federal law; to sue for protections under a state "whistleblower" statute; to sue for breach of express and implied employment contracts; and to sue based on implied covenants of good faith and fair dealing. [Citations omitted.]

3. Model Rule 5.5(b) imposed a similar mandatory duty: "A lawyer shall not . . . assist a person who is not a member of the bar in the performance of activity that constitutes the unauthorized practice of law."

disregarded. Like other non-lawyer employees, an in-house lawyer is dependent upon the corporation for his or her sole income, benefits, and pensions; the lawyer is often governed by the corporation's personnel policies and employees' handbooks; and the lawyer is subject to raises and promotions as determined by the corporation. In addition, the lawyer's hours of employment and nature of work are usually determined by the corporation. To the extent that these realities are ignored, the analysis here cannot hope to present an accurate picture of modern in-house practice.

We also reject *Balla*'s reasoning that recognition of a retaliatory discharge action under these circumstances would have a chilling effect upon the attorney-client relationship and would impair the trust between an attorney and his or her client. This rationale appears to be premised on one key assumption: the employer desires to act contrary to public policy and expects the lawyer to further that conduct in violation of the lawyer's ethical duties. We are simply unwilling to presume that employers as a class operate with so nefarious a motive, and we recognize that when employers seek legal advice from in-house counsel, they usually do so with the intent to comply with the law.

Moreover, employers of in-house counsel should be aware that the lawyer is bound by the Code of Professional Responsibility, and that the lawyer may ethically reveal client confidences and secrets in many cases. Therefore, with respect to the employer's willingness to seek the advice of the lawyer for legally questionable conduct, the nature of the relationship should not be further diminished by the remote possibility of a retaliatory discharge suit. In fact, "[t]here should be no discernible impact on the attorney-client relationship [by recognition of a retaliatory discharge action], unless the employer expects his counsel to blindly follow his mandate in contravention of the lawyer's ethical duty." Therefore, we conclude that little, if any, adverse effect upon the attorney-client relationship will occur if we recognize an action for discharge in violation of public policy.

Finally, we reject *Balla*'s assertion that allowing damages as a remedy for retaliatory discharge would have the effect of shifting to the employer the costs of in-house counsel's adherence to the ethics rules. The very purpose of permitting a claim for retaliatory discharge in violation of public policy is to encourage employers to refrain from conduct that is injurious to the public interest. Because retaliatory discharge actions recognize that it is the *employer* who is attempting to circumvent clear expressions of public policy, basic principles of equity all but demand that the costs associated with such conduct also be borne by the employer.

Indeed, permitting the employer to shift the costs of adhering to public policy from itself to an employee—irrespective of whether the employee is also a lawyer—strikes us as an inherently improper balance "between the employment-at-will doctrine and rights granted employees under well-defined expressions of public policy." If anything, the "public interest is better served [when] in-house counsel's resolve to comply with ethical and statutorily mandated duties is strengthened by providing judicial recourse when an employer's demands are in direct and unequivocal conflict with those duties."

In summary, we find unpersuasive the rationales set forth by *Balla* and other cases which equate the employment opportunities of in-house counsel with those of a lawyer possessing a larger client base. While in-house counsel may be a lawyer, we must further recognize that he or she is also an employee of the corporation, with all of the attendant benefits and responsibilities. Therefore, we hold that a lawyer may generally bring a claim for retaliatory discharge when the lawyer is discharged for abiding by the ethics rules as established by this Court.

PROPER STANDARD TO APPLY IN TENNESSEE

In Tennessee, the elements of a typical common-law retaliatory discharge claim are as follow: (1) that an employment-at-will relationship existed; (2) that the employee was discharged, (3) that the reason for the discharge was that the employee attempted to exercise a statutory or constitutional right, or for any other reason which violates a clear public policy evidenced by an unambiguous constitutional, statutory, or regulatory provision; and (4) that a substantial factor in the employer's decision to discharge the employee was the employee's exercise of protected rights or compliance with clear public policy.

However, as we have noted throughout this opinion, this case does not present the typical retaliatory discharge claim. Consequently, while the special relationship between a lawyer and a client does not categorically prohibit in-house counsel from bringing a retaliatory discharge action, other courts have held that it necessarily shapes the contours of the action when the plaintiff was employed as in-house counsel. For example, the courts in *General Dynamics* and *Stewart* held that a lawyer could pursue a retaliatory discharge claim, but only if the lawyer could do so without breaching the duty of confidentiality. Indeed, the California Supreme Court went so far as to forewarn lawyers that those who revealed confidential information in a retaliatory discharge suit, without a basis for doing so under the ethics rules, would be subject to disciplinary proceedings.

Since 1970, lawyers in this state have been subject to the Tennessee Code of Professional Responsibility, and, at least with respect to the ethical duty of confidentiality, our Code is similar to the ethical provisions relied upon in *General Dynamics* and *Stewart*. The Disciplinary Rules generally require that a lawyer not knowingly reveal the confidences or secrets of a client. However, this rule is subject to some limited exceptions, including when the client consents, when compelled by law or court order, or when necessary to prevent the client from committing a crime. A lawyer may also reveal client confidences and secrets as a defensive measure against "accusations of wrongful conduct," though no exception permits a lawyer to reveal client confidences or secrets "offensively" to establish a claim against a client, except in fee-collection disputes.

If we perceive any shortcomings in the holdings of *General Dynamics* and *Stewart*, it is that they largely take away with one hand what they appear to give with the other. Although the courts in these cases gave in-house counsel an important right of action, their respective admonitions about preserving client confidentiality appear to stop just short of halting most of these actions at the courthouse door. With little imagination, one could envision cases involving important issues of public concern being denied relief merely because the wrongdoer is protected by the lawyer's duty of confidentiality. Therefore, given that courts have recognized retaliatory discharge actions in order to protect the public interest, this potentially severe limitation strikes us as a curious, if not largely ineffective, measure to achieve that goal.

However, some courts following versions of the Model Rules of Professional Conduct have reached different conclusions concerning a lawyer's ability to use confidential information in a retaliatory discharge action. Unlike Disciplinary Rule 4-101(C), Model Rule 1.6(b)(2) permits a lawyer to reveal "information relating to the representation of a client" when the lawyer reasonably believes such information is necessary "to establish a *claim or defense* on behalf of the lawyer in a controversy between the lawyer and the client. . . ." (emphasis added). Although some commentators have asserted that this provision merely permits lawyers to use confidential information in fee-collection disputes as under the Model Code, the plain language of the Model Rule is clearly more broad than these authorities would presume. In fact, at least one state supreme court has held that this language permits in-house counsel to reveal confidential information in a retaliatory discharge suit, at least to the extent reasonably necessary to establish the claim. *See Burkhart*, 5 P.3d at 1041 (stating that a lawyer "does not forfeit his rights simply because to prove them he must utilize confidential information. Nor does the client gain a right to cheat the lawyer by imparting confidences to him." (citation omitted)).

We agree with the approach taken by the Model Rules, and pursuant to our inherent authority to regulate and govern the practice of law in this state, we hereby expressly adopt a new provision in Disciplinary Rule 4-101(C) to permit in-house counsel to reveal the confidences and secrets of a client when the lawyer reasonably believes that such information is necessary to establish a claim or defense on behalf of the lawyer in a controversy between the lawyer and the client. This exception parallels the language of Model Rule of Professional Conduct 1.6(b)(2), and we perceive the adoption of a similar standard to be essential in protecting the ability of in-house counsel to effectively assert an action for discharge in violation of public policy. Nevertheless, while in-house counsel may ethically disclose such information to the extent necessary to establish the claim, we emphasize that in-house counsel "must make every effort practicable to avoid unnecessary disclosure of [client confidences and secrets], to limit disclosure to those having the need to know it, and to obtain protective orders or make other arrangements minimizing the risk of disclosure." Model Rule 1.6 Comment 19.

ANALYSIS OF THE COMPLAINT IN THIS CASE

Having found that in-house counsel are not categorically prohibited from maintaining retaliatory discharge actions against their former employers, we now examine whether the plaintiff in this case has stated such a claim in her complaint. As for the first element, the existence of an at-will employment relationship, the complaint alleges only that the "Plaintiff became employed with Defendant Buckman" initially as a legal assistant and that she "began working as an attorney in Buckman's Legal Department" after becoming licensed to practice law. Although we are unable to determine from the complaint whether this employment relationship is alleged to have been at-will or based upon an employment contract, we will presume that the plaintiff intended to allege an at-will employment relationship. . . .

The next issue, then, is whether the complaint alleges the existence of a "clear public policy which is evidenced by an unambiguous constitutional, statutory, or regulatory provision." To establish this second element, the plaintiff argues that the ethical rules relating to the unauthorized practice of law—such as Disciplinary Rule 3-101(A), which places upon lawyers a mandatory ethical duty "not [to] aid a non-lawyer in the unauthorized practice of law" — are for the protection of the public interest and may serve as the basis for a retaliatory discharge action. We agree.

It cannot seriously be questioned that many of the duties imposed upon lawyers by the Tennessee Code of Professional Responsibility represent a clear and definitive statement of public policy. Indeed, we have previously expressly recognized that specific "provisions of the Code of Professional Responsibility, promulgated by the Supreme Court and authorized by the Tennessee Constitution and statutes, reflect public policy. . . ."

Although we need not conclude today that every provision of the Code of Professional Responsibility reflects an important *public* policy, there can be no doubt that the public has a substantial interest in preventing the unauthorized practice of law. As this Court has acknowledged, "the purpose of regulation[s] governing the unauthorized practice of law is . . . to serve the public right to protection against unlearned and unskilled advice in matters relating to the science of the law." Further, the Court of Appeals has recognized that regulations proscribing the unauthorized practice of law are designed to protect "the public from being advised and represented in legal matters by incompetent and unreliable persons over whom the judicial department could exercise little control." As such, we find here the existence of a clear public policy evidenced by the ethical duty not to aid in the unauthorized practice of law.

To be clear, although the plaintiff was not under a *mandatory* ethical duty to report Ms. Davis's alleged unauthorized practice of law to the Board of Law Examiners, she certainly possessed a *permissive* duty to report Ms. Davis's conduct.[6] . . .

[The court concluded that the complaint alleged that the plaintiff was discharged from her employment and that a "substantial factor" in her discharge was her compliance with her ethical duties.]

Traditional Doctrine Confronts Economic Reality

Crews and other cases upholding retaliatory discharge claims for lawyers (assuming the jurisdiction otherwise recognizes such claims), are driven in part by the economic realities confronting the employed lawyer. Lawyers in their own firm practices are rarely as dependent on a single client as are lawyers who work for a salary. As a result, the traditional right of clients (or really the client's officers) to fire a company's in-house counsel may subject the company to liability. These cases give employed lawyers special protection because they have special vulnerability. As stated above, ACC a professional group devoted to

6. Disciplinary Rule 1-103(A) imposes a mandatory duty to report clear violations of Disciplinary Rule 1-102, which itself prohibits violations of a Disciplinary Rule. However, Rule 1-102 applies only to violations by lawyers, and because Ms. Davis was not yet licensed at the time the plaintiff reported her conduct to the Board of Law Examiners, it appears that the plaintiff's only *mandatory* duty here was to refrain from furthering Ms. Davis's application for admission to the bar under Disciplinary Rule 1-101(B).

the interests of house counsel, had opposed recognition of the claim. If employed lawyers have special rights, corporate clients may view them as posing special dangers, leading the clients to give highly sensitive (and highly interesting) work to outside counsel instead.

It is inaccurate to say, as *Crews* does, that *General Dynamics* and *Stewart* took "away with one hand what they appear to give with the other," through their "admonitions about preserving client confidentiality." For example, while *General Dynamics* did express concern for client information, it also said that "trial courts can and should apply an array of ad hoc measures from their equitable arsenal designed to permit the attorney plaintiff to attempt to make the necessary proof while protecting from disclosure client confidences subject to the privilege." The court then mentioned "sealing and protective orders, limited admissibility of evidence, orders restricting the use of testimony in successive proceedings, and, where appropriate, in camera proceedings" as examples.

The fact that Model Rule 1.6(b)(5) (originally numbered (b)(2)) is broader than its Code equivalent makes it easier to allow retaliatory discharge claims. Note that the Tennessee Supreme Court actually used the occasion of *Crews* to rewrite its Code provision. (The state has since adopted a version of the Model Rules.) Burkhart v. Semitool, Inc., 5 P.3d 1031 (Mont. 2000), after comparing the reasoning in *Balla* with *General Dynamics*, chose to follow the latter. On the issue of client confidences, it wrote: "In comparing the language of Rule 1.6 and DR 4-101(C), it is clear that the language set forth in the Model Rules is extremely broad. While the Comments to Rule 1.6 do not specifically state that a lawyer may reveal client confidences in order to support an employment-related claim, such a statement is not necessary, as the Comments merely state examples of situations in which Rule 1.6 may be applied."

Not all retaliatory discharge claims are based on state law. When the lawyer's claim is federal, she has the additional argument that state ethics rules should not limit her proof. The Third Circuit permitted an in-house lawyer to sue her former employer for retaliatory discharge and sex discrimination under Title VII notwithstanding risks to the client's confidential information. Kachmar v. SunGard Data Systems, Inc., 109 F.3d 173 (3d Cir. 1997). While quoting *General Dynamics* for the proposition that the trial court had "equitable measures at its disposal 'designed to permit the attorney plaintiff to attempt to make the necessary proof while protecting from disclosure client confidences subject to the privilege,'" the court also raised the possibility that the language of Model Rule 1.6(b)(5) could in fact permit the plaintiff lawyer to use client confidences to establish her case. Although the comments to the rule offered, as examples, only fee disputes and the defense of claims against a lawyer, the court concluded that "the Rules do not address affirmative claims for relief under a federal statute and thus we believe they are at best inconclusive on the issue SunGard raises."

Apart from confidentiality concerns prompted by lawsuits against a client, loyalty concerns also arise when the lawyer is still employed by the client. To see how incredibly complex things can get when an employed lawyer sues her current entity client — to see, that is, the apparent inconsistency between the lawyer's fiduciary role and her role as plaintiff — let me tell you a story a lawyer friend presented to me. The facts have been altered but the point remains the same.

My friend was an outside lawyer for a company with branch offices in several states. The company had a general counsel's office at its headquarters and small legal departments in its branch offices. One of the lawyers in a branch office had filed a complaint accusing the company of paying her less because of her sex. Must the very managers whom the lawyer has said have discriminated against her continue to confide in her as the company lawyer? Will refusal to do so risk a claim of retaliation under Title VII? Assume, too, that in her job the lawyer is exposed daily to sensitive information about the salary and benefits of all company personnel. These data are directly relevant to the issues in her claim. Must the company continue to allow her to see this information? What if she can't do her job without it? Assume that the lawyer's special area of expertise in this small office is employment law. It is her responsibility to defend the company against claims of discrimination just like the one she has leveled. Must the company continue to carry her in that role? Assume there are no other positions in her office to which it could transfer her and that, indeed, there is no other area in which she has an equivalent level of expertise. Assume, finally, that the lawyer filed her discrimination claim at the end of a year in which she was twice criticized for poor work, perhaps believing that the criticism was pretextual. She may have anticipated that the company was about to fire her.

Will filing the claim now inoculate her against being fired, because it can be made to look like retaliation? Even if the company believes the criticism is valid? Finally, assume the company does defend by citing the lawyer's poor work compared with other lawyers' work, thereby providing a perfectly valid reason to fire her. How will that defense be adjudicated? Will we have a trial to determine the quality of her legal work, either absolutely or by comparison? Will a lay jury be expected to make that determination?*

A lawyer's ability to use client confidences as "a sword," not merely a "shield," is not unlimited. A cautionary tale is told in Douglas v. DynMcDermott Petroleum Operations Co., 144 F.3d 364 (5th Cir. 1998). The lawyer there, complaining of race discrimination, revealed client confidences outside of an administrative or judicial proceeding. When she was fired, she claimed that it was in retaliation for her discrimination charge. The trial judge entered a jury verdict for the lawyer, concluding that the disclosed confidences were "minimal" and not "substantive." The circuit court was less forgiving:

> Furthermore, Douglas's conduct not only undermined her effectiveness as an employee, but her actions also violated the ethical rules of the legal profession. Here, while employed as in-house counsel for DynMcDermott, Douglas breached her professional duties of confidentiality and of loyalty when she revealed to a third party information relating to the representation of her client. She took no precautions[12] to preserve the attorney-client relationship

* I admit that I stacked the hypo in favor of the company to make my point. Of course, it is also possible that our lawyer has a solid basis for her charge and that firing her is indeed retaliatory. But that would be a different hypo.

12. Even when revealing confidences falls within an exception to the ethical rules, there are appropriate means for revealing confidences that limit the dissemination of information disclosed. They include requesting in camera review, requesting that the court seal the record in any proceeding and obtaining permission to prosecute the action without revealing the true name of either party. See, e.g., Doe v. A Corp., 709 F.2d 1043, 1045 n.1 (5th Cir. 1983); United States v. Scott, 909 F.2d 488, 494 n.12 (11th Cir. 1990) (noting different protective measures attorneys may take to protect client confidences when they suspect a client of intending to commit perjury).

and instead acted with thoughtless indiscretion, demonstrating little regard for the ethical obligations inherent in the legal profession. This dereliction of professional duties meant that DynMcDermott could no longer place full trust in her to keep confidences that she may acquire as its attorney. In short, the trust undergirding the attorney-client relationship was broken and Douglas could no longer function in her role as in-house counsel. . . .

In sum, although the right to oppose unlawful practices under Title VII is a right that, independently, is entitled to great weight in the balancing test, the exercise of that right in violation of the profession's ethical duties of confidentiality and loyalty simply will not counter the weight of the employer-client's rights and the duty owed to the legal profession.

We therefore conclude that when an attorney's Title VII right to oppose her employer-client's allegedly discriminatory practices by disclosing confidential information contrary to the ethical obligations of the profession is balanced against her employer-client's right to ethical representation and the profession's interest in assuring the ethical conduct of its members, the employer's and the profession's interests must prevail. Given the obligations to which an attorney agrees when she joins the profession and when she accepts employment, and the importance of the duties of confidentiality and loyalty to the employer-client and to the integrity of the profession, we hold as a matter of law that conduct that breaches the ethical duties of the legal profession is unprotected under Title VII.

In reaching this holding, we are aware that the trial court determined that there was "minimal disclosure of any substantive information" and, therefore, that any indiscretion on Douglas's part did not warrant much consideration. This conclusion was error because, as we hold today, *any* betrayal of a client's confidences that breaches the ethical duties of the attorney places that conduct outside Title VII's protection. The employer-client need not tolerate baby steps of unethical conduct while anxiously wondering when and if the giant step will occur, and with what consequences. Once the trust between attorney and client is breached in violation of professionally sanctioned duties, Title VII provides no shield from retaliation.[16]

FURTHER READING

The *General Dynamics* court listed accumulated research on lawyer retaliatory discharge claims in its note 5. The text of that note follows:

Despite the fact that no more than a handful of such cases have been reported nationally, scholarly comment on the issues raised in retaliatory discharge tort claims by in-house counsel is disproportionately large. (For a sampling, see Feliu, Discharge of Professional Employees: Protecting Against Dismissal for Acts Within a Professional Code of Ethics (1979) 11 Colum. Hum. Rts. L. Rev.

---

16. As is obvious from our opinion, we do not address violations of Title VII against an attorney that, although arising from the same factual scenario, occur independent of the ethical breach. We only make it clear that an attorney who violates her profession's ethical rules is not entitled to any damages flowing from retaliation taken by her employer-client because of her violative conduct. So long as the conduct actually constituted a violation of the profession's ethically imposed duties, the employer is insulated from liability irrespective of whether it took adverse employment action because the conduct constituted a breach or because the conduct was in opposition to discriminatory employment practices.

149; Wilbur, Wrongful Discharge of Attorneys: A Cause of Action to Further Professional Responsibility (1988) 92 Dick. L. Rev. 777; Abramson, Why Not Retaliatory Discharge for Attorneys: A Polemic (1991) 58 Tenn. L. Rev. 271; Note, A Remedy for the Discharge of Professional Employees Who Refuse to Perform Unethical or Illegal Acts: A Proposal in Aid of Professional Ethics (1976) 28 Vand. L. Rev. 805; Moskowitz, [Employment-at-will and Codes of Ethics: The Professional's Dilemma (1988)] 23 Val. U.L. Rev. 33; Schneyer, Professionalism and Public Policy: The Case of House Counsel (1988) 2 Geo. J. Legal Ethics 449; Note, In-House Counsel's Right to Sue for Retaliatory Discharge (1992) 92 Colum. L. Rev. 389; Giesel, [The Ethics or Employment Dilemma of In-House Counsel (1992)] 5 Geo. J. Legal Ethics 535; Gillers, Protecting Lawyers Who Just Say No (1988) 5 Ga. State U.L. Rev. 1; Reynolds, Wrongful Discharge of Employed Counsel (1988) 1 Geo. J. Legal Ethics 553; Kalish, The Attorney's Role in the Private Organization (1980) 59 Neb. L. Rev. 1; Schneyer, Limited Tenure for Lawyers and the Structure of Lawyer-Client Relations: A Critique of the Lawyer's Proposed Right to Sue for Wrongful Discharge (1980) 59 Neb. L. Rev. 11.

The Rights of Associates

Because lawyers employed by corporations have one client, economic dependency can lead to the dilemma identified here. Associates at law firms may have many clients, but they have a single employer, inviting the same dependency. If an associate is fired because he insists on compliance with ethical obligations, may he sue the firm? New York courts have been among the least generous in recognizing breach-of-contract or retaliatory discharge claims for at-will employees. Sabetay v. Sterling Drug, Inc., 506 N.E.2d 919 (N.Y. 1987); Murphy v. American Home Prods. Corp., 448 N.E.2d 86 (N.Y. 1983). Are lawyers different?

Howard Wieder, a New York law firm associate, asked his firm to let another associate represent him in the purchase of a condominium apartment. Wieder eventually concluded that his colleague had lied to him in the course of the representation. He insisted that the firm report the associate under DR 1-103(A). The Model Rule equivalent is Rule 8.3(a). We will study these rules in chapter 13D. For now you should know that they sometimes require a lawyer to report another lawyer's unethical conduct to disciplinary authorities.

Wieder's insistence ultimately caused the firm to report the other lawyer. Shortly thereafter, however, the firm fired Wieder, who then sued for breach of contract and abusive discharge, contending that he was fired because he had insisted on compliance with the ethics rules. Lower courts dismissed Wieder's complaint. Following are portions of Judge Hancock's opinion for the Court of Appeals in Wieder v. Skala, 609 N.E.2d 105 (N.Y. 1992):

> We agree with plaintiff that in any hiring of an attorney as an associate to practice law with a firm there is implied an understanding so fundamental to the relationship and essential to its purpose as to require no expression: that both the associate and the firm in conducting the practice will do so in accordance with the ethical standards of the profession. Erecting or countenancing disincentives to compliance with the applicable rules of professional conduct, plaintiff contends, would subvert the central professional purpose of his relationship with the firm — the lawful and ethical practice of law.

The particular rule of professional conduct implicated here (DR 1-103[A]), it must be noted, is critical to the unique function of self-regulation belonging to the legal profession. . . . To assure that the legal profession fulfills its responsibility of self-regulation, DR 1-103(A) places upon each lawyer and Judge the duty to report to the Disciplinary Committee of the Appellate Division any potential violations of the Disciplinary Rules that raise a "substantial question as to another lawyer's honesty, trustworthiness or fitness in other respects." . . .

Moreover, as plaintiff points out, failure to comply with the reporting requirement may result in suspension or disbarment. Thus, by insisting that plaintiff disregard DR 1-103(A) defendants were not only making it impossible for plaintiff to fulfill his professional obligations but placing him in the position of having to choose between continued employment and his own potential suspension and disbarment. We agree with plaintiff that these unique characteristics of the legal profession in respect to this core Disciplinary Rule make the relationship of an associate to a law firm employer intrinsically different from that of the financial managers to the corporate employers in *Murphy* and *Sabetay*. The critical question is whether this distinction calls for a different rule regarding the implied obligation of good faith and fair dealing. . . . We believe that it does in this case, but we, by no means, suggest that each provision of the Code of Professional Responsibility should be deemed incorporated as an implied-in-law term in every contractual relationship between or among lawyers. . . .

Plaintiff argues, moreover . . . that the dictates of public policy in DR 1-103(A) have such force as to warrant our recognition of the tort of abusive discharge pleaded in the fifth cause of action. While the arguments are persuasive and the circumstances here compelling, we have consistently held that "significant alteration of employment relationships, such as the plaintiff urges, is best left to the Legislature." We believe that the same rationale applies here.

Judge Gleeson extended *Wieder* in Kelly v. Hunton & Williams, 1999 Westlaw 408416 (E.D.N.Y. 1999). The plaintiff claimed that he was asked to resign after reporting a partner's billing fraud to other partners of the firm. Judge Gleeson upheld the claim although, unlike *Wieder*, Kelly was not yet admitted to the bar and had not threatened to go to the Disciplinary Committee as of the time he was asked to leave. But Illinois, adhering to the dubious logic of Balla v. Gambro, has rejected an attorney's claim that he was wrongfully discharged from his law firm in retaliation for reporting the firm's illegal practices to a senior partner at the firm. As in *Balla*, the court held that the plaintiff, as a licensed lawyer in Illinois, had an ethical duty to report the misconduct. "Therefore, the attorney's ethical obligations serve to adequately protect" the public against the alleged illegal conduct. It was not necessary to provide the lawyer with a remedy for his discharge even if it was retaliatory. Jacobson v. Knepper & Moga, P.C., 706 N.E.2d 491 (1998).

C. SARBANES-OXLEY AND THE RULE 1.13 AMENDMENTS

On July 25, 2002, Congress passed what has come to be known as the Sarbanes-Oxley Act (or SOX informally). The House vote was 423 to 3 and the Senate vote was 99 to 0. The President signed the law on July 30, 2002. Sarbanes-Oxley was the most significant federal legislative response to the corporate scandals in the United States, beginning with the collapse of Enron and including the indictment, conviction (later reversed), and eventual demise of Arthur Andersen; and the troubles at Imclone, Tyco, WorldCom, and HealthSouth, among others.

Section 307 of the Act (15 U.S.C. §7245) was submitted as an amendment by Senators Edwards, Enzi, and Corzine on July 10, 2002. It passed unanimously later that month with little discussion. It provides:

RULES OF PROFESSIONAL CONDUCT FOR ATTORNEYS.

Not later than 180 days after July 30, 2002, the Commission shall issue rules, in the public interest and for the protection of investors, setting forth minimum standards of professional conduct for attorneys appearing and practicing before the Commission in any way in the representation of issuers, including a rule —

(1) requiring an attorney to report evidence of a material violation of securities law or breach of fiduciary duty or similar violation by the company or any agent thereof, to the chief legal counsel or the chief executive officer of the company (or the equivalent thereof); and

(2) if the counsel or officer does not appropriately respond to the evidence (adopting, as necessary, appropriate remedial measures or sanctions with respect to the violation), requiring the attorney to report the evidence to the audit committee of the board of directors of the issuer or to another committee of the board of directors comprised solely of directors not employed directly or indirectly by the issuer, or to the board of directors.

In introducing §307, Senator Edwards (a plaintiff's lawyer in his prior life) said:

The truth is that executives and accountants do not work alone. Anybody who works in corporate America knows that wherever you see corporate executives and accountants working, lawyers are virtually always there looking over their shoulder. If executives and/or accountants are breaking the law, you can be sure that part of the problem is that the lawyers who are there and involved are not doing their jobs. . . .

Let me be a little more specific about what this amendment does and what the responsibility of a lawyer is and should be. If you are a lawyer for a corporation, your client is the corporation and you work for the corporation and you work for the shareholders, the investors in that corporation; that is to whom you owe your responsibility and loyalty. . . .

One of the most critical responsibilities that [corporate] lawyers have is, when they see something occurring or about to occur that violates the law, breaks the law, they must act as an advocate for the shareholders, for the company itself, for the investors. They are there and they can see what is happening. They know the law and their responsibility is to do something about it if they see the law being broken or about to be broken.

This amendment is about making sure those lawyers . . . ensure that the law is being followed.

What do you think of this assumption? Lawyers who work for companies of even moderate size, and certainly lawyers who work at large companies, are likely to know early on if something is amiss. Since the company is the client, the import of §307 and the amendments to Model Rule 1.13 is to compel the lawyer to act to protect the client against the misconduct of its other agents. Some argue that this turns lawyers into cops, in effect deputizing them to carry out the business of law enforcement. While acknowledging that the client must be protected, critics of §307 (and the SEC rules it has spawned) and of the amendments to Model Rule 1.13, contend that they micromanage how lawyers go about protecting their clients. Whether or not that criticism is valid, lawyers who violate the SEC rules risk discipline by the Commission, and lawyers who violate Rule 1.13 risk discipline by the courts of states that have adopted it. And even lawyers who have no principled quarrel with the particular obligations contained in the SEC rules may nevertheless object to their source — the federal government — in the belief that the tradition of state regulation of the bar should not be breached.

The SEC rules implementing §307 can be found at 17 C.F.R. Part 205. In substance, they impose very specific *reporting-up* requirements for certain lawyers. "Reporting up" is shorthand for a duty to go up the corporate chain of command to correct certain perceived illegalities by corporate constituents. The SEC imposed the reporting-up duty on lawyers "appearing and practicing before the commission," a phrase that is expansively defined to include "[t]ransacting any business with the Commission"; representing "an issuer . . . in connection with any Commission investigation [or] inquiry"; providing advice regarding any document if the lawyer "has notice" that it will be filed with the Commission or incorporated in another filed document; and advising on whether information is required to be filed with the Commission. Because the enabling legislation required the Commission to promulgate rules "requiring an attorney to report evidence of a material violation of securities law or breach of fiduciary duty or similar violation by the company or any agent thereof," the reporting-up obligations in the Commission's rules are not limited to the securities law. The Commission defines "breach of fiduciary duty" to include "any breach of fiduciary or similar duty to the issuer recognized under an applicable Federal or State statute or at common law, including but not limited to misfeasance, nonfeasance, abdication of duty, abuse of trust, and approval of unlawful transactions." This is obviously quite broad.

The Commission's rules are detailed with various triggers requiring lawyers to act and react. Here, it suffices to focus on the larger picture. Lawyers who become "aware of evidence of a material violation" of securities law or fiduciary duty or similar law, whether federal or state, must report what they know to the company's chief legal officer or its chief executive officer. The term "evidence of a material violation" is defined, awkwardly, to mean "credible evidence, based upon which it would be *un*reasonable, under the circumstances, for a prudent and competent attorney *not* to conclude that it is reasonably likely that a material violation has occurred, is ongoing, or is about to occur." The Commission was criticized for adopting a definition containing a double negative and that, in the view of some, made reporting too easy to avoid.

In any event, once a report is made, the reporting lawyer and the chief legal officer or chief executive officer have various duties depending upon what a further inquiry, which is mandatory, reveals. The rules contemplate that a substantiated report will ultimately result in corrective action or that the information will be reported to the board of directors, the audit committee of the board, or the independent directors. The rules also permit companies to channel evidence of a material violation to an entity called a qualified legal compliance committee (QLCC). This is a committee consisting of at least one member of the company's audit committee or the equivalent and two independent directors and given responsibility by the company's board for handling reports of evidence of a violation. The idea behind reporting up is that once the top officials, especially independent directors, learn of a serious problem, action will be taken because inaction can create substantial personal liability.

The Commission's rules also permit, but do not require, lawyers appearing and practicing before the commission to reveal the client's confidential information related to the representation to the extent the lawyer "reasonably believes necessary" to prevent the issuer "from committing a material violation that is likely to cause substantial injury to the financial interest or property of the issuer or investors"; to prevent the issuer from committing perjury or a fraud on the commission; or to "rectify the consequences of a material violation by the issuer that caused, or may cause, substantial injury to the financial interest or property of the issuer or investors in the furtherance of which the attorney's services were used." This is a *reporting-out* provision because it permits the lawyer to reveal confidential information to persons outside the corporate client. The permission is in substance the same as the exceptions to confidentiality now contained in Rules 1.6 and 3.3. It is, however, permissive only, whereas the duty to correct fraud on a tribunal under Rule 3.3 is obligatory.

The Commission proposed but never adopted rules that would have mandated reporting out — that is, informing the Commission of material violations of its rules when the issuer has not taken corrective action. Retained attorneys would have been required to withdraw from representing the issuer, notify the Commission within a day, and disaffirm any document filed with the Commission and prepared by the attorney if the attorney "reasonably believes" the document "may be materially false or misleading." Employed lawyers would have had the same obligations except they would not have to quit their jobs. This language echoes the noisy withdrawal provisions of the Model Rules. See page 509. As an alternative, the Commission also proposed a rule that, in effect, would obligate the issuer, not the lawyer, to notify the Commission of its lawyer's withdrawal. Although the noisy withdrawal provision and the alternative were both proposed in January 2003, neither had been adopted as of late 2008 and, absent new scandals, are probably dead letters.

Activity, meanwhile, was proceeding on a parallel track. Anticipating congressional action in light of the corporate scandals, in March 2002 the ABA created a Task Force on Corporate Responsibility. If the ABA and then state courts modified their own rules of professional conduct in a way the SEC approved, the bar could hope that the agency would take a minimalist approach to the congressional mandate in §307. Indeed, the Task Force's recommendations to amend Rules 1.6 and 1.13, which the House of Delegates accepted in August 2003, most likely explains the SEC's forbearance from adopting either version of the mandatory reporting-out obligation. As stated in chapter 2, the amendments to Rule 1.6 expand the exceptions under which a lawyer is permitted to reveal client confidential information to third persons. The amendments to Rule 1.13 are also significant. First, they strengthen the reporting-up obligation. Although reporting up is not obligatory, it is now presumptively required "[u]nless the lawyer reasonably believes that it is not necessary in the best interest of the organization to do so." Previously, reporting up was simply one option available to the lawyer. Of greater consequence, Rule 1.13 now contains its own exception to confidentiality. It permits, but does not require, reporting out if, after reporting up, "the highest authority . . . insists upon or fails to address in a timely and appropriate manner an action, or a refusal to act, that is clearly a violation of law," and if, in addition, "the lawyer reasonably believes that the violation is reasonably certain to result in substantial injury to the organization." Remember that the SEC rules only apply to lawyers appearing and practicing before the Commission (although that term is very broad). Rule 1.13, however, applies to all lawyers for organizational clients, whatever the nature of the work.

FURTHER READING

Sarbanes-Oxley has spawned a mini publishing industry. Two articles from different perspectives (one about the duty of lawyers, the other looking at the criminal law) are Roger Cramton, George Cohen & Susan Koniak, Legal and Ethical Duties of Lawyers After Sarbanes-Oxley, 49 Vill. L. Rev. 725 (2004); and Kathleen Brickey, From Enron to Worldcom and Beyond: Life and Crime After Sarbanes-Oxley, 81 Wash. U. L.Q. 357 (2003). Sung Hui Kim has also written on the lawyer's gatekeeper role in the wake of the corporate malfeasance in the 1990s and early 2000s. Sung Hui Kim, The Banality of Fraud: Re-Situating the Inside Counsel as Gatekeeper, 74 Fordham L. Rev. 983 (2005); and Gatekeepers Inside Out, 21 Geo. J. Legal Ethics 411 (2008). The latter article argues that contrary to popular assumptions, inside lawyers may be more effective than outside counsel at detecting and stopping misconduct.

XI

Judges

The judge should not be young; he should have learned to know evil, not from his own soul, but from late and long observation of the nature of evil in others; knowledge should be his guide, not personal experience.

—Plato, The Republic

Isabella: Yet show some pity.
Angelo: I show it most of all when I show justice;
For then I pity those I do not know,
Which a dismissed offense would after gall;
And do him right that, answering one foul wrong,
Lives not to act another. Be satisfied.
Your brother dies tomorrow; be content.
Isabella: So you must be the first that gives this sentence,
And he, that suffers. O, it is excellent
To have a giant's strength; but it is tyrannous
To use it like a giant.

—Shakespeare, Measure For Measure, 2.03.126-136

Justice should not only be done, but should manifestly and undoubtedly be seen to be done.

—Lord Hewart (1870-1943), in Rex v. Sussex Justices

- *Conflicts and Recusal*
- *Bias On and Off the Bench*

As it does for lawyers, the American Bar Association promulgates a model code of conduct for judges. The ABA adopted the Canons of Judicial Ethics in 1924 and replaced it in 1972 with the Code of Judicial Conduct. The Code itself was substantially amended in 1990 and again in 2007. Nearly every state, the District of Columbia, and the U.S. Judicial Conference have adopted judicial conduct codes based on the ABA models. All jurisdictions also have a mechanism for judicial discipline. Sanctions for code violations can range from private discipline to removal. Discipline cannot, however, be used to remove federal judges appointed under Article III of the Constitution. Impeachment and

585

conviction by Congress is constitutionally required. Nevertheless, discipline short of removal is statutorily contemplated. 28 U.S.C. §351 et seq.

Two circuit courts have held that the Code of Conduct for United States Judges "cannot be the standard for judicial discipline. The Canons are aspirational goals, voluntarily adopted by the judiciary itself. . . . Congress imposed a standard for discipline that is significantly lower than, and conceptually different from, the ideals embodied in the Canons." In re Charge of Judicial Misconduct, 62 F.3d 320 (9th Cir. 1995). See also In re Charge of Judicial Misconduct, 91 F.3d 1416 (10th Cir. 1996). Compare Matter of a Charge of Judicial Misconduct, 85 F.3d 701 (D.C. Cir. 1996), which, while generally subscribing to this proposition, concludes: "Still, there is some indication that judicial councils should be guided in part by the Canons in determining whether a [statutory] violation occurred." And the Judicial Conference of the United States has also written that the Code "may have informational value" on the meaning of §351. Comment, Rule 3, Rules for Judicial Conduct and Judicial Disability Proceedings.

Like lawyer conflicts, judicial conflicts are also enforced outside the disciplinary process through motions for disqualification, or recusal, of a judge based on an alleged conflict of interest. Standards for disqualification appear in Rule 2.11 of the ABA Code of Judicial Conduct. Standards for disqualification may also appear in statutory law. In the federal system, the statutes are 28 U.S.C. §144 and §455. The latter is more detailed and more important. Indeed, the former has almost no role today. The language of §455 is similar to the language of the various ABA Codes because Congress relied on the 1972 Code in writing §455.

Beyond codes and statutes, the Due Process Clause of the Constitution offers a third basis for judicial disqualification. Its standards are, however, less strict than those in the codes and legislation. Due process challenges to a presiding judge most frequently occur in criminal cases. See, e.g., Tumey v. Ohio, 273 U.S. 510 (1927) (judicial income may not depend on fines from convicted persons). But sometimes, as in *Aetna*, discussed below, the clause applies in a civil matter too.

One interesting distinction between ethics codes for lawyers and those for judges is worth noting here. Whereas the Model Rules reject the "appearance of impropriety" as a standard for evaluating a private lawyer's conduct (see page 326), judicial codes continue to be sensitive to appearances. One test for disqualifying a judge, as discussed hereafter, is that the judge's "impartiality might reasonably be questioned." Where a judge at sentencing said that his "object in this case from day one has always been to get back to the public that which was taken from it as a result of the fraudulent activities of this defendant and others," his impartiality was reasonably in question, whether or not he was actually biased, because it appeared that the judge had an agenda "from day one." The remedy was to reverse the conviction and remand the case for a new trial before a different judge. United States v. Antar, 53 F.3d 568 (3d Cir. 1995) ("Crazy Eddie" case) overruled on another point in Smith v. Berg, 247 F.3d 532 (3rd Cir. 2001). See also Canon 2. Why does it make sense, for surely it does, to adhere to an appearance standard for judges and government lawyers but not private lawyers?

This chapter will focus on two broad issues in the behavior of judges. The first, as you have probably guessed, is conflicts of interest. What kind of conflict will prevent a judge from sitting in a matter? We will ask this question initially as a matter of due process, but we will spend most of our time on the conflict standards in the ethics codes and federal law. Just as motions to disqualify lawyers have increased significantly in the last 25 years, so too have motions to recuse a judge, although not nearly as much. Why not? For one thing, ordinarily the judge will herself make the decision. If the motion loses, the loser will be faced with the same judge at trial. That might not be a happy prospect if the motion made allegations of the judge's bias or apparent bias. Separately, recusal motions generally fail. It's harder to disqualify a judge than a lawyer, who will usually be saddled not only with her own conflicts but with the imputed client conflicts of colleagues.

The second issue we cover deals with racism, sexism, homophobia, and similar bias issues. This is an area that has seen much development in the last decade. The 2007 ABA Code speaks to it more clearly than its predecessors. The Senate Judiciary Committee has several times debated whether it should confirm judicial nominees who fail adequately to explain their membership in discriminatory private clubs. See, e.g., Neil Lewis, Committee Rejects Bush Nominee to Key Appellate Court in South, N.Y. Times, Apr. 12, 1991. State commissions have alleged the existence of racism in state court systems. Report of the New York State Judicial Commission on Minorities (1991). Studies of gender bias in the profession and courts have also been extensive. For a list of 34 state task forces that have studied gender bias in the courts, see Marsha S. Stern, Courting Justice: Addressing Gender Bias in the Judicial System, 1996 Ann. Surv. Am. L. 1 (1996). See also the special issue in volume 45 of the Stanford Law Review, July 1993, for articles by Barbara Allen Babcock, Judith Resnik, Deborah Rhode, and others.

The issues here are both more complex and more subtle than whether biased attitudes can be allowed to influence judicial decisions (easy, *no*) or whether judges should be permitted to refer to women lawyers as "girls" or to comment suggestively on their appearance (easy, again, *no*). But should it be unethical for a judge to tell a mildly anti-Semitic or homophobic joke at a private dinner party? What if the judge is Jewish or gay? To attend the nightclub act of a blatantly sexist performer? To belong to a social club restricted to persons of the judge's religious faith or ethnic group? To collect sexually explicit but nonobscene pictures? To march in the parade of a group that relies on the First Amendment to exclude lesbians and gay men from joining under their own banner? See Hurley v. Irish-American Gay, Lesbian and Bisexual Group of Boston, 515 U.S. 557 (1995) (state court's use of public accommodation law to require parade organizers to include gay, lesbian, and bisexual groups in St. Patrick's Day Parade violated organizers' First Amendment rights). Obviously the questions raise issues of judicial freedom of speech, association, and religion, as well as ethical issues.

Ex Parte Communications.   Before moving to conflicts and bias, we should say a few words about the prohibition against ex parte communications. We have, after all, an adversary system. One of its postulates is that all parties get to hear information that other parties give the court — judge or jury — and to reply. With narrow exception, a judge may not let a lawyer or litigant communicate with the judge in the absence of other parties. The ABA Code of Judicial Conduct is quite stern about this. Rule 2.9A forbids a judge, without party consent, to "initiate, permit, or consider ex parte communications, or consider other communications made to the judge outside the presence of the parties or their lawyers. . . ." unless one of several exceptions applies. Lawyers are separately forbidden to communicate ex parte with the judge absent an exception. Model Rule 3.5(b).

Perhaps the most famous report of alleged (and highly improper) ex parte communication in recent American history arose in the trial of Julius and Ethel Rosenberg for treason in 1951. The Rosenbergs were convicted of conspiracy to engage in espionage, and Irving Kaufman, the trial judge, sentenced them to death. They were executed in 1953. Roy Cohn, who is alleged to have had ex parte contacts with Kaufman, was on the prosecutorial team. Kaufman later became Chief Judge of the Second Circuit. Cohn later became an aide to Senator Joseph McCarthy and worked for him during the Army-McCarthy Hearings of 1954. Later still, Cohn became a successful New York lawyer, although his reputation in some legal quarters was less than stellar. The federal government indicted Cohn three times but never convicted him. He died in 1986, but that didn't end his celebrity. Tony Kushner reincarnated Cohn as a character in the highly successful play (and then film) *Angels in America*. Shortly before his death, Cohn was disbarred for cheating private clients. Matter of Cohn, 503 N.Y.S.2d 759 (1st Dept. 1986).

Journalist Sidney Zion, a friend of Cohn, quotes Cohn extensively in his book, *The Autobiography of Roy Cohn* (1988). With regard to the Rosenberg trial, Zion writes that Cohn claimed that "[b]efore, during and after the trial, [U.S. Attorney] Irving Saypol and I were in constant communication with Judge Kaufman." Cohn reportedly said that he "often" talked with Kaufman from phone booths, with Kaufman's secretary telling each "where to be at what hour." And after the Rosenbergs were convicted, Zion writes, Cohn claimed that Kaufman telephoned him for advice on Ethel Rosenberg's sentence, having told Cohn "before the trial started that he was going to sentence Julius Rosenberg to death." In his biography, *Citizen Cohn* (1988), Nicholas von Hoffman quotes an FBI memo dated April 3, 1951, which in turn quotes Cohn's reports of the substance of his conversations with Judge Kaufman during the trial and before sentence.

Whatever one thinks of the Rosenbergs — and recent revelations* now seem to confirm that Julius was guilty but Ethel was not — the perception is widespread that their trial, and certainly their death sentences, fell far below the requirements of due process. Years later, Irving Kaufman was said to bemoan that despite all of his important rulings thereafter, and there were many, the New York Times would still cite his role in the Rosenberg case in the second sentence of his obituary. He was wrong about that. It appeared in the first sentence: "Judge Irving R. Kaufman, who gained national attention in 1951 as the judge who sentenced Julius and Ethel Rosenberg to the electric chair and who wrote landmark decisions in First Amendment, antitrust and civil rights cases for more than 30 years on the Federal bench, died on Saturday night in the Mount Sinai Medical Center." He was 81 years old. New York Times, Feb. 3., 1992.

FURTHER READING

Going beyond (but including) ethics in the narrow sense, Geoffrey Miller takes on the subject of "bad judges" and what to do about them in his article,

---

* Sam Roberts, Rosenbergs' Sons Accept Conclusion That Father Was A Spy, New York Times, Sept. 17, 2008.

Bad Judges, 83 Tex. L. Rev. 431 (2004) (identifying a dozen factors that can make a judge bad, ranging from incompetence and inappropriate behavior to bias and lack of candor).

A. CONFLICTS AND DISQUALIFICATION

"Conflicts in Bush v. Gore?"

In December 2000, a 5-4 Supreme Court majority ended the Florida presidential vote recount and gave George W. Bush the electoral votes necessary to establish his victory over Albert Gore. The popular press identified three Justices whom some believed had conflicts that should have resulted in their disqualification. All three were in the majority. Should these Justices have stepped aside? No one asked them to do so.

1. **Antonin Scalia:** George Bush's lawyer was Theodore Olson, a partner in Gibson, Dunn & Crutcher. Another Gibson partner was Eugene Scalia, Justice Scalia's son. In addition, John Scalia, another son of the Justice, had just joined Greenberg, Traurig, the law firm of Barry Richard, who had represented Mr. Bush in Florida. Joe Conason, writing in The New York Observer, said that it was not "difficult to imagine how greatly the partnership interests of two Scalia offspring would be promoted by a victory for Mr. Olson and Mr. Richard (and their firms) in one of the most important legal cases in history." The Ties That Bind Scalia and Olson, N.Y. Observer, Dec. 18, 2000. Is he right?

2. **Clarence Thomas:** Justice Thomas's wife, Virginia, was at the time gathering resumes for potential Bush administration jobs on behalf of the Heritage Foundation, a conservative think tank. L.A. Times, Dec. 13, 2000. Did Justice Thomas have a conflict?

3. **Sandra Day O'Connor:** According to the Wall Street Journal, "Justice O'Connor, a cancer survivor, has privately let it be known that, after 20 years on the high court, she wants to retire to her home state of Arizona. . . . At an Election Night party . . . the justice's husband, John O'Connor, mentioned to others her desire to step down, according to three witnesses. But Mr. O'Connor said his wife would be reluctant to retire if a Democrat were in the White House and would choose her replacement." Supreme Interests: For Some Justices, the Bush-Gore Case Has a Personal Angle, Wall St. J., Dec. 12, 2000. Did Justice O'Connor have a conflict? (As it happens, Justice O'Connor did not retire until the second Bush term.)

"The Clients of My Daughter Mean Nothing to Me"

"I'm an associate justice of our seven-member state supreme court. The former governor appointed me to this position 11 years ago, and the current governor reappointed me last year. It's a ten-year term. My daughter, Abigail

Casey Benhop, is a lawyer. We have different last names. She practices in our capital city, where I sit. (Which, by the way, is lucky because I get to see her for lunch and on weekends. I get to see the grandchildren too. My colleague Henrietta's kids live in Chattanooga and she's able to fly down there only three or four times a year. But that's not why I called.)

"Abby joined the bar nine years ago and now she's a partner at a good firm in town. Once she became a partner, I stopped sitting on cases in which her firm was trial counsel or is appellate counsel, even if she was not involved. (I never sat on cases in which she was involved at any stage.) Did I have to do that? I tell you, I don't know. Some said yes. Some said no. I'd like to hear what you think. In any event, I said, 'Roy, why create an issue?' And I took my own advice. Sometimes you just have to go with your instinct, especially if it's the conservative approach.

"In our state when a supreme court justice recuses, a lower court appellate judge can be brought up for that case in order to prevent a tie. Abby says there are cases her firm doesn't get because the client wants to be sure I'll sit if the case reaches us. I'm sorry about that, but they get plenty of business. Ethics is ethics, the way I see it.

"Abby's practice is limited to intellectual property work before federal agencies and the federal courts. We almost never get a case raising the issues she deals with. But one of Abby's clients, her biggest client, is Beanstalker, a large manufacturer of gardening equipment that also sells fertilizer, plants, trees, gardening and landscaping books, seeds, and so on.

"Beanstalker is a major company in our state and a big employer. It has an internet presence and sells internationally. It has legal cases that have nothing to do with intellectual property. We see three or four Beanstalker cases on our docket each year and another one or two in which the company is an amicus. Some of these cases involve small amounts of money but they raise important legal issues that can have huge consequences. Some cases involve large sums of money but have no broader legal implications. And . . . well, you see the picture.

"Now I'm wondering if I should continue to sit on Beanstalker cases even where it is not represented by Abby's firm, given the importance of some of the cases to the company and the importance of the company to Abby personally. The clients of my daughter mean nothing to me. I honestly believe that. It will not incline me at all one way or the other. No one has ever sought to recuse me in a Beanstalker case, not yet anyway, and I think that at least some of the lawyers who practice here know the relationships. But I'd rather not wait until that happens, and inevitably it will, before deciding on the right thing to do. One worry I have is that if I expand the scope of my recusal to all Beanstalker cases, I'm imposing on other judges to do the work. Also, the state has an interest in continuity of decisions from a cohesive court. Having lower court judges sit here too often dilutes that. What if my colleagues all recused themselves for the same reason? Three others, including our chief, have children, spouses of children, or their own spouse, practicing law in town. One has all three."

What Judicial Conflicts Violate the Due Process Clause?

In Aetna Life Insurance Co. v. Lavoie, 475 U.S. 813 (1986), the Supreme Court invoked the Due Process Clause to invalidate a state appellate judgment in a civil matter where one of the participating state judges had a direct financial interest in the outcome. The Alabama Supreme Court had affirmed a $3.5 million punitive damage award against Aetna. Justice Embry wrote the 5-4 per curiam opinion. At the time, as Aetna later discovered, Justice Embry was a plaintiff in a state case against other insurance companies. Justice Embry's claim, like the claim in *Aetna*, alleged a bad-faith failure to pay. After the *Aetna* decision, Justice Embry settled his own case for $30,000. The Supreme Court unanimously reversed. After concluding that "Justice Embry's opinion for the Alabama Supreme Court [in the *Aetna* case] had the clear and immediate effect of enhancing both the legal status and the settlement value of his own case," Chief Justice Burger continued:

> We conclude that Justice Embry's participation in this case violated appellant's due process rights. . . . We make clear that we are not required to decide whether in fact Justice Embry was influenced, but only whether sitting on the case then before the Supreme Court of Alabama " 'would offer a possible temptation to the average . . . judge to . . . lead him not to hold the balance nice, clear and true.' " The Due Process Clause "may sometimes bar trial by judges who have no actual bias and who would do their very best to weigh the scales of justice equally between contending parties. But to perform its high function in the best way, 'justice must satisfy the appearance of justice.' "

The Court stressed that Justice Embry had cast the deciding vote. Justice Brennan concurred and Justice Blackmun (joined by Justice Marshall) concurred in the judgment. Both concurring opinions concluded that the result should be the same even if Justice Embry had not cast the deciding vote. Justice Brennan wrote: "The participation of a judge who has a substantial interest in the outcome of a case of which he knows at the time he participates *necessarily* imports a bias into the deliberative process. This deprives litigants of the assurance of impartiality that is the fundamental requirement of due process." While it is rare for the Supreme Court to grant relief on the ground that a judge's interest or bias violated due process, another such case is Bracy v. Gramley, 520 U.S. 899 (1997). Ruling unanimously in an opinion by the Chief Justice, the Court held that a state death row inmate was entitled to discovery on his habeas claim. After Bracy's conviction, Maloney, the judge who had presided at his trial, was himself convicted of accepting bribes in other murder cases. Bracy argued that he should be entitled to discovery to support his theory, for which he had some evidence, that Maloney's bribe-taking in other cases "induced a sort of compensatory bias against *defendants* [like Bracy] who did *not* bribe Maloney. Maloney was biased in this latter, compensatory sense [Bracy argued] to avoid being seen as uniformly and suspiciously 'soft' on criminal defendants." The Court found "good cause" to permit discovery. "Maloney was shown to be thoroughly steeped in corruption through his public trial and conviction. We emphasize, though, that petitioner supports his discovery request by pointing not only to Maloney's conviction for bribe taking in other cases, but also to additional evidence . . . that lends support to his claim that Maloney was actually biased *in petitioner's own case.*" On remand, a divided Seventh Circuit ultimately held that Bracy's theory entitled him to a new sentencing hearing but not a new determination of guilt. Bracy v. Schomig, 286 F.3d 406 (7th Cir. 2002) (en banc). (Thereafter, former Illinois governor Ryan commuted all death sentences in the state.)

Aetna has its limits, as several subsequent lower court opinions reveal. In one, a state appellate judge who participated in a decision affirming a conviction had been the local prosecuting attorney at the time of the conviction, and his name appeared on the state's appeal brief. The Fifth Circuit initially granted a writ of habeas corpus. The petitioner's due process rights were violated, it ruled, whether or not the judge had actually participated in the prosecution personally. The petitioner did not have to show prejudice. Why not? Bradshaw v. McCotter, 785 F.2d 1327 (5th Cir. 1986). On rehearing, the court denied relief because the judge's vote was not necessary for the result. 796 F.2d 100 (5th Cir. 1986). What about the risk that the other judges might have been influenced by their colleague's name on the state's appellate brief and his participation in deliberations?

The Aetna issue will be back in the Court in 2009. Caperton v. Massey Coal Co. asks when a large judicial campaign contribution requires recusal. See page 609.

Ethical and Statutory Disqualification

LILJEBERG v. HEALTH SERVICES ACQUISITION CORP.
486 U.S. 847 (1988)

JUSTICE STEVENS delivered the opinion of the Court.

In 1974 Congress amended the Judicial Code "to broaden and clarify the grounds for judicial disqualification." The first sentence of the amendment provides: "Any justice, judge, or magistrate of the United States shall disqualify himself in any proceeding in which his impartiality might reasonably be questioned...."

I

In November 1981, respondent Health Services Acquisition Corp. brought an action against petitioner John Liljeberg, Jr., seeking a declaration of ownership of a corporation known as St. Jude Hospital of Kenner, Louisiana (St. Jude). The case was tried by Judge Robert Collins, sitting without a jury. Judge Collins found for Liljeberg and, over a strong dissent, the Court of Appeals affirmed. Approximately 10 months later, respondent learned that Judge Collins had been a member of the Board of Trustees of Loyola University while Liljeberg was negotiating with Loyola to purchase a parcel of land on which to construct a hospital. The success and benefit to Loyola of these negotiations turned, in large part, on Liljeberg prevailing in the litigation before Judge Collins.

Based on this information, respondent moved pursuant to Federal Rule of Civil Procedure 60(b)(6) to vacate the judgment on the ground that Judge Collins was disqualified under §455 at the time he heard the action and entered judgment in favor of Liljeberg. Judge Collins denied the motion and respondent appealed. The Court of Appeals determined that resolution of the motion required factual findings concerning the extent and timing of Judge Collins' knowledge of Loyola's interest in the declaratory relief litigation. Accordingly, the panel reversed and remanded the matter to a different judge for such findings. On remand, the District Court found that based on his attendance at Board meetings Judge Collins had actual knowledge of Loyola's interest in St. Jude in 1980 and 1981. The court further concluded, however, that Judge Collins had forgotten about Loyola's interest by the time the declaratory judgment suit came to trial in January 1982. On March 24, 1982, Judge Collins reviewed materials sent to him by the Board to prepare for an upcoming meeting. At that time — just a few days after he had filed his opinion finding for Liljeberg and still within the 10-day period allowed for filing a motion for a new trial — Judge Collins once again obtained actual knowledge of Loyola's interest in St. Jude. Finally, the District Court found that although Judge Collins thus lacked actual knowledge during trial and prior to the filing of his opinion, the evidence nonetheless gave rise to an appearance of impropriety. However, reading the Court of Appeals' mandate as limited to the issue of actual knowledge, the District Court concluded that it was compelled to deny respondent's Rule 60(b) motion.

The Court of Appeals again reversed. The court first noted that Judge Collins should have immediately disqualified himself when his actual knowledge of Loyola's interest was renewed. The court also found that regardless of Judge Collins' actual knowledge, "a reasonable observer would expect that Judge Collins would remember that Loyola had some dealings with Liljeberg and St. Jude and seek to ascertain the nature of these dealings." Such an appearance of impropriety, in the view of the Court of Appeals, was sufficient ground for disqualification under §455(a). . . .

II

Petitioner, John Liljeberg, Jr., is a pharmacist, a promoter, and a half-owner of Axel Realty, Inc., a real estate brokerage firm. In 1976, he became interested in a project to construct and operate a hospital in Kenner, Louisiana, a suburb of New Orleans. In addition to providing the community with needed health care facilities, he hoped to obtain a real estate commission for Axel Realty and the exclusive right to provide pharmaceutical services at the new hospital. The successful operation of such a hospital depended upon the acquisition of a "certificate of need" from the State of Louisiana; without such a certificate the hospital would not qualify for health care reimbursement payments under the federal medicare and medicaid programs. Accordingly, in October 1979, Liljeberg formed St. Jude, intending to have the corporation apply for the certificate of need at an appropriate time.

During the next two years Liljeberg engaged in serious negotiations with at least two major parties. One set of negotiations involved a proposal to purchase a large tract of land from Loyola University for use as a hospital site, coupled with a plan to rezone adjoining University property. The proposed benefits to the University included not only the proceeds of the real estate sale itself, amounting to several million dollars, but also a substantial increase in the value to the University of the rezoned adjoining property. The progress of these negotiations was regularly reported to the University's Board of Trustees by its Real Estate Committee and discussed at Board meetings. The minutes of those meetings indicated that the University's interest in the project was dependent on the issuance of the certificate of need.

[Liljeberg was conducting separate negotiations with HAI, predecessor to respondent Health Services Acquisition Corp. Eventually Liljeberg and HAI entered a contract whose meaning became the subject of the instant action. In essence, the question before Judge Collins was whether, under the contract, Liljeberg or HAI owned St. Jude. This was important because, in the interim, St. Jude had received a certificate of need for the hospital. Only if Liljeberg controlled the certificate would he be able to proceed with his arrangement with Loyola, and would Loyola enjoy the benefits identified in the Court's opinion.]

Respondent filed its complaint for declaratory judgment on November 30, 1981. The case was tried by Judge Collins, sitting without a jury, on January 21 and 22, 1982. At the close of the evidence, he announced his intended ruling, and on March 16, 1982, he filed a judgment (dated March 12, 1982) and his findings of fact and conclusions of law. He credited Liljeberg's version of oral conversations that were disputed and of critical importance in his ruling.

During the period between November 30, 1981, and March 16, 1982, Judge Collins was a trustee of Loyola University, but was not conscious of the fact that the University and Liljeberg were then engaged in serious negotiations concerning the Kenner hospital project, or of the further fact that the success of those negotiations depended upon his conclusion that Liljeberg controlled the certificate of need. To determine whether Judge Collins' impartiality in the Liljeberg litigation "might reasonably be questioned," it is appropriate to consider the state of his knowledge immediately before the lawsuit was filed, what happened while the case was pending before him, and what he did when he learned of the University's interest in the litigation.

After the certificate of need was issued, and Liljeberg and HAI became embroiled in their dispute, Liljeberg reopened his negotiations with the University. On October 29, 1981, the Real Estate Committee sent a written report to each of the trustees, including Judge Collins, advising them of "a significant change" concerning the proposed hospital in Kenner and stating specifically that Loyola's property had "again become a prime location." The Committee submitted a draft of a resolution authorizing a University vice-president "to continue negotiations with the developers of the St. Jude Hospital." At the Board meeting on November 12, 1981, which Judge Collins attended, the trustees discussed the connection between the rezoning of Loyola's land in Kenner and the St. Jude project and adopted the Real Estate Committee's proposed resolution. Thus, Judge Collins had actual knowledge of the University's potential interest in the St. Jude hospital project in Kenner just a few days before the complaint was filed.

While the case was pending before Judge Collins, the University agreed to sell 80 acres of its land in Kenner to Liljeberg for $6,694,000. The progress of negotiations was discussed at a Board meeting on January 28, 1982. Judge Collins did not attend that meeting, but the Real Estate Committee advised the trustees that "the federal courts have determined that the certificate of need will be awarded to the St. Jude Corporation." Presumably this advice was based on Judge Collins' comment at the close of the hearing a week earlier, when he announced his intended ruling because he thought "it would be unfair to keep the parties in doubt as to how I feel about the case."

The formal agreement between Liljeberg and the University was apparently executed on March 19th. The agreement stated that it was not in any way conditioned on Liljeberg's prevailing in the litigation "pending in the U.S. District Court for the Eastern District of Louisiana . . . involving the obtaining by [Liljeberg] of a Certificate of Need," but it also gave the University the right to repurchase the property for the contract price if Liljeberg had not executed a satisfactory construction contract within one year and further provided for nullification of the contract in the event the rezoning of the University's adjoining land was not accomplished. Thus, the University continued to have an active interest in the outcome of the litigation because it was unlikely that Liljeberg could build the hospital if he lost control of the certificate of need; moreover, the rezoning was in turn dependent on the hospital project.

The details of the transaction were discussed in three letters to the trustees dated March 12, 15, and 19, 1982, but Judge Collins did not examine any of those letters until shortly before the Board meeting on March 25, 1982. Thus, he acquired actual knowledge of Loyola's interest in the litigation on March 24, 1982. As the Court of Appeals correctly held, "Judge Collins should have recused himself when he obtained actual knowledge of that interest on March 24."

In considering whether the Court of Appeals properly vacated the declaratory relief judgment, we are required to address two questions. We must first determine whether §455(a) can be violated based on an appearance of partiality, even though the judge was not conscious of the circumstances creating the appearance of impropriety, and second, whether relief is available under Rule 60(b) when such a violation is not discovered until after the judgment has become final.

III

Title 28 U.S.C. §455 provides in relevant part:

(a) Any justice, judge, or magistrate of the United States shall disqualify himself in any proceeding in which his impartiality might reasonably be questioned.

(b) He shall also disqualify himself in the following circumstances: . . .

(4) He knows that he, individually or as a fiduciary, or his spouse or minor child residing in his household, has a financial interest in the subject matter in controversy or in a party to the proceeding, or any other interest that could be substantially affected by the outcome of the proceeding. . . .

(c) A judge should inform himself about his personal and fiduciary financial interests, and make a reasonable effort to inform himself about the personal financial interests of his spouse and minor children residing in his household.

Scienter is not an element of a violation of §455(a). The judge's lack of knowledge of a disqualifying circumstance may bear on the question of remedy, but it does not eliminate the risk that "his impartiality might reasonably be questioned" by other persons. To read §455(a) to provide that the judge must know of the disqualifying facts, requires not simply ignoring the language of the provision — which makes no mention of knowledge — but further requires concluding that the language in subsection (b)(4) — which expressly provides that the judge must *know* of his or her interest — is extraneous. A careful reading of the respective subsections makes clear that Congress intended to require knowledge under subsection (b)(4) and not to require knowledge under subsection (a).[8] Moreover, advancement of the purpose of the provision — to promote public confidence in the integrity of the judicial process — does not depend upon whether or not the judge actually knew facts creating an appearance of impropriety, so long as the public might reasonably believe that he or she knew. . . .

Contrary to petitioner's contentions, this reading of the statute does not call upon judges to perform the impossible — to disqualify themselves based on facts they do not know. If, as petitioner argues, §455(a) should only be applied prospectively, then requiring disqualification based on facts the judge does not know would of course be absurd; a judge could never be expected to disqualify himself based on some fact he does not know, even though the fact is one that perhaps he should know or one that people might reasonably suspect that he does know. But to the extent the provision can also, in proper cases, be applied retroactively, the judge is not called upon to perform an impossible feat. Rather, he is called upon to rectify an oversight and to take the steps necessary to maintain public confidence in the impartiality of the judiciary. If he concludes that "his impartiality might reasonably be questioned," then he should also find that the statute has been violated. This is certainly not an impossible task. No one questions that Judge Collins could have disqualified himself and vacated his judgment when he finally realized that Loyola had an interest in the litigation. The initial appeal was taken from his failure to disqualify himself and vacate the judgment *after* he became aware of the appearance of impropriety, not from his failure to disqualify himself when he first became involved in the litigation and lacked the requisite knowledge.

In this case both the District Court and the Court of Appeals found an ample basis in the record for concluding that an objective observer would have questioned Judge Collins' impartiality. Accordingly, even though his failure to disqualify himself was the product of a temporary lapse of memory, it was nevertheless a plain violation of the terms of the statute.

A conclusion that a statutory violation occurred does not, however, end our inquiry. As in other areas of the law, there is surely room for harmless error committed by busy judges who inadvertently overlook a disqualifying

---

8. Petitioner contends that §455(a) must be construed in light of §455(b)(4). He argues that the reference to knowledge in §455(b)(4) indicates that Congress must have intended that scienter be an element under §455(a) as well. Petitioner reasons that §455(a) is a catchall provision, encompassing all of the specifically enumerated grounds for disqualification under §455(b), as well as other grounds not specified. Not requiring knowledge under §455(a), in petitioner's view, would thus render meaningless the knowledge requirement under §455(b)(4). The requirement could always be circumvented by simply moving for disqualification under §455(a), rather than §455(b).

Petitioner's argument ignores important differences between subsections (a) and (b)(4). Most importantly, §455(b)(4) requires disqualification no matter how insubstantial the financial interest and regardless of whether or not the interest actually creates an appearance of impropriety. See §455(d)(4); In re Cement and Concrete Litigation, 515 F. Supp. 1076 (D. Ariz. 1981), mandamus denied, 688 F.2d 1297 (C.A.9 1982), aff'd by the absence of quorum, 459 U.S. 1191 (1983). In addition, §455(e) specifies that a judge may not accept a waiver of any ground for disqualification under §455(b), but may accept such a waiver under §455(a) after "a full disclosure on the record of the basis for disqualification." Section 455(b) is therefore a somewhat stricter provision, and thus is not simply redundant with the broader coverage of §455(a) as petitioner's argument posits.

circumstance.[9] There need not be a draconian remedy for every violation of
§455(a). It would be equally wrong, however, to adopt an absolute prohibition
against any relief in cases involving forgetful judges.

IV

Although §455 defines the circumstances that mandate disqualification of
federal judges, it neither prescribes nor prohibits any particular remedy for a
violation of that duty. Congress has wisely delegated to the judiciary the task of
fashioning the remedies that will best serve the purpose of the legislation.

In considering whether a remedy is appropriate, we do well to bear in mind
that in many cases — and this is such an example — the Court of Appeals is in a
better position to evaluate the significance of a violation than is this Court. Its
judgment as to the proper remedy should thus be afforded our due consideration. A review of the facts demonstrates that the Court of Appeals' determination that a new trial is in order is well supported.

Section 455 does not, on its own, authorize the reopening of closed litigation.
However, as respondent and the Court of Appeals recognized, Federal Rule of
Civil Procedure 60(b) provides a procedure whereby, in appropriate cases, a
party may be relieved of a final judgment. In particular, Rule 60(b)(6), upon
which respondent relies, grants federal courts broad authority to relieve a party
from a final judgment "upon such terms as are just," provided that the motion is
made within a reasonable time and is not premised on one of the grounds for
relief enumerated in clauses (b)(1) through (b)(5). The Rule does not partic-
ularize the factors that justify relief, but we have previously noted that it provides
courts with authority "adequate to enable them to vacate judgments whenever
such action is appropriate to accomplish justice," while also cautioning that it
should only be applied in "extraordinary circumstances." Rule 60(b)(6) relief is
accordingly neither categorically available nor categorically unavailable for all
§455(a) violations. We conclude that in determining whether a judgment
should be vacated for a violation of §455(a), it is appropriate to consider the
risk of injustice to the parties in the particular case, the risk that the denial of
relief will produce injustice in other cases, and the risk of undermining the
public's confidence in the judicial process. We must continuously bear in
mind that "to perform its high function in the best way 'justice must satisfy
the appearance of justice.'" In re Murchison, 349 U.S. 133, 136 (1955) (citation
omitted).

Like the Court of Appeals, we accept the District Court's finding that while
the case was actually being tried Judge Collins did not have actual knowledge of
Loyola's interest in the dispute over the ownership of St. Jude and its precious

9. Large, multidistrict class actions, for example, often present judges with unique difficulties in
monitoring any potential interest they may have in the litigation. In such cases, the judge is
required to familiarize himself or herself with the named parties and all the members of the
class, which in an extreme case may number in the hundreds or even thousands. This already
difficult task is confounded by the fact that the precise contours of the class are often not defined
until well into the litigation.

Of course, notwithstanding the size and complexity of the litigation, judges remain under a duty
to stay informed of any personal or fiduciary financial interest they may have in cases over which
they preside. See 28 U.S.C. §455(c). The complexity of determining the conflict, however, may have
a bearing on the Rule 60(b)(6) extraordinary circumstance analysis.

certificate of need. When a busy federal judge concentrates his or her full attention on a pending case, personal concerns are easily forgotten. The problem,
however, is that people who have not served on the bench are often all too
willing to indulge suspicions and doubts concerning the integrity of judges.[12]
The very purpose of §455(a) is to promote confidence in the judiciary by avoiding even the appearance of impropriety whenever possible. Thus, it is critically
important in a case of this kind to identify the facts that might reasonably cause
an objective observer to question Judge Collins' impartiality. There are at least
four such facts.

First, it is remarkable that the judge, who had regularly attended the meetings
of the Board of Trustees since 1977, completely forgot about the University's
interest in having a hospital constructed on its property in Kenner. The importance of the project to the University is indicated by the fact that the 80-acre
parcel, which represented only about 40% of the entire tract owned by the
University, was sold for $6,694,000 and that the rezoning would substantially
increase the value of the remaining 60%. The "negotiations with the developers
of the St. Jude Hospital" were the subject of discussion and formal action by the
trustees at a meeting attended by Judge Collins only a few days before the lawsuit
was filed.

Second, it is an unfortunate coincidence that although the judge regularly
attended the meetings of the Board of Trustees, he was not present at the January 28, 1982, meeting, a week after the 2-day trial and while the case was still
under advisement. The minutes of that meeting record that representatives of
the University monitored the progress of the trial, but did not see fit to call to the
judge's attention the obvious conflict of interest that resulted from having a
University trustee preside over that trial. These minutes were mailed to Judge
Collins on March 12, 1982. If the Judge had opened that envelope when he
received it on March 14th or 15th, he would have been under a duty to recuse
himself *before* he entered judgment on March 16.[13]

Third, it is remarkable — and quite inexcusable — that Judge Collins failed to
recuse himself on March 24, 1982. A full disclosure at that time would have

---

12. As we held in Aetna Life Ins. Co. v. Lavoie, 475 U.S. 813 (1986), this concern has
constitutional dimensions. In that case we wrote:

We conclude that Justice Embry's participation in this case violated appellant's due process
rights as explicated in *Tumey* [*v. Ohio*, 273 U.S. 510 (1927)], *Murchison*, and *Ward* [*v. Village of
Monroeville*, 409 U.S. 57 (1972)]. We make clear that we are not required to decide whether in
fact Justice Embry was influenced, but only whether sitting on the case then before the Supreme
Court of Alabama " 'would offer a possible temptation to the average [judge to] lead him not to
hold the balance nice, clear and true.' " . . .

A finding by another judge — faced with the difficult task of passing upon the integrity of a
fellow member of the bench — that his or her colleague merely possessed *constructive* knowledge,
and not *actual* knowledge, is unlikely to significantly quell the concerns of the skeptic.

13. One of the provisions of the contract between Loyola and Liljeberg is also remarkable.
Despite the fact that earlier minutes of the Board make it clear that the University's interest in
serious negotiations with Liljeberg was conditioned upon the certificate of need, the contract
expressly recites that control of the certificate was the subject of pending litigation and then
provides "that this sale shall not be in any way conditioned upon" the outcome of that litigation.
The University, however, retained the right to repurchase the property if Liljeberg was unable to go
forward with the hospital project. If Liljeberg was found not to control the certificate of need, he, at
least arguably, would have been precluded from going forward with the hospital. Moreover, if the
parties simply wanted to make the transaction unconditional, they could have omitted any
reference to the litigation. An objective observer might reasonably question why the parties felt
a need to include this clause.

completely removed any basis for questioning the Judge's impartiality and would have made it possible for a different judge to decide whether the interests — and appearance — of justice would have been served by a retrial. Another 2-day evidentiary hearing would surely have been less burdensome and less embarrassing than the protracted proceedings that resulted from Judge Collins' nonrecusal and nondisclosure. Moreover, as the Court of Appeals correctly noted, Judge Collins' failure to disqualify himself on March 24, 1982, also constituted a violation of §455(b)(4), which disqualifies a judge if he "knows that he, individually or as a fiduciary, . . . has a financial interest in the subject matter in controversy or in a party to the proceeding, or any other interest that could be substantially affected by the outcome of the proceeding." This separate violation of §455 further compels the conclusion that vacatur was an appropriate remedy; by his silence, Judge Collins deprived respondent of a basis for making a timely motion for a new trial and also deprived it of an issue on direct appeal. Fourth, when respondent filed its motion to vacate, Judge Collins gave three reasons for denying the motion,[15] but still did not acknowledge that he had known about the University's interest both shortly before and shortly after the trial. Nor did he indicate any awareness of a duty to recuse himself in March of 1982.

These facts create precisely the kind of appearance of impropriety that §455(a) was intended to prevent. The violation is neither insubstantial nor excusable. Although Judge Collins did not know of his fiduciary interest in the litigation, he certainly should have known. In fact, his failure to stay informed of this fiduciary interest may well constitute a separate violation of §455. See §455(c). Moreover, providing relief in cases such as this will not produce injustice in other cases; to the contrary, the Court of Appeals' willingness to enforce §455 may prevent a substantive injustice in some future case by encouraging a judge or litigant to more carefully examine possible grounds for disqualification and to promptly disclose them when discovered. It is therefore appropriate to vacate the judgment unless it can be said that respondent did not make a timely request for relief, or that it would otherwise be unfair to deprive the prevailing party of its judgment.

If we focus on fairness to the particular litigants, a careful study of [Circuit] Judge Rubin's analysis of the merits of the underlying litigation suggests that there is a greater risk of unfairness of upholding the judgment in favor of Liljeberg than there is in allowing a new judge to take a fresh look at the issues. Moreover, neither Liljeberg nor Loyola University has made a showing of special hardship by reason of their reliance on the original judgment. Finally, although a delay of 10 months after the affirmance by the Court of Appeals would normally foreclose relief based on a violation of §455(a), in this case the entire delay is attributable to Judge Collins' inexcusable failure to disqualify himself on March 24, 1982; had he recused himself on March 24, or even disclosed Loyola's

---

15. These were his three reasons:

First, Loyola University was not and is not a party to this litigation, nor was any of its real estate the subject matter of this controversy. Second, Loyola University is a nonprofit, educational institution, and any benefits [inuring] to that institution would not benefit any individual personally. Finally, and most significantly, this Judge never served on either the Real Estate or Executive Committees of the Loyola University Board of Trustees. Thus, this Judge had no participation of any kind in negotiating Loyola University's real estate transactions and, in fact, had no knowledge of such transactions.

interest in the case at that time, the motion could have been made less than 10 days after the entry of judgment. . . .

The judgment of the Court of Appeals is accordingly affirmed.

CHIEF JUSTICE REHNQUIST, with whom JUSTICE WHITE and JUSTICE SCALIA join, dissenting.

The Court's decision in this case is long on ethics in the abstract, but short on workable rules of law. The Court first finds that 28 U.S.C. §455(a) can be used to disqualify a judge on the basis of facts not known to the judge himself. It then broadens the standard for overturning final judgments under Federal Rule of Civil Procedure 60(b). Because these results are at odds with the intended scope of §455 and Rule 60(b), and are likely to cause considerable mischief when courts attempt to apply them, I dissent.

I

As detailed in the Court's opinion, §455(a) provides that "[a]ny justice, judge, or magistrate of the United States shall disqualify himself in any proceeding in which his impartiality might reasonably be questioned." . . .

Subsection (b) of §455 sets forth more particularized situations in which a judge must disqualify himself. Congress intended the provisions of §455(b) to remove any doubt about recusal in cases where a judge's interest is too closely connected with the litigation to allow his participation. Subsection (b)(4), for example, disqualifies a jurist if he knows that he, his spouse, or his minor children have a financial interest in the subject matter in controversy. Unlike the more open-ended provision adopted in subsection (a), the language of subsection (b) requires recusal only in specific circumstances, and is phrased in such a way as to suggest a requirement of actual knowledge of the disqualifying circumstances.

The purpose of §455 is obviously to inform judges of what matters they must consider in deciding whether to recuse themselves in a given case. The Court here holds, as did the Court of Appeals below, that a judge must recuse himself under §455(a) if he *should have known* of the circumstances requiring disqualification, even though in fact he did not know of them. I do not believe this is a tenable construction of subsection (a). A judge considering whether or not to recuse himself is necessarily limited to those facts bearing on the question of which he has knowledge. To hold that disqualification is required by reason of facts which the judge does *not* know, even though he should have known of them, is to posit a conundrum which is not decipherable by ordinary mortals. While the concept of "constructive knowledge" is useful in other areas of the law, I do not think it should be imported into §455(a).

At the direction of the Court of Appeals, Judge Schwartz of the District Court for the Eastern District of Louisiana made factual findings concerning the extent and timing of Judge Collins' knowledge of Loyola's interest in the underlying lawsuit. Judge Schwartz determined that Judge Collins had no actual knowledge of Loyola's involvement when he tried the case. Not until March 24, 1982, when he reviewed materials in preparation for a Board meeting, did Judge Collins obtain actual knowledge of the negotiations between petitioners and Loyola.

Despite this factual determination, reached after a public hearing on the subject, the Court nevertheless concludes that "public confidence in the impartiality of the judiciary" compels retroactive disqualification of Judge Collins under §455(a). This conclusion interprets §455(a) in a manner which Congress never intended. As the Court of Appeals noted, in drafting §455(a) Congress was concerned with the "appearance" of impropriety, and to that end changed the previous subjective standard for disqualification to an objective one; no longer was disqualification to be decided on the basis of the opinion of the judge in question, but by the standard of what a reasonable person would think. But the facts and circumstances which this reasonable person would consider must be the facts and circumstances *known* to the judge at the time. In short, as is unquestionably the case with subsection (b), I would adhere to a standard of actual knowledge in §455(a), and not slide off into the very speculative ground of "constructive" knowledge.

II

The Court then compounds its error by allowing Federal Rule of Civil Procedure 60(b)(6) to be used to set aside a final judgment in this case. Rule 60(b) authorizes a district court, on motion and upon such terms as are just, to relieve a party from a final judgment, order, or proceeding for any "reason justifying relief from the operation of the judgment." However, we have repeatedly instructed that only truly "extraordinary circumstances" will permit a party successfully to invoke the "any other reason" clause of 60(b). . . .

For even if one accepts the Court's proposition that §455(a) permits disqualification on the basis of a judge's constructive knowledge, Rule 60(b)(6) should not be used in this case to apply §455(a) retroactively to Judge Collins' participation in the lawsuit. In the first place, it is beyond cavil that Judge Collins stood to receive no *personal* financial gain from the transactions involving petitioner, respondent, and Loyola. Judge Collins' only prior tie to the dealings was as a member of Loyola's rather large Board of Trustees and, although Judge Collins was a member of at least two of the Board's subcommittees, he had no connection with the Real Estate subcommittee, the entity responsible for negotiating the sale of the [land in issue]. In addition, the motion to set aside the judgment was made by respondent almost 10 months after judgment was entered in March 1982; although relief under Rule 60(b)(6) is subject to no absolute time limitation, there can be no serious argument that the time elapsed since the entry of judgment must weigh heavily in considering the motion. Finally, and most important, Judge Schwartz determined that Judge Collins did not have actual knowledge of his conflict of interest during trial and that he made no rulings after he acquired actual knowledge.[4] . . .

4. The majority's opinion suggests a number of troubling hypothetical situations, only one of which will demonstrate the difficulties inherent in its decision. Suppose Judge Doe sits on a bench trial involving *X* Corp. and *Y* Corp. The judge rules for *X* Corp., and judgment is affirmed on appeal. Ten years later, officials at *Y* Corp. learn that, unbeknownst to him, Judge Doe owned several shares of stock in *X* Corp. Even in the face of an independent factual finding that Judge Doe had no knowledge of this ownership, the Court's construction of §455(a) and Rule 60(b) would permit the final judgment in *X* Corp.'s favor to be set aside if the "appearance of impartiality" were not deemed wholly satisfied. Such a result will adversely affect the reliance placed on final judgments and will inhibit developments premised on their finality.

Justice O'Connor, dissenting.

For the reasons given by Chief Justice Rehnquist, I agree that "constructive knowledge" cannot be a basis for a violation of 28 U.S.C. §455(a). The question then remains whether respondent is entitled to a new trial because there are other "extraordinary circumstances," apart from the §455(a) violation found by the Fifth Circuit, that justify "relief from operation of the judgment." Although the Court collects an impressive array of arguments that might support the granting of such relief, I believe the issue should be addressed in the first instance by the courts below. I would therefore remand this case with appropriate instructions.

President Carter nominated Judge Collins in 1978. In 1991, Collins was convicted of bribery, conspiracy, and obstruction of justice in connection with his judicial duties. He was sentenced to nearly seven years in prison, but for a while he remained a federal judge and continued to draw his salary *while in prison*. In 1993, to avoid impeachment, he resigned his judgeship. He was disbarred in November 1994. New Orleans Times-Picayune, Nov. 22, 1994.

Liljeberg is about as critical an opinion as one can imagine. Did Justice Stevens believe Judge Collins's assertion that, while trying the case, he did not know of Loyola's interest? The majority wrote that "we accept" the finding in this regard. Are you convinced? But if Judge Collins did not know of Loyola's interest, what then is the harm that the Court's remedy — vacating the judgment — is meant to address? After all, the Fifth Circuit had previously affirmed Judge Collins on the merits of the underlying dispute. Justice Stevens identifies four actual or possible violations of §455: (1) a violation of subsection (a); (2) a violation of subsection (b)(4); (3) a failure to reveal a possible basis for recusal when, after trial, Judge Collins discovered it; and (4) a possible violation of subsection (c). You should be able to articulate the theory behind each of these. To which of them does the Chief Justice respond? How?

What Conflicts Prevent a Judge from Sitting?

Personal Relationships or Interests.   Section 455(b) identifies certain relationships that will automatically disqualify a judge. Other relationships may disqualify the judge under §455(a).

In Cheney v. United States District Court, 542 U.S. 367, decided June 24, 2004, the Supreme Court turned back an effort to require the vice president to reveal the names of members of an energy task force he headed in the early days of the Bush administration. The identity of the members (some of whom may later have been caught up in the scandal surrounding Enron, or so some suspected) became an issue in the 2004 campaign. The trial court had ordered the vice president to reveal the names, and the court of appeals concluded that it lacked appellate jurisdiction to review the order.

Certiorari in the vice president's case was granted on December 15, 2003. On January 17, 2004, the Los Angeles Times reported that "Vice President Dick Cheney and Supreme Court Justice Antonin Scalia spent part of last week duck hunting together at a private camp in Southern Louisiana just three weeks after the Court agreed to take up the vice president's appeal in lawsuits over his handling of the administration's energy taskforce." The national press was all over the story. Late-night comics lampooned Justice Scalia. Editorials from many newspapers criticized the trip. The Sierra Club, one of the two organizations that brought the case against the vice president, asked Justice Scalia to recuse himself, citing 28 U.S.C §455(a). The other organization said it had no concerns about Justice Scalia's impartiality.

In due course, it came to light that Justice Scalia was accompanied on the trip by his son and son-in-law and that the three flew to Louisiana as guests on the vice president's plane (but flew home commercially on a round-trip ticket). In responding to the Sierra Club's recusal motion, Justice Scalia wrote:

> We departed from Andrews Air Force Base at about 10 a.m. on Monday, January 5, flying in a Gulfstream jet owned by the Government. We landed in Patterson, Louisiana, and went by car to a dock where Mr. Carline met us, to take us on the 20-minute boat trip to his hunting camp. We arrived at about 2 p.m., the 5 of us joining about 8 other hunters, making about 13 hunters in all; also present during our time there were about 3 members of Mr. Carline's staff, and, of course, the Vice President's staff and security detail. It was not an intimate setting. The group hunted that afternoon and Tuesday and Wednesday mornings; it fished (in two boats) Tuesday afternoon. All meals were in common. Sleeping was in rooms of two or three, except for the Vice President, who had his own quarters. Hunting was in two- or three-man blinds. As it turned out, I never hunted in the same blind with the Vice President. Nor was I alone with him at any time during the trip, except, perhaps, for instances so brief and unintentional that I would not recall them — walking to or from a boat, perhaps, or going to or from dinner. Of course we said not a word about the present case. The Vice President left the camp Wednesday afternoon, about two days after our arrival. I stayed on to hunt (with my son and son-in-law) until late Friday morning, when the three of us returned to Washington on a commercial flight from New Orleans.

In rejecting recusal, Justice Scalia explained that the vice president was sued only in his official, not his personal, capacity and that friendship should not "affect impartiality in official-action suits." The Sierra Club argued that the vice president's reputation and integrity were on the line in the lawsuit, but Justice Scalia rejected that argument. The only issue before the Court, he wrote, was whether the "Court of Appeals should have asserted mandamus or appellate jurisdiction over the District Court. Nothing this Court says on those subjects will have any bearing upon the reputation and integrity of Richard Cheney." He went on to conclude that even if the vice president lost the case and was forced to disclose the names of the task force members, that still would not affect his reputation and integrity.

> To be sure, there could be political consequences from disclosure of the fact (if it be so) that the Vice President favored business interests, and especially a sector of business with which he was formerly connected. But political consequences are not my concern, and the possibility of them does not convert an official suit into a private one. That possibility exists to a greater or lesser degree in virtually all suits involving agency action.

Justice Scalia supported his ruling by citing a trip Justice Jackson took with President Roosevelt in 1942 and a trip Justice White took with Attorney General Robert Kennedy in 1963. However, he did not mention that the statute the Sierra Club cited as the basis for recusal was passed in 1974. No equivalent statutory language restricted Justices Jackson or White. One might also question whether cases then before the earlier Justices at the time of their trips could affect the reputations of the officials with whom they traveled. Rather, the cases Scalia cited dealt with the power of the Executive Branch generally. Justice Scalia also rejected the allegation that the trip to Louisiana on the vice president's plane, for himself and two family members, constituted a gift requiring recusal. Cheney v. United States District Court, 541 U.S. 913 (2004). (Supreme Court Justices get to decide recusal motions aimed at them. Unlike recusal decisions by other federal judges, there is no further review.)

On the merits, the Supreme Court vacated the decision of the Court of Appeals and remanded the case for further consideration. Five Justices, in an opinion by Justice Kennedy, concluded that the Court of Appeals did have mandamus jurisdiction to review the District Court's discovery order but left it to that court to decide whether to exercise the jurisdiction. Justice Stevens concurred. Justice Thomas, joined by Justice Scalia, filed an opinion dissenting in part. Justice Thomas would have dismissed the case against the vice president outright. Justice Ginsburg dissented, joined by Justice Souter.

For an informed and witty debate over the propriety of Justice Scalia's decision to sit in the *Cheney* case, see Lawrence Fox, I Did Not Sleep With the Vice President, 15 Professional Lawyer No. 2 at 1 (2004) (a title that means to play on Scalia's defense that Cheney had his own bedroom), and the reply by W. William Hodes, Nino Protested Too Much, But Larry Created the Appearance of Politicizing Judicial Ethics, 15 Professional Lawyer No. 3 at 1 (2004). See also Monroe Freedman, Duck-Blind Justice: Justice Scalia's Memorandum in the *Cheney* Case, 18 Geo. J. Legal Ethics 229 (2004).

Can you square Justice Scalia's decision with the next case, also involving a high government official, in which personal relationships did result in removal of a judge? The case is United States v. Tucker, 78 F.3d 1313 (8th Cir. 1996). On motion of Whitewater Independent Counsel Kenneth Starr, Judge Henry Woods of the District Court in Arkansas was removed from the trial of former Arkansas Governor Jim Guy Tucker because of Judge Woods's close relationship with First Lady Hillary Rodham Clinton. Judge Woods had even spent a night in the White House. "For their part, President and Mrs. Clinton have been reported to have expressed continued support for Tucker since his indictment by the grand jury. . . . Moreover, as the Independent Counsel has noted, 'this case will, as a matter of law, involve matters related to the investigation of the President and Hillary Rodham Clinton.'" The Circuit Court cited popular publications, including the Wall Street Journal and The New Yorker, in support of its finding of a "link" between Judge Woods and the Clintons. For his part, Judge Woods questioned the Circuit's analysis:

> Judge Woods today acerbically criticized the court's reversal of his ruling. In the midst of a 78th birthday party for him in his chambers, the judge said he might be the first judge in "Anglo-American history who has been removed from a case on the basis of newspaper accounts, magazine articles and television transcripts."

He paused, waved his arms toward the walls of his chambers to indicate the bookcases packed with legal texts on evidential issues, including one he had written, and said, "But I suppose on the basis of this opinion I will have to expand my library and subscribe to Vanity Fair and The New Yorker."*

Personal interest forced the disqualification of Judge Wayne Alley from trying Timothy McVeigh and Terry Nichols, two men charged in the Oklahoma City bombing case. Here are the Tenth Circuit's reasons: "Judge Alley's courtroom and chambers were one block away from the epicenter of a massive explosion that literally rocked downtown Oklahoma City, heavily damaged the Murrah Building, killed 169 people, and injured many others. The blast crushed the courthouse's glass doors, shattered numerous windows, ripped plaster from ceilings, dislodged light fixtures, showered floors with glass, damaged Judge Alley's courtroom and chambers, and injured a member of his staff, as well as other court personnel and their families." Nichols v. Alley, 71 F.3d 347 (10th Cir. 1995). Does this persuade you that Judge Alley's impartiality might reasonably be questioned within the meaning of §455(a)? Can you reconcile the result with United States v. Harrelson, 754 F.2d 1153 (5th Cir. 1985), where the defendant was charged with killing a federal judge? Recusal of the trial judge was not required even though he had been a judicial colleague of the victim and had eulogized him at his memorial service. Their relationship was collegial. No social relationship existed between the judges or their families.

Judicial "Affairs." In one highly unusual case, a Connecticut Supreme Court justice was suspended without pay for six weeks after sitting on three appeals, including a murder case, argued by a legal aid lawyer with whom he had had a "close personal relationship." David Margolick, A Top Judge in Connecticut Is Suspended, N.Y. Times, Feb. 19, 1994, at 21. And as I write, a Texas death sentence has been stayed and an investigation launched because of allegations that the judge and the prosecutor were having an affair while the capital trial was in progress. According to a defense lawyer, in the ensuing inquiry judge and prosecutor admitted under oath to an affair, but it remains unclear whether the affair was ongoing during the trial. Should that matter? Should a judge preside at a trial where one of the lawyers is a former lover? My vote: No way. And in a criminal case, not even with fully informed consent. James C. McKinley, Jr., Judge and Prosecutor Admit to Affair, Lawyer Says, New York Times, Sept. 9, 2008. See also "Lawyer Relatives" and "Manipulation of Disqualification" later in this chapter.

Source of Knowledge. Section 455(b)(1) requires a judge to disqualify herself if the judge "has a personal bias or prejudice concerning a party." This provision covers *actual* bias. But §455(a) would require disqualification if the judge's impartiality might reasonably be questioned because of *apparent* bias — in other words, people will reasonably believe that the judge is biased, even if the judge is not biased. One question that has arisen is whether §455(a) can require recusal for apparent bias if the apparent bias is based on

---

* Ronald Smothers, Broad Reach of Whitewater Counsel's Inquiry Is Upheld, New York Times, March 16, 1996, p.7, col. 1.

information the judge learns in his judicial capacity — that is, while sitting as a judge. Subsection (b)(1) has long been read to require an extrajudicial source for actual bias. This requirement has been called the "extrajudicial source doctrine." A judge who becomes disposed (or biased) against a party because of what she learns in doing her job — like hearing evidence — will not in this view trigger the statute's actual bias standard. Judges are supposed to form opinions based on what they learn while judging. That's what judging is all about. Disqualification for actual bias, in this view, requires that the source of the judge's bias be something that happened outside of court (extrajudicial).

Lower courts divided, however, on whether the extrajudicial source doctrine also applied to §455(a). Even if a judge cannot be disqualified under §455(b)(1) unless the source of bias is extrajudicial, might she be disqualified under subsection (a) if the source of apparent bias is merely "intrajudicial," on the theory that subsection (a) is broader and more demanding than subsection (b)? The dispute was resolved in Liteky v. United States, 510 U.S. 540 (1994). The Court held that while the extrajudicial source doctrine *does* apply to subsection (a), too, "there is not much doctrine to the doctrine" because the presence of an extrajudicial source for a judge's bias is neither a necessary nor a sufficient cause of disqualification. Justice Scalia's majority opinion relabeled the doctrine the "extrajudicial source factor." The opinion described how the "factor" would work:

> [O]pinions formed by the judge on the basis of facts introduced or events occurring in the course of the current proceedings, or of prior proceedings, do not constitute a basis for a bias or partiality motion unless they display a deep-seated favoritism or antagonism that would make fair judgment impossible. Thus, judicial remarks during the course of a trial that are critical or disapproving of, or even hostile to, counsel, the parties, or their cases, ordinarily do not support a bias or partiality challenge. They *may* do so if they reveal an opinion that derives from an extrajudicial source; and they *will* do so if they reveal such a high degree of favoritism or antagonism as to make fair judgment impossible. An example of the latter (and perhaps of the former as well) is the statement that was alleged to have been made by the District Judge in Berger v. United States, 255 U.S. 22 (1921), a World War I espionage case against German-American defendants: "One must have a very judicial mind, indeed, not [to be] prejudiced against the German Americans" because their "hearts are reeking with disloyalty." *Not* establishing bias or partiality, however, are expressions of impatience, dissatisfaction, annoyance, and even anger, that are within the bounds of what imperfect men and women, even after having been confirmed as federal judges, sometimes display. A judge's ordinary efforts at courtroom administration — even a stern and short-tempered judge's ordinary efforts at courtroom administration — remain immune.

Justice Kennedy concurred in an opinion for himself and three others. Justice Kennedy had no problem with the result in the case but concluded that the majority's reasoning unduly limited the breadth of §455(a), contrary to the holding in *Liljeberg*: "One of the distinct concerns of §455(a) is that the appearance of impartiality be assured whether or not the alleged disqualifying circumstance is also addressed under §455(b)." See also Blanche Road Corp. v. Bensalem Township, 57 F.3d 253 (3d Cir. 1995), overruled on other grounds, 316 F.3d 392 (3d Cir. 2003) (disqualification possible under §455(a) despite absence of an extrajudicial source).

"Judicial Seminars."   In the mid-1970s, corporations that frequently litigate in federal court began contributing to nonprofit organizations, including
law schools, to fund the expenses of federal judges (and sometimes a guest) to
attend "seminars," often at posh resorts at optimal times of the year. Golf was a
popular pastime along with the seminars. Speakers at the seminars would often
advocate perspectives on the law that were favorable to the corporate sponsors.
Judges attending these seminars are required to list their trips as gifts on financial disclosure forms. The propriety of attendance, however, has led to debate.
Does a judge have an obligation to learn the identity of the corporate sponsors?
Does it matter if the seminar is "unbalanced" in favor of or against a particular
perspective? Does it matter whether a judge attending a seminar currently has
on his docket a case in which one of the corporate sponsors is a party or a case
raising a legal issue of great consequence to a nonparty sponsor?

In Nothing For Free: How Private Judicial Seminars Are Undermining Environmental Protections and Breaking the Public's Trust (Community Rights
Counsel 2000), the CRC identified what it perceived to be a certain pattern
between attendance at corporate-sponsored judicial seminars and some
subsequent judicial rulings that favored the broad policy positions of seminar
sponsors. Of course, a pattern, even if present, does not mean causality. But
because conflict rules are concerned with the appearance of impartiality, as well
as its fact, a perception of a connection may be enough to raise concern. On
April 6, 2001, the ABC news show *20/20* broadcast an investigation of corporate-
sponsored judicial seminars based in part on the CRC Report. On the same day,
Senators John Kerry and Russell Feingold issued a statement recalling that in the
prior Congress they had "introduced legislation that would have banned these
private seminars once and for all." The legislation failed, but the senators vowed
to "introduce new legislation in this Congress and this time we will insist on its
passage until the very end." As of 2008, no legislation has passed.

In 2001, the Second Circuit refused to order the disqualification of a district
judge who had attended a seminar (in Montana in September) sponsored by the
Foundation for Research on Economics and the Environment (FREE). Texaco
was a contributor to FREE's general funding, though not to the particular seminar. The judge had recently handled an environmental matter in which Texaco
was a litigant. When the case was remanded to him soon after the seminar
ended, he did not reveal his attendance at the seminar. A former chief executive
of Texaco, who was CEO when the facts of the underlying case occurred, spoke
at the seminar, although not on the subject of the case. Although Judge Winter's
opinion for the circuit court rejected disqualification on the facts before it, he
added "several cautionary notes" on how to think about these questions.

> In particular, we caution judges that recusal may be required after accepting
> meals or lodging from organizations that may receive a significant portion of their
> general funding from litigants or counsel to them — whether or not in connec-
> tion with an unbalanced presentation. The extent of funding is, of course, again a
> matter of judgment, but accepting something of value from an organization
> whose existence is arguably dependent upon a party to litigation or counsel to
> a party might well cause a reasonable observer to lift the proverbial eyebrow.
>
> Moreover, where a presentation concerns issues material to the disposition
> of litigation or involves parties, witnesses, or counsel in particular actions,

the recusal calculus will differ, albeit again without an applicable mechanical standard. Presentations at bar association meetings or law schools may well relate to particularized issues, and recusal should be considered seriously, but on a case-by-case basis. Judges should be wary of attending presentations involving litigation that is before them or likely to come before them without at the very least assuring themselves that parties or counsel to the litigation are not funding or controlling the presentation. See In re Sch. Asbestos Litig., 977 F.2d 764, 781-85 (3d Cir. 1992) (issuing writ of mandamus directing recusal where district judge approved ex parte request by plaintiffs to use money from settlement fund to pay indirectly for conference about crucial scientific issue in that litigation, where plaintiffs' proposed expert witnesses presented their views, and where judge also attended conference with many expenses paid). Where parties or counsel to them fund or control such a presentation, the appearance created bears too great a resemblance to an ex parte contact.

In re Aguinda, 241 F.3d 194 (2d Cir. 2001). The Third Circuit disqualified a judge from hearing a class action case after the judge and his wife attended an expenses-paid conference at which the speakers included 13 of the plaintiffs' probable expert witnesses. In re School Asbestos Lit., 977 F.2d 764 (3d Cir. 1992) (the plaintiffs' lawyers were also the source of funding for the conference).

It is hardly possible to overstate the intensity of the debate over whether rules should limit or even forbid these trips. The simple fact is that judges like to go on them. Judges don't earn *all* that much. The trips can be worth thousands of dollars, especially if a spouse or guest accompanies the judge. And judges ask, rhetorically in their view, "Do you think for one second, even for one second, that I would ever change my decision in any case because I was given a free trip? Do you?" Critics respond that changing a decision is not the issue. That would be bribery. In their view, the issue is not whether a judge is being bought but whether the impartiality of a judge who goes on these trips "might reasonably be questioned" (in the language of the code and the statute) in a case in which a benefactor is a party or has an interest. In their view, it's not a question of payback, but of influence. And they argue that courtroom opponents of companies that fund the trips usually lack the money to stage equivalent events at which they can present their views to a "captive" audience.

The 2007 ABA Code of Judicial Conduct permits reimbursement of "reasonable" expenses for a judge and guest but requires the judge to file a public report of the value within thirty days after the event. Where "technically feasible," the report must be posted on the court's website. Rule 3.14 and 3.15. A comment, which is not binding, provides:

> A judge must assure himself or herself that acceptance of reimbursement or fee waivers would not appear to a reasonable person to undermine the judge's independence, integrity, or impartiality. [Although this sentence is cast in mandatory terms it merely restates the requirements of Rule 1.2.] The factors that a judge should consider when deciding whether to accept reimbursement or a fee waiver for attendance at a particular activity include:
>
> (a) whether the sponsor is an accredited educational institution or bar association rather than a trade association or a for-profit entity;

(b) whether the funding comes largely from numerous contributors rather than from a single entity and is earmarked for programs with specific content;

(c) whether the content is related or unrelated to the subject matter of litigation pending or impending before the judge, or to matters that are likely to come before the judge;

(d) whether the activity is primarily educational rather than recreational, and whether the costs of the event are reasonable and comparable to those associated with similar events sponsored by the judiciary, bar associations, or similar groups;

(e) whether information concerning the activity and its funding sources is available upon inquiry;

(f) whether the sponsor or source of funding is generally associated with particular parties or interests currently appearing or likely to appear in the judge's court, thus possibly requiring disqualification of the judge under Rule 2.11;

(g) whether differing viewpoints are presented; and

(h) whether a broad range of judicial and nonjudicial participants are invited, whether a large number of participants are invited, and whether the program is designed specifically for judges.

The Judicial Conference of the United States, the entity that promulgates rules governing the behavior of federal judges (including the Code of Conduct for U.S. Judges), has also tried to tackle this issue and also opts for "greater transparency," including through posting information on each court's website. For a description of the policy and a list of corporate and other funders and speakers since January 1, 2007, go to http://www.uscourts.gov/disclosure/overview.html.

Is disclosure the correct solution or should the practice be banned entirely? True, some of these seminars have educational value, but then why not give each federal judge an annual budget to attend educational seminars of his or her choosing instead of allowing them to be beneficiaries of high-end corporate generosity? Or is that too cynical?

Further Reading

Douglas Kendall & Jason Rylander, Tainted Justice: How Private Judicial Trips Undermine Public Confidence in the Judiciary, 18 Geo. J. Ethics 65 (2004).

Campaign Contributions. In 2008, the West Virginia Supreme Court decided 3-2 to vacate a $50 million judgment against a company controlled by a man who had spent $3 million on television ads and other support toward the election of one of the justices in the majority. That justice had refused to recuse himself. Dorothy Samuels, The Selling of the Judiciary: Campaign Cash 'in the Courtroom,' New York Times, Apr. 15, 2008 (editorial). In November 2008, the Supreme Court granted review to decide whether the justice's participation violated due process. Caperton v. Massey Coal Co., 08-22. The Times editorial quoted former Supreme Court Justice Sandra Day O'Connor as saying at a Fordham Law School conference, "We put cash in the courtroom, and it's just wrong."*

Why is it wrong? Many state judges run for office. They have campaign committees that seek contributions. Contributors are often lawyers but often, too, they are companies who frequently appear in state court and have an obvious interest in the judicial philosophy of state judges, especially state high court judges, whose state law decisions are final. The costs of running a state supreme court election, once rather cheap and sleepy affairs, have escalated as corporate interests have attempted to influence the composition of these courts and thereby to affect the development of legal doctrines important to their businesses. Often these doctrines concern tort law liability and the measure (and availability) of damages for injuries. The New York Times did an in depth examination of this development in Ohio:

> In the fall of 2004, Terrence O'Donnell, an affable judge with the placid good looks of a small-market news anchor, was running hard to keep his seat on the Ohio Supreme Court. He was also considering two important class-action lawsuits that had been argued many months before.
>
> In the weeks before the election, Justice O'Donnell's campaign accepted thousands of dollars from the political action committees of three companies that were defendants in the suits. Two of the cases dealt with defective cars, and one involved a toxic substance. Weeks after winning his race, Justice O'Donnell joined majorities that handed the three companies significant victories.
>
> Justice O'Donnell's conduct was unexceptional. In one of the cases, every justice in the 4-to-3 majority had taken money from affiliates of the companies. None of the dissenters had done so, but they had accepted contributions from lawyers for the plaintiffs.
>
> Thirty-nine states elect judges, and 30 states are holding elections for seats on their highest courts this year. Spending in these races is skyrocketing, with some judges raising $2 million or more for a single campaign. As the amounts rise, questions about whether money is polluting the independence of the judiciary are being fiercely debated across the nation. And nowhere is the battle for judicial seats more ferocious than in Ohio.
>
> An examination of the Ohio Supreme Court by The New York Times found that its justices routinely sat on cases after receiving campaign contributions from the parties involved or from groups that filed supporting briefs. On average, they voted in favor of contributors 70 percent of the time. Justice O'Donnell voted for his contributors 91 percent of the time, the highest rate of any justice on the court. . . .
>
> Three recent cases, two in Illinois and one in West Virginia, have put the complaints in sharp focus. Elected justices there recently refused to disqualify themselves from hearing suits in which tens or hundreds of millions of dollars were at stake. The defendants were insurance, tobacco and coal companies whose supporters had spent millions of dollars to help elect the justices.
>
> After a series of big-money judicial contests around the nation, the balance of power in several state high courts has tipped in recent years in favor of corporations and insurance companies.

---

* A closely related question — the scope of the First Amendment right of candidates for election to judicial office to tell voters their views on controversial legal issues — is addressed in chapter 15, which focuses on the speech rights of judges and lawyers.

Adam Liptak & Janet Rogers, Campaign Cash Mirrors a High Court's Rulings, New York Times, Oct. 1, 2006.

But Ohio judges are not alone in choosing to rule despite receipt of campaign help from lawyers or parties before them. In Dean v. Bondurant, 193 S.W.3d 744 (Ky. 2006), the Chief Justice of Kentucky, ruling on a recusal motion directed at him, surveyed numerous state court decisions and concluded: "I have yet to find a case that required recusal merely based on a campaign contribution within the state's campaign donation limits." The Chief Justice did step aside, however, because of factors in addition to contributions.

Apart from making all state (or state supreme court) positions appointive rather than elective, which is not about to happen, there seems to be no solution to this problem, short of seriously limiting the amount of campaign contributions, which could pose constitutional problems in itself. See Randall v. Sorrell, 548 U.S. 230 (2006) (contribution limit of $200 in gubernatorial contests and lower limit in other state contests violates First Amendment). And even with low contribution limits, supporters of particular candidates remain free to spend independently to influence the outcome of elections. Besides, does the problem go away, or merely get buried, if the executive (or in a few states, the legislature) appoints judges? At least, with elections, it's out in the open. Candidates can be required to report contributions.

But wait. Is there even a problem here? Critics (like the Times) claim that campaign contributions are at bottom a form of legal bribery. Judges know they will have to run for re-election or retention (many as frequently as every six years), and they know that they may need a big war chest to beat back challengers. So, critics argue, judges will tilt toward favoring the interests that have the money to contribute to their future campaigns. But defenders reply that this argument mixes cause and effect. Judges don't favor the views of moneyed litigants. Rather, the moneyed interests contribute to the candidates whose policy preferences (and remember that judging does involve policy preferences) are likely to favor their legal positions. Whatever you think about judicial elections, the defenders say, so long as we have them, everyone is entitled to contribute money or volunteer time to help candidates whose views of the law they favor. Who's right?

For the several state variations on judicial selection, see the helpful website of the American Judicature Society at http://www.ajs.org/selection/sel_state-select-map.asp.

Employment Interests. A judge was required to recuse himself when a "headhunter" working on his behalf, concerning possible employment after retirement, mistakenly contacted law firms representing opposing parties in an antitrust action pending before him. Pepsico, Inc. v. McMillen, 764 F.2d 458 (7th Cir. 1985). The court said that there was no "actual impropriety," but an objective observer might wonder whether the judge would "at some unconscious level" favor the firm that had not definitively rejected his employment. This result is consistent with Model Rule 1.12(b).

A trial judge was negotiating for a job with the Justice Department while it was trying a criminal case before the judge. The defendant was convicted. The appellate court vacated the conviction and ordered a new trial even though the defendant could show no prejudice. Scott v. United States, 559 A.2d 745 (D.C. 1989).

Consider what the bankruptcy judge did in In re Continental Airlines Corp., 901 F.2d 1259 (5th Cir. 1990). The judge made several important rulings in favor of Continental. Shortly thereafter he granted Continental's law firm a $700,000 fee. A day later he accepted employment with the firm. The bankruptcy judge asserted that he was unaware he would receive an employment offer when he made his rulings and granted the fee award. The Fifth Circuit held that when the offer came in, the bankruptcy judge should have rejected it outright or, if he preferred to consider the offer, he should have recused himself and vacated his rulings. Nevertheless, citing *Liljeberg*, the court concluded that the error was harmless and did not require reversal of the judge's rulings. Three years later, however, in Matter of Continental Airlines, 981 F.2d 1450 (5th Cir. 1993), the same court further explained its conclusion in the appeal of another ruling by the same bankruptcy judge, which it did vacate. The scope of review on the second appeal was for an abuse of discretion, whereas the former ruling was reviewable de novo. Why then the difference in result? In considering whether "the violation of §455(a) constitutes harmless error," the court wrote, "[t]he risk of injustice to the parties is much greater when a court lacks broad powers of review." Do you see why? The court explained that if the later order were not vacated, "the parties may remain subject to an order entered by a judge who has violated [§455(a)], yet has not abused his discretion in entering the order."

A Duty to Sit?   In his memorandum refusing to recuse himself in Laird v. Tatum, 409 U.S. 824 (1972), a case challenging military spying on civilians, Justice Rehnquist observed that "federal courts of appeals that have considered the matter have unanimously concluded that a federal judge has a duty to *sit* where *not disqualified* which is equally as strong as the duty to *not sit* where *disqualified*." (Emphasis in original.) He went on to say that the policy in favor of the "equal duty" concept is stronger in the case of the Supreme Court, for whose members, unlike lower court judges, no substitute is possible and where there is no higher court to review an equally divided bench. The challengers lost 5 to 4, with Justice Rehnquist in the majority for reversal. A 4-4 vote would have affirmed their lower court victory.

The basis for the motion to recuse Justice Rehnquist in *Laird* was testimony he gave on the legality of the spying program when he served as an assistant attorney general. After his decision refusing recusal, Congress amended §455 to add §455(b)(3), which forbids a judge to sit if as a government lawyer he "participated as counsel, adviser or material witness concerning the proceeding or expressed an opinion concerning the merits of the particular case in controversy." Justice Rehnquist's refusal to recuse himself in *Laird* became a subject of inquiry in his 1986 confirmation hearings to be Chief Justice. Jeffrey Stempel pursued the issues thereafter and unearthed facts beyond those adduced at the hearings. His article is cited in Further Readings, page 618.

Laird arose before the 1974 amendments to §455. In United States v. Kelly, 888 F.2d 732 (11th Cir. 1989), the court held that §455 does away with the "duty to sit" doctrine and instead requires judges "to resolve any doubts they may have in favor of disqualification." Chief Justice Rehnquist acknowledged the same effect in a portion of his *Liljeberg* dissent omitted here. In *Kelly*, the judge presided at a bench trial of a criminal case. The wife of a defense witness (Wills) was a friend of the judge's wife. The judge acknowledged that the witness's testimony "created the risk that he might bend over backwards to prove he lacked favoritism toward Wills. . . . Conversely, he stated that if he found Kelly guilty he felt he might jeopardize his wife's friendship with Mrs. Wills." Nevertheless, the judge did not recuse himself. The Eleventh Circuit reversed.

What happens if every judge in a position to hear a case would be disqualified? In United States v. Will, 449 U.S. 200 (1980), several district judges sued the government to recover additional compensation on the ground that inflation had worked a reduction in their salaries in violation of Article III, which provides that the compensation of federal judges "shall not be diminished during their Continuance in Office." If the plaintiffs were successful, all federal judges would benefit from the victory. Nevertheless, the Supreme Court rejected a claim that 28 U.S.C. §455 and the ABA's Code of Judicial Conduct required all federal judges to disqualify themselves, holding that under the "Rule of Necessity, a well-settled principle at common law," a judge having a personal interest in a case not only may but must take part in the decision if the case could not otherwise be heard. Further, in enacting §455, Congress did not intend to alter this principle.

Financial Interests.   A judge must recuse herself under §455(b)(4) if she knows that the judge, her spouse, or minor child residing in the household has a financial interest in a party, "however small." §455(b)(4)(d)(4). Headwaters, Inc. v. Bureau of Land Management, 665 F. Supp. 873 (D. Or. 1987). To enable judges to determine whether they have financial interests in corporate litigants, procedural rules often require corporate parties to list their affiliates, parents, and subsidiaries. See Fed. R. App. P. 26.1.

Because the financial interests of a judge's spouse may force recusal, and because judicial families may have holdings in various kinds of accounts, vigilance and communication are required to avoid ignoring the rule. The retirement account of Justice Ruth Bader Ginsburg's husband, Martin Ginsburg, a tax lawyer and law professor, contained shares in companies whose cases came before the Court 20 times between 1995 and 1997. After these facts were reported by Insight magazine, which discovered them in a review of the financial disclosure forms federal judges are required to file, Mr. Ginsburg made the following statement: "I had not appreciated that stocks held in an I.R.A. account managed by a third party professional raised the concern Insight has highlighted. After reading the article, I promptly instructed Smith Barney to sell all stocks in the I.R.A. account and to invest only in mutual funds." N.Y. Times, July 11, 1997, at 19. What does it matter what Professor Ginsburg "realized"? The rule restricts Justice Ginsburg, not her husband.

The words "however small" in the §455(d)(4) definition of forbidden financial interests have led to absurd results, prompting reform.

In re Cement & Concrete Litigation (cited in footnote 8 of *Liljeberg*) was a multidistrict class action charging a price-fixing conspiracy in the cement industry. The plaintiff class consisted of 210,000 individuals and corporate entities, all of whom were alleged to be users of cement. Judge Muecke of the District Court for the District of Arizona had spent five years presiding over the litigation when certain of the defendants moved to disqualify him because his wife owned shares of stock in seven of the class plaintiffs. Judge Muecke concluded that the class members in which his wife held stock were "parties" within the meaning of §455(b)(4) even though they were not named parties. He further concluded that his wife's stock interest was a "financial interest" within the meaning of that subsection, according to the definition in §455(d)(4). Judge Muecke computed the total value of his wife's financial interest, assuming that the plaintiff class would be entirely successful. Before corporate taxes that interest amounted to $29.70. Nevertheless, Judge Muecke concluded that he had to disqualify himself under the mandatory language of §455 because the definition of "financial interest" included "a legal or equitable interest, however small." (If a ground for disqualification is one of the provisions under §455(b), as in this case, the parties may not waive the disqualification.) Judge Muecke expressed surprise that "Congress did not consider the effect of §455 on the administration of class action litigation," especially since with the

> number of participants in a large class action, it is not an easy matter to deter-mine whether a per se conflict exists. In normal litigation, a judge can simply compare his [family's] holdings with the names on the caption to the com-plaint. In a complex multidistrict class action, the litigation may be well under way before a comprehensive class list can be compiled. To switch judges in mid-stream not only wastes judicial time and energy, but can constitute a substantial administrative burden.

Section 455(f), added in 1988, now permits a judge with a "financial interest" to remain on a matter when "appearance or discovery" of the interest occurred after the matter was assigned to the judge, if the judge has already devoted "substantial judicial time . . . to the matter," and if the interest could not be "substantially affected by the outcome." For an example of the operation of §455(f), where quick disinvestment enabled a judge to continue with a matter, see Kidder, Peabody & Co. v. Maxus Energy Corp., 925 F.2d 556 (2d Cir. 1991).

Lawyer Relatives.   Advisory Opinion No. 58 (1978), issued by a committee of the U.S. Judicial Conference, concerns judicial disqualification in a case in which a relative is employed by a participating law firm. It provides in part:

> We believe the following conclusions find support in the Code [of Judicial Conduct]. A judge is disqualified and should recuse if a relative within the third degree of relationship to the judge or his spouse (a) is a partner in a law firm appearing in the case; or (b) will profit or lose from the judge's action in the case either financially or otherwise, for example, the reputation of the firm would be significantly affected by the litigation.

The Utah Supreme Court disqualified an intermediate appellate judge from hearing an appeal where the appellant was seeking a judgment larger than the jury awarded and counsel fees larger than the trial judge awarded. The appel-lant's lawyer was in a firm whose partners included the judge's father-in-law and brother-in-law. The trial judge had awarded $7,500 in counsel fees, and the firm wanted about $26,000. Regional Sales Agency, Inc. v. Reichert, 830 P.2d 252 (Utah 1992). A comparable situation is presented when the judge's relative has worked on the matter. In re Aetna Casualty & Surety Co., 919 F.2d 1136 (6th Cir. 1990) (en banc), issued mandamus disqualifying a judge and vacating certain of his orders where the judge's daughter, a lawyer, had briefly participated in the matter with a firm representing one of the parties. It did not matter that the daughter had since left the firm. What is the problem if the daughter does not stand to profit financially?

Chief Justice Rehnquist declined to recuse himself in an appeal of the government's antitrust claim against Microsoft Corporation even though his son James, who was in private practice, was then representing an antitrust plaintiff against Microsoft on an hourly basis. James was not involved in the government's antitrust claim, but Rehnquist recognized that a Supreme Court decision in the government's case "could have a significant effect on Microsoft's exposure to antitrust suits in other courts. But, by virtue of this Court's position atop the federal judiciary, the impact of many of our decisions is often quite broad. The fact that our disposition of the pending Microsoft litigation could potentially affect Microsoft's exposure to antitrust liability in other litigation does not, to my mind, significantly distinguish the present situation from other cases that this Court decides." The Chief Justice concluded that "an objective observer" would not perceive an appearance of partiality. He emphasized that the consequence of recusal would be to leave the court with an even number of Justices creating "a risk of affirmance of a lower court decision by an equally divided court." Microsoft Corp. v. United States, 530 U.S. 1301 (2000).

Law Clerks.   A law clerk's career may also lead to disqualification. In Hall v. Small Business Administration, 695 F.2d 175 (5th Cir. 1983), the court (citing §455(a)) reversed a judgment for the plaintiffs in a Title VII sex discrimination case tried before a magistrate, because his "sole law clerk was initially a member of the plaintiff class in this suit, had before her employment with the magistrate expressed herself as convinced of the correctness of its contentions, and accepted employment with its counsel before judgment was rendered." It was "immaterial" that the magistrate asserted he had made up his mind "immediately after the hearing" and before the law clerk worked on [the] case. Accord, Miller Indus. v. Caterpillar Tractor Co., 516 F. Supp. 84 (S.D. Ala. 1980).

But in Hunt v. American Bank & Trust Co., 783 F.2d 1011 (11th Cir. 1986), there was no disqualification ordered where a law clerk did not work on a case in which his prospective employer was counsel, nor did he "even tal[k] with the judge about it to any significant extent." In In re Allied-Signal, Inc., 891 F.2d 967 (1st Cir. 1989), disqualification was rejected where parties before the judge were represented by siblings of two of the judge's law clerks. The proper remedy, said the court, was not disqualification but exclusion of the clerks from the matter. Accord, Reddy v. Jones, 419 F. Supp. 1391 (W.D.N.C. 1976). See also a report of the Committee on Recruitment of Lawyers of the New York City Bar Association on Law Firm Recruitment, Judicial Clerks and Avoidance of Any Appearance of Impropriety, 36 The Record 53 (1981).

Judge's Prior Affiliation.   Section 455(b)(2) and (3) disqualifies a judge based on work the judge (or the judge's law firm) may have done while the judge was in private practice or in government employment. Preston v. United States, 923 F.2d 731 (9th Cir. 1991), presents a variation on this issue. *Preston* was a wrongful death action against the United States, tried before Judge Letts. Preston's estate had also filed a claim against Hughes Aircraft in state court based on the same events. Before his appointment, Judge Letts had been of counsel to Latham & Watkins while the firm represented Hughes in the state court action. After Judge Letts's appointment, Latham represented Hughes in connection with discovery issues in the federal action, but Hughes was not itself a party to the federal action. Hughes had an indemnity agreement that required it to pay any judgment against the United States in the federal case.

After a bench trial, judgment went for the United States, and plaintiffs argued on appeal that Judge Letts should have recused himself. The Ninth Circuit agreed. The fact that Hughes was not a party to the federal action was irrelevant. "Rather, the focus has consistently been on the question whether the relationship between the judge and an interested party was such as to present a risk that the judge's impartiality in the case at bar might reasonably be questioned by the public," within the meaning of §455(a). Here the answer to that question was yes. A client of the trial judge's former law firm, whom the firm had represented on the same underlying facts, "would have faced a potential claim for indemnification by the government" if plaintiffs prevailed. The remedy was a new trial. The court also cited §455(b)(2). Judge Letts had nothing to do with Hughes while he was of counsel to Latham. Why then should he be disqualified?

Manipulation of Disqualification.   Where a litigant selects a lawyer to represent him knowing that the lawyer is a relative of the trial judge and intending thereby to force the trial judge to recuse himself, the result will instead be that the lawyer is disqualified from representing the litigant. So ruled the Fifth Circuit in McCuin v. Texas Power & Light Co., 714 F.2d 1255 (5th Cir. 1983). The court acknowledged that "[f]orum-shopping is sanctioned by our judicial system [and] is as American as the Constitution." Further, the court recognized that "a litigant's motives for selecting a lawyer are not ordinarily subject to judicial scrutiny." Nevertheless, there are limits:

> A lawyer's acceptance of employment solely or primarily for the purpose of disqualifying a judge creates the impression that, for a fee, the lawyer is available for sheer manipulation of the judicial system. It thus creates the appearance of professional impropriety. Moreover, sanctioning such conduct brings the judicial system itself into disrepute. To tolerate such gamesmanship would tarnish the concept of impartial justice. To permit a litigant to blackball a judge merely by invoking a talismanic "right to counsel of my choice" would contribute to skepticism about and mistrust of our judicial system.

An interesting pattern in choice of counsel was identified in Robinson v. Boeing Co., 79 F.3d 1053 (11th Cir. 1996), which affirmed a decision not to permit the defendant to add a particular lawyer to its team where doing so would force the recusal of the judge (his uncle) to whom the case had been assigned. The court did not speculate on motive but an appendix to the opinion revealed many cases in which litigants had employed the same lawyer's firm after the identity of the assigned trial judge became known. In a later case involving the same judge (Clemon), his nephew (Price) was disqualified where the defendant hired Price only after the case had been assigned to his uncle. The client unsuccessfully sought to overturn the disqualification order in mandamus. The district judge who ordered the disqualification (not the uncle) and the circuit court (2-1) discerned a certain pattern. In re BellSouth Corp., 334 F.3d 941 (11th Cir. 2003) ("Price was retained in only four of the 204 cases in which BellSouth was sued in the Northern District of Alabama since 1991. Although the 204 cases were divided among 19 different judges, three of the four Price cases were initially referred to Judge Clemon, forcing his recusal."). Three lawyers were disciplined in Grievance Administrator v. Fried, 570 N.W.2d 262 (Mich. 1997), after the court concluded that they formed co-counsel relationships in criminal cases with the specific purpose of forcing the recusal of particular judges.

Judge's Duty to Reveal.   How can a lawyer know facts of a judge's life that might support a disqualification motion? Some facts may be a matter of public record. Examples are the judge's prior professional affiliations and the information contained in financial disclosure forms. But other facts — like the financial or other interests of close relatives — may not be. A comment to Rule 2.11 of the ABA Code requires judges to "disclose on the record information that the judge believes the parties or their lawyers might reasonably consider relevant to a possible motion for disqualification, even if the judge believes there is no basis for disqualification." This obligation is essential to ensure that a judge's decision to sit is reviewable, isn't it? Recall the Court's criticism of Judge Collins for failure to disclose Loyola's interest in the litigation before him after he learned of it following trial and before expiration of the deadline for a new trial motion (page 599). Section 455(b) says that a judge *shall* disqualify in certain circumstances. Liteky v. United States, 510 U.S. 540 (1994), which construed §455(b)(1) and by implication other parts of subsection (b), placed "the obligation to identify the existence of [disqualifying] grounds upon the judge himself, rather than requiring recusal only in response to a party affidavit." See also Aronson v. Brown, 14 F.3d 1578 (Fed. Cir. 1994) (§455 is "self-executing" and judge must recuse sua sponte when it applies).

Waiver.   Confusion reigns here. Section 455 and the two ABA Codes differ on waiver of judicial conflicts. Section 455 permits waiver of conflicts falling under subsection (a) ("impartiality might reasonably be questioned") but not of those falling under subsection (b) — for example, if the judge's spouse owns ten shares of stock in a litigant. The 1972 Code disallowed waiver where the judge's "impartiality might reasonably be questioned," but permitted waiver of other conflicts that the statute makes nonwaivable. The 1990 and 2007 Codes permit waiver of any conflict except those based on "personal bias." Waiver must follow full disclosure on the record. Waiver provisions have been criticized on two grounds: They give insufficient consideration to the public's interest in the appearance of justice; and even though the trial judge may not be told which of several parties declined to waive, the judge will usually be able to infer the answer, which may harm relationships between that party or its counsel and the judge in other matters. That prospect casts doubt on whether a waiver is really voluntary. Delay in seeking recusal after getting notice of the factual basis can result in denial even where the grounds arise under §455(b) and are therefore not subject to waiver. Summers v. Singletary, 119 F.3d 917 (11th Cir. 1997). That's right, isn't it? Any other rule would invite opportunistic behavior. ("Let's wait to see how he rules, and if we lose we move to recuse.")

FURTHER READING

Thorough treatment of issues discussed here appears in Richard Flamm, Judicial Disqualification (Little, Brown & Company 1996). John Leubsdorf has analyzed judicial disqualification law by examining theories of judging. John Leubsdorf, Theories of Judging and Judge Disqualification, 62 N.Y.U. L. Rev. 237 (1987). See also a critical evaluation of Justice Rehnquist's refusal to recuse himself in Laird v. Tatum: Jeffrey Stempel, Rehnquist, Recusal, and Reform, 53 Brook. L. Rev. 589 (1987). Sherrilyn Ifill, Do Appearances Matter? Judicial Impartiality and the Supreme Court in *Bush v. Gore*, 61 U. Md. L. Rev. 606 (2002), concludes that "several Justices could and should have taken a variety of measures — including but not limited to recusal — that would have diminished the appearance of judicial bias in that case." Note, Disqualifying Elected Judges from Cases Involving Campaign Contributors, 40 Stan. L. Rev. 449 (1988) (authored by Stuart Banner), examines the nearly impossible problems that arise when judges must run for election and raise money to do so. Should the judge whose recusal is sought decide if she is recused? Leslie Abramson, who says not always, tries to identify when the decision-maker should be another judge, in Deciding Recusal Motions: Who Judges the Judges?, 28 Val. U.L. Rev. 543 (1994). Professor Abramson has also suggested that the list of "per se" grounds for disqualification in §455(b) should from time to time be reexamined with a view toward expansion, to add reasons that would cause "average persons" to "feel uncomfortable having their cases presided over by a [particular] judge." Leslie Abramson, Specifying Grounds for Judicial Disqualification in Federal Courts, 72 Neb. L. Rev. 1046 (1993). In yet a third article, Professor Abramson takes on §455(a) and its "appearance of impropriety" standard. Leslie Abramson, Appearance of Impropriety: Deciding When a Judge's Impartiality "Might Reasonably Be Questioned," 14 Geo J. Legal Ethics 55 (2000).

B. EXPRESSIONS OF GENDER, RACIAL, AND OTHER BIAS

"The Judge and the Boy Scouts"

Federal Judge Wilbur Claremont III is a lifetime member of the Boy Scouts, which he supports with contributions and volunteered time. Now, at age 48, he helps run the local Boy Scouts chapter in Sunnyvale, goes on scouting trips with chapter members, and encourages his two sons, Homer and Burke, to be active Scouts. The Boy Scouts do not permit homosexuals to serve as scout masters, and this rule has been upheld by the Supreme Court. Boy Scouts of America v. Dale, 530 U.S. 640 (2000) (First Amendment right of expressive association prevents state from using public accommodations law to require Boy Scouts to admit homosexual man as assistant scout master). On one occasion, when debate over the Scouts' policy was in the news, Judge Claremont wrote a letter to his local newspaper in which he mentioned his lifelong work with the Scouts, did not identify himself as a judge, and endorsed the exclusionary policy. "Understandably, many parents might not let their sons participate in the Scouts if gay men were permitted to serve as scoutmasters, which task can include supervision on overnight camping excursions," he wrote.

Does Judge Claremont's participation in the Boy Scouts violate his obligations under the Code of Judicial Conduct Rule 3.6(a), which forbids "membership in any organization that practices invidious discrimination on the basis of . . . sexual orientation?" The comment, set out more fully below, states that whether an organization practices "invidious discrimination is a complex question," dependent on a number of factors including "whether it is an intimate, purely private organization whose membership limitations could not constitutionally be prohibited."

If Judge Claremont is randomly selected to preside over a class action challenging the state's refusal to recognize same-sex marriages performed out of state and to give these couples the same economic and other benefits the state affords married couples, should he be disqualified to sit on the ground that his "impartiality might reasonably be questioned" under 28 U.S.C. §455(a)?

Judicial and Courtroom Bias

In 1990 the ABA amended the Code of Judicial Conduct and dramatically rewrote or introduced new sections intended to address judicial and courtroom bias. These were expanded in the 2007 Code. See Rules 2.3 and 3.6 and their comments, summarized below but worth reading in full.

IN RE MARRIAGE OF IVERSON
11 Cal. App. 4th 1495, 15 Cal. Rptr. 2d 70 (1992)
SILLS, PRESIDING JUSTICE.

Cheryl Iverson appeals from a judgment dissolving her marriage of 15 years to George Chick Iverson. Primarily she challenges the trial court's finding that a premarital agreement signed by the parties was valid. She also challenges the granting of a protective order limiting discovery and the interpretation of the agreement. Chick cross-appeals from a portion of the judgment directing him to maintain a $1 million life insurance policy in favor of Cheryl.

The oral statement of decision of the judge who presided over the trial of the validity of the premarital agreement—and who acted as trier of fact in that proceeding—is so replete with gender bias that we are forced to conclude Cheryl could not have received a fair trial. Accordingly, we must reverse and direct the matter to be retried before a different judge. All other issues follow in the wake of this determination.

I

Cheryl and Chick separated in April 1987. Shortly thereafter, Cheryl filed this action to dissolve the marriage.

Chick obtained an order to bifurcate the proceeding and try the validity of a premarital agreement each had signed. During the trial, Chick testified he did not want to get married, told Cheryl he did not want to get married, and made it clear to his associates he was perfectly happy not getting married.

Cheryl told a somewhat different story. Chick first brought up the subject of marriage. He asked her to marry him in front of the late actor John Wayne, just after Chick had asked Wayne to be his best man. Marriage was the reason she moved in with Chick. He told her he wanted the couple to live together and be married.

The testimony also differed on the circumstances surrounding Cheryl's signing of the agreement. Chick presented the testimony of Rita Cruikshank, wife of the late William Cruikshank, Chick's attorney. She testified that in June 1972, Cheryl and Chick met on her husband's boat. William Cruikshank read the agreement to them. He asked if they understood what he was reading to them. They answered yes. This happened several times while he was reading the agreement. After he finished, he turned to Cheryl and told her, "Cheryl, I think maybe it's advisable you see another attorney, make sure this is what you want to do." Cheryl said, "No, no, no. Whatever Chick wants." He then handed Cheryl a pen. She signed.

Cheryl testified she never discussed the contents of the agreement with an attorney before she signed it. Nor could she recall ever being advised by any attorney about her rights to property that might be acquired during her marriage to Chick. She had no recollection of ever signing the agreement (though she acknowledged signing it, because her name was on it).

After the testimony was finished, the trial judge noted there was "too much money" involved in the case "for it not to be appealed." He then said, "I want whoever reviews this to be able to have the benefit of my reasoning for how I get to where I got." He then elaborated:

"One of the things that struck me, first of all, was that the petitioner in this case, Cheryl Iverson, only had five or six luncheon dates with Chick Iverson before she decided to move into his home. Now, he sure as heck does not look like John Wayne and he doesn't look like John Derek. And even if we take 17 years off him, I don't think he looks like Adonis.

"And, so, we have a situation in the beginning where we have a girl who has been testified to [sic] was lovely, and is lovely, but who did not have much of an education, and did not have much of a background in business, and did not have much by way of material wealth. Had nothing going for her except for her physical attractiveness. Who, somehow or other, comes to the attention of Mr. Iverson and, after five or six luncheon dates, is invited to move into his home.

"It seems to me that the process of marrying is one in which there is some mutual advantages from the act of getting married, maybe different ones from the act of establishing a relationship, a live-in type, spousal-type relationship.

"But, in light of the testimony that Mr. Iverson had come out of a very unpleasant, very unhappy marriage, his statement that he was reluctant to get married again adds some dimension here. 'Once burned, twice cautious.' He had just gone through a divorce which cost him a million dollars. He does not want to get in one of those things again. He has talked to his important friends in the film industry and other areas, where living together is the common situation rather than marriage. And, so, decides that's the best thing for him. He makes an offer to petitioner, who thinks it's good. And then she moves in.

"I cannot accept the fact that, as she said, he was the one that proposed marriage to her. That would be the last thing that would be on his mind. And why, in heaven's name, do you buy the cow when you get the milk free, as we used to say. And, so, he's getting the milk free. And Cheryl is living with him in his home.

"And the impetus for marriage must be coming from her side, because there's nothing Mr. Iverson is going to get out of it. Marriage is a drag on the market. It's a deprivation of his freedom. He's got everything that he would want out of a relationship with none of the obligations. Now, I am of the opinion that the impetus for the marriage in the home, prior to the incident of the birthday party for John Wayne, came almost entirely from the petitioner in this case, resisted by respondent."

II

We quote the judge's statement at length to show that, in resolving disputed issues of fact, it is reasonably clear that he entertained preconceptions about the parties because of their gender. These perceptions appear to have made it impossible for Cheryl to receive a fair trial.

In the first place, the statement that Cheryl was a "lovely girl" shows gender bias toward her as a witness. The judge did not use a similar description for Chick. The resolution of the credibility issues in this case thus may have been based, at root, on Cheryl's gender and physical attributes. As the validity of the prenuptial issue depended on the resolution of conflicting testimony, this possibility contaminates the subsequent disposition of the case. The day is long past when appellate courts can disregard judicial action rooted in racial or sexual bias as harmless error.

Additionally, use of the word "lovely" reveals gender bias. While the word is usually complimentary, in context here it was used in juxtaposition to "education," "background in business," and "material wealth," to indicate Cheryl's limited credibility as a witness. There is thus more than a faint whiff of " 'romantic paternalism' " in the choice of the word.

Furthermore, it cannot be gainsaid that, whatever the judge's actual gender bias, the description of Cheryl — a woman in her forties — as a "girl" seriously detracts from the appearance of justice. Our Supreme Court has directed that " '[t]he trial of a case should not only be fair in fact, but it should also appear to be fair.' "

Besides the use of language indicating gender bias, the judge also appears to have employed gender-based stereotypes in his decision-making process. His reasoning appears to have been that "lovely" women are the ones who ask wealthy men who do not look like "Adonis" to marry, and therefore Cheryl was not credible when she testified Chick asked her to marry him. The error here is the application of a generality to specific individuals. It is the essence of our system of justice that individuals shall be judged on their own merits, not on some characteristic they happen to share with other people.

Next, the reference to not buying the "cow" when the "milk is free" cannot be countenanced. There is, in the reference, an obvious double standard based on stereotypical sex roles. (Both Chick and Cheryl were living together, but only Chick was seen as benefitting from the relationship, simply because he was a man.) And we hardly need elaborate that in the context in which it was used, the reference was plainly demeaning to Cheryl, analogizing her to a cow. Again we find a "predetermined disposition" to rule against her based on her status as a woman. . . .

The gender bias evidenced in the resolution of the validity of the prenuptial contract contaminated not only that issue but the balance of the case which depended on it. The judgment is therefore reversed and remanded for a new trial on all issues. The Presiding Judge of the Orange County Superior Court is directed to assign the matter to a different judge. . . .

MOORE, ASSOCIATE JUDGE, concurring.

While I concur in the result, I do not join in the zeal of my colleagues in flogging the trial judge for actual bias. I disdain bias of whatever kind. However, I do not agree that the trial court's comments read in context establish actual bias. I am supported in this position by Cheryl's own attorney who, at oral argument, admitted: "I'm not charging the judge with legal bias in terms of was he biased against my client."

Notwithstanding this concession, the majority pounce on the trial judge's comments during the trial's first phase, lift the remarks out of context, and reverse the judgment, concluding the remarks established the trial judge was biased in fact against Cheryl because of her gender. As I shall explain, the grounds employed by the majority are wholly unnecessary. It matters not whether there was actual bias, appearance of bias being sufficient to warrant reversal. . . .

The trial judge's comments in this case gave the appearance of his lack of impartiality. His characterization of Cheryl and his use of the cow metaphor were clearly inappropriate. The average person on the street could well entertain a doubt concerning whether the trial judge was impartial. Inasmuch as that is now the test, the judgment should be reversed.

MATTER OF BOURISSEAU
439 Mich. 1230, 480 N.W.2d 270 (Mich. 1992)
ORDER

On order of the Court, this Court having received the decision of the Judicial Tenure Commission and its recommendation for an order of discipline, we adopt the following findings of the Commission:

1. The respondent is now, and at all pertinent times has been, judge of the Mason County Probate Court.
2. On April 23, 1991, the respondent participated in a telephone interview with a newspaper reporter who solicited his views on the Parental Rights Restoration Act.

3. As a result of that interview, a newspaper article appeared on April 24, 1991. In it, the respondent expressed his displeasure with the enactment of the Act. He also stated that one of the circumstances in which he might permit a minor to have an abortion would be the rape of a white girl by a black man. These remarks were widely disseminated in the news media, and were subsequently criticized as insensitive and racist.

4. Several grievances were filed with the Commission. In reply, the respondent acknowledged making the statements in question, but indicated that it had not been his intention to speak in a racially insensitive manner. He expressed regret for his remarks, and stated that he had not, and would not, base any decision about abortion on the race of the persons involved.

5. Respondent's remarks were offensive, improper, and constituted misconduct in office. They called into question the impartiality of the judiciary, and exposed the judicial system to contempt and ridicule. Such erosion of public confidence in the judiciary is clearly prejudicial to the administration of justice.

We agree with the Commission and the respondent that a public censure is an appropriate response to the respondent's remarks. This order shall stand as this Court's censure.

Catchpole v. Brannon, 42 Cal. Rptr. 2d 440 (Ct. App. 1995), reversed a judge's verdict for the defendants in a case alleging workplace sexual harassment. In a meticulous opinion, the appellate court analyzed the trial judge's use of language and attitude toward the female plaintiff. The court accepted the following definition of "gender bias" from a study by the Judicial Council of California. Gender bias "includes behavior or decision making of participants in the justice system which is based on or reveals (1) stereotypical attitudes about the nature and roles of women and men; (2) cultural perceptions of their relative worth; and (3) myths and misconceptions about the social and economic realities encountered by both sexes." For another study of gender bias in the courts, see Ninth Circuit Gender Bias Task Force, The Effects of Gender in the Federal Courts: The Final Report of the Ninth Circuit Gender Bias Task Force, 67 S. Cal. L. Rev. 745 (1993).

Another California appellate court reversed a judgment in favor of a medical malpractice defendant and remanded the case to a different trial judge in part because of the lower court's recitation of "a veritable litany condemning and impugning the character of undocumented immigrants, including plaintiff, who place a burden upon the taxpayers by obtaining educational, medical, housing, and other services . . . to which they are not entitled, and then add insult to injury by suing the providers, such as the 'good doctor [defendant]' in order to make 'a pot of [undeserved] money.'" Hernandez v. Paicius, 134 Cal. Rptr. 2d 756 (Ct. App. 2003).

Judge Greene was presiding over a criminal case in which a man had been charged with assaulting his estranged wife. The judge "made derogatory remarks about Interact, the battered women's assistance group whose representative was present in court in support of the victim, including the comment that they were 'a one-sided man-hating bunch of females . . . and a pack of she-dogs.' " After the trial, the judge approached the victim in the hall and told her "in the presence of the Interact representative that once his wife had slapped him and that he had 'laid her on the floor and did not have any more problems from her.' " In In re Greene, 403 S.E.2d 257 (N.C. 1991), the court held that these comments violated §2(A), §31(A)(2), and §3(A)(3) of the 1972 Judicial Conduct Code. A further allegation, that Judge Greene had told the victim that "she deserved to be hit and had not been hit that much, [was] not supported by clear and convincing evidence." Judge Greene was censured. Is that sanction too harsh under the circumstances? All of these events occurred after the judge had already found the victim's estranged husband guilty.

The Ninth Circuit Judicial Council publicly reprimanded District Judge Alan McDonald for exchanging offensive notes with a court clerk. In a trial with Hispanic defendants, Judge McDonald passed a note to his court clerk that read: "It smells like oil in here—too many 'greasers.' " In another case, with a black defendant, he wrote "Ah is im po tent!" And in a third case, Judge McDonald referred to labor union representatives in dark suits as "union mafia" and "gangsters." The Judicial Council, after a six-month investigation, concluded that McDonald "is not and was not biased against any ethnic, racial, or religious group." However, the judge had violated standards of conduct by "his practice, and by his condoning the practice among his courtroom staff, of writing and exchanging in open court, notes that could reasonably be interpreted as reflecting bias." The notes "created an appearance of impropriety, undermined the public's confidence in an impartial judiciary, and impugned the dignity and seriousness of the ongoing court proceedings." The Council concluded that "more than a private reprimand is warranted." See The Spokesman Review (Spokane, Wash.), (Sept. 12, 2000).

Sometimes the appearance of bias is quite subtle but the appellate reaction can be strong nonetheless. Consider United States v. Kaba, 480 F.3d 152 (2d Cir. 2007). In sentencing an immigrant for a drug offense, a district judge said:

> What I am hearing, I don't often say that deterrence is a major factor, sometimes it is, but rarer than we might wish, but from what I hear from Ms. Roth [the Assistant U.S. Attorney], it is entirely reasonable to assume that people from the Guinea community are going to say gee, do you hear what happened to [Kaba]? I don't want that to happen to me.
> I hope that [deterrence] has some effect here, that will deter other people from that background from doing what you've done here, and you certainly had the brains not to do it to start with. . . . [The sentence] is one that I don't think people coming here from Guinea are going to want to say I want to put in that kind of time being stupid about American laws. We'll see. Maybe it will have the effect and maybe it won't. . . .
> Ms. Kaba, I suggest that you go around telling people, look, watch yourself here. If you come to this country, it gives you great opportunity to build a restaurant and make a life for yourself, but if you violate our laws, they're going to dump on you. They dumped on me and I'm back here. This is when you are talking from across the Atlantic.

The Second Circuit accepted that the sentencing judge harbored no actual bias toward Kaba. But it reversed for resentencing before a different judge:

> Because " 'justice must satisfy the appearance of justice,' even the appearance that the sentence reflects a defendant's race or nationality will ordinarily require a remand for resentencing."

> The comments of the district court that led to a remand in [*precedent*] resemble those at issue here. In both cases, the district court referred to the publicity a sentence might receive in the defendant's ethnic community or native country and explicitly stated its intention to seek to deter others sharing that national origin from violating United States laws in the future.

Statements Off the Bench

John E. Santora was chief judge of an intermediate Florida appellate court. On December 22, 1991, he gave a recorded interview to the Florida Times-Union, a general circulation newspaper in the area covered by his court. The full text of the interview is published as an appendix to In re Petition for Removal of a Chief Judge, 592 So. 2d 671 (Fla. 1992). A portion follows:*

Question: [Santora had just condemned a recent cross-burning and racial slurs to a Northside black family.] But at the same time, you trace a lot of these [crime] problems back to integration. . . . You have the feeling that . . .

Santora: No, I don't. The people that were doing this [terrorizing a black family] were like you; they grew up with them. As a general rule, they are young people. But, you see, the blacks have come into the school system, which they never were in there before and it was a step forward for them, yet they couldn't cope with it. Because they had a chip on their shoulder—I'm talking about the average—when they went there. And they started the fights, they started the gangs. And the whites retaliated, and they did the same thing. But I never heard of a weapon when I went to school. . . . The three years I was in high school, I never saw a fight, not one, much less somebody with a knife, or a gun or a stick or a club. . . . I never heard a teacher sassed, much less raped. I never saw a girl mistreated by a boy, much less raped. Ever. I never saw a guy hit a girl, or another guy. . . . The teacher said "frog," we jumped. If you didn't, you'd get your butt beat. And we knew it.

But now, it's a different ballgame. . . . Girls are wearing panty hose and miniskirts that would make a guy my age chase them down the hallway. I mean, I never saw anything like that when I was in high school. They look 20 years old, not 15. And that's also causing the blacks, the blacks are playing with those white girls, with the white girls' consent. . . .

Question: Are your thoughts that whites are somehow different?

Santora: When you're trying a case, it doesn't make a difference what your color is.

---

* Ellipses in original.

Question: What about when you're not trying a case?

Santora: You mean my private, personal thoughts? . . . I would not date a black girl. I would not take one home, my mother would kill me. I wouldn't mistreat one. I would not want my children to marry a black or an Asian or a Chinese or a Puerto Rican. I would not want them to. And they know that. I have friends who are black, we all do. You have them in your workplace; I've got 'em in my workplace. The best judicial assistant in this building, one of the best, is a black girl. One of the best, without a doubt. But that's unusual. One of the best judges is black. One of the worst is black. I think that there is a difference between a lot of them that they can't overcome. And it's not all of it their fault. It's the fault of their mothers and their daddies and their ancestors. And our fault. We have been too good to them. We, the United States Congress. Because they make more money by staying home on welfare than they do working. And you can't blame 'em. Why give up $1,500 a month when you can't make but $800 working?

Question: You see that as a black issue, not white?

Santora: Oh yeah, we have whites doing it, but most of them are black. We talk about . . . why is it that 20 percent of the population is black and 45 percent of the prisoners are black. That's because, goddamnit, they're the ones committing the crimes. As I told you earlier, you've got more of those folks involved in drugs than whites, as far as felonies are concerned. I don't know how many of them are using, we have no way of knowing. Every day the Times-Union reports another killing on the Northside. Every day. So they are involved in crime. That's the reason. How do we stop them from being involved in crime? We give them a mama and a daddy to start off with. We give them a home with love and affection in it to start off with. But how do we go about doing that? It's impossible, if that's what they need.

The Florida Supreme Court removed Judge Santora as chief judge, writing:

Because Judge Santora's candid public statements, freely given to a newspaper reporter, have been read by a significant portion of the community as affirmatively embracing and endorsing discriminatory stereotypes that are inimical to the laws of this state, the interests of the judiciary, and the oft-stated policies of this Court, we conclude that his actions have significantly eroded his ability to work effectively with all segments of the community in administering the courts within the Fourth Judicial Circuit in his present office as Chief Judge. We recognize that the residents of the circuit are sharply divided over this issue. It was Judge Santora's actions, however, that led to this divisiveness.

Thereafter the court reprimanded Judge Santora based on the same published remarks. In re Santora, 602 So. 2d 1269 (Fla. 1992). Is a reprimand adequate sanction? Should Judge Santora have been removed from the bench? If you think the reprimand and the demotion from chief judge are legitimate responses to the interview—or if you think harsher penalties were due—what do you say to those who cite Judge Santora's freedom of speech? The judge's statements were off the bench, in an interview with a newspaper. Doesn't a judge have a right to say what he thinks? Can he be punished for doing so?

In answering that question, consider the case of Judge Connie Glen Wilkerson, a George County, Mississippi, Justice Court judge. In March 2002, Judge Wilkerson wrote to a local newspaper that he "got sick [to] my stomach" on learning that California and other states had granted "gay partners the same right to sue as spouses or family members." He also wrote that "gays and lesbians should be put in some type of a mental institute instead of having a law like this passed for them." His letter did not identify him as a judge. A local radio station apparently did recognize his name and a few weeks later broadcast an interview with Judge Wilkerson in which he was identified as a judge. In it, the judge said that although he had never run into anything "like that," he believed that "a person like that's sick, you know. I wouldn't want to punish a fellow for being sick. . . . But I don't think he ought to have . . . extraordinary rights. . . . God didn't put up with it in Sodom and Gomorrah, and that's the part that worries me, you know."

Did Judge Wilkerson violate Canon 2A of the Mississippi Code, which requires a judge to maintain "high standards of conduct so that the integrity and independence of the judiciary may be preserved"? Did he violate Mississippi Canon 4A(1), whose comment says: "Expressions of bias or prejudice by a judge, even outside the judge's judicial activities, may cast reasonable doubt on the judge's capacity to act impartially as a judge," and references in particular "remarks demeaning individuals on the basis of their . . . sexual orientation"? (The comment was added to the Code after the judge's letter but before his radio interview.) Or did Judge Wilkerson have a First Amendment right to speak his mind on the issue? The Mississippi Supreme Court, applying strict scrutiny under the First Amendment, held 4-2 that the letter and interview were constitutionally protected, and it rejected discipline. Mississippi Commission on Judicial Performance v. Wilkerson, 876 So.2d 1006 (Miss. 2004). Why weren't Judge Santora's comments similarly protected by the First Amendment? Does the answer turn on the fact that the bias was directed at a different group in each case? The First Amendment didn't save the Chief Justice of the Alabama Supreme Court, who placed a granite monument containing the Ten Commandments in the rotunda of the courthouse and refused to remove it even when a federal judge ordered him to do so. Chief Justice Moore was found to have violated Canons 1 and 2 of the Code of Judicial Conduct and was removed from the bench. His First Amendment claims were rejected. Matter of Moore, 891 So. 2d 848 (Judicial Inquiry Comm'n 2004).

What the Code Requires

Courtroom Bias.   The 1990 Code imposed obligations on a judge to prevent bias in the courtroom. Section 3(B)(6) said that a judge shall "require lawyers in proceedings before the judge to refrain from manifesting, by words or conduct, bias or prejudice based upon race, sex, religion, national origin, disability, age, sexual orientation or socioeconomic status, against parties, witnesses, counsel or others." The 2007 Code makes a few nonsubstantive language changes; adds gender, ethnicity, marital status, and political affiliation to the list; states that the list is not exclusive; and further forbids "harassment" based on these attributes. Rule 2.3(C). The same requirements apply to judges. Rule 2.3(B). Rule 2.3(D) states that "The restrictions of paragraphs (B) and (C) do not preclude judges or lawyers from making legitimate reference to the listed factors, or similar factors, when they are relevant to an issue in a proceeding."

Marina Angel has analyzed the empirical evidence of judicial sexual harassment and compares remedial efforts with those in the private sector. She calls for "vigorous enforcement" of the Code commentary. Marina Angel, Sexual Harassment by Judges, 45 U. Miami L. Rev. 817 (1991).

Discriminatory Organizations. Canon 2(C) of the 1990 Code stated: "A judge shall not hold membership in any organization that practices invidious discrimination on the basis of race, sex, religion or national origin." The 2007 Code expands the list to include gender, ethnicity, and sexual orientation. A comment requires judges who learn they are members of such organizations to "resign immediately." Rule 3.6(A). Notice that even as expanded this list remains shorter than the one in Rule 2.3 dealing with courtroom bias. Would it violate Rule 3.6(A) for a judge to belong to a social club limited to persons of Irish ancestry? Irish Catholics? Irish Catholic men? Should it? The commentary to the rule states:

> An organization is generally said to discriminate invidiously if it arbitrarily excludes from membership on the basis of race, sex, gender, religion, national origin, ethnicity, or sexual orientation persons who would otherwise be eligible for admission. Whether an organization practices invidious discrimination is a complex question to which judges should be attentive. The answer cannot be determined from a mere examination of an organization's current membership rolls, but rather, depends upon how the organization selects members, as well as other relevant factors, such as whether the organization is dedicated to the preservation of religious, ethnic, or cultural values of legitimate common interest to its members, or whether it is an intimate, purely private organization whose membership limitations could not constitutionally be prohibited.

New York State Club Assn. v. City of New York, 487 U.S. 1 (1988), tells us that the Constitution's guarantee of freedom of association will sometimes override a jurisdiction's antidiscrimination laws. Presumably, then, a judge could be a member of a group whose discrimination is constitutionally protected. Should (could) the Code limit the constitutional rights of judges? A comment to Rule 1.2 does say that "A judge should expect to be the subject of public scrutiny that might be viewed as burdensome if applied to other citizens, and must accept the restrictions imposed by the Code." And the Code's restriction on judicial speech is greater than the First Amendment would tolerate for others. Rule 2.10(A) says that "A judge shall not make any public statement that might reasonably be expected to affect the outcome or impair the fairness of a matter pending or impending in any court. . . ." What if the civil rights law of the judge's jurisdiction does not forbid an organization's exclusionary policy — say a policy that prohibited membership based on sexual orientation or gender — even though it constitutionally could do so? Is the judge forbidden to be a member of that organization?

Some judges have taken issue with the ABA amendments on the ground that they intrude too much on a judge's private life. Bill Graves, a state trial judge in Oklahoma, is one of them. He opposes the addition of gender, ethnicity, and sexual orientation to the definition of exclusionary organizations. In an April 8, 2008, letter to the Bench and Bar Committee (BBC) of the Oklahoma Bar Association, available on various websites, he cited the "liberal, pro-homosexual American Bar Association" and argued:

> The liberties guaranteed by the Constitution's First Amendment do not, according to the ABA and the BBC, include judges. While proposed Rule 3.6 apparently does not prohibit a judge from being a member of a church that objects to homosexuality, it would prohibit association with numerous other organizations which do not subscribe to and discriminate as to the homosexual agenda. These include the Boy Scouts, traditional family groups, the Knights of Columbus, the American Legion, Disabled American Veterans, Veterans of Foreign Wars, the Masons, AWANAs, and Alcoholics Anonymous.
>
> Such a policy curbing freedom of religion, speech, and association as to judges is fraught with constitutional violations. One can only wonder why the ABA and the BBC are promoting the agenda of homosexuals and lesbians at the expense of the constitutional freedoms of judges and the People they represent. In 2002, the U.S. Supreme Court in *Republican Party of Minnesota v. White*, in fact struck down a regulation prohibiting freedom of expression by judges.

Does Judge Graves have a point? Isn't he entitled to associate, in his private life, with exclusionary organizations whose membership policies violate no law? (We look at the Supreme Court's *White* decision in chapter 15.)

Part Four

AVOIDING AND REDRESSING PROFESSIONAL FAILURE

XII

Control of Quality:
Reducing the Likelihood
of Professional Failure

- *Getting Admitted*
- *Temporary Practice*
- *Unauthorized Practice of Law*
- *(But What is Law?)*

A state may try to prevent professional failures, such as malpractice, breach of fiduciary duty, or neglect of client matters, in many ways. When a professional failure nevertheless occurs, various remedies are possible. In this chapter, we look at ways in which a state may try to prevent professional failure. In chapter 13 we address remedial measures. This division is slightly arbitrary. A remedial measure — for example, discipline or a civil action against the lawyer — has a preventive dimension as well as a curative one.

One issue with regard to the preventive measures discussed in this chapter is the relationship between a particular rule and the reduction of risk of professional failure that the rule is meant to accomplish. For example, do residency requirements, bar examinations, or educational prerequisites to bar membership reduce the likelihood of professional error or appreciably increase quality of work? If so, by how much is the likelihood of error reduced or quality improved in relation to the cost of the requirement? A requirement that bar applicants graduate from accredited law schools after three years of study has an enormous cost — in time and money, not to mention anxiety. Well, of course, you know that. Is the cost justified by the higher quality of work that the requirement produces when compared with the quality of work we would have without it? What if law school were only two years? Residency requirements, unauthorized practice laws, and character tests can also be economically analyzed.

A related issue is epistemological. How can we know the answers to these questions? Do we simply accept some things on faith? In the material that follows, courts and other rulemakers must weigh the costs of a particular requirement, including claimed burdens on constitutional rights, against the interests of the jurisdiction that wishes to impose the requirement. How do they conduct the empirical evaluation? What level of constitutional scrutiny do the courts apply?

Certainly, bar applicants cannot be excluded because of race, national origin, sex, sexual orientation, or religion. This was not always so. An infamous Supreme Court decision, for example, upheld Illinois' refusal to admit a married woman to its bar. See Bradwell v. State, 83 U.S. 130 (1872). Just over a century later, the Supreme Court held that Connecticut could not limit bar admission to United States citizens. In re Griffiths, 413 U.S. 717 (1973). However, the Fifth Circuit held that Louisiana could constitutionally exclude nonimmigrant aliens from admission to its bar. A nonimmigrant alien is legally in the United States but not a permanent resident. LeClerc v. Webb, 419 F.3d 405 (5th Cir. 2005) (the plaintiffs were not a suspect class and the rule was rationally related to state's interest in continuity and accountability in legal services); rehearing en banc denied over seven dissents, LeClerc v. Webb, 444 F.3d 428 (5th Cir. 2006).

Nor should we close our eyes to competitive motives. A subtext to any discussion of rules, like those in this chapter, that limit the supply of lawyers or the ability of nonlawyers to compete with lawyers is the economic consequence of the particular rule. A rule making it harder for nonresidents to join a state's bar protects in-state lawyers from competition. Is that (or was it ever) the motive for the prohibition, or is the motive an interest in ensuring quality legal work by reliable lawyers? Or is it both? To what extent should the courts be cognizant of economic motives in analyzing barriers to bar admission? To what extent should such motives be impermissible? Similarly, an expansive definition of the "practice of law" prevents nonlawyers from providing even simple legal advice and service, thereby reducing the supply of talent and increasing the price. Comparable questions can and should be asked about restrictions on pro hac vice admission, on lay investment in or management of law firms (chapter 14), and on ways in which lawyers may market their services (chapter 16).

Here's an introductory passage describing how one might analyze these questions if one is a person disposed to reasoning in legal and economics terms, as its author is. As we shall see in part A2 of this chapter, a state may choose to grant out-of-state lawyers admission to its bar without requiring them to take the bar examination. Lawyers obviously prefer this option. But a state may attach certain conditions to this act of generosity. Indiana admitted lawyers this way on condition that for five years thereafter they "predominantly" practice "in Indiana." (How this requirement was policed is a big question.) The Seventh Circuit upheld Indiana's conditions against equal protection and Commerce Clause challenges. Scariano v. Justices of the Supreme Court of the State of Indiana, 38 F.3d 920 (7th Cir. 1994), rehearing en banc denied, 47 F.3d 173 (7th Cir. 1995). Chief Judge Posner dissented from denial of the motion to rehear en banc as follows:

> The Indiana rule which the panel's decision upholds places a kind of tax on the practice of law in other states by permitting a lawyer to practice in Indiana without taking and passing the Indiana bar exam if the lawyer's practice is more than 50 percent "in Indiana."
>
> To see the effect of the rule, compare, first, two lawyers, each of whom is licensed in Illinois and practices in both Illinois and Indiana. The first lawyer

bills his Illinois clients for 900 hours of work a year and his Indiana clients for the same number. The second lawyer bills his Illinois clients for 500 hours and his Indiana clients for 800. The second lawyer can gain admission to the Indiana bar without taking the Indiana bar exam. The first cannot, even though he has the larger Indiana practice. He will have an incentive to reduce the Illinois component of his practice in order to become eligible to join the Indiana bar without taking the bar exam.

When a state law is obviously protectionist — a tariff would be the clearest example — it is generally found to violate the commerce clause without further ado; in other cases, such as this, the test is whether the benefits of the law in advancing some legitimate interest of the state exceed the costs in impairing free trade among the states. The distortion of the interstate practice of law brought about by the challenged rule is small; for it is limited, as the panel stressed, by the costs (mainly in time) of sitting for the Indiana bar exam. But the benefits are not only slight; they are negligible, because the rule is not designed to promote any legitimate interest of the state.

States have an interest in assuring the minimum competence of the lawyers who practice in their courts and advise their citizens. Most economists would believe that this interest could be best protected by allowing free competition among lawyers. Indiana is not required to subscribe to that belief. It can establish conditions for admission to its bar that are designed, paternalistically, to protect its citizens from falling into the clutches of incompetent or dishonest lawyers. It can, in particular, require as a condition of admission to its bar that lawyers take and pass its bar exam. The challenged rule establishes an alternative condition. The alternative, which is probably designed to give a break to lawyers who practice primarily or even exclusively in Indiana but happen to live in an adjacent state, allows the substitution of practical experience with Indiana law for ability to pass a test.

Or does it? Consider first the not uncommon case of a person who practices law part time. The rule requires that the lawyer seeking to take advantage of it practice "actively" in Indiana, but obviously that does not mean full-time. Suppose the lawyer practices 500 hours a year, 300 of them in Indiana. He would be entitled to admission to the Indiana bar (conditionally, until he had fulfilled the predominance requirement for five consecutive years), even though a lawyer who practiced twice as much in Indiana but more elsewhere would have to take the bar exam. . . .

Consider next the case of a person who practices law in Washington, D.C., and whose major client is Eli Lilly, a large Indiana firm, which the lawyer represents exclusively before the Food and Drug Administration. The lawyer knows no Indiana law; he has never handled a problem involving Indiana law, either for Eli Lilly or for anyone else. But if more than 50 percent of his practice is representing Lilly, he is entitled to be admitted to the Indiana bar without taking the bar exam, because the rule defines the practice of law "in Indiana" to include representing Indiana clients anywhere. . . .

A. ADMISSION TO THE BAR

The United States has a federal system, but there is no general federal bar examination. States (and D.C.) license lawyers. In the nineteenth century, this made much sense. Law firms had their offices in one state; a client's matter rarely crossed state lines or if it did, then not by much. But a system of local licensure does not fit well with twenty-first-century law practice and client need, at least not for some specialists whose clients are national or international, nor for a certain group of clients — i.e., those with national and global problems. Today, large law firms have offices in every region of the country and some have ten or more offices abroad, the better to serve clients who have needs around the nation and the world. Even a firm with only one office may be hired by clients elsewhere because of some specialty. Technology makes cross-border practice easy (think e-mail and satellite), as does the ready accessibility (think Westlaw and Lexis) and increasing uniformity of much commercial law. Yet a New York lawyer is not a lawyer in any other U.S. jurisdiction, and a British or Japanese lawyer is not a lawyer anywhere in the United States. If either lawyer does legal work where she is not admitted, she risks violating rules against the unauthorized practice of law (UPL), which can be a crime. As we shall see, to make matters more complicated, that unauthorized presence may be virtual, not only physical. Yes, you read that right. You can never leave your office and yet be guilty of UPL in a place you've never been if you spend too much time on e-mail and the telephone communicating with others in the distant place.

Without adjustment, our nineteenth-century licensing system could not serve a twenty-first-century economy, and, indeed, it survives only by overlooking how lawyers really behave and by making small doctrinal adjustments along the way, which we discuss in this chapter. More changes are likely in ensuing decades, though prediction of what they may be and when we might expect them is difficult. This is not solely an American problem either. Globalization is affecting law practice and lawyers everywhere. Be that as it may, we proceed to decipher the system we have today (and will have for some time to come) and to learn how we got where we now are.*

1. *Geographical Exclusion*

May a state prohibit a lawyer who lives outside its borders from gaining admission to its bar? That many states once did (and some required a period of residence before an applicant could even take the bar) tells you something about how parochial admission rules once were. They still are, but less so. New Hampshire's geographical exclusion rule is tested in the following case, which might be called the first modest assault on the edifice of rigid state admission rules. A distinct but related question (deferred until part A2) is whether a state may impose restrictions (short of exclusion) on lawyers who live outside the state, when such restrictions are not imposed on in-state lawyers.

---

* I plead guilty to having a strong interest in modernizing the regulatory structure. I was on the ABA Commission that drafted Rule 5.5, discussed later in this chapter, and have begun to think about lawyer regulation in a global economy. See Bar None, American Lawyer (October 2008).

SUPREME COURT OF NEW HAMPSHIRE v. PIPER
470 U.S. 274 (1985)

JUSTICE POWELL delivered the opinion of the Court.

The Rules of the Supreme Court of New Hampshire limit bar admission to state residents. We here consider whether this restriction violates the Privileges and Immunities Clause of the United States Constitution, Art. IV, §2.

I

A

Kathryn Piper lives in Lower Waterford, Vermont, about 400 yards from the New Hampshire border. In 1979, she applied to take the February 1980 New Hampshire bar examination. Piper submitted with her application a statement of intent to become a New Hampshire resident. Following an investigation, the Board of Bar Examiners found that Piper was of good moral character and met the other requirements for admission. She was allowed to take, and passed, the examination. Piper was informed by the Board that she would have to establish a home address in New Hampshire prior to being sworn in.

On May 7, 1980, Piper requested from the Clerk of the New Hampshire Supreme Court a dispensation from the residency requirement. Although she had a "possible job" with a lawyer in Littleton, New Hampshire, Piper stated that becoming a resident of New Hampshire would be inconvenient. Her house in Vermont was secured by a mortgage with a favorable interest rate, and she and her husband recently had become parents. According to Piper, these "problems peculiar to [her] situation . . . warrant[ed] that an exception be made." . . .

On May 13, 1980, the Clerk informed Piper that her request had been denied. She then formally petitioned the New Hampshire Supreme Court for permission to become a member of the bar. She asserted that she was well qualified and that her "situation [was] sufficiently unique that the granting of an exception [would] not result in the setting of any undesired precedent." . . . The Supreme Court denied Piper's formal request on December 31, 1980.[2]

II

A

Article IV, §2 of the Constitution provides that the "Citizens of each State shall be entitled to all Privileges and Immunities of Citizens in the several States."[6] This clause was intended to "fuse into one Nation a collection of

---

2. Piper was not excluded totally from the practice of law in New Hampshire. Out-of-state lawyers may appear pro hac vice in state court. This alternative, however, does not allow the nonresident to practice in New Hampshire on the same terms as a resident member of the bar. The lawyer appearing pro hac vice must be associated with a local lawyer who is present for trial or argument. Furthermore, the decision on whether to grant pro hac vice status to an out-of-state lawyer is purely discretionary. See Leis v. Flynt, 439 U.S. 438, 442 (1979) (per curiam). . . .

6. Under this Clause, the terms "citizen" and "resident" are used interchangeably. See Austin v. New Hampshire, 420 U.S. 656, 662, n.8 (1975). Under the Fourteenth Amendment, of course, "[a]ll persons born or naturalized in the United States . . . are citizens . . . of the State wherein they reside."

independent, sovereign States." Toomer v. Witsell, 334 U.S. 385, 395 (1948). Recognizing this purpose, we have held that it is "[o]nly with respect to those 'privileges' and 'immunities' bearing on the vitality of the nation as a single entity" that a State must accord residents and nonresidents equal treatment. Baldwin v. Fish & Game Commn. [436 U.S. 371, 383 (1978)]. In *Baldwin*, for example, we concluded that a State may charge a nonresident more than it charges a resident for the same elk-hunting license. Because elk-hunting is "recreation" rather than a "means of a livelihood," we found that the right to a hunting license was not "fundamental" to the promotion of interstate harmony.

Derived, like the Commerce Clause, from the fourth of the Articles of Confederation, the Privileges and Immunities Clause was intended to create a national economic union. It is therefore not surprising that this Court repeatedly has found that "one of the privileges which the Clause guarantees to citizens of State A is that of doing business in State B on terms of substantial equality with the citizens of that State." In Ward v. Maryland, 12 Wall. 418 (1871), the Court invalidated a statute under which nonresidents were required to pay $300 per year for a license to trade in goods not manufactured in Maryland, while resident traders paid a fee varying from $12 to $150. Similarly, in *Toomer*, supra, the Court held that nonresident fishermen could not be required to pay a license fee of $2,500 for each shrimp boat owned when residents were charged only $25 per boat. Finally, in Hicklin v. Orbeck, 437 U.S. 518 (1978), we found violative of the Privileges and Immunities Clause a statute containing a resident hiring preference for all employment related to the development of the State's oil and gas resources.

There is nothing in *Ward, Toomer,* or *Hicklin* suggesting that the practice of law should not be viewed as a "privilege" under Article IV, §2. Like the occupations considered in our earlier cases, the practice of law is important to the national economy. As the Court noted in *Goldfarb*, the "activities of lawyers play an important part in commercial intercourse." Goldfarb v. Virginia State Bar, 421 U.S. 773, 788 [1975].

The lawyer's role in the national economy is not the only reason that the opportunity to practice law should be considered a "fundamental right." We believe that the legal profession has a noncommercial role and duty that reinforce the view that the practice of law falls within the ambit of the Privileges and Immunities Clause. Out-of-state lawyers may—and often do—represent persons who raise unpopular federal claims. In some cases, representation by nonresident counsel may be the only means available for the vindication of federal rights. See Leis v. Flynt, 439 U.S. at 450 (Stevens, J., dissenting). The lawyer who champions unpopular causes surely is as important to the "maintenance or well-being of the Union," *Baldwin*, as was the shrimp fisherman in *Toomer* or the pipeline worker in *Hicklin*.

B

The State asserts that the Privileges and Immunities Clause should be held inapplicable to the practice of law because a lawyer's activities are "bound up with the exercise of judicial power and the administration of justice." Its contention is based on the premise that the lawyer is an "officer of the court," who "exercises state power on a daily basis." [The State] concludes that if [it] cannot exclude nonresidents from the bar, its ability to function as a sovereign political body will be threatened.

Lawyers do enjoy a "broad monopoly . . . to do things other citizens may not lawfully do." In re Griffiths, 413 U.S. 717, 731 (1973). We do not believe, however, that the practice of law involves an "exercise of state power" justifying New Hampshire's residency requirement. In In re Griffiths, supra, we held that the State could not exclude an alien from the bar on the ground that a lawyer is an "'officer of the Court who' . . . is entrusted with the 'exercise of actual governmental power.'" We concluded that a lawyer is not an "officer" within the ordinary meaning of that word. 413 U.S. at 728. He "'makes his own decisions, follows his own best judgment, collects his own fees and runs his own business.'" Moreover, we held that the state powers entrusted to lawyers do not "involve matters of state policy or acts of such unique responsibility that they should be entrusted only to citizens."

Because, under *Griffiths*, a lawyer is not an "officer" of the State in any political sense, there is no reason for New Hampshire to exclude from its bar nonresidents. We therefore conclude that the right to practice law is protected by the Privileges and Immunities Clause.

III

The conclusion that [the New Hampshire rule] deprives nonresidents of a protected privilege does not end our inquiry. The Court has stated that "[l]ike many other constitutional provisions, the privileges and immunities clause is not an absolute." Toomer v. Witsell, 334 U.S. at 396. . . . The Clause does not preclude discrimination against nonresidents where (i) there is a substantial reason for the difference in treatment; and (ii) the discrimination practiced against nonresidents bears a substantial relationship to the State's objective. . . . In deciding whether the discrimination bears a close or substantial relationship to the State's objective, the Court has considered the availability of less restrictive means.

The Supreme Court of New Hampshire offers several justifications for its refusal to admit nonresidents to the bar. It asserts that nonresident members would be less likely (i) to become, and remain, familiar with local rules and procedures; (ii) to behave ethically; (iii) to be available for court proceedings; and (iv) to do pro bono and other volunteer work in the State.[18] We find that none of these reasons meets the test of "substantiality," and that the means chosen do not bear the necessary relationship to the State's objectives.

There is no evidence to support the State's claim that nonresidents might be less likely to keep abreast of local rules and procedures. Nor may we assume that a nonresident lawyer — any more than a resident — would disserve his clients by failing to familiarize himself with the rules. As a practical matter, we think that unless a lawyer has, or anticipates, a considerable practice in the New Hampshire

---

18. A former president of the American Bar Association has suggested another possible reason for the rule: "Many of the states that have erected fences against out-of-state lawyers have done so primarily to protect their own lawyers from professional competition." Smith, Time for a National Practice of Law Act, 64 A.B.A. J. 557 (1978). This reason is not "substantial." The Privileges and Immunities Clause was designed primarily to prevent such economic protectionism.

courts, he would be unlikely to take the bar examination and pay the annual dues of $125.[19]

We also find the State's second justification to be without merit, for there is no reason to believe that a nonresident lawyer will conduct his practice in a dishonest manner. . . .

There is more merit to the State's assertion that a nonresident member of the bar at times would be unavailable for court proceedings. In the course of litigation, pretrial hearings on various matters often are held on short notice. At times a court will need to confer immediately with counsel. Even the most conscientious lawyer residing in a distant State may find himself unable to appear in court for an unscheduled hearing or proceeding. Nevertheless, we do not believe that this type of problem justifies the exclusion of nonresidents from the state bar. One may assume that a high percentage of nonresident lawyers willing to take the state bar examination and pay the annual dues will reside in places reasonably convenient to New Hampshire. Furthermore, in those cases where the nonresident counsel will be unavailable on short notice, the State can protect its interests through less restrictive means. The trial court, by rule or as an exercise of discretion, may require any lawyer who resides at a great distance to retain a local attorney who will be available for unscheduled meetings and hearings.

The final reason advanced by [the State] is that nonresident members of its bar would be disinclined to do their share of pro bono and volunteer work. Perhaps this is true to a limited extent, particularly where the member resides in a distant location. We think it is reasonable to believe, however, that most lawyers who become members of a state bar will endeavor to perform their share of these services. This sort of participation, of course, would serve the professional interest of a lawyer who practices in the State. Furthermore, the nonresident bar member, like the resident member, could be required to represent indigents and perhaps to participate in formal legal-aid work.

In summary, the State neither advances a "substantial reason" for its discrimination against nonresident applicants to the bar, nor demonstrates that the discrimination practiced bears a close relationship to its proffered objectives. . . .

JUSTICE WHITE, concurring in the result. . . .

I concur in the judgment invalidating the New Hampshire residency requirement as applied to Appellee Piper.

JUSTICE REHNQUIST, dissenting. . . .

My belief that the practice of law differs from other trades and businesses for Art. IV, §2 purposes is not based on some notion that law is for some reason a

---

19. Because it is markedly overinclusive, the residency requirement does not bear a substantial relationship to the State's objective. A less restrictive alternative would be to require mandatory attendance at periodic seminars on state practice. There already is a rule requiring all new admittees to complete a "practical skills course" within one year of their admission.

New Hampshire's "simple residency" requirement is underinclusive as well, because it permits lawyers who move away from the State to retain their membership in the bar. There is no reason to believe that a former resident would maintain a more active practice in the New Hampshire courts than would a nonresident lawyer who had never lived in the State.

superior profession. The reason that the practice of law should be treated differently is that law is one occupation that does not readily translate across state lines. Certain aspects of legal practice are distinctly and intentionally *nonnational*; in this regard one might view this country's legal system as the antithesis of the norms embodied in the Art. IV Privileges and Immunities Clause. Put simply, the State has a substantial interest in creating its own set of laws responsive to its own local interests, and it is reasonable for a State to decide that those people who have been trained to analyze law and policy are better equipped to write those state laws and adjudicate cases arising under them. The State therefore may decide that it has an interest in maximizing the number of resident lawyers, so as to increase the quality of the pool from which its lawmakers can be drawn. A residency law such as the one at issue is the obvious way to accomplish these goals. Since at any given time within a State there is only enough legal work to support a certain number of lawyers, each out-of-state lawyer who is allowed to practice necessarily takes legal work that could support an in-state lawyer, who would otherwise be available to perform various functions that a State has an interest in promoting.[3]

Nor does the State's interest end with enlarging the pool of qualified lawmakers. A State similarly might determine that because lawyers play an important role in the formulation of state policy through their adversary representation, they should be intimately conversant with the local concerns that should inform such policies. And the State likewise might conclude that those citizens trained in the law are likely to bring their useful expertise to other important functions that benefit from such expertise and are of interest to state governments — such as trusteeships, or directorships of corporations or charitable organizations, or school board positions, or merely the role of the interested citizen at a town meeting. Thus, although the Court suggests that state bars can require out-of-state members to "represent indigents and perhaps to participate in formal legal-aid work," . . . the Court ignores a host of other important functions that a State could find would likely be performed only by in-state bar members. States may find a substantial interest in members of their bar being residents, and this insular interest — as with the opposing interest in interstate harmony represented by Art. IV, §2 — itself has its genesis in the language and structure of the Constitution. . . .

There is yet another interest asserted by the State that I believe would justify a decision to limit membership in the state bar to state residents. The State argues that out-of-state bar members pose a problem in situations where counsel must be available on short notice to represent clients on unscheduled matters. The Court brushes this argument aside, speculating that "a high percentage of nonresident lawyers willing to take the state bar examination and pay the annual dues will reside in places reasonably convenient to New Hampshire," and suggesting that in any event the trial court could alleviate this problem by requiring the lawyer to retain local counsel. . . . Assuming that the latter suggestion does not itself constitute unlawful discrimination under the Court's test, there

3. In New Hampshire's case, lawyers living 40 miles from the state border in Boston could easily devote part of their practice to New Hampshire clients. If this occurred a significant amount of New Hampshire legal work might wind up in Boston, along with lawyers who might otherwise reside in New Hampshire.

nevertheless may be good reasons why a State or a trial court would rather not get into structuring attorney-client relationships by requiring the retention of local counsel for emergency matters. The situation would have to be explained to the client, and the allocation of responsibility between resident and non-resident counsel could cause as many problems as the Court's suggestion might cure.

Nor do I believe that the problem can be confined to emergency matters. The Court admits that even in the ordinary course of litigation a trial judge will want trial lawyers to be available on short notice; the uncertainties of managing a trial docket are such that lawyers rarely are given a single date on which a trial will begin; they may be required to "stand by" — or whatever the local terminology is — for days at a time, and then be expected to be ready in a matter of hours, with witnesses, when the case in front of them suddenly settles. A State reasonably can decide that a trial court should not have added to its present scheduling difficulties the uncertainties and added delays fostered by counsel who might reside one thousand miles from New Hampshire. If there is any single problem with state legal systems that this Court might consider "substantial," it is the problem of delay in litigation — a subject that has been profusely explored in the literature over the past several years. . . . Surely the State has a substantial interest in taking steps to minimize this problem. . . .

The "New Jersey" Problem

After *Piper*, lawyers living anywhere in the country may choose to take bar examinations in any state. The majority did not adopt Justice White's view that the case should be decided on the narrow ground that Piper lived so close to New Hampshire. Footnote 3 of the dissent speculates that if out-of-state lawyers can easily gain admission to the New Hampshire bar, lawyers in Boston might devote part of their practices to New Hampshire legal work. If that consequence were significant, the resident New Hampshire bar would shrink because there would be less work to support it and because New Hampshire lawyers might follow the work to Boston. The implication is that Boston lawyers might be more attractive than New Hampshire lawyers to a large number of New Hampshire clients. So the contest here would appear to be between the possible competitive advantage of Boston lawyers in a free market and the state's wish to curtail the operation of that market to protect its resident bar and thereby to ensure a vibrant New Hampshire bar with a permanent stake in the life of their communities. Are those valid state interests? They are, aren't they? The question is how much weight they can command.

Several states have reason to fear "client flight," and consequent harm to the economic health of their bars, as geographical limitations on bar admission are eliminated and national or regional firms come looking for work. I think the term is "cherry picking" the best cases. (Law firm marketing, see chapter 16, and advances in cheap communication technology facilitate this trend.) New Jersey is a good example because it is sandwiched between the legal and media markets of Philadelphia and New York. New Jersey cannot, after *Piper*, exclude out-of-state lawyers from taking its bar examination, but it can and does condition admission to its bar on passage of the same examination its own lawyers must pass. New Jersey does not grant reciprocity to out-of-state lawyers, which means it does not allow lawyers admitted in another state to be admitted without examination (that is, on motion) in New Jersey, even if the other state offers this opportunity to New Jersey lawyers.

Many states do grant reciprocity, at least for experienced out-of-state lawyers. (According to Chief Justice Rehnquist's dissent in Supreme Court of Virginia v. Friedman (see page 647), 28 states in 1988 did *not* recognize admission on motion.) By 2008, the number had dropped to 21. (This information and other information on bar admission can be found the in the invaluable Comprehensive Guide to Bar Admission Requirements published by the ABA Section on Legal Education and Admission to the Bar and the National Conference of Bar Examiners and available for download at the ABA's website.) A few states grant reciprocity only to designated states in their region of the country — e.g., Oregon grants reciprocity only to lawyers from Washington and Idaho. New York has a reciprocity law. But because New York lawyers were required to take the New Jersey bar examination, while New Jersey lawyers gained comparatively painless motion admission to the New York bar, New York retaliated with a "reverse reciprocity" law (present in other states too) that denies reciprocity admission to out-of-state lawyers whose home states (read New Jersey) do not grant reciprocity to New York lawyers. 22 N.Y.C.R.R. §520.10(a)(1). If the goal was to pressure New Jersey to change its rules, it failed. New Jersey has maintained its position.

2.   *Geographical Restriction*

SUPREME COURT OF VIRGINIA v. FRIEDMAN
487 U.S. 59 (1988)

Justice Kennedy delivered the opinion of the Court.

Qualified lawyers admitted to practice in other States may be admitted to the Virginia bar "on motion," that is, without taking the bar examination which Virginia otherwise requires. The State conditions such admission on a showing, among other matters, that the applicant is a permanent resident of Virginia. The question for decision is whether this residency requirement violates the Privileges and Immunities Clause of the United States Constitution, Art. IV, §2. We hold that it does.

I

Myrna E. Friedman was admitted to the Illinois Bar by examination in 1977 and to the District of Columbia bar by reciprocity in 1980. From 1977 to 1981, she was employed by the Department of the Navy in Arlington, Virginia, as a civilian attorney, and from 1982 until 1986, she was an attorney in private practice in Washington, D.C. In January 1986, she became associate general counsel for ERC International, Inc., a Delaware corporation. Friedman practices and maintains her offices at the company's principal place of business in Vienna, Virginia. Her duties at ERC International include drafting contracts and advising her employer and its subsidiaries on matters of Virginia law.

From 1977 to early 1986, Friedman lived in Virginia. In February 1986, however, she married and moved to her husband's home in Cheverly, Maryland. In June 1986, Friedman applied for admission to the Virginia bar on motion.

The applicable rule, promulgated by the Supreme Court of Virginia pursuant to statute, is Rule 1A:1. The Rule permits admission on motion of attorneys who are licensed to practice in another jurisdiction, provided the other jurisdiction admits Virginia attorneys without examination. The applicant must have been licensed for at least five years and the Virginia Supreme Court must determine that the applicant:

(a)   Is a proper person to practice law.
(b)   Has made such progress in the practice of law that it would be unreasonable to require him to take an examination.
(c)   Has become a permanent resident of the Commonwealth.
(d)   Intends to practice full time as a member of the Virginia bar. . . .

The Clerk wrote Friedman that her request had been denied. He explained that because Friedman was no longer a permanent resident of the Commonwealth of Virginia, she was not eligible for admission to the Virginia bar. . . .

II . . .

A

Appellants concede, as they must, that our decision in *Piper* establishes that a nonresident who takes and passes an examination prescribed by the State, and who otherwise is qualified for the practice of law, has an interest in practicing law that is protected by the Privileges and Immunities Clause. Appellants contend, however, that the discretionary admission provided for by Rule 1A:1 is not a privilege protected by the Clause for two reasons. First, appellants argue that the bar examination "serves as an adequate, alternative means of gaining admission to the bar." In appellants' view, "[s]o long as any applicant may gain admission to a State's bar, without regard to residence, by passing the bar examination," the State cannot be said to have discriminated against nonresidents "as a matter of fundamental concern." Second, appellants argue that the right to admission on motion is not within the purview of the Clause because, without offense to the Constitution, the State could require all bar applicants to pass an examination. Neither argument is persuasive.

We cannot accept appellants' first theory because it is quite inconsistent with our precedents. We reaffirmed in *Piper* the well-settled principle that " 'one of the privileges which the Clause guarantees to citizens of State A is that of doing business in State B on terms of substantial equality with the citizens of that State.' " After reviewing our precedents, we explicitly held that the practice of law, like other occupations considered in those cases, is sufficiently basic to the national economy to be deemed a privilege protected by the Clause. The clear import of *Piper* is that the Clause is implicated whenever, as is the case here, a State does not permit qualified nonresidents to practice law within its borders on terms of substantial equality with its own residents.

Nothing in our precedents, moreover, supports the contention that the Privileges and Immunities Clause does not reach a State's discrimination against nonresidents when such discrimination does not result in their total exclusion from the State. In Ward v. Maryland, 12 Wall. 418 (1871), for example, the Court invalidated a statute under which residents paid an annual fee of $12 to $150 for a license to trade foreign goods, while nonresidents were required to pay $300. Similarly, in *Toomer* [v. Witsell, 334 U.S. 385 (1948)], the Court held that nonresident fishermen could not be required to pay a license fee one hundred times the fee charged to residents. In Hicklin v. Orbeck, 437 U.S. 518 (1978), the Court invalidated a statute requiring that residents be hired in preference to nonresidents for all positions related to the development of the State's oil and gas resources. Indeed, as the Court of Appeals correctly noted, the New Hampshire rule struck down in *Piper* did not result in the total exclusion of nonresidents from the practice of law in that State. [See *Piper*, at n.2.]

Further, we find appellants' second theory — that Virginia could constitutionally require that all applicants to its bar take and pass an examination — quite irrelevant to the question whether the Clause is applicable in the circumstances of this case. A State's abstract authority to require from resident and nonresident alike that which it has chosen to demand from the nonresident alone has never been held to shield the discriminatory distinction from the reach of the Privileges and Immunities Clause. Thus, the applicability of the Clause to the present case no more turns on the legality vel non of an examination requirement than it turned on the inherent reasonableness of the fees charged to nonresidents in *Toomer* and *Ward*. The issue instead is whether the State has burdened the right to practice law, a privilege protected by the Privileges and Immunities Clause, by discriminating among otherwise equally qualified applicants solely on the basis of citizenship or residency. We conclude it has.

B

Our conclusion that the residence requirement burdens a privilege protected by the Privileges and Immunities Clause does not conclude the matter, of course; for we repeatedly have recognized that the Clause, like other constitutional provisions, is not an absolute. The Clause does not preclude disparity in treatment where substantial reasons exist for the discrimination and the degree of discrimination bears a close relation to such reasons. In deciding whether the degree of discrimination bears a sufficiently close relation to the reasons proffered by the State, the Court has considered whether, within the full panoply of legislative choices otherwise available to the State, there exist alternative means of furthering the State's purpose without implicating constitutional concerns.

Appellants offer two principal justifications for the Rule's requirement that applicants seeking admission on motion reside within the Commonwealth of Virginia. First, they contend that the residence requirement assures, in tandem with the full-time practice requirement, that attorneys admitted on motion will have the same commitment to service and familiarity with Virginia law that is possessed by applicants securing admission upon examination. Attorneys admitted on motion, appellants argue, have "no personal investment" in the jurisdiction; consequently, they "are entitled to no presumption that they will willingly and actively participate in bar activities and obligations, or fulfill their public service responsibilities to the State's client community." Second, appellants argue that the residency requirement facilitates enforcement of the full-time practice requirement of Rule 1A:1. We find each of these justifications insufficient to meet the State's burden of showing that the discrimination is warranted by a substantial State objective and closely drawn to its achievement.

We acknowledge that a bar examination is one method of assuring that the admitted attorney has a stake in her professional licensure and a concomitant interest in the integrity and standards of the bar. A bar examination, as we know judicially and from our own experience, is not a casual or lighthearted exercise. The question, however, is whether lawyers who are admitted in other States and seek admission in Virginia are less likely to respect the bar and further its interests solely because they are nonresidents. We cannot say this is the case. While *Piper* relied on an examination requirement as an indicium of the nonresident's commitment to the bar and to the State's legal profession, it does not follow that when the State waives the examination it may make a distinction between residents and nonresidents.

Friedman's case proves the point. She earns her living working as an attorney in Virginia, and it is of scant relevance that her residence is located in the neighboring State of Maryland. It is indisputable that she has a substantial stake in the practice of law in Virginia. Indeed, despite appellants' suggestion at oral argument that Friedman's case is "atypical," the same will likely be true of all nonresident attorneys who are admitted on motion to the Virginia bar, in light of the State's requirement that attorneys so admitted show their intention to maintain an office and a regular practice in the State. This requirement goes a long way toward ensuring that such attorneys will have an interest in the practice of law in Virginia that is at least comparable to the interest we ascribed in *Piper* to applicants admitted upon examination. . . .

Further, to the extent that the State is justifiably concerned with ensuring that its attorneys keep abreast of legal developments, it can protect these interests through other equally or more effective means that do not themselves infringe constitutional protections. While this Court is not well positioned to dictate specific legislative choices to the State, it is sufficient to note that such alternatives exist and that the State, in the exercise of its legislative prerogatives, is free to implement them. The Supreme Court of Virginia could, for example, require mandatory attendance at periodic continuing legal education courses. The same is true with respect to the State's interest that the nonresident bar member does her share of volunteer and pro bono work. A "nonresident bar member, like the resident member, could be required to represent indigents and perhaps to participate in formal legal-aid work."

We also reject appellants' attempt to justify the residency restriction as a necessary aid to the enforcement of the full-time practice requirement of Rule 1A:1. Virginia already requires, pursuant to the full-time practice restriction of Rule 1A:1, that attorneys admitted on motion maintain an office for the practice of law in Virginia. As the Court of Appeals noted, the requirement that applicants maintain an office in Virginia facilitates compliance with the full-time practice requirement in nearly the identical manner that the residency restriction does, rendering the latter restriction largely redundant. The office requirement furnishes an alternative to the residency requirement that is not only less restrictive, but also is fully adequate to protect whatever interest the State might have in the full-time practice restriction. . . .

CHIEF JUSTICE REHNQUIST, with whom JUSTICE SCALIA joins, dissenting. . . .

I think the effect of today's decision is unfortunate even apart from what I believe is its mistaken view of the Privileges and Immunities Clause. Virginia's rule allowing admission on motion is an ameliorative provision, recognizing the fact that previous practice in another State may qualify a new resident of Virginia to practice there without the necessity of taking another bar examination. The Court's ruling penalizes Virginia, which has at least gone part way towards accommodating the present mobility of our population, but of course leaves untouched the rules of those States which allow no reciprocal admission on motion.* Virginia may of course retain the privilege of admission on motion without enforcing a residency requirement even after today's decision, but it might also decide to eliminate admission on motion altogether.

After *Piper* and *Friedman*, What Can a State Do to Discourage Out-of-State Lawyers?

By now you may be wondering whether the effort to make life harder for out-of-state lawyers is motivated by considerations of quality or money. Or perhaps it's just due to habit and a failure of imagination. I'm inclined toward the last explanation, because it's the simplest. People don't think outside the box because it's easier to stay with what you know. You may not even recognize that you're in a box. Inertia as a comfort zone has application beyond our subject, of course, but certainly includes it. Then something happens to upset that reflex. The Supreme Court's decisions on bar eligibility, like those rejecting rules that limit legal advertising and solicitation (see chapter 16), modestly upset the status quo. Opponents of easier admission standards, like opponents of advertising, invoke the theme of law as a profession, not a business, to defend greater state controls, at least over licensure matters. The Supreme Court doesn't disagree that law is a profession. Of course, it is. But the Court has refused to allow states to wave the flag of professionalism to impose conditions on lawyer admission or restrictions on other conduct that ignore constitutional boundaries. Piper won because she passed the New Hampshire bar examination and the state could not treat her differently than it treated its own residents. The Court did not rely on her "possible job" in New Hampshire. Friedman won because her full-time job in Virginia entitled her to the same reciprocity rights as resident Virginia lawyers with full-time Virginia jobs. A third permutation is revealed in Goldfarb v. Supreme Court of Virginia, 766 F.2d 859 (4th Cir. 1985), decided before *Friedman*. Whereas Friedman lived in Maryland and worked in Virginia, Goldfarb lived in Virginia and worked in Washington, D.C. The Fourth Circuit upheld Virginia's in-state work requirement as a condition of reciprocal admission when applied to a Virginia resident. Is that because, this time, Virginia wasn't treating an out-of-stater differently? It was discriminating against its own. Does this

---

* At present, 28 states do not allow reciprocal admission on motion. . . .

decision survive *Friedman*? It has. As mentioned above, the Seventh Circuit upheld an Indiana rule requiring that lawyers admitted on motion spend more than half their professional time for five years advising Indiana clients, although not necessarily about Indiana law or from an office within Indiana. Scariano v. Justices of the Supreme Court of Indiana, 38 F.3d 920 (7th Cir. 1994) (distinguishing *Friedman*). And the Third Circuit agreed in Tolchin v. Supreme Court of the State of New Jersey, 111 F.3d 1099 (3d Cir. 1997). Non-residents who work in the state cannot be treated differently from residents who do.

So what restraints may a state continue to impose? Certainly no case has required (or is ever likely to require) a state to do away with the bar examination for attorneys admitted elsewhere. Motion admission is not a constitutional right; but where allowed, it must be administered constitutionally. It can be denied to everyone so long as the state does not favor its own. And some states do deny it to everyone. Persistently, that has included California and Florida. Why is that, do you think?

3.   Education and Examination

If there is one institution that has resisted all efforts to end it, it is the bar examination. No one seriously believes that a bar examination is a perfect way to test knowledge or ability to practice law. Even those charged with examining bar applicants probably recognize the rough justice the examination delivers. The trouble is, no one has advanced a persuasive substitute or been able to convince state courts and legislatures to do away with it. Wisconsin will admit and Montana once admitted graduates of law schools in the state without examination. See Supreme Court Rule 40.03. The practice has been upheld. Huffman v. Montana Supreme Court, 372 F. Supp. 1175 (D. Mont.), aff'd, 419 U.S. 955 (1974). The fact that these graduates appear to enter the profession and practice law as uneventfully as their much-examined colleagues would seem to provide a "control group" that could be used to study the predictive value of the bar examination. However, no matter how conclusively such a study might prove that the examination does not predict competence, it would be unlikely to lead to repeal of the examination or to persuade a court to declare it unconstitutional.

Again, why is that? The exams test knowledge of subjects that many aspiring lawyers will never need to know, and they do not generally test subjects that many new lawyers will practice (antitrust, federal tax, copyright). The benign answer is that a state has an interest in assuring that those whom it holds out to the public as competent are competent, at some level, and this is the way it has chosen to do so, thank you very much. The exam and the license give the public confidence in lawyers. A less charitable view, which I'm not implying, is that a lot of people make a living from the existence of the bar examination, not to mention the fees states charge for taking one. A still less charitable view, which I'm also not implying, is that the exam is an entry barrier that enables the profession to limit competition.

The fact that one racial group generally does better on a bar examination than another will not invalidate the examination, absent a showing of an intent to discriminate. Richardson v. McFadden, 563 F.2d 1130 (4th Cir. 1977); Tyler v. Vickery, 517 F.2d 1089 (5th Cir. 1975); Pettit v. Gingerich, 427 F. Supp. 282 (D. Md. 1977), aff'd, 582 F.2d 869 (4th Cir. 1978).

Bar examinations have been challenged on nearly every ground imaginable. Plaintiffs have charged that methods of grading were improper, that particular questions were improper, that the format of the examination was improper, that they had a constitutional right to a postexamination hearing, and that they had a constitutional right to see their examination papers and to receive model answers. The annotation at 30 A.L.R. Fed. 934 collects the cases rejecting these and other varieties of challenge. See also Giannini v. Real, 911 F.2d 354 (9th Cir. 1990). One court has held that an applicant has a constitutional right to see an examination paper and a model answer. In re Peterson, 459 P.2d 703 (Alaska 1969). Of course, a state may choose to allow applicants to review their examination papers and some do. See, e.g., 22 N.Y.C.R.R. §6000.7. See also Sutton v. Lionel, 585 F.2d 400 (9th Cir. 1978).

Twenty American jurisdictions limit the number of times an applicant may take the bar examination, from two in Iowa and New Hampshire to six in Utah and Puerto Rico. ABA, Comprehensive Guide to Bar Admission Requirements 2008 (Chart V). In some states, the limit may be waived. The Seventh Circuit upheld Indiana's four-time limit in Poats v. Givan, 651 F.2d 495 (7th Cir. 1981). It relied in part on a Tenth Circuit decision rejecting the plaintiff's claim that he had a right to take the Colorado bar examination a fourth time. Younger v. Colorado State Bd. of Law Examiners, 625 F.2d 372 (10th Cir. 1980). See also Jones v. Board of Commissioners, 737 F.2d 996 (11th Cir. 1984), which, over a dissent, rejected the minority applicants' challenge to a former Alabama rule that limited to five the number of times a person could then sit for the bar examination. The *Jones* court also discussed the relationship between limitations on reexamination and the right to review one's paper, citing Lucero v. Ogden, 718 F.2d 355 (10th Cir. 1983).

Rules requiring applicants for admission to be graduates of accredited law schools have also been upheld. Cline v. Supreme Court of Georgia, 781 F.2d 1541 (11th Cir. 1986) (upholding such a rule despite a "grandparent" clause that exempted students who attended or were then attending nonaccredited schools); Lombardi v. Tauro, 470 F.2d 798 (1st Cir. 1972).

In Hoover v. Ronwin, 466 U.S. 558 (1984), an unsuccessful bar applicant charged that the bar examiners had set the grading scale "with reference to the number of new attorneys they thought desirable, rather than with reference to some 'suitable' level of competence," in violation of the antitrust laws. In a 4-to-3 opinion, the Supreme Court did not address this allegation, concluding instead that the passing score was set pursuant to state authorization and therefore was "immune from antitrust liability under Parker v. Brown, 317 U.S. 341 (1943)." See page 175 for further discussion of the antitrust laws as a limit on rules that regulate lawyers.

4. Character Inquiries

"Shattered Glass"

Did you see the movie of the same name or read Stephen Glass's novel, *The Fabulist*, about a character named Stephen Glass who makes things up. Okay, who lies. I recommend the movie. In the 1990s the real Stephen Glass was in his mid-20s, on the staff of The New Republic, and a night student at Georgetown Law School. He was a remarkably gifted writer who had a knack for discovering riveting stories and providing riveting descriptions that enlivened his reporting. I'm understating. His language skill was off the charts. His work drew attention in and out of journalistic circles. I recall reading his stories with amazement. This can't be true, I thought, while believing every word. (The article about young Republican men misbehaving toward women at a political conference was especially memorable.) But much of what Glass wrote was a lie. Not just little details, but big details, too. In fact, sometimes the entire story was a complete fiction. (The young Republicans story, for example.) He invented all or parts of 27 stories published in the magazine.

Then Glass got tripped up. It was, of course, inevitable. He wrote a story about an event (a meeting of computer geeks) that caught the eye of a reporter at Forbes.com who covered the industry. How had he missed it, the Forbes guy wondered? His editor asked the same question. So the Forbes guy tried to verify Glass's sources without success. The Forbes editor called Glass's editor. Glass then lied to his own editor to cover up the original lies. He created false proof (notes, a fake Web site). But the circle was tightening. Eventually, Glass confessed in the face of overwhelming proof and was fired. The New Republic reviewed everything he wrote for it (not all of it was lies) and published extensive corrections.

Glass eventually passed the New York bar examination, but as of late 2008 failed to gain admission, so far as I can determine. No reputable newspaper or magazine will ever hire Stephen Glass as a reporter, editor, probably not even as a copy boy. (Are there still copy boys?) Today he is finished as a journalist. Should the bar admit him? Not honest enough to be a reporter so try law? Is that the message we want to tell the public? Or is that too harsh? Does there come a time when we can say, if true, that Glass has reformed and may join us? Is there a statute of limitations on his disgrace? If you were on the state's character committee and Glass claimed to have reformed himself, would you let him be a lawyer? Would you be willing to give him a state license and in so doing tell the client population he deserves its trust?

In addition to testing for knowledge, all jurisdictions subject bar applicants to a test of what may loosely be called their "character." Character committees have traditionally considered it their prerogative to inspect at least four aspects of the lives of bar applicants. First is the applicant's mental health. Second is the applicant's honesty and integrity. Third may be the applicant's personal life, including financial probity. Finally, character committees have asked about the applicant's loyalty to the American system of government.

Criticism of the work of character committees has taken many forms. Most critics agree that one or more of the inquiries just listed are appropriate if the focus is sufficiently narrow. Others question the underlying premise of character inquiries, namely that it is possible, based on past conduct, to predict future behavior. See generally Deborah Rhode, Moral Character as a Professional Credential, 94 Yale L.J. 491 (1985). Is the only reason to conduct a character inquiry to determine how the applicant will behave as a lawyer? Or are there other purposes as well? For example, may the state validly exclude persons with "checkered pasts" on the ground that their admission would undermine confidence in the bar? Alternatively, might it be argued that when a state licenses a person to be a lawyer, it is implicitly representing that person to the public as a man or woman of honesty and integrity? If so, doesn't it then have a duty to assure itself that he or she fits that description? And might not a state also conclude that the prospect of a character inquiry will weed out some people who might otherwise consider a legal career?

Character tests have also been criticized on the grounds that they invade the privacy rights of those tested and that they were once used to exclude applicants who were "different from," or not members of the same religious or ethnic groups as, those who dominated the bar. See generally Jerold Auerbach, Unequal Justice 94-101 (1976).

IN RE MUSTAFA
631 A.2d 45 (D.C. 1993)

SULLIVAN, ASSOCIATE JUDGE:

John W. Mustafa II, passed the July 1991 Bar examination and is an applicant for admission to the Bar of the District of Columbia. The Committee on Admissions ("the Committee") recommended that he be admitted to the Bar, despite its finding that Mustafa "converted to his personal use funds entrusted to him for expenditure in a law school program." We conclude, however, that on the record here, particularly the short period of time that has elapsed since his misconduct, Mustafa has failed to establish that he has the good moral character required for admission to the Bar. Accordingly, we deny his application for admission.

I

In [their] third year of law school at the University of California at Los Angeles, Mustafa and Larry Brennan served as co-chief justices of the law school's moot court program, and shared access to and control over the program's checking account.[1] Over a five-month period between October 1990 and February 1991, Mustafa wrote thirteen checks totaling $4,331, approximately $3,510 of which he converted to his personal use.[2] On at least seven occasions, he wrote checks to reimburse himself for expenditures which had been, or would be, reimbursed by the university's accounting department. At other

---

1. The account held student-paid dues of $25.00 each to cover moot court expenses not paid by the university.
2. Mustafa explained that he used the funds principally to pay his rent and other bills, to pay a $1,000 bail for his sister, to lend another sister $750 so she could leave an abusive husband, and to pay expenses for a law student to compete in a Chicago moot court competition. Mustafa also assumed responsibility for approximately $811 which he claimed were legitimate moot court program expenses for which he could provide no documentation.

times he failed to make any notation about the use of the money or falsified the purpose of the checks.[3]

Mustafa admitted to Brennan on June 14, 1991, that he had taken $1,000 from the fund to pay his sister's bail and that he would repay the money from a loan he had arranged from his then-prospective employer. Several days later, Brennan discovered that less than $800 remained in the account, rather than the $1,300 he had expected; Brennan closed the account. On June 25th, Mustafa presented Brennan with a cashier's check for $2,200. On June 28th, Brennan disclosed Mustafa's misconduct to the law school dean; on the same day, Mustafa disclosed his misconduct to a law school professor and to the Committee. After an investigation, the university was satisfied that Mustafa had made full restitution and disposed of the matter by issuing a letter of censure to be placed in his confidential student discipline file for four years. As required by the university, Mustafa disclosed his misconduct to the law firm at which he is presently employed as a law clerk.

Following a hearing, the Committee found that Mustafa always intended to repay the sums taken from the fund, principally because he repaid $1,500 on January 2, 1991, kept an accurate mental record of how much he had taken from the fund, and made full restitution before there was any threatened action by the law school. The Committee was also impressed by Mustafa's honesty and forthrightness before the Committee and during the law school investigation. Moreover, Mustafa's references from two law school professors, three former members of the moot court program board, a former employer, and three partners and two associates from the law firm where Mustafa is employed, were, to the Committee, powerful testimony of his current good character. The Committee unanimously recommended that Mustafa be admitted to the Bar.

II

In order to gain admission to the Bar, an applicant must demonstrate "by clear and convincing evidence, that the applicant possessed good moral character and general fitness to practice law in the District of Columbia" at the time of the applicant's admission. This court will "accept findings of fact made by the Committee unless they are unsupported by substantial evidence of record," will "make due allowance for the Committee's opportunity to observe and evaluate the demeanor of the applicant where relevant," and will "afford the Committee's recommendations some deference. . . ."

Mustafa candidly acknowledges that he, like few others in his position, was placed in a position of trust in handling others' money and that he "failed that test." As the Committee recognized, Mustafa's conduct, while it did not result in a criminal conviction, "was sufficiently serious to require analysis under the principles laid down in [precedent]." Of particular significance is the Committee's finding that Mustafa's conduct "could be considered criminal in nature and would almost invariably have resulted in the disbarment of an attorney

---

3. In particular, on November 28, 1990, he wrote a check to himself for $1,500, stating falsely on the check stub that it was for air fare to a competition in New York. Mustafa returned this amount to the fund via a personal check on January 2, 1991. Again, on February 28, 1991, he wrote a check for $1,500, indicating on the stub that the check was for $75.00 for Girl Scout cookies.

admitted to practice." There is no doubt that an attorney who mismanages the funds of a client will ordinarily face disbarment. Similarly, an attorney convicted of a crime involving moral turpitude faces automatic disbarment. A disbarred attorney would be ineligible to apply for reinstatement for five years. While we do not hold as a matter of law that an applicant for admission to the Bar, like a disbarred attorney, must necessarily wait a minimum of five years from the date of proven misconduct before applying for admission to the Bar, we conclude that on the record here, particularly the relatively short period of time that has elapsed since the date of his misconduct, Mustafa has failed to establish that he has the good moral character required for admission to the Bar.

In reaching this conclusion, we are mindful of Mustafa's outstanding law school record[5] and his appropriate conduct since the embezzlement: he cooperated with the university and the Committee; he has married; and he has volunteered in several community projects since coming to the District of Columbia. . . .

Indeed, on the record here, it appears likely that Mustafa will be able to establish the requisite good moral character at some future time. At present, however, "[o]ur consideration of the entire record leaves us unpersuaded that [Mustafa] now possesses those qualities of truth-speaking, of a high sense of honor, of granite discretion, of the strictest observation of fiduciary responsibility, that have . . . been compendiously described as [the] moral character necessary for the practice of law." In sum, Mustafa has not demonstrated his present fitness for the privilege of membership in the District of Columbia Bar. [Internal quotes omitted.]

[Epilogue: Mustafa was admitted to the California bar in 1994. In 2002, he resigned while facing charges. He was found to have acted fraudulently by converting a fee he should have shared with another lawyer, to have commingled personal and business funds, to have ignored client matters, and to have used funds in his trust account for personal expenses. He claimed to have had family problems during this period. Does this event lend some support to character inquiries?]

Frequently Cited Grounds for Delaying or Denying Admission to the Bar

Criminal Conduct. Criminal conduct has traditionally excluded applicants to the bar, whether or not it has led to conviction. In re Goldman, 206 So. 2d 643 (Fla. 1968). Even an acquittal will not prevent the conduct from being weighed in the admission process. The burden of proof in a criminal case is on the state beyond a reasonable doubt, whereas the burden of showing good moral character may be on the applicant and is in any event lower. See, for example, Siegel v. Committee of Bar Examiners, 514 P.2d 967 (Cal. 1973).

---

5. Mustafa was a staff member and editor of the law review; he was one of two co-chief justices of the moot court program; was named one of twelve outstanding advocates during his second year of law school; and was one of three graduating law students selected by the law school dean, Susan Westerberg Prager, to attend an annual spring donors' dinner. He also participated in several other law school activities.

In Matter of Prager, 661 N.E.2d 84 (Mass. 1996), the applicant certainly turned his life around, but he was denied admission to the bar because over a period of six years he had "organized and led a large-scale international drug smuggling operation" (marijuana). That ended in 1981, but Prager continued to sell marijuana in the United States until he was indicted in 1983. He was a fugitive abroad until 1987. He pled guilty and received a suspended sentence plus probation, which he satisfactorily completed in 1993. He graduated from law school in 1994, clerked for a state supreme court judge in Maine (where he had attended law school), and applied to the Massachusetts bar. In a lengthy opinion, the court concluded that Prager had failed to show that his "admission would not be detrimental to the integrity of the bar or the public interest." What does "integrity of the bar" mean? Should the only question be what Prager would or would not do? The court gave him leave to reapply in five years. See also Matter of N.W.R., 674 So. 2d 729 (Fla. 1996) (admission denied where applicant, while a college student, used a fellow student's mailbox without permission to order credit cards and magazines in the other student's name).

In In re Fine, 736 P.2d 183 (Or. 1987), the court denied admission to a man who, while in college and as part of a political protest, set a bomb that accidentally killed someone. The man was then a fugitive for five and a half years. In re DeBartolo, 488 N.E.2d 947 (Ill. 1986), rejected an applicant partially because he had misrepresented himself as a police officer and also because he had received more than 200 parking tickets in a brief time.

According to the 2008 Comprehensive Guide to Bar Admission Requirements, no state makes every felony a conclusive basis for excluding a bar applicant for all time, although Missouri and Texas require a waiting period of five years after completion of the sentence and Mississippi excludes all felons except those convicted of manslaughter or a tax crime. (Tax and manslaughter? That sounds like the statute was intended to benefit particular individuals, doesn't it?) States examine the nature of the crime, how long ago it occurred, and the applicant's conduct thereafter. In In re Manville, 538 A.2d 1128 (D.C. 1988), the court admitted three applicants who had been convicted, respectively, of manslaughter, attempted armed robbery, and the sale of narcotics. Compare In re Polin, 630 A.2d 1140 (D.C. 1993) (applicant who had been convicted of cocaine conspiracy in 1984 and released from incarceration in 1987 was denied admission to the bar in 1991 but admitted two years later).

Lack of Candor in the Application Process. Fuggedaboutit. This can be deadly. Preapplication conduct that would not result in exclusion can lead to exclusion if the bar applicant consciously omits it from the application. Strigler v. Board of Bar Examiners, 864 N.E.2d 8 (Mass.2007) ("An applicant's failure to answer all of the board's questions candidly, both on the application and at any hearing, is a powerful indication that the applicant lacks the good character required for admission to the bar"). Connecticut denied admission to an applicant where a law school discipline committee found that he had cheated on a closed book exam (even though the dean later reversed the committee's sanction because he found that delay in the process prejudiced the student's ability to defend). The bar committee then found that he was "untruthful" under oath when he testified before the committee about the incident. Matter of Friedman, 824 A.2d 866 (Conn. App. 2003). See also Radtke v. Board of Bar

Examiners, 601 N.W.2d 642 (Wis. 1999) (admission delayed where applicant "omitted a material fact [and] thereby minimized his culpability and responsibility for the termination" from his job as a university lecturer); In re Greenberg, 614 P.2d 832 (Ariz. 1980). If falsity on an application is discovered after admission, the lawyer can be censured, suspended, or disbarred. Carter v. Charos, 536 A.2d 527 (R.I. 1988); Matter of Harper, 645 N.Y.S.2d 846 (2d Dept. 1996) (censure where lawyer failed to reveal that he had been expelled from a graduate law program for plagiarism). The fact that a criminal conviction has been expunged is not generally a ground for omitting it from the application without express permission to do so. In re Watson, 509 N.E.2d 1240 (Ohio 1987); Kentucky Bar Assn. v. Guidugli, 967 S.W.2d 587 (Ky. 1998) (lawyer suspended for failing to reveal misdemeanor conviction on bar application notwithstanding that conviction occurred in juvenile court, where records are sealed). Unless you have a letter from a state bar official on letterhead saying you can omit your expunged or juvenile record, reveal it!

Dishonesty or Lack of Integrity in Legal Academic Settings.   No excuses. By the time you're in law school, expect no sympathy. You can't plead your youth and inexperience. In re Mustafa, supra. Cheating on LSAT, bar, or law school examinations can result in delay or even denial of admission. Radtke v. Board of Bar Examiners, supra, delayed admission where the applicant was guilty of plagiarizing a scholarly article submitted for publication; In re Knight, 208 S.E.2d 820 (Ga. 1974); In re Corrigan, 546 N.E.2d 1315 (Ohio 1989) (applicant may never reapply).

Mental Health

Question:
   Have you, within the past five years, been treated or counseled for a mental, emotional, or nervous disorder? If yes:

(a)   *list dates of treatment;*
(b)   *give names, addresses and telephone numbers of health care providers and hospitals;*
(c)   *describe completely the diagnosis and treatment and the prognosis and provide any other relevant facts.*

Some state bar applications may still contain questions like (or slightly narrower than) this one, and at one time nearly all did. Lawyers have occasionally been excluded from the bar not for anything they did but because of what others predicted they might do based on their mental health history.

   The Americans with Disabilities Act appears to have changed the rules. A handful of opinions have now held that the Act applies to bar applications and that questions like the one posed above are prohibited. In fact, the quoted question is based on one of the more thorough opinions on the issue, Clark v. Virginia Board of Bar Examiners, 880 F. Supp. 430 (E.D. Va. 1995), where Judge Cacheris collects the cases and summarizes the "mental health" inquiry in every

American jurisdiction's bar admission process. (Only seven states, according to *Clark*, made no inquiry into mental health.)

Two interesting statistics are revealed in *Clark*.

First, with applications to the Virginia bar then running at about 2,000 yearly, in the prior 23 years, only 47 Virginia bar applicants answered yes to this question. Yet experts testified that at any given time, about one-fifth of the population "suffers from some form of mental or emotional disorder." This may mean that some applicants lied in answering the question or that law and pre-law students refrain from seeking help because they do not want to have to reveal the details of their problem to strangers or risk delay in bar admission.

Second, the opinion reveals that in the same 23-year period not one Virginia bar applicant had been denied admission based on the fact of mental health treatment. So the question, while demanding highly private information and possibly deterring individuals from seeking treatment, resulted in exclusion of no applicant based on perceived danger.

These issues are further explored in Jon Bauer, The Character of the Questions and the Fitness of the Process: Mental Health, Bar Admissions and the Americans with Disabilities Act, 49 U.C.L.A. L. Rev. 93 (2001).

Financial Probity.   Think student loans. Admission committees and courts inquire about financial irregularities in the applicant's life. Dishonesty or abuse of trust in business or personal financial matters may predict lack of probity as a lawyer. In In re Gahan, 279 N.W.2d 826 (Minn. 1979), the court denied admission to a lawyer from another jurisdiction who had declared bankruptcy while he still owed some $14,000 in student loans. The court acknowledged that the Supremacy Clause prevented it from denying admission *because* Gahan had declared bankruptcy. It rested its decision on the applicant's failure to satisfy his financial obligations during the prebankruptcy period, when he was employed and able to do so. Matter of Anonymous, 549 N.E.2d 472 (N.Y. 1989), held that an application may be rejected because of an inability to handle personal finances, as long as bankruptcy is not the sole reason for the rejection. Matter of C.R.W., 481 S.E.2d 511 (Ga. 1997) (application denied in part because applicant failed to show a satisfactory payment history on two student loans totaling over $35,000).

Applicant's Private Life.   Three decades ago, the Virginia Supreme Court reversed a denial of bar admission where the applicant lived with a man to whom she was not married. "While Cord's living arrangement may be unorthodox and unacceptable to some segments of society, this conduct bears no rational connection to her fitness to practice law." Cord v. Gibb, 254 S.E.2d 71 (Va. 1979).

At one time, applicants to the bar might be denied admission because of their sexual orientation or, if already admitted, might be disbarred for the same reason. Hard to believe? Or maybe not. See State ex rel. Florida Bar v. Kimball, 96 So. 2d 825 (Fla. 1957). Lawrence v. Texas, 539 U.S. 558 (2003), would have put an end to that had the practice not ended decades earlier.

Ability to Speak English.   Bar committees also inquire into "fitness," which does not seem to have a meaning separate from "character," unless it means passing the bar exam. But in Application of Singh, 800 N.E.2d 1112 (Ohio 2003), the court denied an applicant permission to take the bar examination not because of his character but because "deficiencies in speaking and writing English and in comprehending the speech and writing of others [led to] doubts about his fitness to practice law. Communication skills are central to the practice of law." The applicant could reapply after 18 months.

"The Racist Bar Applicant"

Matthew Hale, a 1998 graduate of Southern Illinois University Law School who passed the Illinois bar exam, is an avowed racist and founder of the World Church of the Creator. A character committee of the Illinois Supreme Court rejected Hale's application for admission to the state bar on the ground that his white supremacist views were "diametrically opposed to the letter and spirit" of the Rules of Professional Conduct. A member of Hale's Church, Benjamin Smith, killed two people and wounded nine others in July 1999. All of the victims were black or Asian. Smith then killed himself. Although Hale was not charged with these or any other crimes, he had publicly called for a racial "holy war" of whites against people of color.

The Illinois Supreme Court refused to review the character committee's rejection of Hale's application for bar membership. Justice Heiple dissented on the ground that the denial raises free speech questions under the federal and state constitutions. "In addition," Justice Heiple added, the character committee "merely speculates that [Hale] is 'on a collision course with the Rules of Professional Conduct' and that, if admitted, he will *in the future* 'find himself before the [disciplinary system].' I believe this court should address whether it is appropriate for the Committee to base its assessment of an applicant's character and fitness on speculative predictions of future actionable conduct.

"The question also arises: If all of [Hale's] statements identified by the Committee had been made after obtaining a license to practice law, would he then be subject to disbarment? That is to say, is there one standard for admission to practice and a different standard for continuing to practice? And, if the standard is the same, can already-licensed lawyers be disbarred for obnoxious speech?" In re Hale, 723 N.E.2d 206 (Ill. 1999).

Should a person like Matthew Hale be admitted to practice law in Illinois?* Should an avowed racist who has *not* called for violence be denied admission?

Procedures Regarding Character Inquiry

Applicants to the bar who are denied admission because they lack good moral character are entitled to a hearing, at which they can present evidence and confront the evidence against them. Willner v. Committee on Character & Fitness,

---

* The question can't be asked about Matthew Hale himself. Hale was later convicted of soliciting the murder of a federal judge and obstruction of justice. New York Times, April 27, 2004, at A23.

373 U.S. 96 (1963). The hearing may be held before either an administrative body or a court. If an administrative body makes the determination to exclude the applicant, the scope of court review varies. In In re Willis, 215 S.E.2d 771 (N.C. 1975), the court said that it would not reverse a determination of its board of law examiners if there was substantial evidence in the record supporting the conclusion. Other courts have stressed that the bar examiners' findings are not controlling, although they may be entitled to great weight with the burden on the applicant to show that the examiners' determination was erroneous. Bernstein v. Committee of Bar Examiners, 443 P.2d 570 (Cal. 1968). *Bernstein* also held that reasonable doubts should be resolved in favor of the applicant. The applicant is generally viewed as bearing the burden of showing the presence of good moral character. Siegel v. Committee of Bar Examiners, 514 P.2d 967 (Cal. 1973).

5.   Admission in a Federal System

The fact that we have both federal and state court systems raises some interesting problems. One of these is discipline, which is discussed at page 770. Another is admission. As a general rule, federal courts admit applicants who are members of the bar of the highest court of the state in which that federal court is located. Sometimes the federal court may have rules permitting the admission of lawyers who are not members of the local state bar but who, for example, are employees of the federal government, such as Assistant U.S. Attorneys working in the particular federal district. Admission in these circumstances may last only as long as the lawyer continues in the job. Federal courts also have their own pro hac vice admission procedures. Federal courts reserve the right to conduct character inquiries and in rare cases decline to admit a lawyer who has been admitted in the state in which the federal court sits. In re G. L. S., 745 F.2d 856 (4th Cir. 1984). Judge Dubois reviews the admission rules of all federal district courts in In re Pawlak, 1995 Westlaw 723177 (E.D. Pa. 1995) (denying admission to district court of an attorney who was not a member of the state bar).

Should or must a federal court admit an attorney to its bar even if she is not a member of the bar of the state in which the federal court sits? What if the attorney is interested only in matters within the exclusive jurisdiction of the federal court, and there is no question about the attorney's competence to handle such matters?

In re Roberts, 682 F.2d 105 (3d Cir. 1982), was a challenge to a rule of the federal district court in New Jersey that limited membership in the court's bar to members of the New Jersey bar. The Third Circuit found the limitation rational. It wrote that

> tying district court admission to state bar membership tends to protect the interests of the public. For example, when a choice of either a federal or a state forum is available in a particular case an attorney admitted only to the federal court may choose that forum solely for that reason, possibly disregarding the interests of his client. Moreover, issues of state law are often dispositive in

federal tax cases, further supporting the application of the state bar requirement to lawyers specializing in federal taxation.

See also Matter of North, 383 F.3d 871 (9th Cir. 2004) (federal court in Arizona may condition admission to its bar on "active" membership in Arizona bar).

But a district court may have a more generous rule. The lawyer in Matter of Desilets, 291 F.3d 925 (6th Cir. 2002), was admitted in Texas and had offices in Michigan and Wisconsin even though he was not admitted in either state. He was admitted to the local bankruptcy court in Michigan, however, and the court upheld his right to practice before it. A dissent feared that the decision would portend "a national system for licensing, removing and regulating federal practice," displacing state regulation to that extent. Maybe, and this is surely a question to watch: If a lawyer is admitted to a local federal court in a state but not to the state's own courts, does he have a federal right to open an office in that state? Or may the state prevent it? Desilets doesn't answer that question. The only issue for the court was whether the lawyer could practice in the federal bankruptcy court, not whether he could have a permanent office in Michigan. Compare Office of Disciplinary Counsel v. Marcone, 855 A.2d 654 (Pa. 2004), which distinguished Desilets on this ground when it refused to let a suspended lawyer keep an office in the state despite his plan to limit his practice to federal court, where he was still admitted. Although Marcone concerned a suspended lawyer, its detailed analysis of the federalism issue would apply to any lawyer admitted only in a federal court within a state and who wished to open an office in the state.

Marcone's reasoning did not persuade the Third Circuit, which cited the Supremacy Clause to uphold the right of a Pennsylvania lawyer who was suspended from state practice but still admitted to the local district court to maintain a law office in the state limited to cases, including diversity cases, before the district court. Surrick v. Killion, 449 F.3d 520 (3d Cir. 2006) ("the direct effect of a state regulation prohibiting an attorney from maintaining a law office is the frustration of his or her ability to practice before a federal court"). If the Third Circuit is correct, what does that mean for a state's control of lawyers within its borders? Surrick's facts are unusual. The question arose only because the plaintiff was suspended by the state court but not by the federal court. But the Circuit's reasoning is broad. Surrick, fairly read, would allow federal courts to erect parallel admission systems that grant licenses entitling recipients to open offices for practice before federal courts within a state, including in diversity cases where state substantive law controls, without ever bothering to take a state's bar examination or go before its character committee. Presumably, though, the applicant would have to be admitted somewhere. Although the holding is broad, the case's practical effect is quite narrow. Federal courts are not about to create a parallel licensing system. But what if we move out of the federal/state paradigm and focus solely on state admission? A New York lawyer wishes to move to Florida and open an office limited to the practice of New York law. He does not wish to join the Florida bar. Too bad. He has no Supremacy Clause argument. Gould v. Florida Bar, 2007 Westlaw 4403556 (11th Cir. 2007) (rejecting this very effort).

B.　TRANSIENT LAWYERS AND MULTIJURISDICTIONAL FIRMS: LOCAL INTERESTS CONFRONT A NATIONAL BAR

A client's legal problems do not always stop at a state border. Even when they do, the client may have good reason for seeking the aid of an out-of-state lawyer. Does a lawyer admitted in Oregon have a right to assist a client with legal problems in Nevada if the lawyer is not admitted to practice there? Whether or not the lawyer has that right, does the client have the right to the lawyer's assistance? Think about a criminal defendant in Ohio who wants to hire a prominent New York defense lawyer and cites his Sixth Amendment right to counsel. Does Ohio have to let him? There are other variables here. For example, will the lawyer perform services in connection with a litigation or simply give advice? In either case, does the litigation or the advice encompass federally protected rights of the client or only rights under the law of the state in which the lawyer is not admitted? Does this matter? If the lawyer is helping the client in connection with a litigation, is the litigation in federal or state court? Does this matter? Remember, if an out-of-state lawyer serves a client in a jurisdiction in which he is not admitted, he may be guilty of the unauthorized practice of law or UPL. And the lawyers who help him may be guilty of aiding UPL. Rule 5.5(a). UPL is further discussed at page 690.

One rule is clear. If a lawyer stays in his home jurisdiction, he can advise on the law of any jurisdiction in the world, so long as he is competent to do so. Problems arise only when the lawyer does work "in" a jurisdiction in which he is not admitted (called a "host" jurisdiction). But what does it mean to serve a client "in" a jurisdiction? You have probably never encountered a more ambiguous preposition. Does the lawyer actually have to travel physically to the other jurisdiction and give advice there? Or is it UPL to phone or e-mail advice to a client in the host jurisdiction? (Is your head spinning? I'm not done.) What if a Colorado lawyer gives advice on Colorado law while in Kansas? On federal law? What if the client is a Coloradan or a Texan? The problem is obvious. May the lawyer's geographical location at the time of the advice be the sole test? A test at all? Modern communication technology would make that look ridiculous, wouldn't it? What then should be the test? How can we define the authorized practice of law *in* a multijurisdictional licensing system if we don't know exactly what we want to, and constitutionally are able to, forbid? Further complications — or does it actually simplify things? — are that the laws of all jurisdictions are easily accessible to lawyers anywhere via computer databases, that a good deal of modern law is uniform (or nearly so) nationwide, and that federal and international law is the same everywhere.

This is clearly an area in transition. Not all questions can be answered with certainty, but some can. We are witnessing a delicate balancing between proper, and perhaps sometimes improper, local interests on the one hand and, on the other hand, the reality of a national economy and national interests that need the services of lawyers nationwide and, increasingly, worldwide. Recall the material on residency requirements, which in a different context also required a balance between local and national interests.

It can be argued that restrictive rules in this area are an example of economic protectionism for the local bar. Fence out the competition. But is that too harsh? A benign explanation is the interest in protecting a state's residents against incompetence or dishonesty. Remember, by definition the out-of-state lawyer will not have passed the jurisdiction's bar examination. He may be wholly unfamiliar with local court rules or the nuances of local substantive law. A legal system in any particular geographical and political area has a life and style of its own. Local lawyers and judges have a real interest in ensuring its smooth operation. All of these explanations argue in favor of powers of exclusion, but do they argue too much? Could lawyers in West Texas or North Florida cite them to justify excluding lawyers from East Texas or South Florida from practicing before their courts?

Another state interest is in the honesty of lawyers who practice within the state. Licensed lawyers are subject to the control of the licensing jurisdiction, including its disciplinary systems. What control can a jurisdiction exercise over a lawyer who renders legal advice within its borders — even if on the law of her home state — but who does not belong to its bar? This quandary troubled the court in Kennedy v. Bar Assn., 561 A.2d 200 (Md. 1989). Even if the lawyer is competent to advise in the particular area of law, can he be trusted? Servidone Construction Corp. v. St. Paul Fire & Marine Ins. Co., 911 F. Supp. 560 (N.D.N.Y. 1995) (discussing character issue and holding that unauthorized practice rules are concerned not only with what law is practiced but also where the practice occurs). In trying to understand the state interest here, compare medicine. The human body is the same in Iowa and Virginia. Let's assume that Virginia's standards for licensing doctors are at least as stringent as Iowa's standards. What interest does Iowa have in regulating a Virginia doctor's treatment of an Iowan (or anyone else) in Iowa?

One step that would facilitate interstate practice would be to give states some control over lawyers admitted elsewhere by recognizing what we might call "long-arm discipline." May a state assume disciplinary authority over lawyers whose misconduct causes harm within the state, even if they are admitted elsewhere? A few states have said yes. South Carolina purports to exercise jurisdiction over lawyers who send advertisements or solicitations into South Carolina if those messages violate the state's rules regarding lawyer commercial speech. Sanctions include not only a letter of caution but also the possibility that the lawyer "may be ordered to refund all fees paid to [him] pursuant to any contract of employment arising out of the advertising or solicitation." The lawyer may also be punished for contempt of court and enjoined. Rule 418, South Carolina Rules of Court. In Matter of Murgatroyd, 741 N.E.2d 719 (Ind. 2001), the court said it had "regulatory authority" over California lawyers who mailed allegedly improper solicitations to Indiana residents in which the lawyers sought to be retained for claims arising out of the crash of a military aircraft in Indiana. The matter ended with a consent injunction. Rule 8.5(a) subjects to the disciplinary authority of a jurisdiction any lawyer who "provides or offers to provide any legal services in this jurisdiction." Out-of-state lawyers may also be subject to long-arm civil jurisdiction, which subjects them to suits by clients or third persons. Wendt v. Horowitz, 822 So. 2d 1252 (Fla. 2002) (state can assert jurisdiction over Michigan lawyer and his firm based on their sending communications into Florida even though they never physically entered state).

Long-arm discipline is, however, only a partial solution to a state's interest in protecting its residents and its justice system because a state may not suspend or revoke the license of a lawyer who is not admitted to its bar. These are the most formidable sanctions. Only if the lawyer's home state agrees to give the host state's decisions full faith and credit will the host state be able to impose the full range of sanctions and be more amenable to multijurisdictional practice. Rule 22D of the ABA's Model Rules for Lawyer Disciplinary Enforcement does propose something approaching full faith and credit for disciplinary sanctions (called "reciprocal discipline"), but even it contains four exceptions, one of which is that the "discipline imposed would result in grave injustice or be offensive to the public policy of the jurisdiction."

The question of when an out-of-state lawyer is guilty of unauthorized law practice *in* another state dramatically captured the bar's attention after the California Supreme Court's surprising 1998 decision in Birbrower, Montalbano, Condon & Frank, P.C. v. Superior Court, set out below. The Birbrower firm's work in California was in connection with an impending arbitration there that never took place. Lawyers who engage in transactional work or in dispute resolution that occurs in nonjudicial forums are at greater risk of UPL claims than are lawyers who litigate in court. This is because litigators can request judges to grant them temporary admission to a court's bar for purposes of trying a particular case. Pro hac vice admission, which translates to "for this turn," is discussed below. But even litigators have a problem. The legal work they do in a state may precede filing an action or any request for temporary admission (which may never occcur). Also, lawyers may do legal work in one state for litigation in another state. And lawyers may engage in alternate dispute resolution (like arbitration) in a host state. ADR tribunals have not ordinarily had the power to grant pro hac vice admission. In each of these situations, are the lawyers violating UPL laws?

As you work through this material, keep in mind the several risks lawyers face when they provide unauthorized legal services in jurisdictions where they are not admitted. These risks include criminal prosecution (rare, but it happens), discipline, contempt, injunction, disqualification, and, most common, loss of a fee for the unauthorized work. Think about whether the United States of the twenty-first century needs another way to regulate lawyers, one more compatible with its national economy, and if so what it might be.

We begin with Leis v. Flynt, the culmination of Hustler publisher Larry Flynt's failed effort to retain two New York lawyers to defend him in an Ohio obscenity prosecution. The Supreme Court held that the lawyers had no constitutional right to gain pro hac vice admission. It did not address the rights of clients, which are broader and the subject of both Justice Stevens's dissenting tour of the role of out-of-state lawyers in American history and the ensuing note. Although *Leis* is an important event in the law of interstate practice (and state power to curtail it), you should know that trial judges (especially in federal court) are generous in admitting lawyers pro hac vice if they are in good standing elsewhere, although many courts require the lawyer to associate with local counsel. (What's the valid reason for that requirement? Surely, giving local lawyers a fee is not a valid reason.) *Leis* gives us no indication of why Larry Flynt's New York lawyers encountered resistance in the Ohio trial court. The *Leis* majority didn't require a reason, let alone a good one.

For further reading on rules governing lawyers who practice in other jurisdictions, see Andrew Perlman, A Bar Against Competition: The Unconstitutionality of Admission Rules for Out-of-State Lawyers, 18 Geo. J. Legal Ethics 135 (2004) (arguing that the "protectionism" evidenced by certain hurdles on admission of out-of-state lawyers violates "the Article IV Privileges and Immunities Clause, the Fourteenth Amendment Privileges or Immunities Clause, and the dormant Commerce Clause"); Stephen Gillers, Lessons from the Multijurisdictional Practice Commission: The Art of Making Change, 44 Ariz. L. Rev. 685 (2002); Charles Wolfram, Sneaking Around in the Legal Profession: Interjurisdictional Unauthorized Practice by Transactional Lawyers, 36 S. Tex. L. Rev. 665 (1995); and Carol Needham, Negotiating Multi-state Transactions: Reflections on Prohibiting the Unauthorized Practice of Law, 12 St. Louis U. Pub. L. Rev. 113 (1993).

1. Admissions Pro Hac Vice

LEIS v. FLYNT
439 U.S. 438 (1979)

PER CURIAM.

Petitioners, the judges of the Court of Common Pleas of Hamilton County, Ohio, and the Hamilton County prosecutor, seek relief from a decision of the United States Court of Appeals for the Sixth Circuit. The Court of Appeals upheld a Federal District Court injunction that forbids further prosecution of respondents Larry Flynt and Hustler Magazine, Inc., until respondents Herald Fahringer and Paul Cambria are tendered a hearing on their applications to appear pro hac vice in the Court of Common Pleas on behalf of Flynt and Hustler Magazine. Petitioners contend that the asserted right of an out-of-state lawyer to appear pro hac vice in an Ohio court does not fall among those interests protected by the Due Process Clause of the Fourteenth Amendment. Because we agree with this contention, we grant the petition for certiorari and reverse the judgment of the Sixth Circuit.

Flynt and Hustler Magazine were indicted on February 8, 1977, for multiple violations of Ohio Rev. Code Ann. §2907.31 (1975), which prohibits the dissemination of harmful material to minors. . . .

As this Court has observed on numerous occasions, the Constitution does not create property interests. Rather it extends various procedural safeguards to certain interests "that stem from an independent source such as state law." The Court of Appeals evidently believed that an out-of-state lawyer's interest in appearing pro hac vice in an Ohio court stems from some such independent source. It cited no state-law authority for this proposition, however, and indeed noted that "Ohio has no specific standards regarding pro hac vice admissions. . . ." Rather the court referred to the prevalence of pro hac vice practice in American courts and instances in our history where counsel appearing pro hac vice have rendered distinguished service. We do not question that the practice of courts in most States is to allow an out-of-state lawyer the privilege of appearing upon motion, especially when he is associated with a member of the local bar. In view of the high mobility of the bar, and also the trend toward specialization, perhaps this is a practice to be encouraged. But it is not a right granted either by statute or the Constitution. Since the founding of the Republic, the licensing and regulation of lawyers has been left exclusively to the States and the District of Columbia within their respective jurisdictions. The States prescribe the qualifications for admission to practice and the standards of professional conduct. They also are responsible for the discipline of lawyers.[4]

A claim of entitlement under state law, to be enforceable, must be derived from statute or legal rule or through a mutually explicit understanding. The record here is devoid of any indication that an out-of-state lawyer may claim such an entitlement in Ohio, where the rules of the Ohio Supreme Court expressly consign the authority to approve a pro hac vice appearance to the discretion of the trial court. Even if, as the Court of Appeals believed, respondents Fahringer and Cambria had "reasonable expectations of professional service," they have not shown the requisite *mutual* understanding that they would be permitted to represent their clients in any particular case in the Ohio courts. The speculative claim that Fahringer's and Cambria's reputation might suffer as the result of the denial of their asserted right cannot by itself make out an injury to a constitutionally protected interest. There simply was no deprivation here of some right previously held under state law.

Nor is there a basis for the argument that the interest in appearing pro hac vice has its source in federal law. There is no right of federal origin that permits such lawyers to appear in state courts without meeting that State's bar admission requirements. This Court, on several occasions, has sustained state bar rules that excluded out-of-state counsel from practice altogether or on a case-by-case basis. These decisions recognize that the Constitution does not require that because a lawyer has been admitted to the bar of one State, he or she must be allowed to practice in another. Accordingly, because Fahringer and Cambria did not possess a cognizable property interest within the terms of the Fourteenth Amendment, the Constitution does not obligate the Ohio courts to accord them procedural due process in passing on their application for permission to appear pro hac vice before the Court of Common Pleas of Hamilton County.[5]

---

4. The dissenting opinion relies heavily on dictum in Spanos v. Skouras Theatres Corp., 364 F.2d 161 (2d Cir. 1966). The facts of that case were different from those here, and the precise holding of the court was quite narrow. The court ruled that where a client sought to defend on the ground of illegality against an out-of-state attorney's action for his fee, and where the illegality stemmed entirely from the failure of the client's in-state attorneys to obtain leave for the out-of-state attorney to appear in Federal District Court, the client would not be allowed to escape from the contract through his own default. Id., at 168-169. The balance of the opinion, which declared that "under the privileges and immunities clause of the Constitution no state can prohibit a citizen with a federal claim or defense from engaging an out-of-state lawyer to collaborate with an in-state lawyer and give legal advice concerning it within the state," id., at 170, must be considered to have been limited, if not rejected entirely, by Norfolk & Western R. Co. v. Beatty, 423 U.S. 1009 (1975).

The dissenting opinion also suggests that a client's interest in having out-of-state counsel is implicated by this decision. The court below, however, "did not reach the issue of whether the constitutional rights of Flynt and Hustler Magazine had also been violated," 574 F.2d 874, 877 (6th Cir. 1978), recognizing as it did that a federal court injunction enjoining a state criminal [proceeding] would conflict with this Court's holding in Younger v. Harris, 401 U.S. 37 (1971).

5. The dissenting opinion of Justice Stevens argues that a lawyer's right to "pursu[e] his calling is protected by the Due Process Clause . . . when he crosses the border" of the State that licensed him. Justice Stevens identifies two "protected" interests that "reinforce" each other. These are said

The petition for writ of certiorari is granted, the judgment of the Sixth Circuit is reversed, and the case is remanded for further proceedings consistent with this opinion.

It is so ordered.

JUSTICE WHITE would grant certiorari and set the case for oral argument.

JUSTICE STEVENS, with whom JUSTICE BRENNAN and JUSTICE MARSHALL join, dissenting.

A lawyer's interest in pursuing his calling is protected by the Due Process Clause of the Fourteenth Amendment. The question presented by this case is whether a lawyer abandons that protection when he crosses the border of the State which issued his license to practice.

The Court holds that a lawyer has no constitutionally protected interest in his out-of-state practice. In its view, the interest of the lawyer is so trivial that a judge has no obligation to give any consideration whatsoever to the merits of a pro hac vice request, or to give the lawyer any opportunity to advance reasons in support of his application. The Court's square holding is that the Due Process Clause of the Fourteenth Amendment simply does not apply to this kind of ruling by a state trial judge.[2]

---

to be "the 'nature' of the interest in pro hac vice admissions [and] the 'implicit promise' inhering in Ohio custom."

The first of these lawyers' "interests" is described as that of "discharging [his] responsibility for the fair administration of justice in our adversary system." As important as this interest is, the suggestion that the Constitution assures the right of a lawyer to practice in the court of every State is a novel one, not supported by any authority brought to our attention. Such an asserted right flies in the face of the traditional authority of state courts to control who may be admitted to practice before them. If accepted, the constitutional rule advanced by the dissenting opinion would prevent those States that have chosen to bar all pro hac vice appearances from continuing to do so, and would undermine the policy of those States which do not extend reciprocity to out-of-state lawyers.

The second ground for due process protection identified in the dissenting opinion is the "implicit promise" inherent in Ohio's past practice in "assur[ing] out-of-state practitioners that they are welcome in Ohio's courts. . . ." We recall no other claim that a constitutional right can be created — as if by estoppel — merely because a wholly and *expressly* discretionary state privilege has been granted generously in the past. That some courts, in setting the standards for admission *within their jurisdiction*, have required a showing of cause before denying leave to appear pro hac vice provides no support for the proposition that the Constitution imposes this "cause" requirement on state courts that have chosen to reject it.

2. Although the Court does not address it, this case also presents the question whether a defendant's interest in representation by nonresident counsel is entitled to any constitutional protection. The clients, as well as the lawyers, are parties to this litigation. Moreover, the Ohio trial judge made it perfectly clear that his ruling was directed at the defendants, and not merely their counsel. . . .

A defendant's interest in adequate representation is "perhaps his most important privilege" protected by the Constitution. Powell v. Alabama, 287 U.S. 45, 70 [1932]. Whatever the scope of a lawyer's interest in practicing in other States may be, Judge Friendly is surely correct in stating that the client's interest in representation by out-of-state counsel is entitled to some measure of constitutional protection:

> We are persuaded, however, that where a right has been conferred on citizens by federal law, the constitutional guarantee against its abridgement must be read to include what is necessary and appropriate for its assertion. In an age of increased specialization and high mobility of the bar, this must comprehend the right to bring to the assistance of an attorney admitted in the resident state a lawyer licensed by "public act" of any other state who is thought best fitted for the task, and to allow him to serve in whatever manner is most effective, subject only to valid rules of courts as to practice before them. Indeed, in instances where the federal claim or defense is unpopular, advice and assistance by an out-of-state lawyer may be the only means available for vindication. [Spanos v. Skouras Theatres, 364 F.2d 161, 170 (en banc) (2d Cir. 1966).]

The premises for this holding can be briefly stated. A nonresident lawyer has no right, as a matter of either state or federal law, to appear in an Ohio court. Absent any such enforceable entitlement, based on an explicit rule or mutual understanding, the lawyer's interest in making a pro hac vice appearance is a mere "privilege" that Ohio may grant or withhold in the unrestrained discretion of individual judges. The conclusion that a lawyer has no constitutional protection against a capricious exclusion seems so obvious to the majority that argument of the question is unnecessary. Summary reversal is the order of the day. . . .

I

The notion that a state trial judge has arbitrary and unlimited power to refuse a nonresident lawyer permission to appear in his courtroom is nothing but a remnant of a bygone era. Like the body of rules that once governed parole, the nature of law practice has undergone a metamorphosis during the past century. Work that was once the exclusive province of the lawyer is now performed by title companies, real estate brokers, corporate trust departments, and accountants. Rules of ethics that once insulated the local lawyer from competition are now forbidden by the Sherman Act and by the First Amendment to the Constitution of the United States. Interstate law practice and multistate law firms are now commonplace. Federal questions regularly arise in state criminal trials and permeate the typical lawyer's practice. Because the assertion of federal claims or defenses is often unpopular, "advice and assistance by an out-of-state lawyer may be the only means available for vindication." The "increased specialization and high mobility" of today's Bar is a consequence of the dramatic change in the demand for legal services that has occurred during the past century.

History attests to the importance of pro hac vice appearances. As Judge Merritt, writing for the Court of Appeals, explained:

> Nonresident lawyers have appeared in many of our most celebrated cases. For example, Andrew Hamilton, a leader of the Philadelphia bar, defended John Peter Zenger in New York in 1735 in colonial America's most famous freedom-of-speech case. Clarence Darrow appeared in many states to plead the cause of an unpopular client, including the famous *Scopes* trial in Tennessee where he opposed another well-known, out-of-state lawyer, William Jennings Bryan. Great lawyers from Alexander Hamilton and Daniel Webster to Charles Evans Hughes and John W. Davis were specially admitted for the trial of important cases in other states. A small group of lawyers appearing pro hac vice inspired and initiated the civil rights movement in its early stages. In a series of cases brought in courts throughout the South, out-of-state lawyers Thurgood Marshall, Constance Motley and Spottswood Robinson, before their appointments to the federal bench, developed the legal principles which gave rise to the civil rights movement. . . .

The modern examples identified by Judge Merritt, though more illustrious than the typical pro hac vice appearance, are not rare exceptions to a general custom of excluding nonresident lawyers from local practice. On the contrary, appearances by out-of-state counsel have been routine throughout the country for at least a quarter of a century. The custom is so well recognized that, as Judge Friendly observed in 1966, there "is not the slightest reason to suppose" that a qualified lawyer's pro hac vice request will be denied.

This case involves a pro hac vice application by qualified legal specialists; no legitimate reason for denying their request is suggested by the record. They had been retained to defend an unpopular litigant in a trial that might be affected by local prejudices and attitudes. It is the classic situation in which the interests of justice would be served by allowing the defendant to be represented by counsel of his choice.

The interest these lawyers seek to vindicate is not merely the pecuniary goal that motivates every individual's attempt to pursue his calling. It is the profession's interest in discharging its responsibility for the fair administration of justice in our adversary system. The nature of that interest is surely worthy of the protection afforded by the Due Process Clause of the Fourteenth Amendment.

II

In the past, Ohio has implicitly assured out-of-state practitioners that they are welcome in Ohio's courts unless there is a valid, articulable reason for excluding them. Although the Ohio Supreme Court dismissed respondents' petition for an extraordinary writ of mandamus in this case, it has not dispelled that assurance because it did not purport to pass on the merits of their claim. In my opinion the State's assurance is adequate to create an interest that qualifies as "property" within the meaning of the Due Process Clause.

The District Court found as a fact that Ohio trial judges routinely permit out-of-state counsel to appear pro hac vice. This regular practice is conducted pursuant to the Rules of the Supreme Court of Ohio, Ohio's Code of Professional Responsibility, rules of each local court, and a leading opinion of the Ohio Court of Appeals identifying criteria that should inform a trial judge's discretion in acting on pro hac vice applications. While it is unquestionably true that an Ohio trial judge has broad discretion in determining whether or not to allow nonresident lawyers to appear in his court, it is also true that the Ohio rules, precedents, and practice give out-of-state lawyers an unequivocal expectation that the exercise of that discretion will be based on permissible reasons. . . .

III

Either the "nature" of the interest in pro hac vice admissions or the "implicit promise" inhering in Ohio custom with respect to those admissions is sufficient to create an interest protected by the Due Process Clause. Moreover, each of these conclusions reinforces the other.

The mode of analysis employed by the Court in recent years has treated the Fourteenth Amendment concepts of "liberty" and "property" as though they defined mutually exclusive, and closed categories of interests, with neither shedding any light on the meaning of the other. Indeed, in some of the Court's recent opinions it has implied that not only property but liberty itself does not exist apart from specific state authorization or an express guarantee in the Bill of Rights. In my judgment this is not the way the majestic language of the Fourteenth Amendment should be read.

Justice Stevens's dissent explains the interest in allowing a client to hire an out-of-state lawyer. (The constitutional strength of that interest is another matter.) Out-of-state lawyers were especially important in the 1960s, when northern lawyers went south to do civil rights work. For a striking case illustrating the need for those lawyers at the time and the efforts by prosecutors and local judges to impede them (including by arrest), see Sobol v. Perez, 289 F. Supp. 392 (E.D. La. 1968), cited in the dissent. Here's a snapshot.

Richard Sobol, an Arnold & Porter lawyer who was not admitted in Louisiana, went to the state in the mid-1960s. Sobol worked alongside lawyers admitted in Louisiana. Leander Perez was the powerful district attorney of Plaquemines Parish, where Sobol was doing some of his work. Sobol was about to appear in state court for Gary Duncan, a black man charged with assault. (Gary Duncan's case would later result in the Supreme Court decision applying the Sixth Amendment's jury trial right to the states.) Eugene Leon, the state judge hearing Duncan's case, told Daryl Bubrig, the assistant district attorney, of Sobol's imminent appearance in his court. After Bubrig alerted Perez, "Perez signed a bill of information charging Sobol with practicing law without a license." When Sobol appeared, Judge Leon "issued a bench warrant for [his] arrest." In other words, the judge and the prosecutors cooperated to impede Sobol's civil rights work. As the federal court described the situation in its ruling on Sobol's request for an injunction against prosecution:

> Shortly after leaving the Judge's chambers and while still in the courthouse Sobol was arrested and charged with practicing law without a license. Sobol was incarcerated in the Plaquemines Parish Prison for approximately four hours. He was fingerprinted and photographed several times, his belt and tie were taken away, and his brief case containing all the Duncan case papers was taken over his objection. Bail was set at $1500.00, without his ever appearing before the Judge in regard to it, and Sobol was released upon posting that bond later in the day on February 21, 1967.

In enjoining the prosecution, the court concluded:

> The circumstances surrounding the arrest and charge against Sobol, and the course of the Duncan case, convince us that Sobol was prosecuted only because he was a civil rights lawyer forcefully representing a Negro in a case growing out of the desegregation of the Plaquemines Parish school system.
> . . .
> This prosecution was meant to show Sobol that civil rights lawyers were not welcome in the parish, and that their defense of the Negroes involved in cases growing out of civil rights efforts would not be tolerated. It was meant also as a warning to other civil rights lawyers and to Negroes in the parish who might consider retaining civil rights lawyers to advance their rights to equal opportunity and equal treatment under the Equal Protection Clause of the Fourteenth Amendment.

Recall that Justice Stevens's *Leis* dissent is cited with approval in Justice Powell's majority opinion in *Piper* (holding that a Vermont resident had the right to seek admission to the New Hampshire bar by taking its bar examination) for the proposition that in "some cases, representation by nonresident counsel may be the only means available for the vindication of federal rights" (page 638). But Justice Powell also distinguished *Leis* in *Piper* on the ground that the nonresident who seeks to join a state's bar, unlike the pro hac vice applicant, "must have the same professional and personal qualifications required of resident lawyers" and "is subject to the full force of [the state's] disciplinary rules." How significant are these distinctions?

What About the Client's Interests?

Leis v. Flynt addressed the interests of lawyers. The defendants could not seek federal relief because of the *Younger* abstention doctrine (see note 4 of the majority opinion). Would the defendants have had superior interests? Ford v. Israel, 701 F.2d 689 (7th Cir. 1983), hovered around this question but did not answer it directly. Ford was charged with murder in a Wisconsin state court. He was indigent, but his parents had retained a Chicago lawyer (Grant) to represent him. Wisconsin, however, had a rule that required all nonresident counsel to appear with local counsel. The public defender (Rosen) offered to serve as local counsel, cost free, but the state court ruled that Ford would have to pay for local counsel if he was going to pay for an out-of-state lawyer to try the case. Ford's parents refused to put up the additional money, the Chicago lawyer withdrew, and Rosen was appointed to represent Ford, who was convicted. In a habeas proceeding, Ford challenged the local rule. Judge Posner, rejecting the challenge, acknowledged that it "has about it the air of a guild restriction and may for all we know be motivated by a desire to increase the fees of Wisconsin lawyers." But it wasn't an arbitrary rule, Judge Posner said, and was in fact "less arbitrary in a criminal than in a civil case." Here is why:

> It is a favorite tactic of an unsuccessful criminal defendant to complain, on appeal or in a habeas corpus proceeding, that he did not have effective assistance of counsel at trial; and if his only trial counsel was from out of state, and made errors of criminal procedure that a local counsel would not have made, a basis is laid for a colorable complaint of ineffective assistance of counsel. If as Ford contends Wisconsin must in every criminal case waive its rule requiring retention of local counsel, criminal defendants will find it easier to draw out the proceedings against them by complaining that they were denied effective assistance of counsel — a complaint that can be raised against retained as well as appointed counsel and is judged under the same standards in both types of cases. Cuyler v. Sullivan, 446 U.S. 335, 344-345 (1980). In the present case, it is true, local counsel — Rosen — was willing to serve without fee, and if he had been allowed to do so Ford would have had the counsel of his choice. But Rosen is paid by the state, so it would have meant giving a man who had retained one lawyer another free of charge. The state was not required to do that. The choice was Grant or Rosen; and the state had a reason why it could not be Grant.

So Ford may have had a right to hire out-of-state counsel but Wisconsin had a right to insist on in-state co-counsel. Result: Ford lost. One judge dissented.

Fuller had local counsel to represent him in his criminal case in a New Jersey state court, but he also wanted help from two nonresident lawyers. The trial judge rejected their pro hac vice admission, and Fuller was convicted. In habeas, the Third Circuit held that Fuller had a Sixth Amendment right to out-of-state counsel that could not be arbitrarily denied. The "trial court's wooden approach and its failure to make record-supported findings balancing the right to counsel with the demands of the administration of justice resulted in an arbitrary denial of Fuller's motion." The writ was granted with no requirement that Fuller show harm. Fuller v. Diesslin, 868 F.2d 604 (3d Cir. 1989). See also United States v. Lillie, 989 F.2d 1054 (9th Cir. 1993) overruled on other grounds, United States v. Garrett, 179 F.3d 1143 (9th Cir. 1999) (right to counsel of choice includes right to out-of-state lawyer); United States v. Collins, 920 F.2d 619 (10th Cir. 1990) ("denial of admission pro hac vice in criminal cases implicates the constitutional right to counsel of choice"). United States v. Ries, 100 F.3d 1469 (9th Cir. 1996), using an abuse of discretion standard, upholds a trial judge's refusal of pro hac vice admission in view of the lawyer's identified failures to comply with judicial orders or local rules.

Despite *Leis*'s rejection of the alternate holding in Spanos v. Skouras Theatres Corp. (note 4), some federal courts have continued to recognize a litigant's interest in employing an out-of-state lawyer in a civil matter. Roma Construction Co. v. aRusso, 96 F.3d 566 (1st Cir. 1996) ("where the plaintiffs identified specific, logical reasons for their request, we conclude that the district court's decision [not to admit a second pro hac vice attorney] amounts to an abuse of discretion"). The Eleventh Circuit has gone even further. "Absent a showing of unethical conduct rising to a level that would justify disbarment, the [district] court *must* admit the attorney." Schlumberger Technologies, Inc. v. Wiley, 113 F.3d 1553 (11th Cir. 1997) (emphasis in original).

Lawyers who have been admitted pro hac vice have a right to notice and an opportunity to respond before the status may be revoked. Martens v. Thomann, 273 F.3d 159 (2d Cir. 2001) ("pro hac vice counsel are entitled to the same notice and opportunity to be heard as are admitted counsel prior to being sanctioned"); Kirkland v. National Mortgage Network, Inc., 884 F.2d 1367 (11th Cir. 1989) (once granted, pro hac vice status is a property interest). Revocation of the status is in the discretion of the trial court. Conduct that may warrant revocation includes disregard of a trial judge's rulings, failure to maintain due respect, and violation of local rules of professional conduct. Filppula-McArthur v. Halloin, 622 N.W.2d 436 (Wis. 2001).

2.   *Services Other Than Litigation*

"Local Office, National Practice"

"I was asked to explain my specialty and situation to illustrate a problem for this book. For obvious reasons, I am not going to tell you my real name or where I work. Let's just call me Jill.

"I have a most unusual practice. I represent highly paid executives in negotiations of their compensation packages, usually when they change jobs or get promoted. Even with the current financial crisis (I'm writing in fall 2008) and widespread anger at highly compensated corporate officers, my practice is doing well. The need I fill will always be there.

"I kind of fell into this 19 years ago when a friend asked me to help her mother, who was taking a new position and needed to negotiate terms. That client was a midlevel corporate executive whose entire compensation package was worth maybe $350,000 annually in today's dollars. Many issues are the same even when you add a zero or even two zeroes. These include salary, bonus, triggers for additional compensation based on performance, deferred compensation, tax advice, entertainment accounts, separation clauses (a/k/a "golden parachutes"), and such things as personal shoppers, drivers, use of the company plane, and financial consultants for individual investments. Anyway, I did a good job for my friend's mother, word got around, I got more of this business, and now that's all I do.

"Funny, isn't it? Many of my friends came to their specialty in the same accidental way. I tell my children that beyond talent and a willingness to work hard, success is one-third luck, one-third recognizing luck when it happens, and (maybe most important) one-third resilience in the face of adversity. My screen saver has that quote from Shakespeare, "Sweet are the uses of adversity."

"Anyway, my office is in State X, but my clients are all over the country. I handle their work from my office, using fax, e-mail, phone, and express mail. Sometimes I meet them in their home cities, which is not necessarily the same city as the prospective employer's office. But sometimes it is.

"I have a very tasteful Web site just so people who have heard about me and want to contact me know how. If you Google my name, the Web site comes up first. The work I do for a client is, first, negotiate terms, then I draft the agreement along with the lawyers representing the company. The agreement often says whose law will govern in the event of a dispute, and that's usually the law of the place where the company is located or is incorporated. Almost always, the company pays my fee. In fact, that's a term for which I negotiate. I get my client's approval first, of course, but no client has ever said he would rather pay my fee himself. It can be $150,000 or more because the negotiations and drafting can take months.

"I'm admitted only in X, but I don't think of myself as an X lawyer. My practice is national. In fact, only three times in 19 years were my clients or their employers in X. When I was asked to describe my work for this problem, I was told it was in connection with the *Birbrower* case. I had never heard of that case (I'm not in California). I have since read it. I think it's an awful opinion and totally out of touch with the real world of law practice in the twenty-first century. It reflects a nineteenth-century mindset. I would have expected more realism from that court. I understand that new rules in California have limited its effect, but I don't think they go far enough. So now I'm worried. More than 10 percent of my business takes me to California. Is there anything wrong with what I'm doing under the new rules or under the ABA rule on cross-border practice, Rule 5.5? Is there something I should be doing differently to protect myself?"

The problem of out-of-state practice becomes complex, seemingly intractable, when the lawyer, like our pseudonymous Jill, does not go into court for the client and so cannot be admitted pro hac vice. There is no logical reason (but plenty of practical ones) why states could not create a category of pro hac vice admission for nonlitigation services and few have tried. Pro hac vice admission in court is limited to a pending case. How can we define the scope of pro hac vice admission for out-of-court services? Pro hac vice admission in court envisions a judge who will oversee the out-of-state lawyer's behavior, but equivalent oversight is hardly feasible for out-of-court work. Many lawyers responded to *Birbrower* with shock, first, because what the lawyers there did is common in this highly mobile age; second, because while it appears that the regulatory authorities in California demonstrated no concern with the firm's conduct, the client was nonetheless permitted to use an unauthorized law practice claim as a way to avoid paying a fee; third, because the court held, contrary to what many lawyers believe, that the Birbrower lawyers could not have protected themselves under state law by associating with local counsel; and fourth, and perhaps most alarming, because the court said that the lawyers would be guilty of UPL in California solely through their "virtual" presence in the state from their New York office, via phone, fax, e-mail, or satellite.

BIRBROWER, MONTALBANO, CONDON & FRANK, P.C. v. SUPERIOR COURT
17 Cal. 4th 119, 949 P.2d 1, 70 Cal. Rptr. 2d 304 (1998), cert. denied, 525 U.S. 920 (1998)

CHIN, J.

Business and Professions Code section 6125 states: "No person shall practice law in California unless the person is an active member of the State Bar." We must decide whether an out-of-state law firm, not licensed to practice law in this state, violated section 6125 when it performed legal services in California for a California-based client under a fee agreement stipulating that California law would govern all matters in the representation.

Although we are aware of the interstate nature of modern law practice and mindful of the reality that large firms often conduct activities and serve clients in several states, we do not believe these facts excuse law firms from complying with section 6125. Contrary to the Court of Appeal, however, we do not believe the Legislature intended section 6125 to apply to those services an out-of-state firm renders in its home state. We therefore conclude that, to the extent defendant law firm Birbrower, Montalbano, Condon & Frank, P.C. (Birbrower), practiced law in California without a license, it engaged in the unauthorized practice of law in this state (§6125). We also conclude that Birbrower's fee agreement with real party in interest ESQ Business Services, Inc. (ESQ), is invalid to the extent it authorizes payment for the substantial legal services Birbrower performed in California. If, however, Birbrower can show it generated fees under its agreement for limited services it performed in New York, and it earned those fees under the otherwise invalid fee agreement, it may, on remand, present to the trial court evidence justifying its recovery of fees for those New York services. Conversely, ESQ will have an opportunity to produce contrary evidence. Accordingly, we affirm the Court of Appeal judgment in part and reverse it in part, remanding for further proceedings consistent with this opinion.

I. Background

The facts with respect to the unauthorized practice of law question are essentially undisputed. Birbrower is a professional law corporation incorporated in New York, with its principal place of business in New York. During 1992 and 1993, Birbrower attorneys, defendants Kevin F. Hobbs and Thomas A. Condon (Hobbs and Condon), performed substantial work in California relating to the law firm's representation of ESQ. Neither Hobbs nor Condon has ever been licensed to practice law in California. None of Birbrower's attorneys were licensed to practice law in California during Birbrower's ESQ representation.

ESQ is a California corporation with its principal place of business in Santa Clara County. In July 1992, the parties negotiated and executed the fee agreement in New York, providing that Birbrower would perform legal services for ESQ, including "All matters pertaining to the investigation of and prosecution of all claims and causes of action against Tandem Computers Incorporated [Tandem]." The "claims and causes of action" against Tandem, a Delaware corporation with its principal place of business in Santa Clara County, California, related to a software development and marketing contract between Tandem and ESQ dated March 16, 1990 (Tandem Agreement). The Tandem Agreement stated that "The internal laws of the State of California (irrespective of its choice of law principles) shall govern the validity of this Agreement, the construction of its terms, and the interpretation and enforcement of the rights and duties of the parties hereto." Birbrower asserts, and ESQ disputes, that ESQ knew Birbrower was not licensed to practice law in California.

While representing ESQ, Hobbs and Condon traveled to California on several occasions. In August 1992, they met in California with ESQ and its accountants. During these meetings, Hobbs and Condon discussed various matters related to ESQ's dispute with Tandem and strategy for resolving the dispute. They made recommendations and gave advice. During this California trip, Hobbs and Condon also met with Tandem representatives on four or five occasions during a two-day period. At the meetings, Hobbs and Condon spoke on ESQ's behalf. Hobbs demanded that Tandem pay ESQ $15 million. Condon told Tandem he believed that damages would exceed $15 million if the parties litigated the dispute.

Around March or April 1993, Hobbs, Condon, and another Birbrower attorney visited California to interview potential arbitrators and to meet again with ESQ and its accountants. Birbrower had previously filed a demand for arbitration against Tandem with the San Francisco offices of the American Arbitration Association (AAA). In August 1993, Hobbs returned to California to assist ESQ in settling the Tandem matter. While in California, Hobbs met with ESQ and its accountants to discuss a proposed settlement agreement Tandem authored. Hobbs also met with Tandem representatives to discuss possible changes in the proposed agreement. Hobbs gave ESQ legal advice during this trip, including his opinion that ESQ should not settle with Tandem on the terms proposed.

ESQ eventually settled the Tandem dispute, and the matter never went to arbitration.

[ESQ and the Birbrower firm had a falling out, with the client alleging malpractice and the firm suing for its fee. ESQ claimed that the firm could not collect a fee because of its unauthorized practice. The court pointed out that the parties initially had a contingent fee agreement that was then changed to a flat fee. But while the firm was not clear about which agreement it wished to enforce, nothing turned on it. In California, nearly all fee arrangements must be in writing and here both were.

[In a footnote, the court wrote that, contrary to the trial court's "implied assumption, no statutory exception to section 6125 allows out-of-state attorneys to practice law in California as long as they associate local counsel. . . ." This statement was surprising because it was unnecessary to the decision. Birbrower did not associate with local counsel.

[The lower court refused to enforce the fee agreement but left open the possibility that the firm could collect in quantum meruit without specifying the work that could be so compensated. The court of appeal agreed.]

We granted review to determine whether Birbrower's actions and services performed while representing ESQ in California constituted the unauthorized practice of law under section 6125 and, if so, whether a section 6125 violation rendered the fee agreement wholly unenforceable.

II. Discussion
A. The Unauthorized Practice of Law

The California Legislature enacted section 6125 in 1927 as part of the State Bar Act (the Act), a comprehensive scheme regulating the practice of law in the state. Since the Act's passage, the general rule has been that, although persons may represent themselves and their own interests regardless of State Bar membership, no one but an active member of the State Bar may practice law for another person in California. The prohibition against unauthorized law practice is within the state's police power and is designed to ensure that those performing legal services do so competently.

A violation of section 6125 is a misdemeanor. Moreover, "No one may recover compensation for services as an attorney at law in this state unless [the person] was at the time the services were performed a member of The State Bar."

Although the Act did not define the term "practice law," case law explained it as " 'the doing and performing services in a court of justice in any matter depending therein throughout its various stages and in conformity with the adopted rules of procedure.' " (People v. Merchants Protective Corp. (1922) 189 Cal. 531, 535 [209 P. 363] (Merchants).) *Merchants* included in its definition legal advice and legal instrument and contract preparation, whether or not these subjects were rendered in the course of litigation. . . .

In addition to not defining the term "practice law," the Act also did not define the meaning of "in California." In today's legal practice, questions often arise concerning whether the phrase refers to the nature of the legal services, or restricts the Act's application to those out-of-state attorneys who are physically present in the state.

Section 6125 has generated numerous opinions on the meaning of "practice law" but none on the meaning of "in California." In our view, the practice of law "in California" entails sufficient contact with the California client to render the nature of the legal service a clear legal representation. In addition to a quantitative analysis, we must consider the nature of the unlicensed lawyer's activities in the state. Mere fortuitous or attenuated contacts will not sustain a finding that the unlicensed lawyer practiced law "in California." The primary inquiry is whether the unlicensed lawyer engaged in sufficient activities in the state, or created a continuing relationship with the California client that included legal duties and obligations.

Our definition does not necessarily depend on or require the unlicensed lawyer's physical presence in the state. Physical presence here is one factor we may consider in deciding whether the unlicensed lawyer has violated section 6125, but it is by no means exclusive. For example, one may practice law in the state in violation of section 6125 although not physically present here by advising a California client on California law in connection with a California legal dispute by telephone, fax, computer, or other modern technological means. Conversely, although we decline to provide a comprehensive list of what activities constitute sufficient contact with the state, we do reject the notion that a person automatically practices law "in California" whenever that person practices California law anywhere, or "virtually" enters the state by telephone, fax, e-mail, or satellite. (See e.g., Baron v. City of Los Angeles (1970) 2 Cal. 3d 535, 543 [86 Cal. Rptr. 673, 469 P.2d 353, 42 A.L.R.3d 1036] (Baron) ["practice law" does not encompass all professional activities].) . . .

This interpretation acknowledges the tension that exists between interjurisdictional practice and the need to have a state-regulated bar. As stated in the American Bar Association Model Code of Professional Responsibility, Ethical Consideration EC 3-9, "Regulation of the practice of law is accomplished principally by the respective states. Authority to engage in the practice of law conferred in any jurisdiction is not per se a grant of the right to practice elsewhere, and it is improper for a lawyer to engage in practice where he is not permitted by law or by court order to do so. However, the demands of business and the mobility of our society pose distinct problems in the regulation of the practice of law by the states. In furtherance of the public interest, the legal profession should discourage regulation that unreasonably imposes territorial limitations upon the right of a lawyer to handle the legal affairs of his client or upon the opportunity of a client to obtain the services of a lawyer of his choice in all matters including the presentation of a contested matter in a tribunal before which the lawyer is not permanently admitted to practice."

If we were to carry the dissent's narrow interpretation of the term "practice law" to its logical conclusion, we would effectively limit section 6125's application to those cases in which nonlicensed out-of-state lawyers appeared in a California courtroom without permission. Clearly, neither *Merchants*, nor *Baron*, supports the dissent's fanciful interpretation of the thoughtful guidelines announced in those cases. Indeed, the dissent's definition of "practice law" ignores *Merchants* altogether, and, in so doing, substantially undermines the Legislature's intent to protect the public from those giving unauthorized legal advice and counsel.

Exceptions to section 6125 do exist, but are generally limited to allowing out-of-state attorneys to make brief appearances before a state court tribunal. They are narrowly drawn and strictly interpreted. For example, an out-of-state attorney not licensed to practice in California may be permitted, by consent of a trial judge, to appear in California in a particular pending action.

In addition, with the permission of the California court in which a particular cause is pending, out-of-state counsel may appear before a court as counsel pro hac vice. A court will approve a pro hac vice application only if the out-of-state attorney is a member in good standing of another state bar and is eligible to practice in any United States court or the highest court in another jurisdiction. The out-of-state attorney must also associate an active member of the California Bar as attorney of record and is subject to the Rules of Professional Conduct of the State Bar.

The Act does not regulate practice before United States courts. Thus, an out-of-state attorney engaged to render services in bankruptcy proceedings was entitled to collect his fee.

Finally, California Rules of Court, rule 988, permits the State Bar to issue registration certificates to foreign legal consultants who may advise on the law of the foreign jurisdiction where they are admitted. These consultants may not, however, appear as attorneys before a California court or judicial officer or otherwise prepare pleadings and instruments in California or give advice on the law of California or any other state or jurisdiction except those where they are admitted.

The Legislature has recognized an exception to section 6125 in international disputes resolved in California under the state's rules for arbitration and conciliation of international commercial disputes. This exception states that in a commercial conciliation in California involving international commercial disputes, "The parties may appear in person or be represented or assisted by any person of their choice. A person assisting or representing a party need not be a member of the legal profession or licensed to practice law in California." Likewise, the Act does not apply to the preparation of or participation in labor negotiations and arbitrations arising under collective bargaining agreements in industries subject to federal law.

B.　THE PRESENT CASE

The undisputed facts here show that neither *Baron*'s definition nor our "sufficient contact" definition of "practice law in California" would excuse Birbrower's extensive practice in this state. Nor would any of the limited statutory exceptions to section 6125 apply to Birbrower's California practice. As the Court of Appeal observed, Birbrower engaged in unauthorized law practice in California on more than a limited basis, and no firm attorney engaged in that practice was an active member of the California State Bar. As noted in 1992 and 1993, Birbrower attorneys traveled to California to discuss with ESQ and others various matters pertaining to the dispute between ESQ and Tandem. Hobbs and Condon discussed strategy for resolving the dispute and advised ESQ on this strategy. Furthermore, during California meetings with Tandem representatives in August 1992, Hobbs demanded Tandem pay $15 million, and Condon told Tandem he believed damages in the matter would exceed that amount if the parties proceeded to litigation. Also in California, Hobbs met with ESQ for the stated purpose of helping to reach a settlement agreement and to discuss the agreement that was eventually proposed. Birbrower attorneys also traveled to California to initiate arbitration proceedings before the matter was settled.

As the Court of Appeal concluded, ". . . the Birbrower firm's in-state activities clearly constituted the [unauthorized] practice of law" in California.

Birbrower contends, however, that section 6125 is not meant to apply to any out-of-state attorneys. Instead, it argues that the statute is intended solely to prevent nonattorneys from practicing law. This contention is without merit because it contravenes the plain language of the statute. Section 6125 clearly states that no person shall practice law in California unless that person is a member of the State Bar. The statute does not differentiate between attorneys or nonattorneys, nor does it excuse a person who is a member of another state bar. . . .

Birbrower next argues that we do not further the statute's intent and purpose — to protect California citizens from incompetent attorneys — by enforcing it against out-of-state attorneys. Birbrower argues that because out-of-state attorneys have been licensed to practice in other jurisdictions, they have already demonstrated sufficient competence to protect California clients. But Birbrower's argument overlooks the obvious fact that other states' laws may differ substantially from California law. Competence in one jurisdiction does not necessarily guarantee competence in another. By applying section 6125 to out-of-state attorneys who engage in the extensive practice of law in California without becoming licensed in our state, we serve the statute's goal of assuring the competence of all attorneys practicing law in this state. . . .

Assuming that section 6125 does apply to out-of-state attorneys not licensed here, Birbrower alternatively asks us to create an exception to section 6125 for work incidental to private arbitration or other alternative dispute resolution proceedings. Birbrower points to fundamental differences between private arbitration and legal proceedings, including procedural differences relating to discovery, rules of evidence, compulsory process, cross-examination of witnesses, and other areas. As Birbrower observes, in light of these differences, at least one court has decided that an out-of-state attorney could recover fees for services rendered in an arbitration proceeding. (See Williamson v. John D. Quinn Const. Corp. (S.D.N.Y. 1982) 537 F.Supp. 613, 616 (*Williamson*).)

In *Williamson*, a New Jersey law firm was employed by a client's New York law firm to defend a construction contract arbitration in New York. It sought to recover fees solely related to the arbitration proceedings, even though the attorney who did the work was not licensed in New York, nor was the firm authorized to practice in the state. In allowing the New Jersey firm to recover its arbitration fees, the federal district court concluded that an arbitration tribunal is not a court of record, and its fact-finding process is not similar to a court's process. The court relied on a local state bar report concluding that representing a client in an arbitration was not the unauthorized practice of law. But as amicus curiae the State Bar of California observes, "While in *Williamson* the federal district court did allow the New Jersey attorneys to recover their fees, that decision clearly is distinguishable on its facts. . . . [¶] In the instant case, it is undisputed that none of the time that the New York attorneys spent in California was" spent in arbitration; *Williamson* thus carries limited weight. . . .

We decline Birbrower's invitation to craft an arbitration exception to section 6125's prohibition of the unlicensed practice of law in this state. Any exception for arbitration is best left to the Legislature, which has the authority to determine qualifications for admission to the State Bar and to decide what constitutes the practice of law. Even though the Legislature has spoken with respect to international arbitration and conciliation, it has not enacted a similar rule for private arbitration proceedings. Of course, private arbitration and other alternative dispute resolution practices are important aspects of our justice system. Section 6125, however, articulates a strong public policy favoring the practice of law in California by licensed State Bar members. In the face of the Legislature's silence, we will not create an arbitration exception under the facts presented.[4] . . .

C. COMPENSATION FOR LEGAL SERVICES

Because Birbrower violated section 6125 when it engaged in the unlawful practice of law in California, the Court of Appeal found its fee agreement with ESQ unenforceable in its entirety. Without crediting Birbrower for some services performed in New York, for which fees were generated under the fee agreement, the court reasoned that the agreement was void and unenforceable because it included payment for services rendered to a California client in the state by an unlicensed out-of-state lawyer. The court opined that "When New York counsel decided to accept [the] representation, it should have researched California law, including the law governing the practice of law in this state." The Court of Appeal let stand, however, the trial court's decision to allow Birbrower to pursue its fifth cause of action in quantum meruit.[5] We agree with the Court of Appeal to the extent it barred Birbrower from recovering fees generated under the fee agreement for the unauthorized legal services it performed in California. We disagree with the same court to the extent it implicitly barred Birbrower from recovering fees generated under the fee agreement for the limited legal services the firm performed in New York.

It is a general rule that an attorney is barred from recovering compensation for services rendered in another state where the attorney was not admitted to the bar. The general rule, however, has some recognized exceptions. . . .

[Birbrower argued that even if it was practicing law without authority, it should be able to enforce its agreement under one of several exceptions recognized elsewhere: (1) the exception for litigation in federal court, but the court rejected that argument because the arbitration was not a federal case; (2) the exception for services not involving court appearances, but the court refused to recognize that exception at all; and (3) an exception where the lawyer has revealed to the client his lack of a local license, a kind of waiver argument, which the court also refused to recognize.]

---

4. The dissent focuses on an arbitrator's powers in an attempt to justify its conclusion that an out-of-state attorney may engage in the unlicensed representation of a client in an arbitration proceeding. This narrow focus confuses the issue here. An arbitrator's powers to enforce a contract or "award an essentially unlimited range of remedies" has no bearing on the question whether unlicensed out-of-state attorneys may represent California clients in an arbitration proceeding. Moreover, any discussion of the practice of law in an arbitration proceeding is irrelevant here because the parties settled the underlying case before arbitration proceedings became necessary. Nonetheless, we emphasize that, in the absence of clear legislative direction, we decline to create an exception allowing unlicensed legal practice in arbitration in violation of section 6125.

5. We observe that ESQ did not seek (and thus the court did not grant) summary adjudication on the Birbrower firm's quantum meruit claim for the reasonable value of services rendered. Birbrower thus still has a cause of action pending in quantum meruit.

Therefore, as the Court of Appeal held, none of the exceptions to the general rule prohibiting recovery of fees generated by the unauthorized practice of law apply to Birbrower's activities in California. Because Birbrower practiced substantial law in this state in violation of section 6125, it cannot receive compensation under the fee agreement for any of the services it performed in California. Enforcing the fee agreement in its entirety would include payment for the unauthorized practice of law in California and would allow Birbrower to enforce an illegal contract.

Birbrower asserts that even if we agree with the Court of Appeal and find that none of the above exceptions allowing fees for unauthorized California services apply to the firm, it should be permitted to recover fees for those limited services it performed exclusively in New York under the agreement. In short, Birbrower seeks to recover under its contract for those services it performed for ESQ in New York that did not involve the practice of law in California, including fee contract negotiations and some corporate case research. Birbrower thus alternatively seeks reversal of the Court of Appeal's judgment to the extent it implicitly precluded the firm from seeking fees generated in New York under the fee agreement.

We agree with Birbrower that it may be able to recover fees under the fee agreement for the limited legal services it performed for ESQ in New York to the extent they did not constitute practicing law in California, even though those services were performed for a California client. Because section 6125 applies to the practice of law in California, it does not, in general, regulate law practice in other states. Thus, although the general rule against compensation to out-of-state attorneys precludes Birbrower's recovery under the fee agreement for its actions in California, the severability doctrine may allow it to receive its New York fees generated under the fee agreement, if we conclude the illegal portions of the agreement pertaining to the practice of law in California may be severed from those parts regarding services Birbrower performed in New York. . . .

[The court then reviewed state law on severability of contract and concluded, contrary to the lower courts, that although the agreement could not be enforced for work "in" California, it might not be "entirely illegal, assuming ESQ was to pay Birbrower compensation based in part on work Birbrower performed in New York that did not amount to the practice of law in California."]

Therefore, we conclude the Court of Appeal erred in determining that the fee agreement between the parties was entirely unenforceable because Birbrower violated section 6125's prohibition against the unauthorized practice of law in California. Birbrower's statutory violation may require exclusion of the portion of the fee attributable to the substantial illegal services, but that violation does not necessarily entirely preclude its recovery under the fee agreement for the limited services it performed outside California.

Thus, the portion of the fee agreement between Birbrower and ESQ that includes payment for services rendered in New York may be enforceable to the extent that the illegal compensation can be severed from the rest of the agreement. On remand, therefore, the trial court must first resolve the dispute surrounding the parties' fee agreement and determine whether their agreement conforms to California law. If the parties and the court resolve the fee dispute and determine that one fee agreement is operable and does not violate any state drafting rules, the court may sever the illegal portion of the consideration (the value of the California services) from the rest of the fee agreement. Whether the trial court finds the contingent fee agreement or the fixed fee agreement to be valid, it will determine whether some amount is due under the valid agreement. The trial court must then determine, on evidence the parties present, how much of this sum is attributable to services Birbrower rendered in New York. The parties may then pursue their remaining claims. . . .

KENNARD, J., dissenting:

[The dissent's position was that using the definition of "practice of law" in the *Baron* case, on which the majority also relied, arbitration was not law practice. *Baron* is not entirely clear. *Baron* held that not everything lawyers do is limited only to lawyers. But how do we tell what is from what isn't? *Baron* wrote that "if the application of legal knowledge and technique is required, the activity constitutes the practice of law." But *Baron* also said that conduct should be deemed law practice "if difficult or doubtful legal questions are involved which, to safeguard the public, reasonably demand the application of a trained legal mind."

The dissent viewed *Baron*'s definition as "quite similar" to one proposed by Charles Wolfram of Cornell University Law School, who wrote that the test is "whether the matter handled was of such complexity that only a person trained as a lawyer should be permitted to deal with it." In the balance of its opinion, the dissent analyzed what arbitration required.]

Unlike the majority, I would for the reasons given above adhere to the more narrowly drawn definition of the practice of law that this court articulated in *Baron:* the representation of another in a judicial proceeding or an activity requiring the application of that degree of legal knowledge and technique possessed only by a trained legal mind. Applying that definition here, I conclude that the trial court should not have granted summary adjudication for plaintiffs based on the Birbrower lawyers' California activities. That some or all of those activities related to arbitration does not necessarily establish that they constituted the practice of law, as I shall explain.

As I mentioned earlier, Birbrower's clients had a software development and marketing agreement with Tandem. The agreement provided that its validity, interpretation, and enforcement were to be governed by California law. It also contained an arbitration provision. After a dispute arose pertaining to Tandem's performance under the agreement, Birbrower initiated an arbitration on behalf of its clients by filing a claim with the American Arbitration Association in San Francisco, and held meetings in California to prepare for an arbitration hearing. Because the dispute with Tandem was settled, the arbitration hearing was never held. . . .

Representing another in an arbitration proceeding does not invariably present difficult or doubtful legal questions that require a trained legal mind for their resolution. Under California law, arbitrators are "not ordinarily constrained to decide according to the rule of law. . . ." Thus, arbitrators, " 'unless specifically required to act in conformity with rules of law, may base their decision upon broad principles of justice and equity, and in doing so may expressly or impliedly reject a claim that a party might successfully have asserted in a judicial action.' " They " 'are not bound to award on principles of dry law, but may decide on principles of equity and good conscience, and make their award ex aequo et bono [according to what is just and good].' " For this reason, "the existence of an error of law apparent on the face of the [arbitration] award that causes substantial injustice does not provide grounds for judicial review."

Moreover, an arbitrator in California can award any remedy "arguably based" on "the contract's general subject matter, framework or intent." This means that "an arbitrator in a commercial contract dispute may award an essentially unlimited range of remedies, whether or not a court could award them if it decided the same dispute, so long as it can be said that the relief draws its 'essence' from the contract and not some other source."

To summarize, under this court's decisions, arbitration proceedings are not governed or constrained by the rule of law; therefore, representation of another in an arbitration proceeding, including the activities necessary to prepare for the arbitration hearing, does not necessarily require a trained legal mind.

Commonly used arbitration rules further demonstrate that legal training is not essential to represent another in an arbitration proceeding. Here, for example, Birbrower's clients agreed to resolve any dispute arising under their contract with Tandem using the American Arbitration Association's rules, which allow any party to be "represented by counsel or other authorized representative." Rules of other arbitration organizations also allow for representation by nonattorneys. For instance, the Rules of Procedure of the Inter-American Commercial Arbitration Commission, article IV provides: "The parties may be represented or assisted by persons of their choice." By federal law, this rule applies in all arbitrations between a United States citizen and a citizen of another signatory to the Inter-American Convention on International Commercial Arbitration, unless the arbitrating parties have expressly provided otherwise.

The American Arbitration Association and other major arbitration associations thus recognize that nonattorneys are often better suited than attorneys to represent parties in arbitration. The history of arbitration also reflects this reality, for in its beginnings arbitration was a dispute-resolution mechanism principally used in a few specific trades (such as construction, textiles, ship chartering, and international sales of goods) to resolve disputes among businesses that turned on factual issues uniquely within the expertise of members of the trade. In fact, "rules of a few trade associations forbid representation by counsel in arbitration proceedings, because of their belief that it would complicate what might otherwise be simple proceedings." The majority gives no adequate justification for its decision to deprive parties of their freedom of contract and to make it a crime for anyone but California lawyers to represent others in arbitrations in California. . . .

The majority's attempt to distinguish *Williamson* from this case is unpersuasive. The majority points out that in *Williamson*, the lawyers of the New Jersey firm actually rendered services at the New York arbitration hearing, whereas here the New York lawyers never actually appeared at an arbitration hearing in California. The majority distinguishes *Williamson* on the ground that in this case no arbitration hearing occurred. Does the majority mean that an actual appearance at an arbitration hearing is not the practice of law, but that preparation for arbitration proceedings is? . . .

If *Birbrower* Is the Problem, What Is the Solution?

How tolerant should states be in letting unlicensed lawyers into (or virtually into) their jurisdictions? At one extreme may be the out-of-state lawyer who opens a law office in a state. Even if she is competent in the area of law she wishes to practice, states will still not allow it because, they say, they have interests in protecting state residents against failures other than incompetence. At the other end of the spectrum, routinely allowed, is the lawyer who briefly enters a state to serve a particular home-state client. *Birbrower* falls in between. The lawyers did not open an office in California, but their work had a triple California connection: The client was a California company; its dispute arose under California law; and the arbitration was to be held in California. The court recounts this triple nexus though it does not say that its holding depends on the presence of all three. What if Delaware law applied or if the client were an Arizona company? In addition, the written fee agreement was governed by California law and the Birbrower lawyers made three trips to the state of a few days each. The court said that the sum of these contacts amounted to "extensive practice in this state." It is an understatement to say that this conclusion would come as a great and unpleasant surprise to a great many lawyers.

California and Californians had to expect to pay a price for the *Birbrower* holding. Look at it this way. A week after the decision, Whistler, an Illinois lawyer representing a Chicago client, is concluding the negotiation of a contract with O'Keefe, a California lawyer with a San Francisco client. The contract has an arbitration clause and O'Keefe suggests that the lawyers designate San Francisco as the site of any arbitration. Lots of flights, nice to visit. Earlier, the parties had agreed that California law would govern any dispute, so this seems logical. But now Whistler has to worry that in the event of a dispute, he will not be able to represent his client in California. So he and his client insist on Chicago as the venue. O'Keefe understands Whistler's concern, but she can offer no assurances. Maybe the parties will have to agree to arbitrate in a third state. The result is that California does not get the arbitral business and O'Keefe's California client will have to travel out of state in the event of a dispute.

Perhaps responding to this unpleasantness, the California legislature passed a law that in effect gives arbitrators power to admit out-of-state lawyers pro hac vice for in-state arbitrations. The law was meant to sunset on January 1, 2001, but it was later extended until January 1, 2006, to give a state committee time to study the issue. Eventually, the state supreme court adopted new UPL rules (many times as wordy and less generous than the amended Rule 5.5). California Rules of Court 9.45 through 9.48.

Because the *Birbrower* holding was so shocking to so many, and because it came from a court otherwise acknowledged to be sophisticated about modern law practice, the disappointment had a silver lining. It galvanized the bar into action. Here's what the ABA did. Following *Birbrower*, ABA President Martha Barnett appointed a Commission on Multijurisdictional Practice (MJP) to sort things out. Among other solutions, the commission proposed amendments to Rule 5.5 to create a number of fairly generous "safe harbors" for lawyers who cross state lines (physically or virtually) to represent clients temporarily when pro hac vice admission is not available. Those amendments were adopted in 2002. As of mid-2008, more than two-thirds of U.S. jurisdictions have adopted the amended Rule 5.5 in the same or substantially similar form.

The ABA also adopted the commission's recommended changes to Rule 8.5, which now provides for long-arm discipline (so that a host state will have jurisdiction to discipline an out-of-state lawyer, even one who never physically enters the host state). Rule 8.5 also contains a choice-of-rule rule to determine whose ethics rules will apply to the discipline of a lawyer whose work has touched on more than one jurisdiction (it's not necessarily the host state's rules). Other recommendations of the commission can be found at its Web site: *http://www. abanet.org/cpr/mjp-home.html.* For a discussion of the work of the commission by one of its members, see Stephen Gillers, Lessons from the Multijurisdictional Practice Commission: The Art of Making Change, 44 Ariz. L. Rev. 685 (2002). Cases rejecting the view that representation in an arbitration is the practice of law include Colmar, Ltd. v. Fremantlemedia North America, Inc., 801 N.E.2d 1017 (Ill. App. 2003); and Prudential Equity Group, LLC v. Ajamie, 538 F.Supp.2d 605 (S.D.N.Y. 2008).

Maybe we can learn from the European Union? The EU has 15 countries with different legal systems and traditions. While California and other states fret about the appropriate level of tolerance for lawyers from other U.S. *states,* the EU *nations* have opened their doors with a different model for cooperation:

> This model permits lawyers from any of the EU's fifteen member states to cross jurisdictional boundaries and practice within another EU country. The attorney practices in the other country under his home-state title (e.g., solicitor) and may do so on a permanent basis. The attorney is required only to register in the member country. Upon completion, the attorney may advise clients with regard to home and host state law, international law, and EU law. Registered attorneys are subject to the disciplinary rules of both the home and host countries.
>
> The EU adopted this directive after recognizing the dramatic increase in cross-border activity similar to that of the U.S. The EU model has effectively permitted attorneys to fully assist their clients even though the attorney is not a resident of the country he or she is visiting. While the laws of the member countries may vary considerably from jurisdiction to jurisdiction, the EU has recognized the need for uniformity in a multijurisdictional setting, and the benefits have proven to outweigh the costs of not being grounded in a particular jurisdiction. EU lawyers may now practice in almost all fields of law in the EU community, represent clients on a continuous basis, and form multinational law firms with offices in any desired member state.

Catherine Davis, Approaching Reform: The Future of Multijurisdictional Practice in Today's Legal Profession, 29 Fla. St. U. L. Rev. 1339 (2002). Bravo Old Europe!

Some Other Decisions

Although lawyer unauthorized practice is still a rare issue to surface in court, it does arise and seems to be on the increase. Here are some other interesting cases. See if you can discern a pattern.

- A Minnesota lawyer who advised a North Dakota businessman on federal tax matters could not collect a fee for work done during frequent trips to

North Dakota, but only for work he did in Minnesota. Ranta v. McCarney, 391 N.W.2d 161 (N.D. 1986).

- A lawyer who was not admitted in New York but had an office there was denied a $4 million fee for work done and advice given from his New York office in connection with a matter pending in a federal court in which he *was* admitted. Servidone Construction Corp. v. St. Paul Fire & Marine Ins. Co., 911 F. Supp. 560 (N.D.N.Y. 1995).

- A California lawyer who came to New York at a client's request to assist in a contemplated antitrust action could collect his fee for work done in New York notwithstanding that the matter was settled before he had a chance to seek pro hac vice admission. Spanos v. Skouras Theatres Corp., 364 F.2d 161 (2d Cir. 1966) (cited in both *Leis* opinions).

- Ohio has enjoined lawyers who have opened offices in Ohio though not admitted there, regardless of the law they planned to practice. Cleveland Bar Assn. v. Misch, 695 N.E.2d 244 (Ohio 1998); Cleveland Bar Assn. v. Moore, 722 N.E.2d 514 (Ohio 2000). The state has also disciplined an Ohio lawyer who aided one of these lawyers. Office of Disciplinary Counsel v. Pavlik, 732 N.E.2d 985 (Ohio 2000).

- A Georgia lawyer who, while living in New York, probated a will in surrogate's court without seeking pro hac vice admission was charged with unauthorized practice and pled guilty to a misdemeanor. Thereafter, Georgia suspended him from practice for one year. Matter of Schrader, 523 S.E.2d 327 (Ga. 1999).

- A Colorado lawyer could collect a statutory fee from a California court in connection with advice he gave to a Colorado citizen who was co-executor of the estate of a deceased Californian, notwithstanding that the advice related to California law and that the lawyer may physically and virtually have entered California. The co-executor also had local counsel in California. Estate of Condon, 76 Cal. Rptr. 2d 922 (Ct. App. 1998) (distinguishing *Birbrower*). See also Fought & Co. v. Steel Engineering & Erection, Inc., 951 P.2d 487 (Haw. 1998) (distinguishing *Birbrower*, upholds right of Oregon lawyer to a counsel fee under fee-shifting statute for work performed in Oregon in assisting client's Hawaii counsel in connection with Hawaii litigation).

- A Massachusetts lawyer who practiced transactional law in New Jersey from 1991 to 1998 without becoming a member of the New Jersey bar, then applied for admission, was denied admission for one year because of the unauthorized practice. Matter of Jackman, 761 A.2d 1103 (N.J. 2000).

- A Wisconsin lawyer was reprimanded following denial of a fee in Colorado because of unauthorized practice there. In re Bolte, 699 N.W.2d 914 (Wis. 2005).

- An in-house lawyer based in Ohio who used the designation "general counsel" and "legal counsel" on internal documents and documents sent to outsiders without being a member of the Ohio Bar, was engaged in unauthorized practice, but absent evidence of "a deliberate attempt to mislead," the court permitted her to apply for admission without examination. Application of Stage, 692 N.E.2d 993 (Ohio 1998).

Some Alternatives

As *Birbrower* reveals, the prohibition against lawyers licensed in another state has found exceptions — both textual and judicially created. One of the more significant exceptions is for in-house lawyers — lawyers employed by a corporation or other entity who work only for that entity. These lawyers may find themselves transferred from one jurisdiction to another, often for only a few years at a time, and surely do not relish taking multiple bar examinations or even seeking admission on motion if that is possible. Half the states have special rules allowing these lawyers to advise their employer-clients without gaining formal admission to the bar. About half the states have a special admission category for legal services lawyers.

The idea of multistate-practitioner admissions also finds support in separate admissions systems for lawyers from other nations. For example, New York admits foreign lawyers, without examination, as "legal consultants" on the laws of non-U.S. jurisdictions. A licensed legal consultant is subject to the same disciplinary authority as a lawyer. She may become a partner in a New York law firm, and her foreign law firm may hire American lawyers. See N.Y. Jud. Law §53(6); 22 N.Y. C.R.R. §§521.1 et seq. About 28 other American jurisdictions, including California, Illinois, and the District of Columbia, have similar rules.

C. THE ETHICAL DUTY OF COMPETENCE

Rule 1.1 of the Model Rules ("Competence") states: "A lawyer shall provide competent representation to a client. Competent representation requires the legal knowledge, skill, thoroughness and preparation reasonably necessary for the representation."

The ethical requirement of competence is not often invoked as a basis for discipline. See generally Susan Martyn, Lawyer Competence and Lawyer Discipline: Beyond the Bar?, 69 Geo. L.J. 705 (1981). Although the courts do say that a single instance of incompetence can justify discipline, People v. Yoakum, 552 P.2d 291 (Colo. 1976), State ex rel. Nebraska State Bar Assn. v. Holscher, 230 N.W.2d 75 (Neb. 1975), in fact the cases in which these statements are made generally involve significantly more culpable conduct than a single act of incompetence. Occasionally, however, it does happen that an attorney will be disciplined mainly for incompetence. In Florida Bar v. Gallagher, 366 So. 2d 397 (Fla. 1978), an attorney was publicly reprimanded after he accepted a maritime personal injury claim knowing that "he was neither qualified nor competent to handle" the claim. But even here there was the additional fact that the attorney neglected to "timely file suit on the client's behalf, and the claim was barred by the applicable statute of limitations."

Although rare (see chapter 13E), it does happen that a criminal conviction is reversed because the defense lawyer provided ineffective assistance of counsel within the meaning of the Sixth Amendment. The Sixth Amendment test for effective assistance of counsel is quite hard to prove, meaning that courts tolerate a lot of pretty shoddy work in criminal cases. But when a lawyer is constitutionally ineffective, does the finding of ineffectiveness lead to discipline? Rare though these Sixth Amendment violations are (especially in noncapital cases), ensuing discipline is even more rare. One example is Florida Bar v. Sandstrom, 609 So. 2d 583 (Fla. 1992), where the court did discipline a lawyer who had been found ineffective, while adding that most ineffectiveness cases will not merit discipline. The case before the court, however, involved a "flagrant lack of preparation and such deficient performance by counsel." See also Matter of Wolfram, 847 P.2d 94 (Ariz. 1993).

A competent lawyer may handle matters incompetently not because of the difficulty of the matters, but because he has too many of them. Competence is a function not only of expertise but also of workload, which is especially a problem for lawyers employed in high-volume offices. The lawyer has a duty to decline to accept more work than he can competently handle, but that might not be easy. If the person assigning the work is a lawyer, does that person have an ethical duty not to assign more work than the receiving lawyer can perform well? Yes, according to ABA Opinion 06-441:

> All lawyers, including public defenders and other lawyers who, under court appointment or government contract, represent indigent persons charged with criminal offenses, must provide competent and diligent representation. If workload prevents a lawyer from providing competent and diligent representation to existing clients, she must not accept new clients. If the clients are being assigned through a court appointment system, the lawyer should request that the court not make any new appointments. Once the lawyer is representing a client, the lawyer must move to withdraw from representation if she cannot provide competent and diligent representation. If the court denies the lawyer's motion to withdraw, and any available means of appealing such ruling is unsuccessful, the lawyer must continue with the representation while taking whatever steps are feasible to ensure that she will be able to competently and diligently represent the defendant.
>
> Lawyer supervisors, including heads of public defenders' offices and those within such offices having intermediate managerial responsibilities, must make reasonable efforts to ensure that the other lawyers in the office conform to the Rules of Professional Conduct. To that end, lawyer supervisors must, working closely with the lawyers they supervise, monitor the workload of the supervised lawyers to ensure that the workloads do not exceed a level that may be competently handled by the individual lawyers.

Competence is not only an ethical duty; it is also a legal duty. Incompetence can serve as the basis for a malpractice action, which in most places may be based in tort or contract or both. See chapter 13A. To the extent that the market works, incompetence should also lead to fewer clients, while lawyers whose work is more than competent should have more clients. This assumes, however, that prospective clients get complete information about the lawyers they are planning to hire and know how to interpret it. They don't, of course. Disciplinary decisions may not be public (see page 806), and many malpractice actions are settled out of court, sometimes with a promise of confidentiality or a stipulation sealing the record. Should there be a Web site that consumers can consult to see if their lawyers have been sued for malpractice or charged in a disciplinary matter?

D. CONTINUING LEGAL EDUCATION

Will a requirement that a lawyer continue law study increase competence and decrease risk of professional failure? Many states think so. According to the 2008 Comprehensive Guide to Bar Admission Requirements, more than 40 American jurisdictions have mandatory continuing legal education (CLE) requirements. These plans generally require an average of 10 to 15 hours of approved CLE classes yearly. Most jurisdictions require that two or three of these hours be in legal ethics. (*Yes!*) Failure to obey CLE requirements can result in discipline. In re Yamagiwa, 650 P.2d 203 (Wash. 1982) (suspension); In re Polk, 732 N.W.2d 419 (Wis. 2007) (administrative suspension of license for three years (!) for failure to comply with CLE requirements).

In Verner v. Colorado, 716 F.2d 1352 (10th Cir. 1983), the plaintiff was a Colorado lawyer suspended from practice for failure to comply with the state's CLE requirements. The plaintiff sought, among other relief, to enjoin the enforcement of those allegedly unconstitutional requirements. In rejecting the plaintiff 's claim, the Tenth Circuit wrote:

> As the trial court noted, the basic issue presented is a novel one: whether a state supreme court may constitutionally require attorneys to meet continuing legal education requirements. Ample precedent exists supporting the authority to prescribe minimum levels of legal competency, measured by a bar examination, as a prerequisite to admission to a state bar. A fortiori, a state can require an attorney to take reasonable steps to maintain a suitable level of competency, so long as such requirements have a "rational connection with the [attorney's] fitness or capacity to practice law." We cannot say that the CLE requirements in Colorado have no rational connection to a lawyer's suitability to practice law.

E. SUPERVISORY RESPONSIBILITIES

"I Don't Want to Pry, But . . ."

"I head our firm's corporate department. My name is Spencer Sweet. We do deals with more digits in the bottom line than Ben & Jerry's has flavors. Well, not quite, but you know what I mean. Mistakes can cost millions and we have all sorts of redundancy procedures in place to avoid them. I still have nightmares that someone will misplace a decimal point and it'll happen to us what happened to that New York firm that recorded a mortgage as $92,885 when it was $92,885,000.*

"About a year ago, we hired Catherine Sutton, a lateral from the corporate department of a good firm in Boston. She was moving to Dallas for personal

---

* Prudential Ins. Co. v. Dewey, Ballantine, Bushby, Palmer & Wood, 605 N.E.2d 318 (N.Y. 1992). Dewey, Ballantine was not the firm that made the error.

reasons. I inferred that the personal reasons had more to do with leaving Boston than with choosing Dallas. So be it. I don't especially want to know about my lawyers' private lives.

"Our firm, which has nine offices and 850 lawyers, has solid rules on supervising associate work. We do a lot of it. Also, we are well aware of the growing number of cases that say it's the partnership's ethical and fiduciary duty to do that. Not doing it can mean discipline, but even more daunting, it can mean a malpractice judgment.

"About six months ago, Kitty seemed to begin to go through some lifestyle change. It happened gradually. Her dress, makeup, hairstyle, way of carrying herself, way of talking, all were . . . what can I say, more like she was an art student at the Sorbonne than a corporate lawyer in conservative Dallas. She got a small tattoo on her forearm and another near her ankle. Tasteful, but visible. Also, she began to lose weight, then it leveled off, but she still looks too thin if you ask me. I tell you, if she had presented herself that way at her interviews, I simply would not have hired her.

"I mean, I don't give a whit about her private life. I'm worried about two things. I'm worried that our clients, who are personally very conservative people, will be put off that someone who presents herself the way Kitty does is handling their million dollar deals and has their highly confidential information. And I'm worried, too, that she'll mess up. People from here who've run into Kitty outside the office say the friends she hangs out with are weird. And a couple of people have told me they've seen her high — on something — in public. I'm worried about what Kitty's new 'self' says about her fitness as a lawyer in her stressful and responsible job.

"I have to admit that Kitty's work has been fine so far, though not stellar. She hasn't made any mistakes other than the usual small ones we're all prone to make. She does what we ask her to do and she does it mostly on time. She puts in the time we expect. It's the future I'm worried about.

"When I started here 27 years ago, the firm had 115 lawyers who were all alike and like our clients. We're a bureaucracy now. Personnel management is harder. When our Chairman (based in L.A.) met Kitty at a firm dinner, he asked whose date she was. When I told him what I've told you, he responded, 'Spence, why run the risk of error or of scaring away clients? If we get sued for her errors, the stuff you told me will all come out and show conscious disregard of the risks. And if we spend partner time closely checking her work, who'll pay for that? Give her six months' notice. A year even. Help place her somewhere else. Don't let her have client contact or heavy responsibility in the meantime.' He's got a point. Advise me how to proceed."

Supervisory responsibilities are of two kinds. One appears in Model Rule 5.1(a) and (b). Rule 5.1(a) requires law firm partners to "make reasonable efforts to ensure that the firm has in effect measures giving reasonable assurance that all lawyers in the firm conform to the [Model Rules]." Rule 5.1(b) imposes an equivalent obligation on lawyers with "direct supervisory authority over another lawyer." A partner or supervisory lawyer can be disciplined under these provisions even if she was unaware of another lawyer's misconduct. Indeed, the way the section reads, the failure to install appropriate preventive measures will warrant discipline all by itself. The Rules separately impose a duty to rectify another lawyer's misconduct under certain circumstances. Rule 5.1(c)(2). Parallel preventive and remedial obligations apply in connection with the work of a law office's lay employees. Rule 5.3. See In re Opinion No. 24, 607 A.2d 962 (N.J. 1992) ("attorney who does not properly supervise a paralegal is in violation of the ethical Rules"). A careful analysis of the "three different levels of supervision" mandated in Rule 5.1 appears in Matter of Anonymous Member of the South Carolina Bar, 552 S.E.2d 10 (S.C. 2001).

If the supervising attorney has no reason to suspect misconduct, however, he may not be vicariously liable for discipline. In re Corace, 213 N.W.2d 124 (Mich. 1973), involved an associate who signed the name of an opposing party on a stipulation for adjournment, despite the senior partner's earlier explanation that it was firm practice never to sign another's name. The court held that a partner is not vicariously liable in a disciplinary proceeding if he had no reason to suspect or guard against an associate's violation. But where a lawyer should have known about the actions of an associate under his supervision, he was suspended for 30 days even if he in fact did not know. Matter of Cohen, 847 A.2d 1162 (D.C. 2004) (construing D.C. Rule 5.1(c)(2), which imposes responsibility for the conduct of a subordinate where a lawyer "knows *or reasonably should know* of the conduct. . . ."). (The Model Rules do not have the italicized words.) A lawyer may also be liable in a disciplinary action for violations of partners or associates whom he does not supervise if he knew of or reasonably should have suspected the misconduct. In re Brown, 59 N.E.2d 855 (Ill. 1945); In re Pollack, 536 N.Y.S.2d 437 (1st Dept. 1989).

A failure to supervise that leads to the client's financial loss will also support malpractice liability. Anderson v. Hall, 755 F. Supp. 2 (D.D.C. 1991) (action against law partnership after associate let statute of limitations run out on client's claim). See also the material on vicarious liability in malpractice at page 721.

In 1996, New York became the first state to adopt rules that apply to an entire law firm, not merely individual lawyers. New York Rule 8.4 applies to a "law firm" as well as a lawyer, so that firms as well as lawyers may not violate disciplinary rules, engage in conduct prejudicial to the administration of justice, engage in illegal conduct involving moral turpitude, and so on. New York's 5.1(a) now says that "A law firm shall make reasonable efforts to ensure that all lawyers in the firm conform these Rules" Rule 1.10(e) requires a law firm to keep contemporaneous records of engagements and adopt a system that allows firm lawyers to check for conflicts when "the firm agrees to represent a new client [or] an existing client in a new matter;" or when the "firm hires or associates with another lawyer or an additional party is named or appears in a pending matter." Violation of the record-keeping requirements can lead to discipline even if no client conflict ensues. Rule 1.10(f). The inspiration for this innovation was an article by Professor Ted Schneyer, Professional Discipline for Law Firms?, 77 Cornell L. Rev. 1 (1991). This development is echoed in the 1993 amendments to Rule 11 (see page 431), which allow courts to sanction law firms and lawyers other than those who have signed an offending paper.

F. UNAUTHORIZED PRACTICE OF LAW

States license lawyers to ensure a level of quality and to protect their citizens. One consequence of this barrier to practice is that fewer people are available to provide legal services. As a result, we might expect the cost (as well as the quality) of a particular legal service to be higher than it would be if anyone could offer that service. But what if the service is perfunctory, so the threat to quality is low?

Think about the following questions while reading this section: Shouldn't a consumer of a service be entitled to hire whomever he wishes? For the performance of a service arguably "legal," should the consumer be entitled to take the risk of hiring a person who has not attended law school? On the other hand, doesn't the state have a right to protect people from their own foolishness? Does your answer to this question vary depending upon whether the client wishes to utilize the services of the attorney in a criminal or civil matter? In negotiating and writing a contract? Does it vary depending on whether the state is prepared to provide free counsel to an indigent client in a civil matter?

The bar's monopoly on the provision of legal services might be diluted in two ways. First, we could create an exception. Even though a particular service is considered "legal," we could allow other professionals to perform the service too. Tax accountants, for example, interpret a rather complex statute, the Internal Revenue Code. Second, we could adopt a narrow definition of what constitutes the practice of law. If a service is not defined as legal, a person who is not a lawyer may perform it without being guilty of the unauthorized practice of law.

Traditionally, the definition of the practice of law has been broad. Texas partly defines unauthorized law practice by statute, as follows:

(a) In this chapter the "practice of law" means the preparation of a pleading or other document incident to an action or special proceeding or the management of the action or proceeding on behalf of a client before a judge in court as well as a service rendered out of court, including the giving of advice or the rendering of any service requiring the use of legal skill or knowledge, such as preparing a will, contract, or other instrument, the legal effect of which under the facts and conclusions involved must be carefully determined.

(b) The definition in this section is not exclusive and does not deprive the judicial branch of the power and authority under both this chapter and the adjudicated cases to determine whether other services and acts not enumerated may constitute the practice of law.

(c) In this chapter, the "practice of law" does not include the design, creation, publication, distribution, display, or sale, including publication, distribution, display, or sale by means of an Internet web site, of written materials, books, forms, computer software, or similar products if the products clearly and conspicuously state that the products are not a substitute for the advice of an attorney.

Tex. Govt. Code §81.101. If paragraph (c) seems unusual, the explanation is this: A federal judge in Texas had held that the sale of Quicken Family Lawyer, the computer program that helps users write wills and do simple legal tasks for themselves, was unauthorized law practice, as described at page 698. The legislature quickly overturned the decision by passing paragraph (c).

Who decides whether to create an exception to unauthorized practice rules? Who decides how to define the practice of law? The answer is the courts, with or without some participation by the legislature, depending on the jurisdiction. Recall the "inherent powers" doctrine discussed in chapter 1. It applies in this instance too. Whether or not particular conduct is the practice of law is a question of law, not ethics. Rule 5.5 forbids lawyers to engage in unauthorized law practice or to help another to do so, but it does not define "law practice."

Remember that not only the rights of laypersons but also the rights of out-of-state lawyers depend on these questions of definition and exception. The definitions and exceptions, however, may be differently articulated depending on whether the person who seeks to provide the service is an out-of-state lawyer or a layperson. Why should that be? Remedies may also vary. Out-of-state lawyers are unlikely to be prosecuted, but they do risk losing their fees, as we saw earlier in this chapter.

Unauthorized law practice can occur in two ways. A nonlawyer may render what are deemed to be legal services. That is the focus of the next case. Alternatively, an entity that is not authorized to practice law, say a business corporation, may hire or employ a licensed lawyer and provide his work to another for a fee. In this second category the client is at least guided by counsel licensed in the jurisdiction, but restrictions nevertheless apply because the lawyer is working for an organization that is not authorized to sell legal services. The fear is that the managers of the organization that retains or employs the lawyer to represent its client will control how the lawyer performs her duties. See Eisel v. Midwest Bank Centre, 230 S.W.3d 335 (Mo. 2007) (unauthorized law practice where "Midwest charged the Eisels a document preparation fee for preparing or completing various mortgage loan documents, including promissory notes and deeds of trust"). As discussed in chapter 14, this concern is differently addressed depending on whether the organization is in business for profit.

PROFESSIONAL ADJUSTERS, INC. v. TANDON
433 N.E.2d 779 (Ind. 1982)

PIVARNIK, JUSTICE. . . .

The facts show that defendants Tandon had a fire loss on their mobile home in Terre Haute, Indiana, on December 22, 1976. They had a policy of insurance to cover such loss with defendant USF&G, and filed a claim with that company. USF&G offered to settle the claim for eight-thousand dollars ($8,000), which figure was unacceptable to the Tandons. The Tandons then hired Professional Adjusters, Inc., to handle their claim against USF&G for them. Plaintiff prepared estimates of repair cost, temporary electrical costs, depreciation from actual cash value, replacement of outdoor furniture and fixtures, equipment and carpeting, estimates on unscheduled property with dates of purchase and current value and depreciated value, and a claim for additional living expenses, including projections for completion and repair which [it claims] required the expending of sixty-five hours of time. Professional Adjusters, Inc., then submitted this claim to GAB Service, Inc., which was the adjusting agency of USF&G. In response, Professional Adjusters received from GAB Service, Inc., an offer to settle the claim for substantially more than the original offer of eight-thousand dollars ($8,000). Defendants Tandon, in the meantime, contacted a lawyer and subsequently settled the claim with USF&G. Tandons tendered a check in the amount of five-hundred dollars ($500) to Professional Adjusters, Inc., which was offered as payment, which was refused. . . .

[The relevant statute] provides that before anyone can act as a certified public adjuster he must be issued a certificate of authority by the Commissioner of Insurance of the State of Indiana and succeeding sections of the chapter provide for the mechanics to be employed by the Insurance Commissioner. [The statute also] provides for a written examination for the Commissioner to give applicants to determine the trustworthiness and competence of the applicant and provides that such testing shall include but not be limited to the following areas: "1) the Indiana Insurance Code; 2) inventory and appraisal procedures; 3) building construction; 4) standard fire policy; 5) insurance contracts related to claims on real or personal property; and 6) insurance coverage questions regarding business interruptions, improvements and betterments, replacement cost coverage, concurrent and non-concurrent apportionment, co-insurance and contribution."

[The statute] creates a new type of adjuster heretofore unknown in the insurance field. All of the traditional forms and duties of insurance adjusters are excepted from this statute. Adjusters have traditionally been employees or agents of insurance companies hired by them to attempt to ascertain the nature of a loss under one of their policies and to attempt to settle it in behalf of the company. This was true of independent adjusting agencies that were hired by insurance companies to act as their agents in making an adjustment. Those adjusters who were employees of the company were, of course, agents who acted in full authority to bind the company in settling with its insured. Independent adjusting firms were hired by companies to act as independent appraisers to help the company fix and determine the amount of a loss so that the company could then settle the claim with the insured. This statute proposes to create a public adjuster which represents an insured and receives compensation to act on behalf of that assured to negotiate for and effect the settlement of a claim for loss or damages. It does not limit the activity and authority of the adjuster to appraise the loss and report back to the client the fair value of the claim so that the client can then go forward and settle his claim. It authorizes the adjuster to go forward and to negotiate for and effect that settlement as a direct agent and representative of the insured. This is, pure and simple, the practice of law. In acting as the statute authorizes a public adjuster to act, he is acting as an attorney at law.

In the present case, Professional Adjusters, Inc., made a determination of the loss of Tandons and then submitted this claim to the insurance carrier for negotiation of a settlement. The fact that the negotiations did not reach the stage where there was a bargaining process of offers and counter-offers does not make it any less negotiation. Plaintiff [was] in all ways acting as attorney-at-law for Tandons by submitting a figure which they would deem acceptable for their loss and contemplating in return a response from the insurance carrier that would effect the settlement. [It] expected to receive remuneration in an amount that was contingent upon the amount [it] recovered. As one of the allegations of [its] complaint, the plaintiff alleged: "6. On February 3, 1977, the defendant USF&G formally rejected the proof of loss filed by defendant Tandon on January 10, 1977, and on March 18, 1977, the plaintiff furnished all of the above claim information to GAB Business Service, Inc., the adjusting agent for USF&G pursuant to said contract."

Thus, in [its] complaint, the plaintiff [states] that not only did the contract contemplate that it would be the duty of plaintiff to take the claim forward to USF&G, but [it] alleged that is, in fact, what [it] did. In discussing the subject of the practice of law, this Court stated, in Matter of Perrello, (1979) 270 Ind. 390, 386 N.E.2d 174, 179:

> The core element of practicing law is the giving of legal advice to a client and the placing of oneself in the very sensitive relationship wherein the confidence of the client, and the management of his affairs, is left totally in the hands of the attorney. The undertaking to minister to the legal problems of another, creates an attorney-client relationship without regard to whether the services are actually performed by the one so undertaking the responsibility or are delegated or subcontracted to another. It is the opinion of this Court that merely entering into such relationship constitutes the practice of law.

We further said, in Groninger v. Fletcher Trust Co., (1942) 220 Ind. 202, 207, 41 N.E.2d 140:

> The practice of law is restricted to natural persons who have been licensed upon the basis of established character and competence as a protection to the public against lack of knowledge, skill, integrity, and fidelity. Disbarment procedure is available in the case of those who do not conform to proper practice. The practice of law involves advising or rendering services for another. A natural person may plead his own case in court or do any of the things for himself which if done for another would constitute practicing law. He may discuss the legal aspects of his affairs with other interested parties or with strangers. Either a natural person or a corporation may employ lawyers to do these things.
>
> The very criteria required under [the statute], in its creation of Certified Public Adjusters is knowledge and competency in dealing with rights and liabilities of other persons as required in the ethical considerations in case law heretofore relied upon, but does not require admission to the Bar in this State and therefore does not subject those so acting to the disciplinary rules of this Court. Undertaking the determination of rights and liabilities under an insurance contract and the negotiation of settlements requires the interpretation of the terms of that contract. . . .

[The trial court's dismissal of the complaint is affirmed.]

HUNTER, Justice, dissenting.

I must respectfully dissent from the majority opinion. The majority recognizes the contract at issue is unenforceable [on state contract law grounds]; it is not necessary to reach the question of the statute's constitutionality and it is our duty to so refrain. Furthermore, the legislatively-created occupation of "Public Adjuster" does not constitute "the practice of law"; consequently, it is not within our province constitutionally to abolish the occupation by rendering the statutory package void. If, however, the rationale of the majority is valid, then other occupations created by our legislature also constitute "the practice of law."

The validity of this latter proposition is revealed within the confines of the majority opinion, where it is acknowledged that, traditionally, insurance companies have long employed adjusters "who acted in full authority to bind the company in *settling* with its insured." (Emphasis added.) Indeed, our legislature has expressly granted insurance "administrators" or "designated claim representatives" statutory authority to "settle" claims.

In terms of "the practice of law," there is no valid distinction between the public adjuster and the person who settles claims on behalf of an insurance company. . . . While the insurance company agent may practice the art of settlement with the blessing of his employer, he or she, nonetheless, is engaged in the practice of law, as the majority defines it; to settle a claim, the agent must interpret the contract of insurance, assess the claim of damages, and negotiate the settlement, all with full authority to bind his insurance company. These very considerations are the basis for the majority's conclusion that the public adjuster who exercises his authority . . . engages in "the practice of law." . . .

The statute thus limits the public adjuster's ability to act to those claims in which the opposing party is also represented by an adjuster not licensed to practice law. The remaining portions [of the statute] prohibit the public adjuster from dispensing recommendations regarding legal courses of action; that limitation is consistent with the sole statutory function of the public adjuster, which is to assess the assured's real property loss and attempt to negotiate and settle the claim with the insurer.

Nobody would argue that the act of examining the damaged property and assessing the pecuniary loss constitutes the practice of law. Nor can it be said that the act of negotiating and settling disputes is the practice of law; that art is practiced in various forms by virtually every citizen from our playgrounds to our centers of trade. It is, then, the public adjuster's examination of the assured's contractual terms which carries him into "the practice of law," according to the majority.

That supposition was implicitly rejected by this Court in [precedent], where it was held that real estate brokers and salespersons may utilize legal forms in the contract formation process. The public interest, this Court reasoned, is served by the expeditious handling of some transactions. . . .

Similarly, it should be recognized [that] a public adjuster's assistance in adjusting a claim with the insurer's designated claim representative may well facilitate the expeditious settlement of the dispute, to the benefit of both parties and the public interest. In addition, the availability of trustworthy and competent settlement experts serves the public interest by placing assureds on the same footing as insurance companies, who have always enjoyed the benefits of such services. This latter public policy consideration no doubt prompted the legislature's passage of [of the statute] and should not be ignored by this Court.

Is it any wonder the legal profession is not popular? The majority opinion gives us a rigidly protectionist (but not unique) view of the definition of law practice and of judicial reluctance to let lawmakers (and therefore the democratic process) participate in regulating "legal" services. Insurers in Indiana can use nonlawyer adjusters to negotiate claims; but an insured may not. How can the court possibly defend that discrepancy? Its reason is that the company's adjuster, whether an agent or an employee, has authority to bind the company. In other words he has *more* power than the plaintiff did here. So it's not a problem. See?

No one claimed that the final settlement offer ("substantially" higher than the first offer) was inadequate or that plaintiff failed to do a good job. It was, after all, tested and licensed under the statutory scheme. And what exactly did the plaintiff do that amounted to the practice of law? It merely submitted the claim, and the insurer made an acceptable offer without any negotiation. Yet it was the practice of law because implicitly the adjuster was required to interpret the insurer's contract obligations. I'd wager that trained (and licensed) insurance adjusters are as good as, if not better than, most lawyers at interpreting property insurance contracts. Have you ever looked at one of those policies? Not even the plain English movement has done much to make them comprehensible. Could the adjuster have given its paperwork to the Tandons to submit to the insurer? Or would that still be law practice?

We should, of course, recognize that adjusters generally charge less than lawyers, often 10 to 20 percent of the recovery, whereas lawyers will charge one-third or more. Furthermore, if a client with property damage, like the Tandons, does go to a lawyer, he or she will often need to hire an adjuster as well, to evaluate the cost of repair, and that will be an added charge.

Judges are not uniform on these questions, as you can see in Judge Hunter's dissent. Compare Utah State Bar v. Summerhayes & Hayden, 905 P.2d 867 (Utah 1995), which affirmed an injunction against nonlawyers engaging in "third-party adjusting," but (disagreeing with the Indiana court) allowing them to engage in "first-party adjusting." The former occurs when the adjuster negotiates a victim's claim with a potential defendant's (i.e., the third party's) insurance company. The latter occurs when the adjuster negotiates with the client's own insurer, as in *Tandon*. The former is a tort claim, the latter a contract claim. The court concluded that the distinction should make a difference for unauthorized practice purposes. Why is that? Don't both services require some legal judgment?

The South Carolina Supreme Court permits public adjusters to evaluate losses but (over a dissent) does not allow them to interpret insurance contracts, negotiate coverage disputes, or advise on whether to accept an offer. But they may evaluate the amount of the loss and negotiate that amount with the insurer. These are tasks that do not require interpretation of the contract language. Linder v. Insurance Claims Consultants, Inc., 560 S.E.2d 612(S.C. 2002).

The New Jersey and Washington Supreme Courts have been more generous in allowing nonlawyers to engage in what would traditionally be deemed law practice. Historically, residential house closings in the southern and northern halves of New Jersey have proceeded differently. In the south, it is routine not to use a lawyer. In the north, it is routine to use one. The bar challenged the practice in southern New Jersey, which relied on real estate brokers and title insurance companies to do the necessary paperwork. After sending the issue to a special master to take testimony, the Supreme Court upheld the southern practice, but not without qualms. In a lengthy opinion, In re Opinion No. 26, 654 A.2d 1344 (N.J. 1995), the unanimous court wrote:

> Under our Constitution, this Court's power over the practice of law is complete. We are given the power to permit the practice of law and to prohibit its unauthorized practice. We have exercised that latter power in numerous cases.
>
> The question of what constitutes the unauthorized practice of law involves more than an academic analysis of the function of lawyers, more than a determination of what they are uniquely qualified to do. It also involves a determination of whether nonlawyers should be allowed, in the public interest, to engage in activities that may constitute the practice of law. As noted later, the conclusion in these cases that parties need not retain counsel to perform limited activities that constitute the practice of law and that others may perform them does not imply that the public interest is thereby advanced, but rather that the public interest does not require that those parties be deprived of their right to proceed without counsel. We reach that conclusion today given the unusual history and experience of the South Jersey practice as developed in the record before us. . . .
>
> We believe that parties to the sale of a family home, both seller and buyer, would be better served if each were represented by counsel from the beginning to the end of the transaction, from contract signing through closing. We are persuaded, however, that they should continue to have the right to choose *not* to be represented. They should, of course, be informed of the risks. The record fails to demonstrate that the public interest has been disserved by the South Jersey practice over the many years it has been in existence. While the risks of non-representation are many and serious, the record contains little proof of actual damage to either buyer or seller. Moreover, the record does not contain proof that, in the aggregate, the damage that has occurred in South Jersey exceeds that experienced elsewhere. In this case, the absence of proof is particularly impressive, for the dispute between the realtors and the bar is of long duration, with the parties and their counsel singularly able and highly motivated to supply such proof as may exist. The South Jersey practice also appears to save money. For the record demonstrates what is obvious, that sellers and buyers without counsel save counsel fees. We believe, given this record, that the parties must continue to have the right to decide whether those savings are worth the risks of not having lawyers to advise them in what is almost always the most important transaction they will ever undertake. . . .

The court, however, required brokers to give clients detailed warnings: "We premise our holding on the condition that both buyer and seller be made aware of the conflicting interests of brokers and title companies in these matters and of the general risks involved in not being represented by counsel."

In Cultum v. Heritage House Realtors, Inc., 694 P.2d 630 (Wash. 1985), the question was whether a real estate salesperson who completed "a form earnest money agreement containing a contingency clause" was engaged in the unauthorized practice of law. The preprinted form was essentially an offer to sell at a stated price contingent on a satisfactory report from an examining engineer. The court held that "although the completion of form earnest money agreements might be commonly understood as the practice of law, we believe it is in the public interest to permit licensed real estate brokers or licensed salespersons to complete such lawyer prepared standard form agreements provided that, in doing so, they comply with the standard of care demanded of an attorney." The court continued:

> It should be emphasized that the holding in this case is limited in scope. Our decision provides that a real estate broker or salesperson is permitted to complete simple printed standardized real estate forms, which forms must be approved by a lawyer, it being understood that these forms shall not be used for other than simple real estate transactions which arise in the usual course of the broker's business and that such forms will be used only in connection with real estate transactions actually handled by such broker or salesperson as a broker or salesperson and then without charge for the simple service of completing the forms.

After *Cultum*, the court adopted rules to "authorize certain laypersons to select, prepare, and complete legal documents incident to the closing of real estate and personal property transactions and to prescribe the conditions of and limitations upon such activities." The rules contemplate licensing of "closing officers" who satisfy certain educational and examination requirements. Rule 12, Wash. Local Rules of Court.

The Troubled World of Unauthorized Practice

The supreme courts of each of the states surveyed above agree on one essential fact: *They* decide who can practice law and what law practice is.

Few subjects in the area of lawyer regulation are met with as much lay suspicion as unauthorized practice rules. Why is that? First, it is obvious that these rules can be and are used to restrict the "supply side" of legal services and thereby raise fees. Many people are skeptical of the claim that the profession's motive for guarding its borders is selfless concern for clients. See generally Deborah Rhode's examination of the issue in Policing the Professional Monopoly: A Constitutional and Empirical Analysis of Unauthorized Practice Prohibitions, 34 Stan. L. Rev. 1 (1981).

Second, courts occasionally invalidate legislation that means to help consumers by letting laypersons perform fairly routine work at foreseeably lower costs. (These actions may be brought by lawyers or bar groups.) If the court relies on the argument that the definition of "law practice" is within its inherent power, the public is left with little democratic control (short of a state constitutional amendment) over a major component of their justice systems — the cost and source of advice.

Last, the kinds of "legal" services a layperson may wish to offer will likely be simple, requiring little or no discretion. If a client retains a law firm to provide such a routine service, he may discover that it is mostly performed by a lay employee of the firm anyway, with minimal lawyer supervision. See Florida Opinion 1989-5 (nonlawyer law firm employees may handle real estate closings under certain circumstances). The client may then wonder why he cannot hire a nonlawyer directly and save the overhead.

Constitutional Limitations

Despite the claim of inherent judicial power to define "law practice," several constraints exist. One is the federal Constitution.

In National Revenue Corp. v. Violet, 807 F.2d 285 (1st Cir. 1986), the court reviewed a state law that prohibited anyone but state-licensed lawyers from engaging in debt collection in Rhode Island. The court held that the law unconstitutionally burdened interstate commerce. But see Ferguson v. Skrupa, 372 U.S. 726 (1963) (rejecting due process challenge to Kansas law defining "debt adjustment" as the practice of law).

Sperry v. State ex rel. Florida Bar, 373 U.S. 379 (1963), ruled that state power to regulate the practice of law had to yield to incompatible federal legislation that authorized lay representation in cases before the U.S. Patent Office. By virtue of the Supremacy Clause, Congress could authorize lay agents to provide legal services "reasonably necessary and incident to the preparation and prosecution of patent applications." The Court ruled that the "State maintains control over the practice of law within its borders except to the limited extent necessary for the accomplishment of the federal objectives." Furthermore, the Patent Office "safeguards [citizens from unskilled and unethical practitioners] by testing applicants for registration" and by authorizing practice only before the Patent Office. See also Florida Bar re Advisory Opinion, 571 So. 2d 430 (Fla. 1990) (state court cannot prohibit nonlawyers from preparing and presenting documents to federal agencies that have admitted them to practice).

Efforts to stop publication of books or materials that enable purchasers to represent themselves have generally failed, on the theory that the author is offering general advice and is not addressing the reader's or user's legal situation. In New York County Lawyers' Assn. v. Dacey, 234 N.E.2d 459 (N.Y. 1967), the plaintiff bar association tried to stop Norman Dacey from selling his book, *How to Avoid Probate.* The book purported to instruct readers on how they might go about organizing their assets during their lifetime so that upon death these assets would pass to others without having to be administered under the supervision of a probate court. Probate is a "bread-and-butter" area of practice for lawyers, including general practitioners, possibly explaining the motivation for the lawsuit. The state court of appeals ruled that Dacey was not practicing law simply by selling a book containing information about law. See also Oregon State Bar v. Gilchrist, 538 P.2d 913 (Or. 1975) (do-it-yourself divorce kits).

These cases recognize a First Amendment interest in the underlying activity. *Dacey* specifically relied on the dissent in the lower court, 283 N.Y.S.2d 984 (1st Dept. 1967), which cited the federal and state constitutional guarantees of freedom of speech and press. *Gilchrist* cited the same dissent.

Quicken Family Lawyer Meets Texas UPL Statute:
And the Winner Is . . .

The following tale is not a spoof from The Onion. Unauthorized Practice of Law Committee v. Parsons Technology, Inc., 1999 Westlaw 47235 (N.D. Tex. 1999), offers a pitch-perfect parody of state bar efforts to deny consumers self-help legal material. Plaintiff sought to enjoin the sale of Quicken Family Lawyer in Texas. As the court described it,

> QFL offers over 100 different legal forms (such as employment agreements, real estate leases, premarital agreements, and seven different will forms) along with instructions on how to fill out these forms. QFL's packaging represents that the product is "valid in 49 states, including the District of Columbia"; is "developed and reviewed by expert attorneys"; and is "updated to reflect recent legislative formats." The packaging also indicates that QFL will have the user "answer a few questions to determine which estate planning and health care documents best meet [the user's] needs"; and that QFL will "interview you in a logical order, tailoring documents to your situation." Finally, the packaging reassures the user that "[h]andy hints and comprehensive legal help topics are always available."

The court went on to explain in some detail the volume of information available on QFL and the methodology for interactive use. One notable feature is called "Ask Arthur Miller," which the court says enables the user to select predesignated questions (e.g., "Doesn't a premarital agreement take the romance out of marriage?") and get "either a text-based answer [or] if the user's computer has a CD-ROM player, a sound card and a video card, a sound and video image of Arthur Miller answering the question. . . ." (What makes him an expert on that question?)

Distinguishing *Dacey* and rejecting the Parsons first amendment arguments, the court concluded that Quicken Family Lawyer violated the Texas UPL statute and enjoined its sale. "QFL is far more than a static form with instructions on how to fill in the blanks. For instance, QFL adapts the content of the form to the responses given by the user. QFL purports to select the appropriate health care document for an individual based upon the state in which she lives. The packaging of QFL makes various representations as to the accuracy and specificity of the forms."

The Texas legislature reacted immediately. It amended the state UPL statute to provide that the practice of law "does not include the design, creation, publication, distribution, display, or sale . . . [of] computer software, or similar products if the products clearly and conspicuously state that the products are not a substitute for the advice of an attorney." Tex. Govt. Code Ann. §81.101(c) (1999). Thereafter, the Fifth Circuit vacated the lower court's injunction. Unauthorized Practice of Law Committee v. Parsons Technology, Inc., 179 F.3d 956 (5th Cir. 1999).

XIII

Control of Quality: Remedies for Professional Failure

- *When Clients Can Sue Lawyers*
- *When Third Persons Can Sue*
- *Discipline*
- *When Is Assistance of Counsel Effective?*

A. MALPRACTICE AND BREACH OF FIDUCIARY DUTY

An attorney's negligence is based on an objective standard, and whether the attorney acted in good faith in representing a client has no bearing on liability. Although an attorney is not liable for every mistake that may occur in practice, and an error in judgment does not necessarily constitute a basis for liability, a subjective good faith exercise of judgment or an honest belief will not protect an attorney from an otherwise negligent act or omission.

> — Meyer v. Wagner, Massachusetts Supreme Judicial Court (1999)

Maybe an unscrupulous lawyer could have thrown enough sand in the jury's eyes to avert a judgment for the Weekleys, or at least an award of punitive damages, but unwillingness to do so is not evidence of malpractice. Refusal to violate professional ethics — or even to approach as near to the line as humanly possible — is not professional misconduct. A scrupulous lawyer, a lawyer who takes Law Day rhetoric seriously, who sincerely believes that he has a dual duty, to his client and to the law, and acts on his belief, may lose some clients to his less scrupulous competitors but he should not be deemed to be courting a tort judgment.

> — Transcraft, Inc. v. Galvin, Stalmack, Kirschner & Clark, (7th Cir. 1994)

Errors of judgment do not create liability. No need to get as close "to the line" as possible. Pretty thoughts those, but if the size of my research files is any indication, they may not offer much comfort. No topic in this book has witnessed more growth in the nearly three decades since I began working on the first edition than the doctrines surrounding a lawyer's liability to clients and third parties. In parts A, B, and C of this chapter, we inspect the rules governing lawyer liability to clients (both for malpractice and for breach of fiduciary duty) and to third parties, under any of a disturbing number of traditional and novel theories. Disturbing for lawyers, that is. But is it good for everyone else (including the lawyers who bring the cases)? That's the question for examination, or at least one of them.

Some Statistics. In 2008, the ABA reported that for calendar years 2004 to 2007, the following areas of law accounted for the greatest number of claims against lawyers out of all claims filed (percents are rounded): plaintiff's personal injury (21 percent); real estate (20 percent); family law (10 percent); estate, trust, and probate (9 percent); business transaction/commercial law (5 percent); corporate/business organization (5 percent); collection and bankruptcy (7 percent). All of these areas saw an increase in the absolute number of claims filed since an earlier study for the 1999 to 2003 period. The number of total claims filed rose to 40,486 from 36,844 in the 1999 to 2003 period.

Other indicators show an uptick in successful malpractice claims. Of the 40,974 claims that were *concluded* in the 2003 to 2007 period (as opposed to claims filed), about 21 percent resulted in an insurer's payment to the claimant, the same percent as in the prior four-year period. But the absolute number increased. For 2003 to 2007, 2,678 claims led to payments above $50,000 and 124 claims resulted in payments above $1,000,000. For the 1999 to 2003 period, the numbers, respectively, were 1,914 claims and 56 claims. Similarly, the number of claims that resulted in no payment at all—whether insured or not—decreased from 61 percent in 1999 to 2003 to 51 percent in 2003 to 2007. ABA, Profile of Legal Malpractice Claims 2004-2007 (2008). The study is based on reports from leading malpractice insurance carriers and does not capture claims made against lawyers who are uninsured or insured by carriers who did not report to the ABA.

Here are some more dramatic statistics, the kind that get headlines in the business and law press. According to the New York Law Journal (April 12, 2004, at 1), between 1992 and 2004, many of the country's leading law firms (or their insurers) paid huge settlements to clients or third parties, including these: Kaye Scholer paid $41 million to the RTC, a federal receiver for a failed savings and loan (S&L), in 1992; Jones Day paid $51 million to the RTC in 1993; Paul Weiss paid $45 million to the RTC in 1994; Stroock & Stroock paid $11 million to the RTC in 1995; Brown & Wood (now merged into Sidley & Austin) paid $23 million to Orange County, California, in 1998; Morgan Lewis paid $35 million to the Pennsylvania Insurance Dept. in 1998; Simpson Thatcher paid $19.5 million to a client's shareholders in 2004; and Jenkens & Gilchrist paid $75 million in 2004 to former tax clients who claimed the firm gave them bad advice on illegal tax avoidance schemes.

And the trend continues. The National Law Journal (March 31, 2008) reports:

In the past few years, law firms have faced some of the most aggressive and expensive malpractice and fraud lawsuits over their corporate work, with several seeking more than $100 million in damages. Among them are Mayer Brown, Clifford Chance and Akin Gump Strauss Hauer & Feld.

While some of the suits involve clients with straightforward malpractice claims, an increasing number of suits are being filed by the trustees overseeing the bankruptcy of a law firm's client.

Those cases allege both malpractice and other claims, such as aiding and abetting breach of fiduciary duty. At the same time, large investors — particularly private equity firms and hedge funds — have brought suits against law firms, replacing traditional securities fraud allegations in favor of fraud claims. . . .

The latest suits to target law firms have been filed by the trustees overseeing the bankruptcies of their clients.

Of course, not all of these claims succeed. The fact that they are brought, however, displays an increased willingness to sue lawyers (for big money) and confidence among the plaintiffs' lawyers that their legal theories will support liability — or at least get them past a dispositive motion and lead to settlement. And appreciate that a verdict does not have to be $100 million or more to ruin your life. A verdict of even a few million dollars above a modest malpractice policy (if any) can bankrupt a lawyer and destroy a small firm.

Here are some questions to keep in mind as you look at the issues in this chapter:

Is there a "crisis"?   That word keeps popping up in discussions about increased professional liability. Indeed, the words "malpractice" and "crisis" can seem inseparable. One half expects to see them hyphenated. Nonetheless, what is a crisis for lawyers may not be all bad, and from the consumer perspective it may even look good. Or have some of the cases gone too far?

How will increased liability change lawyers' behavior?   Beyond liability to clients for malpractice, lawyers argue that greater legal exposure to nonclients will make them timid, that they will begin to think of themselves first and their clients second, that they will no longer be as zealous, and that as a result the legal system and justice will suffer. A legitimate concern, to be sure, and most influential in litigation, where lawyers are meant to be gladiators, other parties have lawyers to protect them, and a judge is available to guard against excess. And indeed, rarely are lawyers sued for litigation behavior (putting aside misrepresentations in settlement negotiations; see page 512), though they may be sanctioned for frivolous or abusive conduct. See chapter 7E. Arguments that sanctions chill a lawyer's zeal have not been persuasive. Meanwhile, transactional work occurs not in a public forum but in private, so the prospect of a lawyer's civil liability may help deter bad behavior.

Is there a connection between professionalism and the "crisis"?   Although perhaps it can never be proved in any but an anecdotal way, an increase in civil liability to clients and others may be partly a consequence of the perceived diminution of professionalism (page 15). This risk is in fact cited by those who favor rules that would prevent law firms from owning ancillary businesses (page 852). If the public (read juries and plaintiffs) believe that lawyers are no different from other business people — that the professional label no longer quite fits — and indeed if the bar's behavior offers evidence to support that belief, might we not expect lawyers to be tempting lawsuit targets, no different from anyone else? If a deal turns sour — and investors or purchasers who lose money start looking for someone to sue — lawyers, with their deep pockets, and perhaps large malpractice policies, will appear mighty tempting. That certainly happened after the S&L failures. Several big law firms settled claims for tens of millions of dollars. Complain as they will, lawyers should remember that before they wind up on the defendants' side of the court caption, another lawyer has to put them there.

Is greater liability exposure the result of a decrease in the sanctity of professions generally? Here we encounter several trends. First is the increase in malpractice actions against doctors. By bringing and winning these actions for great sums of money, lawyers made it socially acceptable to sue professionals and to seek large recoveries or settlements. No longer is it seen as thankless to sue someone who tried to help you when you were in trouble. Second is the increase in the liability of accountants to persons who are not in privity with them (in other words, nonclients). By bringing these "third party" actions and persuading courts to adopt doctrines leading to huge recoveries or settlements against accountants, often in class actions, lawyers created the theories (or at least encouraged an attitude) that could easily be turned against the bar. After all, unlike doctors, accountants and lawyers sell similar services (and sometimes, as in the tax area, the same service).

1.   Liability to Clients

"When Sally Left Harry . . ."

Memorandum

"To: New Business Committee
"Fr: Emily Adichie

"Adam Rosini represented Sally Terzakis nearly three years ago when she asked her husband Harry Kovair for a divorce. You know Harry Kovair from the business pages — bald with a close beard, skinny as a string bean. Anyway, Adam is a partner in Rosini, Wattenberg & Yossarian LLP, a nine-lawyer firm that does general civil representation. Sally's divorce ended the way most do — with a settlement agreement. In fact, going to court was pro forma since the couple had agreed on everything beforehand.

"Sally came to see me last Tuesday because she was beginning to have doubts about Adam's work. It seems she was at a party down at the beach last month, and a woman there told her that when *she* got divorced some two years ago, the settlement included half the increased value of property her husband inherited during their marriage. Which apparently was a healthy piece of change. And that got Sally thinking.

"In our state, as you know, property you inherit during the marriage and hold in your own name is not subject to division in the event of divorce. Of that there is no doubt. But for quite some time, it was unclear whether the same exclusion applied to any increase in the value of that property. Say you inherit stock worth $10,000 and two years later, when you divorce, it's worth $12,000. Does your spouse have a claim against the $2,000 gain? That was the question in Sally's case.

"When Sally left Harry, nobody knew the answer for sure. In a case called *Rojinski v. Rojinski*, a trial court in another county of the state had ruled, two years before Sally hired Adam, that the increase was *not* subject to equitable distribution. It was a thorough opinion by a respected judge, and it was affirmed in an intermediate appellate opinion ten months later. Neither opinion was binding in our county (where Sally and Harry lived) because we're in a different judicial district. But both were likely to be influential in our county and in the state supreme court when the issue reached it, as inevitably it would. *Rojinski* settled without reaching the supreme court. Cases from other state high courts went both ways, but mostly they disagreed with *Rojinski*. Most secondary authorities, including a leading law review article, also disagreed. This was the state of things when Sally hired Adam.

"I don't know how much of all this Adam knew or what research he did, except that I do know that he was intimately familiar with *Rojinski* because he represented the successful spouse, the wife. The *Rojinski* court held that the increase in the value of her inheritance was not subject to division. When Adam negotiated Sally's separation agreement, he did not seek half of the increased value of Harry's sizeable real estate inheritance. The increase in value totaled about $3 million. Now, Sally wants to know why she didn't get half of it, like the woman she met at the beach. I should say that Harry had other assets subject to distribution. Sally's share of these was over $4 million. She was left pretty well off.

"The other thing I learned since I met with Sally is that while Adam was her lawyer, his partner Gretchen Baxindell was representing a limited real-estate partnership that was negotiating for a large parcel of land on which to build a shopping center. Harry had a 25 percent interest in the partnership. (Sally did get her share of Harry's interest in the partnership.) I'm sure Sally knew that Gretchen was Adam's partner but she would have had no reason to know that Gretchen was the lawyer for Adam's real-estate partnership.

"Last year, our state supreme court finally addressed the appreciated value question and agreed with *Rojinski* 5-2. Two months later, faster than it does nearly anything else except vote itself pay raises, the legislature overturned the supreme court's decision prospectively, and the governor signed the bill the next day. So we know that if Sally got divorced today, she'd get half of the $3 million increment in the value of Harry's inheritance. But we also know that at the time of her divorce, she would have lost before the supreme court, whose membership hasn't changed in six years, assuming as we must that the judges voted the same way.

"Sally is coming by to see me tomorrow to find out if she has a case against Adam and, if so, whether we're willing to take it. So I would first like to know what you think about that. What would be the theory of liability? Was Adam guilty of malpractice? Was he conflicted? What kind of proof could I use? What were Sally's damages, if any? How can I prove those? Does the fact that Sally would have lost before the state high court if her case had gone there when Adam was her lawyer mean she has no claim against Rosini and his firm?

"I have this further complication. Yesterday, I learned that our partner Dinitia Rodriguez is representing Brenda Cleary in a complicated estate litigation arising out of the death of Brenda's stepfather. Brenda is the executor of the estate. Brenda is also Adam's partner. Does that create a conflict that prevents me from representing Sally without waivers? I did do a conflicts check before meeting with Sally, and I did check both Rosini and his firm, but it never occurred to me to look to see if we were representing any of the other lawyers in the firm personally. Does it matter?

"And as if all this were not complicated enough, if we do have a conflict and don't want to or can't get consents, what do I tell Sally, if anything, about what my research shows thus far with respect to Adam's (and vicariously his firm's) liability? One thing my research confirmed, although I already knew this, is that the statute of limitations on lawyer malpractice and breach of fiduciary duty claims in this jurisdiction is three years, which means Sally has seven weeks and three days to bring any claim or she's sunk."

Once again we confront the "Who is a client?" question. As you know by now, in our new Einsteinian universe of lawyer regulation, this question can no longer be answered with good old Newtonian certainty. Very often, of course, there will be no room to quibble, especially if the purported client has a retainer agreement, monthly statements, and a pile of canceled checks (generally sufficient but by no means necessary conditions for creation of a professional relationship). Occasionally, however, the issue will be fuzzier, as we see in the wonderful *Togstad* case (a law teacher's dream) and the note below.

A lawyer can also be sued by a nonclient on any of a number of theories (which seem to be increasing exponentially). We plumb this trend in part C, which also identifies some untraditional theories for liability to clients. But if lawyers can be liable to nonclients, why the big deal about whether the plaintiff was or was not a client? For two reasons. First, some jurisdictions are hesitant to expand the bases for liability to nonclients fearing that the risk of nonclient liability will detract from the lawyer's loyalty to the client, so the plaintiff is either a client or may be out of court. Second, even in places that give nonclients lots of room to sue lawyers, clients will enjoy yet more room. Lawyers always have fiduciary relationships with their clients, but infrequently with nonclients. And lawyers will *always* owe clients a duty of care in the performance of their legal work; not so with nonclients.

To gain one or both of these advantages of "clienthood," plaintiffs who would not traditionally have been considered clients of a lawyer may attempt to squeeze into a client's shoes, to become client-equivalents, part way between traditional clients and third persons, as discussed in part A2.

As you read *Togstad*, think about the following questions:

1. What is the court's basis for concluding that an attorney-client relationship existed? Who was (were) Miller's client(s)? How did each of the parties try to characterize their conversation so as to encourage the conclusion that there was or was not a professional relationship?

2.   Precisely what did Miller do or fail to do that was wrong? Stated otherwise, on each of the two theories of liability, what could he have done to avoid malpractice liability?

3.   Assume a law firm, after reading *Togstad*, asked you to write a memo to its lawyers specifying office protocols that would allow them to meet with possible new clients without exposing themselves to the fate of Miller's firm. What policies do you recommend?

4.   Do law firms that decline to accept a litigation have a duty to advise on the statute of limitations? Does Emily in the problem above?

TOGSTAD v. VESELY, OTTO, MILLER & KEEFE
291 N.W.2d 686 (Minn. 1980)

PER CURIAM.

This is an appeal by the defendants from a judgment of the Hennepin County District Court involving an action for legal malpractice. The jury found that the defendant attorney Jerre Miller was negligent and that, as a direct result of such negligence, plaintiff John Togstad sustained damages in the amount of $610,500 and his wife, plaintiff Joan Togstad, in the amount of $39,000. Defendants (Miller and his law firm) appeal to this court from the denial of their motion for judgment notwithstanding the verdict or, alternatively, for a new trial. We affirm.

In August 1971, John Togstad began to experience severe headaches and on August 16, 1971, was admitted to Methodist Hospital where tests disclosed that the headaches were caused by a large aneurysm on the left internal carotid artery. The attending physician, Dr. Paul Blake, a neurological surgeon, treated the problem by applying a Selverstone clamp to the left common carotid artery. The clamp was surgically implanted on August 27, 1971, in Togstad's neck to allow the gradual closure of the artery over a period of days. . . .

In the early morning hours of August 29, 1971, a nurse observed that Togstad was unable to speak or move. At the time, the clamp was one-half (50%) closed. Upon discovering Togstad's condition, the nurse called a resident physician, who did not adjust the clamp. Dr. Blake was also immediately informed of Togstad's condition and arrived about an hour later, at which time he opened the clamp. Togstad is now severely paralyzed in his right arm and leg, and is unable to speak.

Plaintiffs' expert, Dr. Ward Woods, testified that Togstad's paralysis and loss of speech was due to a lack of blood supply to his brain. Dr. Woods stated that the inadequate blood flow resulted from the clamp being 50% closed and that the negligence of Dr. Blake and the hospital precluded the clamp's being opened in time to avoid permanent brain damage. Specifically, Dr. Woods claimed that Dr. Blake and the hospital were negligent for (1) failing to place the patient in the intensive care unit or to have a special nurse conduct certain neurological tests every half-hour; (2) failing to write adequate orders; (3) failing to open the clamp immediately upon discovering that the patient was unable to speak; and (4) the absence of personnel capable of opening the clamp. . . .

About 14 months after her husband's hospitalization began, plaintiff Joan Togstad met with attorney Jerre Miller regarding her husband's condition.

Neither she nor her husband was personally acquainted with Miller or his law firm prior to that time. John Togstad's former work supervisor, Ted Bucholz, made the appointment and accompanied Mrs. Togstad to Miller's office. Bucholz was present when Mrs. Togstad and Miller discussed the case.[3]

Mrs. Togstad had become suspicious of the circumstances surrounding her husband's tragic condition due to the conduct and statements of the hospital nurses shortly after the paralysis occurred. One nurse told Mrs. Togstad that she had checked Mr. Togstad at 2 A.M. and he was fine; that when she returned at 3 A.M. by mistake, to give him someone else's medication, he was unable to move or speak; and that if she hadn't accidentally entered the room no one would have discovered his condition until morning. Mrs. Togstad also noticed that the other nurses were upset and crying, and that Mr. Togstad's condition was a topic of conversation.

Mrs. Togstad testified that she told Miller "everything that happened at the hospital," including the nurses' statements and conduct which had raised a question in her mind. She stated that she "believed" she had told Miller "about the procedure and what was undertaken, what was done, and what happened." She brought no records with her. Miller took notes and asked questions during the meeting, which lasted 45 minutes to an hour. At its conclusion, according to Mrs. Togstad, Miller said that "he did not think we had a legal case, however, he was going to discuss this with his partner." She understood that if Miller changed his mind after talking to his partner, he would call her. Mrs. Togstad "gave it" a few days and, since she did not hear from Miller, decided "that they had come to the conclusion that there wasn't a case." No fee arrangements were discussed, no medical authorizations were requested, nor was Mrs. Togstad billed for the interview.

Mrs. Togstad denied that Miller had told her his firm did not have expertise in the medical malpractice field, urged her to see another attorney, or related to her that the statute of limitations for medical malpractice actions was two years. She did not consult another attorney until one year after she talked to Miller. Mrs. Togstad indicated that she did not confer with another attorney earlier because of her reliance on Miller's "legal advice" that they "did not have a case."

On cross-examination, Mrs. Togstad was asked whether she went to Miller's office "to see if he would take the case of [her] husband. . . ." She replied, "Well I guess it was to go for legal advice, what to do, where shall we go from here? That is what we went for." Again in response to defense counsel's questions, Mrs. Togstad testified as follows:

Q. And it was clear to you, was it not, that what was taking place was a preliminary discussion between a prospective client and lawyer as to whether or not they wanted to enter into an attorney-client relationship?

A. I am not sure how to answer that. It was for legal advice as to what to do.

Q. And Mr. Miller was discussing with you your problem and indicating whether he, as a lawyer, wished to take the case, isn't that true?

A. Yes.

---

3. Bucholz, who knew Miller through a local luncheon club, died prior to the trial of the instant action.

On re-direct examination, Mrs. Togstad acknowledged that when she left Miller's office she understood that she had been given a "qualified, quality legal opinion that [she and her husband] did not have a malpractice case."

Miller's testimony was different in some respects from that of Mrs. Togstad. Like Mrs. Togstad, Miller testified that Mr. Bucholz arranged and was present at the meeting, which lasted about 45 minutes. According to Miller, Mrs. Togstad described the hospital incident, including the conduct of the nurses. He asked her questions, to which she responded. Miller testified that "[t]he only thing I told her [Mrs. Togstad] after we had pretty much finished the conversation was that there was nothing related in her factual circumstances that told me that she had a case that our firm would be interested in undertaking."

Miller also claimed he related to Mrs. Togstad "that because of the grievous nature of the injuries sustained by her husband, that this was only my opinion and she was encouraged to ask another attorney if she wished for another opinion" and "she ought to do so promptly." He testified that he informed Mrs. Togstad that his firm "was not engaged as experts" in the area of medical malpractice, and that they associated with the Charles Hvass firm in cases of that nature. Miller stated that at the end of the conference he told Mrs. Togstad that he would consult with Charles Hvass and if Hvass's opinion differed from his, Miller would so inform her. Miller recollected that he called Hvass a "couple days" later and discussed the case with him. It was Miller's impression that Hvass thought there was no liability for malpractice in the case. Consequently, Miller did not communicate with Mrs. Togstad further.

On cross-examination, Miller testified as follows:

Q. Now, so there is no misunderstanding, and I am reading from your deposition, you understood that she was consulting with you as a lawyer, isn't that correct?

A. That's correct.

Q. That she was seeking legal advice from a professional attorney licensed to practice in this state and in this community?

A. I think you and I did have another interpretation or use of the term "Advice." She was there to see whether or not she had a case and whether the firm would accept it.

Q. We have two aspects; number one, your legal opinion concerning liability of a case for malpractice; number two, whether there was or wasn't liability, whether you would accept it, your firm, two separate elements, right?

A. I would say so.

Q. Were you asked on page 6 in the deposition, folio 14, "And you understood that she was seeking legal advice at the time that she was in your office, that is correct also, isn't it?" And did you give this answer, "I don't want to engage in semantics with you, but my impression was that she and Mr. Bucholz were asking my opinion after having related the incident that I referred to." The next question, "Your legal opinion?" Your answer, "Yes." Were those questions asked and were [those answers] given?

Mr. Collins: Objection to this, Your Honor. It is not impeachment. The Court: Overruled.

The Witness: Yes, I gave those answers. Certainly, she was seeking my opinion as
   an attorney in the sense of whether or not there was a case that the firm
   would be interested in undertaking.

Kenneth Green, a Minneapolis attorney, was called as an expert by plaintiffs.
He stated that in rendering legal advice regarding a claim of medical malpractice, the "minimum" an attorney should do would be to request medical authorizations from the client, review the hospital records, and consult with an expert
in the field. John McNulty, a Minneapolis attorney, and Charles Hvass testified as
experts on behalf of the defendants. McNulty stated that when an attorney is
consulted as to whether he will take a case, the lawyer's only responsibility in
refusing it is to so inform the party. He testified, however, that when a lawyer is
asked his legal opinion on the merits of a medical malpractice claim, community
standards require that the attorney check hospital records and consult with an
expert before rendering his opinion.

Hvass stated that he had no recollection of Miller's calling him in October
1972 relative to the Togstad matter. He testified that:

A.   . . . when a person comes in to me about a medical malpractice action,
   based upon what the individual has told me, I have to make a decision as
   to whether or not there probably is or probably is not, based upon that
   information, medical malpractice. And if, in my judgment, based upon
   what the client has told me, there is not medical malpractice, I will so
   inform the client.

Hvass stated, however, that he would never render a "categorical" opinion. In
addition, Hvass acknowledged that if he were consulted for a "legal opinion"
regarding medical malpractice and 14 months had expired since the incident in
question, "ordinary care and diligence" would require him to inform the party
of the two-year statute of limitations applicable to that type of action.

This case was submitted to the jury by way of a special verdict form. The jury
found that Dr. Blake and the hospital were negligent and that Dr. Blake's negligence (but not the hospital's) was a direct cause of the injuries sustained by
John Togstad; that there was an attorney-client contractual relationship between
Mrs. Togstad and Miller; that Miller was negligent in rendering advice regarding
the possible claims of Mr. and Mrs. Togstad; that, but for Miller's negligence,
plaintiffs would have been successful in the prosecution of a legal action against
Dr. Blake; and that neither Mr. nor Mrs. Togstad was negligent in pursuing their
claims against Dr. Blake. The jury awarded damages to Mr. Togstad of $610,500
and to Mrs. Togstad of $39,000. . . .

In a legal malpractice action of the type involved here, four elements must be
shown: (1) that an attorney-client relationship existed; (2) that defendant acted
negligently or in breach of contract; (3) that such acts were the proximate cause
of the plaintiffs' damages; (4) that but for defendant's conduct the plaintiffs
would have been successful in the prosecution of their medical malpractice
claim.

This court first dealt with the element of lawyer-client relationship in the
decision of Ryan v. Long. The *Ryan* case involved a claim of legal malpractice
and on appeal it was argued that no attorney-client relation existed. This court,

without stating whether its conclusion was based on contract principles or a tort theory, disagreed:

> [I]t sufficiently appears that plaintiff, for himself, called upon defendant, as an attorney at law, for "legal advice," and that defendant assumed to give him a professional opinion in reference to the matter as to which plaintiff consulted him. Upon this state of facts the defendant must be taken to have acted as plaintiff's legal adviser, at plaintiff's request, and so as to establish between them the relation of attorney and client.

More recent opinions of this court, although not involving a detailed discussion, have analyzed the attorney-client consideration in contractual terms. . . .

We believe it is unnecessary to decide whether a tort or contract theory is preferable for resolving the attorney-client relationship question raised by this appeal. The tort and contract analyses are very similar in a case such as the instant one,[4] and we conclude that under either theory the evidence shows that a lawyer-client relationship is present here. The thrust of Mrs. Togstad's testimony is that she went to Miller for legal advice, was told there wasn't a case, and relied upon this advice in failing to pursue the claim for medical malpractice. In addition, according to Mrs. Togstad, Miller did not qualify this legal opinion by urging her to seek advice from another attorney, nor did Miller inform her that he lacked expertise in the medical malpractice area. Assuming this testimony is true, as this court must do, we believe a jury could properly find that Mrs. Togstad sought and received legal advice from Miller under circumstances which made it reasonably foreseeable to Miller that Mrs. Togstad would be injured if the advice were negligently given. Thus, under either a tort or contract analysis, there is sufficient evidence in the record to support the existence of an attorney-client relationship.

Defendants argue that even if an attorney-client relationship was established the evidence fails to show that Miller acted negligently in assessing the merits of the Togstads' case. They appear to contend that, at most, Miller was guilty of an error in judgment which does not give rise to legal malpractice. However, this case does not involve a mere error of judgment. The gist of plaintiffs' claim is that Miller failed to perform the minimal research that an ordinarily prudent attorney would do before rendering legal advice in a case of this nature. The record, through the testimony of Kenneth Green and John McNulty, contains sufficient evidence to support plaintiffs' position.

In a related contention, defendants assert that a new trial should be awarded on the ground that the trial court erred by refusing to instruct the jury that Miller's failure to inform Mrs. Togstad of the two-year statute of limitations for medical malpractice could not constitute negligence. The argument continues

---

4. Under a negligence approach it must essentially be shown that defendant rendered legal advice (not necessarily at someone's request) under circumstances which made it reasonably foreseeable to the attorney that if such advice was rendered negligently, the individual receiving the advice might be injured thereby. Or stated another way, under a tort theory, "[a]n attorney-client relationship is created whenever an individual seeks and receives legal advice from an attorney in circumstances in which a reasonable person would rely on such advice." 63 Minn. L. Rev. 751, 759 (1979). A contract analysis requires the rendering of legal advice pursuant to another's request and the reliance factor, in this case, where the advice was not paid for, need be shown in the form of promissory estoppel.

that since it is unclear from the record on what theory or theories of negligence the jury based its decision, a new trial must be granted.

The defect in defendants' reasoning is that there is adequate evidence supporting the claim that Miller was also negligent in failing to advise Mrs. Togstad of the two-year medical malpractice limitations period and thus the trial court acted properly in refusing to instruct the jury in the manner urged by defendants. One of defendants' expert witnesses, Charles Hvass, testified:

Q. Now, Mr. Hvass, where you are consulted for a legal opinion and advice concerning malpractice and 14 months have elapsed [since the incident in question], wouldn't—and you hold yourself out as competent to give a legal opinion and advice to these people concerning their rights, wouldn't ordinary care and diligence require that you inform them that there is a two-year statute of limitations within which they have to act or lose their rights?

A. Yes. I believe I would have advised someone of the two-year period of limitation, yes.

Consequently, based on the testimony of Mrs. Togstad, i.e., that she requested and received legal advice from Miller concerning the malpractice claim, and the above testimony of Hvass, we must reject the defendants' contention, as it was reasonable for a jury to determine that Miller acted negligently in failing to inform Mrs. Togstad of the applicable limitations period.

There is also sufficient evidence in the record establishing that, but for Miller's negligence, plaintiffs would have been successful in prosecuting their medical malpractice claim. Dr. Woods, in no uncertain terms, concluded that Mr. Togstad's injuries were caused by the medical malpractice of Dr. Blake. Defendants' expert testimony to the contrary was obviously not believed by the jury. Thus, the jury reasonably found that had plaintiffs' medical malpractice action been properly brought, plaintiffs would have recovered.

Based on the foregoing, we hold that the jury's findings are adequately supported by the record. Accordingly we uphold the trial court's denial of defendants' motion for judgment notwithstanding the jury verdict. . . .

The Clifford firm accepted a wrongful death case in March 2001. In August 2001, it wrote to the representative of the estate (father of the decedent) to withdraw from the matter. It told the father that the statute of limitations was two years from death. That was wrong. It was one year. Before one year expired, the father consulted a new lawyer, Loran, who, in declining the matter, warned the father that "all lawsuits are limited by a period prescribed by statute." But he did not state the period for the father's claim. When the father next consulted counsel, a year had elapsed and his claim failed. He sued the Clifford firm, which argued, among other things, that Loran's failure to advise on the precise limitations period when he declined the case was a superseding cause of the loss of the claim. The court disagreed. "We do not find any Illinois authority which would impose that burden upon an attorney on the strength of an exploratory meeting which did not result in an acceptance of the case."

Lopez v. Clifford Law Offices, P.C., 841 N.E.2d 465 (Ill.App. 2005). On this reasoning, would Jerre Miller have avoided liability to the Togstads if the case had arisen in Illinois?

What Is the Required Standard of Care?

I sometimes try to understand why *Togstad* ever happened. Why did Miller slip up? The answer I keep coming back to is that he slipped up because he's a nice guy. As I imagine it, Miller agreed, at the request of a friend (now deceased), to meet with Mrs. Togstad to allay her nagging concern that she wasn't doing right by her husband. The visit with Miller gave her the opportunity to get peace of mind. If I'm right — and maybe I'm not, I'm just trying to channel Miller — is there a lesson here? Perhaps it is that the road to malpractice liability can be paved with all of the best intentions? I'm not defending Miller's conduct. I'm just trying to understand it.

As the *Togstad* court wrote, a "mere error of judgment" does not constitute malpractice. Instead the court looked at what "an ordinarily prudent attorney would do before rendering legal advice in a case of this nature" and concluded that Miller failed to do the "minimal research" necessary to satisfy that standard. Ordinary prudence is the standard; here, failure to do the research violated it. A reasonable (but as it turns out, wrong) opinion reached after appropriate legal and factual research may be immune to liability because not every misjudgment is malpractice; but the same conclusion reached with no research can be actionable. Jerry's Enterprises, Inc. v. Larkin, Hoffman, Daly & Lindgren, 711 N.W.2d 811 (Minn. 2006) (citing *Togstad*, court holds that lawyer who failed to do the necessary research cannot claim an exercise of reasonable judgment as a defense to a malpractice claim). *Lesson: Save your research notes.*

Courts follow the *Togstad* description of the generic standard. One court wrote that a lawyer is obligated to exercise "that degree of care, skill, diligence and knowledge commonly possessed and exercised by a reasonable, careful and prudent lawyer in the practice of law in this jurisdiction." Cook, Flanagan & Berst v. Clausing, 438 P.2d 865 (Wash. 1968). An old opinion but the law hasn't changed. See also Cosgrove v. Grimes, 774 S.W.2d 662 (Tex. 1989) (attorney's subjective good faith is no defense if he failed to act as a reasonably prudent lawyer would have acted under the circumstances). Efforts to extend the geographical range, so that the standard includes the profession generally and not lawyers in a particular state, have failed. Kellos v. Sawilowsky, 325 S.E.2d 757 (Ga. 1985) (degree of skill, prudence, and diligence of Georgia lawyers). Chapman v. Bearfield, 207 S.W.3d 736 (2006), adopts a statewide standard for Tennessee.

If a lawyer has persuaded a client to use her services by proclaiming some expertise in a particular field, the client will expect her to know more about the field than a lawyer who makes no such claims, and the lawyer will be judged by the standard of the specialty. What kind of statement will suffice to trigger this higher standard? See Neel v. Magana, Olney, Levy, Cathcart & Gelfand, 491 P.2d 421 (Cal. 1971) (if a lawyer "further specializes within the profession, he must meet the standards of knowledge and skill of such specialists"); Walker v. Bangs, 601 P.2d 1279 (Wash. 1979) (generally, "one who holds himself out as specializing and as possessing greater than ordinary knowledge and skill in a particular field, will be held to the standard of performance of those who hold themselves out as specialists in that area").

Settlement Duties.   The duty of care a lawyer owes a client includes a duty to attempt to effectuate a reasonable settlement where standards of professional care in the jurisdiction should lead the lawyer to conclude that settlement will be the most reasonable way to achieve the client's goals. Mutuelles Unies v. Kroll & Linstrom, 957 F.2d 707 (9th Cir. 1992) (applying California law). When a lawyer does recommend a settlement, he risks liability if he does not do the legal and factual research necessary to determine its adequacy. Meyer v. Wagner, 709 N.E.2d 784 (Mass. 1999) (collecting cases including contrary authority from Pennsylvania). In criminal cases, settlements are called plea bargains. In an unusual case, Boria v Keane, 99 F.3d 492 (2d Cir. 1996), the court wrote:

> There seems to be no Second Circuit decision dealing with the precise question of a criminal defense lawyer's duty when a defendant's best interests clearly require that a proffered plea bargain be accepted, but the defendant, professing innocence, refuses to consider the matter. This lack of specific decision undoubtedly arises from the circumstance that such duty is so well understood by lawyers practicing in this Circuit that the question has never been litigated.
>
> While the Second Circuit may not have spoken, the Strickland [v. Washington] Court [page 811] has indicated how the question should be resolved. Just before starting its discussion of the merits, it observed that it had "granted certiorari to consider the standards by which to judge a contention that the Constitution requires that a criminal judgment be overturned because of the actual ineffective assistance of counsel." Later it pointed to "[p]revailing norms of practice as reflected in American Bar Association standards" as guides "to determining what is reasonable."
>
> The American Bar Association's standard on the precise question before us is simply stated in its Model Code of Professional Responsibility, Ethical Consideration 7-7 (1992): "A defense lawyer in a criminal case has the duty to advise his client fully *on whether a particular plea to a charge appears to be desirable.*" (Emphasis added.)

The defendant in Boria v. Keane had been charged with selling drugs. He was offered a plea bargain of one to three years, turned it down, and was convicted and sentenced to 20 years to life. The court held that the defense lawyer's failure to advise the defendant on the wisdom of accepting the offer — merely deferring to the defendant's rejection — was ineffective assistance of counsel, that the client would likely have accepted the offer if counsel had done his job, and that the remedy was to give the defendant the benefit of the plea offer, which resulted in immediate release after six years in prison.

Fraud and Misrepresentation

It should come as no surprise that a lawyer who defrauds a client will be liable for that conduct. Were it not for Baker v. Dorfman, 239 F.3d 415 (2d Cir. 2000), and Wilson v. Vanden Berg, 687 N.W.2d 575 (Iowa 2004), we might have left it at that. But the facts of these cases are irresistible. In 1994, Ricky Baker retained David Alan Dorfman (who should not be confused with a law professor who shares his first and last name). Dorfman was then 27 years old and two years out of law school. Baker wanted to sue New York City after its health department erroneously diagnosed him as HIV positive. It took nine months for the city to correct the error. Unfortunately, Dorfman failed to file the action before the limitations period expired, and Baker lost his claim against the city. He sued Dorfman. So far the case is quite conventional. But in addition to suing for malpractice, Baker sued for fraud. What was the fraud? Dorfman had lied to Baker about his qualifications for the work. In other words, this was an extreme case of resumé padding. The trial judge listed 13 examples, which the circuit opinion recounts. Among the misrepresentations were the extent of Dorfman's trial experience, the number of his bar memberships, that he had created a graduate law degree in health care law at N.Y.U., and that he had taught at N.Y.U.

The Second Circuit affirmed Baker's judgment for compensatory and punitive damages, including $285,000 for emotional distress. In response to Dorfman's claim that his exaggerations were "mere puffery," Judge Jacobs wrote:

> It can be expected that any professional will convey to potential clients a healthy self-estimation. But as the district court noted, "the evidence at trial established that virtually all of the representations in Dorfman's resumé were either false or grossly misleading, and created the false impression for Baker of an experienced litigator. . . ."
>
> Dorfman knowingly and with intent to deceive made numerous material misrepresentations concerning his experience and expertise. Baker then reasonably relied on those misrepresentations to his obvious detriment. Accordingly, the fraud judgment—and thus the punitive damages award—is affirmed.

Dorfman evaded payment of the judgment for seven more years. In 2007, 13 years after Baker first retained him, a district judge found Dorfman in criminal contempt for avoiding payment orders and sentenced him to two years probation on condition that he honor a new payment schedule. New York Law Journal, Dec. 20, 2007. Dorfman's self-destructive conduct is beyond the comprehension of persons legally trained. But the larger point remains. Overstating your credentials violates your duty to a client. See also Valentine v. Watters, 896 So. 2d 385 (Ala. 2004) (jury may decide that misrepresenting experience in breast implant products liability litigation is a breach of standard of care without need for expert testimony).

The fraud alleged in *Wilson* was different. The plaintiffs hired Vanden Berg, a Mason City lawyer, to pursue a claim against Huff, a local realtor who, they alleged, had misrepresented the size of residential property he sold them. The Wilsons were concerned that personal relationships in town might interfere with Vanden Berg's ability to represent them against Huff, but Vanden Berg assured them that he had no conflict. Later, in the Wilsons' presence, Vanden Berg called Huff and "without identifying himself, began his conversation with Huff by stating 'Hey buddy, what's up?'" Still later, Vanden Berg told the Wilsons to get another lawyer. He could not sue Huff because it "would result in 'potential conflicts with realtors in the area' with whom Vanden Berg worked." The Wilsons sued Vanden Berg in small claims court and recovered compensatory and punitive damages. Upholding the verdict, the supreme court said Vanden Berg's "conduct constituted a willful and wanton disregard for the plaintiffs' [interest and because it also] amounts to fraud, an intentional tort, there was a sufficient factual and legal basis for the court's award of punitive damages." See also Black v. Shultz, 530 F.3d 702 (8th Cir. 2008) (client has claim for harm from "patently false and negligent legal advice," regardless of the merits of the underlying claim, which her lawyer had failed to bring while falsely assuring her that he had done so).

Breach of Fiduciary Duties

Civil liability can be based on conduct other than a failure to exercise the proper standard of care. It can also be based on violation of a duty the lawyer owes the client as a fiduciary. (See chapter 2B.) For example, a fiduciary's duty of loyalty requires him to avoid conflicts of interest. (Ethics rules require the same.) If a client suffers a loss as a result of a lawyer's conflict of interest, the client will be able to recover for breach of fiduciary duty or in malpractice. These theories of recovery are often used interchangeably. That's fine. However, the concepts are not the same. First, as a matter of doctrinal purity, we should realize that only professionals can be guilty of malpractice (as we use the word). A truck driver who crashes may be negligent, but we do not say she is guilty of malpractice. The same for a carpenter who builds a wobbly desk. We reserve the word for professionals: lawyers, doctors, architects, and accountants, among others. Why this should be so — and the criteria for the designation as a profession — may be a product of history and interest group politics. Certainly, the answer cannot be because only members of a profession have expertise far beyond that of their customers, clients, and patients. At least not today. A plumber and an airline pilot clearly have that expertise as well.

Fiduciary duty, however, applies to a much large audience. All agents are fiduciaries and may therefore be guilty of breach of fiduciary duty even if they are not professionals and cannot be guilty of malpractice. An agent who steals or abuses a principal's confidential information breaches fiduciary duty.

The difference can have practical consequences. For example, in Vallinoto v. DiSandro, 688 A.2d 830 (R.I. 1997), the court addressed a jury verdict in favor of a former matrimonial client whose lawyer demanded sexual favors during the representation. She said she complied because she feared the lawyer would otherwise cease to represent her, and she would be unable to find new counsel. However, the plaintiff could show no professional negligence. Her case had not suffered. Further, the complaint had not alleged breach of fiduciary duty. The court acknowledged, as discussed below, that the lawyer's conduct could breach fiduciary duty, had that been alleged. The plaintiff's $225,000 verdict was reversed. (The lawyer was censured in a separate proceeding. Matter of DiSandro, 680 A.2d 73 (R.I. 1996).) We discuss sex with clients as a basis for discipline at page 784.

A fiduciary may not use a client's confidential information to the client's disadvantage. This is an ethical rule too. Rules 1.8(b), 1.9(c)(1). If a lawyer does that, the lawyer will be liable for damages. See Tri-Growth Centre City,

Ltd. v. Silldorf, Burdman, Duignan & Eisenberg, 265 Cal. Rptr. 330 (Ct. App. 1989); Perez v. Kirk & Carrigan, page 32. Breach of fiduciary duty can also occur if a lawyer helps another agent of a client violate the agent's fiduciary duties to the client. In Avianca, Inc. v. Corriea, 705 F. Supp. 666 (D.D.C. 1989), a lawyer for the plaintiff corporation had allegedly helped one of the plaintiff's officers secretly compete with the corporation. See also page 561. Professors Roy Anderson and Walter Steele have unraveled the differences among the various available theories for suing lawyers in their valuable analysis, Fiduciary Duty, Tort and Contract: A Primer on the Legal Malpractice Puzzle, 47 S.M.U. L. Rev. 235 (1994).

But don't think that malpractice and breach of fiduciary duty are hermetically distinct categories in practice. Courts and lawyers often use the former label to subsume any act that would fall within the latter one. Weil, Gotshal & Manges, LLP v. Fashion Boutique of Short Hills, Inc., 780 N.Y.S.2d 593 (1st Dept. 2004) (malpractice charge encompasses allegations of fiduciary breach). Complaints against lawyers often cite both doctrines just to cover all bases.

Is Sex with Clients a Breach of Fiduciary Duty?

TANTE v. HERRING
264 Ga. 694, 453 S.E.2d 686 (1994)

HUNT, CHIEF JUSTICE.

The Herrings retained Tante to pursue a claim for social security disability benefits for Mrs. Herring before the Social Security Administration. During his representation of Mrs. Herring, Tante appeared with her at a hearing before an administrative law judge and wrote a letter brief on her behalf. Thereafter, the administrative law judge issued a favorable award to Mrs. Herring. Tante's subsequent request for attorney fees for his work in representing Mrs. Herring, which request had been approved by both the Herrings, was approved by the administrative law judge.

The issues underlying this appeal involve the Herrings' action against Tante for legal malpractice, breach of fiduciary duty and breach of contract, all pertaining to Tante's adulterous relationship with Mrs. Herring during the period in which he was pursuing the disability claim on her behalf. The Herrings allege that Tante caused physical and mental harm to Mrs. Herring by taking advantage of confidential information regarding her emotional and mental condition to convince her to have an affair with him. The Herrings also allege Tante violated rules and standards of the State Bar of Georgia, violated his fiduciary duty, and breached his contract with the Herrings. . . .

There is no evidence that Tante's conduct of which the Herrings complain had any effect on his performance of legal services under his agreement with the Herrings. Indeed, Tante obtained for Mrs. Herring precisely the results for which he was retained, the recovery of social security disability benefits.

However . . . the Herrings have a claim against Tante for damages for breach of fiduciary duty. That claim is not one for professional malpractice based on negligence involving Tante's performance of legal services, and, therefore, no expert affidavit is required in support of it. The fiduciary duty in this context arises from the attorney-client relationship. Tante was a fiduciary with regard to the confidential information provided to him by his client just as he would have been a fiduciary with regard to money or other property entrusted to him by a client.

Thus, the Herrings' claim is based on Tante's alleged misuse, to his own advantage, of confidential information in medical and psychological reports concerning Mrs. Herring obtained in and solely because of Tante's representation of her. Tante did not controvert the allegations that he took advantage of information contained in Mrs. Herring's confidential medical and psychological reports about her impaired emotional and mental condition, that Tante took advantage of that condition, convincing her to have an affair with him, resulting in physical and mental harm to the Herrings. The Court of Appeals correctly noted that, as a fiduciary with regard to information shared with him by his client, Tante owed his client the utmost good faith and loyalty. By using information available to him solely because of the attorney-client relationship to his advantage and to the Herrings' disadvantage, he breached that fiduciary duty. Accordingly, the Herrings may pursue their claim for damages resulting from that breach.

Herring claimed Tante had "obtained psychological evaluations of Mrs. Herring [identifying] organic brain damage, impaired judgment and impulse control, difficulties in maintaining adequate social functioning, depression, anxiety and feelings of insecurity and inadequacy and an impairment to intellectual functioning which had affected her logical memory, recall and retention of verbal information." He also learned that "she had noticed a severe decrease in her desire for sex."

Tante was separately suspended for 18 months. In re Tante, 453 S.E.2d 688 (Ga. 1994). Of late, debate has centered on when, if ever, it should be an actionable breach of fiduciary duty for an attorney to initiate an intimate personal relationship with a current client. (Pre-existing relationships may continue. You can represent your spouse or partner assuming there are no other problems.) The issue has arisen almost exclusively in divorce cases, when a client may be especially vulnerable to imposition and the lawyer is in a position to ask highly personal questions about the client's marriage. So far as I can determine, these cases have all been filed by women. See page 784 and Rule 1.8(j) for discussion of when this conduct can be the basis for discipline. But ethics aside, when should it be actionable?

One court has refused to find a breach where the client could show no harm to her legal interests as a result of the intimate relationship. The client's mental anguish, humiliation, and shame were not compensable damages. Among the allegations the court assumed to be true was this one:

> [O]n December 10, 1983, [plaintiff] went to defendant's office, at his request, to discuss her case. On this occasion defendant locked his office door and then unzipped his pants. He then requested that plaintiff have oral sex with him. Plaintiff contended that she was "stunned and confused" but that she complied because she was "fearful that he . . . would not advocate for her and her children's interests in her divorce case were she to refuse." Suppressed v. Suppressed, 565 N.E.2d 101 (Ill. App. 1990).

A disciplinary complaint against this lawyer had earlier been dismissed.

McDaniel v. Gile, 281 Cal. Rptr. 242 (Ct. App. 1991), has possibly gone furthest in recognizing an action for breach of fiduciary duty. A lawyer sued his client for legal fees and the client cross-claimed, charging that the lawyer had her fill out a "lengthy and intimate" questionnaire "seeking intimate details of her personal and sexual life." He then repeatedly referred to her answers and made sexual advances toward her. After all were rebuffed, the lawyer allegedly did no work on the client's case and ignored her calls. When she complained, he responded that if she "had played the game the right way" she would know how to reach him immediately.

The court upheld claims for intentional infliction of emotional distress and malpractice. As to the first, the court wrote:

> Defendant had a special relationship with plaintiff in that she was a client and plaintiff was her attorney representing her in a dissolution of marriage proceeding. Plaintiff was in a position of actual or apparent power over defendant. Defendant was peculiarly susceptible to emotional distress because of her pending marital dissolution. Plaintiff was aware of defendant's circumstances. The withholding by a retained attorney of legal services when sexual favors are not granted by a client and engaging in sexual harassment of the client constitute acts of outrageous conduct under these circumstances.

As to the second claim, the court said:

> The facts before this court show that plaintiff not only delayed rendering legal services, but also withheld them and gave substandard services when defendant did not grant him sexual favors. This conduct necessarily falls below the standard of care and skill of members of the legal profession. We specifically do not address whether sexual relations between an attorney and client constitute a per se violation of the fiduciary relationship.

Or maybe *McDaniel* does not mark the outer limits of liability for this misbehavior. The Mississippi Supreme Court upheld a $1.5 million judgment against a lawyer for breach of contract and intentional infliction of emotional distress where the lawyer started an affair with the plaintiff's *estranged* wife while he was representing the couple and their minor son in a medical malpractice case. No expert testimony was needed. Pierce v. Cook, 992 So.2d 612 (Miss. 2008). Do you think this opinion goes too far? What duty to the husband did the affair with his estranged wife violate? (Pierce later married the former Mrs. Cook.)

Moral: Wait until the work is done before getting into bed or, if you can't wait, withdraw from the matter first.

2. Third Parties as "Client-Equivalents"

Some cases have upheld professional liability to third parties by concluding that even though the plaintiff never actually retained or sought to retain the defendant lawyer, nevertheless the plaintiff was entitled to the benefit of the service — and the same duty of care — the lawyer had agreed to provide to the actual client. Lawyers can be liable to third parties on other, more numerous theories, and these are addressed in Part C. The division of cases between this note and those in part C is a bit arbitrary at the margins, but the categories are conceptually distinct. I think so anyway.

The drafting of wills presents the classic fact pattern in which a third party seeks to hold an attorney liable for lack of care in performing a legal service. Edmund hires a lawyer to draft a will leaving a tidy sum of money to his friend Carmela. Edmund dies. It is then discovered that the lawyer failed to include the bequest or drafted it inadequately. Edmund is no longer around to sue the lawyer, so Carmela sues. The lawyer claims that nonclient Carmela was owed no duty.

While some jurisdictions accept this defense (see Victor v. Goldman, 344 N.Y.S.2d 672 (Sup. Ct. 1973), aff 'd, 351 N.Y.S.2d 956 (2d Dept. 1974)), many do not. Blair v. Ing, 21 P.3d 452 (Haw. 2001) (recognizing recovery under negligence or third-party beneficiary theories and citing numerous cases). In Hale v. Groce, 744 P.2d 1289 (Or. 1987), Justice Linde found the intended beneficiary under the will a "classic . . . third-party beneficiary of the lawyer's promise to his client within the rule of Restatement [of Contracts] section 302(1)(b)." In addition, "[b]ecause under third-party analysis the contract creates a 'duty' not only to the promisee, the client, but also to the intended beneficiary, negligent nonperformance may give rise to a negligence action as well." Illinois has held that a lawyer owes a duty of care to a beneficiary in a will if the testator retained the lawyer intending to benefit the beneficiary. McLane v. Russell, 546 N.E.2d 499 (Ill. 1989). Application of this rule is not limited to wills. Williams v. Mordkofsky, 901 F.2d 158 (D.C. Cir. 1990), permitted a corporation to sue a lawyer who had been retained by its shareholders and an affiliated company for the purpose of benefitting the plaintiff. See also Nelson v. Nationwide Mortgage Corp., 659 F. Supp. 611 (D.D.C. 1987); Meighan v. Shore, 40 Cal. Rptr. 2d 744 (Ct. App. 1995) (lawyer who accepted husband's medical malpractice claim had a duty to both husband and wife to advise on wife's loss of consortium claim, relying in part on duty to wife and in part on husband's "community property interest" in wife's recovery); Flaherty v. Weinberg, 492 A.2d 618 (Md. 1985). *Flaherty* contains an especially good review of the law to 1985.

Opinion letters present another (and frequent) circumstance in which a nonclient may have a claim against a lawyer. A client may ask its lawyer to express a legal opinion in order to induce a third party to take action. For example, a business seeking to borrow money from a bank may ask its lawyer to write a letter to the bank stating that the security for the loan is not otherwise encumbered. The bank may insist on the letter. If the lawyer does so, and his opinion is negligent, he will be liable to the bank. Greycas, Inc. v. Proud, 826 F.2d 1560 (7th Cir. 1987) (attorney's letter to client's lender negligently misrepresenting status of collateral creates liability); Prudential Ins. Co. of America v. Dewey, Ballantine, Bushby, Palmer & Wood, 605 N.E.2d 318 (N.Y. 1992): "Gilmartin contends that [Code provisions], regarding the preservation of client loyalty and client confidences, argue against imposing liability on attorneys in these circumstances. However, where, as here, the negligent acts, i.e., the creation of an opinion letter and the transmission of that letter to a third party for the party's own use, were carried out by the lawyer at the client's express direction, the ethical considerations . . . are insufficient reason to insulate attorneys from liability."

Courts that resist creating clientlike duties to third parties often cite the danger to the lawyer-client relationship if the lawyer must also protect the interests of someone else, someone whose interests may not be identical to those of the client. The Minnesota Supreme Court has refused to use a third-party beneficiary theory to create duties to others who would benefit from the lawyer's work for a client (if it were competently performed) unless the third party was a "direct and intended beneficiary of the attorney's services." By "direct" the court meant that the "transaction has [as] a central purpose an effect on the third party and the effect is intended as a purpose of the transaction." By "intended" the court meant that "the attorney must be aware of the client's intent to benefit the third party." McIntosh County Bank v. Dorsey & Whitney, LLP, 745 N.W.2d 538 (Minn. 2008).

3. *Vicarious Liability*

Law partners, like other partners, are responsible for each other's professional failures within the scope of the legal partnership. Kansallis Finance Ltd. v. Fern, 659 N.E.2d 731 (Mass. 1996) (vicarious liability imposed if law firm partner acted to benefit the partnership or if partner "has apparent authority to do the act" alleged); Roach v. Mead, 722 P.2d 1229 (Or. 1986). Whether lawyers who are shareholders in a professional corporation are vicariously liable for the defaults of their co-shareholders generally depends on the jurisdiction's corporation law. The dominant view is that co-shareholders are not personally liable on account of that status alone. Vanderhoof v. Cleary, 725 A.2d 917 (Vt. 1998). The law firm itself remains liable.

When a lawyer borrows money from a client and doesn't pay it back, the lawyer's partners may be sued. The defense might be that borrowing money from a client is not within the scope of a legal partnership, so there is no vicarious liability. This defense lost in Roach v. Mead, supra. The court reasoned that the borrowing lawyer was obligated to tell his client to seek independent legal advice and that the loans should be secured. His failures to do so were "failures of Mead as a lawyer advising his client. Because these failures occurred within the scope of the legal partnership, responsibility for Mead's negligence was properly charged to defendant as Mead's law partner."

In a particularly disquieting case, a lawyer overcharged a client more than $3 million. The client sued the lawyer's partners. The court upheld liability on two theories. First, all partners were liable for a partner's wrongful acts within the scope of the partnership business, even if the other partners were unaware of those acts. Here, billing clients was within the scope of the law firm's business. Second, and more consequential, the co-partners were liable for negligent supervision. The firm had no system in place for identifying the breaches of ethics or dishonest acts of firm lawyers. Dresser Indus., Inc., v. Digges, 1989 Westlaw 139234, 1989 Westlaw 139240 (D. Md. 1989). The client, Dresser Industries, later sued the law firm's malpractice carrier for the overbillings plus interest (a total of more than $4 million). The Fourth Circuit affirmed the judgment against Dresser. The underlying conduct was not within the policy because it was "dishonest" and because the firm, on purchasing the policy, had failed to alert the carrier to "potential claims against it." St. Paul Fire & Marine

Ins. Co. v. Dresser Indus., Inc., 972 F.2d 341 (4th Cir. 1992). *Lesson: Choose your partners wisely. Monitor their behavior.*

In Federal Deposit Insurance Corp. v. Mmahat, 907 F.2d 546 (5th Cir. 1990), a firm partner who was also chairman and general counsel of the board of an S&L directed it to make loans that violated federal regulations. After the S&L failed, the FDIC sued the partner and his firm. The court affirmed a jury finding that the partner had acted as a lawyer, not as chairman, in directing the loans and that the firm was therefore vicariously liable.

Does all this sound scary? Many lawyers think so. When large firms have several offices, nationally and globally, a partner in one city may not cotton to the prospect of being vicariously liable for the misdeeds of a partner half the world away, over whom she has no practical control and whom she may never even have met. Large settlements against big law firms, especially in cases arising out of financial meltdowns, prompted lawyer-inspired legislation in many states permitting law practice in the form of limited liability partnerships (LLPs or, depending on your grammatical purity, L.L.P.s). These work like ordinary partnerships except that partners are personally liable only for their own professional negligence or breach of duty and, potentially, for lawyers they supervise. The partnership, *as an entity*, remains liable for the malpractice of any of its lawyers. The advantage of a limited liability partnership is that in the event of catastrophe, after depletion of the firm's assets (which includes future income) and insurance, only the personal assets of the lawyers whose conduct created the liability (and their negligent supervisors) will be at risk. Is this wise from the perspective of firm collegiality? Is it fair to clients? How explicit should the warning to clients be? See generally Note, Lawyers' Responsibilities and Lawyers' Responses, 107 Harv. L. Rev. 1547 (1994) (discussion of limited liability partnership as one of several professional responses to increased financial exposure).

B. PROVING MALPRACTICE

1. *Use of Ethics Rules and Expert Testimony*

A former client, whether suing in tort or contract, has to prove that the defendant lawyer either violated a duty of care or breached a fiduciary or other duty. How will the plaintiff do that? As in actions against other professionals, very often the plaintiff will call another lawyer to testify that the defendant breached one of these duties. A lay jury ordinarily cannot be expected to know the standard of care of lawyers in the relevant community. If the claim is that the lawyer did not perform competently (even if well-meaning), the expert will be someone familiar with the kind of practice and how lawyers in the state perform in the area. Wastvedt v. Vaaler, 430 N.W.2d 561 (N.D. 1988) (expert needed "to explain whether the failure to explain the ramifications of [a certain clause in an agreement] was a deviation from the appropriate standard of care because that conduct is not a matter within the common knowledge of a lay person"). On the other hand, some defaults are so obviously improper that even a lay juror can say so. That was true about a lawyer's failure to communicate a settlement offer to a client in Rizzo v. Haines, 555 A.2d 58 (Pa. 1989). Wagenmann v. Adams, 829 F.2d 196 (1st Cir. 1987), applying Massachusetts law, concluded that a lawyer "committed malpractice 'so gross or obvious' that expert testimony was not required to prove it." The lawyer, appointed to represent an arrested man, did virtually nothing to secure his release, including failing to interview witnesses. No expert was required in Vandermay v. Clayton, 984 P.2d 272 (Or. 1999), where the former client, who was selling a business, claimed that his lawyer had accepted, and instructed him to sign, an indemnity provision far broader than the client had said he wanted. The jury did not need help in evaluating the failure of a lawyer to follow a client's instructions. In Valentine v. Watters, 896 So. 2d 385 (Ala. 2004), the court held that plaintiff needed no expert to establish liability either for her allegation that her lawyer failed to file a form needed to protect her claim or for her allegation that the defendant had misrepresented his litigation experience. Even if a plaintiff is not obligated to use an expert to establish breach of duty, however, she may want to do so because it will strengthen her case before the jury.

Apart from an expert on the standard of care, a malpractice plaintiff might also (or instead) wish to introduce evidence of the jurisdiction's ethics rules (and an expert to explain the meaning of those rules) where the plaintiff claims that the lawyer's conduct violated one of the rules. The plaintiff might ask her expert witness to talk about the rules or ask the judge to instruct the jury on their requirements. A defendant may want his own expert to say he followed the rules. As the following case shows, judicial receptivity to ethics experts was for a time mixed, but today it is mostly favorable. In an analogous area, ethics rules for judges have been used in cases involving judges. Use of a state's judicial conduct code to cross-examine a judge on trial for bribery and other crimes was upheld in United States v. Grubb, 11 F.3d 426 (4th Cir. 1993). The trial court had properly instructed that violation of code standards is not a crime but that the jury could take any noncompliance "into consideration on the matter of intent . . . absence of mistake, motive, things of that nature."

SMITH v. HAYNSWORTH, MARION, McKAY & GEURARD
322 S.C. 433, 472 S.E.2d 612 (1996)

WALLER, JUSTICE.

This case arises out of respondent, Haynsworth, Marion, McKay & Geurard's (Haynsworth) representation of appellants, Smith and Murray, in a real estate development scheme. Smith and Murray contracted with a developer, Bill Bashor, to purchase lots on Wild Dunes. Bashor planned to develop the lots, then sell them for a profit. Two of the investors in the scheme were partners in the Haynsworth firm. Haynsworth represented Bashor in his acquisition and sale of the lots, as well as in various other legal matters. Haynsworth also represented Smith and Murray in the transaction, with Bashor paying their attorney's fees.

The development scheme fell through and the lots were ultimately foreclosed by the bank. Smith and Murray sued Haynsworth for malpractice. The jury returned a verdict for respondents. . . .

Respondents moved to exclude the testimony of appellant's expert, Professor Gregory Adams, contending his testimony concerning the Rules of Professional Conduct (RPC) . . . was inadmissible, and claiming that Adams was not qualified to give an expert opinion as he was neither a real estate lawyer nor licensed to practice law in South Carolina. The trial court agreed and excluded Professor Adams' testimony. This was error.

A plaintiff in a legal malpractice action must generally establish the standard of care by expert testimony. The parameters of such testimony have, however, been the subject of much debate.

The preamble to the RPC state that "[v]iolation of a Rule should not give rise to a cause of action nor should it create any presumption that a legal duty has been breached."[3] The RPC are silent, however, as to whether or not they are relevant in assessing the duty of care, or whether an expert may base his opinions in reliance thereon. Courts in other jurisdictions are divided.

A majority of courts permit discussion of such a violation at trial as some evidence of the common law duty of care.[4] These courts generally rule that the expert must address his or her testimony to the breach of a legal duty of care and not simply to breach of disciplinary rule. Other courts have held that ethical standards conclusively establish the duty of care and that any violation is negligence per se. A minority find that violation of an ethical rule establishes a rebuttable presumption of legal malpractice. And, finally, a few courts hold that ethical standards are inadmissible in a legal malpractice action. See Hizey v. Carpenter, 119 Wash. 2d 251, 830 P.2d 646, 654.[5]

We concur with the majority of jurisdictions and hold that, in appropriate cases, the RPC may be relevant and admissible in assessing the legal duty of an attorney in a malpractice action. However, we adopt the view taken by the Supreme Court of Georgia in Allen v. Lefkoff, Duncan, Grimes & Dermer, 265 Ga. 374, 453 S.E.2d 719, 721-722 (1995) as follows:

> This is not to say, however, that all of the Bar Rules would necessarily be relevant in every legal malpractice action. In order to relate to the standard of care in a particular case, we hold that a Bar Rule must be intended to protect a person in the plaintiff's position or be addressed to the particular harm.[6]

3. The RPC did not become effective until September 1, 1990. However, their applicability was not challenged at trial. In any event, the Code of Professional Responsibility in effect prior to adoption of the RPC likewise disclaimed the creation of standards of legal malpractice.

4. The theory behind this view is that, since the ethical rules set the minimum standard of competency to be displayed by all attorneys, a violation thereof may be considered as evidence of a breach of the standard of care. Other courts admit this evidence in an analogous manner of admitting statutes, ordinances, or practice codes in defining the duty of care.

5. Even these courts, however, do not restrict an expert's right to base his opinions on the Rules. For example, *Hizey* held that an expert may rely on the disciplinary rules in forming an opinion as to an attorney's failure to conform to an ethical rule so long as the expert addresses the breach of a legal duty, and not simply the breach of an ethical rule. . . . One court has rejected expert testimony where it was based solely on an attorney's violation of ethical rules. Lazy Seven Coal Sales, Inc. v. Stone and Hinds, 813 S.W.2d 400 (Tenn. 1991). That court noted, however, that the Code may be relevant in determining the standard of care and may provide guidance in ascertaining lawyers' obligations.

6. The failure to comply with the RPC should not, however, be considered as evidence of negligence per se. It is merely a circumstance that, along with other facts and circumstances, may be considered in determining whether the attorney acted with reasonable care in fulfilling his legal duties to a client.

Finally, in its written order, the trial court ruled Adams unqualified in any event as he is not licensed to practice law in this state, and is not an expert in the area of real estate law. Appellants contend this ruling effectually establishes a "locality rule" requiring an expert to testify only to local standards governing malpractice.

This Court has abandoned the "locality rule" in the context of medical malpractice and accountants. In the context of legal malpractice, most courts which originally adopted a strict locality rule have expanded the relevant geographical region to create a statewide standard of care. The rationale for this development is that attorneys are generally regulated on a statewide basis, with state rules of procedure and different substantive laws. Accordingly, we adopt the majority view and rule that the standard to be applied in determining legal malpractice issues is statewide.

Further, the fact that Adams is not licensed to practice law in this state does not disqualify him as an expert. Likewise, the fact that Adams is not a real estate lawyer does not prohibit his testimony concerning those ethical obligations which are relevant to appellants' claims. Accordingly, in light of our holding the matter must be reversed and remanded for a new trial. . . .

Because the *Smith* court's focus was whether the proffered testimony was properly excluded, it did not describe the plaintiffs' theories of liability. The facts suggest at least two conflicts. See if you can infer them. Might one of them have hurt Bashor, the other client, too?

Professional conduct rules may also be invoked defensively. That sometimes happens in criminal cases where an accused lawyer will cite the rules, or his allegedly reasonable understanding of what the rules require, in order to rebut an inference of criminal purpose. See, e.g., United States v. Cavin, 39 F.3d 1299 (5th Cir. 1994).

The Restatement §52(2) endorses what *Smith* calls the majority view. The section provides:

Proof of a violation of a rule or statute regulating the conduct of lawyers:

(a) does not give rise to an implied cause of action for professional negligence or breach of fiduciary duty;

(b) does not preclude other proof concerning the duty of care . . . ; and

(c) may be considered by a trier of fact as an aid in understanding and applying the standard [of care] to the extent that (i) the rule or statute was designed for the protection of persons in the position of the claimant and (ii) proof of the content and construction of such a rule or statute is relevant to the claimant's claim.

The Model Rules also recognize the evidentiary use of a rule violation. Paragraph [20] of the Scope says "[S]ince the Rules do establish standards of conduct by lawyers, a lawyer's violation of a Rule may be evidence of breach of the applicable standard of conduct." This language was adopted in 2002 as part of the the Ethics 2000 Commission's work. (Previously, the Rules, like the Model Code, rejected the idea that an ethics code might have any role in civil claims against lawyers.) See also Mainor v. Nault, 101 P.3d 308 (Nev. 2004) (allowing expert to rely on state conflict rules as some evidence of standard of care for lawyers but not as an independent basis for liability, calling this the "majority rule"); Note, The Evidentiary Use of the Ethics Codes in Legal Malpractice: Erasing a Double Standard, 109 Harv. L. Rev. 1102 (1996) ("At the very least, the provisions of a jurisdiction's ethics codes that relate to the facts of a malpractice suit should be admissible in helping to establish the proper standard of care.").

Ethical Violations as a Basis for Reduction or Denial of Fees

HENDRY v. PELLAND
73 F.3d 397 (D.C. Cir. 1996)

TATEL, CIRCUIT JUDGE.

[The Hendrys — a grandmother, two children, and two infant grandchildren — retained the Pelland law firm in connection with certain real estate transactions. The transactions lost money, and the Hendrys sued Pelland. Their expert testified that multiple representation of all five Hendrys without consent was improper because they had conflicting interests. "Viewed most favorably to the Hendrys, this evidence was sufficient for a reasonable jury to find that Pelland violated DR 5-105 [now replaced by Rule 1.7], thereby breaching his fiduciary duty of loyalty." The Hendrys had cited this breach in an effort to recoup the $89,000 in legal fees they had paid Pelland and as a defense to Pelland's claim for $37,000 in unpaid fees. The lower court rejected the Hendrys' disgorgement and fee forfeiture claims.]

We also agree with the Hendrys that, to the extent they sought disgorgement of legal fees, they needed to prove only that Pelland breached his duty of loyalty, not that his breach proximately caused them injury. Although we have found no District of Columbia cases precisely on point, courts in other jurisdictions have held that clients must prove injury and proximate causation in a fiduciary duty claim against their lawyer if they seek *compensatory damages*, not if, as here, they seek only *forfeiture of legal fees*. Even courts that sometimes *do* require a showing of injury and causation in claims seeking only forfeiture of legal fees have stated that it is not necessary when the clients' claim is based, again as here, on a breach of the duty of loyalty. . . .

The different treatment of compensatory damages and forfeiture of legal fees also makes sense. Compensatory damages makes plaintiffs whole for the harms that they have suffered as a result of defendants' actions. Clients therefore need to prove that their attorney's breach caused them injury so that the trier of fact can determine whether they are entitled to any damages. Forfeiture of legal fees serves several different purposes. It deters attorney misconduct, a goal worth furthering regardless of whether a particular client has been harmed. It also fulfills a longstanding and fundamental principle of equity — that fiduciaries should not profit from their disloyalty. And, like compensatory damages, it compensates clients for a harm they have suffered. Unlike other forms of compensatory damages, however, forfeiture reflects not the harms clients suffer from the tainted representation, but the decreased value of the representation itself. Because a breach of the duty of loyalty diminishes the value of the attorney's representation as a matter of law, some degree of forfeiture is thus appropriate without further proof of injury.

We thus conclude that, under District of Columbia law, clients suing their attorney for breach of the fiduciary duty of loyalty and seeking disgorgement of legal fees as their sole remedy need prove only that their attorney breached that duty, not that the breach caused them injury. Because the Hendrys presented evidence that Pelland breached his duty of loyalty by violating DR 5-105, they were entitled to have their fiduciary duty claim for disgorgement of legal fees go to the jury. The district court therefore erred in granting judgment for Pelland and his firm.

In reaching this conclusion, we have not addressed . . . the extent of forfeiture to which the Hendrys might be entitled if, at a new trial, they succeed in proving that Pelland breached his duty of loyalty. Some courts have suggested that attorneys must forfeit all fees earned in their tainted representation of a client; others have ruled that lawyers must forfeit all fees earned in such representation *after* the breach occurred; while still others have held that the extent of forfeiture depends upon the facts and circumstances of the case. . . . [Reversed.]

Fee Forfeiture and Disgorgement

Forfeiture occurs when the lawyer loses the right to collect the fee. Disgorgement occurs when the lawyer has to give back fees he has already gotten. Because either remedy may be available where the lawyer violated an ethical rule, even absent proof of other harm, forfeiture and disgorgement can be powerful remedies. Kirkland & Ellis v. CMI Corp., 1999 Westlaw 92257 (N.D. Ill. 1999) (an alleged conflict of interest may serve as an affirmative defense to a law firm's fee claim even though the same conduct cannot support a counterclaim for damages). The client may have paid (or may owe) the lawyer a lot. Although violation of an ethics rule may not automatically establish a violation of a legal duty, it will threaten the lawyer's right to a fee if the ethics rule is intended to protect the client, as will often be true. First National Bank of Cincinnati v. Pepper, 454 F.2d 626 (2d Cir. 1972) ("[A]n attorney discharged for cause or guilty of professional misconduct in the handling of his client's affairs has no right to payment of fees"); Eriks v. Denver, 824 P.2d 1207 (Wash. 1992) ("The general principle that a breach of ethical duties may result in denial or disgorgement of fees is well recognized").

The same principle appears independently in the Bankruptcy Code, which permits a judge to deny some or all compensation to any professionals, including lawyers, whose interests are adverse to the bankrupt estate at any time during their employment. Matter of West Delta Oil Co., Inc., 432 F.3d 347 (5th Cir. 2005) (all fees denied to attorneys who "had an interest adverse to that of the estate with respect to matters on which they were employed"). In Matter of Taxman Clothing Co., 49 F.3d 310 (7th Cir. 1995), the court denied counsel for a trustee in bankruptcy the requested fees after finding that he had pursued claims even after it became obvious that doing so would cost more than the pursuit would likely bring the estate. "Fees obtained as a consequence of a breach of fiduciary obligation, even a non-willful breach . . . may be retained only if, by analogy to claims for quantum meruit, the fiduciary, notwithstanding his breach, conferred a benefit on his principal," which was not true on the facts before the court.

The *Hendry* court did not resolve the question of whether the alleged breach would result in total or only partial forfeiture. While older cases do not recognize partial forfeiture, see In re Clarke's Estate, 188 N.E.2d 128 (N.Y. 1962) (denying compensation, even absent harm, because "the vice is placing oneself in a position where self interest presents a second master to serve"), recent authority is inclined to calibrate the harm. Bertelsen v. Harris, 537 F.3d 1047 (9th Cir. 2008) (affirming as within his discretion a district judge's refusal to order any fee disgorgement where even assuming multiple ethical violations and breach of fiduciary duty, the fee was reasonable for the results achieved) (2-1 decision); Burrow v. Arce, 997 S.W.2d 229 (Tex. 1999) (establishing criteria for determining the amount, if any, of appropriate forfeiture). Restatement §37, on which *Burrow* relies, also opts for calibration and recognizes forfeiture only in cases of "clear and serious violation of duty to a client." Among the considerations are "the gravity and timing of the violation, its willfulness, its effect on the value of the lawyer's work for the client, any other threatened or actual harm to the client, and the adequacy of other remedies." See also Phansalkar v. Andersen Weinroth & Co., L.P., 344 F.3d 184 (2d Cir. 2003), which, while focusing on New York law, contains an extensive discussion of the "faithless servant doctrine" and the items subject to forfeiture or disgorgement under it.

Hendry also held that the determination of whether forfeiture would be ordered and the amount were jury questions. Burrow v. Arce, supra, concluded that fee forfeiture is an "equitable remedy," to be decided by the trial judge. Many other opinions implicitly assume that the disgorgement remedy is decided by the court.

FURTHER READING

Robert Dahlquist, The Code of Professional Responsibility and Civil Damage Actions Against Attorneys, 9 Ohio N.U. L. Rev. 1 (1982); Jean Faure & R. Keith Strong, The Model Rules of Professional Conduct: No Standard for Malpractice, 47 Mont. L. Rev. 363 (1986); Charles Wolfram, The Code of Professional Responsibility as a Measure of Attorney Liability in Civil Litigation, 30 S.C. L. Rev. 281 (1979); Note, The Rules of Professional Conduct: Basis for Civil Liability of Attorneys, 39 U. Fla. L. Rev. 777 (1987) (authored by Michael Benjamin). For more on the use of experts in legal malpractice actions, see Michael Ambrosio & Denis McLaughlin, The Use of Expert Witnesses in Establishing Liability in Legal Malpractice Cases, 61 Temp. L. Rev. 1351 (1988).

2. *Causation and Defenses*

Traditionally, a tort or contract plaintiff must prove that the tort or breach caused damages and the amount. Where the alleged negligence occurs in connection with litigation, this is usually said to mean that the malpractice plaintiff must prove that "but for" the lawyer's negligence, the plaintiff would have won or done better in the underlying case. Recall *Togstad* at page 707. (We will question whether that requirement is fair. Should Sally Terzakis have to prove that but for Adam Rosini's alleged malpractice, she would have won half the incremental value of Harry Kovair's inheritance in court? If so, she loses, doesn't she? Looking back, we know what would have happened.) Where the negligence arises in a transactional matter, as in the next case, two questions arise: Is the "but for" test still applicable, or can the malpractice plaintiff prevail with a less onerous burden? If the burden remains the same, how do you prove causation in a transactional matter? In the following opinion, the lower court's charge is described in note 2.

VINER v. SWEET

30 Cal. 4th 1232, 70 P.3d 1046 (Cal. 2003)

KENNARD, J.

In a client's action against an attorney for legal malpractice, the client must prove, among other things, that the attorney's negligent acts or omissions caused the client to suffer some financial harm or loss. When the alleged malpractice occurred in the performance of transactional work (giving advice or preparing documents for a business transaction), must the client prove this causation element according to the "but for" test, meaning that the harm or loss would not have occurred without the attorney's malpractice? The answer is yes.

I

In 1984, plaintiffs Michael Viner and his wife, Deborah Raffin Viner, founded Dove Audio, Inc. (Dove). The company produced audio versions of books read by the authors or by celebrities, and it did television and movie projects.

In 1994, Dove went public by issuing stock at $10 a share. In 1995, the Viners and Dove entered into long-term employment contracts guaranteeing the Viners, among other things, a certain level of salaries, and containing indemnification provisions favorable to the Viners. The Viners received a large share of Dove's common stock and all of its preferred cumulative dividend series "A" stock.

Thereafter, Michael Viner discussed with longtime friend David Povich, a partner in defendant law firm Williams & Connolly in Washington, D.C., the possibility of selling the Viners' interest in Dove. In the fall of 1996, Norton Herrick proposed buying the Viners' entire interest in Dove. Attorney Povich assigned the matter to his partner, defendant Charles A. Sweet, a corporate transactional attorney. Sweet was not a member of the California Bar and was not familiar with California law. During the negotiations with Herrick, Sweet learned that under the Viners' employment agreements with Dove, the latter owed the Viners a substantial amount of unpaid dividends on their preferred stock. Sweet also learned that the Viners wanted to preserve their right to engage in the television and movie businesses.

When the negotiations with Herrick were unsuccessful, Ronald Lightstone of Media Equities International (MEI) approached the Viners. Thereafter, in

March 1997, the Viners and MEI entered into an agreement under which MEI was to invest $4 million, and the Viners $2 million, to buy Dove stock. By May 1997, disputes arose, and the parties to the agreement each threatened litigation. That same month, Ronald Lightstone of MEI and Michael Viner, without defendant attorney Sweet's involvement, agreed that MEI would buy the Viner's stock in Dove and the Viners would terminate their employment with Dove.

Defendant attorney Sweet and Lightstone of MEI negotiated the final agreement, which the parties signed on June 10, 1997. The deal consisted of a securities purchase agreement and an employment termination agreement. Under the former, MEI agreed to buy a significant portion of the Viners' stock for more than $3 million. Under the latter agreement, the Viners' employment with Dove was terminated, mutual general releases were given, and Dove was to pay the Viners a total of $1.5 million over five years in monthly payments, with Dove's series "E" preferred stock to be held in escrow for distribution to the Viners if Dove defaulted on the monthly payments to them.

The employment termination agreement contained a noncompetition provision stating that the Viners would not " 'compete' in any way, directly or indirectly, in the audio book business for a period of four years" in any state in which Dove was doing business. The agreement also had a nonsolicitation provision that the Viners would not "directly or indirectly contract with, hire, solicit, encourage the departure of or in any manner engage or seek to employ any author or, for purposes of audio books, reader, currently under contract or included in the Company's book or audio catalogues for a period of four years."

In addition, the employment termination agreement provided that Deborah Raffin Viner would receive "Producer Credit" on audiobook work initiated during her employment with Dove; that Dove would not amend documents to terminate or reduce its obligation to indemnify the Viners; and that disputes would be submitted to arbitration, whose costs were to be split equally between the parties, with attorney fees to the party seeking to enforce the arbitration in court.

Defendant attorney Sweet led the Viners to believe that the employment termination agreement gave them three years of monthly payments by Dove, retained the indemnity protection they had with Dove, and provided credit for work done before their departure from Dove. The Viners also thought that they could use their celebrity contacts for any work that did not compete with Dove's audiobook business and involvement in film and television productions, and that if Dove defaulted on the agreed-upon monthly payments to them, the noncompetition clauses would be voided. The contracts did not so provide.

Later, several arbitration proceedings took place to resolve disputes between the Viners and MEI, including a claim by the Viners that the noncompetition provision of the employment termination agreement violated Business and Professions Code section 16600's restrictions on noncompetition agreements. The arbitrator rejected the claim, and the superior court confirmed the arbitrator's decision.

On June 3, 1998, the Viners brought a malpractice action against Attorney Sweet and the law firm of Williams & Connolly. Presented at trial were these seven claims: (1) Sweet told the Viners that the nonsolicitation clause of the employment termination agreement prohibiting plaintiffs from using their contacts to obtain work in television and movie projects applied only to the book and audiobook parts of Dove's business, but Dove, because the clause was ambiguous, asserted that the clause also encompassed Dove's television and movie projects; (2) Sweet negligently agreed to the noncompetition provision, which violated Business and Professions Code section 16600's restrictions on such provisions; (3) the Viners had asked for an attorney fees provision, but the employment termination agreement disallowed attorney fees in any disputes, permitting them only in enforcing an arbitration award; (4) ambiguous language in the Producer Credit provision caused Dove not to give Deborah Raffin Viner credit as a producer; (5) the Viners lost rights to dividends on Dove's series "A" preferred stock; (6) the employment termination agreement did not contain an indemnity provision providing the same level of protection as the Viners' agreement with Dove; and (7) the series "E" stock afforded inadequate security to the Viners if Dove defaulted on the monthly payments due them under the employment termination agreement.

After deliberating five days, the jury found defendants liable on all seven claims of malpractice, awarding the Viners $13,291,532 in damages. Defendants moved for judgment not withstanding the verdict or in the alternative for a new trial, arguing that the trial court erred in not instructing the jury that the Viners needed to prove they would have received a better deal "but for" defendant attorney Sweet's negligence. The trial court denied both motions.

The Court of Appeal reduced the damage award to $8,085,732, but otherwise affirmed the judgment. . . .

The Court of Appeal distinguished transactional malpractice from litigation malpractice, in which the plaintiff is required to prove the harm would not have occurred without the alleged negligence, and it offered three reasons for treating the two forms of malpractice differently. First, the court asserted that in litigation a gain for one side is always a loss for the other, whereas in transactional work a gain for one side could also be a gain for the other side. Second, the court observed that litigation malpractice involves past historical facts while transactional malpractice involves what parties would have been willing to accept for the future. Third, the court stated that "business transactions generally involve a much larger universe of variables than litigation matters." According to the Court of Appeal, in "contract negotiations the number of possible terms and outcomes is virtually unlimited," and therefore the "jury would have to evaluate a nearly infinite array of 'what-ifs,' to say nothing of 'if that, then whats,' in order to determine whether the plaintiff would have ended up with a better outcome 'but for' the malpractice."

We granted defendants' petition for review, and thereafter limited the issues to whether the plaintiff in a transactional legal malpractice action must prove that a more favorable result would have been obtained *but for* the alleged negligence.[2]

---

2. The trial court refused defendants' requested instruction on "but for" causation. The court did instruct the jury that a cause of an injury "is something that is a substantial factor in bringing about" the harm. Because the Court of Appeal addressed this case as presenting the "pure question of law" of whether the legal requirement of showing "but for" causation applies at all to transactional malpractice cases, and because we limited our review to that issue, we have not framed our discussion in terms of instructional error.

II

Defendants contend that in a transactional malpractice action, the plaintiff must show that *but for* the alleged malpractice, a more favorable result would have been obtained. Thus, defendants argue, the Viners had to show that without defendants' negligence (1) they would have had a more advantageous agreement (the "better deal" scenario), or (2) they would not have entered into the transaction with MEI and therefore would have been better off (the "no deal" scenario). . . .

The Court of Appeal here held that a plaintiff suing an attorney for transactional malpractice need not show that the harm would not have occurred in the absence of the attorney's negligence. We disagree. We see nothing distinctive about transactional malpractice that would justify a relaxation of, or departure from, the well-established requirement in negligence cases that the plaintiff establish causation by showing either (1) *but for* the negligence, the harm would not have occurred, or (2) the negligence was a concurrent independent cause of the harm.

"When a business transaction goes awry, a natural target of the disappointed principals is the attorneys who arranged or advised the deal. Clients predictably attempt to shift some part of the loss and disappointment of a deal that goes sour onto the shoulders of persons who were responsible for the underlying legal work. Before the loss can be shifted, however, the client has an initial hurdle to clear. *It must be shown that the loss suffered was in fact caused by the alleged attorney malpractice.* It is far too easy to make the legal advisor a scapegoat for a variety of business misjudgments unless the courts pay close attention to the cause in fact element, and deny recovery where the unfavorable outcome was likely to occur anyway, the client already knew the problems with the deal, or where the clients' own misconduct or misjudgment caused the problems. It is the failure of the client to establish the causal link that explains decisions where the loss is termed remote or speculative. Courts are properly cautious about making attorneys guarantors of their clients' faulty business judgment." (Bauman, Damages for Legal Malpractice: An Appraisal of the Crumbling Dike and Threatening Flood (1988) 61 Temp. L.Rev. 1127, 1154-1155, fns. omitted, italics added (hereafter Bauman, Damages for Legal Malpractice).

In a litigation malpractice action, the plaintiff must establish that *but for* the alleged negligence of the defendant attorney, the plaintiff would have obtained a more favorable judgment or settlement in the action in which the malpractice allegedly occurred. The purpose of this requirement, which has been in use for more than 120 years, is to safeguard against speculative and conjectural claims. It serves the essential purpose of ensuring that damages awarded for the attorney's malpractice actually have been caused by the malpractice.

The Court of Appeal here attempted to distinguish litigation malpractice from transactional malpractice in order to justify a relaxation of the "but for" test of causation in transactional malpractice cases. One of the distinguishing features, according to the court, was that in litigation a gain for one side necessarily entails a corresponding loss for the other, whereas in transactional representation a gain for one side does not necessarily result in a loss for the other. We question both the accuracy and the relevance of this generalization. In litigation, as in transactional work, a gain for one side does not necessarily result in a loss for the other side. Litigation may involve multiple claims and issues arising from complaints and cross-complaints, and parties in such litigation may prevail on some issues and not others, so that in the end there is no clear winner or loser and no exact correlation between one side's gains and the other side's losses. In addition, an attorney's representation of a client often combines litigation and transactional work, as when the attorney effects a settlement of pending litigation. The "but for" test of causation applies to a claim of legal malpractice in the settlement of litigation even though the settlement is itself a form of business transaction.

Nor do we agree with the Court of Appeal that litigation is inherently or necessarily less complex than transactional work. Some litigation, such as many lawsuits involving car accidents, is relatively uncomplicated, but so too is much transactional work, such as the negotiation of a simple lease or a purchase and sale agreement. But some litigation, such as a beneficiary's action against a trustee challenging the trustee's management of trust property over a period of decades, is as complex as most transactional work.

It is true, as the Court of Appeal pointed out, that litigation generally involves an examination of past events whereas transactional work involves anticipating and guiding the course of future events. But this distinction makes little difference for purposes of selecting an appropriate test of causation. Determining causation always requires evaluation of hypothetical situations concerning what might have happened, but did not. In both litigation and transactional malpractice cases, the crucial causation inquiry is *what would have happened* if the defendant attorney had not been negligent. This is so because the very idea of causation necessarily involves comparing historical events to a hypothetical alternative.

The Viners also contend that the "but for" test of causation should not apply to transactional malpractice cases because it is too difficult to obtain the evidence needed to satisfy this standard of proof. In particular, they argue that proving causation under the "but for" test would require them to obtain the testimony of the other parties to the transaction, who have since become their adversaries, to the effect that they would have given the Viners more favorable terms had the Viners' attorneys not performed negligently. Not so. In transactional malpractice cases, as in other cases, the plaintiff may use circumstantial evidence to satisfy his or her burden. An express concession by the other parties to the negotiation that they would have accepted other or additional terms is not necessary. And the plaintiff need not prove causation with absolute certainty. Rather, the plaintiff need only " 'introduce evidence which affords a reasonable basis for the conclusion that it is more likely than not that the conduct of the defendant was a cause in fact of the result.' "

In any event, difficulties of proof cannot justify imposing liability for injuries that the attorney could not have prevented by performing according to the required standard of care. . . .

For the reasons given above, we conclude that, just as in litigation malpractice actions, a plaintiff in a transactional malpractice action must show that *but for* the alleged malpractice, it is more likely than not that the plaintiff would have obtained a more favorable result.

On remand, the lower court concluded that on five of their seven claims the Viners' trial evidence failed to prove "but for" causation as a matter of law. A dissent thought the Viners were entitled to a new trial so a jury could make this determination as a matter of fact and, independently, to give the Viners a chance to introduce any additional evidence needed to satisfy the state supreme court's new causation requirement. Viner v. Sweet, 12 Cal. Rptr.3d 533 (Cal. App. 2004).

Ruminations on the "But For" Test in Legal Malpractice

The "but for" test is commonly applied in malpractice cases, whether the underlying conduct occurred in connection with transactional work, as in *Viner*, or in litigation. (We saw an example in a transactional matter in Simpson v. James at page 289.) Yet the differences between the two kinds of work have spawned objections to the "but for" test in transactional work. The *Viner* court describes but rejects these objections. It then purports to ameliorate the stringency of its holding by writing that a plaintiff can show "but for" proof with "circumstantial evidence." Just how might a lawyer go about proving circumstantially that absent the defendant's negligence or breach of fiduciary duty the former client, now a plaintiff, would have gotten better terms or would have been better off rejecting the deal it did get? (The court calls these the "better deal" and the "no deal" scenarios.) Imagine that you were the Viners' lawyer on remand (assuming that they had gotten a second chance), what evidence would you introduce?

Where a plaintiff alleges malpractice in litigation, the "but for" test requires her to prove a "case within a case." In the case against her former lawyer (sometimes called the "outer" case), she must prove the malpractice. Then she must prove that, absent the lawyer's mistakes, she would have come out better in the underlying (or "inner") case, the one that the lawyer messed up. If the malpractice plaintiff was the plaintiff in the inner case and lost or if the inner case was never brought because the lawyer missed a deadline, the plaintiff will claim that she should have or would have won the case. If she did win the inner case, she will allege that she would have won even more but for the malpractice. If the malpractice plaintiff was the defendant in the inner case, she will allege that she would have had to pay even less (or nothing) absent counsel's errors.

The "but for" test has also been criticized when the underlying work was litigation. When the malpractice case actually goes to trial, substantial additional time will have elapsed since the original event, making proof of the inner case more difficult or impossible. Further, the malpractice plaintiff may want to prove *not* that she would have won or done better at trial of the inner case but that she would have been able to settle the inner case before trial with a more generous outcome than she received.

Consider a personal injury plaintiff who lost her day in court because her lawyer missed the statute of limitations. The malpractice is clear. The only issue is causation and damages. Rather than prove what she would have recovered at trial, which may have become harder because witnesses disappear and forget, the plaintiff may instead wish to show that the inner case would have settled for a particular sum. She might want to call an expert witness to testify that nearly all personal injury cases in the jurisdiction (at least of her type) do settle and to tell the jury the range of settlements for injuries like the one she suffered. The Restatement of Law Governing Lawyers, §53 comment *b*, would allow a plaintiff to prove a lost settlement opportunity. Garcia v. Kozlov, Seaton, Romanini & Brooks, P.C., 845 A.2d 602 (N.J. 2004), also has a good discussion of the "but for" burden in litigation malpractice cases and possible mitigating devices.

Courts also use the "but for" test when a lawyer is charged with breach of fiduciary duty. Garrett v. Bryan Cave, 211 F.3d 1278 (10th Cir. 2000) (applying Oklahoma and Missouri law). But some courts have relaxed that burden in some fiduciary duty cases, perhaps viewing certain fiduciary breaches as more blameworthy than negligence. These courts apply a "substantial factor" test of causation instead.

In Milbank, Tweed, Hadley & McCloy v. Boon, 13 F.3d 537 (2d Cir. 1994), the court relieved the plaintiff, a former client, from having to "show strict 'but for' causation or proximate cause" where the firm was found to have violated its fiduciary duty by helping the client's former agent consummate the very deal that the client had pursued with the firm's help. The court said that "breaches of a fiduciary relationship in any context comprise a special breed of cases that often loosen normally stringent requirements of causation and damages." Does *Milbank* make sense as a matter of policy? On the one hand, it is now easier to make a lawyer "pay" for conduct that can be viewed as more reprehensible than mere negligence. On the other hand, without "but for" causation, a client can win with a lower standard of proof — i.e., even though he would have suffered the same loss anyway. What should the jury be told to do if the defendant lawyer proves by a preponderance of evidence that the loss would have occurred in any event?

Milbank's treatment of the causation requirement was put in doubt in American Federal Group, Ltd. v. Rothenberg, 136 F.3d 897 (2d Cir. 1998), a case that did not involve a lawyer and that did not cite *Milbank*. But in a footnote, the court identified two lines of fiduciary duty cases in New York. One line imposed the traditional causation requirement ("but for"), and the other applied the "less stringent, 'substantial factor' causation requirement." The court reconciled these cases by reference to the kind of damage the plaintiff was seeking. Where the remedy was compensation for a loss (as in *Milbank*), the stricter (but for) causation rule applied, but where the remedy "being sought is a restitutionary one to prevent the fiduciary's unjust enrichment as measured by his ill-gotten gain," the "substantial factor" standard "may be more appropriate." In other words, in the first category is the client who didn't get as much from, or had to pay more to, a third person because of the lawyer's breach. In the second category is the fiduciary who has cheated the client for his own gain. The lawyer in the second category gets less protection. That's right, isn't it? But if so, it means *Milbank* applied the wrong standard.

Gibbs v. Breed, Abbott & Morgan, 710 N.Y.S.2d 578 (1st Dept. 2000) supports the view that an eased burden applies when fiduciaries abuse their trust for personal gain. "This is because the purpose of this type of action is not merely to *compensate* the plaintiff for wrongs committed . . . [but also] to prevent them, by removing from agents and trustees all inducement to attempt dealing for their own benefit in matters which they have undertaken for others, or to which their agency or trust relates." (Internal quotes omitted.) Otherwise, the "but for" test applies. Weil, Gotshal & Manges, LLP v. Fashion Boutique of Short Hills, Inc., 780 N.Y.S.2d 593 (1st Dept. 2004) (whether the claim is malpractice or breach of fiduciary duty, plaintiff must show "but for" causation "where the injury is the value of the claim lost").

The issue of causation can be especially thorny where the plaintiffs, say shareholders of a corporation or the company itself, charge the company's lawyers (or accountants) with professional negligence in failing to detect and prevent wrongdoing by corporate officers, resulting in a loss or even bankruptcy. The misbehaving officers may have acted unlawfully toward the company (in which case it was a victim) or they may have caused the company to act unlawfully toward others (in which case the company was itself a wrongdoer because the officers' misconduct is imputed to it).

Recall that in the S&L cases, Judge Sporkin asked why the professionals charged to protect the company from the misconduct of its officers failed to do so (page 532). Shareholders (or the company with successor corporate officers or a bankruptcy trustee) may ask the same question and sue the lawyers and accountants for not protecting the company. Assuming the lawyers or accountants negligently failed to detect the illegality, should it matter whether the company was the victim or the imputed victimizer?

The Seventh Circuit has ruled that it should matter. In Cenco, Inc. v. Seidman & Seidman, 686 F.2d 449 (7th Cir. 1982), Judge Posner wrote that "[f]raud on behalf of a corporation is not the same thing as fraud against it." When "top management" causes a company to defraud others, the company is a "participant" in, not a "victim" of, the fraud. As a result, the auditor defendants had a complete defense in a class action shareholder derivative suit. This is called an "in pari delicto" defense.

A year later the Seventh Circuit decided Schacht v. Brown, 711 F.2d 1343 (7th Cir. 1983), which was an action by the Illinois Director of Insurance against three accounting firms, two insurance companies, the former officers and directors of Reserve Insurance Company, and Reserve's parent company. Schacht, who was liquidating Reserve following its insolvency, alleged that the defendants fraudulently concealed, or aided in the concealment of, Reserve's true financial situation while Reserve was "systematically looted of its most profitable and least risky business and more than $3,000,000 in income." As a result, Schacht alleged, Reserve, its policyholders, and creditors suffered losses exceeding $100 million. The accounting firms and the two insurance companies sought to defend against Schacht's complaint on behalf of Reserve by arguing that management's wrongdoing had to be attributed to Reserve itself and therefore to the receiver. The court disagreed. It distinguished Cenco, emphasizing that "[i]n no way can these results be described as beneficial to Reserve." The company was the fatal victim, not the intended beneficiary, of management's unlawful conduct.

The Seventh Circuit has continued to embrace this distinction between the entity as "victim" of an officer's misconduct on one hand, in which case the misconduct is not imputed to the entity when it sues its lawyers or accountants, and the entity as the purported "beneficiary" of the misconduct on the other, in which case the misconduct is imputed and provides a defense in a malpractice case. Eastern Trading Co. v. Refco, Inc., 229 F.3d 617 (7th Cir. 2000). It has been influential, but is it a persuasive, distinction? If a lawyer or accountant has indeed been negligent in failing to detect an officer's illegality, what difference should it make whether the illegality was meant to benefit the company? Does Judge Posner's description of the company as a "participant" to the fraud presume, counterfactually, that shareholders know what management is doing?

Or is his aim to encourage shareholder vigilance? Posner says it is the second. Is it realistic to expect shareholders to monitor the management of publicly held companies in the same manner?

In an odd way, the victim-or-beneficiary issue arose in O'Melveny & Myers v. FDIC, 512 U.S. 79 (1994). A small bank stood to benefit from its owners' fraud, but the scheme failed and so did the bank. The FDIC, as receiver, sued the bank's law firm, O'Melveny, for negligently failing to uncover the fraud. The firm argued that the receiver had no greater rights than the bank and that, under California law, the owners' fraud would be imputed to the bank. But in an alternate holding the Ninth Circuit created a federal common law rule that disallowed imputation when the opposing litigant was the FDIC as receiver. The unanimous Supreme Court found no statutory authority for such a rule and no basis for federal common law. It remanded for application of state law. Concurring for himself and three others, Justice Stevens wrote that even a state that accepted the imputation defense in actions brought by the entity (or in its name) might reject it when the plaintiff is a third party, like a receiver or bankruptcy trustee. "Indeed, a state court might well attach special significance to the fact that the interests of taxpayers as well as ordinary creditors will be affected by the rule at issue in this case." On remand, the Ninth Circuit's huffy per curiam opinion held that under state law the owner's fraud would not be imputed to the receiver and so could not provide a defense. "While a party may itself be denied a right or defense on account of its misdeeds, there is little reason to impose the same punishment on a trustee, receiver or similar innocent entity that steps into the party's shoes pursuant to court order or operation of law." FDIC v. O'Melveny & Myers, 61 F.3d 17 (9th Cir. 1995).

Unlike the Ninth Circuit, two other circuits have allowed law firms to assert in pari delicto defenses, and impute management wrongdoing to a former corporate client, even in actions brought by the company's bankruptcy trustee. Mosier v. Callister, Nebeker & McCullough, 546 F.3d. 1271 (10th Cir. 2008); Gray v. Evercore Restructuring L.L.C., 544 F.3d 320 (1st Cir. 2008).

Causation in Criminal Cases

We come now to a difficult question, difficult because the right answer seems to require an impossible reconciliation of policy with traditional doctrine, because the case law is all over the place, and because of the several independent variables that a jurisdiction might (or might not) adopt in refining its law in the area. Try this experiment.

"Adkins v. Dixon"

Adkins is charged with two serious felonies. He is indigent, so the judge appoints Dixon to represent him. Adkins (who knows a bit of law from a prior incarceration) urges Dixon to move to dismiss the charges on speedy trial grounds, and Dixon does so, but loses. Adkins is then convicted in separate trials and sentenced to two concurrent life terms. Dixon appeals both convictions, but for some reason he makes the speedy trial argument in only one of the two appeals. It wins. But the other conviction is affirmed. Adkins gets a new lawyer and goes to a higher court, which refuses to consider the speedy trial motion on the affirmed conviction because it had not been raised in the lower appellate court. So Adkins is in jail for life. He sues Dixon for malpractice. It is stipulated that both charges should have been dismissed on speedy trial grounds and that Dixon was negligent in omitting that ground in the second appeal. Now what? Should we let Adkins sue Dixon? What are the damages? You are on the state supreme court when this case arrives. Your options include the following.

1. Your court can conclude that there is no difference between criminal and civil cases. If so, then once Adkins proves that but for Dixon's negligence, he would have been acquitted (or convicted of a lesser charge), the malpractice is proved and damages must compensate for any (or any lengthier) incarceration. Result: Dixon pays for Adkins's life in prison.

2. Your court can treat criminal case malpractice differently as a matter of policy and insist that Adkins also prove his factual innocence by a preponderance of the evidence. If he's factually guilty, he loses. His crime, not his lawyer's negligence, is deemed the *legal* cause of his loss, even if not the logical cause.

3. Or your court can require Adkins to have his conviction reversed, or vacated in a collateral proceeding, before it will hear the malpractice issue. (This is sometimes called "exoneration.")

4. Last, your court can require that Adkins meet the hurdles in paragraphs 2 *and* 3. They are not the same test. A person who is factually guilty — i.e., he did it — may be able to have a conviction reversed or vacated for other reasons.

What do you do?

A minority of courts have followed paragraph 1, but the great majority would require Adkins either to prove actual innocence (paragraph 2) or to have his conviction overturned in court (paragraph 3) or both. For a thorough review of all positions, see Canaan v. Bartee, 72 P.3d 911 (Kan. 2003) (holding that the plaintiff had to win exoneration in court, leaving undecided whether he also had to prove actual innocence). See also the several opinions in Ang v. Martin, 114 P.3d 637 (Wash. 2005).

As you read the following materials, consider whether good reasons exist to require proof of actual innocence in addition to judicial exoneration. Or to require judicial exoneration if the client can prove actual innocence. Or maybe you disagree with both alternatives and conclude that courts should adopt the standard in paragraph 1, so a plaintiff like Adkins would win compensatory damages even if he is factually guilty and unexonerated, so long as he can show that but for the lawyer's negligence he would have beat the charges or gotten a lower sentence.

The next case describes an allegation of malpractice that is particularly egregious because the charge is not merely that the lawyer erred, but that he did not communicate a prosecutorial offer that would have avoided any conviction at all. Indeed, the facts permit the inference that this failure *might* have been motivated by an effort to protect another client.

PEELER v. HUGHES & LUCE
909 S.W.2d 494 (Tex. 1995)

ENOCH, JUSTICE. . . .

I

Carol Peeler was an officer of both Hillcrest Equities, Inc. and its wholly-owned subsidiary Hillcrest Securities Corp., Inc. (collectively, "Hillcrest"), a corporation trading in government securities. She and other individuals came under federal criminal investigation by the United States Internal Revenue Service because they were suspected of engineering illegal tax write-offs for wealthy investors. Peeler hired Darrell C. Jordan, a partner with Hughes & Luce, L.L.P., to represent her. She paid Hughes & Luce a $250,000 non-refundable retainer fee and further agreed to pay any hourly fees exceeding that amount.

After nearly four years of investigation and negotiation, a federal grand jury indicted Peeler on twenty-one counts. That grand jury also indicted her husband, and the other Hillcrest principals on various charges. A deal was struck between Peeler and the United States. Peeler signed a plea agreement admitting her guilt to count eighteen — "aiding and assisting the filing of a false and fraudulent U.S. Partnership Return of Income for Byrd Investments." She also appeared before the federal judge, admitting her guilt and further testifying that her admission was freely and voluntarily given. In exchange for this, the United States dropped the balance of the charges against her, dismissed all charges against her husband, and recommended a relatively short prison sentence. She was sentenced to a $100,000 fine, $150,000 in restitution, and five years of probation in lieu of incarceration.

II

This case comes to us in the posture of a summary judgment granted in favor of Jordan and Hughes & Luce. Many of the underlying facts in this case are not in dispute. Where they are, it is Peeler's summary judgment proof that we must accept as true.

Peeler complains that prior to the time she pled guilty, Jordan failed to tell her that the United States Attorney had offered her absolute transactional immunity. In other words, the United States Attorney had offered to not prosecute Peeler for her crime, if she would become a witness and testify against her colleagues. Peeler learned about this offer from a journalist three days after pleading guilty. . . .

III

Generally, to recover on a claim of legal malpractice, a plaintiff must prove that (1) the attorney owed the plaintiff a duty, (2) the attorney breached that duty, (3) the breach proximately caused the plaintiff's injuries, and (4) damages occurred. In the context of a criminal matter, we have not addressed whether the client's criminal conduct is, as a matter of law, the sole proximate or producing cause of the client's eventual conviction and damages, such that a legal malpractice claim may not be brought absent a showing that the plaintiff has been exonerated from the criminal conviction, either by direct appeal, post-conviction relief, or otherwise. . . . Like the court of appeals below, however, nearly every court that has addressed the question of whether a convict may sue his or her attorney holds that, for reasons of public policy, the criminal conduct is the only cause of any injury suffered as a result of conviction.

One court in particular has articulated the public policy considerations at stake:

> [P]ermitting a convicted criminal to pursue a legal malpractice claim without requiring proof of innocence would allow the criminal to profit by his own fraud, or to take advantage of his own wrong, or to found [a] claim upon his iniquity, or to acquire property by his own crime. As such, it is against public policy for the suit to continue in that it "would indeed shock the public conscience, engender disrespect for courts and generally discredit the administration of justice."

State ex rel. O'Blennis v. Adolf, 691 S.W.2d 498, 504 (Mo. Ct. App. 1985) (quoting In re Estate of Laspy, 409 S.W.2d 725 (Mo. Ct. App. 1966) (citations omitted)). As a result, only plaintiffs who have been exonerated are permitted to negate the sole proximate cause bar to their cause of action for professional negligence in these jurisdictions.

There are two states that have refused to impose an "innocence requirement" on convicts pursuing malpractice claims against their former attorneys. But they have done so without fully addressing the policy concerns of the jurisdictions that have adopted the innocence requirement. See Krahn v. Kinney, 43 Ohio St. 3d 103, 105-06, 538 N.E.2d 1058, 1061 (1989); Gebhardt v. O'Rourke, 444 Mich. 535, 510 N.W.2d 900, 908 (1994). These courts entertain the possibility that a defense attorney's negligence may be the legal cause of a client's damages, treating legal malpractice suits against criminal and civil attorneys exactly alike.

IV

Because of public policy, we side with the majority of courts and hold that plaintiffs who have been convicted of a criminal offense may negate the sole proximate cause bar to their claim for legal malpractice in connection with that conviction only if they have been exonerated on direct appeal, through post-conviction relief, or otherwise. While we agree with the other state courts that public policy prohibits convicts from profiting from their illegal conduct, we also believe that allowing civil recovery for convicts impermissibly shifts responsibility for the crime away from the convict. This opportunity to shift much, if not all, of the punishment assessed against convicts for their criminal acts to their former attorneys, drastically diminishes the consequences of the convicts' criminal conduct and seriously undermines our system of criminal justice. We therefore hold that, as a matter of law, it is the illegal conduct rather than the negligence of a convict's counsel that is the cause in fact of any injuries flowing from the conviction, unless the conviction has been overturned.

While urging us to apply the same standard for legal malpractice in the criminal law context as we do in civil contexts, Peeler implicitly differentiates her circumstances from the usual criminal prosecution in that had she received transactional immunity, she would have avoided criminal prosecution altogether, not to mention being indicted in the first place. This argument does not, however, address the public policy principle at issue that convicts may not shift the consequences of their crime to a third party.

Peeler makes much of the notably remarkable affidavit from the prosecuting attorney. He confirms that he had offered transactional immunity to Peeler through Jordan. Peeler also makes much of the personal emotional struggle she experienced over her concern for the care of her young children if both she and her husband were convicted on all counts of the indictment and consequently sentenced to lengthy prison terms. It was because of this admittedly grave and understandable concern that she accepted the deal with the prosecution. True, the constitutional protections conferred upon a citizen accused of a crime (including a right to counsel) emanate from this country's fundamental commitment to individual liberty. But, the purpose of such protections is to protect an innocent accused against an erroneous or overzealous prosecution. The lost opportunity of an admittedly guilty person to escape prosecution because of her lawyer's negligence does not override the public policy against shifting the consequences of a crime to a third party.

We emphasize that Peeler, at no time, even asserts that she did not commit the acts which formed the basis of the matters charged. To the contrary, she conceded in her deposition that she committed many of the acts for which she was indicted, but not prosecuted because of the deal she struck. Furthermore, care for her children ceased to be at risk, because the charges against her husband were dropped and her light prison sentence was probated. While arguably her plea is compelling, it cannot be gainsaid that to allow her suit against her attorneys merely permits cost-shifting of the consequences of her criminal conduct to her lawyer. . . .

The record is silent as to whether Peeler filed a grievance against Jordan. Factual allegations of this nature generally merit review by the State Bar. Nothing in this opinion should be construed as relieving criminal defense attorneys of their responsibility to maintain the highest standards of ethical and professional conduct. Whether public policy prohibits Peeler's suit against her attorney is a question independent of whether her attorney committed acts proscribed by the State Bar's disciplinary code.

Striking what we believe is the proper balance between protecting the strong public policies of preventing convicts from escaping the consequences of, or benefiting financially from, their illegal acts and holding defense attorneys responsible for their professional negligence, we affirm the judgment of the court of appeals.

HIGHTOWER, JUSTICE, concurring.

I concur in the result. However, I write separately to comment on the alleged conduct of Hughes & Luce and Darrell Jordan. According to Peeler's pleadings and her summary judgment proof, Assistant United States Attorney William Alexander contacted Jordan in December 1985 to offer both Peeler and her husband transactional immunity from prosecution in exchange for her cooperation with the government's investigation. IRS agent Ernesto Hernandez and others corroborated Alexander's testimony. According to Peeler, Jordan never communicated any such offer to her. Jordan denies that Alexander ever spoke to him concerning immunity for Peeler and her husband. Subsequently, transactional immunity from prosecution was offered to and accepted by another individual.[2] In January 1989, the government indicted Peeler, her husband and others on various charges. Based on the advice of Jordan and other lawyers, Peeler ultimately pled guilty to one count of the indictment in March 1989.

Even though the Court concludes that Peeler's own conduct is the sole proximate or producing cause of her indictment and conviction, the holding today should not be perceived as condoning the alleged conduct of Hughes & Luce and Jordan which, if true, is reprehensible and unconscionable.

PHILLIPS, CHIEF JUSTICE, delivered a dissenting opinion, joined by GAMMAGE and SPECTOR, JUSTICES.

The Court bases today's holding in large part on its belief that all criminal acts are so reprehensible that permitting someone convicted of a crime to recover against his or her former attorney for professional negligence "would shock the public conscience, engender disrespect for courts and generally discredit the administration of justice." The public morality is thus protected at the expense of shielding all criminal defense attorney malpractice, no matter how egregious, from any redress in the civil justice system. While I agree with the Court's approach in those cases where there is some doubt about the effect of the alleged malpractice, I believe it proves too much in those unusual circumstances where the convicted defendant can offer particularly probative evidence that there would have been no conviction but for the attorney's malpractice. Because Peeler's summary judgment proof, if believed by the finder of fact, would meet this extraordinary burden, I would reverse the judgment of the court of appeals and remand this cause to the trial court for further proceedings.

In most cases the law should not permit a person convicted of a crime to recover for legal malpractice. Allowing any disappointed convicted criminal to sue his or her former attorney would wreak havoc on the orderly administration of justice, impeding the delivery of legal representation guaranteed by the Sixth Amendment to anyone charged with an offense punishable by imprisonment. If the law did not impose a substantial burden on convicted criminals seeking to sue their attorneys for professional negligence, most criminal convictions might simply be a prelude to a civil malpractice suit. Our civil justice system cannot and should not be available to hear such claims.

The Court's position, however, is that any person convicted of a crime must establish his or her innocence in order to maintain a civil malpractice suit. . . .

None of [the cited] cases, however, presents a situation analogous to Peeler's. In particular, in none of those cases would the allegations of malpractice, if true, conclusively have established that the former criminal defendant would have avoided conviction but for the attorney's malpractice. In Glenn v. Aiken, for example, the plaintiff's criminal attorney failed to object to an erroneous jury

---

2. In addition, at least one other defendant was represented by Hughes & Luce.

instruction and the plaintiff was convicted. In the subsequent malpractice trial, the court held that the plaintiff was required to prove his innocence of the underlying criminal charge to establish causation since it was unclear whether the jury in his criminal trial, even if properly instructed, would have acquitted him. Likewise, in Weiner v. Mitchell, Silberberg & Knupp, the plaintiff sued his former criminal attorneys for failing to apprise him of serious conflicts of interest. Reviewing the trial court's dismissal of the plaintiff's suit, the court held that because the plaintiff could not assert his innocence, "all of the various causes of action alleged in tort against defendants . . . founder on the complete lack of proximate causation between the torts alleged . . . and the injuries plaintiff allegedly suffered. . . ."

Here, however, Peeler does not need to establish her innocence in order to prove with a high degree of certainty that her attorney's conduct resulted in her indictment and conviction. If, as Peeler claims, the prosecutor made an offer of transactional immunity which Jordan failed to convey to her, that failure proximately caused her indictment and conviction. Whether Peeler actually committed the crimes with which she was charged is—under these circumstances—irrelevant. Under her version of the facts, she certainly would not have been either indicted or convicted had she known about and accepted the government's offer of transactional immunity. The affidavit offered as summary judgment proof from the prosecutor makes clear that the immunity he discussed with Jordan would have saved Peeler from prosecution for any acts arising out of the transactions under investigation.

Thus, if a plaintiff introduces, as part of his or her case-in-chief, proof of an offer of immunity that is supported by evidence originating with the governmental entity that allegedly made that offer, and further proof both that the offer was not communicated to the defendant and that the defendant would have accepted it, I would allow the plaintiff's action to proceed to the jury. This rule, unlike the Court's, would encourage attorneys to communicate such immunity offers in order to facilitate the conviction of those parties to a crime whom prosecutors believe are most culpable. Summary judgment still would be proper for a convicted criminal's former attorney, however, unless the plaintiff can provide testimony from a current or former prosecutor, an official government document, or some other evidence that meets this stringent burden, together with further proof that the offer would have made a difference but for the attorney's conduct. . . .

Acquittal, Innocence, or Exoneration?

Wiley v. County of San Diego, 966 P.2d 983 (Cal. 1998), like *Peeler*, views the conviction and any punishment to be a legal result of the guilty client's conduct, not the lawyer's negligence. It cites other remedies, including appeal and post-conviction relief, as adequate to address a defense lawyer's incompetence. *Wiley* also relies on Levine v. Kling, 123 F.3d 580 (7th Cir. 1997), where, as Judge Posner archly described it, the plaintiff was seeking damages "to compensate him for the loss of his liberty during the period of his rightful imprisonment."

Not only would this be a paradoxical result, depreciating and in some cases wholly offsetting the plaintiff's criminal punishment, but it would be contrary to fundamental principles of both tort and criminal law. Tort law provides damages only for harms to the plaintiff's legally protected interests . . . and the liberty of a guilty criminal is not one of them. The guilty criminal may be able to obtain an acquittal if he is skillfully represented, but he has no right to that result (just as he has no *right* to have the jury nullify the law, though juries sometimes do that), and the law provides no relief if the "right" is denied him. [Emphasis in original.]

Judge Posner, predicting Illinois law, held that the defendant must first attempt to exhaust his postconviction remedies. "Should he succeed in getting his conviction overturned, he can bring a new malpractice suit . . . though he will have to prove in that suit by a preponderance of the evidence that he was in fact innocent, and not just lucky. If his postconviction attacks on the conviction fail, then he cannot bring a malpractice suit even if he is prepared to present evidence that he was innocent in fact, and his conviction therefore unjust." For this last proposition, Judge Posner relied on collateral estoppel doctrine. The conviction, while it stands, bars the malpractice claim. Not all courts that require proof of actual innocence also require the defendant to overturn his conviction. *Wiley* collects the cases. Although *Wiley* did not require the defendant to overturn his conviction, Coscia v. McKenna & Cuneo, 25 P.3d 670 (Cal. 2001) imposed that requirement three years later: "[W]e hold that an individual convicted of a criminal offense must obtain reversal of his or her conviction, or other exoneration by postconviction relief, in order to establish actual innocence in a criminal malpractice action. . . . [P]ublic policy considerations require that only an innocent person wrongly convicted be deemed to have suffered a legally compensable harm."

Ohio has adopted a minority view on these issues. Consider the following facts. Krahn was charged with three gambling misdemeanors because she had a gambling device in her bar. She retained Kinney to represent her. Unknown to her, Kinney also represented Shaffer, whose company installed and serviced the device. The prosecutor told Kinney that he would dismiss the charge against Krahn if she testified against Shaffer. Kinney did not communicate this offer to Krahn. He instead recommended that she enter a guilty plea, and she did. Krahn cannot establish her actual innocence. She's factually guilty. Nevertheless, the court held that her complaint stated a claim. Krahn v. Kinney, 538 N.E.2d 1058 (Ohio 1989). What should be her theory of recovery? One possibility is that Kinney did not communicate the offer to Krahn because he was protecting Shaffer. Did you notice note 2 in Justice Hightower's concurrence? Hughes & Luce also represented at least one other defendant. The offer Jordan did not transmit would have required Peeler to testify against others. You can see how Peeler might have tried to use Jordan's multiple representation to win her malpractice case if she had been allowed to bring it.

For a long time I thought that *Peeler* was the most indefensible decision in the field, even accepting that options 2 or 3 above stated the right rule in ordinary negligence cases (as does the dissent). I find the dissent's distinction compelling. Now, I have a new candidate for least defensible decision in the field. At least Peeler pled guilty to a crime and was sentenced for it. In Ang v. Martin, supra, the Angs' former counsel had encouraged them to plead guilty in federal court, but then, disenchanted with the advice they were getting, the Angs brought in new lawyers, withdrew their proffered plea (which had never been accepted), went to trial, and were acquitted. They then sued their former counsel for malpractice. The jury found that one of their former lawyers was in fact negligent. But the trial court had also instructed the jury that the Angs also had to prove that they were actually innocent, which they were unable to do. This is a complete confusion of the doctrine. The reason courts may require a criminal malpractice plaintiff to prove innocence is so that the defense lawyer, even if negligent, isn't made to compensate the former client for the sentence and conviction, which is seen to follow from the client's criminal conduct. But the Angs were never convicted of a crime, so there should be nothing for them to prove they didn't do. And of course they weren't seeking compensation for wrongful incarceration but for the harm caused by their first set of lawyers (including, I assume, the fees they paid) in representing them poorly.

Let's go back to Adkins v. Dixon, the hypothetical with which we began this inquiry. The guilty defendant urged his lawyer to assert a speedy trial defense in two felony cases, but the lawyer allegedly failed to preserve the defense for one of the charges. What's your position now? Should Adkins have a claim against Dixon for his negligent failure to assert the defense if that's the only reason that Adkins will now spend his life in prison? If so, should Dixon have to pay for Adkins's life in prison? Or should Adkins first have to get his conviction vacated or prove his innocence or both?

In the actual case, the Virginia Supreme Court rejected Adkins's malpractice claims. "We agree with the defendants' claim that Adkins's actual guilt is a material consideration since courts will not permit a guilty party to profit from his own crime. . . . [W]e think that Adkins's guilt, not Dixon's alleged failure to assert the speedy trial defense, was the proximate cause of the convictions." Adkins v. Dixon, 482 S.E.2d 797 (Va. 1997) (containing a denser but analytically indistinct version of the hypothetical facts and requiring the malpractice plaintiff both to obtain postconviction relief and to prove actual innocence). We know now that the court is using the words "proximate cause" in a special sense. Surely, Dixon's error is the immediate logical cause of Adkins's predicament. So it must be that the words "proximate cause" are policy-laden, as they are in the other cases requiring proof of actual innocence. As a matter of policy, we will not make a negligent lawyer pay for a client's imprisonment for his crime. Adkins's effort to secure postconviction relief in the federal courts was unsuccessful. Adkins v. Murray, 872 F. Supp. 1491 (W.D. Va. 1994), aff'd, 97 F.3d 1446 (4th Cir. 1996).

Keep in mind that although plaintiffs in Peeler's situation may not be able to win a malpractice claim, their lawyer's failure to inform them of the plea bargain may at a minimum suffice to establish ineffective assistance of counsel and vacate the conviction. Cottle v. State, 733 So. 2d 963 (Fla. 1999). Further, if state law demands only that the conviction be vacated, not proof of actual innocence, then a malpractice claim for the conduct alleged in *Peeler* may be available after all. (In addition, couldn't Peeler get back the fee she paid Jordan? She should not have to prove actual innocence for that.)

Stranger Than Fiction Department. Randolph Taylor's Virginia drivers' license was suspended, so he used a moped because he understood that license suspensions did not affect mopeds. Taylor was arrested, and the court appointed

Richard Davis to defend him. Taylor told Davis that the suspension did not apply to mopeds, but Davis allegedly did no research to determine the accuracy of his client's information. At trial, the judge convicted Taylor and sentenced him to jail for 60 days and a fine. Althea Hunt was appointed to represent Taylor on appeal. Taylor told Hunt about the moped exception, but Hunt, allegedly without doing research, told him he was wrong and "that there was no need to appeal."

Taylor was right about the Moped exception. His lawyers, the prosecutor, and the judge were all wrong. Taylor went to jail for committing a noncrime. He eventually had the conviction vacated, then sued his lawyers, citing the "wrongful conviction, incarceration, monetary losses, and other damages." Davis and Hunt, relying on Adkins v. Dixon, supra, successfully moved to dismiss the case because Taylor had "failed to plead that he had obtained postconviction relief." (He had gotten that relief, but the defendants argued that his complaint was deficient because he had failed to "plead" it.) The Virginia Supreme Court reversed. *Adkins* did not apply. When the former client of a criminal defense lawyer "makes allegations . . . which, if true, establish that the plaintiff is actually innocent as a matter of law because the purported offense for which he was convicted did not constitute a crime . . . the plaintiff is not required to plead that he sought and obtained post-conviction relief." Taylor v. Davis, 576 S.E.2d 445 (Va. 2003).

FURTHER READING

The issues here, as I wrote at the outset, are challenging and laden with conflicting policy considerations. The bar seems seriously divided (as are many courts) about the right rule. For further reading, see Rantz v. Kaufman, 109 P.3d 132 (Colo. 2005) (collecting cases and opting for option 2 above); and Therrien v. Sullivan, 891 A.2d 560 (N.H. 2006) (requiring exoneration and proof of actual innocence). Professor Duncan examines the issues here in Meredith Duncan, Criminal Malpractice: A Lawyer's Holiday, 37 Ga. L. Rev. 1251 (2003). She considers the facts of our cases, including *Adkins*, and "suggests reforms to remove the needless impediments that serve to frustrate criminal malpractice claimants' quest within the civil system for relief against their former counsel."

Assigned Counsel

One distinct variety of criminal defense lawyer is the lawyer who works for a public defender's office or like organization that represents indigent defendants. Closely aligned are lawyers in private practice who accept criminal court assignments. The Supreme Court has held that nothing in federal law bestows immunity on defense lawyers in private practice who represent indigent defendants under the Criminal Justice Act of 1964 (which provides for selection of those lawyers and their payment). Ferri v. Ackerman, 444 U.S. 193 (1979). However, where the lawyer defending a criminal case in federal court is employed by the federal public defender, an institutional office used in some federal districts to provide indigent defense services, the rule changes. These lawyers are "employees" of the United States within the meaning of the Federal Tort Claims Act. A former client charging malpractice must sue the United States under the FTCA, not the lawyer. Sullivan v. United States, 21 F.3d 198 (7th Cir. 1994). In California, by contrast, public defenders are liable for malpractice to the same extent as private counsel. Barner v. Leeds, 13 P.3d 704 (Cal. 2000). Florida has refused to afford public defenders quasi-judicial immunity. Schreiber v. Rowe, 814 So. 2d 396 (Fla. 2002) ("the role of public defenders is more analogous to the role of private attorneys than to that of state attorneys," who do enjoy qualified immunity). Elsewhere, public defenders have been held to be absolutely immune from malpractice liability under state law. Dziubak v. Mott, 503 N.W.2d 771 (Minn. 1993).

3. Damages or Injury

"Memorandum to the Court from the Chief Judge"

By coincidence, our docket this month has two cases that pose the same question but from opposite perspectives. Our state has no law on the question so we have to look to underlying policies and the persuasive force of decisions from other jurisdictions, which, as you might expect, go both ways.

In the first case, Talbot v. Skidmore, Talbot had hired Skidmore to sue Mascotti for an intentional tort resulting in personal injury. Skidmore filed a complaint seeking compensatory damages of $300,000 and unspecified punitive damages. To get punitive damages under our precedent, Skidmore would have to prove that Mascotti's conduct was "willful and outrageous," which the complaint alleged. Skidmore duly informed Talbot of a $200,000 settlement offer and even negotiated a $40,000 increase in the offer. He then advised Talbot to accept on the ground that a jury was not likely to be much more generous, and although the case was strong, he said, victory was not certain. It all makes sense except that at no time did Skidmore ever explain to Talbot what punitive damages were, how they were determined and computed, how much they might be, or that by settling she was giving up her claim to them. So although the settlement for the compensatory amount was reasonable standing alone, Talbot did not know that she was giving up the chance to get substantial punitive damages from Mascotti.

In her case against Skidmore, Talbot claimed that Skidmore was guilty of malpractice for failure to inform her about punitive damages and that but for the malpractice, she would have recovered them. The trial jury, instructed on the case within a case principle, did in fact find that if the inner case had gone to trial, Talbot would have recovered $500,000 in punitive damages. The trial court entered judgment in favor of Talbot and against Skidmore for $500,000. Skidmore is now appealing this award. He accepts that his failure was malpractice (which he can hardly deny) and that it caused Talbot to lose some amount of punitive damages. Nevertheless, he says as a matter of policy he should not have to pay the lost punitive damages. He argues that *his* conduct was not willful and outrageous and that he should not have to pay for the outrageous and willful conduct of Mascotti.

Also on our docket is Wiggins v. Belinder, which presents the mirror situation. Wiggins, represented by Belinder, was a defendant in a case called McNeal v.

Wiggins. The jury awarded McNeal $150,000 compensatory damages and $750,000 in punitive damages. But as you know, the legislature recently created a presumption that punitive damages should not exceed three times compensatory damages. If the jury awards more than that, the defendant can move for a reduction. The plaintiff must then rebut the presumption by clear and convincing evidence. A list of statutory factors guide the judge's ruling. Belinder failed to make the appropriate motion and the trial court entered judgment for the full amount. When Belinder realized her error, it was too late. Wiggins then sued Belinder and got a verdict for $300,000. Belinder's appeal makes pretty much the same argument as in our other case. She may have been negligent, she says, but her conduct was not willful and outrageous. As a matter of policy, she argues, she should not have to pay for her client's conduct, which *was* willful and outrageous.

Please come to the conference prepared to take and defend a view on each case. It may be that the plaintiff should prevail in *Talbot* but not *Wiggins* or the opposite, or in both or neither. I don't mean to suggest that the cases should be decided the same way.

The part of a malpractice case concerned with damages or injury draws largely on the law of remedies in tort and contract. We have already seen some damage issues in the preceding material. Essentially, the client has to prove that the lawyer's default caused a loss. To the extent that malpractice plaintiffs may recover only for economic loss, clients who use lawyers for noneconomic problems will have hollow claims if their lawyers act incompetently. Many jurisdictions do decline to recognize noneconomic injuries. See, e.g., Timms v. Rosenblum, 713 F. Supp. 948 (E.D. Va. 1989), aff'd, 900 F.2d 256 (4th Cir. 1990), where the plaintiff charged that the defendants were negligent in a custody matter, as a result of which she lost custody of her children. The court held that the plaintiff could not recover for her emotional distress unless the defendant's behavior was intentional or outrageous or the plaintiff suffered physical injury. Shocked?

However, significant inroads on the reluctance to allow recovery for noneconomic injury have also appeared. In Wagenmann v. Adams, 829 F.2d 196 (1st Cir. 1987), lawyer Healy's professional failures caused his client to spend a night confined in a state mental hospital:

> As a direct and proximate result of Healy's ineffectiveness, the plaintiff was forcibly deprived of his liberty and dispatched to a mental hospital. The fright and suffering incident to such a wrenching dislocation can hardly be overstated. Subsequent to his release, Wagenmann claimed (credibly) to have undergone continuing anguish and to have felt the weight of the stigma attendant to such confinement. He feared that others would learn of it and question his sanity. . . .
>
> Were we to accept the notion that a client's recovery on the grim facts of a case such as this must be limited to purely economic loss, we would be doubly wrong. The negligent lawyer would receive the benefit of an enormous windfall, and the victimized client would be left without fair recourse in the face of

ghastly wrongdoing. Despite having caused his client a substantial loss of liberty and exposed him to a consequent parade of horribles, counsel would effectively be immunized from liability because of the fortuity of the marketplace. That Healy was guilty of malpractice in the defense of commitment proceedings, rather than in the prosecution of a civil claim for damages, is no reason artificially to shield him from the condign consequences of his carelessness. We are not required by the law of the commonwealth, as we read it, to reach such an unjust result.

Other cases that allow damages for emotional distress are Worsham v. Nix, 145 P.3d 1055 (Okla. 2006) (emotional distress on learning that law firm had fraudulently concealed its failure to file claim for which it had been hired); Salley v. Childs, 541 A.2d 1297 (Me. 1988) (also allowing damages for injury to reputation); Cummings v. Pinder, 574 A.2d 843 (Del. 1990) (same); and Bowman v. Doherty, 686 P.2d 112 (Kan. 1984) (also allowing punitive damages). An innocent client who is incarcerated as a result of a lawyer's negligence or neglect will often have little to show by way of economic loss but a great deal of emotional pain. As in *Wagenmann,* courts have recognized this damage. Rowell v. Holt, 850 So. 2d 474 (Fla. 2003) (damages allowed for emotional distress resulting from ten-day incarceration where lawyer had, but failed to provide court with, exculpatory document); Snyder v. Baumecker, 708 F. Supp. 1451 (D.N.J. 1989) (lawyer liable for client's emotional distress caused by incarceration but not for client's resulting unforeseeable suicide). Courts have allowed former clients to collect punitive damages if the lawyer's conduct was especially blameworthy. Metcalfe v. Waters, 970 S.W.2d 448 (Tenn. 1998) (plaintiff must prove "intentional, fraudulent, malicious, or reckless [conduct] by clear and convincing evidence") (collecting cases); Bierman v. Klapheke, 967 S.W.2d 16 (Ky. 1998) (allegation of fraud).

In one unusual case, a widow, whose deceased husband had been a state judge, alleged that she did not remarry because her lawyer told her, wrongly, that if she did she would lose her first husband's pension. Instead she lived with a man who later left her after striking oil (literally). The court held that she stated a claim for the economic losses she suffered as a result of not marrying. These included the interest in the man's assets state law would have given her had they married. Horn v. Croegaert, 542 N.E.2d 1124 (Ill. App. 1989).

One question on which courts have divided is whether the client's recovery ought to be reduced by the fee the lawyer would have earned had she not acted negligently. For example, a client retains a lawyer on a one-third contingency basis in a personal injury action. The lawyer forgets to file the complaint on time. The client sues the lawyer and proves that she would have recovered $30,000 at the trial of the underlying action. Should the judgment be reduced by the $10,000 the lawyer would have received had he acted properly? Yes: Horn v. Wooster, 165 P.3d 69 (Wyo. 2007). No: Campagnola v. Mulholland, Minion & Roe, 555 N.E.2d 611 (N.Y. 1990). Why should the negligent attorney get a fee — via the offset — for a matter he messed up?

Alternatively, should the damages be increased by the amount the client will have to pay the second lawyer to recover against the first lawyer? Are these two questions related? On the issue of recovery of legal fees, courts distinguish between the fees paid to sue the former lawyer, generally disallowed, and fees paid to a new lawyer to avoid or mitigate the harm from the former lawyer's conduct, generally allowed. Rudolf v. Shayne, Dachs, Stanisci, Corker & Sauer, 867 N.E.2d 385 (N.Y. 2007); Gibraltar Sav. v. Commonwealth Land Title Ins. Co., 907 F.2d 844 (8th Cir. 1990). But see Saffer v. Willoughby, 670 A.2d 527 (N.J. 1996) (negligent attorney must pay legal fees of former client in prosecuting legal malpractice claim against former lawyer).

C. BEYOND MALPRACTICE: OTHER GROUNDS FOR ATTORNEY LIABILITY TO CLIENTS AND THIRD PARTIES

"Death and Taxes (and Liability?)"

Anticipating retirement, the Medveds had been searching for rural property when a realtor, Sonny Vikar of Country Dreams Properties, showed them 137 acres and a nineteenth-century colonial that was in need of work but retained original architectural details. And it was big enough to accommodate visits from the Medveds' three children and (so far) eight grandchildren. About 20 of the acres were on flat arable land that Lucius Medved recognized as perfect for the vegetable and flower gardens he planned to grow. The property had been owned by Ezekiel Montforte for 52 years, until his death a few months earlier. Zeke, as he was known, had lived alone after his wife's death eight years earlier. The couple had no children and Zeke left no will, so the property descended by intestacy to Emma Newcastle, the daughter of his wife's sister. Emma and her husband, Otto Shapinksi, lived 2,200 miles away. A month after Emma learned the news of the inheritance, she and Otto visited the property and engaged Sonny Vikar to sell it.

Emma was also named administrator of Zeke's estate. She hired a lawyer from the nearby city, Chandler Pierce of Mulberry, Okoli & Cho LLP, to wind up the estate.

Emma contracted to sell the property to the Medveds for $2.7 million. Chandler Pierce also represented Emma on the sale. The house wasn't worth a great deal, given its disrepair, but the land was valuable because of its location and size and because the county had become popular with second-home buyers following an extension of the interstate a few years earlier.

The Medveds retained attorney Naomi Kell to handle the purchase. Naomi called an agent at Safe-T Title for the title insurance. The agent in turn wrote to Chandler Pierce to find out if all estate taxes had been paid. This was important because if they were not all paid, the IRS or state taxing authorities could levy against the estate's real property, in which case Safe-T, if it insured the title outright (i.e., without a reservation for estate taxes), would be liable. With Emma's permission to reply, Chandler wrote: "This firm has calculated all estate taxes which in our opinion were due. As instructed by the administrator of the estate, Ms. Newcastle, we have paid these sums from estate funds we hold in escrow." Naomi was copied on this correspondence. On getting Chandler's reply, Safe-T Title issued the Medveds a policy insuring the title.

Eight months after the Medveds took title to the property, the IRS determined that the estate's tax return erred in its calculation of the amount of taxes due and levied an additional $317,000 against the estate, which included interest and penalties. The levy became a lien against the Medveds' property. Safe-T Title as the Medveds' title insurer paid the IRS bill.

Safe-T Title then brought an action against Chandler Pierce (and his law firm). The complaint charged negligent misrepresentation in Chandler's reply to Safe-T Title. It alleged, first, that Chandler's statement to Safe-T was false — not all taxes had been paid even if he honestly believed otherwise; second, that the firm's preparation of the estate tax return was negligent; and third, that Chandler and his firm owed Safe-T Title a duty of care when it replied to its inquiry. Separately, Safe-T, as subrogee of the Medveds, also sued Emma Newcastle for violating the warranty of title in the contract of sale and Naomi Kell for malpractice; and Emma cross-claimed against Chandler Pierce for malpractice in failing to properly compute estate taxes, resulting in interest and penalties above what she would have had to pay if he had not erred.

All in all, it was a big mess; but fortunately, our only concern is going to be Safe-T's claim against Chandler and his firm for negligent misrepresentation.

Chandler and his firm moved to dismiss Safe-T's complaint on the ground that the allegations did not state a cause of action. First, they argued that Chandler's statement was true even if the calculation of the estate tax was wrong, so there was no *mis*representation. Second, they argued that Chandler, as counsel to Emma, owed no duty to Safe-T Title, so it had no right to rely on Chandler's reply.

The dramatis personae in the following case are:

Herrigel, a lawyer;
Petrillo, the plaintiff, who had contracted to purchase land from Herrigel's client;
Bachenberg, Herrigel's client;
Rohrer, Herrigel's prior client, who had owned the land before Bachenberg bought it at a sheriff's sale; and
Heritage, the company that did a percolation test when Rohrer owned the land.

Bachenberg is a real estate broker who had tried without success to sell the land for Rohrer before he bought it himself and contracted to sell it to Petrillo. Eventually, after Petrillo's land deal with Bachenberg fell through, Petrillo sued not only Bachenberg but also lawyer Herrigel for return of her deposit and damages. Herrigel was never Petrillo's lawyer. So far as appears, he never met her, talked to her, gave her any document, or even knew her name. Keep your eye on her theory of his liability. Exactly what did Herrigel do that exposed him to liability to his client's buyer? What could he have done to avoid this exposure?

PETRILLO v. BACHENBERG
139 N.J. 472, 655 A.2d 1354 (1995)

POLLOCK, J.

I

In 1987, Rohrer Construction (Rohrer) owned a 1.3-acre tract of undeveloped land in Union Township, Hunterdon County. Herrigel represented Rohrer in the sale of the property. Rohrer hired Heritage Consulting Engineers (Heritage) to perform percolation tests concerning a contract of sale to Land Resources Corporation (Land Resources). Percolation tests reveal, among other things, the suitability of soil for a septic system. Union Township requires two successful percolation tests for municipal approval of a septic system.

In September and October 1987, Heritage provided Rohrer and Herrigel with copies of reports describing two series of percolation tests. The first report, dated September 24, 1987, revealed that of twenty-two tests, only one had been successful. A November 3, 1987, report showed that of eight tests conducted in October, one had been successful.

Rohrer's contract with Land Resources failed. Subsequently, Rohrer listed the property with a local real estate broker, Bachenberg & Bachenberg, Inc. In October 1988, William G. Bachenberg, Jr. (Bachenberg) of Bachenberg & Bachenberg, Inc. asked Herrigel for information concerning the listing. Herrigel told Bachenberg that "he had some perc results," and sent him a two-page document consisting of one page from each of the two Heritage reports. The first page was page one from the September 24, 1987, report; it reflected one successful test and five unsuccessful tests. The second page was culled from the November 3, 1987, report; it listed one successful and one unsuccessful test. Read together, the two pages appear to describe a single series of seven tests, two of which were successful. In fact, the property had passed only two of thirty percolation tests. The document, subsequently described as the "composite report," became part of Bachenberg's sales packet.

Herrigel admits that he possessed both Heritage reports and that he delivered the composite report to Bachenberg. Although Herrigel does not deny that he prepared the composite report, his petition for certification states: "However, there was no evidence given during plaintiff's proofs that Mr. Herrigel had in fact prepared the erroneous two-page report."

Rohrer, which apparently was experiencing financial problems, could not sell the property. In December 1988, Bachenberg and a partner, John Matthews, bought the property at a sheriff's sale for $70,000. In January 1989, Bachenberg discussed with Rohrer the 1987 engineering reports. Rohrer declined to provide those reports to Bachenberg because Bachenberg would not reimburse Rohrer for Heritage's engineering fees.

Bachenberg listed the property for sale at $160,000. In February 1989, Petrillo expressed an interest in purchasing the property to build and operate a child day-care facility. That month, at their first meeting, Bachenberg gave Petrillo a sales packet, which included the composite report.

In June 1989, Petrillo agreed to pay Bachenberg his asking price. Herrigel represented Bachenberg in negotiating the terms of the contract with Petrillo's attorney. Nothing in the record indicates that Herrigel informed Petrillo's attorney of the test results that had been omitted from the composite report. At the insistence of Petrillo's attorney, the contract provided Petrillo with forty-five days to conduct independent soil and water tests, including percolation tests. The contract provided further that Petrillo could rescind if the percolation tests were not satisfactory to her.

In August 1989, Petrillo hired an engineering firm, Canger & Cassera, to conduct soil tests and site planning. Based on the composite report, Canger & Cassera recommended that they start siteplanning work simultaneously with the conduct of percolation tests by a subcontractor, PMK, Ferris & Perricone (PMK). PMK conducted six percolation tests, all of which failed. Consequently, PMK concluded that the site was inadequate for a septic system. Canger & Cassera stopped working on the preliminary site plan. On August 22, 1989, Petrillo notified Bachenberg that the contract was null and void. . . .

The parties could not settle their differences. Bachenberg refused to return Petrillo's $16,000 down payment, claiming that she had breached the contract. Petrillo sued Bachenberg, Matthews, and Herrigel for the return of the down payment and for the costs of her engineering fees. Her complaint alleged claims sounding in breach of contract, fraud, concealment, negligent misrepresentation, and conspiracy. . . .

[The trial court dismissed Petrillo's complaint against Herrigel on the ground that the facts did not show that he owed her a duty. The Appellate Division reversed and the Supreme Court granted review.]

II

As a claim against an attorney for negligence resulting in economic loss, Petrillo's claim against Herrigel is essentially one for economic negligence. Formerly, the doctrine of privity limited such claims by non-clients against attorneys and other professionals. More recently, other doctrines have replaced privity as a means of limiting a professional's duty to a non-client. See, e.g., Biakanja v. Irving, 49 Cal. 2d 647, 320 P.2d 16 (1958) (adopting a "balance of factors" test).

The determination of the existence of a duty is a question of law for the court. Whether an attorney owes a duty to a non-client third party depends on balancing the attorney's duty to represent clients vigorously, with the duty not to provide misleading information on which third parties foreseeably will rely. . . .

Thus, when courts relax the privity requirement, they typically limit a lawyer's duty to situations in which the lawyer intended or should have foreseen that the third party would rely on the lawyer's work. [A] lawyer reasonably should foresee that third parties will rely on an opinion letter issued in connection with a securities offering. The purpose of a legal opinion letter is to induce reliance by others. If an attorney foresees or should foresee that reliance, the resulting duty of care can extend to non-client third parties. . . .

In other contexts, courts have imposed a duty on an attorney who prepares an instrument with the intent that third parties will rely on it. Thus, in Molecular Technology Corp. v. Valentine, 925 F.2d 910, 915-17 (1991), the Sixth Circuit

Court of Appeals determined that a lawyer who prepared a private offering statement for his client's corporate debentures owed a duty of care to potential investors whom the attorney knew, or should have known, would rely on the statement. The court held that Michigan law "imposes a duty in favor of all those third parties who defendant knows will rely on the information and to third parties who defendant should reasonably foresee will rely on the information." . . .

Similarly, section 73 of the proposed Restatement of the Law Governing Lawyers, pertaining to "duty to certain non-clients," provides:

> For the purposes of liability . . . , a lawyer owes a duty to use care . . . :
>
> (2) To a non-client when and to the extent that the lawyer or (with the lawyer's acquiescence) the lawyer's client invites the non-client to rely on the lawyer's opinion or provision of other legal services, the non-client so relies, and the non-client is not, under applicable law, too remote from the lawyer to be entitled to protection. . . . *

We also recognize that attorneys may owe a duty of care to non-clients when the attorneys know, or should know, that non-clients will rely on the attorney's representations and the non-clients are not too remote from the attorneys to be entitled to protection. The Restatement's requirement that the lawyer invite or acquiesce in the non-client's reliance comports with our formulation that the lawyer know, or should know, of that reliance. No matter how expressed, the point is to cabin the lawyer's duty, so the resulting obligation is fair to both lawyers and the public.

III

The imposition on attorneys of defined liability to third parties comports with general principles of tort law. In effect, section 552 of the Restatement (Second) of Torts (1977) imposes pecuniary liability for negligent misrepresentation when an attorney "supplies false information for the guidance of others in their business transactions, . . . if he fails to exercise reasonable care or competence in obtaining or communicating the information." The same section limits liability to loss suffered

> (a) by the person or one of a limited group of persons for whose benefit and guidance he intends to supply the information or knows that the recipient intends to supply it; and
>
> (b) through reliance upon it in a transaction that he intends the information to influence or knows that the recipient so intends or in a substantially similar transaction. . . .

---

* The majority and dissenting opinions refer to §73 of the 1994 draft of the Restatement of Law Governing Lawyers. In the Restatement as adopted, the number of this section is 51. Although some changes were made in the text of the black letter section and in the comment, they are substantially the same as the draft language. The Restatement position is further described at page 769 — Ed.

IV

The objective purpose of documents such as opinion letters, title reports, or offering statements, and the extent to which others foreseeably may rely on them, determines the scope of a lawyer's duty in preparing such documents. . . .

Here, Herrigel did not prepare an opinion letter. Giving Petrillo the benefit of all reasonable inferences, however, we infer that Herrigel extracted information from existing percolation-test reports, created the composite report, and delivered the report to a real estate broker. Our initial inquiry, as with an opinion letter or comparable document, is to ascertain the purpose of the report.

Although Herrigel may have intended that the composite report would demonstrate only that the property had passed two percolation tests, his subjective intent may not define the objective meaning of the report. The roles and relationships of the parties color our assessment. In making that assessment, we cannot ignore the fact that Herrigel is an attorney who, in connection with his client's efforts to sell the property, provided the report to a real estate broker. We infer that when he delivered the report to Bachenberg, Herrigel knew, or should have known, that Bachenberg might deliver it to a prospective purchaser, such as Petrillo. Herrigel did nothing to restrict a prospective purchaser's foreseeable use of the report. In neither the report, a covering letter, nor a disclaimer did Herrigel even hint that the report was anything but complete and accurate.

Significantly, Herrigel's involvement continued after he delivered the report to Bachenberg. After Bachenberg purchased the property, Herrigel acted as his lawyer and negotiated the terms of the contract for the sale of commercial property to Petrillo. Although compiling an engineering report to help a client sell real estate may not be part of a lawyer's stock-in-trade, representing the seller of real estate is a traditional legal service. By representing Bachenberg on the sale to Petrillo, Herrigel confirmed the continuity of his involvement as a lawyer. On these facts, Herrigel's continuing involvement permits the inference that the objective purpose of the report was to induce a prospective purchaser to buy the property. His involvement supports the further inference that Herrigel knew that Bachenberg intended to use the report for that purpose.

Furthermore, a purchaser reading the composite report reasonably could conclude that the property had passed two of seven, not two of thirty, percolation tests. Based on that conclusion, a purchaser reasonably could decide to sign a purchase contract, although the purchaser would not have signed the contract if he or she had seen the complete set of percolation reports. So viewed, Herrigel should have foreseen that Petrillo would rely on the total number of percolation tests in deciding whether to sign the purchase contract. In sum, a jury reasonably could infer that the composite report misrepresented material facts.

By providing the composite report to Bachenberg and subsequently representing him in the sale, Herrigel assumed a duty to Petrillo to provide reliable information regarding the percolation tests. Herrigel controlled the risk that the composite report would mislead a purchaser. Fairness suggests that he should bear the risk of loss resulting from the delivery of a misleading report. We further conclude that Herrigel should have foreseen that a prospective purchaser would rely on the composite report in deciding whether to sign the contract and proceed with engineering and site work.

Herrigel easily could have limited his liability. Most simply, he could have sent complete copies of both reports to Bachenberg. Alternatively, Herrigel could have sent a letter to Bachenberg stating that the property had passed two successful percolation tests as required by Union Township. Or he could have stated either in a letter to Bachenberg or in the composite report that the report evidenced only that the property had yielded two successful percolation tests and that no one should rely on the report for any other purpose. Because Herrigel did nothing to limit the objective purpose of the composite report, he should have foreseen that Petrillo, as a prospective purchaser, would rely on the facts set forth in the report. Accordingly, Herrigel's duty extends to Petrillo. Given Petrillo's concern about percolation, a concern she expressed in the contract, Herrigel's duty includes the obligation to provide information about unsuccessful, as well as successful, percolation tests.

Our decision to affirm the reversal of the judgment of dismissal for Herrigel does not mean that a jury may not return a verdict in his favor. A jury might find that Petrillo was interested only in the fact that the property had passed two percolation tests. Alternatively it could find that the omission of the undisclosed test results was neither material nor misleading. We do not resolve these or other factual issues that may arise on remand. We decide only that a jury should have the opportunity to determine the issue of the effect of Herrigel's alleged negligent misrepresentation.

Our dissenting colleague accepts both our fundamental legal analysis and our conclusion that a jury could find Herrigel to have been negligent. The dissent, however, concludes as a matter of law that Herrigel could not have foreseen that Petrillo would have relied on the composite report when contracting to purchase the property from Bachenberg. Only by ignoring Herrigel's continuous involvement with Bachenberg may the dissent sustain its conclusion.

Contrary to the dissent, a jury reasonably could conclude that when he delivered the report to Bachenberg, Herrigel should have foreseen that Bachenberg, in trying to sell the property, would deliver it to a prospective purchaser. A jury could reach that conclusion notwithstanding the change in Bachenberg's role from agent to principal. As both realtor and investor, Bachenberg's goal was to sell the property. A jury could find that Herrigel should have foreseen that Bachenberg would transmit the composite report to a prospective purchaser, such as Petrillo. Given Herrigel's continuing relationship with Bachenberg, the four-month lapse between Herrigel's delivery of the report to Bachenberg and Bachenberg's delivery to Petrillo is not so great as to render Petrillo's receipt of the report unforeseeable as a matter of law. Neither is the potential class of recipients of the report so vast that we expose Herrigel to boundless risk by recognizing that he owed a duty to Petrillo. Nor is Herrigel, linked by his relationship with Bachenberg, so remote from Petrillo that we can conclude as a matter of law that the chain of events "makes her too remote from Herrigel for him to have foreseen harm to her."

We further disagree with the dissent's unsupported conjecture that recognizing a duty extending from Herrigel to Petrillo will make lawyers less accessible and more defensive. Nor will the duty lead to legal services that are more cumbersome and costly. Recognition of that duty, however, may protect innocent third parties from negligent misrepresentations by lawyers. The recognized duty hardly constitutes lawyers as "guarantors of the accuracy of surveys or other similar experts' reports that they merely transmit." We do not hold that Herrigel guaranteed the accuracy of the tests. Our holding goes no further than to state that Herrigel had a duty not to misrepresent negligently the contents of a material document on which he knew others would rely to their financial detriment. In many situations, lawyers, like people generally, may not have a duty to act, but when they act, like other people, they should act carefully.

The judgment of the Appellate Division is affirmed.

STEIN, J., concurring.

I join the Court's opinion and write separately only to emphasize that in my view the Court's decision effects no material change in the liability of lawyers or other professionals to third parties. Accordingly, the calamitous consequences forecast by our dissenting colleague vastly overstate the effect of our holding and ignore its exceptional factual predicate. . . .

GARIBALDI, J., dissenting.

The majority imposes on an attorney a duty of care to a non-client broader than that imposed on an attorney under the proposed Restatement of the Law Governing Lawyers §73 (Tentative Draft No. 7, 1994), under the Restatement (Second) of Torts §552 (1977), and under our case law. . . . Such an extension will lead to defensive lawyering; it will make legal services more cumbersome, more costly, and less accessible to clients.

I agree with the proposed Restatement of the Law Governing Lawyers §73, pertaining to "duty to certain non-clients," that provides:

> For the purposes of liability . . . , a lawyer owes a duty to use care . . . :
>   (2) To a non-client when and to the extent that the lawyer or (with the lawyer's acquiescence) the lawyer's client invites the non-client to rely on the lawyer's opinion or provision of other legal services, the non-client so relies, and the non-client is not, under applicable law, too remote from the lawyer to be entitled to protection. . . .

I agree with the majority that "[t]he purpose of the legal opinion letter is to induce reliance by others. If an attorney foresees or should foresee that reliance, the resulting duty of care can extend to non-client third parties." . . .

An attorney who undertakes a specific task for a non-client who the attorney knows will rely on that specific task also owes a duty of care to that non-client. As Comment e to section 73 of the proposed Restatement of the Law Governing Lawyers, supra, states:

> When a non-client is invited to rely on a lawyer's services, rather than on the lawyer's opinions, the analysis is similar. For example, if the seller's lawyer at a real-estate closing offers to record the deed for the buyer, the lawyer is subject to liability to the buyer for negligence in doing so, even if the buyer did not thereby become a client of the lawyer and the lawyer, for example, owes the buyer no duty of confidentiality. . . .

This case does not concern a lawyer's legal opinion or the performance of any legal services. Nor does this case concern a non-client for whom an attorney has undertaken a specific legal task. Rather, this case is about an attorney's error in not continuing to follow the whereabouts of a report of a consulting engineering company that was incorrectly collated in his office and sent to the real estate agent of his then-client, but that ended up in the hands of a subsequent non-client, from a subsequent seller of the same property. . . .

Thus Rohrer was the client whom Herrigel was representing when he purportedly gave the two-page report to Bachenberg, Rohrer's realtor. Petrillo was never Rohrer's prospective buyer; she was solely Bachenberg's prospective buyer. By the time Petrillo expressed interest in the property, Bachenberg was no longer the realtor but the seller.

Under section 73 of the proposed Restatement of the Law Governing Lawyers, supra, Herrigel has no duty to Petrillo. Herrigel did not give Petrillo a "legal opinion" or provide "other legal services" to her. Indeed, the negligence charged to Herrigel is not related to either his legal opinion or other legal services. . . .

Herrigel owed no duty of care to Petrillo. She did not rely on his legal opinion. He did not provide her with other legal services nor did he undertake to perform any specific tasks for her. The attenuated chain of events that led to Petrillo having the report makes her too remote from Herrigel for him to have foreseen harm to her. Moreover, as the record demonstrates, Petrillo did not rely on the report. Accordingly, I respectfully dissent.

The Expanding Universe in Professional Liability

> Though we certainly do not suggest that a lawyer by rendering services becomes a partner in his client's misdeeds . . . membership in the legal profession is not a shield against liability for conduct in excess of professional right or duty.
>
> — Hartford Accident and Indemnity Co. v. Sullivan,
> 846 F.2d 377 (7th Cir. 1988)

Hartford Accident cites Wahlgren v. Bausch & Lomb Optical Co., 68 F.2d 660 (7th Cir. 1934) ("One may not use his license to practice law as a shield to protect himself from the consequences of his participation in an unlawful or illegal conspiracy"). *Petrillo* is not your first encounter with legal theories that impose third-party liability on lawyers for professional work. Recall the cases in chapters 9 and 13A2. The following discussion addresses some of the old, new, and newly applied theories that third parties, and sometimes clients, have asserted in actions against lawyers, and theories that lawyers have interposed in defense. Clients, of course, also have recourse to traditional professional negligence claims, as do some nonclients (page 719), although third parties will usually be unable to show entitlement to the full panoply of lawyerly duties to clients.

An early case, Biakanja v. Irving, 320 P.2d 16 (Cal. 1958), adopted a "balancing of various factors" test to decide whether a lawyer has a duty to a non-client. This test does not offer much in the way of predictability, but perhaps stricter categorization is not easily achieved. Efforts to be more precise when more precision is illusory can create greater problems than ambiguity. But it's in the nature of the legal process, isn't it, to make the effort? The Washington Supreme Court, among others, has attempted to itemize the factors encompassed by the balancing test. Trask v. Butler, 872 P.2d 1080 (Wash. 1994), listed the following ingredients:

(1) the extent to which the transaction was intended to benefit the plaintiff;
(2) the foreseeability of harm to the plaintiff;
(3) the degree of certainty that the plaintiff suffered injury;
(4) the closeness of the connection between the defendant's conduct and the injury;
(5) the policy of preventing future harm; and
(6) the extent to which the profession would be unduly burdened by a finding of liability.

Thus . . . the threshold question is whether the plaintiff is an intended beneficiary of the transaction to which the advice pertained. While the answer to the threshold question does not totally resolve the issue, no further inquiry need be made unless such an intent exists.

Here are a few of the more prominent theories for holding lawyers accountable to non-clients. Keep in mind, however, that jurisdictions vary widely on their willingness to recognize third-party claims against lawyers arising out of the work the lawyers do for traditional clients. Contrary to *Trask*, an intent to benefit the plaintiff is not a necessary condition for all theories of liability.

Duty of Care to Third Party. A court might recognize a duty of care to third persons — essentially a duty to avoid malpractice or professional negligence — by viewing the third person as a third-party beneficiary under contract law, as in some of the cases at page 719. Or a court might impose such a duty on a tort theory or by operation of law. The alternate routes are fully plumbed in Leyba v. Whitley, 907 P.2d 172 (N.M. 1995), which adopts the Trask v. Butler test and uses it to "imply in law a term in every agreement between an attorney and personal representative that the agreement is formed with the intent to benefit the statutory beneficiaries of [a wrongful death] action." The court excepted only those situations where the beneficiary is "an adverse party. An adverse party cannot justifiably rely on the opposing lawyer to protect him from harm." In *Lebya*, the lawyers represented the mother of a decedent, as personal representative of her son's estate, in a wrongful death case. After settlement, the lawyers deducted their fee and gave the balance to the mother, who spent it on herself. The mother had no right to the money personally, which by statute belonged to the decedent's son, her grandson, to whom she was legally obliged to distribute it. The court said the lawyers owed a duty of care to the grandson to protect against dissipation of the money.

Consumer Protection Laws. Can a client or third person sue a lawyer under consumer protections laws by claiming that a law office is a business and that these laws purport to regulate the behavior of businesses? Suits under a consumer protection law may offer clients a better chance of, and a greater, recovery (including counsel fees) than if a claim is solely in malpractice.

A thorough treatment of the availability of these laws appears in Crowe v. Tull, 126 P.3d 196 (Colo. 2006). The facts are unusual. A former client claimed that the defendant law firm used extensive advertising, primarily on television, portraying the firm "as highly skilled at negotiating with insurance companies and promised the firm would obtain full value for its clients' personal injury claims." In fact, the plaintiff alleged, the firm was nothing more than a settlement "mill" that "relies on quick settlements of cases with minimal expenditure of effort. . . ." The plaintiff claimed that the firm mishandled his case. The court held that attorneys are liable under the consumer protection law, not only for deceptive advertising but also for the manner in which they represented the plaintiff. In Guenard v. Burke, 443 N.E.2d 892 (Mass. 1982), the plaintiff-client, in connection with an action against her former attorney, was allowed to invoke the benefit of a state law forbidding "unfair or deceptive acts or practices in the conduct of any trade or commerce." The court assumed without discussion that the practice of law was "trade or commerce" within the meaning of the state statute. Unlike a traditional common law malpractice action, the statute provided for multiple damages, attorney's fees, and costs. Taking *Guenard* one step further, Sears, Roebuck & Co. v. Goldstone & Sudalter, P.C., 128 F.3d 10 (1st Cir. 1997), not only permitted a client to sue counsel under the Massachusetts consumer protection law for unfair billing practices, but also held that "[v]iolations of the rules governing the legal profession are . . . relevant in" actions under the statute. Other courts have concluded that consumer protection laws do not apply to a lawyer's act of charging excessive fees. Cripe v. Leiter, 703 N.E.2d 100 (Ill. 1998).

The Supreme Court ruled that the Fair Debt Collection Practices Act applies to a lawyer who "regularly," through litigation, tries to collect consumer debts. Heintz v. Jenkins, 514 U.S. 291 (1995). In Garrett v. Derbes, 110 F.3d 317 (5th Cir. 1997), the defendant was hired by a local phone company to collect delinquent telephone bills. In nine months, he mailed about 639 demand letters to individual customers of the company. Although this work accounted for only one-half of one percent of Derbes's entire law practice, the court held that, given the number of demand letters sent, Derbes "regularly" attempted to collect consumer debts within the meaning of the Act. See also Avila v. Rubin, 84 F.3d 222 (7th Cir. 1996) (attorney violated FDCPA through use of mass-produced letters to student loan debtors because letters bore a facsimile of attorney signature, thereby creating the false impression that they were from him).

Criminal Law.   A lawyer who performs otherwise mundane legal services for a client may be guilty of conspiracy or other crimes in connection with the client's misconduct if the lawyer knows that otherwise legitimate legal services advance the client's criminal goals. In United States v. Ross, 190 F.3d 446 (6th Cir. 1999), attorney Mark Ross was found guilty of drug and money-laundering conspiracies. In part, the evidence against him showed that he had assisted his clients in transferring real property and in posting a cash bond. Both acts advanced the client's crimes. The court found "ample evidence to support a finding that [Ross] knew of and joined in both conspiracies by engaging in money laundering in connection with the [real] property" and "from which the jury could find that Mark Ross knew that drug proceeds would be used to post the bond for Sullivan with the hope that he would not cooperate with the government."

Many a lawyer would be amazed to discover that cheating a client on fees, while perhaps a breach of contract or even fiduciary duty and a basis for discipline, is also a federal felony if the mails or telephone lines are used in the process. Hausmann (whom we earlier encountered in chapter 5A1), was a personal injury lawyer working on a one-third contingency. Expenses (like fees to medical witnesses) came out of the client's share. Hausmann referred clients to a chiropractor (Rise) who gave Hausmann a 20 percent kickback. Over a two-year period, Hausmann netted $77,000 this way. He was indicted for theft of honest services under the federal mail fraud statute. Hausmann and Rise argued that since Rise's fees were reasonable and the clients would not have been entitled to the kickback in any event (the money would otherwise have gone to Rise), the clients suffered "no harm." This might be called the "no harm, no crime" defense, and it usually fails. (Where would the crime of attempt or conspiracy be if it succeeded?) The Seventh Circuit was not impressed:

> This reasoning ignores the reality that Hausmann deprived his clients of their right to know the truth about his compensation: In addition to one third of any settlement proceeds he negotiated on their behalf, every dollar of Rise's effective twenty percent fee discount went to Hausmann's benefit. [The scheme] converted Hausmann's representations to his clients into misrepresentations, and Hausmann illegally profited at the expense of his clients, who were entitled to his honest services. . . .

Fraud and Negligent Misrepresentation. In Banco Popular North America v. Gandi, 876 A.2d 253 (N.J. 2005), the court (citing *Wahlgren*, supra) explained the basis for liability in *Petrillo* this way:

> If the attorney's actions are intended to induce a specific non-client's reasonable reliance on his or her representations, then there is a relationship between the attorney and the third party. Contrariwise, if the attorney does absolutely nothing to induce reasonable reliance by a third party, there is no relationship to substitute for the privity requirement. Indeed, in *Petrillo*, we noted that "when courts relax the privity requirement they typically limit a lawyer's duty to situations in which the lawyer intended or should have foreseen that the third party would rely on the lawyer's work." Put differently, the invitation to rely and reliance are the linchpins of attorney liability to third parties.

Common law or securities claims may be leveled against lawyers as against anyone else, whether by third parties or by former clients. Morganroth & Morganroth v. Norris, McLaughlin & Marcus, P.C., 331 F.3d 406 (3d Cir. 2003) (upholding complaint for creditor fraud that alleged law firm assisted client in avoiding execution of a judgment against client's property); Kline v. First Western Government Securities Inc., 24 F.3d 480 (3d Cir. 1994) (investor's claim against attorneys who wrote opinion letter for issuer); Greycas, Inc. v. Proud, 826 F.2d 1560 (7th Cir. 1987) (attorney's letter to client's lender misrepresenting status of collateral).

Since this is fertile ground for holding lawyers (and other professionals) liable to third parties, let us look at a few more examples. The Tenth Circuit has also upheld a claim against an adverse law firm for fraudulent concealment during discovery, as a result of which the plaintiff allegedly was unable to prove his case at trial. Robinson v. Volkswagenwerk AG, 940 F.2d 1369 (10th Cir. 1991). A lawyer representing the seller of a business who knowingly makes a false statement of fact to the buyer and the buyer's lawyer will have to indemnify the buyer's lawyer for any liability the buyer's lawyer has to the buyer for professional negligence arising out of the failure to discover the fraud. Hansen v. Anderson, Wilmarth & Van Der Maaten, 630 N.W.2d 818 (Iowa 2001) ("once a lawyer responds to a request for information in an arm's-length transaction and undertakes to give that information, the lawyer has a duty to the lawyer requesting the information to give it truthfully," and breach of the duty "supports a claim of equitable indemnity by the defrauded lawyer").

New York was once committed to "privity" before allowing a nonclient plaintiff to sue a lawyer for professional mistakes. But even New York has now recognized that lawyers may sometimes be liable to third parties for negligent misrepresentation. Prudential Ins. Co. v. Dewey, Ballantine, Bushby, Palmer & Wood, 605 N.E.2d 318 (N.Y. 1992). But its holding was limited. It wrote that "in order to provide fair and manageable bounds to what otherwise could prove to be limitless liability," privity or something approaching privity is needed. Relying on precedent concerning the liability of accountants, the court identified "three critical criteria for imposing liability." These were:

> (1) an awareness by the maker of the statement that it is to be used for a particular purpose; (2) reliance by a known party on the statement in furtherance of that purpose; and (3) some conduct by the maker of the statement linking it to the relying party and evincing its understanding of that reliance.

This test echoes §552 of the Restatement (Second) of Torts. Section 552, cited in *Petrillo*, imposes liability for economic loss on a person who negligently supplies false information "for the guidance of others in their business transactions." But the information provider's liability is expressly limited to loss suffered

> (a) by the person or one of a limited group of persons for whose benefit and guidance he intends to supply the information or knows that the recipient intends to supply it; and (b) through reliance upon it in a transaction that he intends the information to influence or knows that the recipient so intends or in a substantially similar transaction.

Negligent misrepresentation claims can also arise in connection with settlement talks. A cautionary tale is found in Slotkin v. Citizens Casualty Co., 614 F.2d 301 (2d Cir. 1979). Don't make this mistake. A child's parents brought a medical malpractice action against the hospital in which the child was born and others, alleging that the child suffered neurological and brain damage as a result of professional negligence at his birth. While the trial was in progress, but before a verdict, the parties settled for $185,000. Counsel for the hospital made certain representations to counsel for the plaintiffs. On one occasion, McGrath, the hospital's lawyer, said that he "knew" the hospital's insurance coverage was $200,000. On another occasion, he said that this was what he had been informed. In agreeing to the settlement, the plaintiffs expressly relied on these statements. It later turned out that the hospital had a separate insurance policy for $1 million in addition to the $200,000 policy to which its counsel was referring. It also turned out that McGrath had access to documents (of which he claimed to be unaware) revealing the excess coverage. After the settlement and after the plaintiffs learned about the additional insurance coverage, they sued the hospital's counsel, among others, alleging fraud and related claims. (Today, after *Prudential* eliminated New York's privity requirement, the claim would likely be or include negligent misrepresentation.) Judgment against the hospital's lawyer was upheld because of his representation that he "knew" the insurance coverage was $200,000.

> McGrath's insistence that the policy limit was $200,000 renders him liable under the New York definition of scienter as "a reckless indifference to error," "a pretense of exact knowledge," or "(an) assertion of a false material fact 'susceptible of accurate knowledge' but stated to be true on the personal knowledge of the representer."

So, even if McGrath truly believed that what he thought he knew was correct, the fact that it turned out to be false subjected him to personal liability under New York law. How could he have protected himself? (*Hint:* Begin your sentence, "My client tells me that. . . .")

Should a lawyer be liable for negligent misrepresentation to persons of whose reliance the lawyer is unaware? Yes, in Michigan, according to Molecular Technology Corp. v. Valentine, 925 F.2d 910 (6th Cir. 1991) (liability extends to persons who lawyers "should reasonably foresee will rely on the information"). With so expansive a potential liability, what can a lawyer do to protect himself? Will a disclaimer work?

Opinion letters offered to a client's adversary (e.g., a lender) are a rich source of potential problems. The general rule that a lawyer will not have a duty of care to a client's adversary does not apply where the lawyer writes a letter that she, or to her knowledge the client, gives the adversary in order to induce particular conduct, like a loan. Mehaffy, Rider, Windholz & Wilson v. Central Bank of Denver, N.A., 892 P.2d 230 (Colo. 1995). You might say that on these facts the lawyer knows exactly what she is getting into. Here the line between professional negligence and negligent misrepresentation begins to blur. Judge Posner recognized as much in Greycas, Inc. v. Proud, supra, where the borrower's lawyer purportedly conducted a U.C.C. search on the collateral and represented to the lender (Greycas) that it was "free and clear of all liens or encumbrances." This was wrong. In fact, the lawyer conducted no search at all. The loan went unpaid, another lender foreclosed on the collateral, and Greycas sued the lawyer for negligent misrepresentation. Judge Posner determined that Illinois law, which applied, would support a professional malpractice claim. Did it matter that Greycas sued for negligent misrepresentation instead? It did not. The lender elected one theory over another. "We know of no obstacle to such an election; nothing is more common in American jurisprudence than overlapping torts." Incidentally, the lawyer was the brother-in-law of the borrower. The lender might have sued for fraud, but did not. Can you guess why it did not?

Abuse of Process

Milberg Weiss Bershad Hynes & Lerach, a [former] New York law firm that [had] grown rich by suing corporate America, agreed to pay $50 million yesterday to its long-time foe, Lexecon, Inc., a Chicago consulting firm which had contended in court that the law firm had tried to destroy its reputation. . . .

After hearing the consultants' contentions that the law firm had abused the legal process to discredit Lexecon, a jury in Federal District Court in Chicago on Monday awarded the consulting firm $45 million in compensatory damages.

Before the jury could decide whether punitive damages should be added to that amount, the two sides [settled] for $50 million.

N.Y. Times, Apr. 14, 1999.

Lexecon's claim rested on Milberg Weiss's decision in 1990 to add Lexecon as a defendant in a securities fraud case against Lincoln Savings and Loan. Lexecon settled that claim for $700,000, about equal to its consulting fees from Lincoln. But thereafter, "Milberg Weiss lawyers brought up the Lincoln Savings case to try to discredit Lexecon's testimony" in other cases. The complaint alleged abuse of process in bringing the 1990 claim, leading to lost profits and a reduced value of Lexecon when it was thereafter sold to Michael Milken.

Lexecon's case against Milberg Weiss received greater attention than most third-party claims against a law firm, not least of all because of Milberg Weiss's prominence and the amount of the settlement. But the case stands as a warning for all lawyers. Anyone, lawyers included, can commit a variety of torts by misusing court process. Because lawyers invoke the power of courts routinely, as part of their work, the risk of violation is greater for them. One common tort (discussed next) is malicious prosecution, which by definition generally requires the prosecution of an action without probable cause and for an improper purpose. Another tort associated with the work of lawyers, as Milberg Weiss discovered, is abuse of process, which one court has defined as occurring when legal process is

> used to attain a collateral objective beyond that anticipated by the process. An ulterior motive does not alone satisfy the requirement for an action in abuse of process; a definite act or threat outside the process is required . . . An abuse of process can occur even though there is probable cause to bring the action and the original action terminates in favor of the plaintiff.

Wilson v. Hayes, 464 N.W.2d 250 (Iowa 1990). The Third Circuit, citing much authority, held that using process (including discovery) "primarily to harass and cause direct injury to an adversary" may be actionable. The "point of liability is reached when 'the utilization of the procedure for the purpose for which it was designed becomes so lacking in justification as to lose its legitimate function as a reasonably justifiable litigation procedure.'" General Refractories Co. v. Fireman's Fund Ins. Co., 337 F.3d 297 (3rd Cir. 2003). The words "primarily" and "so lacking" tell us that a lawyer will not escape liability merely by articulating a legitimate reason for use of the process.

A lawyer who knowingly garnishes exempt assets of a judgment debtor may also be subject to liability. Penalber v. Blount, 550 So. 2d 577 (La. 1989). In one unusual case, a lawyer was charged with undertaking discovery in a civil matter in order to obtain information that would benefit his client in a criminal case arising out of the same events. This allegation stated a claim. Rohda v. Franklin Life Ins. Co., 689 F. Supp. 1034 (D. Colo. 1988).

Malicious Prosecution and Defense. The tort of malicious prosecution is generally established if the plaintiff can show that the defendant brought an action against her, that the plaintiff won that action (or it was settled favorably), that the action was commenced without probable cause, and that the defendant initiated the action with malice. A litigant who brings such an action under these circumstances will be liable for malicious prosecution. So will the lawyer who helps him if that lawyer acts maliciously and without probable cause. See generally Siebel v. Mittlesteadt, 161 P.3d 527 (Cal. 2007) (allegation that lawyers prosecuted claims they knew to be "bogus" to "extract a settlement"); Zamos v. Stroud, 87 P.3d 802 (Cal. 2004) (malicious prosecution to maintain action after learning it lacks any basis). To establish malice on the part of an attorney, the plaintiff will have to show that the attorney's primary purpose in prosecuting the underlying action was improper. Friedman v. Dozorc, 312 N.W.2d 585 (Mich. 1981) (dismissing suit by doctor against lawyers who represented plaintiffs in unsuccessful medical malpractice action).

If there can be malicious prosecution, why can't there be malicious defense? Good question. The New Hampshire Supreme Court (over dissent) decided that symmetry justified recognizing the latter tort and remanded in Aranson v. Schroeder, 671 A.2d 1023 (N.H. 1995), for a determination of whether the lawyer defendants were guilty of malicious defense. The elements of this tort appear to be mirror images of the elements of malicious prosecution: taking an active part in the assertion of a defense with knowledge or notice that it lacks merit and primarily for the purpose of harming another. The proceedings in which the allegedly malicious defense occurred must terminate in favor of the defendant and there must be injury or damage in fact. Compare Wilkinson v. Shoney's, Inc., 4 P.3d 1149 (Kan. 2000) (rejecting malicious defense claims).

Lassoing a Longhorn. I tried to figure out how to include at least a few pages of Seltzer v. Morton, 154 P.3d 561 (Mont. 2007) in this edition. But this remarkable opinion is far too long and the facts far too complicated. Don't get me wrong. The opinion is a careful, indeed a meticulous, treatment of the issues, but it defies sensible editing. So here's a summary, and if you're ever interested in trying to locate the line between legitimate (even impassioned) advocacy and abuse of the justice system, read the whole thing. (Also, read it if you're ever interested in early twentieth-century art from the American West.)

The Montana Supreme Court upheld malicious prosecution and abuse of process claims against Gibson, Dunn & Crutcher LLP (GDP), among others. The jury's punitive damage award against the firm itself was $20 million, reduced to $9.9 million. The case can be read as a textbook example of a firm's failure to manage or perhaps even recognize risk, not to mention intimations of professional hubris. Essentially, on behalf of a man named Morton, the firm tried to get a Montana art appraiser named W. Steve Seltzer to retract his identification of the artist who painted *Lassoing a Longhorn*, a title that could also serve as an ironic description of this tale, with Gibson Dunn in the role of the lassoed longhorn. The painting was done in the early part of the twentieth century. W. Steve Seltzer (and another appraiser, Ginger Renner) identified Seltzer's own grandfather, O. C. Seltzer, as the artist. O. C. Seltzer was a renowned Western artist but not as renowned as his mentor, Charles M. Russell. The painting might be worth twenty times as much to Morton if the painter was Russell, not Seltzer, but because Steve Seltzer and Ginger Renner had already declared the painting a Seltzer, Morton apparently needed them to back off before he could sell it as a Russell.

So as a favor to Morton (see below; this case is not, I assume, the usual staple of Gibson's client inventory), Gladwell, a retired Gibson partner, "sent Seltzer a correspondence resembling a formal litigation interrogatory seeking responses to ten pointed questions regarding the basis of Seltzer's opinion of the painting. The GDC letterhead on which this correspondence was written indicated that GDC was a large international law firm with offices in Irvine, Los Angeles, Century City, San Francisco, and Palo Alto, California; Dallas, Texas; Denver, Colorado; New York, New York; Washington, D.C.; Paris, France; and London, England." This is called throwing your weight around. When this first letter failed to get satisfaction, Gladwell escalated the threat in a second letter to the appraisers containing this paragraph:

> Mr. Morton gave you every chance to withdraw your damaging comments over the better part of eight months during last year. Each of you elected to ignore his pleas or simply dismissed them. You will not have that luxury this time around. We expect immediate cooperation on the drafting of your "withdrawal of opinion" or litigation will be filed without any further discussion. And, given the opportunity afforded you to rectify this wrong, and your refusal to do so, punitive damages will be requested.

Gibson said it would sue Seltzer (and Renner) unless they recanted and paid Morton for his out-of-pocket losses and $50,000 for his "grief and anxiety." This is called really throwing your weight around. In Montana, it may work less well than in Los Angeles. Seltzer refused to back down, and Morton, represented by Gibson, sued him in federal court (diversity) for defamation and other claims. Gibson's case soon fell apart. Basically, Gibson could not prove that the picture was a Russell. The case was dismissed without a trial. Seltzer then sued Gibson and Morton for abuse of process and malicious prosecution. The Montana Supreme Court said Gibson's "use of the judicial system amounts to legal thuggery. This behavior is truly repugnant to Montana's foundational notions of justice and is therefore highly reprehensible." Elsewhere, the court wrote "the fact that [Gibson] utilized the judicial system as a tool to accomplish intimidation and oppression makes this behavior uniquely egregious."

P.S. I think the following explains a lot. Gladwell, the emeritus Gibson partner, could not himself accept the case for the firm. Only a partner could do so. So Gladwell wrote the following to a colleague, who did accept it: "We will probably put in less than 20-30 hours. You will recall that Steve [Morton] is President of the Bob Hope Desert Classic so I want to do it." Talk about faulty predictions. Perhaps the firm expected Seltzer to fold as soon as he saw Gibson's name and demands and, indeed, Seltzer said the litigation caused him "severe emotional distress for approximately 9 months [and] significant physical complications," partly explaining the huge punitive damage award. The lesson, to quote Elihu Root again: "About half the practice of a decent lawyer is telling would-be client that they are damned fools and should stop." Can Morton now sue Gibson for bad advice leading to his personal liability?

Helping Fiduciaries Breach Their Duties.   Lawyers who purposely or negligently assist fiduciaries in violating their fiduciary duties to beneficiaries may be held liable to the beneficiaries. We encountered this issue in chapter 9 on negotiation (see page 507), and chapter 10 on entity representation (page 563). The courts are not consistent here. In Oregon, a lawyer who merely advised a client to act in a way that breached fiduciary duty was not liable to the alleged victim. Reynolds v. Schrock, 142 P.3d 1062 (Or. 2006). By contrast, an Illinois lawyer who negotiated a deal for a client could be liable if the deal were later found to breach the client's fiduciary duty. Thornwood, Inc. v. Jenner & Block, 799 N.E.2d 756 (Ill. App. 2003). Compare Angel, Cohen & Rogovin v. Oberon Inv., N.V., 512 So. 2d 192 (Fla. 1987) (negligently helping fiduciary violate trust does not state claim), with Fickett v. Superior Court, 558 P.2d 988 (Ariz. App. 1976) (contra), and Albright v. Burns, 503 A.2d 386 (N.J. App. 1986) (lawyer "had reason to foresee the specific harm which occurred").

A connected question is whether a lawyer for a fiduciary, such as a trustee or the executor of an estate, owes any duty of care to beneficiaries in the performance of his work. Trask v. Butler, page 759, after applying its newly minted balancing test, concludes that the answer is no. Reaching the same result is Hopkins v. Akins, 637 A.2d 424 (D.C. 1993). The ABA has opined that a lawyer for a fiduciary does not, under the Model Rules, have any greater ethical obligation toward the beneficiary than the lawyer has toward any other third party. ABA Opinion 94-380. Leyba v. Whitley, page 759, although adopting *Trask*'s test, distinguished a personal representative in a wrongful death action from a trustee. "A trustee in the traditional sense has broad discretionary powers over the estate assets and must make difficult investment and distribution decisions. The attorney for the trustee must assist the trustee to make these discretionary decisions. A personal representative under the Wrongful Death Act, by contrast, must simply distribute any proceeds obtained in accordance with the statute and has no discretionary authority. [The] lack of discretionary powers over any wrongful death recovery makes the trust cases inapposite." The court accordingly upheld liability of lawyers representing a personal representative.

Government Lawyers.   In Barrett v. United States, 798 F.2d 565 (2d Cir. 1986), federal lawyers allegedly conspired to prevent an estate from learning the cause of the decedent's death (secret drug experiments conducted on civilians by the Army). As a result, the estate was unaware of potential federal liability for the death. The estate sued the lawyers for concealing the truth. The court upheld liability, rejecting a claim of absolute immunity and on the facts before it also rejecting qualified immunity. In R.J. Longo Construction Co. v. Schragger, 527 A.2d 480 (N.J. App. 1987), township attorneys negligently failed to obtain easements as required by statute. As a result, a private contractor who had won a bid to construct a sewer facility in the township suffered damages when it began construction in the absence of the easements. The contractor sued the government lawyers. The court held that the defendants owed a duty to the plaintiff because of the statutory obligation, despite the absence of an attorney-client relationship.

Inducing Breach of Contract.   If *X* induces *Y* to breach a contract with *Z*, *Z* may be able to sue *X* for interference with *Z*'s contractual rights or for intentional interference with *Z*'s prospective economic advantage. If, however, *X* had a fiduciary relationship with *Y*, *X* might enjoy a privilege that will be a defense to the action. The privilege is based on the agent's duty to protect the principal's interests, a duty that might sometimes require the agent to counsel the principal to break a contract and pay damages. Attorneys are among the fiduciaries who enjoy this privilege. However, the privilege can be lost if the attorney (or other fiduciary) acts from "improper motives," which include furthering his own economic interests. The definition of "improper motives" varies with jurisdictions and sometimes with whether the underlying contract was at will or for a fixed term. Los Angeles Airways, Inc. v. Davis, 687 F.2d 321 (9th Cir. 1982); Duggin v. Adams, 360 S.E.2d 832 (Va. 1987).

Invasion of Privacy.   An Ohio matrimonial lawyer representing a wife in a divorce and custody dispute properly received the psychiatric records of the husband in discovery. The wife's lawyer then shared the records with a prosecutor who had brought charges against the husband for assaulting his wife. The court sustained the husband's claim against the wife's lawyer for breach of privacy. Although the privilege for the records was waived because the husband had placed his parental fitness in issue in the custody matter, the waiver extended no further than that case. The wife's lawyer was not free to further disseminate the records. Hageman v. Southwest General Health Center, 893 N.E.2d 153 (Ohio 2008).

Violation of Escrow Agreement.   When a lawyer agrees to act as an escrow agent — to hold property under an agreement between two or more parties, one of whom is usually the lawyer's client — the lawyer assumes certain obligations to the parties to the agreement that transcend the responsibilities the lawyer owes to the client. If the lawyer violates those responsibilities, he may be liable even though the violation benefited the client. Escrow agreements usually (but not invariably) contemplate holding cash. For example, the lawyer for the seller of a home may hold the buyer's 10 percent down payment in escrow pending the closing on the property. Because the fact of the escrow arrangement gives the lawyer a legal duty to a third party, possibly a party adverse to the client, the client must understand the lawyer's supervening obligations, as must the lawyer.

In Wasmann v. Seidenberg, 248 Cal. Rptr. 744 (Ct. App. 1988), Seidenberg had represented the wife, Barbara, in negotiating a settlement agreement. The husband's lawyer had sent Seidenberg a final draft of the agreement with a deed conveying a piece of realty from Wasmann, the husband, to the wife. The agreement contemplated that in return the wife would pay Wasmann $70,000 for his share of the value of the realty. Wasmann's lawyer instructed Seidenberg that he (Seidenberg) could record the deed "only upon obtaining" the money for Wasmann. Without getting the money, Seidenberg allowed the wife to get the deed. She recorded it. Wasmann then sued the wife and Seidenberg. The court held that Seidenberg owed Wasmann "no professional duty," but that "his acceptance of [the] deed would give rise to a duty of care. The wellspring of this duty is the fiduciary role of an escrow holder." The court continued:

> As officers of the court, attorneys enjoy both privileges and responsibilities, among which is the duty to deal honestly and fairly with adverse parties and counsel. Wasmann and his attorney Hartman reasonably relied on Seidenberg because of his professional status and role as attorney for Barbara. If Seidenberg did not want to be responsible for the deed, he should have promptly returned it to Wasmann. We hold a trier of fact could find any failure to do so was an acceptance of Wasmann's entrustment. Thus, the allegations of acceptance are legally sufficient.
>
> Having accepted the deed from Wasmann, Seidenberg was bound to comply strictly with the escrow instructions. Specifically, he was obligated to prevent recordation of the deed until Barbara deposited into escrow the sum due to Wasmann. Violation of an escrow instruction gives rise to an action for breach of contract; similarly, negligent performance by an escrow holder creates liability in tort for breach of duty.
>
> Wasmann foregoes the contract claim and alleges negligence in Seidenberg's handling of the deed. According to the complaint, ". . . Seidenberg breached said duty [by] . . . negligently and carelessly [allowing] Plaintiff's Grant Deed to be recorded . . . without first obtaining for Plaintiff the sum of $70,000.00, or a note secured by a deed of trust. . . ." The facts pleaded are sufficient to state a cause of action for negligence against Seidenberg. . . .
>
> The complaint not only states facts sufficient to support a cause of action for negligence, but for the alleged constructive fraud as well. This tort "arises from a breach of duty by one in a confidential or fiduciary relationship to another which induces a justifiable reliance by the latter to his prejudice." . . . "A form of such fraud is the nondisclosure by the fiduciary of relevant matters arising from the relationship."
>
> Wasmann alleged Seidenberg not only breached his fiduciary duty by allowing recordation of the deed, but compounded his wrongdoing by failing to disclose this fact, despite repeated inquiries from Wasmann's attorney. Clearly, recordation of the deed was a material fact and suppression of this information worked to benefit Seidenberg's client and to prejudice Wasmann.

See also Virtanen v. O'Connell, 44 Cal.Rptr.3d 702 (Ct. App. 2006), reaching the same conclusions in reliance on *Wasmann.* How might a lawyer protect herself from competing claims of escrow beneficiaries?

Leon v. Martinez, 638 N.E.2d 511 (N.Y. 1994), is a close analogue to the escrow cases. The New York Code required a lawyer to "[p]romptly notify a client or third person of the receipt of funds, securities, or other properties in which the client or third person has an interest." The New York Court of Appeals held that this provision creates an obligation in the lawyer to distribute the third person's property to him. Violation will support a civil action.

The Restatement's Position.   Section 51 of the Restatement, which *Petrillo* quoted in draft, describes the liability of lawyers to a nonclient as follows:
[A lawyer owes a duty to use care] . . .

>   (2) to a nonclient when and to the extent that:
>   (a) the lawyer or (with the laywer's acquiescence) the lawyer's client invites the nonclient to rely on the lawyer's opinion or provision of other legal services, and the nonclient so relies; and

(b) the nonclient is not, under applicable tort law, too remote from the lawyer to be entitled to protection;

(3) to a nonclient when and to the extent that:

(a) the lawyer knows that a client intends as one of the primary objectives of the representation that the lawyer's services benefit the nonclient;

(b) such a duty would not significantly impair the lawyer's performance of obligations to the client; and

(c) the absence of such a duty would make enforcement of those obligations to the client unlikely; and

(4) to a nonclient when and to the extent that:

(a) the lawyer's client is a trustee, guardian, executor, or fiduciary acting primarily to perform similar functions for the nonclient;

(b) the lawyer knows that appropriate action by the lawyer is necessary with respect to a matter within the scope of the representation to prevent or rectify the breach of a fiduciary duty owed by the client to the nonclient, where (i) the breach is a crime or fraud or (ii) the lawyer has assisted or is assisting the breach;

(c) the nonclient is not reasonably able to protect its rights; and

(d) such a duty would not significantly impair the performance of the lawyer's obligations to the client.

FURTHER READING

Ronald Mallen and Jeffrey Smith, Legal Malpractice (5th ed. 2000), is a leading textbook on malpractice. Symposium, The Lawyer's Duties and Liabilities to Third Parties, in the October 1996 issue of the South Texas Law Review, includes articles by Geoffrey Hazard on the privity requirement, John Bauman on the influence of tort law, John Sutton on duties arising out of fiduciary status, John Price on duties to nonclients in estate planning, Russell Pearce on the duty of union lawyers to union members, Edward Carr on opinion letters, and Ellen Pansky on an entity lawyer's responsibilities to entity constituents. Other works that specifically address expanding liability to third parties include Nancy Lewis's conceptual vision in Lawyers' Liability to Third Parties: The Ideology of Advocacy Reframed, 66 Or. L. Rev. 801 (1987), and H. Robert Fiebach's critical perspective in A Chilling of the Adversary System: An Attorney's Exposure to Liability from Opposing Parties or Counsel, 61 Temp. L. Rev. 1301 (1988). See also Note, Attorneys' Negligence and Third Parties, 57 N.Y.U. L. Rev. 126 (1982) (authored by Ellen Eisenberg). The author proposes a "unified approach in determining the duty of attorneys to third parties." She then applies the proposed test to a variety of factual situations.

D.   DISCIPLINE

1.   Purposes of Discipline

Discipline is a remedy for professional failure, but unlike malpractice and other remedies previously reviewed, discipline vindicates the interest in protecting the public and deterring unethical behavior. Discipline does not have the purpose, although it may have the effect, of providing a remedy to the particular individual injured by a lawyer's improper conduct. See In re Robertson, 612 A.2d 1236 (D.C. 1992) (restitution can be a disciplinary remedy, but only to the extent of ordering the return of money or property that the client has paid or entrusted to the lawyer, not as a substitute for a malpractice action). Iowa Supreme Court Board of Professional Ethics and Conduct v. Erbes, 604 N.W.2d 656 (Iowa 2000) (ethics rules "are chiefly intended to provide protection to the public"). An analogy might be to criminal prosecutions. Both civil and criminal actions can derive from the same conduct, but the civil claim belongs to a person or entity, who or which can settle or choose not to pursue it. The criminal case belongs to the sovereign. Indeed, discipline has been called "quasi-criminal." In re Ruffalo, 390 U.S. 544 (1968).

Another distinction between discipline and civil liability lies in the nature of the conduct that can serve as a basis for either. An act that violates the Rules may bring discipline but, as we have seen (page 722), will not necessarily support a civil claim. Similarly, a single negligent act may bring civil liability even though it could not (or as a practical matter would not) support discipline. Of course, there is still a wide area of overlap in which the same conduct will subject a lawyer to both damages and discipline — and sometimes a criminal conviction.

The ABA Standards for Imposing Lawyer Sanctions explains the purpose of lawyer discipline proceedings as follows:

> The purpose of lawyer discipline proceedings is to protect the public and the administration of justice from lawyers who have not discharged, will not discharge, or are unlikely properly to discharge their professional duties to clients, the public, the legal system, and the legal profession.

The Commentary to this provision states:

> While courts express their views on the purpose of lawyer sanctions somewhat differently, an examination of reported cases reveals surprising accord as to the basic purpose of discipline. As identified by the courts, the primary purpose is to protect the public. Second, the courts cite the need to protect the integrity of the legal system, and to insure the administration of justice. Another purpose is to deter further unethical conduct and, where appropriate, to rehabilitate the lawyer. A final purpose of imposing sanctions is to educate other lawyers and the public, thereby deterring unethical behavior among all members of the profession. As the courts have noted, while sanctions imposed on a lawyer obviously have a punitive aspect, nonetheless, it is not the purpose to impose such sanctions for punishment.

Fred Zacharias, The Purposes of Lawyer Discipline, 45 Wm. & Mary L. Rev. 675 (2003), further delves into these questions.

2. Sanctions

While some terms are uniform, there is no national consistency in the labels attached to the escalating types of discipline. "Disbarment" generally refers to indefinite or permanent exclusion from the bar. In New York, for example, a disbarred lawyer may apply for readmission after seven years. 22 N.Y.C.R.R. §603.14(a). In a few jurisdictions, such as New Jersey, disbarment is always permanent. In others, such as Ohio, Kentucky, and California, the court may elect permanent disbarment as the maximum sanction. Of course, the right to reapply by no means guarantees readmission. Jurisdictions use "suspension" to refer to the less harsh sanction of allowing a lawyer to continue as a member of the bar while her right to practice is suspended for a period of time. The periods of time generally are in the range of three months to five years. It is also possible for an attorney to be suspended "until further order of the court" without a specified time limit. Even when a time period is specified, resumption of the right to practice might not be automatic on the termination of the time period. The court might suspend the attorney "for two years and until further order of the court," so that the attorney will have to reapply at the end of two years and show that he or she has stayed out of trouble (and out of the practice of law) for that period.

Censure (or public reprimand) is a near universal punishment. Like disbarment and suspension, the fact of censure is public, though many jurisdictions also provide for private censure (or reprimand) in certain cases. Although the censured lawyer is not removed or suspended from practice, the publicity attached to the censure is seen as significantly unpleasant. In addition, the censure (like all other disciplinary actions) will be considered in determining sanction should the lawyer again be guilty of a professional transgression.

The nomenclature becomes less uniform at this point. Words like "admonition," "warning," and "caution" are among those used in various jurisdictions. They do not carry a consistent import. But whatever words are used, grievance bodies seek to have gradations of responses at their disposal. Some jurisdictions have used "warnings" or similar words to caution a lawyer where discipline is not called for because no rule has been violated, but where the lawyer appears ignorant of the riskiness of his conduct.

California (among other states) developed a novel way to deal with minor infractions. When appropriate, disciplinary authorities will offer to dismiss a matter provided the attorney attends an eight-hour class on legal ethics. Amy Stevens, What Can a Lawyer Learn in One Day in Downtown L.A.?, Wall St. J., May 1, 1991, at A1. For example, one participant had "hired four of the most beautiful women he could find to hang out at a singles bar on the beach near San Diego. They were to pick up married men — and hand out business cards for [the lawyer's] divorce practice." Lawyers who take the course must pass a test consisting of 20 true-or-false questions. The program reports that nobody has ever failed and that recidivism is zero.

Some jurisdictions permit a lawyer under investigation to resign in advance of court-imposed discipline. Many times a lawyer will prefer resignation if the alternative is the virtual certainty of disbarment. In some places, the fact of resignation is not made public, and this may be an added inducement to resign in advance of disbarment. In one case receiving substantial public attention, Richard M. Nixon was disbarred in New York State for conduct in which he engaged while serving as president. In re Nixon, 385 N.Y.S.2d 305 (1st Dept. 1976). Nixon had attempted to resign rather than contest the charges made against him. But his resignation was rejected because it did not contain a sworn acknowledgment that "he could not successfully defend himself on the merits against [the] charges," as required by New York law. A subsequent president, Bill Clinton, negotiated a five-year suspension of his Arkansas law license while he was under investigation for giving false answers in Paula Jones's harassment action against him. See page 406. The five years have passed but Clinton has not sought readmission to any bar as of mid-2008. (Why in the world would he want to?)

3. Disciplinary Systems

Jurisdictions have various ways to provide the staff necessary to run their disciplinary systems. Needed are investigators, lawyers, and judges, in addition to support personnel. A majority of states use employed investigators and employed lawyers to gather evidence and prosecute disciplinary violations. Some of these states may supplement paid staff with volunteer lawyers. A few states are predominantly dependent on volunteer lawyers to investigate and prosecute cases. Most states that rely on volunteers have small lawyer populations, but some, like New Jersey and Texas, have many lawyers.

From time to time the ABA has conducted a formal study of lawyer disciplinary systems. In 1970, a committee headed by former Supreme Court Justice Tom Clark published the first nationwide evaluation of lawyer disciplinary procedures. In 1991, a second evaluation was published. Entitled "Report of the Commission on Evaluation of Disciplinary Enforcement," it assessed the state of lawyer discipline nationwide and made 22 recommendations for improvement. This commission was headed by Dean Robert McKay until his death in 1990. Both reports are available at abanet.org/cpr for those who want to understand the various ways in which jurisdictions have attempted to administer lawyer discipline and the ABA's view of what an ideal disciplinary system should contain.

Private Discipline. When we think of lawyer discipline, we think of systems administered by courts, usually state courts. But increasingly, law firms, especially large ones, are instituting their own disciplinary systems as a way of making clear their intolerance for misbehavior. Knowledge of these systems is necessarily anecdotal. Firms don't broadcast their existence. However, the American Lawyer reported one intriguing incident. Three associates at Shearman & Sterling were suspended for a month without pay for submitting the costs of lunches and dinners to the firm with false statements that summer associates had attended these events. Taking a summer associate to a meal enabled the lawyers to have their own meals reimbursed, thereby providing the motive. Even Shearman associates were unable to muster much sympathy for the offenders. " 'It's ironic,' says one, 'that people who make as much as we make . . . abuse the system.' " "Ghost Busters," Am. Law., Sept. 19, 1999, at 17. In another instance, a Sullivan & Cromwell partner unsuccessfully sought to avoid public discipline for improperly revealing client confidences by arguing that the firm had already punished the same conduct by reducing his income "several hundred thousand dollars a year" for five years. In re Holley, 729 N.Y.S.2d 128 (1st Dept. 2001).

4. Acts Justifying Discipline

Much of this book describes conduct that will support professional discipline. Here we highlight some of the more frequent reasons why lawyers are sanctioned and also some unusual ones.

a. Dishonest and Unlawful Conduct

Dishonesty in its many forms and criminal conduct that may, but need not, involve dishonesty are among the two most frequent reasons for discipline (neglect of client matters is repeatedly cited as the most frequent noncriminal basis). The following case concerns unauthorized withdrawals from an attorney's trust or escrow account. Using escrow money accounts for a substantial amount of discipline nationwide. Lawyers are required to place funds that belong to others, or to which others have a claim, in trust accounts (even if the lawyer also has a claim to the money). It is unethical to commingle trust funds with one's own money and, even worse, to make actual (even if "temporary") use of trust funds. At this point in your career you should read and memorize the substance of Rule 1.15 or its equivalent wherever you plan to practice.

IN RE WARHAFTIG
106 N.J. 529, 524 A.2d 398 (1987)

Per Curiam. . . .

I

The charges filed against respondent were the result of a random compliance audit conducted by the Office of Attorney Ethics pursuant to Rule 1:21-6(c). The audit took place in November and December, 1983, and covered the two-year period ending on October 31st of the same year. The audit findings were summarized in the Board's Decision and Recommendation: "The audit disclosed that respondent continually issued checks to his own order for fees in pending real estate matters. He would replace the 'advance' when the funds were received for the real estate closing."

In one case, a real estate closing occurred on September 19, 1983. Funds totalling $70,722.33 were deposited into respondent's trust account on September 20, 1983. In another case, a real estate closing took place on October 28, 1983. The funds totalling $150,686.27 were deposited into his trust account on October 31, 1983. However, respondent had issued a check to his order for $910 on June 16, 1983, which represented his fee of $455 for each of these two closings. The audit report revealed other instances where respondent similarly took advance fees. . . .

Respondent maintained his own lists of fees taken in advance. This list contained the names of clients and the amounts he anticipated earning from these clients in pending real estate closings. As a closing occurred and the fee was earned, respondent would delete the client's name and fee. When an anticipated closing fell through, respondent would replace the fee he had earlier advanced to himself. . . .

When respondent received notice of the audit, he contacted his accountant who advised him that if his trust account was short he should immediately replace the funds. Respondent borrowed $11,125 from accounts in the names of his two teenage sons and deposited the money into his trust account to cover the withdrawn fees. Respondent made this deposit about five days before the originally scheduled audit date of October 4, 1983.

The auditor was not able to determine which clients' monies respondent had taken because of the size of respondent's real estate practice. Money continually flowed in and out of the trust account. Respondent, at the ethics hearing, maintained that he never failed to make the proper disbursements at the closings and that no one ever lost money as a result of his practice. He discontinued this practice in September 1983 when he received notice of the audit.

At the Ethics Committee hearing, respondent explained that his withdrawal of advance fees from the trust account was necessitated by the "gigantic cash flow burden" he experienced beginning in the early 1980's. Such pressures were the result of a precipitous decline in his real estate practice. At the same time, an additional strain on respondent's finances was created by his wife's having to undergo treatment for cancer, and by his son's need for extensive psychiatric counseling. According to respondent, only a small portion of these expenses was covered by insurance.

Respondent was also questioned at the hearing as to whether he knew, at the time the advance-fee scheme was implemented, that his conduct constituted an ethical violation. Respondent stated:

> I was aware that what I was doing was wrong, and I was also aware that no one was being hurt by what I was doing. And what I was doing, especially by keeping lists like this, was making sure that nobody would get hurt by what I was doing. . . .
>
> My perspective on the taking of the money was it was wrong, it was a violation of the rules. But I was so certain that no one could possibly be hurt by it that I didn't feel that I was stealing, certainly not stealing. . . .

II

In recommending public discipline, the [Disciplinary Review Board] recognized that In re Wilson, 81 N.J. 451, 409 A.2d 1153 (1979), which requires the disbarment of an attorney who knowingly misappropriates his clients' funds, controls the outcome of this case. However, the Board emphasized a perceived distinction between respondent's conduct, which it characterized as the "premature withdrawal of . . . monies to which he had a colorable interest[,]" and the knowing misappropriation described in *Wilson*, supra. Apparently, the Board was persuaded by respondent's contention that while he was aware that he was violating a Disciplinary Rule, he "didn't feel that [he] was stealing. . . ."

The distinction drawn by the DRB cannot be sustained under the *Wilson* rule. As we stated in In re Noonan, 102 N.J. 157, 160, 506 A.2d 722 (1986), knowing misappropriation under *Wilson* "consists simply of a lawyer taking a client's money entrusted to him, knowing that it is the client's money and knowing that the client has not authorized the taking." We have consistently maintained that a lawyer's subjective intent, whether it be to "borrow" or to steal, is irrelevant to the determination of the appropriate discipline in a misappropriation case. In *Wilson*, supra, we articulated the reason for this strict approach:

> Lawyers who "borrow" may, it is true, be less culpable than those who had no intent to repay, but the difference is negligible in this connection. Banks do not rehire tellers who "borrow" depositors' funds. Our professional standards, if anything, should be higher. Lawyers are more than fiduciaries: they are representatives of a profession and officers of this Court.

It is clear that respondent's conduct constituted knowing misappropriation as contemplated by *Wilson*. Through the use of the advance-fee mechanism, he took funds from his trust account before he had any legal right to those monies. These "fees" were taken by respondent before he received any deposits in connection with the relevant real estate closings. Thus, he was effectively borrowing monies from one group of clients in order to compensate himself, in advance, for matters being handled for other clients. Respondent made these withdrawals with full recognition that his actions had not been authorized by his clients, and that he was therefore violating the rules governing attorney conduct. Respondent's unauthorized misappropriation of clients' trust funds for his personal needs cannot be distinguished from the conduct condemned in *Wilson*, supra.

[The court concluded that various mitigating factors were insufficient to prevent disbarment.]

Intentionally taking a client's money without authorization, even if temporarily and intending to return it, will almost always result in serious discipline. In a few jurisdictions, disbarment is nearly automatic. New Jersey has consistently ordered disbarment for knowing misappropriation, even temporarily, of client funds, even small amounts. Matter of Barlow, 657 A.2d 1197 (N.J. 1995) (temporary misappropriation of $2,894.94 results in disbarment). *Warhaftig* and *Barlow* are but two of hundreds of cases a year from American jurisdictions where lawyers, sometimes in financial distress, take or "borrow" client money to get by. Although New Jersey may be the state least tolerant of such conduct, lawyers elsewhere should not expect sympathy. In re Cleland, 2 P.3d 700 (Colo. 2000) ("As we have said numerous times before, disbarment is the presumed sanction when a lawyer knowingly misappropriates funds belonging to a client or a third person."); In re Schoepfer, 687 N.E.2d 391 (Mass. 1997) (if "an attorney intended to deprive the client of funds, permanently or temporarily, or if the client was deprived of funds (no matter what the attorney intended), the standard discipline is disbarment or indefinite suspension"). Random audits of attorney trust accounts, permitted in some jurisdictions, including New Jersey, make this sort of misconduct easier to detect. The violation is ridiculously easy to prove. Nearly all it takes is a subpoena to the lawyer's bank. Banks may also have a duty to notify authorities when a lawyer bounces a check on her business or escrow account. But as the New Jersey Supreme Court has emphasized, the misappropriation must be "knowing," and not accidental or merely negligent. Compare Matter of Konopka, 596 A.2d 733 (N.J. 1991), holding that careless recordkeeping resulting in unintentional use of client funds does not cause automatic disbarment but does violate Rule 1.15, which requires lawyers to protect client property. The sanction in *Konopka* was a six-month suspension.

IN RE AUSTERN
524 A.2d 680 (D.C. 1987)

PRYOR, CHIEF JUDGE. . . .

I

The relevant facts in this case are largely uncontested. The Hearing Committee found that respondent represented Milton Viorst and a corporation largely controlled by Viorst known as Harmony House Corporation. Viorst and Harmony House converted several buildings to condominiums. Respondent's clients were anxious to go to closing on the various condominium units as quickly as possible with a number of prospective purchasers. Several of these prospective purchasers had been tenants in the buildings before the conversion and were actually in possession of their units. However, the work necessary to bring the units into compliance with the District of Columbia Housing Code had not yet been completed to the satisfaction of the prospective purchasers.

On January 27, 1981, the parties met to attempt to close on as many of the units as then had committed purchasers. Respondent was not able to be present at the beginning of this closing because of other commitments. He arrived later in the evening as the closing was continuing; before his arrival, Viorst was represented by one of respondent's partners. During this time, Viorst and the purchasers drafted an escrow agreement in order to facilitate closing on that date.

Despite the fact that the purchasers were suspicious of Viorst and entertained doubts concerning his willingness to complete the repairs necessary to the units, they were willing to go to closing on the condition that Viorst deposit $10,000 into the escrow account. The funds in the account were to be available to complete the work on the units if Viorst or Harmony House did not perform. If Viorst did perform, the escrow funds were to be released back to the sellers upon agreement by all parties that the relevant work had indeed been satisfactorily performed.

For their protection, the purchasers insisted that the escrow account be under the control of two co-escrow agents — respondent, who represented the sellers, and Arnold Spevak, who represented the purchasers and who was also acting as the settlement attorney.

Upon respondent's late arrival at the closing, the substance of the escrow agreement had already been agreed upon by the parties. According to respondent, the escrow agreement had been fully drafted, typed, and signed by all the other parties before he arrived. Respondent testified that he was put under considerable pressure to agree to act as the co-escrow agent and that he ultimately yielded and signed the agreement that same evening.

Notwithstanding respondent's testimony,[3] the Hearing Committee found that the escrow agreement, although dated January 27, 1981, had not been finally typed and signed by respondent until the following day. The Hearing Committee's finding was based upon the testimony of Robert Cohen, who acted as the leader of the group of purchasers. The Board concluded that Cohen's testimony was unequivocal and emphatic that the escrow agreement was signed by all of the parties, including respondent, on the second day of the settlement, January 28, 1981.[4]

After respondent's arrival at the closing, Viorst wrote a check in the amount of $10,000, which was intended to fund the escrow account. The check was exhibited to the purchasers and to their attorney, Spevak. It was decided that respondent, as one of the two escrow agents, would take possession of the check and deposit it. Either before or after respondent gained possession of the check, respondent and Viorst stepped out into the hall, out of earshot of the other parties to the transaction. Viorst then informed respondent that there were no funds in the account upon which the check had been written. Respondent considered the ramifications of this revelation, but took the necessary steps to complete the closing on January 28.

Respondent held the worthless check but did not inform his co-escrow agent about the situation. Subsequently, on March 23, 1981, Viorst received a $10,000 non-refundable deposit from a purchaser in connection with the sale of one of the condominium units. He then gave this deposit check to respondent. Respondent promptly opened an interest-bearing savings account at a local bank into which this check was deposited on March 27, 1981. Respondent did not notify his co-escrow agent that the funds were finally on hand, nor did he ever arrange to have his co-escrow agent obtain signature authority over the account.

It was not until the beginning of April, after the time the funds were actually placed in the escrow account, that one of the purchasers made the first claim against the account. That claim was paid from the account, and there is no question that the $10,000 was properly administered by respondent once it was placed into the account. . . .

While a client is entitled to representation by his attorney for any objective within the bounds permitted by law, see Canon 7, District of Columbia Code of Professional Responsibility, he is not entitled to affirmative assistance by his attorney in conduct that the lawyer knows to be illegal or fraudulent. DR 7-102(A)(7). Generally, a lawyer should abide by a client's decisions concerning the objectives of the representation, and the lawyer can determine the means to accomplish these objectives, so long as the lawyer does not knowingly assist the client to engage in illegal conduct. District of Columbia Ethical Consideration

---

3. Respondent maintained that he signed the escrow agreement the evening of January 27, and agreed to act as the co-escrow agent *before* he was informed by Viorst that his check for the escrow account was worthless. The Hearing Committee found that he signed the agreement at the following day's continuation of the closing, on January 28, *after* he was informed that Viorst's check was worthless.

4. The Board concluded that the testimony of respondent, however, was ambiguous as to when he signed the escrow agreement. The Board concluded that Cohen's clear and emphatic testimony, in contrast, provided ample support in the record for the finding that respondent signed the escrow agreement on January 28, 1981.

7-5; see also ABA Model Rule of Professional Conduct 1.2(a). When the attorney is presented with a situation where the client's wishes call for conduct that is illegal or fraudulent, the attorney is under an affirmative duty to withdraw from representation. DR 2-110(B)(2), DR 7-102(A)(7); Model Rule 1.16(a)(1).

In the instant case, therefore, respondent was under an affirmative duty to withdraw from his representation of Mr. Viorst once he knew that the escrow account Viorst purported to establish to induce settlement was funded with a worthless check. We do not deem crucial the question of whether respondent signed the escrow agreement before rather than after being informed that the check was worthless. In either event, his conduct in furthering the transaction and acquiescing in its fraudulent purpose is violative of DR 1-102(A)(4) and DR 7-102(A)(7).

III

Turning to the issue of an appropriate sanction, the Board rejected the recommendation of the Hearing Committee that respondent receive a reprimand by the Board and concluded that respondent should receive a sanction of public censure by this court. . . .

The Board determined that a public censure by this court would be the most appropriate sanction in this case because the culpability of the conduct at issue here fell short of that in other cases where attorney dishonesty resulted in a brief suspension.

The Board also considered many mitigating factors in this case. It observed that respondent has no prior disciplinary record, and has indeed made notable contributions in the area of legal ethics. The Board also took into account the fact that respondent's conduct was not motivated by the desire for personal gain, and caused no pecuniary injury to the purchasers of the client's units who relied on the escrow account.[9] The Board further observed that respondent's decision making may have been affected by the extreme animosity which existed between him and his client, Mr. Viorst. The Board noted that respondent may have been too anxious to overcompensate for this ill will and "may have bent over backwards in the client's favor" by taking part in the fraudulent transaction, concluding that respondent's participation may have been motivated in part by a desire to bring the troubled attorney-client relationship to a speedy close. . . .

To be sure, no monetary harm befell anyone as a result of respondent's failure to disclose that the check funding the escrow account was worthless. But it is important to remember that for a number of weeks the purpose of the escrow account was in fact defeated. The protection the account was supposed to offer did not exist. Respondent, as co-escrow agent, owed a fiduciary duty to the client's purchasers to protect their investment; instead, he aided his client in inducing the buyers to proceed to settlement although there was no escrow protection. Therefore, considering the gravity of respondent's misconduct, the mitigating factors considered by the Board, and viewing respondent's

9. The Board noted that since this case is not a civil action for damages, the fact that the purchasers actually suffered no injury is immaterial to the consideration of the ethical obligation of an attorney not to assist in fraud or other conduct involving dishonesty or misrepresentation.

violations "in light of all relevant factors," we conclude that the Board's recommended sanction of public censure is appropriate.*

Deceit, Dishonesty, Etcetera

Inflating bills to clients — e.g., billing time that was not actually spent on the client's matter — can lead to criminal prosecution as well as discipline. While this surely goes on at all strata of the profession, every so often a prominent lawyer is discovered to have engaged in the activity and it makes headlines. Underlying documents may reveal the deception or the alleged time may be inconsistent with other events. ("How could you bill eight hours in Chicago and Toronto on the same day?" "How could you have spent four hours in a meeting with Elena when she was in the hospital giving birth that day?") The fraud need not be in misrepresenting time. In re Haskell, 962 P.2d 813 (Wash. 1998) (presenting client with false disbursement bills and misrepresenting the identity of lawyers who worked on the matter warrants two-year suspension).

William Duker, a prominent New York lawyer, pled guilty to federal felonies for falsely billing time to his client, the United States, in connection with his investigations of and lawsuits against other law firms that may have had civil liability to the United States as a result of their representation of failed savings and loan associations. The story of a lawyer who defrauded the government while helping it discover the fraudulent conduct of other lawyers was the kind of "man bites dog" story that landed on page one. Paul Barrett, Cost Crunch: Attorney Was a Critic of Law-Firm Fraud; Now He Faces Prison, Wall St. J., Sept. 30, 1997, at A1. Duker was disbarred. Matter of Duker, 662 N.Y.S.2d 847 (3d Dept. 1997).

Lawyers sometimes defraud their own partners and law firms. This can be done, for example, by seeking reimbursement for false expenses. The money may or may not be charged to the client. It doesn't matter. Courts will routinely visit harsh discipline, usually disbarment, on lawyers who engage in that deception. In re Thompson, 991 P.2d 820 (Colo. 1999) (law firm associate disbarred for keeping $15,000 in client fees that should have been turned over to his firm); In re Greenberg, 714 A.2d 243 (N.J. 1998) (disbarment where "multiple acts of misappropriation" resulted in lawyer taking more than $34,000 from his firm "for his own purposes"); Matter of Shapiro, 644 N.Y.S.2d 894 (1st Dept. 1996) (resignation from bar where lawyer was under investigation because he altered receipts for expenditures, created receipts, and sent bills to clients that contained false descriptions of disbursements); Matter of Welt, 743 N.Y.S.2d 482 (1st Dept. 2002) (same). In recent years, there has been a minor outbreak of such behavior by lawyers at prominent law firms. Here are some headlines from the New York Law Journal: "Ex-Latham Partner Pleads to Fraud Charge" (3-31-2008); "Partner Resigns Over Litany of Misconduct" (from WilmerHale, 8-16-2006); "Billing Clients for Private Calls Ends in Sanction" (Wilkie Farr, 7-31-2006); "Ex-Kronish Lieb Partner Resigns From Bar Over Improper Expenses" (6-19-2002). The amounts are generally quite small compared with the lawyer's

---

* See the material on the responsibility of lawyers when serving as escrow agents at page 768. — ED.

income. This could be the very definition of self-destructive behavior. If discovered, it will likely result in loss of a partnership or job and discipline, including disbarment. Further, the reporting duty described below will usually require the firm to notify the disciplinary committee (as well as any defrauded client). I know from experience that when firms suspect this conduct they bring in the forensic accountants who x-ray the suspected lawyer's financial life going back years down to the penny.

Lying or misleading omissions on a resumé will also bring discipline. Joe McDaniel, not yet admitted to the bar, got a job at Skadden Arps through the use of a false transcript of his law school record. While at Skadden, he altered credit card slips to get reimbursements to which he was not entitled. Skadden discovered his misconduct, and he resigned. McDaniel then gained admission to the New York Bar, but he concealed his Skadden employment, ostensibly to avoid discovery of the reason for his departure. When his misconduct was later discovered, he was disbarred. In re McDaniel, 699 N.Y.S.2d 397 (1st Dept. 1999). See also Matter of Wolmer, 650 N.Y.S.2d 679 (1st Dept. 1996) (public censure of young lawyer, looking for a new job, whose resumé "exaggerated the amount of time he worked at prior legal and investment banking positions . . . and omitted other positions, in an effort to present a more stable employment history").

A lawyer who violates a fiduciary duty owed to a nonclient or deceives a person who is not a client may nevertheless be disciplined. Beery v. State Bar, 739 P.2d 1289 (Cal. 1987). A lawyer may also be disciplined for conduct she engages in as a businessperson. Matter of Nasti, 642 N.Y.S.2d 689 (1st Dept. 1996) (suspension for six months where lawyer while employed as the general manager of a newspaper committed misdemeanor by falsely inflating its circulation figures); In re Lurie, 546 P.2d 1126 (Ariz. 1976). *Lurie* makes the additional point that a lawyer who engages in business continues to be bound by the ethical responsibilities that apply to lawyers.

Authorities diverge on whether a lawyer engages in "deceit" when recording a conversation without the other party's permission. In some states, such conduct would be illegal and therefore unethical. But where the conduct is not illegal, is it unethical? Consider the following views. Gunter represented a man who wanted to get divorced. Gunter told the man to place a wiretap on his home phone, which was in the man's name, in the expectation that they would discover conversations revealing adultery by the man's wife. They didn't. After the tap was discovered, Gunter was charged with violating state wiretap laws but was acquitted. Nonetheless, the Virginia Supreme Court found the conduct deceitful and suspended Gunter. Gunter v. Virginia State Bar, 385 S.E.2d 597 (Va. 1989). By contrast, the ABA, after taking the position in 1974 that nonconsensual recording was deceitful and therefore unethical reversed itself in 2001 and concluded that the conduct is permissible so long as it is not illegal and the lawyer does not affirmatively mislead the person being recorded. A lawyer may even record a conversation with a client without the client's knowledge. Compare Opinion 337 (1974) with Opinion 422 (2001). Compare D.C. Opinion 229 (1992) (if legal, it is ethical surreptitiously to tape meeting among lawyer, client, and federal agency officials).

Although courts are quite strict when lawyers steal law firm or client money, they are remarkably lenient when a lawyer has been convicted of "stealing" the government's money through conscious failure to pay taxes. Even New Jersey, which will disbar a lawyer who takes money from a client or law firm, shows great leniency in tax matters. Matter of Garcia, 574 A.2d 394 (N.J. 1990) (willful failure to file income tax returns warrants public reprimand); Iowa Supreme Court Attorney Disciplinary Bd v. Iversen, 723 N.W.2d 806 (Iowa 2006) (willful failure to file state and federal tax returns for ten years and a state felony tax conviction warrants suspension for at least one year); Attorney Grievance Commn. of Maryland v. Atkinson, 745 A.2d 1086 (Md. 2000) (failure to file and pay federal and state income taxes for 11 years warrants suspension with leave to reapply after one year) (three judges, dissenting, say the penalty is too harsh); Matter of Haugabrook, 606 S.E.2d 257 (Ga. 2004) (one-year suspension of lawyer who pled guilty to two federal tax felonies). Can you reconcile disbarment of the lawyer in *Warhaftig*, page 774, with the lesser sanction of suspension in the tax cases, where the sums are usually much greater? In *Haugabrook* the lawyer was convicted of a federal felony. Warhaftig was convicted of nothing.

A law professor (!) who altered his student evaluations to increase his chances of getting a chair was suspended from practice and resigned his faculty position. Supreme Court Attorney Disciplinary Bd. v. Kress, 747 N.W.2d 530 (Iowa 2008). Plagiarism of 18 pages of a brief from a treatise without citation warranted a six-month suspension. Iowa Supreme Court Bd. of Prof. Ethics & Conduct v. Lane, 642 N.W.2d 296 (Iowa 2002) ("Plagiarism itself is unethical") (court also notes that lawyer applied for a fee of $200 hourly for 80 hours required to "write" the brief).

Private lawyers who conduct "sting" operations to get information they think will help their clients — and which indeed might help their clients — engage in deceit. This conduct is sometimes called pretexting. Matter of Ositis, 366 P.3d 500 (Or. 2002), reprimanded a lawyer who hired an investigator to pose as a journalist and interview a potential adversary of his client in a possible litigation. Two Massachusetts lawyers, one a former assistant state prosecutor who oversaw undercover operations, were disbarred after they used an elaborate pretext (more Keystone Kops than Mission Impossible) in an unsuccessful effort to learn information from a law clerk that they hoped to use to disqualify the judge for whom he worked (they pretended to be interviewing him for a job). In re Curry, 880 N.E.2d 388 (Mass. 2008); In re Crossen, 880 N.E.2d 352 (Mass. 2008).

Prosecutors and other government lawyers who file false documents with the court or instruct witnesses to lie will be disciplined, even if the conduct is part of a government "sting" operation or an effort to protect an undercover informant. People v. Reichman, 819 P.2d 1035 (Colo. 1991); In re Friedman, 392 N.E.2d 1333 (Ill. 1979); In re Malone, 480 N.Y.S.2d 603 (3d Dept. 1984), aff'd, 482 N.E.2d 565 (1985). In *Reichman*, the prosecutor arranged the false arrest of an undercover informant and the filing of fictitious charges in order to "rehabilitate" the informant's credibility among cohorts after it appeared that his dual role had been "compromised." The court censured Reichman for, among other things, engaging in dishonest conduct and conduct prejudicial to the administration of justice: "The respondent's responsibility to enforce the laws in his judicial district grants him no license to ignore those laws or the Code of Professional Responsibility." A prosecutor who was found to have knowingly presented false testimony in a capital case was disbarred in Matter of Peasley, 90 P.3d 764 (Ariz. 2004). As a result of the prosecutor's misconduct, double jeopardy prevented the state from retrying the defendant for a triple homicide. Florida suspended an Assistant U.S. Attorney for a year after she allowed a witness to testify using an alias. The prosecutor was trying to help the witness avoid "a negative impact" her testimony might have on her "personal domestic litigation." But the ruse was discovered and a mistrial declared after jeopardy had attached. The court said that disbarment was the presumptive sanction, but it imposed the suspension because of an unblemished career. Florida Bar v. Cox, 794 So. 2d 1278 (Fla. 2001).

Can you square these results with the fact that prosecutors often oversee police sting operations, whose very aim is to fool others?

b. Neglect and Lack of Candor

Neglect of client matters is a recurrent basis for discipline regardless of the lawyer's motives. (Motives may of course influence the sanction.) The likelihood of discipline increases as the number of neglected matters increases. In Matter of Snow, 530 N.Y.S.2d 886 (3d Dept. 1988), a pattern of neglect of several legal matters resulted in a one-year suspension. The court was especially unimpressed with the lawyer's "attempt to blame his failure to respond to telephone calls or correspondence on his secretary's illness." (This is the disciplinary equivalent of "The dog ate my homework.") A lawyer's failure to provide a defense for a client in a personal injury case resulted in a default judgment of $221,000. Given the serious harm to the client and prior discipline, the lawyer was disbarred. In re Scott, 979 P.2d 572 (Colo. 1999). Neglect should be distinguished from negligence: Sins of omission are more likely to meet with disciplinary committee disapproval than are acts of negligence. Why is that? At the same time, neglect can lead to discipline even if the client is not harmed, since the neglect itself is forbidden.

It is in response to allegations of neglect, often profound neglect, that lawyers will likely present psychological defenses, including dependency on prescribed or illegal substances, depression, and obsessive character traits. These are discussed at page 802.

Neglect, lack of candor, or outright sloppiness in a submission to a court can result in a sanction directly by the court, bypassing the disciplinary committee. In DCD Programs, Ltd. v. Leighton, 846 F.2d 526 (9th Cir. 1988), a lawyer misstated the record from the district court. When ordered to show cause for his misstatements, the lawyer attributed the errors to "neglect in not having more carefully reviewed the record." He also relied on inexperience, since the appeal was his first in federal court. The court wrote:

As this court stated in In re Boucher, 837 F.2d 869 (9th Cir. 1988) [modified at 850 F.2d 597 (9th Cir. 1988)], counsel's professional duty requires scrupulous accuracy in referring to the record. A court should not have to pore over an extensive record as an alternative to relying on counsel's representations. The court relies on counsel to state clearly, candidly, and accurately the record as it in fact exists.

It is not required that the court find intentional conduct in order for an attorney to be disciplined pursuant to Rule 46(c) [of the Federal Rules of Appellate Procedure]. Lack of diligence which impairs the deliberations of the court is sufficient.

The lawyer was suspended for two months. See also Amstar Corp. v. Envirotech Corp., 730 F.2d 1476 (Fed. Cir. 1984), in which a lawyer omitted language when he quoted from the record. The omission was revealed with ellipses, but the quote as edited conveyed a meaning opposite to the meaning imparted by the record as a whole. The court said such behavior reflects a "lack of the candor required by . . . Rule 3.3 . . . , wastes the time of the court and of opposing counsel, and imposes unnecessary costs on the parties and on fellow citizens whose taxes support this court and its staff." The court doubled the costs on appeal as a sanction for this and other conduct. See also the material on Rule 11 and other sanctions in chapter 7. See also *Precision Specialty Metals*, at page 441, which reprimanded a federal government lawyer who used ellipses to eliminate language from a case that undermined her position.

c. Sexual Relations with a Client

In the film *Jagged Edge*, the character played by Glenn Close has an affair with a man she is defending (played by Jeff Bridges) who is charged with murdering his wife. Several times during the trial, Close's skills as a lawyer are (visibly) hampered because of information she learns about her client's relationships with other women. Did Glenn Close's character act unethically in sleeping with her client during the course of the representation? If you think she did, how if at all would you distinguish the situation of a law firm partner who begins an affair with an officer of the firm's corporate client?

In the years since the first edition of this casebook (1985), the courts and bar have begun to pay serious attention to the dangers attendant on lawyer-client sexual relationships. Whereas cases focusing on these issues were once quite rare, now there are many—and a plethora of law review articles too, some of which are cited below. A handful of states have adopted specific rules forbidding lawyers to commence an intimate personal relationship with a client during a representation. Other states have relied on conflict rules or other generic rules to punish such behavior. We are not here talking about sexual assault, which would be a crime as well as a basis for discipline, but rather about supposedly consensual relationships. Can a relationship be truly consensual when a lawyer is representing a client at serious risk and dependent on the lawyer?

Domestic relations work accounts for the great majority of cases in which lawyers have been charged with misconduct for initiating intimate relationships with clients. Criminal and personal injury cases account for most of the rest. But in every reported case of which I am aware, the lawyer has been a man and the client (or, rarely, the client's significant other) has been a woman. Here we are talking about professional discipline. Earlier, we saw that a lawyer who has sex with a client may be liable for civil damages. See page 717.

MATTER OF TSOUTSOURIS
748 N.E.2d 856 (Ind. 2001)

PER CURIAM.

The respondent, James V. Tsoutsouris, engaged in a sexual relationship with his client while he was representing her in a dissolution matter. He claims such a relationship was not improper. Alternatively, he argues that even if it were, it merits only a private reprimand. We disagree and suspend him from the practice of law in Indiana for 30 days. . . .

[A] client hired the respondent in 1994 to represent her in a child support modification action filed by her first husband. The client paid the respondent a total fee of $350. While that child support matter was pending, the client also hired the respondent to represent her in a dissolution action against her second husband. While the respondent was representing the client in the fall of 1994, the respondent and the client began dating and engaged in consensual sexual relations several times. The respondent did not inform the client how a sexual relationship between them might impact his professional duties to her or otherwise affect their attorney/client relationship.

The respondent ended the sexual relationship a few weeks after it began in 1994. The client hired the respondent for a third legal matter in 1996. In 1997, the client sought psychological treatment. One of the subjects discussed during that treatment was her personal relationship with the respondent three years earlier.

In his Petition for Review, the respondent contends his consensual sexual relationship with his client during his representation of her does not violate the Rules of Professional Conduct. He bases that argument on the lack of evidence establishing that his sexual relationship with the client impaired his ability to represent the client effectively. The respondent contends that a sexual relationship between attorney and client in Indiana is professional misconduct only when it affects the quality of the attorney's representation of the client. The respondent also suggests that Indiana law in 1994 was ambiguous with respect to the impropriety of sexual relations between attorney and client. Therefore, he argues a finding of misconduct would be inappropriate because he was unaware of his obligations to avoid sexual contact with his client at the time of such contact.

Rule 1.7(b) prohibits representation of a client if the representation "may be materially limited . . . by the lawyer's own interests." Although the rule contains general exceptions in instances where the lawyer reasonably believes that the representation will not be adversely affected and the client consents after consultation,[2] these exceptions will not generally avail when the "lawyer's own interests" at issue are those related to a lawyer/client sexual relationship. In effect, the respondent argues that sexual relationships between lawyers and clients ought to be authorized unless there is evidence of impaired representation. We decline to adopt that position. . . .

---

2. Although not necessary for our determination, we note that the respondent concedes that he did not inform the client of the possible impact that a sexual relationship could have on their professional relationship and obtain her consent to his continued representation after such consultation.

[In] ABA Formal Ethics Opinion No. 92-364, the ABA made it clear that attorneys should avoid sexual contact with their clients.[3] This position is further bolstered by the recent proposed revisions of the ABA Model Rules of Professional Conduct resulting from a three-year comprehensive study and evaluation by the ABA Commission on Evaluation of the Rules of Professional Conduct (commonly referred to as the "Ethics 2000" Commission). These revisions include a proposed new rule explicitly declaring that "A lawyer shall not have sexual relations with a client unless a consensual sexual relationship existed between them when the client-lawyer relationship commenced." Proposed Model Rule 1.8(j). The proposed rule is further supported by commentary reflecting important policy considerations.[4] The concerns articulated in both ABA Ethics Opinion No. 92-364 and Comment 17 to Proposed ABA Model Rule 1.8 reflect important policy considerations that are of concern to this Court.*

In Matter of Grimm, 674 N.E.2d 551 (Ind. 1996), this Court found an attorney's "sexual relationship with his client during the pendency of dissolution and post-dissolution matters materially limited his representation of her," thereby violating Prof. Cond. R. 1.7(b). We explained:

> In their professional capacity, lawyers are expected to provide emotionally detached, objective analysis of legal problems and issues for clients who

---

3. While the ABA Model Rules of Professional Conduct do not explicitly prohibit a sexual relationship between an attorney and client, we note that such relationships have been unequivocally discouraged, as noted in ABA Ethics Opinion 92-364:

> First, because of the dependence that so often characterizes the attorney-client relationship, there is a significant possibility that the sexual relationship will have resulted from the exploitation of the lawyer's dominant position and influence and, thus, breached the lawyer's fiduciary obligations to the client. Second, a sexual relationship with a client may affect the independence of the lawyer's judgment. Third, the lawyer's engaging in a sexual relationship with a client may create a prohibited conflict between the interests of the lawyer and those of the client. Fourth, a non-professional, yet emotionally charged, relationship between attorney and client may result in confidences being imparted in circumstances where the attorney-client privilege is not available, yet would have been, absent the personal relationship.

> We believe the better practice is to avoid all sexual contact with clients during the representation.

4. Proposed Comment 17 to Rule 1.8 states:

> The relationship between lawyer and client is a fiduciary one in which the lawyer occupies the highest position of trust and confidence. The relationship is almost always unequal; thus, a sexual relationship between lawyer and client can involve unfair exploitation of the lawyer's fiduciary role, in violation of the lawyer's basic ethical obligation not to use the trust of the client to the client's disadvantage. In addition, such a relationship presents a significant danger that, because of the lawyer's emotional involvement, the lawyer will be unable to represent the client without impairment of the exercise of independent professional judgment. Moreover, a blurred line between the professional and personal relationships may make it difficult to predict to what extent client confidences will be protected by the attorney-client evidentiary privilege, since client confidences are protected by privilege only when they are imparted in the context of the client-lawyer relationship. Because of the significant danger of harm to client interests and because the client's own emotional involvement renders it unlikely that the client could give adequate informed consent, this Rule prohibits the lawyer from having sexual relations with a client regardless of whether the relationship is consensual and regardless of the absence of prejudice to the client.

* In 2002, the ABA adopted Rule 1.8(j) and Comment [17]. Indiana adopted both thereafter — ED.

may be embroiled in sensitive or difficult matters. Clients, especially those who are troubled or emotionally fragile, often place a great deal of trust in the lawyer and rely heavily on his or her agreement to provide professional assistance. Unfortunately, the lawyer's position of trust may provide opportunity to manipulate the client for the lawyer's sexual benefit. Where a lawyer permits or encourages a sexual relationship to form with a client, that trust is betrayed and the stage is set for continued unfair exploitation of the lawyer's fiduciary position. Additionally, the lawyer's ability to represent effectively the client may be impaired. Objective detachment, essential for clear and reasoned analysis of issues and independent professional judgment, may be lost. . . .

We hold that the respondent violated Prof. Cond. R. 1.7(b) and prejudiced the administration of justice in violation of Prof. Cond. R. 8.4(d). Given our finding of misconduct, we must determine an appropriate sanction. In doing so, we consider the misconduct, the respondent's state of mind underlying the misconduct, the duty of this court to preserve the integrity of the profession, the risk to the public in allowing the respondent to continue in practice, and any mitigating or aggravating factors. As a mitigating factor only, we find no evidence that the respondent's sexual relationship with his client actually impaired his representation of her. In fact, the client hired the respondent to handle another legal matter for her after the sexual relationship ended but before disciplinary charges were filed against the respondent. Moreover, the respondent has not been disciplined previously during his 33 years of practicing law. Given these mitigating factors, we conclude a 30-day suspension from the practice of law is warranted.

Should Lawyers Be Forbidden to Have Sexual Relations with Clients?

Does this opinion mean that if he explains the risks, a lawyer might be able to begin an intimate relationship with a client? Or should we say (as the Model Rules now do) that the dangers inherent in such relationships are too great to allow even with consent? Can we be comfortable that consent, especially from a matrimonial client, is freely given? Remember, the state here is attempting to control the private conduct of competent adults. How far should we let the state intrude? The lawyer in Vallinoto v. DiSandro, page 716, won his civil case but lost the discipline. Citing conflict rules, the Rhode Island Supreme Court censured him for beginning and continuing an affair with his divorce client. Matter of DiSandro, 680 A.2d 73 (R.I. 1996).

Cases that discipline lawyers for having sex with clients often describe fairly unremarkable facts. The parties somehow drift into an intimate relationship. Most often the lawyer instigates the relationship, but sometimes the client does, or it just happens. In re Halverson, 998 P.2d 833 (Wash. 2000) (even if intimate relationship with matrimonial client was consensual, lawyer, who was former president of the state bar, is suspended for one year). In any event, the courts emphasize the threat to the lawyer's independent professional judgment and the danger, especially in matrimonial or custody matters, to the client's case. The privilege is also endangered, isn't it? Were they talking as lovers or as lawyer and client? Some representative cases are: In re Heard, 963 P.2d 818 (Wash. 1998) (Heard "sexually exploited a [personal injury] client with alcohol problems and who suffered the effects of serious head injuries;" two-year suspension); People v. Good, 893 P.2d 101 (Colo. 1995) (sexual relationship with criminal defendant client); Disciplinary Counsel v. DePietro, 643 N.E.2d 1145 (Ohio 1994) (consensual relationship concurrent with professional relationship results in discipline without need to show harm). Matter of Lewis, 415 S.E.2d 173 (Ga. 1992), suspended a lawyer for three years where the lawyer had engaged in sexual intercourse with a client in a matrimonial matter. The court wrote: "Every lawyer must know that an extramarital relationship can jeopardize every aspect of a client's matrimonial case — extending to forfeiture of alimony, loss of custody, and denial of attorney fees. Thus . . . the admission by Lewis of sexual intercourse with this client authorized the entry of summary judgment against him." The applicable rule prohibited the acceptance of a representation if the lawyer's "exercise of his professional judgment on behalf of his client will be or reasonably may be affected." Given these dangers in matrimonial matters, is it also unwise for a lawyer to represent someone with whom he is already intimate? Rules speak in terms of *commencing* a sexual relationship with a current client. But isn't the lawyer who represents a lover, at least in matrimonial or criminal matters, taking a big risk?

For other instances of discipline, see In re Hoffmeyer, 656 S.E.2d 376 (S.C. 2008) (nine-month suspension, matrimonial client); In re Bourdon, 565 A.2d 1052 (N.H. 1989) (affair with matrimonial client who had minor child); The Florida Bar v. Bryant, 813 So. 2d 38 (Fla. 2002) (lawyer accepted client's offer of sex in exchange for legal services; court holds the conduct "exploited" the professional relationship within the meaning of Florida's rule); Office of Disciplinary Counsel v. Moore, 804 N.E.2d 423 (Ohio 2004) (making unsolicited sexual advances to client " 'perverts the very essence of the lawyer-client relationship' " even where nothing further happened).

Do you support a rule categorically prohibiting the commencement of a sexual relationship between a lawyer and any matrimonial or criminal client? California forbids the commencement of a sexual relationship with a client, but only if the relationship is coercive or the product of undue influence, or if the relationship causes the lawyer to perform legal services incompetently. California Rule 3-120. Oregon may go the furthest of all. Not only does Oregon forbid commencement of a sexual relationship with a current client in any matter, but Oregon lawyers are also forbidden to "have sexual relations with a representative of a current client of the lawyer if the sexual relations would, or would likely, damage or prejudice the client in the representation." Oregon Rule 1.8 (j). What are they getting at? Comment [19] to Mode Rule 1.8 also addresses relationships with client representatives, but in different language: "When the client is an organization, paragraph (j) of this Rule prohibits a lawyer for the organization (whether inside counsel or outside counsel) from having a sexual relationship with a constituent of the organization who supervises, directs or regularly consults with that lawyer concerning the organization's legal matters."

The South Carolina Supreme Court, in Matter of Bellino, 417 S.E.2d 535 (S.C. 1992), gave the following thoughtful justification for forbidding sexual relationships between attorneys and clients, at least in certain matters. Bellino was suspended after he kissed and fondled two matrimonial clients while he was a lawyer in the Marine Corps. The court wrote:

> This case is not about sex or sex abuse. It is about power — the awesome power that comes with the license to practice law — and the abuse thereof. A certain amount of courage is required for a person to make romantic overtures to another person. The fear of rejection is legitimate, and the pain of rejection is real. Some people find ways to cheat and, thereby, avoid the possibility of rejection. One way is by the use of a prostitute. Another and even more reprehensible way is by taking advantage of a weaker person, a person either physically weaker or, as the result of circumstances, less able to say no. This is precisely what Mr. Bellino did. He took advantage of his superior position as an officer in the Marine Corps and as a lawyer. It would be difficult to imagine anyone more vulnerable or more subject to the control of another than the women on whom Mr. Bellino forced himself.

Support for the rule is not unanimous. Professor Linda Fitts Mischler has taken a decidedly skeptical and contrarian view of per se bans on sex between lawyers and clients, charging that they "disempower predominantly female clients, perpetuate stereotypes that historically deprive women of self-determination and foster dependency rather than self-reliance. Nowhere is this deprivation of self-determination more acute than when a per se ban is tailored to apply only to the area of marital and divorce representation." In lieu of bans, Professor Mischler recommends "education and enlightenment of both attorney and client as an effective and lasting solution to the problem of attorney-client sex." Linda Mischler, Reconciling Rapture, Representation, and Responsibility: An Argument Against Per Se Bans on Attorney-Client Sex, 10 Geo. J. Legal Ethics 209 (1997).

In a later article, Professor Mischler questions the New York rule that forbids lawyers to enter into sexual relations with clients but only "in domestic relations matters." Focusing on the issue of "client vulnerability" as a justification for the ban, she writes:

> Almost any client seeking legal counsel will be "vulnerable" to a certain degree. The fact that the attorney has superior legal knowledge creates a power imbalance and a dependency on the part of the client, but whether this power imbalance leads to a full-fledged transference response will depend in part on the predisposition of the client. . . . Emotional vulnerability crops up in a variety of practice settings; consider clients who have been raped or sexually assaulted, those pursuing medical malpractice or wrongful death actions, those involved with immigration proceedings, or those filing for bankruptcy. Criminal and indigent clients also have unique vulnerabilities. The vulnerabilities of some of these clients will be even greater than those of domestic relations clients, rendering the domestic relations classification on the basis of client vulnerability under-inclusive.
>
> Prohibiting domestic relations attorney-client sex on grounds of client vulnerability is also over-inclusive. . . . Because of the myriad possibilities regarding vulnerability, which depend on the procedural posture of the case, as well as the particular personalities and temperaments involved, a per se rule is too broad to be rationally related to the state's interest in protecting clients. Stereotypes about the traditional family and the effects of its demise should not be used as a proxy for vulnerability.

Personal Morals Masquerading as Professional Ethics: Regulations Banning Sex Between Domestic Relations Attorneys and Their Clients, 23 Harv. Women's L.J. 1 (2000).

Courts have uniformly condemned nonconsensual sexual contact between lawyers and clients. See In re Romano, 660 N.Y.S.2d 426 (1st Dept. 1997) (intimate examination of female clients in workers' compensation cases); Courtney v. Alabama State Bar, 492 So. 2d 1002 (Ala. 1986) (attorney who placed arms around minor client's mother, touched her buttocks, and kissed her after office meeting publicly censured); In re Liebowitz, 516 A.2d 246 (N.J. 1985) (taking "sexual advantage" of assigned client warrants public reprimand); In re Gibson, 369 N.W.2d 695 (Wis. 1985) (unsolicited physical advances toward client calls for 90-day suspension). Threatening to withdraw or other harmful consequences to a client's case if the client does not submit to a lawyer's demands will also result in discipline. In re Piatt, 951 P.2d 889 (Ariz. 1997) (even absent specific rule, a lawyer may not "extort sexual conduct from a client").

FURTHER READING

Lawrence Dubin, Sex and the Divorce Lawyer: Is the Client Off Limits?, 1 Geo. J. Legal Ethics 585 (1988); Note, Keeping Sex Out of the Attorney-Client Relationship: A Proposed Rule, 92 Colum. L. Rev. 887 (1992) (authored by John O'Connell); Joanne Pitulla, Unfair Advantage, A.B.A. J., Nov. 1992, at 76. Oregon's rule is analyzed by Professor Caroline Forell in Oregon's "Hands-Off" Rule: Ethical and Liability Issues Presented by Attorney-Client Sexual Contact, 29 Willamette L. Rev. 711 (1993). See also Nancy Goldberg, Sex and the Attorney-Client Relationship: An Argument for a Prophylactic Rule, 26 Akron L. Rev. 45 (1992).

d. The Lawyer's "Private" Life and Conduct Unrelated to Clients

To what extent should a lawyer's behavior unrelated to her law practice be a basis for discipline? What if the behavior is related to practice but unrelated to client representation? As we saw at page 782, tax crimes can result in discipline even though unconnected to law practice, and so can other crimes. Leaving the scene of a fatal automobile accident warrants disbarment. Matter of Tidwell, 831 A.2d 953 (D.C. 2003) (lawyer previously disbarred in New York following felony conviction for same conduct). Louisiana State Bar Assn. v. Bensabat, 378 So. 2d 380 (La. 1979) (conspiracy to import cocaine). Some states mandate disbarment for all felony convictions. Mitchell v. Association of the Bar, 351 N.E.2d 743 (N.Y. 1976) (disbarment of former Attorney General John Mitchell following conviction of a federal felony). Personal use of marijuana has resulted in mild sanctions. In re Anonymous Member of the S.C. Bar, 360 S.E.2d 322 (S.C. 1987) (private reprimand for marijuana use), though even these sanctions are increasingly rare. But see In re Johnson, 500 N.W.2d 215 (S.D. 1993) (government lawyer who represented the state in civil and criminal matters suspended two years after using marijuana recreationally 100 times and cocaine once). Courts are less tolerant of lawyers who are convicted of possessing cocaine and like drugs. Michigan will discipline lawyers who are convicted of drunk driving. Grievance Administrator v. Deutch, 565 N.W.2d 369 (Mich. 1997).

Private consensual sexual activity between *adults* no longer leads to discipline, even though it may offend community standards or violate laws against adultery or fornication. But sex-related behavior in other contexts can result in discipline. An example is sexual harassment of law firm employees. Cincinnati Bar Assn. v. Young, 731 N.E.2d 631 (Ohio 2000); People v. Lowery, 894 P.2d 758 (Colo. 1995). In In re Gelfand, 512 N.E.2d 533 (N.Y. 1987), a New York trial judge (male) was removed from the bench after exhibiting extreme and obsessive behavior toward a lawyer employed by the court (female). The former dean of a law school was publicly reprimanded after he made unwelcome physical contact and verbal communications of a sexual nature with four female staff members, two of whom were also students of the law school. In re Peters, 428 N.W.2d 375 (Minn. 1988).

Increasingly, state courts will discipline lawyers who willfully fail to honor child support obligations. In re Chase, 121 P.3d 1160 (Or. 2005); In re Geer, 858 N.E.2d 388 (Ohio 2006). Dishonesty in private business dealings can support discipline. Oklahoma Bar Ass'n v. Pacenza, 136 P.3d 616 (Okla. 2006). An assistant prosecutor who used an office computer to view pornographic Web sites despite office policies forbidding it was publicly reprimanded. In re Beatse, 722 N.W.2d 385 (Wis. 2006) (he also lied about it).

An associate used his office computer to have sexually explicit exchanges with a police officer pretending to be a 13-year-old girl. After he arranged to meet her for oral sex, he was arrested, fired, and pled guilty to a misdemeanor. What's the right sanction? The referee recommended a six month suspension. The court imposed three years. Two dissenters voted to disbar him. In re Lever, 2008 Westlaw 5396870 (1st Dept. 2008).

Domestic violence or violence toward persons with whom the lawyer is in an intimate or dating relationship will also bring discipline. Lawrence Magid pled guilty to assaulting K. P. "by punching her in the head and face area causing a black eye, knocking her to the ground and kicking her in the neck, head, and lower back. . . ." The sentence was probation. The incident occurred at a private club "frequented by law enforcement personnel. At the time of the incident, respondent was the First Assistant Prosecutor of Gloucester County. [K. P.] was also employed by the Gloucester County Prosecutor's Office and had been dating respondent for several months. As a result of this incident, respondent was discharged from his position in the Prosecutor's Office." Matter of Magid, 655 A.2d 916 (N.J. 1995). What should the sanction be? The court ordered a reprimand, citing Magid's "unblemished professional record" and the fact that it had "not previously addressed the appropriate discipline to be imposed on an attorney who is convicted of an act of domestic violence. . . ." However, the court cautioned lawyers that in the future it "will ordinarily suspend an attorney who is convicted of an act of domestic violence." True to its word, in 1997 the New Jersey Supreme Court suspended each of two lawyers for three months after they pled guilty to assaulting a wife and former wife respectively. Matter of Margrabia, 695 A.2d 1378 (N.J. 1997) (conduct was post-*Magid* so lawyer on notice); Matter of Toronto, 696 A.2d 8 (N.J. 1997) (conduct was pre-*Magid* but there were other aggravating factors).

Other states have also punished domestic violence. "It is patent . . . that an attorney's conduct in engaging in spousal abuse, domestic violence, is viewed by the courts addressing the issue as prejudicial to the administration of justice and maybe even as impacting adversely that attorney's fitness to practice law." Attorney Grievance Commn. of Maryland v. Painter, 739 A.2d 24 (Md. 1999) (holding that suspension is the appropriate sanction absent aggravated assault, which can result in disbarment). A one-year suspension was ordered in People v. Musick, 960 P.2d 89 (Colo. 1998), where the respondent physically assaulted his girlfriend on three separate occasions. Although the assaults resulted in no serious injuries, the court stressed "the complete absence of evidence that the respondent has taken any steps whatsoever to rehabilitate himself or even to recognize that he has a problem." As a condition of reinstatement, Musick would have to "demonstrate that he has completed a certified domestic violence treatment program."

e.   Racist and Sexist Conduct

MATTER OF JORDAN SCHIFF
Docket No. HP 22/92 (Feb. 2, 1993)
Departmental Disciplinary Committee
First Judicial Department New York State Supreme Court
REPORT AND RECOMMENDATIONS OF HEARING PANEL

The charges in this case involve allegations of misconduct during a deposition, in violation of the Code of Professional Responsibility. While serious deposition misconduct is found today among lawyers at all levels of the Bar, and while this respondent is a young lawyer only three years out of law school with no prior history of disciplinary violations, who appears to have been influenced by the improper attitudes of his superiors, his misbehavior was so flagrant that we recommend public censure. He and others must be deterred from such misbehavior in the future.

Respondent's misbehavior occurred at the deposition of a witness named Adamina Morales, in a personal injury case brought by the witness, who was represented by the firm in which Mr. Schiff was an associate, Shapiro & Yankowitz. The deposition, which was held at the Shapiro & Yankowitz offices, was taken by Elizabeth Mark, Esq., of Baumeister & Samuels, a lawyer of approximately Mr. Schiff's age and experience.

During the deposition, Mr. Schiff showered Ms. Mark with sexist obscenities, partly off the record and partly on the record, in pursuance of a generally obstructive pattern of conduct. While Ms. Mark handled the incident professionally, and was not intimidated from carrying out her duty to her client, no lawyer should have to endure such behavior from an adversary.

FACTS

Respondent, a graduate of Stuyvesant High, the University of Michigan and Cardozo Law School, was admitted to practice by the Appellate Division, Second Department on March 16, 1988, and has maintained an office in New York County at all relevant times. The first deposition of respondent's client, Mrs. Morales, was held on August 30, 1989. When the plaintiff filed a supplemental Bill of Particulars on January 18, 1990, adding lumbosacral injuries, defendant requested a supplemental [deposition]. It was at this second [deposition], held March 14, 1991, that Ms. Mark and Mr. Schiff appeared together for the first time, and at which Mr. Schiff misbehaved as charged.

Early in this deposition, a senior partner of Mr. Schiff's firm, Mr. Yankowitz, set a highly improper tone. When Mr. Schiff, after a dispute, rudely told Ms. Mark to "get out of here" and walked out of the room, Mr. Yankowitz thereupon appeared. Ms. Mark attempted on the record to protest Mr. Schiff's actions, and, after hearing Mr. Yankowitz, asked him to stop mischaracterizing what had occurred. Mr. Yankowitz replied:

Mr. Yankowitz: Don't tell me what to do. Ever. It's my office, it's my firm. This is my client. The record is clear. I have made my statement and I have recited what the judge has directed in this case. You don't make the rules, you don't wear a black robe, you are not the judge.

Ms. Mark: Excuse me, first of all, let the record reflect that Mr. Yankowitz is pointing at me, standing and shouting. In the second place, let the record reflect that the court hasn't said a thing about this deposition so you obviously don't know what you are talking about. Finally—

Mr. Yankowitz: Your statements are ludicrous.

Ms. Mark: I am not finished.

Mr. Yankowitz: You have lost your mind, young lady, continue the deposition or leave.

After this example of mentoring at Shapiro & Yankowitz, the deposition proceeded.

Respondent Schiff said to Ms. Mark:

Just do your examination and shut up. Just do your examination already. Enough with the bullshit. Do your examination or I am going to throw you out of the office. Bitch. You are the nastiest person I ever met and I am going to really be all over you during this exam, so you better watch your ass.

Ms. Mark: Mark that for a ruling as well, please. I will be seeking santions for all of this.

Mr. Schiff: Do whatever you want to do. Do whatever you want to do. The judge is sick of you and your firm anyway.

Ms. Mark: Mark that for a ruling.

Mr. Schiff: You give lawyers a bad name. You and your firm give attorneys a bad name, I will tell you that right now. . . .

Ms. Mark: I am not going to sit here and listen to your scatological comments all day.

Mr. Schiff: I know a scatalog when I see one.

Mr. Schiff descended further during discussions which were held off the record but in the presence of the court reporter, Mr. Harold Brown, and the Spanish interpreter, Ms. Nancy Adler, both of whom testified before us. Ms. Mark testified that Mr. Schiff referred to her as a "cunt," an "asshole," and advised her that she should "go home and have babies." This evidence was corroborated in substantial part by the other witnesses.

Mr. Brown, who has been a court reporter since 1967, testified, "I remember him saying something like you're an asshole, Ms. Mark, and you should be home having, making babies. Those are the two that I can specifically remember."

Q: Do you recall Ms. Mark making any offensive remarks off the record?
A: No.
Q: Can you describe their demeanor during the deposition?
A: Well, she was quiet. I felt, I just felt that she was trying to do her job and examine the witness.

When asked on redirect by staff counsel why he remembered what Mr. Schiff said to Ms. Mark when off the record he answered: "It was certainly very unusual. It was, like I say, I do hundreds of depositions a year and I just was frankly shocked." Ms. Adler, the interpreter, when asked if she remembered any off the record remarks made by Mr. Schiff during the deposition answered: "He made some remarks. I don't know, I don't remember if they were off the record. I remember him calling Betsy, I think her name is, bitch and to go home and have babies and something like you're a cunt, you're a bitch, go home and have babies, what are you doing here."

Q: Do you remember Ms. Mark making any offensive remarks off the record?
A: No.

We accept this testimony. We also credit the testimony of Ms. Mark, a 1986 graduate of Mt. Holyoke and 1989 graduate of St. John's Law School, who has been employed by the law firm of Baumeister & Samuels since August, 1989.

Ms. Mark explained why she continued with the deposition after the degrading and vulgar comments had been made to her by respondent. "I had a client to protect and this case was about to be certified for trial."

[A] panel member asked, "Ms. Mark, was there a procedural advantage, to your knowledge, which Mr. Schiff was seeking to achieve by engaging in misconduct?" Her answer was:

> I have no explanation for why these events took place as they did. I felt there was an attempt here to prevent the defense from obtaining relevant information regarding an additional injury that had been alleged in a supplemental Bill of Particulars, and if I had just crawled back to my office and felt bad about what happened and not made my motion, I would not have had benefit of all the information that was uncovered at a supplemental deposition as far as the medical records that were obtained as a result of this and the continued deposition.

DISCUSSION

Not surprisingly, there is a paucity of precedent in disciplinary cases concerning sexual harassment of female attorneys by male adversaries. Possibly this is because those women so victimized are hesitant to complain, perhaps believing that if a woman aspires to have the designation "Attorney-at-Law" on her business card she must be willing to ignore obscene, explicit vulgarities directed at her anatomy and gender. Indeed, in this case, the complaint to the Disciplinary Committee did not come from the victim but rather came by referral from Judge Jane Solomon. However, women attorneys must be assured that humiliating and reprehensible sexual harassment is definitely not a "rite of passage" which must be silently endured, and that should they encounter it in the course of their practice, they must feel confident they can file a complaint, secure in the knowledge that it will be taken very seriously and investigated very thoroughly. . . .

We conclude that respondent, without provocation, chose to degrade and disparage his adversary by using dirty, discriminatory gutter language offensively directed to harass her because of her gender. Moreover, his was not an isolated comment, possibly uttered spontaneously and without intent, but was instead an ongoing calculated rudeness intended to intimidate a female colleague. . . .

In mitigation, respondent apologized to Ms. Mark by letter and at the hearing. Half of the panel gives very little weight to apologies made under pressure of a court order and the disciplinary process. The other half considers the apologies to constitute evidence of contrition.

In aggravation, the record shows that a direction by Judge Postel to apologize to Ms. Mark, which reflected the Court's opinion of respondent's conduct, and the sanctions imposed on Shapiro & Yankowitz by Judge Solomon on May 3 and September 6, 1991, were insufficient warning to convince Mr. Schiff that his conduct was in need of reform. This was evidenced by . . . the transcript of a deposition taken March 17, 1992, in yet another case, where he called Eileen Stegensky, Esq. a "cunt" and . . . a "nasty fucking bitch."

The Panel finds that on the evidence presented to us all charges are sustained. These include: Count I, a violation of DR 7-106(C)(6), Count II, a violation of DR 7-102(A)(1), and Count III, a violation of DR 1-102(A)(7).

The Panel unanimously finds that public censure is the appropriate sanction, because those in the profession must understand that sexual harassment is unacceptable behavior and the public must understand that the profession abhors such behavior and will not condone it. Were it not for respondent's unblemished record and his youth, 28 years, which leaves room to believe that he can mend his ways, and the consideration that he is no longer with the firm that set him such a bad example, our recommendation would be even more severe.

s/ Sheldon H. Elsen,
Chair For the Panel

The court ultimately censured Mr. Schiff, Matter of Schiff, 599 N.Y.S.2d 242 (1st Dept. 1993), writing that his conduct was "inexcusable and intolerable, and violates DR 1-102(A)(7) . . . in that it reflects adversely on his fitness to practice law." A New York court suspended a lawyer for a pattern of sexually offensive comments toward women such as this: The lawyer "frequently consumed peppermint-ball candies in the courthouse and, when offering candies to adversarial female staff attorneys, consistently made sexually offensive comments, such as, 'do you want to suck one of my balls?' When told by female attorneys that they were offended by his remarks, respondent replied, 'If you're so damned refined then why do you understand?'" In re Kahn, 791 N.Y.S.2d 36 (1st Dep't 2005). For another example of sexist behavior, resulting in a monetary sanction, see page 437.

Courts discipline lawyers for racist or sexist conduct in connection with their public roles. In People v. Sharpe, 781 P.2d 659 (Colo. 1989), Sharpe, a deputy district attorney, was prosecuting two men, Borrego and Lucero, for capital murder. In a hallway conversation Sharpe told Lucero's attorney, "I don't believe either one of those chili-eating bastards." The court imposed public censure, stressing the need to "emphasize that lawyers, especially those acting as public officials, must scrupulously avoid statements as well as deeds that could be perceived as indicating that their actions are motivated to any extent by racial prejudice."

At a deposition, New York lawyer Thomas Monaghan criticized the opposing lawyer's pronunciation of certain words. A sample: "This is finished. We are not going any further. Because you, my dear, with all due respect, are not totally aware of what you are saying, and that is frightening. Because not only did you say extablish, you repeatedly said expecially." When the opposing lawyer, an African-American woman, asked Monaghan what he wanted her to do, he said: "I want you to admit on the record, you cannot pronounce two words." At a hearing on a motion for sanctions, Judge Mukasey cited the fact that lawyers, on admission to the court, promise to "abstain from all offensive personality," called Monaghan's conduct "outrageous," and fined him $500. The court referred Monaghan to the federal court's disciplinary committee, where he agreed to accept a public censure "for his race-based abuse of opposing counsel." N.Y.L.J., April 30, 2001, at 7.

A public reprimand and two-year probation were ordered for a lawyer who, among other things, "made demeaning facial gestures and stuck out his tongue at Ms. Berger and Ms. Figueroa . . . told Ms. Figueroa that she was a 'stupid idiot' and that she should 'go back to Puerto Rico' . . . and told Ms. Figueroa that depositions are not conducted under 'girl's rules.' The entire record is replete with evidence of Martocci's verbal assaults and sexist, racial, and ethnic insults. . . ." Florida Bar v. Martocci, 791 So. 2d 1074 (Fla. 2001). See also In re Charges of Unprofessional Conduct, 597 N.W.2d 563 (Minn. 1999) (despite "lack of malice and her apologies and remorse," private admonition of prosecutor who "brought a motion that sought to prohibit an attorney from participating in a case based solely on the color of his skin").

Perhaps Larry Klayman and Paul Orfanedes thought they were engaged in legitimate advocacy when they asked Federal Judge Denny Chin to consider recusing himself in a commercial litigation. Judge Chin had made a critical ruling against their client at a bench trial. The lawyers then suggested that the judge might be biased against them because he was a Clinton appointee of Asian descent and active on behalf of Asian-Americans, while they were involved elsewhere in a highly publicized lawsuit investigating illegal campaign contributions to the Clinton campaign by or through Asians. Judge Chin revoked the lawyers' pro hac vice status, denied any future applications to appear before him pro hac vice, and required them to provide a copy of his opinion whenever they sought pro hac vice status in the Southern District of New York. Judge Chin relied on DR 1-102(A)(5), which forbids conduct "prejudicial to the administration of justice," and DR 7-106(C)(6), which forbids a lawyer to engage in "undignified or discourteous conduct which is degrading to a tribunal." The Second Circuit affirmed. Judge Winter wrote: "Courts have repeatedly held that matters such as race or ethnicity are improper bases for challenging a judge's impartiality. A suggestion that a judge cannot administer the law fairly because of the judge's racial and ethnic heritage is extremely serious and should not be made without a factual foundation going well beyond the judge's membership in a particular racial or ethnic group. Such an accusation is a charge that the judge is racially or ethnically biased and is violating the judge's oath of office." MacDraw, Inc. v. CIT Group Equipment Financing, Inc., 138 F.3d 33 (2d Cir. 1998).

The Model Rules contain no express prohibition on biased conduct or speech in the practice of law. Should they? Some states have amended their ethics rules to contain variously worded prohibitions. Some of these have to do with employment discrimination. Others are broader. For example, Florida Rule 4-8.4(d) forbids lawyers "to knowingly, or through callous indifference, disparage, humiliate, or discriminate against litigants, jurors, witnesses, court personnel, or other lawyers on any basis, including, but not limited to, on account of race, ethnicity, gender, religion, national origin, disability, marital status, sexual orientation, age, socioeconomic status, employment, or physical characteristic." Illinois Rule 8.4(a)(5) is similar. Minnesota Rule 8.4(g) forbids lawyers to "harass a person on the basis of sex, race, age, creed, religion, color, national origin, disability, sexual preference or marital status in connection with a lawyer's professional activities." Other states, including Colorado and New Jersey, have similar provisions.

Close Questions?

As you think about whether the adoption of "anti-bias" ethical rules is or is not a misguided capitulation to political correctness at the expense of free speech, factor in the following three events, all of which received prominent attention in the law press or popular media.

1. In 1993, a criminal defense lawyer, Frank Swan, sent a letter to an assistant U.S. attorney after he was disqualified from representing his client. His letter complained that the disqualification was "neither just nor fair to the defendants." According to the court:

Appended to the letter was a single sheet of paper with the following photocopied words, all enlarged and in capital letters:

MALE LAWYERS PLAY BY THE RULES, DISCOVER TRUTH AND RESTORE ORDER. FEMALE LAWYERS ARE OUTSIDE THE LAW, CLOUD TRUTH AND DESTROY ORDER.

The court continued: "Swan copied the attachment from 'No Way to Treat a Lawyer,' an article from the December 1992 issue of California Lawyer that discussed negative gender stereotyping of female attorneys in movies and television." The Justice Department asked the district judge to punish Swan and she did. She ordered Swan to apologize and she referred the matter to the district court's disciplinary committee. Swan appealed. Representing him was the ACLU. Opposing him was the Justice Department, the California State Bar, and the NOW Legal Defense and Education Fund. The Ninth Circuit reversed, holding that Swan's conduct did not impugn the integrity of the court in violation of local rules; was not an interference with the administration of justice; and could not be punished under a California law prohibiting attorneys from engaging in "offensive personality" because the law was unconstitutionally vague. United States v. Wunsch, 84 F.3d 1110 (9th Cir. 1996).

2. The second event was the decision of the Massachusetts Commission Against Discrimination to fine a female lawyer, Judith Nathanson, because she limited her practice to the representation of women in matrimonial matters. The Commission ruled that by refusing to represent a man in a divorce case, she violated the state's public accommodations law. According to the National Law Journal, the lawyer's

> dilemma highlights the tension between an attorney's duty to provide zealous representation — she argued that she could not represent men as well as she could women — and a lawyer's role in providing services to the public.
>
> Drake University Law School Prof. Sally B. Frank, who successfully sued to force Princeton University's all-male eating clubs to admit women on the ground that they were places of public accommodation, said the same principle applies to law offices. She noted that most of the feminists who would sympathize with Ms. Nathanson would be outraged if a lawyer refused to accept black clients. . . .
>
> Some experts in feminist law, however, argued that it was misguided to compare law offices with other places of public accommodation. . . . St. John's University School of Law Prof. Rosemary C. Salomone said the question centers on to what extent the state can interfere with a private business to foster equality. "That's really a Draconian use of government power to interfere with a professional practice," she said of the decision. Professor Salomone noted that the state has more incentive to intervene if the group has been traditionally disadvantaged. But she questioned whether men going through a divorce fall into this category.

Juliet Eilperin, Female Lawyer Fined for Not Accepting Male Client, Natl. L.J., May 12, 1997, at A7. The rejected client was quite sympathetic. "Mr. Joseph Stropnicky supported his wife through medical school and took care of their children until the youngest one could attend school. By the time the two got divorced, Mr. Stropnicky's wife was earning nearly ten times as much as her husband."

3. Our final exhibit here is a veteran prosecutor's 1987 speech to other prosecutors about how to pick a jury. The speaker was Jack McMahon, who became a candidate for Philadelphia District Attorney against Lynne Abraham in 1997. Mr. McMahon's speech was recorded on videotape. Ms. Abraham released the tape early in the 1997 campaign, focusing intense media attention on Mr. McMahon's conduct and raising the specter of challenges to convictions he had obtained while a prosecutor. Recall that at the time of Mr. McMahon's 1987 speech, the Supreme Court had recently held that a lawyer could not constitutionally exclude potential jurors based on race. Here is part of what McMahon told prosecutors:

> You are there to win. . . . The defense is there to win, too. The only way you're going to do your best is to get jurors that are unfair and more likely to convict

than anybody else in that room, because the defense is doing the exact same thing.

Let's face it: . . . The blacks from the low-income areas are less likely to convict. I understand it. . . . There's a resentment for law enforcement. There's a resentment for authority. And, as a result, you don't want those people on your jury. . . .

My opinion is you don't want smart people . . . because smart people will analyze the hell out of your case. They have a higher standard. They hold you up to a higher standard. They hold the courts up to a higher standard, because they're intelligent people. They take those words reasonable doubt, and they actually try to think about them. . . .

Another factor in selecting blacks: You don't want the real educated ones. This goes across the board — all races. . . . If you're sitting down and you're going to take blacks, you want older black men and women, particularly men. . . .

The other thing is blacks from the South — excellent. . . . I tell you, I don't think you can ever lose a jury with blacks from South Carolina. They are law and order. They are on the cops' side. Those people are good.

Again, my experience, young black women are very bad. There's an antagonism. I guess maybe because they're downtrodden in two respects: They are women, and they're black. So they are downtrodden in two areas, so they somehow want to take it out on somebody, and you don't want it to be you. . . .

You want people of all the same intellectual capabilities, all middle class, same economic backgrounds. That's the ideal jury. You're not going to have some brain surgeon from Chestnut Hill with some nitwit from 33rd and Diamond.

Again, some people say: Well, the best jury is an all-white jury. I don't buy that — particularly with a black defendant. . . . You may get that kind of reverse racism in your case. . . . A jury of eight whites and four blacks is a great jury. . . . You're not going to get any of that racist type of attitude, because a white guy is not going to sit on that jury and say "Oh, these people live like this and that," with three other blacks sitting in the room. . . .

You don't want social workers. That's obvious. They got intelligence, sensitivity, all this stuff. You don't want them. . . .

Teachers are bad, especially young teachers. If you get, like, a white teacher teaching in a black school that's sick of these guys, maybe. That may be one you accept.*

What should we do about this issue? Should Mr. Swan, Ms. Nathanson, or Mr. McMahon be subject to professional discipline?

f. Failure to Report Another Lawyer's Misconduct

"Better Late than Never"

"I'm working with Isadora Rice on an international commodities fraud case. Our client is the Mercury Fund. I'm only here a year, and out of law school

---

* McMahon's Own Words, Philadelphia Inquirer, April 6, 1997, at E4.

two years, and I really lucked out. I get to fly to Europe and Asia to take depositions, well, to watch Isadora take depositions mostly, and to talk to witnesses. These are places I could never afford to visit on my own. Isadora's pretty good about letting me have sightseeing time, too. The case has been in pretrial eight months with a trial date next September.

"Yesterday, on the plane on the way back from Jakarta, Isadora said to me, 'Laura, I need to get your time sheets for the last two months.' 'Sure,' I said, 'is something wrong?' I figured I wasn't being entirely accurate though I try to be. 'No,' she said, 'but I haven't had a chance to do mine and now I've forgotten the half of it. So since we've been working so closely I'll reconstruct mine from yours.' 'Oh,' I said.

"But I started thinking that I do a lot of work she doesn't, and she does a lot of stuff I don't. So how can she possibly reconstruct her time from mine, except very roughly if that? She's going to be guessing a lot. We bill in tenths of hours. And when we send out the quarterly bills — I do the first draft so I know — we send backup time sheets from the computer run which, when a client looks at them, definitely imply that the time is recorded contemporaneously with the work. You know, the same day or maybe the next. And our retainer letters say explicitly that we record time contemporaneously because smart clients insist on it.

"So what do I do about this?"

Rule 8.3(a) requires lawyers to report misconduct of other lawyers under certain circumstances. Lawyers sometimes call this the "squeal rule," which should tell you something about how popular it is. (Judges are under a similar obligation. Code of Judicial Conduct §2.15.) The Rules require reporting misconduct only if it raises "a substantial question as to [another] lawyer's honesty, trustworthiness or fitness as a lawyer." The Code had no such limitation.

The Rules excuse reporting if the basis for a lawyer's knowledge is confidential information as defined in Rule 1.6. It will be unusual for a lawyer to have knowledge of another lawyer's unethical conduct that is *not* based on protected information, won't it? Yet it will happen. Matter of Riehlmann, 891 So.2d 1239 (La. 2005), reprimanded a lawyer who failed to report a close friend's confession that as a prosecutor the friend had once suppressed exculpatory evidence. (Did you get that? The rule requires you to betray a close friend. Indeed, the text would require you to tattle on an adult child, parent, or even a spouse. There is no exception for other privileged relationships.) A lawyer must report knowledge that a colleague has stolen from clients or the firm, for example. Peter Rofes navigates the relationship between the reporting and the confidentiality duties in Another Misunderstood Relation: Confidentiality and the Duty to Report, 14 Geo. J. Legal Ethics 621 (2001). He discerns "a disturbing inability of courts and ethics panels to integrate the confidentiality exception successfully into the decisional and advisory law of the reporting duty" and proposes a detailed reformulation of Rule 8.3(c) to enable lawyers and judges "to work through the thorny issues" created by the current rule.

The duty to report another lawyer's misconduct was honored mostly in the breach, so far as one can tell, until in 1988 the Illinois Supreme Court suspended a lawyer for one year for failure to comply with his Code obligation to report another lawyer's misconduct. In re Himmel, 533 N.E.2d 790 (Ill. 1988). This opinion roused the profession because of the dearth, if not the complete absence, of public discipline (let alone a suspension) for violating the reporting obligation theretofore. So far *Himmel* stands nearly alone. It has started no stampede of court decisions publicly punishing lawyers for failures to report. In Illinois, however, lawyers learning of misconduct by other lawyers have on occasion taken to asking third lawyers to advise whether they have a reporting obligation. Negative advice has sometimes taken the form of letters, inevitably called "*Himmel* letters," which the inquiring lawyer can file away should anyone challenge a decision not to report.

Further, *Himmel* may have contained extenuating circumstances. Himmel represented a client whose funds (about $23,000) had been converted by a lawyer named Casey. Himmel negotiated a deal by which Casey would pay the client $75,000, and the client would not report Casey for discipline or criminal prosecution. Himmel, who stood to get a third of the negotiated sum, was suspended for not reporting Casey. So Himmel did not simply fail to act. He exploited another lawyer's professional exposure as a negotiation tactic that would net him a disproportionate settlement and a large fee. So viewed, *Himmel* is not a "plain vanilla" nonreporting case. The opinion might therefore have caused lawyers less anxiety except that the Illinois court did not rely on these added facets in determining the proper discipline.

Himmel argued that his client did not want him to report Casey. Obviously, a promise not to report was a valuable bargaining chip for the client. Reporting, indeed, might have made it impossible for the client to get anything. (She eventually got about $10,000. Himmel got nothing.) The court held, however, that a defense based on the client's direction had "no legal support."

Himmel's knowledge of Casey's violation was a secret, but not a confidence (because the client gave Himmel the information with a third person present), and therefore it was not protected under the attorney-client privilege. Under the code, which Illinois then had, reporting was obligatory if the lawyer's knowledge was merely an unprivileged secret. Rule 8.3, by contrast, subordinates the reporting duty to all information protected by Rule 1.6. Which result is correct? Under the Rules, may a lawyer use the threat to report misconduct to negotiate a better deal? See page 526. Illinois has since adopted a version of the Model Rules, but its version of Rule 8.3 continues to require reporting if the information is not privileged. Skolnick v. Altheimer & Gray, 730 N.E.2d 4 (Ill. 2000). See also the "Terminology" section of the Illinois rules.

Subordinate lawyers enjoy a "following orders" defense if directed to do something arguably improper, so long as the supervisor's conclusion is "reasonable." Rule 5.2(b). That defense would also seem to relieve the subordinate of the duty to report the supervisor. If, however, a supervisor directs a subordinate lawyer to do something clearly wrong — destroy a subpoenaed letter or perhaps backdate a document — the subordinate will not be able to rely on a "following orders" defense. What's more, the subordinate will be obligated to report the supervisor if she "knows" that the supervisor has proceeded with the unethical plan and her knowledge is not confidential. If the conduct violates a duty to a client, the subordinate's fiduciary obligation will require her to insure that the firm tells the client. Conn. Op. 96-20 (1996) (associate who has learned that another associate has misrepresented information on client bills must, after talking to managing partner, report the other associate; the duty is not delegable); D.C. Opinion 270 (1997) (lawyer who learns that his boss is deceiving clients must ensure that the boss informs the clients of the deception and report the boss without revealing confidential information).

5. Defenses

Earlier editions of this book began this section with these sentences: "Realistically speaking, there are no defenses. Or, rather, there is one: The lawyer did not do it, whatever the 'it' might be. But as a statistical matter, if a case gets as far as a hearing, that defense is not likely to be true." Not so, says, Kenneth M. Mogill, of Mogill, Posner & Cohen in Detroit, and an adjunct professor at Wayne State University Law School. He explains:

> While it's true that in many attorney discipline cases the charges are well-grounded, it is also true that in many the charges are entirely defensible on the facts or the law. In my experience, which includes practicing in this field for many years, it is not at all unusual for the Grievance Commission's charges to be legally or factually flawed: Either the evidence adduced at a hearing fails to support what the Commission asserts or the charges of the formal complaint seek to impose discipline based on a strained and incorrect application of the rules. Even in cases where some charged misconduct is established, it is not unusual for the evidence to be insufficient as to other charged misconduct. In addition, there are from time to time in Michigan substantial legal skirmishes as to the application of otherwise well-settled notions of due process to attorney discipline proceedings, including, inter alia, the scope of a lawyer's First Amendment rights and the application of the void-for-vagueness doctrine.

Point taken. My earlier comments were based on my experience in the 1980s serving on the disciplinary committee in New York City and were, I believe (hope?), factually correct for that time and place. Be that as it may, I don't discount the incidence of overcharging (and other deficiencies) in disciplinary cases, just as happens in criminal prosecutions.

Lawyers commonly cite stress, depression, substance abuse, obsessive-compulsive behavior, or other psychological problems to explain what they characterize as aberrant behavior. These defenses will rarely avoid discipline, but they may affect the sanction. Why should that be? If disciplinary sanctions are intended to protect the public, not punish the lawyer, shouldn't these defenses instead underscore the need for a tough sanction? Another mitigating factor lawyers will submit (if true) is their "unblemished record," a phrase that regularly appears in disciplinary opinions, and a pro bono work history. Courts often credit those factors in determining sanction.

Recall that, in discussing bar admission, we discovered that the Americans with Disabilities Act has been held to limit what bar examiners may ask applicants about prior treatment for psychological problems. The ADA has also been invoked by lawyers charged with disciplinary violations. Here, it has worked less well. Although courts have held that the ADA applies to state disciplinary proceedings against lawyers, its application will not prevent discipline. People v. Reynolds, 933 P.2d 1295 (Colo. 1997). Although *Reynolds* refused to apply the ADA to prevent discipline, it did rely on the lawyer's depression to reduce the severity of the sanction. Similarly, in State v. Busch, 919 P.2d 1114 (Okla. 1996), the court declined to apply the ADA despite the respondent's attention deficit disorder, but it did rely on that syndrome in determining the proper sanction.

Courts are skeptical about allowing a lawyer's alcoholism or substance abuse to reduce the severity of a sanction that might otherwise be appropriate for particular misconduct. After canvassing cases nationwide, Attorney Grievance Commn. of Maryland v. Kenney, 664 A.2d 854 (Md. 1995), cautioned that "absent truly compelling circumstances, alcoholism will not be permitted to mitigate where an attorney commits a violation of ethical or legal rules which would ordinarily warrant disbarment." The court relied on its obligation "to protect the public from being victimized." Similarly, courts have refused to recognize other kinds of substance abuse in mitigation. In re Marshall, 762 A.2d 530 (D.C. App. 2000) (cocaine addiction did not prevent disbarment for misappropriation of client funds and submitting false documents) (collecting cases).

Courts do sometimes entertain claims of depression or other mental disorder in mitigation. Lawyer Disciplinary Bd. v. Dues, 624 S.E.2d 125 (2005) (severe depression mitigates sanction for 39 violations; public reprimand plus certain limits on practice); Cincinnati Bar Assn. v. Stidham, 721 N.E.2d 977 (Ohio 2000) (major "depression [having] severe and debilitating effect on . . . ability to function as an attorney" results in suspension rather than disbarment for mishandling escrow account); Cleveland Bar Assn. v. Knowlton, 689 N.E.2d 538 (Ohio 1998) ("sleep apnea disorder," described as "a disease which causes sleepiness and impairs judgment and ability to concentrate," results in suspension instead of disbarment for misappropriation of client funds). But see Disciplinary Counsel v. Parker, 876 N.E.2d 556 (Ohio 2007) ("narcissistic personality disorder," though recognized, is not a defense to charges of dishonesty and bias and bullying as a municipal court judge); Iowa Supreme Court Board of Professional Ethics and Conduct v. Adams, 623 N.W.2d 815 (Iowa 2001) (court does "not recognize" depression and alcoholism "as an excuse for unethical conduct").

Occasionally, a mental disorder that sounds preposterous partly succeeds. In People v. Lujan, 890 P.2d 109 (Colo. 1995), a lawyer attributed her theft of funds from her law firm to her compulsion to shop. (Yes, that's right.) The court chose to suspend, rather than disbar, her because it was persuaded that her compulsion was real and the product of a serious accident abroad followed by criminal violence against her.

Remember our law professor who surreptitiously changed student evaluations to increase his chance to get a chair? Iowa Supreme Court Attorney Disciplinary Bd. v. Kress, supra. Here is how the court treated his defense of "delirium, due to out of control diabetes, complicated by mental illness."

Once the Board has shown an intentional act of fraud, dishonesty, deceit, or misrepresentation, the affirmative defenses of insanity or mental incapacity are unavailable. While insanity is a recognized defense in criminal proceedings, it is not recognized in attorney disciplinary proceedings. Certainly, where fraudulent, deceitful, or dishonest acts occur, claims that the attorney was acting as a result of mental aberration or amnesia depriving him or her of the ability to distinguish between right and wrong are of no avail. See, e.g., In re Hoover, 155 Ariz. 192, 745 P.2d 939, 945-46 (1987) (holding that manic depressive could not assert as a complete defense his inability to distinguish right from wrong in case involving misappropriation of client funds); La. State Bar Ass'n v. Theard, 222 La. 328, 62 So.2d 501, 503 (1952) (holding that insanity defense was not available where attorney engaged in forgery and conversion of client funds even though he had no recollection of events); In re Houtchens, 555 S.W.2d 24, 26 (Mo.1977) (holding that attorney who converted client funds who suffered from pscyhotemporal epilepsy reflected in periodic amnesia, disorientation, and confusion could not raise defense of severe mental or physical problems); In re Fallick, 247 A.D. 176, 286 N.Y.S. 581, 583 (1936) (holding that a lawyer who converted funds but suffered from mental illness and lapse of memory was subject to sanction). But see In re Conduct of Holman, 297 Or. 36, 682 P.2d 243, 261 (1984) (holding that heavy alcohol abuse and addiction to prescription drugs showed lack of appreciation of ethical violation necessary to support violation of ethical rule prohibiting conduct involving dishonesty).

The principal reason for refusing to accept affirmative defenses based on mental health is the need to protect the public from dishonest acts of lawyers regardless of their mental health status. The primary purpose of attorney discipline is to protect the public, not mete out punishment.

6. *Disciplinary Procedures*

In broad outline, disciplinary procedures are much alike in all jurisdictions. See ABA, Model Rules for Lawyer Disciplinary Enforcement, at abanet.org/cpr. Although many details vary among jurisdictions, the Due Process Clause of the Fourteenth Amendment mandates a certain uniformity. Even when discipline is summarily imposed, as in *DCD Programs*, page 783, the Due Process Clause will entitle the lawyer to certain safeguards, such as notice and (usually) a hearing. The Supreme Court described the notice requirement this way in In re Ruffalo, 390 U.S. 544 (1968):

Disbarment, designed to protect the public, is a punishment or penalty imposed on the lawyer. He is accordingly entitled to procedural due process, which includes fair notice of the charge. It was said in Randall v. Brigham, [74 U.S.] 523, 540 [1868], that when proceedings for disbarment are "not taken for matters occurring in open court, in the presence of the judges, notice should be given to the attorney of the charges made and opportunity afforded him for explanation and defence." Therefore, one of the conditions this Court considers in determining whether disbarment by a State should be followed by disbarment here is whether "the state procedure from want of notice or opportunity to be heard was wanting in due process."

In the present case petitioner had no notice that his employment of Orlando would be considered a disbarment offense until *after* both he and Orlando had testified at length on all the material facts pertaining to this phase of the case. As Judge Edwards, dissenting below, said, "Such procedural violation of due process would never pass muster in any normal civil or criminal litigation."

These are adversary proceedings of a quasi-criminal nature. The charge must be known before the proceedings commence. They become a trap when, after they are underway, the charges are amended on the basis of testimony of the accused. He can then be given no opportunity to expunge the earlier statements and start afresh.

Ruffalo was from Ohio. Another Ohio lawyer, named Zauderer, whom we shall meet again when we discuss marketing by lawyers in chapter 16, placed a newspaper ad to represent persons accused of driving while intoxicated. He also advertised for clients injured by their use of the Dalkon Shield, an intrauterine birth control device. He was charged with misconduct for both ads.

The first ad said the client would not have to pay a fee if he was convicted of DWI. Disciplinary counsel charged that this was a contingent fee, forbidden in criminal matters. The state court eventually upheld discipline for this ad but on another theory, recommended by the board that conducted the hearing: It was misleading because rarely did a DWI charge result in a DWI conviction. Zauderer complained that the change in theories denied him notice. The Supreme Court disagreed in Zauderer v. Office of Disciplinary Counsel, 471 U.S. 626 (1985):

Finally, we address appellant's argument that he was denied procedural due process by the manner in which discipline was imposed on him in connection with his drunken driving advertisement. Appellant's contention is that the theory relied on by the Ohio Supreme Court and its Board of Commissioners as to how the advertisement was deceptive was different from the theory asserted by the Office of Disciplinary Counsel in its complaint. We cannot agree that this discrepancy violated the constitutional guarantee of due process.

Under the law of Ohio, bar discipline is the responsibility of the Ohio Supreme Court. The Board of Commissioners on Grievances and Discipline formally serves only as a body that recommends discipline to the Supreme Court; it has no authority to impose discipline itself. That the Board of Commissioners chose to make its recommendation of discipline on the basis of reasoning different from that of the Office of Disciplinary Counsel is of little moment: what is important is that the Board's recommendations put appellant on notice of the charges he had to answer to the satisfaction of the Supreme Court of Ohio. Appellant does not contend that he was afforded no opportunity to respond to the Board's recommendation; indeed, the Ohio rules appear to provide ample opportunity for response to Board recommendations, and it appears that appellant availed himself of that opportunity.[17]

---

17. Appellant suggests that he was prejudiced by his inability to present evidence relating to the Board's factual conclusion that it was a common practice for persons charged with drunken driving to plead guilty to lesser offenses. If this were in fact the case, appellant's due process objection might be more forceful. But appellant does not—and probably cannot—seriously dispute that guilty pleas to lesser offenses are common in drunken driving cases, nor does he argue that he was precluded from arguing before the Ohio Supreme Court that it was improper for the Board of Commissioners to take judicial notice of the prevalence of such pleas. Under these circumstances, we see no violation of due process in the Ohio Supreme Court's acceptance of the Board's factual conclusions.

In dissent, Justice Brennan, joined by Justice Marshall, wrote that Zauderer had no opportunity to introduce evidence contradicting the theory of liability first adopted by the board and the court after the case had been heard.

With regard to the Dalkon Shield ad, Zauderer said that the client would have to pay a fee only if there were a recovery. But he failed to say that clients would have to pay *costs* in any event. The Ohio rule did not explicitly require lawyers to include this disclaimer in contingent fee ads. Even the Ohio Supreme Court's opinion in Zauderer's own case left the content of the disclaimer requirement unclear. Zauderer therefore complained that he had not been given notice of what he was required to say in his ad. (Zauderer had presented the ad to the disciplinary office for clearance before he ran it, but that office disclaimed authority to advise him.) Justice White characterized the lack of notice as "unfortunate." Citing *Ruffalo*, he wrote that "it may well be that for Ohio actually to disbar an attorney on the basis of its disclosure requirements as they have been worked out to this point would raise significant due process concerns." Nevertheless, the Court saw "no infirmity in a decision to issue a public reprimand." Justices Brennan and Marshall dissented on this point as well.

In addition to a right to notice, other due process rights that must be granted before a state may impose discipline are as follows: (1) an opportunity to confront the evidence against the respondent attorney and to cross-examine witnesses; see Willner v. Committee on Character & Fitness, 373 U.S. 96 (1963); (2) the right to present witnesses and argument on one's own behalf; In re Ginger, 372 F.2d 620 (6th Cir. 1967); (3) the right to assert the privilege against self-incrimination; Spevack v. Klein, 385 U.S. 511 (1967); and (4) the right to have the facts determined and the sanction imposed by an impartial body; see Morrissey v. Brewer, 408 U.S. 471 (1972), and Gagnon v. Scarpelli, 411 U.S. 778 (1973). All jurisdictions appear to give an accused attorney the right to be represented by retained counsel at disciplinary proceedings, although the Supreme Court has never had an opportunity to consider whether this right is constitutionally compelled. Compare In re Gault, 387 U.S. 1 (1967), in which the Court held that a juvenile charged with delinquency has a right to retained or appointed counsel. The Supreme Court has cited *Gault* by analogy in describing the nature of the disciplinary proceeding. *Ruffalo*, 390 U.S. at 551.

The majority view is that the disciplining body has the burden of proving the facts justifying discipline by clear and convincing evidence, although the precise articulation of the standard varies. The minority standard is only a fair preponderance of the evidence. In re Capoccia, 453 N.E.2d 497 (N.Y. 1983). The Fifth Circuit has held that clear and convincing evidence is needed to disbar a lawyer in federal court. In re Medrano, 956 F.2d 101 (5th Cir. 1992). But this is not constitutionally required. In re Barach, 540 F.3d 82 (1st Cir. 2008) (finding the preponderance standard sufficient). Once a finding of probable cause is made, most states now open the disciplinary process to the public, whether or not the lawyer consents. Rules forbidding the complainant publicly to reveal the fact or content of her complaint have been held to violate the First Amendment. R.M. v. Supreme Court, 883 A.2d 369 (N.J. 2005) (also holding that an ethics complaint and statements made in the disciplinary process enjoy absolute immunity); Doe v. Doe, 127 S.W.3d 728 (Tenn. 2004).

7. Discipline in a Federal System

The U.S. Supreme Court has held that "[w]hile a lawyer is admitted into a federal court by way of a state court, he is not automatically sent out of the federal court by the same route." Theard v. United States, 354 U.S. 278 (1957). Each judicial system has "autonomous control over the conduct of [its] lawyers." A state court determination of disbarment, therefore, "is not conclusively binding on the federal courts." See also, In re Barach, supra, which discusses the question in suspending a lawyer from federal court following state suspension.

Although a state court is not obligated to impose the same discipline another state has imposed, it often does. See In re Kaufman, 406 A.2d 972 (N.J. 1979). Occasionally a state or federal court will opt for a different (often lesser) sanction from what a state or federal court previously imposed. In re Weissman, 524 A.2d 1141 (Conn. 1987) (federal discipline, one year; state imposes one month); In re Evans, 533 A.2d 243 (D.C. 1987) (Maryland federal court imposed disbarment; D.C. Court of Appeals imposes public censure); In re McCabe, 583 N.E.2d 233 (Mass. 1991) (no state discipline of lawyer whose five-year suspension in federal court in Louisiana was affirmed by the Fifth Circuit). See also page 658 for discussion of federal/state issues in the context of bar admission.

A rare example of possible conflict between state ethics rules and federal law arose in the discussion of prosecutorial contact with targets of investigations. See page 126. Matter of Howes, 940 P.2d 159 (N.M. 1997), censured a member of the New Mexico bar who violated its "no-contact" rule (Rule 4.2) while acting as an assistant U.S. Attorney in a federal prosecution in the Superior Court of the District of Columbia. You cannot have a case with more federalism issues than that. Compare Rand v. Monsanto Co., 926 F.2d 596 (7th Cir. 1991) (Fed. R. Civ. P. 23 superior to state's prohibition against lawyer assuming court costs).

With the increase in multistate practice, one question that arises is whether a state may discipline an out-of-state lawyer for conduct that may harm a state resident, even if the lawyer is not admitted to that state's bar and never enters the state. Lawyer Disciplinary Board v. Allen, 479 S.E.2d 317 (W. Va. 1996), holds that a state does have the constitutional power to impose discipline on the out-of-state lawyer in these circumstances. In the particular case, discipline was rejected because of the text of the state's jurisdictional rule at the time. But the court left no doubt that even a single improper client solicitation of an in-state resident by an out-of-state lawyer could subject that lawyer to the state's disciplinary machinery. Of course, the forum state may only censure the out-of-state lawyer. It may not suspend or disbar her because she's not a member of its bar. See also cases at page 661.

If a federal lawyer is charged with discipline before a state body for conduct "under color" of his or her federal office, removal to federal court may be available. Kolibash v. Committee on Legal Ethics, 872 F.2d 571 (4th Cir. 1989). The federal court provides a neutral forum for adjudication of the state ethics complaint. In *Kolibash*, the complainant charged that the respondent, a federal prosecutor, had participated in the prosecution of the complainant after having represented him as a private defense lawyer with regard to the same underlying conduct.

Jeffrey Parness examines discipline in a federal system in Enforcing Professional Norms for Federal Litigation Conduct: Achieving Reciprocal Cooperation, 60 Alb. L. Rev. 303 (1996). He finds that "existing norms governing lawyer conduct during federal litigation are poorly enforced, in part because of the lack of reciprocal cooperation between available norm enforcers." He offers "suggestions on achieving better coordination." Confronting a related but distinct issue that has so far escaped solution — exemplified by the battle over the Reno rules and the Thornburgh memorandum (see page 127) — is Bruce Green, Whose Rules of Professional Conduct Should Govern Lawyers in Federal Court and How Should the Rules Be Created?, 64 Geo. Wash. L. Rev. 460 (1996).

E.   CONSTITUTIONAL PROTECTION IN CRIMINAL CASES

The Sixth Amendment guarantees criminal defendants "the assistance of counsel." This guarantee has been interpreted to mean that counsel must be "effective." McMann v. Richardson, 397 U.S. 759 (1970). The right is enjoyed by defendants who retain counsel or have counsel appointed for them. Cuyler v. Sullivan, 446 U.S. 335 (1980). A convicted defendant whose counsel is proved to be ineffective and whose case was prejudiced thereby will be entitled to have the conviction overturned. After Evitts v. Lucey, 469 U.S. 387 (1985), the guarantee of effective assistance of counsel applies to counsel on a first appeal too. The material here describes the standards for determining the effective assistance of counsel and the remedies when those standards are violated. One common basis for a claim of ineffectiveness is that counsel was conflicted. That basis, and the remedies particular to it, were discussed at chapter 5B1 and are referenced again in Strickland v. Washington, below.

Some overlap must be expected between the levels of performance required by the Sixth Amendment, by the law of malpractice, and by the ethical duty of competence, but these are still distinct concepts. The main reason they are distinct is that effective assistance of counsel is a constitutional guarantee and applies uniformly nationwide. Malpractice and ethical rules are determined by each jurisdiction for itself. The constitutional guarantee applies only in criminal cases and protects the defendant only, whereas other mechanisms to encourage or remedy professional defaults apply to all lawyers and in all kinds of cases.

Looking at the issue institutionally, we might expect judges to be more hesitant to find a lawyer's conduct ineffective when the result is that a conviction must be upset and a new trial held (assuming that is still possible) than they will be to allow a jury to award civil damages against a lawyer. Courts might also be expected to be highly deferential toward a criminal defense lawyer's decisions (even, as we shall see, when the decision is to do nothing).

As with malpractice, the ineffectiveness claim, even if proved, will not lead to a remedy unless there is a causal relationship between the professional failure and injury to the client. In malpractice, we have seen that that requirement draws on the common law proximate cause standard (see page 728). In Sixth Amendment challenges (which usually come in a collateral attack on the judgment but may come in a direct appeal as well), the injury requirement generally obligates the convicted defendant to demonstrate, with some degree of confidence, that but for the lawyer's mistakes he would have fared better in the criminal trial or appeal. Where the ineffectiveness claim is based on a conflict, *Cuyler* eased the prejudice burden. Sometimes, we are certain enough of the likelihood of prejudice, either because of experience or for reasons of principle, that the defendant need not prove prejudice at all, as for example when the person defending him was not actually a lawyer.

As you can see, a legal system that guarantees the effective assistance of counsel will have a lot of questions to answer. Imagine that you are hired to create an enlightened criminal justice system for a new society with a federal system. You mean to guarantee the effective assistance of counsel in criminal cases. You will need to answer the following questions, keeping in mind the legitimate interests of the accused and of society (which includes the justice system):

- Who, the convicted defendant or the state, must prove ineffectiveness or its opposite?
- What is the burden of proof? More likely than not? Clear and convincing evidence? Beyond a reasonable doubt?
- What is the standard for ineffectiveness? You can't require perfection because rarely is a trial perfect. Just as a lawyer will not be liable in malpractice for errors of judgment, neither can you make every such error the equivalent of ineffectiveness, even if the error might *conceivably* have made a difference, can you. Nor can you rest on the different ethical or malpractice standards of the various states. A constitution needs a national standard. So what do you do? In answering this question, keep in mind
  (a) why counsel is guaranteed in the first place. You need to know that in order to know if counsel was ineffective;
  (b) the costs to the defendant or society of making the standard too easy or too hard to satisfy; and
  (c) the impossibility of anticipating the many acts or failures to act that may later be challenged as ineffective or the precise contexts in which these acts or failures may arise. The fact that prediction and precision are difficult counsels a general standard. But the fact that many judges will have to apply the standard in a multiplicity of circumstances requires that it have adequate content to guide them and to promote consistency.
- What is the causation requirement? Or maybe you don't need one. Maybe you should just say that if counsel is proved ineffective, the defendant should always get a new trial because it is not possible to know how a trial might have gone had counsel not made the mistake that rose to the level of ineffectiveness. Alternatively, you could (perhaps rebuttably) presume prejudice for some kinds of errors and require proof of it for other kinds. But which errors will fall into which categories? For example, what should the system do if a convicted defendant proves that he "paid" his lawyer with the publication rights to his story? See page 227. Or that his lawyer was actually suspended from practice while defending him? Or that

his lawyer, unaware of a recent case, failed to raise an obvious defense (like a statutory speedy trial right) that would have resulted in dismissal but is now waived? Should a defendant who shows any of these have to show anything else before getting a new trial?

- If you decide that prejudice (along with proof of ineffectiveness) will sometimes be required, you must allocate and identify the burden of proof on prejudice too. Who must prove or disprove prejudice and by what quantum? (Will the answers here turn on the reason for the ineffectiveness?) You will also have to define "prejudice." Should it suffice that without the ineffectiveness the verdict could (would probably?) have been different regardless of factual guilt?

- We have been making a critical and unstated assumption that the way to remedy ineffectiveness in the assistance of counsel in criminal cases is to review the work of counsel *after* the case is over. Is this the best (or only) way to do it? Why not take steps in advance of trial to increase the likelihood that counsel *will be* effective? Of course, your system may already do that to some extent when it licenses attorneys. But maybe you can reduce the risk of ineffectiveness in a more focused way, *immediately* before the event, rather than long before it (back when the lawyer took the bar examination) or when the case is over. By taking preventive measures you may avoid ineffectiveness that would otherwise occur. You also reduce the prospect that a judge may have to upset a conviction and order a new trial, a result that has high institutional costs and that may discourage judges from finding ineffectiveness in the first place, despite serious doubts. Are there good reasons to rely nearly exclusively on case "autopsies" in lieu of pretrial precautions?

That concludes our questions, but before we attempt answers, consider how the courts of appeals defined the standard of ineffectiveness before the 1970s. In Trapnell v. United States, 725 F.2d 149 (2d Cir. 1983), the Second Circuit was faced with a claim of ineffective assistance. It wrote:

> Before examining appellant's specific contentions, we discuss the appropriate standard of competence for a defendant's attorney in a criminal trial. In the Second Circuit, that standard has been governed for over thirty years by the rule laid down in United States v. Wight, 176 F.2d 376, 379 (2d Cir. 1949), cert. denied, 338 U.S. 950 (1950): "A lack of effective assistance of counsel must be of such a kind as to shock the conscience of the court and make the proceedings a farce and mockery of justice." In *Wight*, this court adopted the standard first formulated by Judge Thurman Arnold for the D.C. Circuit in Diggs v. Welch, 148 F.2d 667, 670 (D.C. Cir.), cert. denied, 325 U.S. 889 (1945).

By 1970 every circuit had adopted the "farce and mockery" standard, if indeed it can even be called a standard. But in the next decade every circuit except the Second Circuit moved to a "reasonably competent assistance" test or its equivalent. In *Trapnell*, the Second Circuit joined them. The large majority of state courts also adopted some form of the "reasonably competent assistance" standard. See Note, A Functional Analysis of the Effective Assistance of Counsel, 80 Colum. L. Rev. 1053 (1980) (authored by Bruce Green).

The Supreme Court decided Strickland v. Washington and United States v. Cronic, both below, in 1984. In *Strickland,* the Court answered some of the questions we presented above. In *Cronic,* the Court applied the *Strickland* standard to the recurring problem of a defense lawyer given only a few weeks to prepare a case that the government may have been planning for months or years.

Think about this question as you read: A judge or prosecutor comes to believe that defense counsel is in way over his head, missing evidentiary objections and procedural motions to protect his client. What should she do?

STRICKLAND v. WASHINGTON
466 U.S. 668 (1984)

[The respondent challenged his death sentence on the ground that the lawyer who represented him at the sentencing hearing was constitutionally ineffective. In most states, the sentence in a capital case is decided by a jury. Whoever sentences, a hearing is held at which evidence in mitigation and aggravation is elicited. Because, as Justice O'Connor wrote, a capital sentencing hearing is "like a trial in its adversarial format and in the existence of standards for decision," her opinion for the Court applies both to such hearings and to trials. It expressly does not address the standards of performance at ordinary sentencing hearings. The case is less important for the immediate holding than for its description of a defendant's two burdens when seeking to prove ineffective assistance of counsel and especially for its decision to rely on the assumptions behind the adversary system as the basis for its conclusions. Applying its newly minted test to the case before it, the Court held that defense counsel's choice of the information he would offer at the sentencing hearing were strategic and reasonable and that, in any event, the defendant could not prove prejudice.]

III

A convicted defendant's claim that counsel's assistance was so defective as to require reversal of a conviction or death sentence has two components. First, the defendant must show that counsel's performance was deficient. This requires showing that counsel made errors so serious that counsel was not functioning as the "counsel" guaranteed the defendant by the Sixth Amendment. Second, the defendant must show that the deficient performance prejudiced the defense. This requires showing that counsel's errors were so serious as to deprive the defendant of a fair trial, a trial whose result is reliable. Unless a defendant makes both showings, it cannot be said that the conviction or death sentence resulted from a breakdown in the adversary process that renders the result unreliable.

A

As all the Federal Courts of Appeals have now held, the proper standard for attorney performance is that of reasonably effective assistance. The Court indirectly recognized as much when it stated in McMann v. Richardson, [397 U.S. 759 (1970)], at 770, 771, that a guilty plea cannot be attacked as based on inadequate legal advice unless counsel was not "a reasonably competent attorney" and the advice was not "within the range of competence demanded of attorneys in criminal cases." When a convicted defendant complains of the ineffectiveness of counsel's assistance, the defendant must show that counsel's representation fell below an objective standard of reasonableness.

More specific guidelines are not appropriate. The Sixth Amendment refers simply to "counsel," not specifying particular requirements of effective assistance. It relies instead on the legal profession's maintenance of standards sufficient to justify the law's presumption that counsel will fulfill the role in the adversary process that the Amendment envisions. The proper measure of attorney performance remains simply reasonableness under prevailing professional norms.

Representation of a criminal defendant entails certain basic duties. Counsel's function is to assist the defendant, and hence counsel owes the client a duty of loyalty, a duty to avoid conflicts of interest. From counsel's function as assistant to the defendant derive the overarching duty to advocate the defendant's cause and the more particular duties to consult with the defendant on important decisions and to keep the defendant informed of important developments in the course of the prosecution. Counsel also has a duty to bring to bear such skill and knowledge as will render the trial a reliable adversarial testing process.

These basic duties neither exhaustively define the obligations of counsel nor form a checklist for judicial evaluation of attorney performance. In any case presenting an ineffectiveness claim, the performance inquiry must be whether counsel's assistance was reasonable considering all the circumstances. Prevailing norms of practice reflected in American Bar Association [Standards for Criminal Justice] and the like are guides to determining what is reasonable, but they are only guides. No particular set of detailed rules for counsel's conduct can satisfactorily take account of the variety of circumstances faced by defense counsel or the range of legitimate decisions regarding how best to represent a criminal defendant. Any such set of rules would interfere with the constitutionally protected independence of counsel and restrict the wide latitude counsel must have in making tactical decisions. See United States v. Decoster, 624 F.2d [196 (D.C. Cir. 1979)], at 208. Indeed, the existence of detailed guidelines for representation could distract counsel from the overriding mission of vigorous advocacy of the defendant's cause. Moreover, the purpose of the effective assistance guarantee of the Sixth Amendment is not to improve the quality of legal representation, although that is a goal of considerable importance to the legal system. The purpose is simply to ensure that criminal defendants receive a fair trial.

Judicial scrutiny of counsel's performance must be highly deferential. It is all too tempting for a defendant to second-guess counsel's assistance after conviction or adverse sentence, and it is all too easy for a court, examining counsel's defense after it has proved unsuccessful, to conclude that a particular act or omission of counsel was unreasonable. A fair assessment of attorney performance requires that every effort be made to eliminate the distorting effects of hindsight, to reconstruct the circumstances of counsel's challenged conduct, and to evaluate the conduct from counsel's perspective at the time. Because of the difficulties inherent in making the evaluation, a court must indulge a strong presumption that counsel's conduct falls within the wide range of reasonable professional assistance; that is, the defendant must overcome the presumption that, under the circumstances, the challenged action "might be considered sound trial strategy." There are countless ways to provide effective assistance in any given case. Even the best criminal defense attorneys would not defend a particular client in the same way. See Goodpaster, The Trial for Life: Effective Assistance of Counsel in Death Penalty Cases, 58 N.Y.U. L. Rev. 299, 343 (1983).

The availability of intrusive post-trial inquiry into attorney performance or of detailed guidelines for its evaluation would encourage the proliferation of ineffectiveness challenges. Criminal trials resolved unfavorably to the defendant would increasingly come to be followed by a second trial, this one of counsel's unsuccessful defense. Counsel's performance and even willingness to serve could be adversely affected. Intensive scrutiny of counsel and rigid requirements for acceptable assistance could dampen the ardor and impair the independence of defense counsel, discourage the acceptance of assigned cases, and undermine the trust between attorney and client.

Thus, a court deciding an actual ineffectiveness claim must judge the reasonableness of counsel's challenged conduct on the facts of the particular case, viewed as of the time of counsel's conduct. A convicted defendant making a claim of ineffective assistance must identify the acts or omissions of counsel that are alleged not to have been the result of reasonable professional judgment. The court must then determine whether, in light of all the circumstances, the identified acts or omissions were outside the wide range of professionally competent assistance. In making that determination, the court should keep in mind that counsel's function, as elaborated in prevailing professional norms, is to make the adversarial testing process work in the particular case. At the same time, the court should recognize that counsel is strongly presumed to have rendered adequate assistance and made all significant decisions in the exercise of reasonable professional judgment.

These standards require no special amplification in order to define counsel's duty to investigate, the duty at issue in this case. As the Court of Appeals concluded, strategic choices made after thorough investigation of law and facts relevant to plausible options are virtually unchallengeable; and strategic choices made after less than complete investigation are reasonable precisely to the extent that reasonable professional judgments support the limitations on investigation. In other words, counsel has a duty to make reasonable investigations or to make a reasonable decision that makes particular investigations unnecessary. In any ineffectiveness case, a particular decision not to investigate must be directly assessed for reasonableness in all the circumstances, applying a heavy measure of deference to counsel's judgments.

The reasonableness of counsel's actions may be determined or substantially influenced by the defendant's own statements or actions. Counsel's actions are usually based, quite properly, on informed strategic choices made by the defendant and on information supplied by the defendant. In particular, what investigation decisions are reasonable depends critically on such information. For example, when the facts that support a certain potential line of defense are generally known to counsel because of what the defendant has said, the need for further investigation may be considerably diminished or eliminated altogether. And when a defendant has given counsel reason to believe that pursuing certain investigations would be fruitless or even harmful, counsel's failure to pursue those investigations may not later be challenged as unreasonable. In short, inquiry into counsel's conversations with the defendant may be critical to a proper assessment of counsel's investigation decisions, just as it may be critical to a proper assessment of counsel's other litigation decisions.

B

An error by counsel, even if professionally unreasonable, does not warrant setting aside the judgment of a criminal proceeding if the error had no effect on the judgment. The purpose of the Sixth Amendment guarantee of counsel is to ensure that a defendant has the assistance necessary to justify reliance on the outcome of the proceeding. Accordingly, any deficiencies in counsel's performance must be prejudicial to the defense in order to constitute ineffective assistance under the Constitution.

In certain Sixth Amendment contexts, prejudice is presumed. Actual or constructive denial of the assistance of counsel altogether is legally presumed to result in prejudice. So are various kinds of state interference with counsel's assistance. Prejudice in these circumstances is so likely that case-by-case inquiry into prejudice is not worth the cost. Moreover, such circumstances involve impairments of the Sixth Amendment right that are easy to identify and, for that reason and because the prosecution is directly responsible, easy for the government to prevent.

One type of actual ineffectiveness claim warrants a similar, though more limited, presumption of prejudice. In Cuyler v. Sullivan, 446 U.S., at 345-350, the Court held that prejudice is presumed when counsel is burdened by an actual conflict of interest. In those circumstances, counsel breaches the duty of loyalty, perhaps the most basic of counsel's duties. Moreover, it is difficult to measure the precise effect on the defense of representation corrupted by conflicting interests. Given the obligation of counsel to avoid conflicts of interest and the ability of trial courts to make early inquiry in certain situations likely to give rise to conflicts, see, e.g., Fed. Rule Crim. Proc. 44(c), it is reasonable for the criminal justice system to maintain a fairly rigid rule of presumed prejudice for conflicts of interest. Even so, the rule is not quite the per se rule of prejudice that exists for the Sixth Amendment claims mentioned above. Prejudice is presumed only if the defendant demonstrates that counsel "actively represented conflicting interests" and "that an actual conflict of interest adversely affected his lawyer's performance." Cuyler v. Sullivan, supra, at 350, 348 (footnote omitted).

Conflict of interest claims aside, actual ineffectiveness claims alleging a deficiency in attorney performance are subject to a general requirement that the defendant affirmatively prove prejudice. The government is not responsible for, and hence not able to prevent, attorney errors that will result in reversal of a conviction or sentence. Attorney errors come in an infinite variety and are as likely to be utterly harmless in a particular case as they are to be prejudicial. They cannot be classified according to likelihood of causing prejudice. Nor can they be defined with sufficient precision to inform defense attorneys correctly just what conduct to avoid. Representation is an art, and an act or omission that is unprofessional in one case may be sound or even brilliant in another. Even if a defendant shows that particular errors of counsel were unreasonable, therefore, the defendant must show that they actually had an adverse effect on the defense.

It is not enough for the defendant to show that the errors had some conceivable effect on the outcome of the proceeding. Virtually every act or omission of counsel would meet that test, and not every error that conceivably could have influenced the outcome undermines the reliability of the result of the proceeding. Respondent suggests requiring a showing that the errors "impaired the presentation of the defense." That standard, however, provides no workable principle. Since any error, if it is indeed an error, "impairs" the presentation of the defense, the proposed standard is inadequate because it provides no way of deciding what impairments are sufficiently serious to warrant setting aside the outcome of the proceeding.

On the other hand, we believe that a defendant need not show that counsel's deficient conduct more likely than not altered the outcome in the case. This outcome-determinative standard has several strengths. It defines the relevant inquiry in a way familiar to courts, though the inquiry, as is inevitable, is anything but precise. The standard also reflects the profound importance of finality in criminal proceedings. Moreover, it comports with the widely used standard for assessing motions for new trial based on newly discovered evidence. Nevertheless, the standard is not quite appropriate.

Even when the specified attorney error results in the omission of certain evidence, the newly discovered evidence standard is not an apt source from which to draw a prejudice standard for ineffectiveness claims. This high standard for newly discovered evidence claims presupposes that all the essential elements of a presumptively accurate and fair proceeding were present in the proceeding whose result is challenged. An ineffective assistance claim asserts the absence of one of the crucial assurances that the result of the proceeding is reliable, so finality concerns are somewhat weaker and the appropriate standard of prejudice should be somewhat lower. The result of a proceeding can be rendered unreliable, and hence the proceeding itself unfair, even if the errors of counsel cannot be shown by a preponderance of the evidence to have determined the outcome.

Accordingly, the appropriate test for prejudice finds its roots in the test for materiality of exculpatory information not disclosed to the defense by the prosecution, and in the test for materiality of testimony made unavailable to the defense by Government deportation of a witness. The defendant must show that there is a reasonable probability that, but for counsel's unprofessional errors, the result of the proceeding would have been different. A reasonable probability is a probability sufficient to undermine confidence in the outcome.

In making the determination whether the specified errors resulted in the required prejudice, a court should presume, absent challenge to the judgment on grounds of evidentiary insufficiency, that the judge or jury acted according to law. . . .

In making this determination, a court hearing an ineffectiveness claim must consider the totality of the evidence before the judge or jury. Some of the factual findings will have been unaffected by the errors, and factual findings that were affected will have been affected in different ways. Some errors will have had a pervasive effect on the inferences to be drawn from the evidence, altering the entire evidentiary picture, and some will have had an isolated, trivial effect. Moreover, a verdict or conclusion only weakly supported by the record is more likely to have been affected by errors than one with overwhelming record support. Taking the unaffected findings as a given, and taking due account of the effect of the errors on the remaining findings, a court making the prejudice inquiry must ask if the defendant has met the burden of showing that the decision reached would reasonably likely have been different absent the errors. . . .

[Justice Brennan concurred in the Court's standards. Justice Marshall dissented from both the performance standards and the prejudice standard.]

Inadequate Time to Prepare

UNITED STATES v. CRONIC*
466 U.S. 648 (1984)

[Cronic received a 25-year sentence for mail fraud involving the transfer of more than $9 million. The Court of Appeals reversed on the ground that Cronic was denied the effective assistance of counsel. Cronic's lawyer had been appointed on June 12, 1980. A week later counsel asked for a 30-day continuance of the trial, then scheduled to begin June 30. The trial court granted a 25-day continuance instead. The Supreme Court held that these facts alone could not support a finding of ineffectiveness in the particular case. "This case is not one in which the surrounding circumstances make it unlikely that the defendant could have received the effective assistance of counsel. . . . Respondent can therefore make out a claim of ineffective assistance only by pointing to specific errors made by trial counsel." In the course of his opinion for the Court, Justice Stevens wrote:]

The substance of the Constitution's guarantee of the effective assistance of counsel is illuminated by reference to its underlying purpose. "[Truth]," Lord Eldon said, "is best discovered by powerful statements on both sides of the question." This dictum describes the unique strength of our system of criminal justice. "The very premise of our adversary system of criminal justice is that partisan advocacy on both sides of a case will best promote the ultimate objective that the guilty be convicted and the innocent go free." It is that "very premise" that underlies and gives meaning to the Sixth Amendment. It "is meant to assure fairness in the adversary criminal process." Unless the accused receives the effective assistance of counsel, "a serious risk of injustice infects the trial itself."

Thus, the adversarial process protected by the Sixth Amendment requires that the accused have "counsel acting in the role of an advocate." The right to the effective assistance of counsel is thus the right of the accused to require the prosecution's case to survive the crucible of meaningful adversarial testing. When a true adversarial criminal trial has been conducted — even if defense counsel may have made demonstrable errors — the kind of testing envisioned by the Sixth Amendment has occurred. But if the process loses its character as a confrontation between adversaries, the constitutional guarantee is violated. . . .

While the Court of Appeals purported to apply a standard of reasonable competence, it did not indicate that there had been an actual breakdown of the adversarial process during the trial of this case. Instead it concluded that the

---

* *Cronic* is one of those cases where the name of the litigant resonates with the issue before the court — inadequate time. Loving v. Virginia (striking miscegenation laws) is another example.

circumstances surrounding the representation of respondent mandated an inference that counsel was unable to discharge his duties.

In our evaluation of that conclusion, we begin by recognizing that the right to the effective assistance of counsel is recognized not for its own sake, but because of the effect it has on the ability of the accused to receive a fair trial. Absent some effect of challenged conduct on the reliability of the trial process, the Sixth Amendment guarantee is generally not implicated. Moreover, because we presume that the lawyer is competent to provide the guiding hand that the defendant needs, the burden rests on the accused to demonstrate a constitutional violation. There are, however, circumstances that are so likely to prejudice the accused that the cost of litigating their effect in a particular case is unjustified.

Most obvious, of course, is the complete denial of counsel. The presumption that counsel's assistance is essential requires us to conclude that a trial is unfair if the accused is denied counsel at a critical stage of his trial. Similarly, if counsel entirely fails to subject the prosecution's case to meaningful adversarial testing, then there has been a denial of Sixth Amendment rights that makes the adversary process itself presumptively unreliable. No specific showing of prejudice was required in Davis v. Alaska, 415 U.S. 308 (1974), because the petitioner had been "denied the right of effective cross-examination" which " 'would be constitutional error of the first magnitude and no amount of showing of want of prejudice would cure it.' "

Circumstances of that magnitude may be present on some occasions when although counsel is available to assist the accused during trial, the likelihood that any lawyer, even a fully competent one, could provide effective assistance is so small that a presumption of prejudice is appropriate without inquiry into the actual conduct of the trial. Powell v. Alabama, 287 U.S. 45 (1932), was such a case.*

The defendants had been indicted for a highly publicized capital offense. Six days before trial, the trial judge appointed "all the members of the bar" for purposes of arraignment. "Whether they would represent the defendants thereafter if no counsel appeared in their behalf, was a matter of speculation only, or, as the judge indicated, of mere anticipation on the part of the court." On the day of trial, a lawyer from Tennessee appeared on behalf of persons "interested" in the defendants, but stated that he had not had an opportunity to prepare the case or to familiarize himself with local procedure, and therefore was unwilling to represent the defendants on such short notice. The problem was resolved when the court decided that the Tennessee lawyer would represent the defendants, with whatever help the local bar could provide.

"The defendants, young, ignorant, illiterate, surrounded by hostile sentiment, haled back and forth under guard of soldiers, charged with an atrocious crime regarded with especial horror in the community where they were to be tried, were thus put in peril of their lives within a few moments after counsel for the first time charged with any degree of responsibility began to represent them."

---

* This was the *Scottsboro* case. — Ed.

This Court held that "such designation of counsel as was attempted was either so indefinite or so close upon the trial as to amount to a denial of effective and substantial aid in that regard." The Court did not examine the actual performance of counsel at trial, but instead concluded that under these circumstances the likelihood that counsel could have performed as an effective adversary was so remote as to have made the trial inherently unfair. *Powell* was thus a case in which the surrounding circumstances made it so unlikely that any lawyer could provide effective assistance that ineffectiveness was properly presumed without inquiry into actual performance at trial.

But every refusal to postpone a criminal trial will not give rise to such a presumption. In Avery v. Alabama, 308 U.S. 444 (1940), counsel was appointed in a capital case only three days before trial, and the trial court denied counsel's request for additional time to prepare. Nevertheless, the Court held that since evidence and witnesses were easily accessible to defense counsel, the circumstances did not make it unreasonable to expect that counsel could adequately prepare for trial during that period of time. Similarly, in Chambers v. Maroney, 399 U.S. 42 (1970), the Court refused "to fashion a per se rule requiring reversal of every conviction following tardy appointment of counsel." Thus, only when surrounding circumstances justify a presumption of ineffectiveness can a Sixth Amendment claim be sufficient without inquiry into counsel's actual performance at trial. . . .

Some Reasons for Ineffectiveness Claims

Cronic was remanded to give the defendant a chance to demonstrate specific errors. On remand, the Tenth Circuit found such errors, vacated the conviction, and ordered a new trial. United States v. Cronic, 839 F.2d 1401 (10th Cir. 1988).

The Supreme Court's *Strickland* test means that most ineffectiveness claims will have to be analyzed individually rather than categorically. It should come as no surprise that courts are highly deferential to strategies later attacked as ineffective. If a lawyer chooses to do something and does it, it is rare that he will be found wanting. For example, a lawyer who interviews the alibi witnesses the client has identified, finds their credibility doubtful, and chooses not to call them will not likely be constitutionally deficient even if the decision was tactically misguided.

On the other hand, if the lawyer never bothered to interview the alibi witnesses at all, a Sixth Amendment challenge has a good chance of succeeding. (We saw the same pattern in discipline, where inaction may result in sanction for neglect while errors of commission are usually left to malpractice.) Harris v. Reed, 894 F.2d 871 (7th Cir. 1990), draws this omission/commission distinction and then finds a lawyer ineffective where he failed to interview eyewitnesses whose testimony could have exonerated the accused. The court was not impressed by counsel's purported strategy of relying instead on weaknesses in the state's case.

A lawyer will be constitutionally ineffective if he fails to follow a defendant's express instructions to file a notice of appeal. Failure to consult with a convicted defendant about whether he wants to appeal may, but will not always, constitute ineffectiveness, depending on the context. Roe v. Flores-Ortega, 528 U.S. 470

(2000). A lawyer's failure to investigate and present substantial mitigating evidence at the sentencing phase of a death penalty trial is constitutionally ineffective counsel. Williams v. Taylor, 529 U.S. 362 (2000). The Supreme Court has endorsed the distinction between investigating and then making a (perhaps misguided but not incompetent) strategic decision based on the results of an appropriate investigation, on the one hand, and failing to conduct the investigation needed to make that decision, on the other. It reversed a death sentence in Wiggins v. Smith, 539 U.S. 510 (2003), where counsel did not introduce mitigating evidence — of which there was much — at the penalty phase of the case. While that decision might be tactically defensible if counsel knew about the evidence and then chose not to use it, here counsel made their decision after an inadequate investigation that left them ignorant of the extent of the mitigating evidence. Failure to convey a plea-bargain offer is ineffective counsel. Cottle v. State, 733 So. 2d 963 (Fla. 1999) (also holding that the defendant had no burden to prove that the plea bargain would have been accepted). Failure to counsel a defendant who wishes to reject a plea offer on the wisdom of accepting it is also ineffective. Boria v Keane, 99 F.3d 492 (2d Cir. 1996).

Sometimes, ineffectiveness is attributed to the fact that the defendant's lawyer was in fact not a lawyer. This may be true for several reasons. First, the "lawyer" may have been suspended or disbarred before or during the trial. Second, the "lawyer," though a law school graduate, may never have been admitted to the bar of any jurisdiction. Third, the "lawyer" may never have gone to law school. Decisions in pre-*Strickland* cases varied, but they generally agreed that if the "lawyer" was never admitted to a bar, then the defendant's Sixth Amendment right would have been violated and prejudice would be presumed. See Solina v. United States, 709 F.2d 160 (2d Cir. 1983) (Friendly, J.) (historical discussion of meaning of "counsel"). Citing *Solina* and reviewing case law in the area, United States v. Novak, 903 F.2d 883 (2d Cir. 1990), vacated a conviction where the defense lawyer, though a member of the bar at the time of trial, was later disbarred after the discovery that he had gained admission by fraudulently claiming he was entitled to a waiver of the bar examination requirement.

Another kind of claim is that defense counsel, though indeed a lawyer qualified to practice in the jurisdiction, was for some reason not present during a part of the trial. In Javor v. United States, 724 F.2d 831 (9th Cir. 1984), the lawyer was dozing during "a substantial part of [a multidefendant] trial . . . including some occasions when evidence relevant to the prosecution case against defendant . . . was being elicited." The court held that the defendant's right to counsel had been denied and presumed prejudice. Burdine v. Johnson, 262 F.3d 336 (5th Cir. 2001) (en banc), got a great deal of press attention, perhaps because it was a capital case in which the Fifth Circuit initially upheld the conviction and death sentence even though defense counsel repeatedly slept during the trial. A sharply divided en banc court later vacated the conviction. The defense lawyer in Siverson v. O'Leary, 764 F.2d 1208 (7th Cir. 1985), was not present during jury deliberations, nor when the verdict was returned. The court characterized these events as critical stages of the proceedings. But it found the failure harmless. Wright v. Van Patten, 128 S.Ct. 743 (2008), rejected a collateral attack on a conviction where the defense lawyer appeared at the plea hearing via speaker phone, not in person. The Court held not unreasonable the Wisconsin Supreme Court's conclusion that a speaker phone appearance was consistent with *Cronic's* requirement of presence during every critical stage of the proceeding.

A final way in which counsel may be "absent" is when she is awake in the courtroom but does little or nothing during the trial. Sometimes a court characterizes this conduct (or lack of conduct) as a "silent strategy" and refuses to second-guess counsel. See Warner v. Ford, 752 F.2d 622 (11th Cir. 1985). Other courts have been less charitable. Martin v. Rose, 744 F.2d 1245 (6th Cir. 1984) (lawyer's lack of participation deprived client of effective assistance; no proof of prejudice required). Rompilla v. Beard, 545 U.S. 374 (2005), found ineffectiveness where the defense lawyer failed to review a capital defendant's criminal record (contained in the courthouse file) even though he knew that the prosecutor was going to rely on it in support of a death sentence. As a result, he did not discover mitigating information that he could have presented to the court.

Morris v. Slappy: Effectiveness Does Not Include Rapport

In Morris v. Slappy, 461 U.S. 1 (1983), Slappy's court-appointed lawyer was hospitalized for emergency surgery shortly before Slappy's trial for serious felonies was about to begin. The public defender assigned substitute counsel. On the first day of trial and thereafter, Slappy appeared to protest the change in counsel. There was no claim that the new lawyer was constitutionally ineffective. The trial judge made no effort to ascertain how long the first lawyer would be unavailable. After Slappy was convicted, the Ninth Circuit granted his petition for a writ of habeas corpus on the ground that the Sixth Amendment guaranteed Slappy not merely competent counsel but also "the right to a meaningful attorney-client relationship." The Supreme Court unanimously agreed that the issue had not been preserved for review because Slappy had not made a timely motion for a continuance and to be represented by the first lawyer. Five members of the Court, in an opinion by Chief Justice Burger, went on to consider the merits of Slappy's argument, which they rejected in one sentence: "No court could possibly guarantee that a defendant will develop the kind of rapport with his attorney — privately retained or provided by the public — that the Court of Appeals thought part of the Sixth Amendment guarantee of counsel." Justice Brennan, joined by Justice Marshall, dissented on the merits.

In *Cronic*, Justice Stevens wrote that in response to a claim of ineffective assistance,

> the appropriate inquiry focuses on the adversarial process, not on the accused's relationship with his lawyer as such. If counsel is a reasonably effective advocate, he meets constitutional standards irrespective of his client's evaluation of his performance. [Jones v. Barnes, page 89; Morris v. Slappy.] It is for this reason that we attach no weight to either respondent's expression of satisfaction with counsel's performance at the time of his trial, or to his later expression of dissatisfaction.

Sometimes the rapport may be so bad that the Sixth Amendment right is offended. The Ninth Circuit held that ineffective assistance was established when the client could prove that his appointed lawyer made racial slurs against him and threatened a poor defense unless the client agreed to plead guilty. Frazer v. United States, 18 F.3d 778 (9th Cir. 1994). But an indigent defendant's "distrust" of the assigned public defender was insufficient to win relief on ineffectiveness grounds. Plumlee v. Masto, 512 F.3d 1204 (9th Cir. 2008) (en banc).

The Ineffectiveness Test in a System of Procedural Defaults

Recall that we initially posited an effectiveness standard for a *federal* system. Perhaps our system envisions federal judicial review of state convictions where the state defendant alleges a denial of federal constitutional rights. Call it a petition for a writ of habeas corpus. When we studied the lawyer's status as the client's agent in chapter 2B, we discovered that a lawyer's decisions, even mistaken ones, will generally bind the client. This is the rule in criminal cases too, where a lawyer's failure to raise a defendant's constitutional claims in state court will generally be a procedural default that will prevent the defendant from later raising those claims in a federal collateral attack. This will be true even if counsel's failure was the product of "ignorance or inadvertence," Murray v. Carrier, 477 U.S. 478 (1986), and the defendant was not responsible for it. "[T]he mere fact that counsel failed to recognize the factual or legal basis for a claim, or failed to raise the claim despite recognizing it, does not constitute cause for [excusing] a procedural default."

A defendant will not, however, be bound by a lawyer's procedural default if the lawyer was constitutionally ineffective. So the harder it is to prove ineffectiveness, the more unforgiving will be the system of procedural defaults. How should that fact affect our articulation of the Sixth Amendment standard? Should it matter if the defense lawyer was retained or assigned? (It doesn't.) Should it matter if the case is a capital one? Lawrence v. Florida, 549 U.S. 327 (2007) ("Lawrence argues that his counsel's mistake in miscalculating the limitations period entitles him to equitable tolling. If credited, this argument would essentially equitably toll limitations periods for every person whose attorney missed a deadline. Attorney miscalculation is simply not sufficient to warrant equitable tolling, particularly in the postconviction context where prisoners have no constitutional right to counsel")(capital case), citing Coleman v. Thompson, 501 U.S. 722 (1991) (federal habeas review foreclosed to death row inmate where counsel filed state appeal from state collateral attack *three days late*; ineffective assistance claim rejected because defendant had no constitutional right to counsel on appeal from state collateral attack).

An Ounce of Prevention?

We conclude by returning to the final question posed at page 810: Given what you have just read, would it make sense to incorporate some preventive measures that will reduce the incidence of ineffectiveness? In United States v. Decoster, 624 F.2d 196 (D.C. Cir. 1979) (en banc), dissenting Judge Bazelon, joined by Judge Wright, proposed a more active role for the trial judge in criminal cases as a way of guarding against ineffective assistance of counsel. The majority characterized Judge Bazelon's suggestion as constituting a "drastic overhaul" and concluded that he had not "made a case" for it. Following is a portion of Judge Bazelon's lengthy dissent. What do you think of his proposal?

> Because, as this case demonstrates, ineffective representation is often rooted in inadequate preparation, a first step that a trial judge can take is to refuse to allow a trial to begin until he is assured that defense counsel has conducted the necessary factual and legal investigation. The simple question, "Is defense ready?" may be insufficient to provide that assurance. Instead, we should consider formalizing the procedure by which the trial judge is informed about the extent of counsel's preparation. Before the trial begins — or before a guilty plea is accepted — defense counsel could submit an investigative checklist certifying that he has conducted a complete investigation and reviewing the steps he has taken in pretrial preparation, including what records were obtained, which witnesses were interviewed, when the defendant was consulted, and what motions were filed. Although a worksheet alone cannot assure that adequate preparation is undertaken, it may reveal gross violations of counsel's obligations; at a minimum, it should heighten defense counsel's sensitivity to the need for adequate investigation and should provide a record of counsel's asserted actions for appeal.
>
> The trial judge's obligation does not end, however, with a determination that counsel is prepared for trial. Whenever during the course of the trial it appears that defense counsel is not properly fulfilling his obligations, the judge must take appropriate action to prevent the deprivation of the defendant's constitutional rights. "It is the judge, not counsel, who has the ultimate responsibility for the conduct of a fair and lawful trial."
>
> My colleagues fear that judicial "inquiry and standards [may] tear the fabric of [our] adversary system." But for so very many indigent defendants, the adversary system is already in shreds. Indeed, until judges are willing to take the steps necessary to guarantee the indigent defendant "the reasonably competent assistance of an attorney acting as his diligent conscientious advocate," we will have an adversary system in name only. The adversary system can "provide salutary protection for the rights of the accused" only if both sides are equally prepared for the courtroom confrontation.
>
> Some of my colleagues are also concerned that a wide-ranging inquiry into the conduct of defense counsel would transform the role of the trial judge. To emphasize the supposed hazards of such a result, the majority refers to the warning of Judge Prettyman in Mitchell v. United States [259 F.2d 787 (D.C. Cir.), cert. denied, 358 U.S. 850 (1958)]: "If the trial judge were required, after a trial has been concluded, to judge the validity of the trial by appraising defense decisions, he would also be under an obligation to protect those rights of an accused as the trial progressed." Yet this is the very role that the Constitution has assigned the trial judge. His is the ultimate responsibility for ensuring that the accused receives a fair trial, with all the attendant safeguards of the Bill of Rights. It is no answer to say that defense counsel will fulfill the function of protecting the accused's interest; the very essence of the defendant's complaint is that he has been denied effective assistance of counsel. The trial judge simply cannot "stand idly by while the fundamental rights of a criminal defendant are forfeited through the inaction of ill-prepared counsel."

Judge Bazelon's recommendations have not found support in the Supreme Court. Justice O'Connor (page 812) cites the ABA Standards for Criminal

Justice, but she eschews adoption of a "set of rules" for defense counsel, in part because they "would interfere with the constitutionally protected independence of counsel and restrict the wide latitude counsel must have in making tactical decisions." She fears that such rules would also "distract counsel from the over-riding mission of vigorous advocacy of the defendant's cause," citing the *Decoster* majority opinion. Conversely, apprehension about intruding upon a defense lawyer's tactical judgments or professional relationship with the accused disappear if after trial the defendant brings an ineffectiveness claim. Then, obviously, the professional relationship is over, and the defendant is inviting the court to review counsel's conduct.

Is Justice O'Connor justified in her concerns? Would Judge Bazelon's inquiry unduly intrude on a defense lawyer's performance? The great majority of criminal defendants are represented by appointed lawyers because they are unable to afford their own. Consequently, they have no choice of counsel. They must accept whomever the state assigns unless they can convince a court that there is good reason for a change. How, if at all, should this fact affect the analysis?

Systemic defects in the methods of appointing lawyers to represent indigents have occasionally led to prophylactic judicial intervention on the ground that the defects were likely to result in inadequate representation. In an unusual case, State v. Smith, 681 P.2d 1374 (Ariz. 1984), an Arizona county fulfilled its obligation to provide counsel to indigent defendants by requesting bids from all attorneys in the county. In 1982 to 1983 the county accepted the four lowest bidders (ranging from $24,000 to $34,400), each of whom was expected to handle one-quarter of the total case load, without limit. Bids were accepted without regard to the background or capabilities of the bidding attorney. The costs of investigators, paralegals, secretaries, and the like were expected to be assumed by the bidding attorney. The Arizona Supreme Court held the system in violation of the state and federal Constitutions because it resulted in an attorney being "so overburdened [that he] cannot adequately represent all his clients properly and be reasonably effective." The court faulted the system because it

> does not take into account the time that the attorney is expected to spend . . . does not provide for support costs [and] fails to take into account the competency of the attorney [and] the complexity of each case. . . . Even though in the instant case [this court does] not find inadequate representation, so long as the County . . . fails to take into account the items listed above, there will be an inference that the adequacy of representation is adversely affected by the system.

See also Recorder's Court Bar Assn. v. Wayne Circuit Court, 503 N.W.2d 885 (Mich. 1993) (fixed fee system for paying counsel for indigents in Wayne County held unreasonable); State v. Young, 172 P.3d 138 (N.M. 2007) (low compensation in complicated capital case denies effective counsel). For discussion of these issues, see Note, (Un)Luckey v. Miller: The Case for a Structural Injunction to Improve Indigent Defense Services, 101 Yale L.J. 481 (1991) (authored by Rodger Citron); Comment, Quality Control for Indigent Defense Contracts, 76 Cal. L. Rev. 1147 (1988) (authored by Meredith Nelson).

FURTHER READING

Professor Vivian Berger has written a thorough and critical analysis of the Supreme Court's work in this area, reviewing the cases discussed here and others. Vivian Berger, The Supreme Court and Defense Counsel: Old Roads, New Paths — A Dead End?, 86 Colum. L. Rev. 9 (1986). For the pre-*Strickland* views of a federal district judge, see William Schwarzer, Dealing with Incompetent Counsel — The Trial Judge's Role, 93 Harv. L. Rev. 633 (1980). Finally, two investigators, Professors Michael McConville and Chester Mirsky, have published a mammoth empirical study, unprecedented in scope, of the adequacy of representation of New York City indigents. Michael McConville & Chester Mirsky, Criminal Defense of the Poor in New York City, 15 N.Y.U. Rev. L. & Soc. Change 581 (1986-1987).

XIV

Control of Quality: Lay Participation in Law Business (and Law Firm Ancillary Services)

> At issue is the basic right to group legal action, a right first asserted in this Court by an association of Negroes seeking the protection of freedoms guaranteed by the Constitution. The common thread running through our decisions in NAACP v. Button, *Trainmen*, and *United Mine Workers* is that collective activity undertaken to obtain meaningful access to the courts is a fundamental right within the protection of the First Amendment.
>
> —Justice Black in United Transportation Union v.
> State Bar of Michigan (1971)

- *First Amendment Rights of Public Interest Firms and Unions*
- *Lay Investment in or Management of Law Firms*
- *Litigation Funding Companies*
- *Ancillary Legal Services*

This chapter could be subtitled: "Beware Nonlawyers. They Will Tempt You From the Straight and Narrow and Ruin Your Life. Beware."

In the mid-1920s, a group of people in Illinois organized the Motorists' Association of Illinois as a not-for-profit corporation. The association hired a staff of lawyers. The only work of the lawyers was to represent the 50,000 members of the association, without charge, in connection with certain court proceedings arising out of the operation of their automobiles. Each member of the association paid an annual membership fee. The Chicago Bar Association did not like this arrangement. (Why not?) It petitioned the court to forbid the motorists' group from continuing in business. The bar association contended that the motorists' group was practicing law without a license. True, the lawyers themselves were licensed to practice law in Illinois, but the motorists' association, which was providing legal services to its membership, was not licensed and so was allegedly in violation of the unauthorized practice statute. The Illinois Supreme Court agreed. Not only did it hold that the motorists' association was practicing law without a license, but the court went even further. It held that the state legislature was without power to allow the association to do so, since only the court could decide who was, and who was not, fit to engage in the practice of law. People ex rel. Chicago Bar Assn. v. Motorists' Assn., 188 N.E. 827 (Ill. 1933). See the discussion of the negative inherent powers doctrine, page 7. It is *possible* (but only possible) that if a similar effort were mounted today, the result would differ, at least in some states. This chapter will show why.

From an economic point of view, tolerance for group practice plans will likely affect the cost of legal services. If a hundred consumers interested in purchasing iPods or Toyotas offered to make all purchases from a single retailer, they would be able to command a much lower price than if each walked in separately. Group purchasing power should also work where the product is legal services. By hiring a relatively small number of attorneys on salary, the Illinois motorists could have reduced the cost of representation from what each would have to pay to retain a private lawyer. Doesn't the same principle explain why large corporations employ dozens or hundreds of lawyers on salary to represent and counsel the corporation, which is certainly permitted? Employed (salaried) lawyers are way cheaper than paying an outside law firm hundreds of dollars hourly for the same services. What's the difference between the a corporate employer and the Illinois association? There is a factual difference, of course, but should it make a legal difference? Today, the goal of the Illinois motorists (to manage legal costs) is addressed through insurance, which carries transaction costs (profit for the insurer, administrative costs). But, as we'll see, the same fundamental questions arise even there: May insurance companies do in defending its insureds what the Motorists' Association of Illinois could not do for its members — that is, hire salaried lawyers?

Although the material in this chapter is sometimes analyzed as raising "unauthorized practice" issues, in fact these issues are different from those present in the material on unauthorized practice at page 690. The earlier material mostly addressed competency risks that arise when persons who are not members of a state's bar perform work labeled the "practice of law." (Whether the work *should* be so labeled is a separate question.) By contrast, in the following pages we discuss legal work performed by lawyers admitted in the particular jurisdiction. There is no competency problem. But the lawyer will be working with, through, or under an organization or person not qualified to practice law. In other words, because the *vehicle* through which the legal service is delivered is not a law firm, regulators worry about the quality of the work. Why should that be? What difference does it make whether a lawyer works for a traditional law firm or some other kind of entity, like a motorists' association or an insurance company? Or even Wal-Mart? What if a big retailer offered customers legal services through hired lawyers, working out of cubicles located between the optometrist and the beauty salon? Get a will with your haircut or manicure.

When courts refuse to allow organizations whose owners or managers include nonlawyers to employ lawyers to work for the entity's clients, no matter how small the ownership interest or how modest the managerial authority, they may say it's because the organization is engaged in the unauthorized practice of law, although it is not a law firm. This tells us little. Nor does it explain why non-lawyers are excluded from owning or managing organizations that *are* law firms. Why can't Skadden Arps go public?

Sometimes courts and opponents of lay participation in the law industry (so to speak) will be more specific. They will cite the risk of a conflict of interest or a threat to confidentiality. Does lay participation increase those dangers, thereby justifying the ban? How great a risk do such conflicts pose? Why isn't the risk as great in a traditional law firm? In other contexts, we tolerate equivalent risks of conflict between the interests of lay intermediaries and the interests of clients. Consider, for example, the position of a corporation's house counsel who reports to an executive vice president. The lawyer depends on the good will of management for her job and assignments, but her client is the company. (See page 529.) Conflicts aside, what risks to the confidentiality of client information does lay management or ownership present? Nonlawyer law firm employees routinely get client confidences. Page 57.

Distrust of lay influence on lawyers especially threatened the work of public interest law offices, like the NAACP and the ACLU, and the lawyers who worked for them. These offices may include nonlawyer managers and board members. Unions that helped their members secure low cost legal counsel for routine matters, like worker's compensation claims, were also stymied by the ban on lay participation in the law industry. Both vehicles — public interest organizations and unions — had to fight to establish constitutional protection for their activities. Both had to overcome adversaries who cited client protection as their only concern. Many believed the true motives of these adversaries were instead political or financial. As a result of much litigation in the middle of the twentieth century, our tolerance for risks of conflicts of interest or to confidentiality now depends on the context in which the questions arise. Is the organization's goal political change (Part A1), cost-sharing (Part A2), or profit (Part B)? Which goal creates the greatest threat to the profession's core values? Which should receive the greatest protection?

Lines have blurred in two directions. Not only may nonlawyers seek to own or run organizations that sell or provide legal services (whether called "law firms" or something else), but law firms may seek to expand into areas that are, strictly speaking, not the practice of law. Here, tolerance for expansion has been greater, but not without expressions of anxiety. Blurred lines can disturb tranquility and the sense of (professional) identity. Some perceive threats to professionalism if law firms are permitted to offer services that are "ancillary" to the practice of law. These threats are viewed as especially heightened if the services are tendered in association with nonlawyers. For example, a law firm may offer clients and others legislative lobbying or economic forecasting services, either directly or through a separate business that the firm may (or may not) co-own with lobbyists or economists. Part C examines whether dangers that supposedly arise when nonlawyers own interests in or manage law firms resurface if lawyers market ancillary services, whether or not in affiliation with other professionals.

In reading the balance of this chapter, keep two themes in mind. Each theme has been prominent in discussion of these issues. First, the decision to allow lay participation in the provision of legal services for profit has potentially enormous economic consequences, both in terms of the cost of those services and the identity of those who share in the wealth. The full ramifications of changes in this area cannot possibly be anticipated. But it should not go unnoticed that if lay interests (and private capital) can compete with traditional law firms in buying legal talent (i.e., lawyers) and selling their knowledge to clients, competition on the "supply" side will grow. Second, money aside, any erosion of a clear distinction between the "law business" and "other business" will, in ways unpredictable, affect how lawyers think of themselves and how the public thinks of the bar. Who should make the decision about the degree of erosion we will tolerate? Lawyers? Judges? Legislators? These are not static, historical questions. Tolerance for (even acceptance of) lay participation in some parts of the law business has increased over the last half century, especially in the United Kingdom and Australia.

Spurred by the debate over multidisciplinary practice (page 849), Grace Giesel examines an antecedent question: Why do we forbid corporations to hire lawyers to represent the clients of the corporation? Ordinarily, the practice of law for profit can only be done through law partnerships or professional corporations or associations. But why? Professor Giesel questions whether the prohibition ever made sense, but even if it "had validity or served a beneficial purpose in the early years of the century, much has changed. These changes call the doctrine into question." In a lucid analysis going back to the origins of the prohibition, Professor Giesel concludes that "too much has changed for the corporate practice of law doctrine, lacking a solid rationale and logic, to continue to contribute to or control debate about changes and developments in the legal services market." Giesel, Corporations Practicing Law Through Lawyers: Why the Unauthorized Practice of Law Doctrine Should Not Apply, 65 Mo. L. Rev. 151 (2000).

The questions here are structural. They are not about what one lawyer owes one client in one representation. They are about who owns and can dispense the product called legal services. The answers have potentially enormous consequences to the rule of law (and access to advice), but the questions are not much discussed by lawyers, and the subject may be overlooked in some courses, given the need to address more immediate issues. So omission is no reflection on your syllabus. I have often omitted this chapter. But I'll never eliminate it. The topic is too important. Even if it's not assigned, you might want to spend a couple of discretionary hours with chapter 14.

Legislative History

The intriguing and revealing legislative history of these issues was characterized early on by fierce resistance to any lay participation in the delivery of legal services. Whether this hostility is best explained by perception of danger to clients (the stated reason), protection of professional identity, or economic fears is anyone's guess. Probably all three. But judicial and public criticism of that resistance ultimately forced a partial turnaround, though not a full about-face.

A draft of the Code of Professional Responsibility permitted a lawyer to participate in group legal services sponsored by a "professional association, trade association, labor union, or other bona fide, non-profit organization which, as an incident to its primary activities, furnishes, pays for, or recommends legal services furnished to its members or beneficiaries." In 1969, the ABA House of Delegates rejected the draft as too liberal. The final text permitted lawyers to participate in group legal services sponsored by a "non-profit organization . . . but *only* in those instances and *to the extent* that controlling constitutional interpretation at the time of the rendition of the services *requires* the allowance of such legal services activities, and only if [additional] conditions, unless prohibited by such interpretations, are met." (Emphasis added.)

This begrudging conclusion, reached after the decisions in NAACP v. Button, *Trainmen,* and *United Mine Workers,* all set out below, reveals that the organized bar was prepared to approve group practice only so far as the Constitution commanded it. Lawyers did not want "managed care" for clients.

Efforts were made to liberalize the restriction. In 1974, a more permissive provision passed, and the text of DR 2-103(D)(4) appeared in its final form. Early drafts of this rule had prohibited what have come to be known as "closed panel plans." These are plans under which a small number of lawyers, generally employed on a salary basis by the plan, are available to the beneficiaries of the plan. By contrast, an "open panel plan" is one in which the plan pays all or part of the fees of independent counsel selected by the beneficiary of the plan from a large (or the entire) pool of local lawyers. Closed panel plans, like the one attempted by the Motorists' Association of Illinois, tend to make legal services cheaper than open panel plans. Do you see why? DR 2-103(D)(4)(a) as adopted allowed closed panel plans but only if they are not for profit. DR 2-103(D)(4)(e) required that any such plan allow a beneficiary to hire an outside lawyer if he "so desires." The plan also had to provide the beneficiary with "appropriate relief" if the beneficiary decides to choose other counsel because representation by the plan's counsel "would be unethical, improper or inadequate under the circumstances." These encumbrances, especially given their ambiguities, made group plans more difficult to set up.

Many believed that the success of group legal services depended on the ability to use closed panel plans. Many lawyers argued against closed panel plans not, they maintained, because of the impact on fees or possible loss of clients, but rather because it was important for a client to be able to select his own lawyer, whose allegiance and loyalty were solely to the client, not to the operators of the plan. (Can't a plan member do that anyway?) DR 2-103(D)(4)(e) represented a vague compromise between these opposing views. For an article tracing the history of the development of this rule, see Note, Prepaid Legal Plans: A Glimpse of the Future, 47 Tenn. L. Rev. 148 (1979) (authored by Pamela Reeves).

In addition to DR 2-103(D)(4), separate provisions of the Model Code affected group legal practice by forbidding a lawyer to aid in the unauthorized practice of law (including by an organization), to divide a legal fee with a "nonlawyer," or to form a partnership with a "nonlawyer." DR 3-101, DR 3-102, and DR 3-103. Presumably DR 3-101 is not violated by a lawyer's affiliation with an organization that meets the requirements of DR 2-103(D)(4).

The Rules of Professional Conduct have a separate history. Notably, the January 1980 draft of the Model Rules provided as follows:

[7.5] A lawyer shall not practice with a firm in which an interest is owned or managerial authority is exercised by a nonlawyer, unless services can be rendered in conformity with the Rules of Professional Conduct. The terms of the relationship shall expressly provide that (a) there is no interference with the lawyer's independence of professional judgment or with the client-lawyer relationship; and (b) the confidences of clients are protected. . . .

The June 1982 draft continued this language substantially unchanged. But the Model Rules as finally adopted dropped it, and while there is still no direct equivalent to DR 2-103(D)(4), much of DR 3-101, DR 3-102, and DR 3-103 is now contained in Model Rules 5.4 and 5.5. See also DR 5-107, incorporated in part in Rule 5.4. What legitimate interest of the bar is served by provisions like Rules 5.4 and 5.5? What are the economic consequences of these rules, whether or not intended?

With regard to the last question, the following event has assumed mythic status in the history of lawyer regulation, although it is not a myth. It actually happened. Professor Geoffrey Hazard, who was the Reporter for the Kutak Commission (see page 10), described how it came to pass that proposed Rule 7.5 was dropped from the Model Rules pretty much on the eve of their adoption. "During the debate," he reported, "someone asked if [the] proposal would allow Sears, Roebuck to open a law office. When they found out it would, that was the end of the debate." David Kaplan, Want to Invest in a Law Firm?, Natl. L.J., Jan. 19, 1987. Yet do the Rules as adopted effectively exclude Sears? The Model Rules seem to permit lay participation in legal delivery systems, whether or not for profit, so long as the organizers do not make the strictly formal error of calling their business a law firm or a professional corporation. However, the courts may still declare the activity unauthorized law practice, as Illinois did with the Motorists' Association, in which case participation in the practice is also unethical.

A. NONPROFIT ENTITIES AND INTERMEDIARIES

1. Public Interest Organizations

The civil rights movement of the middle third of the twentieth century presented the first serious challenges to state laws aimed at curtailing lay influence in the attorney-client relationship. And for good reason. The movement was largely spearheaded by organizations that were run by lay people. The state laws made it difficult if not impossible for them to use litigation to advance their goals. Virginia had such a law. Although the state presented its statute as a neutral effort to protect clients, the timing of the law — it was passed soon after Brown v. Board of Education — belied that claim in the eyes of many. *Button* addresses but does not rely on a finding of segregationist motives, and as a result it attained broader influence than if it had. *Button*, though often overlooked today, in fact laid the foundation for the emergence of public interest law firms, which pursue social and political change in the courts. *Button* (and subsequent decisions) free those firms to behave in ways still forbidden to traditional firms. We'll see another example of this in *Primus* at page 942. *Primus*, which protected an ACLU cooperating lawyer against charges of improper solicitation, is very much the child of *Button*.

Button also introduces you to the common law offenses of champerty, barratry, and maintenance, ill-defined doctrines that continue to have an unpredictable (and, some argue, unfortunate) influence on innovations in the delivery of legal services. They are discussed in the ensuing note.

NAACP v. BUTTON
371 U.S. 415 (1963)

Justice Brennan delivered the opinion of the Court. . . .

[The NAACP sought to enjoin enforcement of certain Virginia laws. The NAACP's Virginia chapter, or Conference, had for over ten years "concentrated upon financing litigation aimed at ending racial segregation in the public schools of the Commonwealth." To this end, the association provided attorneys, whom it paid, to represent litigants challenging segregated schooling. "The actual conduct of assisted litigation is under the control of the attorney, although the NAACP continues to be concerned that the outcome of the lawsuit should be consistent with NAACP's policies. A client is free at any time to withdraw from an action."

In 1956, the Virginia legislature passed certain laws that would have made it more difficult for the NAACP to represent school desegregation plaintiffs. A federal court invalidated three chapters of these laws and ordered the NAACP to go to state court for authoritative interpretations of two remaining chapters. The state courts voided one of these chapters but upheld Chapter 33, which prohibited solicitation by "an agent for an individual or an organization which retains a lawyer in connection with an action to which it is not a party and in which it has no pecuniary right or liability." The Virginia Supreme Court of Appeals held that this amendment prohibited the NAACP's agents from soliciting persons to serve as plaintiffs in challenges to segregated education. Without plaintiffs, of course, no case could be brought. The law stymied the NAACP's ability to find plaintiffs. The Supreme Court granted review.]

II . . .

A

We meet at the outset the contention that "solicitation" is wholly outside the area of freedoms protected by the First Amendment. To this contention there are two answers. The first is that a State cannot foreclose the exercise of constitutional rights by mere labels. The second is that abstract discussion is not the only species of communication which the Constitution protects; the First Amendment also protects vigorous advocacy, certainly of lawful ends, against governmental intrusion. In the context of NAACP objectives, litigation is not a technique of resolving private differences; it is a means for achieving the lawful objectives of equality of treatment by all government, federal, state and local, for the members of the Negro community in this country. It is thus a form of political expression. Groups which find themselves unable to achieve their objectives through the ballot frequently turn to the courts. . . . And under the conditions of modern government, litigation may well be the sole practicable avenue open to a minority to petition for redress of grievances.

We need not, in order to find constitutional protection for the kind of cooperative, organizational activity disclosed by this record, whereby Negroes seek through lawful means to achieve legitimate political ends, subsume such activity under a narrow, literal conception of freedom of speech, petition or assembly. For there is no longer any doubt that the First and Fourteenth Amendments protect certain forms of orderly group activity. . . .

The NAACP is not a conventional political party; but the litigation it assists, while serving to vindicate the legal rights of members of the American Negro community, at the same time and perhaps more importantly, makes possible the distinctive contribution of a minority group to the ideas and beliefs of our society. For such a group, association for litigation may be the most effective form of political association.

B . . .

We read the decree of the Virginia Supreme Court of Appeals in the instant case as proscribing any arrangement by which prospective litigants are advised to seek the assistance of particular attorneys. No narrower reading is plausible. We cannot accept the reading suggested on behalf of the Attorney General of Virginia on the second oral argument that the Supreme Court of Appeals construed Chapter 33 as proscribing control only of the actual litigation by the NAACP after it is instituted. . . .

We conclude that under Chapter 33, as authoritatively construed by the Supreme Court of Appeals, a person who advises another that his legal rights have been infringed and refers him to a particular attorney or group of attorneys (for example, to the Virginia Conference's legal staff) for assistance has committed a crime, as has the attorney who knowingly renders assistance under such circumstances. There thus inheres in the statute the gravest danger of smothering all discussion looking to the eventual institution of litigation on behalf of the rights of members of an unpopular minority. . . . We cannot close our eyes to the fact that the militant Negro civil rights movement has engendered the intense resentment and opposition of the politically dominant white community of Virginia; litigation assisted by the NAACP has been bitterly fought. In such circumstances, a statute broadly curtailing group activity leading to litigation may easily become a weapon of oppression, however evenhanded its terms appear. Its mere existence could well freeze out of existence all such activity on behalf of the civil rights of Negro citizens. . . .

We hold that Chapter 33 as construed violates the Fourteenth Amendment by unduly inhibiting protected freedoms of expression and association. In so holding, we reject two further contentions of respondents. The first is that the Virginia Supreme Court of Appeals has guaranteed free expression by expressly confirming petitioner's right to continue its advocacy of civil rights litigation. But in light of the whole decree of the court, the guarantee is of purely speculative value. As construed by the court, Chapter 33, at least potentially, prohibits every cooperative activity that would make advocacy of litigation meaningful. If there is an internal tension between proscription and protection in the statute, we cannot assume that, in its subsequent enforcement, ambiguities will be resolved in favor of adequate protection of First Amendment rights. . . .

C

The second contention is that Virginia has a subordinating interest in the regulation of the legal profession, embodied in Chapter 33, which justifies limiting petitioner's First Amendment rights. Specifically, Virginia contends that the NAACP's activities in furtherance of litigation, being "improper solicitation" under the state statute, fall within the traditional purview of state regulation of professional conduct. However, the State's attempt to equate the activities of the NAACP and its lawyers with common-law barratry, maintenance and champerty, and to outlaw them accordingly, cannot obscure the serious encroachment worked by Chapter 33 upon protected freedoms of expression. The decisions of this Court have consistently held that only a compelling state interest in the regulation of a subject within the State's constitutional power to regulate can justify limiting First Amendment freedoms. . . .

However valid may be Virginia's interest in regulating the traditionally illegal practices of barratry, maintenance and champerty, that interest does not justify the prohibition of the NAACP activities disclosed by this record. Malicious intent was of the essence of the common-law offenses of fomenting or stirring up litigation. And whatever may be or may have been true of suits against government in other countries, the exercise in our own, as in this case, of First Amendment rights to enforce constitutional rights through litigation, as a matter of law, cannot be deemed malicious. Even more modern, subtler regulations of unprofessional conduct or interference with professional relations, not involving malice, would not touch the activities at bar; regulations which reflect hostility to stirring up litigation have been aimed chiefly at those who urge recourse to the courts for private gain, serving no public interest. . . .

Objection to the intervention of a lay intermediary, who may control litigation or otherwise interfere with the rendering of legal services in a confidential relationship, also derives from the element of pecuniary gain. Fearful of dangers thought to arise from that element, the courts of several States have sustained regulations aimed at these activities. We intimate no view one way or the other as to the merits of those decisions with respect to the particular arrangements against which they are directed. It is enough that the superficial resemblance in form between those arrangements and that at bar cannot obscure the vital fact that here the entire arrangement employs constitutionally privileged means of expression to secure constitutionally guaranteed civil rights.[26] There has been no showing of a serious danger here of professionally reprehensible conflicts of interest which rules against solicitation frequently seek to prevent. This is so partly because no monetary stakes are involved, and so there is no danger that the attorney will desert or subvert the paramount interests of his client to enrich himself or an outside sponsor. And the aims and interests of NAACP have not been shown to conflict with those of its members and non-member Negro litigants. . . .

Resort to the courts to seek vindication of constitutional rights is a different matter from the oppressive, malicious, or avaricious use of the legal process for purely private gain. Lawsuits attacking racial discrimination, at least in Virginia, are neither very profitable nor very popular. They are not an object of general competition among Virginia lawyers; the problem is rather one of an apparent dearth of lawyers who are willing to undertake such litigation. There has been neither claim nor proof that any assisted Negro litigants have desired, but have been prevented from retaining, the services of other counsel. We realize that an

26. Compare [ABA] Opinion 148, n.13, 19, at 312 (1957): "The question presented, with its implications, involves problems of political, social and economic character that have long since assumed the proportions of national issues, on one side or the other [of] which multitudes of patriotic citizens have aligned themselves. These issues transcend the range of professional ethics."

NAACP lawyer must derive personal satisfaction from participation in litigation on behalf of Negro rights, else he would hardly be inclined to participate at the risk of financial sacrifice. But this would not seem to be the kind of interest or motive which induces criminal conduct.

We conclude that although the petitioner has amply shown that its activities fall within the First Amendment's protections, the State has failed to advance any substantial regulatory interest, in the form of substantive evils flowing from petitioner's activities, which can justify the broad prohibitions which it has imposed. . . .

Reversed.

[JUSTICE DOUGLAS concurred. JUSTICE WHITE concurred in part and dissented in part.]

JUSTICE HARLAN, joined by JUSTICES CLARK and STEWART, dissenting. . . .

I

At the outset the factual premises on which the Virginia Supreme Court of Appeals upheld the application of Chapter 33 to the activities of the NAACP in the area of litigation, as well as the scope of that court's holding, should be delineated.

First, the lawyers who participate in litigation sponsored by petitioner are, almost without exception, members of the legal staff of the NAACP Virginia State Conference. (It is, in fact, against Conference policy to give financial support to litigation not handled by a staff lawyer.) As such, they are selected by petitioner, are compensated by it for work in litigation (whether or not petitioner is a party thereto), and so long as they remain on the staff, are necessarily subject to its directions. As the Court recognizes, it is incumbent on staff members to agree to abide by NAACP policies.

Second, it is equally clear that the NAACP's directions, or those of its officers and divisions, to staff lawyers cover many subjects relating to the form and substance of litigation. . . .

In short, as these and other materials in the record show, the form of pleading, the type of relief to be requested, and the proper timing of suits have to a considerable extent, if not entirely, been determined by the Conference in coordination with the national office.

Third, . . . the present record establishes that the petitioner does a great deal more than to advocate litigation and to wait for prospective litigants to come forward. In several instances, especially in litigation touching racial discrimination in public schools, specific directions were given as to the types of prospective plaintiffs to be sought, and staff lawyers brought blank forms to meetings for the purpose of obtaining signatures authorizing the prosecution of litigation in the name of the signer.

Fourth, there is substantial evidence indicating that the normal incidents of the attorney-client relationship were often absent in litigation handled by staff lawyers and financed by petitioner. Forms signed by prospective litigants have on occasion not contained the name of the attorney authorized to act. In many cases, whether or not the form contained specific authorization to that effect, additional counsel have been brought into the action by staff counsel. There were several litigants who testified that at no time did they have any personal dealings with the lawyers handling their cases nor were they aware until long after the event that suits had been filed in their names. This is not to suggest that the petitioner has been shown to have sought plaintiffs under false pretenses or by inaccurate statements. But there is no basis for concluding that these were isolated incidents, or that petitioner's methods of operation have been such as to render these happenings out of the ordinary. . . .

III

The interest which Virginia has here asserted is that of maintaining high professional standards among those who practice law within its borders. This Court has consistently recognized the broad range of judgments that a State may properly make in regulating any profession. But the regulation of professional standards for members of the bar comes to us with even deeper roots in history and policy, since courts for centuries have possessed disciplinary powers incident to the administration of justice.

The regulation before us has its origins in the long-standing common-law prohibitions of champerty, barratry, and maintenance, the closely related prohibitions in the Canons of Ethics against solicitation and intervention by a lay intermediary, and statutory provisions forbidding the unauthorized practice of law. The Court recognizes this formidable history, but puts it aside in the present case on the grounds that there is here no element of malice or of pecuniary gain, that the interests of the NAACP are not to be regarded as substantially different from those of its members, and that we are said to be dealing here with a matter that transcends mere legal ethics — the securing of federally guaranteed rights. But these distinctions are too facile. They do not account for the full scope of the State's legitimate interest in regulating professional conduct. For although these professional standards may have been born in a desire to curb malice and self-aggrandizement by those who would use clients and the courts for their own pecuniary ends, they have acquired a far broader significance during their long development.

First, with regard to the claimed absence of the pecuniary element, it cannot well be suggested that the attorneys here are donating their services, since they are in fact compensated for their work. Nor can it tenably be argued that petitioner's litigating activities fall into the accepted category of aid to indigent litigants. The reference is presumably to the fact that petitioner itself is a nonprofit organization not motivated by desire for financial gain but by public interest and to the fact that no monetary stakes are involved in the litigation.

But a State's felt need for regulation of professional conduct may reasonably extend beyond mere "ambulance chasing." . . .

Underlying this impressive array of relevant precedent is the widely shared conviction that avoidance of improper pecuniary gain is not the only relevant factor in determining standards of professional conduct. Running perhaps even deeper is the desire of the profession, of courts, and of legislatures to prevent any interference with the uniquely personal relationship between lawyer and client and to maintain untrammeled by outside influences the responsibility which the lawyer owes to the courts he serves.

When an attorney is employed by an association or corporation to represent individual litigants, two problems arise, whether or not the association is organized for profit and no matter how unimpeachable its motives. The lawyer becomes subject to the control of a body that is not itself a litigant and that, unlike the lawyers it employs, is not subject to strict professional discipline as an officer of the court. In addition, the lawyer necessarily finds himself with a divided allegiance — to his employer and to his client — which may prevent full compliance with his basic professional obligations. . . .

Second, it is claimed that the interests of petitioner and its members are sufficiently identical to eliminate any "serious danger" of "professionally reprehensible conflicts of interest." Support for this claim is sought in our procedural holding in NAACP v. Alabama ex rel. Patterson, 357 U.S. 449, 458-459 [1958]. But from recognizing, as in that case, that the NAACP has standing to assert the rights of its members when it is a real party in interest, it is plainly too large a jump to conclude that whenever individuals are engaged in litigation involving claims that the organization promotes, there cannot be any significant difference between the interests of the individual and those of the group.

The NAACP may be no more than the sum of the efforts and views infused in it by its members; but the totality of the separate interests of the members and others whose causes the petitioner champions, even in the field of race relations, may far exceed in scope and variety that body's views of policy, as embodied in litigating strategy and tactics. Thus it may be in the interest of the Association in every case to make a frontal attack on segregation, to press for an immediate breaking down of racial barriers, and to sacrifice minor points that may win a given case for the major points that may win other cases too. But in a particular litigation, it is not impossible that after authorizing action in his behalf, a Negro parent, concerned that a continued frontal attack could result in schools closed for years, might prefer to wait with his fellows a longer time for good-faith efforts by the local school board than is permitted by the centrally determined policy of the NAACP. Or he might see a greater prospect of success through discussions with local school authorities than through the litigation deemed necessary by the Association. The parent, of course, is free to withdraw his authorization, but is his lawyer, retained and paid by petitioner and subject to its directions on matters of policy, able to advise the parent with that undivided allegiance that is the hallmark of the attorney-client relation? I am afraid not. . . .

Third, it is said that the practices involved here must stand on a different footing because the litigation that petitioner supports concerns the vindication of constitutionally guaranteed rights.[12]

But surely state law is still the source of basic regulation of the legal profession, whether an attorney is pressing a federal or a state claim within its borders.

---

12. It is interesting to note the Court's reliance on [ABA] Opinion 148, Opinions of the Committee on Professional Ethics and Grievances, American Bar Assn. This opinion, issued in 1935 at the height of the resentment in certain quarters against the New Deal, approved the practice of the National Lawyers Committee of the Liberty League in publicly offering free legal services (without compensation from any source) to anyone who was *unable* to *afford* to challenge the constitutionality of legislation which he believed was violating his rights. The opinion may well be debatable as a matter of interpretation of the Canons. But in any event I think it wholly untenable to suggest (as the Court does in its holding today) that a contrary opinion regarding *paid* services to *nonindigent* litigants would be unconstitutional.

The true question is whether the State has taken action which unreasonably obstructs the assertion of federal rights. Here, it cannot be said that the underlying state policy is inevitably inconsistent with federal interests. The State has sought to prohibit the solicitation and sponsoring of litigation by those who have no standing to initiate that litigation themselves and who are not simply coming to the assistance of indigent litigants. Thus the state policy is not unrelated to the federal rules of standing — the insistence that federal court litigants be confined to those who can demonstrate a pressing personal need for relief. . . .

Maintenance, Barratry, Champerty, and Change: What Did *Button* Decide?

The Common Law Background. *Button*'s importance to public interest law in particular, and delivery of legal services generally, can hardly be overstated. To understand why, we need to provide a little more context. Virginia argued that its regulation was a traditional effort to prevent the kinds of evils condemned by the common law offenses of barratry, champerty, and maintenance. These terms no longer have precise meanings, assuming they ever did. Maintenance, according to Lord Denning, is "improperly stirring up litigation and strife by giving aid to one party to bring or defend a claim without just cause or excuse." In re Trepca Mines, Ltd., [1963] 3 All E.R. 351 (C.A.). A person lacked just cause, according to the *Button* majority, if there was "malicious intent," which was absent if the maintaining party's motives were charitable. "Champerty has been described as the unlawful maintenance of a suit, where a person without an interest in it agrees to finance the suit, in whole or in part, in consideration for receiving a portion of the proceeds of the litigation. . . . The ancient prohibition against champerty arose in feudal England. More recently the doctrine has been viewed as a check on frivolous or unnecessary litigation, or a mechanism to encourage the settlement of disputes without recourse to litigation." Saladini v. Righellis, 687 N.E.2d 1224 (Mass. 1997). "Barratry (or barretry) is the offense of frequently exciting and stirring up quarrels and suits between other individuals." Osprey, Inc. v. Cabana Ltd. Partnership, 532 S.E.2d 269 (S.C. 2000).

As should be clear, these doctrines have no clear boundaries, making them wild cards in any efforts to change the traditional way lawyers are organized and funded. Further, they rest on a view that litigation, if not quite an evil, can be used abusively and, in any event, should be discouraged. As the *Button* majority saw it, the doctrines themselves were being used abusively — to deny unpopular litigants access to the courts. A few cases, including *Saladini* and *Osprey*, have held that the doctrines will no longer be recognized. The *Saladini* court wrote:

> We have long abandoned the view that litigation is suspect, and have recognized that agreements to purchase an interest in an action may actually foster resolution of a dispute. . . . We also no longer are persuaded that the champerty doctrine is needed to protect against the evils once feared: speculation in lawsuits, the bringing of frivolous lawsuits, or financial overreaching by a party of superior bargaining position. There are now other devices that more effectively accomplish these ends.

But the doctrines live on elsewhere. For one thing, some states have statutes that preserve the basic idea behind the common law offenses so courts in those states are not free to abolish them. For example, §489 of New York's Judiciary Law forbids a person or entity to "solicit, buy or take an assignment of, or be in any manner interested in buying or taking an assignment of a bond, promissory note, bill of exchange, book debt, or other thing in action, or any claim or demand, with the intent and for the purpose of bringing an action or proceeding thereon." Bluebird Partners, L.P. v. First Fidelity Bank, N.A., 731 N.E.2d 581 (N.Y. 2000), construes the statute to require that "intent to sue on [the] claim must at least have been the primary purpose for, if not the sole motivation behind, entering into the transaction."* Even where the offenses are not statutory, courts may prefer to let the legislature decide whether to abolish them. Toste Farm Corp. v. Hadbury, Inc., 798 A.2d 901 (R.I. 2002) (upholding civil damage claim for maintenance against a law firm).

The Constitutional Context. As you see in *Button*, the analysis changes when the party whose conduct is alleged to constitute champerty or maintenance is able to claim constitutional protection for its activities. Much of what we shall see in the material on legal advertising (chapter 16), as well as in this chapter, is suspicion of these common law offenses when they appear to interfere with interests protected by the First and Fourteenth Amendments. Certainly the common law offenses can be and have been used to stifle the flow of information to people about their rights and the means (financial and human) to vindicate them. The question *Button* asked was when state interest in the policies underlying the common law offenses will (or will not) justify this interference.

When *Button* reached the Supreme Court, the single remaining issue was whether Virginia could prohibit the NAACP from using agents to solicit plaintiffs whom lawyers, paid by the NAACP, would then represent in school desegregation cases. But neither the majority opinion nor the dissent was able to avoid a larger question: May NAACP lawyers, working for a lay organization, represent

---

* *Bluebird* explains the fascinating etymology of the word "champerty."

The "champerty" concept is based on a type of French feudal tenure in land, a "champart," in which the fee for use of the land was neither in money nor ordinary service in kind. The tenant-by-champart was a partial owner of the land bound to share any rents and profits with the grantor, but the grantor took the risk that the crops might fail and that there would be no return. Anyone who then obtained a legal interest in that grant of land would also take a share of the profits in champart (see, Radin, Maintenance By Champerty, 24 Cal. L. Rev. 48, 61-62 [1935]).

"Champerty," as a term of art, grew out of this practice to describe the medieval situation where someone bought an interest in a claim under litigation, agreeing to bear the expenses but also to share the benefits if the suit succeeded. The most important litigation of that era was over land, and a person who bought lawsuits could acquire a partial interest in landed estates — an estimable power play. The taint on the process arose because the purchase price was usually far below the value of the potential land acquisition — a transaction suffused with speculation related to the "sin" of usury and its concomitant legal prohibitions. The champerty transaction, however, evaded the strict prohibitive laws involving usury (see, id., at 60-61, 67).

Even as the feudal system faded, English law retained the word "champart" as a metaphor to indicate a disapproval of lawsuits brought "for part of the profits" of the action (see, id., at 63; see also, Winfield, The History of Maintenance and Champerty, 35 L.Q. Rev. 50 [1919]).

plaintiffs in these cases under any circumstances, even if the plaintiffs had not been solicited? Both opinions identify the state's interest as avoidance of conflicts between the interests of the lawyers' employer (the NAACP) and the interests of the plaintiffs, who were their clients. But the majority and dissent disagree about the likelihood of actual conflict. The opinions also disagree about the scope of constitutional protection for the arrangement and the amount of deference the Court should give to the state's professed concern about divided loyalties. Finally, the opinions disagree about motives — both Virginia's and the NAACP's. Should motive be a consideration?

The majority believes that Virginia is motivated by hostility to desegregation lawsuits, doesn't it? How does it know that? The dissent, by contrast, accepts Virginia's claim that all it wants to do is maintain "high professional standards among those who practice law within its borders." Chapter 33 was, after all, not unlike antisolicitation provisions in just about all jurisdictions at the time. As for the NAACP's motives, the fact that they were not pecuniary influenced Justice Brennan to conclude that there was small risk of an actual conflict between the client and the NAACP as sponsor of the action. Justice Harlan was not as impressed by the absence of a pecuniary motive. He's right, isn't he? Doesn't history teach us that political motives can be at least as strong an influence on deeds (and misdeeds) as financial ones? Maybe even stronger. Even so, can we nevertheless defend *Button* on the ground that the Constitution at least is more protective of political motives than commercial ones? After all, the First Amendment protects the right to petition the government, which includes the courts. It doesn't protect the right to make money.

It will not always be possible to distinguish the pecuniary from the political. Fee-shifting statutes in civil liberties cases, like 42 U.S.C. §1988, enacted after *Button*, raise the prospect that today a politically motivated sponsor of litigation (or even a private firm) will also hope to be the beneficiary of sizeable court-ordered fees. (It may even count on the fees to survive.) For example, Shearman & Sterling and the ACLU sought court-ordered fees of $6.15 million for representing Shannon Faulkner, who successfully challenged exclusion of women from a state-supported military college in South Carolina. Richard Schmitt, Fee for All: Citadel and ACLU Are at It Again, Wall St. J., Aug. 6, 1997, at A1. Does that prospect change the constitutional balance?

In re Primus, page 942, held that it does not change the balance when the question was the extent of First Amendment protection for a public interest lawyer's solicitation of a client in a fee-shifting case. But protection of First Amendment motives did not impress the Missouri Supreme Court when the issue was not whether a lawyer could solicit or represent clients as an employee of a public interest organization, but whether a nonlaw firm like the ACLU has a First Amendment right to receive a court-ordered legal fee. ACLU/Eastern Missouri Fund v. Miller, 803 S.W.2d 592 (Mo. 1991), was an action between an ACLU chapter and one of its (former) staff lawyers to determine who would get to keep a legal fee awarded by a federal judge in an action sponsored by the ACLU and handled by the staff lawyer. The plaintiff in the federal case had assigned the fee to the ACLU. When the staff lawyer pocketed the money, the ACLU sued him in state court. The Missouri Supreme Court denied the ACLU's First Amendment right to receive a legal fee, summarily rejecting its reliance on *Primus* and *Button.* It held that a state law prohibiting lawyers from sharing legal fees with laypersons prevented the ACLU from getting the money. *Miller* did not address the Supremacy Clause issue — whether §1988, the source of judicial power to award the fee, superseded state law — but addressed only whether *Missouri's* fee-splitting ban violated the First Amendment rights of the ACLU on these facts. Rhode Island Training School v. Martinez, 465 F.Supp.2d 131 (D.R.I. 2006), held that under the Supremacy Clause the federal fee-shifting statute entitled the ACLU to counsel fees despite a Rhode Island rule to the contrary. ABA Opinion 93-374 read the Model Rules to reject the Missouri noncompromise. In 2002, that conclusion was preserved in Model Rule 5.4(a)(4), but the entity receiving the fee must be nonprofit.

See generally on these issues Roy Simon's careful sifting of the interests in Fee Sharing Between Lawyers and Public Interest Groups, 98 Yale L.J. 1069 (1989).

2. *Labor Unions*

In due course, and inevitably, the subject shifted from political change to modest financial ones, from civil rights to money. It happened because of labor unions, which emerged as a second "lay intermediary" between lawyers and clients. Unions too had to struggle to earn the constitutional right to assist their members in gaining low-cost legal aid. The opponents this time were state bar groups (aided by state courts). Newsman Fred Friendly used to say, "When someone says it's not about the money, it's about the money." And so it was. As in *Button*, opposition to the union agenda was also couched in neutral terms, but it was broader and may have been even more intense than the forces arrayed against the NAACP. The contest is told in a trilogy of Supreme Court cases. The bar did not come out looking good.

Take note of several distinctions between unions and organizations like the NAACP and the ACLU. First, unions are seeking to provide lawyers for their members, whereas the NAACP in *Button* was offering legal help to persons who may have had no affiliation with the organization. Second, the underlying legal claims of union members have been routine — mainly workers' compensation or disability claims — unlike the constitutional rights that the NAACP and ACLU try to vindicate. Third, a prime goal of union plans has been to control the legal costs of pursuing a claim, not to win judicial recognition for the claim in the first place. The right is clear and usually statutory. The only question is whether the claimant has a case. For all of these reasons, the economic threat to the lawyers who relied on these cases for their income is (or was) quite real. And the response proved it.

A year after *Button*, the Supreme Court decided Brotherhood of Railroad Trainmen v. Virginia ex rel. Virginia State Bar, 377 U.S. 1 (1964). The union's Department of Legal Counsel advised injured members not to settle claims without consulting counsel. The department also recommended particular counsel, who the union believed were "legally and morally competent to handle injury claims for members." Lawyers were recommended based on a plan that divided the country into 16 regions. The union president designated a firm in each region, which the president could also remove from the plan. The union would recommend that an injured member retain the firm designated for the particular region. Virginia enjoined this practice.

The Supreme Court reversed, in an opinion by Justice Black, holding that

> the First and Fourteenth Amendments protect the right of the members through their Brotherhood to maintain and carry out their plan for advising workers who are injured to obtain legal advice and for recommending specific lawyers. . . . And, of course, lawyers accepting employment under this constitutionally protected plan have a like protection which the State cannot abridge.

Justice Stewart did not participate. Justice Clark, joined by Justice Harlan, dissented. Justice Clark pointed to the 25-percent kickbacks that designated lawyers had been required to give the union until 1959. He doubted that the union had "sincerely reformed," but even if it had, he anticipated that the Court's opinion would "encourage further departures from the high standards set by canons of ethics . . . and [would] be a green light to other groups who for years have attempted to engage in similar practices." Distinguishing *Button* and sharply disagreeing with Justice Black, he wrote that "[p]ersonal injury litigation is not a form of political expression."

Here's a little-known fact that should tell you something about the expected economic consequences of *Trainmen* (bad for lawyers, good for workers). After the decision, 48 bar associations joined the ABA in an unsuccessful motion for rehearing! Note, Group Legal Services and the Organized Bar, 10 Colum. J.L. & Soc. Probs. 228 (1974) (authored by Norman Riedmueller).

That was chapter one in this story. Three years later the Court decided United Mine Workers, District 12 v. Illinois State Bar Assn., 389 U.S. 217 (1967). The union had now raised the pecuniary stakes substantially. It employed a lawyer on a salary basis to handle members' workers' compensation claims before a state commission. (Union members formerly had retained individual counsel and had paid 40 or 50 percent of their recoveries in attorney's fees.) Again Justice Black reversed a lower court opinion enjoining the practice. Citing the First Amendment, *Button*, and *Trainmen*, he wrote: "The litigation in question is, of course, not bound up with political matters of acute social moment . . . but the First Amendment does not protect speech and assembly only to the extent it can be characterized as political." The Court held that it was of no consequence that the rights at issue in *Trainmen* were created by Congress while those in the present case were created by the state.

Justice Harlan dissented:

> The union lawyer has little contact with his client. He processes the applications of injured members on a mass basis. Evidently, he negotiates with the employer's counsel about many claims at the same time. The State was entitled to conclude that, removed from ready contact with his client, insulated from interference by his actual employer, paid a salary independent of the results achieved, faced with a heavy caseload, and very possibly with other activities competing for his time, the attorney will be tempted to place undue emphasis upon quick disposition of each case. . . . He might be led, so the State might consider, to compromise cases for reasons unrelated to their own intrinsic merits, such as the need to "get on" with negotiations or a promise by the employer's attorney of concessions relating to other cases. The desire for quick disposition also might cause the attorney to forgo appeals in some cases in which the amount awarded seemed unusually low.

Notice the conjecture in Justice Harlan's dissent. He speaks of temptation. He uses the word "might" three times in this one excerpt. But he is correct, isn't he? These bad things *might* happen. Then again they might not. The question, however, is whether the union members have asserted a constitutional interest — i.e., to more cheaply petition the courts through a salaried lawyer — that Justice Harlan's plausible conjecture cannot override, at least not without some solid empirical proof.

The third and final chapter in our story was written in 1971. By this time, Justice Black is entirely fed up. His impatience with state efforts to obstruct the full reach of his earlier opinions is now self-evident, as shown by the quote at the start of this chapter. (After the three union cases, what do you think of the validity of the *Motorists' Association* case at page 825?)

UNITED TRANSPORTATION UNION v. STATE BAR OF MICHIGAN
401 U.S. 576 (1971)

JUSTICE BLACK delivered the opinion of the Court.

The Michigan State Bar brought this action in January 1959 to enjoin the members of the Brotherhood of Railroad Trainmen [later merged into the petitioner] from engaging in activities undertaken for the stated purpose of assisting their fellow workers, their widows and families, to protect themselves from excessive fees at the hands of incompetent attorneys in suits for damages under the Federal Employers' Liability Act. The complaint charged, as factors relevant to the cause of action, that the Union recommended selected attorneys to its members and their families, that it secured a commitment from those attorneys that the maximum fee charged would not exceed 25% of the recovery, and that it recommended Chicago lawyers to represent Michigan claimants. The State Bar's complaint appears to be a plea for court protection of unlimited legal fees. The Union's answers admitted that it had engaged in the practice of protecting members against large fees and incompetent counsel; that since 1930 it had recommended, with respect to FELA claims, that injured member employees, and their families, consult attorneys designated by the Union as "Legal Counsel"; that prior to March 1959, it had informed the injured members and their families that the legal counsel would not charge in excess of 25% of any recovery; and that Union representatives were reimbursed for transporting injured employees, or their families, to the legal counsel offices.

The only evidence introduced in this case was the testimony of one employee of the Association of American Railroads in 1961 that from 1953 through 1960 a large number of Michigan FELA claimants were represented by the Union's designated Chicago legal counsel. Based on this evidence and the Union's admissions set out above, the state trial court in 1962 issued an order enjoining the Union's activities on the ground that they violated the state statute making it a misdemeanor to "solicit" damage suits against railroads. . . .

In affirming the trial court decree, . . . the Michigan Supreme Court gave our holding in *Trainmen* the narrowest possible reading. . . . The Michigan Supreme Court failed to follow our decisions in *Trainmen, United Mine Workers,* and

NAACP v. Button, upholding the First Amendment principle that groups can unite to assert their legal rights as effectively and economically as practicable. When applied, as it must be, to the Union's activities reflected in the record of this case, the First Amendment forbids the restraints imposed by the injunction here under review for the following among other reasons.

First. The decree approved by the Michigan Supreme Court enjoins the Union from "giving or furnishing legal advice to its members or their families." Given its broadest meaning, this provision would bar the Union's members, officers, agents, or attorneys from giving any kind of advice or counsel to an injured worker or his family concerning his FELA claim. In *Trainmen* we upheld the commonsense proposition that such activity is protected by the First Amendment. Moreover, the plain meaning of this particular injunctive provision would emphatically deny the right of the Union to employ counsel to represent its members, a right explicitly upheld in *United Mine Workers* and NAACP v. Button. . . .

Second. The decree also enjoins the Union from furnishing to any attorney the names of injured members or information relating to their injuries. The investigation of accidents by Union staff for purposes of gathering evidence to assist the injured worker or his family in asserting FELA claims was part of the Union practice upheld in *Trainmen.* It would seem at least a little strange now to hold that the Union cannot communicate that information to the injured member's attorney.

Third. A provision of the decree enjoins the members of the Union from "accepting or receiving compensation of any kind, directly or indirectly, for the solicitation of legal employment for any lawyer, whether by way of salary, commission or otherwise." The Union conceded that prior to 1959, Union representatives were reimbursed for their actual time spent and out-of-pocket expenses incurred in bringing injured members or their families to the offices of the legal counsel. Since the members of a union have a First Amendment right to help and advise each other in securing effective legal representation, there can be no doubt that transportation of injured members to an attorney's office is within the scope of that protected activity. To the extent that the injunction prohibits this practice, it is invalid under *Trainmen, United Mine Workers,* and NAACP v. Button.

Fourth. . . . Our Brother Harlan appears to concede that the State Bar has neither alleged nor proved that the Union has engaged in the past, is presently engaging, or plans to engage, in the sharing of legal fees. Nonetheless, he suggests that the injunction against such conduct is justified in order to remove any "temptation" for the Union to participate in such activities. We cannot accept this novel concept of equity jurisdiction that would open the courts to claims for injunctions against "temptation," and would deem potential "temptation" to be a sufficient basis for the issuance of an injunction. Indeed, it would appear that jurisdiction over "temptation" has heretofore been reserved to the churches. . . .

Fifth. Finally, the challenged decree bars the Union from controlling, directly or indirectly, the fees charged by any lawyer. The complaint alleged that the Union sought to protect its members from excessive legal fees by securing an agreement from the counsel it recommends that the fee will not exceed 25% of the recovery, and that the percentage will include all expenses incidental to investigation and litigation. The Union in its answer admitted that prior to 1959 it secured such agreements for the protection of its members.

United Mine Workers upheld the right of workers to act collectively to obtain affordable and effective legal representation. One of the abuses sought to be remedied by the Mine Workers' plan was the situation pursuant to which members "were required to pay forty or fifty per cent of the amounts recovered in damage suits, for attorney fees." The Mine Workers dealt with the problem by employing an attorney on a salary basis, thereby providing free legal representation for its members in asserting their claims before the state workmen's compensation board. The Union in the instant case sought to protect its members against the same abuse by limiting the fee charged by recommended attorneys. It is hard to believe that a court of justice would deny a cooperative union of workers the right to protect its injured members, and their widows and children, from the injustice of excessive fees at the hands of inadequate counsel. Indeed, the Michigan court was foreclosed from so doing by our decision in *United Mine Workers*.

In the context of this case we deal with a cooperative union of workers seeking to assist its members in effectively asserting claims under the FELA. But the principle here involved cannot be limited to the facts of this case. At issue is the basic right to group legal action, a right first asserted in this Court by an association of Negroes seeking the protection of freedoms guaranteed by the Constitution. The common thread running through our decisions in NAACP v. Button, *Trainmen*, and *United Mine Workers* is that collective activity undertaken to obtain meaningful access to the courts is a fundamental right within the protection of the First Amendment. However, that right would be a hollow promise if courts could deny associations of workers or others the means of enabling their members to meet the costs of legal representation. That was the holding in *United Mine Workers, Trainmen*, and NAACP v. Button. The injunction in the present case cannot stand in the face of these prior decisions.

Reversed.

[Justice Stewart took no part in the decision of this case. Justice Harlan concurred in part and dissented in part. Justice White, with whom Justice Blackmun joined, concurred in part and dissented in part.]

Not all change has come from Supreme Court fiat. On occasion, state high courts have created exceptions to their own rules forbidding lay intermediaries. An enlightened example is In re 1115 Legal Service Care, 541 A.2d 673 (N.J. 1988). The petitioner was a prepaid legal service program funded by employers under a collective bargaining agreement with a labor union. In New Jersey, the program employed lawyers to serve union members. Elsewhere it retained law firms. The state supreme court upheld the right of the program to practice this way and to do so in its own name. It emphasized that

[i]ndividual attorneys providing legal services remain professionally responsible and accountable for their conduct. No control over the rendition of legal services is retained or exerted by non-lawyers. No profits generated by the practice of law enure to the organization itself. The practice of law under the aegis of the plan . . . is in no way inconsistent with or inimical to the regulatory standards governing the legal profession.

B. FOR-PROFIT ENTERPRISES

"Can Viktor Be Our Partner?"

"My name is Olga Denov. I am a partner in a three-person law office whose clients are émigrés from the former Soviet Union. We help them with most every legal problem they have — immigration, landlord, credit, government benefits, employment — except criminal, which we refer. My parents and I came here from Moscow when I was eight. My two partners, one was born here to émigré parents and one was born in Estonia. We make a modest living. Sometimes we'll represent a person for nothing or next to nothing. He'll prosper and continue to hire us. As you might infer, we see ourselves as public interest lawyers who happen to work in a for-profit law firm.

"Much of what our clients need is not strictly speaking legal advice or help, or not only that. They need the sort of help that social workers are well trained to give and often better able than lawyers. Like navigating government bureaucracies, helping new arrivals get settled, kids in school, medical care, ESL lessons, opening a bank account. Even simple things like learning the currency. My friend Viktor Portnoi is a social worker with a non-profit humanitarian group. Sometimes he helps us out, but he's got his own clients. I asked Viktor if he'd be interested in coming to work at our firm. Our need for a social worker has grown significantly in the last year. We're also on the lookout for a new lawyer (must speak Russian). Viktor said yes, he is interested.

"I do not want Viktor to be our employee. I don't want to be his boss. His skills and knowledge in an allied field are as good or better than mine. I want him to have a stake in the firm. It won't much matter to his income, but it will matter to his pride, sense of belonging, and identification with our mission. It also gives him more credibility with the people he deals with. And it shows respect for his contribution. Much of what Viktor will do will resemble what we do, though of course he cannot practice law. He will work on his own where a client needs only his help, and he will work with one of us when a client needs legal help, too. Can we do this?"

Should We Let Nonlawyers Own Law Firms or Non-Law Firms Sell Legal Services to the Public?

We have so far discussed nonprofit organizations that are not seeking to earn a profit from the work a lawyer does for a client. The constitutional protection afforded such arrangements can be seen to depend on the issues they seek to raise and their nonprofit status (*Button*) or on the right of the intermediary's members to pool their resources to reduce the cost of legal help in vindicating legal rights (the union cases) or both. If we remove these two characteristics, what constitutional protection remains? May a state legitimately forbid lay ownership or managerial control of entities that market routine legal services for a profit?

As we saw above (page 828), the Code was especially hostile to lay participation in the delivery of legal services. Although this hostility softened over time, it was not because lawyers had become enamored of the idea but because the

Supreme Court's decisions in *Button* and the union cases weakened the earlier broad prohibitions. The ABA's amendments to the Code barely went further than the Constitution required. Efforts to make the Model Rules explicitly receptive to lay participation in for-profit law offices (at the owner or management level) were defeated by the "Sears" question (page 830). Sensitivity (hypersensitivity?) to the specter of lay influence is not limited to ownership or management. The ABA also forbids a lawyer who handles a fee-shifting case for a corporate employer to give the employer any part of the court-awarded fee beyond what it costs the employer for the lawyer's services in the matter. ABA Opinion 95-392. The ABA opinion distinguishes Opinion 93-374, page 840, on the ground that risk of interference with the lawyer's independent professional judgment is "unlikely" when the lawyer's employer is a nonprofit organization. Once again, we see differences depending on whether the motives are profit or some "higher" goal.

A hybrid situation is presented when an insured person calls upon her insurance company to defend her against a claim covered by the policy. Often, the company will retain outside counsel, which ordinarily presents no problem unless the company is reserving its rights to deny coverage. See page 299. But insurance companies, like other organizations, realize that the cost of providing a defense can be substantially reduced if they use employed lawyers or a "captive" law firm. A captive law firm is one that has been created by the insurance company to do its defense work only. While an insurance company that provides a defense through a retained lawyer is doing what it contracted to do, can it be that an insurance company that uses an employed lawyer or a captive law firm for this work engages in unauthorized practice? Some courts have said yes, even where the insurance company will pay all of any judgment or settlement. See, e.g., Gardner v. North Carolina State Bar, 341 S.E.2d 517 (N.C. 1986). This distinction is woefully formal and easy to mock as in reality a way to make more work for lawyers. It is also costly because it ratchets up legal fees and insurance defense costs and therefore premiums. Other courts have allowed the practice. Cincinnati Ins. Co. v. Wills, 717 N.E.2d 151 (Ind. 1999) (in a thorough discussion, court identifies eight state courts that have permitted the arrangement and only two that have not; court then rejects challenge to use of employed lawyers or captive law firm and further rejects claim that such arrangements necessarily entail conflicts of interest); American Home Assurance Co. v. Unauthorized Practice of Law Committee, 121 S.W.3d 831 (Tex. App. 2003) (upholding practice, citing fact that 18 states also do so and only Kentucky and North Carolina do not). ABA Opinion 430 (2003) finds no ethical impediment to the arrangement.

The usual reason offered to oppose lay ownership or managerial authority in an organization that sells legal services for profit is that laypersons might use their power over the entity's lawyers (whether fellow owners or employees) to cause them to disserve clients so as to maximize profits for the enterprise. This risk arises if the layperson's income depends on the profitability of the enterprise and she has power within the organization to get her way. But wait a minute. Why isn't the same risk present whether the owner is a lawyer or a layperson? Are we assuming that lawyers are more trustworthy than laypeople? Or less interested in money? Is it because lawyers can be disciplined if they cause another lawyer to disserve a client, whereas the bar has no equivalent authority over lay owners? (Civil claims would still be possible.) If the need for regulatory control is the answer, why isn't it sufficient that we retain regulatory control over the lawyer? What reason do we have to suppose that lawyers will risk discipline and allow themselves to be corrupted by the lay profiteer?

The tone of the preceding sentences is decidedly skeptical. Is it perhaps too dismissive? Not every ethical rule that excludes competition and, predictably, raises the cost of legal services is necessarily unwise. Even if the motives behind the rule are not wholly selfless, the rule may still serve a valid purpose. Can't a state legislature or court validly apprehend excessive risk in a law firm or other organization that includes nonlawyer owners and sells legal services for a profit?

Litigation Funding Companies

The common law offenses of champerty and maintenance have lately been invoked in an effort to prevent a new kind of commercial enterprise — investing in law suits. Here's the idea. Nina is a personal injury plaintiff. She has a claim that her lawyer values at $300,000, give or take 10 percent. (By studying hundreds of jury verdicts in any jurisdiction, insurance companies and experienced lawyers can predict, within a margin of error, what a jury is likely to do in a particular case.) Because of pretrial procedures and crowded court calendars, Nina's lawyer tells her that she's not likely to come close to trial for two years. Nor is she likely to get a realistic settlement offer until then. But what if Nina needs money for medical bills, lost income, and the expenses of daily living? Nina's lawyer cannot lend her the money (see page 229). Or maybe Nina doesn't *need* the money but doesn't want to wait. She'd like to "sell" part of her claim now. Who will buy?

Along comes a company that invests in claims it thinks have a good chance of producing a settlement or judgment. It will give Nina $25,000 now, but only if she agrees that she will repay the first $75,000 of any award. The company will have no right to control the litigation or to learn attorney-client confidences. It will just wait to see what happens. If Nina loses, she repays nothing. For the company, it's an investment, made after calculating the risk of nonrecovery against the likelihood of recovery (and the amount). For the plaintiff, it's cash when she needs it or wants it. Any problem?

These companies have been springing up lately and, predictably, their business plans have been challenged in court as illegal. The challenge may come from a state regulator. Or it may come from another direction. Say Nina takes the $25,000 and settles a year later for $250,000. The company wants its cut, but Nina offers only $25,000 and interest, which amounts to much less than the additional $50,000 the company demands. She asks the court to declare the contract void as against public policy.

In Rancman v. Interim Settlement Funding Corp., 789 N.E.2d 217 (Ohio 2003), the court held that just such an investment in a plaintiff's claim was champerty and maintenance and void in Ohio. More than a dozen companies in the same line of business as the funding companies in *Rancman* filed amicus briefs in their support. But the court said no: "The advances sub judice constitute champerty because FSF and Interim [the investors] sought to profit from Rancman's case. They also constitute maintenance because FSF and Interim each purchased a share of a suit to which they did not have an independent interest; and because the agreements provided Rancman with a disincentive to settle her case." The court added that the contract before it "promotes speculation in lawsuits."

The court's point about effect on settlement (certainly a legitimate concern for the court) is the only part of the opinion that actually offers a policy justification, as opposed to reasoning by labels. The facts are these: In April 1999, FSF advanced

> $6,000 to Rancman in exchange for the first $16,800 she would recover if the case was resolved within 12 months, $22,200 if resolved within 18 months, or $27,600 if resolved within 24 months. If the case was not resolved in Rancman's favor, she had no obligation under the contract. . . . In September 1999, Interim advanced an additional $1,000 to Rancman, which was secured by the next $2,800 she expected to collect on her claim. The Interim agreement was also without recourse if Rancman did not recover in the State Farm action. Rancman settled her case against State Farm for $100,000 within 12 months of entering the agreement with FSF. Rancman refused payment on the contracts.

Here's the court's analysis:

> The $6,000 advance . . . gave FSF the right to the first $16,800 of the settlement after fees, expenses, and superior liens, if the State Farm case settled within 12 months. If there had not been any superior liens on Rancman's settlement and her attorney had charged a 30 percent contingency fee, Rancman would not have received any funds from a settlement of $24,000 or less. This calculation gives Rancman an absolute disincentive to settle for $24,000 or less because she would keep the $6,000 advance regardless of whether she settles with State Farm and would not receive any additional money from a $24,000 settlement. . . .
>
> Under the same facts, the $1,000 Interim advance would provide a settlement disincentive of an additional $4,000. Thus, with no liens and a 30 percent attorney fee, the $7,000 advanced to Rancman effectively bars her from considering a settlement offer of up to $28,000.
>
> These advances also affect settlement offers greater than $28,000. Suppose Rancman decides that she will settle for nothing less than $80,000 minus attorney fees. Because of the obligation to repay the advances, she would refuse to settle until State Farm offers $98,000.[2] If the settlement advance agreements are enforced, Rancman must receive an $18,000 premium on a settlement offer to have the same incentive to settle that she would have had if she had not entered into the agreements with FSF and Interim. This can prolong litigation and reduce settlement incentives — an evil that prohibitions against maintenance seek to eliminate.

Is the court saying anything more than that Rancman had sold part of her interest in her claim and would have to accept the consequences of her choices,

---

2. This number is the combination of the $80,000 Rancman desires plus the $10,800 and $1,800 premiums she must pay to FSF and Interim, respectively, together with attorney fees on these premiums.

just as with any investment? Or is the court saying that those consequences affect the court's calendar and the court is not prepared to allow the arrangement for that reason? Given calendar delay and the usual economic disparities between injured plaintiffs and defendants or their insurers, can it also be said that these arrangements level the litigation playing field? Let's say economic need will force a plaintiff like Rancman to settle for half of what her claim is worth if trial is delayed (and the defendant may know that and may seek to delay the trial in any legitimate way it can). Why is forcing the plaintiff to accept a deep discount settlement better public policy than letting the plaintiff sell part of her claim on a contingent basis with the chance to net more in the end? If, as the court seemed to believe, litigation funding can be abusive, why isn't the correct answer regulation? For example, the court emphasizes that the return on the funders' investment (assuming it was not nothing) could exceed 180 percent per annum. Maybe that's too high. Maybe the plaintiff is not—we should assume she is not—in a good bargaining position. Why then isn't the solution to limit the return to a percentage that is high enough to make litigation funding economically attractive but not so high as to be abusive?

Here is another way to look at it. Traditionally, a plaintiff has always been able to sell her claim, hasn't she, but there has been only one possible buyer: the defendant. The defendant had no competition in the market for the plaintiff's claim. Litigation funding enables the plaintiff to sell just *part* of a claim to someone else in the hope of netting more in the end. Ohio refuses to let her do that even if her decision to spread the risk is counseled and financially reasonable.

Rancman is the most prominent high state court decision to address litigation funding. Its unsatisfying explanation for an outright ban has not, so far as I can tell, shut down the industry (except in Ohio). Companies are still offering money to plaintiffs to enable them to prosecute their claims—and not only individual plaintiffs, but also companies that may not otherwise choose, or be able, to invest in the cost of litigation. The impediments are notable—the vague common law offenses, usury laws, gambling laws, unauthorized practice rules, rules against splitting legal fees, and rules about assigning legal claims—but apparently not insurmountable (except in Ohio) since the deals keep getting made. For a discussion of the issues and citation to other decisions, see Julia McLaughlin, Litigation Funding: Charting a Legal and Ethical Course, 31 Vermont L. Rev. 615 (2007) (weighing the dangers and value of litigation funding, reviewing the case law, and recommending legislation to regulate the industry).*

Multidisciplinary Practice (MDP)

Currently, the rules of professional conduct in every American jurisdiction except the District of Columbia prohibit law partnerships between lawyers and

---

* An intermediate appellate court in North Carolina rejected *Rancman's* champerty analysis but found other problems with the legality of the agreement before it, including usury and unfair trade practices. Odell v. Legal Bucks LLC, 665 S.E.2d 767 (N.C. 2008).

nonlawyers and prohibit lawyers from sharing legal fees with nonlawyers. The District of Columbia permits law firms to include nonlawyer partners and to share legal fees with them under certain conditions — see D.C. Rule 5.4(b) — but even D.C. does not allow lawyer-nonlawyer partnerships unless the "sole purpose" of the entity is "providing legal services to the clients." For a brief time, it looked like the prohibition might give way, however modestly. In August 1998, ABA President Phillip S. Anderson appointed a Commission on Multidisciplinary Practice (the MDP Commission) to "study and report on the extent to which and the manner in which professional service firms operated by accountants and others who are not lawyers are seeking to provide legal services to the public." The commission's qualified recommendations favoring multidisciplinary practice (i.e., lawyers and nonlawyers, through entities that are not law firms) were debated at the ABA's August 1999 Annual Meeting, but the reception was cool. Maybe "frigid" better describes it. The Florida Bar proposed a resolution that the ABA "make no change, addition or amendment to the Model Rules of Professional Conduct which permits a lawyer to offer legal services through a multidisciplinary practice unless and until additional study demonstrates that such changes will further the public interest without sacrificing or compromising lawyer independence and the legal profession's tradition of loyalty to clients." That resolution passed by the lopsided vote of 304 to 98.

In May of 2000, the ABA's MDP Commission issued a new report that remained generally favorable to MDPs but with stricter conditions than the 1999 report. This report immediately encountered broad and strong opposition, including an alternative recommendation cosponsored by four state bars that squarely opposed any change in the ABA Model Rules that would permit multidisciplinary practice. At the ABA's 2000 Annual Meeting, the ABA House of Delegates soundly rejected the MDP Commission's recommendation. Instead, the delegates voted overwhelmingly (by a margin of 314 to 106) in favor of the alternative recommendation that condemned MDPs, articulated the "core values" of the legal profession, rejected the MDP Commission's report, and discharged the MDP Commission "with gratitude."

MDP Commission's Final (Rejected) Recommendation:

RESOLVED, that the American Bar Association amend the Model Rules of Professional Conduct consistent with the following principles:

1. Lawyers should be permitted to share fees and join with non-lawyer professionals in a practice that delivers both legal and nonlegal professional services (Multidisciplinary Practice), provided that the lawyers have the control and authority necessary to assure lawyer independence in the rendering of legal services. "Nonlawyer professionals" means members of recognized professions or other disciplines that are governed by ethical standards.
2. This Recommendation must be implemented in a manner that protects the public and preserves the core values of the legal profession, including competence, independence of professional judgment, protection of confidential client information, loyalty to the client through the avoidance of conflicts of interests, and *pro bono publico* obligations.

3. Regulatory authorities should enforce existing rules and adopt such additional enforcement procedures as are needed to implement these principles and to protect the public interest.
4. The prohibition on nonlawyers delivering legal services and the obligations of all lawyers to observe the rules of professional conduct should not be altered.
5. Passive investment in a Multidisciplinary Practice should not be permitted.

FURTHER READING

The MDP proposal engendered substantial debate at conferences, in bar associations, and in law reviews. Perhaps that's because the proposal raised fundamental questions about the nature of the profession and the work of lawyers. (MDPs are allowed in some other countries.) The ABA's rejection of rules that would tolerate some degree of multidisciplinary practice will not, of course, end the discussion and may even continue it. Articles that skillfully analyze the issues include Mary Daly, Choosing Wise Men Wisely: The Risks and Rewards of Purchasing Legal Services from Lawyers in a Multidisciplinary Partnership, 13 Geo. J. Legal Ethics 217 (2000) (by the Reporter for the MDP Commission); John Dzienkowski & Robert Peroni, Multidisciplinary Practice and the American Legal Profession: A Market Approach to Regulating the Delivery of Legal Services in the Twenty-First Century, 69 Fordham L. Rev. 83 (2000); Laurel Terry, A Primer on MDPs: Should the "No" Rule Become a New Rule?, 72 Temple L. Rev. 869 (1999) (Professor Terry has studied multidisciplinary practice in Western Europe and was the source of substantial data for the MDP Commission). See also Stephen Gillers, The Anxiety of Influence, 27 Fla. St. U. L. Rev. 123 (1999).

Reciprocal Referral Agreements

New York State, while opposing MDPs, has amended its rules to permit cooperative business arrangements between lawyers and nonlawyers. New York Rule 5.8 provides that a "lawyer or law firm may enter into and maintain a contractual relationship with a nonlegal professional or nonlegal professional service firm for the purpose of offering to the public, on a systematic and continuing basis, legal services performed by the lawyer or law firm as well as other nonlegal professional services" so long as the nonlegal service providers have no "ownership or investment interest in, or managerial or supervisory right, power or position in connection with the practice of law by the lawyer or law firm," the lawyer does not share legal fees with the nonlawyer, and the lawyer does not receive or give any monetary or other benefit for getting or receiving a referral.

The ABA has also amended its rules to authorize cooperation between lawyers and other professionals. But unlike New York's verbose provision, the ABA's streamlined rule states the requirements in some 50 words: Lawyers and nonlawyer professionals can refer clients to each other if their "agreement is not exclusive" and "the client is informed of the existence and nature of the agreement." Model Rule 7.2(b)(4). Why forbid exclusivity?

C. MAY A LAW FIRM OWN AN ANCILLARY BUSINESS?

Washington, D.C.'s Howrey & Simon and its army of more than 50 nonlawyer consultants likely represents the largest single group of ancillary staffers, says managing partner Ralph Savarese.

Starting in the early 1980s, Howrey created three separate partnerships that are still wholly owned by the law firm. The units, which bill on an hourly basis, help manage its complex business litigation practice and assist its clients in their own strategic planning efforts.

Howrey's Capital Environmental . . . has 10 scientists and other specialists to provide its in-house lawyers and their clients with risk analysis and assessments of likely cleanup costs.

Capital Accounting . . . is staffed with 15 accountants who help litigants measure their potential exposure to damages. Capital Economics . . . has more than 30 economists and accountants to do mergers-and-acquisitions market analysis.

Darryl Van Duch, Bullish on Spinoffs, Natl. L.J., Aug. 10, 1998, at A1.

Jones Day, Perkins Coie, and Arnold & Porter also started ancillary businesses. An ancillary business is a certain kind of nonlaw business owned by a law firm, whether operated as a subsidiary of the firm or wholly in-house. Nonlawyers may co-own or manage it. Jones Day's business provided intellectual property consulting. Arnold & Porter's ancillary businesses advised on lobbying and management, real estate development, and banking and finance. Perkins Coie's subsidiary advised on environmental matters and international trade. Clients of the ancillary business may or may not be law clients of the firm. The attractiveness of owning an ancillary business, and thereby providing the firm with an additional profit center, seems to have increased after the ABA rejected rule changes that would have permitted MDPs. ABA J., Feb. 2001, at 50. ("Since the ABA's rejection of multidisciplinary practices, more law firms are branching out into law-related businesses.")

What makes a business "ancillary" is its logical or functional connection to the firm's legal services. A law firm that owns a restaurant does not have an ancillary business, but a construction law firm whose ancillary business offers architectural or engineering services does.

When a business ancillary to the practice of law is owned or controlled by lawyers, possibly along with laypersons, critics point to various dangers: conflicts of interest with law clients, domination of lawyers by the lay owners or managers of the business, confusion about whether the customer of the business is also a client of the firm, unethical marketing of legal services by using the business as a "front," and threats to the confidentiality of client information if a business client mistakenly assumes its communication is privileged.

Many lawyers vehemently oppose ancillary businesses and support an ethical rule that will prohibit most of them. "What will happen [if they proliferate] is that the profit motive will become the sole motive, not the client's best interest," predicted Dennis Block, a prominent New York lawyer. Thomas Gibbons, Branching Out, A.B.A. J., Nov. 1989, at 70. However, James Jones, then of Arnold

& Porter in Washington, D.C., said the goal was not profit but client service in a more complex world. "The lawyer's role used to be fairly well defined, and one could distinguish ... between 'legal' matters ... and 'business' matters. Increasingly, however, the distinction ... is often quite blurred. Today's lawyer is almost as likely to be focusing on economic, scientific, financial or political questions as on strictly legal issues."

The differences of opinion, sometimes sharp, on the issue of law firm ancillary businesses split the ABA. The tale is worth briefly unraveling. It tells us several things: how a professional organization works; how ethics rules come and go; and how disparate are the views of what a lawyer is or should be. So here it is:

The Rise and Fall and Humble Return of Model Rule 5.7

Responding to a growing trend, the ABA's Litigation Section advocated significant curtailment of ancillary businesses, citing threats to independent professional judgment, the quality of legal work, the reputation of the profession, and the profession's obligations to society. This last threat posits that the legal profession is "unique ... with special obligations different from any other profession or occupation," which ancillary businesses will vitiate.

The Litigation Section would have allowed law firms to offer clients nonlaw services but only if "incidental to, in connection with, and concurrent to, the provision of legal services by the law firm to such clients." Further, the nonlaw services would have to be performed by "employees of the law firm itself and not by a subsidiary or other affiliate of the law firm."

Are the Litigation Section's fears reasonable? Should they lead to a per se rule? Lawrence Fox, then a member of the section's governing council, wrote in Restraint Is Good in Trade, Natl. L.J., Apr. 29, 1991, at 17:

> [T]he ancillary business movement introduces non-lawyers into positions of influence and control of the profession. All the safeguards one can imagine do not overcome the reality that those who come to prominence and success in the operations of the ancillary business will end up with real power in the governance of the overall enterprise. Quite simply, money talks, and dependence on money changes perspectives in a way that people of the utmost good will cannot overcome. . . .
>
> Also disquieting is the possibility that, if lawyers enter other fields of endeavor, non-lawyer enterprises such as Household Finance, Coldwell Banker, American Express and WalMart are likely to wish to add legal services to their array of consumer products. As lawyers cloak their drive for financial hegemony in arguments such as "it's a public service to offer the public one-stop shopping," it becomes a very small leap, if a leap at all, to argue that these other non-law-firm, non-lawyer-controlled entities are entitled to an equal opportunity to provide this "public service," particularly when law firms seek to offer the services to non-clients of the firm and/or without any relation to the provision of legal services.

Fox anticipated further that ancillary businesses will "expose the profession to levels of liability that have been unheard of until now" and will undermine its "entitlement to self-regulation." Since Fox wrote, ancillary businesses have pro-liferated and his predictions have not come true. Score another goal for empir-ical testing.

The ABA's Standing Committee on Ethics and Professional Responsibility and its Special Coordinating Committee on Professionalism rejected a per se rule, instead favoring specific amendments to the Model Rules aimed at protect-ing customers of these businesses. The Standing Committee reported that its research "has been unable to discover any evidence of actual harm to clients, the public or the profession, arising from lawyers' participation in ancillary business activities." The Litigation Section did not seem to dispute this empirical asser-tion. Rather it appeared to rely on normative principles, behavioral assump-tions, intuition, and considerations of appearance. Should we require empirical support before an ethics rule is used to forbid otherwise lawful con-duct? We don't require it now, do we?

The Standing Committee introduced a proposal that would have permitted ancillary businesses so long as lawyers took certain precautions to guard against conflicts of interest, violation of solicitation rules, and protection of client con-fidences. The Litigation Section, by contrast, proposed to ban all ancillary ser-vices when offered by entities outside the law firm. Provision of these services within a firm would be permissible only under the limited circumstances described above.

The alternative proposals of the Standing Committee and the Litigation Section were presented in August 1991 to the ABA House of Delegates, which adopted the Litigation Section's proposal by a close vote. The result became (former) Model Rule 5.7. James Jones, whose comments in support of ancillary businesses were quoted earlier, was reported to have "played down the impor-tance of the vote," predicting: "In most states, this proposal will not be adopted."

Jones was right. In its short life Rule 5.7 won no adoptions. But then the rule never made it past age one. The ABA House of Delegates repealed it, again by a narrow vote. Nothing happened for nearly two years. Then in February 1994 the House of Delegates adopted Rule 5.7 as it currently reads. What does the rule actually tell lawyers? To be careful? That the Model Rules apply to their law-related work for clients unless they take care to separate that work from their legal work? Wouldn't a conscientious lawyer do what Rule 5.7 commands even if there were no such rule? But given this rule, may lawyers legitimately complain if nonlaw businesses (like banks and accounting firms) want to provide lawyers to help their clients with legal problems? Gary Munneke explores the debate sur-rounding law firm ancillary businesses and "proposes a resolution to this con-troversy that both ensures the long-term growth of the legal services industry and fosters professionalism." Gary Munneke, Dances with Nonlawyers: A New Per-spective on Law Firm Diversification, 61 Fordham L. Rev. 559 (1992). Interpret-ing its own rule, the California State Bar has also permitted lawyers to provide clients with nonlegal services, either directly or through an entity in which the lawyer has an ownership interest, so long as conflict and confidentiality obliga-tions are observed and no legal fees are divided with nonlawyers. California Opinion 1995-141.

Part Five

FIRST AMENDMENT RIGHTS OF LAWYERS AND JUDICIAL CANDIDATES

XV

Free Speech Rights of Lawyers and Judicial Candidates

- *Talking to the Press About Your Cases*
- *Criticizing Judges*
- *Speech Rights of Judicial Candidates*

Lawyers enjoy First Amendment protection for two kinds of speech. Like everyone else, though with at least two important exceptions, lawyers may criticize government, including courts and judges, and speak about public issues. The two exceptions? A lawyer enjoys less freedom than others do to speak publicly about her own cases. Also, lawyers may sometimes be disciplined for false accusations against judges. The subject of this chapter is traditional free speech issues as they affect lawyers and judges. The First Amendment also protects a lawyer's commercial speech — speech that markets legal services — which is the subject of chapter 16.

Some crimes in the orbit of the administration of justice are often, though not necessarily, committed through speech. Consider contempt of court or obstruction of justice. Lawyers who commit these crimes may be punished even if they are advocating their clients' interests at the time. One kind of court sanction is punishment through summary (or direct) contempt. The court imposes an immediate sanction without traditional procedural protections. After a review of authorities, the Georgia Supreme Court concluded that criminal contempt requires, first, "that the attorney's statements and attendant conduct either actually interfered with or posed an imminent threat of interfering with the administration of justice;" and second, "that the attorney knew or should have known that the statements and attendant conduct exceeded the outermost bounds of permissible advocacy." These findings must be made beyond a reasonable doubt. In re Jefferson, 657 S.E.2d 830 (Ga. 2008).

Cases vary on their tolerance for the use of this summary remedy. Some examples:

- The Supreme Court, without briefing or oral argument, affirmed summary contempt against a lawyer who, after hearing the judge instruct other lawyers in the case not to ask witnesses questions that would reveal certain information to the jury, asked two such questions. The trial court found that the conduct "permanently prejudiced the jury in favor of [the lawyer's] client." Pounders v. Watson, 521 U.S. 982 (1997).

- At a bench conference, Fawer responded to a sarcastic comment of an opposing lawyer by saying "Go kiss my ass, okay?" He refused the judge's request for an apology. At a later bench conference, Fawer said, "Judge, I don't want to deal with this idiot." Apology declined. At a third bench conference, after the judge had overruled Fawer's objection, he replied, "Ah, shit." Contempt upheld. United States v. Ortlieb, 274 F.3d 871 (5th Cir. 2001).
- In In re Dodson, 572 A.2d 328 (Conn. 1990), summary contempt was affirmed where, immediately after imposition of sentence, the defense lawyer interrupted the court to say that the sentence was "totally outrageous" and had "no basis."
- Matter of Daniels, 570 A.2d 416 (N.J. 1990), affirmed summary contempt where a defense lawyer twice responded to adverse rulings by laughing, rolling his head, and throwing himself back on his seat. The lawyer's behavior was said to threaten the "dignity" and the "authority" of the court.
- Activist lawyer William Kunstler was summarily found guilty of criminal contempt after he continued to address the court following the judge's instruction to call the next case. Kunstler was representing one of the defendants in the "Central Park jogger" case. Among other things, he said to the judge: "You are a disgrace to the bench." Kunstler v. Galligan, 571 N.Y.S.2d 930 (1st Dept.), aff 'd without opinion, 587 N.E.2d 286 (N.Y. 1991).

By contrast, courts have held that summary contempt was not the appropriate method for punishing all statements that are "crude" or "vulgar." One must also look to the effect on the tribunal. "Summary punishment for direct contempt 'is warranted only when essential to the orderly administration of justice.'" Commonwealth v. Diamond, 703 N.E.2d 1195 (Mass. 1999) (summary contempt rejected where lawyer said to his opponent in court: "If you want discovery, you're going to get discovery up the ass."). See also Williams v. Williams, 721 A.2d 1072 (Pa. 1998) (summary contempt rejected where lawyer, after an adverse ruling, said about the judge, within hearing of others in court: "He's such a fucking asshole.").

Aside from contemptuous conduct in court, lawyer free speech issues tend to arise in two factual contexts, both of which we will address: first, when a lawyer speaks to the press about a pending or impending litigation with which the lawyer is or was associated; and second, when a lawyer criticizes a judge or the court's performance in her case. This chapter is also about the speech rights of candidates for judicial office. Specifically, it addresses a judicial candidate's constitutional right to tell voters his or her views on legal questions that will come before the candidate if elected. Traditionally, the electoral statements of judicial candidates (who may or may not be sitting judges) have been heavily restricted. The Supreme Court changed all that in 2002, but in doing so left important questions unanswered.

The issues in this chapter, and many others, including speech issues that arise in bar admission and lawyer discipline, are discussed in Professor W. Bradley Wendel's 139-page opus, Free Speech for Lawyers, 28 Hastings Const. L.Q. 305

(2001). Professor Wendel writes that he does "not aim just to criticize reported cases, but rather to show how the regulation of lawyers' speech fits within the various doctrinal complexities that characterize First Amendment law and within the ethical norms that govern the practice of law." He concludes, however, "that decisions by courts considering free speech arguments by lawyers are surprisingly out of touch with the mainstream of constitutional law. While generally applicable First Amendment law is astonishingly protective of expression . . . the decisions of courts in lawyer-speech cases cluster around the opposite extreme."

A. PUBLIC COMMENT ABOUT PENDING CASES

"What Can I Say?"

"My name is Margaret McClellan, and I represent Cameron Wykoff, who, as you know, unless you've been living on the moon the last two months, is charged with murdering a woman at his Malibu estate. Wykoff, though not a household name nationally, is legendary and exceedingly wealthy as a songwriter and promoter in L.A. The dead woman, Kelsey Anne Bird, is — well, was — a B-movie actress in her early forties, still getting parts, mostly as the mistress of a married guy or the older sister of the female lead. She was quite fetching when she was in her twenties, and even as she aged the camera loved her. She resembled Paulette Goddard in Chaplin's *Modern Times.* You know, the gamine look. A dash of young girl, a dash of danger and abandon. She carried it off well.

"Cameron vaguely knew Bird as people in the industry always vaguely know each other. He ran into her at a party last month. At about midnight she accompanied him, willingly of course, back to his estate. At about 4 A.M. that morning, he called the police to say that Bird had killed herself on his veranda with one of his licensed firearms, a valuable nineteenth-century collector's item that Cameron had removed from a locked case to show Bird. Cameron collects antique weapons. The D.A. claims Cameron murdered her either intentionally or recklessly.

"It's not true, of course. For one thing, Cameron had no motive. For another thing, he's quite skilled with firearms, so it could not have been a reckless act. We have a strong case. I know how to try it. That's not why I'm talking to you.

"The case is all over the press and on cable practically 24/7. Greta has dedicated her Fox show to it most nights, using the usual talking heads — lawyers and former cops who can only guess about the facts. That doesn't stop them from speaking with authority, of course, as if they know something, which they definitely do not. Their comments are hostile to Cameron, although they take care first to pay pro forma respect to the presumption of innocence. Believe me, on cable, the presumption is guilt or you lose the audience. And then there's Nancy Grace, a former prosecutor. I swear you'd think she'd never met an innocent defendant. She doesn't even pretend to be neutral in my humble opinion. Her sneer alone insinuates proof beyond a reasonable doubt.

"Look, I'm sounding more critical than I have a right to be. Most of the talking heads are my friends. I've been on these shows myself and probably will be again. It's fun. You get recognized on the street and good tables at crowded restaurants. It attracts clients. But when you're on the tube pretending to be omniscient, you're really just guessing based on stories in the tabloids or the supermarket weeklies. Or Drudge. Or some blog. Or nothing but your imagination, very often.

"And that's my problem. Any actual facts they have are almost all coming out of law enforcement, which leaks like a colander. I'm not blaming the D.A.'s office, necessarily. I assume prosecutors will be circumspect, at least most of them. But cops, paralegals, crime lab people, clerks, secretaries. They each have access to pieces of this case and are occupationally inclined to view the evidence harshly. The crime reporters are buddies with this group and have been for years. Cases come and go, but the press and the law enforcement people stay put. The press knows how to massage egos and reward cooperation with friendly coverage. The law enforcement crowd knows how to use the press (not for attribution, of course) to slime defendants and create a bad climate for the future trial. We're talking about relationships going back years, decades. All the negative publicity you're seeing is coming out of those relationships.

"My own mother asked me yesterday how I could defend 'that bastard.' My own mother! She's a cable junkie, and she's already convicted Cameron. And she's one of the fair-minded ones, given what her daughter does for a living. But it's people like my retired mother that will be on the jury for this three-month trial. Even casual cable watchers will see a lot of this story between now and the trial six months from now. They'll all swear to decide fairly on the evidence, of course, and they'll mean it, too. But who knows how this garbage, coming month after month, is going to affect the jurors? I'm not happy and neither is my client.

"Cameron, who's out on $5 million bail, says to me, 'Don't they call you for a response?' Sure they do. They have to. Press ethics, right? But what can I say? You tell me. As I read the rules my hands are tied, or I mean my lips are sealed. What can I say? An example: The story leaked that according to the police lab report, the gun was fired from ten feet away, which if true totally undermines suicide. But it's not true according to our investigation. Am I allowed to explain why it's wrong if I choose to go public with my theory?

"Another thing, even more troublesome. When this sort of case breaks the tabs and cable get all over the defendant's life. They talk to former girlfriends and wives, unhappy former business partners, the kid he bullied in ninth grade, neighbors who say things like *he was strange, kept to himself, never fit in, didn't say 'good morning' after I said 'good morning,' rarely smiled, I kept my distance.* They report what he did when he got drunk in college. I mean, they stop at nothing. They quote 'informed sources.' There are always 'informed sources.' Everyone has done things they'd rather forget. Friends can say he's a nice guy but 'nice guy' doesn't sell. One tab reported that a former unnamed girlfriend stopped seeing Cameron because he liked rough sex and it scared her. That's what the public is hearing. None of it will get into evidence.

"Well, I have a few choice bits of information I can tell about Ms. Bird, believe me. Items that will support our claim of suicide. Episodes in her romantic life, medical records, a 911 tape, overdoses, financial problems. I'm not getting into details. But let's just say that maybe I should bring her down a little, so the public, or the part that will sit on the jury, realizes early on that we're not dealing with an untroubled soul of angelic proportions. Unlike the stuff coming out about Cameron, some of this will be admissible at trial to show Bird's state of mind. Suicidal.

"Cameron has a publicity team, of course. He'd rather I make the public statements because I'm more credible than a flack. But he says if I can't, would I just consult with the flacks to help them decide what *they'll* say and how to put it? I'm considering it, but I don't know. It's also why I'm here."

Laurie Cohen had a source. When the United States was investigating Michael Milken for securities law violations in the 1980s, Cohen, a Wall Street Journal reporter, wrote frequent stories, attributed to unidentified sources, revealing bits and pieces of the government's case. Laurie Cohen won't identify her source. Many assumed it was the prosecutor's office, congressional staffers, or a federal agency like the SEC, and that the source's motive was to pressure Milken to plead guilty, which he eventually did. Milken's lawyers decried the leaks and, with the court's aid, tried but failed to trace them. Milken, not without funds, had his own public relations team, which had mixed success trying to rebut the leaks. Milken's case was one of many in recent years that were pre-tried, in part at least, in the media. Recall, too, the rape case against William Kennedy Smith. Smith's 1991 trial made headlines because of his middle name. The media had no trouble reporting on its progress even, apparently, without cooperation from his defense lawyer, Roy Black, who claims to have a firm policy against talking to reporters about his cases. Be that as it may, the first prize for pretrial publicity still belongs, hands down, to California's 1995 prosecution of O. J. Simpson for the murder of his former wife, Nicole Brown Simpson, and her friend, Ronald Goldman. You will be interested to know that California, apparently alone among jurisdictions, did not then have some form of the ABA rule restricting pretrial publicity (Rule 3.6 or DR 7-107). It has since adopted a substantially equivalent rule. Cal. Rule 5-120.

Beyond the risk of discipline or contempt, lawyers must be aware of other dangers when they speak publicly. As discussed at page 881, they may be sued for defamation. Earlier (page 68), we saw that a lawyer's status as a client's agent may mean that her statements are attributable to the client as a vicarious admission. Further, some courts have rejected claims of privilege for conversations between counsel and a client's public relations agent. See page 58.

Some trial judges seek to reduce the incidence of pretrial comment, attributed or not, by issuing "gag" orders that forbid the lawyers, their clients, and persons working with either to talk to the media, except perhaps to repeat matters of public record or to state the general nature of a charge or defense. A gag order has double value. Unlike legal ethics rules, a gag order restrains both lawyers and nonlawyers, most notably investigative agencies and clients. And because violation of a gag order can result in a criminal contempt conviction, it may get more respect than underenforced ethics rules.

Gag orders have three problems, which also plague ethical rules forbidding public comments: (1) Although violations are easy to detect (there's the news story, after all), violators are hard to identify, especially if the source is in a government agency, where hundreds of people may have access to the information; (2) investigation and prosecution may be the job either of the very agency whose personnel are suspect or of prosecutors who work closely with it; and (3) appellate courts differ in their tolerance for gag orders. Compare United States v. Brown, 218 F.3d 415 (5th Cir. 2000) (in prosecution of prominent Louisiana political figure, upholding gag order forbidding public comment that "could interfere with a fair trial or prejudice any defendant, the government, or the administration of justice") and United States v. Cutler, 58 F.3d 825 (2d Cir. 1995) (holding Bruce Cutler in contempt for violating gag order in prosecution of his client John Gotti), with United States v. Salameh, 992 F.2d 445 (2d Cir. 1993) (vacating gag order as overly broad prior restraint in trial of persons accused of 1993 World Trade Center bombing) and New York Times Co. v. Rothwax, 533 N.Y.S.2d 73 (1st Dept. 1988) (reversing gag order in trial of Joel Steinberg for murder of "daughter" Lisa). You will not have failed to notice that gag orders are prevalent in those very cases that the media find irresistible.

May a gag order gag the litigants as well as the lawyers? Judge Vinson thought so in United States v. Hill, 893 F. Supp. 1039 (N.D. Fla. 1994). Hill was charged with violating a federal act protecting abortion clinics. The judge took "judicial notice that the crime for which the defendant in this case is accused has received extensive local and national publicity, and that such publicity will almost certainly continue." The gag order applied to the defendant and counsel.

Some judges have suggested that the First Amendment is more tolerant of orders that gag prosecutors or other government lawyers. See United States v. Simon, 664 F. Supp. 780 (S.D.N.Y. 1987), aff'd sub nom. In re Dow Jones & Co., 842 F.2d 603 (2d Cir. 1988); Levine v. United States Dist. Court, 764 F.2d 590 (9th Cir. 1985) (Sneed, J., concurring); In re Axelrod, 549 A.2d 653 (Vt. 1988). They're right, aren't they? Responding to the general perception that law enforcement leaks threaten greater harm to a defendant's hope for a fair trial than defense leaks pose for the state, John Barrett proposes a remedy in The Leak and the Craft: A Hard Line Proposal to Stop Unaccountable Disclosures of Law Enforcement Information, 68 Fordham L. Rev. 613 (1999) (part of a symposium issue on the Independent Counsel investigation of President Clinton).

To understand this subterranean world a little better, consider, in each case and generally, the motives of each side for revealing information to the media. (What were Dominic Gentile's motives in the case following?) Also, which side is likely to have greater media contacts? Which side generally has more to gain if a case escapes public attention? How will publicity affect judges?

Wait a minute. How many sides are there? If you said two, count again. This play has a third part: Laurie Cohen's. And if ever there was a time when courts could hope to try cases out of the full glare of media attention, 24-hour cable news and the Web have changed all that, putting aside, as we must, the quality of the analysis (or lack thereof) or the newsworthiness of the trials (same). For the fact is, pre- or post-cable, some cases are big news. The press was going to cover the prosecutions of O. J. Simpson, Martha Stewart, L'il Kim, Michael Milken, Lewis Libby (Cheney's chief of staff), Michael Jackson, Puff Daddy, Timothy McVeigh, Oliver North, Kobe Bryant, and Scott Peterson, come what may. (How else would you know some of those names?) A lawyer on such a case must conjure with publicity, like it or not. How long will a defense lawyer be able to say "no comment" if, day after day, news stories tilt in favor of the prosecution because no one will speak for the defendant? Unlike Michael Milken, most clients cannot afford a press agent. It's the lawyer or no one.

Rules in every jurisdiction limit what lawyers may say about pending matters. The ABA Model Rule is 3.6. See also Rule 3.8(f), which requires prosecutors to use "reasonable care" to prevent law enforcement personnel from making statements to the press that the prosecutor may not and tells prosecutors that, with narrow exception, they must "refrain from making extrajudicial comments that have a substantial likelihood of heightening public condemnation of the accused." (Chapter 8 set out a case in which a court refused to dismiss a complaint against a prosecutor and her employer, New York City, alleging that the prosecutor's extrajudicial statements denied the plaintiff a fair trial. See page 476.) Further, Rule 5.3 requires a lawyer to supervise nonlegal personnel.

Notice that the rule applies in civil as well as criminal cases and whether the fact finder is a judge or jury. Efforts to limit the rule to criminal cases or jury trials (or both) have not succeeded. Should they? As it happens, nearly all debate about the proper scope of these rules focuses on criminal cases. But not exclusively. The Michigan Supreme Court sharply divided in Maldonado v. Ford Motor Co., 719 N.W.2d 809 (Mich. 2006), in upholding a trial judge's dismissal of a sexual harassment claim after the plaintiff and her lawyers repeatedly publicized inadmissible information although the judge had warned them not to do so. The dissents relied in part on the First Amendment and used aggressive language in characterizing the majority opinion that, as we see in part B below, if used by a lawyer about a judge would invite discipline. The dissents called the majority's reasoning an "acrobatic effort," "disingenuous," and the product of "whim," among other characterizations.

In *Gentile*, below, the Supreme Court directly addressed the First Amendment ramifications of ethical rules forbidding comment on pending cases. The Court had avoided the constitutional issue three decades prior. In re Sawyer, 360 U.S. 622 (1959), vacated discipline because the record did not establish a violation of the ethics rule. As Justice Kennedy tells you, Nevada's rule in *Gentile* was almost identical to Model Rule 3.6 as it originally read. The rule was amended after *Gentile* to conform to the case, as discussed hereafter. But one part of the rule has not changed. The rule forbids public comments that "will have a substantial likelihood of materially prejudicing an adjudicative proceeding." But the rule also allows certain statements "notwithstanding" this possibility. The Court had to construe both provisions. The Court upheld the "substantial likelihood" test against First Amendment challenge but split 5-4 on the meaning of that term. The Court also split 5-4 on whether Gentile's speech fell within one of safe-harbor provisions in the rule. Justice O'Connor was the swing vote both times. The post-*Gentile* changes reworded those provisions modestly and also added what is now Rule 3.6(c) and (d) and Rule 3.8(f).

I wish *Gentile* were shorter and the Court's holding clearer. Perhaps someday the Court will revisit the issue and offer better guidance. But until then, *Gentile* is the leading case on the extent to which rules like Rule 3.6 can silence lawyers from making public statements about their cases. For an analysis of *Gentile*'s issues, using as a backdrop the O. J. Simpson murder trial, certainly our most flagrant modern experience with extrajudicial comment, see Kevin Cole & Fred

Zacharias, The Agony of Victory and the Ethics of Lawyer Speech, 69 S. Cal. L. Rev. 1627 (1996).

GENTILE v. STATE BAR OF NEVADA
501 U.S. 1030 (1991)

JUSTICE KENNEDY announced the judgment of the Court and delivered the opinion of the Court with respect to Parts III and VI, and an opinion with respect to Parts I, II, IV, and V in which JUSTICE MARSHALL, JUSTICE BLACKMUN, and JUSTICE STEVENS join.

Hours after his client was indicted on criminal charges, petitioner Gentile, who is a member of the Bar of the State of Nevada, held a press conference. He made a prepared statement, which we set forth in Appendix A to this opinion, and then he responded to questions. We refer to most of those questions and responses in the course of our opinion.

Some six months later, the criminal case was tried to a jury and the client was acquitted on all counts. The State Bar of Nevada then filed a complaint against petitioner, alleging a violation of Nevada Supreme Court Rule 177, a rule governing pretrial publicity almost identical to ABA Model Rule of Professional Conduct 3.6. . . .

[The Nevada Disciplinary Board recommended that Gentile be privately reprimanded. Gentile waived confidentiality and appealed to the Nevada Supreme Court, which affirmed. Gentile, represented by American University Law Professor Michael Tigar, took his free speech claims to the Supreme Court.]

I . . .

B

We are not called upon to determine the constitutionality of the ABA Model Rule of Professional Conduct 3.6 (1981), but only Rule 177 as it has been interpreted and applied by the State of Nevada. Model Rule 3.6's requirement of substantial likelihood of material prejudice is not necessarily flawed. Interpreted in a proper and narrow manner, for instance, to prevent an attorney of record from releasing information of grave prejudice on the eve of jury selection, the phrase substantial likelihood of material prejudice might punish only speech that creates a danger of imminent and substantial harm. A rule governing speech, even speech entitled to full constitutional protection, need not use the words "clear and present danger" in order to pass constitutional muster. . . .

The drafters of Model Rule 3.6 apparently thought the substantial likelihood of material prejudice formulation approximated the clear and present danger test. See ABA Annotated Model Rules of Professional Conduct 243 (1984) ("formulation in Model Rule 3.6 incorporates a standard approximating clear and present danger by focusing on the likelihood of injury and its substantiality"). . . .

The difference between the requirement of serious and imminent threat found in the disciplinary rules of some States and the more common formulation of substantial likelihood of material prejudice could prove mere semantics. Each standard requires an assessment of proximity and degree of harm. Each may be capable of valid application. Under those principles, nothing inherent in Nevada's formulation fails First Amendment review; but as this case demonstrates, Rule 177 has not been interpreted in conformance with those principles by the Nevada Supreme Court.

II

Even if one were to accept respondent's argument that lawyers participating in judicial proceedings may be subjected, consistent with the First Amendment, to speech restrictions that could not be imposed on the press or general public, the judgment should not be upheld. The record does not support the conclusion that petitioner knew or reasonably should have known his remarks created a substantial likelihood of material prejudice, if the Rule's terms are given any meaningful content. . . .

A. PRE-INDICTMENT PUBLICITY

On January 31, 1987, undercover police officers with the Las Vegas Metropolitan Police Department (Metro) reported large amounts of cocaine (four kilograms) and travelers' checks (almost $300,000) missing from a safety deposit vault at Western Vault Corporation. The drugs and money had been used as part of an undercover operation conducted by Metro's Intelligence Bureau. Petitioner's client, Grady Sanders, owned Western Vault. John Moran, the Las Vegas sheriff, reported the theft at a press conference on February 2, 1987, naming the police and Western Vault employees as suspects.

Although two police officers, Detective Steve Scholl and Sergeant Ed Schaub, enjoyed free access to the deposit box throughout the period of the theft, and no log reported comings and goings at the vault, a series of press reports over the following year indicated that investigators did not consider these officers responsible. Instead, investigators focused upon Western Vault and its owner. Newspaper reports quoted the sheriff and other high police officials as saying that they had not lost confidence in the "elite" Intelligence Bureau. From the beginning, Sheriff Moran had "complete faith and trust" in his officers.

The media reported that, following announcement of the cocaine theft, others with deposit boxes at Western Vault had come forward to claim missing items. One man claimed the theft of his life savings of $90,000. Western Vault suffered heavy losses as customers terminated their box rentals, and the company soon went out of business. The police opened other boxes in search of the missing items, and it was reported they seized $264,900 in United States currency from a box listed as unrented.

Initial press reports stated that Sanders and Western Vault were being cooperative; but as time went on, the press noted that the police investigation had failed to identify the culprit and through a process of elimination was beginning to point toward Sanders. Reports quoted the affidavit of a detective that the theft was part of an effort to discredit the undercover operation and that business records suggested the existence of a business relation between Sanders and the targets of a Metro undercover probe.

The deputy police chief announced the two detectives with access to the vault had been "cleared" as possible suspects. According to an unnamed "source close to the investigation," the police shifted from the idea that the thief had planned to discredit the undercover operation to the theory that the thief had unwittingly stolen from the police. The stories noted that Sanders "could not be reached for comment."

The story took a more sensational turn with reports that the two police suspects had been cleared by police investigators after passing lie detector tests. The tests were administered by one Ray Slaughter. But later, the FBI arrested Slaughter for distributing cocaine to an FBI informant, Belinda Antal. It was also reported that the $264,900 seized from the unrented safety deposit box at Western Vault had been stored there in a suitcase owned by one Tammy Sue Markham. Markham was "facing a number of federal drug-related charges" in Tucson, Arizona. Markham reported items missing from three boxes she rented at Western Vault, as did one Beatrice Connick, who, according to press reports, was a Colombian national living in San Diego and "not facing any drug related charges." (As it turned out, petitioner impeached Connick's credibility at trial with the existence of a money laundering conviction.) Connick also was reported to have taken and passed a lie detector test to substantiate her charges. Finally, press reports indicated that Sanders had refused to take a police polygraph examination. The press suggested that the FBI suspected Metro officers were responsible for the theft, and reported that the theft had severely damaged relations between the FBI and Metro.

B.   THE PRESS CONFERENCE

Petitioner is a Las Vegas criminal defense attorney, an author of articles about criminal law and procedure, and a former Associate Dean of the National College for Criminal Defense Lawyers and Public Defenders. Through leaks from the police department, he had some advance notice of the date an indictment would be returned and the nature of the charges against Sanders. Petitioner had monitored the publicity surrounding the case, and, prior to the indictment was personally aware of at least 17 articles in the major local newspapers, the Las Vegas Sun and Las Vegas Review-Journal, and numerous local television news stories which reported on the Western Vault theft and ensuing investigation. Petitioner determined, for the first time in his career, that he would call a formal press conference. He did not blunder into a press conference, but acted with considerable deliberation.

1.   Petitioner's Motivation

As petitioner explained to the disciplinary board, his primary motivation was the concern that, unless some of the weaknesses in the State's case were made public, a potential jury venire would be poisoned by repetition in the press of information being released by the police and prosecutors, in particular the repeated press reports about polygraph tests and the fact that the two police officers were no longer suspects. Respondent distorts Rule 177 when it suggests this explanation admits a purpose to prejudice the venire and so proves a violation of the Rule. Rule 177 only prohibits the dissemination of information that one knows or reasonably should know has a "substantial likelihood of materially prejudicing an adjudicative proceeding." Petitioner did not indicate he thought he could sway the pool of potential jurors to form an opinion in advance of the trial, nor did he seek to discuss evidence that would be inadmissible at trial. He sought only to counter publicity already deemed prejudicial. The Southern Nevada Disciplinary Board so found. It said petitioner attempted

> (i) to counter public opinion which he perceived as adverse to Mr. Sanders, (ii) . . . to refute certain matters regarding his client which had appeared in the media, (iii) to fight back against the perceived efforts of the prosecution to poison the prospective juror pool, and (iv) to publicly present Sanders' side of the case.

Far from an admission that he sought to "materially prejudic[e] an adjudicative proceeding," petitioner sought only to stop a wave of publicity he perceived as prejudicing potential jurors against his client and injuring his client's reputation in the community.

Petitioner gave a second reason for holding the press conference, which demonstrates the additional value of his speech. Petitioner acted in part because the investigation had taken a serious toll on his client. Sanders was "not a man in good health," having suffered multiple open-heart surgeries prior to these events. And prior to indictment, the mere suspicion of wrongdoing had caused the closure of Western Vault and the loss of Sanders' ground lease on an Atlantic City, New Jersey, property.

An attorney's duties do not begin inside the courtroom door. He or she cannot ignore the practical implications of a legal proceeding for the client. Just as an attorney may recommend a plea bargain or civil settlement to avoid the adverse consequences of a possible loss after trial, so too an attorney may take reasonable steps to defend a client's reputation and reduce the adverse consequences of indictment, especially in the face of a prosecution deemed unjust or commenced with improper motives. A defense attorney may pursue lawful strategies to obtain dismissal of an indictment or reduction of charges, including an attempt to demonstrate in the court of public opinion that the client does not deserve to be tried.

2. Petitioner's Investigation of Rule 177

Rule 177 is phrased in terms of what an attorney "knows or reasonably should know." On the evening before the press conference, petitioner and two colleagues spent several hours researching the extent of an attorney's obligations under Rule 177. He decided, as we have held, see Patton v. Yount, 467 U.S. 1025 (1984), that the timing of a statement was crucial in the assessment of possible prejudice and the Rule's application.

Upon return of the indictment, the court set a trial date for August 1988, some six months in the future. Petitioner knew, at the time of his statement, that a jury would not be empaneled for six months at the earliest, if ever. He recalled reported cases finding no prejudice resulting from juror exposure to "far worse" information two and four months before trial, and concluded that his proposed statement was not substantially likely to result in material prejudice.

A statement which reaches the attention of the venire on the eve of voir dire might require a continuance or cause difficulties in securing an impartial jury, and at the very least could complicate the jury selection process. As turned out to be the case here, exposure to the same statement six months prior to trial would not result in prejudice, the content fading from memory long before the trial date.

In 1988, Clark County, Nevada had a population in excess of 600,000 persons. Given the size of the community from which any potential jury venire would be drawn and the length of time before trial, only the most damaging of information could give rise to any likelihood of prejudice. The innocuous content of petitioner's statement reinforces my conclusion.

3.   The Content of Petitioner's Statement

[The following transcript of Gentile's press conference statement, which appears as Appendix A to Justice Kennedy's opinion, is printed out of order for fuller understanding of Kennedy's opinion.]

APPENDIX A — PETITIONER'S OPENING REMARKS
AT THE PRESS CONFERENCE OF FEBRUARY 5, 1988.

Mr. Gentile: I want to start this off by saying in clear terms that I think that this indictment is a significant event in the history of the evolution of sophistication of the City of Las Vegas, because things of this nature, of exactly this nature have happened in New York with the French Connection case and in Miami with cases — at least two cases there — have happened in Chicago as well, but all three of those cities have been honest enough to indict the people who did it; the police department, crooked cops.

When this case goes to trial, and as it develops, you're going to see that the evidence will prove not only that Grady Sanders is an innocent person and had nothing to do with any of the charges that are being leveled against him, but that the person that was in the most direct position to have stolen the drugs and money, the American Express Travelers' checks, is Detective Steve Scholl.

There is far more evidence that will establish that Detective Scholl took these drugs and took these American Express Travelers' checks than any other living human being.

And I have to say that I feel that Grady Sanders is being used as a scapegoat to try to cover up for what has to be obvious to people at Las Vegas Metropolitan Police Department and at the District Attorney's office.

Now, with respect to these other charges that are contained in this indictment, the so-called other victims, as I sit here today I can tell you that one, two — four of them are known drug dealers and convicted money launderers and drug dealers; three of whom didn't say a word about anything until after they were approached by Metro and after they were already in trouble and are trying to work themselves out of something.

Now, up until the moment, of course, that they started going along with what detectives from Metro wanted them to say, these people were being held out as being incredible and liars by the very same people who are going to say now that you can believe them.

Another problem that you are going to see develop here is the fact that of these other counts, at least four of them said nothing about any of this, about anything being missing until after the Las Vegas Metropolitan Police Department announced publicly last year their claim that drugs and American Express Travelers' c[h]ecks were missing.

Many of the contracts that these people had show on the face of the contract that there is $100,000 in insurance for the contents of the box. If you look at the indictment very closely, you're going to see that these claims fall under $100,000.

Finally, there were only two claims on the face of the indictment that came to our attention prior to the events of January 31 of '87, that being the date that Metro said that there was something missing from their box.

And both of these claims were dealt with by Mr. Sanders and we're dealing here essentially with people that we're not sure if they ever had anything in the box.

That's about all that I have to say.

Petitioner was disciplined for statements to the effect that (1) the evidence demonstrated his client's innocence, (2) the likely thief was a police detective, Steve Scholl, and (3) the other victims were not credible, as most were drug dealers or convicted money launderers, all but one of whom had only accused Sanders in response to police pressure, in the process of "trying to work themselves out of something." He also strongly implied that Steve Scholl could be observed in a videotape suffering from symptoms of cocaine use. Of course, only a small fraction of petitioner's remarks were disseminated to the public, in two newspaper stories and two television news broadcasts.

The stories mentioned not only Gentile's press conference but also a prosecution response and police press conference. The chief deputy district attorney was quoted as saying that this was a legitimate indictment, and that prosecutors cannot bring an indictment to court unless they can prove the charges in it beyond a reasonable doubt. Deputy Police Chief Sullivan stated for the police department, "We in Metro are very satisfied our officers (Scholl and Sgt. Ed Schaub) had nothing to do with this theft or any other. They are both above reproach. Both are veteran police officers who are dedicated to honest law enforcement." In the context of general public awareness, these police and prosecution statements were no more likely to result in prejudice than were petitioner's statements, but given the repetitive publicity from the police investigation, it is difficult to come to any conclusion but that the balance remained in favor of the prosecution.

Much of the information provided by petitioner had been published in one form or another, obviating any potential for prejudice. The remainder, and details petitioner refused to provide, were available to any journalist willing to do a little bit of investigative work.

Petitioner's statements lack any of the more obvious bases for a finding of prejudice. Unlike the police, he refused to comment on polygraph tests except to confirm earlier reports that Sanders had not submitted to the police polygraph; he mentioned no confessions and no evidence from searches or test results; he refused to elaborate upon his charge that the other so-called victims were not credible, except to explain his general theory that they were pressured to testify in an attempt to avoid drug-related legal trouble, and that some of them may have asserted claims in an attempt to collect insurance money.

C. EVENTS FOLLOWING THE PRESS CONFERENCE

Petitioner's judgment that no likelihood of material prejudice would result from his comments was vindicated by events at trial. While it is true that Rule 177's standard for controlling pretrial publicity must be judged at the time a statement is made, ex post evidence can have probative value in some cases. Here, where the Rule purports to demand, and the Constitution requires, consideration of the character of the harm and its heightened likelihood of occurrence, the record is altogether devoid of facts one would expect to follow upon any statement that created a real likelihood of material prejudice to a criminal jury trial.

The trial took place on schedule in August 1988, with no request by either party for a venue change or continuance. The jury was empaneled with no apparent difficulty. The trial judge questioned the jury venire about publicity. Although many had vague recollections of reports that cocaine stored at Western Vault had been stolen from a police undercover operation, and, as petitioner had feared, one remembered that the police had been cleared of suspicion, not a single juror indicated any recollection of petitioner or his press conference.

At trial, all material information disseminated during petitioner's press conference was admitted in evidence before the jury, including information questioning the motives and credibility of supposed victims who testified against Sanders, and Detective Scholl's ingestion of drugs in the course of undercover operations (in order, he testified, to gain the confidence of suspects). The jury acquitted petitioner's client, and, as petitioner explained before the disciplinary board,

> when the trial was over with and the man was acquitted the next week the foreman of the jury phoned me and said to me that if they would have had a verdict form before them with respect to the guilt of Steve Scholl they would have found the man proven guilty beyond a reasonable doubt.

There is no support for the conclusion that petitioner's statement created a likelihood of material prejudice, or indeed of any harm of sufficient magnitude or imminence to support a punishment for speech.

III

As interpreted by the Nevada Supreme Court, the Rule is void for vagueness, in any event, for its safe harbor provision, Rule 177(3), misled petitioner into thinking that he could give his press conference without fear of discipline. Rule 177(3)(a) provides that a lawyer "may state without elaboration . . . the general nature of the . . . defense." Statements under this provision are protected "[n]otwithstanding subsection 1 and 2(a-f)." By necessary operation of the word "notwithstanding," the Rule contemplates that a lawyer describing the "general nature of the . . . defense" "without elaboration" need fear no discipline, even if he comments on "[t]he character, credibility, reputation or criminal record of a . . . witness," and even if he "knows or reasonably should know that [the statement] will have a substantial likelihood of materially prejudicing an adjudicative proceeding."

Given this grammatical structure, and absent any clarifying interpretation by the state court, the Rule fails to provide " 'fair notice to those to whom [it] is directed.' " Grayned v. City of Rockford, 408 U.S. 104, 112 (1972). A lawyer seeking to avail himself of Rule 177(3)'s protection must guess at its contours. The right to explain the "general" nature of the defense without "elaboration" provides insufficient guidance because "general" and "elaboration" are both classic terms of degree. In the context before us, these terms have no settled usage or tradition of interpretation in law. The lawyer has no principle for determining when his remarks pass from the safe harbor of the general to the forbidden sea of the elaborated.

Petitioner testified he thought his statements were protected by Rule 177(3). A review of the press conference supports that claim. He gave only a brief opening statement, and on numerous occasions declined to answer reporters' questions seeking more detailed comments. . . .

The prohibition against vague regulations of speech is based in part on the need to eliminate the impermissible risk of discriminatory enforcement, for history shows that speech is suppressed when either the speaker or the message is critical of those who enforce the law. The question is not whether discriminatory enforcement occurred here, and we assume it did not, but whether the Rule is so imprecise that discriminatory enforcement is a real possibility. The inquiry is of particular relevance when one of the classes most affected by the regulation is the criminal defense bar, which has the professional mission to challenge actions of the State. Petitioner, for instance, succeeded in preventing the conviction of his client, and the speech in issue involved criticism of the government.

IV

The analysis to this point resolves the case, and in the usual order of things the discussion should end here. Five Members of the Court, however, endorse an extended discussion which concludes that Nevada may interpret its requirement of substantial likelihood of material prejudice under a standard more deferential than is the usual rule where speech is concerned. It appears necessary, therefore, to set forth my objections to that conclusion and to the reasoning which underlies it.

Respondent argues speech by an attorney is subject to greater regulation than speech by others, and restrictions on an attorney's speech should be assessed under a balancing test that weighs the State's interest in the regulation of a specialized profession against the lawyer's First Amendment interest in the kind of speech that was at issue. The cases cited by our colleagues to support this balancing involved either commercial speech by attorneys or restrictions upon release of information that the attorney could gain only by use of the court's discovery process. Neither of those categories, nor the underlying interests which justified their creation, were implicated here. Petitioner was disciplined because he proclaimed to the community what he thought to be a misuse of the prosecutorial and police powers. Wide-open balancing of interests is not appropriate in this context.

A

Respondent would justify a substantial limitation on speech by attorneys because "lawyers have special access to information, including confidential statements from clients and information obtained through pretrial discovery or plea negotiations" and so lawyers' statements "are likely to be received as especially authoritative." Rule 177, however, does not reflect concern for the attorney's special access to client confidences, material gained through discovery, or other proprietary or confidential information. We have upheld restrictions upon the release of information gained "only by virtue of the trial court's discovery processes." Seattle Times Co. v. Rhinehart, [467 U.S. 20 (1984)], at 32. And *Seattle Times* would prohibit release of discovery information by the attorney as well as the client. Similar rules require an attorney to maintain client confidences. See, e.g., ABA Model Rule of Professional Conduct 1.6 (1981).

This case involves no speech subject to a restriction under the rationale of *Seattle Times*. Much of the information in petitioner's remarks was included by explicit reference or fair inference in earlier press reports. Petitioner could not have learned what he revealed at the press conference through the discovery process or other special access afforded to attorneys, for he spoke to the press on the day of indictment, at the outset of his formal participation in the criminal proceeding. We have before us no complaint from the prosecutors, police, or presiding judge that petitioner misused information to which he had special access. And there is no claim that petitioner revealed client confidences, which may be waived in any event. Rule 177, on its face and as applied here, is neither limited to nor even directed at preventing release of information received through court proceedings or special access afforded attorneys. It goes far beyond this. . . .

V

Even if respondent is correct, and as in *Seattle Times* we must balance "whether the 'practice in question [furthers] an important or substantial governmental interest unrelated to the suppression of expression' and whether 'the limitation of First Amendment freedoms [is] no greater than is necessary or essential to the protection of the particular governmental interest involved,' " the Rule as interpreted by Nevada fails the searching inquiry required by those precedents.

A

Only the occasional case presents a danger of prejudice from pretrial publicity. Empirical research suggests that in the few instances when jurors have been exposed to extensive and prejudicial publicity, they are able to disregard it and base their verdict upon the evidence presented in court. Voir dire can play an important role in reminding jurors to set aside out-of-court information, and to decide the case upon the evidence presented at trial. All of these factors weigh in favor of affording an attorney's speech about ongoing proceedings our traditional First Amendment protections. Our colleagues' historical survey notwithstanding, respondent has not demonstrated any sufficient state interest in restricting the speech of attorneys to justify a lower standard of First Amendment scrutiny.

Still less justification exists for a lower standard of scrutiny here, as this speech involved not the prosecutor or police, but a criminal defense attorney. Respondent and its amici present not a single example where a defense attorney has managed by public statements to prejudice the prosecution of the State's case. Even discounting the obvious reason for a lack of appellate decisions on the topic — the difficulty of appealing a verdict of acquittal — the absence of anecdotal or survey evidence in a much-studied area of the law is remarkable.

The various bar association and advisory commission reports which resulted in promulgation of ABA Model Rule of Professional Conduct 3.6 (1981), and other regulations of attorney speech, and sources they cite, present no convincing case for restrictions upon the speech of defense attorneys. The police, the prosecution, other government officials, and the community at large hold innumerable avenues for the dissemination of information adverse to a criminal defendant, many of which are not within the scope of Rule 177 or any other regulation. By contrast, a defendant cannot speak without fear of incriminating himself and prejudicing his defense, and most criminal defendants have insufficient means to retain a public relations team apart from defense counsel for the sole purpose of countering prosecution statements. These factors underscore my conclusion that blanket rules restricting speech of defense attorneys should not be accepted without careful First Amendment scrutiny.

B

Respondent uses the "officer of the court" label to imply that attorney contact with the press somehow is inimical to the attorney's proper role. Rule 177 posits no such inconsistency between an attorney's role and discussions with the press. It permits all comment to the press absent "a substantial likelihood of materially prejudicing an adjudicative proceeding." Respondent does not articulate the principle that contact with the press cannot be reconciled with the attorney's role or explain how this might be so.

Because attorneys participate in the criminal justice system and are trained in its complexities, they hold unique qualifications as a source of information about pending cases. "Since lawyers are considered credible in regard to pending litigation in which they are engaged and are in one of the most knowledgeable positions, they are a crucial source of information and opinion." Chicago Council of Lawyers v. Bauer, 522 F.2d 242, 250 (CA7 1975). To the extent the press and public rely upon attorneys for information because attorneys are well informed, this may prove the value to the public of speech by members of the bar. If the dangers of their speech arise from its persuasiveness, from their ability to explain judicial proceedings, or from the likelihood the speech will be believed, these are not the sort of dangers that can validate restrictions. The First Amendment does not permit suppression of speech because of its power to command assent.

One may concede the proposition that an attorney's speech about pending cases may present dangers that could not arise from statements by a nonparticipant, and that an attorney's duty to cooperate in the judicial process may prevent him or her from taking actions with an intent to frustrate that process. The role of attorneys in the criminal justice system subjects them to fiduciary obligations to the court and the parties. An attorney's position may result in some added ability to obstruct the proceedings through well-timed statements to the press, though one can debate the extent of an attorney's ability to do so without violating other established duties. A court can require an attorney's cooperation to an extent not possible of nonparticipants. A proper weighing of dangers might consider the harm that occurs when speech about ongoing proceedings forces the court to take burdensome steps such as sequestration, continuance, or change of venue.

If as a regular matter speech by an attorney about pending cases raised real dangers of this kind, then a substantial governmental interest might support additional regulation of speech. But this case involves the sanction of speech so innocuous, and an application of Rule 177(3)'s safe harbor provision so begrudging, that it is difficult to determine the force these arguments would carry in a different setting. The instant case is a poor vehicle for defining with precision the outer limits under the Constitution of a court's ability to regulate an attorney's statements about ongoing adjudicative proceedings. At the very least, however, we can say that the Rule which punished petitioner's statement represents a limitation of First Amendment freedoms greater than is necessary or essential to the protection of the particular governmental interest, and does not protect against a danger of the necessary gravity, imminence, or likelihood.

The vigorous advocacy we demand of the legal profession is accepted because it takes place under the neutral, dispassionate control of the judicial system. Though cost and delays undermine it in all too many cases, the American judicial trial remains one of the purest, most rational forums for the lawful determination of disputes. A profession which takes just pride in these traditions may consider them disserved if lawyers use their skills and insight to make untested allegations in the press instead of in the courtroom. But constraints of professional responsibility and societal disapproval will act as sufficient safeguards in most cases. And in some circumstances press comment is necessary to protect the rights of the client and prevent abuse of the courts. It cannot be said that petitioner's conduct demonstrated any real or specific threat to the legal process, and his statements have the full protection of the First Amendment.

VI

The judgment of the Supreme Court of Nevada is reversed.

CHIEF JUSTICE REHNQUIST delivered the opinion of the Court with respect to parts I and II, and delivered a dissenting opinion with respect to part III in which JUSTICE WHITE, JUSTICE SCALIA, and JUSTICE SOUTER have joined. . . .

I

[The opinion highlights these additional parts of the press conference in which Gentile responded to questions:

. . . because of the stigma that attaches to merely being accused — okay — I know I represent an innocent man. . . . The last time I had a conference with you, was with a client and I let him talk to you and I told you that that case would be dismissed and it was. Okay?

I don't take cheap shots like this. I represent an innocent guy. All right? . . .

[The police] were playing very fast and loose. . . . We've got some video tapes that if you take a look at them, I'll tell you what, [Detective Scholl] either had a hell of a cold or he should have seen a better doctor.]

II . . .

Petitioner maintains . . . that the First Amendment to the United States Constitution requires a State, such as Nevada in this case, to demonstrate a "clear and present danger" of "actual prejudice or an imminent threat" before any discipline may be imposed on a lawyer who initiates a press conference such as occurred here. He relies on decisions such as Nebraska Press Assn. v. Stuart, 427 U.S. 539 (1976), Bridges v. California, 314 U.S. 252 (1941), Pennekamp v. Florida, 328 U.S. 331 (1946), and Craig v. Harney, 331 U.S. 367 (1947), to support his position. . . .

Respondent State Bar of Nevada points out, on the other hand, that none of these cases involved lawyers who represented parties to a pending proceeding in court. It points to the statement of Holmes, J., in Patterson v. Colorado, 205 U.S. 454, 463 (1907), that "[w]hen a case is finished, courts are subject to the same criticism as other people, but the propriety and necessity of preventing interference with the course of justice by premature statement, argument or intimidation hardly can be denied." Respondent also points to a similar statement in Bridges, supra, at 271: "The very word 'trial' connotes decisions on the evidence and arguments properly advanced in open court. Legal trials are not like elections, to be won through the use of the meeting-hall, the radio, and the newspaper."

These opposing positions illustrate one of the many dilemmas which arise in the course of constitutional adjudication. The above quotes from Patterson and Bridges epitomize the theory upon which our criminal justice system is founded: The outcome of a criminal trial is to be decided by impartial jurors, who know as little as possible of the case, based on material admitted into evidence before them in a court proceeding. Extrajudicial comments on, or discussion of, evidence which might never be admitted at trial and ex parte statements by counsel giving their version of the facts obviously threaten to undermine this basic tenet.

At the same time, however, the criminal justice system exists in a larger context of a government ultimately of the people, who wish to be informed about happenings in the criminal justice system, and, if sufficiently informed about those happenings, might wish to make changes in the system. The way most of them acquire information is from the media. The First Amendment protections of speech and press have been held, in the cases cited above, to require a showing of "clear and present danger" that a malfunction in the criminal justice system will be caused before a State may prohibit media speech or publication about a particular pending trial. The question we must answer in this case is whether a lawyer who represents a defendant involved with the criminal justice system may insist on the same standard before he is disciplined for public pronouncements about the case, or whether the State instead may penalize that sort of speech upon a lesser showing.

It is unquestionable that in the courtroom itself, during a judicial proceeding, whatever right to "free speech" an attorney has is extremely circumscribed. An attorney may not, by speech or other conduct, resist a ruling of the trial court beyond the point necessary to preserve a claim for appeal. Even outside the courtroom, a majority of the Court in two separate opinions in the case of In re Sawyer, 360 U.S. 622 (1959), observed that lawyers in pending cases were subject to ethical restrictions on speech to which an ordinary citizen would not be. There, the Court had before it an order affirming the suspension of an attorney from practice because of her attack on the fairness and impartiality of a judge. The plurality opinion, which found the discipline improper, concluded that the comments had not in fact impugned the judge's integrity. Justice Stewart, who provided the fifth vote for reversal of the sanction, said in his separate opinion that he could not join any possible "intimation that a lawyer can invoke the constitutional right of free speech to immunize himself from even-handed discipline for proven unethical conduct."

He said that "[o]bedience to ethical precepts may require abstention from what in other circumstances might be constitutionally protected speech." The four dissenting Justices who would have sustained the discipline said:

> Of course, a lawyer is a person and he too has a constitutional freedom of utterance and may exercise it to castigate courts and their administration of justice. But a lawyer actively participating in a trial, particularly an emotionally charged criminal prosecution, is not merely a person and not even merely a lawyer. . . .
>
> He is an intimate and trusted and essential part of the machinery of justice, an "officer of the court" in the most compelling sense.

Likewise, in Sheppard v. Maxwell, [384 U.S. 333 (1966),] where the defendant's conviction was overturned because extensive prejudicial pretrial publicity had denied the defendant a fair trial, we held that a new trial was a remedy for such publicity, but

> we must remember that reversals are but palliatives; the cure lies in those remedial measures that will prevent the prejudice at its inception. The courts must take such steps by rule and regulation that will protect their processes from prejudicial outside interferences. Neither prosecutors, counsel for defense, the accused, witnesses, court staff nor enforcement officers coming under the jurisdiction of the court should be permitted to frustrate its function. *Collaboration between counsel and the press as to information affecting the fairness of a criminal trial is not only subject to regulation, but is highly censurable and worthy of disciplinary measures.* (Emphasis added.)

We expressly contemplated that the speech of *those participating before the courts* could be limited.[5] This distinction between participants in the litigation and strangers to it is brought into sharp relief by our holding in Seattle Times Co. v.

_____

5. The Nevada Supreme Court has consistently read all parts of Rule 177 as applying only to lawyers in pending cases, and not to other lawyers or nonlawyers. We express no opinion on the constitutionality of a rule regulating the statements of a lawyer who is not participating in the pending case about which the statements are made. . . .

Rhinehart. There, we unanimously held that a newspaper, which was itself a defendant in a libel action, could be restrained from publishing material about the plaintiffs and their supporters to which it had gained access through court-ordered discovery. In that case we said that "[a]lthough litigants do not 'surrender their First Amendment rights at the courthouse door,' those rights may be subordinated to other interests that arise in this setting," and noted that "on several occasions [we have] approved restriction on the communications of trial participants where necessary to ensure a fair trial for a criminal defendant." . . .

We think that the quoted statements from our opinions in In re Sawyer, and Sheppard v. Maxwell, rather plainly indicate that the speech of lawyers representing clients in pending cases may be regulated under a less demanding standard than that established for regulation of the press in Nebraska Press Assn. v. Stuart and the cases which preceded it. Lawyers representing clients in pending cases are key participants in the criminal justice system, and the State may demand some adherence to the precepts of that system in regulating their speech as well as their conduct. As noted by Justice Brennan in his concurring opinion in *Nebraska Press*, which was joined by Justices Stewart and Marshall, "[a]s officers of the court, court personnel and attorneys have a fiduciary responsibility not to engage in public debate that will redound to the detriment of the accused or that will obstruct the fair administration of justice." Because lawyers have special access to information through discovery and client communications, their extrajudicial statements pose a threat to the fairness of a pending proceeding since lawyers' statements are likely to be received as especially authoritative. We agree with the majority of the States that the "substantial likelihood of material prejudice" standard constitutes a constitutionally permissible balance between the First Amendment rights of attorneys in pending cases and the State's interest in fair trials.

When a state regulation implicates First Amendment rights, the Court must balance those interests against the State's legitimate interest in regulating the activity in question. The "substantial likelihood" test embodied in Rule 177 is constitutional under this analysis, for it is designed to protect the integrity and fairness of a State's judicial system, and it imposes only narrow and necessary limitations on lawyers' speech. The limitations are aimed at two principal evils: (1) comments that are likely to influence the actual outcome of the trial, and (2) comments that are likely to prejudice the jury venire, even if an untainted panel can ultimately be found. Few, if any, interests under the Constitution are more fundamental than the right to a fair trial by "impartial" jurors, and an outcome affected by extrajudicial statements would violate that fundamental right. Even if a fair trial can ultimately be ensured through voir dire, change of venue, or some other device, these measures entail serious costs to the system. Extensive voir dire may not be able to filter out all of the effects of pretrial publicity, and with increasingly widespread media coverage of criminal trials, a change of venue may not suffice to undo the effects of statements such as those made by petitioner. The State has a substantial interest in preventing officers of the court, such as lawyers, from imposing such costs on the judicial system and on the litigants.

The restraint on speech is narrowly tailored to achieve those objectives. The regulation of attorneys' speech is limited — it applies only to speech that is substantially likely to have a materially prejudicial effect; it is neutral as to points of view, applying equally to all attorneys participating in a pending case; and it merely postpones the attorneys' comments until after the trial. While supported by the substantial state interest in preventing prejudice to an adjudicative proceeding by those who have a duty to protect its integrity, the Rule is limited on its face to preventing only speech having a substantial likelihood of materially prejudicing that proceeding.

III . . .

Gentile also argues that Rule 177 is void for vagueness because it did not provide adequate notice that his comments were subject to discipline. The void-for-vagueness doctrine is concerned with a defendant's right to fair notice and adequate warning that his conduct runs afoul of the law. Rule 177 was drafted with the intent to provide "an illustrative compilation that gives fair notice of conduct ordinarily posing unacceptable dangers to the fair administration of justice." The Rule provides sufficient notice of the nature of the prohibited conduct. Under the circumstances of his case, petitioner cannot complain about lack of notice, as he has admitted that his primary objective in holding the press conference was the violation of Rule 177's core prohibition—to prejudice the upcoming trial by influencing potential jurors. Petitioner was clearly given notice that such conduct was forbidden, and the list of conduct likely to cause prejudice, while only advisory, certainly gave notice that the statements made would violate the Rule if they had the intended effect.

The majority agrees with petitioner that he was the victim of unconstitutional vagueness in the regulations because of the relationship between §3 and §§1 and 2 of Rule 177. Section 3 allows an attorney to state "the general nature of the claim or defense" notwithstanding the prohibition contained in §1 and the examples contained in §2. It is of course true, as the majority points out, that the word "general" and the word "elaboration" are both terms of degree. But combined as they are in the first sentence of §3, they convey the very definite proposition that the authorized statements must not contain the sort of detailed allegations that petitioner made at his press conference. No sensible person could think that the following were "general" statements of a claim or defense made "without elaboration": "the person that was in the most direct position to have stolen the drugs and the money . . . is Detective Steve Scholl"; "there is far more evidence that will establish that Detective Scholl took these drugs and took these American Express Travelers' checks than any other living human being"; "[Detective Scholl] either had a hell of a cold, or he should have seen a better doctor"; and "the so-called other victims . . . one, two—four of them are known drug dealers and convicted money launderers." Section 3, as an exception to the provisions of §§1 and 2, must be read in the light of the prohibitions and examples contained in the first two sections. It was obviously not intended to negate the prohibitions or the examples wholesale, but simply intended to provide a "safe harbor" where there might be doubt as to whether one of the examples covered proposed conduct. These provisions were not vague as to the conduct for which petitioner was disciplined; "[i]n determining the sufficiency of the notice a statute must of necessity be examined in the light of the conduct with which a defendant is charged."

Petitioner's strongest arguments are that the statements were made well in advance of trial, and that the statements did not in fact taint the jury panel. But the Supreme Court of Nevada pointed out that petitioner's statements were not only highly inflammatory — they portrayed prospective government witnesses as drug users and dealers, and as money launderers — but the statements were timed to have maximum impact, when public interest in the case was at its height immediately after Sanders was indicted. Reviewing independently the entire record, we are convinced that petitioner's statements were "substantially likely to cause material prejudice" to the proceedings. While there is evidence pro and con on that point, we find it persuasive that, by his own admission, petitioner called the press conference for the express purpose of influencing the venire. It is difficult to believe that he went to such trouble, and took such a risk, if there was no substantial likelihood that he would succeed.

While in a case such as this we must review the record for ourselves, when the highest court of a State has reached a determination "we give most respectful attention to its reasoning and conclusion." The State Bar of Nevada, which made its own factual findings, and the Supreme Court of Nevada, which upheld those findings, were in a far better position than we are to appreciate the likely effect of petitioner's statements on potential members of a jury panel in a highly publicized case such as this. The board and Nevada Supreme Court did not apply the list of statements likely to cause material prejudice as presumptions, but specifically found that petitioner had intended to prejudice the trial,[6] and that based upon the nature of the statements and their timing, they were in fact substantially likely to cause material prejudice. We cannot, upon our review of the record, conclude that they were mistaken.

Several amici argue that the First Amendment requires the State to show actual prejudice to a judicial proceeding before an attorney may be disciplined for extrajudicial statements, and since the board and Nevada Supreme Court found no actual prejudice, petitioner should not have been disciplined. But this is simply another way of stating that the stringent standard of *Nebraska Press* should be applied to the speech of a lawyer in a pending case, and for the reasons heretofore given we decline to adopt it. An added objection to the stricter standard when applied to lawyer participants is that if it were adopted, even comments more flagrant than those made by petitioner could not serve as the basis for disciplinary action if, for wholly independent reasons, they had no effect on the proceedings. An attorney who made prejudicial comments would

6. Justice Kennedy appears to contend that there can be no material prejudice when the lawyer's publicity is in response to publicity favorable to the other side. Justice Kennedy would find that publicity designed to counter prejudicial publicity cannot be itself prejudicial, despite its likelihood of influencing potential jurors, unless it actually would go so far as to cause jurors to be affirmatively biased in favor of the lawyer's client. In the first place, such a test would be difficult, if not impossible, to apply. But more fundamentally, it misconceives the constitutional test for an impartial juror — whether the "juror can lay aside his impression or opinion and render a verdict on the evidence presented in Court." Murphy v. Florida, 421 U.S. 794, 800 (1975). A juror who may have been initially swayed from open-mindedness by publicity favorable to the prosecution is not rendered fit for service by being bombarded by publicity favorable to the defendant. The basic premise of our legal system is that law suits should be tried in court, not in the media. A defendant may be protected from publicity by, or in favor of, the police and prosecution through voir dire, change of venue, jury instructions and, in extreme cases, reversal on due process grounds. The remedy for prosecutorial abuses that violate the rule lies not in self-help in the form of similarly prejudicial comments by defense counsel, but in disciplining the prosecutor.

be insulated from discipline if the government, for reasons unrelated to the comments, decided to dismiss the charges, or if a plea bargain were reached. An equally culpable attorney whose client's case went to trial would be subject to discipline. The United States Constitution does not mandate such a fortuitous difference. . . .

JUSTICE O'CONNOR concurring.

I agree with much of The Chief Justice's opinion. In particular, I agree that a State may regulate speech by lawyers representing clients in pending cases more readily than it may regulate the press. . . .

For the reasons set out in Part III of Justice Kennedy's opinion, however, I believe that Nevada's rule is void for vagueness. Subsection (3) of Rule 177 is a "safe harbor" provision. . . . Gentile made a conscious effort to stay within the boundaries of this "safe harbor." In his brief press conference, Gentile gave only a rough sketch of the defense that he intended to present at trial — i.e., that Detective Scholl, not Grady Sanders, stole the cocaine and traveler's checks. When asked to provide more details, he declined, stating explicitly that the ethical rules compelled him to do so. Nevertheless, the disciplinary board sanctioned Gentile because, in its view, his remarks went beyond the scope of what was permitted by the Rule. Both Gentile and the disciplinary board have valid arguments on their side, but this serves to support the view that the Rule provides insufficient guidance. As Justice Kennedy correctly points out, a vague law offends the Constitution because it fails to give fair notice to those it is intended to deter and creates the possibility of discriminatory enforcement. . . .

QUESTIONS ABOUT GENTILE

1. Why, exactly, did Gentile win? After *Gentile,* the ABA deleted the words "general nature of" and reworked the language of the safe harbor quoted at page 870.
2. If we assume that voir dire can discover and eliminate pretrial prejudice — an assumption that courts routinely make in response to defense motions to change venue — what legitimate state interest supports a curb on a lawyer's public statements? Or perhaps we should reverse the question: If in fact voir dire will remedy prejudice, why do lawyers engage in "spin control" in the first place?
3. In perhaps his most remarkable paragraph, Justice Kennedy wrote (page 867):

    > An attorney's duties do not begin inside the courtroom door. . . . [A]n attorney may take reasonable steps to defend a client's reputation and reduce the adverse consequences of indictment . . . including an attempt to demonstrate in the court of public opinion that the client does not deserve to be tried.

    Could an "activist" lawyer have put it better? Can it be that four Supreme Court Justices (but only four!) were prepared to vest lawyers with the right, perhaps the duty, to advocate for their clients in public? If that position is correct (is it correct?), why have a pretrial publicity rule at all?

4. Rule 3.6 prohibits certain statements that "have a substantial likelihood of materially prejudicing an adjudicative proceeding." The ABA has repeatedly rejected a "clear and present danger" test. The Third Circuit invoked its supervisory powers to require district courts within its jurisdiction to use the ABA standard. United States v. Wecht, 484 F.3d 194 (3d Cir. 2007). (The case reports that only three states — Illinois, New Mexico, and Oklahoma — have a test offering more protection to speech.) In a Model Rules jurisdiction, that means that a lawyer prepared to make a statement must also be prepared to predict the reasonable likelihood of the effect of that statement on any subsequent trial. How is a lawyer to know in advance? How can a disciplinary committee know in retrospect if a statement violated this standard at the time it was made? *Gentile* envisions that a statement may violate Rule 3.6 even if no trial is ever held, perhaps because of a plea bargain or a settlement. Does that make sense? (It does, doesn't it, because in part the bargain or settlement may have been the product of the publicity.)

5. *Gentile* construed the Nevada rule to apply only to lawyers who speak about matters with which they are associated, not to all lawyers. After *Gentile*, Rule 3.6 was narrowed to cover only a lawyer "who is participating or has participated in the investigation or litigation of a matter." In other words, the rule would not restrict the speech of individuals who happen to be lawyers and who comment on a pending or impending matter, like the "talking heads" in the problem at the start of this section. What First Amendment protection applies then? Should lawyers who sound off about a case with which they have no connection (which seemed to be true for about half the bar during the O. J. Simpson and Scott Peterson trials) enjoy as much protection as the general public? Why?

Defamation Claims

Even if gag orders and professional conduct rules do not stop a lawyer from speaking publicly about a pending or impending case, the risk of a defamation action might. Litigation breeds animosity and on occasion may lead to inflammatory statements about the character or conduct of an opposing lawyer or client. An adversary may also see tactical value in suing an opposing lawyer for libel or slander.

Lawyers often have a strong defense to such claims. The Restatement of Torts and American jurisdictions recognize an absolute litigation privilege. Because the privilege is absolute, no claim of defamation can be based on any statement a lawyer utters within the scope of the privilege, regardless of the lawyer's alleged motive, even if thoroughly malicious. This is rather dramatic protection. The Iowa Supreme Court explained the policy behind it: "The judicial proceedings privilege is based upon a public policy of giving attorneys, as officers of the court, the utmost freedom in their efforts to secure justice for their clients." Kennedy v. Zimmermann, 601 N.W.2d 61 (Iowa 1999). However, immunity only protects a statement made "in communications preliminary to a proposed judicial proceeding, or in the institution of, or during the course and as part of, a judicial proceeding in which [the lawyer] participates as counsel, if it has some relation to the proceeding." Restatement of Law (Second) of Torts §586 (1977). "A statement falls outside the privilege only if it is 'so palpably irrelevant to the subject matter of the controversy that no reasonable man can doubt its irrelevancy or impropriety.'" Hugel v. Milberg, Weiss, Bershad, Hynes & Lerach, LLP, 175 F.3d 14 (1st Cir. 1999). Statements during settlement discussions are within the privilege. Oesterle v. Wallace, 725 N.W.2d 470 (Mich. 2006).

One court upheld the privilege where the alleged libel appeared in a draft petition that counsel sent to people they were soliciting to be clients. Samson Investment Co. v. Chevaillier, 988 P.2d 327 (Okla. 1999). The privilege will protect statements in correspondence sent to a potential adversary threatening litigation, Messina v. Krakower, 439 F.3d 755 (D.C. Cir. 2006), but not if the statement is extraneous to the claim. Nguyen v. Proton Technology Corp., 81 Cal. Rptr. 2d 392 (Ct. App. 1999) (mention in a letter that an employee of the opponent had an alleged criminal record held extraneous and outside the privilege). Nor will the privilege apply if the demand letter is "excessively published," which means if it is sent to persons who are not "necessary to resolve the dispute or further the objectives of the proposed litigation." Krouse v. Bower, 20 P.3d 895 (Utah 2001) (letter was not excessively published when sent by counsel for dissident condominium owners to lawyer for condominium association with copies to all homeowners where letter alleged possible violation of fiduciary duties and fraud by officers of the association; other homeowners "had a clear legal interest in the subject matter of the letter and the threatened lawsuit"). Publication fell outside the privilege, however, where the defendant lawyers allegedly sent a memorandum containing false accusations of dishonesty about the plaintiff lawyers to two lawyers who had no client interest in the case. Edelman, Combs & Latturner v. Hinshaw & Culbertson, 788 N.E.2d 740 (Ill. App. 2003).

Defamation and Technology.   What if a law firm believes that a consumer product is dangerous but doesn't know who may be using it? The firm may be tempted to advertise for prospective clients on the internet or in newspapers. Prospective clients, after all, might look for lawyers by Googling the name of the product and other key words ("lawyer," "defect" "lawsuit"). On the other hand, posting information on the internet risks disparaging the product to the world, not just prospective clients.

A Tennessee firm faced this dilemma. It believed a product used in wood-frame construction might be defective. It did not know the identities of the purchasers, so it advertised to find them. The ads (on the Web and in a newspaper) were fairly tame. They did not flat out say the product was bad, but only (in a newspaper) that buyers "may have certain rights and be entitled to monetary compensation"; and (more aggressively, on the firm's Web site) that the firm was "investigating the accelerated corrosion due to defectively manufactured screws and fasteners. ..." The maker sued for defamation. Answering a certified question from the federal district court, the Tennessee Supreme Court held that the litigation privilege would apply to these efforts to find clients. "In some situations attorneys may have no practical means of discerning in advance whether the recipients of the communication have an interest in the proposed proceeding. In that event, the attorney can only communicate with those having the ability and desire to join the proposed litigation by publishing the statement to a wider audience, which may include uncon-nected individuals." Simpson Strong-Tie Co., Inc. v. Stewart, Estes & Donnell, 232 S.W.3d 18 (Tenn. 2007).

This is pretty strong stuff given the reach of the internet. Would it make sense also to require that the solicitation's description of the product be as neutral as possible consistent with the firm's goal of finding possible clients? For example, the content of the newspaper ad ("may have certain legal rights") should do the trick without resorting to the language on the firm's Web site ("investigating accelerated corrosion").

With the media's migration to the web, it bears emphasis that the litigation privilege does not protect statements to the media. Bochetto v. Gibson, 860 A.2d 67 (Pa. 2004) ("As Gibson's act of sending the complaint to [reporter] Dudick was an extrajudicial act that occurred outside of the regular course of the judicial proceedings and was not relevant in any way to those proceedings, it is plain that it was not protected by the judicial privilege") (two dissenting judges see "no principled distinction, for defamation purposes, between the filed public com-plaint and the copy of it provided to the press"); Rothman v. Jackson, 57 Cal. Rptr. 2d 284 (Ct. App. 1996) (permitting defamation action against singer Michael Jackson and his lawyers based on press conference in which the defen-dants allegedly accused plaintiff, a lawyer, of making "false accusations against Jackson in order to extort money from him"). An earlier California case, Shahvar v. Superior Court, 30 Cal. Rptr. 2d 597 (Ct. App. 1994), had recognized a defamation action against a lawyer who faxed a copy of his civil complaint to a newspaper, which thereafter published its charges. In response, the California legislature extended the litigation privilege to include dissemination of court papers to the media. Cal. Civ. Code §47(d). However, no privilege protects statements that violate the ethical rule on pretrial publicity, a court order, or confidentiality duties imposed by law. In other states, too, state law may protect accurate reporting to the press, which one court read to include posting a complaint on the internet. Amway Corp. v. Procter & Gamble Co., 346 F.3d 180 (6th Cir. 2003) (Michigan law).

B. PUBLIC COMMENT ABOUT JUDGES AND COURTS

1. Criticizing the Administration of Justice

A *multiple-choice question*: Robert Snyder, Esquire, (a) wanted to be some kind of hero, (b) held fast on a matter of principle, (c) foolishly hurt his reputation for no transcendent value, (d) should grow up, (e) all or none of the above, (f)?

Snyder practiced in North Dakota. The district court appointed him to rep-resent a defendant under the Criminal Justice Act (CJA), which authorizes (modest) government compensation to lawyers so appointed. When the case ended, Snyder claimed $1,898 under the meager government rates. The district court approved $1,796, about 5 percent less. Not bad. But the law required circuit court approval of amounts above $1,000. The chief judge of the circuit returned Snyder's claim with a request for more information. Snyder supplied it, but the chief judge found it wanting. Snyder, apparently losing patience or not wishing to spend more (uncompensated) time, or both, then wrote a letter to the district judge's secretary in which he said:

> In the first place, I am appalled by the amount of money which the federal court pays for indigent criminal defense work. The reason that so few attorneys in Bismarck accept this work is for that exact reason. We have, up to this point, still accepted the indigent appointments, because of a duty to our profession, and the fact that nobody else will do it.
>
> Now, however, not only are we paid an amount of money which does not even cover our overhead, but we have to go through extreme gymnastics even to receive the puny amounts which the federal courts authorize for this work. We have sent you everything we have concerning our representation, and I am not sending you anything else. You can take it or leave it.
>
> Further, I am extremely disgusted by the treatment of us by the Eighth Circuit in this case, and you are instructed to remove my name from the list of attorneys who will accept criminal indigent defense work. I have simply had it.
>
> Thank you for your time and attention.

Now begins the battle of the wills. The district judge discussed the letter with the chief judge who, irritated by its tone, questioned Snyder's fitness to practice in the federal courts but offered to drop the matter if Snyder apologizes. Snyder would not apologize and was ordered to show cause why he should not be suspended, not because of the tone of his letter, mind you, but because of his professed "refusal" to accept further CJA assignments. Snyder responded that many lawyers did not accept CJA assignments and that theretofore his firm had taken 15 percent of the CJA assignments in the district. (A remarkably high number, I might add.)

A hearing was held. Over Snyder's protest, it focused not on Snyder's refusal to accept future assignments, the subject of the show cause order, but returned once again to the tone of Snyder's letter. Snyder was given ten days to "reconsider" his tone. He did not. Instead he reconsidered CJA assignments. He said he'd accept them if all lawyers in his district were required to do so. The chief judge once again asked Snyder "to apologize for the letter that you wrote." Snyder replied:

> I cannot, and will never, in justice to my conscience, apologize for what I consider to be telling the truth, albeit in harsh terms. . . .
>
> It is unfortunate that the respective positions in the proceeding have so hardened. However, I consider this to be a matter of principle, and if one stands on a principle, one must be willing to accept the consequences.

Well, at least he acknowledged the "harsh terms," but that did not satisfy the court. Citing Snyder's "contumacious conduct," the Eighth Circuit suspended him from practice in all federal courts in the circuit for six months. Readmission was contingent on reapplication (and presumably an apology). Rehearing en banc was denied, the court writing that the "gravamen of the situation is that [Snyder's letter] became harsh and disrespectful to the Court." Stop here. "Contumacious" means "stubbornly disobedient" in my dictionary (*Merriam*

Webster's Collegiate). Was Snyder that? Is this a case of lèse majesté, i.e., an offense against the dignity of the ruler?

The Supreme Court granted review and, in an opinion by Chief Justice Burger, unanimously reversed the suspension. In re Snyder, 472 U.S. 634 (1985). (Justice Blackmun did not participate.) Avoiding Snyder's First Amendment claim, the Court held that the record did not establish a basis for suspension under Rule 46 of the Federal Rules of Appellate Procedure, which authorizes suspension for conduct "unbecoming a member of the bar." The Court said that the remedy for Snyder's failure to augment the information in his fee application was denial of a fee, not discipline, and continued:

> The record indicates the Court of Appeals was concerned about the tone of the letter; petitioner concedes that the tone of his letter was "harsh," and, indeed it can be read as ill-mannered. All persons involved in the judicial process — judges, litigants, witnesses, and court officers — owe a duty of courtesy to all other participants. The necessity for civility in the inherently contentious setting of the adversary process suggests that members of the bar cast criticisms of the system in a professional and civil tone. However, even assuming that the letter exhibited an unlawyerlike rudeness, a single incident of rudeness or lack of professional courtesy — in this context — does not support a finding of contemptuous or contumacious conduct, or a finding that a lawyer is "not presently fit to practice law in the federal courts." Nor does it rise to the level of "conduct unbecoming a member of the bar" warranting suspension from practice.

Catch that phrase, "a single incident." What does it portend? Does any legitimate state interest support a lower level of First Amendment protection for lawyers who criticize the justice system rudely and often?

For the Eighth Circuit's parting shot, in its remand order vacating the suspension, see In re Snyder, 770 F.2d 743 (8th Cir. 1985).

2. *Criticizing Particular Judges*

Judges are public officials. The Supreme Court has held that public officials who sue for defamation must prove falsity and "actual malice" — defined as knowledge of a statement's falsity or reckless (that is, conscious) disregard for its truth. Harte-Hanks Communications, Inc. v. Connaughton, 491 U.S. 657 (1989); New York Times Co. v. Sullivan, 376 U.S. 254 (1964). Does the same standard apply before a lawyer may be disciplined for public criticism of a judge? *Gentile* gave less First Amendment protection to lawyers who make pretrial statements about their own pending or impending cases than the rest of the world enjoys. Does the same diminished protection apply when a lawyer's criticism of a judge turns out to be false?

The following case tells the story of Elizabeth Holtzman, former comptroller of New York City, former Brooklyn district attorney, former member of the House Judiciary Committee during the Watergate investigation, and twice a candidate for U.S. senator. She did not fare as well as Gentile and Snyder. Why not?

MATTER OF HOLTZMAN
78 N.Y.2d 184, 577 N.E.2d 30, 573 N.Y.S.2d 39,
cert. denied, 502 U.S. 1009 (1991)

PER CURIAM. . . .

The charge of misconduct that is relevant to this appeal was based on the public release by petitioner, then District Attorney of Kings County, of a letter charging Judge Irving Levine with judicial misconduct in relation to an incident that allegedly occurred in the course of a trial on criminal charges of sexual misconduct (Penal Law §130.20), and was reported to her some six weeks later. Specifically, petitioner's letter stated that:

> Judge Levine asked the Assistant District Attorney, defense counsel, defendant, court officer and court reporter to join him in the robing room, where the judge then asked the victim to get down on the floor and show the position she was in when she was being sexually assaulted. . . . The victim reluctantly got down on her hands and knees as everyone stood and watched. In making the victim assume the position she was forced to take when she was sexually assaulted, Judge Levine profoundly degraded, humiliated and demeaned her.

The letter, addressed to Judge Kathryn McDonald as Chair of the Committee to Implement Recommendations of the New York State Task Force on Women in the Courts, was publicly disseminated after petitioner's office issued a "news alert" to the media.

Following a dispute over the truth of the accusations, Robert Keating, as Administrative Judge of the New York City Criminal Court, conducted an investigation into the allegations of judicial misconduct. His report, dated December 22, 1987, concluded that petitioner's accusations were not supported by the evidence. Upon receipt of the report, Albert M. Rosenblatt, then Chief Administrative Judge, referred the matter to the Grievance Committee for inquiry as to whether petitioner had violated the Code of Professional Responsibility.

Some six months later, the Grievance Committee sent petitioner a private Letter of Admonition in which it stated that "the totality of the circumstances presented by this matter require that you be admonished for your conduct." Petitioner's misconduct, the Committee concluded, violated DR 8-102(B), DR 1-102(A)(5), (6) and EC 8-6 of the Code of Professional Responsibility.

In July 1988, after petitioner requested a subcommittee hearing, she was served with three formal charges of misconduct under DR 8-102(B) and DR 1-102(A)(5) and (6). Charge One alleged that petitioner had engaged in conduct that adversely reflected on her fitness to practice law in releasing a false accusation of misconduct against Judge Levine. . . . Only Charge One is in issue on this appeal.

The conduct set forth in Charge One, allegedly demonstrating petitioner's unfitness to practice law, included release of the letter to the media (1) prior to obtaining the minutes of the criminal trial, (2) without making any effort to speak with court officers, the court reporter, defense counsel or any other person present during the alleged misconduct, (3) without meeting with or discussing the incident with the trial assistant who reported it [in memoranda], and (4) with the knowledge that Judge Levine was being transferred out of the Criminal Court, and the matter would be investigated by the Court's Administrative Judge as well as the Commission on Judicial Conduct (to which the petitioner had complained). . . .

Petitioner relies primarily on two arguments. First, she asserts that the allegations concerning Judge Levine's conduct were true or at least not demonstrably false. Second, petitioner asserts that her conduct violates no specific disciplinary rule and further that DR 1-102(A)(6), if applicable, is unconstitutionally vague. These contentions are without merit.

The factual basis of Charge One is that petitioner made false accusations against the Judge. This charge was sustained by the Committee and upheld by the Appellate Division, and the factual finding of falsity (which is supported by the record) is therefore binding on us.

As for the contention that petitioner's conduct did not violate any provision of the Code, DR 1-102(A)(6) provides that a lawyer shall not "[e]ngage in any other conduct that adversely reflects on [the lawyer's] fitness to practice law." As far back as 1856, the Supreme Court acknowledged that "it is difficult, if not impossible, to enumerate and define, with legal precision, every offense for which an attorney or counsellor ought to be removed" (Ex Parte Secombe, 60 U.S. [19 How.] 9, 14 [1856]). Broad standards governing professional conduct are permissible and indeed often necessary.

Such standards are set forth in Canon 1 and particularly in DR 1-102. An earlier draft of the Code listed "conduct degrading to the legal profession" as a basis for a finding of misconduct under DR 1-102, but this provision was replaced by the "fitness" language of DR 1-102(A)(6) and the "prejudicial to the administration of justice" standard of DR 1-102(A)(5) (see, Annotated Code of Professional Responsibility, Textual and Historical Notes, at 12). The drafters of the Code refined the provisions to provide attorneys with proper ethical guidelines. Were we to find such language impermissibly vague, attempts to promulgate general guidelines such as DR 1-102(A)(6) would be futile.

Rather than an absolute prohibition on broad standards, the guiding principle must be whether a reasonable attorney, familiar with the Code and its ethical strictures, would have notice of what conduct is proscribed.

Applying this standard, petitioner was plainly on notice that her conduct in this case, involving public dissemination of a specific accusation of improper judicial conduct under the circumstances described, could be held to reflect adversely on her fitness to practice law. Indeed, her staff, including the person assigned the task of looking into the ethical implications of release to the press, counseled her to delay publication until the trial minutes were received.

Petitioner's act was not generalized criticism but rather release to the media of a false allegation of specific wrongdoing, made without any support other than the interoffice memoranda of a newly admitted trial assistant, aimed at a named Judge who had presided over a number of cases prosecuted by her office. Petitioner knew or should have known that such attacks are unwarranted and unprofessional, serve to bring the Bench and Bar into disrepute, and tend to undermine public confidence in the judicial system.

Therefore, petitioner's conduct was properly the subject of disciplinary action under DR 1-102(A)(6), and it is of no consequence that she might be charged with violating DR 8-102(B) based on this same course of conduct. Indeed, in the present case there are factors that distinguish petitioner's conduct from that prohibited under DR 8-102(B) — most notably, release of the false charges to the media — and make it particularly relevant to her fitness to practice law.

Petitioner contends that her conduct would not be actionable under the "constitutional malice" standard enunciated by the Supreme Court in New York Times Co. v. Sullivan (376 U.S. 254 [1964]). Neither this Court nor the Supreme Court has ever extended the *Sullivan* standard to lawyer discipline and we decline to do so here.

Accepting petitioner's argument would immunize all accusations, however reckless or irresponsible, from censure as long as the attorney uttering them did not actually entertain serious doubts as to their truth. Such a standard would be wholly at odds with the policy underlying the rules governing professional responsibility, which seeks to establish a "minimum level of conduct below which no lawyer can fall without being subject to disciplinary action." (Code of Professional Responsibility, Preliminary Statement.)

Unlike defamation cases, "professional misconduct, although it may directly affect an individual, is not punished for the benefit of the affected person; the wrong is against society as a whole, the preservation of a fair, impartial judicial system, and the system of justice as it has evolved for generations." It follows that the issue raised when an attorney makes public a false accusation of wrongdoing by a Judge is not whether the target of the false attack has been harmed in reputation; the issue is whether that criticism adversely affects the administration of justice and adversely reflects on the attorney's judgment and, consequentially, her ability to practice law.

In order to adequately protect the public interest and maintain the integrity of the judicial system, there must be an objective standard of what a reasonable attorney would do in similar circumstances. It is the reasonableness of the belief, not the state of mind of the attorney, that is determinative.

Petitioner's course of conduct satisfies any standard other than "constitutional malice," and therefore Charge One must be sustained.*

The two charges the court did not address prohibited "conduct prejudicial to the administration of justice" and "knowingly [making] a false accusation against a judge or other adjudicatory officer." These two provisions are continued in the Model Rules in somewhat different form. Rule 8.4(d) and Rule 8.2(a). The "fitness to practice law" provision on which the court upheld Holtzman's discipline is not in the Model Rules. The closest analogue is Rule 8.4(b), which defines as misconduct commission of a "criminal act that reflects adversely on the lawyer's honesty, trustworthiness or fitness as a lawyer in other respects." Holtzman's act was not, of course, criminal.

* Chief Judge Wachtler did not participate. — Ed.

QUESTIONS ABOUT HOLTZMAN

1. In a public statement issued after the decision, Holtzman said: "The court's decision is a blow to those who value freedom of speech and who care about the treatment of rape victims by the courts." N.Y.L.J., July 2, 1991, at 1. Is she right?

2. Should Holtzman's position as D.A. give her a greater obligation to "get it right" than that imposed on others who criticize judges?

3. Does the court's standard — "whether a reasonable attorney, familiar with the Code and its ethical strictures, would have notice of what conduct is proscribed" — give adequate notice of the conduct proscribed by DR 1-102(A)(6)? Compare *Gentile. Holtzman* was decided four days after *Gentile,* but the *Holtzman* court did not cite it. Why did the court ignore the *Gentile* vagueness analysis?

4. In any event, why wasn't a memorandum from a lawyer on her staff — albeit a "newly admitted" one — a sufficient basis for Holtzman's response?

5. Take a look at the court's view of what it would mean to accept Holtzman's reliance on New York Times v. Sullivan. Is it correct that if the subjective *New York Times* defense were available, then a "reckless" attorney would escape responsibility for false accusations against judges, as the court says? *New York Times* would not protect a knowingly false statement or a statement made with reckless disregard for its truth or falsity. *New York Times* dealt with First Amendment defenses to defamation claims. Most (but not all) courts to address the question, like *Holtzman,* reject a subjective test when the issue is not defamation but professional ethics. In re Cobb, 838 N.E.2d 1197 (Mass. 2005), collects the cases and opts for an objective test, which asks what a reasonable lawyer would believe. Further, while public officials or public figures who bring defamation cases have the burden of proving the subjective *New York Times* malice standard, Philadelphia Newspapers, Inc. v. Hepps, 475 U.S. 767 (1986), Holtzman seems to have had the burden of proving what a reasonable lawyer would believe under the circumstances. The Florida Bar v. Ray, 797 So.2d 556 (2001).

Other Examples of Lawyers Criticizing Judges and Justice

Less than two months before *Holtzman,* another prosecutor was reprimanded for a different kind of statement. After losing a case in an intermediate appellate court, the prosecuting attorney of Missouri's St. Louis County, George Westfall, said this (in a television interview) of the judge who wrote the opinion: (1) his reasons were "somewhat illogical and I think even a little bit less than honest"; (2) he "has really distorted the statute and I think convoluted logic to arrive at a decision that he personally likes"; (3) the decision "means that [the judge] made up his mind before he wrote the decision, and just reached the conclusion that he wanted to reach."

Missouri has Rule 8.2. The Missouri court, like the New York court, said the reference should be to what a reasonable attorney would know or believe, not

Westfall's own state of mind. The interest in protecting the public, the admin-istration of justice, and the profession made a purely subjective test inappropri-ate. Matter of Westfall, 808 S.W.2d 829 (Mo. 1991). Chief Justice Blackmar wrote a lengthy dissent ("We should proceed very carefully when we are asked to censor or censure political speech.").

Should it matter that judges sometimes use abusive language in characteriz-ing the reasoning of other judges? After all, why should lawyers be held to a higher standard? Matter of Wilkins, 777 N.E.2d 714 (Ind. 2002), modified, 782 N.E.2d 985 (Ind. 2003), is an interesting specimen of this phenomenon (yet others appear hereafter). In a note in a brief, Wilkins questioned the legal and factual accuracy of the lower court opinion and wrote that "one is left to wonder whether [the court] was determined to find for [the opposing party] and then said whatever was necessary to reach that conclusion (regardless of whether the facts or the law supported its decision)." The majority said this statement vio-lated Rule 8.2(a), which forbids a lawyer to make statements that are knowingly false or in reckless disregard of the truth "concerning the qualifications or integrity of a judge. . . ." The court rejected Wilkins's argument that his state-ment deserved First Amendment protection. The dissent, although finding Wilkins's language "tasteless," could not "see how this footnote differs from the charges occasionally leveled by judges at other judges." It cited a dissent where Justice Scalia wrote that "[s]eldom has an opinion of this Court rested so obviously upon nothing but the personal views of its members," and Justice Scalia's statement in another case that Justice O'Connor's position was "irrational" and "cannot be taken seriously."

Dominic Gentile's comments did not have to be proved to be a "clear and present danger" to the administration of justice before he could be sanctioned. It was enough if his remarks created "a substantial likelihood of materially prejudicing an adjudicative proceeding." But what if a lawyer criticizes a judge without reference to an "adjudicative proceeding" or, as in *Holtzman*, the proceeding is over so prejudice to it is impossible? That difference didn't help D.A. Holtzman, but it did save Stephen Yagman, who was accused of mak-ing various harsh statements about a federal district judge, including that he was "drunk on the bench" and "dishonest." The Ninth Circuit reversed federal discipline on the ground that Yagman's comments were not shown to present a clear and present danger to the administration of justice.

> When lawyers speak out on matters unconnected to a pending case, there is no direct and immediate impact on the fair trial rights of litigants. Information the lawyers impart will not be viewed as coming from confidential sources, and will not have a direct impact on a particular jury venire.

Standing Committee on Discipline v. Yagman, 55 F.3d 1430 (9th Cir. 1995) (2-1 decision) (also applying an objective version of the *New York Times* standard). Matter of Green, 11 P.3d 1078 (Colo. 2000), purports to follow *Yagman* but then applies a subjective, rather than an objective, standard for malice. The opinion goes on to hold that the lawyer's allegation that a judge was a "racist and bigot" was not a statement of fact at all, but "of opinion based upon fully disclosed and uncontested facts," and therefore absolutely protected by the First Amendment. Disagreeing with the *Yagman* approach is Matter of Palmisano, 70 F.3d 483 (7th Cir. 1995) ("To the extent [*Yagman*] may hold that attorneys are entitled to excoriate judges in the same way, and with the same lack of investigation, as persons may attack political officeholders, it is inconsistent with *Gentile* and our own precedents.").

William Kunstler, whose in-court statement to the presiding judge ("You are a disgrace to the bench.") resulted in a contempt citation (page 858), was also charged with professional misconduct and censured. In re Kunstler, 606 N.Y.S.2d 607 (1st Dept. 1993). In United States District Court v. Sandlin, 12 F.3d 861 (9th Cir. 1993), a lawyer was suspended from practice after he wrongly accused the district judge of altering the transcript of a proceeding before her.

A reprise to the Michigan Supreme Court is required here. Recall the harsh language of the dissents in its *Maldonado* decision (page 863). In another bitterly divided opinion, the same court upheld discipline of Geoffrey Fieger (who you may recall represented Dr. Kevorkian a/k/a Dr. Death). Fieger said the following on his radio show after three intermediate appellate court judges reversed a $15 million verdict for his client: "Hey Michael Talbot, and Bandstra, and Markey [the judges], I declare war on you. You declare it on me. I declare it on you. Kiss my ass, too." He referred to them as "three jackass court of appeals judges" and when someone else used the word "innuendo," Fieger said "I know the only thing that's in their endo should be a large, you know, plunger the size of, you know, my fist." Fieger was reprimanded for violating a Michigan rule (which is not in the Model Rules) that requires lawyers to be courteous and civil. Grievance Administrator v. Fieger, 719 N.W.2d 123 (Mich. 2006). Later, a federal judge declared these rules unconstitutional, though the federal court had no authority to vacate Fieger's discipline. Fieger v. Michigan Supreme Court, 2007 Westlaw 2571975 (E.D. Mich. 2007). The Sixth Circuit then vacated Feiger's victory for lack of standing. 553 F.3d 955 (6th Cir. 2009).

Now we come to the "What Got Into Them?" Department. Exhibit One: A judge issued an injunction against Louis Waller's client and then recused himself. In an application to the new judge seeking to vacate the injunction, Waller began his legal memorandum this way: "Comes defendant, by counsel, and respectfully moves the Honorable Court, much better than that lying incompetent asshole it replaced if you graduated from the eighth grade. . . ." Fast forward. The court suspended Waller for six months. Kentucky Bar Assn. v. Waller, 929 S.W.2d 181 (Ky. 1996).

Exhibit Two is Richard Golub. Golub represented Sandra Jennings, who sued the movie star William Hurt, claiming to be his common-law wife. In a trial before Justice Jacqueline Silbermann, without a jury, Hurt won. Although Golub had been respectful and courteous to the court throughout the trial, his loss prompted him to charge that Justice Silbermann was "star-struck" and "madly in love" with Hurt. "Let five judges who are men decide this, not one woman who's impressed by a movie star," Golub remarked on filing his appeal. (The appellate court—five men—affirmed.) In discipline, Golub admitted that his comments violated the Code. He was censured (by five male judges). In re Golub, 597 N.Y.S.2d 370 (1st Dept. 1993).

Exhibit Three: In a newspaper interview, an Indiana prosecutor said the following about a judge in his own county: "Her arrogance is exceeded only by her ignorance." "Whenever [the judge] says anything, I can see a [political figure's] lips moving." "She doesn't have any comprehension of what's going on with respect to [certain] cases and she refuses to learn." The prosecutor agreed to a public reprimand, which the court imposed. Two dissenting judges thought the penalty was too mild. Matter of Reed, 716 N.E.2d 426 (Ind. 1999).

C. JUDICIAL CAMPAIGN SPEECH

"I Got These Questionnaires"

"My name is Marta Rojas. I'm a lawyer in private practice. I am running for an elected spot on the state high court. I've been in practice 23 years and active in the bar association. I do a lot of pro bono work on immigrant rights, especially Hispanic men and women because Spanish is my first language. All around I think I'm a pretty good citizen of the profession and of my state.

"In connection with my campaign, I got questionnaires from three different groups. One is from a right-to-life group. It lists a bunch of statements and asks me to say whether I agree, disagree, am undecided, or decline to answer. One statement is: 'I believe that the unborn child is biologically human and alive and that the right to life of human beings should be respected at every stage of their biological development.' Another is 'I believe that no provision of the state constitution is intended to protect a right to abortion.'

"A second questionnaire is from a tort reform group. It asks me whether I agree with the following statement, among others: 'Some state high courts have interpreted their state constitutions to forbid punitive damages at greater than three times actual damages. Our state constitution imposes at least as severe a limit on punitive damages in our courts.'

"A final questionnaire is from a gay rights group. Among other things, I am asked to say whether I agree with the following statement: 'The state constitution protects the right to gay marriage.' And this one: 'Gay men and lesbians have a constitutional right to adopt children.'

"Now, I have tentative or strongly held views on some of the statements in these questionnaires and no view on other statements, but I'd just as soon not say what any of them are. Some of my opponents may state their views. I'm not asking for your campaign advice. I know I don't have to reply. My question is can I reply under our state code of judicial conduct, which is the same as the 2007 ABA Code? And if I do respond to a question and get elected, am I thereby disqualified from any appeal raising that issue?"

A majority of American jurisdictions elect some or all of their trial and appellate judges. In this, they vary from the federal model. Whether election or appointment is the better policy, or whether the answer depends on the particular judicial position, is not on the table here. There is no doubt that states can choose election. But for decades, states have also limited the campaign speech of judicial candidates in ways that the First Amendment would not tolerate for candidates for political office. The limitations, though somewhat differently worded, drew on provisions of the ABA's various Codes of Judicial Conduct and appeared in the states' judicial conduct codes.

The following opinion addresses the constitutionality of one limitation, called the announce clause (which the Ginsburg opinion capitalizes; Scalia's does not). The clause forbids a candidate to "announce his or her views on disputed legal or political issues." Another clause, called the pledges and promises clause, was not before the Court in this case nor since. But it figures in Justice Ginsburg's dissent. It prohibits judicial candidates from making "pledges or promises of conduct in office other than the faithful and impartial performance of the duties of the office." The precise meaning of and difference between the two clauses is not clear, and this may explain some of the differences between the majority opinion and the dissents. Has Justice Ginsburg, for example, so limited the scope of the announce clause's prohibitions that they are in effect no broader than the pledges and promises clause and therefore easier to uphold?

After *White*, states scrambled to rewrite their judicial conduct codes either without further prompting or in response to local court challenges. That effort was still ongoing at the end of 2008. We address one change below. That is the language that the ABA adopted in its new (2007) Code of Judicial Conduct in an effort to bring the code into compliance with *White*.

You should know, too, that litigation over the First Amendment rights of judicial candidates did not end with *White*. On remand, a seriously divided Eighth Circuit, in banc, overturned Minnesota's rule that prohibited judicial candidates from soliciting campaign contributions from large groups and from signing letters soliciting contributions. The court also overturned a rule that limited candidates from seeking or accepting political party endorsements (Minnesota's judicial elections are nonpartisan) and from identifying themselves "as members of a political organization." Republican Party of Minnesota v. White, 416 F.3d 738 (8th Cir. 2005).

For other examples of the issue in the lower courts, compare the different rulings on the meaning of the pledges and promises clause in In re Watson, 794 N.E.2d 1 (N.Y. 2003) (censuring judge who in campaign speech promised to "work with" and "assist" police and others in law enforcement), with Pennsylvania Family Institute v. Celluci, 521 F.Supp.2d 351 (E.D. Pa. 2007) (rejecting *Watson's* reading of the clause as inadequate to solve its overbreadth problem and accepting a construction that would prohibit only "pledging, promising, or committing to decide an issue or a case in a particular way once elected judge"). Debate over the validity and meaning of this clause will continue.*

REPUBLICAN PARTY OF MINNESOTA v. WHITE
536 U.S. 765 (2002)

JUSTICE SCALIA delivered the opinion of the Court.

The question presented in this case is whether the First Amendment permits the Minnesota Supreme Court to prohibit candidates for judicial election in that State from announcing their views on disputed legal and political issues.

---

* Incidentally, and purely as an aside, the entire Court in *White* agrees that state supreme court judges, at least, make law through their rulings and could not avoid doing so. The conservatives are even more emphatic about this role. Keep that in mind next time you hear a candidate for political office say he or she will appoint judges who apply the law, not make it. —ED.

I

Since Minnesota's admission to the Union in 1858, the State's Constitution has provided for the selection of all state judges by popular election. Since 1912, those elections have been nonpartisan. Since 1974, they have been subject to a legal restriction which states that a "candidate for a judicial office, including an incumbent judge," shall not "announce his or her views on disputed legal or political issues." This prohibition, promulgated by the Minnesota Supreme Court and based on Canon 7(B) of the 1972 American Bar Association (ABA) Model Code of Judicial Conduct, is known as the "announce clause." Incumbent judges who violate it are subject to discipline, including removal, censure, civil penalties, and suspension without pay. Lawyers who run for judicial office also must comply with the announce clause.

In 1996, one of the petitioners, Gregory Wersal, ran for associate justice of the Minnesota Supreme Court. In the course of the campaign, he distributed literature criticizing several Minnesota Supreme Court decisions on issues such as crime, welfare, and abortion. A complaint against Wersal challenging, among other things, the propriety of this literature was filed with the Office of Lawyers Professional Responsibility, the agency which, under the direction of the Minnesota Lawyers Professional Responsibility Board, investigates and prosecutes ethical violations of lawyer candidates for judicial office. The Lawyers Board dismissed the complaint; with regard to the charges that his campaign materials violated the announce clause, it expressed doubt whether the clause could constitutionally be enforced. Nonetheless, fearing that further ethical complaints would jeopardize his ability to practice law, Wersal withdrew from the election. In 1998, Wersal ran again for the same office. Early in that race, he sought an advisory opinion from the Lawyers Board with regard to whether it planned to enforce the announce clause. The Lawyers Board responded equivocally, stating that, although it had significant doubts about the constitutionality of the provision, it was unable to answer his question because he had not submitted a list of the announcements he wished to make. Shortly thereafter, Wersal filed this lawsuit in Federal District Court against respondents, seeking, inter alia, a declaration that the announce clause violates the First Amendment and an injunction against its enforcement. Wersal alleged that he was forced to refrain from announcing his views on disputed issues during the 1998 campaign, to the point where he declined response to questions put to him by the press and public, out of concern that he might run afoul of the announce clause. Other plaintiffs in the suit, including the Minnesota Republican Party, alleged that, because the clause kept Wersal from announcing his views, they were unable to learn those views and support or oppose his candidacy accordingly. The parties filed cross-motions for summary judgment, and the District Court found in favor of respondents, holding that the announce clause did not violate the First Amendment. Over a dissent by Judge Beam, the United States Court of Appeals for the Eighth Circuit affirmed.

II

Before considering the constitutionality of the announce clause, we must be clear about its meaning. Its text says that a candidate for judicial office shall not "announce his or her views on disputed legal or political issues."

We know that "announc[ing] . . . views" on an issue covers much more than promising to decide an issue a particular way. The prohibition extends to the candidate's mere statement of his current position, even if he does not bind himself to maintain that position after election. All the parties agree this is the case, because the Minnesota Code contains a so-called "pledges or promises" clause, which separately prohibits judicial candidates from making "pledges or promises of conduct in office other than the faithful and impartial performance of the duties of the office,"—a prohibition that is not challenged here and on which we express no view.

There are, however, some limitations that the Minnesota Supreme Court has placed upon the scope of the announce clause that are not (to put it politely) immediately apparent from its text. The statements that formed the basis of the complaint against Wersal in 1996 included criticism of past decisions of the Minnesota Supreme Court. One piece of campaign literature stated that "[t]he Minnesota Supreme Court has issued decisions which are marked by their disregard for the Legislature and a lack of common sense." It went on to criticize a decision excluding from evidence confessions by criminal defendants that were not tape-recorded, asking "[s]hould we conclude that because the Supreme Court does not trust police, it allows confessed criminals to go free?" It criticized a decision striking down a state law restricting welfare benefits, asserting that "[i]t's the Legislature which should set our spending policies." And it criticized a decision requiring public financing of abortions for poor women as "unprecedented" and a "pro-abortion stance." Although one would think that all of these statements touched on disputed legal or political issues, they did not (or at least do not now) fall within the scope of the announce clause. The Judicial Board issued an opinion stating that judicial candidates may criticize past decisions, and the Lawyers Board refused to discipline Wersal for the foregoing statements because, in part, it thought they did not violate the announce clause. The Eighth Circuit relied on the Judicial Board's opinion in upholding the announce clause, and the Minnesota Supreme Court recently embraced the Eighth Circuit's interpretation.

There are yet further limitations upon the apparent plain meaning of the announce clause: In light of the constitutional concerns, the District Court construed the clause to reach only disputed issues that are likely to come before the candidate if he is elected judge. The Eighth Circuit accepted this limiting interpretation by the District Court, and in addition construed the clause to allow general discussions of case law and judicial philosophy. The Supreme Court of Minnesota adopted these interpretations as well when it ordered enforcement of the announce clause in accordance with the Eighth Circuit's opinion.

It seems to us, however, that—like the text of the announce clause itself—these limitations upon the text of the announce clause are not all that they appear to be. First, respondents acknowledged at oral argument that statements critical of past judicial decisions are not permissible if the candidate also states that he is against stare decisis. Thus, candidates must choose between stating their views critical of past decisions and stating their views in opposition to stare decisis. Or, to look at it more concretely, they may state their view that prior decisions were erroneous only if they do not assert that they, if elected, have any power to eliminate erroneous decisions. Second, limiting the scope of the clause to issues likely to come before a court is not much of a limitation at all. One would hardly expect the "disputed legal or political issues" raised in the course of a state judicial election to include such matters as whether the Federal Government should end the embargo of Cuba. Quite obviously, they will be those legal or political disputes that are the proper (or by past decisions have been made the improper) business of the state courts. And within that relevant category, "[t]here is almost no legal or political issue that is unlikely to come before a judge of an American court, state or federal, of general jurisdiction." Third, construing the clause to allow "general" discussions of case law and judicial philosophy turns out to be of little help in an election campaign. At oral argument, respondents gave, as an example of this exception, that a candidate is free to assert that he is a " 'strict constructionist.' " But that, like most other philosophical generalities, has little meaningful content for the electorate unless it is exemplified by application to a particular issue of construction likely to come before a court — for example, whether a particular statute runs afoul of any provision of the Constitution. Respondents conceded that the announce clause would prohibit the candidate from exemplifying his philosophy in this fashion. Without such application to real-life issues, all candidates can claim to be "strict constructionists" with equal (and unhelpful) plausibility.

In any event, it is clear that the announce clause prohibits a judicial candidate from stating his views on any specific nonfanciful legal question within the province of the court for which he is running, except in the context of discussing past decisions — and in the latter context as well, if he expresses the view that he is not bound by stare decisis.

Respondents contend that this still leaves plenty of topics for discussion on the campaign trail. These include a candidate's "character," "education," "work habits," and "how [he] would handle administrative duties if elected." Indeed, the Judicial Board has printed a list of preapproved questions which judicial candidates are allowed to answer. These include how the candidate feels about cameras in the courtroom, how he would go about reducing the caseload, how the costs of judicial administration can be reduced, and how he proposes to ensure that minorities and women are treated more fairly by the court system. Whether this list of preapproved subjects, and other topics not prohibited by the announce clause, adequately fulfill the First Amendment's guarantee of freedom of speech is the question to which we now turn.

III

As the Court of Appeals recognized, the announce clause both prohibits speech on the basis of its content and burdens a category of speech that is "at the core of our First Amendment freedoms" — speech about the qualifications of candidates for public office. The Court of Appeals concluded that the proper test to be applied to determine the constitutionality of such a restriction is what our cases have called strict scrutiny; the parties do not dispute that this is correct. Under the strict-scrutiny test, respondents have the burden to prove that the announce clause is (1) narrowly tailored, to serve (2) a compelling state interest. In order for respondents to show that the announce clause is narrowly tailored, they must demonstrate that it does not "unnecessarily circumscrib[e] protected expression."

The Court of Appeals concluded that respondents had established two interests as sufficiently compelling to justify the announce clause: preserving the impartiality of the state judiciary and preserving the appearance of the impartiality of the state judiciary. Respondents reassert these two interests before us, arguing that the first is compelling because it protects the due process rights of litigants, and that the second is compelling because it preserves public confidence in the judiciary. Respondents are rather vague, however, about what they mean by "impartiality." Indeed, although the term is used throughout the Eighth Circuit's opinion, the briefs, the Minnesota Code of Judicial Conduct, and the ABA Codes of Judicial Conduct, none of these sources bothers to define it. Clarity on this point is essential before we can decide whether impartiality is indeed a compelling state interest, and, if so, whether the announce clause is narrowly tailored to achieve it.

A

One meaning of "impartiality" in the judicial context — and of course its root meaning — is the lack of bias for or against either party to the proceeding. Impartiality in this sense assures equal application of the law. That is, it guarantees a party that the judge who hears his case will apply the law to him in the same way he applies it to any other party. This is the traditional sense in which the term is used. It is also the sense in which it is used in the cases cited by respondents and amici for the proposition that an impartial judge is essential to due process. Tumey v. Ohio, 273 U.S. 510, 523, 531-534 (1927) (judge violated due process by sitting in a case in which it would be in his financial interest to find against one of the parties); Aetna Life Ins. Co. v. Lavoie, 475 U.S. 813, 822-825 (1986) (same); Ward v. Monroeville, 409 U.S. 57, 58-62 (1972) (same); Johnson v. Mississippi, 403 U.S. 212, 215-216 (1971) (per curiam) (judge violated due process by sitting in a case in which one of the parties was a previously successful litigant against him); Bracy v. Gramley, 520 U.S. 899, 905 (1997) (would violate due process if a judge was disposed to rule against defendants who did not bribe him in order to cover up the fact that he regularly ruled in favor of defendants who did bribe him); In re Murchison, 349 U.S. 133, 137-139 (1955) (judge violated due process by sitting in the criminal trial of defendant whom he had indicted).

We think it plain that the announce clause is not narrowly tailored to serve impartiality (or the appearance of impartiality) in this sense. Indeed, the clause is barely tailored to serve that interest at all, inasmuch as it does not restrict speech for or against particular parties, but rather speech for or against particular issues. To be sure, when a case arises that turns on a legal issue on which the judge (as a candidate) had taken a particular stand, the party taking the opposite stand is likely to lose. But not because of any bias against that party, or favoritism toward the other party. Any party taking that position is just as likely to lose. The judge is applying the law (as he sees it) evenhandedly.

B

It is perhaps possible to use the term "impartiality" in the judicial context (though this is certainly not a common usage) to mean lack of preconception in favor of or against a particular legal view. This sort of impartiality would be concerned, not with guaranteeing litigants equal application of the law, but rather with guaranteeing them an equal chance to persuade the court on the legal points in their case. Impartiality in this sense may well be an interest served by the announce clause, but it is not a compelling state interest, as strict scrutiny requires. A judge's lack of predisposition regarding the relevant legal issues in a case has never been thought a necessary component of equal justice, and with good reason. For one thing, it is virtually impossible to find a judge who does not have preconceptions about the law. As then-Justice Rehnquist observed of our own Court: "Since most Justices come to this bench no earlier than their middle years, it would be unusual if they had not by that time formulated at least some tentative notions that would influence them in their interpretation of the sweeping clauses of the Constitution and their interaction with one another. It would be not merely unusual, but extraordinary, if they had not at least given opinions as to constitutional issues in their previous legal careers." Laird v. Tatum, 409 U.S. 824, 835 (1972) (memorandum opinion). Indeed, even if it were possible to select judges who did not have preconceived views on legal issues, it would hardly be desirable to do so. "Proof that a Justice's mind at the time he joined the Court was a complete tabula rasa in the area of constitutional adjudication would be evidence of lack of qualification, not lack of bias." Ibid. The Minnesota Constitution positively forbids the selection to courts of general jurisdiction of judges who are impartial in the sense of having no views on the law. Minn. Const., Art. VI, §5 ("Judges of the supreme court, the court of appeals and the district court shall be learned in the law"). And since avoiding judicial preconceptions on legal issues is neither possible nor desirable, pretending otherwise by attempting to preserve the "appearance" of that type of impartiality can hardly be a compelling state interest either.

C

A third possible meaning of "impartiality" (again not a common one) might be described as openmindedness. This quality in a judge demands, not that he have no preconceptions on legal issues, but that he be willing to consider views that oppose his preconceptions, and remain open to persuasion, when the issues arise in a pending case. This sort of impartiality seeks to guarantee each litigant, not an equal chance to win the legal points in the case, but at least some chance of doing so. It may well be that impartiality in this sense, and the appearance of it, are desirable in the judiciary, but we need not pursue that inquiry, since we do not believe the Minnesota Supreme Court adopted the announce clause for that purpose.

Respondents argue that the announce clause serves the interest in openmindedness, or at least in the appearance of openmindedness, because it relieves a judge from pressure to rule a certain way in order to maintain consistency with statements the judge has previously made. The problem is, however, that statements in election campaigns are such an infinitesimal portion of the public commitments to legal positions that judges (or judges-to-be) undertake, that this object of the prohibition is implausible. Before they arrive on the bench (whether by election or otherwise) judges have often committed themselves on legal issues that they must later rule upon. See, e.g., Laird, supra, at 831-833 (describing Justice Black's participation in several cases construing and deciding the constitutionality of the Fair Labor Standards Act, even though as a Senator he had been one of its principal authors; and Chief Justice Hughes's authorship of the opinion overruling Adkins v. Children's Hospital of D.C., 261 U.S. 525 (1923), a case he had criticized in a book written before his appointment to the Court). More common still is a judge's confronting a legal issue on which he has expressed an opinion while on the bench. Most frequently, of course, that prior expression will have occurred in ruling on an earlier case. But judges often state their views on disputed legal issues outside the context of adjudication — in classes that they conduct, and in books and speeches. Like the ABA Codes of Judicial Conduct, the Minnesota Code not only permits but encourages this. That is quite incompatible with the notion that the need for openmindedness (or for the appearance of openmindedness) lies behind the prohibition at issue here.

The short of the matter is this: In Minnesota, a candidate for judicial office may not say "I think it is constitutional for the legislature to prohibit same-sex marriages." He may say the very same thing, however, up until the very day before he declares himself a candidate, and may say it repeatedly (until litigation is pending) after he is elected. As a means of pursuing the objective of openmindedness that respondents now articulate, the announce clause is so woefully underinclusive as to render belief in that purpose a challenge to the credulous.

Justice Stevens asserts that statements made in an election campaign pose a special threat to openmindedness because the candidate, when elected judge, will have a particular reluctance to contradict them. That might be plausible, perhaps, with regard to campaign promises. A candidate who says "If elected, I will vote to uphold the legislature's power to prohibit same-sex marriages" will positively be breaking his word if he does not do so (although one would be naïve not to recognize that campaign promises are — by long democratic tradition — the least binding form of human commitment). But, as noted earlier, the Minnesota Supreme Court has adopted a separate prohibition on campaign "pledges or promises," which is not challenged here. The proposition that judges feel significantly greater compulsion, or appear to feel significantly greater compulsion, to maintain consistency with nonpromissory statements made during a judicial campaign than with such statements made before or after the campaign is not self-evidently true. It seems to us quite likely, in fact, that in many cases the opposite is true. We doubt, for example, that a mere statement of position enunciated during the pendency of an election will be regarded by a judge as more binding — or as more likely to subject him to popular disfavor if reconsidered — than a carefully considered holding that the judge set forth in an earlier opinion denying some individual's claim to justice. In any event, it suffices to say that respondents have not carried the burden imposed by our strict-scrutiny test to establish this proposition (that campaign statements are uniquely destructive of openmindedness) on which the validity of the announce clause rests.

Moreover, the notion that the special context of electioneering justifies an abridgment of the right to speak out on disputed issues sets our First Amendment jurisprudence on its head. "[D]ebate on the qualifications of candidates" is "at the core of our electoral process and of the First Amendment freedoms," not at the edges. "The role that elected officials play in our society makes it all the more imperative that they be allowed freely to express themselves on matters of current public importance. . . . It is simply not the function of government to select which issues are worth discussing or debating in the course of a political campaign." We have never allowed the government to prohibit candidates from communicating relevant information to voters during an election.

Justice Ginsburg would do so — and much of her dissent confirms rather than refutes our conclusion that the purpose behind the announce clause is not openmindedness in the judiciary, but the undermining of judicial elections. She contends that the announce clause must be constitutional because due process would be denied if an elected judge sat in a case involving an issue on which he had previously announced his view. She reaches this conclusion because, she says, such a judge would have a "direct, personal, substantial, and pecuniary interest" in ruling consistently with his previously announced view, in order to reduce the risk that he will be "voted off the bench and thereby lose [his] salary and emoluments." But elected judges — regardless of whether they have announced any views beforehand — always face the pressure of an electorate who might disagree with their rulings and therefore vote them off the bench. Surely the judge who frees Timothy McVeigh places his job much more at risk than the judge who (horror of horrors!) reconsiders his previously announced view on a disputed legal issue. So if, as Justice Ginsburg claims, it violates due process for a judge to sit in a case in which ruling one way rather than another increases his prospects for reelection, then — quite simply — the practice of electing judges is itself a violation of due process. It is not difficult to understand how one with these views would approve the election-nullifying effect of the announce clause. They are not, however, the views reflected in the Due Process Clause of the Fourteenth Amendment, which has coexisted with the election of judges ever since it was adopted.

Justice Ginsburg devotes the rest of her dissent to attacking arguments we do not make. For example, despite the number of pages she dedicates to disproving this proposition, we neither assert nor imply that the First Amendment requires campaigns for judicial office to sound the same as those for legislative office. What we do assert, and what Justice Ginsburg ignores, is that, even if the First Amendment allows greater regulation of judicial election campaigns than legislative election campaigns, the announce clause still fails strict scrutiny because it is woefully underinclusive, prohibiting announcements by judges (and would-be judges) only at certain times and in certain forms. We rely on the cases involving speech during elections only to make the obvious point that this underinclusiveness cannot be explained by resort to the notion that the First Amendment provides less protection during an election campaign than at other times.[11]

---

11. Nor do we assert that candidates for judicial office should be compelled to announce their views on disputed legal issues. Thus, Justice Ginsburg's repeated invocation of instances in which nominees to this Court declined to announce such views during Senate confirmation hearings is pointless. That the practice of voluntarily demurring does not establish the legitimacy of legal compulsion to demur is amply demonstrated by the unredacted text of the sentence she quotes in part, post from Laird v. Tatum, 409 U.S. 824, 836, n. 5 (1972): "*In terms of propriety, rather than disqualification,* I would distinguish quite sharply between a public statement made prior to nomination for the bench, on the one hand, and a public statement made by a nominee to the bench." (Emphasis added.)

But in any case, Justice Ginsburg greatly exaggerates the difference between judicial and legislative elections. She asserts that "the rationale underlying unconstrained speech in elections for political office — that representative government depends on the public's ability to choose agents who will act at its behest — does not carry over to campaigns for the bench." This complete separation of the judiciary from the enterprise of "representative government" might have some truth in those countries where judges neither make law themselves nor set aside the laws enacted by the legislature. It is not a true picture of the American system. Not only do state-court judges possess the power to "make" common law, but they have the immense power to shape the States' constitutions as well. Which is precisely why the election of state judges became popular.[12]

IV

To sustain the announce clause, the Eighth Circuit relied heavily on the fact that a pervasive practice of prohibiting judicial candidates from discussing disputed legal and political issues developed during the last half of the 20th century. It is true that a "universal and long-established" tradition of prohibiting certain conduct creates "a strong presumption" that the prohibition is constitutional: "Principles of liberty fundamental enough to have been embodied within constitutional guarantees are not readily erased from the Nation's consciousness." The practice of prohibiting speech by judicial candidates on disputed issues, however, is neither long nor universal.

At the time of the founding, only Vermont (before it became a State) selected any of its judges by election. Starting with Georgia in 1812, States began to provide for judicial election, a development rapidly accelerated by Jacksonian democracy. By the time of the Civil War, the great majority of States elected their judges. We know of no restrictions upon statements that could be made by judicial candidates (including judges) throughout the 19th and the first quarter of the 20th century. Indeed, judicial elections were generally partisan during this period, the movement toward nonpartisan judicial elections not even beginning until the 1870's. Thus, not only were judicial candidates (including judges) discussing disputed legal and political issues on the campaign trail, but they were touting party affiliations and angling for party nominations all the while.

---

12. Although Justice Stevens at times appears to agree with Justice Ginsburg's premise that the judiciary is completely separated from the enterprise of representative government ("[E]very good judge is fully aware of the distinction between the law and a personal point of view"), he eventually appears to concede that the separation does not hold true for many judges who sit on courts of last resort. ("If he is not a judge on the highest court in the State, he has an obligation to follow the precedent of that court, not his personal views or public opinion polls.") Even if the policy making capacity of judges were limited to courts of last resort, that would only prove that the announce clause fails strict scrutiny. "[I]f announcing one's views in the context of a campaign for the State Supreme Court might be" protected speech, then — even if announcing one's views in the context of a campaign for a lower court were not protected speech — the announce clause would not be narrowly tailored, since it applies to high- and low-court candidates alike. In fact, however, the judges of inferior courts often "make law," since the precedent of the highest court does not cover every situation, and not every case is reviewed. Justice Stevens has repeatedly expressed the view that a settled course of lower court opinions binds the highest court.

The first code regulating judicial conduct was adopted by the ABA in 1924. It contained a provision akin to the announce clause: "A candidate for judicial position . . . should not announce in advance his conclusions of law on disputed issues to secure class support. . . ." The States were slow to adopt the canons, however. "By the end of World War II, the canons . . . were binding by the bar associations or supreme courts of only eleven states." J. MacKenzie, The Appearance of Justice 191 (1974). Even today, although a majority of States have adopted either the announce clause or its 1990 ABA successor, adoption is not unanimous. Of the 31 States that select some or all of their appellate and general-jurisdiction judges by election, see American Judicature Society, Judicial Selection in the States: Appellate and General Jurisdiction Courts (Apr. 2002), 4 have adopted no candidate-speech restriction comparable to the announce clause, and 1 prohibits only the discussion of "pending litigation." This practice, relatively new to judicial elections and still not universally adopted, does not compare well with the traditions deemed worthy of our attention in prior cases.

* * *

There is an obvious tension between the article of Minnesota's popularly approved Constitution which provides that judges shall be elected, and the Minnesota Supreme Court's announce clause which places most subjects of interest to the voters off limits. (The candidate-speech restrictions of all the other States that have them are also the product of judicial fiat.) The disparity is perhaps unsurprising, since the ABA, which originated the announce clause, has long been an opponent of judicial elections. . . . That opposition may be well taken (it certainly had the support of the Founders of the Federal Government), but the First Amendment does not permit it to achieve its goal by leaving the principle of elections in place while preventing candidates from discussing what the elections are about. "[T]he greater power to dispense with elections altogether does not include the lesser power to conduct elections under conditions of state-imposed voter ignorance. If the State chooses to tap the energy and the legitimizing power of the democratic process, it must accord the participants in that process . . . the First Amendment rights that attach to their roles."

The Minnesota Supreme Court's canon of judicial conduct prohibiting candidates for judicial election from announcing their views on disputed legal and political issues violates the First Amendment. Accordingly, we reverse the grant of summary judgment to respondents and remand the case for proceedings consistent with this opinion.

It is so ordered.

JUSTICE O'CONNOR, concurring.

I join the opinion of the Court but write separately to express my concerns about judicial elections generally. Respondents claim that "[t]he Announce Clause is necessary . . . to protect the State's compelling governmental interes[t] in an actual and perceived . . . impartial judiciary." I am concerned that, even aside from what judicial candidates may say while campaigning, the very practice of electing judges undermines this interest.

We of course want judges to be impartial, in the sense of being free from any personal stake in the outcome of the cases to which they are assigned. But if judges are subject to regular elections they are likely to feel that they have at least some personal stake in the outcome of every publicized case. Elected judges cannot help being aware that if the public is not satisfied with the outcome of a particular case, it could hurt their reelection prospects. Even if judges were able to suppress their awareness of the potential electoral consequences of their decisions and refrain from acting on it, the public's confidence in the judiciary could be undermined simply by the possibility that judges would be unable to do so.

Moreover, contested elections generally entail campaigning. And campaigning for a judicial post today can require substantial funds. See Schotland, Financing Judicial Elections, 2000: Change and Challenge, 2001 L. Rev. Mich. State U. Detroit College of Law 849, 866 (reporting that in 2000, the 13 candidates in a partisan election for 5 seats on the Alabama Supreme Court spent an average of $1,092,076 on their campaigns); American Bar Association, Report and Recommendations of the Task Force on Lawyers' Political Contributions, pt. 2 (July 1998) (reporting that in 1995, one candidate for the Pennsylvania Supreme Court raised $1,848,142 in campaign funds, and that in 1986, $2,700,000 was spent on the race for Chief Justice of the Ohio Supreme Court). Unless the pool of judicial candidates is limited to those wealthy enough to independently fund their campaigns, a limitation unrelated to judicial skill, the cost of campaigning requires judicial candidates to engage in fundraising. Yet relying on campaign donations may leave judges feeling indebted to certain parties or interest groups. Even if judges were able to refrain from favoring donors, the mere possibility that judges' decisions may be motivated by the desire to repay campaign contributors is likely to undermine the public's confidence in the judiciary . . .

JUSTICE KENNEDY, concurring . . .

I adhere to my view . . . that content-based speech restrictions that do not fall within any traditional exception should be invalidated without inquiry into narrow tailoring or compelling government interests. The speech at issue here does not come within any of the exceptions to the First Amendment recognized by the Court. . . .

Minnesota may choose to have an elected judiciary. It may strive to define those characteristics that exemplify judicial excellence. It may enshrine its definitions in a code of judicial conduct. It may adopt recusal standards more rigorous than due process requires, and censure judges who violate these standards. What Minnesota may not do, however, is censor what the people hear as they undertake to decide for themselves which candidate is most likely to be an exemplary judicial officer. Deciding the relevance of candidate speech is the right of the voters, not the State. The law in question here contradicts the principle that unabridged speech is the foundation of political freedom . . .

JUSTICE STEVENS, with whom JUSTICE SOUTER, JUSTICE GINSBURG, and JUSTICE BREYER join, dissenting. . . .

The limits of the Court's holding are evident: Even if the Minnesota Lawyers Professional Responsibility Board (Board) may not sanction a judicial candidate for announcing his views on issues likely to come before him, it may surely advise the electorate that such announcements demonstrate the speaker's unfitness for judicial office. If the solution to harmful speech must be more speech, so be it. The Court's reasoning, however, will unfortunately endure beyond the next election cycle. By obscuring the fundamental distinction between campaigns for the judiciary and the political branches, and by failing to recognize the difference between statements made in articles or opinions and those made on the campaign trail, the Court defies any sensible notion of the judicial office and the importance of impartiality in that context.

The Court's disposition rests on two seriously flawed premises — an inaccurate appraisal of the importance of judicial independence and impartiality, and an assumption that judicial candidates should have the same freedom " 'to express themselves on matters of current public importance' " as do all other elected officials. Elected judges, no less than appointed judges, occupy an office of trust that is fundamentally different from that occupied by policymaking officials. Although the fact that they must stand for election makes their job more difficult than that of the tenured judge, that fact does not lessen their duty to respect essential attributes of the judicial office that have been embedded in Anglo-American law for centuries.

There is a critical difference between the work of the judge and the work of other public officials. In a democracy, issues of policy are properly decided by majority vote; it is the business of legislators and executives to be popular. But in litigation, issues of law or fact should not be determined by popular vote; it is the business of judges to be indifferent to unpopularity. . . .

Of course, any judge who faces reelection may believe that he retains his office only so long as his decisions are popular. Nevertheless, the elected judge, like the lifetime appointee, does not serve a constituency while holding that office. He has a duty to uphold the law and to follow the dictates of the Constitution. If he is not a judge on the highest court in the State, he has an obligation to follow the precedent of that court, not his personal views or public opinion polls. He may make common law, but judged on the merits of individual cases, not as a mandate from the voters . . .

JUSTICE GINSBURG, with whom JUSTICE STEVENS, JUSTICE SOUTER, and JUSTICE BREYER join, dissenting. . . .

I

The speech restriction must fail, in the Court's view, because an electoral process is at stake; if Minnesota opts to elect its judges, the Court asserts, the State may not rein in what candidates may say.

I do not agree with this unilocular, "an election is an election," approach. Instead, I would differentiate elections for political offices, in which the First Amendment holds full sway, from elections designed to select those whose office it is to administer justice without respect to persons. Minnesota's choice to elect its judges, I am persuaded, does not preclude the State from installing an election process geared to the judicial office.

Legislative and executive officials serve in representative capacities. They are agents of the people; their primary function is to advance the interests of their constituencies. Candidates for political offices, in keeping with their representative role, must be left free to inform the electorate of their positions on specific issues. Armed with such information, the individual voter will be equipped to cast her ballot intelligently, to vote for the candidate committed to positions the voter approves. Campaign statements committing the candidate to take sides on contentious issues are therefore not only appropriate in political elections, they are "at the core of our electoral process," for they "enhance the accountability of government officials to the people whom they represent."

Judges, however, are not political actors. They do not sit as representatives of particular persons, communities, or parties; they serve no faction or constituency. "[I]t is the business of judges to be indifferent to popularity." They must strive to do what is legally right, all the more so when the result is not the one "the home crowd" wants.[1] . . .

II . . .

[T]he Court ignores a crucial limiting construction placed on the announce clause by the courts below. The provision does not bar a candidate from generally "stating [her] views" on legal questions; it prevents her from "publicly making known how [she] would decide" disputed issues. That limitation places beyond the scope of the Announce Clause a wide range of comments that may be highly informative to voters. Consistent with the Eighth Circuit's construction, such comments may include, for example, statements of historical fact ("As a prosecutor, I obtained 15 drunk driving convictions"); qualified statements ("Judges should use sparingly their discretion to grant lenient sentences to drunk drivers"); and statements framed at a sufficient level of generality ("Drunk drivers are a threat to the safety of every driver"). What remains within the Announce Clause is the category of statements that essentially commit the candidate to a position on a specific issue, such as "I think all drunk drivers should receive the maximum sentence permitted by law." . . .

The announce clause is thus more tightly bounded, and campaigns conducted under that provision more robust, than the Court acknowledges. Judicial candidates in Minnesota may not only convey general information about themselves, they may also describe their conception of the role of a judge and their views on a wide range of subjects of interest to the voters. Further, they may discuss, criticize, or defend past decisions of interest to voters. What candidates may not do — simply or with sophistication — is remove themselves from the constraints characteristic of the judicial office and declare how they would decide an issue, without regard to the particular context in which it is presented,

---

1. In the context of the federal system, how a prospective nominee for the bench would resolve particular contentious issues would certainly be "of interest" to the President and the Senate in the exercise of their respective nomination and confirmation powers, just as information of that type would "interest" a Minnesota voter. But in accord with a longstanding norm, every Member of this Court declined to furnish such information to the Senate, and presumably to the President as well. Surely the Court perceives no tension here; the line each of us drew in response to preconfirmation questioning, the Court would no doubt agree, is crucial to the health of the Federal Judiciary. But by the Court's reasoning, the reticence of prospective and current federal judicial nominees dishonors Article II, for it deprives the President and the Senate of information that might aid or advance the decision to nominate or confirm. The point is not, of course, that this "practice of voluntarily demurring" by itself "establish[es] the legitimacy of legal compulsion to demur," (emphasis omitted). The federal norm simply illustrates that, contrary to the Court's suggestion, there is nothing inherently incongruous in depriving those charged with choosing judges of certain information they might desire during the selection process.

sans briefs, oral argument, and, as to an appellate bench, the benefit of one's colleagues' analyses. Properly construed, the Announce Clause prohibits only a discrete subcategory of the statements the Court's misinterpretation encompasses. . . .

III

Even as it exaggerates the reach of the Announce Clause, the Court ignores the significance of that provision to the integrated system of judicial campaign regulation Minnesota has developed. Coupled with the Announce Clause in Minnesota's Code of Judicial Conduct is a provision that prohibits candidates from "mak[ing] pledges or promises of conduct in office other than the faithful and impartial performance of the duties of the office." Although the Court is correct that this "pledges or promises" provision is not directly at issue in this case, the Court errs in overlooking the interdependence of that prohibition and the one before us. In my view, the constitutionality of the Announce Clause cannot be resolved without an examination of that interaction in light of the interests the pledges or promises provision serves.

A . . .

Prohibiting a judicial candidate from pledging or promising certain results if elected directly promotes the State's interest in preserving public faith in the bench. When a candidate makes such a promise during a campaign, the public will no doubt perceive that she is doing so in the hope of garnering votes. And the public will in turn likely conclude that when the candidate decides an issue in accord with that promise, she does so at least in part to discharge her undertaking to the voters in the previous election and to prevent voter abandonment in the next. The perception of that unseemly quid pro quo — a judicial candidate's promises on issues in return for the electorate's votes at the polls — inevitably diminishes the public's faith in the ability of judges to administer the law without regard to personal or political self-interest.[4] Then-Justice Rehnquist's observations about the federal system apply with equal if not greater force in the context of Minnesota's elective judiciary: Regarding the appearance of judicial integrity, "[one must] distinguish quite sharply between a public statement made prior to nomination for the bench, on the one hand, and a public statement made by a nominee to the bench. For the latter to express any but the most general observation about the law would suggest that, in order to obtain favorable consideration of his nomination, he deliberately was announcing in advance, without benefit of judicial oath, briefs, or argument, how he would decide a particular question that might come before him as a judge." Laird v. Tatum, 409 U.S. 824, 836, n. 5 (1972) (memorandum opinion).

---

4. The author of the Court's opinion declined on precisely these grounds to tell the Senate whether he would overrule a particular case: "Let us assume that I have people arguing before me to do it or not to do it. I think it is quite a thing to be arguing to somebody who you know has made a representation in the course of his confirmation hearings, and that is, by way of condition to his being confirmed, that he will do this or do that. I think I would be in a very bad position to adjudicate the case without being accused of having a less than impartial view of the matter."

B

The constitutionality of the pledges or promises clause is thus amply supported; the provision not only advances due process of law for litigants in Minnesota courts, it also reinforces the authority of the Minnesota judiciary by promoting public confidence in the State's judges. The Announce Clause, however, is equally vital to achieving these compelling ends, for without it, the pledges or promises provision would be feeble, an arid form, a matter of no real importance.

Uncoupled from the Announce Clause, the ban on pledges or promises is easily circumvented. By prefacing a campaign commitment with the caveat, "although I cannot promise anything," or by simply avoiding the language of promises or pledges altogether, a candidate could declare with impunity how she would decide specific issues. Semantic sanitizing of the candidate's commitment would not, however, diminish its pernicious effects on actual and perceived judicial impartiality. To use the Court's example, a candidate who campaigns by saying, "If elected, I will vote to uphold the legislature's power to prohibit same-sex marriages," will feel scarcely more pressure to honor that statement than the candidate who stands behind a podium and tells a throng of cheering supporters: "I think it is constitutional for the legislature to prohibit same-sex marriages." Made during a campaign, both statements contemplate a quid pro quo between candidate and voter. Both effectively "bind [the candidate] to maintain that position after election." And both convey the impression of a candidate prejudging an issue to win votes. Contrary to the Court's assertion, the "nonpromissory" statement averts none of the dangers posed by the "promissory" one. (Emphasis omitted).

By targeting statements that do not technically constitute pledges or promises but nevertheless "publicly mak[e] known how [the candidate] would decide" legal issues, the Announce Clause prevents this end run around the letter and spirit of its companion provision. No less than the pledges or promises clause itself, the Announce Clause is an indispensable part of Minnesota's effort to maintain the health of its judiciary, and is therefore constitutional for the same reasons . . .

In 2007, the ABA changed its Code of Judicial Conduct to satisfy *White*. The new code eliminates the announce clause and offers an expanded pledges and promises clause with commentary. Rule 4.1(A)(13) says that a judicial candidate (whether via election or appointment) shall not

> in connection with cases, controversies, or issues that are likely to come before the court, make pledges, promises, or commitments that are inconsistent with the impartial performance of the adjudicative duties of judicial office.

The same limitation is applied to sitting judges in Rule 2.10(B). The code's terminology provides:

> "Impartial," "impartiality," and "impartially" mean absence of bias or prejudice in favor of, or against, particular parties or classes of parties, as

well as maintenance of an open mind in considering issues that may come before a judge.

Commentary to Rule 4.1 explains:

[11] The role of a judge is different from that of a legislator or executive branch official, even when the judge is subject to public election. Campaigns for judicial office must be conducted differently from campaigns for other offices. The narrowly drafted restrictions upon political and campaign activities of judicial candidates provided in Canon 4 allow candidates to conduct campaigns that provide voters with sufficient information to permit them to distinguish between candidates and make informed electoral choices . . .

[13] The making of a pledge, promise, or commitment is not dependent upon, or limited to, the use of any specific words or phrases; instead, the totality of the statement must be examined to determine if a reasonable person would believe that the candidate for judicial office has specifically undertaken to reach a particular result. Pledges, promises, or commitments must be contrasted with statements or announcements of personal views on legal, political, or other issues, which are not prohibited. When making such statements, a judge should acknowledge the overarching judicial obligation to apply and uphold the law, without regard to his or her personal views . . .

[15] Judicial candidates may receive questionnaires or requests for interviews from the media and from issue advocacy or other community organizations that seek to learn their views on disputed or controversial legal or political issues. Paragraph (A)(13) does not specifically address judicial responses to such inquiries. Depending upon the wording and format of such questionnaires, candidates' responses might be viewed as pledges, promises, or commitments to perform the adjudicative duties of office other than in an impartial way. To avoid violating paragraph (A)(13), therefore, candidates who respond to media and other inquiries should also give assurances that they will keep an open mind and will carry out their adjudicative duties faithfully and impartially if elected. Candidates who do not respond may state their reasons for not responding, such as the danger that answering might be perceived by a reasonable person as undermining a successful candidate's independence or impartiality, or that it might lead to frequent disqualification. See Rule 2.11.

Rule 2.11(A)(5) requires a judge to disqualify himself or herself if "[t]he judge, while a judge or a judicial candidate, has made a public statement, other than in a court proceeding, judicial decision, or opinion, that commits or appears to commit the judge to reach a particular result or rule in a particular way in the proceeding or controversy."

What do you think of these changes? The ABA has obviously chosen a double strategy. First, it decided not to back down any further than *White* required. It did this even though some lower court activity suggested that the pledges and promises clause, which the ABA retained, might not survive *White's* analysis. Second, the ABA used the risk of disqualification as a safety net. Even if the prohibition in the new pledges and promises clause might not satisfy the First Amendment, whether facially or in particular cases, the judge who speaks may be disqualified from sitting if his speech commits or appears to commit him to rule in a particular way. While there may be a constitutional right to speak, there is no constitutional right not to be disqualified. What advice would you give to Marta Rojas, the judicial candidate in "I Got These Questionnaires," set out above?

The Fall 2008 issue of the Georgetown Journal of Legal Ethics has several articles on the issues in this section. See also Stephen Gillers, "If Elected, I Promise (_____)" — What Should Judicial Candidates Be Allowed to Say?, 35 Indiana L. Rev. 725 (2002) (arguing that the pre-*White* ABA rules made little sense even apart from First Amendment considerations).

XVI

Marketing Legal Services

- *Commercial Speech Protection for Lawyer Marketing*
- *The Supreme Court's Methodology*
- *Sprecial Rules for Public Interest Lawyers*

"I'm Back on My Feet"

A firm wants to hire an actor to perform the following script for an advertisement to be shown on cable television:

> My debts were piling up after I was laid off, and it looked certain that I was going to lose my home and car. I didn't know what to do. I called Crutch & Bly because I had seen their ads on TV. I made an appointment to see a lawyer who told me about bankruptcy. I didn't think it was for me at first, but I didn't want to lose all I had worked for. The lawyer told me I'd be able to keep my house and some of my savings. I decided to go ahead. I managed to keep my house and most of my savings. The plant began rehiring and I'm now back on my feet. I owe a lot to Crutch & Bly.

Then another voice would come on, also that of an actor, saying:

> Bankruptcy isn't for everyone, but sometimes it's the right choice. Crutch & Bly will show you how it works, answer your questions, and help you decide if it's for you. Give them a call. They might be able to help.

Is this ad protected by the First Amendment? Is it truthful even though the actors are pretending to be what they're not: a real client and a real lawyer describing a real matter? Let's say the firm has actual clients who are in the first actor's precise situation but who are not as telegenic. And let's assume that the second actor is recognizable, perhaps someone who plays a lawyer on a popular television show. If Crutch & Bly came to you before broadcasting the ad, which lines, if any, would you advise the law firm to change or delete? Why? If the First Amendment would not protect a firm's wish to use actors or a dramatization, do you think a jurisdiction's rules should forbid either?

If you are the average reader of this book, a second- or third-year law student, you won't recall a time without legal advertising. Lawyers' ads may not be as common as those for airlines, cell phones, or banks, but you've probably seen or heard hundreds of legal advertisements in your life — in the classified sections of newspapers, on radio and television, in glossy business magazines — and thought nothing of it. Yet for most of the last century, legal advertising was banned, with a few extremely narrow exceptions. A lawyer whose career straddles the watershed year 1977 may still be amazed at the changes, and some will also wonder if it has all been for the good.

It is easy for a teacher to choose to dispense with this chapter, particularly if your course is only two credits, with such important topics as confidentiality and conflicts competing for attention. And I am always tempted to shorten it. But each time I try, I am reminded of its complexity. (Nevertheless, I did manage to cut a bit this time.) Reading this material will evoke several resonances with lessons elsewhere in this book and in other courses. In short, the lawyer marketing material (which incorporates both traditional advertising and solicitation of specific clients) presents a kind of case study. The subject encompasses the methodology of constitutional analysis, particularly the extent to which federal courts should defer to state claims of legitimate regulatory interests; First Amendment jurisprudence in the area of commercial speech; differing views on what it means to be a professional; the effect of an interest in money on professionalism; the effect of advertising on the desire for wealth and the image of lawyers; how the Supreme Court uses or misuses empirical information; and even the economic interpretation of law.

Three interlocking trends will keep the rules that regulate law firm marketing in the news and a subject of discussion for the profession. The first is the continuing growth of national and international law firms. Second is the expanding American lawyer population, which intensifies competition and encourages advertising (tasteful or not). Third, internet Web sites (and perhaps technology yet unknown) make lawyer marketing easy, cheap, and even respectable. But these trends do not mean that issues of lawyer advertising will soon see the level of court attention we witnessed in the final quarter of the last century. After the Supreme Court opened the First Amendment door a few inches in 1977, it and lower courts, as well as state rulemaking bodies, all struggled to identify boundaries for this new freedom. By century's end, that activity had subsided, especially in court, perhaps because the contesting parties (on one side, those who wanted greater freedom for lawyers to sell their services; on the other, those who found the phenomenon unprofessional at best, repulsive at worst, or just economically threatening) had reached something close to a standoff. How long it will last no one can say.

Before we launch into the story at hand, consider these two anecdotes from opposite ends of the profession:

I gave a speech at a very traditional law firm not long ago, and afterwards, I got to talking to a woman in its marketing department, as the firm called it. "How many people worked in that department?" I asked. "Thirty," she said. "For the entire firm?" "No, just in the New York office." The firm has offices in a dozen world cities.

Some firms like to liven up their print ads with pictures. Catches the eye, don't you know. Some firms want those pictures to be of an animal whose presumed qualities the firm would like the public to associate with its lawyers. So no cocker spaniels. But how about a lion? A bear? A shark? A pit bull? A panther? It fell to the

Florida Supreme Court to decide whether to allow the pit bull (the other creatures have all been tolerated except the shark). The court held that the pit bull (and an 800 number that spelled out "pit bull") violated Florida rules against characterizing the quality of the lawyer's services and permitting only information objectively relevant to hiring counsel. The Florida Bar v. Pape, 918 So.2d 240 (Fla. 2005).

The year to start the constitutional journey is 1977, but to put that journey in context, we must recount an event that occurred 14 years earlier.

A. DEFINING THE BORDERS: *BATES* AND *OHRALIK*

For many, success comes too late or not at all. For some lawyers at the New York firm of Olwine Connelly, it came too early.

In 1962, Life magazine published a gushy article about the firm ("A Day in the Life of a Wall Street Law Firm") with the help of some Olwine partners and associates. The article, accompanied by photographs, described the firm as "blue chip" and one that enjoyed "the cream of corporate business." The participating partners were censured for fostering "self-interest publicity," but the associates were let off because the case was one of first impression. In re Connelly, 240 N.Y.S.2d 126 (1st Dept. 1963).*

Vindication, of sorts, came 14 years later. Bates v. State Bar of Arizona, 433 U.S. 350 (1977), said advertising by lawyers was commercial speech entitled to First Amendment protection. *Bates* is usually credited (or blamed) for all those late-night television (and similar) ads for legal services. But the rationale and effect of *Bates* was not limited to advertising. By freeing lawyers to talk to the media and to publish books and articles that in a prior age would be condemned as "self-laudatory," *Bates* invited broad efforts in public relations and self-promotion. These efforts in turn facilitated growth of the "legal press" and increased attention on lawyers by the popular press, because lawyers could now freely discuss their work with reporters. (The National Law Journal and The American Lawyer both began publication after *Bates*.) Today, law firms compete for media attention. Many hire or retain outside public relations experts; as noted above, large firms have marketing professionals on staff. An article like the one about Olwine Connelly would today be "to die for."

The point here is that there is more to legal marketing than "PERSONAL BANKRUPTCY/$299." In a stratified and increasingly competitive profession, we should expect many varieties of self-promotion. Lawyers will aim at the audience containing their potential client population and will do so in commensurate style. So while some resort to the Yellow Pages, billboards, and matchbook covers ("Don't Perish in Jail/Call Bogart for Bail"), others choose more sophisticated venues. For example, Baker & McKenzie, one of the world's largest law firms, profiled itself in a six-page color ad in California Lawyer magazine. One partner reflected that the ad "brought us enormous recognition, which

---

* Olwine Connelly closed shop many years later, but not because of the disciplinary opinion. Rather, it fell victim to economic trends that saw the demise of many medium-sized New York law firms in the 1970s and 1980s.

inevitably leads to business." Wall St. J., Sept. 17, 1990. Brobeck, Phleger and Harrison (now defunct) advertised on CNN. Here is how Crain Communications described one ad (Feb. 5, 2001):

> In one spot, titled "Glider plane," a plane glides around a Gerber daisy suspended above a snowfield and then passes by a nattily dressed businessman. In the next image, the plane is reflected in the sunglasses of a young woman standing in aqua blue water. At that point, the plane starts to lose altitude but a hand comes out of the sky to lift the plane and send it soaring.

And there is more like that: Bingham McCutchen had an ad that featured "a computer-generated image of a grizzly bear holding an infant, meant to signal the tough but tender skills of its litigators." A previous ad showed a "zebra chasing a lioness, with the message: 'Great lawyers will find a way to turn the tables in your favor.' " Karen Donovan, Images to Help Law Firms Recast Their Image, New York Times, Sept. 13, 2007. Squire, Sanders & Dempsey found another way to generate goodwill and name recognition. It funded a traveling exhibition of Winslow Homer paintings to celebrate the firm's centennial. A.B.A. J., May 1998, at 34. Prominent law firms like O'Melveny & Myers and Pilsbury Winthrop have made donations to National Public Radio, entitling them to on-air acknowledgment by name (just before "and members like you").

A personal favorite of mine is the campaign of Womble, Carlyle, Sandridge & Rice of North Carolina. According to the New York Times (Nov. 15, 2001, at A1), the firm "illustrates its slogan, 'Our lawyers mean business,' with a bulldog. The mascot, named Winston, has appeared on airport billboards, coffee cups, T-shirts and mouse pads." A lawyer at the firm explained that "if the idea is to be noticed and get name recognition, it's certainly done that for us." The same story reports that (nonlawyer) client development people at some firms come from advertising, accounting, consulting, and consumer products companies, with some earning partner-level salaries.

What is it with lawyers and animals? The Dallas firm Bickel & Brewer saw value in identifying itself with nonhuman creatures, but it chose very different mascots. The city zoo had asked local businesses to pay for an animal's upkeep in return for public acknowledgment. As reported in Corporate Legal Times (May 1994):

> [T]he way Marschall I. Smith chose Dallas-based Bickel & Brewer, a litigation boutique, has to rank as one of the strangest. "I picked them," says Smith, general counsel of IMC Fertilizer Group Inc., Northbrook, Ill., "on the basis of a Business Week article that mentioned they were sponsoring the reptile house at the Dallas Zoo.
>
> "The theme of their sponsorship was 'Adopt a snake,' and the deal was, if you adopted a snake you could name it after your favorite lawyer. They had written this little blurb about how snakes and lawyers have a lot in common. They are both misunderstood, both play an important role, things like that. So I figured anyone with that kind of a sense of humor couldn't be all bad. I decided to talk to them, even though they had this Rambo litigators' reputation, which is not exactly the culture I want."

But we're getting ahead of the story. Let us begin with the ad that started it all. It was headlined "Do You Need A Lawyer? Legal Services At Very Reasonable Fees."

There was a drawing of the scales of justice and a list of services and costs (e.g., uncontested divorce $175; change of name $95; individual bankruptcy $250).

Arizona gave these six reasons why it could forbid all legal advertising, including this ad: Legal ads (1) would have an "adverse effect on professionalism" and encourage "commercialization," (2) were inherently misleading, (3) would stir up litigation, (4) would increase the cost of legal services, (5) would encourage shoddy work, and (6) were difficult to monitor against abuse. The Supreme Court rejected each of these blanket claims, examined the specific ad before it, and held it protected as commercial speech. But the Court also said that a state could prohibit false, deceptive, or misleading ads; might be able to require a warning or disclaimer in legal ads; and could possibly restrict quality claims because they were hard to verify or measure.

Of Arizona's six reasons, it is the first that still resonates today: the idea that professionalism (good) is at war with commercialization (bad) and that advertising advances the latter (very bad), with the result that lawyers become consumed with making more money than the lawyer next door, leading inexorably to a change in the culture of practice, all to the detriment of clients and the justice system (really awful). In response to these claimed threats, Justice Blackmun wrote:

> But we find the postulated connection between advertising and the erosion of true professionalism to be severely strained. At its core, the argument presumes that attorneys must conceal from themselves and from their clients the real-life fact that lawyers earn their livelihood at the bar. We suspect that few attorneys engage in such self-deception. And rare is the client, moreover, even one of modest means, who enlists the aid of an attorney with the expectation that his services will be rendered free of charge. . . .
>
> Moreover, the assertion that advertising will diminish the attorney's reputation in the community is open to question. Bankers and engineers advertise, and yet these professions are not regarded as undignified. In fact, it has been suggested that the failure of lawyers to advertise creates public disillusionment with the profession. The absence of advertising may be seen to reflect the profession's failure to reach out and serve the community: Studies reveal that many persons do not obtain counsel even when they perceive a need because of the feared price of services or because of an inability to locate a competent attorney. Indeed, cynicism with regard to the profession may be created by the fact that it long has publicly eschewed advertising, while condoning the actions of the attorney who structures his social or civic associations so as to provide contacts with potential clients.
>
> It appears that the ban on advertising originated as a rule of etiquette and not as a rule of ethics. Early lawyers in Great Britain viewed the law as a form of public service, rather than as a means of earning a living, and they looked down on "trade" as unseemly. Eventually, the attitude toward advertising fostered by this view evolved into an aspect of the ethics of the profession. But habit and tradition are not in themselves an adequate answer to a constitutional challenge. In this day, we do not belittle the person who earns his living by the strength of his arm or the force of his mind. Since the belief that lawyers are somehow "above" trade has become an anachronism, the historical foundation for the advertising restraint has crumbled.

Bates evaluated a newspaper ad. The Court took no position on ads on the "electronic broadcast media." In his conclusion, Justice Blackmun tried to limit the reach of the opinion to the ad in question, but the next decades proved it to be no limit at all:

> The constitutional issue in this case is only whether the State may prevent the publication in a newspaper of appellants' truthful advertisement concerning the availability and terms of routine legal services. We rule simply that the flow of such information may not be restrained, and we therefore hold the present application of the disciplinary rule against appellants to be violative of the First Amendment.

Four Justices dissented.

Bates refused to credit the state's prediction of the harms legal advertising would bring. While some of the evils the state identified were within its power to prevent, there were other, less intrusive ways to prevent them. The status of a legal ad as commercial speech, entitled to limited First Amendment protection, led the Court to require proof of harm more focused than Arizona's general anxiety. More than three decades later, we can ask whether Arizona's fears (and those of many other states) have come to pass. The law world does seem more commercial now, but is that because of lawyer marketing or other forces? And does legal practice merely seem more commercial (because we see the ads) or because it is more commercial in fact? And last, has some heightened interest in the moneymaking side of practice (if there is one) harmed professionalism, however defined? Can these things be measured?

A year after *Bates* the Court was highly deferential to Ohio's reasons for curtailing a different kind of speech promoting a lawyer's services. How would you (how did the Court) explain the difference?

OHRALIK v. OHIO STATE BAR ASSN.
436 U.S. 447 (1978)

Justice Powell delivered the opinion of the Court.

In Bates v. State Bar of Arizona, this Court held that truthful advertising of "routine" legal services is protected by the First and Fourteenth Amendments against blanket prohibition by a State. The Court expressly reserved the question of the permissible scope of regulation of "in-person solicitation of clients — at the hospital room or the accident site, or in any other situation that breeds undue influence — by attorneys or their agents or 'runners.'" Today we answer part of the question so reserved, and hold that the State — or the Bar acting with state authorization — constitutionally may discipline a lawyer for soliciting clients in person, for pecuniary gain, under circumstances likely to pose dangers that the State has a right to prevent.

I

Appellant, a member of the Ohio Bar, lives in Montville, Ohio. . . . On February 13, 1974, . . . appellant learned . . . about an automobile accident that had taken place on February 2 in which Carol McClintock, a young woman with whom appellant was casually acquainted, had been injured. Appellant [visited]

Ms. McClintock's parents, [who] explained that their daughter had been driving the family automobile on a local road when she was hit by an uninsured motorist. Both Carol and her passenger, Wanda Lou Holbert, were injured and hospitalized. In response to the McClintocks' expression of apprehension that they might be sued by Holbert, appellant explained that Ohio's guest statute would preclude such a suit. When appellant suggested to the McClintocks that they hire a lawyer, Mrs. McClintock retorted that such a decision would be up to Carol, who was 18 years old and would be the beneficiary of a successful claim.

Appellant proceeded to the hospital, where he found Carol lying in traction in her room. After a brief conversation about her condition,[1] appellant told Carol he would represent her and asked her to sign an agreement. Carol said she would have to discuss the matter with her parents. She did not sign the agreement, but asked appellant to have her parents come to see her.[2] Appellant also attempted to see Wanda Lou Holbert, but learned that she had just been released from the hospital. He then departed for another visit with the McClintocks.

[A]ppellant [first] detoured to the scene of the accident, where he took a set of photographs. He also picked up a tape recorder, which he concealed under his raincoat before arriving at the McClintocks' residence. Once there, [a]ppellant discovered that the McClintocks' insurance policy would provide benefits of up to $12,500 each for Carol and Wanda Lou under an uninsured-motorist clause. . . . The McClintocks . . . told appellant that Carol had phoned to say that appellant could "go ahead" with her representation. Two days later appellant returned to Carol's hospital room to have her sign a contract, which provided that he would receive one-third of her recovery. . . .

[A]ppellant [later] visited Wanda Lou at her home, without having been invited. He again concealed his tape recorder and recorded most of the conversation with Wanda Lou. . . . [A]ppellant told Wanda Lou that he was representing Carol and that he had a "little tip" for Wanda Lou: the McClintocks' insurance policy contained an uninsured-motorist clause which might provide her with a recovery of up to $12,500. The young woman, who was 18 years of age and not a high school graduate at the time, replied to appellant's query about whether she was going to file a claim by stating that she really did not understand what was going on. Appellant offered to represent her, also, for a contingent fee of one-third of any recovery, and Wanda Lou stated "O.K."[4]

Wanda's mother attempted to repudiate her daughter's oral assent the following day. . . . Appellant insisted that Wanda had entered into a binding agreement. A month later Wanda confirmed in writing that she wanted neither

---

1. Carol also mentioned that one of the hospital administrators was urging a lawyer upon her. According to his own testimony, appellant replied: "Yes, this certainly is a case that would entice a lawyer. That would interest him a great deal."

2. Despite the fact that appellant maintains that he did not secure an agreement to represent Carol while he was at the hospital, he waited for an opportunity when no visitors were present and then took photographs of Carol in traction.

4. Appellant told Wanda that she should indicate assent by stating "O.K." which she did. Appellant later testified: "I would say that most of my clients have essentially that much of a communication. . . . I think most of my clients, that's the way I practice law."

In explaining the contingent-fee agreement, appellant told Wanda Lou that his representation would not "cost [her] anything" because she would receive two-thirds of the recovery if appellant were successful in representing her but would not "have to pay [him] anything" otherwise.

to sue nor to be represented by appellant. She requested that appellant notify the insurance company that he was not her lawyer, as the company would not release a check to her until he did so. Carol also eventually discharged appellant. Although another lawyer represented her in concluding a settlement with the insurance company, she paid appellant one-third of her recovery[6] in settlement of his lawsuit against her for breach of contract.

[After a disciplinary hearing, the Supreme Court of Ohio affirmed the finding that appellant had violated DR 2-103(A) and DR 2-104(A) of the Code, and suspended him indefinitely.]

The decision in *Bates* was handed down after the conclusion of proceedings in the Ohio Supreme Court. We noted probable jurisdiction in this case to consider the scope of protection of a form of commercial speech, and an aspect of the State's authority to regulate and discipline members of the bar, not considered in *Bates*. We now affirm the judgment of the Supreme Court of Ohio.

II . . .

A

Appellant contends that his solicitation of the two young women as clients is indistinguishable, for purposes of constitutional analysis, from the advertisement in *Bates*. Like that advertisement, his meetings with the prospective clients apprised them of their legal rights and of the availability of a lawyer to pursue their claims. According to appellant, such conduct is "presumptively an exercise of his free speech rights" which cannot be curtailed in the absence of proof that it actually caused a specific harm that the State has a compelling interest in preventing. But in-person solicitation of professional employment by a lawyer does not stand on a par with truthful advertising about the availability and terms of routine legal services, let alone with forms of speech more traditionally within the concern of the First Amendment. . . .

B

The state interests implicated in this case are particularly strong. In addition to its general interest in protecting consumers and regulating commercial transactions, the State bears a special responsibility for maintaining standards among members of the licensed professions. "The interest of the States in regulating lawyers is especially great since lawyers are essential to the primary governmental function of administering justice, and have historically been 'officers of the courts.'" While lawyers act in part as "self-employed businessmen," they also act "as trusted agents of their clients, and as assistants to the court in search of a just solution to disputes." . . . The substantive evils of solicitation have been stated over the years in sweeping terms: stirring up litigation, assertion of fraudulent claims, debasing the legal profession, and potential harm to the solicited client in the form of overreaching, overcharging, underrepresentation, and misrepresentation. The American Bar Association, as amicus curiae, defends the rule against solicitation primarily on three broad grounds: It is said that the prohibitions embodied in

_____

6. Carol recovered the full $12,500 and paid appellant $4,166.66. She testified that she paid the second lawyer $900 as compensation for his services.

DR 2-103(A) and 2-104(A) serve to reduce the likelihood of overreaching and the exertion of undue influence on lay persons, to protect the privacy of individuals, and to avoid situations where the lawyer's exercise of judgment on behalf of the client will be clouded by his own pecuniary self-interest.[19]

[A]ppellant has conceded that the State has a legitimate and indeed "compelling" interest in preventing those aspects of solicitation that involve fraud, undue influence, intimidation, overreaching, and other forms of "vexatious conduct." . . .

III

Appellant's concession that strong state interests justify regulation to prevent the evils he enumerates would end this case but for his insistence that none of those evils was found to be present in his acts of solicitation. He challenges what he characterizes as the "indiscriminate application" of the Rules to him and thus attacks the validity of DR 2-103(A) and DR 2-104(A) not facially, but as applied to his acts of solicitation. And because no allegations or findings were made of the specific wrongs appellant concedes would justify disciplinary action, appellant terms his solicitation "pure," meaning "soliciting and obtaining agreements from Carol McClintock and Wanda Lou Holbert to represent each of them," without more. Appellant therefore argues that we must decide whether a State may discipline him for solicitation per se without offending the First and Fourteenth Amendments.

We agree that the appropriate focus is on appellant's conduct. . . . But appellant errs in assuming that the constitutional validity of the judgment below depends on proof that his conduct constituted actual overreaching or inflicted some specific injury on Wanda Holbert or Carol McClintock. His assumption flows from the premise that nothing less than actual proved harm to the solicited individual would be a sufficiently important state interest to justify disciplining the attorney who solicits employment in person for pecuniary gain.

Appellant's argument misconceives the nature of the State's interest. The Rules prohibiting solicitation are prophylactic measures whose objective is the prevention of harm before it occurs. The Rules were applied in this case to discipline a lawyer for soliciting employment for pecuniary gain under circumstances likely to result in the adverse consequences the State seeks to avert. In such a situation, which is inherently conducive to overreaching and other forms of misconduct, the State has a strong interest in adopting and enforcing rules of conduct designed to protect the public from harmful solicitation by lawyers whom it has licensed.

The State's perception of the potential for harm in circumstances such as those presented in this case is well founded. The detrimental aspects of face-to-face

---

19. A lawyer who engages in personal solicitation of clients may be inclined to subordinate the best interests of the client to his own pecuniary interests. Even if unintentionally, the lawyer's ability to evaluate the legal merit of his client's claims may falter when the conclusion will affect the lawyer's income. A valid claim might be settled too quickly, or a claim with little merit pursued beyond the point of reason. These lapses of judgment can occur in any legal representation, but we cannot say that the pecuniary motivation of the lawyer who solicits a particular representation does not create special problems of conflict of interest.

selling even of ordinary consumer products have been recognized and addressed by the Federal Trade Commission, and it hardly need be said that the potential for overreaching is significantly greater when a lawyer, a professional trained in the art of persuasion, personally solicits an unsophisticated, injured, or distressed lay person.[24] Such an individual may place his trust in a lawyer, regardless of the latter's qualifications or the individual's actual need for legal representation, simply in response to persuasion under circumstances conducive to uninformed acquiescence. Although it is argued that personal solicitation is valuable because it may apprise a victim of misfortune of his legal rights, the very plight of that person not only makes him more vulnerable to influence but also may make advice all the more intrusive. Thus, under these adverse conditions the overtures of an uninvited lawyer may distress the solicited individual simply because of their obtrusiveness and the invasion of the individual's privacy, even when no other harm materializes. Under such circumstances, it is not unreasonable for the State to presume that in-person solicitation by lawyers more often than not will be injurious to the person solicited.

The efficacy of the State's effort to prevent such harm to prospective clients would be substantially diminished if, having proved a solicitation in circumstances like those of this case, the State were required in addition to prove actual injury. Unlike the advertising in *Bates*, in-person solicitation is not visible or otherwise open to public scrutiny. Often there is no witness other than the lawyer and the lay person whom he has solicited, rendering it difficult or impossible to obtain reliable proof of what actually took place. This would be especially true if the lay person were so distressed at the time of the solicitation that he could not recall specific details at a later date. If appellant's view were sustained, in-person solicitation would be virtually immune to effective oversight and regulation by the State or by the legal profession, in contravention of the State's strong interest in regulating members of the Bar in an effective, objective, and self-enforcing manner. It therefore is not unreasonable, or violative of the Constitution, for a State to respond with what in effect is a prophylactic rule. . . .

Accordingly, the judgment of the Supreme Court of Ohio is affirmed.

[Justice Marshall concurred in part and in the judgment. Justice Rehnquist concurred in the judgment for the reasons contained in his dissent in In re Primus (page 942). Justice Brennan did not participate.]

A Prophylactic Rule

Ohralik is the only lawyer advertising case in the Supreme Court to uphold a permanent and categorical ban on a type of communication — in-person

---

24. Most lay persons are unfamiliar with the law, with how legal services normally are procured, and with typical arrangements between lawyer and client. To be sure, the same might be said about the lay person who seeks out a lawyer for the first time. But the critical distinction is that in the latter situation the prospective client has made an initial choice of a lawyer at least for purposes of a consultation; has chosen the time to seek legal advice; has had a prior opportunity to confer with family, friends, or a public or private referral agency; and has chosen whether to consult with the lawyer alone or accompanied.

solicitation. You should recognize the theory that enabled the Court to do that despite *Bates*. But *Orhalik* has itself been narrowed. In Edenfield v. Fane, 507 U.S. 761 (1993), Fane, an accountant, had successfully built a practice advising small- and medium-sized businesses in New Jersey. He often obtained clients through "direct, personal, uninvited solicitation," which New Jersey allowed. Fane moved to Florida, which prohibited that conduct, and he challenged the prohibition. Eight Justices held it unconstitutional. Only Justice O'Connor dissented. How did the Court treat *Ohralik?* Justice Kennedy's opinion said:

> While *Ohralik* discusses the generic hazards of personal solicitation, the opinion made clear that a preventative rule was justified only in situations "inherently conducive to overreaching and other forms of misconduct." . . . Unlike a lawyer, a CPA is not "a professional trained in the art of persuasion." A CPA's training emphasizes independence and objectivity, not advocacy. The typical client of a CPA is far less susceptible to manipulation than the young accident victim[s] in *Ohralik*. Fane's prospective clients are sophisticated and experienced business executives who understand well the services that a CPA offers. In general, the prospective client has an existing professional relation with an accountant and so has an independent basis for evaluating the claims of a new CPA seeking professional work.
>
> The manner in which a CPA like Fane solicits business is conducive to rational and considered decisionmaking by the prospective client, in sharp contrast to the "uninformed acquiescence" to which the accident victims in *Ohralik* were prone. While the clients in *Ohralik* were approached at a moment of high stress and vulnerability, the clients Fane wishes to solicit meet him in their own offices at a time of their choosing. If they are unreceptive to his initial telephone solicitation, they need only terminate the call. Invasion of privacy is not a significant concern. . . .

See also Tennessee Secondary School Athletic Ass'n v. Brentwood Academy, 551 U.S. 291 (2007) ("we have not been chary of invalidating state restrictions on solicitation and commercial advertising in the absence of the acute risks associated with in-person legal solicitation").

What is left of *Ohralik* after *Edenfield?* May lawyers do what accountant Fane did? Which lawyers? Falanga v. State Bar of Georgia, 150 F.3d 1333 (11th Cir. 1998), recognizes the distinction between *Ohralik* and *Edenfield* and upholds the state rule forbidding a personal injury lawyer's in-person solicitation of "poor and uneducated individuals."

B. DEFINING THE CENTER: *ZAUDERER* AND *SHAPERO*

Bates and *Ohralik* define the boundaries to the debate over legal advertising (sometimes elevated to "law firm marketing," sometimes disparaged as "crass self-promotion"). The nature of the legal inquiry has remained similar whatever the particular challenge. We first ask if the speech is commercial speech. If instead it is traditionally protected speech, such as in *Button*, page 831, or

In re Primus, page 942, the constitutional protection is greater. If it is commercial speech, we next ask if it is of a type of communication so conducive to evils the state can prevent that it may be banned categorically. That's *Ohralik.* If the state has not attempted a categorical ban but some form of regulation, we ask what showing the state must make to justify the regulation, whether it has done so, and whether there exists a less intrusive way to accomplish the state's goal.

1.   *Targeted Advertisements*

ZAUDERER v. OFFICE OF DISCIPLINARY COUNSEL
471 U.S. 626 (1985)

JUSTICE WHITE delivered the opinion of the Court. . . .

I . . .

In the spring of 1982, appellant placed an advertisement in 36 Ohio newspapers publicizing his willingness to represent women who had suffered injuries resulting from their use of a contraceptive device known as the Dalkon Shield Intrauterine Device. The advertisement featured a line drawing of the Dalkon Shield accompanied by the question, "DID YOU USE THIS IUD?" The advertisement then related the following information:

> The Dalkon Shield Interuterine [sic] Device is alleged to have caused serious pelvic infections resulting in hospitalizations, tubal damage, infertility, and hysterectomies. It is also alleged to have caused unplanned pregnancies ending in abortions, miscarriages, septic abortions, tubal or ectopic pregnancies, and full-term deliveries. If you or a friend have had a similar experience do not assume it is too late to take legal action against the Shield's manufacturer. Our law firm is presently representing women on such cases. The cases are handled on a contingent fee basis of the amount recovered. If there is no recovery, no legal fees are owed by our clients.

The ad concluded with the name of appellant's law firm, its address, and a phone number that the reader might call for "free information."

The advertisement was successful in attracting clients: appellant received well over 200 inquiries regarding the advertisement, and he initiated lawsuits on behalf of 106 of the women who contacted him as a result of the advertisement. The ad, however, also aroused the interest of the Office of Disciplinary Counsel. On July 29, 1982, the Office filed a complaint against appellant charging him with a number of disciplinary violations arising out of [the] Dalkon Shield advertisements. . . .

II

There is no longer any room to doubt that what has come to be known as "commercial speech" is entitled to the protection of the First Amendment, albeit to protection somewhat less extensive than that afforded "noncommercial speech." . . .

Our general approach to restrictions on commercial speech is also by now well-settled. The States and the Federal Government are free to prevent the dissemination of commercial speech that is false, deceptive, or misleading or that proposes an illegal transaction. Commercial speech that is not false or deceptive and does not concern unlawful activities, however, may be restricted only in the service of a substantial governmental interest, and only through means that directly advance that interest. Our application of these principles to the commercial speech of attorneys has led us to conclude that blanket bans on price advertising by attorneys and rules preventing attorneys from using nondeceptive terminology to describe their fields of practice are impermissible, but that rules prohibiting in-person solicitation of clients by attorneys are, at least under some circumstances, permissible. To resolve this appeal, we must apply the teachings of these cases to three separate forms of regulation Ohio has imposed on advertising by its attorneys: prohibitions on soliciting legal business through advertisements containing advice and information regarding specific legal problems; restrictions on the use of illustrations in advertising by lawyers; and disclosure requirements relating to the terms of contingent fees.

III

We turn first to the Ohio Supreme Court's finding that appellant's Dalkon Shield advertisement (and his acceptance of employment resulting from it) ran afoul of the rules against self-recommendation and accepting employment resulting from unsolicited legal advice. Because all advertising is at least implicitly a plea for its audience's custom, a broad reading of the rules applied by the Ohio court (and particularly the rule against self-recommendation) might suggest that they forbid all advertising by attorneys — a result obviously not in keeping with our decisions in *Bates* and In re R. M. J. [455 U.S. 191 (1982)]. But the Ohio court did not purport to give its rules such a broad reading: it held only that the rules forbade soliciting or accepting legal employment through advertisements containing information or advice regarding a specific legal problem.

The interest served by the application of the Ohio self-recommendation and solicitation rules to appellant's advertisement is not apparent from a reading of the opinions of the Ohio Supreme Court and its Board of Commissioners. The advertisement's information and advice concerning the Dalkon Shield was, as the Office of Disciplinary Counsel stipulated, neither false nor deceptive: in fact, they were entirely accurate. The advertisement did not promise readers that lawsuits alleging injuries caused by the Dalkon Shield would be successful, nor did it suggest that appellant had any special expertise in handling such lawsuits other than his employment in other such litigation. Rather, the advertisement reported the indisputable fact that the Dalkon Shield has spawned an impressive number of lawsuits and advised readers that appellant was currently handling such lawsuits and was willing to represent other women asserting similar claims. In addition, the advertisement advised women that they should not assume that their claims were time-barred — advice that seems completely unobjectionable in light of the trend in many States toward a "discovery rule" for determining when a cause of action for latent injury or disease accrues. The State's power to prohibit advertising that is "inherently misleading" thus cannot justify Ohio's decision to discipline appellant for running advertising geared to persons with a specific legal problem.

Because appellant's statements regarding the Dalkon Shield were not false or deceptive, our decisions impose on the State the burden of establishing that prohibiting the use of such statements to solicit or obtain legal business directly advances a substantial governmental interest. The extensive citations in the opinion of the Board of Commissioners to our opinion in [*Ohralik*] suggest that the Board believed that the application of the rules to appellant's advertising served the same interests that this Court found sufficient to justify the ban on in-person solicitation at issue in *Ohralik*. We cannot agree. Our decision in *Ohralik* was largely grounded on the substantial differences between face-to-face solicitation and the advertising we had held permissible in *Bates*. In-person solicitation by a lawyer, we concluded, was a practice rife with possibilities for overreaching, invasion of privacy, the exercise of undue influence, and outright fraud. In addition, we noted that in-person solicitation presents unique regulatory difficulties because it is "not visible or otherwise open to public scrutiny." These unique features of in-person solicitation by lawyers, we held, justified a prophylactic rule prohibiting lawyers from engaging in such solicitation for pecuniary gain, but we were careful to point out that "in-person solicitation of professional employment by a lawyer does not stand on a par with truthful advertising about the availability and terms of routine legal services."

It is apparent that the concerns that moved the Court in *Ohralik* are not present here. Although some sensitive souls may have found appellant's advertisement in poor taste, it can hardly be said to have invaded the privacy of those who read it. More significantly, appellant's advertisement — and print advertising generally — poses much less risk of overreaching or undue influence. Print advertising may convey information and ideas more or less effectively, but in most cases, it will lack the coercive force of the personal presence of a trained advocate. In addition, a printed advertisement, unlike a personal encounter initiated by an attorney, is not likely to involve pressure on the potential client for an immediate yes-or-no answer to the offer of representation. Thus, a printed advertisement is a means of conveying information about legal services that is more conducive to reflection and the exercise of choice on the part of the consumer than is personal solicitation by an attorney. Accordingly, the substantial interests that justified the ban on in-person solicitation upheld in *Ohralik* cannot justify the discipline imposed on appellant for the content of his advertisement.

Nor does the traditional justification for restraints on solicitation — the fear that lawyers will "stir up litigation" — justify the restriction imposed in this case. In evaluating this proffered justification, it is important to think about what it might mean to say that the State has an interest in preventing lawyers from stirring up litigation. It is possible to describe litigation itself as an evil that the State is entitled to combat: after all, litigation consumes vast quantities of social resources to produce little of tangible value but much discord and unpleasantness. "[A]s a litigant," Judge Learned Hand once observed, "I should dread a lawsuit beyond almost anything else short of sickness and death."

But we cannot endorse the proposition that a lawsuit, as such, is an evil. Over the course of centuries, our society has settled upon civil litigation as a means for redressing grievances, resolving disputes, and vindicating rights when other means fail. There is no cause for consternation when a person who believes in good faith and on the basis of accurate information regarding his legal rights that he has suffered a legally cognizable injury turns to the courts for a remedy: "we cannot accept the notion that it is always better for a person to suffer a wrong silently than to redress it by legal action." [*Bates.*] That our citizens have access to their civil courts is not an evil to be regretted; rather, it is an attribute of our system of justice in which we ought to take pride. The State is not entitled to interfere with that access by denying its citizens accurate information about their legal rights. Accordingly, it is not sufficient justification for the discipline imposed on appellant that his truthful and nondeceptive advertising had a tendency to or did in fact encourage others to file lawsuits.

The State does not, however, argue that the encouragement of litigation is inherently evil, nor does it assert an interest in discouraging the particular form of litigation that appellant's advertising solicited. Rather, the State's position is that although appellant's advertising may itself have been harmless — may even have had the salutary effect of informing some persons of rights of which they would otherwise have been unaware — the State's prohibition on the use of legal advice and information in advertising by attorneys is a prophylactic rule that is needed to ensure that attorneys, in an effort to secure legal business for themselves, do not use false or misleading advertising to stir up meritless litigation against innocent defendants. Advertising by attorneys, the State claims, presents regulatory difficulties that are different in kind from those presented by other forms of advertising. Whereas statements about most consumer products are subject to verification, the indeterminacy of statements about law makes it impractical if not impossible to weed out accurate statements from those that are false or misleading. A prophylactic rule is therefore essential if the State is to vindicate its substantial interest in ensuring that its citizens are not encouraged to engage in litigation by statements that are at best ambiguous and at worst outright false.

The State's argument that it may apply a prophylactic rule to punish appellant notwithstanding that his particular advertisement has none of the vices that allegedly justify the rule is in tension with our insistence that restrictions involving commercial speech that is not itself deceptive be narrowly crafted to serve the State's purposes. . . . The State's argument, then, must be that . . . there are some circumstances in which a prophylactic rule is the least restrictive possible means of achieving a substantial governmental interest.

We need not, however, address the theoretical question whether a prophylactic rule is ever permissible in this area, for we do not believe that the State has presented a convincing case for its argument that the rule before us is necessary to the achievement of a substantial governmental interest. The State's contention that the problem of distinguishing deceptive and nondeceptive legal advertising is different in kind from the problems presented by advertising generally is unpersuasive.

The State's argument proceeds from the premise that it is intrinsically difficult to distinguish advertisements containing legal advice that is false or deceptive from those that are truthful and helpful, much more so than is the case with other goods or services. This notion is belied by the facts before us: appellant's statements regarding Dalkon Shield litigation were in fact easily verifiable and completely accurate. Nor is it true that distinguishing deceptive from nondeceptive claims in advertising involving products other than legal services is a comparatively simple and straightforward process. A brief survey of the body of caselaw that has developed as a result of the Federal Trade Commission's efforts to carry out its mandate under §5 of the Federal Trade Commission Act to eliminate "unfair or deceptive acts or practices in ... commerce," 15 U.S.C. §45(a)(1), reveals that distinguishing deceptive from nondeceptive advertising in virtually any field of commerce may require resolution of exceedingly complex and technical factual issues and the consideration of nice questions of semantics. In short, assessment of the validity of legal advice and information contained in attorneys' advertising is not necessarily a matter of great complexity; nor is assessing the accuracy or capacity to deceive of other forms of advertising the simple process the State makes it out to be. The qualitative distinction the State has attempted to draw eludes us. . . .

IV

[The Court subjected the State's restriction on illustrations in legal advertising to the same First Amendment test it used to protect the text of the ad itself. The Court rejected the argument that prohibiting the illustration of the Dalkon Shield could be justified on the ground that "some members of the population may find [it] embarrassing or offensive." It also rejected the argument that the use of illustrations in lawyer ads "creates unacceptable risks that the public will be misled, manipulated, or confused." The Court was "not persuaded that identifying deceptive or manipulative uses of visual media in advertising is so intrinsically burdensome that the State is entitled to forego that task in favor of the more convenient but far more restrictive alternative of a blanket ban on the use of illustrations."]

V

Appellant contends that assessing the validity of the Ohio Supreme Court's decision to discipline him for his failure to include in the Dalkon Shield advertisement the information that clients might be liable for significant litigation costs even if their lawsuits were unsuccessful entails precisely the same inquiry as determining the validity of the restrictions on advertising content discussed above. In other words, he suggests that the State must establish either that the advertisement, absent the required disclosure, would be false or deceptive or that the disclosure requirement serves some substantial governmental interest other than preventing deception; moreover, he contends that the State must establish that the disclosure requirement directly advances the relevant governmental interest and that it constitutes the least restrictive means of doing so. Not surprisingly, appellant claims that the State has failed to muster substantial evidentiary support for any of the findings required to support the restriction.

Appellant, however, overlooks material differences between disclosure requirements and outright prohibitions on speech. In requiring attorneys who advertise their willingness to represent clients on a contingent-fee basis to state that the client may have to bear certain expenses even if he loses,

Ohio has not attempted to prevent attorneys from conveying information to the public; it has only required them to provide somewhat more information than they might otherwise be inclined to present. We have, to be sure, held that in some instances, compulsion to speak may be as violative of the First Amendment as prohibitions on speech. . . .

But the interests at stake in this case are not of the same order as those discussed in [prior cases]. Ohio has not attempted to "prescribe what shall be orthodox in politics, nationalism, religion, or other matters of opinion or force citizens to confess by word or act their faith therein." The State has attempted only to prescribe what shall be orthodox in commercial advertising, and its prescription has taken the form of a requirement that appellant include in his advertising purely factual and uncontroversial information about the terms under which his services will be available. Because the extension of First Amendment protection to commercial speech is justified principally by the value to consumers of the information such speech provides, appellant's constitutionally protected interest in *not* providing any particular factual information in his advertising is minimal. Thus, in virtually all our commercial speech decisions to date, we have emphasized that because disclosure requirements trench much more narrowly on an advertiser's interests than do flat prohibitions on speech, "warning[s] or disclaimer[s] might be appropriately required . . . in order to dissipate the possibility of consumer confusion or deception."

[The Court upheld Ohio's requirement that contingent fee advertisements specify that the client might in any event be liable for costs. But the Court reversed Zauderer's reprimand insofar as it was based on his use of an illustration and his offer of legal advice in the advertisement. Justice Powell took no part in the consideration or decision of the case. Justices Brennan and Marshall concurred in part. They generally agreed that a state may require a lawyer to disclose that a client, regardless of the case's outcome, would ultimately be liable for costs, but dissented on procedural grounds from the Court's decision to uphold the discipline here. (See page 804 for a discussion of procedures in lawyer discipline.)]

[Justice O'Connor, joined by Chief Justice Burger and Justice Rehnquist, dissented from the Court's conclusion in Part III. "In my view," Justice O'Connor wrote, "the use of unsolicited legal advice to entice clients poses enough of a risk of overreaching and undue influence to warrant Ohio's rule." She continued, sounding a theme that would resurface in her 1988 *Shapero* dissent (page 932):]

Merchants in this country commonly offer free samples of their wares. Customers who are pleased by the sample are likely to return to purchase more. This effective marketing technique may be of little concern when applied to many products, but it is troubling when the product being dispensed is professional advice. Almost every State restricts an attorney's ability to accept employment resulting from unsolicited legal advice. At least two persuasive reasons can be advanced for the restrictions. First, there is an enhanced possibility for confusion and deception in marketing professional services. Unlike standardized products, professional services are by their nature complex and diverse.

Faced with this complexity, a layperson may often lack the knowledge or experience to gauge the quality of the sample before signing up for a larger purchase. Second, and more significantly, the attorney's personal interest in obtaining business may color the advice offered in soliciting a client. As a result, a potential customer's decision to employ the attorney may be based on advice that is neither complete nor disinterested. . . .

In my view, a State could reasonably determine that the use of unsolicited legal advice "as bait with which to obtain agreement to represent [a client] for a fee," *Ohralik*, 436 U.S. at 458, poses a sufficient threat to substantial state interests to justify a blanket prohibition. As the Court recognized in *Ohralik*, the State has a significant interest in preventing attorneys from using their professional expertise to overpower the will and judgment of laypeople who have not sought their advice. While it is true that a printed advertisement presents a lesser risk of overreaching than a personal encounter, the former is only one step removed from the latter. When legal advice is employed within an advertisement, the layperson may well conclude there is no means to judge its validity or applicability short of consulting the lawyer who placed the advertisement. This is particularly true where, as in appellant's Dalkon Shield advertisement, the legal advice is phrased in uncertain terms. A potential client who read the advertisement would probably be unable to determine whether "it is too late to take legal action against the . . . manufacturer" without directly consulting the appellant. And at the time of that consultation, the same risks of undue influence, fraud, and overreaching that were noted in *Ohralik* are present.

The State also has a substantial interest in requiring that lawyers consistently exercise independent professional judgment on behalf of their clients. Given the exigencies of the marketplace, a rule permitting the use of legal advice in advertisements will encourage lawyers to present that advice most likely to bring potential clients into the office, rather than that advice which it is most in the interest of potential clients to hear. . . . Ohio and other States afford attorneys ample opportunities to inform members of the public of their legal rights. Given the availability of alternative means to inform the public of legal rights, Ohio's rule against legal advice in advertisements is an appropriate means to assure the exercise of independent professional judgment by attorneys. A State might rightfully take pride that its citizens have access to its civil courts, while at the same time opposing the use of self-interested legal advice to solicit clients. . . .

2.   Targeted Mail

The immediate issue in the next case was whether a state could prohibit lawyers from sending solicitations by mail to persons known to need legal assistance. These mailings are called "targeted" because they are aimed at a particular population and not prospective clients generally. Are recipients known to need the offered service in greater need of protection? (And if so, won't this subgroup be included within a nontargeted recipient population anyway?) The case is especially interesting because of Justice O'Connor's argument for overturning *Bates*.

SHAPERO v. KENTUCKY BAR ASSN.
486 U.S. 466 (1988)

JUSTICE BRENNAN announced the judgment of the Court and delivered the opinion of the Court as to Parts I and II and an opinion as to Part III in which JUSTICE MARSHALL, JUSTICE BLACKMUN, and JUSTICE KENNEDY join.

This case presents the issue whether a State may, consistent with the First and Fourteenth Amendments, categorically prohibit lawyers from soliciting legal business for pecuniary gain by sending truthful and nondeceptive letters to potential clients known to face particular legal problems.

I

In 1985, petitioner, a member of Kentucky's integrated Bar Association, applied to the Kentucky Attorneys Advertising Commission for approval of a letter that he proposed to send "to potential clients who have had a foreclosure suit filed against them." The proposed letter read as follows:

> It has come to my attention that your home is being foreclosed on. If this is true, you may be about to lose your home. Federal law may allow you to keep your home by *ORDERING* your creditor [sic] to *STOP* and give you more time to pay them.
>
> You may call my office anytime from 8:30 A.M. to 5:00 P.M. for *FREE* information on how you can keep your home.
>
> Call *NOW*, don't wait. It may surprise you what I may be able to do for you. Just call and tell me that you got this letter. Remember it is *FREE*, there is *NO* charge for calling.

[Ultimately the Kentucky Supreme Court held that the letter violated Rule 7.3 of the Model Rules, which, as it *then* read, prohibited mail solicitation that was targeted to persons known to need legal services if a "significant motive for the lawyer's doing so is the lawyer's pecuniary gain."]

II . . .

Our lawyer advertising cases have never distinguished among various modes of written advertising to the general public. Thus, Ohio could no more prevent Zauderer from mass-mailing to a general population his offer to represent women injured by the Dalkon Shield than it could prohibit his publication of the advertisement in local newspapers. Similarly, if petitioner's letter is neither false nor deceptive, Kentucky could not constitutionally prohibit him from sending at large an identical letter opening with the query, "Is your home being foreclosed on?," rather than his observation to the targeted individuals that "It has come to my attention that your home is being foreclosed on." The drafters of Rule 7.3 apparently appreciated as much, for the Rule exempts from the ban "letters addressed or advertising circulars distributed generally to persons . . . who are so situated that they might in general find such services useful."

The court below disapproved petitioner's proposed letter solely because it targeted only persons who were "known to need [the] legal services" offered in his letter, rather than the broader group of persons "so situated that they might in general find such services useful." Generally, unless the advertiser is inept, the latter group would include members of the former. The only reason to disseminate an advertisement of particular legal services among those persons who are "so situated that they might in general find such services useful" is to reach individuals who *actually* "need legal services of the kind provided [and advertised] by the lawyer." But the First Amendment does not permit a ban on certain speech merely because it is more efficient; the State may not constitutionally ban a particular letter on the theory that to mail it only to those whom it would most interest is somehow inherently objectionable.

The court below did not rely on any such theory. Rather, it concluded that the State's blanket ban on all targeted, direct-mail solicitation was permissible because of the "serious potential for abuse inherent in direct solicitation by lawyers of potential clients known to need specific legal services." By analogy to *Ohralik*, the court observed:

> Such solicitation subjects the prospective client to pressure from a trained lawyer in a direct personal way. It is entirely possible that the potential client may feel overwhelmed by the basic situation which caused the need for the specific legal services and may have seriously impaired capacity for good judgment, sound reason and a natural protective self-interest. Such a condition is full of the possibility of undue influence, overreaching and intimidation.

Of course, a particular potential client will feel equally "overwhelmed" by his legal troubles and will have the same "impaired capacity for good judgment" regardless of whether a lawyer mails him an untargeted letter or exposes him to a newspaper advertisement — concededly constitutionally protected activities — or instead mails a targeted letter. The relevant inquiry is not whether there exist potential clients whose "condition" makes them susceptible to undue influence, but whether the mode of communication poses a serious danger that lawyers will exploit any such susceptibility.

Thus, respondent's facile suggestion that this case is merely "*Ohralik* in writing" misses the mark. In assessing the potential for overreaching and undue influence, the mode of communication makes all the difference. Our decision in *Ohralik* that a State could categorically ban all in-person solicitation turned on two factors. First was our characterization of face-to-face solicitation as "a practice rife with possibilities for overreaching, invasion of privacy, the exercise of undue influence, and outright fraud." [Citing *Zauderer.*] Second, "unique . . . difficulties," [id.] would frustrate any attempt at state regulation of in-person solicitation short of an absolute ban because such solicitation is "not visible or otherwise open to public scrutiny." Targeted, direct-mail solicitation is distinguishable from the in-person solicitation in each respect.

Like print advertising, petitioner's letter — and targeted, direct-mail solicitation generally — "poses much less risk of overreaching or undue influence" than does in-person solicitation. [*Zauderer.*] Neither mode of written communication involves "the coercive force of the personal presence of a trained advocate" or the "pressure on the potential client for an immediate yes-or-no answer to the offer of representation." [Id.] Unlike the potential client with a badgering advocate breathing down his neck, the recipient of a letter and the "reader of an advertisement . . . can 'effectively avoid further bombardment of [his] sensibilities simply by averting [his] eyes.'" A letter, like a printed advertisement (but unlike a lawyer), can readily be put in a drawer to be considered later, ignored, or discarded. In short, both types of written solicitation "conve[y] information about legal services [by means] that [are] more conducive to reflection and the exercise of choice on the part of the consumer than is personal solicitation by an attorney." [Id.] Nor does a targeted letter invade the recipient's privacy any more than does a substantively identical letter mailed at large. The invasion, if any, occurs when the lawyer discovers the recipient's legal affairs, not when he confronts the recipient with the discovery.

Admittedly, a letter that is personalized (not merely targeted) to the recipient presents an increased risk of deception, intentional or inadvertent. It could, in certain circumstances, lead the recipient to overestimate the lawyer's familiarity with the case or could implicitly suggest that the recipient's legal problem is more dire than it really is. Similarly, an inaccurately targeted letter could lead the recipient to believe she has a legal problem that she does not actually have or, worse yet, could offer erroneous legal advice.

But merely because targeted, direct-mail solicitation presents lawyers with opportunities for isolated abuses or mistakes does not justify a total ban on that mode of protected commercial speech. The State can regulate such abuses and minimize mistakes through far less restrictive and more precise means, the most obvious of which is to require the lawyer to file any solicitation letter with a state agency, giving the State ample opportunity to supervise mailings and penalize actual abuses. The "regulatory difficulties" that are "unique" to in-person lawyer solicitation [*Zauderer*] — solicitation that is "not visible or otherwise open to public scrutiny" and for which it is "difficult or impossible to obtain reliable proof of what actually took place" — do not apply to written solicitations. The court below offered no basis for its "belie[f] [that] submission of a blank form letter to the Advertising Commission [does not] provid[e] a suitable protection to the public from overreaching, intimidation or misleading private targeted mail solicitation." Its concerns were presumably those expressed by the ABA House of Delegates in its comment to Rule 7.3:

> State lawyer discipline agencies struggle for resources to investigate specific complaints, much less for those necessary to screen lawyers' mail solicitation material. Even if they could examine such materials, agency staff members are unlikely to know anything about the lawyer or about the prospective client's underlying problem. Without such knowledge they cannot determine whether the lawyer's representations are misleading.

The record before us furnishes no evidence that scrutiny of targeted solicitation letters will be appreciably more burdensome or less reliable than scrutiny of advertisements. As a general matter, evaluating a targeted advertisement does not require specific information about the recipient's identity and legal problems any more than evaluating a newspaper advertisement requires like information about all readers. If the targeted letter specifies facts that relate to particular recipients (e.g., "It has come to my attention that your home is being foreclosed on"), the reviewing agency has innumerable options to minimize mistakes. It might, for example, require the lawyer to prove the truth of the fact stated (by supplying copies of the court documents or material that led the lawyer to the fact); it could require the lawyer to explain briefly how she discovered the fact and verified its accuracy; or it could require the letter to bear a label identifying it as an advertisement or directing the recipient how to report inaccurate or misleading letters. To be sure, a state agency or bar association that reviews solicitation letters might have more work than one that does not. But "[o]ur recent decisions involving commercial speech have been grounded in the faith that the free flow of commercial information is valuable enough to justify imposing on would-be regulators the costs of distinguishing the truthful from the false, the helpful from the misleading, and the harmless from the harmful." [*Zauderer.*]

III

[Justice Brennan acknowledged that the "First Amendment overbreadth doctrine does not apply to professional advertising." Consequently, even if Kentucky's rule would reach constitutionally protected ads, the State was still free to argue that Shapero's ad was "unworthy of . . . protection." But the Court then rejected Kentucky's arguments that Shapero's use of capital letters or his statement, "It may surprise you what I may be able to do for you," deprived his letter of First Amendment protection. On remand the State was "free to raise" other arguments.

Justice Brennan's opinion was for a plurality of four. Justices White and Stevens, concurring and dissenting in part, were "of the view that the matters addressed in Part III should be left to the state courts in the first instance."]

JUSTICE O'CONNOR, with whom CHIEF JUSTICE REHNQUIST and JUSTICE SCALIA join, dissenting. . . .

II . . .

A standardized legal test has been devised for commercial speech cases. Under that test, such speech is entitled to constitutional protection only if it concerns lawful activities and is not misleading; if the speech is protected, government may still ban or regulate it by laws that directly advance a substantial governmental interest and are appropriately tailored to that purpose. See Central Hudson Gas & Electric Corp. v. Public Service Commn. of New York, 447 U.S. 557 (1980). Applying that test to attorney advertising, it is clear to me that the States should have considerable latitude to ban advertising that is "*potentially* or demonstrably misleading," In re R. M. J., 455 U.S. 191 (1982) (emphasis added), *as well as* truthful advertising that undermines the substantial governmental interest in promoting the high ethical standards that are necessary in the legal profession.

Some forms of advertising by lawyers might be protected under this test. Announcing the price of an initial consultation might qualify, for example, especially if appropriate disclaimers about the costs of other services were included. Even here, the inherent difficulties of policing such advertising suggest that we should hesitate to interfere with state rules designed to ensure that adequate disclaimers are included and that such advertisements are suitably restrained. . . .

III

The roots of the error in our attorney advertising cases are a defective analogy between professional services and standardized consumer products and a correspondingly inappropriate skepticism about the States' justifications for their regulations. In *Bates*, for example, the majority appeared to demand conclusive proof that the country would be better off if the States were allowed to retain a rule that served "to inhibit the free flow of commercial information and to keep the public in ignorance." Although the opinion contained extensive discussion of the proffered justifications for restrictions on price advertising, the result was little more than a bare conclusion that "we are not persuaded that price advertising will harm consumers." Dismissing Justice Powell's careful critique of the implicit legislative fact-finding that underlay its analysis, the *Bates* majority simply insisted on concluding that the benefits of advertising outweigh its dangers. In my view, that policy decision was not derived from the First Amendment, and it should not have been used to displace a different and no less reasonable policy decision of the State whose regulation was at issue.

Bates was an early experiment with the doctrine of commercial speech, and it has proved to be problematic in its application. Rather than continuing to work out all the consequences of its approach, we should now return to the States the legislative function that has so inappropriately been taken from them in the context of attorney advertising. The *Central Hudson* test for commercial speech provides an adequate doctrinal basis for doing so, and today's decision confirms the need to reconsider *Bates* in the light of that doctrine.

Even if I agreed that this Court should take upon itself the task of deciding what forms of attorney advertising are in the public interest, I would not agree with what it has done. The best arguments in favor of rules permitting attorneys to advertise are founded in elementary economic principles. Restrictions on truthful advertising, which artificially interfere with the ability of suppliers to transmit price information to consumers, presumably reduce the efficiency of the mechanisms of supply and demand. Other factors being equal, this should cause or enable suppliers (in this case attorneys) to maintain a price/quality ratio in some of their services that is higher than would otherwise prevail. Although one could probably not test this hypothesis empirically, it is inherently plausible. Nor is it implausible to imagine that one effect of restrictions on lawyer advertising, and perhaps sometimes an intended effect, is to enable attorneys to charge their clients more for some services (of a given quality) than they would be able to charge absent the restrictions.

Assuming, *arguendo*, that the removal of advertising restrictions should lead in the short run to increased efficiency in the provision of legal services, I would not agree that we can safely assume the same effect in the long run. The economic argument against these restrictions ignores the delicate role they may play in preserving the norms of the legal profession. While it may be difficult to defend this role with precise economic logic, I believe there is a powerful argument in favor of restricting lawyer advertising and that this argument is at the very least not easily refuted by economic analysis.

One distinguishing feature of any profession, unlike other occupations that may be equally respectable, is that membership entails an ethical obligation to temper one's selfish pursuit of economic success by adhering to standards of conduct that could not be enforced either by legal fiat or through the discipline of the market. There are sound reasons to continue pursuing the goal that is implicit in the traditional view of professional life. Both the special privileges incident to membership in the profession and the advantages those privileges give in the necessary task of earning a living are means to a goal that transcends the accumulation of wealth. That goal is public service, which in the legal profession can take a variety of familiar forms. This view of the legal profession need not be rooted in romanticism or self-serving sanctimony, though of course it can be. Rather, special ethical standards for lawyers are properly understood as an appropriate means of restraining lawyers in the exercise of the unique power that they inevitably wield in a political system like ours.

It is worth recalling why lawyers are regulated at all, or to a greater degree than most other occupations, and why history is littered with failed attempts to extinguish lawyers as a special class. See generally R. Pound, The Lawyer from Antiquity to Modern Times (1953). Operating a legal system that is both reasonably efficient and tolerably fair cannot be accomplished, at least under modern social conditions, without a trained and specialized body of experts. This training is one element of what we mean when we refer to the law as a "learned profession." Such knowledge by its nature cannot be made generally available and it therefore confers the power and the temptation to manipulate the system of justice for one's own ends. Such manipulation can occur in at least two obvious ways. One results from overly zealous representation of the client's interests; abuse of the discovery process is one example whose causes and effects (if not its cure) is apparent. The second, and for present purposes the more relevant, problem is abuse of the client for the lawyer's benefit. Precisely because lawyers must be provided with expertise that is both esoteric and extremely powerful, it would be unrealistic to demand that clients bargain for their services in the same arms-length manner that may be appropriate when buying an automobile or choosing a dry cleaner. Like physicians, lawyers are subjected to heightened ethical demands on their conduct towards those they serve. These demands are needed because market forces, and the ordinary legal prohibitions against force and fraud, are simply insufficient to protect the consumers of their necessary services from the peculiar power of the specialized knowledge that these professionals possess.

Imbuing the legal profession with the necessary ethical standards is a task that involves a constant struggle with the relentless natural force of economic self-interest. It cannot be accomplished directly by legal rules, and it certainly will not succeed if sermonizing is the strongest tool that may be employed. Tradition and experiment have suggested a number of formal and informal mechanisms, none of which is adequate by itself and many of which may serve to reduce competition (in the narrow economic sense) among members of the profession. A few examples include the great efforts made during this century to improve the quality and breadth of the legal education that is required for admission to the bar; the concomitant attempt to cultivate a subclass of genuine scholars within the profession; the development of bar associations that aspire to be more than trade groups; strict disciplinary rules about conflicts of interest and client abandonment; and promotion of the expectation that an attorney's history of voluntary public service is a relevant factor in selecting judicial candidates.

Restrictions on advertising and solicitation by lawyers properly and signifi-cantly serve the same goal. Such restrictions act as a concrete, day-to-day remin-der to the practicing attorney of why it is improper for any member of this profession to regard it as a trade or occupation like any other. There is no guarantee, of course, that the restrictions will always have the desired effect, and they are surely not a sufficient means to their proper goal. Given their inevitable anticompetitive effects, moreover, they should not be thoughtlessly retained or insulated from skeptical criticism. Appropriate modifications have been made in the light of reason and experience, and other changes may be suggested in the future.

In my judgment, however, fairly severe constraints on attorney advertising can continue to play an important role in preserving the legal profession as a gen-uine profession. Whatever may be the exactly appropriate scope of these restric-tions at a given time and place, this Court's recent decisions reflect a myopic belief that "consumers," and thus our nation, will benefit from a constitutional theory that refuses to recognize either the essence of professionalism or its fragile and necessary foundations. In one way or another, time will uncover the folly of this approach. I can only hope that the Court will recognize the danger before it is too late to effect a worthwhile cure.

The Response to *Shapero*

The ABA responded to *Shapero* by rewriting Rule 7.3 to permit targeted direct mail to potential clients. However, where the communication is aimed at a person "known to be in need of legal services in a particular matter," the words "Advertising Material" must appear "on the outside envelope, if any, and at the beginning and ending of any recorded or electronic communica-tion," unless the recipient is a lawyer, a member of the lawyer's family, or some-one with whom the lawyer has a "prior professional relationship."

Some jurisdictions go much further in describing the limits on targeted solic-itation, specifying the type size, ink color, and location(s) of the word "adver-tisement" and requiring the lawyer to reveal how she obtained the recipient's name. Some rules require the lawyer to tell the recipient to disregard the letter if the recipient already has a lawyer on the matter. (Why should that be? Maybe the client is unhappy with his lawyer.) Other rules, with necessary adjustment, apply specifically to e-mail contacts. Examples of these and other limits on written or electronic solicitation by lawyers include the versions of Rule 7.3 in Florida, Louisiana, and South Carolina, all of which can be found either in statutory supplements to casebooks or online.

As we know from *Ohralik*, accident victims are most likely to be viewed as in special need of protection from lawyer solicitation. Florida adopted a rule for-bidding lawyers to solicit accident victims or their survivors by mail for 30 days after the occurrence of the accident. The rule was challenged as a violation of *Shapero* and commercial speech cases generally. The case drew much attention because if any two of the four post-*Shapero* Justices — Souter, Ginsburg, Thomas, and Breyer (but especially Breyer, who had not yet voted in a high Court lawyer marketing case) — agreed with the *Shapero* dissenters, *Bates* could be overruled. The Supreme Court upheld the Florida rule in Florida Bar v. Went For It, Inc.,

515 U.S. 618 (1995), with the *Shapero* dissenters and Justices Thomas and Breyer in the five-person majority. However, the Court not only did not overturn *Bates,* it seemed to accept the lawyer advertising decisions through *Shapero*, while distinguishing them.

What state interest justified Florida's 30-day ban? Although Florida asserted various interests in earlier stages of the litigation, in the end it relied solely on its right to protect the reputation of its legal profession, as the Court explained:

> Because direct mail solicitations in the wake of accidents are perceived by the public as intrusive, the Bar argues, the reputation of the legal profession in the eyes of Floridians has suffered commensurately. The regulation, then, is an effort to protect the flagging reputations of Florida lawyers by preventing them from engaging in conduct that, the Bar maintains, "is universally regarded as deplorable and beneath common decency because of its intrusion upon the special vulnerability and private grief of victims or their families."

The Bar's evidence of Floridians' view of solicitation of accident victims was statistical and anecdotal. For example, a "survey of Florida adults commissioned by the Bar indicated that Floridians 'have negative feelings about those attorneys who use direct mail advertising.'" The anecdotal evidence was drawn from newspaper articles quoting Florida residents. One article described a resident who "was 'appalled and angered by the brazen attempt' of a law firm to solicit him by letter shortly after he was injured and his fiancee was killed in an auto accident." Is that enough evidence, or should even a temporary ban on commercial speech require more proof?

In upholding the restriction, the Court stressed that it was "limited to a brief period" and that lawyers had other ways to make their availability known to clients, including through television, radio, newspapers, and other media. (This was the Court's first clear protection for the electronic media, which were excluded from the *Bates* holding.) The Tenth Circuit relied on the Supreme Court's emphasis on the temporary nature of the Florida ban to invalidate New Mexico's permanent ban on direct-mail contact of personal injury victims and their families. Revo v. Disciplinary Board of the Supreme Court for the State of New Mexico, 106 F.3d 929 (10th Cir. 1997).

Since *Went For It* was decided, courts have addressed other temporary bans and found them wanting. A Maryland rule required lawyers to wait 30 days after a charging document was filed before communicating with a criminal accused or a person charged with a traffic infraction that carries a period of incarceration. Ficker v. Curran, 119 F.3d 1150 (4th Cir. 1997), invalidated the rule. Distinguishing *Went For It*, the court held that the state's poll results did not show that the reputation of the profession suffered when lawyers contacted criminal defendants. Further, unlike personal injury actions, where a person ordinarily has years to sue, a criminal accused is already in litigation and needs a lawyer quickly. "Defendants can lose rights if unrepresented for thirty days after arrest."

The United States Congress has relied on *Went For It* to limit contact with victims of airline accidents or their families. In 1996, Congress passed legislation forbidding "unsolicited communication concerning a potential action for personal injury or wrongful death . . . by an attorney . . . or any potential party to the litigation to an individual injured in the accident, or to a relative of an individual involved in the accident, before the 45th day following the date of the accident." 49 U.S.C. §1136(g)(2). Notice the words "or any potential party to the litigation." This is a salutary addition often omitted from rules forbidding lawyers to contact accident victims. To whom does it refer?

C. DEFINING THE METHODOLOGY

The Supreme Court's methodology in legal marketing cases raises interesting questions about governance and craft. Actually, we find two competing methodologies, nicely captured in the *Shapero* majority and dissent. Both methodologies have to identify how much weight to give the speaker's First Amendment interests. Both have to identify how much respect to give the purported dangers the state anticipates and wishes to prevent. And both have to identify how much deference to give to the means a state has chosen to use to prevent those dangers. Any decision requires empirical assumptions about both human motivation and the causal relationship between the state's means and its goals. How does the Court get this information? Lurking about these issues is a further riddle, eloquently addressed in Justice O'Connor's *Shapero* dissent: the relationship between legal marketing and professionalism. Is there a relationship? Who decides? If there is one, what *constitutional* difference should it make?

How Does the Court Know Things?

In *Ohralik*, the Court appeared willing to allow states categorically to forbid in-person solicitation for profit, although it could have stopped short of that holding and rested instead on Ohralik's abusive tactics. At one point it seemed the Court might issue a more limited ruling. Justice Powell, distinguishing *Bates*, wrote that the state, "having proved a solicitation in circumstances like those of this case" need not also prove actual injury. But elsewhere Justice Powell made it clear that Ohralik could be disciplined under a "prophylactic" rule regardless of the specific circumstances of the case.

If *Ohralik* contained an ambiguity, *Shapero* resolved it in favor of state power to adopt a prophylactic rule. Justice Brennan characterized the "decision in *Ohralik*" as holding "that a State could categorically ban all in-person solicitation." Even Justice Marshall, who in his *Ohralik* concurrence wrote that the Court's decision was "limited" and depended on the "circumstances" contained in "this record," joined the *Shapero* majority.

Edenfield v. Fane weakened *Ohralik*, but by how much? We do not yet know. Given the result in *Shapero*, the *Ohralik* prophylactic authority, even broadly read, is as a practical matter less momentous. Do you see why? But *Edenfield* now challenges the scope of even that authority. The *Ohralik* opinion contains many uses of "likely" and "may." How does the Court know that in-person solicitation is as dangerous as it says it is? How does the Court know that the conduct in *Shapero* is not as dangerous as Kentucky (and many other states) believed it to be? What assumptions is the Court making about motivations

and especially about how money influences the behavior of lawyers? Compare
Village of Schaumburg v. Citizens for a Better Environment, 444 U.S. 620
(1980), which also reviewed a state law that made certain assumptions about
money and behavior. A village ordinance barred door-to-door and on-the-street
solicitations of contributions to charities unless the charities used at least 75
percent of their receipts for "charitable purposes," defined to exclude the cost
of solicitation. In striking the ordinance, the Court suggested that there were
less intrusive methods for protecting privacy interests, such as the ordinance's
provision permitting homeowners to bar solicitors from their property by
posting signs reading "No Solicitors or Peddlers Invited." Are the decisions
in Schaumburg and Ohralik compatible?

The Schaumburg Court contrasted Ohralik in response to the village's contention that the ordinance furthered the goal of preventing fraud. The Court said
that that goal could be "better served by measures less intrusive than a direct
prohibition on solicitation," such as through a penal law. "Unlike the situation
in Ohralik . . . charitable solicitation is not so inherently conducive to fraud and
overreaching as to justify its prohibition." Is the Court really saying that lawyers
are more prone to dishonesty than people who canvass for charities, justifying
greater intrusion on the lawyers' First Amendment rights? How does the Court
know that? Justice O'Connor (appointed after Schaumburg) seems to believe that
the Court is not equipped to evaluate the relative risks inherent in legal advertising; accordingly, she counsels deference and would give the states greater (but
not unfettered) discretion to fashion rules limiting lawyer advertising.

One big difference between the conduct in Ohralik and Shapero is the state's
ability to prove overreaching or fraud. In Ohralik, the substance of the in-person
conversation would not usually be preserved. It would instead be a matter of
dispute among the participants—a credibility contest. In Shapero, at the very
least the letter the lawyer sent will be available as evidence in the event of a
disciplinary proceeding. Another difference between the two cases is in the
degree of privacy invasion. In-person solicitation is more intrusive than a letter.

Aside from privacy invasion, the justifications usually advanced to prohibit
in-person solicitation by lawyers for profit are the danger of overreaching and
the potential conflict between the interests of the lawyer and the prospective
client. Yet aren't these risks present in all client-lawyer relationships, no
matter how the lawyer happens to meet up with the client? What reason is
there to believe the risks are greater when a lawyer solicits a client in person?
Justice Powell deals with the empirical quandary this way in note 19 of Ohralik:
After acknowledging that particular lawyer-client conflicts can arise whether
or not the lawyer personally solicits the client, he writes "we cannot say that
the pecuniary motivation of the lawyer who solicits a particular representation
does not create special problems of conflict of interest." Catch the double
negative. If the Court "cannot say" that something "does not create" problems, why is it upholding a limitation on speech, even commercial speech?
And what is the basis for what the Court "cannot say"? The experiences of the
Justices? The record? Intuition?

Florida Bar v. Went For It approached empiricism from a different direction.
It relied on two surveys to justify deference to the 30-day moratorium on solicitation of accident victims by mail. But these surveys were pretty soft. While they
purported to show public disapproval of such solicitation, they amounted to

little more than some newspaper quotes of individuals who were unhappily solicited and poll conclusions like these: "A random sampling of persons who received direct-mail advertising from lawyers in 1987 revealed that 45% believed that direct-mail solicitation is 'designed to take advantage of gullible or unstable people'; 34% found such tactics 'annoying or irritating'; 26% percent found it 'an invasion of your privacy'; and 24% reported that it 'made you angry.'" If the public is truly hostile to lawyer direct-mail advertising, shouldn't we expect the effort to be unsuccessful, in which case lawyers won't employ it? The empiricism approved in *Went For It* raised the likelihood that future proponents of advertising restrictions might try to satisfy their First Amendment burden of proof with surveys of public attitudes coupled with the now-recognized state interest in protecting the bar's good reputation. But that doesn't seem to have happened.

Professionalism and Money

What is the relationship between professionalism and money? So much of the current debate revolves around this question. Recall Roscoe Pound's definition of "profession" as "a group pursuing a learned art as a common calling in the spirit of public service" (page 15). Recall, however, that Justice Blackmun was not terribly impressed with Arizona's argument in *Bates* that advertising would encourage commercialization at the expense of professionalism. Nevertheless, that argument will not go away. It persists in legal literature and at bar meetings. So let's investigate it. At what point, if any, does the pursuit of money diminish professionalism? Are permissive rules on legal marketing likely to lead us to that point?

Justice O'Connor makes two assumptions in her *Shapero* dissent, a definitional or normative one and a causal one. She writes first that membership in a profession "entails an ethical obligation to temper one's selfish pursuit of economic success" and second that "fairly severe constraints on attorney advertising" will "act as a concrete, day-to-day reminder to the practicing attorney of why it is improper for any member of this profession to regard it as a trade or occupation like any other." Accordingly she questions the *Bates* decision.

Justice O'Connor's definitional assumption is in accord with Roscoe Pound's: At some level, pursuit of a profession and pursuit of wealth are inconsistent. Do you accept that definition of "professionalism"? What are the consequences of rejecting it? One consequence might be to deny lawyers the right of self-regulation, such as it is — the right, with deference from the courts and legislatures, to write their own code of ethics. The Preamble to the Model Rules, after pointing out that "[t]he legal profession is largely self-governing," stresses the profession's "responsibility to assure that its regulations are conceived in the public interest and not in furtherance of parochial or self-interested concerns of the bar." The Preamble then warns that "[t]o the extent that lawyers meet the obligations of their professional calling, the occasion for government regulation is obviated." Professor Nancy Moore has questioned, among other things, the accuracy of the equation between professionalism and the public interest, and the wisdom of continued self-regulation. Nancy Moore, Professionalism Reconsidered, 1987 Am. B. Found. Res. J. 773.

What do you think of Justice O'Connor's second (empirical) prediction that strict rules against legal advertising will remind lawyers that they are not in a "trade or occupation like any other," or so a state may properly conclude? Many share her view that as advertising increases, professionalism declines. The cases from *Bates* forward, and the prominence of lawyer marketing efforts thereby occasioned, have caused something of a professional identity crisis. One result has been the report of the ABA Commission on Professionalism, which cautions lawyers not to make "the acquisition of wealth a principal goal of law practice" and urges "good sense and high standards" in legal ads. Another ABA commission has proposed "aspirational goals" in legal ads, intended to assure that the ads are "dignified" and "tasteful."

As Justice O'Connor recognizes, it is not possible to *prove* that an increase in legal advertising comes at the expense of professionalism (or leads to a heightened concern with wealth), though the relationship may have some intuitive appeal. The *Shapero* dissenters believe the causality sufficiently probable to render it a legitimate state interest (to which the Court should defer), which will in turn support "fairly severe constraints on attorney advertising" despite the First Amendment.

Opponents of this view argue that such restrictions discriminate against those consumers who are unlikely to know that they have a legal problem or to know which lawyer to see when they do. Wealthy and corporate clients do not need ads to know these things. (Has a lawyer ever been disciplined for in-person solicitation of the corporate vice president during a round of golf?: "You know, Linda, we have a fellow in our securities department who ...") Critics also argue that in any event an interest in money is not so bad. It increases the chances that rights will be vindicated. Given the contingent fee (see page 168), a lawyer's economic self-interest may inspire the search for clients who may be unaware of their legitimate claims — claims that, if asserted, will benefit the clients *and* enrich the lawyer. Critics of contingent fees and class actions have a different view. For them, advertising permits lawyers to attract clients with weak claims who are willing, cost-free, to gamble on a lawsuit. Even worse, because class clients are said to be illusory or "notational," class litigation is seen as mainly serving the economic interests of lawyers. Especially worrisome is the power of internet ads. Susan Adams, "Lawsuit.com: The Internet Is Fast Becoming a Fertile Breeding Ground for Litigation," *Forbes*, Dec. 1, 1997.

FURTHER READING

Numerous articles and studies on legal advertising have been published since the *Bates* decision. One noteworthy study by the Federal Trade Commission concluded that legal advertising has reduced the cost of legal services and that a "false or deceptive" standard for lawyer advertising would present no greater problems than for other kinds of advertising. FTC Staff Report, Improving Consumer Access to Legal Services: The Case for Removing Restrictions on Truthful Advertising (1984). Louise Hill argues that "categorical proscriptions on in-person solicitation ... lack a firm historical basis and constitute a violation of the first amendment." She attempts to demonstrate that "significantly less restrictive and more precise alternatives exist to safeguard the states' concern that the public be protected from the coercive force of a trained advocate." Louise Hill, Solicitation by Lawyers: Piercing the First Amendment Veil, 42 Me. L. Rev. 369 (1990). Other publications include Frederick Moss's article, The Ethics of Law Practice Marketing, 61 Notre Dame L. Rev. 601 (1986), which addresses nearly every conceivable way in which a lawyer and a firm might seek to make their availability known. For a study of the effects of lawyer advertising on quality and price, see Timothy Muris and Fred McChesney, Advertising and the Price and Quality of Legal Services: The Case for Legal Clinics, 1979 Am. B. Found. Res. J. 179, and Fred McChesney and Timothy Muris, The Effect of Advertising on the Quality of Legal Services, 65 A.B.A. J. 1503 (1979). The authors compared the quality and price of routine legal services provided by the legal clinic of Jacoby & Meyers, which advertises, with those of traditional firms. See also Geoffrey Hazard, Russell Pearce, and Jeffrey Stempel, Why Lawyers Should Be Allowed to Advertise: A Market Analysis of Legal Services, 58 N.Y.U. L. Rev. 1084 (1983).

D. SOLICITATION BY PUBLIC INTEREST AND CLASS ACTION LAWYERS

"I Need to Make Contact"

"Laws in my state require the local school board to pay for the special education needs of children with disabilities, including emotional and learning disabilities. I'm an expert in those laws. The laws also provide that the legal fees of the child (or his or her parents) will be paid by the state if it is determined that the claim 'has merit.' The determination is made by an administrative law judge and there is an appeal to the courts. Many parents whose children have emotional or learning problems are unaware of these laws or their scope. The state does nothing to publicize them, and the school boards have no incentive either because they are required to pay two-thirds of the cost of the educational benefits and my counsel fees.

"I have many friends who are teachers who tell me about students who, in their view, would benefit from special education programs, some of which can be quite expensive. But the parents don't know. I would like to call these parents and explain the situation. I realize I could write to them, too, but the rules here say my envelope has to have ADVERTISEMENT on it in 18-point red capital letters. So you know where those go. The trash. I read *Ohralik* and I also read *Primus* [below] and frankly I don't fit into either case. I would like to phone these parents and explain the situation, but I fear I would end up like Ohralik. Or at least I would like to send a letter without ADVERTISEMENT on the envelope, even though this is targeted direct mail. Can I do either? Does my particular practice afford me the greater protection that the Supreme Court gave Edna Smith Primus? "Thank you for your advice.

"Samantha Kelso"

The precise holding of In re Primus, below, decided the same day as *Ohralik* (page 916), has now been overshadowed by *Shapero* (page 929), which would protect Primus's letter even if her motive was pecuniary gain. But *Primus* makes a larger and more important point, one that remains vital for public interest lawyers: States have much less power to regulate client solicitation when a lawyer's motive is political rather than financial. We encountered the same distinction in NAACP v. Button, page 831, where the question was the constitutionality of a state law that prohibited the NAACP from soliciting school desegregation plaintiffs. In *Button*, the focus was on the lay status of the intermediary and the danger of conflicts between the interests of the client and the interests of the NAACP, which sponsored the litigation. In *Primus*, the focus was on the legality of the solicitation itself. As in *Button*, *Primus* assumes that it is possible to determine motives and that Primus's were good while Ohralik's were not, constitutionally speaking. That assumption gives Justice Rehnquist, the sole dissenter, a nifty rhetorical platform on which to juxtapose *Primus* and *Ohralik*. Rule 7.3, written after *Primus* (and revised after *Shapero*), continues the use of motive to determine the permissible scope of client solicitation.

IN RE PRIMUS
436 U.S. 412 (1978)

JUSTICE POWELL delivered the opinion of the Court.
We consider on this appeal whether a State may punish a member of its Bar who, seeking to further political and ideological goals through associational activity, including litigation, advises a lay person of her legal rights and discloses in a subsequent letter that free legal assistance is available from a nonprofit organization with which the lawyer and her associates are affiliated. Appellant, a member of the Bar of South Carolina, received a public reprimand for writing such a letter. . . .

I

Appellant, Edna Smith Primus, is a lawyer practicing in Columbia, S.C. During the period in question, she was associated with the "Carolina Community Law Firm," and was an officer of and cooperating lawyer with the Columbia branch of the American Civil Liberties Union (ACLU). She received no compensation for her work on behalf of the ACLU, but was paid a retainer as a legal consultant for the South Carolina Council on Human Relations (Council), a nonprofit organization with offices in Columbia.

During the summer of 1973, local and national newspapers reported that pregnant mothers on public assistance in Aiken County, S.C., were being sterilized or threatened with sterilization as a condition of the continued receipt of medical assistance under the Medicaid program. Concerned by this development, Gary Allen, an Aiken businessman and officer of a local organization serving indigents, called the Council requesting that one of its representatives come to Aiken to address some of the women who had been sterilized. At the Council's behest, appellant, who had not known Allen previously, called him and arranged a meeting in his office in July 1973. Among those attending was Mary Etta Williams, who had been sterilized by Dr. Clovis H. Pierce after the birth of her third child. Williams and her grandmother attended the meeting because Allen, an old family friend, had invited them and because Williams wanted "[t]o see what it was all about. . . ." At the meeting, appellant advised those present, including Williams and the other women who had been sterilized by Dr. Pierce, of their legal rights and suggested the possibility of a lawsuit.

Early in August 1973, the ACLU informed appellant that it was willing to provide representation for Aiken mothers who had been sterilized. Appellant testified that after being advised by Allen that Williams wished to institute suit against Dr. Pierce, she decided to inform Williams of the ACLU's offer of free legal representation. Shortly after receiving appellant's letter, dated August 30, 1973[6] — the centerpiece of this litigation — Williams visited Dr. Pierce to discuss the progress of her third child who was ill. At the doctor's office, she encountered his lawyer and at the latter's request signed a release of liability in the doctor's favor. Williams showed appellant's letter to the doctor and his lawyer, and they retained a copy. She then called appellant from the doctor's office and

---

6. Written on the stationery of the Carolina Community Law Firm, the letter stated:

August 30, 1973

Mrs. Marietta Williams
347 Sumter Street
Aiken, South Carolina 29801

Dear Mrs. Williams:

You will probably remember me from talking with you at Mr. Allen's office in July about the sterilization performed on you. The American Civil Liberties Union would like to file a lawsuit on your behalf for money against the doctor who performed the operation. We will be coming to Aiken in the near future and would like to explain what is involved so you can understand what is going on.

Now I have a question to ask of you. Would you object to talking to a women's magazine about the situation in Aiken? The magazine is doing a feature story on the whole sterilization problem and wants to talk to you and others in South Carolina. If you don't mind doing this, call me *collect* at 254-8151 on Friday before 5:00, if you receive this letter in time. Or call me on Tuesday morning (after Labor Day) *collect.*

I want to assure you that this interview is being done to show what is happening to women against their wishes, and is not being done to harm you in any way. But I want you to decide, so call me collect and let me know of your decision. This practice must stop.

About the lawsuit, if you are interested, let me know, and I'll let you know when we will come down to talk to you about it. We will be coming to talk to Mrs. Waters at the same time; she has already asked the American Civil Liberties Union to file a suit on her behalf.

Sincerely,
s/Edna Smith
Edna Smith
Attorney-at-law

announced her intention not to sue. There was no further communication between appellant and Williams.

[The Supreme Court of South Carolina issued Primus a public reprimand for her letter to Mrs. Williams.]

II

This appeal concerns the tension between contending values of considerable moment to the legal profession and to society. Relying upon NAACP v. Button, and its progeny, appellant maintains that her activity involved constitutionally protected expression and association. In her view, South Carolina has not shown that the discipline meted out to her advances a subordinating state interest in a manner that avoids unnecessary abridgment of First Amendment freedoms. Appellee counters that appellant's letter to Williams falls outside of the protection of *Button*, and that South Carolina acted lawfully in punishing a member of its Bar for solicitation. . . .

III

In NAACP v. Button, the Supreme Court of Appeals of Virginia had held that the activities of members and staff attorneys of the National Association for the Advancement of Colored People (NAACP) and its affiliate, the Virginia State Conference of NAACP Branches (Conference), constituted "solicitation of legal business" in violation of state law. . . .

This Court reversed:

> We hold that the activities of the NAACP, its affiliates and legal staff shown on this record are modes of expression and association protected by the First and Fourteenth Amendments which Virginia may not prohibit, under its power to regulate the legal profession, as improper solicitation of legal business violative of [state law] and the Canons of Professional Ethics.

The solicitation of prospective litigants, many of whom were not members of the NAACP or the Conference, for the purpose of furthering the civil-rights objectives of the organization and its members was held to come within the right " 'to engage in association for the advancement of beliefs and ideas.' "

Since the Virginia statute sought to regulate expressive and associational conduct at the core of the First Amendment's protective ambit, the *Button* Court insisted that "government may regulate in the area only with narrow specificity." . . . The Court concluded that "although the [NAACP] has amply shown that its activities fall within the First Amendment's protections, the State has failed to advance any substantial regulatory interest, in the form of substantive evils flowing from [the NAACP's] activities, which can justify the broad prohibitions which it has imposed."

Subsequent decisions have interpreted *Button* as establishing the principle that "collective activity undertaken to obtain meaningful access to the courts is a fundamental right within the protection of the First Amendment." . . . Without denying the power of the State to take measures to correct the substantive evils of undue influence, overreaching, misrepresentation, invasion of privacy, conflict of interest, and lay interference that potentially are present in solicitation of prospective clients by lawyers, this Court has required that "broad rules framed to protect the public and to preserve respect for the administration of justice" must not work a significant impairment of "the value of associational freedoms."

IV

We turn now to the question whether appellant's conduct implicates interests of free expression and association sufficient to justify the level of protection recognized in *Button* and subsequent cases. . . .

Although the disciplinary panel did not permit full factual development of the aims and practices of the ACLU, the record does not support the state court's effort to draw a meaningful distinction between the ACLU and the NAACP. From all that appears, the ACLU and its local chapters, much like the NAACP and its local affiliates in *Button*, "[engage] in extensive educational lobbying activities" and "also [devote] much of [their] funds and energies to an extensive program of assisting certain kinds of litigation on behalf of [their] declared purposes." The court below acknowledged that " 'the ACLU has only entered cases in which substantial civil liberties questions are involved. . . . ' " It has engaged in the defense of unpopular causes and unpopular defendants and has represented individuals in litigation that has defined the scope of constitutional protection in areas such as political dissent, juvenile rights, prisoners' rights, military law, amnesty, and privacy. For the ACLU, as for the NAACP, "litigation is not a technique of resolving private differences"; it is "a form of political expression" and "political association."

We find equally unpersuasive any suggestion that the level of constitutional scrutiny in the case should be lowered because of a possible benefit to the ACLU. The discipline administered to appellant was premised solely on the possibility of financial benefit to the organization, rather than any possibility of pecuniary gain to herself, her associates, or the lawyers representing the plaintiffs in the Walker v. Pierce litigation,[21] [another sterilization lawsuit against Dr. Pierce]. It is conceded that appellant received no compensation for any of the activities in question. It is also undisputed that neither the ACLU nor any lawyer associated with it would have shared in any monetary recovery by the plaintiffs in Walker v. Pierce. If Williams had elected to bring suit, and had been represented by staff lawyers for the ACLU, the situation would have been similar to that in *Button*, where the lawyers for the NAACP were "organized as a staff and paid by" that organization.

Contrary to appellee's suggestion, the ACLU's policy of requesting an award of counsel fees does not take the case outside of the protection of *Button*. [I]n a case of this kind there are differences between counsel fees awarded by a court and traditional fee-paying arrangements which militate against a presumption that ACLU sponsorship of litigation is motivated by considerations of pecuniary gain rather than by its widely recognized goal of vindicating civil liberties.

21. Appellee conjectures that appellant would have received increased support from private foundations if her reputation was enhanced as a result of her efforts in the cause of the ACLU. The decision below acknowledged, however, that the evidence did not support a finding that appellant solicited Williams on her own behalf. . . .

Counsel fees are awarded in the discretion of the court; awards are not drawn from the plaintiff's recovery, and are usually premised on a successful outcome; and the amounts awarded often may not correspond to fees generally obtainable in private litigation. . . . And even if there had been an award during the period in question, it would have gone to the central fund of the ACLU. Although such benefit to the organization may increase with the maintenance of successful litigation, the same situation obtains with voluntary contributions and foundation support, which also may rise with ACLU victories in important areas of the law. That possibility, standing alone, offers no basis for equating the work of lawyers associated with the ACLU or the NAACP with that of a group that exists for the primary purpose of financial gain through the recovery of counsel fees.

Appellant's letter of August 30, 1973, to Mrs. Williams thus comes within the generous zone of the First Amendment protection reserved for associational freedoms. The ACLU engages in litigation as a vehicle for effective political expression and association, as well as a means of communicating useful information to the public. As *Button* indicates, and as appellant offered to prove at the disciplinary hearing, the efficacy of litigation as a means of advancing the cause of civil liberties often depends on the ability to make legal assistance available to suitable litigants. . . .

V

South Carolina's action in punishing appellant for soliciting a prospective litigant by mail, on behalf of the ACLU, must withstand the "exacting scrutiny applicable to limitations on core First Amendment rights. . . ." South Carolina must demonstrate "a subordinating interest which is compelling," and that the means employed in furtherance of that interest are "closely drawn to avoid unnecessary abridgment of associational freedoms." . . .

B . . .

Where political expression or association is at issue, this Court has not tolerated the degree of imprecision that often characterizes government regulation of the conduct of commercial affairs. The approach we adopt today in *Ohralik*, that the State may proscribe in-person solicitation for pecuniary gain under circumstances likely to result in adverse consequences, cannot be applied to appellant's activity on behalf of the ACLU. Although a showing of potential danger may suffice in the former context, appellant may not be disciplined unless her activity in fact involved the type of misconduct at which South Carolina's broad prohibition is said to be directed.

The record does not support appellee's contention that undue influence, overreaching, misrepresentation, or invasion of privacy actually occurred in this case. Appellant's letter of August 30, 1973, followed up the earlier meeting — one concededly protected by the First and Fourteenth Amendments — by notifying Williams that the ACLU would be interested in supporting possible litigation. The letter imparted additional information material to making an informed decision about whether to authorize litigation, and permitted Williams an opportunity, which she exercised, for arriving at a deliberate decision. The letter was not facially misleading; indeed, it offered "to explain what is involved so you can understand what is going on." The transmittal of this letter—as contrasted with in-person solicitation—involved no appreciable invasion of privacy; nor did it afford any significant opportunity for overreaching or coercion. Moreover, the fact that there was a written communication lessens substantially the difficulty of policing solicitation practices that do offend valid rules of professional conduct. The manner of solicitation in this case certainly was no more likely to cause harmful consequences than the activity considered in *Button*.

Nor does the record permit a finding of a serious likelihood of conflict of interest or injurious lay interference with the attorney-client relationship. Admittedly, there is some potential for such conflict or interference whenever a lay organization supports any litigation. That potential was present in *Button*, in the NAACP's solicitation of non-members and its disavowal of any relief short of full integration. But the Court found that potential insufficient in the absence of proof of a "serious danger" of conflict of interest, or of organizational interference with the actual conduct of the litigation. . . .

The State's interests in preventing the "stirring up" of frivolous or vexatious litigation and minimizing commercialization of the legal profession offer no further justification for the discipline administered in this case. The *Button* Court declined to accept the proffered analogy to the common-law offenses of maintenance, champerty, and barratry, where the record would not support a finding that the litigant was solicited for a malicious purpose or "for private gain, serving no public interest." The same result follows from the facts of this case. And considerations of undue commercialization of the legal profession are of marginal force where, as here, a nonprofit organization offers its services free of charge to individuals who may be in need of legal assistance and may lack the financial means and sophistication necessary to tap alternative sources of such aid.

At bottom, the case against appellant rests on the proposition that a State may regulate in a prophylactic fashion all solicitation activities of lawyers because there may be some potential for overreaching, conflict of interest, or other substantive evils whenever a lawyer gives unsolicited advice and communicates an offer of representation to a layman. Under certain circumstances, that approach is appropriate in the case of speech that simply "propose[s] a commercial transaction." See *Ohralik*. In the context of political expression and association, however, a State must regulate with significantly greater precision.

VI

The State is free to fashion reasonable restrictions with respect to the time, place, and manner of solicitation by members of its Bar. The State's special interest in regulating members of a profession it licenses, and who serve as officers of its courts, amply justifies the application of narrowly drawn rules to proscribe solicitation that in fact is misleading, overbearing, or involves other features of deception or improper influence. As we decide today in *Ohralik*, a State also may forbid in-person solicitation for pecuniary gain under circumstances likely to result in these evils. And a State may insist that lawyers not solicit on behalf of lay organizations that exert control over the actual conduct of any ensuing litigation. Accordingly, nothing in this opinion should be read to fore-close carefully tailored regulation that does not abridge unnecessarily the associational freedom of nonprofit organizations, or their members, having characteristics like those of the NAACP or the ACLU. . . .

JUSTICE REHNQUIST, dissenting.

In this case and the companion case of *Ohralik*, the Court tells its own tale of two lawyers: One tale ends happily for the lawyer and one does not. . . .

If Albert Ohralik, like Edna Primus, viewed litigation " 'not [as] a technique of resolving private differences,' " but as " 'a form of political expression' and 'political association,' " for all that appears he would be restored to his right to practice. And we may be sure that the next lawyer in Ohralik's shoes who is disciplined for similar conduct will come here cloaked in the prescribed mantle of "political association" to assure that insurance companies do not take unfair advantage of policyholders.

This absence of any principled distinction between the two cases is made all the more unfortunate by the radical difference in scrutiny brought to bear upon state regulation in each area. Where solicitation proposes merely a commercial transaction, the Court recognizes "the need for prophylactic regulation in furtherance of the State's interest in protecting the lay public." On the other hand, in some circumstances "[w]here political expression or association is at issue," a member of the Bar "may not be disciplined unless her activity in fact involve[s] the type of misconduct at which South Carolina's broad prohibition is said to be directed."

. . . I believe that constitutional inquiry must focus on the character of the conduct which the State seeks to regulate, and not on the motives of the individual lawyers or the nature of the particular litigation involved. . . .

While *Button* appears to permit such individual solicitation for political purposes by lay members of the organization, it nowhere explicitly permits such activity on the part of lawyers. . . .

A State may reasonably fear that a lawyer's desire to resolve "substantial civil liberties questions" may occasionally take precedence over his duty to advance the interests of his client. It is even more reasonable to fear that a lawyer in such circumstances will be inclined to pursue both culpable and blameless defendants to the last ditch in order to achieve his ideological goals. Although individual litigants, including the ACLU, may be free to use the courts for such purposes, South Carolina is likewise free to restrict the activities of the members of its Bar who attempt to persuade them to do so.

I can only conclude that the discipline imposed upon *Primus* does not violate the Constitution, and I would affirm the judgment of the Supreme Court of South Carolina.

Communication with Class Members

Before *Shapero* afforded First Amendment protection to direct-mail solicitation, there was some question whether a lawyer who brought a class action could seek to communicate with potential class members (before class certification) by targeted mail. Today, after *Shapero*, two questions remain: Despite *Ohralik*, does the First Amendment afford class action lawyers additional protection for in-person solicitation of class members? Despite *Shapero*, may a court order a class action lawyer not to contact potential class members through the mail?

In Gulf Oil Co. v. Bernard, 452 U.S. 89 (1981), the plaintiffs had brought a class action charging the defendant with employment discrimination based on race. The trial judge, relying on Federal Rule of Civil Procedure 23(d), had granted the defendant's motion for an order restraining "all communications concerning the class action between parties or their counsel and any actual or potential class member who was not a formal party, without the prior approval of the court." The Supreme Court held that the trial court had abused its discretion in restraining the communications. It acknowledged that such communications created a "potential for abuse," which provides a trial judge with "both the duty and the broad authority to exercise control over a class action and to enter appropriate orders governing the conduct of counsel and parties." On the other hand, orders restraining communications with class members may make it difficult for counsel and the class representatives to represent the class effectively. Justice Powell wrote for a unanimous Court:

> Because of these potential problems, an order limiting communications between parties and potential class members should be based on a clear record and specific findings that reflect a weighing of the need for a limitation and the potential interference with the rights of the parties. Only such a determination can ensure that the court is furthering, rather than hindering, the policies embodied in the Federal Rules of Civil Procedure, especially Rule 23. In addition, such a weighing — identifying the potential abuses being addressed — should result in a carefully drawn order that limits speech as little as possible, consistent with the rights of the parties under the circumstances.

An order forbidding contact with class members clashed with one group's public interest agenda in Gates v. Cook, 234 F.3d 221 (5th Cir. 2000). After prisoners in Mississippi filed a pro se federal complaint alleging inadequate medical care for HIV-positive inmates, a district judge appointed Welch, a solo practitioner, to represent them. The court later entered a consent decree certifying a prisoner class and settling the action. Some members of the class objected to the terms of the settlement. Over the next four years, class members dissatisfied with Welch's work in enforcing the settlement contacted the National Prison Project (NPP) of the ACLU. Eventually, every member of the prisoner class sought to have the NPP substituted as class counsel. The district judge denied the request and enjoined NPP lawyers from contacting class members. In a 2-1 ruling, the Fifth Circuit reversed, citing *Gulf Oil*: "The order in this case bars all contact between NPP attorneys and class members regarding the subject matter of the class action. . . . The order is not narrowly drawn nor is it justified by any factual findings. . . ." The court overturned the no-contact order and also directed that NPP counsel be substituted for Welch.

ABA Opinion 07-445 concludes that the Model Rules do not forbid plaintiff's or defendant's counsel from contacting potential class members. Once the class is certified, defense counsel are bound by Rule 4.2 (no-contact rule). Separately, a court may forbid defense contact with members of a certified class during the opt-out period. Consider Kleiner v. First National Bank of Atlanta, 751 F.2d 1193

(11th Cir. 1985), a class action against a bank for interest overcharges. The trial judge instructed defense counsel not to contact plaintiff class members during a period within which the members had to decide whether to opt out of the class. (Recall the "no-contact" rule in chapter 3A.) After reading *Gulf Oil*, and despite the court order, the bank's counsel concluded that the bank could solicit opt-outs so long as it did so truthfully and without coercion (many of the potential class members were bank customers and dependent on the bank for loans). The bank began a telephone campaign. Its lawyer helped. The campaign identified 2,800 borrowers, with nearly $700 million in loans, who agreed to opt out, although some may have intended to do so in any event.

When the district judge learned of the campaign, she imposed fines and costs totaling more than $100,000 against counsel and the bank, disqualified counsel from continuing to represent the bank, and ruled that the customers who had chosen to opt out would be permitted to rejoin the class after entry of judgment (in other words, after seeing who won). The Eleventh Circuit affirmed (with minor exception on procedural grounds), rejecting the bank's First Amendment claim based on Gulf Oil Co. v. Bernard:

> *Bernard* was a classic case of noncommercial speech which directly implicated the doctrine of prior restraint. In the domain of commercial speech, as discussed, the Supreme Court had issued repeated admonitions against the wholesale incorporation of the law of prior restraint. We therefore judge petitioners' prior restraint argument under a relaxed standard of scrutiny better suited to the hardiness of commercial speech. . . .
>
> The trial court's order was narrowly drawn to avoid suppressing utterances worthy of first amendment protection. As a directive addressed to counsel for the Bank, the ambit of the order was restricted to communications regarding the litigation. The order thus did not impinge on the Bank's ability to speak with customers about routine business matters unrelated to the lawsuit. Since defense counsel had an ethical duty to refrain from discussing the litigation with members of the class as of the date of class certification, if not sooner, the order in no way tread on legitimate communications by counsel.
>
> Similarly, we discern no less restrictive alternative to the district judge's order. The purpose of the directive was to filter news of the opportunity for exclusion through the impartial and open medium of court-supervised notice. As such, the order implemented the preview screening which the Supreme Court has commended as a constitutional substitute for a complete ban on communications.

Table of Cases

Principal cases are in italics.

951

Table of Cases

Table of Cases

Table of Cases

Table of Cases

Table of Codes, Rules, and Restatement Provisions

Index